Barcelona

P9-AOX-606

TO ✈, Ⓜ Espanya

SANT ANTONI

EL RAVAL

CIUTAT VELLA

BARRI GOTIC

LA RIBERA

POBLE SEC

BARCELONETA

MONTJUIC

PARC DE LA CIUTADELLA

Parc Zoològic

Parc Zoològic

VILA OLÍMPICA

C. Sardenya
C. Sicilia
C. de Nápols
C. Casp
C. Roger de Flor
Corts Catalanes
PLAÇA TETUAN
Passeig de Sant Joan
C. Bailén
C. Girona
D'Ali-Bei
Carrer de Bruc
Carrer de Roger de Llúria
Ronda Sant Pere
Carrer de Trafalgar
Passeig de Gràcia
Pg. Gràcia
PLAÇA DE CATALUNYA
El Corte Inglés
PLAÇA URQUINAONA
Urquinaona
C. Comtal
C. de Fontanella
Ronda Universitat
Universitat
C. Bergara
C. Pelai
C. Elisabets
MACBA
C. Valldonzella
C. Fortuny
C. Carme
Palau de la Virreina
C. Ferlandina
Ribera Baja
Ribera Alta
Peu de la Creu
L'Hospital
S. Antón Abad
Casanova
Villarroel
Comte d'Urgell
C. Comte Borrell
C. Viladomat
C. Tamarit
C. Manso
C. Parlament
Mercat de Sant Antoni
Ronda de Sant Pau
M. Campo Sagrado
Aldana
Parallel
Blai
Calàbria
Poble Sec
Floridablanca
Av. Mistral
Rocafort
C. Sepúlveda
Gran Via Corts Catalanes
Avinguda del Paral·lel
Entença
Vilamarí
Pg. de l'Exposició
Teatre Grec
Fundació Miró
TO OLYMPIC STADIUM
TO CASTELL MONTJUIC
Funicular
Cable Car
Magallanes
Pg. de Montjuïc
Lleida
Jose Carner
Passeig
Cable Car

Trains to Airport (Old Train Station)
C. Ribas
Arc de Triomf
Av. Vilanova
Almogàvers
Buenaventura Muñoz
Av. Meridiana
C. Wellington
Passeig Pujades
Museu de Zoologia
Museu D'Art Modern
Passeig Lluís Companys
Passeig de Picasso
C. Fussina
C. Comerç
Estació de França
Passeig Circumvallació
Ronda Litoral
Mercat del Born
Museu Picasso
Av. Marquès d'Argentera
Carrer de Princesa
Carrer Montcada
Banys Vells
Mallarés
Argenteria
Llotja
Pg. Isabel II
Barceloneta
Palau de la Música
C. Francesc Cambó
Via Laietana
Av. Catedral
Portal de l'Àngel
Sta. Anna
C. Canuda
Portaferrissa
C. Comtessa
C. Petritxol
Catedral
Esglésià del Pi
C. Boqueria
Mercat de la Boqueria
Las Ramblas
Liceu
Teatre Liceu
La Unió
PLAÇA REIAL
C. Ferran
C. Jaume I
Ajuntament
Església Sta. Maria del Mar
C. Ferran
C. S. Miquel
D'en Arai
C. Ample
La Mercè
C. Mercè
Passeig de Colom
C. Escudellers
La Pau
Els Dels
J. A. Clavé
Drassanes
Monument a Colom
Arc del Teatre
Avda. de les Drassanes
Avinguda de la Rambla
Carrer de Sant Pau
Carrer Nou
Cabanes St.
Moll de la Fusta
Maremàgnum
Multicines
Cine IMAX
Aquarium
Marina-Port Vell
Harbor

Buses to Airport
Buses & Trains to Airport

300 yards
300 meters

N

Madrid Metro

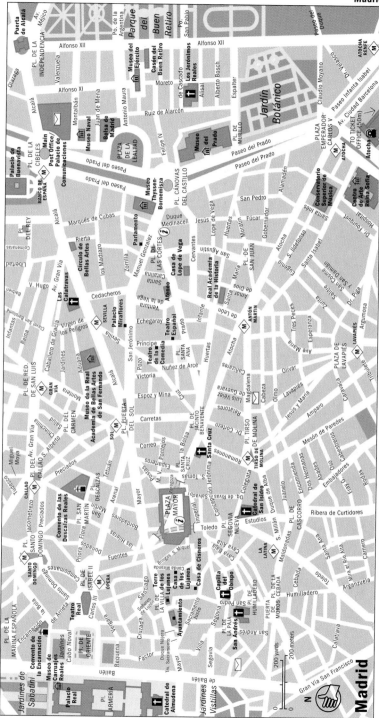

Madrid

Barcelona Metro

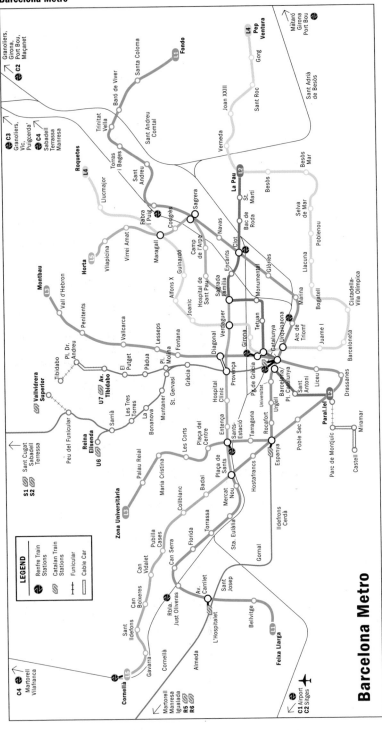

Barcelona Metro

◪ Let's Go writers travel on your budget.

"Guides that penetrate the veneer of the holiday brochures and mine the grit of real life."

—*The Economist*

"The writers seem to have experienced every rooster-packed bus and lunar-surfaced mattress about which they write."

—*The New York Times*

"All the dirt, dirt cheap."

—*People*

◪ Great for independent travelers.

"The guides are aimed not only at young budget travelers but at the independent traveler; a sort of streetwise cookbook for traveling alone."

—*The New York Times*

"Flush with candor and irreverence, chock full of budget travel advice."

—*The Des Moines Register*

"An indispensible resource, *Let's Go*'s practical information can be used by every traveler."

—*The Chattanooga Free Press*

◪ Let's Go is completely revised each year.

"Only *Let's Go* has the zeal to annually update every title on its list."

—*The Boston Globe*

"Unbeatable: good sightseeing advice; up-to-date info on restaurants, hotels, and inns; a commitment to money-saving travel; and a wry style that brightens nearly every page."

—*The Washington Post*

◪ All the important information you need.

"*Let's Go* authors provide a comedic element while still providing concise information and thorough coverage of the country. Anything you need to know about budget traveling is detailed in this book."

—*The Chicago Sun-Times*

"Value-packed, unbeatable, accurate, and comprehensive."

—*Los Angeles Times*

Let's Go

SPAIN & PORTUGAL

INCLUDING MOROCCO

2001

Meredith Lea Petrin editor
Marla B. Kaplan associate editor
Tova Carlin associate editor

researcher-writers
Luis Rego
Jennifer Y. Hyman
Alexandra Price
Marcella Prieto
Iciar P. Garcia
David Modigliani
Lauren Klein

Theadora W. Sakata map editor

St. Martin's Press ⋈ New York

Maps by David Lindroth copyright © 2001, 2000, 1999, 1998, 1997, 1996, 1995, 1994, 1993, 1992, 1991, 1990, 1989, 1988 by St. Martin's Press.

Distributed outside the USA and Canada by Macmillan.

ISBN: 0–312-24690-0

First edition
10 9 8 7 6 5 4 3 2 1

Let's Go: Spain & Portugal, Including Morroco is written by Let's Go Publications, 67 Mount Auburn Street, Cambridge, MA 02138, USA.

Let's Go® and the thumb logo are trademarks of Let's Go, Inc.
Printed in the USA on recycled paper with biodegradable soy ink.

CONTENTS

MAPS

ABOUT LET'S GO

FORTY-ONE YEARS OF WISDOM

As a new millennium arrives, *Let's Go: Europe*, now in its 41st edition and translated into seven languages, reigns as the world's bestselling international travel guide. For over four decades, travelers criss-crossing the Continent have relied on *Let's Go* for inside information on the hippest backstreet cafes, the most pristine secluded beaches, and the best routes from border to border. In the last 20 years, our rugged researchers have stretched the frontiers of backpacking and expanded our coverage into Asia, Africa, Australia, and the Americas. This year, we've introduced a new city guide series with books on San Francisco and our hometown, Boston. Now, our seven city guides feature sharp photos, more maps, and an overall more user-friendly design. We've also returned to our roots with the inaugural edition of *Let's Go: Western Europe*.

It all started in 1960 when a handful of well-traveled students at Harvard University handed out a 20-page mimeographed pamphlet offering a collection of their tips on budget travel to passengers on student charter flights to Europe. The following year, in response to the instant popularity of the first volume, students traveling to Europe researched the first full-fledged edition of *Let's Go: Europe*, a pocket-sized book featuring honest, practical advice, witty writing, and a decidedly youthful slant on the world. Throughout the 60s and 70s, our guides reflected the times. In 1969 we taught travelers how to get from Paris to Prague on "no dollars a day" by singing in the street. In the 80s and 90s, we looked beyond Europe and North America and set off to all corners of the earth. Meanwhile, we focused in on the world's most exciting urban areas to produce in-depth, fold-out map guides. Our new guides bring the total number of titles to 51, each infused with the spirit of adventure and voice of opinion that travelers around the world have come to count on. But some things never change: our guides are still researched, written, and produced entirely by students who know first-hand how to see the world on the cheap.

HOW WE DO IT

Each guide is completely revised and thoroughly updated every year by a well-traveled set of nearly 300 students. Every spring, we recruit over 200 researchers and 90 editors to overhaul every book. After several months of training, researcher-writers hit the road for seven weeks of exploration, from Anchorage to Adelaide, Estonia to El Salvador, Iceland to Indonesia. Hired for their rare combination of budget travel sense, writing ability, stamina, and courage, these adventurous travelers know that train strikes, stolen luggage, food poisoning, and marriage proposals are all part of a day's work. Back at our offices, editors work from spring to fall, massaging copy written on Himalayan bus rides into witty, informative prose. A student staff of typesetters, cartographers, publicists, and managers keeps our lively team together. In September, the collected efforts of the summer are delivered to our printer, who turns them into books in record time, so that you have the most up-to-date information available for your vacation. Even as you read this, work on next year's editions is well underway.

WHY WE DO IT

We don't think of budget travel as the last recourse of the destitute; we believe that it's the only way to travel. Living cheaply and simply brings you closer to the people and places you've been saving up to visit. Our books will ease your anxieties and answer your questions about the basics—so you can get off the beaten track and explore. Once you learn the ropes, we encourage you to put *Let's Go* down now and then to strike out on your own. You know as well as we that the best discoveries are often those you make yourself. When you find something worth sharing, please drop us a line. We're Let's Go Publications, 67 Mount Auburn St., Cambridge, MA 02138, USA (email: feedback@letsgo.com). For more info, visit our website, www.letsgo.com.

RESEARCHER-WRITERS

Iciar Garcia   *Northwestern Spain, Castilla y León, and Northern Portugal*

After spending last summer completing the Camino de Santiago, Iciar came to *Let's Go* armed with impressive regional knowledge. Galician cousins in tow (or driving the car), she buffed up our history, did wonders for La Coruña and even drew us pictures of her favorite beach. Winner of the smallest handwriting award, Iciar overwhelmed us with fantastic detail and piles of brochures.

Jennifer Hyman   *Barcelona, the Balearic Islands, and the Eastern Coast*

It's quite possible that Jenn was actually born to cover this route. Arguably the most enthusiastic researcher in the 2001 series, she made us green with envy when she called from Ibiza, and her Barcelona copy was nothing short of pure poetry. Jenn's unbelievable tan might finally fade after a few months, but we have a hunch that the string of broken hearts she's left in Spain are going to last a lot longer.

Lauren Klein   *Morocco*

After learning the necessity of loose clothing, Lauren covered Morocco without a hitch. Unless, of course, you count almost getting arrested for photographing a policeman, nearly falling off a precariously tilted camel's back, or getting wrapped up in a stow-away conspiracy. A generous gentleman in Aït Benhaddour offered to buy Lauren with 100 camels, but we say her grit and wit are priceless.

David Modigliani   *Extremadura, Madrid, and the Canary Islands*

A veteran of *Let's Go Australia 2000*, David came back for more, this time in search of his Latin roots. Madrid quickly reminded him that fashion codes are not universal, but he willingly donned the appropriate tight black gear, fought past sickness and computer trouble, and blessed the capital city with the most concise, funniest writing we've seen this summer. Travelers to the Canaries will probably spend the rest of 2001 praising his ferry schedule and perceptive town write-ups.

Marcella Prieto   *Andalucía*

We almost couldn't believe it, but Marcella really did love the scorching heat of southern Spain as much as she loves the art of flamenco. From wining and dining with guitarists in Córdoba to an encounter with thieves in Marbella, Marcella flew effortlessly through the good and the bad of Andalucía, totally revamping Sevilla nightlife and giving us a sharp-eyed low-down on everything from Antonio Banderas's favorite beachtown to the tiniest mountain villages of Las Alpujarras.

Alexandra Price   *Northeastern Spain and Castilla la Mancha*

Alex may have permanently white knuckles from navigating the narrow, precarious roads in the Spanish Pyrenees, but not once did she let such a minor inhibition prevent her from writing copious, detailed descriptions—we thank her to from the bottom of our editing hearts for such thoughtful coverage advice. Alex took fact-checking to impressive levels as well, even following a few hostel owners right into the bars during the Running of the Bulls...where else to find them, after all?

Luis Rego   *Portugal*

Portugal has never seen such a precise researcher—we actually swooned over Luis's detailed map corrections. Undaunted by the fact that everything in Lisbon was under construction, Luis polished off the capital city, pulled together complicated bus links, and put the port into our Porto coverage. Not two weeks later, he was back in the office earning himself a reputation as Let's Go sharpest-eyed proofer. We only wish we could have put him in more than one place at once.

HOW TO USE THIS BOOK

Welcome to *Let's Go Spain, Portugal, and Morocco 2001*, otherwise known affectionately as **SPAM** (**S**pain, **P**ortugal, **A**ndorra, **M**orocco). Unlike our namesake, the famed mystery meat, we want you to know exactly what you're ingesting. So without further ado, here are the key features of the guide.

INTRODUCTION. The first chapter of this book—**Discover Spain, Portugal, and Morocco**—provides you with an overview of travel in the three countries, including **Suggested Itineraries** that give you an idea of what you shouldn't miss and how long it will take to see it. The **Essentials** section outlines the practical information you will need to prepare for and execute your trip. Each country has its own **Life and Times** chapter with a general introduction to the country's history, art, culture, and food, as well as a brief country-specific Essentials section.

THE "MEAT". Coverage of Spain begins with **Madrid**, and moves from there into the provinces that make up **Central Spain**, then down to **Andalucía**, beginning an outward spiral that eventually ends in **Northwestern Spain**. From there it is on to **Spain's Islands, Portugal**, and finally **Morocco**. The black tabs in the margins will help you to navigate between chapters quickly and easily. Each chapter begins with a regional intro, and each town and city is broken down into several sections: **Orientation and Practical Information, Accommodations, Food, Sights, Nightlife**, and **Entertainment**. For smaller towns, categories occasionally get thrown together.

APPENDIX. The appendix contains **climate charts**, a **time-travel chart**, phrasebooks for Spanish, Portuguese, Arabic, and French, information on **time zones**, and a **glossary** with useful words for traveling and eating in Spain, Portugal, and Morocco.

A FEW NOTES ABOUT LET'S GO FORMAT

TRANSPORTATION. *Let's Go* follows a "travel-away-from" layout: the transportation section for each city/town is designed mainly to tell you how to get *away* from there to new destinations. Also, most transportation links lead only to equal-sized or larger cities, so to get to a small town from a larger one you should look for the connecting bus/train line under the smaller town's transportation section.

RANKING ESTABLISHMENTS. In each section (accommodations, food, etc.), we list establishments in order from best to worst. This is true for **sights** as well, unless we explicitly say that we are organizing by walking tour or convenience. Our absolute favorites are denoted with a Let's Go thumbs-up (◙).

PHONE CODES AND TELEPHONE NUMBERS. In Morocco, the **phone code** for each region, city, or town appears opposite the name of that region, city, or town, and is denoted by the ☎ icon. Spain and Portugal do not have separate regional phone codes. **Phone numbers** in text are also preceded by the ☎ icon.

GRAYBOXES AND WHITEBOXES. Grayboxes at times provide interesting cultural insight, at times simply crude humor. In any case, they usually attempt to be amusing, so enjoy. **Whiteboxes**, on the other hand, provide important practical information, such as warnings (▶), helpful hints, and further resources (▶).

So go. Have fun. We hope you'll love these countries as much as we do.

ACKNOWLEDGMENTS

SPAM THANKS: Esti, Thea, Melissa R., and Fiore for so many late nights, Nick for kickball, burgers and even asparagus, Anne for the tough-guy act, Amélie for helping out, our RWs for getting it done, Luis for proofing, Kate for her chopping expertise, Marly for being so generous,and France for making us laugh.

MEREDITH THANKS: Kate D., for far more than I can write here—may there be gallons of *sangría* to come. mc seas, creature of the night, for being my brother-away-from-home. Alex, for sincerity and listening. It's *never* too late to achieve "greatness"! Andrea for Radiohead and Club Go, Ann and Popper for late-night food, Mica for vent-sessions, Anna for talks, Esti for being so mellow, Team France for adopting me, and Alice, Bede, Marc, Paul, Matt R. and Windom for good times. Tova for perspective, and Marla (or was it Co.?) for working so hard and wearing a snowsuit. Mais for making me so damn happy, my roommates and family for always being there even when I wasn't, and Papa Bear for that first plane ticket to Madrid.

TOVA THANKS: Ma famille bien sur, comme toujours, Daniel for being my inspiration. The best beast for always being there, I will too. Tom for always being so patient, making me laugh and not biting my ass. Mer for putting up with me and my stoopid questions. Marla for having the best hair and an even better smile. Katie and Mi for finally getting yo' butts here. Su, Liz and Cath for the world's most rockin' roomates. Chung for letting me be your damsel in distress. Megs and Ann, thank god you were doing this too. Emmy because. Bethpretty. Schnee for you. Zach for hanging out and dancing.

MARLA THANKS: Mere for busting her butt (literally) to get this all done. Tova for her energy and laughter. Mica and Megan for keeping me on my toes, and for putting together an awesome PEB book. Katy, Charlie, and the Pfoho girls for making me look forward to the summer's end; my friends at home for making me hope it never would. Sra. Timberlake for making me love Spanish. Dad for all the rides and for being so understanding (even if I never did clean my room), and Jonah for being an awesome brother. Mom, who's out there somewhere watching over me.

Editor
Meredith Petrin
Associate Editors
Tova Carlin, Marla Kaplan
Managing Editor
Esti Iturralde
Map Editor
Thea Sakata

Publishing Director
Kaya Stone
Editor-in-Chief
Kate McCarthy
Production Manager
Melissa Rudolph
Cartography Manager
John Fiore
Editorial Managers
Alice Farmer, Ankur Ghosh, Aarup Kubal, Anup Kubal
Financial Manager
Bede Sheppard
Low-Season Manager
Melissa Gibson
Marketing & Publicity Managers
Olivia L. Cowley, Esti Iturralde
New Media Manager
Jonathan Dawid
Personnel Manager
Nicholas Grossman
Photo Editor
Dara Cho
Production Associates
Sanjay Mavinkurve, Nicholas Murphy, Rosalinda Rosalez
Matthew Daniels, Rachel Mason, Daniel Visel, Dan Williams
Office Coordinators
Sarah Jacoby, Chris Russell

Director of Advertising Sales
Cindy Rodriguez
Associate Sales Executives
Adam Grant, Rebecca Rendell

President
Andrew M. Murphy
General Manager
Robert B. Rombauer
Assistant General Manager
Anne E. Chisholm

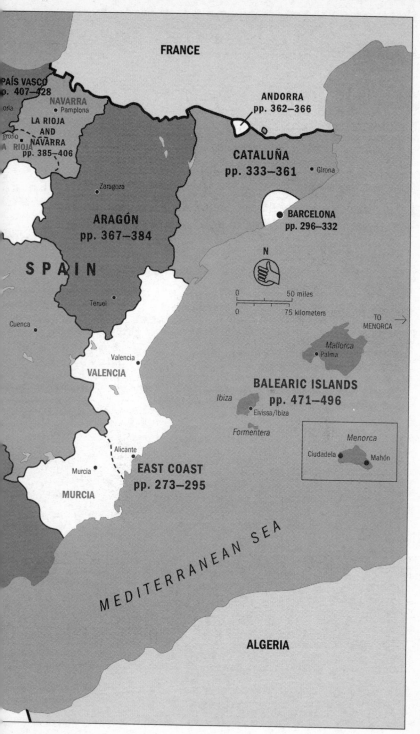

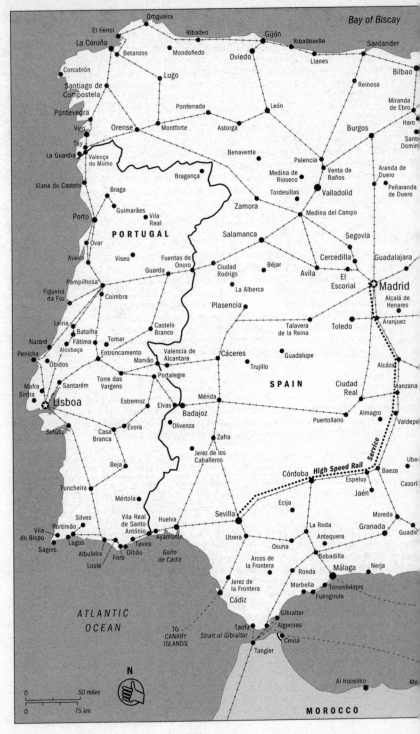

XIV

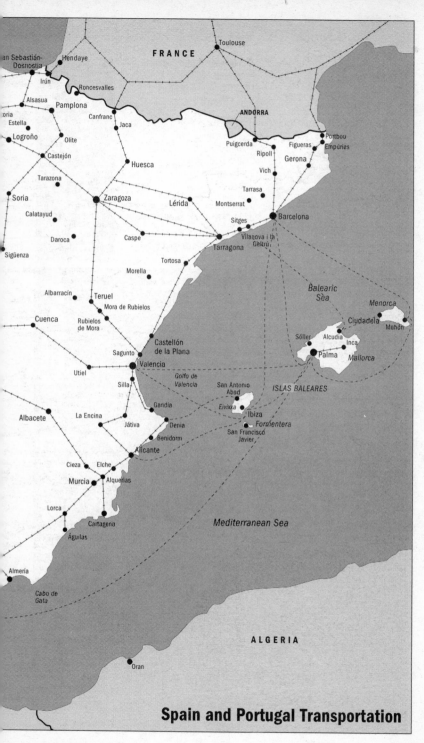

Spain and Portugal Transportation

Youth Hostel

San Eugenio - Las Arenas

No twins , only dormitories
No curfew
Máximum age 30 Years Old
Near the Beach
Near the Discos
Near the University
Youth ambience
Barbecue posibilities
Bonfire posibilities
Interior garden

Your contribution will help the
mantemance of an orphanage and
a charity house for young homeless.

24 Eugenia Viñes St. Bus 32, last stop, cross the street ,move to
Just in front of 1st Pavía St.   the left and just in the corner by the beach

Free ½ h. Internet access **Showing this ticket**
(This offer is only valid during your hostel´s stay)

Beach

1.000 pts. (+- 6$) per night
Showing your Let´s Go Book

Free ½ h. Internet access **Showing this ticket**
(This offer is only valid during your hostel´s stay)

Beach

1.000 pts. (+- 6$) per night
Showing your Let´s Go Book

Free

INTERNET
Eugenia Viñes St. 24
Bus 32 (Last Stop)
(cross the street and turn to the left side
until the corner by the beach)
Just in front of 1 Pavía St.
Valencia

Free

Free

INTERNET
Eugenia Viñes St. 24
Bus 32 (Last Stop)
(cross the street and turn to the left side
until the corner by the beach)
Just in front of 1 Pavía St.
Valencia

Free

DISCOVER SPAIN, PORTUGAL, AND MOROCCO

SPAIN

Spain is a budget traveler's dream. Inexpensive and politically stable, it is a country where art, architecture, beaches, and nightlife vie for supremacy. The people have an irresistible gusto for life that they are eager to share, and regional diversity assures something for everyone. Art lovers flock to northern Spain to see trend-setting Barcelona, the coastline that inspired Dalí, and Bilbao's shining new Guggenheim museum. Adventure-seekers trek through the winding Pyrenees, and architectural enthusiasts explore the Baroque cathedrals of northwestern Spain, the Modernist creations of Antoni Gaudí, and the Arab-influenced buildings of Andalucía, Spain's southernmost region. Flamenco, bullfighting and *tapas*, Spain's most unique cultural expressions, also hail from the south, while Madrid, Barcelona and Ibiza do enough insane, all-night partying to make up for every quiet rural village in the country. Spain is the perfect destination for first-time travelers, for seasoned adventurers, for families with young children, or for college students in search of that "craziest summer ever." You can do Spain in a week, a month, or a year. But you must do it at least once.

PORTUGAL

Sandwiched between Spain and the Atlantic Ocean, Portugal is the forgotten country of Western Europe. Most people know that it colonized Brazil, invented sugary-sweet port wine and hosted Expo '98 (which, incidentally, was a disaster) But there is much more to discover in Portugal—like Spain, its greatest strength lies in its diversity. Lisbon, the capital and largest city, has the country's most impressive imperial monuments, while the southern Algarve boasts spectacular beaches and the wildest nightlife. Northern Coimbra has the electric energy of a university town, and Porto surpasses Lisbon in sophisticated elegance. Portugal's small interior towns have a certain timeless feel, with medieval castles overlooking rushing rivers and peaceful town squares. But perhaps most unique about the country is its wild northern hinterlands, where some villages have not changed in nearly a millennium; the land in Trás-Os-Montes is among the most pristine in all of Europe.

MOROCCO

Morocco is an experience that goes beyond common expectations of hustlers, drugs, and prostitutes, or of snake charmers and carpet sellers. It is, above all, a land of extremes, characterized by the snow-capped peaks of the Atlas mountains and the hot sun on golden sand dunes, by industrialized coastal cities and isolated desert towns, by the sheer insanity of Marrakesh's Djemâa el-Fna and the peaceful seclusion of Essaouira's beaches. European backpackers come to Morocco to "see Africa," but they stay for the medinas (large outdoor markets where you can buy everything from a camel to a toothbrush to fresh orange juice), the excursions (treks on foot, four-wheel-drive, and camel into endless dunes or up North Africa's highest peak), and the wealth of architectural history (towering mosques, crumbling kasbahs, and Roman ruins).

COUNTRY FACTS

SPAIN	PORTUGAL	MOROCCO
Population: 39,371,000	**Population:** 9,964,000	**Population:** 27,225,463
Size: 504,784 sq. km	**Size:** 92,389 sq. km	**Size:** 458,730 sq. km
Capital: Madrid	**Capital:** Lisbon	**Capital:** Rabat
Currency: peseta (pta)	**Currency:** escudo ($)	**Currency:** dirham (dh)

...AND FIGURES

Pork produced annually per resident of Spain: 67kg (147 lb.)

Coastline per resident of Portugal: 1.8km

Desert per resident of Morocco: 1504 sq. km

Ratio of yearly tourists to actual residents of Spain: 9 to 8

Amount of cork Portugal produces annually: Enough to keep the entire population afloat—with each person wearing a 40lb. backpack.

What Humphrey Bogart was paid to make the film *Casablanca*: $4, 583

WHEN TO GO

Summer is **high season** (*temporada alta*) for coastal and interior regions in Spain, Portugal, and Morocco; winter is high season for ski resorts and the Canary Islands. In many parts of Spain and Portugal, high season extends back to **Semana Santa** (Holy Week; April 9-15 in 2001) and includes festival days. Tourism on the Iberian Peninsula reaches its height in August; the coastal regions overflow while inland cities empty out, leaving closed offices, restaurants, and lodgings.

Traveling in the **off-season** (*temporada baja*) has many advantages, most noticeably lighter crowds and lower prices. Many hostels cut their prices by 50% or more, and reservations are seldom necessary. But while major cities and university towns may burst with vitality, many smaller seaside towns virtually shut down, and tourist offices and sights cut their hours nearly everywhere. During Ramadan in Morocco (December), there will be little activity outside the sacred realm. For a temperature chart, see **Climate,** p. 727. For a chart detailing all the festivals in Spain, see p. 73, in Portugal p. 535, and in Morocco p. 667.

WHAT TO DO

The best thing about traveling to Spain, Portugal, and Morocco is the diversity of things to do and see; these are just some of the most popular reasons people come to the Iberian Peninsula. For more specific regional attractions, see the **Highlights of the Region** section at the beginning of each chapter.

IT'S IN THE BLOOD

Spain, Portugal, and Morocco are *alive*. Two millennia of invading cultures have come and gone from this corner of Europe, and the result is a vibrant, if confused, *alegría* (joy). The region bursts at the seams. You can see it in Madrid's famous flea market (p. 120), in the happy chaos of Fez's outdoor medina (p. 683), in the sidewalk cafes of downtown Lisbon (p. 536), and above all in Spain's spectacular festivals. During *Carnaval* in Cádiz (p. 229), Valencia's *Las Fallas* (p. 276), Sevilla's *Feria de Abril* (p. 192), and Pamplona's infamous *San Fermines* (p. 396), there is no denying the Spaniards' overwhelming cultural exuberance.

Still, like all passions, it is not entirely manic. Iberia's poignant expressions of heartbreak are often as blood-quickening as its celebrations. The ritually tragic expressions inherent in *flamenco* and *fado* bring tears to the eyes of even the most macho of bullfighters, who in turn create tragedies of life-and-death on the bloody sand. Actual tragedy on a larger scale has scarred Spain for a good part of this century—Picasso's powerfully cryptic *Guernica* (p. 110) and the propagandistic Valley of the Fallen (p. 124) give travelers a taste of the pain of fascism. All of this inherited emotional activity demands a break now and then. The thin-aired reverence of Montserrat (p. 333) and the calm to be found in a rowboat in the Retiro (p. 106) or on a surreal bench in Parc Güell (p. 323) inspire contemplative relaxation; more untouched than the rest of Europe is touched, Portugal's Trás-os-Montes (p. 647) will make even the most devout urbanites kiss the ground.

ARCHITECTURE

From traditionally conservative to unconventionally decadent, the buildings and monuments of Iberia form a collage of architectural styles. The remains of ancient civilizations are everywhere—from the Celtiberian tower of O Castro de Baroña (p. 454) and the ruins of the Roman Augusta Emerita at Mérida (p. 186) to the Torre D'en Gaumés Talayotic settlement in Menorca (p. 484). Hundreds of years of Moorish occupation have left a powerful mark on Granada's spectacular Alhambra (p. 259), Córdoba's Mezquita (p. 218), and Sintra's Castelo dos Mouros (p. 565), among others, and the Catholic church has poured immense amounts of money into the construction of some of the world's most ornate religious complexes, ranging from the pastiche of the Convento de Cristo (p. 613) to the imposing El Escorial (p. 122), from which the Inquisition was conducted. Spain's magnificent cathedrals can be Gothic (p. 146 and p. 165), Plateresque, built on top of mosques, or just plain bizarre, as with Gaudí's magnificent, still-unfinished Sagrada Familia in Barcelona (p. 321), a brilliant climax of the Modernista style. The quest for truly modern architecture will continue into the next millennium; most recently it has manifested itself in Santiago Calatrava's sensational bridges in Sevilla and Mérida, Lisbon's expansive Park of Nations (p. 556), Bilbao's shining Guggenheim Museum (p. 420) and Valencia's huge Ciudad de las Artes y las Ciencias (p. 281).

NATURE

Iberia's best-kept secret is its national parks and mountain chains, which range from green wildlife reserves to soaring, snowy peaks. Dozens of popular climbs explore tiny Andorra's glacial valleys, rolling forests, and wild meadows (p. 364.) In northern Spain, the Parque Nacional de Ordesa (p. 381) maintains well-cut trails through jagged rock faces, rushing rivers, and thundering waterfalls, and the Parc Nacional d'Agüestortes (p. 334) hides 50 ice-cold mountain lakes in its 10,000 hectares (24,700 acres) of towering peaks and valleys. Northern Portugal's Parque Natural de Montesinho (p. 649) is probably the most isolated, untouched land in all of Europe; the villages nestled within the park borders have hardly changed since the 8th century. Farther south, city-bored *madrileños* hike in the Sierra de Guadarrama (p. 124) and nature-lovers are drawn to Andalucía's huge Parque Nacional Coto de Doñana (p. 226), which protects nearly 25,000 hectares (60,000 acres) of land for threatened wildlife. Las Alpujarras (p. 269), the southern slopes of the Sierra Nevada, are perfect for hiking among Spain's famous white towns, and trails in Mallorca (p. 471) and the Canary Islands (p. 495) offer a unique opportunity to see mountains and miles of sea at the same time. In Morocco, ambitious explorers can trek to the top of the Djebal Toubkal, North Africa's highest peak (p. 717) or take camel trips into the dunes of Erfoud (p. 726) or M'Hamid (p. 722).

BEACHES

It would be a shame to spend your *entire* time in Spain, Portugal and Morocco beach-hopping, but if you were to insist, there's enough tempting coastline to fill even the most passionate ocean-lover's itinerary. Marc Chagall deemed the red-cliffed, rocky shores of Tossa de Mar (p. 341) "Blue Paradise." San Sebastián's (p. 405) calm, voluptuous Playa de la Concha has been an elite vacation destination for decades. The beaches of Galicia (p. 447) curve around miles of crystal-green, misty inlets, one of which has inspired a pagan cult, the "Ninth Wave.'" The Balearic and Canary Islands are a constant display of blackened, glistening bodies maximizing every inch of coastline, and southern Spain's infamous Costa del Sol (p. 242) brings tourists to its scorched Mediterranean bays by the plane-load. The eastern Costa Blanca (p. 291) mixes small-town charm with ocean expanses, and the looming cliffs and turquoise waters of Portugal's southern Algarve adorn hundreds of postcards. In Morocco, windsurfers flock to the ex-pirate cove Essaouira (p. 704) and sun-bathers escape the desert on the pristine sands of Agadir (p. 707).

NIGHTLIFE

Nightlife in Spain, Portugal, and Morocco can be relaxing, sipping a cold beer in a local bar or people-watching in the town square. But it can also be an experience of unabashed hedonism, the closest Dionysus has come to leaving the forest. Madrid (p. 112) has earned international renown as the "city that never sleeps"—its late-night clubs are so popular that highways are as jammed at 5am as they are at 5pm. Barcelona (p. 298) boasts the world's only mall complex made of discos (complete with escalators), as well as its own outdoor disco theme park, the Poble Espanol. Residents of Sevilla (p. 192) gather by the hundreds to drink and dance in the breezy air along the Guadalquivir River, and only on Ibiza (p. 487), the jetset's favorite party island, do clubs *open* at 4pm to catch crowds still going from the night before. Student-packed Salamanca (p. 151) is a crazed, international game of "find-your-fling," and Lagos, Portugal (p. 569) has more bars per square meter than any town in the world. Need we say more?

■ LET'S GO PICKS

BEST PLACE TO GET YOURSELF KILLED: Pamplona (S), on the horns of a stampeding bull (p. 396), or if you prefer, **Ciutadella** (S), under the hooves of a wild horse (p. 484).

BEST AFTER-AFTER-HOURS CLUB: Bora Bora, in Ibiza (S)—don't bother coming until late afternoon (p. 487), and you best not be sober.

BEST UNFINISHED BUILDING: La Sagrada Familia, Gaudí's masterpiece in Barcelona (S). 117 years under construction, and counting (p. 321).

BEST PLACE TO BE RIPPED OFF: Tangier (M)—who ever knew you had so many "friends" eager to help??? (p. 668)

BEST 5AM FOOD: Churros con choco-late (S), hands down. Hangovers have never felt this good.

BEST PLACE TO GET HIGH: Chefcha-ouen (M, p. 675) birthplace of much *hashish*, or gazing at the **Purple Isles** (M), once home to Jimi Hendrix (p. 707).

BEST MESSY FESTIVAL: La Tomatina, in tiny Buñol (S). For two hours every August, the entire town has a massive, juicy tomato war. No joke.

BEST PLACE TO TAN IN YOUR BIRTHDAY SUIT: The southern edge of Formentera (S), the Balearics' semi-deserted island paradise (p. 493).

BEST RELIGIOUS MONUMENT MADE OF DEAD PEOPLE: 5000 unwitting skeletons went into the making of the macabre **Capella de Ossos (Chapel of Bones)** in Évora (P, p. 585).

BEST TOILET: The velvet-covered baby seat in Aranjuez's **Palacio Real** (S). Even potty-training is easy for royalty. (p. 125).

BEST PLACE TO PICK UP A HOTTIE BACKPACKER: Lagos (P), playground of too many tanned Kiwi and Australian 20-somethings to count (p. 569).

BEST FRESH-SQUEEZED ORANGE JUICE: Fez (M), in the medina, for a mere 20 cents a pop (p. 683).

SUGGESTED ITINERARIES

SPAIN, PORTUGAL, AND MOROCCO (5 WEEKS) Start off in **Madrid** (4 days, 4 nights, p. 75), with daytrips to the austere palace of **El Escorial** (p. 122) and the medieval streets of **Toledo** (p. 127). Visit the university town of **Salamanca** (1 day, p. 151) and cross the border into **Portugal,** heading up to the unpretentious **Porto** (2 days, p. 627). Continue down the coast to the beach resort of **Figueira da Foz** (2 days, p. 621). Hit the sights, sounds, and cafes of **Lisbon** (2 days, 3 nights, p. 536) with a daytrip to the town of **Sintra** (1 day, p. 563). To the south lies Algarve; stop in **Lagos** (2 days, p. 569) to dance the night away. Catch your shut-eye on the 7hr. bus from Lagos to **Sevilla** (2 days, p. 192) and prepare for a romantic stroll along the Guadalquivir River. Delve deeper into its Arab roots and take a ferry from **Algeciras** to **Tangier, Morocco** (1 day, p. 668). Move on quickly to the imperial cities of **Fez** (2 days, p. 683) and **Marrakesh** (2 days, p. 709) which are much more enchanting. Stop by the coastal capital **Rabat** (1 day), and then swing back through Sevilla and Algeciras to **Córdoba, Spain** (2 days, p. 213), with its gargantuan Mezquita, and **Granada** (2 days, p. 259) home to the world-famous Alhambra. Head up the Mediterranean Coast to **Valencia** (1 day, p. 276), where the food—*paella* and oranges—rivals the new planetarium as Valencia's top attraction. Onwards to **Barcelona** (3 days, p. 298), one of Europe's most vibrant cities. After a tour of bizarre Modernista architecture and raging nightlife, sun on the beaches in **Tossa de Mar** (1 day, p. 341), visit the monastery in **Montserrat** (1 day, p. 333), or the Dalí museum in **Figueres** (1 day, p. 352). Continue on to **San Sebastián** (2 days, p. 405) and **Bilbao** (1 day, p. 416), home to the new Guggenheim Museum, before concluding your tour back in Madrid.

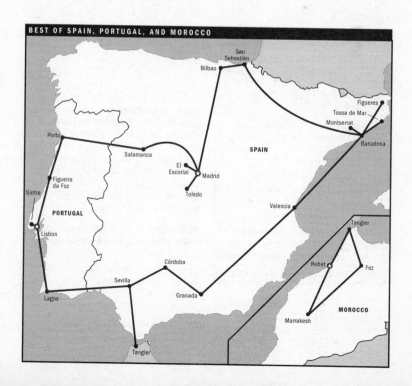

BEST OF SPAIN, PORTUGAL, AND MOROCCO

THE BEST OF SPAIN (3 WEEKS)

Begin in **Madrid** (4 days, 4 nights, p. 75), with daytrips to **El Escorial** (p. 122) and **Toledo** (p. 127). Then speed out to **Córdoba** (2 days, p. 213), and on to **Sevilla** (2 days, p. 192). Board the bus to the peaceful *pueblo blanco* (white town) of **Arcos de la Frontera** (1 day, p. 228) before heading south to the tanning fields of Spain's Costa del Sol. Layover in **Marbella** (1 day, p. 247) for raging nightlife and celebrity-watching. Peaceful beaches and relaxation await in **Nerja** (1 day, p. 249). Head inland to the cobblestoned streets and world-renowned Alhambra in **Granada** (2 days, p. 259). Cruise the the coast down to **Valencia** (1 day, p. 276). Indulge your athleticism with watersports on the beaches in **Gandía** (1 day, p. 286). Venture up the coast to Spain's jewel, **Barcelona** (2 days, p. 298), a pleasure for art and nightlife lovers alike. Worthwhile daytrips in Cataluña abound: partake of **Tossa de Mar's** beaches (1 day, p. 341), breathtaking mountain views from **Montserrat** (1 day, p. 333), or saying Hello Dalí in **Figueres** (1 day, p. 352). Hop a bus ride to the beaches and *tapas* of **San Sebastián** (2 days, p. 405). Finally, it's on to **Bilbao** (1 day, p. 416), home of the incredible Guggenheim museum.

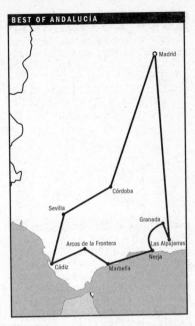

BEST OF ANDALUCÍA

THE BEST OF ANDALUCÍA (2 WEEKS)

Depart Madrid on the high-speed AVE train to **Córdoba** (2 days, p. 213), to tour the Mezquita mosque-turned-cathedral. Hop back on the AVE to **Sevilla** (2 days, p. 192) for prime sight-seeing. A quick trip down to Costa del Luz yeilds the soft-sanded beaches of **Cádiz** (2 days, p. 229). Move into the heart of Andalucía and the classic *pueblo blanco* **Arcos de la Frontera** (1 day, p. 228). Party with the beautiful people in the Costa del Sol resort town of **Marbella** (1 day, p. 247); rejuvenate on the peaceful beaches of **Nerja** (2 days, p. 249). Continue inland to **Granada** (2 days, p. 259), where the Alhambra and Albacín are sights for sore eyes. Fresh air awaits in the mountain town of **Alpujarras** (1 day, p. 269). Ride the rails back to Madrid.

BEST OF SPAIN

THE BEST OF PORTUGAL (2 WEEKS)

Begin in the busy capital **Lisbon** (2 days, 3 nights, see p. 536) and daytrip to fairy tale **Sintra** (1 day, see p. 563) Head down to the infamous beach-and-bar town **Lagos** (2-3 days, see p. 569) and spend an afternoon in **Sagres,** once considered the end of the world. Check out the creepy bone chapel in **Évora** (1 day, see p. 585) and the mysterious convent in **Tomar** (1 day, see p. 611). Bake on the beach in **Figueira da Foz** (1-2 days, see p. 621) then move on to the university town **Coimbra** (2 days, see p. 614). Finish in **Porto** (2 days, see p. 627), home of, you guessed it, sweet port wine.

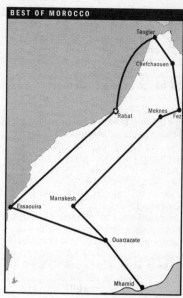

BEST OF MOROCCO

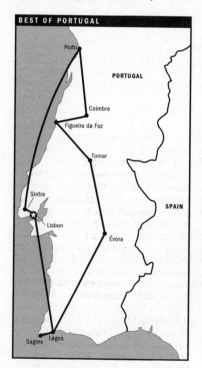

BEST OF PORTUGAL

THE BEST OF MOROCCO (2 WEEKS)

From Spain, hop on a ferry from Spanish **Algeciras** to **Tangier.** Not the highlight of Morocco, it's best viewed briefly. (1 day, p. 668). Make a quick departure to **Chefcha-oun** (1 day, see p. 675) for sweet relaxation. Experience the enchanting imperial cities of **Fez** (2 days, see p. 683), **Meknes** (2 days, see p. 676), and **Marrakesh** (2 days, seen p. 709). Probe deeper into the desserts in **Ouarzazate** (1 day, see p. 719). Back track through Marrakesh to beachside **Essaouira** (2 days, see p. 704) and travel up the coast to the capital **Rabat** (1 day, see p. 694) before ending in Tangier.

ESSENTIALS

DOCUMENTS AND FORMALITIES

ENTRANCE REQUIREMENTS

Passport (p. 9). Required for all citizens of United Kingdom, Canada, Australia, New Zealand, South Africa, Ireland and the United States.

Visa (p. 10). Required in addition to a passport for South Africans going to Spain, Portugal, and Morocco, and for Australians going to Portugal.

Work Permit (p. 48). Required for all foreigners planning to work in Spain, Portugal, and Morocco.

Driving Permit (p. 40). Required for all those planning to drive in Spain, Portugal, and Morocco.

CONSULAR SERVICES AT HOME

Questions concerning visas and passports go to consulates, not embassies (which handle weightier matters).

SPANISH

Australia: Embassy: 15 Arkana St., **Yarralumla,** ACT 2600. Mailing address: P.O. Box 9076, Deakin, ACT 2600 (☎ (02) 62 73 35 55; fax 62 73 39 18). **Consulates:** Level 24, St. Martins Tower, 31 Market St., **Sydney,** NSW 2000 (☎ (02) 92 61 24 33 or 92 61 24 43; fax 92 83 16 95); 540 Elizabeth St., 4th fl., **Melbourne,** VIC 3000 (☎ (03) 93 47 19 66 or 93 47 19 97; fax 93 47 73 30).

Canada: Embassy: 74 Stanley Ave., **Ottawa,** ON K1M 1P4 (☎ (613) 747-2252; fax 744-1224). **Consulates:** 1 Westmount Sq., Suite 1456, **Montreal,** PQ H3Z 2P9 (☎ (514) 935-5235; fax 935-4655); Simtoe Place, 200 Front St., Suite 2401, P.O. Box 15, **Toronto,** ON M5V 3K2 (☎ (416) 977-1661; fax 593-4949).

Ireland: Consulate: 17A Merlyn Park, Ballsbridge, **Dublin** 4 (☎ (01) 269 1640; fax 269 1854).

New Zealand: Embassy: Refer to Embassy in Australia.

South Africa: Embassy: 169 Pine St., Arcadia, P.O. Box 1633, **Pretoria** 0083 (☎ (012) 344 3875; fax 343 4891). **Consulate:** 37 Shortmarket St., **Cape Town** 8001 (☎ (012) 222 415; fax 222 328).

UK: Embassy: 39 Chesham Pl., **London** SW1X 8SB (☎ (020) 7235 5555; fax 7259 5392). **Consulates:** 20 Draycott Pl., **London** SW3 2RZ (☎ (020) 7589 8989; fax 7581 7888); Suite 1A, Brook House, 70, Spring Gardens, **Manchester** M2 2BQ (☎ (016) 1236 1233; fax 1228 7467); 63 N. Castle St., **Edinburgh** EH2 3LJ (☎ (013) 1220 1843, 1220 1439, or 1220 1442; fax 1226 4568).

US: Embassy: 2375 Pennsylvania Ave. NW, **Washington, D.C.** 20037 (☎ (202) 728-2330; fax 728-2308). **Consulates:** 150 E. 58th St., 30th fl., **New York,** NY 10155 (☎ (212) 355-4080; fax 644-3751); **others** in Boston, Chicago, Houston, Los Angeles, Miami, New Orleans, Puerto Rico, San Francisco, and Washington, D.C. www.spainemb.org.

PORTUGUESE

Australia: Embassy: 23 Culgoa Circuit, **O'Malley,** ACT 2603; mailing address P.O. Box 9092, Deakin, ACT 2600 (☎ (02) 62 90 17 33; fax 62 90 19 57). **Consulate:** Level 9 #30, Clarence St., **Sydney,** NSW 2000; mailing address P.O. Box 3309 (☎ (02) 92 62 59 91; fax 92 62 59 91).

Canada: Embassy: 645 Island Park Dr., **Ottawa,** ON K1Y OB8 (☎ (613) 729-0883; fax 729-4236). **Consulates:** 2020 University, Suite 1725, **Montréal,** QU H3A 2A5 (☎ (514) 499-0621 or 499-0359; fax 499-0366); 438 University Ave., Suite 1400, **Toronto,** ON M5G 2K8 (☎ (416) 217-0966 or 217-0971; fax 217-0973); 700 W. Pender St., Suite 904, **Vancouver,** BC V6C 1G8 (☎ (604) 688-6514; fax 685-7042).

New Zealand: Embassy: Refer to Embassy in Australia. **Consulates:** 33 Garfield St., Painell **Auckland** 5 (☎ (09) 309 1454; fax 308 9061); 21 Marion St., **Wellington** 1; mailing address P.O. Box 1024 (☎ (04) 382 6650; fax 382 6659).

South Africa: Embassy: 599 Leyds St., Mucklenuk, **Pretoria** (☎ (012) 341 2340; fax 341 3975). **Consulates:** Barclays Sq., 296 Walker St., Sunnyside, **Pretoria,** (☎ (012) 341 5522; fax 341 5690); Diamond Corner Building, 68 Eloff St., 3rd fl., **Johannesburg** (☎ (011) 293 8206; fax 333 9009); 320 W. St., 16th fl., P.O. Box 315, **Durban** (☎ (031) 305 7511; fax 304 6036).

UK: Embassy: 11 Belgrave Sq., **London** SW1X 8PP (☎ (020) 7235 5331; fax 7245 1287). **Consulate:** Silver City House, 62 Brompton Rd., **London** SW3 1BJ (☎ (020) 7581 8722; fax 7581 3085).

US: Embassy: 2125 Kalorama Rd. NW, **Washington, D.C.** 20008 (☎ (202) 328-8610; fax 462-3726). **Consulates:** 630 5th Ave., 8th fl., Suite 801, **New York,** NY 10111 (☎ (212) 246-4580 or 246-4582; fax 459-0190); **others** in Boston, Chicago, Coral Gables (FL), Houston, Honolulu, Los Angeles, Newark, New Bedford (MA), New Orleans, Philadelphia, Providence, San Francisco, San Juan (PR), Waterbury (CT), and Washington, D.C.

MOROCCAN

Australia: Embassy: 11 West St., Unit #2, **North Sydney,** NSW 2060 (☎ (02) 99 22 49 99; fax 99 23 10 53; email maroc@magna.com.au).

Canada: Embassy: 38 Range Rd., **Ottawa,** ON K1N 8J4 (☎ (613) 236-7391 or 236-7392; fax 236-6164). **Consulate:** 1010 Sherbrooke West St., Suite 1510, **Montreal,** QU H3A 2R7 (☎ (514) 288-8750; fax 288-4859).

South Africa: Embassy: 799 Shoeman St., **Pretoria** (☎ (012) 343 0230; fax 343 0613).

UK: Embassy: 49 Queens Gate Gardens, **London** SW7 5NE (☎ (020) 7581 5001; fax 7225 3862).

US: Embassy: 1601 21st St. NW, **Washington, D.C.** 20009 (☎ (202) 462-7979; fax 265-0161). **Consulates:** 10 East 40th. St., 23rd fl., **New York,** NY 10016 (☎ (212) 213-9644; fax 779-7441); 1821 Jefferson Place NW, **Washington, D.C.** 20036 (☎ (202) 462-7979; fax 452-0106).

CONSULAR SERVICES ABROAD

Foreign embassies and consulates located in Spain, Portugal, and Morocco are listed in the individual **Essentials** sections for each country (**Spain** p. 54, **Portugal** p. 521, **Morocco** p. 662). Consulates give legal advice and medical referrals and can readily contact relatives back home. In extreme cases, they may offer emergency financial assistance.

PASSPORTS

REQUIREMENTS. Citizens of Australia, Canada, Ireland, New Zealand, South Africa, the UK, and the US need valid passports to enter Spain, Portugal, and Morocco and to re-enter their own countries. For citizens of some countries, neither Spain, Portugal, nor Morocco allows entrance if the holder's passport expires in under six months; check with the appropriate consulate or embassy to see if this applies to you.

PHOTOCOPIES. Be sure to photocopy the page of your passport with your photo, passport number, and other identifying information, as well as any visas, travel insurance policies, plane tickets, or traveler's check serial numbers. Carry one set of copies in a safe place, apart from the originals, and leave another set at home. Consulates also recommend that you carry an expired passport or an official copy of your birth certificate in a part of your baggage separate from other documents.

ESSENTIALS

ESSENTIALS

LOST PASSPORTS. If you lose your passport, immediately notify the local police and the nearest embassy or consulate of your home government. To expedite its replacement, you will need to know all information previously recorded and show ID and proof of citizenship. In some cases, a replacement may take weeks to process, and it may be valid only for a limited time. Any visas stamped in your old passport will be irretrievably lost. In an emergency, ask for immediate temporary traveling papers that will permit you to re-enter your home country. Your passport is a public document belonging to your nation's government. You may have to surrender it to a foreign government official, but if you don't get it back in a reasonable amount of time, inform the nearest consulate of your home country.

NEW PASSPORT. File any new passport or renewal applications well in advance of your departure date. Most passport offices offer rush services for a steep fee. Citizens living abroad who need a passport or renewal should contact the nearest consular service of their home country.

Australia: Info ☎ 13 12 32; email passports.australia@dfat.gov.au; www.dfat.gov.au/passports. Apply for a passport at a post office, passport office (in Adelaide, Brisbane, Canberra, Darwin, Hobart, Melbourne, Newcastle, Perth, or Sydney), or overseas diplomatic mission. Passports AUS$128 (32-page) or AUS$192 (64-page); valid for 10 years. Children AUS$64 (32-page) or AUS$96 (64-page); valid for 5 years.

Canada: Canadian Passport Office, Department of Foreign Affairs and International Trade, Ottawa, ON K1A OG3 (☎ (613) 994-3500 or (800) 567-6868; www.dfait-maeci.gc.ca/passport). Applications available at passport offices, Canadian missions, and post offices. Passports CDN$60; valid for 5 years (non-renewable).

Ireland: Pick up an application at a *Garda* station or post office, or request one from a passport office. Then apply by mail to the Department of Foreign Affairs, Passport Office, Molesworth St., Dublin 2 (☎ (01) 671 1633; fax 671 1092; www.irlgov.ie/iveagh), or the Passport Office, Irish Life Building, 1A South Mall, Cork (☎ (021) 27 25 25). Passports IR£45; valid for 10 years. Under 18 or over 65 IR£10; valid for 3 years.

New Zealand: Send applications to the Passport Office, Department of International Affairs, P.O. Box 10526, Wellington, New Zealand (☎ (0800) 22 50 50 or (4) 474 8100; fax (4) 474 8010; www.passports.govt.nz; email passports@dia.govt.nz). Standard processing time is 10 working days. Passports NZ$80; valid for 10 years. Children NZ$40; valid for 5 years. 3 day "urgent service" NZ$160; children NZ $120.

South Africa: Department of Home Affairs. Passports are issued only in Pretoria, but all applications must still be submitted or forwarded to the nearest South African consulate. Processing time is 3 months or more. Passports around SAR80; valid for 10 years. Under 16 around SAR60; valid for 5 years. For more information, check out www.usaembassy.southafrica.net/VisaForms/Passport/Passport2000.html.

United Kingdom: Info ☎ (0870) 521 0410; www.open.gov.uk/ukpass/ukpass.htm. Get an application from a passport office, main post office, travel agent, or online (for UK residents only) at www.ukpa.gov.uk/forms/f_app_pack.htm. Then apply by mail or in person at a passport office. Passports UK£28; valid for 10 years. Under 15 UK£14.80; valid for 5 years. The process takes about 4 weeks; faster service (by personal visit to the offices listed above) costs an additional £12.

United States: Info ☎ (202) 647-0518; www.travel.state.gov/passport_services.html. Apply at any federal or state courthouse, authorized post office, or US Passport Agency (in most major cities); see the "US Government, State Department" section of the telephone book or a post office for addresses. Processing takes 3-4 weeks. New passports US$60; valid for 10 years. Under 18 US$40; valid for 5 years. Passports may be renewed by mail or in person for US$40. Add US$35 for 3-day expedited service.

TOURIST VISAS

As of August 2000, citizens of South Africa need a visa—a stamp, sticker, or insert in your passport specifying the purpose of your travel and the permitted duration of your stay—in addition to a valid passport for entrance to Spain, Portugal, or

GONE EUROPE. The idea of European unity has come a long way since 1958, when the European Economic Community (EEC) was created in order to promote solidarity and cooperation between its six founding states. Since then, the EEC has become the European Union (EU), with political, legal, and economic institutions spanning 15 member states: Austria, Belgium, Denmark, Finland, France, Germany, Greece, Ireland, Italy, Luxembourg, the Netherlands, Portugal, Spain, Sweden, and the UK.

What does this have to do with the average non-EU tourist? Well, 1999 established **freedom of movement** across 14 European countries—the entire EU minus Denmark, Ireland, and the UK, but plus Iceland and Norway. This means that border controls between participating countries have been abolished, and visa policies harmonized. While you're still required to carry a passport (or government-issued ID card for EU citizens) when crossing an internal border, once you've been admitted into one country, you're free to travel to all participating states. Britain and Ireland have also formed a **common travel area,** abolishing passport controls between the UK and the Republic of Ireland. For more important consequences of the EU for travelers, see The Euro (see p. 14) and European Customs and EU customs regulations (see p. 13).

Morocco; citizens of Australia need a visa to enter Portugal but not Morocco or Spain; and citizens of Canada, Ireland, the UK, the US, and New Zealand do not need visas to enter Spain, Portugal or Morocco. Visas vary in cost based on the length of stay and can only be obtained with extensive documentation on your planned activity in the country. Applications are available at the nearest consulate or embassy for the country to which you are traveling. In some cases they can also be filed in the foreign country (Morocco even requires that some applications be filed within Morocco itself), but generally speaking visa applications must be filed in your home country. Before departing, check with your local embassy or consulate of Spain, Portugal or Morocco for more detail on obtaining visas, as well as for the most recent information on entrance requirements. US citizens can also consult www.pueblo.gsa.gov/cic_text/travel/foreign/foreignentryreqs.html.

For more information on work and study visas, see **Alternatives to Tourism,** p.54.

IDENTIFICATION

When you travel, always carry two or more forms of identification on your person, including at least one photo ID; a passport combined with a driver's license or birth certificate is usually adequate. Many establishments, especially banks, may require several IDs in order to cash traveler's checks. Never carry all your forms of ID together; split them up in case of theft or loss. It is useful to bring extra passport-size photos to affix to the various IDs or passes you may acquire along the way.

STUDENT AND TEACHER IDENTIFICATION. The **International Student Identity Card (ISIC),** the most widely accepted form of student ID, provides discounts on sights, accommodations, food, transport, and even swimming pools. The ISIC is preferable to an institution-specific card (such as a university ID), although school cards are increasingly accepted in the large cities. All cardholders have access to a 24-hour emergency helpline for medical, legal, and financial emergencies (in North America call ☎ (877) 370-ISIC, elsewhere call US collect ☎ +1 (715) 345-0505), and US cardholders are also eligible for insurance benefits (see **Insurance,** p. 23). Most student travel agencies issue ISICs. The card costs AUS$15, CDN$15, or US$20. Applicants must be degree-seeking students of a secondary or post-secondary school and must be of at least 12 years of age. Because of the proliferation of fake ISICs, some services (particularly airlines) require additional proof of student identity, such as a school ID or a letter attesting to your student status, signed by your registrar and stamped with your school seal. The **International Teacher Identity Card (ITIC)** offers the same insurance coverage as well as similar but limited discounts. The fee is AUS$13,

UK£5, or US$20. For more info, contact the **International Student Travel Confederation (ISTC),** Herengracht 479, 1017 BS Amsterdam, Netherlands (☎ +31 (20) 421 28 00; fax 421 28 10; email istcinfo@istc.org; www.istc.org). The International Student Travel Confederation issues a discount card to travelers who are 26 years old or under, but are not students. This one-year **International Youth Travel Card** (**IYTC;** formerly the **GO 25** Card) offers many of the same benefits as the ISIC. Most organizations that sell the ISIC also sell the IYTC (US$20).

TOURIST BOARDS

SPANISH
Spain's official tourist board operates an extensive website at www.tourspain.es. It also has offices in Canada, the US, and the UK.

> **Canada:** Tourist Office of Spain, 2 Bloor Street West, Suite 3402, Toronto, ON M4W 3E2 (☎ (416) 961-3131; fax (416) 961-1992).

> **UK:** Spanish National Tourist Office, 22-23 Manchester Square, London W1M 5AP (☎ (171) 486 8077; fax (171) 486 8034; info.londres@tourspain.es).

> **US:** Tourist Office of Spain, 666 Fifth Avenue, 35th fl., New York, NY 10103 (☎ (212) 265-8822; fax (212) 265-8864). Additional offices in Chicago, IL (☎ (312) 642-1992), Beverly Hills, CA (☎ (323) 658-7188), and Miami, FL (☎ (305) 358-1992).

PORTUGUESE
The official Portuguese tourism website is located at www. portugalinsite.pt. There are also offices in Canada, the US, and the UK.

> **Canada:** Portuguese Trade and Tourism Commission, 60 Bloor St. West, Suite 1005, Toronto, ON M4W 3B8 (☎ (416) 921-7376; fax (416) 921-1353; iceptor@idirect.com).

> **United Kingdom:** Portuguese Trade and Tourism Office, 22-25A Sackville Street, 2nd-4th Floor, London W1X 2LY (☎ (20) 7474 1441; fax (20) 7494 1441, iceplond@aol.com).

> **United States:** Portuguese National Tourist Office, 590 Fifth Ave., 4th fl., New York, NY 10036 (☎ (212) 354-4403; fax (212) 764-6137, www.portugal.org). Additional office in Washington D.C. (☎ (202) 331-8222).

MOROCCAN
The official website for tourism in Morocco is www.tourism-in-morocco.com. There are also tourist offices located in Australia, Canada, and the US.

> **Australia:** Moroccan National Tourist Office, 2/11 West St., North Sydney NSW 2060 (☎ (02) 9922 4999; fax (02) 9923 1053; maroc@magna.com.au).

> **Canada:** Moroccan National Tourist Office, Place Montreal Trust, Suite 2450, 1800, Ave. McGill College, Montreal QC H3A 3J6 (☎ (514) 842-8111; fax (514) 842-5316).

> **United States:** Moroccan National Tourist Office, 20 East 46th St., Suite 1201, New York NY 10017 (☎ (212) 557-2520; fax (212) 949-8148). Additional office in Lake Buena Vista, FL (☎ (407) 827-5337).

CUSTOMS

Upon entering Spain, Portugal, or Morocco, you must declare certain items from abroad and pay a duty on the value of those articles that exceeds the allowance established by the country's customs service. Note that goods and gifts purchased at **duty-free** shops abroad are not exempt from duty or sales tax at your point of return and thus must be declared as well; "duty-free" merely means that you need not pay a tax in the country of purchase. Duty-free allowances were abolished for travel between EU member states on July 1, 1999, but still exist for those arriving from outside the EU. Upon returning home, you must similarly declare all articles acquired abroad and pay a duty on the value of articles in excess of your home country's allowance. In order to expedite your return, make a list of any valuables brought from home and register them with customs before traveling abroad. Also be sure to keep receipts for all goods acquired abroad. Spain and Morocco both have value-added taxes which can be redeemed upon leaving the country. See the **Essentials** sections for **Spain** (see p. 54) and **Morocco** (see p. 662) for more info.

EUROPEAN CUSTOMS. As well as freedom of movement of people within the EU (see p. 11), travelers can also take advantage of the freedom of movement of goods. This means that there are no customs controls at internal EU borders (i.e., you can take the blue customs channel at the airport), and travelers are free to transport whatever legal substances they like as long as it is for their own personal (non-commercial) use—up to 800 cigarettes, 10L of spirits, 90L of wine (60L of sparkling wine), and 110L of beer. You should also be aware that **duty-free** was abolished on June 30, 1999, for travel between EU member states; however, travelers between the EU and the rest of the world still get a duty-free allowance when passing through customs.

FURTHER RESOURCES

Australia: Australian Customs National Information Line (in Australia call ☎ (01) 30 03 63, from elsewhere call +61 (2) 6275 6666; www.customs.gov.au).

Canada: Canadian Customs, 2265 St. Laurent Blvd., Ottawa, ON K1G 4K3 (☎ (800) 461-9999 (24hr.) or (613) 993-0534; www.revcan.ca).

Ireland: Customs Information Office, Irish Life Centre, Lower Abbey St., Dublin 1 (☎ (01) 878 8811; fax 878 0836; taxes@revenue.iol.ie; www.revenue.ie/customs.htm).

New Zealand: New Zealand Customhouse, 17-21 Whitmore St., Box 2218, Wellington (☎ (04) 473 6099; fax 473 7370; www.customs.govt.nz).

South Africa: Commissioner for Customs and Excise, Privat Bag X47, Pretoria 0001 (☎ (012) 314 9911; fax 328 6478; www.gov.za).

United Kingdom: Her Majesty's Customs and Excise, Passenger Enquiry Team, Wayfarer House, Great South West Road, Feltham, Middlesex TW14 8NP (☎ (020) 8910 3744; fax 8910 3933; www.hmce.gov.uk).

United States: US Customs Service, 1330 Pennsylvania Ave. NW, Washington, D.C. 20229 (☎ (202) 354-1000; fax 354-1010; www.customs.gov).

MONEY

CURRENCY AND EXCHANGE

As a general rule, it's cheaper to convert money in Spain, Portugal, or Morocco than at home. However, you should bring enough foreign currency to last for the first 24 to 72 hours of a trip to avoid being penniless should you arrive after bank hours or on a holiday. Travelers from the US can get foreign currency from the comfort of home: **International Currency Express** (☎ (888) 278-6628) delivers foreign currency or traveler's checks overnight (US$15) or second-day (US$12) at competitive exchange rates.

When changing money abroad, try to go only to banks or change bureaus that have at most a 5% margin between their buy and sell prices. Since you lose money with every transaction, **convert large sums** (unless the currency is depreciating rapidly), **but no more than you'll need.**

If you use traveler's checks or bills, carry some in small denominations (the equivalent of US$50 or less) for times when you are forced to exchange money at disadvantageous rates, but bring a range of denominations since charges may be levied per check cashed. Store your money in a variety of forms; ideally, you will at any given time be carrying some cash, some traveler's checks, and an ATM and/or credit card. All travelers should also consider carrying some US dollars (or French francs in Morocco, about US$50 worth), which are often preferred by local tellers. Throwing around dollars for preferential treatment may be offensive, especially in Morocco, and it can attract thieves. It may also mark you as a foreigner and invite locals to jack up prices.

THE EURO Since 1999, the official currency of 11 members of the European Union—Austria, Belgium, Finland, France, Germany, Ireland, Italy, Luxembourg, the Netherlands, Portugal, and Spain—has been the euro. (As of January 2001, Greece will be admitted as well.) But you shouldn't throw out your francs, pesetas, and Deutschmarks just yet; actual euro banknotes and coins won't be available until January 1, 2002, and the old national currencies will remain legal tender for six months after that (through July 1, 2002).

While you might not be able to pay for a coffee and get your change in euros yet, the currency has some important—and positive—consequences for travelers hitting more than one euro-zone country. For one thing, money-changers across the euro-zone are obliged to exchange money at the official, fixed rate (see below), and at no commission (though they may still charge a small service fee). So now you can change your guilders into escudos and your escudos into lire without losing fistfuls of money on every transaction. Second, euro-denominated travelers cheques allow you to pay for goods and services across the euro-zone, again at the official rate and commission-free. The exchange rate between euro-zone currencies was permanently fixed on January 1, 1999 at 1 EUR = 40.3399 BEF (Belgian francs) = 1.95583 DEM (German marks) = 166.386 ESP (Spanish pesetas) = 6.55957 FRF (French francs) = 0.787564 IEP (Irish pounds) = 1936.27 ITL (Italian lire) = 200.482 PTE (Portuguese escudos). For more info, see www.europa.eu.int.

See the individual **Essentials** sections for **Spain** (see p. 54), **Portugal** (see p. 521) and **Morocco** (see p. 662) for currency exchange charts including local currency and US dollars, Canadian dollars, British pounds, Irish pounds, Australian dollars, New Zealand dollars, South African Rand, and European Union Euros.

TRAVELER'S CHECKS

Traveler's checks (**American Express** and **Visa** are the most recognized) are one of the safest and least troublesome means of carrying funds. Several agencies and banks sell them for a small commission. Each agency provides refunds if your checks are lost or stolen, and many provide additional services, such as toll-free refund hotlines abroad, emergency message services, and stolen credit card assistance.

While traveling, keep check receipts and a record of which checks you've cashed separate from the checks themselves. Also leave a list of check numbers with someone at home. Never countersign checks until you're ready to cash them, and always bring your passport (or a copy) with you to cash them. If your checks are lost or stolen, immediately contact a refund center to be reimbursed; they may require a police report verifying the loss or theft. Ask about toll-free refund hotlines and the location of refund centers (there are more in Spain than in Portugal, or Morocco) when purchasing checks, and always carry emergency cash.

American Express: Call ☎ (800) 251 902 in Australia; in New Zealand ☎ (0800) 441 068; in the UK ☎ (0800) 521 313; in the US and Canada ☎ (800) 221-7282. Elsewhere call US collect ☎ +1 (801) 964-6665; www.aexp.com. From Spain call toll-free ☎ (900) 994-426; from Portugal toll-free ☎ (0800) 844-080; and from Morocco ☎ (441) 273 35 71 00. Traveler's checks are available at 1-2% commission at AmEx offices, 1-4% at banks, and commission-free at AAA offices (see p. 28). *Cheques for Two* can be signed by either of 2 people traveling together.

Citicorp: In the US and Canada call ☎ (800) 645-6556; from Spain call ☎ (900) 97 44 30; from Portugal call ☎ (800) 844 140; and from Morocco and anywhere else call US collect ☎ +1 (813) 623-1709. Traveler's checks available at 1-2% commission. Call 24hr.

Thomas Cook MasterCard: In the US and Canada call ☎ (800) 223-7373; in the UK call ☎ (0800) 62 21 01; elsewhere call UK collect ☎ +44 (1733) 31 89 50. Checks available in 13 currencies at 2% commission. There are no Thomas Cook offices in Spain; banks accept their checks but will charge commission. In Portugal Marcus & Harting will cash checks commission-free in Faro, Lisbon, and the Algarve. In Morocco, Credit de Maroc will cash commission-free.

Visa: In the US call ☎ (800) 227-6811; in the UK call ☎ (0800) 89 50 78; elsewhere call UK collect ☎ +44 (1733) 31 89 49. Call for the location of their nearest office.

CREDIT CARDS

Where they are accepted, credit cards often offer superior exchange rates—up to 5% better than the retail rate used by banks and other currency exchange establishments. Credit cards may also offer services such as insurance or emergency help, and are sometimes required to reserve hotel rooms or rental cars. **MasterCard** and **Visa** are the most welcomed; **American Express** cards work at some ATMs and at AmEx offices and major airports. However, budget travelers will probably find that few of the establishments they frequent will accept credit cards; aside from the occasional splurge, you will probably use your credit card for emergencies only.

Credit cards are also useful for **cash advances,** which allow you to instantly withdraw pesetas, escudos, or dirhams from associated banks and ATMs throughout the country you are traveling in. However, transaction fees for all credit card advances (up to US$10 per advance, plus 2-3% extra on foreign transactions after conversion) tend to make credit cards a more costly way of withdrawing cash than ATMs or traveler's checks. In an emergency, however, the transaction fee may prove worth the cost. To be eligible for an advance, you'll need to get a **Personal Identification Number (PIN)** from your credit card company (see **Cash (ATM) Cards,** below). Be sure to check with your credit card company before you leave home, though; some companies have started to charge a foreign transaction fee.

CREDIT CARD COMPANIES. Visa (US ☎ (800) 336-8472) and **MasterCard** (US ☎ (800) 307-7309) are issued in cooperation with banks and other organizations. **American Express** (US ☎ (800) 843-2273) has an annual fee of up to US$55. AmEx cardholders may cash personal checks at AmEx offices abroad, access an emergency medical and legal assistance hotline (24hr.; in North America call ☎ (800) 554-2639, elsewhere call US collect +1 (202) 554-2639), and enjoy American Express Travel Service benefits (including plane, hotel, and car rental reservation changes; baggage loss and flight insurance; mailgram and international cable services; and held mail). The **Discover Card** (in US call ☎ (800) 347-2683, elsewhere call US +1 (801) 902-3100) offers small cashback bonuses on most purchases. These services are convenient, but beware that AmEx and Discover are only accepted about 20-40% of the time in Spain and Portugal, and even less in Morocco.

CASH (ATM) CARDS

Cash cards—popularly called ATM cards—are widespread in Spain, Portugal, and Morocco. Depending on the system that your home bank uses, you can most likely access your personal bank account from abroad. ATMs get the same wholesale exchange rate as credit cards, but there is often a limit on the amount of money you can withdraw per day (around US$500), and unfortunately computer networks sometimes fail. There is typically also a surcharge of US$1-5 per withdrawal. Be sure to memorize your PIN code in numeric form since machines elsewhere often don't have letters on their keys. Also, if your PIN is longer than four digits, ask your bank whether you need a new number.

The two major international money networks are **Cirrus** (US ☎ (800) 424-7787) and **PLUS** (US ☎ (800) 843-7587). To locate ATMs around the world, call the above numbers, or consult www.visa.com/pd/atm or www.mastercard.com/atm.

Visa TravelMoney is a system allowing you to access money from any Visa ATM, widespread throughout Spain, Portugal, and Morocco. You deposit an amount before you travel (plus a small administration fee), and you can withdraw up to that sum. The cards, which give you the same favorable exchange rate for withdrawals as a regular Visa, are especially useful if you plan to travel through many countries. In the US, call ☎ (877) 394-3347 to activate a card; from Spain ☎ (900) 95 11 25; from Portugal ☎ (0800) 81 14 26, and from Morocco and anywhere else call collect ☎ (410) 581-9091. **Road Cash** (US ☎ (877) 762-3227; www.roadcash.com) issues cards in the US with a minimum US$300 deposit.

GETTING MONEY FROM HOME

AMERICAN EXPRESS. Cardholders can withdraw cash from their checking accounts at any of AmEx's major offices and many representative offices (up to US$1000 every 21 days; no service charge, no interest). AmEx "Express Cash" withdrawals from any ATM are automatically debited from the cardholder's checking account or line of credit. Green card holders may withdraw up to US$1000 in any seven-day period (2% transaction fee; minimum US$2.50, maximum US$20). To enroll in Express Cash, cardmembers may call ☎ (800) 227-4669 in the US. Elsewhere call the US collect ☎ +1 (336) 668-5041 or call the following national numbers directly: in Spain, ☎ (900) 99 44 26; in Portugal ☎ (0800) 84 40 80; and in Morocco ☎ (441) 273 57 16 00.

WESTERN UNION. Travelers from the US, Canada, and the UK can wire money abroad through Western Union's international money transfer services. In the US, call ☎ (800) 325-6000; in Canada, ☎ (800) 235-0000; in the UK, ☎ (0800) 833 833. To wire money within the US using a credit card, call ☎ (800) CALL-CASH (225-5227). The rates for sending cash are generally US$10-11 cheaper than with a credit card, and the money is usually available at the place you're sending it to within an hour. To locate the nearest Western Union location, consult www.westernunion.com.

US STATE DEPARTMENT (US CITIZENS ONLY). In dire emergencies only, the US State Department will forward money within hours to the nearest consular office, which will then disburse it according to instructions for a US$15 fee. Contact the Overseas Citizens Service, American Citizens Services, Consular Affairs, Room 4811, US Department of State, Washington, D.C. 20520 (☎ (202) 647-5225; nights, Sundays, and holidays ☎ 647-4000; http://travel.state.gov).

COSTS

The cost of your trip will vary considerably, depending on where you go, how you travel, and where you stay. The single biggest cost of your trip will probably be your round-trip **airfare** to Spain, Portugal or Morocco (see p. 30). Before you go, spend some time calculating a reasonable per-day **budget** that will meet your needs. To give you a general idea, a bare-bones day (camping or sleeping in cheap hostels, buying food at supermarkets) in Spain would cost about US$35, in Portugal about US$25, and in Morocco about US$18. A slightly more comfortable day (sleeping in nicer hostels, eating one or two meals a day in restaurants, going out at night) would run US$50 in Spain, US$40 in Portugal, and US$30 in Morocco. For a luxurious day, the sky's the limit. Also, don't forget to factor in emergency reserve funds (at least US$200) when planning how much money you'll need.

Money From Home In Minutes.

If you're stuck for cash on your travels, don't panic. Millions of people trust Western Union to transfer money in minutes to 176 countries and over 78,000 locations worldwide. Our record of safety and reliability is second to none. For more information, call Western Union: USA 1-800-325-6000, Canada 1-800-235-0000. Wherever you are, you're never far from home.

www.westernunion.com

WESTERN UNION | MONEY TRANSFER

The fastest way to send money worldwide.

ESSENTIALS

TIPS FOR STAYING ON A BUDGET

Considering that saving just a few dollars a day over the course of your trip might pay for days or weeks of additional travel, the art of penny-pinching is well worth learning. Learn to take advantage of freebies: for example, museums will typically be free once a week or once a month, and cities often host free open-air concerts or cultural events (especially in the summer). Bring a sleepsack (see p. 24) to save on sheet charges in hostels, and do your laundry in the sink (unless you're explicitly prohibited from doing so). You can split accommodations costs (in hotels and some hostels) with trustworthy fellow travelers; multi-bed rooms almost always work out cheaper per person than singles. The same principle works for cutting down the cost of restaurant meals. You can also buy food in supermarkets instead of eating out; you'd be surprised how tasty (and cheap) varied sandwiches can be.

TIPPING, BARGAINING AND TAXES

See the individual **Essentials** sections for **Spain** (see p. 54), **Portugal** (see p. 521), and **Morocco** (see p. 662) for specifics on tipping, bargaining and taxes in each country.

SAFETY AND SECURITY

The following section is intended as a general guide; refer to the **Essentials** sections of **Spain** (p.67), **Portugal** (p.539) and **Morocco** (p.662) for more detailed info.

EXPLORING. To avoid unwanted attention, try to blend in as much as possible. Respecting local customs (in many cases, dressing more conservatively) may placate would-be hecklers. Familiarize yourself with your surroundings before setting out, and carry yourself with confidence; if you must check a map on the street, duck into a shop. If you are traveling alone, be sure someone at home knows your itinerary, and **never admit that you're traveling alone.**

GETTING AROUND. If you are using a **car,** learn local driving signals and wear a seatbelt. Children under 40 lbs. should ride only in a specially designed carseat, available for a small fee from most car rental agencies. Study route maps before you hit the road, and if you plan on spending a lot of time on the road, you may want to bring spare parts. If your car breaks down, wait for the police to assist you. For long drives in desolate areas, invest in a cellular phone and a roadside assistance program (see p. 40). Be sure to park your vehicle in a garage or well-traveled area, and use a steering wheel locking device in larger cities. **Sleeping in your car** is one of the most dangerous (and often illegal) ways to get your rest. For info on the perils of **hitchhiking,** see p. 42.

SELF DEFENSE. There is no sure-fire way to avoid all the threatening situations you might encounter when you travel, but a good self-defense course will give you concrete ways to react to unwanted advances. **Impact, Prepare, and Model Mugging** can refer you to local self-defense courses in the US (☎ (800) 345-5425) and Vancouver (☎ (604) 878-3838). Workshops (2-3hr.) start at US$50; full courses run US$350-500.

FINANCIAL SECURITY

PROTECTING YOUR VALUABLES. Spain and parts of Portugal are quite heavily touristed; along with that naturally comes a thriving pickpocket trade. Morocco is notorious for the prevalence of theft, even from hostel rooms and other supposedly secure places. But there are a few steps you can take to minimize the financial risk associated with traveling. First, **bring as little with you as possible.** Leave expensive watches, jewelry, cameras, and electronic equipment (like your Discman) at home; chances are you'd break them, lose them, or get sick of lugging them around any-

TRAVEL ADVISORIES. The following government offices provide travel information and advisories by telephone, by fax, or via the web:

Australian Department of Foreign Affairs and Trade: ☎ (2) 6261 1111; www.dfat.gov.au.

Canadian Department of Foreign Affairs and International Trade (DFAIT): In Canada call (800) 267-6788, elsewhere call ☎ +1 (613) 944-6788; www.dfait-maeci.gc.ca. Call for their free booklet, *Bon Voyage... But.*

New Zealand Ministry of Foreign Affairs: ☎ (04) 494 8500; fax 494 8511; www.mft.govt.nz/trav.html.

United Kingdom Foreign and Commonwealth Office: ☎ (020) 7238 4503; fax 7238 4545; www.fco.gov.uk.

US Department of State: ☎ (202) 647-5225, auto faxback (202) 647-3000; http://travel.state.gov. For *A Safe Trip Abroad,* call (202) 512-1800.

ESSENTIALS

way. Second, buy a few combination **padlocks** to secure your belongings either in your pack—which you should **never leave unattended**—or in a hostel or train station locker. Third, **carry as little cash as possible;** instead carry traveler's checks and ATM or credit cards, keeping them in a money belt—not a "fanny pack"—along with your passport and ID cards. Fourth, **keep a small cash reserve separate from your primary stash.** This should entail about US$50 (or the equivalent in French francs in Morocco) sewn into or stored in the depths of your pack, along with your traveler's check numbers and important photocopies. Be particularly careful on **buses** and **trains;** horror stories abound about determined thieves who wait for travelers to fall asleep. Carry your backpack in front of you where you can see it. Use good judgment in selecting a train compartment: never stay in an empty one, and use a lock to secure your pack to the luggage rack. Try to sleep on top bunks with your luggage stored above you (if not in bed with you), and keep important documents and other valuables on your person.

CON ARTISTS AND PICKPOCKETS. Among the more colorful aspects of large cities are con artists. They often work in groups, and children are among the most effective. They possess an innumerable range of ruses. Beware of certain classics: nice young men (or several) wanting to introduce themselves to the beautiful foreign lady, sob stories that require money, rolls of bills "found" on the street, or mustard spilled (or saliva spit) onto your shoulder to distract you while your bag is snatched. Don't ever hand over your passport to someone whose authority you question (ask to accompany them to a police station if they insist). Beware of pickpockets in city crowds, especially on public transportation. Also, be alert in public telephone booths. If you must say your calling card number, do so very quietly; if you punch it in, make sure no one can look over your shoulder.

DRUGS

Recreational drugs are illegal in Spain, Portugal, and Morocco. Possession of small amounts of marijuana sometimes goes unpunished in Spain and Portugal, but any attempt to buy or sell will definitely land you in jail or with a heavy fine. Morocco is infamous as a supplier of hashish to the Iberian Peninsula; don't be surprised if you are stopped and searched on your way into Spain. The Moroccan government enforces drug laws more strictly than most, and foreigners with drugs have regularly been arrested and faced severe punishment.

HEALTH

Common sense is the simplest prescription for good health while you travel. Travelers complain most often about their feet and their gut, so take precautionary measures: drink lots of fluids to prevent dehydration and constipation, wear sturdy, broken-in shoes and clean socks, and use talcum powder to keep your feet dry.

BEFORE YOU GO

Preparation can help minimize the likelihood of contracting a disease and maximize the chances of receiving effective health care in the event of an emergency. For tips on packing a basic **first-aid kit** and other health essentials, see p. 24.

In your **passport,** write the names of any people you wish to be contacted in case of a medical emergency, and also list any allergies or medical conditions of which you would want doctors to be aware. Matching a prescription to a foreign equivalent is not always easy, safe, or possible. If you know you are going to be taking medicine during your trip, take the time to find its foreign equivalent before leaving.

IMMUNIZATIONS AND PRECAUTIONS. Travelers over two years old should be sure that the following vaccines are up to date: MMR (for measles, mumps, and rubella); DTaP or Td (for diptheria, tetanus, and pertussis); OPV (for polio); HbCV (for haemophilus influenza B); and HBV (for Hepatitis B), although HBV is really only recommended for stays nearing six months. Adults traveling to Morocco on trips longer than four weeks should consider getting a Hepatitis A (or immune globulin) and typhoid vaccine four to six weeks before leaving. See the **Essentials** section for Morocco (p.539) for more specific information on staying healthy during a stay in North Africa. For recommendations on immunizations and prophylaxis, consult the CDC (see below) in the US or the equivalent in your home country, and be sure to check with a doctor for guidance.

USEFUL ORGANIZATIONS AND PUBLICATIONS. The US **Centers for Disease Control and Prevention (CDC;** ☎ (877) FYI-TRIP; www.cdc.gov/travel), is an excellent source of information for travelers, and maintains an international fax information service. The CDC's comprehensive booklet *Health Information for International Travelers,* an annual rundown of disease, immunization, and general health advice, is free on the website or US$22 via the Government Printing Office (☎ (202) 512-1800). The **US State Department** (www.travel.state.gov) compiles Consular Information Sheets on health, entry requirements, and other issues for various countries. The **British Foreign and Commonwealth Office** also gives health warnings for individual countries (www.fco.gov.uk).

MEDICAL ASSISTANCE ON THE ROAD. The following section offers general advice about medical help while traveling; see the **Essentials** sections for **Spain** (p. 54), **Portugal** (p. 521), and **Morocco** (p. 662) for more detailed info on each country.

Those with medical conditions (diabetes, allergies to antibiotics, epilepsy, heart conditions) may want to obtain a stainless-steel **Medic Alert** ID tag (first-year US$35, US$15 annually thereafter), which identifies the condition and gives a 24-hour collect-call number. Contact the Medic Alert Foundation, 2323 Colorado Ave, Turlock, CA 95382, USA (☎ (800) 825-3785; www.medicalert.org).

ON THE ROAD

ENVIRONMENTAL HAZARDS

Neither Spain, Portugal, nor Morocco has a very extreme climate; the biggest environmental threat for most travelers is the sun. Stay aware of how much time you're spending lying on Spanish beaches or sweating in Moroccan sand dunes.

Heat exhaustion and dehydration: Heat exhaustion, characterized by dehydration and salt deficiency, can lead to fatigue, headaches, and wooziness. Avoid it by drinking plenty of fluids, eating salty foods (e.g. crackers), and avoiding dehydrating beverages (e.g. alcohol, coffee, tea, and caffeinated soda). Continuous heat stress can eventually lead to heatstroke, characterized by a rising temperature, severe headache, and cessation of sweating. Victims should be cooled off with wet towels and taken to a doctor.

Sunburn: If you are planning on spending time near water, in the desert, or in the snow, you are at risk of getting burned, even through clouds. Apply sunscreen liberally.

High altitude: Allow your body a couple of days to adjust to less oxygen before exerting yourself. Note that alcohol is more potent and UV rays are stronger at high elevations.

INSECT-BORNE DISEASES

Be aware of insects in wet or forested areas, especially while hiking and camping. **Mosquitoes** are most active from dusk to dawn. Wear long pants and long sleeves, tuck your pants into your socks, and buy a mosquito net. Use insect repellents, such as DEET, and soak or spray your gear with permethrin (licensed in the US for use on clothing). Consider natural repellents that make you smelly to insects, like vitamin B-12 or garlic pills. To stop the itch after being bitten, try Calamine lotion or topical cortisones (like Cortaid), or take a bath with a half-cup of baking soda or oatmeal. **Ticks**—responsible for Lyme and other diseases—can be particularly dangerous in forested regions (in parts of northern Spain, for instance). Pause periodically while walking to brush off ticks using a fine-toothed comb on your neck and scalp. Do not try to remove ticks by burning them or coating them with nail polish remover or petroleum jelly.

Malaria: Extremely limited risk, only in some rural parts of Morocco. The incubation period varies from 6-8 days to as long as months. Early symptoms include fever, chills, aches, and fatigue, followed by high fever and sweating, sometimes with vomiting and diarrhea. See a doctor for any flu-like sickness that occurs after travel in a risk area. Left untreated, malaria can cause anemia, kidney failure, coma, and death. To reduce the risk of contracting malaria, use mosquito repellent, particularly in the evenings and when visiting forested areas, and take oral prophylactics, like **mefloquine** (sold under the name Lariam) or **doxycycline** (ask your doctor for a prescription).

Tick-borne encephalitis: A slight risk in the few forested areas of Spain and Portugal. A viral infection of the central nervous system transmitted during the summer by tick bites (primarily in wooded areas) or unpasteurized dairy products. While a vaccine is available in Europe, the immunization schedule is impractical, and the risk of contracting the disease is relatively low, especially if precautions are taken against tick bites.

Lyme disease: Also a slight risk in forested areas of Spain and Portugal. A bacterial infection carried by ticks and marked by a circular bull's-eye rash of 2 in. or more. Later symptoms include fever, headache, fatigue, and aches and pains. Antibiotics are effective if administered early. Left untreated, Lyme can cause problems in joints, the heart, and the nervous system. If you find a tick attached to your skin, grasp the head with tweezers as close to your skin as possible and apply slow, steady traction. Removing a tick within 24 hours greatly reduces the risk of infection.

FOOD- AND WATER-BORNE DISEASES

Prevention is the best cure: be sure that everything you eat is cooked properly and that the water you drink is clean. Peel your fruits and veggies and avoid tap water (including ice cubes and anything washed in tap water, like salad). Watch out for food from markets or street vendors that may have been cooked in unhygienic conditions. Other culprits are raw shellfish, unpasteurized milk, and sauces containing raw eggs. Buy bottled water, or purify your own water by bringing it to a rolling boil or treating it with **iodine tablets.** Always wash your hands before eating, or bring a quick-drying purifying liquid hand cleaner. Your bowels will thank you.

Traveler's diarrhea: Results from drinking untreated water or eating uncooked foods; a temporary (and fairly common) reaction to the bacteria in new food ingredients. Symptoms include nausea, bloating, urgency, and malaise. Try quick-energy, non-sugary foods with protein and carbohydrates to keep your strength up. Over-the-counter anti-diarrheals (e.g. Immodium) may counteract the problems, but can complicate serious infections. The most dangerous side effect is dehydration; drink 8 oz. of water with ½ tsp. of sugar or honey and a pinch of salt, try uncaffeinated soft drinks, or munch on salted crackers. If you develop a fever or your symptoms don't go away after 4-5 days, consult a doctor. Consult a doctor for treatment of diarrhea in children.

Dysentery: Results from a serious intestinal infection caused by certain bacteria. The most common type is bacillary dysentery, also called shigellosis. Symptoms include bloody diarrhea (sometimes mixed with mucus), fever, and abdominal pain and tenderness. Bacillary dysentery generally only lasts a week, but it is highly contagious.

ESSENTIALS

Amoebic dysentery, which develops more slowly, is a more serious disease and may cause long-term damage if left untreated. Seek medical help immediately. Dysentery can be treated with the drugs norfloxacin or ciprofloxacin (commonly known as Cipro). If you are traveling in Morocco (especially rural regions) consider obtaining a prescription before you leave home.

Hepatitis A: A viral infection of the liver acquired primarily through contaminated water. Symptoms include fatigue, fever, loss of appetite, nausea, dark urine, jaundice, vomiting, aches and pains, and light stools. The risk is highest in rural areas and the countryside, but it is also present in urban areas. Ask your doctor about the vaccine (Havrix or Vaqta) or an injection of immune globulin (IG; formerly called gamma globulin).

Parasites: Microbes, tapeworms, etc. that hide in unsafe water and food. **Giardiasis,** for example, is acquired by drinking untreated water from streams or lakes all over the world, including Spain, Portugal, and Morocco. Symptoms include swollen glands or lymph nodes, fever, rashes or itchiness, digestive problems, eye problems, and anemia. Boil water, wear shoes, avoid bugs, and eat only cooked food.

Typhoid fever: Some risk in Morocco, especially in rural areas. Caused by the salmonella bacteria; while mostly transmitted through contaminated food and water, it may also be acquired by direct contact with another person. Symptoms include fever, headaches, fatigue, loss of appetite, constipation, and sometimes a rash on the abdomen or chest. Antibiotics can treat typhoid, but a vaccination is usually recommended.

OTHER INFECTIOUS DISEASES

Rabies: Really only a risk for those who may be exposed to wild or domestic animals during their travel. Transmitted through the saliva of infected animals; fatal if untreated. If you are bitten, wash the wound thoroughly, seek immediate medical care. A rabies vaccine, which consists of 3 shots given over a 21-day period, is only semi-effective.

Hepatitis B: A viral infection of the liver transmitted via bodily fluids or needle-sharing. Vaccinations are recommended for health-care workers, sexually-active travelers, and anyone planning to seek medical treatment abroad. The 3-shot vaccination series must begin 6 months before traveling.

Hepatitis C: Like Hep B, but the mode of transmission differs. IV drug users, those with occupational exposure to blood, hemodialysis patients, and recipients of blood transfusions are at the highest risk, but the disease can also be spread through sexual contact or sharing items like razors and toothbrushes that may have traces of blood on them.

AIDS, HIV, STDS

For detailed information on **Acquired Immune Deficiency Syndrome (AIDS)** in Spain, Portugal, and Morocco, call the **US Centers for Disease Control's** 24-hour hotline at ☎ (800) 342-2437, or contact the **Joint United Nations Programme on HIV/AIDS (UNAIDS),** 20 av. Appia 20, CH-1211 Geneva 27, Switzerland (☎ +41 (22) 791 36 66, fax 791 41 87). Council's brochure, *Travel Safe: AIDS and International Travel,* is available at all Council Travel offices and on their website (www.ciee.org/Isp/safety/travelsafe.htm). Spain, Portugal, and Morocco may deny long-term residence to those who test HIV-positive, but they generally do not deny tourist, student and work visa applications on the basis of HIV status, even when medical tests are required (as they usually are to obtain a Spanish visa). Contact the nearest consulate of Spain, Portugal, or Morocco.

Sexually transmitted diseases (STDs) such as gonorrhea, chlamydia, genital warts, syphilis, and herpes are easier to catch than HIV and can be just as deadly. **Hepatitis B** and **C** are also serious STDs (see **Other Infectious Diseases,** above). Though condoms may protect you from some STDs, oral or even tactile contact can lead to transmission. Warning signs include swelling, sores, bumps, or blisters on sex organs, the rectum, or the mouth; burning and pain during urination and bowel movements; itching around sex organs; swelling or redness of the throat; and flu-like symptoms. If these symptoms develop, see a doctor immediately.

WOMEN'S HEALTH

Women traveling in unsanitary conditions are vulnerable to **urinary tract** and **bladder infections,** common and very uncomfortable bacterial conditions that cause a burning sensation and painful (sometimes frequent) urination. To try to avoid these infections, drink plenty of vitamin-C-rich juice and clean water, and urinate frequently, especially right after intercourse. Untreated, these infections can lead to kidney infections, sterility, and even death. If symptoms persist, see a doctor.

Vaginal yeast infections may flare up in hot and humid climates. Wearing loosely fitting trousers or a skirt and cotton underwear will help, as will over-the-counter remedies like Monostat or Gynelotrimin. Bring supplies from home if you are prone to infection, as it may be embarrassing, if not difficult, to explain your predicament to a foreign druggist. In a pinch, some travelers use a natural alternative such as a plain yogurt and lemon juice douche. Since **tampons, pads,** and reliable **contraceptive devices** are sometimes hard to find when traveling, you should consider bringing supplies with you.

Abortions are illegal in Spain, Portugal, and Morocco, but women considering an **abortion** while traveling can contact the **International Planned Parenthood Federation (IPPF),** Regent's College, Inner Circle, Regent's Park, London NW1 4NS (☎ (020) 7487 7900; fax 7487 7950; www.ippf.org), for guidance. In the US and Canada, the National Abortion Federation Hotline, (US ☎ (800) 772-9100, Canada ☎ (800) 424-2280; M-F 9am-7pm) provides referrals.

INSURANCE

Travel insurance generally covers four basic areas: medical or health problems, property loss, trip cancellation or interruption, and emergency evacuation. Although your regular insurance policies may well extend to travel-related accidents, you may consider purchasing travel insurance if the cost of potential trip cancellation or interruption is greater than you can absorb. Prices for travel insurance purchased separately generally run about US$50 per week for full coverage, while trip cancellation or interruption may be purchased separately at a rate of about US$5.50 per US$100 of coverage.

Medical insurance (especially university policies) often covers costs incurred abroad; check with your provider. **US Medicare** does not cover foreign travel. **Canadians** are protected by their home province's health insurance plan for up to 90 days after leaving the country; check with the provincial Ministry of Health or Health Plan Headquarters for details. **Homeowners' insurance** (or your family's coverage) often covers theft during travel and loss of travel documents (passport, plane ticket, railpass, etc.) up to US$500.

ISIC and **ITIC** (see p. 11) provide basic insurance benefits, including US$100 per day of in-hospital sickness for up to 60 days, US$3000 of accident-related medical reimbursement, and US$25,000 for emergency medical transport. Cardholders have access to a toll-free 24-hour helpline for medical, legal, and financial emergencies overseas (US and Canada ☎ (800) 626-2427, elsewhere call US collect ☎ +1 (713) 267-2525). **American Express** (US ☎ (800) 528-4800) grants most cardholders automatic car rental insurance (collision and theft, but not liability) and ground travel accident coverage of US$100,000 on flight purchases made with the card.

INSURANCE PROVIDERS. Council and **STA** (see p. 33) offer a range of plans that can supplement your basic coverage. Other private insurance providers in the **US and Canada** include: **Access America** (☎ (800) 284-8300); **Berkely Group/Carefree Travel Insurance** (☎ (800) 323-3149; www.berkely.com); **Globalcare Travel Insurance** (☎ (800) 821-2488; www.globalcare-cocco.com); and **Travel Assistance International** (☎ (800) 821-2828; www.worldwide-assistance.com). Providers in the **UK** include **Campus Travel** (☎ (018) 6525 8000) and **Columbus Travel Insurance** (☎ (020) 7375 0011). In **Australia,** try **CIC Insurance** (☎ 9202 8000).

ESSENTIALS

PACKING

Pack light: lay out only what you absolutely need, then take half the clothes and twice the money. The less you have, the less you have to lose (or store, or carry on your back). Any extra space left will be useful for any souvenirs or items you might pick up along the way. If you plan to do a lot of hiking, also see **Outdoors**, p. 26. If you plan to cover most of your itinerary by foot, a sturdy **frame backpack** is unbeatable. (For the basics on buying a pack, see p. 26.) Toting a **suitcase** or **trunk** is fine if you plan to live in one or two cities and explore from there, but a very bad idea if you're going to be moving around a lot. In addition to your main piece of luggage, a **daypack** (a small backpack or courier bag) is a must.

CLOTHING. No matter when you're traveling, it's a good idea to bring a warm jacket or wool sweater, a rain jacket (Gore-Tex is both waterproof and breathable), sturdy shoes or hiking boots, and thick socks. Flip-flops or waterproof sandals are crucial for grubby hostel showers. You may also want a nicer outfit than your jeans and t-shirt uniform. If you plan to visit any religious or cultural sites, remember that you'll need something besides tank tops and shorts to be respectful. For Spain, Portugal, and Morocco, especially if traveling during the summer, bringing cool, light clothing is a wise idea, as temperatures tend to soar.

SLEEPSACK. Some hostels require that you either provide your own linen or rent sheets from them. Save cash by making your own sleepsack: fold a full-size sheet in half the long way, then sew it closed along the long side and one short side.

CONVERTERS AND ADAPTERS. In Spain and Portugal, electricity is 220 volts AC; most of Morocco runs on 220V as well, though some smaller towns still have 110V outlets. **Americans** and **Canadians** should buy an **adapter** (which changes the shape of the plug) and a **converter** (which changes the voltage; US$20). Don't make the mistake of using only an adapter (unless appliance instructions explicitly state otherwise). **New Zealanders** and **South Africans** (who both use 220V at home) as well as **Australians** (who use 240/250V) won't need a converter, but will need a set of adapters to use anything electrical.

TOILETRIES. Toothbrushes, towels, cold-water soap, deodorant, razors, tampons, and condoms are often available, but may be difficult to find, so bring extras along. **Contact lenses** may be expensive and difficult to find, so bring enough extra pairs and solution for your entire trip. Also bring your glasses and a copy of your prescription in case you need emergency replacements.

FIRST-AID KIT. For a basic first-aid kit, pack bandages, aspirin or other painkillers, antibiotic cream, a thermometer, a Swiss Army knife, tweezers, moleskin, decongestant, motion-sickness remedy, diarrhea or upset-stomach medication (Pepto Bismol or Immodium), an antihistamine, sunscreen, insect repellent, burn ointment, and a syringe for emergencies (get an explanatory letter from your doctor).

FILM. Film and developing in Spain, Portugal, and Morocco can get expensive, so consider bringing along enough film for your entire trip and developing it at home. Less serious photographers may want to bring a **disposable camera** or two rather than an expensive permanent one. Despite disclaimers, airport security X-rays *can* fog film, so buy a lead-lined pouch at a camera store or ask security to hand inspect it. Always pack it in your carry-on luggage, since higher-intensity X-rays are used on checked luggage.

OTHER USEFUL ITEMS. For safety purposes, you should bring a **money belt** and small **padlock**. Quick repairs of torn garments can be done on the road with a needle and thread; also consider bringing electrical tape for patching tears. Doing your **laundry** by hand (where it is allowed) is both cheaper and more convenient than doing it at a laundromat—bring detergent, a small rubber ball to stop up the sink, and string for a makeshift clothes line. **Other things** you're liable to forget: an umbrella; sealable **plastic bags** (for damp or dirty clothes, soap, food, shampoo, and other spillables); an **alarm clock**; safety pins; rubber bands; a flashlight; earplugs; garbage bags; and a small **calculator**.

ACCOMMODATIONS

For more specific information on accommodations, see the **Essentials** sections for **Spain** (p. 70), **Portugal** (p. 532), and **Morocco** (p. 665).

HOSTELS

Hostels are generally dorm-style accommodations, often in single-sex large rooms with bunk beds, although some hostels do offer private rooms for families and couples. They sometimes have kitchens and utensils for your use, bike or moped rentals, storage areas, and laundry facilities. There can be drawbacks: some hostels close during certain daytime "lockout" hours, have a curfew, don't accept reservations, impose a maximum stay, or, less frequently, require that you do chores. See the **Essentials** sections for Spain, Portugal, and Morocco for more country-specific information on accommodations.

HOSTELLING INTERNATIONAL

Joining the youth hostel association in your own country (listed below) automatically grants you membership privileges in **Hostelling International (HI)**, a federation of national hosteling associations, which offer accommodations at significantly cheaper prices than private lodgings. HI hostels are scattered throughout Spain and Portugal (though not Morocco) and many accept reservations via the **International Booking Network** (Australia ☎ (02) 9261 1111; Canada ☎ (800) 663-5777; England and Wales ☎ (1629) 58 14 18; Northern Ireland ☎☎ (1232) 32 47 33; Republic of Ireland ☎ (01) 830 1766; New Zealand ☎ (09) 379 4224; Scotland ☎ (541) 55 32 55; US ☎ (800) 909-4776). HI's umbrella organization's web page (www.iyhf.org), which lists the web sites and phone numbers of all national associations, can be a great beginning to researching hosteling in a specific region. Other comprehensive websites include www.hostels.com and www.eurotrip.com/accommodation.

Most HI hostels also honor **guest memberships**—you'll get a blank card with space for six validation stamps. Each night you'll pay a nonmember supplement (one-sixth the membership fee) and earn one guest stamp; get six stamps, and you're a member. Some receptionists may need to be reminded of the policy. Most student travel agencies (see p. 33) sell HI cards, as do all of the national hosteling organizations listed below. All prices listed below are valid for **one-year memberships** unless otherwise noted.

Australian Youth Hostels Association (AYHA), 422 Kent St., Sydney NSW 2000 (☎ (02) 9261 1111; fax 9261 1969; www.yha.org.au). AUS$49, under 18 AUS$14.50.

Hostelling International-Canada (HI-C), 400-205 Catherine St., Ottawa, ON K2P 1C3 (☎ (800) 663-5777 or (613) 237-7884; fax 237-7868; email info@hostellingintl.ca; www.hostellingintl.ca). CDN$25, under 18 CDN$12.

An Óige (Irish Youth Hostel Association), 61 Mountjoy St., Dublin 7 (☎ (1) 830 4555; fax 830 5808; email anoige@iol.ie; www.irelandyha.org). IR£10, under 18 IR£4.

Youth Hostels Association of New Zealand (YHANZ), P.O. Box 436, 173 Cashel St., Christchurch 1 (☎ (03) 379 9970; fax 365 4476; email info@yha.org.nz; www.yha.org.nz). NZ$40, ages 15-17 NZ$12, under 15 free.

Hostels Association of South Africa, 3rd fl. 73 St. George's St. Mall, P.O. Box 4402, Cape Town 8000 (☎ (021) 424 2511; fax 424 4119; email info@hisa.org.za; www.hisa.org.za). SAR50, under 18 SAR25, lifetime SAR250.

Scottish Youth Hostels Association (SYHA), 7 Glebe Crescent, Stirling FK8 2JA (☎ (01786) 89 14 00; fax 89 13 33; www.syha.org.uk). UK£6, under 18 UK£2.50.

Youth Hostels Association (England and Wales) Ltd., Trevelyan House, 8 St. Stephen's Hill, St. Albans, Hertfordshire AL1 2DY, UK (☎ (01727) 85 52 15; fax 84 41 26; www.yha.org.uk). UK£12, under 18 UK£6, families UK£24.

Hostelling International Northern Ireland (HINI), 22-32 Donegall Rd., Belfast BT12 5JN, Northern Ireland (☎ (01232) 32 47 33; fax 43 96 99; email info@hini.org.uk; www.hini.org.uk). UK£7, under 18 UK£3.

Hostelling International-American Youth Hostels (HI-AYH), 733 15th St. NW, #840, Washington, D.C. 20005 (☎ (202) 783-6161 ext. 136; fax 783-6171; email hiayh-serv@hiayh.org; www.hiayh.org). US$25, under 18 free.

HOTELS, GUESTHOUSES, AND PENSIONS

Hotel singles in Spain cost about US$20 per night, doubles US$35-40. In Portugal rates run US$20-30. You'll typically share a hall bathroom; a private bathroom will cost extra, as may hot showers. Some hotels offer "full pension" (all meals) and "half pension" (no lunch). Smaller **guesthouses** and **pensions** are often cheaper than hotels. If you make **reservations** in writing, indicate your night of arrival and the number of nights you plan to stay. The hotel will send you a confirmation and may request payment for the first night. Not all hotels take reservations, and few accept checks in foreign currency. Enclosing two International Reply Coupons will ensure a prompt reply (each US$1.05; available at any post office).

DORMS

Many **colleges and universities** open their residence halls to travelers when school is not in session; some do so even during term-time. These dorms are often close to student areas—good sources for information on things to do—and are usually very clean. Getting a room may take a couple of phone calls and require advanced planning, but rates tend to be low, and many offer free local calls. See listings within individual towns.

CAMPING AND THE OUTDOORS

For more specific information on camping, see the **Essentials** sections of **Spain** (p. 71), **Portugal** (p. 533), and **Morocco** (p. 666).

CAMPING AND HIKING EQUIPMENT

Good camping equipment is both sturdy and light. Camping equipment is generally more expensive in Australia, New Zealand, and the UK than in North America.

Sleeping Bag: Most sleeping bags are rated by season ("summer" means 30-40°F at night; "four-season" or "winter" often means below 0°F). Sleeping bags are made either of **down** (warmer and lighter, but more expensive, and miserable when wet) or of **synthetic** material (heavier, more durable, and warmer when wet). Prices may range from US$80-210 for a summer synthetic to US$250-300 for a good down winter bag. **Sleeping bag pads** include foam pads (US$10-20), air mattresses (US$15-50), and Therm-A-Rest self-inflating pads (US$45-80). Bring a **stuff sack** to store your bag and keep it dry.

Tent: The best tents are free-standing (with their own frames and suspension systems), set up quickly, and only require staking in high winds. Low-profile dome tents are the best all-around. Good 2-person tents start at US$90, 4-person at US$300. Seal the seams of your tent with waterproofer, and make sure it has a rain fly. Other tent accessories include a **battery-operated lantern**, a **plastic groundcloth**, and a **nylon tarp.**

Backpack: Internal-frame packs mold better to your back, keep a lower center of gravity, and flex adequately to allow you to hike difficult trails. **External-frame packs** are more comfortable for long hikes over even terrain, as they keep weight higher and distribute it more evenly. Make sure your pack has a strong, padded hip-belt to transfer weight to your legs. Any serious backpacking requires a pack of at least 4000 cu. in. (16,000cc), plus 500 cu. in. for sleeping bags in internal-frame packs. Sturdy backpacks cost anywhere from US$125-420—this is one area in which it doesn't pay to economize. Either buy a **waterproof backpack cover,** or store all of your belongings in plastic bags inside your pack.

Boots: Be sure to wear hiking boots with good **ankle support.** They should fit snugly and comfortably over 1-2 pairs of wool socks and thin liner socks. Break in boots over several weeks first in order to spare yourself from painful and debilitating blisters.

Other Necessities: Synthetic layers, like those made of polypropylene, and a **pile jacket** will keep you warm even when wet. A **"space blanket"** will help you retain your body heat and doubles as a groundcloth (US$5-15). Plastic **water bottles** are virtually shatter- and leak-proof. Bring **water-purification tablets** for when you can't boil water. Although most campgrounds provide campfire sites, you may want to bring a small **metal grate** or **grill** of your own. For those places that forbid fires or the gathering of firewood (this includes virtually every organized campground in Europe), you'll need a **camp stove** (the classic Coleman starts at US$40) and a propane-filled **fuel bottle** to operate it. Also don't forget a **first-aid kit, pocketknife, insect repellent, calamine lotion,** and **waterproof matches** or a **lighter.**

WILDERNESS SAFETY

Stay warm, stay dry, and stay hydrated. The vast majority of life-threatening wilderness situations can be avoided by following this simple advice. Prepare yourself for an emergency, however, by always packing raingear, a hat and mittens, a first-aid kit, a reflector, a whistle, high energy food, and extra water for any hike. Dress in wool or warm layers of synthetic materials designed for the outdoors; never rely on cotton for warmth, as it is absolutely useless when wet.

Hiking in Morocco, particularly the desert, requires extra precaution. Beware of **snakes, scorpions**, and other desert creatures, such as the palm rat, whose bite is often poisonous and occasionally deadly. If you run low on water, do not try to ration it; one of the most common incidents of death or dehydration in the desert comes from hikers who try to save their water for later. The Moroccan **sun** is also very strong; wear protective clothing and sunblock to avoid dizziness and headaches, signs of **heatstroke.**

KEEPING IN TOUCH

MAIL

See the individual **Essentials** sections for **Spain** (see p. 54), **Portugal** (see p. 521), and **Morocco** (see p. 662) for more detailed information about mailing from abroad. Sending airmail to Spain from the US requires between four and seven days. To Portugal, allow seven to 10 days. Airmail to Morocco usually requires around two weeks, but it could either go more quickly or much more slowly. Mailing from European locations to any of these countries is a few days faster; from Australia, New Zealand, or South Africa, a couple of days slower. Mail sent to smaller towns will take longer. Envelopes should be marked "air mail" or "par avion." There are several ways to arrange pick-up of letters sent to you while you are abroad.

GENERAL DELIVERY

Mail can be sent internationally through *Lista de Correos* in Spain, *Posta Restante* in Portugal, or *Poste Restante* in Morocco. The mail will go to a special desk in the central post office, unless you specify a post office by street address or postal code. As a rule, it is best to use the largest post office in the area, and mail may be sent there regardless of what is written on the envelope. It is usually safer and quicker to send mail express or registered. When picking up your mail, bring a form of photo ID, preferably a passport. There is generally no surcharge; if there is a charge, it should not exceed the cost of postage. If the clerks insist there is nothing for you, have them check under your first name as well. Mark the envelope "HOLD" and address it with the last name capitalized and underlined, as follows:

Spain: <u>DUBNER</u>, Joe; Lista de Correos; City Name; Postal Code; SPAIN; AIR MAIL.

Portugal: <u>HERMAN</u>, PeeWee; Posta Restante; Post Office Street Address; City Name; Postal Code; PORTUGAL; AIR MAIL.

Morocco: It is best to send mail to a major hotel or AmEx office instead. If you want to try, mail should be addressed as follows: <u>COLBURN</u>, Katherine; Poste Restante; Post Office Address; City Name; MOROCCO; AIR MAIL.

AMERICAN EXPRESS. AmEx's travel offices throughout Iberia and Morocco will act as a mail service for cardholders if you contact them in advance. Under this free **Client Letter Service,** they will hold mail for up to 30 days and forward upon request. Address the letter in the same way shown above. Some offices will offer these services to non-cardholders (especially those who have purchased AmEx Travelers Cheques), but you must call ahead to make sure. *Let's Go* lists AmEx office locations for most large cities. AmEx also has a free complete list (☎ 800-528-4800).

OTHER OPTIONS. If regular airmail is too slow, **Federal Express** (US ☎ (800) 247-4747; Spain 900 10 08 71; Portugal 913 29 99 00; Morocco 212 254 21 33) can get a letter from New York to Madrid in two days for a whopping US$50; rates among non-US locations are similarly expensive (London to Madrid, for example, costs upwards of US$45). For a cheaper alternative, try **DHL** (US ☎ (800) 225-5345; Spain 902 12 24 24; Portugal 18 10 00 80; Morocco 297 20 20), which can get a document from New York to Madrid in one to two days for US$39. By **US Express Mail,** a letter from New York would arrive within four days and would cost US$19.

Surface mail is by far the cheapest and slowest way to send mail. It takes one to three months to cross the Atlantic and two to four to cross the Pacific—appropriate for sending large quantities of items you won't need to see for a while. When ordering books and materials from abroad, always include one or two **International Reply Coupons (IRCs)**—a way of providing the postage to cover delivery. IRCs should be available from your local post office and those abroad (US$1.05).

TELEPHONES

CALLING SPAIN, PORTUGAL, OR MOROCCO FROM HOME
Let's Go lists the city **telephone code** under **Practical Information** in Portugal, and Morocco. Spain no longer has city or area codes. The bracketed 0 for Morocco codes is necessary only if you are calling from a different area code within the same country. If you are calling from another country, you will not need to dial the parenthesized number. For example, we have listed the telephone code for Asilah as (0)9. To reach Asilah from elsewhere in Morocco, dial 01, then the number. To reach Asilah from another country, dial 1, then the number. **Portugal has just changed access to its telephone system** by adding a 2 to all previous city codes. See the **Essentials** section for **Portugal** (p.539) for more information on the change. **To place a direct international call,** dial:

1. The international access code of your home country. **International access codes** include: Australia 0011; Ireland 00; New Zealand 00; South Africa 09; UK 00; US 011. Country and city codes are sometimes listed with a zero in front (e.g., 033), but after dialing the international access code, drop successive zeros (e.g., with an access code of 011, dial 011 33).

2. The **country code:** Spain 034, Portugal 351, Morocco 212.

3. For Portugal or Morocco, the city code (see the city's **Practical Information** section).

4. The local number.

CALLING FROM SPAIN, PORTUGAL, OR MOROCCO
For more country-specific information about telephones abroad, see the **Essentials** sections of **Spain** (p. 71), **Portugal** (p. 533), or **Morocco** (p. 666). Most useful communication information (including **international access codes, calling card numbers, country codes, operator** and **directory assistance,** and **emergency numbers**) is also listed on the inside back cover of this book.

Wherever possible, use a **calling card** (see below) for international phone calls, as the long-distance rates for national phone services are often exorbitant. You can usually make direct international calls from pay phones, but if you aren't using a calling card you may need to drop your coins as quickly as your words. Where available, prepaid phone cards and occasionally major credit cards can be used for direct international calls, but they are still less cost-efficient. Look for pay phones in public areas, especially train stations, as private pay phones are often more expensive. Although incredibly convenient, in-room hotel calls invariably include an arbitrary and sky-high surcharge (as much as US$10).

The expensive alternative to dialing direct or using a calling card is using an international operator to place a **collect call.** An English-speaking operator from your home nation can be reached by dialing the appropriate service provider listed above; they will typically place a collect call even if you don't have one of their phone cards.

CALLING CARDS

Setting up a calling card account is probably your best and cheapest bet for making calls from overseas. Calls are billed either collect or to your account. **MCI WorldPhone** also provides access to MCI's Traveler's Assist, which gives legal and medical advice, exchange rate information, and translation services. Other phone companies provide similar services to travelers. **To obtain a calling card** from your national telecommunications service before you leave home, contact the appropriate company below.

Australia: Telstra Australia Direct (☎ 13 22 00).

Canada: Bell Canada **Canada Direct** (☎ (800) 565-4708).

Ireland: Telecom Éireann **Ireland Direct** (☎ (800) 25 02 50).

New Zealand: Telecom New Zealand (☎ (0800) 00 00 00).

South Africa: Telkom South Africa (☎ 09 03).

UK: British Telecom **BT Direct** (☎ (800) 34 51 44).

US: AT&T (☎ (888) 288-4685), **Sprint** (☎ (800) 877-4646), or **MCI** (☎ (800) 444-4141).

PLACING INTERNATIONAL CALLS. To call Spain from home or to place an international call from Spain, dial:

1. The **international dialing prefix.** To dial out of **Australia,** dial 0011; **Canada** or the **US,** 011; the **Republic of Ireland, New Zealand,** or the **UK,** 00; **South Africa,** 09; **Spain,** 07.
2. The **country code** of the country you want to call. To call **Australia,** dial 61; **Canada** or the **US,** 1; the **Republic of Ireland,** 353; **New Zealand,** 64; **South Africa,** 27; the **UK,** 44.
3. The **city** or **area code.** *Let's Go* lists the phone codes for cities and towns in Portugal and Morocco opposite the city or town name, alongside the following icon: ☎. If the first digit is a zero (e.g., 09 for Tangier), omit it when calling from abroad (e.g., dial 011 212 9 from Canada to reach Tangier).
4. The **local number.**

CALLING WITHIN SPAIN, PORTUGAL, AND MOROCCO

The simplest way to call within the country is to use a coin-operated phone. **Prepaid phone cards** (available at newspaper kiosks and tobacco stores), which carry a certain amount of phone time depending on the card's denomination, usually save time and money in the long run. The computerized phone will tell you how much time, in units, you have left on your card. Another kind of prepaid telephone card comes with a Personal Identification Number (PIN) and a toll-free access number. Instead of inserting the card into the phone, you call the access number and follow the directions on the card. These cards can be used to make international as well as domestic calls. Phone rates tend to be highest in the morning, lower in the evening, and lowest on Sunday and late at night.

ESSENTIALS

TIME DIFFERENCES

Greenwich Mean Time (GMT) is five hours ahead of New York time, eight hours ahead of Vancouver and San Francisco time, two hours behind Johannesburg time, ten hours behind Sydney time, and twelve hours behind Auckland time. Some countries ignore **daylight savings time,** and fall and spring switchover times vary.

Spain is two hours ahead of GMT in the summer during daylight savings time, and one hour ahead during the winter. Portugal keeps daylight savings time as well, and is one hour behind Spain year round (one hour ahead of GMT in summer and at GMT in winter). Morocco does not change time; they are always on GMT.

EMAIL AND INTERNET

Email is an attractive communication option and increasingly easy to access in Spain, Portugal, and Morocco. Though in some places it's possible to forge a remote link with your home server, in most cases this is a much slower (and thus more expensive) option than taking advantage of free **web-based email accounts** (e.g., www.hotmail.com and www.yahoo.com). Travelers with laptops can call an Internet service provider via a **modem.** Long-distance phone cards specifically intended for such calls can defray normally high phone charges; check with your long-distance phone provider to see if it offers this option. **Internet cafes** and the occasional free Internet terminal at a public library or university are listed in the **Orientation and Practical Information** sections of major cities.

GETTING THERE

For country-specific information on traveling, travel organizations, and travel discounts within Spain, Portugal, and Morocco, see the **Getting There and Around** sections for **Spain, Portugal,** and **Morocco.** Much of the following general information refers to planning your trip to and from these countries and for general European travel.

Fares on all modes of transportation are either "single" (one-way) or "return" (round-trip). "Period returns" require you to return within a specific number of days; "day return" means you must return on the same day. Unless stated otherwise, *Let's Go* always lists single fares. Round-trip fares on trains and buses are generally 75% above the one-way fares.

BY PLANE

When it comes to airfare, a little effort can save you a bundle. If your plans are flexible enough to deal with the restrictions, courier fares are the cheapest. Tickets bought from consolidators and standby seating are also good deals, but last-minute specials, airfare wars, and charter flights often beat these fares. The key is to hunt around, to be flexible, and to ask persistently about discounts. Students, seniors, and those under 26 should never pay full price for a ticket.

DETAILS AND TIPS

Timing: Airfares to Spain, Portugal, and Morocco peak between mid-June and early September; holidays are also expensive. Midweek (M-Th morning) round-trip flights run US$40-50 cheaper than weekend flights, but they are generally more crowded and less likely to permit frequent-flier upgrades. Traveling with an "open return" ticket can be pricier than fixing a return date when buying the ticket and paying later to change it.

Route: Round-trip flights are by far the cheapest; "open-jaw" (arriving in and departing from different cities) tickets tend to be pricier. Patching one-way flights together is the most expensive way to travel.

Round-the-World (RTW): If Spain, Portugal, or Morocco is only 1 stop on a more extensive globe-hop, consider a RTW ticket. Tickets usually include at least 5 stops and are valid for about a year; prices range US$1200-5000. Try **Northwest Airlines/KLM** (US ☎ (800) 447-4747; www.nwa.com) or **Star Alliance,** a consortium of 13 airlines including United Airlines (US ☎ (800) 241-6522; www.star-alliance.com).

Gateway Cities: Flights between capitals or regional hubs will offer the cheapest fares. The cheapest gateway cities in Spain, Portugal, and Morocco are typically Madrid, Lisbon, and either Rabat or Casablanca.

Boarding: Confirm international flights by phone within 72hr. of departure. Most airlines require that passengers arrive at the airport at least 2hr. before departure. One carry-on item and 2 checked bags is the norm for non-courier flights.

BUDGET AND STUDENT TRAVEL AGENCIES

While knowledgeable agents specializing in flights to Spain, Portugal, and Morocco can make your life easy and help you save, they may not spend the time to find you the lowest possible fare—they get paid on commission. Students and under-26ers holding **ISIC and IYTC cards** (see p. 11), respectively, qualify for big discounts from student travel agencies.

usit world (www.usitworld.com). Over 50 **usit campus** branches in the UK (www.usitcampus.co.uk), including 52 Grosvenor Gardens, **London** SW1W 0AG (☎ (0870) 240 1010); **Manchester** (☎ (0161) 273 1721); and **Edinburgh** (☎ (0131) 668 3303). Nearly 20 **usit now** offices in Ireland, including 19-21 Aston Quay, O'Connell Bridge, **Dublin** 2 (☎ (01) 602 1600; www.usitnow.ie), and **Belfast** (☎ (02890) 327 111; www.usitnow.com). Affiliated offices are also in both Spain and Portugal, including Plaza Callao 3, **Madrid** (☎ 915 31 10 00) and Rua Camilo Castelo Branco, 20, **Lisbon** (☎ (21) 352 59 86). Offices also in Athens, Auckland, Brussels, Frankfurt, Johannesburg, Luxembourg, Paris, Sofia, and Warsaw.

Council Travel (www.counciltravel.com). US offices include: Emory Village, 1561 N. Decatur Rd., **Atlanta**, GA 30307 (☎ (404) 377-9997); 273 Newbury St., **Boston**, MA 02116 (☎ (617) 266-1926); 1160 N. State St., **Chicago**, IL 60610 (☎ (312) 951-0585); 931 Westwood Blvd., Westwood, **Los Angeles**, CA 90024 (☎ (310) 208-3551); 254 Greene St., **New York**, NY 10003 (☎ (212) 254-2525); 530 Bush St., **San Francisco**, CA 94108 (☎ (415) 566-6222); 424 Broadway Ave E., **Seattle**, WA 98102 (☎ (206) 329-4567); and 3301 M St. NW, **Washington, D.C.** 20007 (☎ (202) 337-6464). **For US cities not listed,** call ☎ (800) 2-COUNCIL (226-8624). In the UK, 28A Poland St. (Oxford Circus), **London**, W1V 3DB (☎ (020) 7437 7767).

CTS Travel, 44 Goodge St., **London** W1 (☎ (020) 7636 0031; email ctsinfo@ctstravel.com.uk).

STA Travel, 6560 Scottsdale Rd. #F100, Scottsdale, AZ 85253 (☎ (800) 777-0112; fax (602) 922-0793; www.sta-travel.com). A student and youth travel organization with over 150 offices worldwide. Ticket booking, travel insurance, railpasses, and more. US offices include: 297 Newbury St., **Boston**, MA 02115 (☎ (617) 266-6014); 429 S. Dearborn St., **Chicago**, IL 60605 (☎ (312) 786-9050); 7202 Melrose Ave., **Los Angeles**, CA 90046 (☎ (323) 934-8722); 10 Downing St., **New York**, NY 10014 (☎ (212) 627-3111); 4341 University Way NE, **Seattle**, WA 98105 (☎ (206) 633-5000); 2401 Pennsylvania Ave., Ste. G, **Washington, D.C.** 20037 (☎ (202) 887-0912); and 51 Grant Ave., **San Francisco**, CA 94108 (☎ (415) 391-8407). In the UK, 11 Goodge St., **London** WIP 1FE (☎ (020) 7436 7779 for North American travel). In New Zealand, 10 High St., **Auckland** (☎ (09) 309 0458). In Australia, 366 Lygon St., **Melbourne** Vic 3053 (☎ (03) 9349 4344). In Spain, STA's affiliate, **Barcelo Viajes,** can help STA travelers. Offices include: Princesa 3, **Madrid** (☎ 915 58 19); Paz 38, **Valencia** (☎ 963 51 47 84).

Travel CUTS (Canadian Universities Travel Services Limited), 187 College St., **Toronto**, ON M5T 1P7 (☎ (416) 979-2406; fax 979-8167; www.travelcuts.com). 40 offices across Canada. Also in the UK, 295-A Regent St., **London** W1R 7YA (☎ (020) 7255 1944).

Wasteels, Platform 2, Victoria Station, London SW1V 1JT (☎ (020) 7834 7066; fax 7630 7628; www.wasteels.dk/uk). A huge chain in Europe, with 203 locations. Sells the Wasteels BIJ tickets, which are discounted (30-45% off regular fare), 2nd-class international point-to-point train tickets with unlimited stopovers for those under 26 (sold only in Europe). Locations in Spain, Portugal, and Morocco are: Plaza de Cataluna, **Barcelona** (☎ 933 01 18 81); Blasco de Garay, 13, **Madrid** (☎ 915 43 12 03); Rua dos Caminhos de Ferro, 90, **Lisbon** (☎ (21) 886 97 93); 25 Rue Leon l'Africain, **Casablanca** (☎ (02) 314 060); 45 Bd. Mohamed V, **Meknes** (☎ (05) 523 062).

ESSENTIALS

ESSENTIALS

COMMERCIAL AIRLINES

The commercial airlines' lowest regular offer is the **APEX** (Advance Purchase Excursion) fare, which provides confirmed reservations and allows "open-jaw" tickets. Generally, reservations must be made seven to 21 days ahead of departure, with seven- to 14-day minimum-stay and up to 90-day maximum-stay restrictions. These fares carry hefty cancellation and change penalties (fees rise in summer). Book peak-season APEX fares early; by May you will have a hard time getting your desired departure date. Use **Microsoft Expedia** (expedia.msn.com) or **Travelocity** (www.travelocity.com) to find the lowest published fares, then use the resources outlined here to try and beat those fares. Low-season fares should be appreciably cheaper than the **high-season** (mid-June to early Sept.) ones listed here.

TRAVELING FROM NORTH AMERICA

Basic round-trip fares to Madrid range from roughly US$300-750. Standard commercial carriers like those listed below will probably offer the most convenient flights, but they may not be the cheapest, unless you find a special promotion or ticket war or book far in advance. Foreign or discount airlines often offer better deals that are best found through the Internet or a budget travel agent.

American Airlines (☎ (800) 433-7300; www.aa.com).

Delta (☎ (800) 221-1212; www.delta-air.com).

Swiss Air (☎ (800) 221-4750; www.swissair.com).

TWA (☎ (800) 892-4141; www.twa.com).

United (☎ (800) 241-6522; www.ual.com).

TRAVELING FROM THE UK AND IRELAND

Because of the myriad carriers flying from the British Isles to the continent, we only include discount airlines or those with cheap specials here. The **Air Travel Advisory Bureau** in London (☎ (020) 7636 5000; www.atab.co.uk) provides referrals to travel agencies and consolidators that offer discounted airfares out of the UK.

Aer Lingus: Ireland ☎ (01) 886 88 88; www.aerlingus.ie. Return tickets from Dublin, Cork, Galway, Kerry, and Shannon to Madrid (IR£102-244).

British Midland Airways: UK ☎ (0870) 607 05 55; www.britishmidland.com. Departures from throughout the UK. London to Madrid (UK£98).

easyJet: UK ☎ (0870) 600 00 00; www.easyjet.com. London to Barcelona and Madrid, (UK£47-136). Online tickets.

Go-Fly Limited: UK ☎ (0845) 605 43 21, elsewhere call UK ☎ +44 (1279) 66 63 88; www.go-fly.com. A subsidiary of British Airways. From London to Barcelona, Lisbon, Madrid (return UK£53-180).

TRAVELING FROM AUSTRALIA AND NEW ZEALAND

Singapore Air: Australia ☎ 13 10 11, New Zealand ☎ 0800 808 909; www.singaporeair.com. Flies from Auckland, Sydney, Melbourne, and Perth to various destinations in Western Europe.

TRAVELING FROM SOUTH AFRICA

Air France: ☎ (011) 880 80 40; www.airfrance.com. Johannesburg to Paris; connections throughout Europe.

British Airways: ☎ (0860) 011 747; www.british-airways.com/regional/sa. Cape Town and Johannesburg to Europe from SAR3400.

Lufthansa: ☎ (011) 484 47 11; www.lufthansa.co.za. From Cape Town, Durban, and Johannesburg to Madrid and Barcelona.

AIR COURIER FLIGHTS

Those who travel light should consider courier flights. Couriers help transport cargo on international flights by using their checked luggage space for freight. Generally, couriers must travel with carry-ons only and must deal with complex flight restrictions. Most flights are round-trip only, with short fixed-length stays (usually one week) and a limit of a one ticket per issue. Most of these flights also operate only out of major gateway cities, mostly in North America. Courier flights to Spain are common; those to Portugal or Morocco are scarcer. Generally, you must be over 21. In summer, the popular destinations usually require an advance reservation of about two weeks (you can usually book up to 2 months ahead). Super-discounted fares are common for "last-minute" flights (3-14 days ahead).

TRAVELING FROM NORTH AMERICA

Round-trip courier fares from the US to Spain run about US$200-500. Most flights leave from New York, Los Angeles, San Francisco, or Miami in the US; and from Montreal, Toronto, or Vancouver in Canada. The first four organizations below provide their members with lists of opportunities and courier brokers worldwide for an annual fee (typically US$50-60). Alternatively, you can contact a courier broker (such as the last three listings) directly; most charge registration fees, but a few don't. Prices quoted below are round-trip.

Air Courier Association, 15000 W. 6th Ave. #203, Golden, CO 80401 (☎ (800) 282-1202; elsewhere call US +1 (303) 215-9000; www.aircourier.org). Ten departure cities throughout the US and Canada to Madrid (high-season US$150-360). One-year US$64.

International Association of Air Travel Couriers (IAATC), 220 South Dixie Highway #3, PO Box 1349, Lake Worth, FL 33460 (☎ (561) 582-8320; fax 582-1581; www.courier.org). From 9 North American cities to Western European cities, including Madrid. One-year US$45-50.

Global Courier Travel, PO Box 3051, Nederland, CO 80466 (www.globalcourier-travel.com). Searchable online database. Six departure points in the US and Canada to Madrid. One-year US$40, 2 people US$55.

NOW Voyager, 74 Varick St. #307, New York, NY 10013 (☎ (212) 431-1616; fax 219-1753; www.nowvoyagertravel.com). To Madrid (US$499-699). Usually one-week max. stay. One-year US$50. Non-courier discount fares also available.

FROM THE UK AND IRELAND

Although the courier industry is most developed from North America, there are limited courier flights in other areas. The minimum age for couriers from the **UK** is usually 18. **Brave New World Enterprises,** P.O. Box 22212, London SE5 8WB (email guideinfo@nry.co.uk; www.nry.co.uk/bnw) publishes a directory of all the companies offering courier flights in the UK (UK£10, in electronic form UK£8). **Global Courier Travel** (see above) also offer flights from London and Dublin to continental Europe. **British Airways Travel Shop** (☎ (0870) 606 11 33; www.british-airways.com/travelqa/booking/travshop/travshop.shtml) arranges flights from London to destinations in continental Europe (specials as low as UK£60; no registration fee).

STANDBY FLIGHTS

Traveling standby requires considerable flexibility in arrival and departure dates and cities. Standby flights to Spain are common, but are rarely an option for travelers to Portugal or Morocco. Companies dealing in standby flights sell vouchers rather than tickets, along with the promise to get to your destination (or near your destination) within a certain window of time (typically 1-5 days). You call in before your specific window of time to hear your flight options and the probability that you will be able to board each flight. You can then decide which flights you want to try to make, show up at the appropriate airport at the appropriate time, present your voucher, and board if space is available. Vouchers can usually be bought for both one-way and round-trip travel. You may receive a monetary refund only if every available flight within your date range is full; if you opt not to take an available (but perhaps less convenient) flight, you can only get credit toward future travel. Carefully read agreements with any company offering standby flights as tricky fine print can leave you in a lurch. To check on a company's service record in the US, call the Better Business Bureau (☎ (212) 533-6200). It is difficult to receive refunds, and clients' vouchers will not be honored when an airline fails to receive payment in time. One established standby company in the US is **Airhitch,** 2641 Broadway, 3rd fl., New York, NY 10025 (☎ (800) 326-2009; fax 864-5489; www.airhitch.org) and Los Angeles, CA (☎ (888) 247-4482), which offers one-way flights to Europe from the Northeast (US$159), West Coast and Northwest (US$239), Midwest (US$209), and Southeast (US$189). Intracontinental connecting flights within the US or Europe cost US$79-139. Airhitch's head European office is in **Paris** (☎ +33 01 47 00 16 30); there's also one in **Amsterdam** (☎ +31 (20) 626 32 20).

TICKET CONSOLIDATORS

Ticket consolidators, or **"bucket shops,"** buy unsold tickets in bulk from commercial airlines and sell them at discounted rates. The best place to look is in the Sunday travel section of any major newspaper (such as the *New York Times*), where many bucket shops place tiny ads. Call quickly, as availability is typically extremely limited. Not all bucket shops are reliable, so insist on a receipt that gives full details of restrictions, refunds, and tickets, and pay by credit card (in spite of the 2-5% fee) so you can stop payment if you never receive your tickets. For more info, see www.travel-library.com/air-travel/consolidators.html or pick up Kelly Monaghan's *Air Travel's Bargain Basement* (Intrepid Traveler, US$8).

TRAVELING FROM THE US AND CANADA

Travel Avenue (☎ (800) 333-3335; www.travelavenue.com) rebates commercial fares to or from the US (5% for over US$550) and will search for cheap flights from anywhere for a fee. **NOW Voyager,** 74 Varick St., #307, New York, NY 10013 (☎ (212) 431-1616; fax 219-1793; www.nowvoyagertravel.com) arranges discounted flights, mostly from New York, to Barcelona and Madrid. Other consolidators worth trying are **Airfare Busters** (☎ (800) 232-8783; www.af.busters.com); **Interworld** (☎ (305) 443-4929; fax 443-0351); **Pennsylvania Travel** (☎ (800) 331-0947); **Rebel** (☎ (800) 227-3235; email travel@rebeltours.com; www.rebeltours.com); **Cheap Tickets** (☎ (800) 377-1000; www.cheaptickets.com); and **Travac** (☎ (800) 872-8800; fax (212) 714-9063; www.travac.com). Yet more consolidators on the web include the **Internet Travel Network** (www.itn.com); **SurplusTravel.com** (www.surplustravel.com); **Travel Information Services** (www.tiss.com); **TravelHUB** (www.travelhub.com); and **The Travel Site** (www.thetravelsite.com). Keep in mind that these are just suggestions to get you started in your research; *Let's Go* does not endorse these agencies. As always, be cautious, and research companies before you hand over your credit card number.

TRAVELING FROM THE UK, AUSTRALIA, AND NEW ZEALAND

In London, the **Air Travel Advisory Bureau** (☎ (020) 7636 5000; www.atab.co.uk) can provide names of reliable consolidators and discount flight specialists. From Australia and New Zealand, look for consolidator ads in the travel section of the *Sydney Morning Herald* and other papers.

CHARTER FLIGHTS

Charters are flights a tour operator contracts with an airline to fly extra loads of passengers during peak season. Charter flights fly less frequently than major airlines, make refunds particularly difficult, and are almost always fully booked. Schedules and itineraries may also change or be canceled at the last moment (as late as 48 hours before the trip, and without a full refund), and check-in, boarding, and baggage claim are often much slower. However, they can also be cheaper.

Discount clubs and **fare brokers** offer members savings on last-minute charter and tour deals. Study contracts closely; you don't want to end up with an unwanted overnight layover. **Travelers Advantage,** Stamford, CT, US specializes in European travel and tour packages. (☎ (800) 548-1116; www.travelersadvantage.com. US$60 annual fee includes discounts, newsletters, and cheap flight directories.)

BY TRAIN

Trains in Spain and Portugal are generally comfortable, convenient, and reasonably swift. Second-class travel is pleasant, and compartments, which seat two to six, are great places to meet fellow travelers. Trains, however, are not always safe; for safety tips, see below. For long trips make sure you are in the correct car, as trains sometimes split at crossroads. Towns listed in parentheses require a train switch at the town listed immediately before the parenthesis.

You can either buy a **railpass,** which allows you unlimited travel within a particular region for a given period of time, or rely on buying individual **point-to-point** tickets as you go. Almost all countries give students or youths (usually defined as anyone under 26) direct discounts on regular domestic rail tickets, and many also sell a student or youth card that provides 20-50% off all fares for up to a year.

RESERVATIONS. While seat reservations are required only for selected trains (usually on major lines), you are not guaranteed a seat without one (usually US$3-10). Reservations are available on major trains as much as two months in advance, and Europeans often reserve far ahead of time; you should strongly consider reserving during peak holiday and tourist seasons (at the very latest a few hours ahead). It will be necessary to purchase a **supplement** (US$10-50) or special fare for high speed or quality trains such as Spain's AVE.

OVERNIGHT TRAINS. Night trains have their advantages—you won't waste valuable daylight hours traveling, and you will be able to forego the hassle and considerable expense of securing a night's accommodation. However, night travel has its drawbacks as well: discomfort and sleepless nights are the most obvious; the scenery probably won't look as enticing in pitch black, either. **Sleeping accommodations** on trains differ from country to country, but typically you can either sleep upright in your seat (for free) or pay for a separate space. **Couchettes** (berths) typically have four to six seats per compartment (about US$20 per person); **sleepers** (beds) in private sleeping cars offer more privacy and comfort, but are considerably more expensive (US$40-150). If you are using a railpass valid only for a restricted number of days, inspect train schedules to maximize the use of your pass: an overnight train or boat journey uses up only one of your travel days if it departs after 7pm (you need only write in the next day's date on your pass).

SHOULD YOU BUY A RAILPASS? Railpasses were conceived to allow you to jump on any train in Europe, go wherever you want whenever you want, and change your plans at will. In practice, it's not so simple. You still must stand in line to validate your pass, pay for supplements, and fork over cash for seat and couchette reservations. More importantly, railpasses don't always pay off. If you are planning to spend extensive time on trains, hopping between big cities, a railpass would probably be worth it. But in many cases, especially if you are under 26, point-to-point tickets may prove a cheaper option.

 JUST SAY NO If you are planning on traveling in just Spain and Portugal, do not buy a Eurailpass or Europass. Train travel in these countries is less expensive than the rest of Europe, where passes can save you from paying for expensive train fares. A Eurailpass/Europass only makes sense for those planning on traveling in other European countries as well.

EURAILPASS. Eurail is **valid** in most of Western Europe: Austria, Belgium, Denmark, Finland, France, Germany, Greece, Hungary, Italy, Luxembourg, the Netherlands, Norway, Portugal, the Republic of Ireland, Spain, Sweden, and Switzerland. It is **not valid** in the UK. Standard **Eurailpasses,** valid for a consecutive given number of days, are most suitable for those planning on spending extensive time on trains every few days. **Flexipasses,** valid for any 10 or 15 (not necessarily consecutive) days in a two-month period, are more cost-effective for those traveling longer distances less frequently. **Saverpasses** provide first-class travel for travelers in groups of two to five (prices are per person). **Youthpasses** and **Youth Flexipasses** provide parallel second-class perks for those under 26.

EURAILPASSES	15 days	21 days	1 month	2 months	3 months
1st class Eurailpass	US$554	US$718	US$890	US$1260	US$1558
Eurail Saverpass	US$470	US$610	US$756	US$1072	US$1324
Eurail Youthpass	US$388	US$499	US$623	US$882	US$1089

EURAIL FLEXIPASSES	10 days in 2 months	15 days in 2 months
1st class Eurail Flexipass	US$654	US$862
Eurail Saver Flexipass	US$556	US$732
Eurail Youth Flexipass	US$458	US$599

Passholders receive a timetable for major routes and a map with details on possible ferry, steamer, bus, car rental, hotel, and Eurostar discounts. Passholders often also receive reduced fares or free passage on many bus and boat lines.

EUROPASS. The Europass is a slimmed-down version of the Eurailpass: it allows five to 15 days of unlimited travel in any two-month period within France, Germany, Italy, Spain, and Switzerland. **First-Class Europasses** (for individuals) and **Saverpasses** (for people traveling in groups of 2-5) range from US$348/296 per person (5 days) to US$728/620 (15 days). **Second-Class Youthpasses** for those ages 12-25 cost US$233-513. For a fee, you can add **additional zones** (Austria/Hungary; Belgium/Luxembourg/Netherlands; Greece Plus, including the ADN/HML ferry between Italy and Greece; and/or Portugal): US$60 for one associated country, US$100 for two. You are entitled to the same **freebies** afforded by the Eurailpass (see above), but only when they are within or between countries that you have purchased. Plan your itinerary before buying a Europass: it will save you money if your travels are confined to three to five adjacent Western European countries, or if you only want to go to large cities, but would be a waste if you plan to make lots of side-trips. If you're tempted to add many days and associate countries, consider a Eurailpass.

SHOPPING AROUND FOR A EURAIL OR EUROPASS. Eurailpasses and Euro-passes are designed by the EU itself, and are purchasable only by non-Europe-ans almost exclusively from non-European distributors. These passes must be sold at uniform prices determined by the EU. However, some travel agents tack on a US$10 handling fee, and others offer certain bonuses with purchase, so shop around. Also, keep in mind that pass prices usually go up each year, so if you're planning to travel early in the year, you can save cash by purchasing before January 1 (you have three months from the purchase date to validate your pass in Europe).

It is best to buy your Eurail- or Europass before leaving; only a few places in major European cities sell them, and at a marked-up price. You can get a replacement for a lost pass only if you have purchased insurance on it under the Pass Protection Plan (US$10). Eurailpasses are available through travel agents, student travel agencies like STA and Council (see p. 33), and **Rail Europe,** 500 Mamaroneck Ave., Harrison, NY 10528 (US ☎ (888) 382-7245, Canada ☎ (800) 361-7245, UK ☎ (0990) 84 88 48; www.raileurope.com) or **DER Travel Services,** 9501 W. Devon Ave. #301, Rosemont, IL 60018 (US ☎ (888) 337-7350; www.dertravel.com).

INTERRAIL PASS. If you have lived for at least six months in one of the European countries where InterRail Passes are valid, they prove an economical option. There are eight InterRail **zones,** one of which includes Spain, Portugal, and Morocco. The **Under 26 InterRail Card** allows either 14 days or one month of unlimited travel within one, two, three, or all eight zones; the cost is determined by the number of zones the pass covers (UK£159-259). If you buy a ticket including the zone in which you claim residence, you must still pay 50% fare for tickets inside your own country. Passholders receive **discounts** on rail travel, Eurostar journeys, and most ferries to Ireland, Scandinavia, and the rest of Europe. Most exclude **supplements** for high-speed trains. For info and ticket sales in Europe contact **Student Travel Center,** 24 Rupert St., 1st fl., London W1V 7FN (☎ (020) 74 37 81 01; www.student-travel-centre.com). Tickets are also available from travel agents or major train stations throughout Europe.

DISCOUNTED TICKETS

For travelers under 26, **BIJ** tickets (Billets Internationals de Jeunesse; a.k.a. **Wasteels, Eurotrain,** and **Route 26**) are a great alternative to railpasses. Available for international trips within Europe as well as most ferry services, they knock 20-40% off regular second-class fares. Tickets are good for 60 days after purchase and allow a number of stopovers along the normal direct route of the train journey. Issued for a specific international route between two points, they must be used in the direction and order of the designated route and must be bought in Europe. The equivalent for those over 26, **BIGT** tickets provide a 20-30% discount on 1st- and 2nd-class international tickets for business travelers, temporary residents of Europe, and their families. Both types of tickets are available from European travel agents, at Wasteels or Eurotrain offices (usually in or near train stations), or directly at the ticket counter in some nations. For more info, contact **Wasteels,** Plaza de Cataluna, **Barcelona** (☎ 933 01 18 81); Blasco de Garay, 13, **Madrid** (☎ 915 43 12 03); Rua dos Caminhos de Ferro, 90, **Lisbon** (☎ (21) 886 97 93).

BY BUS

Though European trains and railpasses are extremely popular, in many cases buses prove a better option. In Spain, the bus and train systems are on par; in Portugal, bus networks are more extensive, efficient, and often more comfortable. In Morocco, buses are the easiest way to get around, even though some run somewhat infrequently. Please see the Essentials sections of Spain (see p. 54), Portugal (see p. 521), and Morocco (see p. 662) for details on country specific bus travel.

BY CAR

Cars offer speed, freedom, access to the countryside, and an escape from the town-to-town mentality of trains. Unfortunately, they also insulate you from the *esprit de corps* of rail traveling. Although a single traveler won't save by renting a car, four usually will. If you can't decide between train and car travel, you may benefit from a combination of the two; Rail Europe and other railpass vendors offer rail-and-drive packages for both individual countries and all of Europe.

Before setting off, know the laws of the countries in which you'll be driving. The **Association for Safe International Road Travel (ASIRT)** can provide more specific information about road conditions. It is located at 5413 West Cedar Lane #103C, Bethesda, MD 20814 (☎ (301) 983-5252; fax 983-3663; email asirt@erols.com; www.asirt.org). Western Europeans use unleaded gas almost exclusively.

INTERNATIONAL DRIVING PERMIT (IDP). If you plan to drive a car while in the region, you should have an International Driving Permit (IDP), though Spain, Portugal, and Morocco allow travelers to drive with a valid American or Canadian license for a few months. It may be a good idea to get an IDP anyway, in case you're in a situation (e.g. an accident or being stranded in a smaller town) where the police do not speak English; information on the IDP is printed in 10 languages, including Spanish, French, Portuguese, and Arabic.

Your IDP, valid for one year, must be issued in your own country before you depart; AAA affiliates cannot issue IDPs valid in their own country. To get an IDP you must be at least 18 years old, have a valid driver's license, two passport pictures, and another form of identification. When on the road you will always be asked to present your driver's license with the IDP.

Australia: Royal Automobile Club (RAC) or National Royal Motorist Association (NRMA) if in NSW or the ACT (☎ (08) 9421 4444; www.rac.com.au/travel). Permits AUS$15.

Canada: Contact any Canadian Automobile Association (CAA) branch office or write to CAA, 1145 Hunt Club Rd., #200, K1V 0Y3. (☎ (613) 247-0117; www.caa.ca/CAAInternet/travelservices/internationaldocumentation/idptravel.htm). Permits CDN$10.

Ireland: Contact nearest Automobile Association (AA) office or write to the UK address below. The Irish Automobile Association, 23 Suffolk St., Rockhill, Blackrock, Co. Dublin (☎ (01) 677 9481), honors most foreign automobile memberships. Permits IR£4.

New Zealand: Contact your local Automobile Association (AA) or their main office at Auckland Central, 99 Albert St. (☎ (9) 377 4660; www.nzaa.co.nz). Permits NZ$8.

South Africa: Contact the Travel Services Department of the Automobile Association of South Africa at P.O. Box 596, 2000 Johannesburg (☎ (11) 799 1400; fax 799 1410; http://aasa.co.za). Permits SAR28.50.

UK: To visit your local AA Shop, contact the **AA Headquarters** (☎ (0990) 44 88 66), or write to: The Automobile Association, International Documents, Fanum House, Erskine, Renfrewshire PA8 6BW. To find the location nearest you that issues the IDP, call (0990) 50 06 00 or (0990) 44 88 66. Permits UK£4.

US: Visit any American Automobile Association (AAA) office or write to AAA Florida, Travel Related Services, 1000 AAA Drive (mail stop 100), Heathrow, FL 32746 (☎ (407) 444-7000; fax 444-7380). You don't have to be a member to buy an IDP. Permits US$10.

CAR INSURANCE. Most credit cards cover standard insurance. If you rent, lease, or borrow a car, you will need a **green card,** or **International Insurance Certificate,** to certify that you have liability insurance and that it applies abroad. Green cards can be obtained at car rental agencies, car dealers (for those leasing cars), some travel agents, and some border crossings. Rental agencies may require you to purchase theft insurance in countries that they consider to have a high risk of auto theft. If you have a collision abroad, the accident will show up on your domestic records if you report it to your insurance company. Ask your rental agency about Spain, Portugal, or Morocco.

RENTALS. You can **rent** a car from a US-based firm (Alamo, Avis, Budget, or Hertz) with European offices, from a European-based company with local representatives (Europcar), or from a tour operator (Auto Europe, Europe By Car, and Kemwel Holiday Autos) which will arrange a rental for you from a European company at its own rates. Multinationals offer greater flexibility, but tour operators often strike better deals. Most available cars will have standard transmission—cars with automatic transmission are difficult to find and much more expensive. Reserve well before leaving for the region and pay in advance if at all possible. It is always significantly less expensive to reserve a car from the US than from Spain, Portugal, or Morocco. Ask your airline about special fly-and-drive packages; you may get up to a week of free or discounted rental. Minimum age in Spain and Portugal is usually 25 with the larger agencies (Hertz, Avis) and 21 at smaller, local businesses. Minimum age in Morocco is almost always 21. At most agencies, all that's needed to rent a car is a US license and proof that you've had it for a year, although in Spain, you may need an international driver's license (see above).

BY BICYCLE

Today, biking is one of the key elements of the classic budget Eurovoyage. With the proliferation of mountain bikes, you can do some serious natural sightseeing. If you are nervous about striking out on your own, **Blue Marble Travel** (in Canada ☎ (519) 624-2494; in Paris ☎ (01) 42 36 02 34; in US ☎ 800-258-8689 or (973) 326-9533; www.bluemarble.org) offers bike tours designed for adults aged 20 to 50.

Many airlines will count your bike as your second piece of luggage, and a few charge extra. The additional fee runs about US$60-110 each way. Bikes must be packed in a cardboard box with the pedals and front wheel detached; airlines sell bike boxes at the airport (US$10). Most ferries let you take your bike for free or for a nominal fee. You can always ship your bike on trains, though the cost varies.

Riding a bike with a frame pack strapped on it or your back is about as safe as pedaling blindfolded over a sheet of ice; panniers are essential. The first thing to buy, however, is a suitable **bike helmet** (US$25-50). U-shaped **Citadel** or **Kryptonite locks** are expensive (starting at US$30), but the companies insure their locks against theft of your bike for one to two years. For mail order equipment, **Bike Nashbar**, 4111 Simon Rd., Youngstown, OH 44512 (☎ 800-627-4227; www.nashbar.com), beats all competitors' offers and ships anywhere in the US or Canada.

Renting a bike beats bringing your own if your touring will be confined to one or two regions. *Let's Go* lists bike rental shops for most larger cities and towns. Some youth hostels rent bicycles for low prices. Some train stations rent bikes and often allow you to drop them off elsewhere; check train stations throughout the region for similar deals.

BY MOPED AND MOTORCYCLE

Motorized bikes don't use much gas, can be put on trains and ferries, and are a good compromise between the high cost of car travel and the limited range of bicycles. In Spain, they are an extremely popular method of transportation for locals, and they can be a fun alternative for tourist daytrips. However, they're uncomfortable for long distances, dangerous in the rain, and unpredictable on rough roads and gravel. Always wear a helmet, and never ride with a backpack. If you've never been on a moped, the windy roads of the Pyrenees and the congested streets of Madrid are not the place to start.

Before renting, ask if the quoted price includes tax and insurance, or you may be hit with an unexpected additional fee. Avoid handing your passport over as a deposit; if you have an accident or mechanical failure you may not get it back until you cover all repairs. Pay ahead of time instead.

ESSENTIALS

BY THUMB

 HITCHHIKERS BEWARE. *Let's Go* strongly urges you to consider seriously the risks before you choose to hitch. We do not recommend hitching as a safe means of transportation, and none of the information presented here is intended to do so. Women traveling alone should never hitch.

No one should hitch without careful consideration of the risks involved. Hitching means entrusting your life to a random person who happens to stop beside you on the road and risking theft, assault, sexual harassment, and unsafe driving. In spite of this, there are gains to hitching. Favorable hitching experiences allow you to meet local people and get where you're going, especially in areas where public transportation is sparse or unreliable. The choice, however, remains yours.

Where one stands is vital. Experienced hitchers pick a spot outside of built-up areas, where drivers can stop, return to the road without causing an accident, and have time to look over potential passengers as they approach. Hitching (or even standing) on super-highways is usually illegal: one may only thumb at rest stops or at the entrance ramps to highways. Finally, success will depend on what one looks like. Successful hitchers travel light and stack their belongings in a compact but visible cluster. Most Europeans signal with an open hand, rather than a thumb; many write their destination on a sign in large, bold letters and draw a smiley-face under it. Drivers prefer hitchers who are neat and wholesome. No one stops for anyone wearing sunglasses.

Safety issues are always imperative, even for those who are not hitching alone. Safety-minded hitchers avoid getting in the back of a two-door car and never let go of their backpacks. They will not get into a car that they can't get out of again in a hurry. If they ever feel threatened, they insist on being let off, regardless of where they are. Acting as if they are going to open the car door or vomit on the upholstery will usually get a driver to stop. Hitchhiking at night can be particularly dangerous; experienced hitchers stand in well-lit places, and expect drivers to be leery of nocturnal thumbers (or open-handers).

SPECIFIC CONCERNS

WOMEN TRAVELERS

Women exploring on their own inevitably face some additional safety concerns, but it's easy to be adventurous without taking undue risks. If you are concerned, consider staying in hostels which offer single rooms that lock from the inside or in religious organizations with rooms for women only. Communal showers in some hostels are safer than others; check them before settling in. Stick to centrally located accommodations and avoid solitary late-night treks or metro rides.

When traveling, always carry extra money for a phone call, bus, or taxi. **Hitching** is never safe for lone women, or even for two women traveling together. Choose train compartments occupied by other women or couples; ask the conductor to put together a women-only compartment if he or she doesn't offer to do so first. Look as if you know where you're going (even when you don't) and approach older women or couples for directions if you're lost or feel uncomfortable.

Generally, the less you look like a tourist, the better off you'll be. Dress conservatively, especially in rural areas. Trying to fit in can be effective, but dressing to the style of an obviously different culture may cause you to be ill at ease and a conspicuous target. Wearing a conspicuous **wedding band** may help prevent unwanted overtures. Some travelers report that carrying pictures of a "husband" or "children" is extremely useful to help document marriage status. Even a mention of a husband waiting back at the hotel may be enough in some places to discount your potentially vulnerable, unattached appearance.

Your best answer to verbal harassment is no answer at all; feigning deafness, sitting motionless, and staring straight ahead at nothing in particular will do a world of good that reactions usually don't achieve. The extremely persistent can sometimes be dissuaded by a firm, loud, and very public "Go away!" in the appropriate language. In Morocco, however, it is more advisable to simply ignore the advances, as local women do; rebuffs, or any kind of reaction, are often construed as coy or playing hard to get. Don't hesitate to seek out a police officer or a passerby if you are being harassed. Memorize the emergency numbers in places you visit, and consider carrying a whistle or airhorn on your keychain. A self-defense course will not only prepare you for a potential attack, but will also raise your level of awareness of your surroundings as well as your confidence (see **Self Defense,** p. 18). Also be sure you are aware of the specific health concerns that women face when traveling (see p. 23). Refer to the **Essentials** section for Morocco (p.539) for more information on traveling as a woman there.

OLDER TRAVELERS

Senior citizens are eligible for a wide range of discounts on transportation, museums, movies, theaters, concerts, restaurants, and some accommodations. If you don't see a senior citizen price listed, ask, and you may be delightfully surprised.

ElderTreks, 597 Markham St., Toronto, ON M6G 2L7 (☎ (800) 741-7956 or (416) 588-5000; fax 588-9839; email eldertreks@eldertreks.com; www.eldertreks.com). Adventure travel programs for the 50+ traveler.

Elderhostel, 75 Federal St., Boston, MA 02110, USA (☎ (617) 426-7788 or (877) 426-2166; email registration@elderhostel.org; www.elderhostel.org). Organizes 1- to 4-week "educational adventures" all over the world for those 55+.

The Mature Traveler, P.O. Box 50400, Reno, NV 89513, USA (☎ (775) 786-7419, credit card orders (800) 460-6676). Deals, discounts, and travel packages for the 50+ traveler. Subscription$30.

Walking the World, P.O. Box 1186, Fort Collins, CO 80522, USA (☎ (970) 498-0500; fax 498-9100; email walktworld@aol.com; www.walkingtheworld.com), organizes trips for 50+ travelers to a variety of destinations, including Spain and Portugal.

FURTHER READING

No Problem! Worldwise Tips for Mature Adventurers, Janice Kenyon. Orca Book Publishers (US$16).

A Senior's Guide to Healthy Travel, Donald L. Sullivan. Career Press (US$15).

Unbelievably Good Deals and Great Adventures That You Absolutely Can't Get Unless You're Over 50, Joan Rattner Heilman. Contemporary Books (US$13).

BISEXUAL, GAY, AND LESBIAN TRAVELERS

Attitudes toward homosexuality in Spain, Portugal, and Morocco vary by region. Gay and lesbian travelers may feel out of place in the smaller, rural areas of Spain and Portugal, given the countries' strong Catholic religious heritage, but overt homophobia is extremely rare. The larger cities, especially Lisbon, Barcelona and Madrid, have well-developed gay men's scenes, and the lesbian scene is also growing rapidly. In Spain, Sitges and Ibiza in particular are internationally renowned as gay party destinations, and Madrid hosts annual Gay & Lesbian Pride marches. Most Spanish newsstands carry the *Guía Gay Visado,* a publication dedicated to gay bars, discos, and contacts in Spain; the Portuguese website www.portugalgay.pt offers similar listings in Portuguese and English.

There is no gay community in Morocco. Lesbianism is almost unheard of and unrecognized; male homosexuality, while quite widespread in private, is considered unmanly and is illegal under Islamic and civil law.

Listed below are contact organizations, mail-order bookstores and publishers which offer materials addressing some specific concerns. **The International Gay and Lesbian Travel Association** website in particular offers good links to Spanish and Portuguese gay websites.

International Gay and Lesbian Travel Association, 4331 N. Federal Hwy., #304, Fort Lauderdale, FL 33308, USA (☎ (954) 776-2626; fax 776-3303; www.iglta.com). An organization of over 1350 companies serving gay and lesbian travelers worldwide. Includes links to a growing number of country and city-specific websites.

International Lesbian and Gay Association (ILGA), 81 rue Marché-au-Charbon, B-1000 Brussels, Belgium (☎/fax +32 (2) 502 24 71; www.ilga.org). Not a travel service; provides political information, such as homosexuality laws of individual countries.

FURTHER READING

Spartacus International Gay Guide. Bruno Gmunder Verlag. (US$33).

Damron Men's Guide, Damron's Accommodations, and *The Women's Traveller.* Damron Travel Guides (US$14-19). For more info, call US ☎ (415) 255-0404 or (800) 462-6654 or check their website (www.damron.com).

Ferrari Guides' Gay Travel A to Z, Ferrari Guides' Men's Travel in Your Pocket, Ferrari Guides' Women's Travel in Your Pocket, and *Ferrari Guides' Inn Places.* Ferrari Guides (US$14-16). For more info, call ☎ (602) 863-2408 or (800) 962-2912 or try www.q-net.com.

The Gay Vacation Guide: The Best Trips and How to Plan Them, Mark Chesnut. Citadel Press (US$15).

TRAVELERS WITH DISABILITIES

Those with disabilities should inform airlines and hotels of their disabilities when making arrangements for travel; some time may be needed to prepare special accommodations. Call ahead to restaurants, hotels, parks, and other facilities to find out about accessibility.

Wheelchair accessibility varies widely in Iberia but is generally inferior to that in the United States. Access in Morocco is minimal. In Spain and Portugal, handicapped access is common in modern and big city museums. Check out www.geocities.com/Paris/1502 for general information on traveling for the disabled.

USEFUL ORGANIZATIONS

Mobility International USA (MIUSA), P.O. Box 10767, Eugene, OR 97440, USA (☎ (541) 343-1284 voice and TDD; fax 343-6812; email info@miusa.org; www.miusa.org). Sells *A World of Options: A Guide to International Educational Exchange, Community Service, and Travel for Persons with Disabilities* (US$35).

Moss Rehab Hospital Travel Information Service (☎ (215) 456-9600 or (800) CALL-MOSS; email netstaff@mossresourcenet.org; www.mossresourcenet.org). An information resource center on travel-related concerns for those with disabilities.

Society for the Advancement of Travel for the Handicapped (SATH), 347 Fifth Ave., #610, New York, NY 10016 (☎ (212) 447-7284; www.sath.org). An advocacy group that publishes the quarterly travel magazine *OPEN WORLD* (free for members, US$13 for nonmembers). Also publishes a wide range of info sheets on disability travel facilitation and destinations. Annual membership US$45, students and seniors US$30.

FURTHER READING

Wheelchair Through Europe, Annie Mackin. Graphic Language Press (US ☎ (760) 944-9594; email niteowl@cts.com; US$13).

MINORITY TRAVELERS

Spanish people suffer from little interaction with other races. Infrequent incidents of racism are rarely violent or threatening, just a little awkward. They occur out of naiveté or ignorance, and eagerness when meeting a non-Caucasian foreigner is most often curiosity rather than insensitivity. Portugal, with its rich ethnic composition, is actively anti-racist, and minority travelers generally have little to fear. Moroccan culture is more culturally and racially mixed; visitors are defined more by their foreign ways than by their skin color.

TRAVELERS WITH CHILDREN

Family vacations often require that you slow your pace, and always require that you plan ahead. When deciding where to stay, remember the special needs of young children; when you choose a hostel, call ahead and make sure it's child-friendly. If you rent a car, make sure the rental company provides a car seat for younger children. Be sure that your child carries some sort of ID in case of an emergency or in case he or she gets lost.

Museums, tourist attractions, accommodations, and restaurants often offer discounts for children. Children under two generally fly for 10% of the adult airfare on international flights (this does not necessarily include a seat). International fares are usually discounted 25% for children from two to 11. Finding a private place for **breast feeding** is often a problem while traveling, so pack accordingly.

FURTHER READING

Backpacking with Babies and Small Children, Goldie Silverman. Wilderness Press (US$10).

Take Your Kids to Europe, Cynthia W. Harriman. Globe Pequot (US$17).

How to Take Great Trips with Your Kids, Sanford and Jane Portnoy. Harvard Common Press (US $10).

Have Kid, Will Travel: 101 Survival Strategies for Vacationing With Babies and Young Children, Claire and Lucille Tristram. Andrews and McMeel (US$9).

DIETARY CONCERNS

Spain and Portugal can be difficult places to visit as a strict vegetarian; in Spain in particular meat or fish is featured in the vast majority of popular dishes. Most restaurants serve salads, however, and there are also many egg-, rice- and bean-based dishes that can be requested without meat. Be careful, though, as some servers may interpret a "vegetarian" order to mean "with tuna instead of ham." Eating as a vegetarian in Morocco is slightly easier, as bean-based stews and *couscous* (a form of pasta) dishes are extremely widespread.

The North American Vegetarian Society, P.O. Box 72, Dolgeville, NY 13329, USA (☎ (518) 568-7970; email navs@telenet.com; www.navs-online.org), publishes information about vegetarian travel, including *Transformative Adventures, a Guide to Vacations and Retreats* (US$15).

If it's **kosher,** chances are it's difficult to find in Spain, Portugal, and Morocco. If you are strict in your observance, you may have to prepare your own food on the road. **The Jewish Travel Guide,** which lists synagogues, kosher restaurants, and Jewish institutions in over 100 countries, is available in Europe from Vallentine Mitchell Publishers, Newbury House 890-900, Eastern Ave., Newbury Park, Ilford, Essex IG2 7HH, UK (☎ (020) 8599 8866; fax 8599 0984) and in the US (US$16.95 + US$4 S&H) from ISBS, 5804 NE Hassallo St., Portland, OR 97213 (☎ (800) 944-6190).

ALTERNATIVES TO TOURISM

For an extensive listing of "off-the-beaten-track" and specialty travel opportunities, try the **Specialty Travel Index,** 305 San Anselmo Ave., #313, San Anselmo, CA 94960, USA (☎ (888) 624-4030 or (415) 455-1643; www.spectrav.com; US$6). **Transitions Abroad** (www.transabroad.com) publishes a bimonthly on-line newsletter for work, study, and specialized travel abroad.

STUDYING ABROAD

Spain is one of the most popular destinations in the world for study-abroad students. To find out more, contact US university programs and youth organizations that set students up at Spanish universities and language centers. Ask for the names of recent participants in the programs, and get in touch with them. Many of the programs cluster around Madrid and Sevilla. If you are fluent, enroll directly in a Spanish college (non-Spanish students have practically taken over Salamanca, for example). While Portugal is not as common a destination for study abroad, most universities in **Portugal** open their gates to foreign students, and foreigners can enter language and cultural studies programs at most of them. Study abroad is rare in **Morocco,** though it is somewhat common in Rabat.

Studying in **Spain** or **Portugal** requires a good deal of regulatory paperwork. Students planning to stay longer than three months must obtain a visa from their national consulate. Those students studying only for the summer (i.e., for less than three months) need only a passport. Individual universities and programs have their own requirements, most of which involve a basic knowledge of Spanish and a minimum grade point average.

UNIVERSITIES

Most American undergraduates enroll in programs sponsored by US universities. However, if your Spanish or Portuguese is already good, local universities can be much cheaper than an American university program, though it can be hard to receive academic credit. Schools that offer study abroad programs to foreigners are listed below.

American Institute for Foreign Study, College Division, River Plaza, 9 West Broad St., Stamford, CT 06902, USA (☎ (800) 727-2437, ext. 5163; www.aifsabroad.com). Organizes programs for high school and college study in universities in Spain.

Central College Abroad, Office of International Education, 812 University, Pella, IA 50219, USA (☎ (800) 831-3629 or (515) 628-5284; studyabroad.com/central). Offers semester- and year-long programs in Spain. US$25 application fee.

School for International Training, College Semester Abroad, Admissions, Kipling Rd., P.O. Box 676, Brattleboro, VT 05302, USA (☎ (800) 336-1616 or (802) 258-3267; www.sit.edu). Semester- and year-long programs in Spain and Portugal run US$9500-12,900. Also runs the **Experiment in International Living** (☎ (800) 345-2929; fax (802) 258-3428; email eil@worldlearning.org), 3- to 5-week summer programs that offer high-school students cross-cultural homestays, community service, ecological adventure, and language training in Spain and Portugal and cost US$1900-5000.

Council on International Educational Exchange (CIEE), 205 East 42nd St., New York, NY 10017 (☎ (888) 268-6245 or (800)-407-8839; www.ciee.org/study) sponsors work, volunteer, academic, and internship programs in Spain and Portugal.

Beaver College Center for Education Abroad, 450 S. Easton Rd., Glenside, PA 19038, USA (☎ (888) 232-8379; www.beaver.edu/cea). Operates programs in Spain and Portugal. Costs range from $1900 (summer) to $20,000 (full-year).

LANGUAGE SCHOOLS

These programs are run by foreign universities, independent international or local organizations, and divisions of local universities. They generally cost anywhere from US$1000 per month and usually include food and lodging.

Eurocentres, 101 N. Union St. #300, Alexandria, VA 22314, USA (☎ (800) 648-4809 or (703) 684-1494; www.eurocentres.com) or in Europe, Head Office, Seestr. 247, CH-8038 Zurich, Switzerland (☎ +41 (411) 485 50 40; email info@eurocentres.com). Language programs for beginning to advanced students with homestays in Spain and Portugal run approximately US$1132 a month.

Language Immersion Institute, 75 South Manheim Blvd., The College at New Paltz, New Paltz, NY 12561, USA (☎ (914) 257-3500; www.newpaltz.edu/lii). 2-week summer language courses and some overseas courses in Spanish. Program fees are about US$295 for a weekend or US$750 per 2 weeks.

FURTHER READING AND RESOURCES
www.studyabroad.com

Academic Year Abroad 2000/2001 and *Vacation Study Abroad 2000/2001*. Institute of International Education Books (US$45 and US$43).

Peterson's Study Abroad 2001 and *Summer Study Abroad 2001*. Peterson's (US$30).

WORKING ABROAD

Obtaining a work permit in Spain is a complicated process. EU citizens, if they intend to stay for more than three months, must apply for a residence card (*tarjeta de residencia*) within 30 days of arrival. Application can be made at a regional police headquarters or a Foreigner's Registration Office, and you will need a contract of employment, three photos, and a passport. Non-EU citizens must first obtain a *visado especial* from the Spanish embassy in their country of residence, which requires a copy of the employment contract and a medical certificate. Portugal's regulations are similar, although both EU and non-EU citizens can obtain a work permit with a residence visa.

The most commonly available jobs continue to be in the areas of teaching (particularly English) and child care (especially *au pair* services, but also as private tutors). While jobs in those areas are generally available year-round (with September the best time to look for a teaching job), other, more tourist-specific jobs will often open up in the early summer. One favorite of seasoned work-travelers is "touting," which involves enticing tourists to enter a certain restaurant or club.

In **Spain,** the national employment service (*Oficinas de Empleo*) has a monopoly on the job-finding market, and is probably the best place to begin a search. Many seasoned travelers, however, go straight to a particular town's Yellow Pages

(*Las Paginas Amarillas*) or even go door-to-door in the town in which they are staying. In **Portugal,** the English-language weekly newspaper *Anglo-Portuguese News* carries job advertisements. In **Morocco,** your best bet is to contact your national consulate for a list of schools with openings.

European Union citizens can work in Spain and Portugal, and if your parents were born in an EU country, you may be able to claim the right to a work permit. Friends in Spain or Portugal can often help expedite work permits or arrange work-for-accommodations swaps.

AU PAIR ORGANIZATIONS

Accord Cultural Exchange, 750 La Playa, San Francisco, CA 94121, USA (☎ (415) 386-6203); www.cognitext.com/accord). US$40 application fee.

InterExchange, 161 Sixth Ave., New York, NY 10013 (☎ (212) 924-0446; fax 924-0575; www.interexchange.org). Participants must speak the local language.

Childcare International, Ltd., Trafalgar House, Grenville Pl., London NW7 3SA (☎ (020) 8906 3116; fax 8906 3461; www.childint.co.uk). UK£100 application fee.

TEACHING ENGLISH

International Schools Services, Educational Staffing Program, P.O. Box 5910, Princeton, NJ 08543, USA (☎ (609) 452-0990; www.iss.edu). Recruits teachers and administrators for American and English schools in Spain and Portugal. US$150 application fee.

Office of Overseas Schools, US Department of State, Room H328, SA-1, Washington, D.C. 20522 (☎ (202) 261-8200; fax 261-8224; www.state.gov/www/about_state/schools/). Keeps a comprehensive list of schools abroad and agencies that arrange placement for Americans to teach abroad.

VOLUNTEERING

Volunteer jobs are readily available, and many provide room and board in exchange for labor. You can sometimes avoid high application fees by contacting the individual workcamps directly.

Earthwatch, 680 Mt. Auburn St., Box 403, Watertown, MA 02272, USA (☎ (800) 776-0188 or (617) 926-8200; www.earthwatch.org). Arranges 1- to 3-week programs in Spain to promote conservation of natural resources. Programs average US$1600.

Habitat for Humanity International, 121 Habitat St., Americus, GA 31709, USA (☎ (800) 334-3308; www.habitat.org). Offers international opportunities in Portugal to live with and build houses in a host community. Costs range US$1200-3500.

Peace Corps, Office of Volunteer Recruitment and Selection, 1111 20th St. NW, Washington, D.C. 20526 (☎ (800) 424-8580; www.peacecorps.gov). Opportunities in 78 developing nations including Spain, Portugal, and Morocco. Volunteers must be US citizens ages 18+ willing to make a 2-year commitment. A bachelor's degree is usually required.

Service Civil International Voluntary Service (SCI-IVS), 814 NE 40th St., Seattle, WA 98105, USA (☎/fax (206) 545-6585; www.sci-ivs.org). Arranges placement in workcamps in Spain, Portugal and Morocco for those 18+ (in the US for those 16+). Registration fee US$65-150.

Volunteers for Peace, 1034 Tiffany Rd., Belmont, VT 05730, USA (☎ (802) 259-2759; www.vfp.org). Arranges placement in workcamps in Spain, Portugal or Morocco. Annual *International Workcamp Directory* US$20. Registration fee US$200. Free newsletter.

FURTHER READING

How to Get a Job in Europe, Robert Sanborn. Surrey Books (US$22).

Work Abroad: The Complete Guide to Finding a Job Overseas, Clayton Hubbs. Transitions Abroad (US$16).

Teaching English Abroad, Susan Griffin. Vacation Work (US$17).

Overseas Summer Jobs 2001, Work Your Way Around the World, and *The Directory of Jobs and Careers Abroad.* Peterson's (US$17-18 each).

OTHER RESOURCES

Let's Go tries to cover all aspects of budget travel, but we can't put *everything* in our guides. Listed below are books and websites that can serve as jumping off points for your own research.

USEFUL PUBLICATIONS

The Broadsheet, monthly magazine aimed at English speakers in Madrid. Features current cultural and social events, as well as news. Commercially oriented. Web edition www.thebroadsheet.com.

Canarian Weekly, the first weekly news magazine of the Canary Islands. Free at over 500 locations. Web edition www.canarianweekly.com.

Focus Magazine, monthly online magazine about the Mediterranean world. Includes information on Morocco. www.focusmm.com.au/~focus.

Contemporary Spain: A Handbook, Christopher Ross. Broad and informative discussion of Spanish politics, culture, society, and travel. Edward Arnold (US$19).

Culture Shock! Morocco An extremely helpful guide to the salient cultural characteristics of Morocco, the differences between this culture and ours, and how to manage those differences.

Simple Etiquette in Spain, Victoria McGuinness. Beginner's guide to Spanish customs and manners. Paul Norbury (US$7).

Morocco: Sahara to the Sea, Mary Cross. Overview of Moroccan culture and history, as well as current events and travel information. Abbeville Press (US$20).

THE WORLD WIDE WEB

Almost every aspect of budget travel (with the most notable exception, of course, being experience) is accessible via the web. Even if you don't have Internet access at home, seeking it out at a public library or at work would be well worth it; within 10 minutes at the keyboard, you can make a reservation at a hostel in Spain, Portugal, or Morocco, get advice on travel hotspots from other travelers who have just returned, or find out how much a train from Madrid to Barcelona costs.

Listed here are some budget travel sites to start off your surfing; other relevant web sites are listed throughout the book. Because website turnover is high, use search engines (such as www.yahoo.com) to strike out on your own. But in doing so, keep in mind that most travel web sites simply exist to get your money.

All About Spain (www.red2000.com/spain/index.html) has an excellent photo tour of Spain, traveler's yellow pages, and information on major regions and cities.

Arab Net (www.arab.net/morocco/morocco_contents.html) has good historical, cultural, and tourist information on Morocco, including a list of links.

CIA World Factbook: www.odci.gov/cia/publications/factbook/index.html. Statistics on Spanish, Portuguese and Moroccan geography, government, economy, and people.

CyberSpain (www.cyberspain.com) has a wide variety of tourist and cultural info as well as links to other good sites inside and outside of Spain.

Foreign Language for Travelers: www.travlang.com. Provides free online translating dictionaries and lists of phrases.

MadridMan (www.madridman.com) is a site devoted entirely to the city of Madrid, with tons of useful info for visitors as well as history, culture, and current events sections.

Maroc.net (www.maroc.net) In French and English, this highly informative site includes Moroccan City guides, reviews of national museums, and articles on traditional costume as well as current events.

Morocco Today (www.morocco-today.com/indexnm) is a comprehensive source of information on Moroccan current events, government, and society.

Portugal-info (www.portugal-info.net), an excellent source for all types of information, from photos to wine descriptions to portuguese personals.

Sí, Spain (www.SiSpain.org), run by the Spanish Ministry of Foreign affairs, offers cultural and historical info, tourist info, and another great set of links.

Spanish Culture (spanishculture.miningco.com/culture/spanishculture). Offers a great set of links including everything cultural from Spanish proverbs to bullfighting to Flamenco music. Many of the links are in Spanish.

Spain Tourism (www.tourspain.es/inicioi.htm). Run by the national tourist office, this site is rife with cultural and practical information including stats on national parks, museums, and links to the biggest Spanish newspapers online. In French, English, Spanish and German.

Tourism in Morocco (www.tourism-in-Morocco.com) has helpful information on all aspects of traveling to and within Morocco, plus city-specific info.

TravelPage: www.travelpage.com. Links to official tourist office sites throughout Spain, Portugal, and Morocco.

Turespaña (www.tourspain.es) is the official Spanish tourism site. It offers reams of national and city-specific info, an information request service, helpful links on all aspects of travel, and a nifty festival locator.

Xacobeo 99 (www.xacobeo.es) is the Camino de Santiago's official website.

Microsoft Expedia (expedia.msn.com) has everything you'd ever need to make travel plans on the web: compare flight fares, look at maps, make reservations. FareTracker, a free service, sends you monthly mailings about the cheapest fares to any destination.

Shoestring Travel (www.stratpub.com), an alternative to Microsoft's monolithic site, is budget travel e-zine that features listings of home exchanges, links, and accommodations information.

AND OUR PERSONAL FAVORITE...

Let's Go: www.letsgo.com. Our recently revamped website features photos and streaming video, info about our books, a travel forum buzzing with stories and tips, and links that will help you find everything you could ever want to know about Spain, Portugal or Morocco.

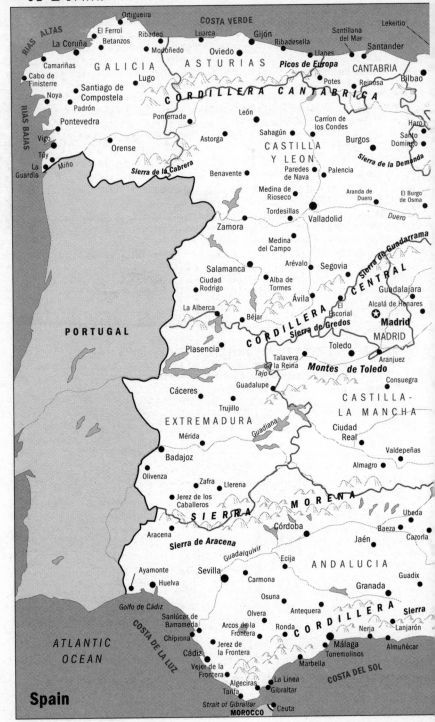

Spain

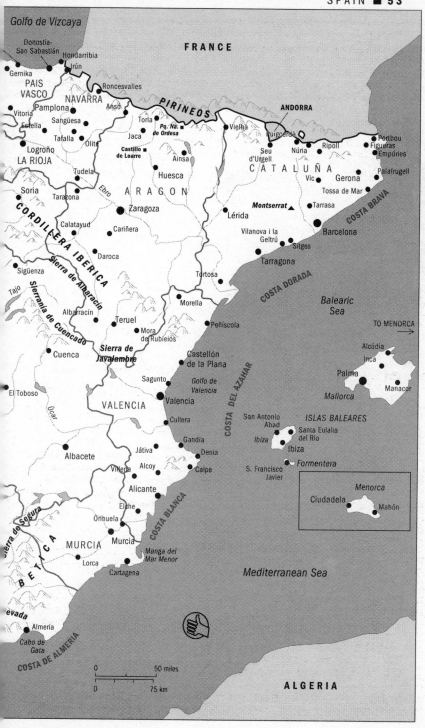

SPAIN

US$1 = 187.4PTAS	100PTAS = US$0.53
CDN$1 = 127PTAS	100PTAS = CDN$0.79
EUR€1 = 166.4PTAS	100PTAS = EUR€0.60
UK£1 = 272.6PTAS	100PTAS = UK£0.37
IR£1 = 211.3PTAS	100PTAS = IR£0.45
AUS$1 = 108.2PTAS	100PTAS = AUS$0.92
NZ$1 = 80.2PTAS	100PTAS = NZ$1.25
SAR1 = 26.9PTAS	100PTAS = SAR3.73
MOR 1DH = 17.3PTAS	100PTAS = MOR 5.81DH
POR 1$ = 0.83PTAS	100PTAS = POR 120.49$

PESETAS

 Country Code: 34. International dialing prefix: 00.

LIFE AND TIMES

With a history that spans over 50 constitutions, an endless array of amorphous kingdoms controlled by indigenous Iberians, Celts, Romans, Visigoths, Arabs, and French, and an empire that spread to the Americas, Spain can only be described, imprecisely, as a *mestizo* (mixed) culture.

HISTORY AND POLITICS

Spain has been colonized by a succession of civilizations who have left their cultural mark—**Basque** (considered indigenous), **Tartesian, Iberian, Celtic, Greek, Phoenician,** and **Carthaginian**—before the **Romans** dropped in with a vengeance in the 3rd century BC. In close to seven centuries, the Romans drastically altered the face and character of Spain, introducing Rome's language, architecture, roads, irrigation techniques, and use of grapes, olives, and wheat. A slew of Germanic tribes, including Swabians and Vandals, swept over Iberia in the early 5th century, but the **Visigoths,** newly converted Christians, emerged above the rest. The Visigoths established their court at Barcelona in 415 and effectively ruled Spain for the next three hundred years, although more as a collection of politically disorganized, fragmented tribes than as a unified whole.

THE MOORISH OCCUPATION (711-1492). Following Muslim unification and their victory tour through the Middle East and North Africa, a small force of Arabs, Berbers, and Syrians invaded Spain in 711. Practically welcomed by the divided Visigoths, the Moors encountered little resistance, and the peninsula soon fell under the dominion of the caliphate of Damascus. These events precipitated the infusion of Muslim influence. The Moors set up their Iberian capital in Córdoba, and during Abd al Rahman III's rule (936-976), some considered Spain the wealthiest and most cultivated country in the world. Abd al Rahman's successor, the dictator Al Mansur (976-1013), snuffed out all opposition within his extravagant court, and undertook a series of military campaigns that climaxed with the destruction of Santiago de Compostela, a Christian holy city, in 997.

Christian resistance was never completely crushed, however. In fact, most Spaniards today point to the 718 victory of Asturian lord Don Pelayo over a Muslim army in Covadonga, Asturias, as the starting point of the Christian **Reconquista** (Reconquest) of Spain. It took more than 750 years for the Christian kingdom to fully expel the Moors from Iberia, however, and tension between the two ruling forces was never completely continuous; most of the time, in fact, both peoples lived in peace. The turning point in Muslim-Christian relations came when Al Mansur died, leaving a power vacuum in Córdoba. At this point, caliphate holdings shattered into petty states called *taifas* and with power less centralized, Christians were finally able to gain the upper hand. For the most part, Christian rulers were tolerant of Muslims and Jews, and syncretic culture and art styles developed. Countless Moorish structures were ruined toward the end of the *Reconquista*, though, and some were renovated into churches (like Córdoba's Mezquita).

THE CATHOLIC MONARCHS (1469-1516). In 1469, the marriage of **Fernando de Aragón** and **Isabel de Castilla** joined Iberia's two mightiest Christian kingdoms. By 1492, the dynamic duo had captured Granada (the last Moorish stronghold) and shuttled off Columbus to explore the New World. By the 16th century, the pair's strong leadership made Spain the world's most powerful empire. The Catholic Monarchs introduced the **Inquisition** in 1478, executing and then burning heretics, principally Jews (even those who had converted earlier). The Inquisition had dual aims: to strengthen the authority of the Church and to unify Spain. In approximately 50 years of rule, the Catholic Monarchs heightened Spain's position as a world economic, political, and cultural power—made all the more enduring by lucrative conquests in the Americas.

THE HABSBURG DYNASTY (1516-1713). The daughter of Fernando and Isabel, **Juana la Loca** (the Mad), married **Felipe el Hermoso** (the Fair) of the powerful Habsburg dynasty. Mr. Handsome (who died playing *cesta punta*, or "jai alai") and Mrs. Crazy (who refused to believe that he had died and dragged his corpse through the streets) produced **Carlos I** (Charles V, 1516-1556), who reigned as the last Roman Emperor over an immense empire comprising modern-day Holland, Belgium, Austria, Spain, parts of Germany and Italy, and the American colonies.

But trouble was brewing in the Protestant Netherlands (then called the Low Countries and Flanders). After Carlos I died, his son **Felipe II** (1556-1598) was left holding the bag full of rebellious territories. More conservative than his father, he still would not stand pat, annexing Portugal after its ailing King Henrique died in 1580. One year later, the Dutch declared their independence from Spain, and Felipe began warring with the Protestants, spurring an embroilment with England. The war with the British ground to a halt when Sir Francis Drake and bad weather undid Spain's **Invincible Armada** in 1588. Much of his European empire sapped, Felipe retreated to his grim, newly built palace, El Escorial, and remained there through the last decade of his reign.

SPAIN

JEWISH EXPERIENCE IN SPAIN
For centuries, **Jews** were peacefully settled throughout Iberia. A 15th-century rabbi noted that the Jews in Castilla "have been the most distinguished in all the realms of the dispersion: in lineage, in wealth, in virtues, in science." Yet in 1369, **Enrique de Trastámara** defeated his half-brother **Pedro el Cruel** (a legendary Richard III type) at Montiel, inaugurating the Trastámara dynasty that was to bring forth **Isabel la Católica**. Always a bit precarious, tolerance in Castilla was replaced by Christian rigidity akin to the scene in 14th-century France. The 1391 pogroms started soon after, as thousands of Jews were massacred and many more forcibly converted. Even those who did convert, called *conversos*, were persecuted and tortured. Paradoxically, *conversos* could rise to the high ranks of political, ecclesiastical, and intellectual institutions and become connected with Christian aristocratic and merchant classes. Catholic saint and author **Teresa of Avila** (1515-1582), for example, was the child of a *converso*, as was **Luis de Santángel,** the Isabel's secretary and a principal supporter of Columbus. The mass conversion led to a complex situation as a "tainted" upper class desperately disavowed its Semitic heritage by such tactics as devising false genealogies. As a result, *converso* culture became neither entirely Jewish nor Christian.

Felipe III (1598-1621), preoccupied with religion and the finer aspects of life, allowed his favorite adviser, the Duque de Lerma, to pull the governmental strings. In 1609, Felipe III and the Duke expelled nearly 300,000 of Spain's remaining Moors. **Felipe IV** (1621-1665) painstakingly held the country together through his long, tumultuous reign. In the beginning of his rule, the impressionable young king was manipulated by the **Conde Duque de Olivares**, but Felipe wisened up as he settled in, and dismissed Olivares in 1643. Emulating his great-grandfather Carlos I, Felipe IV discerningly patronized the arts (painter Diego Velázquez and playwrights Lope de Vega and Calderón de la Barca were in his court) and architecture (the Buen Retiro in Madrid), and donned extravagant black garb. Then the **Thirty Years' War** (1618-1648) broke out over Europe, and defending Catholicism drained Spain's resources. It ended with the marriage of Felipe IV's daughter, María Teresa, and Louis XIV of France. Felipe's successor **Carlos II** (1665-1700), known as the *"hechizado"* (bewitched), was epileptic and impotent, the product of generations of inbreeding. From then on, little went right: Carlos II died, Spain fell into a depression, and cultural bankruptcy ensued.

BOURBONS, CONSTITUTIONS, AND LIBERALS (1713-1930). The 1713 Treaty of Utrecht seated **Felipe V** (1713-1746), a Bourbon grandson of **Louis XIV,** on the Spanish throne. The king built huge, showy palaces (to mimic Versailles in France) and cultivated a flamboyant, debauched court. Despite his undisciplined example, the Bourbons who followed Felipe ably administered the Empire, at last beginning to regain control of Spanish-American trade lost to northern Europeans. They also constructed scores of new canals and roads, organized settlements, and instituted agricultural reform and industrial expansion. **Carlos III** (1759-1788) was probably Madrid's finest "mayor," founding academies and generally beautifying the capital. Spain's global standing recovered enough for it to team with France to help the American colonies gain independence from Britain, aid that was symbolized by Captain Gálvez' heroically engineered victories in the American South.

Napoleon then invaded Spain (1808-1814) as part of his world domination kick. The French occupation ended, ironically enough, when the Protestant Brits beat up the Corsican's troops at Waterloo (1814). This victory led to the restoration of arch-reactionary **Fernando VII** (1814-1833), who sought to revoke the progressive Constitución de Cádiz of 1812. Galvanized by Fernando's ineptitude and inspired by liberal ideas in the new constitution, most of Spain's Latin American empire soon threw off its yoke. Domestically, parliamentary liberalism was restored in 1833 upon Fernando VII's death and survived the conservative challenge of the **Carlist Wars** (1833-1840); it would dominate Spanish politics until **Primo de Rivera's** mild dictatorship in the 1920s. Rapid industrialization and prosperity marked 19th-century Spain. It was during this period that the wealth produced by Catalunya's industrial-inspired *Renaixença* (Renaissance) financed Barcelona's **Modernista** movement in architecture and design. But Spain's defeat to the US in the 1898 **Spanish-American War** cost the Spanish the Philippines, Puerto Rico, Cuba, and dreams of empire, and much of Spain remained indigent and agricultural.

THE SECOND REPUBLIC AND NATIONAL TRAGEDY (1931-1975). In April 1931, **King Alfonso XIII** (1902-1931), disgraced by his support for Rivera's dictatorship, shamefully fled Spain, thus giving rise to the **Second Republic** (1931-1936). Republican Liberals and Socialists established safeguards for farmers and industrial workers, granted women's suffrage, assured religious tolerance, and chipped away at traditional military dominance. National euphoria, however, faded fast. The 1933 elections split the Republican-Socialist coalition, in the process increasing the power of right wing and Catholic parties in the parliamentary *Cortes*. Military dissatisfaction led to a heightened profile of the Fascist *Falange* (founded by Rivera's son José), which further polarized national politics. By 1936, radicals, anarchists, Socialists, and Republicans had formed a loose, federated alliance to win the next elections. But the victory was short-lived. Once **Generalísimo Francisco**

Franco snatched control of the Spanish army, militarist uprisings ensued, and the nation plunged into war. The three-year **Civil War** (1936-1939) ignited worldwide ideological passions. Germany and Italy dropped troops, supplies, and munitions into Franco's lap, while the stubbornly isolationist US and liberal European states were slow to aid the Republicans. Although Franco enjoyed popular support in Andalucía, Galicia, Navarra, and parts of Castilla, the Republicans controlled population and industrial centers. The Soviet Union, somewhat indirectly, called for a **Popular Front** of Communists, Socialists, and other leftist sympathizers to battle Franco's fascism. But soon after, the West abandoned the coalition, and aid from the Soviet Union waned as Stalin began to see the benefits of an alliance with Hitler. Without international aid, Republican forces found themselves cut off from necessary supplies and food, and began to surrender to the Nationalists. All told, bombings, executions, combat, starvation, and disease took nearly 600,000 lives, and in 1939 Franco's forces marched into Madrid and ended the war.

FRANCO AND NATIONAL TRAGEDY (1939-1975). Brain-drain (as leading scientists, artists, and intellectuals emigrated or were assassinated en masse), worker dissatisfaction, student unrest, regional discontent, and international isolation characterized the first decades of Franco's dictatorship. Several anarchist and nationalist groups, notably the Basque ETA, resisted the dictatorship throughout Franco's reign, often via terrorist acts. In his old age, Franco tried to smooth international relations by joining NATO and encouraging tourism, but the "national tragedy" (as it was later called) did not officially end until Franco's death in 1975. **King Juan Carlos I** (1975-), grandson of Alfonso XIII and nominally a Franco protégé, carefully set out to undo Franco's damage. In 1978, under centrist premier Adolfo Suárez, Spain adopted a new constitution in a national referendum that led to the restoration of parliamentary government and regional autonomy.

TRANSITION TO DEMOCRACY (1975-2000). The post-Franco years have been marked by progressive social change. Divorce was finally legalized in 1981 and women now vote more and comprise over 50% of universities' ranks. Problems may still plague Spain, but violent regionalists remain in the minority. Most, in fact, seem satisfied with the degree of regional autonomy. By the early 1980s, many regions controlled everything but foreign relations.

Charismatic **Felipe González** led the PSOE (Spanish Socialist Worker's Party) to victory in the 1982 elections. González opened the Spanish economy and championed consensus policies, overseeing Spain's integration into the European Community (EC; now the EU) in 1986. Despite unpopular economic stands, González was reelected in 1986 and continued a program of massive public investment. The years 1986 to 1990 were outstanding for Spain's economy, as the nation enjoyed an average growth rate of 3.8% a year. By the end of 1993, recession set in. In 1993, González and the PSOE only barely maintained a majority in Parliament over the increasingly popular conservative Partido Popular (PP). Revelations of large-scale corruption led to a resounding Socialist defeat at the hands of the Partido Popular in the 1994 European parliamentary elections. Negative attention triggered losses in regional elections in the President's homeland and traditional Socialist stronghold, Andalucía. A second cascade of high-profile scandals in late 1994 further destabilized the PSOE government. Most damaging of these scandals was the arrest of four interior ministry officials charged with organizing an illegal undercover organization, GAL (Anti-terrorist Liberation Groups), in the 1980s to combat Basque separatists; González himself was eventually pestered into admitting his complicity in GAL "death squads." **José María Aznar** led the PP into power after González's support eroded and has managed to maintain a delicately balanced coalition with the support of the Catalan and Canary Islands regional parties. There was a point in mid-1999 when the PSOE seemed on the verge of regaining the majority, but it achieved the worst results in 20 years in the 2000 elections while the PP won an absolute majority, returning Aznar to office once again.

SPAIN

CURRENT EVENTS. The last two years have seen mixed progress in one of Spain's most pressing areas of concern, Basque nationalism and terrorism. On September 12, 1998, the federal government issued the **Lizarra Declaration,** which called for an open dialogue between all parties (including the militant ETA) and was endorsed by the Basque National Party (PNV). Six days later, ETA publicly declared a truce with the national government. Moreover, the newest Basque president, **Juan José Ibarretxe,** gained the support of Euskal Herritarok (the political wing of ETA) and the federal government, and pledged to maintain and strengthen the peace. On December 3, 1999, however, ETA publicly declared an end to the 14-month cease-fire due to lack of progress with negotiations. The past year has since seen a return of periodic terrorist murders of PP and PSOE members, journalists, and army officers, as well as numerous instances of arson. The cry of "Basque yes, ETA no" has been growing stronger as Basque nationalists themselves split over the issue of terrorism, and the problem has become a central focus point for government officials like Aznar as he begins his new term in office.

On a brighter note, the Spanish economy is currently in good and improving shape. Over the past four years, unemployment has dropped from 23% to 15% with the creation of two million new jobs—half of the total employment increase for the entire European Union during that time. Aznar describes visions of "a new Spain" and plans to reduce unemployment even further, draw more women into the workforce, and improve the faltering birthrate by restructuring family and work arrangements. He has repeatedly emphasized his dedication to extensive labor and economic reforms in order to ensure continued growth, and given his strong political stature, there is little to suggest that he will not succeed.

LANGUAGE

Spain's four regional languages and their various dialects differ far more than just cosmetically, although some spelling variations are merely superficial. **Castilian** *(castellano),* spoken almost everywhere, is Spain's official language. **Catalan** *(catalá)* is spoken in all of Catalunya and has given rise through permutations to **Valencian** *(valenciá),* the regional tongue of Valencia in the east, and **Mallorquín,** the principal dialect of the Balearic Islands. The once-Celtic northwest corner of Iberia gabs in **Galician** *(gallego),* closely related to Portuguese. Although more prevalent in the countryside than cities, Galician is now spreading among the young, as is **Basque** *(euskera),* spoken in País Vasco and northern Navarra. All of these languages have standardized grammars and literary traditions, both oral and written. Regional television broadcasts, native film industries, strong political associations, and extensive schooling have saved these from extinction.

City and provincial names in this text are usually listed in Castilian first, followed by the regional language in parentheses, where appropriate. We have found it most useful, however, to adhere to common usage, and if a town is almost exclusively referred to according to its regional name, then we have written it as such. Information within cities (i.e. street or plaza names), on the other hand, is listed in the regional language. Generally, when traveling throughout Spain, Castilian names will suffice and are universally understood. However, it is wise within the specific regions to exercise politeness and respect towards the native language.

Let's Go provides a **phrasebook, glossary,** and **pronunciation guide** in the back of the book for all terms used recurrently throughout the text (see p. 727).

THE ARTS

PAINTING

Over its long history, Spanish painting has seen a series of luminaries separated by several lulls. Flemish, French, and Italian influences have often predominated, but such heavy hitters as El Greco, Diego Velázquez, Francisco Goya, and Pablo Picasso have forged a dazzling, distinctive, and hugely influential body of work.

SPAIN

EARLY AND RENAISSANCE. In the 11th and 12th centuries, fresco painters and manuscript illuminators decorated churches and their libraries along the Camino de Santiago and in León and Toledo. **Pedro Berruguete's** (1450-1504) use of traditional gold backgrounds in his religious paintings exemplifies the Italian-influenced style of early Renaissance works. Not until after Spain's imperial ascendance in the 16th century did painting reach its **Golden Age** (roughly 1492-1650). Felipe II imported foreign art and artists in order to jump-start native production and embellish his palace, El Escorial. Although he supposedly came to Spain seeking a royal commission, Cretan-born Doménikos Theotokópoulos, known as **El Greco** (1541-1614), was rejected by Felipe II for his intensely personal style. Confounding his contemporaries, El Greco has received newfound appreciation in the 20th century for his haunting, elongated figures and dramatic use of light and color. Setting up camp in Toledo, El Greco graced the Church of Santo Tomé with his masterpiece *The Burial of Count Orgaz* (1586-1588).

Felipe IV's foremost court painter, **Diego Velázquez** (1599-1660), is generally considered one of the world's greatest artists. Whether depicting Felipe IV's family or lowly court jesters and dwarves, Velázquez painted with naturalistic precision; working slowly and meticulously, he captured light with a virtually photographic quality. Nearly half of this Sevillian-born artist's works reside in the Prado, notably his famous *Las Meninas* (1656; see **Museo del Prado**, p. 109). Other noteworthy Golden Age painters include **José de Ribera** (1591-1652), **Francisco de Zurbarán** (1598-1664), and **Bartolomé Esteban Murillo** (1618-1682). Each treated religious subjects with a distinctive vision: Italian-born Ribera took a realistic and even crude approach, Sevillian Zurbarán painted for monastic orders in a fittingly austere style, and Murillo depicted Catholic dogma with idealism and sentimentality.

FROM MODERN TO AVANT-GARDE. During the era of Spain's waning power, **Francisco de Goya** (1746-1828) ushered European painting into the modern age. Hailing from provincial Aragón, Goya rose to the position of official court painter under the degenerate Carlos IV. Not bothering with flattery, Goya's depictions of the royal family come closer to caricature, as can attest Queen María Luisa's haughty, cruel jawline in Goya's famous *The Family of Charles IV* (1800). After an earlier Neoclassical period during which Goya stuck to smiling scenes of upper class gaiety, his later paintings graphically protest the lunacy of warfare. His series of etchings *The Disasters of War* (1810-1814), which includes the landmark *El dos de mayo* and *El tres de mayo*, records the horrific Napoleonic invasion of 1808. Deaf and despondent in his later years, Goya painted more nightmarish and wildly fantastic visions, inspiring expressionist and surrealist artists of the next century. The Prado museum has an full room of his chilling *Black Paintings* (1820-1823).

It is hard to imagine an artist who has had as profound an effect upon 20th-century painting as Andalucian-born **Pablo Picasso** (1881-1973). A child prodigy, Picasso headed for Barcelona, then a hothouse for Modernist architecture and political activism. Bouncing back and forth between Barcelona and Paris, Picasso in 1900 inaugurated his Blue Period, characterized by somber depictions of society's outcasts. His permanent move to Paris in 1904 initiated his Rose Period, during which he probed into the curiously engrossing lives of clowns and acrobats. With his French colleague Georges Braque, he founded **Cubism,** a method of painting objects simultaneously from multiple perspectives. His gigantic 1937 mural *Guernica* portrays the bombing of that Basque city by Nazi planes in cahoots with Fascist forces during the Spanish Civil War (see **The Tragedy of Guernica,** p. 422). A vehement protest against violence and fascism, *Guernica* now resides in the Centro de Arte Reina Sofia in Madrid.

Catalan painter and sculptor **Joan Miró** (1893-1983) created simplistic, almost child-like shapes in bright, primary colors. His haphazard, undefined squiggles became a statement against the authoritarian society of the post-Civil War years. By contrast, fellow Catalan **Salvador Dalí** (1904-1989) scandalized high society and leftist intellectuals in France and Spain by supporting the Fascists. Dalí's name is virtually synonymous with **Surrealism.** The wildly mustached painter tapped into dreams and the unconscious for odd images like the melting clocks in *The Persistence of Memory* (1931). His haunting *Premonition of the Civil War* (1936), subtitled *Soft Construction with Boiled Beans*, envisioned war as a distorted monster of putrefying flesh. A self-congratulatory fellow, Dalí founded the Teatro-Museo Dalí in Figueres, the second-most visited museum in Spain after the Prado.

Since Franco's death in 1975, a new generation of artists has thrived. With new museums in Madrid, Barcelona, Valencia, Sevilla, and Bilbao, Spanish painters and sculptors once again have a national forum for their work. Catalan **Antonio Tapiès** constructs collages out of unusual and unorthodox materials and is a founding member of the self-proclaimed "Abstract Generation," while **Antonio López García** has distinguished himself for his hyperrealist paintings. Upstarts include abstract artist **José María Sicilia**, sculptor **Susana Solano**, and **Miguel Barceló**, whose portraits resemble swarms of black flies.

ARCHITECTURE

Spanish architecture is as impressive and wildly diverse as the various civilizations that have called the Iberian peninsula home. Continental trends tended to arrive here late, only to be transformed into distinct Spanish shapes and forms.

ANCIENT AND EARLY MODERN. Scattered **Roman ruins** testify to six centuries of colonization. Highlights include some of the finest remains in existence: the aqueduct in Segovia, the theater in Mérida, and the town of Tarragona. Other vestiges of the Roman past lie at the ruined towns of Itálica (near Sevilla), Sagunto (near Valencia), and Empúries (near Palafrugell).

After the invasion of 711, the **Moors** constructed mosques and palaces throughout southern Spain. Because the Koran forbade human and animal representation, architects lavished their buildings with stylized geometric designs, red-and-white horseshoe arches, ornate tiles, courtyards, pools, and fountains. The spectacular 14th-century **Alhambra** in Granada and the **Mezquita** in Córdoba, one-time capital of the Muslim empire, epitomize the Moorish style.

The combination of Islam and Christianity created two architectural movements unique to Spain: **Mozarabic** and **Mudéjar**. The former describes Christians under Muslim rule (Mozarabs) who adopted Arab devices like the horseshoe-shaped arch and the ribbed dome. The more common Mudéjar architecture was created by Moors in the years between Christian resurgence (11th century) and the Reconquista (1492). Extensive use of brick and elaborately carved wooden ceilings typify Mudéjar style, which reached its height in the 14th century with **alcazars** (palaces) in Sevilla and Segovia and **synagogues** in Toledo and Córdoba.

The first Gothic cathedral in Spain was Burgos (1221), followed closely by Toledo and León. The **Spanish Gothic** style, like those elsewhere in Europe, brought experimentation with pointed arches, flying buttresses, slender walls, airy spaces, and stained-glass windows. There were variations, though: the Catalan style, for example, employed internal wall supports rather than external buttresses. Other Spanish riffs on the French original include centrally placed *coros* (choirs) and oversized *retablos* (brightly colored carved pieces placed above the high altar). The Gothic period also inspired many of Spain's countryside castles.

THE RENAISSANCE. New World riches inspired the **Plateresque** ("in the manner of a silversmith") style, a flashy extreme of Gothic that transformed wealthier parts of Spain. Intricate stonework and extravagant use of gold and silver splashed 15th- and 16th-century buildings, most notably in Salamanca, where the university practically drips with ornamentation. In the late 16th century, **Italian Renaissance** innovations in perspective and symmetry arrived in Spain to sober up the Plateresque style. **El Escorial** (1563-1584), Felipe II's grand palace, was designed by one of Spain's most prominent architects, Juan de Herrera, and best exemplifies unadorned Renaissance buildings.

Opulence seized center stage once again in 17th- and 18th-century **Baroque** Spain. The Chirruguera brothers pioneered this style—called, appropriately, **Chirrugueresque**—which is equal parts ostentatious, ornamental, and difficult to pronounce. Wildly elaborate works with extensive sculptural detail and twisted columns help set this period apart in Spanish architecture.

In the late 19th and early 20th centuries, Catalunya's **Modernistas** burst on the scene in Barcelona, led by the eccentric genius of **Antoni Gaudí, Luis Domènich i Montaner,** and **José Puig y Caldafalch.** Modernista structures defied any and all previous standards with their voluptuous curves and abnormal textures. The new style was inspired partly by Mudéjar relics but far more so by organic forms and unbridled imagination. Spain's outstanding architectural tradition continues to this day with such trend-setters as **Josep María Sert, Ricardo Bofill, Rafael Moneo,** and **Santiago Calatrava,** who has become the most recent sensation with his steel-and-crystal buildings and unmistakable bridges in Sevilla, Mérida, and Bilbao.

LITERATURE

Spain's literary tradition first blossomed in the late Middle Ages (1000-1500). The 12th-century *Cantar de Mío Cid* (Song of My Cid), Spain's most important epic poem, chronicles national hero El Cid's life and military triumphs, from his exile from Castilla to his return to grace in the king's court. Fernando de Rojas's *La Celestina* (1499), a tragicomedy most noted for its strong, witch-like female character, helped pave the way for picaresque novels like *Lazarillo de Tormes* (1554) and *Guzmán de Alfarache* (1599), rags-to-riches stories about mischievous boys (*pícaros*) with mostly good hearts. This literary form surfaced during Spain's **Golden Age.** Poetry particularly thrived in this era. Some consider the sonnets and romances of **Garcilaso de la Vega** the most perfect ever written in Castilian. Along with his friend **Joan Boscán,** Garcilaso introduced the "Italian" (or Petrarchan) sonnet to Iberia. **Francisco de Quevedo** also contributed to the rebirth of sonnets, treating erotic themes with a sardonic twist. The reverent **Santa Teresa de Ávila** and **San Juan de la Cruz** blessed Spain with mystical autobiographical and poetic writings. This period also bred outstanding dramas, including works from **Calderón de la Barca** and **Lope de Vega,** who wrote nearly 2000 plays. Both espoused the Neoplatonic view of love, claiming it changes one's life dramatically and eternally. **Miguel de Cervantes'** two-part *Don Quijote de la Mancha* (1605-1615)—often considered the world's first novel—is the most famous work of Spanish literature. Cervantes relates the hilarious parable of the hapless Don and his servant Sancho Panza, who think themselves bold *caballeros* (knights) out to save the world.

The 18th century brought a period of economic and political decline accompanied by a belated Enlightenment movement; one of the movement's most important figures was José Cadalso, author of the *Cartas Marruecas* (1789). The 19th century inspired contrasting variety, including the biting journalistic prose of **Mariano José de Larra, José Zorrilla's** romantic poem *Don Juan Tenorio* (1844) (a reworking of Tirso de Molina's *El burlador de Sevilla*), **Benito Pérez Galdos's** prolific realism, and the naturalistic novels of **Leopoldo Alas ("Clarín").** Essayist **Miguel de Unamuno** (whose novel *El árbol de la ciencia* is still the most-sold book in Spain) and cultural critic **José Ortega y Gasset** led the **Generación del '98;** reacting to Spain's defeat in the Spanish-American War (1898), these nationalistic authors argued, through essays and novels, that each individual must spiritually and ideologically attain internal peace before society can do the same. These authors heavily influenced the **Generación del 1927,** a group of experimental lyric poets who wrote Surrealist and avant-garde poetry. This group included **Jorge Guillén, Federico García Lorca** (assassinated at the start of the Civil War), **Rafael Alberti,** and **Luis Cernuda.**

In the 20th century, the Nobel Committee has honored playwright and essayist **Jacinto Benavente y Martínez** (1922), poet **Vicente Aleixandre** (1977), and novelist **Camilo José Cela** (1989; author of *La Familia de Pascal Duarte* (1942)). Female writers, like **Mercè Rodoreda** and **Carmen Martín Gaite,** have likewise earned critical acclaim. As Spanish artists are again migrating to Madrid, just as they did in the early part of the century, an avant-garde spirit—known as La Movida—has been reborn in the capital. **Ana Rossetti** and **Juana Castro** led a new generation of erotic poets into the 80s. This newest group of poets represents the first time in the panorama of Spanish literature that women have taken a place at the forefront. Recent years have also seen an ever-increasing consolidation of the literature of Spain's minority languages: Basque, Galician, and especially Catalan.

MUSIC

Flamenco, one of the cultural aspects for which Spain is most famous, is a combination of *cante jondo* (melodramatic song), guitar, and dancing. It originated among Andalucian gypsies and has continued as an extremely popular tradition that today captivates audiences all over the world. While it is possible to buy all manner of flamenco recordings, nothing compares to seeing a live performance; the spontaneity of the singing and the improvisation for which the best performers are famous is what gives flamenco music its soul. **Paco de Lucía** (1947-) is one of the most well known names associated with the tradition; his recent experimentation with jazz and new styles has irritated some purists. **Andrès Segovia** (1893-1987) was the seminal force in the development of the guitar as a concert instrument; his goal was to invest the guitar with the same renown as the violin and the cello.

Pablo Casals (1876-1973), Spanish cellist, conductor, composer, pianist, and humanitarian, was one of the most influential musicians of the 20th century. To promote world peace, Casals composed the oratorio *The Manger* (1960), which he conducted throughout the world. Singer **Camarón de la Isla**, who died young in 1992, maintains a devoted following throughout the peninsula. Barcelona-born **José Carreras** and **Plácido Domingo**, of "three Tenors" fame, are recognized as two of the world's finest opera singers. Singer-songwriters voiced underground discontent during the Franco years and became outwardly famous for it afterwards. **Joan-Manuel Serrat** is perhaps the biggest name; other singers of note are **Albert Pla, María del Mar Bonet, Luis Llach,** and **Ana Belén**. While American rock is coveted by youth throughout Spain, there is considerable national pride in Spanish rock, which is plentiful and widespread. **Mecano** hypnotizes audiences around the world, and disco-goers dance all night long to pulsing **bakalao** (comparable to American house). Barcelona band **El Último de la Fila** and big-forum **Héroes del Silencio** are well worth a listen. **Ella Baila Sola** tops the best-selling charts, and other popular groups and soloists are **Presuntos Implicados, Los Rodríguez,** and **Manolo Tena**. And we cannot forget **Julio Iglesias**, beloved the world over.

FILM

One of the greatest influences on Spanish film was not a filmmaker, but a politician: Franco's regime of censorship (1939-1975) defined Spanish film both during and after his rule. Early success, at least, did not elude Spanish cinema. Spain's first film, *Ría en un Café* (directed by Fructuos Gelabert), dates to 1897, and director **Segundo de Chomón** is recognized world-wide as a pioneer of early cinema. The Surrealist **Luis Buñuel**, close friends with **Salvador Dalí**, produced several early classics, most notably *Un Chien Andalou* (1929). Later, in exile from Francoist Spain, he produced a number of brilliantly sardonic films including *Belle du Jour* (1967). Meanwhile, in Spain itself, Franco's censorship stifled most creative tendencies and left the public with nothing to watch but cheap westerns *(chonzos)* and bland spy flicks. As government supervision slacked in the early 1970s, Spanish cinema showed signs of life, led by **Carlos Saura's** dark and subversive hits such as *El Jardín de las Delicias* (1970) and *Cría Cuervos* (1975).

In 1977, in the wake of Franco's death, domestic censorship laws were revoked, bringing artistic freedom along with financial hardship for Spanish filmmakers, who found their films shunned domestically in favor of newly permitted foreign films. Internationally, however, depictions of the exuberant excesses of a super-liberated Spain found increasing attention and respect. **Pedro Almodóvar's** *La ley de deseo* (1986), featuring **Antonio Banderas** as a gay man, perhaps best captures the risqué themes of transgression and sexuality most often treated by contemporary Spanish cinema. Almodóvar's *Mujeres al borde de un ataque de nervios* (1988) expresses post-Franco disillusion in an unrefined yet fashion-conscious Madrid. Almodóvar, probably the best known Spanish director of them all, has accumulated a long list of international awards, most recently crowned by a 2000 Oscar for his movie *Todo sobre mi madre*. Other directors to look for in Spain include **Bigas Luna**, director of the controversial *Jamón Jamón* (1992), **Fernando Trueba, Vicente Aranda, Victor Érice,** and **Pilar Micó**. Trueba's *Belle Epoque* won an Oscar in 1994, exemplifying Spanish cinema's ongoing rise in global respect.

BULLFIGHTING

A visit to Spain would not be complete without the experience of a bullfight. The national spectacle that is bullfighting dates, in its modern form, to the early 1700s. With bullfighting growing in popularity, Roman amphitheaters like those in Sevilla and Córdoba were rebuilt and embellished, and bulls began to be bred to possess aggressive instincts. The techniques of the modern bullfighter (*matador*) were developed around 1914 by Juan Belmonte, considered one of the greatest matadors of all time (others include Joselito, Manolete, and Cristina, the first female matador). Belmonte made bullfighting both more exciting and more dangerous by emphasizing closeness to the horns and intricate capework over the kill itself.

A bullfight is divided into three principal stages: in the first, *picadors* (lancers on horseback) pierce the bull's neck muscles to lower his head for the kill; next, assistants on foot thrust *banderillas* (decorated darts) into his back to enliven the tiring animal for the final stage; finally, the matador has ten minutes to kill his opponent with a sword between the shoulder blades. He can be granted up to five extra minutes if necessary, but after that the bull is taken out alive, much to the matador's disgrace. On the other hand, if the matador has shown special skill and daring, the audience waves white handkerchiefs to implore the bullfight's president to reward him with the coveted ears (and, very rarely, the tail).

Although bullfighting has always had its critics—the Catholic church in the 17th century felt that the risks made it equivalent to suicide—the late 20th century has seen an especially strong attack from animal rights' activists and social workers who feel that the prospect of social mobility leads too many young men to premature deaths. Whatever its merits and faults, however, bullfighting is an essential element of the Spanish national consciousness, and will almost certainly continue to be one. For an American take on the myth, meaning, and *machismo* of the bullfight, check out Ernest Hemingway's accounts in *Death in the Afternoon* (1932) and *The Sun Also Rises* (1926).

FOOD AND DRINK

Spanish food has tended to receive less international attention than the country's beaches, bars, and discos. Taste often ranks above appearance, preparation is rarely complicated, and many of the best meals are served not in expensive restaurants but in private homes or streetside bars. All of this has begun to change as Spanish food becomes increasingly sophisticated and cosmopolitan, but fresh local ingredients are still an integral part of the cuisine; consequently it varies according to each region's climate, geography, and history. Most experts, in fact, argue that one can only speak of Spanish food in regional terms.

REGIONAL FARE

Andalucian cuisine is the one of the oldest in all of Spain—it was through Sevilla that New World products like corn, peppers, tomatoes and potatoes first entered Europe. Andalucians have since mastered the art of *gazpacho*, a cool, tomato-based soup perfectly suited to the hot southern climate. The area is also known for its *pescadito frito* (fried fish), *rabo de toro* (bull's tail), egg yolk desserts, sherry wines, and excellent *tapas* (see below). Spain's best cured ham, *jamón ibérico*, (as opposed to the more common *jamón york*) comes from the town of Jabugo, where black-footed Iberian pigs gain a special flavor from daily oak acorn feasts.

SPAIN

Sheep share space with more of these prized pigs in nearby **Extremadura,** where a pastoral lifestyle has lent itself to hearty stews *(cocidos)*, cheeses, and unique breadcrumb-based meals *(migas)*. This type of dry-land "shepherd's cuisine" dominates throughout central Spain. **Castilla-La Mancha** is famous for its sheep's milk *queso manchego*, the most widely eaten cheese in Spain, and lamb and roasted game are an essential part of menus here and in **Castilla y Léon**. *Escabeche*, an Arab tradition of sautéing with lemon or vinegar, has become a Castilian specialty, as has *tortilla de española* (potato omelette) and *menestra de verduras*, a delicious vegetable mix. **Madrid** rivals Andalucía with its *tapas* offerings and is also renowned for the heavy *cocido madrileño*, a mix of meats, marrow, and sausages with cabbage, carrots, and potatoes.

Further north, **Galicia** surpasses every other region with its 800 miles of coastline; most Galician shellfish dishes are prepared simply to emphasize freshness. Octopus, spider crab, and mussels are particularly popular here, as is *empanada gallega*, the Galician pastry filled with everything from pork to chicken to fish. In **Asturias,** dried beans rule the kitchen; *fabada asturiana*, a bean and sausage stew, is the best-known dish. Apples, cider, and cow's milk are also especially good here. **Cantabrian** sardines, tuna, and anchovies are among the best in Spain. Food in the **País Vasco** rivals that of Catalunya in national prominence. Particularly popular dishes include *bacalao* (salted codfish), *angulas* (baby eels), and squid prepared in its own ink. It was also in Basque country that Spain's first gastronomic society was founded on January 1, 1900; these all-male cooking groups have grown increasingly popular over the past century and now number over 1,000.

In **Catalunya,** the Roman trilogy of olives, vineyard, and wheat dominates, and seafood, grilling, and unique sauces are key elements of many meals. **Aragonese** cuisine reflects the huge size of the region and ranges from cured hams to egg dishes to candied fruits. **Navarra** boasts the best red peppers in Spain, as well as the famous Roncal cheese; cooked game, sausages, and caldron stews are popular here. **La Rioja** is known for its pork, vegetables and above all wine. **Valencia,** on the East Coast, has been the home of *paella* and oranges ever since Arab short-grain rice and American oranges were introduced to the area. Less than 200 years old, *paella* has evolved from a simple vegetable-rice dish to an increasingly elaborate mix of seafood, vegetables, poultry, and meats, often cooked in communal settings.

Tapas, small bite-sized dishes, are a popular alternative to full meals. Generally eaten with drinks or as a mid-morning or late-night snack, *tapas* range in price, size, and content, but essentially every component of Spanish cuisine makes some appearance in tapa form. Their name comes from the verb *tapar*, "to cover"—it is speculated that they started out as the ham, cheese, or bread used to top wineglasses in the mid-18th-century to protect them from flies. From that humble beginning they have grown to be a major part of Spanish culinary and social culture. *Tortilla española* and *tortilla francesa* (plain egg omelette) are particularly common snack foods, as are *bocadillos* (thick baguette sandwiches) and *sandwiches* (white bread sandwiches that are often grilled).

MEALS AND DINING HOURS

Spaniards start their day with a continental breakfast of coffee combos or thick, liquid chocolate and *bollos* (rolls), *churros* (lightly fried fritters), or other pastries. Mid-morning they often have another *café* with a *tapa* to tide them over to the main meal of the day, *la comida*, generally eaten around 2 or 3pm. This traditionally consists of several courses: an appetizer of soup or salad; a main course of meat, fish, or a twist like *paella;* and a dessert of fruit, cheese, or some sweets. Children sometimes eat another small meal in the late afternoon; occasionally adults too will indulge in this *merienda* with cold cuts, cheese, or sausage, usually at the end of an early evening walk through the neighborhood. Supper at home, *la cena*, tends to be light, usually a sandwich or tortilla consumed around 8pm. Eating-out starts anywhere between 9pm and midnight. Going out for *tapas* is an integral part of the Spanish lifestyle; groups of friends will often spend several hours moving from bar to bar drinking, eating, and socializing leisurely.

EATING OUT

While some restaurants are open from 8am to 1 or 2am, most serve meals from 1 or 2 to 4pm only and in the evening from 8pm until midnight. Some hints: eating at the bar is cheaper than at tables, and the check won't be brought to your table unless you request it. *("La cuenta, por favor.")* Service in Spain is for the most part notoriously slow and at times frustrating; don't expect subservient, over-eager bus-boys. Most city tourist offices rate nearby *restaurantes* on a fork system, five forks meaning gourmet. Full *restaurante* meal prices range from about 800ptas to perhaps 1800ptas in a four-forker. *Cafeterías* are ranked by cups, one to three. Also, many *bar-restaurantes* (and some *hostales*) have cozy *comedors* (dining rooms) on the premises. Diners will repeatedly come across three options. **Platos combinados** (combination platters) include a main course and side dishes on a single plate, plus bread and sometimes a drink. The **menú del día**—two or three dishes, bread, wine/beer/mineral water, and dessert—is Spaniards' common choice for the *comida*, a good deal at roughly 800-1500ptas. Generally, you'll have several options, although advertised items are periodically not available. Those dining **á la carte** choose from individual entrees. Large *tapas*, often comparable in size to entrees, are called *raciones*. A full meal ordered dish by dish typically runs twice as much, if not more, than the complete *menú*.

DRINKS

Spanish **wine** is uniformly good. When in doubt, the *vino de la casa* (house wine) is an economical, often delectable choice. Also good are *vino tinto* (red wine), *vino blanco* (white wine), or *rosado* (rosé). For a taste, get a *chato* (small glass). Mild, fragrant reds are Spain's best vintages, but the corps of fine wines is vast. La Mancha's **Valdepeñas** are light, dry reds and whites, consumed without long aging. Catalunya's whites and **cavas** (champagnes) and Aragón's Cariñena wines pack bold punches. **Sidra** (alcoholic cider) from Asturias and País Vasco, and **sangría** (a red-wine punch with sliced peaches and oranges, seltzer, sugar, and a dash of brandy) are delicious alcoholic options. A popular light drink is *tinto de verano*, a cool mix of red wine and carbonated mineral water. **Jerez (sherry),** Spain's most famous wine, hails from Jerez de la Frontera in Andalucía. Try the dry *fino* and *amontillado* as aperitifs, or finish off a rich supper with the sweet *dulce*. The *manzanilla* produced in Sanlúcar has a salty aftertaste, ascribed to the region's salt-filled soil.

Wash down your *tapas* with a *caña (de cerveza)*, a normal-sized draft-beer. A *tubo* is a little bigger than a *caña*, and small beers go by different names—*corto* in Castilla, *zurito* in Basque. Pros refer to **mixed drinks** as *copas*. Beer and Schweppes is a **clara**. A **calimocho,** popular with young crowds, mixes Coca-Cola and red wine. Older drinkers prefer **sol y sombra** (brandy and anise).

Spain whips up numerous non-alcoholic quenchers as well, notably **horchata de chufa** (made by pressing almonds and ice together) and the flavored crushed-ice **granizados**. Shun the machine-made versions of either drinks—they don't do either justice. Coffee and milk, though, *do* mix. *Café solo* means black coffee; add a touch of milk for a *nube;* a little more and it's a *café cortado;* half milk, half coffee and you have *café con leche*, probably the most popular breakfast drink.

THE MEDIA

NEWSPAPERS AND MAGAZINES. *ABC*, palpably conservative and pro-monarchist, is the oldest national daily paper. It jostles with the more liberal *El País* for Spain's largest readership. *El Mundo* is a younger left-wing daily renowned for its investigative reporting. Barcelona's *La Vanguardia* maintains a substantial Catalan audience, while *La Voz de Galicia* dominates the northwest. *Diario 16*, the more moderate counterpart to *El Mundo*, publishes the popular newsweekly *Cambio 16*, whose main competition is *Tiempo. Hola*, the original *revista del corazón* (magazine of the heart), caters to Spain's love affair with aristocratic titles, Julio Iglesias, and "beautiful" people. The nosier, less tasteful tabloid *Semana* has gossip galore and readers aplenty.

TELEVISION. Channel surf to the state-run TVE1 and La2 or private stations Tele5 and Antena3. Each region has its own network, broadcast in the local vernacular. In Madrid, the local channel is TeleMadrid (TM3). Canal Plus is Spain's top-notch HBO equivalent. It appears scrambled during movies but features free sitcoms and music videos on Sunday mornings. Tune in to news at 3 and 8:30pm on most stations. Programming includes well-dubbed American movies, sports, steamy Latin American *telenovelas* (soaps), game shows (such as the popular and dangerous *Juego de la Oca*, or *Game of the Goose*), jazzed-up documentaries, and cheesy three-hour variety extravaganzas. View fab American series like *Baywatch* and *Seinfeld* and Spanish equivalents. If all else fails, *fútbol* games and bullfights are guaranteed to hold your attention. Check newspapers for listings.

SPORTS

¡Viva España! True to form, the beat and the glory go on for Spanish sports. **Miguel Indurain,** a Basque hero and Spain's most decorated athlete, may not have been able to win a sixth straight *Tour de France* title before his retirement, but he is remembered fondly by his fanatical fans. Several Spaniards, including old favorites like **Arancha Sanchez-Vicario** and **Conchita Martínez** and up-and-comers like **Carlos Moya** and **Alex Corretja,** have made their names in tennis. Golfer **Chema Olazabal** is one of the world's best, with two Green Jackets in his closet to prove it, but the recent successes of **Seve Ballesteros** and **Sergio García,** "El Niño," have really brought the sport to national attention. As with cuisine, regional specialties spice the sports scene, including *cesta punta* (known internationally as *jai alai*) from Basque country, wind surfing along the southern coast, and skiing in the Sierra Nevadas and the Pyrenees. But the most popular sport is of course *fútbol*, a uniting passion for Spaniards; championship wins send fans into the streets for hours, even days, with painted faces, flags waving from cars, and extended disco hours. Their pride is well-warranted: despite a shocking early knock-out in the first round of the 1998 World Cup, the Spanish national team ranks with the finest in Europe. City teams are also powerful: in May 2000, Real Madrid won its 8th European League championship, beating Valencia in a first-ever same-country final match.

RECOMMENDED READING

English-speaking scribes have penned several top-notch Spanish travel narratives. Richard Ford's witty, 19th-century account, *Handbook for Travellers in Spain and Readers at Home*, remains a fan-favorite. Most time-honored classics are region-specific, including Washington Irving's *Tales of the Alhambra*, Bloomsbury Circle-expatriate Gerald Brenan's *South from Granada*, Robert Graves' Mallorcan stories, and Laurie Lee's *As I Walked Out One Midsummer Morning*. For native flavor, read Nobel prize-winning Camilo José Cela's *Journey to the Alcarria*, based on rural Castilla.

FICTION, SPANISH AND FOREIGN. Start with *Poema del Mio Cid* and Cervantes's *Don Quijote*. Among the most popular modern novelists are the moving Carmen Laforet *(Nada)*, post-modern Juan José Millás *(El desorden de tu nombre)*, lyrical Esther Tusquet *(El mismo mar de todos los veranos)*, and amusing Manuel Vázquez Montalbán *(Murder in the Central Committee)*. Spain has also inspired a number of prominent American and British authors. Ernest Hemingway immortalized bullfighting, *machismo*, and Spain itself in *The Sun Also Rises* and *For Whom the Bell Tolls*. Graham Greene takes a walk (via a priest, all around Spain) on the lighter side in the humorous *Monsignor Quijote*.

ART AND ARCHITECTURE. The definitive work on Spanish art history is Bradley Smith's *Spain: A History in Art*. For late 20th-century art, check out William Dyckes' *Contemporary Spanish Art*. The standard text on Spanish architecture is Bernard Bevan's *History of Spanish Architecture*. For the latest (1980s and 90s) scoop, peruse Anatzu Zabalbeascoa's *The New Spanish Architecture*. Fred Licht's collection of essays, *Goya*, is a must-read for fans of the artist, and books on Picasso, Dalí, and Gaudí can be found with minimal fuss.

HISTORY AND CULTURE. Written in 1968, James Michener's best-seller *Iberia* continues to captivate audiences with its thoroughness, insight, and style. *Barcelona*, by Robert Hughes, delves deep into the culture of Catalunya. George Orwell's *Homage to Catalonia*, a personal account of the Civil War, rivals *Iberia* and *Barcelona* in quality and fame. A handful of other historians and works stand out—Richard Fletcher's comprehensive *Moorish Spain*, J.H. Elliot's masterful *Imperial Spain 1469-1716*, and Raymond Carr (*Spain 1808-1975*) and Stanley Payne (*The Franco Regime 1936-1975*) on the modern era. For a Spaniard's take on Spanish history, try Juan Lalaguna's *A Traveller's History of Spain* (part of the international Traveller's History series).

ESSENTIALS

The information in this section is mostly designed to help travelers get their bearings once they are in Spain. For information about general **travel preparations** (including passports and permits, money, health, packing, international transportation, and more), consult the **Essentials** section at the beginning of this book. Essentials also has important information about alternatives to tourism (**work** and **study** programs in Spain; see p. 46) and for those with specific concerns: **women travelers** (p. 42); **older travelers** (p. 43); **bisexual, gay, and lesbian travelers** (p. 43); **travelers with disabilities** (p. 44); **minority travelers** (p. 44); **travelers with children** (p. 45); and travelers with **dietary concerns** (p. 45).

GETTING THERE AND GETTING AROUND

Transportation to and within Spain is quite good. The easiest, quickest, and often cheapest method of entering Spain is by plane, although Barcelona is well-connected to the European rail system. Despite a romanticized view of European train travel, buses offer the most extensive coverage and are the best option for short trips. Trains are good for longer journeys within Spain, as domestic flights can be somewhat pricey. Spain's islands are accessible by both plane and ferry. For more specific information on island travel, see **Balearic Islands** (p. 54) and **Canary Islands** (p. 495). For general information on traveling in Europe, see **Getting There**, p. 30.

BY PLANE

All major international airlines offer service to Madrid and Barcelona, most serve the Balearic and Canary Islands, and many serve Spain's smaller cities. **Iberia** (in US and Canada ☎ (800) 772-4642; in UK ☎ (020) 7830 0011; in Spain ☎ 902 400 500; in South Africa ☎ (11) 884 92 55; in Ireland ☎ (1) 407 30 17; www.iberia.com) serves all domestic locations and all major international cities. **Aviaco**, a subsidiary of Iberia, covers only domestic routes. Ask about youth and other discounts— youth under 12 often get a 25% discount, and Iberia usually offers a range of ticket types with different restrictions and prices. Some fares purchased in the US require a 21-day minimum advance purchase.

Iberia's two less-established domestic competitors often offer cheaper fares and are worth looking into. **Air Europa** (in US ☎ (888) 238-7672 or (718) 244-6016; in Spain ☎ 902 30 06 00; www.air-europa.com) flies out of New York City and most European cities to Madrid, Málaga, Tenerife, and Santiago de Compostela. Discounts available for youth and senior citizens. No service Wednesdays or Sundays during the summer. **SpanAir** (in US ☎ (888) 545-5757; in Spain ☎ 902 13 14 15; fax 971 49 25 53; www.spanair.com) also offers international and domestic flights.

SpanAir Spain Pass: good for flying to any airport within Spain, including Mallorca and Menorca. No minimum stay; maximum stay 3 months. Reservations must be made before arriving in Spain. Valid for 1 year. Under 12 65% discount. 3 tickets US$195, 4 tickets US$240, 5 tickets US$295. Additional tickets US$50. **SpanAir Spain Pass B** is the same as Spain Pass A, but also includes Lanzarote, Gran Canaria, or Tenerife. 3 tickets US$245, 4 tickets US$290, 5 tickets US$345. Additional tickets US$50.

SPAIN

Iberia VisitSpain Airpass: 4 one-way coupons good for all mainland airports and the Balearic Islands. Reservations must be made before arriving in Spain. Maximum stay 60 days. Oct. 1-June 14 US$240 (US$299 with Canaries added); June 15-Sept. 30 US$260 (US$349 with Canaries).

BY TRAIN

Spanish trains are clean, relatively punctual, and reasonably priced, but tend to bypass many small towns. Spain's national railway is **RENFE** (www.renfe.es). Avoid *tranvía, semidirecto,* or *correo* trains—they are very slow.

AVE (Alta Velocidad Española): High-speed trains dart between Madrid and Sevilla (hitting Ciudad Real and Córdoba). AVE trains soar above others in comfort and price, not just speed. The 10am and noon trains are cheapest; student discounts are available.

Talgo: Sleek trains zip passengers in air-conditioned compartments from Madrid to Málaga, Cádiz/Huelva, or Algeciras. It's more comfortable, possibly faster, and twice as pricey as *Cercanías-Regionales* trains.

Talgo 200: *Talgo* trains on AVE tracks. These currently service only Madrid-Málaga and Madrid-Cádiz/Huelva. Changing a Talgo 200 ticket carries a 20% fine.

Intercity: Cheaper than Talgo, but fewer stops. A/C and comfy. 5 lines: Madrid-Valencia, Madrid-Zaragoza-Barcelona, Madrid-Alicante, Madrid-Zaragoza-Logroño-Pamplona, and Madrid-Murcia-Cartagena.

Estrella: A pretty slow night train that has *literas* (bunks).

Cercanías: Commuter trains from large cities to suburbs and towns, with frequent stops.

Regional: Like *cercanías* but older; multi-stop, cheap rides to small towns and cities.

There is absolutely no reason to buy a Eurail pass if you are planning on traveling just within Spain and Portugal. Trains are cheap, so a pass saves little money. For the most part buses are an easier and more efficient means of traveling around Spain. There are several passes that cover travel within Spain. Ages 4-11 are half-price; children under 4 are free. You must purchase railpasses at least 15 days before departure. Call 1-800-4Eurail in the US or go to www.raileurope.com.

Spain Flexipass offers 3 days of unlimited travel in a 2-month period. 1st-class US$200; 2nd-class US$155. Each additional rail-day (up to 7) US$35 for 1st-class, US$30 for 2nd-class.

Iberic Railpass is good for 3 days of unlimited 1st-class travel in Spain and Portugal for US$205. Each additional rail-day (up to 7) US$45.

Spain Rail n' Drive Pass is good for 3 days of unlimited 1st-class train travel and 2 days of unlimited mileage in a rental car within a 2-month period. Prices US$255-365, depending on how many people are traveling and the type of car. Up to 2 additional rail-days and extra car days are also available, and a 3rd and 4th person can join in the car using only a Flexipass.

BY BUS

Bus routes, far more comprehensive than the rail network, provide the only public transportation to many isolated areas and almost always cost less than trains. They are generally quite comfortable, although leg room may be limited and few buses have bathrooms on board. For those traveling primarily within one region, buses are probably the best method of transport.

Spain has numerous private companies; the lack of a centralized bus company may make itinerary planning an ordeal. Companies' routes rarely overlap; it's unlikely that more than one will serve your intended destination. We list below the major national companies, along with the phone number of the Madrid or Barcelona office; you will likely use other companies for travel within a region.

ALSA (☎ 91 528 28 03). Serves Madrid, Galicia, Asturias, and Castilla y León. Also to Portugal, Morocco, France, Italy, and Poland.

Auto-Res/Cunisa, S.A. (☎ 91 551 72 00). From Madrid to Castilla y León, Extremadura, Galicia, and Valencia.

Julia Via Internacional (☎ 91 490 40 00). Runs throughout Iberia and Western Europe, and to Morocco.

Linebús (☎ 93 265 07 00). Runs to France, the UK, Netherlands, Italy, and Morocco.

SAIA (International Autocares) (☎ 91 530 76 00). Runs to Belgium, Germany, France, Netherlands, and Andorra.

Samar, S.A. (☎ 91 468 48 39). To Aragón, Toulouse (in France), Andorra, and Portugal.

BY CAR

For more info on renting and driving a car, see p. 40. Spain's highway system connects major cities by four-lane *autopistas* with plenty of service stations. Fast may be in vogue, but **speeders beware:** police can "photograph" the speed and license plate of your car, and issue a ticket without pulling you over. Purchase **gas** in super (97-octane), normal (92-octane), diesel, and unleaded. Prices are astronomical by North American standards: about 130-140ptas per liter. **Renting** a car in Spain is considerably cheaper than in many other European countries. You may want to check with **Atesa,** Spain's largest national rental agency. The Spanish automobile association is **Real Automóbil Club de España (RACE),** C. José Abascal, 10, Madrid (☎ 91 447 32 00; fax 91 447 79 48).

BY THUMB

In Spain, hitchers report that Castilla and Andalucía offer little more than a long, hot wait, and that hitchhiking out of Madrid is virtually impossible. The Mediterranean Coast and the islands are much more promising. Approaching people for rides at gas stations near highways and rest stops purportedly gets results. *Let's Go* does not recommend hitchhiking.

MONEY

Banking hours in Spain from June through September are generally Monday through Friday 9am to 2pm; from October to May, banks are also open Saturday 9am to 1pm. Some banks are open in the afternoon as well. **Banco Central Hispano** often provides good rates, especially on traveler's checks. The following rates are from August 2000. For more information on money, see p. 13.

Tipping is not very common in Spain. In restaurants, all prices include service charge. Satisfied customers occasionally toss in some spare change—usually no more than 5%—but this is purely optional. Many people give train, airport and hotel porters a 100pta coin per bag, while taxi drivers sometimes get 5-10%. **Bargaining** is really only common at flea markets and with street vendors.

Spain has a 7% **Value Added Tax,** known as IVA, on all restaurant and accommodations. The prices listed in *Let's Go* include IVA unless otherwise mentioned. Retail goods bear a much higher 16% IVA, although listed prices are usually inclusive. Non-EU citizens who have stayed in the EU fewer than 180 days can claim back the tax paid on purchases at the airport. Ask the shop where you have made the purchase to supply you with a tax return form.

SAFETY

EMERGENCY ☎112	Local police: 091. National police: 092. Medical: 061.

Spain has a low crime rate, but visitors can always fall victim to tourist-related crimes. For general safety tips, see p. 18. Tourists should take particular care in Madrid, especially in El Centro, and in Barcelona around Las Ramblas.

Also of concern to the traveler in the northwestern corner of Spain is Basque terrorism, a highly controversial issue both domestically and internationally. ETA, whose name stands for Basque Homeland and Freedom in the Basque language, has been blamed for the deaths of some 800 people in the past 32 years (see p. 57).

SPAIN

Its separatist aims have been concentrated toward the pulling away of the Basque region as its own country, distinct from Spain and France. Their political activity has taken the form of bombings and political assassinations. In 1998, the government issued the Lizarra Declaración, which called for an open dialogue between all involved parties, and ETA publicly declared a truce eight days later. However, the cease-fire has ended, and as of June 2000 there have been several recent political assassinations. While there may be some risk to the traveler, the attacks are very targeted and are not considered random terrorism.

HEALTH

There are no particular health risks associated with traveling in Spain. For general information on travel-related **health** concerns, see p. 19. The public health care system in Spain is very reliable; in an emergency, seek out the *urgencias* (emergency) section of the nearest hospital. For smaller concerns, it is probably best to go to a private clinic to avoid the frustration of long lines. Expect to pay cash up front (though most travel insurance will pick up the tab later) and bring your passport and other forms of identification. A single visit to a clinic in Spain can cost anywhere from US$40 to US$100, depending upon the service. Ask the tourist office, your consulate or your accommodation for help finding a doctor or clinic.

Farmacias in Spain are also very helpful. A duty system has been set up so that at least one *farmacia* is open at all times in each town; look for a lighted green cross. Spanish pharmacies are not the place to find your cheap summer flip-flops or greeting cards, but they sell contraceptives, common drugs and many prescription drugs; they can answer simple medical questions and help you find a doctor.

ACCOMMODATIONS

YOUTH HOSTELS

Red Española de Albergues Juveniles (REAJ), C. José Ortega y Gasset, 71, Madrid 28006 (☎ 91 347 77 00; fax 91 401 81 60), the Spanish Hostelling International (HI) affiliate, runs 165 youth hostels year-round. Prices depend on location (typically some distance away from town center) and services offered, but are generally 1500-2500ptas for guests under 26 and higher for those 26 and over. Breakfast is usually included; lunch and dinner are occasionally offered at an additional charge. Hostels usually lockout around 11:30am, and have curfews between midnight and 3am. As a rule, don't expect much privacy—rooms typically have from four to 20 beds in them. To reserve a bed in high season (July-Aug. and during *fiestas*), call well in advance. A national **Youth Hostel Card** is usually required (see **Hostels**, p. 25). HI cards are also available from Spain's main youth travel company, **TIVE**. Occasionally, guests can stay in a hostel without one and pay extra, or pay 300ptas extra per night for six nights to become a member.

PENSIONES AND HOSTALES

COULD *LET'S GO* BE WRONG? The prices quoted in *Let's Go* were gathered during the summer of 2000; there is a good chance that they will increase by up to 500ptas by the end of 2001. Don't refuse to pay the owner's price simply because it is more than that quoted in the book. *Let's Go* may update annually, but unfortunately prices update annually as well. On the other hand, if the price is substantially more (over 1000ptas), ask other guests what they are paying to make sure you are getting charged the proper amount.

Spanish accommodations have many aliases, distinguished by the different grades of rooms. The cheapest and barest options are **casas de huéspedes** and **hospedajes**, while **pensiones** and **fondas** tend to be a bit nicer. All are basically just boarding houses. Higher up the ladder, **hostales** generally have sinks in bedrooms and provide sheets and lockers, while **hostal-residencias** are similar to hotels in overall quality. The government rates *hostales* on a two-star system; even establishments receiving one star are typically quite comfortable. The system also fixes each *hostal*'s prices, posted in the lounge or main entrance. *Hostal* owners invariably dip below the official rates, especially in the off season (Sept.-May). In most cases, the owner lives in the same building.

The highest-priced accommodations are **hoteles,** which have a bathroom in each room but are usually too expensive for the budget traveler. The cream of the crop are the beautiful **Paradores Nacionales**—castles, palaces, convents, and historical buildings that have been converted into luxurious hotels that often are interesting sights in their own right. For a *parador*, 12,000ptas per night is a bargain.

Frequently owners will ask to copy your passport number when you check in, and in some cases they will keep it until you pay your bill. Always ask to see a room and verify the price before paying. Haggling for prices, especially in small inns, is common practice. Single rooms in cities are hard to come by, so solo travelers may have to pay for a double.

If you have any trouble (with rates or service), ask for the **libro de reclamaciones** (complaint book), which by law must be produced on demand. The argument will usually end immediately, since all complaints must be forwarded to the authorities within 48 hours. Report any problems to tourist offices who may help resolve disputes for you. In our listings, **full bath** or **bath** refers to a shower and toilet, while **shower** means just a shower stall in the room. Most rooms that we list have winter heating, as Spanish winters (particularly in the north and in the mountains) can be quite chilly; when a listing says "heat in winter" it is to differentiate it from the other accommodations in the area, which are probably unheated. Air-conditioning (A/C) is mentioned when it is available.

In less-touristed areas, **casas particulares** (private residences) may sometimes be the only option. **Casas rurales** (rural cottages) and **casas rústicas** (farmhouses), officially referred to as *agroturismo*, have overnight rates from 1000 to 3500ptas. Both are common in northern Asturias and Castilla y León. In the Pyrenees and Picos de Europa, there are several **refugios,** rustic mountain huts for hikers.

CAMPING

In Spain, **campgrounds** are generally the cheapest choice for two or more people. Most charge separate fees per person, per tent, and per car; others charge for a *parcela*—a small plot of land—plus possible per-person fees. Although it may seem like an inexpensive option, prices can get high for lone travelers, and even for pairs. Campgrounds are categorized on a three-class system, with rating and prices based on amenity quality. Like hostels, they must post fees within view of the entrance. They must also provide sinks, showers, and toilets. Ritzier ones may have playgrounds, grocery stores, cafes, restaurants, post offices, bike or moped rentals, or pools. Most tourist offices provide info on official areas, including the hefty *Guía de campings*. Reservations are usually necessary in the summer.

KEEPING IN TOUCH

Some useful **communication information** (including international access codes, calling card numbers, country codes, operator and directory assistance, and emergency numbers) is listed on the **inside back cover.**

TELEPHONES. The central Spanish phone company is Telefónica. Phone booths are marked by signs that say *Teléfono público* or *Locutorio;* most bars have pay phones, though they are often only coin-operated. The best way to make local calls is with a phone card, issued in denominations of 1000 and 2000ptas and sold at tobacconists (*estancos* or *tabacos*, identifiable by brown signs with yellow lettering and tobacco leaf icons) and most post offices. American Express and Diner's Club cards now work as phone card substitutes in most pay phones. International calls can be made using phone cards but are very expensive; the best way to call home is with an international calling card issued by your phone company. Numbers for obtaining calling cards from home are in the **Essentials** section (see p. 28).

FAX. Most Spanish post offices have **fax services.** Some photocopy shops and telephone offices *(Telefónica)* also offer fax service, but they tend to charge more than post offices (whose rates are standardized by the government), and faxes can only be sent, not received. Cybercafes are also becoming increasingly popular places to send faxes at cheap rates.

MAIL. Air mail *(por avión)* takes five to eight business days to reach the US or Canada; service is faster to the UK and Ireland and slower to Australia and New Zealand. Standard postage is 115ptas to North America. **Surface mail** *(por barco)*, while considerably less expensive than air mail, can take over a month, and packages will take two to three months. **Registered** or **express mail** *(registrado* or *certificado)*, is the most reliable way to send a letter or parcel home, and takes four to seven business days (letter postage 237ptas). Spain's **overnight mail** is not worth the added expense, since it is not exactly "overnight." For better service, try private companies such as DHL, UPS, or the Spanish company SEUR; look under *mensajerías* in the yellow pages. Their reliability does, however, come at a high cost. **Stamps** are sold at post offices and tobacconists *(estancos* or *tabacos)*. Mail letters and postcards from the yellow mailboxes scattered throughout most cities, or from the post office in small towns.

EMAIL. Email is easily accessible within Spain and much quicker and more reliable than the regular mail system. An increasing number of bars offer Internet access for a fee of 600-1000ptas per hour. Cybercafes are listed in most towns and all cities. In small towns, if internet access is not listed, your best bet is to check the library or the tourist office (where occasionally travelers may get access for a small fee). The website www.tangaworld.com lists nearly 200 cybercafes across Spain by location and name.

EMBASSIES AND CONSULATES

Embassies and consulates are usually open Monday through Friday, mornings and evenings, with *siestas* in between. Many consulates are only open in the mornings. Call for specific hours.

Australian Embassy: Santa Engracia, 120, **Madrid** 28003 (☎ 91 441 93 00; fax 91 442 53 62; email information@embaustralia.es; www.embaustralia.es). **Consulates:** Gran Vía Carlos III, 98, 9th fl., **Barcelona** 08028 (☎ 93 330 94 96; fax 93 411 09 04); Federico Rubio, 14, **Sevilla** 41004 (☎ 95 422 09 71; fax 95 421 11 45).

British Embassy: C. Fernando el Santo, 16, **Madrid** 28010 (☎ 91 700 82 00; fax 91 700 83 11). **Consulate-General:** Edificio Torre, Av. Diagonal, 477, 13th fl., **Barcelona** 08036 (☎ 93 366 62 00; fax 93 366 62 21; email brconbcn@alba.mssl.es). **Consulates:** Centro Colón, Marqués de la Ensenada, 16, 2nd fl., **Madrid** 28004 (☎ 91 308 52 01; fax 91 308 08 82); Alameda de Urquijo, 2, 8th fl., **Bilbao** 48008 (☎ 94 415 76 00; fax 94 416 76 32); Pl. Mayor, 3D, **Palma de Mallorca** 07002 (☎ 971 71 24 45; fax 971 71 75 20); Av. Isidor Macabich, 45, 1st. fl., Apartavo 307, **Ibiza** 07800 (☎ 971 30 18 18; fax 971 30 19 72); Pl. Calvo Sotelo, 1/2, **Alicante** 03001 (☎ 96 521 60 22; fax 96 514 05 28); Po. Pereda, 27, **Santander** 39004 (☎ 942 22 00 00; fax 942 22 29 41); Edificio Eurocom, Bloque Sur, **Málaga** 29006 (☎ 95 235 23 00; fax 95 235 92 11); Edificio Cataluña, C. Luis Morote, 6, 3rd fl., **Las Palmas** 35007 (☎ 928 26 25 08; fax 928 26 77 74).

Canadian Embassy: C. Núñez de Balboa, 35, **Madrid** 28001 (☎ 91 423 32 50; fax 91 423 32 51; http://info.ic.gc.ca/Tourism). **Consulates:** Elisenda de Pinos, 8 **Barcelona** 08034 (☎ 93 204 27 00; fax 93 204 27 01); Edificio Horizonte, Pl. Malaguita, 2, 1st fl., **Málaga** 29016 (☎ 95 222 33 46; fax 95 222 40 23; email concon@microcad.es).

Irish Embassy: Po. Castellana, 46, 4th fl., **Madrid,** 28046 (☎ 91 576 35 00 or 91 435 16 77; email irlmad@ibm.net). **Consulate:** Gran Via Carlos III, 94, **Barcelona** 08028 (☎ 93 451 90 21; fax 93 411 29 21).

New Zealand Embassy: Pl. Lealtad, 2, 3rd fl., **Madrid** 28014 (☎ 91 523 02 26; fax 91 523 01 71). **Consulate:** Travesera de Gracia, 64, 4th fl., **Barcelona** 08006 (☎ 93 209 03 99; fax 93 202 08 90).

South African Embassy: Claudio Coello, 91, 6th fl., **Madrid** 28006 (☎ 91 435 66 88; fax 91 577 74 14; email sudafrica@arrakkis.es). **Consulates:** Teodora Lamadrid, 7-11, **Barcelona** 08022 (☎ 93 418 64 45; fax 93 418 05 38; email sudafrica@ceisei.es); Las Mercedes, 31, Las Arenas, **Bilbao** 48930 (☎/fax 94 464 11 24); Franchy y Roca, 5, 6th fl., **Las Palmas de Gran Canaria** 35007 (☎ 928 22 60 04; fax 928 22 60 15).

US Embassy: C. Serrano, 75, **Madrid** 28006 (☎ 91 587 22 00; fax 91 587 22 39). **Consulate General:** Pg. Reina Elisenda de Moncada, 23, **Barcelona** 08034 (☎ 93 280 22 27; fax 93 205 52 06). **Consulates:** Po. Delicias, 7, **Sevilla** 41012 (☎ 95 423 18 85; fax 95 423 20 40); Edificio Arca, C. Los Martínez de Escobar, 3, Oficina 7, **Las Palmas** 35007 (☎ 928 27 12 59; fax 928 22 58 63); C. Paz, 6, Local 5, **Valencia** 46003 (☎ 96 351 69 73; fax 96 352 95 65); Cantón Grande, 6-8 E, **La Coruña** 15003 (☎ 981 21 32 33; fax 981 22 88 08); Av. Jaume II, 26, Entresuelo H1, **Palma de Mallorca** 07012 (☎ 971 72 26 60; fax 971 71 87 55).

HOLIDAYS

Festivals and holidays are a large part of Spanish culture. They can transform the quietest towns into huge parties overnight; they also result in closed establishments, higher prices, and scarce accommodations. The list here is for major festivals only; practically every village in Spain has its own local festivals. The dates listed below are valid for the year 2001 only.

DATE	FESTIVAL	LOCATION
January 1	New Year's Day	National
January 6	Epiphany	National
February 15-25	Carnaval	National, but especially in Cádiz (p. 229) and Cataluya (p. 337)
mid-March	Las Fallas	Valencia (p. 276)
April 9-15	Festival of Religious Music	Cuenca (p. 139)
April 9-15	Semana Santa (Holy Week)	National
April 12	Maundy Thursday	National (except Valencia and Cataluya)
April 13	Good Friday	National
April 15	Easter	National
April 23	Festa di Sant Jordi (St. George's Day)	Barcelona (p. 298)
late April to early May	Feria de Abril (April Fair)	Sevilla (p. 194)
May 1	May Day/Fiesta del Trabajo (Labor Day)	National
May	Feria del Caballo (Horse Fair)	Jerez de la Frontera (p. 222)
early to mid-May	Concurso de Patios Cordoboses (Patio Festival)	Córdoba (p. 213)
2nd half of May	San Isidro Festival	Madrid (p. 119)
June 11	Romería del Rocío (Rocio Pilgrimage)	El Rocío and Sevilla (p. 194)
June 22	Corpus Christi	National, with special celebrations in Toledo, La Laguna (near Tenerife), and Granada (p. 259)
June 20-29	Festival de San Juan (Festival of St. John)	Alicante (p. 287)
June 23	Noche de Sant Joan	National
June 29	Batalla del Vino	Haro (p. 389)
July	Festival Cueva de Nerja	Nerja (p. 249)

DATE	FESTIVAL	LOCATION
June to July	International Guitar Festival	Córdoba (p. 213)
June to July	International Music and Dance Festival	Granada (p. 259)
July 6-14	San Fermines (Running of the Bulls)	Pamplona (Iruña) (p. 390)
mid- to late July	Festival de Jazz	San Sebastián (p. 405)
July 25	Día de Santiago Apóstal (Feast of St. James the Apostle)	National, but especially in Santiago de Compostela
July to August	Festival de Música d'Estiu	Ciutadella (p. 484)
July to August	International Jazz Festival	Sitges (p. 335)
July to August	Festival de Jazz de la Costa Brava	Callela (p. 346)
July to August	Festival de Teatro Clásico	Mérida (p. 186)
August 8-16	Semana Grande	Spain's northern coast
August 15	La Asunción (Feast of the Assumption)	National
mid-August	Moros y Cristianos	Across Valencia province
September 11	Fiesta Nacional de Catalunya	Barcelona (p. 332)
September 21-30	Festival International de Cine (International Film Festival)	San Sebastián (p. 405)
September to November	Festivales de Otoños	Madrid (p. 119)
October 12	Fiesta Nacional de España (National Day)	National
mid-October	Festival Internacional de Cine Fantástico de Sitges (International Film Festival of Fantastic Cinema)	Sitges (p. 335)
November 1	All Saints Day	National
December 6	Día de la Constitución (Constitution Day)	National
December 8	La Inmaculada Concepción (Feast of the Immaculate Conception)	National
December 25	Navidad (Christmas)	National
December 31	New Year's Eve	National

MADRID

There are a few minutes, in the orange light of Madrid's early morning, when the city finally seems to sleep. Just moments later, steel shutters blink open and the streets once again fill with an unending stream of pedestrians and cars. Life between meals is lived on the go. While tourists inundate the city, spending their days absorbing its "Old World" monuments, world-renowned museums, and raging nightlife, Madrid's population of 4.5 million roams the labyrinthine neighborhoods, living life with a simple and energetic joy.

Madrid's history does not read like that of rival European capitals. Although the city witnessed the coronation of Fernando and Isabel, Madrid did not gain importance until Habsburg King Felipe II moved the court here in 1561. Despite being far from vital ports and rivers, it immediately became a seat of wealth, culture, and imperial glory, serving as the center of Spain's 16th- and 17th-century Golden Age of literature, art, and architecture. In the 18th century, Madrid witnessed a Neoclassical rebirth as King Carlos III embellished the city with wide, tree-lined boulevards and scores of imposing buildings. In the 19th century, however, Madrid was scarred by the Peninsular Wars against Napoleon, the bloody inspiration for some of Francisco de Goya's most famous canvases.

In 1939, Madrid was the last city, save Valencia, to fall in the Spanish Civil War. Though it was hostile to Franco's nationalism, the city was forced to serve as the center of his government. This time, its location—smack in the center of the country—was considered its greatest strength. With Franco's death nearly 40 years later came an explosion known as *La Movida* ("Shift" or "Movement"). After decades of totalitarian repression, Madrid burst out laughing and crying in a breathtaking, city-wide release of inhibition. A 200,000-strong student population took to the streets and stayed there—they haven't stopped moving yet.

Today Madrid continues to serve as Spain's political, intellectual and cultural center. It is not as cosmopolitan as Barcelona nor as charming as Sevilla, but it is undeniably the *capital*—the wild, pulsating heart of Spain. Students, families and artists alike flock to the city in pursuit of their dreams, and Madrid continues to grow. Even its very architecture, with modern skyscrapers and shining industrial spaces expanding from narrow alleys and ancient plazas, seems to epitomize the mix of rich history and passion for the present that so defines all of Spain.

HIGHLIGHTS OF MADRID

Felipe IV's magnificent park, **Retiro** (see p. 106)

Three of the world's great museums: the **Museo del Prado** (see p. 109), the **Centro de Arte Reina Sofía** (see p. 110), and the **Museo Thyssen-Bornemisza** (see p. 111).

The **cafes** along Po. Prado by day (see p. 107); the **bars** in Pl. Santa Ana by night (see p. 104)m; and the **clubs** in El Centro, Malasaña, and Chueca by morning (see p. 112).

The striking **Valle de los Caídos** and its somber history (see p. 124).

◼ GETTING THERE AND AWAY

All flights land at **Aeropuerto Internacional de Barajas,** 30 minutes northeast of Madrid. A branch of the **regional tourist office** in the international arrivals area has maps and info. (☎ 91 305 86 56. Open M-F 8am-8pm, Sa 8am-1pm). Branches of the **Brújula accommodations service,** located in the airport and at the Bus-Aeropuerto stop, can help visitors find places to stay (see p. 89).

Madrid Overview

N

0
0

1/2 mile
1/2 kilometer

M30

TO AEROPUERTO DE BARAJAS

AV. DE LA PAZ

PARQUE DE LAS AVENIDAS

ALFONSO XIII

PROSPERIDAD

CARTAGENA

AV. AMÉRICA

AV. DE AMÉRICA

López de Hoyos

C. Francisco

Auditorio Nacional

CRUZ DEL RAYO

CONCHA ESPINA

C. Príncipe de Vergara

C. Costa Rica

COLOMBIA

Av. Pío XII

C. Costa Rica

Av. Pío XII

Av. Pío XII

Estación de Chamartín

D. PASTRANA

C. Agustín Foxá

C. Mateo

Po. la Habana

Av. Alberto Alcocer

Av. Concha Espina

Po. la Habana

C. de Joaquín Costa

REP. ARGENTINA

C. María de Molina

C. Diego de León

US

Museo Lázaro Galdiano

GLORIETA DE EMILIO CASTELAR

C. CASTELAR

CHAMARTÍN

Po. la

PL. DE CASTILLA

CASTILLA

VALDEACEDERAS

CUZCO

PL. DE CUZCO

Castelana

Australia

PL. DE LIMA

LIMA

Po. la Castelana

Calle de Orense

Av. del General Perón

Estación de Nuevos Ministerios

NUEVOS MINISTERIOS

C. Raimundo Fernández Villaverde

RÍOS ROSAS

C. Ríos Rosas

C. José Abascal

ALONSO CANO

Po. General Martínez Campos

IGLESIA

C. Santa Engracia

CANAL

C. Bravo Murillo

TETUÁN

ESTRECHO

ALVARADO

C. CAMINOS

C. Bravo Murillo

Av. de Filipinas

C. Cea Bermúdez

Av. Pablo Iglesias

Av. Reina Victoria

BUENO

C. Francisco de Sales

C. Guzmán el Bueno

C. Francos Rodríguez

Po. Juan XXIII

METROPOLITANO

C. Isaac Peral

CIUDAD UNIVERSITARIA

CIUDAD UNIVERSITARIA

Av. la Complutense

Av. la Puerta de Hierro

Arco de la Victoria

Av. de Séneca

Museo de América

MONCLOA

Av. de la Victoria

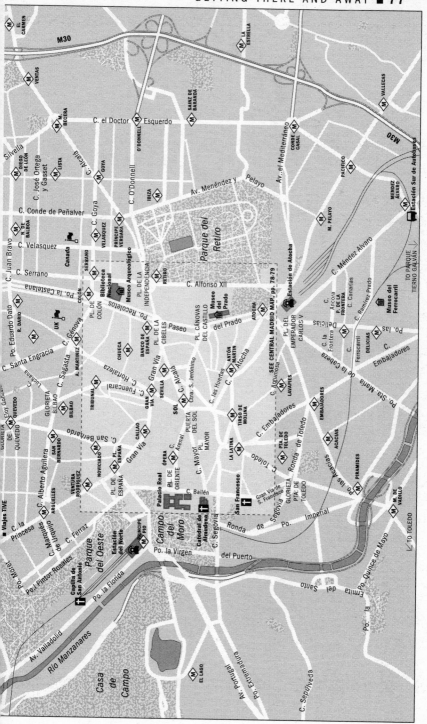

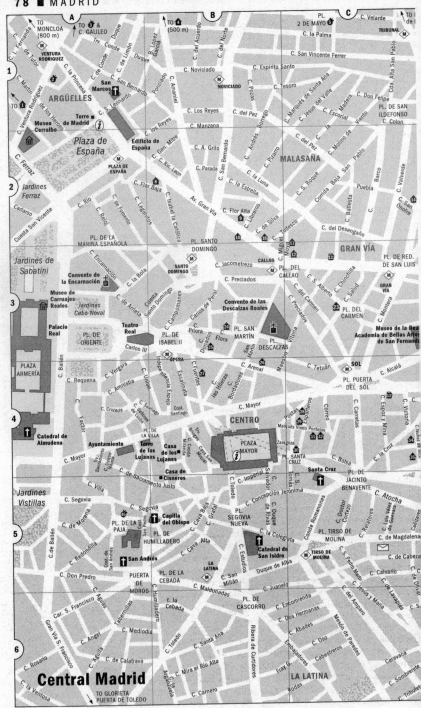

Central Madrid

TO GLORIETA
PUERTA DE TOLEDO

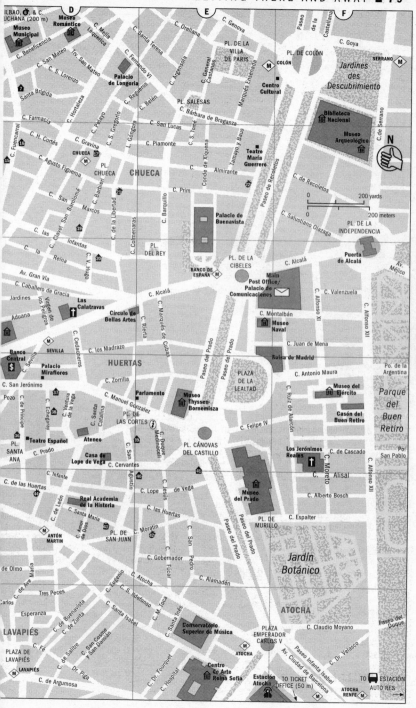

Central Madrid

🔺 ACCOMMODATIONS

Albergue Juvenil Santa Cruz de Marcenado (HI), 4	B1	Hostal-Residencia María, 11	C3
Hostal A. Nebrija, 8	B2	Hostal-Residencia Miño, 26	B4
Hostal Abril, 15	D2	Hostal-Residencia Mondragón, 37	D4
Hostal Acapulco, 23	C3	Hostal-Residencia Regional, 36	D4
Hostal Aguilar, 37	D4	Hostal-Residencia Rios, 1	A1
Hostal Alcante, 26	B4	Hostal-Residencia Rober, 25	B3
Hostal Armesto, 39	E4	Hostal-Residencia Santa Cruz, 30	C4
Hostal Esparteros, 29	C4	Hostal-Residencia Sud-Americana, 41	E5
Hostal Excelsior, 10	B2	Hotel Mónaco, 19	D2
Hostal Gonzalo, 40	E5		
Hostal Internacional, 38	D4	🍎 FOOD THUMB-PICKS	
Hostal Lauria, 10	B2	Ananias, 3	A1
Hostal Leones, 34	C4	Arepas con Todo, 6	D1
Hostal Lorenzo, 20	D3	Café Gijón, 22	E2
Hostal Madrid, 28	C4	Casa Alberto, 44	D5
Hostal Margarita, 18	B2	Cáscaras, 2	A1
Hostal Medieval, 16	D2	Champagneria Gala, 42	E5
Hostal Paz, 24	B3	El 26 de Libertad, 21	D2
Hostal Palacios, 14	C2	El Estragón, 45	A5
Hostal Portugal, 24	B3	La Gata Flora, 5	C1
Hostal R. Rodríguez, 35	C4		
Hostal Ribadavia, 14	C2		
Hostal Villar, 36	D4	🌙 NIGHTLIFE THUMB-PICKS	
Hostal-Residencia Alibel, 12	C3	Acuarela, 17	D2
Hostal-Residencia Carreras, 36	D4	El Café de Sheherezade, 43	D5
Hostal-Residencia Cruz-Sol, 30	C4	Joy Eslava, 33	C4
Hostal-Residencia Domínguez, 7	D1	Sugar Hill, 13	C3
Hostal-Residencia Encarnita, 31	C4		
Hostal-Residencia Lamalonga, 9	B2		
Hostal-Residencia Lido, 38	D4		
Hostal-Residencia Los Arcos, 32	C4		
Hostal-Residencia Luz, 27	B4		

The **Barajas metro line,** inaugurated in June 1999, connects the airport to all of Madrid (130ptas). From the airport, follow signs to the metro. Take line 8 to Mar de Cristal, and switch to line 4 (Las Musas). Changing to line 2 at the Goya stop will bring you to Sol, smack in the middle of Madrid's best accommodations and sights. Another option is the green **Bus-Aeropuerto** (look for "EMT" signs just outside the doors), which leaves from the national and international terminals and runs to the city center (every 25min. 4:45am-6:17am; every 15min. 6:17am-10pm; every hr. 10pm-1:45am; 385ptas). The bus stops underground beneath the Jardines del Descubrimiento in **Plaza de Colón** (M: Colón). After surfacing in Pl. Colón, walk toward the neo-Gothic statue that overlooks the **Paseo de Recoletos** on the opposite side of the gardens. The Colón metro station (brown line, L4) is across the street. Fleets of **taxis** swarm the airport. Taxi fare to central Madrid should cost around 3000ptas, including the 400pta airport surcharge.

AIRLINES

Iberia: Santa Cruz de Marcenado, 2 (☎ 91 587 81 56). M: San Bernardo. Open M-F 9:30am-2pm and 4-7pm. 24hr. reservations and info (☎ 902 40 05 00). **Aviaco,** C. Maude, 51 (☎ 91 554 36 00), is a domestic affiliate. International affiliates, **Tap Air Portugal** (☎ 91 542 06 02) and **Portugalia** (☎ 902 100 145) fly to Portugal.

Air France: Pl. España, 18, 5th fl. (☎ 91 330 04 02; reservations ☎ 91 330 04 40). M: Pl. España. Open M-F 9am-5pm.

American Airlines: C. Pedro Texeira, 8, 5th fl. (☎ 91 597 25 85). M: Santiago Berna-beu. Open M-F 9am-5:30pm. Reservations (☎ 91 597 20 68) open M-F 9am-6:30pm, Sa 9am-2pm.

British Airways: C. Serrano, 60 (☎ 91 577 69 59). M: Serrano. Open M-F 9am-5pm. Reservations (☎ 91 376 96 66) open M-F 9am-7pm.

Continental: C. Leganitos, 47, 9th fl. (☎ 91 559 27 10). M: Pl. España. Open M-F 9am-6pm. Reservations open M-F 9am-7pm.

Lufthansa: Cardenal Marcelo Española, 2 (☎ 91 302 94 26; reservations ☎ 90 222 01 01), located outside city limits.

USAir: Santa Cruz de Marcenado, 31 (☎ 91 541 55 58). M: San Bernardo.

BY TRAIN

Two *Largo Recorrido* (long distance) **RENFE** stations, **Madrid-Chamartín** and **Madrid-Atocha,** connect Madrid to the rest of Europe. Call RENFE (☎ 91 328 90 20) for reservations and info. **RENFE Main Office,** C. Alcalá, 44, at Gran Vía (M: Banco de España) sells tickets. Schedules and **AVE** (☎ 91 534 05 05) and **Talgo** tickets are also available. Open M-F 9:30am-8pm.

Estación Chamartín: (24hr. ☎ for international destinations 93 49 01 122; domestic destinations ☎ 90 224 02 02, Spanish only), Agustín de Foxá. M: Chamartín. Bus #5 runs to and from Sol (45min.); the stop is just beyond the lockers. Ticket windows open 8:30am-10:30pm. Chamartín services both international and domestic destinations. Most *cercanías* (local) trains leave from Chamartín; many stop at Atocha. To: **Barce-lona** (7hr., 10 per day 7am-12:50am, 6,585ptas); **Lisbon** (10hr., 10:45pm, 6,700ptas); **Paris** (13hr., 7pm, 19,300ptas); and **Nice** (22hr., 10am, 21,000ptas). Chamartín is a mini-mall of useful services, including a **tourist office** (☎ 91 315 99 76; open M-F 8am-8pm, Sa 9am-1pm), currency exchange, accommodations service, post office, car rental, police, and **lockers** (400-600ptas).

Estación Atocha: (☎ 91 328 90 20). M: Atocha. Ticket windows open 6:30am-11:30pm. No international service. Trains to: **Andalucía, Castilla-La Mancha, Extrem-adura, Valencia, Castilla y León, Sierra de Guadarrama,** and **El Escorial.** AVE service (☎ 91 534 05 05) to **Córdoba** (1¾hr., 16 per day 7am-10pm, 5100-7200ptas; cheaper on the Málaga route than the Sevilla route) and **Sevilla** (2½hr., 19 per day 7am-10pm, 8400-9900ptas). The cast-iron atrium of the original station has been turned into a simulated rainforest. Art galleries, boutiques, restaurants, and cafes serve as additional diversions. **Luggage storage** (400-600ptas) is by the rainforest.

BY BUS

Numerous private companies, each with its own station and set of destinations, serve Madrid; many buses pass through the **Estación Sur de Autobuses.** The Pl. Mayor tourist office has a comprehensive two-sided photocopy of most relevant inter-city bus information. Search for your destination below. (For more general information, see **By Bus,** p. 68.)

Estación Sur de Autobuses: C. Méndez Alvaro (☎ 91 468 42 00 or 91 468 45 11). M: Méndez Álvaro. Info booth open daily 7am-11pm. **Empresa Galiano Continental** (☎ 91 527 29 61) to **Toledo** (1hr.; M-Sa every 30min. 6:30am-10pm, Su every 30min. 8:30am-midnight; 585ptas). **Empresa Larrea** (☎ 91 539 00 05). To: **Avila** (2hr.; M-F 8 per day 7:15am-8pm, Sa-Su 3 per day 10am-8pm; 930ptas, round-trip 1485ptas). **Empresa Autominibus Urbanos,** (☎ 91 530 46 06) to **Aranjuez** (1hr.; M-F about every hr. 7am-11pm, Sa 13 per day 8am-10pm, Su 9 per day 9am-10pm; 415ptas).

Estación Auto Res: Pl. Conde de Casal, 6 (☎ 91 551 72 00). M: Conde de Casal. To: **Trujillo** (3¼hr., 11-12 per day 8am-1am, 2035ptas, round-trip 3665ptas; express 3hr., 2435ptas, round-trip 4465ptas); **Cáceres** (4¾hr., 7-9 per day 8am-1am, 2420ptas, round-trip 3665ptas; express 3½hr., 2630ptas, round-trip 4760ptas); **Mérida** (4¼hr., 9 per day 8am-1am, 2420ptas, round-trip 4360ptas; express 4hr., 3305ptas, round-trip 6060ptas); **Badajoz** (5¼hr., 9-10 per day 8am-1am, 3245ptas, round-trip 5845ptas; express 4½hr.,

3795ptas, round-trip 6945ptas); **Cuenca** (2½hr., 8-10 per day 6:45am-10pm, 1325ptas, round-trip 2385ptas; express 2hr., 1650ptas, round-trip 3035ptas); **Salamanca** (3-3¼hr., 7 per day 8:30am-10pm, 1480ptas, round-trip 2665ptas; express: 2½hr., 14-15 per day 7am-9:30pm, 2250ptas, round-trip 4000ptas); and **Valencia** (4hr., 13 per day 7am-1am, 2875ptas, round-trip 5175ptas; express 3175ptas, round-trip 5775ptas).

Estación Empresa Alacuber: (☎ 91 376 01 04), on Po. Moret. M: Moncloa. To: **El Pardo** (20min., every 15min. 6am-1:30am, 140ptas).

Estación Empresa Continental Auto: C. Avenida de América, 34 (☎ 745 63 00). M: Cartagena. To: **Alcalá de Henares** (40min.; M-Sa every 15min. 6:23am-11pm, Su every 30min. 7-9am and every 20min. 9am-11pm; 260ptas, round-trip 445ptas) and **Guadalajara** (1hr., every hr. 7am-midnight, 575ptas).

Estación Empresa Larrea: Po. Florida, 11 (☎ 91 530 48 00). M: Príncipe Pío (via extension from M: Ópera). To: **Ávila** (2hr., 4 per day 7:15am-8pm, 910ptas).

Estación Herranz: on C. Princesa, in the Intercambio de Moncloa. M: Moncloa. To: **El Escorial** (50min., every 15min. 7am-9pm, 420ptas) and **Valle de los Caídos** (20min., El Escorial 3:15pm, returns 5:30pm, 1030ptas), via El Escorial.

Estación La Sepulvedana: Po. Florida, 11 (☎ 91 530 48 00). M: Príncipe Pío (via extension from M: Ópera). To: **Segovia** (1½hr., about every 30min. 6:30am-10:15pm, 825ptas, round-trip 1310ptas) and **Ávila** (1½hr., M-F 8 per day 6am-7pm, Sa-Su 3 per day 10am-7pm, 930ptas).

BY THUMB AND RIDESHARE

Hitchhiking is legal only on minor routes. The Guardia Civil de Tráfico picks up highway hitchhikers and deposits them at nearby towns or on a bus. No official organization arranges shared journeys; hitchers often try the message boards listed on p. 86 for rideshare offers. *Let's Go* does not recommend hitchhiking.

⌐ GETTING AROUND

MAPS

The *Plano de Madrid* (street map) and the *Plano y Guía de Transportes* (public transportation map), free at city tourist offices, are fantastic. **El Corte Inglés** (see p. 86) also offers convenient one-page maps of Madrid. For a comprehensive map with street index, purchase the *Almax* map (650ptas) at any newsstand.

METRO

Safe, speedy, and spotless, Madrid's metro puts most major subway systems to shame. Trains run frequently; only on Sundays and late at night is the wait more than five minutes. Green timers hanging above most platforms show the amount of time since the last train departed. The free *Plano del Metro* (available at any ticket booth) and the wall maps of the metro and surrounding neighborhoods (posted in every station) are clear and helpful. All stations also have signs with schedules and fare information.

Ten lines connect Madrid's 164 stations, 40 of which are brand new as of last year. Lines are distinguished by color and number. An individual metro ticket costs 135ptas, but savvy riders opt for the **bonotransporte** (ticket of 10 rides for either the metro or bus system) at 705ptas. Buy both at machines in any metro stop, *estanco* (tobacco shop), or newsstand. For more details, call **Metro info** (☎ 91 580 19 80) or ask at any ticket booth. Remember to hold on to your ticket or pass until you leave the metro—riding without one incurs an outrageous fine.

Trains run every day from 6am to 1:30am. Violent crime in the metro stations is almost unheard of, and women usually feel safe traveling alone. Do watch out for pickpockets in crowded cars. If you feel uncomfortable, avoid empty cars and ride in sight of the conductor. At night avoid the stations to the north, which tend to be less frequented. Metro stations Chueca, Gran Vía, Sol, Tirso de Molina, La Latina, and Plaza de España surface in areas that can be intimidating after midnight.

BUS

Buses in Madrid cover areas inaccessible by the metro and are a great way to see the city while getting where you need to be. Like the metro, the bus system is exceptionally organized. Most stops are clearly marked, but if you want extra guidance in finding routes and stops, try the handy *Plano de los Transportes*, free at the tourist office, or *Madrid en Autobús*, also free at bus kiosks.

The fare is 135ptas. 10-ride *bonotransporte* passes are sold at newsstands and *estancos* for 705ptas. Buses run from 6am to 11:30pm. From 11:30pm until 3am, the night bus service, *buho* (owl), travels from Pl. Cibeles to the outskirts every 30 minutes; from 3-6am, they run every hour. Night buses (N1-N20), the cheapest form of transportation for late-night revelers, are listed in a special section of the *Plano*. Buses stop all along the marked routes, not just in Pl. Cibeles. For more information, call **Empresa Municipal de Transportes** (☎ 91 406 88 10; Spanish only).

TAXI

Madrid is filled with taxis around the clock. If one does not appear when you need it, or if you want to summon one to your door, call ☎ 91 445 90 08 or 91 447 32 32. A green *libre* sign in the window or a lit green light indicates availability. The base fare is 190ptas, plus 50-75ptas per kilometer. Common fare supplements include: airport (400ptas); bus and train stations (125ptas); luggage charge (50ptas per bag); Sundays and holidays (6am-11pm, 125ptas); nighttime (11pm-6am, 125ptas). The fare from the city center to the airport is 2500-3000ptas, depending on traffic.

If you have a complaint or think you've been overcharged, demand a *recibo oficial* (official receipt) and *hoja de reclamaciones* (complaint form), which the driver is required to supply. Take down the license number, route taken, and fare charged. Drop off the forms and information at the **Ayuntamiento (City Hall)**, Pl. Villa, 4 (☎ 91 447 07 15 or 91 447 07 14), to request a refund.

To request **taxi service for the disabled,** call ☎ 91 547 85 00 or 91 547 86 00. Rates are identical to those of other taxis. If you leave possessions in a taxi, visit or call the **Negociado de Objetos Perdidos,** Pl. Legazpi, 7. (☎ 91 588 43 46. Open M-F 9am and 2pm.) Drivers are obligated to turn in items left behind within 48 hours.

CAR RENTAL

There is no reason to rent a car in Madrid. If congested traffic and nightmarish parking don't unnerve you, aggressive drivers and annoying mopeds will. Don't drive unless you're planning to zoom out of the city, and even then bus and train fares will be cheaper. Tobacco shops sell parking permits. If driving to destinations outside of Spain, a larger car rental chain is your best bet. The tourist office has a complete list of car rental companies. For more info, see **Car Rental,** p. 83.

Europcar, Estación de Atocha, AVE terminal (☎ 91 530 01 94; reservations ☎ 91 721 12 22; www.europcar.com), near the rainforest. M: Atocha Renfe. Cheapest car 8200ptas per day, 49,800ptas per week. Unlimited mileage. Minimum age 21. Open daily 8am-midnight. Other offices in Madrid include the airport (☎ 393 72 35).

Avis, Estación de Atocha, AVE terminal (☎91 530 01 68; reservations ☎ 91 348 03 48), near the rainforest. M: Atocha Renfe. Cheapest car 12,300ptas per day, 61,000ptas per week. Unlimited mileage. With more than 3 days, drop off in other cities free. Minimum age 23. Open daily 8am-midnight. Other offices in Madrid include Gran Vía, 60 (☎ 91 548 42 03) and the airport (☎ 91 393 72 22).

MOPED RENTAL

Popular with Madrid's residents, mopeds are swift and easy to park. A lock and helmet are necessary. Rent from **Motocicletas Antonio Castro,** C. Conde Duque, 13 (☎ 91 542 06 57). M: San Bernardo. A Honda costs 4500ptas per day (8am-8pm) or 19,500ptas per week, including unlimited mileage and insurance. Deposit of 40,000ptas required (IVA not included). Renters must be at least 18; for anything larger than 125cc (for highway use, for example), an International Driver's Permit is required. For smaller mopeds any driver's license is sufficient. (Open M-F 8am-1:30pm and 5-8pm, Sa 9-11am.)

MADRID

⚜ ORIENTATION

The "Kilómetro 0" sign in front of the police station in **Puerta del Sol** marks the intersection of eight of Madrid's most celebrated streets, and the starting point of the country's major highways. To make Madrid's infinite plazas and serpentine streets more navigable, the city is broken down into five major neighborhoods: **Centro, Huertas, Malasaña and Chueca, Bilbao,** and **Argüelles.**

Most of Madrid's prominent sights, including the **Ópera** and **Plaza Mayor,** radiate from Sol in the Centro. Just west of Sol off C. Mayor, Plaza Mayor is the hub of activity for tourists and *madrileños* alike; the plaza houses both contemporary cafes and the churches and historical buildings of **Habsburg Madrid,** also known as **Madrid de los Asturias.** Farther west of Sol, by way of C. Arenal, lies the reigning monument of **Bourbon Madrid,** the Palacio Real. This section of Madrid, also known as **Ópera,** hosts fantastic gardens and churches.

To the east of Sol lies **Huertas,** once the literary district and now the center of cafe and theater life, as well as the best nightlife in the city. Huertas is bordered by C. Alcalá to the north, Po. Prado to the east, Sol to the west, and C. Atocha to the south. Centered around **Plaza Santa Ana,** Huertas is crowded with some of the best budget accommodations in the city, as well as some of the best *tapas* bars. It is also the ideal starting point for exploring the city's three great museums (see **Museums,** p. 109) or the lush **Parque del Buen Retiro** (p. 106).

Also south of Sol and west of Huertas is the area around metro stops **La Latina** and **Tirso de Molina,** which has less prestige and fewer tourists than the rest of Old Madrid. **El Rastro,** a gargantuan ancient flea market, is staged here every Sunday morning. Farther south lies **Lavapiés,** a working-class neighborhood.

North of Sol, the grand avenue **Gran Vía** is the commercial center of Madrid, scarring the horizon with skyscrapers and fast-food joints. Linked to C. de Fuencarral, it acts as the southern border of **Malasaña** and **Chueca,** full of über-cool restaurants and shops. Beyond Gran Vía and east of Malasaña and Chueca lies modern Madrid. Running the length of Madrid from **Atocha** in the south to **Plaza de Castilla** in the north, **Paseo del Prado, Paseo de Recoletos,** and **Paseo de la Castellana** pass the Prado, the fountains at the **Plazas Cibeles** and **Colón,** and the elaborate skyscrapers beyond Pl. Colón, including the twin towers of the **Puerta de Europa.**

The area northwest of Sol holds the **Plaza de España** and the tall **Torre de Madrid,** the pride of 1950s Spain. Still farther northwest of Sol lie **Argüelles** and **Bilbao,** energetic neighborhoods spilling over from **Moncloa.** Both are student districts, filled with cheap eateries and neon nightclubs.

Madrid is much safer than other major European cities, but Sol, Pl. España, Pl. Chueca, and Malasaña's Pl. Dos de Mayo are still intimidating late at night. As a general rule, avoid the parks and quiet residential streets after dark and always watch out for thieves and pickpockets in crowds. Clever scams in Madrid are as plentiful as your *pesetas.*

READ THIS The **Guía del Ocio,** available behind the counter of any news kiosk, should be your first purchase in Madrid (125ptas). It has concert, theater, sports, cinema, and TV schedules. It also lists exhibits, restaurants, bars, and clubs. Although it is in Spanish, the alphabetical listings of clubs and restaurants are invaluable even to non-speakers. The *Guía* comes out on Thursday or Friday, so be sure that you are buying an up-to-date copy instead of last week's issue. For an English magazine with articles on new finds in and around the city, pick up *In* **Madrid,** distributed free at tourist offices and many restaurants. Live Music and Nightlife sections are basically an English translation of the *Guía.* **The Broadsheet,** free at bookstores, is a no-frills listing of English classifieds. This self-proclaimed "lifesaver for English speakers in Madrid" is geared toward long-term residents. The weekly **Segundamano,** on sale at kiosks, is essential for apartment or roommate seekers. COGAM publishes **Entiendes...?** which addresses gay issues in Spain and lists activities and nightspots for every town in Spain (see p. 87). **Minerva** keeps you up-to-date on the art scene.

⑦ PRACTICAL INFORMATION

TOURIST AND FINANCIAL SERVICES

Tourist Offices: English is spoken at all tourist offices. Those planning trips outside the Comunidad de Madrid can visit region-specific offices within Madrid; ask the tourist offices below for their addresses. **Municipal,** Pl. Mayor, 3 (☎ 91 366 54 77 or 91 588 16 36; fax 91 366 54 77). M: Sol. Hands out indispensable city and transportation maps and a complete guide to accommodations, as well as *In Madrid* and *Enjoy Madrid,* monthly activities and information guides. Open M-F 10am-8pm, Sa 10am-2pm and 3-8pm. **Regional/Provincial Office of the Comunidad de Madrid,** main office: Duque de Medinacelia, 2 (☎ 91 429 49 51). Brochures, transportation info, and maps for towns in the Comunidad. **Secondary office** at Mercado Pta. de Toledo, Ronda de Toledo 1, stand #3134 (☎ 91 364 18 75). M: Pta. de Toledo. In a gallery with large banners on a plaza across from the metro station. Open M-F 9am-7pm, Sa 9:30am-1:30pm. **Other offices** at Estación Chamartín (see **By Train,** p. 81) and the airport (see **By Plane,** p. 30). Megastore **El Corte Inglés** has **free maps** and information (see p. 86).

⬛ General Info Line: ☎ 010. 20ptas per min. Run by the Ayuntamiento. They'll tell you anything about Madrid, from police locations to zoo hours. Ask for *inglés* and they will transfer you to an English-speaking operator. Outside Madrid dial ☎ 901 300 600.

Websites: www.madridman.com; www.iberica.com; www.red2000.com/spain/madrid.

Tours: Read the fine print before signing on. The following are given in English. **Pullmantur,** Pl. Oriente, 8 (☎ 91 541 18 05 or 91 541 18 06). M: Ópera. Bus tour of Madrid with stops at Casa de Campo and, yes, Planet Hollywood. (2½hr., 3pm, 2800ptas.) Also offers excursions to outlying areas. **Trapsatur,** San Bernardo, 23 (☎ 91 542 63 20). M: Santo Domingo. **Juliá Tours,** Gran Vía, 68 (☎ 91 559 96 05). M: Pl. de España. Offers tours of Andalucía, Portugal, and Morocco.

Budget Travel: Viajes TIVE, C. Fernando el Católico, 88 (☎ 91 543 74 12). M: Moncloa. Exit the metro at C. Isaac Peral, walk straight down C. Arcipreste de Hita, and turn left on C. Fernando el Católico; it is on your left. ISIC 700ptas, HI card 1800ptas. Organizes group excursions and language classes. Lodgings and student residence info. English spoken. Open M-F 9am-2pm, Sa 9am-noon. Arrive early to avoid long lines. If you don't need tickets try **Comunidad de Madrid, Dirección General de Juventud,** C. Gran Vía, 10 (☎ 91 580 42 42; www.comadrid.es/inforjoven). M: Banco de España. Offers many of the same services as TIVE, which it controls, but does not sell tickets. Open M-F 9am-2pm and 5-8pm; in Aug. mornings only. **ASATEJ Group,** Fernando el Católico, 60 (☎ 91 543 47 61; www.asatej.com/iberica). M: Arguelles. Offers student airfares, tours, car rental, bus passes, and other student travel needs. **USIT,** Pl. Callao, 3 (☎ 902 25 25 75 or 902 32 52 75; www.unlimited.com). Part of a travel megaplex with other services. Arranges trips, car rentals, and documentation. **MasCota Viajes,** Gran Vía 88 (☎ 91 541 26 13; mascotacentral@teleline.es). Specializes in adventure travel, but does local and international too. Open M-F 10am-2pm and 5-8pm.

Currency Exchange: Banco Central Hispano charges no commission on cash or traveler's checks and offers the best rates on AmEx traveler's checks. **Main branch,** Pl. Canalejas, 1 (☎ 91 558 11 11). M: Sol. From Sol, follow C. San Jerónimo to Pl. Canalejas. Open Apr.-Sept. M-F 8:30am-2:30pm, Sa 8:30am-1pm; Oct.-Mar. M-Th 8:30am-4:30pm, F 8:30am-2:30pm, Sa 8:30am-1pm. **Banks** usually charge 1-2% commission (min. charge 500ptas). Booths in Sol and Gran Vía, open as late as 2am and on weekends, have poor rates and are not a good deal for cashing traveler's checks, despite their charging commission. On the other hand, for small-denomination bills they may be the best option. **ATMs** are everywhere in Madrid. **Servi Red, Servi Caixa,** and **Telebanco** machines accept bank cards with one or more of the Cirrus, PLUS, EuroCard, and NYCE logos. For more information, see **Cash Cards,** p. 15.

American Express: Pl. Cortés, 2 (☎ 91 322 54 52; info ☎ 91 322 54 00). M: Sevilla. From the metro stop, take a right on C. Alcala, another right down C. Cedacero and a left on C. San Jerónimo; it's on the left. The office has Agencia de Viajes written in big letters on the windows. Offers currency exchange (no commission on cash or AmEx traveler's checks; 750ptas set fee for non-AmEx traveler's checks), will hold mail for 30 days, and can help send and receive wired money. In an emergency, will cash personal checks up to US$1000 for cardholders. Open M-F 9am-5:30pm, Sa 9am-noon. 24hr. Express Cash machine outside. To report or cancel lost traveler's checks, call toll free ☎ 900 99 44 26. To report other problems, call ☎ 900 94 14 13. Both lines 24hr.

LOCAL SERVICES

Message Boards: Tons of cheap travel tickets and rideshare offers at **TIVE** travel agency (see p. 85). Mostly rideshares at **Albergue Juvenil Santa Cruz** (see p. 93).

Luggage Storage: Barajas Airport. Follow the signs to *consigna*. 1 day 425ptas, 2-15 days 530-740ptas per day, after day 15 105-210ptas per day. **Estación Chamartín.** Self-serve, automatic lockers in the *consigna* area by the bus stop. Lockers 400-600ptas per day. Open daily 6:30am-12:30am. **Estación Atocha.** Same services, prices, and hours. Exit the *largo recorrido* area and the lockers are to the left. **Estación Sur de Autobuses.** Bags checked (800ptas).

El Corte Inglés: C. Preciados, 3 (☎ 91 379 80 00). M: Sol. **C. Goya, 76** (☎ 91 432 93 00). M: Goya. **C. Princesa, 56** (☎ 91 454 60 00). M: Argüelles. **C. Raimundo Fernández Villaverde, 79** (☎ 91 556 23 00). M: Nuevos Ministerios. Various other locations in Madrid, and around Spain. Giant chain of department stores with the official motto: "A place to shop. A place to dream." If you need it, they've got it: handy maps, beauty parlor, cafeteria-restaurant, supermarket, telephones, tapes and CDs, books in English, electronics, and fawning salespeople. Currency exchange with no commission but mediocre rates. Open M-Sa 10am-9:30pm, Su 11am-9pm.

English-Language Periodicals: International edition dailies and weeklies available at kiosks everywhere, especially on the Gran Vía, Paseos del Prado, Recoletos, and Castellana, and around Pta. Sol. If you're dying for the *New York Times* (425ptas), try one of the **VIPS** restaurants (see **Red-Eye Establishments,** p. 95).

Language Service: Forocio (*Fo*reign *Ocio*), C. Mayor, 6, 4th fl. (☎ 91 522 56 77). An organization dedicated to bringing foreigners and natives together to share languages and good times. Sponsors weekly international parties and organizes group trips to other parts of Spain. Open daily 10am-8pm.

Libraries: Bibliotecas Populares (info ☎ 91 445 98 45). 1 large branch at M: Puerta de Toledo (☎ 91 366 54 07). English-language periodicals. Open M-F 8:30am-8:45pm. **Washington Irving Center,** C. Marqués Villamagna, 8 (☎ 91 587 22 00). M: Serrano or Colón. From the station, walk up C. Serrano and turn left on C. Marqués de Villamagna. Good selection of American magazines and books. Anyone over 16 can check books out for 2 weeks by filling out a form. Allow 1 week for processing. Open M-F 2-6pm.

Religious Services: Our Lady of Mercy English-Speaking Parish, C. Alfonso XIII, 165 (☎ 91 416 90 09), at Pl. Habana. Sunday mass in English 11am, followed by coffee and donuts. **Immanuel Baptist Church,** C. Hernández de Tejada, 4 (☎ 91 407 43 47). English services Su 11am and 7pm. **Community Church of Madrid,** C. Bravo Murillo, 85. M: Cuatro Caminos. At the Colegio El Porvenir. Multi-denominational Protestant services in English Su 10am. **British Embassy Church of St. George,** C. Núñez de Balboa, 43 (☎ 91 576 51 09). M: Velázquez. Services Su 8:30, 10, and 11:15am. **Sinagoga Beth Yaacov,** C. Balmes, 3 (☎ 91 591 31 31), near Pl. Sorolla. M: Iglesia. Services F 8pm, Sa 9:15am. Kosher restaurant can be reserved. Passport sometimes required. Spanish only. **Centro Islámico,** C. Alonso Cano, 3 (☎ 91 448 05 54). M: Iglesia. Services and language classes. Open M-F 10:45am-2pm.

Women's Services: Instituto de la Mujer (☎ 91 347 80 00). **Ministerio de Asuntos Sociales** (☎ 900 19 10 10). **Librería de Mujeres,** C. San Cristóbal, 17 (☎ 91 521 70 43; www.unapalabraotra.org/libreriamujeres.html), near Pl. Mayor. M: Sol. From Sol, C. San Cristóbal is the second left off C. Mayor. The shop's motto: *"Los libros no muerden, el feminismo tampoco."* ("Books don't bite, neither does feminism.") Books and gifts, but more of a resource for Spanish speakers. Helpful with finding local support and discussion groups. Open M-F 10am-2pm and 5-8pm.

Gay and Lesbian Services: Colectivo de Gais y Lesbianas de Madrid (COGAM), C. Fuencarral, 37 (☎/fax 91 523 00 70). M: Gran Vía. A volunteer organization, always buzzing with activity. Provides a wide range of services and activities of interest to gays, lesbians, and bisexuals. English usually spoken. Free screenings of gay-interest movies, COGAM youth group (25 and under), and HIV-positive support group (☎ 91 522 45 17; M-F 6-10pm). Reception daily M-Sa 5-9pm. Free counseling M-Th 7-9pm. Library open daily 7-9pm. Once every 2 months, COGAM publishes *Entiendes...?,* a magazine in Spanish about gay issues that also lists activities and nightspots for every town in Spain. **Berkana Librería Gai y Lesbiana** has guidebooks, contact information, and listings (see **Books,** p. 120). Most entertainment guides list gay and lesbian clubs. **GAI-INFORM,** a gay info line (☎ 91 523 00 70), provides information in Spanish (and sometimes French and English) about gay associations, leisure activities, and health issues. The same number has info on sports, workshops in French and English, dinners, and on **Brujulai,** COGAM's weekend excursion group. Open daily 5-9pm.

Laundromat: Lavandería, C. Cervantes 1. M: Puerta del Sol or Banco de España. From Pl. Santa Ana follow C. Prado, turn right on C. León and then left onto C. Cervantes. Wash 400ptas, dry 100ptas for 9min. Open M-Sa 9am-8pm. **Lavandería Donoso Cortés,** C. Donoso Cortés, 17 (☎ 91 446 96 90). M: Quevedo. From the metro, walk down C. Bravo Murillo to C. Donoso Cortés. Self-service wash 600ptas, detergent 60ptas. Open M-F 9am-2pm and 3:30-8pm, Sa 9am-2pm. **Lavandería Automática SIDEC,** C. Don Felipe, 4. M: Tribunal. Wash 600ptas, detergent 25ptas. Open M-F 10am-9pm. **Maryland,** C. Meléndez Valdés, 52 (☎ 91 543 30 41). M: Argüelles. Go up C. Princesa and turn right on C. Hilarión, which intersects C. Meléndez Valdés. Wash and detergent 800ptas. Open M-F 10am-2pm and 5-8pm, Sa 10:30am-1:30pm.

EMERGENCY AND COMMUNICATIONS

Emergency: ☎ 112 (new; for all emergencies). ☎ 091 or 092 (national, local police).

Police: C. Luna, 17 (☎ 91 521 12 36). M: Callao. From Gran Vía, walk down C. Arenal. Forms in English available. To report crimes committed in the **metro,** go to the office in the Sol station (☎ 91 521 09 11). Open daily 8am-11pm. **Guardia Civil** (☎ 062 or 91 534 02 00). **Protección Civil** (☎ 91 537 31 00).

Crisis Lines: Poison Control (24hr. ☎ 91 562 04 20). **Rape Hotline** (☎ 91 574 01 10). Open M-F 10am-2pm and 4-7pm (other times machine-recorded instructions).

Help Lines: AIDS Info Hotline (☎ 900 11 10 00). Open M-F 10am-10pm. **Detox** (☎ 900 16 15 15). English spoken. Open daily 9am-9pm. **Alcoholics Anonymous,** C. Juan Bravo, 40-bis, 2nd fl. (English ☎ 91 309 19 47; Spanish crisis line ☎ 91 341 82 82). M: Núñez de Balboa. 20ptas per min. **English-Language Helpline** (☎ 91 559 13 93), offers confidential help from trained volunteers. Open daily 7-11pm. 20ptas per min.

Late-Night Pharmacy: Dial ☎ 098 to find the nearest one. One located at **C. Mayor, 59** (☎ 91 548 00 14), near M: Sol. Listings of the nearest on-duty pharmacy are also posted in all pharmacy windows.

First Aid Stations: Scattered about the city, all open 24hr. C. Navas de Tolosa (☎ 91 521 00 25); General Ricardos, 14 (☎ 92 471 03 50); Avenida del Paseo de Extremadura, 147 (☎ 91 464 76 32).

Hospitals: Prompt appointments are hard to obtain, but public hospitals don't require advance payment. Emergency rooms are the best option for immediate attention. US insurance is not accepted as payment, but get a receipt and your insurance may pick up the tab when you get home. General emergency examination runs 18,000-24,000ptas. For non-emergency concerns, **Anglo-American Medical Unit,** Conde de Aranda, 1, 1st fl. (☎ 91 435 18 23), is quick and friendly. M: Serrano or Retiro. Doctors, dentists, and optometrists. Run partly by British and Americans. Regular personnel on duty 9am-8pm. Not an emergency clinic. Initial visit 9000ptas for students, 10,000-15,000ptas for non-students. V, MC, AmEx. Embassies and consulates also keep lists of English-speaking doctors in private practice. **Hospital Clínico San Carlos** (☎ 91 330 30 00), on Pl. Cristo Rey. M: Moncloa. Open 24hr.

MADRID

Emergency Clinics: In a **medical emergency**, dial ☎ 061. **Equipo Quirúrgico Municipal No. 1**, C. Montesa, 22 (☎ 91 588 51 00). M: Manuel Becerra. **Hospital Ramón y Cajal** (☎ 91 336 80 00), Ctra. Colmenar Viejo. Bus #135 from Pl. Castilla.

Post Office: Palacio de Comunicaciones, C. Alcala, 51 on Pl. Cibeles (☎ 902 19 71 97). M: Banco de España. Enormous, ornate palace on the far side of the plaza from the metro. Info (main vestibule) open M-Sa 8:30am–9:30pm. Windows open M-Sa 8:30am-9:30pm, Su 9am-2pm for stamp purchases, certified mail (main door), telex and **fax** service. Receive **Poste Restante** (Lista de Correos) at windows 80-82; passport required. Send packages at door N (enter from C. Montlaban). Postal Express is at door K (enter from Po. del Prado). **Postal Code:** 28080.

Internet Access: New Internet centers are surfacing everywhere. While the average is 500ptas per hr., many opportunists are starting small shops in apartments and charging less than 300ptas per hr.; keep a lookout for them.

■ **Euronet**, C. Mayor, 1, 4th fl., office 11 (☎ 655 021 793). M: Sol. Take the elevator up and buzz the office. A magical little room run by Mariano and Facundo, boyhood friends from Argentina; friendly service and U2 songs abound. Unbeatably low 250ptas per hr., 150ptas for 30min. Open daily 10am-11pm.

Interpublic, C. San Jerónimo 18, 1st fl. M: Sol. Airy room with international decor. 199ptas for 30min., 299ptas per hr. Open daily 9:30am-midnight.

Internet Silico, C. Fernando el Católico, 80 (☎ 91 549 33 50). M: Moncloa. 200ptas for 10min., 500ptas per hr. Scanner. English spoken.

Net Café, C. San Bernardo, 81 (☎ 91 444 40 35). M: San Bernardo. Flat screens under glass tables. 45min. with each 500ptas of drinks. Pay the difference and watch those drunk emails fly.

Natura, Gran Vía, 16 (☎ 91 521 75 73). A combination of Vitamina, a health-drink joint, with Café Cinho, a coffee spot. Internet downstairs 500ptas per 30min. Fresh fruit drinks 550ptas.

La Casa de Internet, C. Luchana, 20 (☎ 91 446 55 41). M: Bilbao. 900ptas per hr., 700ptas with student ID. Open M-Sa noon-2am, Su 4pm-2am.

Cestein, C. Leganitos, 11 (☎ 91 548 27 75). M: Pl. de España. 400ptas for 30min., 700ptas per hr. Open M-F 8am-10pm, Sa 10am-2pm.

Telephones: Information ☎ 1003. No English spoken. 10ptas per min. (For further information, see **Keeping in Touch**, p. 27.)

▌▘ ACCOMMODATIONS

The demand for rooms in Madrid is always high and increases dramatically in summer. But never fear—the city is filled with hostels. Prices average about 2600ptas per person for a basic hostel room, a bit more for a two-star hostel, and slightly less for a bed in a *pensión*. Accommodation prices may decrease significantly in the low season (Oct.-Apr.). Try negotiating the price if you plan on staying awhile.

In Madrid, the difference between a one-star *hostal* and a *pensión* is often minimal. A room in a one- or two-star *hostal* has at least the basics: bed, closet space, desk with chair, sink and towel, window, light fixture, fake flowers, a lock on the door, and the occasional religious icon. Winter heating is standard, air-conditioning is not. Unless otherwise noted, communal bathrooms (toilet and shower) are the norm. Most places accept reservations, but none require them. Reservations are, however, recommended in summer and on weekends year-round, especially in the Puerta del Sol area and at the first place *Let's Go* lists in each district. Hostels in Madrid are generally well-kept and comfortable. Owners are usually accustomed to opening the doors, albeit groggily, at all hours or providing keys for guests, but ask before club-hopping into the wee hours; late-night lockouts or confrontations with irate owners are never fun. *Pensiones* are like boarding houses: they sometimes have curfews and often host guests staying for longer periods of time. Towels and sheets are provided but not always changed daily. The best deals are found outside central locations, and Madrid's stellar public transportation makes virtually any place central.

Socialite travelers should be aware that there are few common spaces of any sort in Madrid's (mostly residential) hostels; you're much more likely to meet fellow travelers in the streets than in your accommodation.

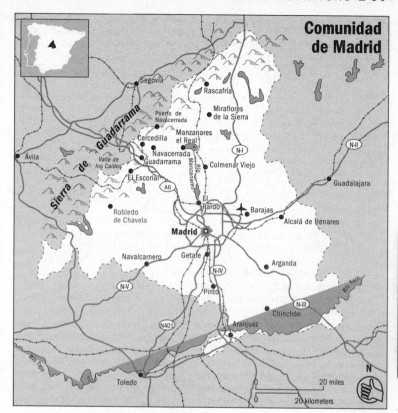

Comunidad de Madrid

RESERVATIONS SERVICE

Viajes Brújula: Estación Atocha (☎ 91 539 11 73), at the AVE terminal (open daily 8am-10pm). For 400ptas, they make reservations with any participating locale in Spain. You must go in person. You pay a deposit of one-third of the room price, which is then subtracted from the price of the accommodation. Not every establishment is signed up with Brújula (no HI youth hostels); nevertheless, it's a good deal and a safe bet if you are tired and need a bed. English spoken. Another office at the **airport bus terminal** (☎ 91 575 96 80) in Pl. Colón (open daily 8am-10pm).

EL CENTRO: SOL, ÓPERA, AND PLAZA MAYOR

Puerta del Sol is the center of the city in the center of the country. All roads converge here (it's Spain's km 0) and most visitors ramble through at least once. Signs indicating *hostales* and *pensiones* stick out from flower-potted balconies and decaying facades on narrow, sloping streets. For better deals in quieter spots, stray several blocks from Sol. Don't be afraid to climb that extra flight of stairs; prices drop the higher up you go. The following listings fall in the area between the Sol and Ópera metro stops. Price and location in the Centro are as good as it gets, especially if you are planning to brave the nightlife. Buses #3, 25, 39, and 500 serve Ópera; buses #3, 5 (from Atocha), 15, 20, 50, 51, 52, 53, and 150 serve Sol.

■ **Hostal Paz,** C. Flora, 4, 1st and 4th fl. (☎ 91 547 30 47). M: Ópera. Don't be deterred by the dark street, parallel to C. Arenal, off C. Donados or C. Hileras. Peaceful rooms sheltered from street noise are lavished with comfort-enhancers; wonderful owners, hand-held climate control, satellite TV, A/C, spotless, spacious bathrooms. Reservations advised. Laundry 1200ptas. Singles 2500ptas; doubles 3800-4300ptas; triples 5700ptas. V, MC.

🔲 **Hostal-Residencia Luz,** C. Fuentes, 10, 3rd fl. (☎ 91 542 07 59 or 91 559 74 18; fax 91 542 07 59), off C. Arenal. M: Ópera. 12 sunny, newly redecorated rooms ooze with comfort: hardwood floors, elegant furniture, beautiful curtains and bedspreads. Satellite TV, fax, and public phone. Laundry 1000ptas. Don't pay the 1000ptas extra for a private bath; the (gorgeous) common ones are cleaned more often than you will use them. Singles 2500ptas; doubles 3700ptas; triples 5500ptas. Discounts for longer stays.

Hostal Esparteros, C. Esparteros, 12, 4th fl. (☎/fax 91 521 09 03). Cheap, small, sparkling rooms with balcony or large windows (no fans). The best owner in Madrid speaks English and ensures a terrific stay. Laundry 1000ptas. Singles 2000-2200ptas, with bath 2700ptas; doubles 3200ptas, with bath 3700ptas; triples 4400ptas, with bath 5500ptas. Discounts for longer stays.

Hostal-Residencia Rober, C. Arenal, 26, 5th fl. (☎ 91 541 91 75). M: Ópera. Wide carpeted hallways lead to carpeted or hardwood rooms vying for cleanest in the capital. Brilliant balcony views down Arenal. Smoking strictly prohibited. All 14 pristine rooms have their own tiny TVs and A/C. Singles with shower 3600ptas, with bath 4500ptas; doubles with bath 5700ptas; triples with bath 7000ptas.

Hostal Madrid, C. Esparteros, 6, 2nd fl. (☎ 91 522 00 60; fax 91 532 35 10). M: Sol. Off C. Mayor. The backpacker's equivalent of a 5-star hotel. Spacious rooms with shiny wood floors and large windows. All have TVs, telephones, enormous closets with safes, A/C, and new bathrooms. Reservations 4 days ahead advised. Singles 6500ptas; doubles 9500ptas; triple with balcony 12,000ptas. V, MC, AmEx.

Hostal Alcante, C. Arenal, 16, 2nd fl., on the right. Spacious rooms, with elegant new wooden furniture, TV, heat, and A/C. Singles 2800-3000ptas, with bath 4000ptas; doubles 5500ptas, with bath 6000ptas; triples with bath 7500ptas. V, MC.

Hostal-Residencia Cruz-Sol, Pl. Santa Cruz, 6, 3rd fl. (☎ 91 532 71 97). M: Sol. A good deal. Last year's renovations left modern rooms with parquet floors, double-paned windows, safes, heat, phones, and A/C. Laundry 1000ptas. Singles 3500ptas, with bath 4000ptas; doubles 6000-7000ptas; triples 8500ptas; quads 9000ptas. V, MC.

Hostal-Residencia Santa Cruz, Pl. Santa Cruz, 6, 2nd fl. (☎/fax 91 522 24 41). M: Sol. Palatial lounge gives way to servant-sized rooms. Renovations, including A/C, on the way. Tiny, sinkless singles 2200-3500ptas; doubles 4200ptas, with bath 5200ptas; triples 6000ptas, with bath 6200ptas. V, MC, AmEx.

Hostal-Residencia Miño, C. Arenal, 16, 2nd fl. (☎ 91 531 50 79 or 91 531 97 89). M: Ópera. Don't be deterred by the deer's head by the entrance; decoration is homier within. Diverse rooms range from large with hardwood floors and balconies to small with vinyl underfoot. Avoid the rooms overlooking C. Arenal, where closed windows shut off air circulation. Singles 3000-3400ptas; doubles 4800ptas, with bath 5500ptas; triples with bath 6900ptas.

Hostal Portugal, C. Flora, 4, (☎ 91 559 40 14). M: Ópera. Great location and cheap prices make up for tired rooms. Like its namesake, the hostel is quickly becoming a favorite with Americans. English spoken. Singles 2500; doubles 4500ptas.

Hostal-Residencia Los Arcos, C. Marqués Viudo de Pontejos, 3, 2nd fl. (☎ 91 522 59 76). Calm, friendly spot with ample rooms and clean baths. Central lounge. Mattresses not quite up to par. Singles with bath 4000ptas; doubles with bath 6000ptas.

Hostal-Residencia Encarnita, C. Marqués Viudo de Pontejo, 7, 4th fl. (☎ 91 531 90 55). M: Sol. Above the María del Mar. Typical hostel charm: dim rooms, soft beds, cheap nature posters, friendly family. Room TVs. Hot showers 200ptas, cold showers 100ptas. Singles 1500ptas; doubles 2600ptas, with bath 2900ptas; triples 3900ptas.

HUERTAS

Although *madrileños* have never settled on a nickname for this neighborhood, the area between C. San Jerónimo and C. de las Huertas is generally referred to as Huertas. Once a seedy neighborhood—and a Hemingway hangout—Huertas has shaped up into a cultural hotbed of food and drink. Though quieter than El Centro and Malasaña and Chueca, Pl. Santa Ana offers some of the best bars in Madrid, and C. Ventura de la Vega some of the best restaurants. It's centrally located—Sol, Pl. Mayor, *el triángulo del arte,* and the Atocha train station are all within walking distance. Sol-bound buses stop near accommodations on C. Príncipe, C. Núñez de Arce, and C. San Jerónimo; buses #14, 27, 37, and 45 run along Po. Prado. The metro stops are Sol and Antón Martín.

Hostal Aguilar, C. San Jerónimo, 32, 2nd fl. (☎ 91 429 59 26 or 91 429 36 61; fax 91 429 26 61). M: Sol. More than 50 clean, modern rooms with vast bathrooms, telephones, A/C, and TVs. Elegantly sparse lounge with deep couches. A great place to meet a young crowd. Singles 4000ptas; doubles 6000ptas; triples 8000ptas. 2000ptas per extra person. V, MC.

Hostal-Residencia Mondragón, C. San Jerónimo, 32, 4th fl. (☎ 91 429 68 16). M: Sol. Two sisters keep guests happy in this many-halled spot where Spain's 1st motion picture was filmed in 1898 (see p. 62). Ask for a room off the gardenia-filled terrace that overlooks the street. Hot water runs only in communal bathrooms. The best value around. Singles 2000ptas; doubles 3000ptas; triples 3900ptas.

Hostal Villar, C. Príncipe, 18, 1st-4th fl. (☎ 91 531 66 00; fax 91 521 50 73). M: Sol. From the metro, walk down C. San Jerónimo and turn right on C. Príncipe. The 1970s stormed through this building, leaving in their wake 46 decidedly brown rooms. Comfortable, with TVs, phones, and A/C. Lounge for the young crowd. Singles 2650ptas, with bath 3200ptas; doubles 3500ptas, with bath 4800ptas; triples 4900ptas, with bath 6720ptas; quads 6300ptas, with bath 8640ptas. V, MC, AmEx.

Hostal Gonzalo, C. Cervantes, 34, 3rd fl. (☎ 91 429 27 14; fax 91 420 20 07). M: Antón Martín. Off C. León, which is off C. Atocha. A budget traveler's dream: newly renovated rooms have pristine baths, firm beds, TVs, and fans in summer. Leather-plush lounge. Singles 4800ptas; doubles 5800ptas; triples 7500pts. V, MC, AmEx.

Hostal-Residencia Sud-Americana, Po. Prado, 12, 6th fl. (☎ 91 429 25 64), across from the Prado. M: Antón Martín or Atocha. Eight rooms, all with faux-leather armchairs, some with balconies. Airy doubles facing the Prado have incredible views of the Paseo. Singles 2600ptas; doubles 5000ptas; triples 7000ptas.

Hostal-Residencia Lido, C. Echegaray, 5, 2nd fl. (☎ 91 429 62 07). M: Sol. Off C. San Jerónimo near Pl. Canalejas. The rickety steps don't keep guests away. Caring owner has big-windowed rooms, some with balconies. Avoid the windowless single. TV lounge. Long-term guests preferred. Ask to use kitchen. Breakfast 350ptas. Singles 2500ptas; doubles 4000ptas. Monthly: singles 45,000ptas; doubles 75,000-80,000ptas.

Hostal Internacional, C. Echegaray, 5, 2nd fl. (☎ 91 429 62 09 or 91 429 81 51). Across the hall from Lido; more bang for more buck. Simple rooms have heat and A/C. Common baths are plush and plentiful. Spacious TV lounge. Kitchen use intended for long-term guests, but attainable for all. Singles 3000ptas; doubles 4000ptas, with bath 5000ptas. Monthly: singles 40,000-50,000ptas.

Hostal Leones, C. Núñez de Arce, 14, 2nd fl. (☎ 91 531 08 89). A classic hostel with narrow hallways, spartan rooms, and spotless bathrooms. Discount with *Let's Go*. Singles 2250ptas; doubles 3900ptas, with bath 4500ptas (IVA not included).

Hostal R. Rodríguez, C. Núñez de Arce, 9, 3rd fl. (☎ 91 522 44 31), off Pl. Santa Ana. M: Sol. Reception decor makes even the cheapest of travelers feel like royalty. Clean shared baths, but watch out for cramped triples. 24hr. reception. English spoken. Spacious singles 3300ptas; doubles 5,000-6,000ptas; triples 8000ptas. V, MC, AmEx.

Hostal-Residencia Carreras, C. Príncipe, 18, 3rd fl. (☎/fax 91 522 00 36). M: Antón Martín, Sol, or Sevilla. Off C. San Jerónimo, between Pl. Santa Ana and Canalejas. Cheap and spacious rooms lit by fluorescent bulbs. Rooms in the annex next door have modern baths. Small, central lounge. Singles 2500-3500ptas, with bath 4500ptas; doubles 4000-4500ptas, with bath 5000ptas; triples 6000-6300ptas, with bath 6900ptas (IVA not included). Advance payment required. V, MC, AmEx.

Hostal Armesto, C. San Agustín, 6, 1st fl. (☎ 91 429 90 31). M: Antón Martín. In front of Pl. Cortés. Tastefully decorated with pink bedspreads, this small hostel offers a quiet night's sleep. Some rooms have garden view; all have private baths, TVs, A/C. Older crowd. Singles 5500ptas; doubles 6500ptas; triples 7500ptas. V, MC, AmEx.

Hostal-Residencia Regional, C. Príncipe, 18, 4th fl. (☎ 91 522 33 73). M: Antón Martín, Sol, or Sevilla. In the same building as Carreras. Cavernous showers. No A/C means stuffy rooms in summer. Singles 2500-3500ptas; doubles 3500-4500ptas; triples 5500ptas.

GRAN VÍA

The neon lights of Broadway and the Champs-Élysées have met their match in Gran Vía. It glows and pulsates with the sharp lights of sex shops, McDonald's, and five-star hotels, in a 24-hour parade of flashing cars, swishing skirts, and stack-heeled shoes. *Hostal* signs scatter the horizon, but accommodations here tend to be overpriced and less comfortable than in other areas. This is not a street you want to be returning to late at night; El Centro and Huertas provide safer bargains. Buses #1, 2, 44, 46, 74, 75, 133, 146, 147, and 148 reach Callao; buses #1, 2, 3, 40, 46, 74, 146, and 149 service both Pl. España and Callao. The closest metro stops are Gran Vía and Callao.

Hostal A. Nebrija, Gran Vía, 67, 8th fl., elevator A (☎ 91 547 73 19). M: Pl. España. A grandson continues his grandparents' tradition with pleasant and spacious rooms in a very tidy building, heavily furnished in classic style. Four rooms with huge windows reveal the best hostel views in Madrid; call ahead to reserve one. Singles 3300ptas; doubles 4500ptas; triples 6300ptas. V, MC, AmEx.

Hostal Margarita, Gran Vía, 50, 5th fl. (☎/fax 91 547 35 49). M: Callao. Stucco walls, light wood shutters, and baby-blue beds make for an airy feel. Rooms tastefully sparse, with big windows, pretty bathrooms, TVs, and telephones; some with street views. Huge, plush lounge and big kitchen. Laundry 1200ptas. Reservations wise. Singles 3400ptas; doubles 5100ptas, with bath 5400ptas; triples with bath 6900ptas. V, MC.

Hostal-Residencia Lamalonga, Gran Vía, 56, 2nd fl. (☎ 91 547 26 31 or 91 547 68 94). M: Santo Domingo. Chandeliers light the way to gentle rooms. Large bathrooms and decadently wide halls compete for the sparkle award. All rooms have TVs, baths, and telephones. Singles 4500ptas; doubles 6500ptas; triples 8500ptas. 10% discount for stays over 5 days. V, MC.

Hostal-Residencia María, Miguel Moya, 4, 2nd fl. (☎ 91 522 44 77). M: Callao. Located just off Pl. Callao. Large rooms with hardwood floors, just beyond the electric din of Gran Vía; many face an interior patio. All with TVs and private baths, some with fans. Singles 4000ptas; doubles 5600ptas; triples 8400ptas. V, MC.

Hostal-Residencia Alibel, Gran Vía, 44, 8th fl. (☎ 91 521 00 51). M: Callao. Well-lit rooms with great views off tired hallways. Doubles 5000-5500ptas, with bath 6000ptas; triples 8000ptas. V, MC.

Hostal Excelsior, Gran Vía, 50, 2nd fl. (☎ 91 547 34 00; fax 91 547 34 08). 35 bare, standard rooms, some with balconies, some with views, others with TVs. If you don't get a good one, it may not be worth it. Sunny TV salon. Special rates for big groups. Singles 3210ptas, with bath 3960ptas; doubles with bath 6206ptas; triples with bath 8345ptas; quads with bath 9950ptas. V, MC, AmEx.

Hostal Acapulco, C. Salud, 13, 4th fl. (☎ 91 531 19 45; fax 91 532 23 29). Inexplicably named, unmistakably quality spot, great for older travelers, families, or luxury seekers. Gorgeous rooms have bath, A/C, phone, mini-fridge, and TV. Singles 5000ptas; doubles 7000ptas; quads 9000ptas; prices fall Nov.-Dec. V, MC, AmEx.

Hostal Lauria, Gran Vía, 50, 4th fl. (☎/fax 91 541 91 82). M: Callao. Green carpeted halls lead to standard rooms with baths and TVs. Large single beds. Big TV salon with stereo. English spoken. Singles 4280ptas; doubles 6200ptas; triples 7500ptas. V, MC.

MALASAÑA AND CHUECA

Split down the middle by C. Fuencarral, Malasaña and Chueca are both hard-core party pits for Madrid's alternative youth. Hostels and *pensiones* are almost as abundant as the clubs and boutiques and are usually located above the first floor of old buildings. Unless techno helps you sleep, make sure your room has sound-proof windows. Chueca is hip, fun, funky, and largely gay, but can be dangerous, especially for solo travelers. Buses #3, 40, and 149 run along C. Fuencarral and Hortaleza. Metro stops Chueca, Gran Vía, and Tribunal serve the area.

Hostal Palacios and **Hostal Ribadavia,** C. Fuencarral, 25, 1st-3rd fl. (☎ 91 531 10 58 or 91 531 48 47). M: Gran Vía. Run by the same cheerful family. Palacio (1st and 2nd fl.) offers large, tiled rooms with elegant modern furniture. Ribadavia (3rd fl.) is older but still has comfortable rooms, all with new TVs. They'll hold luggage for free. Singles 2500ptas, with bath 3500ptas; doubles 4000ptas, with bath 5000ptas; triples 6000ptas, with bath 7000ptas; quads with bath 9000ptas. V, MC, AmEx.

Hostal Lorenzo, C. las Infantas, 26, 3rd fl. (☎ 91 521 30 57; fax 91 532 79 78). M: Gran Vía. Tastefully decorated rooms are pricey but have all the amenities: bathrooms, TVs, telephones, A/C, music, and chandeliers. Sound-proof windows muffle daytime traffic and the nighttime revelry below. Bored? Turning the knob by the bed produces music through ceiling speakers. Some good plaza views. A slightly older crowd. Breakfast 350ptas. Reservations recommended. Singles 5500ptas; doubles 7500ptas; triples 9500ptas (IVA not included). V, MC, AmEx.

Hostal Abril, C. Fuencarral, 39, 4th fl. (☎ 91 531 53 38). M: Tribunal or Gran Vía. Brand new doors and granite floors; some fluorescent lighting. Singles 2000-2300ptas; doubles 3500ptas, with bath 3800ptas; triples with bath 5200ptas.

Hostal-Residencia Domínguez, C. Santa Brígida, 1 (☎/fax 91 532 15 47). M: Tribunal. Go down C. Fuencarral toward Gran Vía, turn left on C. Santa Brígida, and climb up a flight. Modern bathrooms are almost as big as the rooms, which are bare except for TVs; ask for one of the new rooms on the 3rd fl. Hospitable young owner ready with tips on local nightlife. English spoken. Heat and A/C. Singles 2500ptas, with bath 3500ptas; doubles with bath 4900ptas.

Hostal Medieval, C. Fuencarral, 46, 2nd fl. (☎ 91 522 25 49). M: Tribunal. On the corner of C. Augusto Figueroa. No medieval decor here except the lackluster bathrooms; just pleasant peach walls and geraniums. TV lounge, with complimentary nuts, honors the royal couple and Real Madrid. Singles 3000ptas; doubles 4500ptas, with bath 5500ptas; triples 6500ptas. V, MC.

Hotel Mónaco, C. Barbieri, 5 (☎ 91 552 46 30; fax 91 521 16 01). M: Chueca or Gran Vía. Once a brothel catering to Madrid's high society, this hotel still encourages naughtiness with a mix of class and funk. Frescoes of Eve-like temptresses prod the imagination while hundreds of mirrors and *palacio*-sized beds allow the reality. Each room is a different adventure, all with baths. Green-lit lounge and a lively bar/cafeteria area. Slightly older crowd. Be ready to lighten your wallet. Simple singles 7490ptas; doubles 10,700ptas; triples 13,500ptas; quads 15,000ptas. V, MC, AmEx.

ELSEWHERE

Near the **Chamartín** train station budget lodgings are rare, as is the case in most of the residential districts located away from the city center. Near the **Atocha** train station are a handful of hostels, the closest of which are down Po. Santa María de la Cabeza. The tourist office in Pl. Mayor has a full list of lodgings.

Albergue Juvenil Santa Cruz de Marcenado (HI), C. Santa Cruz de Marcenado, 28 (☎ 91 547 45 32; fax 91 548 11 96). M: Argüelles. From the metro, walk 1 block down C. Alberto Aguilera away from C. Princesa, turn right on C. Serrano Jóve, then left on C. Santa Cruz de Marcenado. Modern, recently renovated facilities near the student district mostly house traveling college students. The 72 beds fill quickly, even in winter. Message board and lounge for late-night card playing. English spoken. Rooms have cubbies; recommended lockers are outside the rooms (200ptas extra). Breakfast included. Sheets (but no towels) provided. 3-day max. stay. 1:30am curfew is strictly enforced. Quiet hours after midnight. Reception daily 9am-1:30pm. Reserve a space (by mail, fax, or in person only) in advance, or arrive early and pray. Closed Christmas and New Year's. An HI (YHA) card is required and can be purchased for 1800ptas. Dorms 1200ptas; over 26 yrs. 1820ptas.

Hostal-Residencia Rios, C. Juan Álvarez Mendizábal, 44, 4th fl. (☎ 91 559 51 56). M: Ventura Rodríguez. From the metro, face the green shrubbery, walk 3 blocks up C. Princesa (to your left) to C. Rey Francisco, go 3 blocks to J. A. Mendizábal, and turn left again. Nothing fancy; just clean, cheap, comfortable rooms close to the park, some with A/C (1000ptas). Microwave. Singles 1800ptas, doubles with shower 3600ptas.

MADRID

CAMPING

Tourist offices can provide info about the 13 campsites within 50km of Madrid. Similar info is in the *Guía Oficial de Campings* (official camping guide), a big book which they gladly let you look through but don't give away (most bookstores carry it). The *Mapa de Campings* shows the location of every official campsite in Spain. Also ask for the brochure *Hoteles, Campings, Apartamentos*, which lists hotels, campsites, and apartments in and around Madrid. For further camping info, contact the *Consejería de Educación de Juventud* (☎ 91 522 29 41).

Camping Osuna (☎ 91 741 05 10; fax 91 320 63 65), on Av. Logroño. M: Canillejas. From the metro cross the pedestrian overpass, walk through the parking lot, and turn right along the freeway. Pass under 2 bridges (the 1st a freeway and the 2nd an arch) and look for campground signs on the right. If loaded down with bags, grab the #101 bus from the metro toward Barajas and ask for the campsite. Showers, laundromat, even a supermarket, bar, and restaurant in high season. 690ptas per person, per tent, and per car. 625ptas for electricity. (IVA not included.)

Camping Alpha (☎ 91 695 80 69; fax 91 683 1659), on a tree-lined site 12.4km down the Ctra. de Andalucía in Getafe. M: Legazpi. From the metro station take bus #447, which stops next to the Nissan dealership (10min., every 30min. until 10pm, 185ptas). Ask the driver to let you off at the pedestrian overpass near the Amper building. Cross the bridge and walk 1½km back toward Madrid along a busy highway. Alpha has a pool, showers, laundry, and just about every other amenity. 695ptas per person, 680ptas per tent and per car. (IVA not included.)

◘ FOOD

In Madrid, it's not hard to fork it down without forking over too much. You can't walk a block without tripping over at least five *cafeterías*, where a sandwich, coffee, and dessert sell for around 600ptas. Vegetarians should check out the *Guía del Ocio*, which has a complete listing of Madrid's vegetarian havens under the section *Otras Cocinas*, or the website www.mundovegetariano.com. Even carnivores may appreciate a veggie meal or two, given Madrid's indulgence in fatty meats and fried preparation.

For a full meal at a *restaurante*, one step up from the typical *cafetería*, expect to spend at least 1100ptas. Most restaurants offer a *menú del día*, which includes bread, one drink, and one choice from each of the day's selections for appetizers, main courses, and desserts. For 1000-1500ptas, it is a fantastic way to fill up. (If you don't want this, but a menu in the English sense, ask for *la carta*.) Keep in mind the following essential buzz words for quicker, cheaper *madrileño* fare: *bocadillo* (a sandwich on a long, hard role, 350-450ptas); *sandwich* (a sandwich on sliced bread, ask for it *a la plancha* if you want it grilled, 300ptas); *croissant* (with ham and cheese, 250ptas); *ración* (a large *tapa*, served with bread 300-600ptas); and *empanada* (a puff pastry with meat fillings, 200-300ptas). See the **Glossary** p. 730, for additional useful translations.

In general, *restaurantes* are open from 1 to 4pm and 8pm to midnight; in the following listings, this is the case unless otherwise noted. More casual establishments such as *mesones*, *cafeterías*, *bares*, *cafés*, *terrazas*, and *tabernas* serve drinks and foodstuffs all day until midnight, though some are closed on Sundays.

FOOD SHOPPING

Groceries: Dia and **Simago** are the cheapest city-wide supermarket chains. More expensive are **Mantequerías Leonesas, Expreso,** and **Jumbo.** Every **El Corte Inglés** (see p. 86) has a huge food market with an excellent selection (it shows in the price), located either on the basement or top floor.

Markets: Mercado de San Miguel, a covered market on Pl. San Miguel, off the northwest corner of Pl. Mayor, sells the finest seafood and produce in the city at high prices. Open M-F 9:30am-2:30pm and 5:15-8:15pm, Sa 9am-2:30pm. **Mercado de la Cebada,** at the intersection of C. Toledo and C. San Francisco, is less expensive. Open M-Sa 8am-2pm and 5:30-8pm.

Specialty Shops: Pastry shops are everywhere. The sublime **Horno La Santiagüesa,** C. Mayor, 73, sells everything from *roscones de reyes* (sweet bread for the Feast of the Epiphany) to *empanadas* and pastries doused in rich chocolate. Open M-Sa 8am-9pm, Su 8am-8pm. **Horno San Onofre,** C. San Onofre, 4, off C. Fuencarral, serves sumptuous fruit tarts and *suspiros de modistilla* (seamstress's sighs), a *madrileño* specialty. Open M-Sa 9am-9pm, Su 9am-8pm. Homesick Americans will love **Taste of America,** Pl. Cortes, 7 (☎/fax 91 420 41 73), an American grocery store complete with brownie mix and macaroni and cheese. Open M-Sa 10am-9pm, Su 10:30am-9pm.

Red-Eye Establishments: *Guía del Ocio* lists late-night eateries under *Cenar a última hora.* The chain **VIPS,** at Gran Vía, 43 (☎ 91 542 15 78; M: Callao); Serrano, 41 (M: Serrano); Calle Princesa, 5 (M: Ventura Rodríguez); Fuencarral 101 (M: Tribunal); and other scattered locations is a standard late-night option. A diner with cushioned booths, average service, and overpriced burgers with cheese fries. VIPS also carries English books and magazines, records, and canned food. Open daily 9am-3am. **7-Eleven** stores are scattered about in Ópera, Alonso Martínez (C. Mejía Lequerida), and Av. America. **Hot & Cool,** C. Gaztambide in Moncloa-Argüelles, serves fresh *bocadillos* until 3am on weekends. **Street vendors** also sell cheap *bocadillos* late night on weekends.

EL CENTRO: SOL, ÓPERA, AND PLAZA MAYOR

Tourists overrun this area. Typical fare abounds, and prices run high. Streets off M: Ópera teem with crowded cafes, markets, and restaurants. Places with menus in several different languages are tourist traps. Cruise to nearby Pl. Santa Ana for better deals, but don't miss the Museo del Jamón. The surrounding streets, especially those through the **Arco de los Cuchilleros** in the southwest corner of Pl. Mayor, house old specialty shops and renowned *mesones.* Head here for garlicky *tapas* and pitchers of *sangría* served in a festive, albeit touristy, atmosphere.

Museo del Jamón, C. San Jerónimo, 6 (☎ 91 521 03 46). M: Sol. 5 other much-loved locations throughout the city, including one at C. Mayor 7 (☎ 91 531 45 50). Dodge hooves and shanks at the sterile, metallic downstairs bar or head upstairs to the dining room (open at 1pm) for a sampling of the chef's specialties (600-1160ptas). Succulent Iberian ham is served up in every form you could possibly desire, but the chicken is also good. Bocadillos from 175ptas. *Menú* 1000ptas. Generous combo plates 650-950ptas. Open M-Th 9am-12:30pm, F-Sa 9am-1am, Su 10am-12:30pm. V, AmEx.

El Cuchi, C. Cuchilleros, 3 (☎ 91 366 44 24). Just outside Plaza Mayor, this is better and cheaper than the restaurants inside it. Delicious, authentic Mexican food in a festive setting. Before asking for bread, check the basket hanging from the ceiling above your head. Entrees 900-2900ptas. Open M-Sa 1pm-1am, Su 1-4pm and 8pm-midnight.

Casa Lhardy, C. San Jerónimo, 8 (☎ 91 521 33 85), at C. Victoria. M: Sol. For dinner, get decked out and bring your wallet; this gorgeous restaurant, replete with original wallpaper and woodwork, is 150 years old and the house specialty *cocido* (3800ptas) is famous. For a great deal, in style, join budget hounds on the ground floor for cognac, sherry, *consommé* (250ptas each), and Madrid's best hors d'oeuvres, served from an original silver cabinet. Gourmet foodstuffs for sale. Open M-Sa 1-3:30 and 8:30-11:30pm, Su 1-3:30pm. V, MC, AmEx.

Matador Parilla, C. De La Cruz, 13 (☎ 91 522 35 95), off C. San Jerónimo, 13. They'll grill just about any meat or vegetable for you at this bull-and-*torero*-themed spot—and will have a rowdy good time while they're at it. 5 different 1-person *menús* 1400-2300ptas each. 2-person grilled extravaganza 4000-5100ptas. Pizzas 750-900ptas. Pastas 700ptas. Salads 450-600ptas. Open Su and Tu-Th 1-4:30pm and 8pm-midnight, F-Sa 1-4:30pm and 8pm-1am.

HUERTAS

Pl. Santa Ana is perfect for killing a couple of hours with a drink and snack. Green, shady, and generally happy, it's a popular place among locals. **Calles Echegaray, Ventura de la Vega,** and **Manuel Fernández González** are the best food streets; quality is high and prices are low. As the evening grows and wine flows, these streets become the first stop of a night out in Madrid.

■ **Casa Alberto,** C. Huertas, 18 (☎ 91 429 93 56). M: Antón Martín. Patrons spill out into the night air to wait for a spot at the bar. Interior dining room decorated with bullfighting and Cervantine relics; Cervantes wrote the second part of "El Quijote" here. The *tapas* are all original house recipes. Try the *gambas al ajillo* (shrimp in garlic and hot peppers; 1600ptas) or the filled canapes (275-350ptas). Sit-down dinner is too pricey. Open Tu-Sa 10am-1:30am, Su 10am-4pm. V, MC, AmEx.

Bar Pizza, C. Leon, 8 (☎ 91 420 12 98), off C. del Prado. Offering much more than pizza, this place is hands down the best cheap lunch in the area. A shockingly good *menú* (950ptas, available M-F) includes a selection of exquisite desserts. Most entrees 950ptas. Open Su-M and W-Th 1:30-4:30pm and 8:30pm-1am, Tu 8:30pm-1am, F-Sa 1:30-5:30pm and 8:30pm-2am.

Restaurante Integral Artemisa, C. Ventura de la Vega, 4 (☎ 91 429 50 92), off C. San Jerónimo. M: Sol. Elegant veggie food served in a long, mellow dining area with A/C. Bulletin board at the entrance informs of yoga and other New Age activities. Non-veggie entrees 1500-2000ptas. Salads 1000ptas. Veggie entrees around 1400ptas. *Menú* 1200ptas. Open daily 1:30-4pm and 9pm-midnight. V, MC, AmEx.

Gula Gula, C. Infante 5 (☎ 91 522 87 64), off C. Echegaray near C. Huertas. M: Antón Martín. Elegant, artsy dining room with white cloth-covered seats is mellow by lunch and outrageous by night. All-you-can-eat buffet with salads, chicken, rice and pasta, a soup, and hot dishes (1500ptas at lunch; cold buffet plus an ordered hot dish 2800ptas at dinner). Dinner served in 2 seatings (9 and 11:30pm). Waiters more exotic than the food perform themed drag, strip, and cabaret shows after the meal. Make reservations for weekend dinners a week ahead. Open daily 1-5pm and 9pm-3am. V, MC, AmEx.

Restaurante Luarques, C. Ventura de la Vega, 16 (☎ 91 429 61 74). Royal treatment in service, food, and decor, without the cost of a king's ransom. *Menú* surpasses all others at its price level (1500ptas). Open Tu-Su 2-4:30 and 9-11:30pm. V, MC.

LAVAPIÉS, LA LATINA AND ATOCHA

The neighborhoods south of Sol, bounded by C. Atocha and C. Toledo, are residential and working class. No caviar or champagne here, but you'll find plenty of *menús* for around 1000ptas and can get even better bargains by eating a la carte. **Calle Agurrosa** at Lavapiés has some funky outdoor eateries, and there are good restaurants up the hill toward Huertas.

■ **El Estragón,** Pl. de la Paja, 10 (☎ 91 365 89 82). M: La Latina. From the metro, follow C. Duque de Alba, turn right through to Pl. Puerta de Moros and leave the church on your right; it's on the far side of Pl. de la Paja. Perhaps the best medium-priced restaurant—of any kind—in Madrid, with vegetarian food that could turn the most die-hard carnivores to switch-hitters. Multiple levels ensure an intimate dining experience. Delicious and creative *menú* (M-F 1200ptas; Sa-Su and evenings 2475ptas). Open daily 1-4pm and 8pm-1am. V, MC, AmEx.

■ **Champagneria Gala,** C. Moratín, 22 (☎ 91 429 25 62). Down the hill on Moratín from C. Atocha. The funky *paella* buck stops here, with decor as colorful and varied as its pan-cooked, rice-based dishes. *Menú* (1750ptas) offers choice of *paella*, along with the usual salad, bread, wine, and dessert. Eat in under the high, lit roof of the vine-covered interior garden, or at the bright orange tables in the front room. Make reservations on weekends. Open daily 1:30-5pm and 9pm-12:30am.

El Granero de Lavapiés, C. Argumosa, 10 (☎ 91 467 76 11), off the plaza. M: Lavapiés. For 16 years, frescoes, inventive vegetarian specials, and fresh bread have kept this hideaway packed with locals. Vegetarian *menú* M-Sa 1200ptas. Open daily 1-4pm.

La Farfalla, C. Santa María, 17 (☎ 91 369 46 91). M: Antón Martín. One block from the metro along C. Huertas; look for the butterfly above the entrance. La Farfalla's specialty is Argentine-style grilled meat, but don't miss their thin-crust pizzas (750ptas). Open for dinner Su-Th 9:30pm-3am, F-Sa 9:30pm-4am. V, MC, AmEx.

GRAN VÍA

If you came to Spain to escape fast-food chains, stay clear of Gran Vía. Luckily, **Calle Fuencarral** is lined with cheap eateries.

Costa Del Sol, C. Tres Cruces, 6 (☎ 91 522 02 82 or 91 531 01 79). M: Gran Vía. Off Gran Vía, opposite C. Valverde. Unlike its namesake, this place is virtually tourist-free. The worn front hides a ship-shape restaurant with gargantuan, delicious meals for remarkably low prices. *Raciones* 450-750ptas. House's special *sangría* 950ptas per liter. Lunchtime *menú* 950ptas. Open daily 1-5pm and 7pm-midnight.

Museo Chicote, C. Gran Vía, 12 (☎ 91 532 97 80). M: Gran Vía. Lose yourself in the green leather booths amidst pictures of Spanish stars. Don't miss the museum of rare liquor bottles. Breakfast is the best deal, with coffee and fresh pastries (240-400ptas). Lunchtime *menú* 1200ptas. Open M-Sa 8am-12:30am. Lunch served 1-4pm.

MALASAÑA AND CHUECA

Malasaña and Chueca, both above Gran Vía, are divided in atmosphere along C. Hortaleza. Closer to the Ópera, Malasaña's restaurants often feature new and adventurous menus filled with vegetarian options. Young locals congregate in hordes in **Plaza 2 de Mayo** on warm evenings. From its central plaza at the metro stop, Chueca's flamboyantly gay district boasts an assortment of colorful, fun places to wine and dine before a night of debauchery.

MALASAÑA

La Gata Flora (☎ 91 523 10 26), C. 2 de Mayo, 1, across the street at C. San Vicente Ferrer, 33. M: Noviciado or Tribunal. You can't miss the pink exterior. Young people plus good, cheap food makes for a fun scene; most eat outside in the packed plaza. *Menú* 1075ptas. Pizzas 850-1000ptas. Luscious salads 700-900ptas. Stuffed pitas 550ptas. *Sangría* 600-900ptas. Open daily Su-Th noon-1am, F-Sa noon-3am. V, MC.

El Tazumal, C. Madera, 36 (☎ 91 522 79 82). M: Tribunal. From the station, walk down to C. Espíritu Santo, turn right, then left on C. Madera. Tasty and unique cuisine from El Salvador in a down-home setting. Try the national favorite, *pupusas* (loosely described as small, thick tortillas; 275ptas) with cheese or meat. Large combo plates 1100-1600ptas. Entrees 275-1300ptas. Open W-M 1:30-4:30pm and 8pm-midnight.

La Granja Restaurante Vegetariano, C. San Andrés, 11 (☎ 91 532 87 93), off Pl. 2 de Mayo. M: Tribunal. Warm atmosphere with plants, tiles, and pottery. Entrees 700-800ptas. Salads 700-800ptas. Lunchtime *menú* 975ptas. Open W-M 1:30-4:30pm and 9pm-midnight. Visa.

CHUECA

El 26 de Libertad, C. Libertad, 26 (☎ 91 522 25 22), off C. las Infantas. M: Chueca. Innovative and exotic Spanish cuisine. Lunchtime *menú* (1300ptas) is fantastic. Dinner is served in a yellow room whose cheeriness helps you swallow the price (3000ptas before tax). A red-walled bar offers a selection of wines throughout the day (200-250ptas per glass). Open M-Th 1-4pm and 8pm-midnight, F-Sa 1-4pm and 9pm-12:30am, Su 1-4pm. V, MC, AmEx.

La Sacristía, C. San Marcos, 8 (☎ 91 522 09 45). M: Gran Vía or Chueca. Colored, textured walls create a pleasant cave-like tavern where delicious creations and 60 types of *bacalao* are served. The chef prides himself on original *tapas* (200-800ptas) and pizzas (1000ptas). Lunchtime *menú* (M-F 1300ptas, Sa-Su 2000ptas). Dinner *menú* changes weekly (M-Th only, 2500ptas). Open M-Sa 1-4pm and 8pm-1am, Su 8pm-1am.

La Carreta, C. Barbieri, 10 (☎ 91 532 70 42 or 91 521 60 97), off C. las Infantas. M: Gran Vía or Chueca. Small, friendly spot specializing in Argentinian, Uruguayan, and Chilean meals. Lunch *menú* 1500ptas. Entrees around 1300ptas. If your budget allows, try the delicious Martín Fierro dessert (990ptas), named after the Argentinian national novel. Occasional tango performances on weekends. Reservations recommended. Open daily 1:30-5pm and 9pm-5am. V, MC, AmEx.

La Gastroteca, Pl. de Chueca, 8 (☎ 91 532 25 64 or 91 522 88 04). M: Chueca. Another of Madrid's new imaginative kitchens. Look for the French owners in a mock-Egyptian portrait above the bar. Elegant dark-wood interior with menu to match. Creative appetizers around 1500ptas. Entrees 2400-2980ptas. Open M-F 2-3:30pm and 9pm-1:30am, Sa 9pm-1:30am.

Restaurante Zara, C. las Infantas, 5 (☎ 91 532 20 74), off C. Hortaleza. M: Gran Vía. Young locals swarm this island of colorful Cuban cuisine and checkered tablecloths. Daily "tropical" specials 1500ptas. Meat entrees 700-1500ptas. *Menú* 2500ptas. Open M-F. V, MC, AmEx.

Chez Pomme, C. Pelayo, 4 (☎ 91 532 16 46), off C. Augusto Figueroa. M: Chueca. Quiet, artsy spot. Delicious, creative salads 750-930ptas. Light *menú* 1000ptas. Friendly service. Open M-Th 1:30-4 and 8:30-11:30pm, F-Sa 1:30-4pm and 8:30pm-midnight.

BILBAO

The area north of Glorieta de Bilbao, in the "V" formed by C. Fuencarral and C. Luchana and including Pl. Olavide, is the ethnic food extravaganza of Madrid; it overflows with bars, clubs, cafes, and restaurants of all nationalities. Most serve splendid, cheap *tapas* to the youthful crowd that swarms the area at night. Lunch gets pricier farther north in a more gentrified area. The metro stop is Bilbao.

☒ **Arepas con Todo,** C. Hartzenbusch, 19 (☎ 91 448 75 45), off C. Cardenal Cisneros, which is off C. Luchana. This classic Colombian restaurant really does have *todo*: with a different *menú* (1600-2000ptas) every night of the month, and 60 fixed dishes (1800-2400ptas), only the live music repeats itself. Low hanging lights and festively dressed waitresses. For dinner, make reservations. Open M-W 2pm-1am. V, MC.

Tanger, C. Cardenal Cisneros, 11 (☎ 91 594 44 61). Middle-Eastern and Moroccan dishes, such as tahini-sauced meat (1000-1200ptas) and salads (350-550ptas) are served in a fantastic, mirrored dining room, replete with low, backless seats and engraved wooden tables. Those with back problems might head elsewhere. Midday *menú* 1100ptas. Pitas to go 450ptas. Open Tu-Su 12:30pm-2am.

Pizza Buona, C. Hartzenbusch, 19 (☎ 91 445 78 68), off C. Cardenal Cisneros, which is just off C. Luchana. M: Bilbao. An Italian restaurant decked out in patriotic green, red, and white, on a German-named street in the heart of Spain. Tasty, greasy pizzas 625-925ptas. Down the street, at C. Harzenbusch, 9, a new installment of the same restaurant has refined decor, piano shows Th-Sa, and an expanded menu. White-sauce pizzas 1000ptas. Midday *menú* 1200ptas. Meat options from 1275ptas. Both open Su-Th 1-5pm and 8pm-midnight, F-Sa 1-5pm and 8pm-1am. V, MC, AmEx.

Collage, C. Olid, 6. (☎ 91 448 45 62), off C. Fuencarral. M: Bilbao. A Swedish chef mixes and matches in style. Don't let the understated decor fool you; the meals here explode with flavors, as Swedish reindeer and various fish meet soy sauce and chili. Only the hip need enter, and bring a full wallet. Entrees 1650-2850ptas. Open Su-M 1:30-4pm, Tu-Sa 1:30-4pm and 8:30-midnight. V, MC, AmEx.

Bar Samara, C. Cardenal Cisneros, 13 (☎ 91 448 80 56). M: Bilbao. Bills itself as Egyptian, but offers Middle Eastern staples. Narrow bar fills with college students after dark. The hieroglyphically decorated dining room offers a quiet dinner. Hummus, *baba ghanoush,* and *tajine* salads 575-600ptas. Kebabs and other entrees 1675-2225ptas. Open M 8:30-11:30pm, Tu-Su 2-4pm and 8:30-11:30pm.

ARGÜELLES

Argüelles is a middle-class neighborhood near the Ciudad Universitaria. It's geared toward locals rather than tourists and is therefore full of inexpensive markets, moderately priced restaurants, and informal neighborhood bars. Check out the quiet *terrazas* on C. Pintor Rosales, overlooking the park.

☒ **Cáscaras,** C. Ventura Rodríguez, 7 (☎ 91 542 83 36). M: Ventura Rodríguez. Sleek interior enhances the dining experience. Popular for *tapas, pinchos,* and ice-cold Mahou beer in the early afternoon and evening. Vegetarian entrees 800-985ptas. Tortillas 745-955ptas. Salads 735-895ptas. Non-vegetarian fare as well. Open M-F 7am-1am, Sa-Su 10am-1am. V, MC, AmEx.

▩ **Ananias,** C. Galileo, 9 (☎ 91 448 68 01). Swirling waiters serve Castilian food prepared with love in this friendly down-home spot. Authentic *torero* paraphernalia covers the walls in the front room, while finer diners and regulars enjoy the elegance of the back room. The *rabo de toro* (1300ptas) is not to be missed. Busy on Su. Starters 500ptas, entrees 1000-2500ptas.

La Crêperie, Po. Pintor Rosales, 28 (☎ 91 548 23 58). M: Ventura Rodríguez. The cherub decorations are almost as sweet as the dessert crepes (370-645ptas). Eat the affordable lunch and dinner crepes (535-805ptas) on the chic Po. Rosales *terraza*. Open Su-Th 1:30-4:15pm and 8pm-1am, F-Sa 1:30-4:15pm and 8pm-1:30am.

La Vaca Argentina, Po. Pintor Rosales, 52 (☎ 91 559 66 05). M: Moncloa or Argüelles. Near the Rosaleda. Famous for its regional steak specialties and infamous for the cowhide wallpaper that reminds you what you're eating. Dine in the dark interior or under the shaded awning. Scrumptious and tender fillets 1100-4500ptas. Salads 600-750ptas. *Menú* 2750ptas. Open daily 1-4:30pm and 9pm-12:30am. V, MC, AmEx.

TAPAS

Not so long ago, bartenders in Madrid used to cover *(tapar)* drinks with saucers to keep the flies out. Later, servers began putting little sandwiches on top of the saucers, and there you have it: *tapas.* Hopping from bar to bar gobbling *tapas* is an active alternative to a full sit-down meal and a fun way to sample food you might never dream of even trying. Most *tapas* bars (a.k.a. *tascas* or *tabernas*) are open noon to 4pm and 8pm to midnight or later. Some, like **Museo del Jamón** (see p. 95), double as restaurants, and many cluster around **Plaza Mayor** (beware the tourist traps!) and **Plaza Santa Ana,** which is the place to be on Sundays.

La Toscana, C. Manuel Fernández González, 10-12 (☎ 91 429 60 31), at C. Ventura de la Vega. M: Sol. Despite the antique lettering and wrought iron, the *tapas* are anything but medieval. Spacious bar area jam-packed on weekends. Try the *morcilla* (200ptas), but don't ask what you're eating until you're done. Most *tapas* around 800ptas. Open Th-Tu noon-4pm and 8pm-midnight.

Casa Amadeo, Pl. de Cascorro, 18 (☎ 91 365 94 39). M: La Latina. The jovial owner of 60 years supervises making of house specialty *caracoles* (snails; small plate 700ptas, big plate 1500ptas) and *chorizo* (sausage) made with snails (750ptas). *Raciones* 350-900ptas. Wild Sunday nights. Open M-F 10:30am-4pm and 7-10:30pm, Su 7-11pm.

La Trucha, C. Núñez de Arce, 6 (☎ 91 429 58 33). M: Sol. Cramped but cheap. Their fresh vegetables and daily specials are popular with locals. Impressive selection of seasonal veggies (800-1500ptas), but don't skip the stewed bull's tail (*rabo de toro*). Entrees 200-2500ptas. Open M-Sa 12:30-4pm and 7:30pm-midnight. V, MC, AmEx.

La Princesita, C. Princesa, 80 (☎ 91 543 30 47). M: Argüelles. From open to closing, students crowd the bar to enjoy regional specialties, including *queso de Cabrales* (goat cheese; 150ptas). Open M-Sa 10am-11:30pm.

Cafetería-Restaurante El Encinar del Bierzo, C. Toledo, 82 (☎ 91 366 23 89). M: La Latina. A neighborhood landmark. House specialties *conejo al ajillo* (rabbit with garlic, 2000ptas) and *gambas a la plancha* (fried shrimp, 1100ptas). *Menú* 1100ptas, 1300ptas on Su. Open daily 1-4:30pm and 9pm-11:30pm.

CAFES

Coffee in Madrid's cafes may be expensive (200-450ptas), but included in the price are atmosphere, history, and image. It's customary to linger for an hour or two in these historic cafes, an economical way to soak up a little of Madrid's culture and finally write those postcards you bought a few days ago. You won't be bothered with the check until you ask.

▩ **Café Gijón,** Po. Recoletos, 21 (☎ 91 521 54 25). M: Colón. On its 100th anniversary in 1988, Gijón was designated a historic site for its intellectual significance. It has long since been a favorite of the literati. Check out how smart you look in the mirrors and forget how much that cup of coffee costs. Open daily 9am-1:30am.

TAPAS So finally you've found a hostel, only been lost twice, and are ready to experience the *madrileño* lifestyle. Clearly, it's time for some drinks and *tapas*. The only problem is, what the hell are you going to order? To the untrained reader, *tapas* menus are often cryptic and undecipherable—if the bar has even bothered to print any. To make sure you don't end up eating the stewed parts of the oxen you rode in on, just keep the following words in mind. Servings come in three sizes: *pincho* (normally eaten with toothpicks between sips of beer), *tapa* (small plate), or *ración* (sizable, meal portion). *Aceitunas* (olives), *albondigas* (meatballs), *anchoas* (anchovies), *callos* (tripe), *chorizo* (sausage), *croquetas* (croquettes), *gambas* (shrimp), *jamon* (ham), *patatas alioli y bravas* (potatoes with sauces), *pimentoes* (peppers), *pulpo* (octopus), and *tortillla* (omelette) comprise any basic menu. More adventurous travelers should try *morcilla* (blood sausage) or *sesos* (cow's brains). Bartenders will often offer tastes of *tapas* with your drink and strike up a conversation in the spirit of Madrid's generosity and charm. To ensure full treatment and local respect, the house *cerveza* is always a good choice. *Sangría*, a mixture of wine and fruit juices, seems innocent but is very sharp—natives drink it by the jar and box in the sweltering summers.

Café Círculo de Bellas Artes, C. Alcalá, 42 (☎ 91 360 54 00). M: Banco de España. Tourists rest weary museum feet outside and enjoy a reasonably priced snack. Beer 350-500ptas. Sandwiches 400-600ptas. For a 100ptas cover, lounge on leather couches beneath high frescoed ceilings and fabulous crystal lights. Expensive drinks deter starving artist types. Coffee or tea 200ptas. Open M-F 9am-1am, Sa-Su 9am-3am. V, MC, AmEx.

Café de Oriente, Pl. Oriente, 2 (☎ 91 547 15 64). M: Ópera. A beautiful, old-fashioned cafe catering to a ritzy, older crowd. Spectacular view of the Palacio Real from the *terraza*, especially at night when a spotlight illuminates the palace. Prices are significantly cheaper inside than on the patio. Coffee 200ptas, specialty coffees 540-840ptas. Open Su-Th 8:30am-1:30am, F-Sa 8:30am-1:30am.

Salon Del Prado, C. Del Prado, 4 (☎ 91 429 33 61). M: Sol. Head left down C. San Jerónimo, right down C. Príncipe to Pl. Santa Ana, and left on C. Del Prado. Interior as cool as the *granizado de limón* (frozen lemon drink; 350ptas) it serves up. A corner piano sees use in the evenings. M-Th 2pm-2am, F-Sa 2pm-3am, Su 2pm-1am.

Eucalipto, C. Argumosa, 4. M: Lavapiés. You need not be a koala to enjoy the freshest fruit drinks around (400-550ptas). Spike up the night with a daiquiri (600-650ptas) and enjoy a fantastic fruit salad for 2 (1000ptas), outside with a young, hip, crowd. Open daily M-Th 6pm-2am, F-Sa 6pm-3am, Su 2pm-midnight.

Nuevo Café Barbieri, C. Av. María, 45 (☎ 91 527 36 58). M: Lavapiés. Intellectuals lurk in this crumbling cafe amid curling paint, long mirrors, and dusty red drapes. Art films in the back room some winter nights—pick up a schedule. Coffee 250ptas. Open Su-Th 3pm-2am, F-Sa 3pm-3am.

Café Comercial, Glorieta de Bilbao, 7 (☎ 91 531 34 52). M: Bilbao. Traditional cafe with high ceilings, cushioned chairs, and huge mirrors perfect for people-watching. Frequented by artists and Republican aviators alike. The first anti-Franco protests took place here. Sandwiches and *canapes* from 350ptas. Coffee 160ptas at the bar, 260ptas at a table. The upstairs **Cybercafé Comercial** reflects its move to the 21st century with coin-operated computers. 100ptas per 8min., 500ptas per hr. Open Su-Th 8am-12:45am, F-Sa 8am-1:45am.

🎦 SIGHTS

You need good shoes to walk around in.
    — A shoemaker

Madrid, large as it may seem, is a walker's city. Its fantastic public transportation system should be used as little as possible. Although the word *paseo* refers to a major avenue—such as *Paseo de la Castellana* or *Paseo del Prado*—it literally means "a stroll." Do just that from Sol to Cibeles and from the Plaza Mayor to the Palacio Real—sights will kindly introduce themselves. The city's art and architecture and its culture and atmosphere convince wide-eyed walkers that it was once the capital of the world's greatest empire. While Madrid is perfect for walking, it also offers some of the world's best places to stop strolling. Whether soothing tired feet after perusing the *triángulo de arte* or suffering from a hangover after a night in Chueca, there's nothing better than a shady sidewalk cafe.

For hard-core visitors with a checklist of destinations, the municipal tourist office's *Plano de Transportes* map, which marks monuments as well as bus and metro lines, is indispensable. In the following pages, sights are arranged by neighborhood, offering opportunities for extensive walking tours in each district. Each section has a designated center from which all directions are given. If you are trying to design a walking tour of the entire city, it is best to begin in El Centro, the self-evident nucleus of Madrid. The neighborhoods naturally fall in geographical order from there; a good day of sightseeing might move from historic Madrid, to the cafes of Huertas, to the celebrated *paseos*, to a stroll through the Retiro. El Pardo falls last, as it is a separate trip—buses to its palace and pastures leave from Moncloa. To truly experience the monuments, you should also try to enjoy Madrid's unhurried pace—in between sights, stop, relax, and people-watch.

EL CENTRO

The area known as El Centro, spreading out from the Puerta del Sol ("Gate of the Sun"), is the gateway to the history and spirit of Madrid. Although several rulers carved the winding streets, the Habsburg and Bourbon families left the Centro's most celebrated monuments. As a result, the Centro is divided into two major sections: Madrid de los Habsburgs and Madrid de los Borbones. All directions are given from the Puerta del Sol. For convenience, the metro stop closest to each sight (often not M: Sol) is also listed.

PUERTA DEL SOL

Kilómetro 0—the origin of six national highways fanning out to the rest of Spain—marks the country's physical and psychological center in the most chaotic of Madrid's numerous plazas, Puerta del Sol. Sol blazes all day and night with the lights of taxis, bars, street performers, and newsstands. A web of pedestrian-only tributaries originating at the Gran Vía leads a rush of consumers down a gallery of stores, funneling them into Sol.

It was not until the late 19th century that Sol became the true nucleus of Madrid. In the 16th century, an eastward-facing gate, known as the Gateway to the Sun, stood in Puerta del Sol. Today, government buildings dominate the plaza, where citizens and tourists alike converge upon *El oso y el madroño*, a bronze statue of a bear and a strawberry tree, now a symbol of Madrid. On New Year's Eve, citizens congregate in Sol to gobble up one grape per chime as the clock strikes midnight.

HABSBURG MADRID

"Old Madrid," the city's central neighborhood, is the most densely packed with both monuments and tourists. In the 16th century, the Habsburgs built **Plaza Mayor** and the **Catedral de San Isidro** from scratch. Many of Old Madrid's buildings, however, date from much earlier, some as far back as the Moorish empire. When Felipe II moved the seat of Castilla from Toledo to Madrid (then only a town of 20,000) in 1561, he and his descendants commissioned the court architects (including Juan de Herrera) to update many of Madrid's buildings to the latest styles. After only a century of development and expansion, Madrid more than doubled in population. Today, central Madrid, from the celebrated street of Alcalá to the iron verandas of Plaza Mayor, still reflects the power of the Habsburgs and the architecture of Juan de Herrera.

PLAZA MAYOR. In 1620, Pl. Mayor was completed for Felipe III; his statue, installed in 1847, still graces the plaza's center. Though designed by Juan de Herrera, the architect of the austere El Escorial, Pl. Mayor is much softer in style. Its elegant arcades, spindly towers, and pleasant verandas are defining elements of the "Madrid style" of architecture, which inspired architects across the city and throughout the country. With lances of exaggerated length, 17th-century nobles on horseback spent Sunday afternoons chasing bulls in the plaza. The nobility had such a jolly time that eventually everyone joined in the fun. Citizens, on foot and armed with sticks, also began running hither and thither after those pesky bulls. The tradition came to be known as a *corrida*, from the verb *correr* (to run).

Toward evening, Pl. Mayor awakens as *madrileños* resurface, tourists multiply, and cafe tables fill with lively patrons. Live performances of flamenco and music are a common treat. While the cafes are a nice spot for a drink, food is overpriced; save dinner for elsewhere. On Sunday mornings, the plaza holds a rare coin and stamp sale, marking the starting point of **El Rastro** (see p. 120). During the annual **Fiesta de San Isidro** (May 15-22, see p. 119), the plaza explodes with celebration. *(From Pta. Sol, walk down C. Mayor. The plaza is on the left. M: Sol.)*

CATEDRAL DE SAN ISIDRO. This cathedral, which commemorates San Isidro, protector of crops and patron saint of Madrid, has had a turbulent history. It was designed in the Jesuit Baroque style at the beginning of the 17th century, and in 1769 San Isidro's remains were brought here. During the Civil War rioting workers burned the exterior and damaged much of the cathedral—only the primary nave and a few Baroque decorations remain from the original. San Isidro, which has since been restored, reigned as *the* cathedral of Madrid from the late 19th century until the Catedral de la Almudena (see p. 103) was consecrated in 1993. *(From the Pta. Sol, take C. Mayor to Pl. Mayor, cross the plaza, and exit onto C. Toledo. The cathedral is located at the intersection of C. Toledo and C. Sacramento. M: Latina. Open for mass only.)*

PLAZA DE LA VILLA. When Felipe II made Madrid the capital of his empire in 1561, most of the town huddled between Pl. Mayor and the Palacio Real, stretching north to today's Ópera and south to Pl. Puerta de Moros; Pl. Villa marks the heart of what was once Old Madrid. Though only a handful of medieval buildings remain, the plaza still features a stunning courtyard (surrounding the statue of Don Alvara de Bazón), beautiful tile-work, and eclectic architecture. The horseshoe-shaped door on C. Codo is one of the few examples of Gothic-Mudéjar left in Madrid, and the 15th-century **Torre de los Lujanes** (on the left when looking from C. Mayor) is the sole remnant of the once lavish residence of the Lujanes family. Across the plaza is the 17th-century **Ayuntamiento (Casa de la Villa),** designed in 1640 by Juan Gómez de Mora as both the mayor's home and the city jail. Inside is Goya's *Allegory of the City of Madrid* (1819). The neighboring **Casa de Cisneros,** a 16th-century Plateresque house, also served as a government building when Habsburg officials annexed it for the city's growing bureaucracy. *(From Pta. Sol, go down C. Mayor, past Pl. Mayor. The plaza is on the left. M: Sol.)*

RÍO MANZANARES. Past the Pta. Toledo, the Río Manzanares, Madrid's notoriously puny river, snakes its way around the city. The broad Baroque **Puente de Toledo** (a triumphal arch commissioned by Joseph Bonaparte to celebrate his brother Napoleon) makes up for the river's inadequacies. Sandstone carvings on both sides of the bridge depict San Isidro and his family. The austere **Puente de Segovia,** which fords the river along C. Segovia, was conceived by Juan de Herrera. Both bridges afford gorgeous views and are popular with young couples. *(To reach Puente de Toledo from Pta. Sol, go down C. Mayor, through the Pl. Mayor, and onto C. Toledo; follow Toledo to the bridge. For the Puente de Segovia, take C. Mayor from Pta. Sol, turn left on C. de Bailén, and right on C. Segovia, which crosses the river. M: Sol.)*

OTHER SIGHTS. As the legend goes, the **Iglesia de San Andrés** began as a Mudéjar mosque. A 17th-century overhaul, commissioned by Felipe IV, infused the original structure with Baroque intricacies and brought the sarcophagus of San Isidro to the **Capilla de San Isidro.** *(From Pta. Sol, go down C. Mayor, through the Pl. Mayor onto C. Toledo, and right on C. Duque de Alba. Open for mass only.)* The **Parque de las Vistillas,** named for the tremendous *vistillas* (views) of Palacio Real, Nuestra Señora de la Almudena, and the surrounding countryside, provides a stunning photo-op. Take precaution, as it can be dangerous at night. *(Located in the Pl. Gabriel Miró. From Pta. Sol, go down C. Mayor, turn left on C. Bailén, and then right on C. Morería into the plaza.)*

BOURBON MADRID

Weakened by plagues and political losses, the Habsburg era in Spain ended with the death of Carlos II in 1700. Felipe V, the first of Spain's Bourbon monarchs, ascended the throne in 1714 after the 12-year War of Spanish Succession. Bankruptcy, industrial stagnation, and widespread moral disillusionment compelled Felipe V to embark on a crusade of urban renewal. His successors, Fernando VI and Carlos III, fervently pursued the same ends, with wonderful results. Today, the lavish palaces, churches, and parks that remain are the most touristed in Madrid; a walk around them will require planning and patience.

PALACIO REAL. The impossibly luxurious Palacio Real lounges at the western tip of central Madrid, overlooking the Río Manzanares. Felipe V commissioned Giovanni Sachetti to replace the Alcázar, which had burned down in 1734, with a palace that would dwarf all others; he succeeded. When Sachetti died, Filippo Juvara took over the project, basing his new facade on Bernini's rejected designs for the Louvre. The shell took 40 years to build, and the decoration of its 2000 rooms (with a vast collection of porcelain, tapestries, furniture, armor, and art) dragged on for over a century. When Alfonso XIII abdicated in 1931, the Second Republic abandoned the costly construction. Today, the unfinished palace is only used by King Juan Carlos and Queen Sofía on special occasions. Although only a fragment is complete, the palace stands as one of Europe's most grandiose residences.

The palace's most impressive rooms are decorated in the Rococo style. The **Salón de Gasparini,** site of the king's ceremonial dressing before the court, houses Goya's portrait of Carlos IV and a Mengs ceiling fresco. The **Salón del Trono** (Throne Room) also contains a ceiling fresco, painted by Tiepolo, outlining the qualities of the quintessential ruler. The **Real Oficina de Farmacia** (Royal Pharmacy) features crystal and china receptacles used to hold royal medicines, and the **Biblioteca** shelves first editions of *Don Quijote.* Also open to the public is the **Real Armería** (Armory), which displays the swords of El Cid, the armor of Carlos V and Felipe II, and other medieval weapons and instruments of torture. Look for the hundreds of extravagant chandeliers, almost all gifts from 19th-century French monarchs, and the 250 ornate timepieces that remain from Carlos IV's collection of 450. *(From Pta. Sol, take C. Mayor, and turn right on C. Bailén. M: Sol. Open Apr.-Sept. M-Sa 9am-6pm, Su 9am-3pm; Oct.-Mar. M-Sa 9:30am-5pm, Su 9am-2pm. 900ptas, with tour 1000ptas; students 400ptas, with tour 100ptas. EU citizens free W. Arrive early to avoid lines and skip M, when it is one of the only sights open.)*

CATHEDRAL DE LA ALMUDENA. Take a break from the cherub-filled frescoes of most cathedrals in Spain for refreshingly ultra-modern decor. Begun in 1879 and finished a century later, this cathedral—especially its interior—is a stark contrast to the gilded Palacio Real. After a 30-year hibernation, the building received a controversial face-lift. The reasons for the controversy are immediately apparent, as the cathedral's frescoes and stained glass windows contain a discordant mix of traditional and abstract styles. The simplicity of the gray stone walls clash with the ceiling panels, where brilliant colors and sharp geometric shapes bring a modern tie-rack to mind. *(From Pta. Sol, go down C. Mayo and turn right on C. Bailén; the cathedral is just before the Palacio Real. Closed during mass. Open M-Sa 1-7pm. Free.)*

PLAZA DE ORIENTE. A minor architectural miscalculation was responsible for this sculpture park. Most of the statues were designed for the palace roof, but because they were too heavy, they were instead placed in this shady plaza. An equestrian statue of Felipe IV, sculpted by Pietro Tacca, dominates the plaza; other notable structures include the Teatro Real, inaugurated by Isabel II. Elegant *terrazas* encompass the plaza, offering an opportunity to treat yourself to a pricey coffee. *(From Pta. Sol, take C. Arenal to the plaza.)*

MADRID

OTHER SIGHTS. The **Jardines de Sabatini,** just to the right if you are facing the palace, is the romantic's park of choice. On the other hand, the view from the center of the **Campo de Moro,** opened to the public just 13 years ago, is straight out of a fairy-tale. (*Enter from the side opposite the Palace. Both are free.*)

HUERTAS
The area east of Sol is a wedge bounded by C. de Alcalá to the north, C. Atocha to the south, and Po. Prado to the east. From the wedge's western apex at Sol, a myriad of streets slope downward, outward, and eastward toward various points along Po. Prado. **Carrera de San Jerónimo** splits the wedge a bit north of center, running directly from Sol down to Pl. Cánovas de Castillo. Huertas's sights, from authors' houses to famous cafes, are reflections of its artistic past. Home to Cervantes, Góngora, Quevedo, Calderón, and Moratín at its heyday during the "Siglo de Oro" (see **Literature,** p. 61), Huertas enjoyed a fleeting return to literary prominence when Hemingway frequented the neighborhood in the 1920s. **Plaza Santa Ana** and its *terrazas* are the center of this old literary haunt; all directions in this section start from there.

CASA DE LOPE DE VEGA. Although Golden Age writers Lope de Vega and Miguel de Cervantes were bitter rivals, Vega's 17th-century house is ironically located on C. Cervantes. (Odder still, Cervantes is buried on C. Lope de Vega.) A prolific playwright and poet, Lope de Vega spent the last 25 years of his life, and wrote over two-thirds of his plays, in this house. Highlights include the simple garden described in his works and the library filled with crumbling books. Among the more interesting tidbits revealed on the mandatory tour are the little tokens of affection Vega would leave for his daughters. (*C. Cervantes, 11. With your back to Pl. Santa Ana, turn left on C. Prado, right on C. León, and left on C. Cervantes.* ☎ *91 429 92 16. Open Tu-F 9:30am-2pm, Sa 10am-2pm. 200ptas, students 100ptas. W free.*)

CÍRCULO DE BELLAS ARTES. Designed by Antonio Palacios, this building encloses two stages and several studios for lectures and workshops run by prominent artists. The Círculo is the energetic hub of much of Madrid's art, sponsoring and organizing performances and shows around the city. Many facilities are for *socios* (members) only, but exhibition galleries for all media are open to the public. If you have a few hours to spare and some spiffy threads stashed away, your few (100) extra *pesetas* will buy you entrance and reward you with a sublime taste of a decadent lifestyle. (*C. Alcalá, 42. From Pl. Santa Ana, go up C. del Príncipe, cross C. San Jerónimo, and continue towards C. Alcalá. Turn right on C. Alcalá; the building is on the right. Hours and admission vary with exhibitions. For information on the cafe, see p. 100.*)

OTHER SIGHTS. Juan de Villanueva's simple **Real Academia de la Historia** houses a magnificent old library, another example of Madrid-style architecture. (*At the intersection of C. León and C. Huertas. From Pl. Santa Ana, take C. Príncipe and turn left on C. Huertas.*) Also impressive are the **Palacio Miraflores** and the **Palacio del Marqués de Ugena** designed by the premier 18th-century architect, Pedro de Ribera. (*Palacio Miraflores, C. San Jerónimo, 15. Palacio de Marqués de Ugena, Pl. Canalejas, 3.*)

GRAN VÍA
Urban planners paved the Gran Vía in 1910 to link C. Princesa with Pl. Cibeles. After Madrid gained wealth as a neutral supplier during World War I, the city funneled much of its earnings into making the Gran Vía one of the world's great thoroughfares. Today, movie theaters and fast-food joints line the most Americanized street in Madrid. Still, Gran Vía is a sight in itself—be sure to stroll (quickly) among the shops and skyscrapers.

At Gran Vía's highest elevation in **Plaza de Callao** (M: Callao), C. Postigo San Martín splits off southward, where you'll find the famed **Monasterio de las Descalzas Reales** (see p. 112). Westward from Pl. Callao (left when facing the conspicuous sex shop), the Gran Vía makes its descent toward **Plaza de España** (M: Pl. España), where a statue commemorates Spain's most prized fictional duo: Cervantes' Don Quijote and Sancho Panza (riding horseback and muleback, respectively). Next to Pl. España are two of Madrid's tallest skyscrapers, the **Telefónica building** (1929) and the **Edificio de España** (1953). Louis S. Weeks of the Chicago School designed the Telefónica building, the tallest concrete building in existence at the time (81m), and Franco's architect designed the Edificio de España. Tucked between the two skyscrapers on C. San Leonardo is the small **Iglesia de San Marcos,** a Neoclassical church composed of five intersecting ellipses—this Euclidean dream of a church doesn't have a single straight line.

MALASAÑA AND CHUECA

The area between **Calle de Fuencarral** and **Calle de San Bernardo** is home to some of Madrid's most avant-garde architecture and current art exhibitions. Though not packed with historic monuments, the labyrinthine streets provide many spontaneous, undocumented "sights," from platform-shoe stores to street performers—they are an ultra-modern, funkafied relief for travelers weary of crucifixes and brushstrokes. By night, these districts bristle with Madrid's alternative scene.

IGLESIA DE LAS SALESAS REALES. Bourbon King Fernando VI commissioned this church in 1758 at the request of his wife, Doña Bárbara. The Baroque-Neoclassical domed church is clad in granite, with facade sculptures by Alfonso Vergaza and a dome painting by the brothers González Velázquez. The church's ostentatious facade and interior prompted critics to pun on the queen's name: "Barbaric queen, barbaric tastes, barbaric building, barbarous expense," they said, giving rise to the expression *"¡qué bárbaro!"* Today, the expression refers to absurdity, extravagance, or just plain craziness. For nightlife in surrounding streets that defines *¡qué bárbaro!,* see p. 112. *(M: Chueca. From the metro stop, turn right on C. de Gravina and left on Conde de Xiquena.)*

ARGÜELLES

The 19th century witnessed the growth of several neighborhoods around the core of the city, north and northwest of the Palacio Real. Today, the area known as Argüelles and the zone surrounding **Calle San Bernardo** form a cluttered mixture of elegant middle-class houses, student apartments, and bohemian hangouts, all brimming with cultural activity. Heavily bombarded during the Civil War, Argüelles inspired Chilean poet Pablo Neruda, then a resident, to write *España en el corazón.* Directions in this section are given from the Argüelles metro stop.

TEMPLO DE DEBOD. Built by Pharaoh Zakheramon in the 4th century BC, it's the only Egyptian temple in Spain. In appreciation of Spanish archaeologists who helped rescue monuments from the floods of the Aswan dam, the Egyptian government shipped the temple stone by stone to Spain. The temple and two of its three original gateways stand in a peaceful haven in the **Parque de la Montaña.** *(M: Argüelles. From the metro, walk down C. Princesa and turn right on C. Ventura Rodriguez into the Parque de la Montaña; the temple is on the left.* ☎ *91 409 61 65. Open in summer Tu-Su 10am-1:45pm and 6-7:45pm; off-season Tu-F 10am-2pm and 4-6pm, Sa-Su 10am-2pm. 300ptas, students 150ptas. W and Su free.)*

ERMITA DE SAN ANTONIO DE LA FLORIDA. Although out of the way, the Ermita is worth the trouble. It contains Goya's pantheon—a frescoed dome arches above his buried corpse. Curiously enough, Goya's skull, apparently stolen by a phrenologist, was missing when the corpse arrived from France. *(M: Príncipe Pío. From the metro, go left on C. de Buen Altamirano, walk through the park, and turn left on Po. Florida; the Ermita is at the end of this street.* ☎ *91 542 07 22. Open Tu-F 10am-2pm and 4-8pm, Sa-Su 10am-2pm. Free.)*

CASA DEL CAMPO. Shaded by pines, oaks, and cypresses, families and joggers roam the city's largest park by day. Early morning reveals evidence of questionable nighttime activities; it's wise to stay away after dark. Inside the amusement park **Parque de Atracciones,** you can relive your childhood on the roller coaster. *(M: Argüelles. Walk up C. Princesa and through the park.* ☎ *91 463 29 00. Open Su-F noon-11pm, Sa noon-midnight.)* The **Zoo/Aquarium** is five minutes away. *(*☎ *91 512 37 70. M-F 10:30am-9pm, Sa-Su 10:30am-9:30pm. 1615ptas, children under 8 1300ptas.)*

OTHER SIGHTS. Parque del Oeste is a large, sloping park known for the **Rosaleda** (rose garden) at its bottom. A yearly competition determines which award-winning rose will be added to the permanent collection. *(M: Moncloa. From the metro, take C. Princesa. Open daily 10am-8pm.)* A prime example of Fascist Neoclassicism, the arcaded **Cuartel General del Aire (Ejército del Aire)** commands the view on the other side of Arco de la Victoria (by the Moncloa metro station). The complex was to form part of the "Fachada del Manzanares" urban axis linking Moncloa, the Palacio de Oriente, San Isidro, and the Iglesia de San Francisco. The building looks suspiciously like El Escorial. **Museo de América** (see p. 111) is a bit farther down the avenue, past the **Arco de Moncloa**. The **Faro de Moncloa** is a 92m high metal tower near the museum that offers views of the city. From the tower, you can see El Escorial on a clear day. *(Open M-F. 200ptas to ascend the Faro de Moncloa.)*

RETIRO

Felipe IV intended the 300-acre **Parque del Buen Retiro,** once a hunting ground, to be a *buen retiro* (nice retreat). Today it's full of palm-readers, soccer players, and sunbathers. The northeast corner of the park swells with medieval monastic ruins and waterfalls. On weekends, the promenades fill with musicians, families, and young lovers; on summer nights (when only the north gate remains open), the lively bars and cafes fill with teenagers, families, and couples. It is easily accessible from the Retiro metro stop, and all directions are given from there. Avoid venturing alone into the park after dark. *(M: Retiro.)*

ESTANQUE GRANDE. A rectangular lake in the middle of the park, the Estanque Grande is popular among (often shirtless) rowers. The lake has been the social center of the Retiro ever since aspiring caricaturists, fortune-tellers, sunflower-seed vendors, and drug pushers first parked their goods along its marble shores. *(M: Retiro. With your back to the metro stop, turn right on C. Alcalá and walk until you reach Pta. Alcalá; enter the park on Av. Mejico which leads to the lake. Boat rentals daily 9:30am-8:30pm. Paddle boats 560ptas for 4 people. Motorboats 155ptas per person.)*

PALACIO DE CRISTAL. Built by Ricardo Velázquez to exhibit Philippine flowers, this exquisite steel-and-glass structure hosts a variety of art shows, with subjects ranging from Bugs Bunny to Spanish portraiture. A popular sight for fashion photographers, the Palacio de Cristal may provide a backdrop for models feeding the swans. *(Open Tu-Sa 11am-2pm and 5-8pm, Su 10am-2pm. Admission varies, but often free.)*

PALACIO DE VELÁZQUEZ. A place where all artists should dream of having their art displayed, this Velázquez creation has billowing ceilings, marble floors, and ideal lighting. The Palacio de Velázquez exhibits works in conjunction with the Museo de Arte Reina Sofía (see p. 110). *(From the metro, turn right on C. Alcalá, walk through Pta. Alcalá, pass the Estanque, and turn left on Po. Venezuela. ☎ 91 575 62 45. Open M-Sa 11am-8pm, Su 11am-6pm. Free.)*

OTHER SIGHTS. Bullets from the 1921 assassination of prime minister Eduardo Dato permanently scarred the eastern face of **Puerta de Alcalá** (1778), outside the Retiro's Puerta de la Independencia. To the south, the **Casón del Buen Retiro** faces the park (see p. 110); behind it sits the **Museo del Ejército** (see p. 112). The two buildings are remnants of Felipe IV's palace, which burned down in 1764.

EL PARDO

Built as a hunting lodge for Carlos I in 1547, El Pardo was enlarged by generations of Habsburgs and Bourbons. Though Spain's growing capital eventually engulfed El Pardo, it still stands as one of Spain's greatest country palaces. El Pardo gained attention in 1940 when Franco decided to make it his home; he resided here until his death in 1975. Although politics have changed, the palace is still the official reception site for distinguished foreign visitors who wine, dine, and decide the fate of millions among gorgeous Renaissance and Neoclassical furniture and chandeliers. Renowned for its collection of tapestries—several of which were designed by Goya—the palace also holds a Velázquez painting and Ribera's *Techo de los hombres ilustres (Ceiling of the Illustrious Men).* You can also see the bedroom cabinet in which Franco kept Santa Teresa's silver-encrusted hand. Entrance to the palace's **capilla** and the nearby **Casita del Príncipe,** created by Juan de Villanueva (of Museo del Prado fame), is free. *(Take bus #601 from the stop in front of the Ejército del Aire building above M: Moncloa; 15min., 150ptas. Palace open Apr.-Sept. M-F 9:30am-6pm, Su 9:25am-1:40pm; Oct.-Mar. M-F 10:30am-5pm, Su 9:55am-1:40pm. Compulsory 45min. guided tour in Spanish. 650ptas, students 250ptas. W free for EU citizens.)*

⚡ THE PASEOS: A WALKING TOUR

The most striking feature on any map of Madrid is the one grand avenue that splits the city in two, running from Madrid-Atocha in the south to Madrid-Chamartín in the north. Madrid's great thoroughfare is really three fused segments (from south to north: Po. Prado, Po. Recoletos, and Po. Castellana) that represent three eras of urban expansion. Carlos III, the city's urban visionary, laid the Po. Prado from 1775 to 1782. The road connects Atocha to Pl. Cibeles, passing the Museo del Prado, the Thyssen-Bornemisza, and the Ritz Hotel along the way. Along Po. Recoletos, extending from Pl. Cibeles to Pl. Colón, the newest members of the *clase alta* (upper class) congregate at luxuriously shaded *terrazas.* Contemporary Madrid stretches further north along Po. Castellana (lined with bank buildings from the 1970s and 80s) to Pl. Castilla's twin towers (Puerta de Europa). In the summer, a late afternoon stroll along the *paseos* should include a stop at one of the fabulous chic cafes of the Po. Castellana. Strolls along Po. Prado and Po. Recoletos combine well with a tour of Huertas or the Retiro; even a walk to the post office in Pl. Cibeles can incorporate the majority of the sights along the *paseos.*

PASEO DEL PRADO

Modeled after the Piazza Navona in Rome, Paseo del Prado marks the center of Madrid's art district. Virtually every major museum is in the vicinity of this "museum mile," known as the *triángulo de arte.* Directly across from the **Estación de Atocha,** the **Centro de Arte Reina Sofía** (see p. 110), home to Picasso's *Guernica,* vogues with its glass elevators in Pl. Emperador Carlos V.

Walking up Po. Prado, you'll pass the **Jardín Botánico** on the right. Opened during Carlos III's reign, the garden showcases over 30,000 species of plants, ranging from traditional roses to medicinal herbs. Just about anyone will appreciate the garden's vast collection of imported trees, bushes, and flowers. *(Open daily in summer 10am-9pm; in winter 10am-6pm; in spring and fall 10am-7pm. 200ptas, students 100ptas.)* Next to the Jardín Botánico is the world-renowned **Museo del Prado** (see p. 109) and behind it, on C. Ruiz de Alarcón, stands the **Iglesia de San Jerónimo,** Madrid's royal church. Built by Hieronymite monks and re-endowed by the Catholic Monarchs, the church has witnessed a few joyous milestones, including the coronation of Fernando and Isabel and the marriage of King Alfonso XIII. These days, only the highest of high-society weddings grace the church. *(Open daily 8am-1:30pm and 5-8:30pm.)* Back on Po. Prado, to the north in Pl. Lealtad, stands the **Obelisco a los Mártires del 2 de Mayo,** filled with the ashes of those who died in the 1808 uprising against Napoleon. Its four statues represent Constancy, Virtue, Valor, and Patriotism, and the flame burns continuously in honor of the patriots. Behind the memorial sits the colonnaded Greco-Roman-style **Bolsa de Madrid** (Stock Exchange), designed by Repullés. Ventura Rodríguez's **Fuente de Neptuno,** in Pl. Cánovas de Castillo, is one of three aquatic masterpieces along the avenue.

The arts of the Po. Prado transform into the Po. Recoletos at the tulip-encircled **Plaza de Cibeles.** Madrid residents successfully protected this emblem of their city (best viewed at dusk) during Franco's bomb raids by covering it with a pyramid of sandbags. To the right are the **Museo Naval** *(entrance at Po. Prado, 5; ☎ 91 379 52 99; open Tu-Su 10am-1:30pm; free)* and the eye-popping **Palacio de Comunicaciones** (see p. 88), where you can mail your letters in true style. Antonio Palacios and Julián Otamendi of Otto Wagner's Vienna School designed the neo-Baroque structure in 1920. On the northeastern corner of the intersection (behind black gates) is the former **Palacio de Linares,** a 19th-century townhouse built for Madrid nobility. Long abandoned by its former residents and proven by a team of "scientists" to be inhabited by ghosts, it was transformed into the **Casa de América,** with a library and lecture halls for the study of Latin American culture and politics. It sponsors art exhibitions, tours of the palace, and guest lectures.

PASEO DE RECOLETOS

Continuing north toward the brown **Torres de Colón** (Columbus Towers), you'll pass the **Biblioteca Nacional,** where the sleek **Museo del Libro** displays treasures from the monarchy's collection, including a first-edition copy of *Don Quijote.* *(Entrance at #20. Open Tu-Sa 10am-9pm, Su 10am-2pm. Free.)* Behind the library lies the huge **Museo Arqueológico Nacional** (see p. 112). The museum entrance is on C. Serrano, an avenue lined with expensive boutiques in the posh **Barrio de Salamanca.**

The museum and library huddle just beyond the modern **Plaza Colón** (M: Colón) and the adjoining **Jardines del Descubrimiento** (Gardens of Discovery). At one side loom huge clay boulders, inscribed with odd trivia about the New World, including Seneca's prediction of the discovery, the names of all the mariners on board the caravels, and citations from Columbus's diary. From a thundering fountain in the center of the plaza rises a neo-Gothic spire to Columbus. Concerts, lectures, ballets, and plays are performed in the **Centro Cultural de la Villa,** the underground municipal art center underneath the statue and the waterfall. (☎ *91 575 60 80.)*

PASEO DE LA CASTELLANA

Nineteenth- and early 20th-century aristocrats dislodged themselves from Old Madrid to settle along Paseo de la Castellana. During the Civil War, Republican forces used the mansions as barracks. Most were torn down in the 1960s when banks and insurance companies commissioned new innovative structures. Competition begot architectural excellence, offering the lowly pedestrian a rich man's spectacle of architecture and fashion. Some notables include: Moneo's **Bankinter,** #29, the first to integrate rather than demolish a townhouse; **Banco Urquijo,** known as "the coffeepot"; the Sevillian-tiled **Edificio ABC,** #34, the former office of the conservative, monarchical newspaper; the pink **Edificio Bankunion,** #46; **Banca Catalana Occidente,** #50 (on Glorieta de Emilio Castelar near the US Embassy), which looks like an ice cube on a cracker; and the famous **Edificio La Caixa,** #61.

Just south of the American Embassy, between Pl. Colón and Glorieta de Emilio Castelar and under the C. Juan Bravo overpass, is an **Open-air Sculpture Museum** displaying works by Miró, González, and Chillida. Look up—the works are hanging from the bridge as well.

A number of intimate private museums, including the **Museo Lázaro Galdiano** (see p. 111), are located just off Po. Castellana. At **Plaza de Lima** (M: Lima) is the 110,000-seat **Estadio Santiago Bernabéu,** home to the beloved **Real Madrid,** winner of its 8th European League championship in May 2000. Farther north, the **Puerta de Europa,** consisting of two 27-story leaning towers connected by a tunnel, dominates Pl. Castilla (M: Pl. Castilla). They were designed by American John Bergee as a doorway to the city.

SEX IN THE CIBELES The Plaza de Cibeles, with its infamous marble fountain, has been Madrid's physical and spiritual axis since its construction in 1781. Depicting the fertility goddess's triumph over the emblematic Castilian lions, the fountain's image of Cybele has long captivated citizens. Legend has it that the fleet-footed Atalanta, one of Cybele's maids, would take as her lover only the man who could outrun her. No man was up to the challenge until one cunning suitor instructed his cohorts to scatter golden apples (as distractions) in Atalanta's path. The goddess Cybele, watching the prank, was overcome with wrath at men's evil ways. So, after punishing the plotters by turning them into lions, she hitched them up to her own carriage. This assertion of power and sexuality charmed Madrid, resulting in the proverb *"mas popular qué Cibeles"* (more popular than Cybele).

🏛 MUSEUMS

Madrid's great museums need no introduction. If you plan on visiting the three famous ones, your best bet is the **Paseo del Arte** ticket (1275ptas), which grants admission to the Museo del Prado, Museo Thyssen-Bornemisza, and Centro de Arte Reina Sofía. The pass is on sale at all three museums.

MUSEO DEL PRADO

Po. Prado at Pl. Cánovas del Castillo. M: Banco de España. ☎ *91 420 37 68 or 91 330 28 00; www.museoprado.mcu.es. Open Tu-Sa 9am-7pm, Su 9am-2pm. 500ptas, students 250ptas. Sa after 2:30pm and Su free.*

The Prado is Spain's pride and joy, as well as one of Europe's finest museums. In 1785, architect Juan de Villanueva began construction of the Neoclassical building, following Carlos III's order for a museum of natural history and sciences. In 1819 Fernando VII transformed it into the royal painting archive; the museum's 7000 pieces are the result of hundreds of years of Bourbon art collecting. The walls are filled with Spanish and foreign masterpieces, including a comprehensive selection from the Flemish and Venetian schools.

The museum is well-organized: each room is numbered and described in the museum's free guide. The sheer quantity of paintings means you'll have to be selective—walk past the rooms of imitation Rubens and Rococo cherubs and into the groves of the masters. The museum's guidebooks help you sift through the floors and offer extensive art history and criticism (100-3000ptas).

DIEGO VELÁZQUEZ. The second floor houses Spanish and Italian works from the 16th and 17th centuries. The most notable of these are an unparalleled collection of works by Diego Velázquez (1599-1660), court painter and interior decorator for Felipe IV (portraits of the foppish monarch abound). Because of their unforgiving realism and use of light, Velázquez's works resonate even in the 20th century. Several of his most famous paintings are here, including *Las hilanderas (The Tapestry Weavers), Los borrachos (The Drunkards)*, and *La fragua de Vulcano (Vulcan's Forge)*. With *Las lanzas (The Spears or The Surrender of Breda)*, Velázquez began to experiment with spatial perspective, developing the technique to imply continuous movement in the canvas. Smoke from a recent battle clears in the background as an anxious horse dominates the foreground. Velázquez's technique, called illusionism, climaxed in his magnum opus *Las meninas (The Maids of Honor)*, since dubbed an "encounter" rather than a painting. The "snapshot quality" of the figures transformed painting in the 17th century.

FRANCISCO GOYA. In 1785, Francisco de Goya y Lucientes (1746-1828) became the court portraitist. Perhaps the most interesting aspect of his works is that he managed to depict the royal family so unflatteringly and satirically without being expelled from court. Some suggest that he manipulated light and shadow to focus the viewer's gaze on the figure of the queen (rather than the centrally located king) in *La familia de Carlos IV*—a discreet way of supporting contemporary popular opinion about the true power behind the monarchy. The stark *Dos de Mayo* and *Fusilamientas de Tres de Mayo*, which depict the terrors of the Revolution of 1808, may be Goya's most recognized works. Also notable is the expressionless woman in *La maja vestida* and *La maja desnuda*. Perhaps the most evocative pieces in the Goya collection are the *Pinturas Negras (Black Paintings)*. These paintings were aptly named for the darkness of both the colors and the subject matter—Goya painted them in the house where he lived at the end of his life, deaf and alone. *Saturno devorando a su hijo (Saturn Devouring His Son)* stands out among the *Pinturas Negras*, a reminder from an ailing artist that time eventually destroys its creations. Goya violently captures the moment when Saturn eats his children upon hearing a prophesy that one of them would overthrow him.

ITALIAN, FLEMISH, AND OTHER SPANISH ARTISTS . The Prado also displays many of **El Greco's** (Doménikos Theotokópoulos, 1541-1614) religious paintings. *La Trinidad (The Trinity)* and *La adoración de los pastores (The Adoration* *of the Shepherds)* are characterized by El Greco's luminous colors, elongated figures, and mystical subjects. On the second floor are other works by Spanish artists, including **Murillo's** *Familia con pájaro pequeño (Family with Small Bird)*, **Ribera's** *El martirio de San Bartholomeo (Martyrdom of Saint Bartholomew)*, and **Zurbarán's** *La inmaculada.*

The Prado has a formidable collection of **Italian** works, including **Titian's** portraits of Carlos I and Felipe II and **Raphael's** *El cardenal desconocido (The Unknown Cardinal).* **Tintoretto's** rendition of the homicidal seductress Judith and her hapless victim Holofernes, as well as his *Washing of the Feet* are here as well. Some minor **Botticellis** and a slew of his imitators are also on display. Among the works by **Rubens,** *The Three Graces* and *The Adoration of the Magi* best reflect his voluptuous style.

As a result of the Spanish Habsburgs' control of the Netherlands, the **Flemish** holdings are also top-notch. **Van Dyck's** *Marquesa de Legunes* is here, as well as works by **Albrecht Durer.** Especially harrowing is **Peter Breughel the Elder's** *The Triumph of Death*, in which death drives a carriage of skulls on a decaying horse. **Hieronymus Bosch's** moralistic *The Garden of Earthly Delights* is a favorite, with detailed depictions of hedonism and the destiny that awaits its practitioners.

CASÓN DEL BUEN RETIRO. Three minutes from the Prado sits the Casón del Buen Retiro. Once part of Felipe IV's Palacio del Buen Retiro, the Casón was destroyed in the Napoleonic wars. The rebuilt version normally houses the Prado's 19th- and 20th-century works, currently on loan to the Reina Sofía. *(C. Alfonso XXII, 28. ☎ 91 330 28 60. Closed for renovations until at least 2002.)*

MUSEO NACIONAL CENTRO DE ARTE REINA SOFÍA

C. Santa Isabel, 52, opposite Estación Atocha at the south end of Po. Prado. M: Atocha. ☎ 91 467 50 62. Open M and W-Sa 10am-9pm, Su 10am-2:30pm. 500ptas, students 250ptas. Sa after 2:30pm and Su free.

Since Juan Carlos I decreed this renovated hospital a national museum in 1988, the Reina Sofía's collection of **20th-century art** has grown steadily. The second and fourth floors are a maze of permanent exhibits charting the Spanish avant-garde and contemporary movements. Rooms dedicated to Juan Gris, Joan Miró, and Salvador Dalí display Spain's vital contributions to the Surrealist movement. Miró's works show a sparse, colorful abstraction, while Dalí's paintings, including *Monumental Imperial a la Mujer Niña* and *El Enigma Sin Fin*, portray the artist's Freudian nightmares and sexual fantasies.

Picasso's masterwork *Guernica* is the centerpiece of the Reina Sofía's permanent collection. It depicts the Basque town bombed by the Germans at Franco's request during the Spanish Civil War. Picasso denounced the bloodshed in a huge, colorless work of contorted, agonized figures. The screaming horse in the center represents war, and the twisted bull—an unmistakable national symbol—symbolizes Spain. When asked by Nazi officials whether he was responsible for this work, Picasso answered, "No, you are." He gave the canvas to New York's Museum of Modern Art on the condition that they return it to Spain when democracy was restored. In 1981, five years after Franco's death, *Guernica* was delivered to Madrid's Casón del Buen Retiro. The subsequent move to the Reina Sofía sparked an international controversy—Picasso's other stipulation had been that the painting hang only in the Prado, to affirm his equivalent status with artists like Titian and Velázquez. Today, Basques want the painting relocated to the Guggenheim in Bilbao, but Madrid art officials declare it too delicate to move. The Reina Sofía surrounds *Guernica* with its preliminary sketches and a myriad of other Picasso paintings and sculptures, testimony to his breadth of talent. Two other works of note are *Woman in Blue* and *Painter with Model.*

The first and third floors of the Reina Sofía hold changing exhibitions of world-class contemporary art and photography. Throughout the museum, free laminated descriptions of each room are available at the room entrance.

▨ MUSEO THYSSEN-BORNEMISZA

On the corner of Po. Prado and C. San Jerónimo. M: Banco de España. Bus #6, 14, 27, 37, or 45. ☎ 91 369 01 51; mtb@museothyssen.org; www.museothyssen.org. Open Tu-Su 10am-7pm. No one admitted after 6:30pm. 700ptas, seniors and students with ISIC 400ptas, under 12 free.

Unlike the Prado and the Reina Sofía, the Thyssen-Bornemisza covers a wide range of periods and media, with exhibits ranging from 14th-century canvases to 20th-century sculptures. The museum is housed in the 18th-century Palacio de Villahermosa and contains the former collection of Baron Heinrich Thyssen-Bornemisza. The baron donated his collection in 1993, and today the museum, with over 775 pieces, is the world's most extensive private showcase. To view the collection in chronological order and observe the evolution of styles and themes, begin on the top floor and work your way down.

The top floor is dedicated to the **Old Masters** collection, which includes such notables as Hans Holbein's austere *Portrait of Henry VIII* and El Greco's *Annunciation*. The organization of the Thyssen-Bornemisza provokes natural comparisons across centuries—note how the representation of the body evolves from Lucas Cranach's *The Nymph of the Spring* to Titian's *Saint Jerome in the Desert* to Anthony van Dyck's *Portrait of Jacques Le Roy*. In both variety and quality, the Thyssen-Bornemisza's **Baroque** collection, including pieces by Caravaggio, José de Ribera, and Claude Lorraine, overshadows that of the Prado.

The movement from the dark canvases of the top floor to the vibrant ones below reflects the revolutionary command of light and the arbitrary use of color that became popular in the 17th century. In the 17th-century Dutch works, such as Frans Hals's *Family Group in a Landscape*, artists began to master the use of natural light to illuminate subjects. The **Impressionist** and **Post-Impressionist** collections explode with texture and color—look for works by Renoir, Manet, Pisarro, Degas, Monet, van Gogh, Toulouse-Lautrec, Cézanne, and Matisse. Though less well-known, the **Expressionist** artists are also well-represented, with noteworthy works by Nolde, Marc, and Beckmann.

The highlight of the tour is the museum's **20th-century** collection. The modern artists represented include Picasso, Léger, Mondrian, Miró, Kandinsky, Gorky, Pollack, Rothko, Dalí, Hopper, Chagall, Ernst, Klee, and O'Keefe, among others.

OTHER MUSEUMS

▨ MUSEO DE LA REAL ACADEMIA DE BELLAS ARTES DE SAN FERNANDO.

The collection of Old Masters in this beautiful museum is surpassed only by the Prado. Goya's *La Tirana* and Velázquez's portrait of Felipe IV are masterpieces; the Raphael and Titian collections are also excellent. Other attractions include a room dedicated to Goya (a former academy director) and 17th-century canvases by Ribera, Murillo, Zurbarán, and Rubens. The top floor also has Picasso sketches. The **Calcografía Real** (Royal Print and Drawing Collection), in the same building, houses Goya's studio and organizes temporary exhibitions. *(Alcalá, 13. ☎ 91 522 14 91. M: Sol or Sevilla. Open Tu-F 9am-7pm, Sa-M 9am-2:30pm. 400ptas, students 200ptas. W and Oct. 12, May 18, Dec. 6 free.)*

▨ MUSEO DE AMÉRICA.

This under-appreciated museum recently reopened after painstaking renovations; it is now a must-see. It documents the cultures of America's pre-Columbian civilizations and the effects of the Spanish conquest with detail, insight, and dedication to making it come alive. Artifacts include solid gold Columbian ornaments and Maya treasures. The renovations added state-of-the-art multimedia exhibits. *(Av. Reyes Católicos, 6, next to the Faro de Moncloa. ☎ 91 549 26 41. M: Moncloa. Open Tu-Sa 10am-3pm, Su 10am-2:30pm. 500ptas, students 250ptas. Su free.)*

MUSEO LÁZARO GALDIANO.

Among the riches of this private collection are an overwhelming display of Italian Renaissance bronzes and Celtic and Visigoth brasses. The paintings include Leonardo da Vinci's *The Savior* and Hieronymous Bosch's *Ecce Homo*, as well as works by the Spanish trifecta: El Greco, Velázquez and Goya. *(C. Serrano, 122. Turn right off Po. Castellana onto C. María de Molina. ☎ 91 561 60 84. M: Rubén Darío. Open Sept.-July Tu-Su 10am-2pm. 500ptas. W free.)*

MADRID

MONASTERIO DE LAS DESCALZAS REALES. In 1559 Juana of Austria, Felipe II's sister, converted the former royal palace into a convent; today it is home to 26 Franciscan nuns who watch over Juana's tomb. The **Salón de Tápices** contains 10 renowned tapestries based on cartoons by Rubens, as well as Santa Ursula's jewel-encrusted bones and *El viaje de Santa Ursula y las once mil vírgenes* (*The Journey of Santa Ursula and the Eleven Thousand Virgins*). *(Pl. Descalzas, between Pl. Callao and Pta. de Sol. ☎ 91 559 74 04. M: Callao or Sol. Open Tu-Th and Sa 10:30am-12:45pm and 4-5:45pm, F 10:30am-12:45pm, Su 11am-1:45pm. 700ptas, students 300ptas. W free for EU citizens.)*

MUSEO ARQUEOLÓGICO NACIONAL. The history of the Western world is on display in this huge museum. Amongst other astounding items from Spain's past is the country's most famous archaeological find, *Dama de Elche*, a 4th-century funerary urn. Outside stands a replica of the Altamira caves and their Paleolithic paintings. The museum also houses Moorish ivories from Andalucía and golden Visigoth crowns. *(C. Serrano 13, behind the Biblioteca Nacional. ☎ 91 577 79 12. M: Serrano. Open Tu-Sa 9:30am-8:30pm, Su 9:30am-2:30pm. 500ptas, students 250ptas. Sa after 2:30pm and Su free.)*

CONVENTO DE LA ENCARNACIÓN. Designed by Juan de Herrera's disciple Juan de Gómez (the architect of Pl. Mayor), the convent houses about 1500 relics of saints, including a vial of San Pantaleón's blood, believed to liquify every year on July 27. According to the legend, if the blood does not liquify, disaster will strike Madrid. The permanent collection contains pieces by José de Ribera and Goya's brother-in-law, Francisco Bayeu. *(Pl. Encarnación, off C. Bailén just east of Palacio Real. ☎ 91 542 00 59. M: Ópera. Open Tu-Th and Sa 10:30am-12:45pm and 4-5:45pm, Su 11am-1:45pm. 425ptas, students 225ptas. W free for EU citizens.)*

MUSEO DEL EJÉRCITO. In this stately fragment of the Palacio del Buen Retiro stands a vast collection of military paraphernalia. Each room is dedicated to a different period or conquest; the most famous contains a fragment of the sword Columbus plunged into the ground when he discovered the New World. *(C. Méndez Núñez, 1, just north of Casón del Buen Retiro. ☎ 91 522 89 77. M: Retiro or Banco de España. Open Tu-Su 10am-2pm. 100ptas, students 50ptas, under 18 free. Sa free.)*

MUSEO CERRALBO. This palatial residence-turned-museum displays an eclectic collection of period furniture and ornamentation. The music room has a Louis XVI-style French piano, and the chapel houses El Greco's *The Ecstasy of Saint Francis*. *(C. Ventura Rodríguez, 17. ☎ 91 547 36 46. M: Ventura Rodríguez. Open Tu-Sa 9:30am-2:30pm, Su 10am-2pm. 400ptas, students 200ptas. W and Su free.)*

MUSEO ROMÁNTICO. Housed in a 19th-century mansion built by a disciple of Ventura Rodríguez, this museum is an exquisite time capsule of the Romantic period's decorative arts. *(C. San Mateo, 13. ☎ 91 448 10 71. M: Alonso Martínez. Open Sept.-July Tu-Sa 9am-3pm, Su 10am-2pm. 400ptas, students 200ptas. Su free.)*

◪ NIGHTLIFE

Simply put, *madrileños* like to party. Whether on a *terraza* in the summer or in a *barrio* bar in the winter, the night hours are characterized by a steady stream of pedestrian traffic as revelers meander from place to place. Proud of their nocturnal offerings—they'll tell you with a straight face that they were bored in Paris or New York—*madrileños* insist that no one goes to bed until they've "killed the night" and, in some cases, a good part of the following morning.

An average night includes several neighborhoods and countless venues; half the party is the in-between. A typical evening might start in the *tapas* bars of Huertas, moving to a first-session disco in Malasaña, and then to the wild parties of Chueca. Some clubs don't even bother opening until 4 or 5am; the only (relatively) quiet nights of the week are Sunday and Monday.

THE RIGHT TO PARTY After 40 years of Franco-imposed repression, Madrid was a cultural explosion waiting to happen. Franco's death in 1975 served as a catalyst for change; not a day passed before every newspaper printed a pornographic photo on its front page. *El Destapeo* ("the uncorking" or "uncovering" which followed Franco's regime) and *La Movida* ("the Movement," which took place a few years later) exploded in Madrid, inspiring political diversity, apolitical revelry, and eccentricity of all kinds. Filmmaker Pedro Almodóvar became a reflection of the movement and its most famous member, creating farcical films about loony grandmothers, outgoing young women, unapologetic homosexuals, and eclectic students. Gradually, *La Movida* became too much for the city. Artists and club-rats were forced to give up their favorite pastimes for practical jobs—no one could afford to keep up the careless and eccentric lifestyle that *La Movida* represented. Remnants of *La Movida* are still visible, however, in today's outrageous clubs, ambitious bars, and in the excitement of young *madrileños* planning to *ir de marcha* ("to party," literally "to go marching").

For clubs and discos, life begins around 2am. Many discos have "afternoon" sessions for teens (7pm-midnight; cover 250-1000ptas), but the "night" sessions (lasting until dawn) are when people really let their hair down. The *entrada* (cover) often includes a drink and can be as high as 2000ptas; men may be charged up to 500ptas more than women, if women are charged at all. Keep an eye out for *invitaciones* and *oferta* cards—in stores, restaurants, tourist publications, tourist offices, and in the streets—that offer discounts or free admission.

For the most up-to-date info on what's going on, scan Madrid's entertainment guides (see **Read This**, p. 84). The *Guía del Ocio* is an indispensable tool, featuring the latest information about virtually all of Madrid's nighttime establishments.

EL CENTRO: SOL, ÓPERA, AND PLAYA MAYOR

In the middle of Madrid and at the heart of the action are the grandiose and flamboyant clubs of El Centro. With multiple floors, swinging lights, cages, and discoballs, they fulfill even the wildest club-rat's expectations. The mainstream clubs found among these streets are often tourist hotspots; as a result, a night of fun here is the most expensive in the city. El Centro includes more territory than Madrid's other neighborhoods, so make a plan and bring a map.

■ **Joy Eslava,** C. Arenal, 11 (☎ 91 366 37 33). M: Sol or Ópera. A massive, black 3-tiered theatre-turned-disco featuring 3 bars, laser lights, and live dance shows. Because of its prominent location, Joy Eslava is packed with international tourists grooving to disco, techno, R&B, and salsa. Bust a move on the vast, central dance floor or sip drinks from the recesses of surrounding seats above. Best to come around 2am, and dress well. Cover, including 1 drink, M-Th 2000ptas, F-Su 2500ptas. Open M-Th 11:30pm-5:30am, F-Su 7pm-6am.

Mad Café Club, Virgen del los Peligros, 4 (☎ 91 532 62 28), off C. de Alcalá. M: Sevilla. The metallic decor reflects the light of hundreds of candles. Chic artists come here to lounge on pillows and dance to jazz and techno. Open daily 10pm-morning.

Heaven, C. Veneras, 2 (☎ 91 548 20 22). M: Santo Domingo. Heavenly drag performances and underwordly parties for a primarily gay crowd. Special "Groove Sundays." Drinks 650-900ptas. Cover 1000-1500ptas, includes 1 drink. Open 1:30am-dawn.

El Barbu, C. Santiago, 3 (☎ 91 542 56 98), across C. Mayor from the Ayuntamiento. M: Sol or Ópera. Chill to lounge music in a brick 3-room interior. Th bring visual effects. Open Tu-Sa 8pm-3am. Su bring the transformation to "8th," a rave-like setting with popular local DJs (10:30pm-5:30am; 1000ptas).

Kathmandú, C. Señores de Luzón, 3 (☎ 91 541 52 53), a right off C. Mayor from Puerta del Sol, after Pl. Mayor and facing the Ayuntamiento. M: Sol. Jammed with locals dancing to high-energy techno and acid jazz. Cover 600-1000ptas, includes 1 drink. Open Th 11pm-5am, F-Sa 11pm-6am.

Azúcar, Po. Reina Cristina, 7 (☎ 91 501 61 07). M: Atocha. Sweet, sweet salsa. No sneakers. Salsa classes daily 9:30-11pm; call ahead. Cover 1200ptas, includes 1 drink; Sa 1800ptas, includes 2 drinks. Open M-Sa 11:00pm-5am, Su 9pm-dawn.

Refugio, C. Dr. Cortezo, 1 (☎ 91 869 40 38). M: Tirso de Molina. Don't miss the club— it's the first door on the left. Steel doors covered in steel vines lead to an outrageous gay scene. W nights bring *Naturaleza,* when clothes are, ahem, not allowed. Cover 1000ptas, includes 1 drink. Open W-Sa 11:30pm-dawn.

▨ HUERTAS

Within Huertas lies **Plaza Santa Ana,** brimming with *terrazas,* bars, and live street music. Many bars convert to clubs as the night unfolds, spinning house and techno on intimate dance floors. With its variety of styles, minus the sketchy scenes some- times found in other neighborhoods, Huertas is simply the best place to party. Be sure to check out the larger *discotecas* on **Calle Atocha.** Most locals begin their evenings here and emerge from Malasaña and Chueca (see p. 115) in the morning.

DISCOTECAS

Kapital, C. Atocha, 125 (☎ 91 420 29 06), a block off Po. Prado. M: Atocha. Take the metro—it's the safest way here. One of the most extreme results of *la Movida,* this *macro-discoteca* tries even harder than its glittered 20-something clientele. From hip- hop to house, open *terraza* to cinema, 7 floors of over-stimulation have necessitated a ground-floor directory. Dress to impress (the bouncer). Cover 2000ptas, includes 1 drink. Drinks 1000ptas. Open Th 12:30-6am, F-Sa 6-11pm and 12:30-6am.

Villa Rosa, Pl. Santa, 15 (☎ 92 429 21 27). American pop meets Moorish architecture in this Alhambra-inspired disco, which sports 4 bars, frescoed and tiled walls, and a raised dance floor. Open M-Sa 11pm-5am.

No Se Lo Digas a Nadie, C. Ventura de la Vega, 7 (☎ 91 369 17 27), next to Pl. Santa Ana. M: Sevilla. Don't be thrown off by the art exhibition sign; head through the garage doors onto the packed dance floor. Drinks 500-800ptas. Open W-Sa until 3:30am.

BAR-MUSICALES

Cardamomo, C. Echegaray, 15 (☎ 91 369 07 57). M: Sevilla. Flamenco music spins all night in this brick-walled, designer-lit bar. A local crowd dances flamenco occasionally, but come W nights to see a professional show. Open 9pm-4am.

La Comedia, C. Príncipe, 16 (☎ 91 521 51 64). M: Sevilla. Americans feel at home in a crowd dancing to hip-hop, R&B, and reggae. Hit up DJ Jay with requests; he spins to please. Beer 500ptas. Drinks 900ptas. Open daily 9pm-4am.

Café Jazz Populart, C. Huertas, 22 (☎ 91 429 84 07). With walls covered in old trum- pets, clarinets, and basses, this intimate scene hosts local and foreign talent. Live jazz, blues, reggae, and flamenco. Mostly 30-something crowd. Shows Su-W 11pm, F-Sa 11pm and 12:30am. Open Su-Th 6pm-12:30am, F-Sa 6pm-3am.

Café Central, Pl. Angel, 10 (☎ 91 369 41 43), off Pl. Santa Ana. M: Antón Martín or Sol. Art Deco meets old-world cafe in one of Europe's top-10 jazz venues. An older audience. Beer 300-500ptas. Cover 1200-2500ptas. Shows nightly. Open daily 1:30pm-3:30am.

La Boca del Lobo, C. Echegaray, 11 (☎ 91 429 70 13). M: Sevilla. The wolf on the sign won't eat you, but waterfall mirrors in the bathrooms may drench you. Live shows of reg- gae, funk, blues and rock bands hit this bi-leveled joint, drawing a varied crowd. Cover 1000ptas. Open daily 10pm-dawn.

BARS

▨ **El Café de Sheherezade,** C. Santa María, 18, a block from C. Huertas. M: Antón Martín. Recline on opulent pillows while sipping exotic infusions in a dark, mellow, bohemian atmosphere. Surrounded by Middle Eastern music and decor, groups cluster around personal *pipas* (pipes, 800-1200ptas) that filter sweet, incense-like smoke through whiskey or water. Open daily 7pm-5am.

Trocha, C. Huertas, 55 (☎ 91 429 78 61). M: Antón Martín or Sol. Come here for Brazilian *capirinhas* (lime, ice, rum, and sugar drinks; 725ptas at the bar, 750ptas seated). The delicious and potent drinks (ask for *flor de caña*) are served in a chill setting with jazz tunes, jazz decor, and cushioned wicker couches. Open Su-Th 8pm-3am, F-Sa 8pm-4am.

Mauna Loa, Pl. Santa Ana, 13 (☎ 91 429 70 62). M: Sevilla or Sol. Feels like Hawaii—birds fly freely between low chairs and the scantily clad dance to upbeat tunes. *Fuerte volcano* drinks 825-1650ptas. Open Su-Th 7pm-2am, F-Sa 7pm-3am.

O'Neil's, C. Príncipe, 12 (☎ 91 521 20 30), just off Pl. Santa Ana. Irish pubs are actually a routine stop during most Spaniards' nights, and this is one of the best. Two huge floors, featuring 4 bars, smooth pints, church pews, and other creative Irish decor. Mixed crowd of locals and English speakers. Pints 650ptas, half-pints 350ptas. Open Su-Th midnight-2am, F-Sa midnight-3am.

Viva Madrid, C. Manuel Fernández González, 7 (☎ 91 429 36 40), a sidestreet off C. Echegaray. M: Sol or Sevilla. *"Lo mejor del mundo"* (the best of the world) is the humble motto of this daytime cafe/nighttime foray, a longtime local favorite. Classic architecture, classy clientele, stuffy air, and late 80s-early 90s American rock and funk tunes. Beer 400ptas. Cocktails 1000ptas. Open Su-Th 12:30pm-2am, F-Sa 12:30pm-3am.

Naturbier, Pl. Santa Ana, 9 (☎ 91 429 39 18). M: Sol or Sevilla. Locals pour in for the excellent locally brewed *bier,* inspired by their motto "beer is important to human nutrition." Superior lager 300-700ptas; it gets cheaper as you progress to the innermost of the 3 bars. Open daily 11am-2am.

GRAN VÍA

Even the side streets of Gran Vía never sleep, pulsating in the early morning to the bass beats of flashy, boisterous landmark clubs. Subtlety has never been a strong point for this area, nor is it exactly known for its safety; a mix of sketchy tourists and sketchier locals makes the Gran Vía less than ideal for late-night wandering.

▧ **Sugar Hill,** C. Mesonero Romanos, 13 (☎ 91 532 15 24). M: Gran Vía or Callao. Named after the original, this is the only real hip-hop club in town. Those in the know arrive around 3:30am to a packed dance floor. Cover 1500ptas, includes 1 drink. Drinks 1000ptas. Open Sa only 12:45-5:30am. The same team runs **Bash,** Pl. Callao, 4. Open W only midnight-5:30am.

Goa After Club, C. Mesonero Romanos, 13 (☎ 91 531 48 27). M: Callao or Gran Vía. After-hours party features high-energy techno and even higher-energy clubbers after Sugar Hill (and sanity) departs. The intoxicated, sleep-deprived crowd dances so hard, you won't believe your eyes. Drinks 700-1000ptas. Cover 1000ptas, includes 1 drink. Open Sa-Su 6-10am.

MALASAÑA AND CHUECA

The dark cafes and darker clubs of Malasaña and Chueca filter jazz and techno into the night and early morning. Known for their bohemian crowds, Malasaña's hotspots radiate from **Plaza 2 de Mayo** and **Calle San Vincente Ferrer.** People are high on life, drugs, and booze; be wary at night. **Calle de Pelayo** is the main drag in flamboyant and gay Chueca. The safest walking route at night is up C. Fuencarral from Gran Vía and right on C. Augusto Figueroa.

▧ **Acuarela,** C. Gravina, 8, off C. Hortaleza. M: Chueca. A welcome alternative to the club scene. Buddhas and candles surround antique furniture grouped into enclaves. Spend hours just chilling. Liqueur 500ptas. Open Su-Th 3pm-2am, F-Sa 3pm-4am.

Café del Toro, C. San Andrés, 38 (☎ 91 445 37 52). M: Bilbao. Past the bar, find a mock outdoor cafe, replete with street awnings, mock storefronts (including the helpful "Casa Baños Municipal"), and cobblestone. Gazebo-like stage hosts live entertainment every night, from acoustic music to stand-up comedy (200ptas added to bill). Grab the monthly program. Beer 300ptas. Drinks 600-800ptas. Open Su-Th 7pm-3am, F-Sa 7pm-3:30am.

Café la Palma, C. La Palma, 62 (☎ 91 522 50 31). M: San Bernardo or Noviciado. Eclectic, funky, friendly crowd in a laid-back setting. Lounge in the comfy pillow room or take in the occasional live music on the stage in back. Beer 350ptas. Mixed drinks 700ptas. Open daily 4pm-3:30am.

Midday, C. Amaniel, 13 (☎ 91 547 25 25). M: Noviciado. The after-hours club for Madrid's beautiful people. Techno and house. Open Su 9am-3pm.

Black & White, C. Libertad, 34 (☎ 91 531 11 41). M: Chueca. A lively disco/bar with room to chat, mingle, and groove on packed dance floors. 2 floors of male fun for a gay crowd. W is international exchange night. Beer 500ptas. Mixed drinks 1000ptas. Open Su-Th 9pm-5am, F-Sa 9pm-6am.

Vía Láctea, C. Velarde, 18 (☎ 91 466 75 81). M: Tribunal. This pink-lit elongated club is packed 8-9pm, when soft drinks and beer on tap are 100ptas each. After midnight, a late 20s crowd gets groovy between the counter-lined walls. The loudspeakers might leave you deaf. Beer 350-450ptas. Open daily 8pm-3am.

La Tetera de la Abuela, C. Espíritu Santo, 19. M: Noviciado. "Granny's Teapot." Granny brews some wicked, uh, tea. Open Su-Th 7:30pm-1am, F-Sa 7:30pm-2am.

Davai, C. Flor Baja, 1 (☎ 91 547 57 11). M: Pl. España or Callao. 2 packed floors of dancers swinging to jungle, house, and tight jazz. Open daily 11pm-5am.

Rick's, C. Clavel, 8 (☎ 91 531 91 86). M: Chueca. Mostly gay men lounge in Chueca's hottest bar. A confused but comfortable setting—have cocktails at the bar, dance between gold columns, or play a heated game of foosball in the back room. Look good, be happy. Beer 600-900ptas. Open daily 11pm-morning.

Café Figueroa, C. Augusto Figueroa, 17 (☎ 91 521 16 73), on the corner of C. Hortaleza. M: Chueca. Smoke-filled, pink-walled cafe is lit by dim chandeliers. Mostly gay clientele. Beer 300-425ptas. Coffee 250-450ptas. Open Su-Th 2:30pm-1am, F-Sa 2:30pm-2:30am.

Star's Cafe, C. Marqués de Valdeiglesias, 5 (☎ 91 522 27 12). M: Chueca. A stylish cafe during the week, a vivacious dance club on the weekends. Come well-dressed and don't forget your cell phone. Open Su-Th 10am-2pm, F-Sa 10am-4am.

El Truco, C. Gravina, 10 (☎ 91 532 89 21). M: Chueca. Classy bar featuring local artists' works. Lesbian-friendly. Open Su-Th 8pm-2am, F-Sa 9pm-4am. Same owners run **Escape,** a club down the street. Both are strong enough for a man, but designed particularly for a woman. Open F-Sa midnight-7am.

Bolero Terraza, Po. Castellana, 33 (☎ 91 554 91 51). M: Rubén Darío. If you had your SUV in Madrid, you would drive it to this ultra-fashionable, yuppie *terraza*. Outside seating centered around a bar. Drinks 1000ptas. Open daily 7:30pm-3am.

BILBAO

In the student-filled streets radiating from **Glorieta de Bilbao,** it's easy to find a cheap drink and even easier to find someone to drink it with. Although discos are plentiful, *terrazas* are packed late into the night with boisterous customers sipping icy Mahou on Pl. Olavide, C. Fuencarral, and C. Luchana.

Vaivén, Travesía de San Mateo, 1 (☎ 91 523 14 87). M: Tribunal. Swivel hips with the best at this exclusive salsa club, crawling with well-dressed locals. Mid-week concerts. Beer 600ptas. Mixed drinks 1000ptas. Open daily 9pm-4am.

Clamores Jazz Club, C. Albuquerque, 14 (☎ 91 445 79 38), off C. Cardenal Cisneros. M: Bilbao. Swanky, pink neon setting and some of Madrid's more interesting jazz. The cover (500-1500ptas) gets slipped into the bill if you're there for the live jazz, starting around 10:30, every night but M. Open Su-Th 7pm-3am, F-Sa 7pm-4am.

Barnon, C. Santa Engracia, 17 (☎ 91 447 38 37). M: Alonso Martínez or Tribunal. Barnon actually bars many from its hip-hop scene: those who aren't as cool as the owner, Real Madrid's stud *fútbol* forward. The right duds, however, make a VIT(ourist) a VIP. Open Su-Th 10pm-3am, F-Sa 10pm-4am.

Big Bamboo, C. Barquillo, 42 (☎ 91 562 88 38). M: Alonso Martínez. Walk 3 blocks east of C. Pelayo on C. Gravina and turn left on C. Barquillo. A friendly, international club that jams to smooth reggae. Open 10:30pm-6am, F-Sa 10:30pm-7am.

MONCLOA

No more pencils, no more books, no more teachers' dirty looks: Moncloa is Madrid's student party zone. High-schoolers dominate the streets, sporting their favorite tight jeans, halter tops, denim jackets, and little black bags. The area is packed during grad week and mid-year school vacations but clears out weekdays in June (when exams hit) and everyday in August (during family vacations).

Unless you're Lolita, or looking for one, there are only two reasons to leave Madrid's better nighttime neighborhoods for Moncloa: **Los Bajos** and its incredibly **cheap drinks.** A virtual concrete megaplex of diminutive bars, with three tiers and two enormous courtyards, Los Bajos is more of a phenomenon than a nightspot. Even more than in the rest of Madrid, the real party here is among the swirling crowds outside. Visits to bars are barely long enough to down your drink, which in most cases is a *chupito* (shot) anyway—at 150ptas, they're hard to turn down.

Bars in Los Bajos are usually only open Friday and Saturday nights and generally close by 1 or 2am. They tend to be slightly grimy, if homey, and dance floors are small. If you want to join the students in a super-cheap start to your night, keep an eye out for **Atenea,** the spot with the best *cerebros* (brain) shot in Moncloa, **Orion,** an old-school Metallica bar with beer, B.O., and bad boys past their prime, or **Comix,** home of the *Agítame el Coco* (Shake My Head) shot, infamous for turning your mind into a cocktail mixer (don't swallow until the end).

To get to Los Bajos from M: Moncloa, cross C. Isaac Peral in front of the Plaza de Moncloa, passing under the gate onto C. Gatzambide, 35. A popular Moncloa bar not in Los Bajos is the **Patato Bar,** C. Hilavion Eslava, a loud, welcoming student hotspot with super-cheap beer and fiesty *sangría.* (At C. Fernando el Católico. M: Moncloa. Open daily until 1am.)

🎵 ENTERTAINMENT

Anyone interested in the latest on live entertainment—from music to dance to theater—should stop by the **Círculo de Bellas Artes,** C. Marquez de Casa Riera, 2 (☎ 91 360 54 00; fax 91 523 13 06; presa@c-bellasartes.es), at C. Alcala, 47; M: Sevilla or Banco de España. The six-floored building not only houses performance venues and art exhibits, but also serves as an organizing center for events throughout Madrid; it has virtually all current information on performances. Their monthly magazine, *Minerva,* is indispensable.

MUSIC

In summer, Madrid sponsors free concerts, ranging from classical and jazz to bolero and salsa, at Pl. Mayor, Lavapiés, Oriente, and Villa de París; check the *Guía del Ocio* for the current schedule. Many nightspots also have live music.

The **Auditorio Nacional,** C. Príncipe de Vergara, 146, home to the National Orchestra, features Madrid's best classical performances. (☎ 91 337 01 00. M: Cruz del Rayo. 800-4200ptas.) The **Fundación Juan March,** C. Castelló, 77, hosts a university lecture series (Tu-W 7:30pm) and sponsors free weekend concerts. (☎ 91 435 42 40. M: Núñez de Balboa.) **Teatro Monumental,** C. Atocha, 65, is home to Madrid's Symphonic Orchestra. Reinforced concrete—a Spanish invention—was first used in its construction in the 1920s, so be prepared for unusual acoustics. (☎ 91 429 81 19. M: Antón Martín.) For opera and *zarzuela* (Spanish light opera), head for the ornate **Teatro de la Zarzuela,** C. Jovellanos, 4, modeled on Milan's La Scala. (☎ 91 524 54 00. M: Banco de España.) The grand 19th-century granite **Teatro de la Ópera** (☎ 91 559 35 51), in Pl. Ópera, is the city's principal venue for classical ballet. Most theaters shut down in July and August.

Flamenco in Madrid is tourist-oriented and expensive. A few nightlife spots are authentic (see **Cardamomo,** p. 114), but they too are pricey. **Casa Patas,** C. Cañizares, 10 (☎ 91 369 04 96), is good quality for a bit less than usual; call for prices. **Café de Chinitas,** C. Torija, 7, is as overstated as they come. Shows start at 10:30pm and midnight, but the memories last forever—or at least they should, given the price.

(☎ 91 547 15 01 or 91 547 15 02. M: Santo Domingo. Cover 4000ptas and up.) At **Corral de la Morería,** C. Morería, 17, by the Viaducto on C. Bailén, shows start at 10:45pm and last until 2am. (☎ 91 365 84 46. M: La Latina. Cover 4000ptas, includes one drink.) **Teatro Albéniz,** C. Paz, 11, hosts an annual *Certamen de Coreografía de Danza Española y Flamenco* that features original dance and music, including extraordinary flamenco. (☎ 91 521 99 98. M: Sol. Tickets 700-2000ptas.)

FILM

In summer, the city sponsors free movies and plays, all listed in the *Guía del Ocio* and the entertainment supplements of Friday's newspapers. In July, look out for the **Fescinal,** a film festival at the Parque de la Florida.

Most cinemas show three films per day, at around 4:30, 7:30, and 10:30pm. Tickets cost 850ptas. Some cinemas offer weekday-only matinee student discounts for 600ptas. Wednesday (sometimes Monday instead) is *día del espectador*, when tickets cost around 500ptas—show up early. Check the *versión original (V.O. subtitulada)* listings in the *Guía del Ocio* for English movies subtitled in Spanish. Three excellent movie theaters cluster near M: Ventura Rodríguez, between Pl. España and Argüelles. **Princesa,** C. Princesa, 3 (☎ 91 541 41 00), shows mainstream Spanish films and subtitled foreign films. The theater/bar **Alphaville,** C. Martín de los Héroes, 14 (☎ 91 559 38 36), behind Princesa and underneath the patio, shows current alternative and mainstream Spanish titles. **Renoir,** C. Raimundo Fernández Villaverde, 10 (☎ 91 541 41 00), a few doors down by the popcorn vendor, shows highly acclaimed recent films, many foreign and subtitled. The state-subsidized *filmoteca española* in the Art Deco **Ciné Doré,** C. Santa Isabel, 3, is Madrid's finest repertory cinema. (☎ 91 549 00 11. M: Antón Martín. Tickets 200-400ptas.)

THEATER

Huertas, east of Sol, is Madrid's theater district. In July and August, Pl. Mayor, Lavapiés, and Villa de París frequently host plays as theaters move outdoors. For a complete listing of theaters and shows, consult the *Guía del Ocio*. Seeing a play in Madrid is an entertaining way to participate in traditional culture and to practice your Spanish. Theater-goers should consult the well-illustrated magazines published by state-sponsored theaters, such as **Teatro Español,** C. Príncipe, 25 (☎ 91 429 62 97; M: Sol), **Teatro de la Comedia,** C. Príncipe, 14 (☎ 91 521 49 31; M: Sevilla), and the superb **Teatro María Guerrero,** C. Tamayo y Baus, 4 (☎ 91 319 47 69; M: Colón). Tickets can be purchased at theater box offices or at ticket agencies (**FNAC** ☎ 91 595 62 00; **Librería Crisol** ☎ 91 322 47 00; **TelEntrada** ☎ 902 38 33 33.)

FÚTBOL

Spaniards obsess over *fútbol* (soccer to Americans). If either **Real Madrid** or **Atlético de Madrid** wins a match, count on streets clogged with honking cars. Every Sunday and some Saturdays between September and June, one of these two teams plays at home. Real Madrid plays at **Estadio Santiago Bernebéu,** Po. Castellana, 104 (☎ 91 457 11 12; M: Lima). Atlético de Madrid plays at **Estadio Vicente Calderón,** C. Virgen del Puerto, 67 (☎ 91 366 47 07; M: Pirámides or Marqués de Vadillos). Tickets cost 3000-7000ptas. Those dead set on seeing a match should try to buy tickets well in advance. If tickets are sold out, scalpers lurk around the stadium a few days before the game. For the big games (Atlético vs. Real, or either team vs. F.C. Barcelona, *La Barça*), key tournament matches in April and May, or the summer *Copa del Rey* and *Copa de Europa* games, scalpers are usually the only option.

RECREATIONAL SPORTS

For **bicycle rental,** try **Karacol Sport,** C. Tortosa, 8, M: Atocha (☎ 91 539 96 33). For **cycling info** and bicycle repair, spin over to **Usera Bike,** C. Usera, 26, M: Usera. (☎ 91 475 02 19. Open M-F 9am-2pm and 5-8pm, Sa 9am-2pm.) **Swimmers** splash in the outdoor pools at: **Casa de Campo,** on Av. Angel next to M: Lago (☎ 91 463 00 50); the indoor **Municipal de La Latina,** Pl. Cebada, 2, M: La Latina; and **Peñuelas,** on C. Arganda (☎ 91 474 28 08), M: Delicias or bus #18. (All pools 520ptas, ages 4-13

250ptas. Open daily 10:30am-8pm.) Gallop over to the **Hipódromo de Madrid**, Ctra. de La Coruña, km 7800 (☎ 91 357 16 82), for **horse-racing**. Call the **Oficina de Información Deportiva** (sports information; ☎ 91 463 55 63) for more information on outdoor recreation in Madrid. The tourist office's *Plano de las Instalaciones Deportivos Muncipales* lists areas open to the public.

BULLFIGHTS

Bullfighters are either loved or loathed. So too are the bullfights themselves. Nevertheless, bullfights are a Spanish tradition, and locals joke that they are the only things in Spain ever to start on time. Hemingway-toting Americans and true fans clog Pl. de Ventas for the events.

From May 15 to 22 every year, the **Fiestas de San Isidro** provide a *corrida* (bullfight) every day with top *matadores* and the fiercest bulls. The festival is nationally televised; those without tickets can crowd into bars. There are also bullfights every Sunday in summer from March to October; they occur less frequently during the rest of the year. Look for posters in bars and cafes (especially on C. Victoria, off C. San Jerónimo). **Plaza de las Ventas,** C. Alcalá, 237, east of central Madrid, is the biggest ring in Spain. (☎ 91 356 22 00. M: Ventas.) A seat runs 450-15,200ptas, depending on whether it's in the sun (*sol*) or shade (*sombra*); shade is more expensive. Tickets are usually available the Friday and Saturday before and the Sunday of the bullfight. **Plaza de Toros Palacio de Vista Alegre,** a new ring in town, hosts bullfights and other cultural events. (☎ 91 422 07 80. M: Vista Alegre. Ticket window open M-F 10am-2pm and 5-8pm.) For younger *toreros*, **Saturday** fun, and the old college try, all at a **lesser price,** head to the **bullfighting school,** which has its own *corridas*. (☎ 91 470 19 90. M: Batán. Open Sa 7pm. Tickets 1000ptas, children 500ptas.) If you're intrigued by the lore but not the gore, head to the **Museo Taurino,** C. Alcalá, 237, at Pl. Monumental de Las Ventas. The museum displays a remarkable collection of capes, bullfighters' outfits, and posters of famous *corridas*. (☎ 91 725 18 57. Open M-F 9:30am-2:30pm, on fight days 10am-1pm. Free.)

FESTIVALS

The brochure *Las Fiestas de España,* available at tourist offices and the bigger hotels, contains historical background and general information on Spain's festivals. Madrid's **Carnaval** (February 15-25 in 2001) was inaugurated in the Middle Ages and prohibited during Franco's dictatorship. Now, however, the city bursts with street fiestas, dancing, and processions. In late April, the city bubbles with the renowned **International Theater Festival.** Around May 15, the **Fiestas de San Isidro,** in honor of Madrid's patron saint, bring concerts, parades, and Spain's best bullfights. Throughout the summer, the city sponsors the **Veranos de la Villa,** an outstanding and varied set of cultural activities, including free classical music concerts, movies in open-air settings, plays, art exhibits, an international film festival, opera, *zarzuela* (light Spanish opera), ballet, and sports. The **Festivales de Otoño** (Autumn Festivals), from September to November, also bring an impressive array of music, theater, and film. On November 1, **Todos los Santos** (All Saints Day), an International Jazz Festival, brings great musicians to Madrid. The **Día de la Constitución** (Day of the Constitution, or National Day) on December 6 heralds the arrival of the National Company of Spanish Classical Ballet in Madrid. Tourist offices have all the information.

SHOPPING

Most stores in Madrid open from 10am to 2pm and 5 to 8pm. Some have begun to stay open on Saturday afternoon and during lunch. By law, *grandes almacenes* (department stores) may open only the first Sunday of every month, a vestige of the country's Roman Catholic heritage. Many small boutiques close in August, when practically everyone flees to the coast. **Inal** publishes a yearly *Guía Esencial para vivir en Madrid,* which includes descriptions of most stores. For funky gear and pure entertainment, check out **Chueca's** boutiques; you can even find Madrid's crazy bright street-cleaning uniforms at **Azules de Vergara, S.L.,** C. Fuencarral, 150. (☎ 91 448 78 10. M: Quevedo. Open M-F 9:30am-1:30pm and 4:30-8pm, Sa 9:30am-1:30pm.)

MALLS

La Vaguada (M: Barrio del Pilar; bus #132 from Moncloa), in the northern neighborhood **Madrid-2**, is Madrid's first experiment in super-malls. It offers everything the homesick could want: 350 shops, including the Body Shop, Burberry's, a food court with Kentucky Fried Chicken and trusty McDonald's, multi-cinemas and a bowling alley (open daily 10am-10pm). By far the poshest shopping mall is the **Galería del Prado**, Pl. Cortes, located beneath the Hotel Palace and across the Castellana from the Ritz. (M: Banco de España. Open M-Sa 10am-9pm.) And of course, there's always the unavoidable **El Corte Inglés** (see p. 86).

▓ EL RASTRO (FLEA MARKET)

For hundreds of years, El Rastro has been a Sunday morning tradition in Madrid. From Pl. Mayor and its Sunday stamp and coin market, walk down C. Toledo to Pl. Cascorro (M: La Latina), where the market begins, and follow the crowds to the end, at the bottom of C. Ribera de Curtidores. In El Rastro you can find anything, from pots to jeans to antique tools to pet birds. Although the main street is a labyrinth of cheap jewelry, incense, and sunglasses, each side street has its own concert of vendors and wares. Antique-sellers contribute their peculiar mustiness to C. del Prado. *Tapas* bars and small restaurants line the streets and provide an air-conditioned respite. The flea market is a pickpocket paradise, so leave your camera in your room and turn that backpack into a frontpack. Police are everywhere if you have any problems. El Rastro is open Sundays and holidays from 9am to 2pm.

BOOKS

FNAC, C. Preciados, 28 (☎ 91 595 62 00). M: Callao. The best music and book selection in town. Books in English on 3rd fl. Open M-Sa 10am-9:30pm, Su noon-9:30pm.

Booksellers, C. José Abascal, 48 (☎ 91 442 79 59 or 91 442 81 04). M: Gregorio Marañón. A vast array of new books in English, plus American and English magazines. Open M-F 9:30am-2pm and 5-8pm, Sa 10am-2pm.

Librería de Mujeres, C. San Cristóbal, 17 (☎ 91 521 70 43), near Pl. Mayor. International bookstore. English spoken. (See **Women's Services**, p. 86.)

Berkana Librería Gai y Lesbiana, C. Gravina, 11 (☎/fax 91 532 13 93). M: Chueca. Gay and lesbian bookstore with loads of contact info for foreigners and a free map of gay Madrid. Open M-F 10:30am-2pm and 5-8:30pm, Sa noon-2pm and 5-8:30pm.

Altair, C. Gaztambide, 31. M: Moncloa or Argüelles. Comprehensive travel bookstore, with the world's best travel guides and others. Open M-Sa 10am-2pm and 4:30-8pm.

COMUNIDAD DE MADRID

The Comunidad de Madrid is an autonomous administrative region shaped like an arrowhead and pointing right at the heart of Castilla y León. Historically, this area, along with Madrid and Castilla La Mancha, was known as Castilla La Nueva (New Castile). The small towns make interesting and refreshing daytrips from the city.

ALCALÁ DE HENARES

Residents of Alcalá (pop. 165,000) pride themselves on their town's distinguished offspring, Miguel de Cervantes, their university's famed alumni, including Golden Age authors Francisco de Quevedo and Lope de Vega, and the city's exceptional Renaissance architecture. All three draw numerous daytrippers from Madrid.

▓▓ ORIENTATION AND PRACTICAL INFORMATION. To get to the main square, **Plaza de Cervantes**, from the train station, turn left as you exit and then bear right onto Po. Estación. After Vía Complutense (about 5 blocks down), take the first right onto C. Libreros and the plaza will be on your left. The **train station** (☎ 91 563 02 02) is located on Po. Estación. **Cercanías** trains run to and from Madrid's

Estación Atocha (35min., every 10min., round-trip 640ptas). The **Continental-Auto bus station,** Av. Guadalajara, 5 (☎ 91 888 16 22), runs between Alcalá and Madrid (45min., every 15min., 350ptas). To reach the city center from the bus station, turn right on Av. Guadalajara and continue as it turns into C. Libreros. The **tourist office,** Callejón de Santa María, 1, at Pl. Cervantes, has a list of sites and a detailed map of Alcalá, as well as a list of accommodations. (☎ 91 889 26 94. Open daily June and Aug. 10am-2pm and 5-7:30pm; Mar.-May 10am-2pm and 4-6:30pm; July and Sept. Tu-Su 10am-2pm and 5-7:30pm.) **Banco Central Hispano,** Pl. Cervantes, 4, has an **ATM.** Services include: **emergency** (☎ 112); **ambulance** (☎ 061); and **police** (☎ 91 881 92 63). The **post office,** Pl. Cervantes, 5, is inside Banco Argentina. (☎ 91 219 71 97. Open M-F 8:30am-7pm, Sa 9:30am-1pm.) The **postal code** ranges 28801 to 28807.

▐▐ **ACCOMMODATIONS AND FOOD.** Some of the least expensive rooms lie within **Hostal Jacinto,** Po. Estación, 2, 2nd staircase, 1-D, three blocks from the train station. Firm beds, floral bedspreads, TVs, and an unusual selection of art grace this hostel. (☎/fax 91 889 14 32. Singles 2800ptas; doubles 5000ptas, with bath 5500ptas; triples 6000ptas.) For food, Alcalá's famed *almendras garrapiñadas* (honey- and sugar-coated almonds) beg to be tried. More sustenance awaits at **Mesón Las Cuadras de Rocinante,** C. Carmen Calzado, 1, off C. Mayor, which specializes in sandwiches named after Don Quijote and compatriots. If it's good enough for Don Quijote's horse, it's good enough for you. (☎ 91 880 08 88. 325-500ptas; huge, delicious, and cheap entrees 400-1800ptas. Open daily 11am-midnight). For fantastically cheap *menús,* turn left on C. Mayor from Pl. Cervantes, and check out the restaurants on the right side of the street.

▣ **SIGHTS.** The huge **Plaza de Cervantes,** blessed with a statue of its namesake and filled with cafes and rose bushes, bursts with color in summer. At the end of the plaza opposite C. Libreros lie the **Ruinas de Santa María,** the remains of a 16th-century church destroyed during the Civil War. In the surviving Capilla del Oidor, art exhibits surround the fountain where Cervantes was christened. (Open Tu-Su noon-2pm and 6-9pm. Free.) Just east of Pl. Cervantes in Pl. San Diego sits the **Colegio Mayor de San Ildefonso** (☎ 91 889 04 00), center of the once illustrious humanist university which is now the only one in the world listed as a World Heritage site. Founded by Cardinal Cisneros in 1499, it opened for classes in 1508. In the **Paraninfo,** where doctorates were once awarded, the king now presents the "Premio Cervantes," Spain's most prestigious literary award. The Paraninfo and **Capilla de San Ildefonso** both have spectacular Mudéjar ceilings, crafted wood pieces held together by pressure. (By tour only, M-F 11:30am, 12:30, 1:30, and 5:30pm; Sa-Su 11, 11:45am, 12:30, 1:15, 2, 5, 5:45, 6:30, 7:15 and 8pm; 350ptas.) The town's **Catedral Magistral,** at the intersection of C. Mayor and C. de Escritorios, is one of two in the world with this title; to be so named each priest must be a university magistrate. (Open M-Sa 9-11am and 6-8pm, Su 9am-12:45pm and 6-9pm. Free.)

Down C. Mayor from Pl. Cervantes is the **Casa de Cervantes,** the reconstructed house where the author was born. Currently under expansion, the house displays a variety of period furniture and editions of *Don Quijote* in languages Cervantes never knew. (☎ 91 889 96 54. Open Tu-Su 10:15am-1:30pm and 4-6:30pm. Free.) The **Convento de San Bernardo,** at Pl. Palacio a block north of the cathedral, hides a gorgeous 17th-century elliptical interior behind a simple facade. (Required tour meets in the courtyard and leaves M-F 1:45 and 6pm; Sa 12:30, 1:30, 5, 5:45, 6:30, 7:15, and 8pm; Su 1:30, 5, 5:45, 6:30, 7:15, and 8pm. 350ptas.)

SAN LORENZO DEL ESCORIAL

They called it the eighth wonder of the world and they were right. San Lorenzo's El Escorial—half monastery and half mausoleum—is the most popular daytrip from Madrid. Although Felipe II constructed El Escorial for himself and for God, today, the complex, with its magnificent library, palaces, frescoes, and art treasures, seems as though it were made for tourists. Do not go on Monday, when the whole complex and most of the town is closed. When in the area, don't miss the impressive Valle de los Caídos. Daytrips are especially popular during the Festivals of San Lorenzo (Aug. 10-20), when parades of giant figures line the streets and fireworks fill the sky, and on Romería a la Ermita de la Virgen de Gracia, the second Sunday in September, when folk dancing contests fill the forest of Herría.

▚ PRACTICAL INFORMATION. Autocares Herranz buses, which prove the easiest way to travel, leave from **Madrid's** Moncloa **Metro station** (50min., every 15min. 7am-9pm, round-trip 805ptas) and whisk travelers to El Escorial's Plaza Virgen de Gracia, the center of town. The **Autocares Herranz** office, C. Rey, 27 (☎ 91 896 90 28), sells tickets to Madrid. El Escorial's **train station** (☎ 91 890 07 14; RENFE info ☎ 91 328 90 20), on Ctra. Estación, is 2km from town. Trains run to **Madrid-Atocha** and **Madrid-Chamartín** (1hr., every 20min. 5:57am-10:17pm, round-trip 810ptas).

From C. Rey, with your back to the bus station, turn right, follow the street, and turn right up C. Floridablanca to get to the **tourist office,** C. Floridablanca, 10. (☎ 91 890 15 54. Open M-F 10am-2pm and 3-5pm, Sa 9:55am-1:55pm.) To get to the tourist office from the train station, take the shuttle to Pl. Virgen de Gracia and go right on C. Florida Blanca. For the **newer office,** C. Grimaldi, 2, continue up C. Floridablanca and turn left onto C. Pasaje Grimaldi. (☎ 91 890 53 13. Open M-Th 11am-6pm, F-Su 10am-7pm.) In an **emergency** call ☎ 112 or the **police** (☎ 91 890 52 23).

▚▚ ACCOMMODATIONS AND FOOD. Since rooms fill up quickly in July and August and are almost impossible to find during festivals (Aug. 10-20), it is best to visit El Escorial as a daytrip. However, if you are going to stay over, there are several budget options. From the bus stop to **Hostal Vasco,** Pl. Santiago, 11, walk up C. Rey two blocks and turn right. The hostel has a terrace on the plaza, and some rooms have balconies overlooking the bustle below. In the evenings, the shadows of the monastery provide amazing views. (☎ 91 890 16 19. Doubles 4400ptas, with bath 4900ptas.) To reach the **Residencia Juvenil "El Escorial" (HI),** C. Residencia, 14, from C. Rey near Pl. Virgen Gracia, turn right on C. Tozas, left onto C. Claudio Coello, left onto Po. Unamuno and right onto C. Residencia. (☎ 91 890 59 24; fax 91 890 06 20. Breakfast included; lunch and dinner available. HI card required. Reservations accepted. 1200ptas per person, 1600ptas with dinner, 2000 with lunch and dinner; over 26 1700ptas, 2200ptas, and 2700ptas respectively. V, MC.) To sleep under the stars, head to **Camping Caravaning El Escorial,** at M-600 km 3.5. (☎ 91 890 24 12. 700ptas per person, per tent, and per car.) The center's cafes are busy throughout the day. **Alaska,** Pl. San Lorenzo 4, serves a lunch *menú* (1400ptas) on cushioned chairs in a shady plaza. (☎ 91 980 40 02. Open daily 1-4pm and 8:30-11pm.) Purchase wine, cheese, and other **groceries** at the **Mercado Público,** C. Rey, 7, two blocks off C. Floridablanca (open M-Sa 9am-2pm and 6-9pm).

EL ESCORIAL

☎ 91 890 59 03, 91 890 59 04, or 91 866 02 38. Complex open Apr.-Sept. Tu-Su 10am-7pm; Oct.-Mar. Tu-Su 10am-6pm. Last admission to palaces, pantheons, and museums is 1hr. before closing. Monastery 900ptas, students 400ptas, guided tour 1000ptas. English tours available. W free for EU citizens. Casitas 1500ptas.

THE MONASTERY

The **Monasterio de San Lorenzo del Escorial,** a gift from Felipe II to God, his people, and himself, was meant to commemorate his victory over the French at the battle of San Quintín in 1557 and includes a royal monastery and mausoleum. He commissioned Juan Bautista de Toledo to design the complex in 1561; when he died in 1567, Juan de Herrera inherited the job. Except for the Panteón Real and minor additional work, the monastery was finished in just 21 years. According to tradition, Felipe oversaw much of the work from a chair-shaped rock, **Silla de Felipe II** (Felipe's Chair), 7km from the site.

Considering the resources that Felipe II commanded, the building is noteworthy for its austerity, symmetry, and simplicity; Felipe described it as "majesty without ostentation." Fulfilling the *desornamentado* style, the monastery is pieced together with granite hewn from the surrounding quarries. The entire structure is built around a gridiron pattern. Four massive towers pin the corners, and a great dome surmounts the towers of the central basilica, giving the ensemble a pyramidal shape. At Felipe II's behest, steep slate roofs—the first of their kind in Spain—were introduced from Flanders. Slate spires lend grace to the grim structure, further mellowed by the glowing *piedra de Colmenar* stone. Variations of this Habsburg style (or *estilo herrerense*) of unadorned granite and red brick, slate roofs, and corner towers, appear throughout Spain—particularly in Madrid and Toledo.

GALLERIES AND LIVING QUARTERS. To avoid the worst of the crowds, enter El Escorial by the traditional gateway on the west side (C. Floridablanca), where you'll encounter a collection of Flemish tapestries and paintings. The collection exudes much of the same severity as the monastery, with dark paintings like El Greco's *Martirio de San Mauricio y la Legión* and Roger van der Weyden's glowing-ember *Calvary*. The adjacent **Museo de Arquitectura** and Pintura has an outstanding exhibition comparing the construction of El Escorial to other related structures; there is also a display of wooden models of 16th-century machinery. Though masterpieces by Bosch, Dures, El Greco, Titian, Tintoretto, Velázquez, Zurbarán, Van Dyck, and others hang from the walls, the majority of the collection now lies in Madrid's Prado Museum.

The **Palacio Real,** lined with *azulejos* (tiles) from Toledo, includes the **Salón del Trono (Throne Room)** and two dwellings: Felipe II's spartan 16th-century apartments and the more luxurious 18th-century rooms of Carlos III and Carlos IV. Pastoral images cover the **Puertas de Marguetería,** German doors made from 18 different types of trees, some from as far as North America. The long **Sala de Batallas (Battle Room)** links the two parts of the palace with commanding frescoes by Italian artists Grabelo and Castello. Castile and Spain's greatest victories—including Juan II's 1431 triumph over the Muslims at Higueruela, Felipe's II's two successful expeditions in the Azores, and the Battle of San Quintín—are detailed on the walls and ceiling. Maps line the walls; the last one on the right portrays the world, as (mis)understood by the 16th century Europeans. Downstairs, in the royal chambers, Felipe II's miniscule bed attests to his (relative) asceticism.

LIBRARY. The **biblioteca** (library) on the second floor holds numerous priceless books and manuscripts (though several fires have reduced the collection). Alfonso X's *Cantigas de Santa María*, the Book of Hours of the Catholic monarchs, Saint Teresa's manuscripts and diary, the gold-scrolled *Aureus Codex* (by German Emperor Conrad III, 1039), and an 11th-century *Commentary on the Apocalypse* by Beato de Liébana are just a small selection of the manuscripts. Frescos of history's most prized academic figures cover the ceiling.

BASILICA. The lower main cloister leads to the cool, magnificent basilica. Marble steps lead up to an altar adorned by two groups of elegant sculptures. The figures on the left represent assorted relatives of Felipe II, including parents Carlos I and Isabel, daughter María, and sisters María (Queen of Hungary) and Leonor (Queen of France). Those on the right depict Felipe II with his three wives and his son Carlos. The **Coro Alto** (High Choir) has a magnificent ceiling fresco of an angel-filled heaven. The **cloister** shines under Titian's fresco of the martyrdom of St. Lawrence.

PANTHEONS. The nearby **Panteón Real,** filled with tombs of past monarchs, glistens with intricate gold and marble designs completed in 1654. Felipe II ordered that its design allow for mass to be conducted over his father's tomb. The connecting **Pudreria,** where bodies would dry before being buried, is thankfully out of commission. Two centuries later, the **Panteón de los Infantes** was constructed for the same purpose, and has space for over 50 babies. Rumors run that many of the royalty's illegitimate children, including a son of Charles V, lie within the crypts.

THE CASITAS

Commissioned by the Prince of Asturias, who later became Carlos IV, the **Casita del Príncipe** has a splendid collection of ornaments, including chandeliers, lamps, rugs, furniture, clocks, tapestries, china, and engraved oranges. The French roughed up the *casita* during the Napoleonic invasions, but many rooms were redecorated by Fernando VII in the then-popular Empire style. To get to the *casita*, follow the right side of the Ctra. Estación to the corner of the monastic complex, turn the corner, and fork left. (Open Sa-Su 10:30am-1pm and 3:30-6:30pm. Schedule may expand; call ☎ 91 890 5903 or check at the tourist office.) Three kilometers toward Ávila sits the simpler **Casita del Infante**, commissioned by Carlos's brother, Gabriel de Borbón, in the mid-16th century.

NEAR EL ESCORIAL: EL VALLE DE LOS CAÍDOS

In a once untouched valley of the Sierra de Guadarrama, 8km north of El Escorial, Franco forced prisoners to build the overpowering monument of Santa Cruz del Valle de los Caídos (Valley of the Fallen) as a memorial to those who gave their lives in the Civil War. Although ostensibly a monument to both sides, the massive granite cross (150m tall and 46m wide) implicitly honors only those who died "serving Dios and España," (i.e. the fascist Nationalists); many of the Republican prisoners-of-war died under the grueling conditions of its construction. To climb to the base of the cross, use the stairs adjacent to the automatic lift or follow the paved road up to the trailhead just past the monastery on the right (40min. up). Apocalyptic tapestries line the eerie cave-like **basilica**, which contains the ghost of fascist architecture, and death-angels carry swords and angry light fixtures. Behind the chapel walls lie a multitude (9 levels) of the dead. The high altar, located directly underneath the mammoth cross with its mammoth statues, is testimony to modern Spain's view of Franco—although Franco lies buried underneath, there is no mention of his tomb in tourist literature. El Valle de los Caídos is accessible only via El Escorial. (Mass daily 11am. Open daily June-Aug. 9:30am-7pm; Sept.-May 10am-6pm. 800ptas, seniors and students 350ptas. W free for EU citizens. Funicular to the cross 350ptas.) **Autocares Herranz** runs one bus to the monument (15min., leaves El Escorial Tu-Su 3:15pm and returns 5:30pm, round-trip plus admission 1030ptas, funicular not included).

CERCEDILLA

The Sierra de Guadarrama is a pine-covered mountain range halfway between Madrid and Segovia. *La Mujer Muerta* (The Dead Woman) to the west, the *Sierra de la Maliciosa* (Mountain of the Evil Woman) to the east, and the less-imaginatively-named *Siete Picos* (Seven Peaks) draw both summer and winter visitors who come to hike and ski, basing themselves in the Sierras' canopied hamlets.

Cercedilla, a picturesque chalet town full of budget accommodations and blessed with great weather, is the ideal base for venturing into the Sierras. In the summer, cooler temperatures and a relaxed pace lure hot and tired city-dwellers; in the winter, skiers revel in the nearby resorts. For those weary of Madrid's sights, Cercedilla has no monuments, churches, or museums, and the most exciting event in the town's history is its mention in Quevedo's 17th century novel, *El buscón*.

◧ **PRACTICAL INFORMATION.** Cercedilla makes an easy daytrip from Madrid. The **train station** (☎ 91 852 00 57), at the base of the hill on C. Emilio Serrano, sends trains to: **Puerto de Navacerrada** (30min., every hr. 9:35am-7:35pm, 130ptas); **Los Cotos** (45min., every hr. 9:35am-7:35pm, 495ptas); **Segovia** (45min., 8-9 per day 7:27am-9:23pm, 330ptas); **El Escorial** (1hr., 9 per day 7:30am-12:22am, 160ptas); and **Madrid-Atocha** (1½hr., over 30 per day 6:07am-10:59pm, 485ptas). To get to town from the station, go uphill, fork right at the top, and continue straight at the train tracks (15-20min.). Find info at the **Consejería de Medio Ambiente** (see **Hiking**, below). For **Cta. Las Dehesas**, go straight uphill and stay left at the fork. The **bus station**, Av. José Antonio, 2 (☎ 91 852 02 39), across from the Ayuntamiento, sends buses to **Madrid** (M-F 29 per day 6am-8:45pm, Sa 15-17 per day 6:20am-8:45pm, Su 17 per day 8:30am-9:30pm; 430ptas, 735ptas round-trip). Services include: **emergency** (☎ 112); **police**(☎ 91 852 02 00); and the **Centro Médico** (☎ 91 852 04 97).

▐▛▌ ACCOMMODATIONS AND FOOD. On Ctra. Las Dehesas, two youth hostels afford views of the Sierras. The **Villa Castora (HI)** is closest to the train station, about 1km up Ctra. Las Dehesas on the left (20min.), and offers a terrace and pool in summer. (☎ 91 852 03 34; fax 91 852 24 11. All rooms with private bath. Reception open daily 8am-10pm. Reservations recommended 15 days in advance and only accepted M-F 8am-3pm. Rooms and 3 meals 2000ptas, with 2 meals 1600ptas, only breakfast 1200ptas; over 26 years old, 2889ptas, 2354ptas, 1819ptas respectively.) **Las Dehesas (HI)**, closer to the trails and tucked back among the trees just beyond the Agencia del Medio Ambiente on Ctra. las Dehesas (30min.), has more peaceful and idyllic rooms. (☎ 91 852 01 35; fax 91 852 1836. Parlor games, soccer field, TV. Rates identical to Villa Castora.) HI cards, required at both, are available on the spot for 1800ptas. **Hostal Longinos,** near the train station, is a more expensive option. A restaurant and fountained courtyard accompany decadent rooms, all with private baths, TVs, and phones. (☎ 91 852 15 11. Doubles 6300ptas.) **Camping,** which is strictly controlled throughout the Sierra de Guadarrama, is prohibited within Cercedilla's town limits. A list of campsites is available at the **Conserjería del Medioambiente** (see **Hiking,** below). **Supermarket Gigante,** C. Doctor Cañados, 2, is in the town center off Av. Generalísimo. (☎ 91 852 00 13. Open M-Sa 9:30am-2pm and 5:30-9pm, Su 9:30am-2pm.) **Restaurants** peddle inexpensive *bocadillos* and *raciones* in the town itself. Several restaurants on Ctra. las Dehesas offer Sierra views and finer food for a higher price tag.

▐▟ HIKING. The **Consejería de Medio Ambiente,** Ctra. las Dehesas, a wooden chalet 2km up the road, on the right (30min. from the train station), functions as a tourist office and offers hiking information. (☎/fax 852 22 13. Open daily 10am-6pm.) The free leaflet *Sendas* (self-guided trails) is especially useful. From July to September, themed all-day hikes leave Saturday and Sunday at 10:30am from the train station with a scenic ride on the old train up to Los Cotos; they return at 5:30pm. (Call ahead and bring a lunch. 10-person min. 800ptas per group.) Most of the hiking around Cercedilla begins up the **Carretera las Dehesas,** uphill from the train station. The **Calzada Romana,** atop the carretera, offers hiking along an ancient Roman road that once connected Madrid to Segovia.

NEAR CERCEDILLA: PUERTO DE NAVACERRADA AND LOS COTOS

A magnet for outdoorsy types year-round, **Puerto de Navacerrada** offers bland **skiing** in the winter (Dec.-Apr.) and beautiful **hiking** in the summer. Backpackers in search of challenging overnight hikes often take the popular **Camino Schmid,** a 7km trail which goes from Navacerrada to Cercedilla. For hiking information, try **Deporte y Montaña** (☎ 91 852 10 86 or 91 852 14 35), near the train station. To head straight for the trails, exit the train station, turn left at the highway, and turn left again (off the road) at the large intersection marking the pass. The dirt path leads uphill to several trailpaths through the pine forests (25min.). A **train** leaves for Navacerrada from the Cercedilla station (30min.; every hr. 9:35am-7:35pm; 130ptas, from Madrid 485ptas). **Los Cotos** is another popular winter resort. For information, try the **Parque Nacional Peñalara,** near the train station. **Valdesqui** (☎ 91 515 59 39) is a ski resort in nearby **Rascafria.** For more information on winter sports, consult the tourist office in Madrid or call the resorts. The extension from Cercedilla to Navacerrada stops here as well (40min., every hr. 9:35am-7:45pm).

ARANJUEZ

Two rivers converge at the heart of green Aranjuez (pop. 42,000). Once a getaway for generations of Habsburg and Bourbon royalty, Aranjuez still maintains pastoral elegance, thanks to its dazzling gardens and palaces. Famed for its strawberries and asparagus, this small city is pleasing both to the eyes and to the stomach.

▐▘ TRANSPORTATION. Trains go to: **Toledo** (30min., 10 per day 7:20am-9:12pm, 400ptas); **Madrid** (45min.; *cercanías* to Atocha every 15min. 5:40am-11:30pm, *regionales* to Chamartín 11 per day 5:56am-9:50pm; 385-485ptas); **Cuenca** (2hr., 4-5 per day 6:10am-8:14pm, 1000ptas). **AISA** runs from the **bus station,** C. Infantas, 16 (☎ 91 891 01 83), to **Madrid's Estación Sur de Autobuses** (45min.; M-F every 15min. 6am-9pm, Sa every 30min. 7:45am-9pm, Su 10 per day 8am-10pm; 405ptas). For **taxis,** call ☎ 91 891 11 39.

🚺 ORIENTATION AND PRACTICAL INFORMATION. From the **train station** (☎ 91 891 02 02) it's a 10-minute walk to the town center. With your back to the station, turn right, walk to the end of the street, then turn left onto Ctra. Toledo. Follow the road to the right (when you can see the palace), left at the fork, and go under an arch. Municipal bus L2 stops outside the station and on C. Stuart (M-F every 30min., Sa-Su every hr., 105ptas). The **tourist office,** in Pl. San Antonio, supplies maps and brochures. (☎ 91 891 04 27. Open June-Sept. Tu-Su 10am-2pm and 4-6pm; Oct.-May Tu-Sa 10am-1pm and 3-5pm, Su 10am-2pm.) Services include: **emergency:** ☎ 112; **police,** C. Infantas, 36 (☎ 91 891 00 22) and the **post office,** C. Peña Redonda, 3, off C. Capitán Gómez (☎ 91 891 11 32. Open M-F 8:30am-2:30pm, Sa 9:30am-1pm). The **postal code** is 28300. For **Internet** access, head to **Habana Café,** Ctra. Andalucía, 11, right down the street from the tourist office. (250ptas per 15min., 400ptas per 30min., 700ptas per hr. Open daily 7pm-1am.)

🍴🛏 ACCOMMODATIONS AND FOOD. Accommodations in Aranjuez tend to be both costly and luxurious. **Hostal Infantas,** Av. Infantas, 4-6, features a hotel-like entrance with hotel-like rooms and a top-notch reception. All rooms have TV, phones and A/C. (☎ 91 891 13 41; fax 91 891 66 43. Singles 1900ptas, with shower 2900ptas, with full bathroom 3500ptas; doubles 3500ptas, with shower 5600ptas, with full bathroom 6200ptas; triples with shower 7200ptas, with bath 8200ptas. V, MC.) **Camping Soto del Castillo,** across Río Tajo and off the highway to the right (2km from palace—watch for the signs), sits amid lush fields. (☎ 91 891 13 95. Electricity 525ptas; 625ptas per person, 525ptas per car, 550-675ptas per tent.)

The town's **strawberries** and **asparagus** have been famous for centuries. Nowadays, many of Aranjuez's strawberries are actually grown in other areas of Spain and sold to unsuspecting tourists as *fresón con nata* (strawberries with cream; 350-450ptas) at kiosks and cafes throughout town. The imitations are enormous compared to real Aranjuez strawberries, which are on the smaller side. Aranjuez's restaurants are plentiful and expensive. Don't miss the masterful decor and cuisine of owners Roberto and Felipe at **Brigantino,** C. de los Cuarteles, 14. From the end of C. Infantas, turn right on C. Foso and make the first left. Excellent Italian dishes await on tiled tables under a frescoed ceiling. (☎ 91 801 17 51. Pastas 1000-1200ptas, pizzas 825-950ptas. Open W-Su noon-4:30pm and 8pm-12:30am, Tu 8pm-12:30am. V, MC.)

📷 SIGHTS. The River Tajo and its tributary, the Jarama, water the palace's beautiful **🌳gardens.** River walkways run from the **Jardín de la Isla,** which sprouts banana trees and a mythological statue garden, to the huge **Jardín del Príncipe,** originally created for the amusement of Carlos IV. (Both open daily June-Sept. 8am-8:30pm; Oct.-May 8am-6:30pm. Free.) Inside the park, the **Casa del Labrador,** a mock laborer's cottage, is full of Neoclassical decorative arts. It also houses the queen's private quarters, overflowing with such knick knacks as Roman mosaics from Mérida and sketches of Madrid embroidered in silk. The **Casa de Marinos,** once the quarters of the Tajo's sailing squad, stores royal gondolas. (☎ 91 891 03 05. Both open June-Aug. Tu-Su 10am-6:15pm; Sept.-May Tu-Su 10am-5:15pm. Casa del Labrador 500ptas, students 225ptas. Casa de Marinos 325ptas, students 225ptas.)

The stately **Palacio Real,** splendid in white brick, was originally designed by Juan de Herrera—chief architect of El Escorial—under the direction of Felipe II. In subsequent years, both Felipe VI and Carlos III had the palace enlarged and embellished to suit their own tastes. Room after opulent room displays Vatican marble mosaics, crystal chandeliers, and mirrors from La Granja. Flemish tapestries and ornate French clocks abound. The Oriental **porcelain room,** with three-dimensional wallpaper and Rococo ceramic work, and the Mozarabic **smoking room,** which bears a striking resemblance to the Alhambra, are particularly remarkable. Keep an eye out for the velvet-covered baby's toilet and dumbbells at the end of the tour. (Open Apr.-Sept. Tu-Sa 10am-6:15pm; Oct.-Mar. Tu-Sa 10am-5:15pm. Compulsory 30min. tour in Spanish. 650ptas, students 250ptas. EU citizens free W.)

CENTRAL SPAIN

CASTILLA LA MANCHA

Cervantes chose to set Don Quijote's adventures in La Mancha (*manxa* means parched earth in Arabic) in an effort to evoke a cultural and material backwater. While Castilla La Mancha is indeed one of Spain's least developed regions, no fantasy of the Knight of the Sad Countenance is needed to transform the austere beauty of this battered, windswept plateau. Its tumultuous history, gloomy medieval fortresses, and awesome crags provide enough food for the imagination.

Long ago, this region was at the center of conflicts between Christians and Muslims. When Christian forces arrived in Muslim Spain, La Mancha became the domain of the military orders Santiago, Calatrava, Montesa, and San Juan, which were modeled after such crusading institutions as the Knights Templar, a society of powerful warrior-monks. In the 14th and 15th centuries, the region saw fearsome struggles between the kingdoms of Castilla and Aragón. All this warring left La Mancha in a state of utter destruction.

The region is Spain's largest wine-producing area (Valdepeñas and Manzanares are popular table wines), and its abundant olive groves and excellent hunting influence many local recipes. Stews, roast meats, and game are all *manchego* staples. *Gazpacho manchego* (a hearty stew of rabbit, lamb, chicken, and pork) and *queso manchego* (Castile's beloved cheese) are both indigenous specialties.

> **HIGHLIGHTS OF CASTILLA LA MANCHA**
>
> **Toledo,** glorious former capital of the Holy Roman, Visigothic, and Muslim empires, especially its **cathedral,** one of Spain's best (see below).
> **Cuenca's** famed **casas colgadas** (hanging houses; see p. 135).

 LOCAL FESTIVALS IN CASTILLA LA MANCHA
Toledo's celebration of *Corpus Christi* (June 18 in 2001) is one of the most extravagant in all of Spain. The internationally renowned *Festival of Religious Music* takes place in **Cuenca** the week after *Semana Santa*. **Almagro** draws thousands of performers and theater-lovers to its Golden-Age theater with the annual *Festival Internacional de Teatro Clásico de Almagro* (July 6-30 in 2001).

TOLEDO

For Cervantes, Toledo was a "rocky gravity, glory of Spain and light of her cities." Cossío called it "the most brilliant and evocative summary of Spain's history." To the architecture-lover, Toledo is paradise. Toledo has been successively a Roman settlement, capital of the Visigoth kingdom, stronghold of the Emirate of Córdoba, and imperial city under Carlos V. To the military historian, Toledo is equally interesting, as it produced swords for most of medieval Europe and conquistadors such as Francisco Pizarro. Modern-day Toledo (pop. 65,000) may be marred by armies of tourists and caravans of kitsch, but it remains a treasure trove of Spanish culture. The city's numerous churches, synagogues, and mosques share twisting alleyways, emblematic of a time when Spain's three religions coexisted peacefully. Visitors pay monetary homage to Toledo's Damascene swords and knives, colorful pottery, and almond-paste marzipan.

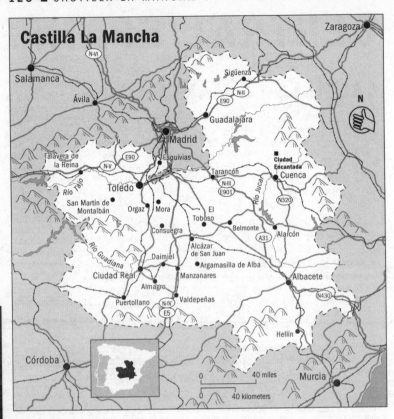

Castilla La Mancha

TRANSPORTATION

Trains: Po. Rosa, 2 (☎ 925 22 30 99), in an exquisite neo-Mudéjar station opposite the Puente de Azarquiel. One line only runs to **Madrid** (1½hr., 10-20 per day M-F 6:30am-9:42pm, Sa-Su 8:30am-9:42pm; 775ptas), sometimes via **Aranjuez** (35min., 9 per day 6:30am-8:56pm, 330ptas).

Buses: (☎925 21 58 50), 5min. from the city gate. From Pl. Zocodóver, take C. Armas. Serviced by various companies. **T. Galiano Continental** (☎ 925 22 36 41) runs to **Madrid** (1½hr.; every 30min. M-Sa 6am-10pm, Su 8:30am-11:30pm; 585ptas). **ALSINA** (☎ 925 22 39 15 or 925 22 12 17) to **Valencia** (M-F 3pm, 2300ptas).

Public Transportation: Buses #5 and 6 stop to the right of the train station and across the street from the bus station; both head to Pl. Zocodóver (120ptas).

Taxis: ☎925 25 50 50 or 925 22 70 70.

Car Rental: Avis (☎ 925 21 45 35 or 925 21 57 94), on C. Venancio González 9, and **Hertz** (☎ 925 25 38 90), at the train station.

ORIENTATION AND PRACTICAL INFORMATION

Toledo is an almost unconquerable maze of narrow streets where pedestrians and cars battle for sovereignty. To get to Plaza de Zocodóver in the town center, take bus #5 or 6 (120ptas) from the stop on the right after you exit the train station. From the bus station, exit from the restaurant, head straight toward the traffic circle, and take the first right along the steep highway that surrounds the city. From the train station, *do not* take the big bridge across the Tajo. Instead, turn right after leaving the station and follow the left fork uphill to a smaller bridge, Puente de Alcántara. Cross the bridge to the stone staircase (through a set of arches); after climbing the stairs, turn left and continue upward, veering right at C. Cervantes to Pl. Zocodóver. Despite the well-labeled streets, you will probably get lost in Toledo. Enjoy it—it's the best way to discover the town's beauty.

Tourist Office: (☎ 925 22 08 43; fax 925 25 26 48), just outside the Puerta Nueva de Bisagra, on the north side of town. From Pl. Zocodóver, take C. Armas, the main street (which changes names several times), downhill and through the gates (Puertas de Bisagra); the office is across the intersection (10min.). From the train station, turn right and take the busy right-hand fork across the bridge (Puente de Azarquiel); follow the city walls until you reach the plaza. The office is across the road, outside the walls. Open M-Sa 9am-7pm and Su 9am-3pm. There is a **second office** in Pl. Ayuntamiento (☎ 925 25 40 30), opposite the cathedral. English spoken. Open Tu-Su 10:30am-2:30pm and 4:30-7pm.

Currency Exchange: Banco Central Hispano, C. Comercio, 47 (☎ 925 22 98 00). Open Apr.-Sept. M-F 8:30am-2:30pm; Oct.-Mar. M-F 8:30am-2:30pm, Sa 8:30am-1pm.

Luggage Storage: At the **bus station** (100-200ptas), open daily 8am-11:30pm. At the **train station** (400ptas), open daily 7am-9:30pm.

Emergency: ☎ 112. **Police:** (☎ 925 21 34 00), Av. Portugal.

Pharmacy: (☎ 925 22 17 68), Pl. Zocodóver. List of late-night pharmacies posted.

Hospital: Hospital Virgen de la Salud (☎ 925 26 92 00), Av. Barber.

Post Office: C. Plata, 1 (☎ 925 22 36 11), off Pl. Zocodóver via C. Comercio. **Lista de Correos.** Open M-F 8:30am-8:30pm, Sa 9am-2pm. **Postal Code:** 45070.

Internet Access: Scorpions (☎ 925 21 25 56), on C. Pintor Matías Moreno. 100ptas per 5min. Open daily noon-midnight. V, MC, AmEx.

ACCOMMODATIONS

Toledo is chock-full of accommodations, but finding a bed during the summer can be a hassle, especially on weekends. If you run into trouble, try the tourist office.

Residencia Juvenil San Servando (HI), Castillo San Servando (☎ 925 22 45 54, reservations ☎ 925 26 77 29), uphill from the train station (10min.). Cross the street from the station, turn left and then immediately right up Callejón del Hospital. When the steps reach a road, turn right and then right again, following the signs to Hospital Provincial (10min.). The steep walk uphill just past the hospital leads to a 14th-century castle—that's not for you; you're going to the annex. Attractive, monumental building has 48 rooms, each with 4 bunk beds, some with views. Pool in summer, and a TV room. Sheets included. Laundry 500ptas. Reception open 7-9:40am, 10am-7:40pm and 8-11:50pm. Curfew 12:30am. Dorms 1200ptas, over 26 1400ptas. Closed various times throughout the year—call ahead.

Pensión Castilla, C. Recoletos, 6 (☎ 925 25 63 18). From Pl. Zocodóver, head up C. Sillería, go diagonally left through Pl. San Agustín, and take a right. The comfortable rooms feature high, wood-beamed ceilings and are furnished with good beds. Singles 2200ptas; doubles with bath 3900ptas.

Pensión Descalzos, C. Descalzos, 30 (☎ 925 22 28 88), down the steps off Po. San Cristóbal. Recently refurbished, high-class hostel with some stunning views of the surrounding hills. Light modern rooms all have TV, A/C, full bath, and phone. Breakfast 225-800ptas. Apr.-Oct. singles 3690ptas; doubles 5900ptas. Oct.-Mar. singles 3500ptas; doubles 5600ptas. IVA not included. V, MC.

Pensión Nuncio Viejo, C. Nuncio Viejo, 19, 3rd fl. (☎ 925 22 81 78), the street leading off the cathedral. The 7 rooms may be cramped but they're light and clean, and waits for the common bathroom are rare. The motherly owner is a great cook. Meals 950ptas. Singles 1900ptas; doubles 3900ptas, with bath 4400ptas.

Pensión Segovia, C. Recoletos, 2 (☎ 925 21 11 24), located around the bend from Pensión Castilla. Simple rooms with decent beds. You may have to wait on occasion for the bathrooms. Singles 2200ptas; doubles 3000ptas; triples 4500ptas.

Camping El Greco (☎ 925 22 00 90), 1.5km from town on the road away from Madrid (C-502). Bus #7 (from Pl. Zocodóver) stops at the entrance. Wooded, shady site between the river and an olive grove. 550ptas per person (children 450ptas), 570ptas per tent, 550ptas per car (IVA not included.) Pool, bar, supermarket. **Circo Romano,** Av. Carlos III, 19, through Puerta de Bisagra, to the left and then the 2nd "spoke" off the traffic circle as you walk to the right. Closer but noisier. Popular pool area. Restaurant and bar. (☎ 925 22 04 42. 550ptas per person, 570ptas per tent, 550ptas per car.)

🍴 FOOD

Toledo grinds almonds into marzipan of every shape and size, from colorful fruity nuggets to half-moon cookies; *pastelerías* beckon on every corner. If your pocket allows, dining out in Toledo can be a pleasant culinary experience (*menús* 1400-1600ptas). Alternatively, buy fresh fruit and the basics at **Frutería-Pan,** C. Real Arrabal 24, opposite the tourist office (open daily 9am-10pm). The **market** takes place in the nondescript building on Pl. Mayor, behind the cathedral (open July-Sept. 9am-2pm and 5-8pm; Oct.-June M-Sa 8:30am-2pm).

Pastucci, C. Sinagoga, 10 (☎ 925 21 48 66), where pizzas and pastas are the name of the game. From Pl. Zocodóver take C. Comercio; keep to the right and turn right through the underpass. Periwinkle walls, lots of light, and cheerful atmosphere. Pastas 850-975ptas. Salads 625-975ptas. Pizzas 900ptas. Open daily 12:15pm-midnight. V, MC.

Restaurante-Mesón Palacios, C. Alfonso X El Sabio, 3 (☎ 925 21 59 72), off C. Nuncio Viejo. A popular escape from the heat, with a cool, dim interior. Two daily *menús* loaded with meat, fish, and egg options (1000 or 1700ptas). English menu available. Entrees 1200-2000ptas. Open M-Sa 1-4pm and 7-11pm, Su 1-4pm. V, MC, AmEx.

🗺 SIGHTS

Toledo has an excellent collection of museums, churches, synagogues, and mosques, making the city almost impossible to see in just one day. Within its fortified walls, which are attributed to 7th-century King Wamba, Toledo's major attractions form a belt around its middle. An east-west tour, beginning in Pl. Zocodóver, is mostly downhill. Most sights are closed on Mondays.

◼ CATHEDRAL. Built between 1226 and 1498, Toledo's grandiose cathedral boasts five naves, delicate stained glass, and unapologetic ostentation; it is also the seat of the Primate of Spain. Noteworthy pieces include the 14th-century Gothic *Virgen Blanca* by the entrance, El Greco's *El Espolio*, and Narciso Tomés's *Transparente*, a Spanish-Baroque whirlpool of architecture, sculpture, and painting. In the **Capilla Mayor,** the massive Gothic altarpiece stretches to the ceiling. The tomb

---

EL GRECO'S THREE MISTAKES
Upon a visit to the sacristy of Toledo's cathedral, the eye is quickly drawn to the large El Greco painting at the end of the room. El Greco painted *El Espolio*—his first painting—specifically for the cathedral, although neither party had thought to negotiate costs before the completion of the work. The cathedral's clergy were unhappy with the painting due to three mistakes El Greco had inadvertently made. The first is an anachronism: the scene depicts the point in the Bible at which the Roman soldiers are about to remove Jesus' gown, but the soldier standing to his left is wearing distinctly 16th-century armor. El Greco's second mistake was painting three women in the bottom left corner; according to the New Testament, no women were present at that moment. The clergy's final complaint was that the artist painted ordinary men's heads above the head of Jesus; even in art, Christ is more holy than mere humans. The two parties went to court over the matter, eventually working out a compromise. In the end, El Greco won something more valuable than money—the court battle threw him into the spotlight, earning him a slew of new commissions and spreading his reputation.

CENTRAL SPAIN

Toledo

▲ ACCOMMODATIONS
Pensión Castilla, 6
Pensión Descalzos, 12
Residencia Juvenil San Servando (HI), 3
Pensión Nuncio Viejo, 10
Pensión Segovia, 5

● FOOD
Frutería-Pan, 1
Market, 11
Pastucci, 9
Restaurante-Mesón Palacios, 7

■ NIGHTLIFE
Bar La Abadía, 4
Enebro, 8
Zaida, 2

CENTRAL SPAIN

of Cardinal Mendoza, founder of the Spanish Inquisition, lies to the left. Beneath the dome is the **Capilla Mozárabe,** the only place where the ancient Visigoth mass (in Mozarabic) is still held. The **treasury** flaunts interesting ornamentations, including a replica of one of Columbus's ships and a 400-pound, 16th-century gold monstrosity lugged through the streets during the annual Corpus Christi procession. The **sacristy** is home to 18 El Grecos and 2 Van Dycks, along with the portraits of every archbishop of Toledo. The red hats hanging from the ceiling mark the cardinals' tombs. *(At Arco de Palacio, southwest of Pl. Zocodóver.* ☎ *925 22 22 41. Open July-Aug. M-Sa 10:30am-7pm, Su 2-6pm; Sept.-June M-Sa 10:30am-6pm, Su 2-6pm. 700ptas. Tickets sold at the store opposite the entrance, open daily 8am-8pm. Respectable dress required.)*

■ **ALCÁZAR.** Toledo's most formidable landmark, the Alcázar has been a stronghold of Romans, Visigoths, Moors, and Spaniards and each of these groups has rebuilt the structure according to their own necessities and architectural tastes. Much of the building was reduced to rubble during the Civil War, when Fascist troops besieged by Republicans used the Alcázar as their refuge. Don't miss the room that details Colonel Moscardó's refusal to surrender the Alcázar, even at the cost of his son's life. You can also visit the dark, windowless basement refuge where over 500 civilians hid during the siege. The rooms above ground have been turned into a national military museum complete with armor, swords, guns, knives, and… dried plants. *(Cuesta Carlos V, 2, a block down from Pl. Zocodóver.* ☎ *925 22 30 38. Open Tu-Su 9:30am-2pm. 200ptas. EU citizens free W.)*

EL GRECO. Greek painter Doménikos Theotokópoulos (more commonly known as El Greco) spent most of his life in Toledo. Many of his works are displayed throughout town, but the majority of his masterpieces have long since been carted off to the Prado and other big-name museums. On the west side of town, the **Iglesia de Santo Tomé** houses El Greco's famous *El entierro del Conde de Orgaz (The Burial of Count Orgaz).* The stark figure staring out from the back is El Greco himself, and the boy is his son, Jorge Manuel, who built Toledo's city hall. *(Pl. Conde.* ☎ *925 25 60 98. Open daily June-Aug. 10am-7pm; Sept.-May 10am-6pm. 200ptas.)* Downhill and to the left lies the **Casa Museo de El Greco.** This oddly arranged museum has 19 works by El Greco, including a copy of the *Vista y plano de Toledo* (Landscape of Toledo), a detailed painting of the city. *(C. Samuel Levi, 3.* ☎ *925 22 40 46. Open Tu-Sa 10am-2pm and 4-6pm, Su 10am-2pm. 200ptas; students, under 18, and over 65 free. Sa and Su afternoons free.)* Outside handsome Puerta Nueva de Bisagra on the way to Madrid, 16th-century **Hospital Tavera** displays five El Grecos as well as several works by his mentor, Titian. *(Cardenal Tavera, 2.* ☎ *925 22 04 51. Open daily 10:30am-1:30pm and 3:30-6pm. 500ptas.)*

THE OLD JEWISH QUARTER. Samuel Ha Leví, diplomat and treasurer to Pedro el Cruel, built the **Sinagoga del Tránsito** (1366). Its simple exterior hides an extraordinarily ornate sanctuary with Mudéjar plasterwork and an *artesonado* (intricately designed wood) ceiling. The walls are crawling with Hebrew inscriptions, mostly taken from psalms. Inside, the **Museo Sefardí** is packed with artifacts, including a Torah (parts of which are over 400 years old) and a beautiful set of Sephardic wedding costumes. *(C. Samuel Levi.* ☎ *925 22 36 65. Open Tu-Sa 10am-2pm and 4-6pm, Su 10am-2pm. 400ptas, students and under 18 200ptas. Free Sa after 4pm and Su.)* **Sinagoga de Santa María la Blanca** (1180), down the street to the right, was originally built to be a mosque, but was then purchased by Jews and used as the city's principal synagogue; in 1492 it was converted into a church. Now secular, the Moorish arches and a tranquil garden make for a pleasant retreat. *(*☎ *925 22 72 57. Open daily June-Aug. 10am-2pm and 3:30-7pm; Sept.-May 10am-2pm and 3:30-6pm. 200ptas.)*

MONASTERIO DE SAN JUAN DE LOS REYES. At the far western edge of the city, with views of the surrounding hills and Río Tajo, stands the Franciscan Monasterio de San Juan de los Reyes, commissioned by Isabel and Fernando to commemorate their victory over the Portuguese in the Battle of Toro (1476). The light-filled cloister, covered with the initials of the *Reyes Católicos,* mixes Gothic and Mudéjar architecture. An eclectic combination that contrasts with the very Gothic Plateresque church interior. The Catholic monarchs had planned to use the church as their burial place but changed their minds after their victory over Granada. *(*☎ *925 22 38 02. Open daily June-Aug. 10am-2pm and 3:30-6pm; Sept.-May until 5pm. 200ptas.)*

REMEMBERING SEPHARAD When Toledo fell to Alfonso VI in 1085, Jewish culture blossomed under his tolerant reign. Jewish poets (including Yehuda Ha Leví), doctors, translators, and bankers rose to prominence, occasionally intermarrying with noble Christian families and serving in royal courts. This period of *toledancia*—a pun on Toledo and tolerance—did not last. Mounting nationalism and anti-Semitism during the 1492 Inquisition led to persecution, forced conversion, expulsion, and, at times, even holocaust. Today, only two of eight synagogues remain in what was once Spain's largest Jewish community (Sepharad). Jews of *toledano* descent, some of whom still speak *Ladino*, a variation on 15th-century Spanish, have recently reappeared: a Jewish-American woman made headlines when she entered a Toledo home with the same key her ancestors had used 500 years before.

OTHER SIGHTS. Toledo was the seat of Visigoth rule and culture for three centuries prior to the 711 Muslim invasion. The **Museo del Taller del Moro,** on C. Bulas near Iglesia de Santo Tomé, features outstanding woodwork, plasterwork, and tiles. *(Taller de Moro, 200. ☎ 925 22 45 00. Open Tu-Sa 10am-2pm and 4-6:30pm, Su 10am-2pm. 100ptas.)* The exhibits at the **Museo de los Concilios y de la Cultura Visigótica** pale in comparison to their beautiful setting in a 13th-century Mudéjar church. *(C. San Clemente, 4. ☎ 925 22 78 72. Open Tu-Sa 10am-2pm and 4-6:30pm, Su 10am-2pm. 100ptas, students 50ptas.)* The impressive and untouristed **Museo de Santa Cruz** (1504) exhibits a handful of El Grecos in its eclectic art collection. Oddly enough, it also holds the remains from archaeological digs throughout the province. *(C. Cervantes, 3, off Pl. Zocodóver. ☎ 925 22 10 36. Open M 10am-2pm and 4-6:30pm, Tu-Sa 10am-6:30pm, Su 10am-2pm. 200ptas, students 100ptas.)*

🐱🎵 NIGHTLIFE AND ENTERTAINMENT

For **nightlife**, try C. Santa Fé, east of Pl. Zocodóver, through the arch. It's filled to the brim with beer and local youth. Look for **Enebro,** tucked away on small Pl. Santiago Caballeros off C. Cervantes whose claim to fame is free *tapas* in the evenings. *(☎ 925 22 21 11. Beer 300ptas. No cover. Open until 3am.)* C. Sillería and C. Alfileritos, west of Pl. Zocodóver, are home to more upscale bars and clubs, including **Bar La Abadía,** Nuñez de Arce, 5, with its cavernous stone-walled basement and well-dressed clientele. *(☎ 925 25 11 40. Open M-Th 8am-midnight, F-Su noon-midnight).* **Zaida,** in the Centro Comercial Miradero, downhill on C. Armas, is a perennial hot spot for dancing. Primped 20-somethings pour in around midnight. *(No cover. Open daily 9pm-5am.)* Toledo goes crazy for **Corpus Christi** (8th Su after Easter), when citizens parade the streets with the cathedral's gold monstrance.

🚌 DAYTRIPS FROM TOLEDO

CONSUEGRA (1¼HR.)

Samar buses (☎ 925 22 39 15) leave from the Toledo bus station (1¼hr.; M-F 11 per day 9:15am-7:30pm, Sa 4 per day 9am-5:30pm, Su 3 per day 10:30am-11pm; 545ptas). Buses return to Toledo from C. Castilla de la Mancha (1¼hr.; M-F 9 per day 6:10am-5:55pm, Sa 4 per day 7:10am-1:25pm, Su 3 per day 7:10am-6:10pm). Buy tickets from the driver when returning from Consuegra; in Toledo, buy them at the ticket office.

Of all Manchegan villages, tiny **Consuegra** provides perhaps the most raw material for an evocation of Quijote's world. The village **castle,** called *Crestería Manchega* by locals, was a Roman, then Arab, then Castilian fortress. It keeps erratic hours, but the view of the surrounding plains justifies a climb any time. El Cid's only son, Diego, died in the stable; you can visit a lavish monument in his honor near the Ayuntamiento. Though small, Consuegra is home to a palace, a Franciscan convent, and a Carmelite monastery. Learn more at the **Museo de Consuegra,** next to the Ayuntamiento. *(☎ 925 47 37 31. Hours not fixed. 100ptas.)* Plan around inconvenient bus departure times so you don't have to spend the night.

DRIVING SOUTH

The following places are not on a public transportation route, but Don Quijote buffs will love them, and they break up the monotony of driving through dry, sun-scorched plains.

A hop, skip, and a jump south of Toledo lands you at the small **San Martín de Montalbán,** home to an amazing castle poised on an enormous pile of gray granite rocks and leaning out over an abysmal gorge of the River Torión. The castle was first Visigothic territory, then an Arab fortress, and later an enclave of the cabalistic Knights Templar. Legend has it that a buried treasure is hidden inside the walls.

Cervantes freaks come to La Mancha to follow in the footsteps of the writer and his characters. Cervantes met and married Catalina de Palacios in the main church in **Esquivias** in 1584 and supposedly began writing his masterpiece while imprisoned in the **Cueva del Medrano,** in the town of **Argamasilla de Alba.** It was in **El Toboso,** 100km southeast of Toledo, that Quijote fell in love with Dulcinea. El Toboso is also home to the **Casa Cervantes,** which displays Cervantes memorabilia, including translations of *Don Quijote* in 30 different languages. (Pl. Cervantes. ☎ 925 52 01 61. Open Sa 10am-2pm. Visits by appointment M-F. 925ptas.)

ALMAGRO

Theater buffs and city slickers seeking quiet and solace will find sleepy Almagro appealing. For most of the year, the life of this small town (pop. 9000) belongs to the locals. But for three weeks in July, a classical theater festival of international renown attracts hundreds of visitors to walk down the cobblestone streets alongside the brightly whitewashed houses and 16th-century theatrical monuments.

📠 **TRANSPORTATION. Trains** run to: **Ciudad Real** (15min., 4 per day 8:41am-9:01pm, 290ptas); **Aranjuez** (2hr., 2 per day, 1605ptas); and **Madrid-Atocha** (2¾hr., 4 per day 9:20am-9:50pm, 1790ptas). Change at Ciudad Real for Córdoba, Sevilla, Granada, Valencia, and other major cities. **Buses** (☎ 926 86 02 50), which are cheaper and more convenient, stop at a brick building at the far end of Ejido de Calatrava, left of the Hospedería Municipal de Almagro. **AISA** buses leave for **Ciudad Real,** the connection point for most other major cities (20min.; M-F 8 per day 8am-6:15pm, Sa 3 per day 9:15am-2:30pm; 230ptas) and **Madrid** (2¼hr., M-F 5 per day 7am-4pm, 1600ptas). The bus station is closed on Sundays. The schedule is not well-documented, so it is advisable to always check the transportation listings.

📠📱 **ORIENTATION AND PRACTICAL INFORMATION.** The train station (☎ 926 86 02 76) is outside the city center, at the end of the tree-lined Po. Estación. To get from the station to the Plaza Mayor, walk down Po. Estación and turn left onto C. Rondo de Calatrava; turn right onto C. Madre de Dios (a sign points to the Centro Urbano), which becomes C. Feria and leads to the plaza. To get to Pl. Mayor from the bus station, turn left on C. Madre de Dios (follow the sign to the Centro Urbano) and take the road straight to the plaza.

The **tourist office,** C. Bernardas, 2, is inside the newly renovated Palacio del Conde de Valdeparaíso, though only the courtyard and tourist office are open to the public. From Pl. Mayor, take a right on C. Mayor de Carnicerías and another right on C. Bernardas. No one speaks English, but they do have brochures for the entire region of Castilla La Mancha and the only contemporary map of Almagro. (☎ 926 86 07 17. Open Apr.-June and Sept. Tu-F 10am-2pm and 5-8pm, Sa 11am-2pm and 5-8pm, Su 11am-2pm; July-Aug. same hours except Tu-F and Sa 6-9pm; Oct.-Mar. same hours except Tu-F 5-7pm, Sa 10am-2pm and 4-6pm.) A **Banco Central Hispano** sits at the corner of Pl. Mayor and C. Mayor de Carnicerías. (☎ 902 24 24 24. Open Apr.-Sept. M-F 8:30am-2:30pm; Oct.-Mar. same hours plus Sa 8:30am-1pm.) An **ATM** is right outside the bank. Fresh fruits and veggies are sold at the outdoor **market.** From the Pl. Mayor, walk down C. de San Agustín for one block. Turn left on C. Mercado until you arrive at the entrance (open Tu-W and F-Su 8am-2pm). In an **emergency,** call ☎ 926 86 00 33; **police** are at C. Mercado, 1 (☎ 609 01 41 36), adjacent to Pl. Mayor. Find the **Centro de Salud (health clinic)** at C. Mayor de Carnicerías, 11 (☎ 926 86 10 26). **Public telephones** can be found inside the tourist office. The **post office** is on C. Mayor de Carnicerías across from Caja Rural. (☎ 926 86 00 52. Open M-F 8:30am-2:30pm, Sa 9:30am-1pm.) The **postal code** is 13270.

▌▛▟ ACCOMMODATIONS AND FOOD. The spacious, dark hallways and high ceilings of **Hospedería Municipal de Almagro,** Ejido de Calátrava (☎ 926 88 20 87; fax 926 88 21 22), resemble the austere decor of the monastery to which it is attached. Most rooms overlook a grand courtyard filled with singing birds, though the voices of diners below can be heard just as well. Clean bathrooms, phones, and TVs provide for a comfortable stay. Make reservations months ahead for the theater festival. (Aug.-June singles with bath 3000ptas; doubles with shower 4000ptas, with bath 5000ptas. July singles 3500ptas.; doubles with bath 5000ptas, with shower 6000ptas. V, MC.) Pl. Mayor has many restaurants with outdoor seating. Locals stop to snack or have lunch at **La Encajera,** C. Mercado 1. The dining room is reserved for special events in the evenings. From Pl. Mayor, follow C. de San Agustín to C. Mercado and turn left. (☎ 926 86 07 97. *Menú* 1000ptas.)

▟▛ SIGHTS AND ENTERTAINMENT. Every July, prestigious theater companies and players from around the world descend on Almagro for the **Festival Internacional de Teatro Clásico de Almagro** (July 6-30 in 2001). Daily performances of Spanish and international classics take place in the Corral de Comedias, Teatro Hospital de San Juan de Dios, Teatro Municipal, Claustro de los Domínicos, Teatro Infantil, Teatro en la Calle, and Seminarios. The **box office** is in the Palacio de los Medrano, C. San Agustín, 7. (☎ 902 10 12 12. Open May-June Th 11am-1:30pm; July daily 11:30am-2pm and 7-10:30pm.) There are daily shows in July at 10:45pm; tickets are 1700-2300ptas (Tu half-price) and should be purchased before the festival. (V, MC accepted by phone.) The festival also has an office in Madrid at C. Principe, 14 (☎ 91 521 07 20), and the 2001 program is listed at www.festivaldealmagro.com.

The center of Almagro, the **Plaza Mayor,** is also the cultural hub. There you can find the **Corral de Comedias,** an open-air multilevel theater resembling Shakespeare's Globe. This theater is the only one left intact from the "Golden Age" of Spanish drama. Here, performers act out the works of such literary masters as Cervantes and Lope de Vega. (☎ 926 86 15 39. Open Apr.-June and Sept. Tu-F 10am-2pm and 5-8pm, Sa 11am-2pm and 5-8 pm, Su 11am-2pm and 4-6pm; July-Aug. same hours except Tu-F 6-9pm, Sa 10am-2pm and 6-9pm, Su 5-7pm; Oct.-Mar. same hours except Tu-F 5-7pm, Sa 10am-2pm and 4-6pm, Su 6-8pm. 1200ptas.) Directly across the plaza from the *corral* and through some arches, the new **Museo Nacional del Teatro** displays the history of Spanish drama. (☎/fax 926 88 22 44. Open Apr.-June and Sept. Tu-F 10am-2pm and 4-6pm, Sa 11am-2pm and 5-8 pm, Su 11am-2pm; July-Aug. same hours except Tu-F 6-9pm, Sa 6-8pm; Oct.-Mar. same hours except Tu-F 5-7pm, Sa 4-6pm. 400ptas, groups 200ptas, seniors and under 18 free. Sa afternoon and Su free.) The final stop on the theater tour is the **Teatro Municipal,** C. San Agustín, 20. Follow C. San Agustín out of Pl. Mayor and look for a crimson building on the right. Inside is a renovated theater as well as a collection of elaborate costumes. (☎ 926 86 13 61. Open Apr.-June and Sept. Tu-F 10am-2pm and 5-8pm, Sa 11am-2pm and 5-8pm, Su 11am-2pm; July-Aug. same hours except Tu-F 6-9pm, Sa 10am-2pm and 6-9pm; Oct.-Mar. same hours except Tu-F 5-7pm, Sa 10am-2pm and 4-6pm. Museo Nacional ticket allows entrance to all three sights.)

CUENCA

Cuenca (pop. 47,000) owes its fame to its location. Perched atop a hill, the vertical city is surrounded by two rivers and the stunning rock formations they have created. These natural boundaries have served the city well; Muslims and then Christians settled in Cuenca because it was nearly impenetrable. Yet Cuenca strains against its borders, forcing much of the city's modern commercial life to spill down the hill into New Cuenca. The enchanting old city, however, safeguards most of Cuenca's unique charm, including the famed *casas colgadas* (hanging houses) that dangle high above the Río Huécar.

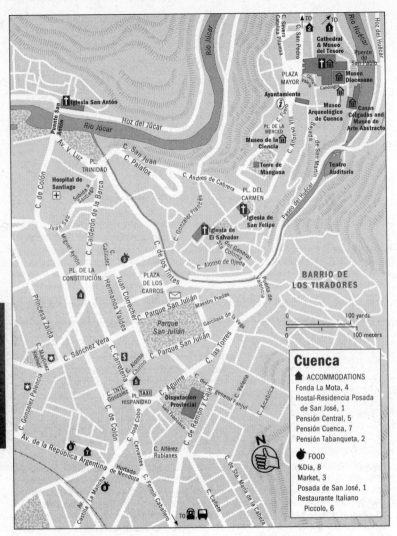

Cuenca

🏠 ACCOMMODATIONS

Fonda La Mota, 4
Hostal-Residencia Posada
de San José, 1
Pensión Central, 5
Pensión Cuenca, 7
Pensión Tabanqueta, 2

🍴 FOOD

%Dia, 8
Market, 3
Posada de San José, 1
Restaurante Italiano
Piccolo, 6

⎘ TRANSPORTATION

Trains: (☎ 902 24 02 02), Po. Ferrocarril, in the new city. To: **Aranjuez** (2hr., 5-6 per day 7:05am-6:55pm, 1020ptas); **Madrid** (2½-3hr., 5-6 per day 7:05am-6:55pm, 1405ptas); and **Valencia** (3-4hr., 4 per day 7:40am-6:40pm, 1545ptas).

Buses: (☎ 969 22 70 87; call **Auto Res** at ☎ 969 22 11 84 for prices), C. Fermín Caballero. To **Madrid** (2½hr.; 7 per day M-Sa 7:30am-8pm, Su 7:30am-10pm; 1325-1615ptas). **AISA** to **Toledo** (3hr., M-F 5:30am, 1620ptas). **SIAL** to **Barcelona** (3½hr., M-Sa 9:30am, 4320ptas).

Taxis: Radio-Taxi (☎ 969 23 33 43). From the train station to Pl. Mayor 500-600ptas.

✈ ⑦ ORIENTATION AND PRACTICAL INFORMATION

When you exit the train station, the back of the bus station is right in front of you; head up the steps to C. Fermín Caballero and turn right. To get to Plaza Mayor in the old city from either station, go left until you hit the first bus shelter and catch bus #1 or 2; the old city's the last stop (every 20min.; 7:20am-10:10pm, July-Aug. until 11pm; 85ptas). To reach Pl. Mayor by foot, take a left from the bus station along C. Fermín Caballero, which becomes C. Cervantes, then C. José Cobo, and finally (after passing through Pl. Hispanidad) **Calle Carretería,** the town's main drag. From here, turn right on C. Fray Luis de León and head upward; it's a grueling walk to Pl. Mayor and the old city (20-25min.).

Municipal Tourist Office (☎ 969 23 21 19), Pl. Mayor, opposite the Ayuntamiento. Brochures, maps, hiking and excursion routes, an interactive computer, and lots of info about the events in town. Some English spoken. Open daily July-Aug. 10:30am-2pm and 4:30-7:30pm; Sept.-June every day 10am-2pm and 4-6:30pm.

Currency Exchange: Banco Central Hispano, C. Carretería, 23 (☎ 969 211 726). **ATM.** Apr.-Sept. M-F 8:30am-2:30pm; Oct.-Mar. M-F 8:30am-2:30pm, Sa 8:30am-1pm.

Luggage Storage: At the **train station** (400ptas per day; open daily 7am-9:30pm) and the **bus station** (200ptas per day; open daily M-F 7am-10pm, Sa-Su 7am-9pm).

Emergency: ☎ 112. **Police:** ☎ 091 or 092. C. Martínez Kleyser, 4 (☎ 969 22 48 59).

Pharmacy: Farmacia Castellanos, C. Cervantes, 20 (☎ 969 21 23 37), located at the corner of C. Alferez Rubianes. A list of late-night pharmacies posted in the window.

Post Office: Parque de San Julián, 16 (☎ 969 22 90 16). Open M-F 8:30am-8:30pm, Sa 9:30am-2pm. Smaller **branch** with fewer services right next to **RENFE** station. Open M-F 8:30am-2:30pm, Sa 9:30am-1pm. **Postal Code:** for the large post office, 16004.

Internet Access: La Repro, C. Jorge Torner, 39 (☎ 969 24 01 36). From the bus station, take C. Fermín Caballero toward the city center; turn right at the 1st stop light, walking up C. Julio Larrañaga 1 block. It's on the corner at the 1st left. 200ptas per 20min., 400ptas per 20min.-1hr. Open M-F 9:30am-2pm and 5-8:30pm, Sa 10:30am-2pm.

▌ ACCOMMODATIONS

The lack of cheap accommodations in the old city is made up for by the abundance in the new city. Slightly pricier rooms on the hill tempt with spectacular views. Both tourist offices have a complete list of places to stay.

▨ **Hostal-Residencia Posada de San José,** C. Julián Romero, 4 (☎ 969 21 13 00; fax 969 23 03 65), a block up from the cathedral. Cash in that extra traveler's check for cushy beds, historic echoes (it's a 17th-century convent), and gorgeous views. Rustic, attractive rooms with modern, tiled baths. Let loose with *sangría* (850ptas) on the terrace. Singles 2600ptas, with full bath 4400ptas; doubles 4400ptas, with bath 8600ptas; triples 5900ptas, with bath 11,600ptas. IVA not included. V, MC, AmEx.

▨ **Pensión Tabanqueta,** C. Trabuco, 13 (☎ 969 21 12 90). Head up C. San Pedro from the cathedral; it turns into C. Trabuco after Pl. Trabuco. Rooms on the side of the gorge have a fabulous view, sinks, and cheerful covers. The bar below with its popular terrace shouldn't be missed. One single 2000ptas; doubles 4000ptas; triples 6000ptas.

Pensión Cuenca, Av. República Argentina, 8, 2nd fl. (☎ 969 21 25 74), in the new city. Take C. Fermín Caballero from the bus station to the intersection; the street to the left is C. Hurtado de Mendoza, which becomes Av. República Argentina. Smallish rooms have good beds, new furniture, and sinks. Amiable owners almost as great as the TV lounge. Singles 1800ptas, with shower 2100ptas; doubles 2700ptas, with shower 3800ptas.

Fonda La Mota, Pl. Constitución, 7, 1st fl. (☎ 969 22 55 67), at the end of C. Carretería. Cheerful modern rooms have sparkling bathrooms, new mattresses, and TVs. Breakfast 250ptas. Doubles with sink 4000ptas, with bath 5500ptas. Singles occasionally available in winter.

Pensión Central, C. Alonso Chirino, 7, 2nd fl. (☎ 969 21 15 11), off C. Carretería. Clean, old-fashioned rooms with big windows and high ceilings. Be prepared to wait in line for the common bathroom. Breakfast 200ptas. Lunch or dinner 900ptas. July-Aug. singles 1800ptas; doubles 3000; triples 4300ptas. Sept.-June singles 1600ptas; doubles 2700ptas; triples 4000ptas.

🍴 FOOD

Restaurants around Pl. Mayor are expensive and mediocre. Budget eateries line C. Cervantes and C. República Argentina, but the cafes off C. Fray Luis de León are even cheaper. *Resoli*, a liqueur of coffee, sugar, orange peel, and eau-de-vie, and *alajú*, a nougat of honey, almonds, and figs, will give you something to smile about. The **market** is on C. Fray Luis de León (open daily 8:30am-2pm). **Groceries** are available at **%Día,** Av. Castilla La Mancha at Av. República Argentina (open M-Th 9:30am-2pm and 5:30-8:30pm, F-Sa 9am-2:30pm and 5:30-9pm).

Posada de San José, C. Julián Romero, 4 (☎ 969 21 13 00). Interior with wood beams, earthenware pots, and an outdoor wood terrace with spectacular views. Soak in the ambiance with delicious regional *tapas* or a great salad for 2 (900ptas). Wonderful *pisto* (stew made of tomatoes, peppers, and onions; 575ptas). *Bocadillos* and omelettes 400-600ptas. Open Tu-Su 8am-11am and 7-11pm. V, MC, AmEx.

Restaurante Italiano Piccolo, Av. República Argentina, 14 (☎ 969 23 20 35). The old photos and prints that cover the walls of this cheerful *trattoria* will bring you back to another era. Wide range of great pizzas 850-1100ptas. Pastas 875-1200ptas. *Menú* 1350ptas (M-F, lunch only). Open Th-Tu. V, MC, AmEx.

👁 SIGHTS

▨ **CASAS COLGADAS.** Cuenca draws its fame from the gravity-defying *casas colgadas* (see **Living on the Edge,** below) that dangle over the riverbanks as precariously today as they did six centuries ago. In his memoirs, Surrealist filmmaker Luis Buñuel recalls a pre-war visit to one of the *casas*, in which he spied birds flying beneath the toilet seat. Walk across the Puente de San Pablo bridge (not for anyone suffering from vertigo) at sunset to get a spectacular view of the *casas* and the surrounding cliffs. Two hiking trails along the Hoz del Júcar and Hoz del Huécar (the steep river gorges on either side of the narrow old city) present fantastic views of perched Cuenca. Maps are available from the municipal tourist office.

MUSEO DE ARTE ABSTRACTO ESPAÑOL. Inside one of the *casas*, the award-winning Museo de Arte Abstracto Español displays important works by the wacky and internationally-renowned "Abstract Generation" of Spanish painters. All pieces were chosen by artist Fernando Zóbel, one of the school's major figures. The well-designed museum exhibits works by Canogar, Tápies, Chillida, and Zóbel himself. Don't miss the "White Room" upstairs. Striking views of the gorge are an added plus. *(Pl. Ciudad de Ronda. ☎ 969 21 29 83. Open Tu-F and holidays 11am-2pm and 4-6pm, Sa 11am-2pm and 4-8pm, Su 11am-2:30pm. 500ptas, students 250ptas.)*

LIVING ON THE EDGE Very little is known about Cuenca's unique 14th-century *casas colgadas*. They were supposedly built to house kings; one is even named Casa del Rey. Casa de la Sirena, the only other remaining original hanging house, got its name from the siren-like screams emitted by a Cuenca *señorita* when she flung herself out of the window after her son was killed by her lover. Despite their striking appearance, the *casas* did not become famous until recently. Indeed, the *casas* were completely run down when the city of Cuenca decided to rehabilitate them early in this century, transforming them into magnificent museums. Now one of Central Spain's greatest tourist attractions, they draw thousands of visitors each year.

CATHEDRAL. The cathedral, constructed under Alfonso VIII six years after he conquered Castile, dominates Pl. Mayor. A perfect square, 25m on each side, it is the only Anglo-Norman Gothic cathedral in Spain. A Spanish Renaissance facade and tower were added in the 16th and 17th centuries, only to be torn down when deemed aesthetically inappropriate. A 1724 fire prevented a subsequent attempt to build a front, leaving the current exterior incomplete and strangely reminiscent of a Hollywood set. Wonderfully colorful stained-glass windows illuminate the entrance like a sunset. Inside, the **Museo del Tesoro** houses some late medieval psalters and much gold jewelry. More impressive is the **Sala Capitular** and its delightful ceiling. (Cathedral open June-Aug. 11am-2pm and 4-6pm; Sept.-May 10:30am-2pm and 4-6pm. Mass 9:20am. Free. Museum open Tu-Su daily 11am-2pm and 4-6pm. 200ptas.)

OTHER SIGHTS. Down C. Obispo Valero, the **Museo Arqueológico de Cuenca** is a treasure trove of archaeological finds, including Roman mosaics, ceramics, coins, and excellent Visigoth jewelry. (☎ 969 21 30 69. Open Tu-Sa 10am-2pm and 5-7pm, Su 11am-2pm. 200ptas, students 100ptas.; Sa afternoon and Su free.) Perhaps the most beautiful of the museums along this street is the **Museo Diocesano**, whose exhibits include Juan de Borgoña's altarpiece from local Convento de San Pablo, many colossal Flemish tapestries, splendid rugs, and two El Grecos—Oración del huerto and Cristo con la cruz. (☎ 969 22 42 10. Open July-Aug. Tu-Sa 11am-2pm and 5-8pm, Su 11am-2pm; Sept.-June Tu-Sa 11am-2pm and 4-6pm, Su 11am-2pm. 300ptas.)

🎵 ENTERTAINMENT

New Cuenca's nighttime bar scene extends into the wee hours of the morning. Several bars with loud music and young, snazzily dressed crowds line small C. Galíndez, off C. Fray Luis de León, a long, dark walk down the hill from Old Cuenca; a taxi will be about 500ptas. Check out the bar under **Pensión Tabanqueta** on C. Trabuco. For more nightlife, take the winding street/staircase just off Pl. Mayor across from the cathedral toward the Río Júcar, where you'll encounter an army of empty bottles. Cuenca rings with song during the **Festival of Religious Music,** a famous international celebration the week before Semana Santa.

SIGÜENZA

Perched on a hill in what seems to be the middle of nowhere, sleepy Sigüenza (pop. 5000) is small-town Spain at its best. Pinkish stone buildings and red-roofed houses cluster around a storybook Gothic cathedral and castle, and tourists come in trickles rather than droves. During the Civil War, the Republicans seized the cathedral and the Nationalists the castle, making for one hell of a shoot-out. Fortunately, Sigüenza's medieval architecture has been painstakingly restored.

🛈 PRACTICAL INFORMATION. The **train station** (☎ 949 39 14 94 or 608 62 38 85) is at the end of Av. Alfonso VI. Trains run to: **Soria** (30min., 5 per day 9:51am-8:38pm, 800ptas); **Madrid** (1½-2hr., 11 per day 5:19am-8pm, 1700ptas); and **Zaragoza** (2hr., 3 per day 10am-4pm, 2200ptas). For a **taxi** call ☎ 949 39 14 11. To get to the **tourist office** follow Av. Alfonso VI to the first intersection after the Parque de la Alameda, which is on the left. The office is just around the corner to the left in the restored Ermita and has a list of accommodations. (☎ 949 34 70 07. Open Tu-F 10am-2pm and 4:30-7pm, Sa-Su 9am-2:30pm and 4:30-7pm.) Across the intersection sits **Banco Hispano Central,** Av. Calvo Siteco, 9 (open M-F 8:30am-2:30pm). **Store luggage** at the train station until midnight (300ptas). Services include: **emergency** (☎ 949 30 00 19); **Red Cross** (☎ 949 39 13 33), Ctra. Madrid; **police** (☎ 949 39 01 95), Ctra. de Atienzo; and the **post office,** C. Villaviciosa, 10, off Pl. Hilario Yabén. (☎ 949 39 08 44. Open M-F 8:30am-2:30pm, Sa 9:30am-1pm.) The **postal code** is 19250.

ACCOMMODATIONS AND FOOD. Although you can "do" Sigüenza in a couple of hours, it can be a fun place to spend the night. **Pensión Venancio,** C. San Roque, 3, is charming. From the station, follow Av. Alfonso VI, turn left at the first intersection onto Av. Pio XII, then take the first right. (☎ 949 39 03 47. Singles 2400ptas; doubles 3400ptas; triples 5400ptas.) Cheap places to eat are everywhere. **Restaurante El Mesón,** Roman Pascual, 14, has entrees for 400-1700ptas. (☎ 949 39 06 49. Open 11:30am-3:30pm. Visa.) **Canfran Muela,** C. Cardenal Mendoza, 2, sells groceries (open M-Sa 9am-2pm and 5-8pm).

SIGHTS. The tourist office offers guided tours of the city, including entrance to all parts of the cathedral, for 800ptas. From the bottom of the hill, two buildings jut out from Sigüenza's low skyline: the cathedral and the fortified **castle,** a 12th-century castle-turned-*parador* (luxury hotel). Restored in the 1970s, the castle merits an uphill stroll through the cobblestone streets, if just to peek in at the luxuriously decorated *parador,* and enjoy a marvelous view. To get to the magnificent **cathedral,** follow Av. Alfonso VI uphill (it changes to C. Humilladero), then take a left onto C. Cardenal Mendoza. Work on the cathedral began in the mid-12th century and continued until the 16th century; it combines Romanesque, Mudéjar, Plateresque, and Gothic styles. One of the structure's most renowned features is the 15th-century Tumba del Doncel, commissioned by Isabel in memory of a favorite page who died fighting the Muslims in Granada. The sacristy's elaborate Renaissance ceiling boasts 304 stone portraits carved by Alanso de Covarrubias. The faces belong to Christians and Moors, monks and countesses, dandies and dames. The adjoining chapel houses an El Greco, *Anunciación,* and a ceiling so magnificent that the church has a mirror on the floor to help you view it. (☎ 619 36 27 15. Open May-Nov. M-F 11am-1:30pm and 4:30-6:30pm, Sa-Su 10:30am-1:30pm and 5:30-6:30pm. Tours in Spanish 11am, noon, 12:45, 4:30, and 5:45pm. 300ptas. No entry during services unless you wish to participate.) Opposite the cathedral, the small **Museo de Arte Antiguo** (Museo Diocesano) has medieval and early modern religious works, including a Ribera and a Zurbarán. (☎ 949 39 10 23. Open Apr.-Sept. Tu-F noon-2pm and 4-5pm, Sa-Su 11am-2pm and 5-7pm. 200ptas.)

CASTILLA Y LEÓN

Castilla y León's hilltop cities emerge like islands from a sea of burnt sienna, as ridge-top homesteads, long and low, surrender to intricate stone masterpieces above. The monuments—the majestic Gothic cathedrals of Burgos and León, the slender Romanesque belfries along León's Camino de Santiago, the intricate sandstone of Salamanca, and the proud city walls of Ávila—have emblazoned themselves as regional and national images.

Well before Castilla's famous 1469 confederation with Aragón, when Fernando of Aragón and Isabel of Castilla were united in world-shaking matrimony, it was clear that Castilla had its act together. In the High Middle Ages, the region emerged from obscurity to lead the Christian charge against Islam. Castilian nobles, sanguine from the spoils of combat, introduced the concept of a unified Spain (under Castilian command, of course), and *castellano* ("Spanish") became the dominant language throughout the nation. Imperious León, Castilla's comrade in arms, though chagrined to be lumped with Castilla in a 1970s provincial reorganization, has much in common with its co-province.

Castilian gastronomy favors red meats and vegetables such as potatoes (which can be grown in relatively cold climates). One favorite is *cocido castellano*, a stew of beef, ham, potatoes, sausage, carrots, and garlic. Castilians also tend to get hyperbolically excited about their lamb dishes.

HIGHLIGHTS OF CASTILLA Y LEÓN

Segovia's impressive **Alcázar** (palace) and hulking **aqueduct** (see below).

The spectacular manicured **gardens** at **La Granja** (see p. 147).

Ávila, the best preserved medieval walled city in Europe (see p. 147).

The lovely Plateresque architecture of the **University of Salamanca** (see p. 155).

Burgos's imposing **Gothic cathedral,** Spain's biggest and best (see p. 174).

LOCAL FESTIVALS IN CASTILLA Y LEÓN

Women take over the town for a day during **Segovia's** *Fiestas de Santa Agueda,* one big men-parodying party (Feb. 5). **Ávila** carries giant effigies on parade to honor Santa Theresa (week of Oct. 15), and the *Fiestas de Verano* bring singing, dancing, fireworks, and a bullfight to the quiet town. From September 8 to 21, festivals and exhibitions flood **Salamanca,** which also continues to remember *Lunes de Agua,* a medieval celebration in honor of the return of the town prostitutes after their Lent banishment. **Valladolid** hosts an *International Cinema Week* in October, **Burgos** brings out a 12th-century banner stolen from the Moors to celebrate *Corpus Christi,* and **Soria's** version of *Fiestas de San Juan* includes a unique twist: running with bulls and eating them that same night.

SEGOVIA

Legend has it that the devil built the famed aqueduct in Segovia (pop. 55,000) in one night, in an effort to win the soul of a Segovian water-seller named Juanilla. When the shocked Juanilla woke up to find the aqueduct almost completed, she prayed to the Virgin Mary, who made the sun rise a bit earlier in order to foil the Devil's scheme. Segovia's aqueduct may not have won Juanilla's soul, but it has intrigued visitors ever since Roman times. During its period of greatest prosperity, in the 12th and 13th centuries, Segovia had the most Romanesque monuments in Europe, and the remaining cathedrals and castles represent Castilla at its finest. The surrounding countryside can be breathtaking, and old-town character oozes from Segovia's twisted alleys, fruit stands, and footpaths. As always, pleasure has its price; prices for food and accommodations are much higher here than in Madrid. On the far side of the Sierra de Guadarrama, Segovia is close enough to the capital to be a daytrip but definitely warrants a longer stay.

⎡ TRANSPORTATION

Trains: (☎ 921 42 07 74), Po. Obispo Quesada. Only one line, the Segovia-Madrid regional. To **Madrid** (2hr., 9 per day, 850ptas) and **Villalba** (1hr.; 550ptas; halfway along the same line, transfer point for El Escorial, Ávila, León, and Salamanca). The bus is usually a better bet unless you're coming directly from the Madrid airport.

Buses: Estacionamiento Municipal de Autobuses, Po. Ezequiel González, 12 (☎ 921 42 77 07), at the corner of Av. Fernández Ladreda. To: **La Granja** (20min., 10-14 per day 7:40am-9:30pm, round-trip 210ptas); **Ávila** (1hr.; M-F 6 per day 7:45am-7:30pm, Sa-Su 10:30am and 2pm 555ptas); **Madrid** (1½hr., every 30min. 6:30am-10:15pm, 825ptas); **Valladolid** (2hr.; M-F 11 per day, Sa-Su 6-8 per day, 9am-9pm; 870ptas); and **Salamanca** (3hr., 3 per day, 1280ptas).

Public Transportation: Transportes Urbanos de Segovia, Pl. Mayor, 8 (☎ 921 46 03 29). Buses 100ptas.

Taxis: Radio Taxi (☎ 921 44 50 00). Taxis pull up by the train and bus stations.

Car Rental: Avis, C. José Zorrilla, 123 (☎ 921 42 25 84).

◼◪ ORIENTATION AND PRACTICAL INFORMATION

To get to **Plaza Mayor,** the city's historic center and site of the **tourist office,** take any bus from the train station (100ptas). On weekdays, some buses go only as far as Po. del Salón, in which case go left up the steps of **Puerta del Sol,** turn right on C.

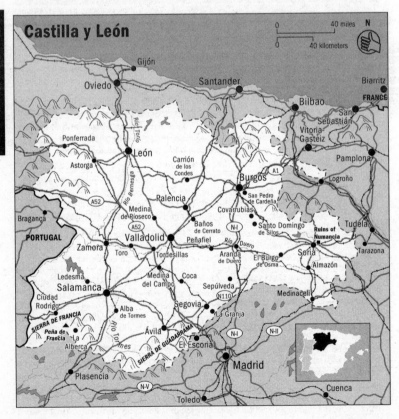

Castilla y León

Judería Vieja, and make the first left onto C. Isabel La Católica up to the plaza. For the fastest route from the **bus station** to Pl. Mayor, make a left from the station onto C. Ezekiel González and walk until you get to the first round intersection with a statue. Turn right onto C. Puente de Sancti Spiritus, and take the stairs up to the park. Cross the park and go up the steps of Pta. Sol. Turn right on C. Judería Vieja, and make the first left onto C. Isabel La Catolica up to the plaza (15min.).

The city is impossible to navigate without a map. Locals describe it as the "Stone Ship," with the Alcázar as the bow, the aqueduct the stern, and the cathedral the towering mainmast. Both Pl. Mayor (10min.) and the Alcázar (20min.) are uphill from Pl. de Azoguejo, next to the **aqueduct.** Pedestrian thoroughfare **Calle Isabel la Católica-Calle Juan Bravo-Calle Cervantes** runs between Pl. Mayor and Pl. Azoguejo.

Tourist Office: Regional Office, Pl. Mayor, 10 (☎ 921 46 03 34; fax 921 46 03 30), in front of the bus stop on the corner opposite the cathedral. Complete info on accommodations, bus and train schedules, and sights posted in the windows. Indispensable map. Open M-F 10am-2pm and 5-7pm, Sa-Su 10am-2pm and 5-8pm. **Municipal Office,** Pl. Azoguejo, 1 (☎ 921 46 11 36; fax 921 46 04 92), at the foot of the steps leading to the top of the aqueduct. Open daily 10am-8pm.

Currency Exchange: Find **banks** on Av. Fernández Ladreda and **ATMs** on Pl. Azoguejo.

Luggage Storage: Lockers at the **train station** (400ptas). Open daily 5:45am-10pm.

Emergency: Municipal Police, C. Guadarrama, 26 (☎ 921 43 12 12).

Medical Services: Hospital Policlínico, C. San Agustín, 13 (☎ 921 41 90 65).

Post Office: Pl. Dr. Laguna, 5 (☎ 921 43 16 11), up C. Cronista Lecea from Pl. Mayor. **Lista de Correos.** Open M-F 8:30am-8:30pm, Sa 9:30am-2pm. **Postal Code:** 40001.

Internet Access: Neociber, C. Santa Isabel, 10 (☎ 921 41 27 68), across from the "Sek-Tagore" sign. 100ptas for 15min., 400ptas per hr. Open M-Th 10:30am-2pm and 4-11pm, F-Sa 10:30am-2pm and 4pm-2am.

▚ ACCOMMODATIONS

Segovia graces many an itinerary, so finding a hostel during the summer can be difficult, especially on weekends. The tourist office's list of accommodations is valuable, but be prepared to pay 3500ptas or more for a single. The *pensiones* are significantly cheaper, but rooms tend to be on the less comfortable side of "basic."

Hostal Juan Bravo, C. Juan Bravo, 12, 2nd fl. (☎ 921 46 34 13), on the main thoroughfare in the old town, near Iglesia de San Martín. According to the owner, Segovia and her hostel both qualify as paradise. Given Juan Bravo's bright, newly renovated rooms, built-in closets, and spotless bathrooms, she might be right. Singles 4300-4700ptas; doubles 3900-4200ptas, with bath 4300-4700ptas; triples 5805-6345ptas. V, MC.

Residencia Juvenil "Emperador Teodosio" (HI), Av. Conde de Sepulveda, 4 (☎ 921 44 11 11 or 44 10 47). From the train station, go right, cross the street, and walk along Po. Obispo Quesada, which soon becomes Av. Conde de Sepúlveda (10min.). The hostel is on the left. From the bus station, go right on C. Ezequiel González, which becomes Av. Conde de Sepúlveda (10min.). The hostel is on the right. Modern amenities and hotel-like doubles and triples, all with private baths, make it nearly impossible to get a room. Same-day reservations only. 3-night max. stay. Dorms 1000ptas, with full meals 2200ptas; over 26 1450ptas, with full meals 3000ptas. Open July 1-Aug. 15.

Hostal Don Jaime, Ochoa Ondategui, 8 (☎ 921 44 47 87). Simple, modern rooms. Breakfast 375ptas. Singles 3200ptas; doubles 4500ptas, with bath 5600ptas; triples with bath 7000ptas. V, MC.

Pensión Ferri, C. Escuderos, 10 (☎ 921 46 09 57), off Pl. Mayor. 5 clean, small, centrally located rooms. Showers 300ptas. Singles 1600ptas; doubles 2500ptas.

CENTRAL SPAIN

Camping Acueducto, Ctra. Nacional, 601, km 112 (☎/fax 921 42 50 00), 2km toward La Granja. Take the AutoBus Urbano from Pl. Azoguejo to Nueva Segovia (100ptas). 2nd-class campsite. Hot showers. Laundry machines. July-Aug. 575ptas per person, per tent, and per car; Sept.-June 535ptas each.

☼ FOOD

Steer clear of Pl. Mayor, Pl. Azoguejo, and all signs on worn "medieval" parchment. *Sopa castellana* (soup with bread, eggs, and garlic), *cochinillo asado* (roast suckling pig), lamb, and *croquetas* are regional specialities. The many sights and steps of Segovia are ideal for picnicking; **fruit and vegetable stands** dot C. Juan Bravo and its neighboring streets, and a **market** graces Pl. de la Reina Dona Juana every Thursday morning until 2:30pm. Buy discount **groceries** at **%Día,** C. Fernández Jiménez, 3, off C. Fernández Ladreda (open M-Th 9:30am-2pm and 5:30-8:30pm, F-Sa 9am-2:30pm and 5:30-9pm).

■ **Restaurante La Almuzara,** C. Marqués del Arco, 3 (☎ 921 46 06 22), past the cathedral toward the Alcázar. Excellent vegetarian restaurant. Big salads 600-1400ptas. Entrees around 1100ptas. Open W-Su noon-5pm and 8pm-midnight, Tu 8pm-midnight.

Bar-Meson Cueva de San Esteban, C. Vadelaguila, 15 (☎ 921 46 09 82), off Pl. Esteaban and C. Escuderos. Swords, shields and meat deck the walls, while incredibly cheap and carefully prepared Castilian food covers the plates. Entrees 675ptas and up. Lunch *menú* 900ptas (IVA not included). Open daily 10am-11pm.

◉ SIGHTS

Segovia rewards the wanderer. Whether palace, church, house, or sidewalk, almost everything deserves close observation. Look for *esgrafía*, lacy patterns on the facades of buildings. Watching the summer sunset from the walls surrounding the Alcázar is a must. Also be sure to explore the northern parts of town, outside the walls and away from the Alcázar. For a long, relaxing walk, tour the less frequented monasteries and churches along the Río Eresma.

■ **AQUEDUCT.** Segovia's serpent-like aqueduct, built by the Romans around 50 BC to pipe in water for thirsty legions from the Río Frío 18km away, commands the entrance to the old city. Supported by 128 pillars that span 813m and reach a height of 28.9m near Pl. Azoguejo, the two tiers of 163 arches were constructed out of some 20,000 blocks of granite—without any mortar to hold them together. This spectacular feat of engineering, restored by the monarchy in the 15th century, can transport 30 liters of water per second and was used until the late 1940s. Construction has recently been started to restore the aqueduct to working form. *(From Pl. Mayor, go down C. Infanta Isabel, right on C. Herrería, and take C. Canalejas to Pl. del Seminario. Then go right on C. Conde de Gazola, left on C. Obispo Gandasegui and down the stone stairs.)*

■ **ALCÁZAR.** The Alcázar, an extremely well-preserved classic late-medieval castle, dominates the far northern end of the old quarter. The surrounding countryside and Queen Eugenia's gardens beg to be photographed. Fortifications have occupied this site since the time of the Celts, due to its strategic location at the intersection of two rivers. Alfonso X, who allegedly believed he was God, took the original 11th-century fortress and beautified it. Successive monarchs added to the Alcázar's grandeur, and the final touches were added for the 1774 coronation of Isabel I as Queen of Castilla. Tapestries, armor, thrones, sculptures, and paintings fill the castle, and the incredible ceilings will leave you with a stiff neck. The walls of the *Sala de Reyes* (royal room) are adorned with wood- and gold-inlaid friezes of monarchs. In the *Sala de Solio* (throne room), the inscription above the throne reads: *"tanto monta, monta tanto"* (she mounts, as does he). Get your mind out of the gutter—this means simply that Fernando and Isabel had equal authority as sovereigns. The strong and the restless climb the 140 steps up a nausea-inducing spiral staircase to the top of

CENTRAL SPAIN

C. de San Gabriel
TO MADRID
Santa Isabel
Soldado Español
C. de los Vargas
C. de Santa Catalina
C. de Antonio Coronel
C. de S. Lorenzo
San Lorenzo
C. del Pozo
C. del Tab.
C. de Padre Claret
Av. de Padre Claret
San Justo
Ochoa Ondátegui
PL. DE DIAZ SANZ
C. Mon Almira
C. de gascos
Via Roma
Via Roma
Acueducto Romano
C. Las Morenas
Monasterio de Santa Cruz la Real
C. de Encharpiedra
C. Cañuelo Zúñiga
C. Cardenal Zúñiga
San Juan de los Caballeros & Museo Zuloaga
Los Zuloaga
C. Taray
C. San Agustín
San Sebastián
Seminario Conciliar
PL. DEL AZOGUEJO
i
C. Ruiz de Alda
C. San Francisco
C. Gobr. F. Jiménez
Av. Fernández Ladreda
C. A. Marinas
C. de Los Molinos
Po. de la Alameda
Río Eresma
C. Doctor Velasco
C. San Bartolomé
C. San Nicolás
San Nicolás
C. D. Laguna
San Facundo
PL. DOCTOR LAGUNA
C. San Quirce
La Trinidad
C. Trinidad
C. Cabrerita
C. Colón
Herrería
Infanta Isabel
C. Martín Higuera
C. Pérez
Macranoja
C. Hildefonso Rodríguez
Museo de Arte Contemporáneo E. Vicente
PL. DEL SEMINARIO
Angosta
Grabador Espinosa
Casa de los Picos
Torreón de Lozoya
PL. ESPEJOS
Juan Bravo
San Martín
Palacio del Conde Alpuente
C. San Millán
San Millán
C. de Cervantes
C. de la Ochoa
C. de Sto. Domingo de Silos
Po. E. González
C. de la Piedad
Camino de la Piedad
Puente Sancti Espíritus
Paseo del Salón
Conista Lecea
Convento Corpus Cristi
Isabel la Católica
Judería Vieja
PL. MAYOR
Capuchinos Baja
PL. DE SAN ESTEBAN
C. Valdeláguila
C. Escuderos
Catedral
Puerta del Sol
Po. Los Tilos
C. San Valentín
Cuesta de Los Hoyos
Casa Museo de Antonio Machado
C. Marqués del Arco
C. del Pozuelo
Cuesta Doctoral
San Genebo
San Juan de la Cruz
Puerta de Santiago
Po. S. Domingo de Santiago
C. Puerta de Santiago
C. Velasco
San Andrés
PL. DE LA MERCED
Museo de Holografía
Museo de Segovia
C. Velarde
C. Daoiz
Rda. Don Juan
Po. de la Alameda
C. Caída del Nieve
La Fábrica de la Moneda
C. la Vía
C. Marqués de Viana
C. San Juan de la Cruz
La Vera Cruz
Vera Cruz
C. de San Marcos
Cta. de Zamarramaja
PL. DE LA REINA VICTORIA EUGENIA
Alcázar
Arroyo Clamores
Cuesta de los Hoyos

Segovia

N

200 yards
200 meters

Segovia

▲ ACCOMMODATIONS
Hostal Don Jaime, 3
Hostal Juan Bravo, 2
Pensión Ferri, 1
Residencia Juvenil "Emperador Teodosio" (HI), 4

the *Torre de Juan II* (80m high), which affords a marvelous view of Segovia and the surrounding amber plains. The **Museo Real Colegio de Artillería,** commemorates the period (1764-1862) in which the Alcázar was used as a artillery training school. Canons, tools, charts, and models abound. *(From the Pl. Mayor, follow C. Marqués del Arco and its continuation and walk through the park.* ☎ *921 46 07 59. Open daily Apr.-Sept. 10am-7pm; Oct.-Mar. 10am-6pm. 400ptas, seniors 250ptas.)*

CATHEDRAL. In 1525, Charles V commissioned the construction of a cathedral to replace the 12th-century one destroyed in the "Revolt of the Comunidades." This new one, he hoped, would tower over the Pl. Mayor. When it was finished 200 years later, with 23 chapels and a silver and gold treasury, the cathedral earned the nickname "The Lady of all Cathedrals." The *Sala Capitular*, hung with well-preserved 17th-century tapestries, displays a silver-and-gold chariot and an incredible number of crucifixes, chalices, and candelabra. Don't miss the intricate sculptures on the altarpiece, crafted by the Baroque master Sabatini. *(☎ 921 46 22 05. Cathedral open daily Apr.-Oct. 9am-7pm, Nov.-Mar. 9:30am-6pm. 300ptas.)*

MUSEUMS. The elegant two-year-old **Museo de Arte Contemporáneo Esteban Vincente,** Pl. de las Bellas, is a joy to visit. It holds a permanent collection of Esteban Vincente's works, as well as prestigious exhibitions of contemporary art. Vincente, son of Segovia, spent time with Lorca and Buñuel in Madrid, Picasso in France, and Rothko and Pollack in New York, painting and sculpting as the avant garde evolved. *(Just above Pl. de San Martín, which is off C. de Cervantes.* ☎ *921 46 20 10. Open Tu-Sa 11am-2pm and 4-7pm; Su and festivals 11am-2pm. 400ptas, students and seniors 250ptas.)* Ceramics fans should not miss the **Museo Zuloaga,** Pl. Colmenares, a church/palace/museum that was once the home and workshop of Daniel Zuloaga, an early 20th-century artist whose tile murals grace many of Madrid's walls. It now holds some of his work—paintings, tiles, and incredible ceramics. His unusual chapel-turned-kiln is still intact. *(☎ 921 46 33 48. open Tu-F 10am-2pm and 5-7pm, Sa-Su 10am-2pm. 200ptas, free Sa-Su.)*

◼ **CASA-MUSEO DE ANTONIO MACHADO.** Though significantly more humble than the palace, this museum holds its own among Segovia's historic treasures. The poet's 13-year residence (1919-1932) has been left untouched, replete with original manuscripts and portraits (including one by Picasso) on the walls. The curator gives personal tours. *(C. Desamparados, 5. From Pl. Mayor, go down C. Marqués del Arco and right on C. Desamparados. Open W-Su 11am-2pm and 4:30-7:30pm. 200ptas, W free.)*

OUTSIDE THE WALLS. A walk away from the city past the meandering Eresma River offers a welcome change of pace. Do be prepared, however, for a grueling uphill trek back to the city. Be sure to see **Iglesia de la Vera Cruz,** a mysterious 12-sided basilica built by the cabalistic Knights Templar in 1208. *(Follow C. Pozo de la Nieve, on the left with your back to the Alcázar, and head down the 2nd stone staircase to Po. San Juan de la Cruz. From there it is a 20min. walk.* ☎ *921 43 14 75. Open Apr.-Sept. Tu-Su 10:30am-1:30pm and 3:30-7pm; Oct.-Mar. Tu-Su 10:30am-1:30pm and 3:30-6pm. 200ptas.)*

LA MUJER MUERTA According to local folklore, the picturesque mountain silhouette south of Segovia known as **La Mujer Muerta (The Dead Woman)** commemorates a bloody but moving turn of events. *La mujer,* the wife of a chief, was widowed when her twin sons were but young boys. As only one of the two could inherit his father's rule, the mother grew fearful of impending fratricide once the children came of age. She offered her life to God as a sacrifice, hoping this act would save both her sons. Unfortunately it settled nothing. On a summer's day years later, as the two young men prepared to fight each other for supremacy, it suddenly began to snow. By the time the storm dissipated, a snow-capped mountain had materialized upon the scene of the proposed battleground. As all soon acknowledged, it was the resting body of the twins' mother. *Segovianos* insist that two small clouds float closer to the mountain at dusk—the two sons kissing their mother good night.

♫ ENTERTAINMENT

Packed with bars and cafes, Pl. Mayor is the center of Segovian nightlife. Pl. Azoguejo and C. Carmen, near the aqueduct, are filled with bars as well, though they are mostly frequented by the high school set. Club headquarters are at C. Ruiz de Alda, off Pl. Azoguejo. **Sabbat,** Po. del Salón, fills the *paseo* with long lines and techno. For decent jazz, locals head to **El Saxo Bar,** C. del Seminario, 2.

From June 24-29, Segovia celebrates a **fiesta** in honor of San Juan and San Pedro. According to local lore, the sun reflects the general joy and intoxication by rising in circles. During the festival there are free open-air concerts on Pl. Azoguejo and dances and fireworks on June 29. Three kilometers northwest of Segovia, **Zamarra-mala** hosts the **Fiestas de Santa Agueda** on February 5. Women parody men to commemorate an abortive sneak attack on the Alcázar in which the townswomen tried to distract the castle guards with wine and song. They take over the town's administration for a day, dress in beautiful, old-fashioned costumes, and parade the streets. After three days, they torch the "Pelele," a doll symbolic of local men.

⚑ DAYTRIP FROM SEGOVIA

LA GRANJA DE SAN ILDEFONSO (20MIN.)

The easiest way to get to La Granja is by bus from Segovia (20min., 10-14 per day, 210ptas round-trip). From the bus stop, walk up the hill and through the ornate gates. Signs from there will guide you to the palace and gardens.

The royal palace of La Granja, 9km southeast of Segovia, is the most extravagant of Spain's four royal summer retreats (the others are El Pardo, El Escorial, and Aranjuez). Felipe V, the first Bourbon King of Spain and grandson of Louis XIV, detested the Habsburgs' austere El Escorial. Nostalgic for Versailles, in which he spent his royal childhood, he commissioned La Granja in the early 18th century, choosing the sight based on its hunting and gardening potential. A fire destroyed the living quarters in 1918, but the structure was rebuilt in 1932 to house one of the world's finest collections of Flemish tapestries. The most notable display is the nine-tapestry series entitled *The Honours* by Pierre van Aelst; it was said to be an allegory of Emperor Charles' moral development. (☎ 921 47 00 19. Open daily June-Sept. Tu-Su 10am-6pm; Oct.-Mar. Tu-Sa 10am-1:30pm and 3-5pm, Su 10am-2pm; Apr.-May Tu-F 10am-1:30pm and 3-5pm, Sa-Su 10am-6pm. Mandatory guided tours depart every 15min. 700ptas, students 300ptas. W free for EU citizens.) Outside the palace building are the manicured █**gardens,** designed by Frenchman René Carlier. Cool pathways, impressive flowerbeds, and undisturbed nooks and crannies fill the gardens, but even they are no match for the decadent *Cascadas Nuevas,* an ensemble of illuminated fountains, pools, and pavilions that represents the continents and four seasons. (Fountains turned on W and Sa-Su at 5:30pm. Gardens W and Sa-Su 375ptas, students 200ptas; M-Tu and Th-F free.) At the **Real Fabrica de Cristales,** also outside the palace, visitors can follow the evolution of the wine bottle. (☎ 921 47 17 12. Open daily Apr.-Sept. 11am-8pm; Oct.-Mar. 11am-7pm. 400ptas, seniors and students 200ptas.)

ÁVILA

There are two things that draw tourists to Ávila (pop. 50,000), and it's hard to tell which is better preserved: the 2.5km of magnificent 12th-century stone walls, or the centuries-old relics of super-nun Santa Teresa de Jesús. Museums and monuments depict her divine visitations and ecstatic visions in exhaustive detail, and Ávila's inhabitants have taken the heroine as their patron saint, naming everything from pastries to driving schools after her and celebrating her day (Oct. 15) for a full week with parades of giant effigies. That and the late July *Fiesta de Verano* aside, though, Santa Teresa would have been pleased at the remarkable peace of Ávila life. The inner walls are something of a time warp, untouched by pollution, advertisements, or the blare of tourist traffic, and they are well worth at least a daytrip from Segovia or Madrid.

⌐ TRANSPORTATION

Trains: (☎ 920 25 02 02), on Av. José Antonio. To: **El Escorial** (1hr., 7 per day, 575ptas); **Villalba**, for transfer to **Segovia** (1hr., 16 per day, 1020ptas); **Valladolid** (1½hr., 7 per day, 1050-1600ptas); **Madrid** (1½-2hr.; 20-25 per day, fewer on weekends; 900-1550ptas); and **Salamanca** (1¾hr., 3 per day, 855ptas).

Buses: Av. Madrid, 2 (☎ 920 22 01 54), at Av. Portugal on the northeast side of town. To: **Segovia** (1hr.; M-F 7 per day 6:30am-8:30pm, Sa 9am and 12:45pm, Su 10am and 6:45pm; 555ptas); **Madrid** (1½hr.; M-F 8 per day 6am-7pm, Sa-Su 3 per day 10am-7pm; 930ptas); and **Salamanca** (1½hr.; M-Sa 4 per day 9:15am-10pm, Su 6pm and 10pm; 700ptas).

Taxis: Pl. Santa Teresa (☎ 920 21 19 59) and at the train station (☎ 920 22 01 49). From the train station to Pl. Santa Teresa 350ptas, plus 25ptas per piece of luggage.

▟⁊ ORIENTATION AND PRACTICAL INFORMATION

The tangled city has two main squares: **Plaza de la Victoria** (known to locals as Pl. del Mercado Chico) inside the city walls, and **Plaza de Santa Teresa** just outside. Pl. Santa Teresa is the social center and the best place to find a meal. In general, stick to the labeled streets; unidentified twisting alleys will probably lead you outside of town. To get to Pl. Santa Teresa from the **train station**, head straight on Av. José Antonio as you exit the station, turn right on Av. del Dieciocho, left on Av. Madrid, and left on C. Duque de Alba, which will lead you into the plaza (15min.). From the **bus station,** cross the intersection across from the station, and follow the length of the park straight to get on C. Duque de Albe, which feeds right into Pl. Santa Teresa (10min.). Municipal bus #1 (75ptas) runs to Pl. Victoria from the stop near the train station, one block toward town.

Tourist Office: Pl. Catedral, 4 (☎ 920 21 13 87; fax 920 25 37 17), opposite the cathedral entrance. From Pl. Santa Teresa, go through the main gate and take your 2nd right onto C. Alemania. Friendly, bilingual staff. Maps of city tours. Lists daily town activities and live performances. Open M-F 9am-2pm and 5-7pm, Sa-Su 10am-2pm and 5-8pm.

Emergency: ☎ 112. **Police:** Av. Inmaculada, 11 (☎ 920 21 11 88).

Medical Services: Hospital Provincial, Jesús del Gran Poder, 42 (☎ 920 35 72 00). **Ambulance:** ☎ 920 22 14 00.

Post Office: Pl. Catedral, 2 (☎ 920 21 13 54), to the left when facing the cathedral entrance. Open M-F 8:30am-8:30pm, Sa 9:30am-2pm. **Postal Code:** 05001.

Internet Access: Arroba@25, C. Ferreol Hernández. 1 (☎ 920 35 23 90), on the corner of Pl. de Italia. From Pl. Santa Teresa, take a left off C. San Millán. 400ptas per hr.

⌐ ACCOMMODATIONS

Ávila's walls surround numerous comfortable, affordable accommodations. Those near the cathedral and Pl. Santa Teresa fill up in the summer, so call early.

Pensión Continental, Pl. Catedral, 6 (☎ 920 21 15 02; fax 920 25 16 9), next to the tourist office. Wooden-floored rooms, all with phones, some with TV, some overlooking the plaza. Rustic TV lounge. Singles 2200ptas; doubles 3700ptas, with bath 4500ptas; triples 5500ptas; 6-room suite 11,500ptas (IVA not included). V, MC, AmEx.

Hostal Casa Felipe, Pl. Victoria, 12, (☎ 920 21 39 24), near the cathedral. Clean halls and well-lit rooms with colorful bedspreads, TVs, and sinks. Many have balconies overlooking the plaza. Rooms without baths have private bathrooms in the hall. July-Oct. singles 2600ptas; doubles 4500ptas, with bath 5500ptas; prices decrease Nov.-June.

Hostal Jardín, C. San Segundo, 38. Behind the namesake garden await large rooms, all with TVs, phones, and bedside reading lights. Slightly musty air, but it may just be the old piano on the landing. July-Sept. breakfast 400ptas. Singles 2675ptas, with bath 3745-4280ptas; doubles 3785ptas, with bath 4875-5350ptas. V, MC.

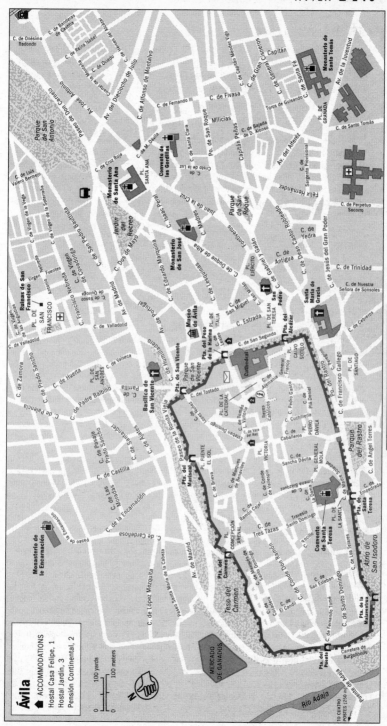

CENTRAL SPAIN

Ávila

▲ ACCOMMODATIONS
Hostal Casa Felipe, 1
Hostal Jardín, 3
Pensión Continental, 2

0   100 yards
0   100 meters

FOOD

Budget sandwich shops cluster around Pl. Victoria. The most affordable restaurant area is C. San Segundo, off Pl. Santa Teresa, although the *terrazas* on the plaza are perfect for people-watching and an after- dinner *café con leche*. The city has won fame for its *ternera de Ávila* (veal) and *mollejas* (sweetbread), and the *yemas de Santa Teresa* or *yemas de Ávila*, local confections made of egg yolk and honey, are divine. Every Friday, the **mercado** in Pl. Victoria sells cheap produce from 10am to 2pm. The **supermarket**, C. Juan José Martín, 6, has all the basics. Heading away from Pl. Santa Teresa, turn left off C. Duque de Alba just after the Monasterio de San José (open M-Sa 9:45am-2pm and 5-8pm).

Restaurante El Grande, Pl. Santa Teresa, 8 (☎ 920 22 30 83). A festive, busy family-style restaurant with outdoor seating on the plaza. Delicious Castilian cuisine. *Raciones* 375-800ptas. *Menú* 1350ptas. Open daily 1-4pm and 8-10:30pm (later on weekends).

Gran Muralla, C. San Segundo, 18 (☎ 920 25 02 26). Flashy Chinese restaurant with hanging lanterns and a 3-D mountain. Cheap, plentiful, and tasty food. Lunch *menú* 765ptas. Entrees 490-940ptas. Open daily 11:30am-4:30pm and 7:30pm-12:30am.

Bocatti, C. San Segundo, 26 (☎ 920 25 10 80). A 50s-inspired sub shop with checkered tiles, Americana on the walls, and Elvis on the jukebox. Cold and hot sandwiches on freshly baked bread 295-490ptas. Open daily 12:30-4:30pm and 6pm-midnight.

 SIGHTS

■ THE CITY WALLS (LAS MURALLAS)

Ávila's historic inner city is guarded by Spain's oldest and best-preserved medieval walls. Construction of the 2500 battlements, 88 towers, and six gates began in 1090, although most were completed in the next century; it was this concentrated burst of activity that gave the walls their unusual uniformity. The most imposing of the towers, **Cimorro,** doubles as the cathedral's bold apse. On the inside, in the corner to the right of the cathedral, are the outlines of two windows and two balconies—all that remains of a former Alcázar. If you want to walk on the walls (200m are open to the public), start from the Puerta del Alcázar. *(With your back to Pl. Santa Teresa it is directly in front of you. Open June-Aug. Tu-Su 11am-1:30pm and 5-7:30pm; Sept.-May Tu-Su 10:30am-3:30pm. 200ptas.)*

The best view of the walls and of Ávila itself is from the **Cuatro Postes,** a four-pillared structure past the Río Adaja, 1.5km out on the highway to Salamanca. It was here that Santa Teresa was caught by her uncle as she and her brother tried to flee to the Islamic south. *(From Pl. Santa Teresa, walk through the inner city and out the Puerta del Puente. Cross the bridge and follow the road to your right for about 1km. Total walk 25min.)*

INSIDE THE WALLS

CATHEDRAL. Some believe that the profile of the huge cathedral looming over the watchtowers inspired Santa Teresa's famous metaphor of the soul as a diamond castle. Begun in the second half of the 12th century, Ávila's is the oldest Spanish cathedral in the transitional style between Romanesque and Gothic. Look for the **Altar de La Virgen de la Caridad,** where 12-year-old Santa Teresa prostrated herself after the death of her mother. Behind the main altar is the alabaster **tomb** of Cardinal Alonso de Madrigal, an Ávilan bishop and prolific writer whose dark complexion won him the title "El Tostado" (The Toasted). The nickname spread, and during the Golden Age it actually became popular to call any literary windbag *un tostado.*The cathedral **museum** displays enormous *libros de canti* (hymnals) that make you feel like Alice in Wonderland, and Juan de Arfe's silver, six-leveled **Custodia del Corpus,** complete with swiveling bells. *(From Pl. Santa Teresa, walk through the Puerta; take the first right onto C. Cruz Vieja, which leads to the cathedral. ☎ 920 21 16 41. Open daily Apr.-Oct. 10am-1pm and 3:30-6pm; Nov.-Mar. 10am-1:30pm and 3:30-5:30pm. 300ptas.)*

OTHER SIGHTS. Santa Teresa's admirers built the 17th-century **Convento de Santa Teresa** on the site of her birthplace and childhood home. *(From Pl. Santa Teresa, go left on C. San Segundo, right on Po. Rastro, and right through Pta. Santa Teresa. Open daily May-Sept. 9:30am-1:30pm and 3:30-9pm; Oct.-Apr. 9:30am-1:30pm and 3:30-8:30pm.)* The **Sala de Reliquias,** a small building near the convent, holds some intriguing Santa Teresa relics, including her right ring finger, the sole of her sandal, and the cord she used to flagellate herself. *(Open daily 9:30am-1:30pm and 3:30-7:30pm. Free.)*

OUTSIDE THE WALLS

MONASTERIO DE LA ENCARNACIÓN. A short distance outside the city walls lies the Monasterio de la Encarnación, where Santa Teresa lived for 30 years. The mandatory guided tour visits Santa Teresa's tiny cell and the small rooms where nuns observed their guests through little barred windows. Santa Teresa had her mystical encounter with the child Jesus on the **main staircase.** Ask for the brochure for a dramatic re-creation of the scene and a transcript of their dialogue. Upstairs from the cloister, a **museum** features a collection of personal effects given to the convent by wealthier nuns as bribes to procure entrance. *(Po. Encarnación, northwest of the city. Open daily June-Aug. 10am-1pm and 4-7pm, Sept.-May 10am-1pm and 3:30-6pm. 150ptas. Tour in Spanish lasts 10-15min.)*

MONASTERIO DE SANTO TOMÁS. The Monasterio de Santo Tomás was built some distance from the city walls as a summer refuge for Fernando and Isabel and a seat of the Inquisition. Inside the church and in front of the *retablo* (altarpiece) is the tomb of Prince Don Juan, Fernando and Isabel's only son, who died in 1497 at the age of 19. To the right (when facing the altar) is the **Capilla de I Santo Cristo,** where Santa Teresa came to pray and confess. Also here are three contrasting cloisters: the Tuscan **Cloister of the Noviciate,** the Gothic **Cloister of Silence,** and the Renaissance-Transition **Cloister of the Kings.** *(Pl. Granada, 1. At the end of C. Jesús del Gran Poder (or Av. Alferéz Provisional). Church open daily 8am-1pm and 4-8pm. Museum open daily 11am-12:45pm and 4-7pm. Cloisters 100ptas. Museum 200ptas. Church free.)*

SALAMANCA

Even at the turn of the millennium, old-town Salamanca maintains a distinctly medieval feel. It is a place of burning sandstone arches, glowing Plateresque facades, cobblestoned streets, and tall, graceful bell towers. The outer city has all the amenities of a prosperous metropolis, but social life still centers on Alberto Churriguera's famous Plaza Mayor, and the true jewel of the city is its 13th-century university. During medieval times, La Universidad de Salamanca was grouped with those of Bologne, Paris, and Oxford as one of the "four leading lights of the world." Countless eminent Spanish intellectuals have graced its hallowed halls, including Antonio de Nebrija, Fernando de Rojas, and Miguel de Unamuno. Students continue to add energy and character to the city today, and its many study-abroad programs ensure an international clientele, particularly in the summer when the city comes alive with numerous feasts, fairs, and concerts.

▐ TRANSPORTATION

Trains: (☎ 923 12 02 02), Po. de la Estación. Walk up C. Toro away from Plaza Mayor, take a right onto Av. de Mirat, then a left onto Po. de la Estación. **RENFE Office,** Pl. Libertad, 10 (☎ 902 24 02 02). Open M-F 9am-2pm and 5-8pm. 2 regional lines. To: **Ávila** (1¾hr., 2 per day 6:45am-5:45pm, regional 865ptas, intercity 1095ptas); **Palencia** (2hr., 1:45pm, 1265ptas); **Valladolid** (2hr., 4 per day 7am-8pm, regional 865ptas, intercity 1600ptas); **Burgos** (3hr., 4-5 per day 2:25am-7:50pm, 2400ptas); Madrid (2½hr., 4 per day 7:45am-7:40pm, 2130ptas); **Lisbon** (6hr., 4:40am, 4800ptas); and **Barcelona** (11½hr., 8am and 7:50pm, regional 5800ptas, intercity 6100ptas).

Buses: Av. Filiberto Villalobos, 71-85 (☎ 923 23 67 17). Info window open M-F 8am-8:30pm, Sa 9am-2:30pm and 4:30-6:30pm, Su 10am-2pm and 4-7:30pm. To: **Ciudad Rodrigo** (1hr.; M-F 12 per day 7:15am-9:30pm, Sa 6 per day 8:30am-6pm; 735ptas);

Zamora (1hr.; M-F 22 per day 6:40am-10:35pm, Sa 10 per day 7:45am-8:30pm; 530ptas); **Ávila** (1½hr., 4-5 per day 6:30am-8:30pm, 700ptas); **Valladolid** (1½hr.; M-Sa 6-8 per day 8am-8pm, F until 10pm, Su 4 per day 10:30am-10pm; 940ptas); **Segovia** (3hr.; M-Sa 7am and 5:30pm, Su 8:45pm; 1280ptas); **Madrid** (regular 3hr.; M-Sa 7 per day 7:30am-8:30pm; Su 7 per day 8:30am-8:30pm; 1460ptas; express 2½hr., 14-15 per day, 1480ptas); **León** (2½hr.; M-F 3 per day 11am-6:30pm, Sa 11am, Su 10pm; 1160ptas); **Cáceres** (4hr.; M-F 5-6 per day 7am-5pm, F until 7pm, Sa 4 per day 9:30am-6:30pm, Su 3 per day 9:30am-9:30pm; 1705ptas); **Barcelona** (11hr., 7:30am and noon, 6415ptas). Also to: La Alberca, Bilbao, Burgos, Valencia, Sevilla, Mérida, Trujillo, Badajoz, Santiago de Compostela, and Santander.

Taxis: Auto-Taxi (24hr. ☎ 923 25 00 09) and **Radio Taxi** (24hr. ☎ 923 25 00 00).

Car Rental: Avis, Po. Canalejas, 49 (☎ 923 26 97 53). Open M-F 9:30am-1:30pm and 4-7pm, Sa 9am-1:30pm. **Europcar,** Po. Canalejas, 123 (☎ 923 26 90 41). Open M-F 9am-1:30pm and 4:30-7:30pm, Sa 9am-1:30pm.

■✴⑦ ORIENTATION AND PRACTICAL INFORMATION

Majestic **Plaza Mayor** is the social and geographic center of town. Most sights and budget hostels lie south of the plaza around R. Mayor; areas to the north tend to be newer and more expensive. Farther north, beyond **Plaza de España,** are working-class districts. The **Universidad** is south of Pl. Mayor, near **Plaza de Anaya.** From the train station, either catch bus #1 (100ptas) to Gran Vía, which is a block from Pl. Mercado (next to Pl. Mayor), or, with your back to the station, turn left down Po. Estación to Pl. España and walk down C. Azafranal (or C. Toro) to Pl. Mayor (20min.). From the bus station, either catch bus #4 to Gran Vía or walk down C. Filiberto Villalobos, cross busy Av. Alemania/Po. San Vicente, and go down C. Ramón y Cajal. Keep the park on your left; at the end (just after the Iglesia de la Purísima), head left and then right on C. Prior, which runs to Pl. Mayor (20min.)

Tourist Office: Municipal, Pl. Mayor, 14 (☎ 923 21 83 42). Large, helpful office. Open M-Sa 9am-2pm and 4:30-6:30pm, Su 10am-2pm and 4:30-6:30pm. **Provincial** (☎ 923 26 85 71; fax 923 26 24 92), R. Mayor, at the Casa de las Conchas. Open M-F 10am-2pm and 5-7pm, Sa-Su 10am-7pm. **Information booths** open occasionally July-Sept. Students distribute maps, information, and hostel listings from booths in Pl. Anaya, the train station, and the bus station. **Café Alcaraván,** C. Compañía, 12, and **Restaurante El Bardo** (see **Food,** p. 154) have message boards offering rideshares, language trades, and rooms to rent.

Budget Travel: TIVE, Po. Carmelitas (also known as Av. Alemania), 83 (☎ 923 26 77 31). Student services, but no ticket sales. Long lines—go early. Open M-F 9am-2pm. **Juventus Travel,** Pl. Libertad, 4 (☎ 923 25 29 90). Open M-F 9am-2pm.

Currency Exchange: ATMs on C. Toro and Rua Mayor. **Banco Central Hispano,** 35-37 Rua Mayor (☎ 923 26 87 56) and 20-22 Gran Via (☎ 923 21 54 83).

Luggage Storage: At the train station (300ptas) and bus station (90ptas per item).

Gay and Lesbian Services: Colectivo de Gais y Lesbianas de Salamanca has a telephone line (☎ 923 24 64 71) staffed M 7-9pm; answering machine will assure that your needs are met at any time.

Emergency: ☎ 112. **Police: local** ☎ 092 and **national** ☎ 091 or 923 26 53 11.

Hospital: Hospital Clínico Universitario, Paseo San Vicente, 182 (☎ 923 29 11 00).

Post Office: Gran Vía, 25-29 (☎ 923 27 04 11). Lista de Correos. Open M-F 8:30am-8:30pm and Sa 9:30am-2pm. **Postal Code:** 37001.

Internet Access: Informática Abaco Bar, C. Zamora, 7 (☎ 923 26 15 89), near Pl. Mayor. 150ptas for 15min; after 9pm 150ptas for 30min., 250ptas per hr. Open M-F 9:30am-2am, Sa-Su 11am-2am. **Navega,** C. Zamora, 70 (☎ 923 28 11 21). Walk down from **Abaco Bar** toward Po. Carmelitas on C. Zamora. Open daily 11am-2am; specials after 10pm, 150ptas for 30min. and 300ptas per hr.

CENTRAL SPAIN

Salamanca

🏠 ACCOMMODATIONS

Hostal Emperatriz, 17
Pensión Bárez, 18
Pensión Estefanía, 20
Pensión Las Vegas, 16
Pensión Marina, 14
Pensión Villanueva, 12

🍎 FOOD

Champion, 1
El Ave, 21
Il Caffé di Roma, 13
Heladería Italianos, 4
La Dehesa, 9
La Parilla de la Carreja, 3
Restaurante El Bardo, 19

🍷 NIGHTLIFE

Birdland, 2
Café Moderno, 11
Café Novelty, 8
Camelot, 5
El Corillo Café, 15
Gatsby, 6
Pub Rojo y Negro, 7
Submarino, 10

ACCOMMODATIONS

Thanks to floods of student visitors, reasonably priced *hostales* and *pensiones* pepper the streets of Salamanca (especially off Pl. Mayor and C. Meléndez). Try to make reservations in advance, especially during July and August, when Salamanca becomes overrun by hostel-hungry students and tourists.

Pensión Estefanía, C. Jesús, 3-5 (☎ 923 21 73 72 or 923 24 87 48), off Pl R. Mayor. Experience the glory of Estefanía. Showers 150ptas. Singles 2000ptas; doubles with private shower 3500ptas; triples with shower 4800ptas. Cash only.

Pensión Marina, C. Doctrinos, 4, 3rd fl. (☎ 923 21 65 69), between C. Compañía and C. Prado. If you're traveling in a group of 2 and don't mind the 3-floor hike, this place is perfect. Showers 200ptas. Doubles with bath 3000ptas. Cash only.

Pensión Bárez, C. Meléndez, 19, 1st fl. (☎ 923 21 74 95). Romantic windows in several large, simple rooms. Generous owners provide TV lounge. Large rooms make adding extra beds (1300 per person) no problem. Two full bathrooms for the floor. Showers 150ptas. Singles 1500ptas; doubles 3500ptas; triples 4500ptas. V, MC.

Pensión Las Vegas, C. Meléndez, 13, 1st fl. (☎ 923 21 87 49). Accessible by R. Mayor and R. Antigua. You'll find cushy mattresses and TVs at a reasonable price. Reservations recommended during July and Aug. Singles 2000ptas; doubles 3000ptas, with bath 4000ptas.; triples with bath 4800ptas.

Pensión Villanueva, C. San Justo, 8, 1st fl. (☎ 923 26 88 33). Exit Pl. Mayor via Pl. Poeta Iglesias, cross the street, and take the first left. Let Sra. Manuela share her local lore and gossip. Soft beds and spacious rooms. Reservations only accepted for F-Su. Singles 1600ptas, with shower 1700ptas; doubles 3200ptas, with shower 3600; triples 4500ptas. Extra beds available at 1500ptas per person. Cash only.

Hostal Emperatriz, R. Mayor, 18 (☎/fax 923 21 91 56). This expensive 1-star hostel offers some serious competition to the 2-star hotel next door. Spacious rooms include full bathroom and telephone. Try to get a room facing R. Mayor for a great view. Laundry service available. Breakfast 300ptas. Singles 3500ptas; doubles 5000ptas; triples 6750ptas; quads 8000ptas. V, MC.

Camping: Regio (☎ 923 13 88 88), on Ctra. Salamanca, 4km toward Madrid. Albertur buses leave from the Gran Vía every 30min. near Pl. de San Julián. A 1st-class site with hot showers. Pool, tennis courts, restaurants, and currency exchange in a luxury tourist complex next door. 450ptas per person, 850ptas per tent and 450ptas more per car. V, MC. **Don Quijote** (☎ 923 20 90 52) on Ctra. Salamanca, 4km toward Aldealengua. Minivans leave from the Gran Vía every hour near La Riojana. A small, 2nd-class campsite. 400ptas per person and per tent, 375ptas per car.

FOOD

Cafes and restaurants surrounding Pl. Mayor provide cuisine as varied and unique as their patrons, but often have inflated prices. Instead, seek out back-alley spots where a full meal costs a little over 1000ptas. Typical *salmantino* dishes include *chanfaina*, a type of beef stew, and *tostón asado* (roasted baby pork). **Champion,** on C. Toro, 64, has a downstairs supermarket (open M-Sa 9:30am-8:30pm).

Restaurante El Bardo, C. Compañía, 8 (☎ 923 21 90 89), between the Casa de Conchas and the Clerecía. Traditional Spanish food, reasonable prices, and a lively bar make El Bardo appealing to tourists and locals. Meat dishes 1400-1900ptas. Vegetarian *paella* 1100ptas. Open daily 1:30-4:30 and 9:30-11:30pm, bar until 1am. V, MC.

La Parrilla de la Calleja, C. Ventura Ruiz Aguilera, 2 (☎ 923 27 19 29). Exit Pl. Mayor on C. Toro and take the first right. Enjoy your meal in the greenhouse courtyard or the rustic brick interior. Dishes are cooked to perfection in a firewood oven. Meat dishes 2000ptas. Salads 1000ptas. *Menú* 4000ptas. Open daily 8:30pm-midnight.

Restaurante La Dehesa—El Oso y El Madroño, Pl. del Angel, 1 (☎ 923 27 10 10). Exit Pl. Mayor through Pl. del Poeta Iglesias, walk alongside the Mercado to P. del Angel. Delicious local specialities at reasonable prices. Seafood dishes 750-1800ptas. Open daily 1:30-4pm and 8:30pm-midnight. Closed Su nights. V, MC, AmEx.

El Ave Bar & Restaurant, C. Libreros, 24 (☎ 923 26 45 11), just outside the University's Patio de Escuelas Menores. A culinary oasis for budget travelers. Salads 300-600ptas. Sandwiches 275-450ptas. Various *platos combinados* 725ptas. *Menú del día* 1100ptas. Su-Th 8am-midnight, F-Sa 9pm-2am. V, MC.

👁 SIGHTS

▓ PLAZA MAYOR. Salamanca's Plaza Mayor is considered one of the most beautiful squares in Spain and is undeniably one of the best people-watching sites. Designed by Alberto Churriguera (see **Architecture,** p. 60) and built between 1729 and 1755, the plaza comprises 88 towering arches, the **Ayuntamiento,** and three pavilions dedicated to historical figures. The **Pabellón Real**, to the right of the Ayuntamiento, honors the Spanish monarchy (and quite controversially includes the 20th-century dictator Franco among them); the **Pabellón del Sur,** in front of the Ayuntamiento, is dedicated to famous Spanish conquistadors; and the **Pabellón del Oeste,** to the left of the Ayuntamiento, pays homage to important *salmantinos* like San Juan de Sahagún, Santa Teresa, Cervantes, and Unamuno. Before the pavilions were built the square served as the town bullring; even today, the plaza is occasionally filled with sand and used for bullfights during feasts. Locals probably wouldn't mind a premature release of some of those bulls during the summer, when the plaza floods with wide-eyed tourist groups and flashing cameras.

▓ THE UNIVERSITY. The focal point of Salamanca, the great university, established in 1218, is best entered from the **Patio de las Escuelas,** left off C. Libreros. The statue here portrays Fray Luis de León, a university professor and one of the most respected literati of the Golden Age. A Hebrew scholar and classical Spanish stylist, Fray Luis was arrested by the Inquisition for translating Solomon's *Song of Songs* into Castilian and for preferring the Hebrew version of the Bible to the Latin one. After five years of imprisonment, he returned to the university and began his first lecture, *"Como decíamos ayer..."* ("As we were saying yesterday..."). The university's entryway is one of the best examples of Spanish Plateresque, a style named after the work of *plateros* (silversmiths). The central medallion represents Fernando and Isabel. Look for the hidden frog in the detailed facade. Legend promises finders will be blessed with good luck and even marriage.

> **TALK ABOUT SOME PRESSURE...** Look closely at the walls of the University and Cathedral and you'll see faded red scrawlings on the sandstone; this is not graffiti. Eight hundred years ago, students of the University of Salamanca used to attend class in the Old Cathedral. They would come to the church the night before their final exam to pray for success; the rigorous oral test (in logic and rhetoric) was then administered the next day in the same place, in front of *La Capilla de Santa Bárbara,* now known as *La Capilla del Estudiante.* Those who were fortunate enough to pass left the Cathedral through the main entrance, to shouts of congratulations from the throng of anxious *salmantinos* waiting outside. Those who failed left the building in shame, through a set of smaller doors in the back. Later that evening, the town would host a bullfight in honor of the new graduates; the fresh blood of the bull was then mixed with a flour paste and used to paint the names of the new doctors on the University and Cathedral walls as an external symbol of the fountain of knowledge that sprang forth from Salamanca.

The old lecture halls inside are open to the public. **Aula Fray Luis de León** has been left in more or less its original state; students in medieval times considered the hard benches luxurious, as most students then sat on the floor. A plaque bears Unamuno's famous love poem to the students of Salamanca. The **Paraninfo** (auditorium) contains Baroque tapestries and a portrait of Carlos IV attributed to Goya. Fray Luis is buried in the 18th-century **chapel**. The **Antigua Biblioteca** (oldest library in Europe) is the most spectacular room of all, located atop a magnificent Platteresque staircase displaying statues and historic books. Salamancan souvenir shops often reproduce the sign in the library that threatens excommunication for those who steal or damage books. And, of course, don't miss the room of fossilized turtles, apparently the second most important such collection in the world.

On the exterior patio are the **Escuelas Menores,** with a smaller version of the main entryway's Plateresque facade. (If you look closely, you'll notice some of the angels are in rather "compromising" positions.) Inside, the **University Museum** preserves the **Cielo de Salamanca,** the library's famous 15th-century fresco of the zodiac, painted on the ceiling by the celebrated Gallego brothers, Francisco and Fernando. Take a peek at the intricate strongbox with its many locks. *(From Pl. Mayor follow R. Mayor, veer right onto R. Antigua, then left onto C. Libreros; the university is on the left.* ☎ *923 29 44 00. Museum* ☎ *923 29 12 25. Open M-F 9:30am-1:30pm and 4-7:30pm, Sa 9:30am-1:30pm and 4-7pm, Su 10am-1:30pm. 300ptas, students and seniors 150ptas. Tickets sold until 30min. before closing.)*

■ **CASA MUSEO DE UNAMUNO.** Miguel de Unamuno, Rector of the University at the beginning of this century, is revered as one of the founding figures of the Spanish literary movement known as the "Generation of '98." Unamuno passionately opposed dictatorship and encouraged his students to do so as well. His stand against General Primo de Rivera's 1923 *coup d'état* led to his dismissal from the rector's post; he was triumphantly reinstated some years later. Unamuno's intricate origami and thoughts on his birth make up some of the more intriguing exhibits. *(To the right of the university's main entrance.* ☎ *923 29 44 00, ext. 1196. Open July-Sept. Tu-F 9:30am-1:30pm, Sa-Su 10am-1:30pm; Oct.-June Tu-F 9:30am-1:30pm and 4-6pm, Sa-Su 10am-2pm. Research room open M-F 9am-2pm. Mandatory tour in Spanish every 30min., 300ptas. Ring bell if house appears closed.)*

CATEDRAL NUEVA. Rome wasn't built in a day, and neither was this. In fact, it took 220 years (1513-1733) to construct this striking Gothic Spanish cathedral. While several subsequent architects decided to retain the original late-Gothic style, they could not resist adding touches from later periods, most notably its Baroque tower, one of the tallest in Spain. Restorers from the 20th century succumbed to the same temptation, adding an astronaut, a bull, and even a demon eating ice cream to the side entrance's facade. Every All Saints Day (Nov.1) a midnight feast is held to commemorate the tower's miraculous survival of the infamous Lisbon earthquake of 1755. The festivities commence with El Mariquelo, a local dressed in traditional salmantino garb, literally scaling the tower wall to the very top. There he plays a traditional song on his *gaita* (Galician bagpipe) and beats the *tamboril* (drum) to mark the official beginning of the festivities. *(From Pl. Mayor, walk down R. Mayor into Pl. Anaya; the New Cathedral is in front of you. Open daily Apr.-Sept. 9am-2pm and 4-8pm; Oct.-Mar. 9am-1pm and 4-6pm. Free.)*

CATEDRAL VIEJA. The smaller Catedral Vieja (1140) was built in the Romanesque style. Apocalyptic angels separate the sinners from the saved inside the arresting cupola. The oldest original part of the cathedral is the **Capilla de San Martín,** with brilliantly colored frescoes dating from 1242. Look for the image of the Virgen de la Vega, patron saint of Salamanca. The **Capilla de Santa Bárbara,** also called the Capilla del Título, was what students used to face as they took their final exams. Other points of interest include a document signed by El Cid Campeador and the crucifix he held at his death. The **cathedral museum** features a paneled ceiling by Fernando Gallego and houses the Mudéjar Salinas organ (one of the oldest in Europe). Be sure to check out the famed **Patio Chico,** behind the cathedral, where students congregate to chat and play music. It is ideal for getting a splendid view of both cathedrals. *(Museum* ☎ *923 21 74 76. Cathedral open daily Apr.-Sept. 9am-2pm and 4-8pm; Oct.-Mar. 9am-1pm and 4-6pm. Cathedral, cloister, and museum 300ptas.)*

CASA DE LAS CONCHAS. From Pl. Mayor, exit onto R. Mayor (through the archway opposite the clock). Follow this street until you reach a second plaza with a water fountain. Take a right and note the face of the building on your right. Yup, those are shells. The 15th-century Casa de las Conchas (House of Shells), with over 300 sandstone scallop halves, is one of Salamanca's most famous landmarks. Pilgrims who journeyed to Santiago de Compostela (see p. 447) traditionally wore shells to commemorate their visit to the tomb of St. James the Apostle (in Spanish, Santiago). The owner of the *casa*, a knight of the Order of Santiago, created this monument to honor the renowned pilgrimage. The building now serves as a public library and houses the provincial tourist office. (☎ 923 26 93 17. Open M-F 9am-9pm, Sa 10am-2pm and 5-8pm, Su 10am-2pm and 5-8pm. Free.)

LA CLERECÍA. Directly across from the Conchas is the Clerecía (Royal College of the Holy Spirit), the private faculty of the Universidad de Salamanca. When Saint Ignatius of Loyola, founder of the Jesuits, arrived in Salamanca in the early 17th century, he was imprisoned for 20 days for heresy. Once the Jesuits were finally recognized by the Church, Loyola decided to claim retribution for his mistreatment by creating an enormous church and college of the Jesuit Order. Founded in 1611 with the financial aid of Queen Margarita de Austria (Felipe III's wife), the college actually owes its name to King Carlos III, who expelled the Jesuits from Spain and made the institute property of the Real Clerecía. The building has a unique U-shaped groundplan, allowing visitors to peer over the Cloister of Studies into the lower gallery and courtyard. Unfortunately, its proximity to Casa de las Conchas makes it difficult to appreciate the beautiful outer facade. Legend has it that the Jesuits leveled every house in the area to build the college; the Casa de las Conchas was the only one that would not let itself be bought, despite the Jesuits' shady offer of one gold coin for every sandstone shell. (☎ 923 26 46 60. Open for mass M-Sa 1:15 and 7pm, Su noon. Free.)

CASA LIS MUSEO ART NOUVEAU Y ART DECO. This house may look bizarre from the outside, but it verges on the fantastical once you pass the door. Salamancan industrialist Miguel de Lis collaborated with modernist architect Joaquín Vargas to design the building, which now showcases Lis's eclectic art collection. The exhibit includes rare lace shawls and a fan signed by Salvador Dali and Marlene Dietrich, among others. Don't miss the room of porcelain dolls or the *Criselefantinas*, statues of marble and gold inspired by Russian ballet and Asian dance. (C. Gibraltar, 14, behind the cathedrals. ☎ 923 12 14 25. Open Apr.1-Oct.15 Tu-F 11am-2pm and 5pm-9pm, Sa-Su 11am-9pm; Oct. 16-Mar.31 Tu-F 11am-2pm and 4-7pm, Sa-Su 11am-8pm. 300ptas.)

MUSEO DE SALAMANCA. The Museo occupies a beautiful 15th-century building that was once home to Alvarez Albarca, physician to Fernando and Isabel. Along with the Casa de las Conchas, this structure is among Spain's most important examples of 15th-century architecture. To a certain extent, the building upstages the art inside, though the museum does have an intriguing collection of painting and sculpture as well as some temporary exhibits in archaeology and ethnology. Its most important canvases are Juan de Flandes's portrait of Saint Andrew and Luis de Morales's *Llanto por Cristo muerto*, both from the 16th century, and Vaccaro's *Inmaculada*. (☎ 923 21 22 35. Open Tu-F 9:45am-1:45pm and 4:45-7:15pm, Sa 10:15am-1:45pm and 4:45-7:15pm, Su 10:15am-1:15pm. 200ptas.)

CONVENTO DE SAN ESTEBAN. While on a fundraising endeavor, Columbus spent time in one of Salamanca's most dramatic monasteries, the Convento de San Esteban. During the afternoon, its facade becomes a solid mass of light depicting the stoning of St. Stephen and the crucifixion of Christ. The beautiful **Claustro de los Reyes (Kings's Cloister),** with its Gothic interior and Plateresque exterior, is visibly the product of two different eras. José Churriguera's central altarpiece (1693) is a masterpiece of Spanish Baroque. Also worth seeing is the **Panteón de los Teólogos,** home to the remains of the most decorated Dominican theologians of the University. (☎ 923 21 50 00. Downhill from the cathedrals. Open daily Apr.-Sept. 9am-1:30pm and 4-8pm; Oct.-Mar. 9:30am-1:30pm and 4-5:30pm. 200ptas.)

CENTRAL SPAIN

LA TUNA... MORE FRAT THAN FISH In Spain, it's not dolphins who are threatened by the "tuna industry." According to legend, it is young women who need to watch out, lest their hearts be captured unawares by a charming bard. *Las tunas* are university student music bands dating back to King Alfons X the Wise, in 1215. Originally founded by students who needed to earn money for their studies, they have become a form of social competition in modern universities, as well as paid entertainment for private parties and high-class restaurants. To become *tunos*, candidates *(pardillos)* must prove their wit and artistic ability in a series of tests culminating with a bowl of The Soup of Charity, a painfully fiery concoction mixed by veteran tunos. The chosen ones take an oath over a tambourine, the symbol of the tuna, and are given a tuna sash and nickname for life.

CONVENTO DE LAS DUEÑAS. Formerly the palace of a court official, this convent has one of the most elegant cloisters in Salamanca. Medallions adorning the walls depict famous Salamancans, while scenes from Dante's *Divina Comedia* line the columns on the second floor. Nuns sell holy candies on the first floor. (☎ *923 21 54 42. Near Convento de San Esteban. Open daily Apr.-Sept. 10:30am-1pm and 4:30-7pm; Oct.-Mar. 10:30am-1pm and 4:30-5:30pm. 200ptas, students 100ptas.)*

HUERTO DE CALIXTO Y MELIBE. This peaceful, romantic garden is named in honor of the tragic star-crossed lovers Calixto and Melibea, protagonists of Fernando de Rojas' famous play, *La Celestina.* The garden boasts a statue of La Celestina herself—the brothel mistress who aided Calixto in winning the noble Melibea—surrounded by beautiful exotic flowers. A perfect place for a midafternoon rest from sightseeing. *(Walk down C. Arcediano, off Patio Chico behind the Catedral Vieja. Ahead to the right upon exiting the Casa Lis. Open daily 10am-6pm. Free)*

PUENTE ROMANO. This 2000-year-old Roman bridge spanning the scenic Río Tormes was once part of an ancient Roman road called the *Camino de la Plata* (Silver Way). The *Camino* ran from Mérida in Extremadura to Astorga and was heavily traveled during the Roman occupation of Spain. In medieval times, the *Camino de la Plata* was the route most Andalucian and Castilian Christians took to complete their pilgrimage to Santiago de Compostela. The bridge is guarded at its near end by a headless granite bull called the **Toro Ibérico.** Though it dates back to pre-Roman times, the bull gained fame in the 16th century when it appeared in *Lazarillo de Tormes,* the prototype of the picaresque novel and a predecessor of *Don Quijote;* in one episode the novel's short hero gets his head slammed into the bull's stone ear after he cheats his employer.

🎵🎭 ENTERTAINMENT AND NIGHTLIFE

Plaza Mayor is *the* social center of Salamanca. Day and night it is packed with locals, students, and tourists who come to lounge in its cafes, watch the sunset, or take a stroll. At night, members of various local college or graduate-school **tunas** (medieval-style student troubadour groups) often finish their rounds here. Dressed in traditional black capes, they strut around the plaza with guitars, mandolins, *bandurrias,* and tambourines, serenading women. Student nightlife is also concentrated on the **Gran Vía, C. Bordadores,** and side streets. Spacious discos/bars, or *pafs,* blast music into the wee hours of the morning. **C. Prior** and **C. Rua Mayor** are full of bars; locals gather in the charming *terrazas* on **Pl. de la Fuente,** off Av. Alemania. More intense partying occurs off **C. Varillas,** where *chupiterías* (bars that mostly serve shots) take precedence over *pafs.*

Camelot, C. Bordadores, 3 (☎ 923 21 21 82). Medieval chic. This monastery-turned-club is a stop on the **Gatsby** and **Cum Laude** (C. Prior) club-hopping routes. Beer 400-500ptas. Mixed drinks 900ptas. Open Su-Th 10pm-3am, F-Sa 10pm-5:30am.

Café Moderno, Gran Vía, 75 (☎ 923 26 01 47). This popular bar attracts much of the post-theater crowd. Despite its "modern" title, the cafe is actually an old-fashioned pub serving as a dance club. Participate in one of the frequent games (like Wheel of Fortune) while dancing to American top-40 hits. Beer 300ptas. Mixed drinks 500-650ptas. Open Su-W 4pm-3am, Th 4pm-3:30am, F-Sa 4pm-4:30am.

Submarino, C. San Justo, 27 (☎ 923 16 02 64), off Gran Vía. Built to resemble the inside of a submarine. Mixed gay and straight clientele grooves to techno beats under black lights. M-Th the 2nd drink is free until 2:30am. Beer 350ptas. Mixed drinks 500-700ptas. Open M-Th 9pm-4am, F-Sa 9pm-5am.

Gatsby, C. Bordadores, 6 (☎ 923 21 72 74) Across the street from Camelot, this club is famous for its themed parties. Come on a "beach" night and you can swim in their inflatable pool. Beer 300ptas. Sangría 350ptas. Shots 250ptas. Mixed drinks 700ptas. Specials nearly every night. Open Su-Th 10pm-4am, F-Sa 7pm-6:30am.

Birdland, C. Azafranal, 57 (☎ 923 26 13 57), by Pl. España. Drink to modern funk jazz. Small tables by large windows overlooking the square make Birdland a good nest for couples or just an intense conversation. Beer 250-400ptas. Mixed drinks 500-1000ptas. Open Su-Th 4pm-3am, F-Sa 4pm-4:30am.

Pub Rojo y Negro, C. Espoz y Mina, 22 (☎ 923 26 67 73). Scrumptious coffee, liqueur, and ice cream in an old-fashioned setting catering to older couples. Traditional Spanish music and flamenco on the dance floor in the back salon. Ice cream 200-1100ptas. Beer 375ptas. Mixed drinks 575ptas. Open Su-Th noon-3am and F-Sa noon-5am.

Café Novelty, on Pl. Mayor. The oldest cafe in town and a popular meeting place for students and professors. Even Miguel de Unamuno was a regular. Beer 200ptas. Mixed drinks 400ptas. Open daily until 2am.

Lugares, a free, slim pamphlet distributed at the tourist office and at some bars, lists everything from movies and special events to bus schedules. Posters at the **Colegio Mayor** (Palacio de Anaya) advertise university events, free films, and student theater. During the summer, Salamanca sponsors the **Verano Cultural de Salamanca,** with silent movies, contemporary Spanish cinema, pop singers, and theater groups. On June 12, in honor of San Juan de Sahagún, there is a **corrida de toros** charity event in **La Plaza de Toros** en Plaza Glorieta to the northeast of old city. From September 8 to 21, Salamanca indulges in festivals and exhibitions, most honoring the bullfight that has made the region's *ganaderías,* or bull farms, the best in all of Spain. This is also a fun place to be during *Semana Santa,* with local traditions like **Lunes de Aguas,** celebrated the Monday after Easter. This feast remembers the tradition of banishing local prostitutes across the river during the 40 days of Lent; they used to return triumphantly on *Lunes de Quasimodo,* when eager *salmantinos* would picnic along the bridge to await their arrival.

🔁 DAYTRIPS FROM SALAMANCA

CIUDAD RODRIGO(1¼HR.)

Ciudad Rodrigo is most accessible by bus; trains are infrequent and the station is 35min. from the old city. Buses come from Salamanca (1¼hr.; M-F 12 per day 6:45am-7:30pm, Sa 7 per day 7:15am-5:45pm, Su 5 per day 9am-8pm; 735ptas).

The honey-colored stonework of Ciudad Rodrigo, a sleepy medieval town just 27km from Portugal, can be seen glistening from the surrounding plains. It is named for Conde Rodrigo Gonzalez Girón, the count who brought the site back to life in 1100 after the destruction of the Moorish invasions. The old city's flower-covered walls enclose intricate 18th-century defenses, a quirky cathedral and other masonry treasures. The ▪cathedral is the town's masterpiece. Originally a Romanesque church commissioned by Fernando II of León, it was later modified in the 16th-century Gothic style. The **coro** (choir) was the masterpiece of Rodrigo Alemán, who worked on it from 1498 to 1504. Look for the sculptor's signature—a carving of his head hidden among the rest of the carvings. The two 16th-century organs star in a series of concerts every August. The cathedral's **claustro** (cloister) alone merits a trip to Ciudad Rodrigo. The columns are covered with figures doing everything from making love to playing peek-a-boo, even flirting with cannibalism. The cathedral's **museum** is filled with strange but interesting pieces, including an ancient clavichord, the cathedral's "ballot box," richly embroidered robes and slippers worn by bishops and priors, and Velázquez's *Llanto de Adán y Eva por Ariel muerto*. (Cathedral open daily 10am-1pm and 4-7pm. Free. Cloister and museum open daily 10am-1pm and 4-6pm. 200ptas. Tours in Spanish.) Also of note is the 14th- and 15th-century **Castillo de Enrique de Trastámara**, built by Gonzalo Arias de Genizaro. Ciudad Rodrigo was once the site of a bloody face-off between Trastámara and Pedro I El Cruel; today the castle serves as a more tranquil *parador de turismo* (luxury hotel) and affords a good view of the Río Agueda and surrounding countryside. The **bus station** (☎ 923 46 10 09) is on C. Campo de Toledo. From the station entrance, take a left (with the station behind you) and then the second right (uphill), and pass through the stone arch; the **tourist office,** Pl. Amayuelas, 6, is immediately on your left, across the street and before the cathedral. (☎ 923 46 05 61. Open M-F 9am-2pm and 5-7pm, Sa-Su 10am-2pm and 5-7pm.)

ALBA DE TORMES(30MIN.)

Buses run to Alba de Tormes from Salamanca (30min., 8-12 per day, 190ptas).

Santa Teresa left her heart in Alba de Tormes. In fact, it's in a big urn, along with her body, in the lovely **Convento de la Anunciación,** which she founded in 1571. In her autobiography, she writes that her heart was pierced by an angel of the Lord with a fiery dart and after repeated stabbings, she was left "on fire with the great love of God." Her heart and the convent lie in Plazuela de Santa Teresa, two blocks from peaceful Pl. Mayor. If you'd like a tour, ask a guide at the **Museo Teresiano** across the street. The museum holds other parts of Santa Teresa and bits of San Juan de la Cruz. (Open daily 10am-1:30pm and 4:30-7pm. Donation requested.) A few blocks down from Pl. Mayor is the **Castillo de los Duques de Alba,** remnants of a 15th- to 16th-century structure which was excavated from 1991-1993. The castle displays Renaissance frescoes and an archaeological exhibit of the uncovered remains. Long wires hooked to the castle's top appear to provide a clothesline for locals. (Open July-Aug. Sa-Su; Sept.-June tourist office staff can let you in.) Though small, Alba de Tormes also boasts seven churches, monasteries, and convents, plus a neo-Gothic basilica. The **tourist office,** C. Lepanto, 4 is quite helpful when open, but hours are not fixed. (☎ 923 30 08 98. Open daily June-Aug. about 11am-1pm and 4:30-6:30pm; Sept.-May 10:30am-2pm and 4-6:30pm.)

LA ALBERCA AND PEÑA DE FRANCIA(1½HR.)

Empresa V. Cosme (☎ 923 30 02 71) runs buses from Salamanca to La Alberca (1½hr.; M-F 2 per day, Sa 12:30pm, Su 9:30am).

Three mountain ranges to the south conceal some delightful small towns on the plains of Castilla y León and Extremadura. **La Alberca,** a charming, rustic village, was the first rural town in the country to be named an official National Historic-Artistic Monument (1940). Every August 15th, the village honors the Holy Virgin with the *Ofertorio,* a colorful display of regional dress and folkloric tradition.

Above La Alberca in the Sierra de Francia looms the province's highest peak, **Peña de Francia** (1723m). Determined souls can scale the mountain from La Alberca. For more information about La Alberca or Peña de Francia, contact the **tourist office.** (C. Lepanto, 4. ☎ 923 41 52 91 ext. 15. Open June-Sept. M-F 10am-1pm and 5-7pm, Sa 10am-1pm and 4-6pm, Su 10am-1pm.)

ZAMORA

Although it was one of the most powerful cities in medieval Castile, provincial Zamora (pop. 65,000) has not seen much action since the 12th century, when Sancho II died here during his attempt to subdue his rebellious sister Doña Urraca and consolidate his hold on the House of Castile. Although she had been passed over in her father's will in favor of Sancho, Urraca managed to steal away her brother's inheritance by threatening to sleep with every man in the House of Castile if the kingdom was not passed to her. Vestiges of this illustrious and shocking past attract some history buffs—but not too many of them.

TRANSPORTATION. Trains leave from the station (24hr. ☎ 980 52 11 10) at the end of C. Alfonso Peña. Among other places, trains go to: **Valladolid** (1½hr., 8:34am and 7:40pm, 1000ptas) and **Madrid** (3hr., 2-3 per day 2:35am-6:20pm, 3400ptas). **Buses** depart from C. Alfonso Peña, 3 (☎ 980 52 12 81 or 980 52 12 82), to: **Valladolid** (1½hr.; M-F 7 per day 7am-8pm, Sa 5 per day 8:30am-6pm, Su 3 per day 8:30am-8pm; 775ptas); **León** (2hr.; M-F 7 per day 7am-7:30pm, Sa 4 per day 10:15am-5pm, Su 4 per day 10:15am-11pm; 1160ptas); **Madrid** (3½hr.; M-Sa 6 per day 7am-8pm, Su 6 per day 10:30am-9pm; 2415-2715ptas); and **Bragança, Portugal** (2hr.; 3 per week M and W 4pm, F 12:15am; 2495ptas).

ORIENTATION AND PRACTICAL INFORMATION. The train and bus stations are both a 15-minute walk from Pl. Mayor. Upon exiting the train station, go straight through the rotary onto C. Alfonso Peña (which becomes Av. Tres Cruces). Continue to Pl. Alemania and turn left onto C. Alfonso IX. Walk two blocks and turn right on **Calle de Santa Clara**, a major pedestrian street that leads to Pl. Mayor. From the front entrance of the bus station, turn right and then turn right again along the side of the station. Go left onto C. Alfonso Peña and follow the directions from the train station. The **tourist office,** C. Santa Clara, 20, has brochures, maps, and a hostel guide. (☎ 980 53 18 45; fax 980 53 38 13. Open M-F 9am-2pm and 5-7pm, Sa 10am-2pm and 5-8pm.) **Luggage storage** is available in the bus station (90ptas per bag; open daily 7am-midnight) and **train station** (300ptas per bag; open 24hr.). In an **emergency** call ☎ 112 or the **police** (☎ 980 54 87 26).

ACCOMMODATIONS AND FOOD. If you're spending the night in Zamora, **Pensión Fernando III**, Pl. Fernando III, 2, has large, clean sunlit rooms, all with sinks; bathrooms are down the hall. From the bus station entrance, take the first two rights and then the first left uphill off C. Alfonso Peña onto C. Brahones. (☎ 980 52 36 83. Singles 1250-1530ptas; doubles 2550-2850ptas; triples 4500ptas.) If you'd rather be near Pl. Mayor, try **Pensión Balborraz**, on C. Balborraz. From the tourist office, walk down C. Santa Clara toward Pl. Mayor and turn left onto C. Balborraz just before the plaza. Rooms are somewhat dim and have no heat. (☎ 980 51 55 19. Singles 1500ptas; doubles 2400ptas.) Most restaurants in Zamora cluster near C. Santa Clara and around Pl. Mayor, particularly on C. Herreros.

SIGHTS AND ENTERTAINMENT. Zamora's foremost monument is its mostly Romanesque **cathedral** (1135), a stocky building topped with a Byzantine dome. Take a moment to observe the detail and complexity of the main altar, made of marble, gold, and silver. Don't miss the golden angels on the baby blue background above. Inside the cloister, the **Museo de la Catedral** features the priceless 15th-century **Black Tapestries.** These gruesome tapestries tell the story of the Trojan War, depicting, among other things, numerous warriors and princesses right before they were decapitated. (☎ 980 53 06 44. Cathedral open daily 9am-2pm and 4-6pm. Mass daily at 10am, also Sa 6pm and Su 1pm. Free. Museum open Apr.-Sept. Tu-Sa 11am-2pm and 5-8pm, Su 11am-2pm; Oct.-Mar. Tu-Sa 11am-2pm and 4-6pm, Su 11am-2pm. 300ptas.) Grab an afternoon picnic in the quiet, charming Parque del Castillo next to the museum. **Roman walls** uphill from the cathedral command a fine view of the mighty Río Duero. Look back toward the city center at the **Iglesia de San Isidoro;** gargoyle-like storks often perch there.

Eight handsome **Romanesque churches** remain within the walls of the old city, each gleaming in the wake of recent restoration. If you suspect they all look the same, drop by the intricately carved porch of the romantic **La Magdalena.** The luminescent marble-veined windows in **Iglesia San Juan** and the bright green-and-orange organ in **Iglesia San Ildefonso** are also worth a look. (All open July-Oct. Tu-Sa 10am-1pm and 5-8pm; Nov.-June F-Sa 10am-2pm, Su 4:30-6:30pm. Free.) **Iglesia Santa María La Nueva** was the site of one of Zamora's most significant historical events, *El Motín de la Trucha*, in 1158; villagers set the church on fire (with Zamoran nobility inside) to protest a law giving noblemen priority over plebians in buying trout. May sound silly, but the event was one of the first in a series that led to the rise of the bourgeois throughout Spain. To get to the church, walk down C. Santa Clara until you get to Pl. de Viriato, then make a left. The **Museo de Semana Santa,** in sleepy Pl. Santa María la Nueva, is a rare find. Hooded mannequins stand guard over elaborately sculpted floats from the turn of the century. These mannequins were used during the *romerías*, processions honoring *Semana Santa;* Zamora has one of the most decorated Easter celebrations in all of Spain. To reach the museum from Pl. Mayor, take C. Sacramento and turn right on C. Barandales. (☎ 980 53 22 95. Open M-Sa 10am-2pm and 5-8pm, Su 10am-2pm. 300ptas.)

The best entertainment in Zamora are the occasional festivals that take over the main plaza, especially during Holy Week, or *Semana Santa*. Nightlife centers on the bars on C. Herreros. The local hangout **Mesón Los Abuelos,** C. Herreros, 30, plays mostly Spanish pop music and salsa; you'd be hard-pressed to find any real *abuelos* (grandfathers) in this youth-filled dance club. (Open daily noon-3am.)

LEÓN

Images of lions are everywhere in León and residents of the city refer to themselves as *leonés*, close to the Spanish word for lions. Strangely enough, though, the city's name has nothing to do with lions—it stems rather from *legio* (Latin for legion), a name that the Seventh Roman Legion gave the town in AD 68. During the Middle Ages, the city was as an important stop on the pilgrim's route to Santiago de Compostela, and it served as an essential defense point against Moorish invaders during the *Reconquista*. Today León is a bustling provincial capital and university town. The city itself is best known for its cathedral, whose spectacular blue stained-glass windows have earned León the nickname *La Ciudad Azul* (The Blue City). Proud *leoneses* boast that their cathedral is the finest in of all Spain; they may very well be right, but León's beautiful museums, historic churches and serene riverside park are just as much of a reason to spend a few days here.

▛ TRANSPORTATION

Trains: RENFE, Av. Astorga, 2 (☎ 987 27 02 02). With Pl. Guzmán el Bueno behind you, cross the river and continue on Av. Astorga until the station is on the left. Open 24hr. Trains to: **Astorga** (45min., 12 per day 1:50am-8:29pm, 700ptas); **Palencia** (1½hr., 17 per day 12:15am-9:42pm, 1065ptas); **Valladolid** (2½hr., 3 per day 8:50am-8:35pm, 1450-2100ptas); **Madrid** (4½hr., 8 per day 7:10am-3:55am, 3380ptas); **La Coruña** (7hr., express 4½hr.; 3 per day 4:05am-2:02pm; 3900ptas); **Barcelona** (9½hr., 3 per day 1:20pm-1:25am, 5800-7500ptas); **Gijón** (3hr., 8 per day 8:55am-4:45am, 1125ptas). **FEVE,** Av. Padre Isla, 48 (☎ 987 22 59 19), north of Pl. Santo Domingo sends trains to local destinations. A full train and bus schedule is printed daily in *Diario de León* (110ptas).

Buses: Estación de Autobuses (☎ 987 21 00 00), Po. Ingeniero Saenz de Miera. Info open M-Sa 7:30am-9pm. To: **Astorga** (40min.; M-F 16 per day 6:30am-9:20pm; Sa 7 per day 9:30am-8:30pm; Su 6 per day 9:30am-8:30pm; 405ptas); **Valladolid** (2hr., 8 per day 2:30am-10:30pm, 1070ptas); **Zamora** (2½hr.; M-F 5 per day 8am-6pm, Sa 4 per day 8am-5pm, Su 4 per day 10:15am-7pm; 1160ptas); **Madrid** (4½hr.; M-F 12 per day 2:30am-10:30pm, Sa-Su 8 per day 2:30am-7:30pm; 2665ptas); and **Santander** (5hr., F 3:30pm and Su 7:30pm, 2680ptas).

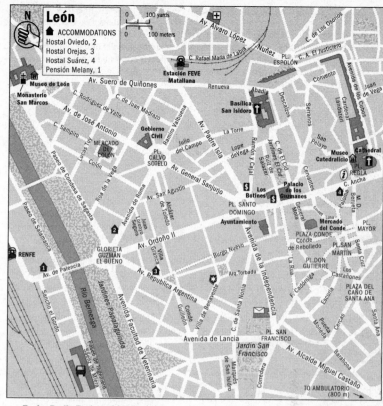

León

♠ ACCOMMODATIONS
Hostal Oviedo, 2
Hostal Orejas, 3
Hostal Suárez, 4
Pensión Melany, 1

Taxis: Radio Taxi (☎ 987 26 14 15).

Car Rental: Hertz, Plaza San Marcos, 6 (☎ 987 23 19 99). Must be at least 25 and have had a license for 1 year or more. Open M-F 9am-2pm and 4-7pm, Sa 9am-1pm.

✳️🛈 ORIENTATION AND PRACTICAL INFORMATION

Most of León, including the old city and modern commercial district, lies on the east side of the **Río Bernesga.** The bus and train stations are across the river in the west end. Av. Palencia (a left out of the bus station or right out of the train station) leads across the river to **Plaza Guzmán el Bueno,** where, after the Glorieta Guzmán Bueno rotary, it becomes **Avenida de Ordoño II** and leads to León's cathedral. Av. Ordoño II then bisects the new city and at Pl. Santo Domingo becomes **Calle Ancha,** which splits the old town in two. Look for the path of little gold shells laid on the pedestrian street in commemoration of the Pilgrimage to Santiago de Compostela.

Tourist Office: Pl. Regla, 3 (☎ 987 23 70 82; fax 987 27 33 91), in front of the cathe-dral. Free city maps, regional brochures, and accommodations guide. English spoken. Open M-F 9am-2pm and 5-7:30pm, Sa-Su 10am-2pm and 4:30-8:30pm.

Budget Travel: TIVE, C. Arquitecto Torbado, 4 (☎ 987 20 09 51), just off Pl. Cortes. ISIC cards 500ptas. HI cards 1800ptas. Open M-F 9am-2pm.

Currency Exchange: Banco Central Hispano, Pl. Santo Domingo (☎ 987 27 38 90 or 987 22 55 00). Follow Av. Ordoño II into the plaza. Open M-F 8:30am-2:30pm.

Luggage Storage: At the **train station,** lockers 400ptas. Open 24hr. At the **bus station,** 25ptas per bag. Open M-F 9am-2pm and 6-8pm, Sa 9am-2pm.

English Bookstore: Pastor, Pl. Santo Domingo, 4 (☎ 987 22 58 56). Follow Av. Ordoño II into the plaza. Open M-F 10am-1:30pm and 4:15-8pm, Sa 10am-1:45pm.

Emergency: ☎ 112. **Police:** ☎ 091 or 092. C. Villa Benavente, 6 (☎ 987 20 73 12).

Medical Services: Hospital Virgen Blanca (☎ 987 23 74 00).

Post Office: (☎ 987 23 90 79; fax 987 87 60 78), Jardín San Francisco. From Pl. Santo Domingo, go down Av. Independencia; the post office is opposite Parque San Francisco on the left. Lista de Correos and **fax** service available. Open M-F 8:30am-8:30pm, Sa 9:30am-2pm **Postal Code:** 24004.

Internet Access: Locutorio La Rúa, C. La Rúa, 8 (☎ 987 23 01 06). Take C. Ancha from Pl. Santo Domingo and turn right on C. La Rúa. 500ptas per hr. Open M-F 9:30am-2:30pm and 4:30-11pm, Sa 10am-2pm and 5-9:30pm). **Haddock Bar,** (☎ 987 20 92 56), C. Santiesteban y Osorio. From Pl. Santo Domingo, walk down Av. Ordoño II. At Glorieta Guzmán El Bueno rotary, make a left onto Av. Facultad de Veterinari, another left onto C. Bernardo del Carpio, and then the first left onto C. Santiesteban and Osorio. 500ptas per hr.; drinks, dancing and music in the background. Open daily 4pm-6am.

▌ ACCOMMODATIONS

Budget beds are fairly easy to come by in León, thanks to the yearly influx of pilgrims on their way to Santiago, but hostels and pensiones do tend to fill during the June fiestas. Look on **Av. de Roma, Av. Ordoño II,** and **Av. República Argentina,** which lead into the new town from Pl. Guzmán el Bueno. Pensiones are also scattered on the streets by the train and bus stations, though these establishments are less centrally located and are surrounded by empty streets that can be intimidating at night. Check the tourist office map for more locations.

Hostal Orejas, Av. República Argentina, 28 (☎ 987 25 29 09), off Pl. Guzmán el Bueno. Large windows illuminate each brand-new room, complete with bath, shower, cable TV and free Internet access. A little pricey, but well worth the stretch. Singles 5500ptas; doubles 6500ptas. Extra beds available for 1500ptas each.

Hostal Oviedo, Av. Roma, 26, 2nd fl. (☎ 987 22 22 36), off Pl. Guzmán el Bueno. Friendly and accommodating proprietors offer large, well-maintained rooms, many with sinks and terraces. Expect to see lots of Americans. Heated in winter. Public telephone. Singles 2000ptas; doubles 3500ptas; triples 5500ptas.

Hostel Suárez, C. Ancha, 7 (☎ 987 25 42 88). Prime location, seconds away from the cathedral. Large windows make for great people-watching. Kitchen. No heat. Doubles 3000ptas; triples 3500ptas. Open Apr.-Nov. Cash only.

Pensión Melany, Av. de Palencia, 4, 1st fl. (☎ 987 24 10 75), up Av. Palencia, directly in front of the train station. Only a few steps from the train and bus stations, this pension offers bargain prices and a prime location for travelers. Old, dim rooms have comfy beds. 10min. walk to the cathedral. Singles 1700ptas; doubles 2700ptas.

▌ FOOD

Inexpensive eateries fill the area near the cathedral and on the small streets off C. Ancha; also check Pl. San Martín, near Pl. Mayor. Meat-lovers will rejoice as many variations of pork top the local menus. In June, León's 3500km of trout-fishable streams draw the **International Trout Festival.** Fresh produce in all shapes and sizes is available at the **Mercado Municipal del Conde,** Pl. Conde, off C. General Mola. (Open M-Sa 9am-3:30pm). For groceries, try **Día Auto Servicion** in Pl. Picara Justina, on Av. República Argentina. (Open M-Sa 9:30am-2:15pm and 5-8:15pm.)

Calle Ancha, C. Ancha, 11 (☎ 987 21 01 83). Between C. General Mola and C. Conde Lun, a 2min. walk from the cathedral. Satisfy your hunger with fresh veggies, quiche, fish, or pizzas made to order by chef Esther in a modern, hip setting. The *menú económica* (950ptas) comes with a bottle of wine. Vegetarian dishes available. Open daily 12-4pm and 9:15pm-midnight, F-Sa until 3:30am. V, MC.

Cafetería-Restaurante Catedral, C. Mariano Domínguez Berrueta, 17 (☎ 987 21 59 18), to the right when facing the cathedral. Monumental portions make the 1300pta *menú* a great bargain. Salads 500-700ptas. Sandwiches 400-1200ptas. Open M and Th-Sa 1:30-4pm and 8pm to midnight; Tu, W, and Su 8-11pm. V, MC.

Zalacain, C. la Rúa, 24 (☎ 987 21 08 21). Walk down C. Ancha when facing the cathedral and take a right onto C. la Rúa. Classic vegetarian specialities and pleasant outdoor seating. *Menú del día* 995ptas. Salads 500-925ptas. Meat dishes 1100-1950ptas. Open M-Sa 12:30-4pm and 7:30pm-midnight, Su 12:30-4pm. V, MC.

■ SIGHTS

■ **CATHEDRAL.** The 13th-century Gothic cathedral, *La Pulchra Leonina*, is arguably the most beautiful cathedral in Spain. It is also one of Spain's best examples of Gothic architecture. The exceptional facade depicts smiling saints amidst bug-eyed monsters munching on the damned. But the real attractions are the rose windows with their spirals of saints, the vivid stained-glass interior, and the glass gardens with tiny faces and luminous petals. The cathedral's museum displays gruesome wonders, including a skeleton, a "Statue of Death," and a sculpture depicting the skinning of a saint. *(☎ 987 87 57 70. Cathedral open daily 8:30am-1:30pm and 4-8pm, until 7pm in winter. Free. Museum open M-F 9:30am-2pm and 4-7pm, Sa 9:30am-12:30pm and 4-6:30pm. 500ptas. Claustro 100ptas. Guides are required for much of the visit.)*

BASÍLICA SAN ISIDORO. The Basílica San Isidoro was dedicated in the 11th century to San Isidoro of Sevilla. After his death his remains were brought from Muslim-dominated Andalucía to the Christian stronghold of León. The corpses of countless royals rest in the impressive Panteón Real, where the ceilings are covered by vibrant 12th-century frescoes. The unusual Annunciation and medieval agricultural calendar are particularly noteworthy. Admission to the pantheon includes entrance to the library, which houses a 10th-century handwritten Bible, and to the treasury, home of Doña Urraca's famous agate chalices. *(Open July-Aug. M-Sa 9am-8pm, Su 9am-2pm; Sept.-June M-Sa 9am-1:30pm and 4-7pm, Su 9am-2pm. 400ptas.)*

OTHER SIGHTS. The **Museo de León** displays an extensive archaeological collection with pieces dating from the Paleolithic era. *(☎ 987 24 50 61. Pl. San Marcos. Open Oct.-April Tu-Su 10am-2pm and 4:30-8pm; May-Sept. 10am-2pm and 5-8:30pm. Closed Su afternoon. 200ptas. Free Su morning.)* . **Los Botines,** in Pl. Santo Domingo, is one of the few buildings outside of Cataluña designed by Antoni Gaudí. The relatively restrained structure still contains hints of the style that would emerge later in his life (see **Barcelona,** p. 298). It now serves as the Caja de España bank.

♫ ▥ ENTERTAINMENT AND NIGHTLIFE

Unfortunately, most of the city's best clubs are only accessible by cab. Try **Oh León!** or **La Tropicana. Baroque** is also a local favorite. For nearby bars, discos, and techno music, head to the *barrio húmedo* (drinker's neighborhood) around **Plaza de San Martín.** To get to the *barrio,* walk up C. Ancha toward the cathedral and take a right on Legión Condor (which becomes Platerías Candiles). Take a right where the street ends, and head left. Almost all the bars here are open until 2am daily and until 5-6am on Friday and Saturday. **El Bacanal** attracts crowds to its Caravaggio-covered walls. *(☎ 987 21 38 51. Beers 150ptas. Drinks 600ptas.)* Mellower music, pastel walls, and actual breathing space characterize **El Robote** (across the square). After 2am, the crowds weave to **Calle Lancia** and **Calle Conde de Guillén,** both heavily populated with discos and bars. Plenty of hip cafes line **Calle Ancha. El Gran Café** (☎ 987 27 23 01), on C. Cervantes one block off C. Ancha, delivers live jazz nightly to a chic clientele. The red velvet seating area and saloon upstairs both overlook the street below. *(Beers 300ptas. Mixed drinks 500ptas.)* **La Gargola** has cushy yellow-striped sofas and tall, translucent orange shades. For more romantic, secluded spots, explore C. La Paloma and the narrow streets around the cathedral.

Festivals commemorating **San Juan** and **San Pedro** occur from June 21 to 30. Highlights include a *corrida de torros* (bullfight) and the feast days of San Juan on June 25 and San Pedro on June 30. King Juan Carlos I and his wife Sofía attend the fiestas and the cathedral's **International Organ Festival** every year.

🚌 DAYTRIP FROM LEÓN

ASTORGA (45 MIN.)

RENFE runs trains to Astorga from León (45min., 8 per day, 400ptas). Buses make the trip more frequently (40min., 16 per day, 405ptas).

Astorga reached its peak in the 15th century as an important stopping point on both *La Ruta de la Plata*, the Roman silver route, and *El Camino Francés*, the pilgrim's path toward Santiago de Compostela that begins in the French Pyrenees. In the early 17th century it became one of world's main centers of chocolate making. Hershey Inc. and friends took care of *that* claim to fame by the late 19th century, but a few die-hards still produce bars of authentic *chocolate de Astorga*.

Today Astorga is perhaps most distinguished by its fanciful ▧Palacio Episcopal, designed by Antoni Gaudí in the late 19th century. Gaudí built the palace to replace the one which burned down in 1886, but no bishop has actually dared live there since, perhaps because it seems more like a giant drip-castle than a home. Now the palace houses the fascinating **Museo de los Caminos,** dedicated to the various paths toward Santiago de Compostela that converge in 2000 year-old Astorga. (☎ 987 61 88 82. Open daily June-Sept. 10am-1:30pm and 4-7:30pm; Oct.-May 11am-2pm and 3:30-6:30pm. 500ptas.) The **cathedral,** opposite Gaudí's palace, is definitely worth a quick visit, though it'll be a bit of a let-down for those coming from León. Pay special attention to the detailed 18th-century facade and the beautiful choir loft. The cathedral's **museum** has ten rooms filled with religious relics. (Cathedral open daily June-Sept. 9:30-10:30am and 5-6:30pm; Oct.-May 9:30-10:30am and 4:30-6pm. Free. Museum open daily June-Sept. 10am-2pm and 4-8pm; Oct.-May 11am-2pm and 3:30-6:30pm. 250ptas, 400ptas for a joint ticket to the Museo de los Caminos.) Kids and sweet-tooths should stop by the **Museo de Chocolate** and other equally sugary museums just outside the city walls. Visiting without buying a box of the famous *La Viuda de León* pastries just might classify as a sin; check with local nuns to be sure.

To get to the town center from the RENFE **train station** (☎ 987 84 21 22), Pl. Estación, follow C. Pedro de Castro across Puerta de Rey. A large building (Casa Granell) is on the right. Pass the wall, turn right onto Los Sitios, and walk to the palace. The **bus station** (☎ 987 61 91 00), on Av. Ponferrada across from the Palacio Episcopal, is close to the town's sights. To get to the **tourist office,** stand with your back to the palace gate and face the plaza (with the cathedral on the right). The gray tourist office is right in front of you, just beyond the plaza. (Open M-Sa 10am-2pm and 4-7:30pm, Su 10:30am-2pm.) **Luggage storage** is available at the train station (400ptas) and the bus station (25ptas).

VALLADOLID

For nearly 300 years, Valladolid was the most important town in the Kingdom of Castile; when Fernando and Isabel were married here in 1469, it stood at the forefront of Spanish politics, finance, and culture. Explorers Magellan and El Cano came here to discuss their plans for voyages that would circumvent the newly discovered round world. Miguel de Cervantes, creater of the romantic hero Don Quijote, lived here, and infamous discoverer Christopher Columbus died here in 1506. Close to a century later, shady dealings by minister Conde Duque de Lerma brought the glory days to an end. In return for a whopping bribe, Lerma took Valladolid (then capital of Castile) out of the running for capital of Spain. Madrid won, and history moved on. Yet today, Valladolid makes up for its lack of national status with an impressive sculpture museum and endearing quirks. Fountains are lit in day-glo pink and green, architecture from the 1970s challenges graceful Renaissance forms, and on certain summer days, Supermarket Simago blasts American music on the main pedestrian thoroughfare while locals hum along.

TRANSPORTATION

Flights: Villanubla Airport, León Highway (N-601), km 13 (☎ 983 41 54 00). Taxi to airport 1800-2000ptas. Daily trips to Barcelona and Paris. Summer service to the Balearic Islands (June-Oct.). Info open daily 8am-8pm. **Iberia,** C. Gamazo, 17 (☎ 983 30 06 66 or 983 30 26 39). Open M-F 9:30am-1:30pm and 4-7pm, Sa 9:30am-1:30pm.

Trains: Estación del Norte (☎ 983 30 35 18, 983 30 75 78, or 902 24 02 02), C. Recondo, at the end of Campo Grande. Info (☎ 983 20 02 02 or 902 24 02 02) open daily 7am-8pm. Ticket windows open 7am-last train. To: **Zamora** (2hr., 8:36am, 1020ptas); **Burgos** (1¾-2½hr., 8-10 per day 1:42am-8:01pm, 975-1070ptas); **León** (2-3hr., 8-10 per day 1:42am-9:01pm, 1265ptas); **Salamanca** (1¾-2¾hr., 8-10 per day 3am-10:02pm, 850ptas); **Madrid** (3-3¾hr., 18-21 per day 12:20am-9:05pm, 1900ptas); **Santander** (3-6hr., 7 per day 1:42am-6:43pm, 1935ptas); **San Sebastián** (5hr.; 1:42, 3:41am, 12:25pm; 3060ptas); **Oviedo** (4-5½hr; 1:42, 10:27am, 5:25pm; 3100ptas); **Bilbao** (4hr.; 1:42, 6:55, 11:47am; 1800ptas); **Barcelona** (9¾-11hr., 9:18 and 9:30am, 5700ptas); **Paris** (11hr., 9:20pm, 13,500ptas); **Lisbon/Oporto** (7¾hr., 3am, 6300ptas).

Buses: Puente Colgante, 2 (☎ 010 or 983 23 63 08). Info open daily 8am-10pm. From the train station, turn left and follow C. Recondo, which borders the train tracks, becoming C. Puente Colgante. The bus station is just past the underpass (5min.). To: **Zamora** (1½hr.; M-F 7 per day 8:30am-8:15pm, Sa 5 per day 8:30am-6pm, Su 8:30am, 3, and 8pm; 795ptas); **Burgos** (1¾-2¾hr., 5-7 per day 9:45am-9:45pm, 1045ptas); **León** (2hr., 8-9 per day 12:45am-9:45pm, 1090ptas); **Madrid** (2¼hr., 17-18 per day 12:30am-9:30pm, 1580ptas); **Oviedo** (3¼-4¼hr., 4 per day 12:30am-6:30pm, 2185ptas); **San Sebastián** (6hr., 1:35 and 5:30pm, 2840ptas); **Barcelona** (10hr.; 9:45am, 12:15, and 9:45pm; 6010ptas); and **Santiago** (8hr., 2:25pm, 3760ptas). **ALSA** info open M-Sa 6am-10pm, Su 8am-10pm.

Taxis: (24hr. ☎ 983 29 14 11 or 983 20 77 55). Stands at both transportation stations.

ORIENTATION AND PRACTICAL INFORMATION

The **bus** and **train stations** sit on the southern edge of town. To get from the bus station to the **tourist office,** turn left on Paseo del Arco de Ladrillo and then veer off the busy street onto C. Laprillo. Walk through the stone archway, which cuts through the wooded park Campo Grande and ends at Pl. Zorrilla; the tourist office is straight across on the right side of C. Santiago. From there, walk down C. Santiago to get to the **Plaza Mayor.** The **cathedral** is a 10-minute walk from Pl. Mayor (on the right as you face the Ayuntamiento).

Tourist Office: C. Santiago, 19 (☎ 983 34 40 13). Maps, museum info, and numerous booklets and brochures. English spoken. Open daily 9am-2pm and 5-7pm.

Budget Travel: TIVE, Edificio Administrativo de Uso Múltiple, 3rd fl. (☎ 983 35 45 63). From Pl. Zorrilla, take C. María de Molina to C. Doctrinos. Follow it across Puente Isabel la Católica and past the parking lot. Open M-F 9am-2pm.

Currency Exchange: At the **bus station** and **Banco Central Hispano,** on the corner of Av. Acera Recoletos and C. Perú, 6 (☎ 983 30 63 40). Open M-F 8:30am-2:30pm.

Luggage Storage: At **Estación del Norte** (lockers 300ptas). At the **bus station** (50ptas per bag). Open M-Sa 8am-10pm.

Emergency: ☎ 112. **National Police:** C. Felipe II, 11 (☎ 983 35 70 66). **Local Police:** ☎ 983 42 61 07. **Guardia Civil:** Av. de Soria, 3 (☎ 983 30 49 00).

CENTRAL SPAIN

Medical Services: Hospital Pío del Río Hortega (☎ 983 42 04 00), C. Santa Teresa. Some doctors speak English. **Red Cross** (☎ 983 22 22 22).

Post Office: (☎ 902 19 71 97 or 983 33 03 95), Pl. Rinconada. From Pl. Mayor, take C. Jesús. **Faxes** and **Lista de Correos.** Open M-F 8:30am-8:30pm, Sa 8:30am-2pm. **Postal Code:** 47001.

Internet Access: Intermática Perú, C. Perú, 14 (☎ 983 21 71 28). 300ptas for 30min., 500ptas per hr. **Café Segafredo,** Po. de Zorilla, 47 (☎ 983 33 80 63). 600ptas per hr. Open Su-Th 8am-midnight, F until 1am, Sa until 2:30am.

▶ ACCOMMODATIONS

Cheap lodgings, all with winter heating, are easy to come by. Though a little dark and scary, the streets off Av. Acera Recoletos near the train station are packed with hostels, as are the streets near the cathedral and behind Pl. Mayor at Pl. Val.

Pensión Dos Rosas, C. Perú, 11, 2nd fl. (☎ 983 20 74 39). From the train station, walk up Av. Acera Recoletos and turn right on C. Perú. Perfumed singles sport shiny crimson bedsheets; doubles are spacious and sunny. Bathrooms down the hall. Portable heaters in winter. Singles 1650ptas; doubles 2900ptas; triples 4100ptas.

Pensión Dani, C. Perú, 11, 1st fl. (☎ 983 30 02 49), below Dos Rosas. The owners of Dos Rosas and Dani are sisters, and you can tell; Dani offers equally clean, spacious rooms, with windows and TVs. Singles 1650ptas; doubles 2900ptas; triples 4200ptas.

Fonda Vianesa, C. Montero Calvo, 1 (☎ 983 30 58 92). Walk down C. Santiago with the fountain at your back. Dark, unsettling halls, but the tiny rooms are clean and the location near Plaza Mayor is a definite plus. Singles 1500ptas; doubles 2500ptas.

▶ FOOD

Competition keeps prices down, making even the most elegant of restaurants accessible to budget diners. Eateries abound between Pl. Mayor and Pl. Val; explore the area near the cathedral for *tapas*. The **Mercado del Val,** on C. Sandoval in Pl. Val, has fresh foods (open M-Sa 6am-3pm). **Supermarket Champion,** C. Santiago, 15, has a wide array of groceries (open M-Sa 9:30am-9:15pm).

Casa San Pedro Regalad, Pl. Ochavo, 1 (☎ 983 34 45 06 or 983 35 46 36), on the corner of C. Platerías, 2 blocks from Pl. Mayor. Descend into the cavernous depths of this 16th-century *bodega* to enjoy elegant dining. *Menú* M-F 1100ptas. Open daily 1:30-3:30pm and 8-11:30pm. V, MC, AmEx.

Restaurante Chino Gran Muralla, C. Santa María, 1 (☎ 983 34 23 07), off C. Santiago, north of Pl. Zorrilla. Look for the hanging dragons. Warm greetings at the door, good Chinese eats inside. *Menú* 685-950ptas. Open daily 11:30am-5pm and 7pm-12:30am.

▶ SIGHTS

■ **MUSEO NACIONAL DE ESCULTURA.** The Museo Nacional de Escultura in the **Colegio de San Gregorio** offers the thrill of 20 churches in one convenient location. More than 20 rooms chart the region's religious art history through transplanted segments of now-destroyed monasteries and churches, including figurines, tableaux, sculpted choirs, and intricate ceilings. *(Cardenas de San Gregorio in front of Pl. Federico Wattenberg, off Pl. de San Pablo, 1. ☎ 983 25 03 75 or 983 25 40 83. Open Tu-Sa 10am-2pm and 4-6pm, Su 10am-2pm. 400ptas, students with ID 200ptas. Under 18 and over 65 free. Sa afternoon and Su free.)*

CATHEDRAL. The cathedral was designed by Juan de Herrera, the creator of El Escorial. The extensive **Museo Diocesano,** inside, is worth a visit for its original model of the basilica; its many statues of Jesus, Mary, and the saints; and its gruesome Jesus with real matted hair. *(C. Arribas, 1, in Pl. Universidad. ☎ 983 30 43 62. Cathedral and museum open M-F 10am-2pm and 5-8pm, Sa-Su 10am-2:30pm. Museum closed Su. Cathedral free. Museum 400ptas.)*

CASA DE CERVANTES. Supposedly the writer wrote part of his epic "El Quijote" while living here from 1603-1606. There is an amusing collection of old books and furniture, but the medieval bed-warmer is the only real highlight. (☎ 983 33 88 10. *C. Castro, off Pl. de Madrid. Open Tu-Sa 9:30am-3:30pm, Su 10am-3pm. 400ptas, students with ID 200ptas. Under 18 and over 65 free. Su free.)*

🎵 ENTERTAINMENT

Valladolid's cafes and bars are lively, though nothing to write home about. A student crowd fills the countless bars on C. Paraíso. For pubs, go to Pl. San Miguel and C. Santa María near the Iglesia Santa María la Antigua. Later on, cafes on C. Vincente Meliner, near Pl. Dorado, draw an older crowd. **Tiutiu,** on Pl. Marti Monsó (to the left of Pl. Mayor when facing Ayuntamiento), deserves its title as most popular bar in Valladolid. **The Black Rose** is a great place to down a few, but the absence of Guinness in this reportedly "Irish" bar is as much of a mystery as its name. (Beer 300ptas. Mixed drinks 600-700ptas.) Discotecas **Charlot,** on C. Espiritu Santo off Río Pisuerga, and **La Rosaleda** (☎ 983 34 12 44), on Av. Ramón Pradera, across the Río Pisuerga off Av. Salamanca, play thumping beats (both open 8pm-8am). **Discoteca Mambo,** on C. San Felipe Neri, 1-3 (☎ 983 21 29 55) and **Club 38,** on C. Mayor, 30 (☎ 983 74 52 82), are also both dance hotspots (both open 7pm-late).

With over 12 movie theaters, Valladolid has one of the highest cinema-to-people ratios in all of Spain. If you can, catch **International Cinema Week** (Oct. 21-31). Find movie schedules and info on the city's first-division soccer team, **Real Valladolid,** in *El Monde de Valladolid* or *El Norte de Castilla.* The week of September 21 marks the **Fiesta Mayor,** which features bullfights, carnivals, and parades.

PALENCIA

In the late 14th century, local townswomen resisted the English attack during the siege of the Duke of Lancaster, and Palencia (pop. 82,000) took a vaulted position as a symbol of Spanish pride. Today the city's charm is rooted in its lovely streets and public gardens, combined with a historical origin shrouded in the myths spun by 11th-century monks, Pilgrims en route to Santiago, and eager local politicians. Though low on pizazz, Palencia will please any traveler craving a healthy dose of Romanesque and Visigothic architecture.

📧 **TRANSPORTATION. Trains** (☎ 979 74 30 19 or 902 24 02 02) steam from Parque Los Jardinillos to: **Valladolid** (45min., 12 per day 7:33am-9:15pm, 410-1100ptas); **Burgos** (1hr., 9 per day, 1200ptas); **León** (1¼hr., 11 per day 8:10am-9:35pm, 945-1700ptas); **Madrid** (3-5hr., 14 per day 2:24am-8:30pm, 2415-3600ptas); **La Coruña** (8hr.; 2:52am, 1, and 4pm; 4600ptas); **Barcelona** (8½-9hr.; 1:30am, 2:21, and 10:55pm; 5300ptas); **Santander** (3-3¾hr., 8 per day 3:56am-7:52pm, 1545-2400ptas); **Salamanca** (2½hr., 8am and 1:10pm, 1900-2265ptas); **Hendaya via Bilbao** (3¾hr. to Bilbao, 4½hr. to Hendaya; 4:07pm; 2500-3100ptas). The **bus station** is just to the right of the train station, down the street along Parque Jardinillos. (☎ 979 74 32 22. Info booth open M-F 8am-10:30pm, Sa-Su 8am-1:30pm and 5-10:30pm.) To: **Carrión de los Condes** (30min.; M-Sa 8am, 1:30, and 6pm, F also 7:30pm, Su 11am and 7:15pm; 315ptas); **Valladolid** (45min.; M-F every hr. 7am-10pm, Sa 6 per day 8am-7:30pm, Su 11am, 4, and 9pm; 385ptas); **Burgos** (1½hr.; M-F 4-5 per day 9am-7:15pm, Sa 9am; 720ptas); **Madrid** (4hr., 6-7 per day 3:30am-7:30pm, 1885ptas).

📋 **PRACTICAL INFORMATION.** The **train** and **bus stations,** next to the **Parque Los Jardinillos,** lie just above **Calle Mayor,** the main pedestrian artery and shopping zone. The bus station has **luggage storage** for 100ptas per day (open M-F 9:30am-7pm, Sa 9:30am-2pm) and the train station for 300ptas per day (open 24hr.). The **tourist office,** C. Mayor, 105, distributes free maps. (☎ 979 74 00 68; fax 979 70 08 22. Open M-Sa 10am-2pm and 5-7pm.) Change currency at **Banco Central Hispano,** C.

Mayor, 37. (☎ 979 74 35 00. Open M-F 8:30am-2:30pm.) In an **emergency** dial ☎ 112 or **local police** (☎ 979 74 76 77). For health services, contact the **Clínica Virgen de la Salud**, Av. Simón Nieto, 31 (☎ 979 74 77 00). There are two **post offices:** the one at Pl. León, 1 (☎ 979 74 21 80; fax 979 74 22 60), sends and receives **faxes;** the second office (☎ 979 74 21 77), next to the train station, provides **Lista de Correos.** (Both open M-F 8:30am-8:30pm, Sa 9:30am-2pm.) The **postal code** is 34001.

█▐█ ACCOMMODATIONS AND FOOD. Plenty of reasonably priced hostels with clean, plain rooms line side streets off C. Mayor. At the HI youth hostel, **Victorio Macho**, C. Dr. Fleming, the complex includes a common room with TV, kitchen and dining hall, and athletic facilities. Bus B from Los Jardinillos (every 15min., 65ptas) saves trekkers a hike. (☎ 979 72 04 62; fax 979 72 98 73. HI members only. Breakfast 100-150ptas. 1000ptas, over 26 1450ptas. Open July-Aug. 15. Call ahead.) **Pensión Gredos,** C. Valentín Calderón, 18, three blocks down and a left off C. Mayor from Pl. León, has comfy beds and a small patio. (☎ 979 70 28 33 or 609 29 46 84. Breakfast 350ptas; lunch and dinner 1000ptas each. Singles 1800ptas; doubles 3500ptas; triples 4800-6000ptas.) Numerous restaurants and *tapas* bars line the streets just off C. Mayor. At █**Bar-Restaurante El Coso,** C. Eduardo Dato, 8, off Pl. León, posters of matadors and bloody bulls line the walls and a stuffed bull's head watches diners eat. (☎ 979 74 67 58. Gourmet regional meat dishes 400-1600ptas. *Bocadillos* 500ptas.)

▣█ SIGHTS AND FESTIVALS. Palencia's biggest attraction is its 14th-century Gothic cathedral, **Santa Iglesia de San Antolín,** in Plaza de la Inmaculada, where 14-year-old Catherine of Lancaster married 10-year-old Enrique III in 1388. Built between the 14th and 16th centuries with predominantly Gothic features, the cathedral boasts a precious sandstone and pastel interior. During the tour, guides illuminate the various altars and then lead visitors down a stone staircase to the spooky **Cripta de San Antolín,** a 7th-century sepulchre. The cathedral's **museum** houses El Greco's famed *San Sebastián* and some spectacular 16th-century Flemish tapestries—not to mention a tiny caricature of Carlos V. (Cathedral ☎ 979 70 13 47. Open M-Sa 9am-1:30pm and 4-6:30pm, Su 9am-1:30pm. Free. Tours in Spanish daily 10:30am and 4pm. 100ptas. Museum open M-Sa 10:30am-1pm and 4-6pm. 300ptas.) Of the other churches in town, the favorite of El Cid fans is **Iglesia de San Miguel,** on C. General Mola, which runs parallel to the river. According to legend, it was here that El Campeador wed Doña Jimena. Its most notable feature is the 13th-century Gothic tower graced with tall openwork windows. (☎ 979 74 07 69. Open daily 9:30am-1:30pm and 6-8pm.) Also of interest is the **Cristo de Otero** to the north of town in "El Cristo" district. This 20m high stone sculpture, called "Christ on the Hillcock," was erected in 1930 by local artist Victorio Macho. At the foot of the statue lies the **Church of Santo Toribio,** originally built into the rock.

For such a small city, Palencia has more than its share of *fiestas*. On the **Baptism of Baby Jesus** (Jan. 1), an ancient carol is sung and godmothers throw sweets and presents from the balcony at Iglesia de San Miguel. On April 16th, Palencia celebrates the **Feast of Santo Toribio** with a pilgrimage to the rock church at the foot of El Cristo de Otero. To remember and atone for the stoning of the saint when he came to Palencia in the 5th century to preach, the mayor and city chancellors "stone" all those who take part in the festivities with pieces of bread and cheese.

DAYTRIP FROM PALENCIA: CARRIÓN DE LOS CONDES (30MIN.)

Buses (☎ 979 74 32 22) carry day-trippers to Carrión from Palencia (30min.; M-Sa 8am, 1:30, 6:30, and 8:30pm, Su 8am and 7:15pm; 315ptas).

Forty kilometers north of Palencia on the Camino de Santiago, the tiny riverside town of Carrión (pop. 1000) hides some incredible sights. On the south side of 12th-century **Iglesia de Santa María** (☎ 979 88 00 72) is a depiction of the legendary tribute of four Carrión maidens to Moorish conquerors. Supposedly, Santa María

foiled the transaction by sending four menacing bulls to gore the Moors. On the far •
side of the Río Carrión looms the secularized **Monasterio de San Zoilo.** Faces of
saints and Popes stare down from the ornate arches of its Renaissance cloister,
now partially open to the public. Near the exit are the tombs of the notorious
Infantes de Carrión. In the *Cantar del Mío Cid,* they married, deflowered, beat,
and then abandoned El Cid's daughters in the middle of the forest. (☎ 979 88 00 49.
Open daily in summer 10:30am-2pm and 4-8pm. 200ptas.) Carrión's hidden treasure is the **Convento de Santa Clara,** also known as **Las Clarisas.** To see the
museo, ring the bell and ask the keeper to let you in. (☎ 979 88 01 34. Open Tu-Su
10:30am-1pm and 4:30-7pm. 200ptas.) Carrión's **tourist office** is in a wood-frame hut
across from Café-Bar España, where the bus stops (hours vary).

BURGOS

Burgos lives in the shadow of its overwhelming history and its Gothic cathedral.
Founded in 884 by Count Diego Rodríguez Porcellos under the reign of King Alfonso III,
the city was created for purely strategic military reasons. During its 500 years as the capital of Castile, Burgos witnessed the birth of both the extraordinary cathedral and Rodrigo Díaz de Vivar, better known as El Cid Campeador, the national hero of Spain
(actually born in the nearby town of Vivar). Nine centuries after El Cid's banishment
from town, General Franco stationed his fascist headquarters here. Today's Burgos is
significantly more relaxed—by day natives share the galeria-lined streets and duck-filled
riverbanks with history-seeking tourists and international pilgrims following the Camino
de Santiago, while at night they hit the bars for Burgos's black pudding and Ribera de
Duero wines, then welcome sunrise from alley pubs and neon-flushed *discotecas.*

▬ TRANSPORTATION

Trains: (☎ 947 20 35 60), at the end of Av. Conde de Guadalhorce across the river from
Pl. Castilla. A 10min. walk southwest from the city center or a 500pta taxi ride. Info
open daily 7am-10pm. **RENFE,** C. Moneda, 21 (☎ 947 20 35 60). Open M-F 9am-1pm
and 4-7pm, Sa 9am-1pm. To: **Palencia** (45min., 8 per day 2:07am-8:20pm, 515-
1200ptas); **Valladolid** (1-2hr., 10-12 per day 1:44am-11:07pm, 975-1700ptas);
Logroño (2-2¾hr., 4 per day 2:17am-11:40pm, 2000ptas); **León** (2-3hr., 6 per day
2:07am-8:20pm, 2100ptas); **Madrid** (3-5½hr., 8 per day 2:20am-11:07pm, 3060-
3500ptas); **San Sebastián** (3-3½hr., 9 per day 3:17am-6:44pm, 2095-2500ptas); **Bilbao** (2½-4hr., 5 per day 3:17am-6:44pm, 2000ptas); **Santiago** (7½hr., 12:13pm,
4600ptas); and **Barcelona** (9-13¾hr., 7 per day 2:17am-11:40pm, 5000ptas).

Buses: C. Miranda, 4 (☎ 947 28 88 55), down C. de Madrid off Pl. Vega, on the south
side of the river. To: **Vitoria-Gasteiz** (1¾hr., 9 per day 7:15am-3:15am, 950ptas); **Valladolid** (2hr.; M-Sa 10:15 and 10:45am, M also 7am; 1045ptas); **Santander** (2¾hr.,
5 per day 7:30am-3:15am, 1350ptas); **Bilbao** (2-3hr., 7 per day 7:15am-6pm,
1420ptas); **Madrid** (2¾hr., 10:15pm, 1950ptas); **León** (3½hr., M-Sa 10:45am,
1700ptas); **Santiago** (7hr., 11am and 12:25am, 4625ptas); and **Barcelona** (7½hr.,
M-Sa 4 per day 8am-11pm, 5085ptas).

Taxis: Radio Taxi (☎ 947 27 77 77 or 947 48 10 10). 24hr. service. Taxis gather by Pl.
de Santo Domingo de Guzmán, Pl. de Vega, and Pl. de Conde Jordana.

Car Rental: Hertz, C. General Mola, 5 (☎ 947 20 16 75), on the block parallel to C.
Miranda near Pl. Vega. Min. age 25. Small cars with unlimited mileage 11,000ptas per
day, longer rentals less. Open M-F 9am-2pm and 4-7pm, Sa 9am-1pm. V, MC, AmEx.

■▪▪ ORIENTATION AND PRACTICAL INFORMATION

The Río Arlanzón splits Burgos into north and south. The **train** and **bus stations** are
on the south side, while the **cathedral** and all other sights of interest are located to
the north. From the train station, follow Av. Conde de Guadalhorce across the
river and take the first right onto Av. Generalísimo Franco, which turns into Po.

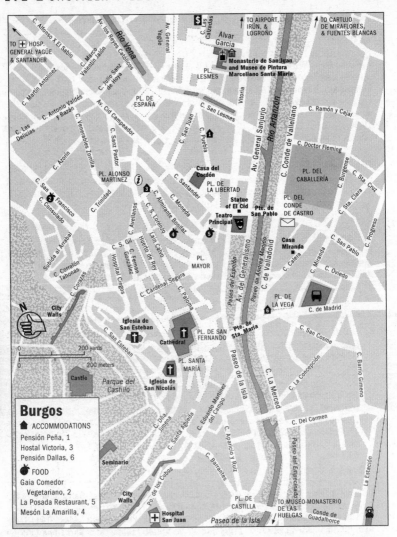

Burgos

▲ ACCOMMODATIONS
Pensión Peña, 1
Hostal Victoria, 3
Pensión Dallas, 6

🍎 FOOD
Gaia Comedor
  Vegetariano, 2
La Posada Restaurant, 5
Mesón La Amarilla, 4

Espolón farther down. From the bus station, follow C. Madrid through Pl. Vega and across the river. Upstream, along the *paseo* at C. Santander, stands a large statue of El Cid. The **Plaza José Antonio** (or **Plaza Mayor**) is between the cathedral and the tourist office.

Tourist Office: Pl. Alonso Martínez, 7 (☎ 947 20 31 25; fax 947 27 65 29). Open M-F 9am-2pm and 5-7pm, Sa-Su and holidays 10am-2pm and 5-8pm.

Budget Travel: TIVE, C. General Yagüe, 20 (☎ 947 20 98 81), off Pl. España. English spoken. Student IDs 700ptas. Open M-F 9am-2pm.

Currency Exchange: Banco Central Hispano, on Plaza de España, 6 (☎ 947 20 52 45). Open M-F 8:30am-1pm. For **ATMs,** hunt down Telebanco or SirviRed signs.

Luggage Storage: Lockers at the **train station** (400ptas). 24hr. At the **bus station** (200-325ptas per bag). Open daily 9am-8pm. After 8pm, inquire in a hotel.

Laundromat: Limpieza Alba, Pl. de España, 7 (☎ 947 27 21 33).

Emergency: ☎ 112. **Guardia Civil:** ☎ 062 or 947 22 11 00. **Police:** ☎ 947 28 88 39.

Pharmacy: Farmacia Natividad Combarro Rodríguez, C. San Juan, 25 (☎ 947 20 12 89). Open M-F 9am-2pm and 4-7:30pm, Sa 9am-2pm.

Medical Services: Ambulance ☎ 947 28 18 28. **Hospital General Yagüe,** Av. El Cid Campeador, 96 (☎ 947 28 18 00).

Telephones: Locutorio Telefónico (☎ 947 26 42 28), Plaza Alonso Martínez, near the tourist office. **Fax** service. Open daily 10am-3pm and 4-11pm.

Post Office: Pl. Conde de Castro, 1 (☎ 947 26 27 50, info ☎ 902 19 71 97). El Cid points the way across the river from Pl. Primo de Rivera; the post office is the big building at the first intersection. **Lista de Correos.** Open M-F 8:30am-8:30pm, Sa 9:30am-2pm. **Postal Code:** 09070.

Internet Access: Café Cabaret Ciber-Café, C. Puebla, 21 (☎ 947 20 27 22). 500ptas for 30min. 300ptas for each additional 30min. Printing 10ptas per page. Open Su-Th 5pm-2am, F-Sa 4pm-4am. **Olivetti Center,** on Pl. Alonso Martínez, next to the tourist office. 800ptas per hr. Open M-F 8am-3am.

ACCOMMODATIONS

For cheap hostels, scout the streets near Pl. Alonso Martínez, north of the river. The C. San Juan area is also dotted with reasonably priced hostels. Reservations are crucial for the festivals in June and July and are advisable in August.

Pensión Peña, C. Puebla, 18, 2nd fl. (☎ 947 20 63 23). From Pl. España, take C. San Lesmes; C. Puebla is the 3rd right. 8 small, elegant rooms with big windows. Restaurant downstairs. Laundry service. Singles 1600-1700ptas; doubles 2800-2900ptas.

Pensión Dallas, Pl. Vega, 1-6 (☎ 947 20 54 57). From the bus station, walk toward the cathedral and look right before crossing C. Valladolid. Communal baths. Rooms can be a bit dark. Winter heating. Shower 300ptas. Singles 2000ptas; doubles 4000ptas.

Hostal Victoria, C. San Juan, 3 (☎/fax 947 20 15 42). From El Cid's statue, walk up C. Santander past Plaza Calvobotelo and turn right onto C. San Juan. Public phone and luggage storage. Singles 2400-2800ptas; doubles 3700-400ptas; triples 5000-6000ptas; extra bed 1700ptas.

Camping Fuentes Blancas (☎ 947 48 60 16). The "Fuentes Blancas" bus leaves from Pl. España (July-Sept. 15 9:30am, 12:30, 4:15, 7:15pm; 75ptas). 540ptas per person, 475ptas per tent and per car. Open Apr.-Sept.

FOOD

Burgos natives take pride in their delicious *queso de Burgos* (cheese) and *morcilla*, a sausage made from tripe, blood, and rice. The area around Pl. Alonso Martínez teems with restaurants serving these staples, while C. San Lorenzo is *tapas* heaven. **Mercado de Abastos (Norte),** near Pl. España, and the smaller **Mercado de Abastos (Sur),** on C. Miranda next to the bus station, sell fresh meat and bread. (Both open M-Sa 7am-3pm; Mercado Norte reopens F 5:30am-8pm.) **Spar Supermercado,** on C. Concepción, between C. Hospital Militar and C. San Cosme, has picnic goods. (☎ 947 26 00 07. Open M-F 9am-2pm and 5-8pm, Sa 9am-2pm).

La Posada, Pl. Santo Domingo de Guzmán, 18 (☎ 947 20 45 78), behind the El Cid statue. A shrine to Spain's most valiant matadors. Try the vegetable plate of the day. Entrees 1200-4000ptas. *Menú* 1800ptas. Open daily 1-4pm and 9-11pm. V, MC.

Gaia Comedor Vegetariano, C. San Francisco, 31 (☎ 947 23 76 45), behind La Iglesia de San Gil. Gazpacho, salads, asparagus *crêpes*, rice sushi, and creamy vegetables fill a light, flavorful *menú* (1000ptas). Info on tai chi and yoga. Open M-Sa 1:30-4pm.

Mesón la Amarilla, C. San Lorenzo, 26 (☎ 947 20 59 36), between Pl. Mayor and Pl. Alonso Martínez. Try the mild and sweet *queso de Burgos con miel* (400ptas). *Raciones* 500-950ptas. *Platos combinados* 1100-1600ptas. *Menú* 1400ptas. Open daily 9:30am-4pm and 7pm-2am. V, MC.

CENTRAL SPAIN

◎ SIGHTS

■ **CATHEDRAL.** The spires of Burgos's magnificent Gothic cathedral rise high above the city. Though the first stone was set in the 13th century by *Reconquista* hero Fernando III (El Santo), the cathedral gained additions during the following three centuries. As a result, the 13th-century Gothic north facade appears stark when compared to the intricate 15th-century towers and the beautiful 16th-century stained-glass dome of the **Capilla Mayor.** Another curious inhabitant of the cathedral is the eerily lifelike **papamoscas** (fly-catcher), high up near the main door in the central aisle. As it tolls the hours, the strange creature opens its mouth and gulps, much to the joy of onlookers below. *(☎ 947 20 47 12. Open daily 9:30am-1pm and 4-7pm. 400ptas, students 250ptas, children 100ptas.)*

■ **MUSEO-MONASTERIO DE LAS HUELGAS REALES.** The Museo-Monasterio de las Huelgas Reales, built by King Alfonso VIII in 1188, is slightly out of the way, but certainly worth the trip. Once a summer palace for Castilian kings and later an elite convent for Cistercian nuns, the monastery has been closely associated with Spanish royalty since the Middle Ages; the abbess of Las Huelgas has traditionally served as a personal advisor to the king. Inside the monastery, the **Museo de Telas** (Textile Museum) houses the burial wardrobe of Fernando de Cerda (1225-1275) and family. *(Take the "Barrio del Pilar" bus from Pl. España to the Museo stop (75ptas). ☎ 947 20 56 87. Open Apr.-Sept. Tu-Sa 10:30am-1:15pm and 3:30-5:45pm, Su 10:30am-2:15pm; Oct.-Mar. Tu-Sa 11am-1:15pm and 3:30-5:45pm, Su 10:30am-2:15pm. 650ptas, students and under 14 250ptas, under 5 free. W free.)*

CASTLE. Atop a hill high above the cathedral, the ruins of a medieval castle preside over Burgos. Napoleonic troops demolished sections of the walls and building, which are still undergoing reconstruction. The bleached castle rocks offer an astounding view of the red roofs of Burgos and the surrounding countryside. *(From Museo del Retablo, climb the 200 steps.)*

MUSEO DE PINTURA MARCELIANO SANTA MARÍA. This renovated museum among the ruins of the **Monasterio de San Juan** stands chock-full of Burgalese paintings. One of the galleries is devoted to the work of the Romantic painter who gives the museum its name, while the other displays contemporary exhibits. *(Follow C. Vitoria away from El Cid's statue and take the 2nd left. ☎ 947 20 56 87. Open M-Sa 10am-1:50pm and 5-7:50pm, Su 10am-1:50pm. 25ptas; students with ID and senior citizens free.)*

CASA MIRANDA. This sprawling 16th-century mansion houses works of provincial Burgalese art as well as local historical artifacts. Included in the exhibit are the remains of Cluny, a piece of the front facade of the monastery at Santo Domingo de Silos, and the sepulchre of Don Juan de Padilla. *(C. Calera, 25. ☎ 947 26 58 75. Open Tu-F 10am-2pm and 4-7:30pm, Sa 10am-2pm and 4:45-8:15pm, Su 10am-2pm. 200ptas; under 18, senior citizens, and students with ID free. Sa-Su free.)*

CASA DEL CORDÓN. The restored Casa del Cordón—named for the Franciscan Friar's rope belt that hangs from the doorway—was built by Castilian constables in the 15th century. Here Columbus met with Fernando and Isabel after his second trip to America and here Felipe el Hermoso (the Handsome) breathed his last ragged breath after an exhausting game of *pelota* (jai-alai). Upon his death, his wife Juana dragged his corpse through the streets, earning her nickname, Juana la Loca (the Mad). *(On C. Santander, on the other side of the statue of El Cid, on the right.)*

CHURCHES. Across from the cathedral stands the **Iglesia de San Nicolás,** adorned with 15th- and 16th-century Hispano-Flemish paintings and altars. *(Pl. Santa María. ☎ 047 20 70 95. Open July-Sept. M-Sa 9am-2pm and 4-8pm; Oct.-Apr. Tu-F 6:30-7:30pm, Sa 9:30am-2pm and 5-7pm, Su 9am-2pm and 5-6pm. Free.)* Altarpiece fans should head to the **Iglesia de San Esteban/Museo del Retablo.** Eighteen 16th- to 18th-century altars depict the life of Christ and various saints. *(C. Pozo Seco. ☎ 947 27 37 52. Open Tu-Sa 10:30am-2pm and 4:30-7pm, Su 10:30am-2pm. 200ptas, students 100ptas.)*

EL CID CAMPEADOR Although Rodrigo Díaz de Vivar (a.k.a. El Cid), Spain's real-life epic hero, was not born in Burgos itself, some of the most celebrated incidents of his life took place here. After the cathedral, the **Estatua del Cid** in Pl. General Primo de Rivera is Burgos's most revered landmark. Díaz de Vivar ("Cid" comes from the Arabic for lord) won his fame through bold exploits at home and in battle against Moors and Christians. Despite the statue's inscription and the legends behind him, El Cid was no traditional Christian hero. A particularly successful mercenary, he spent much of his life exiled from a number of Christian states whose nobles he had outraged; he was even known to ally himself with Muslims. All the same, El Cid is thought to be the most famous Castilian of all time, and the medieval epic poem celebrating his life, *Cantar de Mío Cid* (c. 1140), is considered the first great work of Castilian literature. Tradition compels Burgos's boys to climb the statue and fondle the testicles of El Cid's horse, ensuring their own strength, courage, and fame.

🎵 ENTERTAINMENT

Party-seekers inundate Burgos after dark. By midnight C. Avellanos (across from Pl. Alonso Martínez, near the tourist office) fills with night owls, and as C. Avellanos simmers down, the crowds move onto nearby C. Huerto del Rey. If you have to hit the sack early on a Saturday night, wake up Sunday and join the crowds still dancing at *discotecas* along C. San Juan. Nightlife switches into overdrive the last week in June, when Burgos honors its patron saints with concerts, parades, fireworks, bullfights, and dances. The day after **Corpus Christi,** citizens parade through town with the *Pendón de las Navas*, a banner captured from the Moors in 1212.

Twenty, Pl. Huerto del Rey, 20 (☎ 947 26 46 92). Easily the most popular—and definitely the most crowded—stop on the Huerto del Rey clubhopping route. Beer 300ptas. Mixed drinks 600-800ptas. Open M-Sa 7pm-5am, Su 7pm-midnight.

Bésame Mucho, off Pl. Lesmes, more widely known as Pl. de las Bernardas. The biggest and rowdiest crowd in the area's club scene. Get your groove going with the blasting dance music, then have a few drinks next door at the equally popular **Club QVO.** Beer 300ptas. Mixed drinks 500ptas. Open daily 10pm-6am, but things really start at 2am.

Okra, C. Francisco, 7 (☎ 947 27 15 24). Burgos's gay hotspot offers a simple dance floor and bar. Mixed drinks 600ptas. Open Su-W 6pm-2:30am, Th-Sa 6pm-4am.

Kiss, Pl. Huerto del Rey, 8 (☎ 947 27 49 80). Ample dance floor and a wide array of music. Arrive after 1am for the liveliest crowd. Beer 200ptas. Open Th-Sa 10pm-5am.

Pub Tastos, Pl. Huerto del Rey, 7. Cheap liquor keeps backpackers dancing until dawn. Arrive after 1am. Beer 250ptas. Mixed drinks 450ptas. Open daily 7pm-5am, later F-Sa.

ᴾ DAYTRIP FROM BURGOS

SANTO DOMINGO DE SILOS (1½HR.)

To get from Burgos to Santo Domingo de Silos (50km) by car, take N-234 toward Salas de los Infantes to Hortigüela. From there, C-110, which borders the Arlanza River, will pass the monastery of San Pedro de Arlanza before arriving at Covarrubias; from there it is a short 17km. A bus runs to Santo Domingo from Burgos (1½hr.; departs Burgos M-Th 5:30pm, F 6:30pm, Sa 2pm; departs Santo Domingo M-Th and Sa 8:30am; 630ptas).

Since 1993, the Benedictine monks of Santo Domingo de Silos (pop. 380) have sold 5 million recordings, including the Gregorian chant album that reached #1 on global charts. In the **Abadía de Santo Domingo de Silos,** listeners are transported back in time as black-cloaked monks chant along with the organ and the soothing echoes of their own voices. You can sit in at morning song at high mass at 9am (Su at noon), vespers at 7pm (Th in summer at 8pm), and *compline* at 9:40pm. (☎ 947 39 00 68. Open Tu-Sa 10am-1pm and 4:30-6pm, Su-M 4:30-6pm. 250ptas.) Perhaps

CENTRAL SPAIN

more interesting than the monastery itself are the **museum** and **cloister** next door, whose highlights include an ancient pharmacy of 300-year-old chemicals, skulls, and preserved animal parts. Beyond Santo Domingo de Silos, the sole option for entertainment is hiking in the hills. Ask for directions to **La Yecla** (2.5km from Silos) where a precarious walkway leads through a narrow gorge above a small waterfall. Rooms are easy to find in this friendly (though pricey) little town, a good thing since visitors without cars are almost obligated to stay the night. **Hostal Cruces,** Plaza Mayor, 20, offers clean, sunny rooms with baths. (☎ 947 39 00 64. Singles 3000ptas; doubles 5000ptas.) Near the bus station, **Hostal Santo Domingo,** C. Santo Domingo, 15, has comfortable, well-kept rooms with full baths, phones, and TVs. (☎ 947 39 00 53. Singles 3500-5500ptas; doubles 4900-9500ptas.)

SORIA

Though modern development has encroached upon provincial Soria (pop. 34,000), the city preserves a leisurely pace. Black-bereted men tote bundles of local bread past Romanesque churches, and Soria's inhabitants still religiously observe the evening *paseo*, strolling and chatting with friends and neighbors before dinner. Although the city proper is best used as a base for exploring surrounding towns, two intriguing architectural anomalies on the outskirts of town, the Monasterio de San Juan de Duero and the Ermita San Saturio, are well worth seeing.

☞ TRANSPORTATION

Trains: Estación El Cañuelo (☎ 975 23 02 02), Carretera de Madrid. Shuttle buses run from Pl. Mariano Granados to the train station 30min. before train departure times (50ptas). To **Alcalá de Henares** (2¾hr., 2-3 per day 7:40am-7:35pm, 1490ptas) and **Madrid** (3hr., 2-3 per day 7:40am-7:35pm, 1900ptas).

Buses: (☎ 975 22 51 60), Av. Valladolid, at Av. Gaya Nuño. Shuttle bus from Pl. Mariano Granados (every hr. on the ½hr. 9:30am-2:30pm, 30ptas). Info 9am-7pm and 8-10pm. Most tickets available 30min. before departure, except on holidays when seats may be reserved several days before. **Therpasa** (☎ 975 22 51 60) goes to **Tarazona** (1hr., 3-6 per day 7:30am-9pm, 545ptas) and **Zaragoza** (2¼hr.; M-Sa 3-6 per day 7:30am-9pm, Su 6pm and 9pm; 1075ptas). **La Serrana** (☎ 975 24 09 13) to **Burgos** (2½hr., 1-3 per day 7am-6:30pm, 1250ptas). **Linecar** (☎ 975 23 00 33) goes to **Zaragoza** (2½hr.; 2-3 per day M-F 9:45am-9:30pm, Sa 1:10-9:30pm, Su 1-9:30pm; 1100ptas) and **Valladolid** (3hr.; 2-3 per day M-Sa 9:40am-7pm, Su 11am-7pm; 1460ptas). **Continental Auto** (☎ 975 22 44 01). To: **Logroño** (1½hr.; 7-8 per day M-Th and Sa 11am-9:45pm, F and Su 11am-12:15am; 825ptas); **Pamplona** (2hr.; 3-7 per day M-Th and Sa 10:45am-9:45pm, F and Su 10:45am-12:15am; 1485ptas); and **Madrid** (2½hr.; 6-8 per day M-Th and Sa 8:15am-8:45pm, F 8:15am-11:45pm, Su 9:15am-11:45pm; 1780-2900ptas).

Taxis: (☎ 975 22 30 34 or 975 22 17 18). Stands at Pl. Mariano Granados and bus station. To ruins of Numancia 1800ptas.

Car Rental: Europcar, C. Angel Terrel, 3-5 (☎ 975 22 05 05), off C. Sagunto. Min. age 21; must have valid license, credit card, and passport. 9790ptas per day, 48,070ptas per week (plus IVA). Open M-F 9:30am-1:30pm and 4:30-8pm, Sa 10:30am-1pm.

✦☞ ORIENTATION AND PRACTICAL INFORMATION

To get to the city center from the **bus station,** take either the shuttle bus (see **Buses,** below) or walk for 15 minutes. From the traffic circle outside the station, signs on Av. Valladolid point the way downhill to the *centro ciudad.* Keep walking for about five blocks, then bear right at the fork, after the traffic light, onto Po. Espolón, which borders the **Parque Alameda.** When the park ends you'll see central

Here's your ticket to freedom, baby!

Plaza Mariano Granados directly in front of you. To get to the center from the **train station,** either take the shuttle or turn left onto C. Madrid and follow the signs to *centro ciudad*. Continue on C. Almazán as it bears left and becomes Av. Mariano Vicen; follow for about six blocks (veering left on C. Alfonso VIII at the next fork) until you reach Pl. Mariano Granados (20min.). From the side of the plaza opposite the park, C. Marqués de Vadillo leads to pedestrian **Calle El Collado,** the main shopping street that cuts through the old quarter to **Plaza Mayor.**

Tourist Office: (☎/fax 975 21 20 52; www.sorianitelaimaginas.com), Pl. Ramón y Cajal, on the side of Pl. Mariano Granados opposite the park. It's the glass hut set back from the street. Ask for the *Ruta de los Poetas* map. Open M-F 9am-2pm and 5-7pm, Sa-Su 10am-2pm and 5-8pm.

Currency Exchange: Banco Hispano Central, C. Collado, 56 (☎ 975 22 02 25), off Pl. Ramón Bento Aceño. Open May-Sept. M-F 8:30am-2:30pm; Oct.-Apr. M-F 8:30am-2:30pm, Sa 8:30am-1pm.

Luggage Storage: At the **bus station.** 1st day 75ptas, 25ptas each additional day. Open daily 9am-7pm and 8-10pm.

Emergency: ☎ 112. **Municipal Police:** ☎091, 092, or 975 21 18 62.

Medical Services: Hospital General (☎ 975 23 43 00), Po. Santa Barbara.

Post Office: Po. Espolón, 6 (☎ 975 22 13 99), off Pl. Mariano Granados. Open M-F 8:30am-8:30pm, Sa 9:30am-2pm. **Postal Code:** 42071.

▌ ACCOMMODATIONS

Affordable hostels fill the streets around Pl. Olivo and Pl. Salvador, both near Pl. Mariano Granados. Reservations, necessary during the *fiestas* in the last week of June, are also wise mid-July through mid-September.

Residencia Juvenil Antonio Machado (HI), Pl. José Antonio, 1 (☎ 975 22 00 89). From Pl. Mariano Granados, take C. Nicolás Rabal until you reach Pl. José Antonio, or turn right at the stoplight coming from the bus station. This is your cheapest option in Soria if you can snag one of the 16 beds. No reservations. 3-night max. stay. Curfew 11:30pm. HI members only. Open July-Aug. 15. Dorms 1000ptas, over 26 1450ptas.

Pension Ersogo, C. Alberca, 4 (☎ 975 21 35 08). Facing Pl. Mariano Granados, with your back to the park, head diagonally through Pl. Ramón y Cajal and take the 1st right on C. Alberca. Ring the bell on the right-hand door on the 2nd fl. Friendly owners keep 7 well-lit rooms neat and tidy. Singles 2200ptas; doubles 3300ptas; triples 4600ptas.

Casa Diocesana Pío XII, C. San Juan, 5 (☎ 975 21 21 76). The tall building set back from the street. From Pl. Marciano Granados, go up C. El Collado and right on C. San Juan. July-Aug. singles 1800-2850ptas; doubles 2625-3950ptas. Sept.-June singles 1400-2400ptas; doubles 2275-3500ptas.

Camping Fuente la Teja (☎ 975 22 29 67), 2km from town on Ctra. Madrid (km 233). Swimming pool. 425ptas per person and per car, 475ptas per tent (IVA not included). Open *Semana Santa* to Sept.

▌ FOOD

Soria's specialties include *chorizo* and *migas* (fried bread crumbs); the region's butter is celebrated throughout Spain. C. M. Vicente Tutor is peppered with bars and inexpensive restaurants. Buy fresh produce, meat, and fish at the small **market** in Pl. Bernardo Robles on C. Estudios, left off C. Collado (open M-Sa 8:30am-2pm). Cruise the **supermarket** aisles at **SPAR,** Av. Mariano Vicen, 29, 4 blocks from Pl. Mariano Granados toward the train station (open M-Sa 9am-2pm and 5:30-8:30pm).

Nueva York, C. Collado, 14 (☎ 975 21 27 84), 1 block past Pl. San Esteban. A great place to satisfy your sweet-tooth. Lunch platters 800-995ptas. Breakfast served until 12:30pm. Open daily June-Aug. 8am-10pm; Sept.-May 8am-9:30pm. Visa.

La Parilla, C. Tejera, 20 (☎ 975 21 41 52). Facing the park from Pl. Mariano Granados, take a right on C. Ferial and continue 3 blocks up the hill to C. Tejerat. Popular daily *menú* (1275ptas). Full menu available with broader range of entrees (1100-1800ptas). Open M-Sa 1-3:30pm and 8:30-11pm.

◎ SIGHTS

The great 20th-century poet Antonio Machado once likened the **Río Duero** to a drawn bow which forms an arc around Soria. To find the river from Pl. Mariano Granados, walk past the sign for Restaurant Nueva York and straight down C. Zapatería. Halfway down the hill, C. Zapatería changes to C. Real; follow this road to Pl. San Pedro, and the bridge lies straight ahead.

▧ ERMITA DE SAN SATURIO. Soria's biggest draw is actually across the river and is well worth the trek. The 17th-century Ermita de San Saturio, built into the side of a cliff, is a heavenly retreat where light seeps into the caves through stained-glass windows. *(1.5km downstream. Turn right with the road after crossing the bridge. Open May-Sept. Tu-Su 10:30am-2pm and 4:30-7pm; Oct.-Apr. Tu-Su 10:30-6:30pm. Free.)*

MONASTERIO SAN JUAN DE DUERO. The Monasterio San Juan de Duero sits tranquilly by the river, amid cottonwoods and grass. The church itself, dating from the 12th century, is quite simple. The remarkable, graceful arches, which combine Romanesque and Islamic styles, are all that remain of the 13th-century cloister. Inside, a small museum displays medieval artifacts. *(Turn left after crossing the bridge. Museum ☎ 975 23 02 18. Open June-Aug. Tu-Sa 10am-2pm and 5-9pm, Su 10am-2pm; Sept.-Oct. and Apr.-May Tu-Sa 10am-2pm and 4-7pm, Su 10am-2pm; Nov.-Mar. Tu-Sa 10am-2pm and 3:30-6pm, Su 10am-2pm. 100ptas; under 18, over 65, and students free; Sa-Su free.)*

MUSEO NUMANTINO. The Museo Numantino shows off the impressive Celto-Iberian and Roman artifacts excavated from nearby Numancia. *(Po. Espolón, 8. ☎ 975 22 13 97. Open June-Sept. Tu-Sa 9am-2pm and 5-9pm, Su 10am-1pm; Oct.-May Tu-Sa 9am-8:30pm, Su 10am-1pm. 200ptas; under 18, over 65, and students free; Sa-Su free.)*

♫ ENTERTAINMENT

Early evening finds revelers of all ages crowded into **Pl. Ramón Benito Aceña** and the smaller **Pl. San Clemente,** both off C. Collado. Late-night festivities center at the disco-bars grouped around the intersection of Rota de Calatañazer and C. Cardenal Frías, near Pl. Toros. Many Spanish fiestas involve watching bulls and eating, but Soria ingeniously combines the two during the five-day **Fiesta de San Juan** (beginning the first W after June 24th)—each day starts with a running of the bulls and ends with eating them in local restaurants.

🏛 DAYTRIPS FROM SORIA

RUINS OF NUMANCIA (15MIN.)

Getting to Numancia without a car can be a problem. There is a bus to Garray, 1km from the ruins (15min., M-F 5:45pm, 90ptas), but it doesn't return until 2:15pm the next day.

Archaeology fans will enjoy the ruins of Numancia, a hilltop settlement 7km north of Soria that dates back more than 4000 years. The Celto-Iberians had settled here by the 3rd century BC, and tenaciously resisted Roman conquest. It took 10 years of the Numantian Wars and the direction of Scipio Africanus to dislodge them. Scipio erected a system of walls 9km long, 3m tall, and 2½m thick to encircle the town and starve its residents. After his victory, he kept 50 survivors as trophies, sold the rest into slavery, burned the city, and divided its lands among his allies. Numancia, however, lived on as a metaphor for patriotic heroism in Golden Age and Neoclassical tragedies, and the ruins, though battered, are still worth a visit. Highlights include the foundations of the Roman houses and the underground wells. All excavated artifacts now hang at the Museo Numantino in Soria. (☎ 975 18 07 12. Open June-Aug. Tu-Sa 10am-2pm and 5-9pm, Su 10am-2pm; Sept.-Oct. and Apr.-May Tu-Sa 10am-2pm and 4-8pm, Su 10am-2pm; Nov.-Mar. Tu-Sa 10am-2pm and 3:30-6pm, Su 10am-2pm. 100ptas, under 18, over 65, and students free. Sa-Su free.) If you find yourself needing a bed, check **Pensión Goyo,** C. Ramón Benito Aceña, 5. (☎ 975 25 21 11. Singles 4000ptas; doubles 7500ptas.)

EL BURGO DE OSMA (50MIN.)

Gonzalo Ruiz (☎ 975 22 20 60) sends buses to and from Soria (50min.; M-Sa 3:30pm and 6:30pm, Su 10:30am; 485ptas).

El Burgo de Osma (pop. 5100) is only worth the trip for those with a car, but those who explore past the town's gritty exterior and venture into the streets around the cathedral will be richly rewarded. Two of the more attractive buildings are the **Hospital de San Agustín** and **Casa Consistorial** in Pl. Mayor. Monk Don Pedro de Osma erected the magnificent 13th-century Gothic **cathedral** on the site of an earlier church. The cathedral's two **museums** have an important collection of codices, including a richly illuminated Beato de Liébana commentary on the Apocalypse and a 12th-century charter considered one of the earliest written examples of Castilian vernacular. (☎ 975 34 03 22. Open Tu-Su 10am-1pm and 4-7pm. Free; tour of museums 350ptas.)

CENTRAL SPAIN

EXTREMADURA

The aptly named Extremadura is a land of harsh beauty and cruel extremes. Arid plains bake under the intense summer sun, relieved by scattered patches of glowing sunflowers. Yet the traveler who braves the Extremaduran plains is rewarded with stunning ruins and intimate, peaceful towns. Compared to the hectic pace of nearby Madrid, life in Extremadura is slow and less modern, as though the region's rich history dominated its character in the present as well.

These are the lands that hardened New World conquistadors like Hernán Cortés and Francisco Pizarro, but Extremadura itself has remained unexplored by most Spaniards. Mérida's Roman ruins and the hushed ancient beauty of Trujillo and Cáceres, however, are drawing more and more admirers, and maps and brochures have begun to fill tourist offices throughout the region.

The region's hearty pastoral cuisine is especially appealing; local specialties include rabbit, partridge, lizard with green sauce, wild pigeon with herbs, and *migas* (fried bread) with hot chocolate. Thick *cocido* (chick pea stew) warms *extremeños* in winter, while the many varieties of gazpacho (including an unusual white one) cool in the summer.

HIGHLIGHTS OF EXTREMADURA

Panoramic views from the towers of a **10th-century Arab castle** in **Trujillo** (see p. 186).

The colossal **Teatro Romano** and other Roman ruins at **Mérida** (see p. 184).

The eerie nooks and crannies of **Cáceres's old city** (see p. 180).

LOCAL FESTIVALS IN EXTREMADURA

Cáceres celebrates the *WOMAD* with music, dancing and food during the first or second weekend of May. The *Fiesta de San Fernando* fills the town with food and drink booths the last weekend of May. In **Trujillo,** catch the *Fiesta de Virgen de la Victoria* (last weekend of August). **Mérida** is famous for its *Festival de Teatro Clásico,* some of Europe's finest theater and dance performed among Roman ruins (July-August). It celebrates its own *Feria* the first week of September as well. Join in the revelry in **Badajoz** during *La Feria* (the week of June 24th) and *Los Carnivales de Badajoz* (second week of February).

CÁCERES

Founded by Romans in 34 BC, this thriving provincial capital (pop. 80,000) is the closest Extremadura comes to a big city. One of Spain's eight World Heritage Cities, Cáceres fulfills both the mind and the party-urge. Between the 14th and 16th centuries, rival noble families vied for social and political control, each building a miniature palace to demonstrate their power and wealth. As a result, the old city is a wonderful maze of palaces, museums, and churches. Although Cáceres's newer areas are less interesting, the *Parque del Príncipe* and a healthy nightlife provide ample amusement for a short stay. You can also use the city as a base for exploring the rest of Extremadura. From Cáceres it is possible to enter Portugal by bus or train through Badajoz, or by train via Valença de Alcántara.

▐ TRANSPORTATION

Trains: (☎ 927 23 50 61), on Av. Alemania, 3km from the old city across the highway from the bus station. Info window open daily 6am-10pm. To: **Mérida** (1hr., 4-6 per day, 1300ptas); **Badajoz** (2hr., 3 per day, 1800ptas); **Madrid** (4hr., 5 per day 9am-10:30pm, 2420ptas); **Lisbon** (6hr., 3am, 4475ptas); **Sevilla** (4hr., 8:15am, 2300ptas).

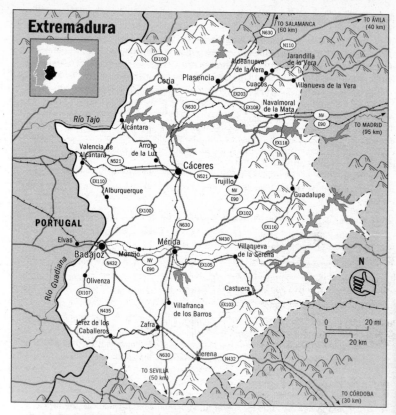

Extremadura

TO SALAMANCA (60 km)
TO ÁVILA (40 km)
TO MADRID (95 km)
TO SEVILLA (50 km)
TO CÓRDOBA (30 km)

Río Tajo
Río Guadiana
PORTUGAL

Coria · Plasencia · Aldeanueva de la Vera · Jarandilla de la Vera · Cuacos · Villanueva de la Vera · Navalmoral de la Mata · Alcántara · Valencia de Alcántara · Arroyo de la Luz · Cáceres · Trujillo · Guadalupe · Alburquerque · Elvas · Badajoz · Montijo · Mérida · Villanueva de la Serena · Olivenza · Castuera · Jerez de los Caballeros · Zafra · Villafranca de los Barros · Llerena

EX109 · N630 · EX203 · EX108 · NV E90 · EX118 · N521 · NV E90 · EX102 · EX116 · N521 · EX110 · EX100 · N630 · N430 · EX105 · EX103 · N432 · EX107 · N435 · N630 · N432 · N110 · N630

N
0   20 mi
0   20 km

Buses: (☎ 927 23 25 50), on Ctra. Sevilla, across from the train station, 3km from the old city. Info window open M-F 7:30am-11:30pm, Sa-Su 8:30am-11:30pm. Fewer buses on weekends. To: **Madrid** (4-5hr., 8 per day, 2420ptas); **Sevilla** (4hr., 5-7 per day, 2900ptas); **Salamanca** (4hr., 3-6 per day, 1705ptas); **Badajoz** (1½hr., 4-5per day, 850-1100ptas); **Mérida** (1hr., 2-3 per day, 675ptas); **Trujillo** (45min., 7-10 per day, 385ptas); **Valencia de Alcántara** (2½hr., 2-3 per day, 975ptas); **Valladolid** (5½hr., 3-4 per day, 2670ptas).

Taxis: Stands at Pl. Mayor and bus and train stations. **Radio Taxi** (☎ 927 23 23 23).

Car Rental: Avis (☎ 927 23 57 21), in the bus station. On the right when you face the station from the outside. One-day rental around 12,000ptas. Cheapest on weekends. Minimum age 23. M-F 9am-1pm and 4:30-7:30pm (in winter 5-8pm); Sa 9am-1pm.

✳ 🛈 ORIENTATION AND PRACTICAL INFORMATION

Both Cáceres's old and new cities lead out from the **Plaza Mayor** (a.k.a. Plaza General Mola), flanked by the **Ciudad Monumental** (old city) and the commercial street **Avenida de España.** The plaza is 3km from the **bus** and **train stations,** which face each other across the rotary intersection of Av. de la Hispanidad and Av. Alemania. To get to the center of town make your way to Av. Alemania (with your back to the bus station, take a right, a left onto Av. de la Hispanidad, and a right at the intersection; with your back to the train station take a left at the intersection). Bus #1 stops on the right, just past the green gas station. Take it to the last stop, Pl. Obispo Galarza (80ptas). Go right upon exiting the bus (facing the bus stop) and take the first left (down the steps). Continue straight through intersections with C. Parras and C. Moret, then take the second left (onto C. Pintores) down into Pl. Mayor. Bus #2 stops on Av. Hispanidad, around the corner to the right as you emerge from the bus station, and runs to **Plaza de América**, hub of the new downtown area (80ptas). From there, "Ciudad Monumental" signs point up the tree-lined Av. España (Po. Canovas) toward Pl. Mayor. When the *avenida* ends, follow C. San Pedro to the right. When this runs into the Pl. de San Juan, take C. Pintores to the Pl. Mayor.

Tourist Office: Pl. Mayor, 10 (☎ 927 62 50 47). English spoken. Open M-F 9:30am-2pm and 4-6:30pm, Sa-Su 9:30am-2pm; in summer M-F 9:30am-2pm and 5-7:30pm, Sa-Su 9:30am-2pm. The **Patronato de Turismo** (☎ 927 25 55 97), C. Amargura, in the Palacio de Caravajal, within the old city, has good maps of the monuments. From Pl. Mayor, pass under Arco de la Estrella into the old city and continue straight until you face the Catedral. It's opposite the left side. Same hours as the tourist office.

Currency Exchange: Banks line Av. España and the streets leading to Pl. Mayor.

Luggage Storage: At the train station (400ptas per day) and bus station (75ptas per item per day).

Emergency: ☎ 112. **Police: Municipal** (☎ 927 24 84 24), C. General Margallo.

Late-Night Pharmacy: Four in Pl. Mayor, all with the *farmacias de guardia* (24-hr. pharmacies) list posted in the window.

Hospital: Hospital Provincial (☎ 927 25 68 00), on Av. España, off Pl. Mayor.

Post Office: (☎ 927 22 50 71) on C. Miguel Primo de Rivera, off Av. España on the left from Pl. de América. Open for stamps and Lista de Correos M-F 8:30am-8:30pm, Sa 9:30am-2pm. **Postal Code:** 10071.

Internet Access: Ciberjust, C. Diego M. Crehuet, 7 (☎ 927 62 72 74). Loud rock music, but a nice set-up. From Pl. Mayor take C. Pintores to Pl. San Juan; continue down C. Rosa de Luna to Pl. Marron. C. Diego M. Carhuet is your third left. 500ptas per hr. or 400ptas per hr. with 1000ptas pre-paid. Open daily 10am-2am.

▟ ACCOMMODATIONS

Hostales and *pensiones* line Pl. Mayor and are scattered throughout the new city. Prices are somewhat higher than in larger cities and may rise during festivals. Make reservations in advance for summer weekends. All have 24-hour reception.

Pensión Carretero, Pl. Mayor, 22 (☎ 927 24 74 82). With your back to the tourist office, it's in the far right corner of the plaza. Simple, cavernous rooms; best bang for your buck. Spacious TV lounge. No winter heating. Singles 2000ptas; doubles 3500ptas; triples 4500ptas; quads 6000ptas. V, MC.

Pensión Castilla, Rios Verdes, 3 (☎ 927 24 44 04). From Pl. Mayor take C. General Ezponda (opposite the tourist office), and then the first right. Friendly live-in owner will do your laundry mama-style for a small fee. Good for a slightly quieter night near the old city. Singles 2000ptas; doubles 4000ptas.

Hostal Residencia Almonte, C. Gil Cordero, 6 (☎ 927 24 09 25; fax 927 24 86 02). Head away from Pl. Mayor on Av. España; C. Gil Cordero is right off Pl. de América. A central 90-room monster with luxuries in every room (full bath, TV, phone, fluffy towel, and firm bed). Parking garage for three lucky cars 500ptas. Singles 2890ptas; doubles 4494ptas; triples 5620ptas.

Pension Marquez, Gabriel y Galán, 2 (☎ 927 24 99 60), off Pl. Mayor, opposite the town hall. The owner's adjoining space and colorful bedspreads give Marquez a homey feel, but the cars exiting Pl. Mayor underneath may have you wanting to exit your room. No winter heating. Doubles 3000ptas; triples 4500ptas.

Camping: Ciudad de Cáceres, Ctra. Nacional, 630, km 549.6 (☎ 927 23 04 03). A first-class site, 5min. drive or 20min. walk from Cáceres, east toward Salamanca. Showers, washing machines. 490ptas per person and per car; 460ptas per tent and per child.

THE THINGS WE DO FOR LOVE Legend has it that the daughter of the Moorish King of Cáceres fell head over heels for the Christian conqueror, Alfonso IX, who was vying for control over Cáceres. Alfonso was badly disadvantaged, but his sweetheart gave him the keys to the walled city, enabling a successful surprise attack. Every April 22, the day before St. George's Day (the patron saint of the city), the legend is reenacted by citizens of Cáceres who break into groups of Christians and Moors and act out the battle, throwing a dragon into fake flames at the end.

FOOD

Like every Pl. Mayor, the one in Cáceres is full of restaurants and cafes serving up cheap *bocadillos* (400-600ptas), *raciones* (300-600ptas), and *menús* (900-1200ptas). Explore the side streets for less-touristed local bars and pastry shops. For groceries, hit up the big **Hiper Tambo**, C. Alfonso IX, 25. From Pl. de America follow the left side of Av. de España to its extension. (☎ 927 21 17 71. Open M-Sa 9:30am-9pm.) **El Toro,** C. General Ezponda, 2, just off Pl. Mayor, serves yuppified Spanish cuisine in an attractive terra-cotta setting, complete with marble floors. (☎ 927 22 90 34. Entrees 700-2500ptas. *Menú* 1200 or 1800ptas. Open Tu-Su.)

SIGHTS AND ENTERTAINMENT

BARRIO ANTIGUO. Golden, stork-filled old Cáceres is home to one of the most varied architectural ensembles in Europe. Roman, Arabic, Gothic, Renaissance, and even Inca influences (via the conquistadors) have all left their mark. The main attraction is the neighborhood as a whole, since most buildings don't open their doors to tourists; the best way to experience the barrio antiguo is to allow yourself to wander among the curving walls and birds' nests. The area is small, but a tourist office map will come in handy. *(From Pl. Mayor, take the stairs to the left of the tourist office to the Arco de la Estrella, the entrance into the walled old city.)*

CATEDRAL DE SANTA MARÍA. A statue of San Pedro de Alcántara, one of Extremadura's two patron saints, eyes the plaza from a corner pedestal of the Catedral de Santa María. His shiny toes are a result of the myth that anyone who rubs them will have good luck. The cathedral itself, built between 1229 and 1547, is Romanesque and Gothic, with a Renaissance ceiling. *(Open daily for mass. Free.)*

CASA Y TORRE DE LAS CIGUEÑAS. Historically, Cáceres's aristocracy resolved their disputes with violence, and the monarchs removed all battlements and spires from local lords' houses as punishment. Due to Don Golfín's loyalty to the ruling family, his Casa y Torre de las Cigueñas (House and Tower of the Storks) was the only one allowed to keep its battlements. Storks nest on its spires every spring. *(From the Arco, take a right up the hill, a left onto C. del Arco de Santa Ana, a right, and a quick left onto C. Condes. Pass through Pl. de San Mateo to Pl. de San Pablo. La Casa is on your left.)* Nearby **Convento de San Pablo** is late Gothic eye-candy for architecture buffs. *(To the left of Casa y Torre de las Cigueñas.)*

MUSEO DE CÁCERES. A must see. Inside the Casa de las Veletas (House of Weathervanes), Museo de Cáceres houses a tiny, brilliant who's who of Spanish art, featuring originals by El Greco, Picasso, Mir, recent abstractionist stars, and ever-changing exhibitions. Also called Museo Arqueológico Provincial, it displays Celtiberian stone animals, Roman and Visigothic tombstones, and crafts. *(Across from the Casa y Torre de las Cigueñas. ☎ 927 24 72 34. Open Tu-Sa 9am-2:30pm, Su 10:15am-2:30pm. 200ptas, students free.)*

OTHER SIGHTS. The 16th-century **Casa Del Sol** is the most famous of Cáceres's numerous mansions; its crest is the city's emblem. The **Casa de Toledo-Moctezuma** was built by the grandson of the Aztec princess Isabel Moctezuma (Tecuixpo Istlaxochitl)

CENTRAL SPAIN

to represent a unification of the old and new worlds. *(In Pl. de San Mateo, to the left as you enter the Arco de la Estrella.)* In another Golfín-owned palace, the **Palacio de los Golfines de Arriba,** Francisco Franco was proclaimed head of the Spanish state and General of its armies on October 26, 1936. *(Sandwiched by C. Olmos and C. Adarve de Santa Ana.)*

ENTERTAINMENT. Weekend revelers crowd the **Plaza Mayor** and its environs or stroll along **C. Pizarro,** which is dotted with live-music bars. Later at night, the party moves to the area called **La Madrala,** near Pl. Albatros in the new city. From the Pl. Mayor, take Av. España, make a right on Primo de Rivera, cross the intersection onto C. Dr. Fleming, and take a right into La Madrala.

⚑ DAYTRIP FROM CÁCERES

GUADALUPE (2½HR.)

Transportation to and from Guadalupe can be somewhat tricky; most visitors arrive on tour buses or in their own cars. Buses run to and from Cáceres (somewhat irregularly; call Empresa Mirat ☎ 927 23 25 50), Madrid (4hr., 1 per day, 2500ptas), and Trujillo (2hr., 2 per day). Bus schedules sometimes force an overnight stay in Guadalupe, but the pleasant calm can be a nice relief from bigger cities.

Two hours east of Trujillo and four hours southwest of Madrid, Guadalupe rests on a mountainside in the Sierra de Guadalupe. Particularly for pilgrims and backpackers, the **Real Monasterio de Santa María de Guadalupe,** with its eclectic history and decadent architecture, is a worthy daytrip. The fairy-tale monastery has even been nicknamed "the Spanish Sistine Chapel." In 1340 at the Battle of Salado, Alfonso XI, supposedly aided by the Virgin Mary, defeated a much superior Muslim army. As a token of his gratitude, he commissioned the lavish Real Monasterio. Years later it became customary to grant licenses for foreign expeditions on the premises; in fact, Columbus finalized his contract with Fernando and Isabel here. To pay homage to the city, he named one of the islands he discovered Guadalupe (now known as Turugueira). The hour-long tour allows visitors to admire the **museum** containing embroidered ecclesiastical finery, the Gothic and Mudejar **cloisters,** and the towering **basilica** (whose *retablo* was designed by El Greco's son). The most prominent object in the basilica is the **icon of the Virgin,** which is made of wood, blackened with age, and cloaked in gold and silver robes. (Monastery open daily 3:30-6:30pm; in summer 9:30am-1pm and 3:30-6:30pm. 300ptas.)

The **tourist office** in **Plaza Mayor** posts information on the door; follow signs from the bus station (open Tu-Su 10am-2pm and 5-7pm). Travelers looking for food or beds should head to Pl. Mayor. For those who get stuck in Guadalupe, dreamy **Hostal Cerezo,** Gregorio López, 12, has airy, peaceful rooms with clean baths and TV. (☎ 927 36 73 79. Singles 3000ptas; doubles 5000ptas; triples 6500ptas; 7% IVA not included. V, MC.) If you have some extra time, be sure to sample local cuisine and liqueurs; the monks had strict rules about the quality of cooking, and their devotion to food is still evident in the town's best dishes.

NEAR CÁCERES

▨ TRUJILLO

The gem of Extremadura, hill-perched Trujillo (pop. 10,000), is an unspoiled joy, often called the "Cradle of Conquistadors." Over 600 explorers and plunderers of the New World, including Peru's conqueror Francisco Pizarro and the Amazon's first explorer, Francisco de Orellana, hailed from here. Scattered with medieval palaces, Roman ruins, Arabic fortresses, and churches of all eras, Trujillo is a hodgepodge of histories and cultures. Its most impressive monument is its highest, the 10th-century Moorish castle which commands a stunning panoramic view of surrounding plains. Twentieth-century residents take pride in the well-preserved beauty of their churches, palace, and castle, adorning them with lovely gardens and flowering vines.

🔁 ORIENTATION AND PRACTICAL INFORMATION. The **bus station** (☎ 927 32 12 02) is at the corner of C. de las Cruces and C. del M. de Albayada; look for the **AutoRes** sign. Buses offer access to many nearby cities and towns, including **Cáceres** (45min., 6-10 per day, 485ptas), **Madrid** (2½hr., 10 per day, 2435ptas), and **Badajoz** (2hr., 10 per day, 1250ptas). To get to the Plaza Mayor (15min.), turn left as you exit the station (up C. de las Cruces), right on C. de la Encarnación, following signs to the tourist office, then left on C. Chica; turn left on C. Guía and right on C. Burgos, continuing onto the Plaza. The tourist office is across the plaza and posts information in its windows when closed. English spoken. (☎ 927 32 26 77. Open daily 10am-2pm and 4-8pm.) **Currency exchange** is available at **Banco Central Hispano,** Pl. Mayor, 25 (☎ 927 24 24 24). In a **medical emergency** call ☎ 927 32 20 16; **police,** C. Carniceria, 2 (☎ 927 32 01 04 or 927 32 10 16), just off Pl. Mayor. The **post office,** Po. Ruiz de Mendoza, 28, is on the way from the station to Pl. Mayor. (☎ 927 32 05 33. Open M-F 9am-2:30pm, Sa 9:30am-1pm.) The **postal code** is 10200.

🖺🖵 ACCOMMODATIONS AND FOOD. The pleasant **Pensión Boni,** C. Mingo de Ramos, 11 is off Pl. Mayor to the right of the church. Close to the plaza without the noise, Boni has airy patio rooms and a comfy TV lounge. The claustrophobic, however, should avoid the showers. (☎ 927 32 16 04. Singles 2000ptas; doubles 3000 ptas, with bath 4500ptas; triple with full bath and A/C 7500ptas.) Enjoy the luxuries of a real hotel down the hill from Pl. Mayor at the spotless **Hostal Trujillo,** C. de Francisco Pizarro, 4-6; from the bus station, turn left on C. de las Cruces, right on C. de la Encarnación, and right onto C. de Francisco Pizarro. All of the rooms have a full bath and TV and there is a brand new bar and restaurant next door. (☎ 927 32 26 61. Singles 3210ptas; doubles 5560ptas; triples 6420ptas.)

The best spot for a meal in Trujillo is a shaded table in the interior garden of ▓**Meson Alberca,** C. Victoria, 8. Enjoy the three-course *menú*, replete with bread and wine (1650ptas) and dishes like *migas* and gazpacho, in this tourist-less sanctum of the old city. (☎ 927 32 22 32. Open Su-T and Th-Sa, 11am-midnight.) For an indoor experience, try **Mesón-Restaurante La Troya,** Pl. Mayor, 8-12, decorated in the style of a typical Spanish house with local *artesania* (crafts). The three-course *menú* is 2000ptas. (☎ 927 32 13 64. Open daily 1-4:30 and 9-11:30pm.)

🔯 SIGHTS. Unlike those in Badajoz, Trujillo's monuments successfully blend with the Plaza Mayor and new city; an afternoon stroll around the old city may be the best in Extremadura. All sights cost 200ptas and are open daily, 9am-2pm and 4:30-7pm, except where indicated otherwise here. If you have time to spend, buy a "bono" ticket at the tourist office (800ptas) which gets you in everywhere. The **Plaza Mayor** was the inspiration for the Plaza de Armas in Cuzco, Perú, which was constructed after Francisco Pizarro defeated the Incas. Palaces, arched corridors, and sprawling cafes surround the central fountain and the **Estatua de Pizarro.** The gift of an American admirer of Pizarro, the bronze statue was erected in 1927 and, like the plaza, has a twin in Perú.

Festooned with stork nests, **Iglesia de San Martín** dominates the northeastern corner of the plaza. The church has several historic tombs, but contrary to local lore, Francisco de Orellana does not rest here. (Evening and Sunday mass not open to the public. Free entrance.) Across the street, the seven chimneys of the **Palacio de los Duques de San Carlos** reputedly symbolize the religions conquered by Spaniards in the New World. (Open daily 10am-1pm and 4:30-6:30pm. 100pta donation requested.) To get to the **Iglesia de Santiago,** which offers a terrific bell-tower view of the Castillo, take C. Ballesteros (above the tourist office) into the walled city, and two hard rights.

The Gothic **Iglesia de Santa María** is located even farther up the hill. According to legend, the giant soldier Diego García de Paredes picked up the fountain (now located next to the rear door) at age 11 and carried it to his mother; the giant was buried here after he twisted his ankle and fell to his death. (Commonly known as the "Extremaduran Samson," the giant is referenced in chapter 32 of Cervantes' *Don Quijote.*) The church's 25-panel Gothic altar-piece was painted by master Fernando Gallego. To the left of the church is the restored **Museo de la Coria,** which explores the relationship between Extremadura and Latin America, both in the past and future (open Sa-Su 11:30am-2pm). To get to the **Casa-Museo de Pizarro**, walk uphill on the stone road to the right of the Iglesia de Santa María. The bottom floor of the house is a reproduction of the living quarters of a 15th-century nobleman), and the top floor is dedicated to the life and times of Francisco Pizarro.

At the top of the hill are the spectacular ruins of a ▧**10th-century Arab castle.** Pacing the battlements and ramparts is like playing in your best Lego creation; a field-fresh breeze complements a view of the unspoiled landscape, with Trujillo on one side and fields scattered with ancient battlements on the others. Inside the castle's intact walls lie remnants of its *aljibe* (cistern) and the entrance to the lower-level dungeons. During summer, beautiful wildflowers hide behind the outer walls.

MÉRIDA

For quality Roman ruins per square foot, it doesn't get any better than Mérida (pop. 60,000), which warrants at least a day's visit. As a reward for services rendered to the Roman Empire, in 26 BC, Augustus Caesar gave a heroic group of veteran legionnaires a new city in Lusitania, a province comprised of Portugal and part of Spain. The veterans chose a lovely spot surrounded by several hills on the banks of the Río Guadiana and founded their new home, which they named "Augusta Emerita." Not content to rest on their laurels and itching to gossip with fellow patricians in Sevilla and Salamanca, soldiers proceeded to build the largest bridge in Lusitania, now the Puente Romano. The nostalgic crew adorned their "little Rome" with baths, aqueducts, temples, a hippodrome, an arena, and a famous amphitheater. Mérida's modern inhabitants have put arches to good work themselves: the arch-supported Puente Romano is upstream of the arch-supported highway and downstream of the arch-suspended Puente Lusitania. Modern Mérida not only copied the Romans' buildings, but also complemented them with walkways, small plazas, and the world-class Museo Romano. In July and August, the spectacular *Festival de Teatro Clásico* presents some of Europe's finest classical and modern theater and dance, performed among the ruins.

▛ TRANSPORTATION

Trains: (☎ 924 31 81 09), C. Cardero. Info window open daily 7am-11pm. To: **Cáceres** (1hr., 4 per day, 500-1200ptas); **Badajoz** (1hr., 7 per day, 400-1100ptas); **Zafra** (1hr., 2 per day, 400ptas); **Madrid** (4hr., 4 per day, 2800-4100ptas); **Sevilla** (4½hr., 1 per day, 1650ptas). For trains to **Lisbon,** transfer in Cáceres.

Buses: (☎ 924 37 14 04), Av. Libertad, in the *Polígono Nueva Ciudad.* Info booth open M-F 7am-11pm, Sa-Su 7am-1pm and 3:15-11pm. To: **Cáceres** (1hr., 2 per day, 675ptas); **Badajoz** (1hr., 10 per day, 610ptas); **Zafra** (1¼hr., 8 per day, 600ptas); **Sevilla** (3hr., 14 per day, 1600ptas); **Salamanca** (5hr., 4 per day, 2185ptas); **Madrid** (5½hr., 8 per day, 2760-3790ptas); **Valladolid** (6hr., 3 per day, 3350ptas); **Burgos** (9hr., 1 per day, 4200ptas); and **Barcelona** (12hr., 1 per day, 6425ptas).

Taxis: Teletaxi (24hr. ☎ 924 31 57 56).

Car Rental: Avis (☎ 924 37 33 11 or 909 26 32 32), at the bus station. Mid-sized car 10,000ptas per day, 53,000ptas per week. IVA and insurance included. Must be 23 to rent. Open M-F 9am-1pm and 5-8pm, Sa 9am-1pm.

▟ ORIENTATION AND PRACTICAL INFORMATION

Plaza de España, the town center, is two blocks up from the Puente Romano and easily accessible from the **Teatro Romano.** The cafes and shops around the plaza quickly transform into quiet residential neighborhoods, and streets often lose their signs. From the **bus station** to Pl. España, cross the suspension bridge **(Puente de Lusitania)** in front of the station and turn right on Av. de Roma. Walk along the river until you reach the Puente Romano, then turn left on C. Puente, which leads straight into Pl. España (20min.). To get to Pl. España from the **train station,** take C. Cardero (on your left as you exit the station) and its continuation, C. Camilo José Cela. Bear right onto C. Felix Valverde Lillo, and follow it to Pl. España (5-10min.).

Tourist Office: (☎ 924 26 32 32), on C. P.M. Plano, across the street from the Museo Romano and to the left as you exit the Teatro. From Pl. España, the town center, head up C. Santa Eulalia, which becomes a pedestrian shopping street, then bear right (as the hill peaks) on C. J. Ramon Melida at the little circle with the statue. The tourist office is at the end of the street to the right (10 min.). Friendly staff doles out small maps, theater schedules, and lists of accommodations, as well as info about the rest of Extremadura. Open in summer M-F 9am-1:45pm and 4-6:30pm, Sa-Su 9:30am-1:45pm; the rest of the year M-F 9am-1:45pm and 5-7:15pm, Sa-Su 9:30am-1:45pm.

Luggage Storage: At the **bus station** (100ptas per day) and **train station** (400ptas).

Emergency: ☎ 112. **Police:** (☎ 924 31 24 58) on C. Vespiano.

Medical Services: Residencia Sanitaria de la Seguridad Social Centralita (☎ 924 38 10 00). From Pl. España, follow the C. John Lennon, curving right onto C. Graciano. Follow this through its multiple name changes; the hospital is on your right after Pl. de Toros. **Emergency:** ☎ 924 38 10 18.

Post Office: (☎ 924 31 24 58; fax 924 30 24 56), Pl. Constitución. From Pl. España, take C. Félix Valverde Lillo, your first left onto C. Trajano, a right onto C. Cardenas and follow it to the plaza. Open for **Lista de Correos** M-F 8:30am-8:30pm, Sa 9:30am-1pm. **Postal Code:** 06800.

Internet Access: Café Internet, C. Banos, 25 (☎ 924 38 86 58). Turn right on C. Z. Vincente from Pl. España, left on C. Sagasta, and right on C. Banos—it's on the left. Merida's urbanization reflected in loud music and fast screens. Special drink deals if you use over 30min. 175ptas per 30min., 300ptas per 1hr. 150ptas per extra 30min.

ACCOMMODATIONS

Mérida gets crowded with visor-sporting tourists, but there are plenty of centrally located budget accommodations. Most don't accept credit cards.

Pensión El Arco, C. Cervantes, 16 (☎ 924 31 83 21 or 30 32 70). Follow C. Santa Eulalia up from Pl. España; C. Cervantes is on the left. The gregarious owner of this *pensión* fills his reception area with signed photos of royalty (Clintons included); his rooms will have you feeling like budget king or queen. Singles 2000ptas; doubles 3000ptas.

Hostal-Residencia Senero, C. Holguín, 12 (☎ 924 31 72 07). From Pl. España take the winding street just to the left of Hotel Emperatriz until it ends by bisecting C. Holguín. Clean and comfortable with space-saving baths and quieter rooms than the Pl. España allows. Rooms vary, some with bath and A/C. Apr.-Sept. singles 2200-3500ptas; doubles 4800-5800ptas. Oct.-Mar. singles 2000-3000; doubles 4000-4800ptas.

Hostal Salud, C. Vespasiano, 41 (☎/fax 924 31 22 59). From the train station follow C. Cardero to the 1st intersection and take a sharp right onto C. Marquesa de Pinares. C. Vespasiano is your 3rd left. From Pl. España, take C. Felix Lillo, the 2nd left onto C. Mor de Vargas, and the 3rd left onto C. Almendralejo. C. Vespasiano is your 1st right. Typical rooms, all with TV and full bath, some with A/C and heat. Singles 2800ptas; doubles 4800-5800ptas; Oct.-Mar. singles 2500ptas; doubles 4000-4800ptas. V, M, AmEx.

Hostal Nueva España, Av. Extremadura, 6 (☎ 924 31 33 56 or 924 31 32 11). From the train station turn left off C. Cardero onto Av. Extremadura. Closets are huge; you may have to hide in them to escape traffic noise. Private baths are spotless. Singles 3200ptas; doubles 5700ptas; triples 7700ptas. Parking garage 900ptas per car.

BULLBOARDS Staring glassy-eyed out the window of your preferred mode of transportation, you may notice rather unusual monuments along the highway: massive, black paper cut-outs of solitary bulls. Once upon a time (in the 1980s) these cut-outs were advertisements for *Soberano Coñac* (cognac). In the early 1990s, however, billboards were prohibited on national roads. A plan was drafted to take the bulls down, but Spaniards protested, as the lone bull towering along the roadside had become an important national symbol. After considerable clamoring and hoofing, the bulls were painted black and left to loom proudly against the horizon. The familiar shape now decorates t-shirts and pins in souvenir shops, but the real thing is still impressive. Keep your eyes peeled as you whiz through the countryside.

FOOD

Plaza de España is filled with outdoor cafes, but they tend to be overpriced; buying food and picnicking is the cheapest way to go. The **market** is on C. San Francisco, which connects C. Félix Valverde Lillo and C. Santa Eulalia; take C. Félix Valverde Lillo from Pl. España; C. San Francisco is your second right. (Open M-Sa 8am-2pm.) For **groceries,** try **EcoStop** (☎ 924 31 11 51), on C. Cabo Verde. From the tourist office, head down C. J. Ramón Melida, take a right down Trav. Museo, your second right (onto C. Mariano José de Larra), left onto C. Reyes Huertas, second right onto C. Pontezuelas and follow it to a T intersection with C. Cabo Verde. Relax and sip a beer (125ptas) at **Casa Benito,** C. San Francisco, 3, between C. Santa Eulalia and C. Lillo; to the left as you face the market. (☎ 924 31 55 00. *Tapas* 100-500ptas, *bocadillos* 400-800ptas. Open daily noon-midnight.)

SIGHTS

Roman edifices crumble slowly and beautifully, and the remains of ancient monuments permeate Mérida like holes in Swiss cheese. Over the wide, shallow Río Guadiana, the striking Puente Romano, one of the Romans' largest bridges, is still the main entrance into town. The **combined ticket** to visit the Teatro Romano, the Anfiteatro Romano, the Casa del Mitreo, the Casa del Anfiteatro, and Alcazaba is the cheapest way to see all the monuments. (800ptas, EU students 400ptas, Saturday afternoons and Sunday mornings free.) June through September, the Roman ruins are all open daily 9:30am-1:45pm and 5-7:15pm. October through May they are open 9:30am-1:45pm and 4-6:15pm.

MUSEO NACIONAL DE ARTE ROMANO. Enormous, elegant galleries under brick arches house all the Roman memorabilia you could ask for. Generous space allows for wonderful thematic and chronological organization of statues, dioramas, coins, remains of wall paintings and other relics. The **Cripta** displays parts of an Augusta Emerita street found when the museum was beginning construction. *(Follow C. Santa Eulalia from Pl. España; turn right on C. Juan Ramón Melida. ☎ 924 31 16 90. Open Tu-Sa 10am-2pm and 4-6pm, Su and holidays 10am-2pm; in summer Tu-Sa 10am-2pm and 5-7pm, Su and holidays 10am-2pm. 400ptas, students 200ptas. Sa afternoon and Su free.)*

TEATRO ROMANO. The spectacular *teatro* was a gift from Agrippa, a Roman administrator, to the city in 16 BC. The 6000 seats face a *scaenaefrons*, an incredible marble colonnade built upstage. **Teatro Clásico** performances take place here. *(Located in a park across the street from the Museo Nacional. ☎ 924 31 25 30. Staffed daily noon-2pm and 7:30-11:30pm. Performances July-Aug. 10:45pm. Tickets 700-3500ptas.)*

ANFITEATRO ROMANO. The most popular entertainment at the time was found in the 16,000-seat *anfiteatro*. Inaugurated in 8 BC, the *anfiteatro* was used for contests between any combination of animals and men, so long as there was blood. *(Separate admission 600ptas.)*

CIRCO ROMANO. Near the theater complex is the Circo Romano, or hippodrome. The most famous Lusitanian racer, Diocles, got his start here; he ended his career with a whopping 1462 victories. Once filled with spectators, the arena (capacity 30,000) is now a quiet public park. *(From outside the ruins, follow the curve of the road to the right, turn left on C. Cabo Verde over the train tracks, and turn right on Av. Juan Carlos.)*

CASA DEL MITREO AND CASA DEL ANFITEATRO. These ruins of Roman homes showcase some of the world's finest Roman mosaics. Take special note of the Casa del Mitreo's **Mosaico Cosmológico,** which depicts the ancient Romans' conception of the world and the forces of nature. *(For Casa del Mitreo, walk down Po. Alvarez with Teatro Romano on your left and take a right on Vía Ensarele; Casa del Anfiteatro is to the left of the anfiteatro with your back to the entrance.)*

OTHER RUINS. The **Alcazaba,** a Moorish fortress, was built with materials discarded by the Visigoths to guard the Roman bridge. Go for the view of the river and Puente Romano—aside from a cistern filled with river water, not much else remains. *(Located down the banks of the Guadiana and near Pl. España.)* At the end of C. Rambla Mártir Santa Eulalia stand the **museo, basílica,** and **iglesia,** all commemorating a martyred child, Santa Eulalia. During the course of repairs to the church in 1990 (it was originally constructed in the 6th century, turned over to the Arabs in 875, and rebuilt in 1230 during the *Reconquista*), layers of ruins were uncovered. These newly discovered ruins include Roman houses dating from the 3rd to 1st centuries BC, a 4th-century necropolis, and a basilica dedicated to Santa Eulalia. *(From Pl. España, take C. Santa Eulalia and bear left onto the rambla. Museum and basilica open daily in summer 10am-1:45pm and 5-7:15pm; off-season 4-5:45pm. They are part of the combined ticket to the Roman ruins. Church open daily during services at 8:30am and 8pm. Free.)*

🏛 DAYTRIP FROM MÉRIDA

ZAFRA (1HR.)

Call ☎ 924 55 39 07 to confirm bus schedules to and from Mérida, Sevilla and Cáceres.

Known as "little Sevilla" for its gaiety and resemblance to the famous Andalucian city, Zafra is one of the better known *pueblos blancos*, the series of glowing whitewashed villages scattered throughout Extremadura and Andalucía. (For more information on *pueblos blancos*, see **Ruta de los Pueblos Blancos,** p. 228.) Zafra is home to charming plazas and 17th- and 18th-century mansions like the **Casa de los Marqueses de Solanda,** a Renaissance Alcázar, but most of the "sights" don't hold up against the rest of Extremadura. If you're in the area, drop your bags at the Zafra station (50ptas), swing through town for an hour or two between buses and be sure to check out **Convent de Santa Clara** for sweet confections from sweet ladies. Exiting the bus station, cross the street and head straight down Av. Principe until it ends in a T with C. López Asme. Take a left and follow the bend around the Alcázar, leaving it on your right. Pl. de España is on your left. The **tourist office** at Pl. de España, 30, will give you a map and info in English. (☎ 924 55 10 36. Open M-F 9:30am-2pm and 4:30-7pm, Sa-Su 10am-2pm. Zafra has a **train station** (☎ 924 55 02 15), but it's a hike from town.

BADAJOZ

Badajoz (pop. 120,000) is little more than a necessary stop en route to or from Portugal. The contemporary art museum is well worth the visit if you're in the area, but while the Moorish ruins and 13th-century cathedral provide for an afternoon distraction, the neglected new city offers little but industrial pollution. Its proximity to Portugal has rendered it the site of countless border disputes; the border is 7km to the west, and Elvas, Portugal, lies 11km beyond. However, settlement since prehistoric times has certainly developed Badajoz's nightlife. Street parties erupt in the evening in the Plaza de España, and jealous Portuguese revelers often cross the border to partake in the fun.

⌐ TRANSPORTATION

Flights: Aeropuerto de Badajoz (☎ 924 21 04 00), Carretera Madrid-Lisboa, 10km east of the city. Small national airport serves Palma, Mallorca, and Tenerife, with **AirEuropa** and **Futuro** terminals. From Pl. España, walk down C. Zurbarán; turn left on Av. Ronda del Pillar and cross the bridge out of the city. A cab makes more sense (2000ptas).

Trains: (☎ 924 27 11 70), Av. Carolina Coronado. It's probably easier to take a bus. To get from the train station to Pl. Libertad, take bus #1. Info booth open daily 6am-9pm. To: **Mérida** (1½hr., 7 per day, 400-1200ptas); **Zafra** (2 per day via Mérida, 925ptas); **Cáceres** (2½hr., 4 per day, 850-1900ptas); **Madrid** (5hr., 2 per day, 4000-4500ptas); **Lisbon** (5½hr., 1per day, 2635ptas); **Barcelona** (2 per day, 6800-8300ptas).

Buses: C. José Rebollo López, 2 (☎ 924 25 86 61). Info booth open daily 7:45am-1am. Buses #3, 6a, 6b, and 9 run between the station and Pl. Libertad (100ptas). To: **Zafra** (1hr., 9-10 per day, 745ptas); **Mérida** (1½hr., 4-10 per day, 610ptas); **Cáceres** (1½hr., 3 per day, 1000ptas); **Trujillo** (2hr., 10 per day, 1215ptas); **Madrid** (4hr., 8-10 per day, 3245ptas); **Sevilla** (4½hr., 3-5 per day, 1745ptas); **Salamanca** (5hr., 3 per day, 2745-2945ptas); **Lisbon** (6hr., 3-6 per day, 2025ptas).

Taxis: At bus and train stations and Pl. de España. **Radio-Taxi** (24hr. ☎ 924 24 31 01).

✦🛈 ORIENTATION AND PRACTICAL INFORMATION

Plaza de España is the heart of Badajoz, bridging the narrow streets of the old town and the more commercial neighborhoods near **Plaza Libertad**. From Pl. España, C. Juan de Ribera leads to Pl. Libertad (5min.) and the tourist office. Between Pl. de España and Pl. Libertad is **Plaza San Francisco** (also right off C. Juan Ribera), where the **post office, supermarket,** and **restaurants** surround a small park. Pl. de España is across the unsightly Río Guadiana from the **train station.** To get from the train station to the center of town, follow Av. Carolina Coronado straight to the Puente de Palmas, cross the bridge, and go straight on C. Prim and its continuation. Turn left on C. Juan de Ribera to get to Pl. de España, right to get to Pl. Libertad (35min.). The #1 bus takes you from the train station to Pl. Libertad, stopping directly across from the **tourist office.** To Pl. de España from the **bus station,** turn left, take a quick right, and then turn left on C. Damión Tellez Lafuente. It becomes C. Fernando Cazadilla, passes through Pl. Constitución, becomes first Av. Europa and then C. Pedro de Valdivia, and runs uphill to the plaza (20min.).

Tourist Office: Pl. Libertad, 3 (☎ 924 22 27 63). City maps and glossy brochures in multiple languages, but staff does not speak English. Open M-F 9:30am-2pm and 5-7:30pm (winter 4-6:30pm), Sa-Su 9:45am-2pm. For tips on nightlife, visit the **Oficina de Información Juvenil,** Pasaje de San Juan, 2P (☎ 924 21 00 88). On the right as you walk up C. San Juan from Pl. de España.

Luggage Storage: In the bus station (50ptas per item) and train station (400ptas).

Emergency: ☎ 112. **Police:** (☎ 924 23 02 53) on Av. Ramón y Cajal. From Pl. Libertad, take Av. Ramón y Cajal. Located at the far corner, near C. Dosmos.

Hospital: Hospital Provincial, Pl. Minayo, 2 (☎ 924 22 47 43). From Pl. de España, walk toward Pl. San Francisco on C. Juan de Ribera; it's on your left before the plaza.

Post Office: Pl. San Francisco, 4 (☎ 924 22 02 04). Main entrance on Pl. San Francisco. **Lista de Correos.** M-F 8:30am-8:30pm, Sa 9am-2pm. **Postal Code:** 06001.

⌐ ACCOMMODATIONS

Most hostels are near Pl. España; they are scarce, however, so keep an eye out.

Pension Pintor, C. Arco-Agüero, 26 (☎ 924 22 42 28). From Pl. de España go down C. Ramón Albarran, take your second left onto C. Martín Cansado, and your 1st left onto C. Arco-Agüero. Spartan but spacious rooms. A tiny dog with a very loud bark guards the clean, tiled bathroom. Singles 1700ptas; doubles-3400ptas; triples 4800ptas.

Hostal Niza, C. Arco-Agüero, 45 (☎ 924 22 38 81). In the heart of Badajoz; from Pl. de España go down C. Ramón Albarran, take your 2nd left onto C. Martin Cansado and your first right onto C. Arco-Argüero. Reception is across the street at **Hostal Niza II,** Niza I's nicer, more expensive sister. Large rooms, and an owner eager to provide maps, brochures, and history. On weekends, ask for an interior room to block out the sounds of traffic and the party train. Singles 1700ptas; doubles 3200ptas; triples 4800ptas.

Hostal Beatriz, C. Abril, 20 (☎/fax 924 23 35 56). For a quieter, slightly upscale spot head downhill from Pl. España on C. Juan de Ribera, take your 3rd right onto C. J.C. Rey de España, and your 5th left onto C. Abril. Comfortable rooms and a TV/VCR room, but tougher on the wallet. Singles with sink 2835ptas; doubles with sink 4535ptas.

FOOD

For cafes and restaurants, check around **Plazas España, Libertad,** and especially **San Francisco.** For **groceries,** try **Simago,** next to the post office on Pl. San Francisco. (Open M-Sa 9:15am-9:15pm. V, MC.) **El Tronco**, C. Muñoz Torrero, 16, right off Pl. España (with your back to the cathedral) serves typical Extremaduran fare. With yellow stucco on the outside and antlers and tile floors inside, the decor is as eclectic as the crowd. Young and old mingle at the bar for drinks and *tapas.* (☎ 924 22 20 76. *Menú* 1250ptas. Open Tu-Sa 9am-4pm and 8pm-2am.) For shockingly good food from across the Mediterranean at the right price, try **Restaurante La Buena Pasta,** C. Muñoz Torrero, 3. Pastas run 700-800ptas, and pizzas 950ptas, in a romantic setting. (☎ 924 26 13 11. Open daily 1-4pm and 8:30-midnight.)

SIGHTS AND ENTERTAINMENT

In 1995, Badajoz inaugurated its ◪**Museo Extremeño e Iberoamericano de Arte Contemporáneo**. Its five floors exhibit recent works from Spain, Portugal, and Latin America, contrasting the distinct cultures of these regions. The permanent collection includes a few controversial creations like Marta María Pérez Bravo's photograph of a woman's breasts as a communion offering. Carefully presented exhibitions change frequently. From Pl. de España, head down C. Juan Ribera, continuing as it turns into Av. Europa. The museum is on your left after Pl. Constitución. (☎ 924 26 03 84. Open Tu-Sa 10:30am-1:30pm and 6-9pm, Su 10:30am-1:30pm; off-season Tu-Sa 10:30am-1:30pm and 5-8pm, Sun 10:30am-1:30pm. Free.)

The old quarter of Badajoz, around **Plaza de España** and **Plaza San Francisco,** is rich with history. The 13th-century **cathedral** in Pl. de España, a converted mosque, is a visual reminder of passing time, with one Romanesque, one Gothic, and one Plateresque window. The ruins of the **Alcazaba,** a Moorish citadel, stand at the top of the hill. For a tour of the old city and the ruins, take C. San Juan up the hill from Pl. de España, and veer left on C. M. Zancudo to enter **Plaza Alta.** Continue through the plaza and across the C. S. de Figueroa to reach the top. (Open Tu-Su 10am-3pm. 200ptas; EU citizens, students, and under 21 free.) Nearby is the **Torre del Apéndiz,** nicknamed Torre de Espantaperros ("to shoo away Christian dogs"), which served as the Alcazaba's watchtower and has become the city's emblem.

Badajoz nightlife draws partiers from neighboring towns and even Portugal. Most of the action takes place in the streets, rather than the clubs. **Calle de San Blas,** off Pl. de España, fills with teens passing around *minis* (large glasses) of *cerveza* or cider (325ptas), and 20-somethings gather in **Calle Zurbarán,** also off Pl. de España. Around 2am, the party shifts to the pubs of **Plaza Conquistadores** and continues into the morning. To get there from Pl. Libertad, head away from the tourist office on Av. de Huelva. Be careful in the area above Pl. España.

CENTRAL SPAIN

ANDALUCÍA

Andalucía derives its spirit from an intoxicating amalgam of cultures. The ancient kingdom of Tartessus—the same Tarshish mentioned in the Bible for its fabulous troves of silver—grew wealthy off the Sierra Nevada's rich ore deposits. The Greeks and Phoenicians established colonies and traded up and down the coast, and the Romans later cultivated wheat, olive oil, and wine from the fertile soil watered by the Guadalquivir. In the 5th century AD, the Vandals flitted through the region on their way to North Africa leaving little more than a name—Vandalusia (House of the Vandals). The Moors provided a more enduring influence. Arriving in AD 711 and establishing a yet unbroken link to Africa and the Muslim world, they bequeathed the region with far more than the flamenco music and gypsy ballads proverbially associated with southern Spain.

Under Moorish rule, which lasted until 1492, Sevilla and Granada reached the pinnacle of Islamic arts, and Córdoba matured into the most culturally influential Islamic city. The Moors preserved, perfected, and blended Roman architectural techniques with their own, creating a style that became distinctively and uniquely Andalucian. Intriguing patios, garden oases with fountains and fish ponds, and alternating red brick and white stone were its hallmarks. Two descendant peoples, the Mozarabs, or "Muslim-like" Christians, and later the Mudéjares, Moors conquered by Christians, made further architectural impacts, the former with horseshoe arches and the latter with intricate wooden ceilings. More importantly, the mingling of Roman and Moorish influences helped spark the European Renaissance, merging Classical wisdom and science with that of the Arab world.

Andalucía has been the source of many popular images of Spanish culture, sent the world over by advertising campaigns. Bullfighting, flamenco, white-washed villages, sherry *bodegas*, sandy beaches, and the blazing sun are much of what the region offers tourists. But beyond these attractions lie Spain's most vivacious and warm-hearted residents. Despite (or perhaps because of) the poverty and high unemployment in their homeland, Andalucians have always maintained a passionate, unshakable dedication to living the good life. The never-ending *festivales, ferias,* and *carnavales* of Andalucía are world-famous for their extravagance.

HIGHLIGHTS OF ANDALUCÍA

Watching **Granada's** incredible sunsets from the legendary **Alhambra** (see p. 264).

Sevilla's jaw-dropping Gothic cathedral and insane outdoor nightlife (see below).

Córdoba's sprawling, brilliant **Mezquita** (see p. 218).

Baeza, a taste of quintessential Andalucía (p. 272).

Desolate and beautiful **Cabo de Gata** (p. 252).

LOCAL FESTIVALS IN ANDALUCÍA

During *Semana Santa* in **Sevilla,** thousands of hooded penitents guide extravagant, candle-lit floats through the streets. Three weeks later, the town erupts into the week-long *Feria de Abril,* one of Spain's biggest parties. In mid-June, hundreds of Sevillians commemorate the *Romería del Rocío* with an 80km pilgrimage and traditional dancing and singing. **Córdoba** holds its unique *Festival de los Patios* in early May and an *International Guitar Festival* every summer. The *Fiestas de Otoño* in **Jerez** (mid-Sept.-mid-Oct.) feature the world's largest horse parade. **Málaga's** *Feria de Agosto,* complete with a huge sardine bake, is another of Andalucía's biggest celebrations. **Mojácar** reenacts the Moorish invasion during the *Fiestas de Moros y Cristianos,* and **Granada** is famous for its annual international theater, music and dance festivals.

Andalucía

N

PORTUGAL

MOROCCO

40 miles
40 kilometers

ATLANTIC OCEAN

MEDITERRANEAN SEA

Golfo de Cádiz

COSTA DE LA LUZ

COSTA DEL SOL

COSTA TROPICAL

COSTA DE ALMERÍA

Murcia
Lorca
Águilas
Mojácar
Carboneras
Vélez Rubio
Huércal-Overa
Níjar
E15
El Cabo
Cabo de Gata
Almería
Golfo de Almería
Roquetas de Mar
Úbeda
Cazorla
Quesada
Parque Natural de Cazorla, Segura y Las Vilas
Úbeda
Baza
Guadix
Laroles
Ugíjar
Órgiva
Trevélez
Capileira
SIERRA NEVADA
Mulhacén
LAS ALPUJARRAS
Salobreña
Almuñécar
Nerja
Cuevas de Nerja
Granada
Pico Veleta
Baeza
Jaén
Linares
Río Guadiana
NIV
A92
Córdoba
Montilla
Antequera
Villanueva de la Concepción
El Torcal
Garganta del Chorro
Álora
Ronda
Mijas
Torremolinos
Fuengirola
Málaga
N331
N340
Marbella
San Pedro de Alcántara
Estepona
La Línea de la Concepción
Gibraltar
Algeciras
Tarifa
Strait of Gibraltar
Tangier
Ceuta
Medina Azahara
Almodóvar del Río
Écija
Estepa
Osuna
Olvera
Setenil
Benaoján
Cueva de la Pleta
Gaucín
Algatocín
Cueva de la Pileta
Arcos de la Frontera
Bornos
Utrera
Carmona
Itálica (Roman Ruins)
Sevilla
Santiponce
El Pedroso
Constantina
Cazalla de la Sierra
Zufre
Aracena
Valverde del Camino
Huelva
Punta Umbría
Matalascañas
Almonte
Parque Nacional de Doñana
Río Guadalquivir
A49
Sanlúcar de Barrameda
Chipiona
Rota
El Puerto de Santa María
Cádiz
San Fernando
Chiclana de la Frontera
Vejer de la Frontera
Jerez de la Frontera
Ayamonte
Villa Real de Santo Antonio
A92

ANDALUCÍA

SEVILLA

If Spain's three great cities were siblings, Sevilla would be the beloved, giggling baby sister who can do no wrong. Once the site of a Roman acropolis founded by Julius Caesar, capital of the Moorish empire, and focal point of the Spanish Renaissance, today Sevilla is the charming guardian angel of traditional Andalucian culture, by far the best place to get a taste of "quintessential" southern Spain.

Flamenco, *tapas*, and bullfighting are at their best here, and the city's cathedral is among the most impressive in Spain. But it is the infectious, vivacious spirit of the city that really draws visitors: Sevilla's yearly *Semana Santa* and *Feria de Abril* celebrations are among the most exorbitant in all of Europe, and in the summer gregarious crowds gather by the hundreds to drink and dance along the mellow Guadalquivir River. (Though not even they can escape the blistering heat that has earned the town its nickname as the "frying pan of Spain.")

Sevilla has always had a powerful effect upon its visitors. Since the 16th century, Spaniards have been saying *"Qui no ha visto Sevilla no ha visto maravilla"* ("he who has not seen Sevilla has not seen a marvel"). *Carmen, Don Giovanni,* and *The Barber of Seville* are only a few of the artistic works that the city has inspired. Santa Teresa denounced it as the work of the devil, and less pious Jean Cocteau included it with Venice and Peking in his trio of magical cities.

✈ GETTING THERE AND AWAY

BY PLANE

All flights depart and land at **Aeropuerto San Pablo** (☎ 954 44 90 00), 12km out of town on Ctra. Madrid. A taxi ride between the airport and the town center costs about 2000ptas. **Los Amarillos** (☎ 954 98 91 84) runs a bus from outside the Hotel Alfonso XIII at the Pta. Jerez (6:15am-11pm, M-F every 30-45min., Sa-Su every hr., 350ptas). **Iberia**, C. Guaira, 8 (☎ 954 22 89 01; nationwide ☎ 902 400 500; open M-F 9am-1:30pm) books flights to **Madrid** (45min., 6 per day) and **Barcelona** (55min., 6 per day), as well as international destinations.

BY TRAIN

Most train service is centralized in the modern **Estación Santa Justa** (☎ 954 41 41 11), on Av. Kansas City. Services include an info booth, luggage storage, a telephone office, a cafeteria, and an ATM. Buses C1 and C2 link Santa Justa and the Prado de San Sebastián bus station. They stop on Av. Kansas City, to the left as you exit the train station. In town, the **RENFE** office, C. Zaragoza, 29, is near Pl. Nueva. (☎ 954 54 02 02. Open M-F 9am-1:15pm and 4-7pm.) International bookings must be made at this office.

> **AVE** trains run to: **Córdoba** (45min., 17 per day 6:30am-9pm, 2400-2800ptas); **Madrid** (2½hr., 20 per day 6:30am-9pm, 8400-9900ptas); and **Cádiz** (1½hr., 2 per day 1:20 and 7:30pm, 1600-2100ptas).

> **Talgo** trains run to: **Huelva** (1½hr., 3 per day 8:50am-8:20pm, 1000ptas); **Córdoba** (1½hr., 6 per day 7:50am-7:50pm, 1090ptas); **Antequera** (2hr., 5 per day 7am-6pm, 2000ptas); **Cádiz** (2hr., 12 per day 6:35am-9:30pm, 1300ptas); **Jaén** (2hr., 1 per day 6:46pm, 2200ptas); **Málaga** (2½hr., 5 per day 7:40am-9:10pm, 2130ptas); **Granada** (3hr., 5 per day 7am-6pm, 2660ptas); **Cáceres** (5½hr., 4:30pm, 3000ptas); **Almería** (5½hr., 3 per day 7am-6pm, 4200ptas); **Valencia** (8½hr., 4 per day 8:11am-9:50pm, 5300ptas); and **Barcelona** (12hr., 6 per day 8:20am-9:50pm, 6400ptas).

BY BUS

The old bus station at **Prado de San Sebastián,** C. Manuel Vázquez Sagastizabal, (☎ 954 41 71 11), mainly serves Andalucía. Buses C1 and C2 link Estación Santa Justa and Prado de San Sebastián. Look carefully for the station, as it is not immediately visible, or marked, from the street.

Transportes Alsina Graells (☎ 954 41 88 11). Open daily 6:30am-11pm. To: **Córdoba** (2hr., 10-13 per day 8am-9pm, 1225ptas); **Málaga** (2½hr., 10-12 per day 7am-midnight, 1850ptas); **Granada** (3hr., 9 per day 8am-11pm, 2400ptas); **Jaén** (4hr., 3-4 per day 7:30am-6pm, 2120ptas); **Nerja** (4½hr., 6pm, 2300ptas); **Almería** (7hr., 6 per day 7am-midnight, 3780ptas); and **Murcia** (8hr., 3 per day 8am-11am, 4630ptas).

Transportes Comes (☎ 954 41 68 58). Open M-Sa 6:30am-9:30pm, Su 7:15am-10:30pm. To: **Cádiz** (1½hr., 12 per day 7am-8:45pm, 1385ptas); **Jerez de la Frontera** (2hr., 7 per day 11am-8pm, 890ptas); **El Puerto de Santa María** (2hr., 2 per day 1075ptas); **Tarifa** (3hr., 4 per day 9am-8pm, 2075ptas); and **Algeciras** (3½hr., 4 per day 9am-8pm, 2100ptas).

Los Amarillos (☎ 954 98 91 84). Open M-F 7:30am-2pm and 2:30-8pm, Sa-Su 7:30am-2pm and 2:30pm-8pm. To: **Arcos de la Frontera** (2hr., 2 per day 8am and 4:30pm, 940ptas); **Sanlúcar** and **Chipiona** (2hr., 5-10 per day 7am-9pm, 920-1010ptas); **Ronda** (2½hr., 3-5 per day 7am-5pm, 1335ptas); **Marbella** (3hr., 1-2 per day 8am-8pm, 975ptas); and **Fuengirola** (3½hr., 1-2 per day 8am-8pm, 2245ptas).

Enatcar-Bacoma (☎ 902 42 22 42). Open daily 9:30am-9pm. To **Valencia** (10hr., 2 per day 9am and 4:30pm, 6485ptas) and **Barcelona** (16hr., 4:30pm, 9755ptas).

The newer bus station at **Plaza de Armas,** on the river bank at the Puente del Cachorro, serves destinations beyond Andalucía, including Portugal and other European countries. Services include an ATM, a cafeteria, and luggage storage. (☎ 954 90 77 37. Open daily 5:30am-1:30am). Buses C1, C2, C3, and C4 stop nearby.

Socibus (☎ 954 90 11 60 or 902 22 92 92; fax 954 90 16 92). Open daily 8:30am-12:45am. To **Madrid** (6hr., 15 per day 1pm-midnight, 2745ptas) and **Lagos** (6hr., 1 daily Jan.-May Th-Su, June-Oct. Tu-Su; 8:30am or 4pm; from 2590ptas).

Damas (☎ 954 90 80 40). Open M-F 8am-1:30pm and 4:30-10:45pm, Sa-Su 10:30am-1:30pm and 8-10:45pm. To: **Huelva** (1¼hr., 16-21 per day, 900ptas); **Badajoz** (3½hr., 3-4 per day 6:45am-8pm, 1700ptas); and **Lisbon** (9hr., 1 per day noon or 1:35pm, 4800ptas).

Alsa Internacional (☎ 954 90 78 00 or 902 42 22 42). July-Sept. 1000ptas more. Under 26 and seniors 10% discount, under 12 50% discount. Sa, and Th July-Sept, 1 per day to: **Toulouse** (21hr., 12,500ptas); **Lyon** (28hr., 18,000ptas); **Geneva** (30hr., 19,600ptas); **Zurich** (31hr., 22,300ptas). In Spain, daily 6:30am-9pm, to: **Cáceres** (4¼hr., 5 per day, 5255ptas); **Salamanca** (9½hr., 5 per day, 3735ptas); and **León** (13hr., 3 per day, 5255ptas).

⌐ GETTING AROUND

To reach El Centro from the train station, catch bus #32 to Plaza de la Encarnación, several blocks north of the cathedral. To get directly to Barrio Santa Cruz from the train station, take bus C-2 and transfer to C-3 at the Jardines del Valle; it will drop you off at the Jardines de Murillo. Walk right one block past the Jardines de Murillo; C. Santa María la Blanca will be on your left. From the bus station at Prado de San Sebastián, it is easiest to walk. Upon exiting the station, take a right on Av. Carlos V Enramadilla and follow it through Pl. Juan de Austria onto C. San Fernando. Continue along C. San Fernando to Puerta de Jerez and turn right onto Av. de la Constitución, which leads directly to the cathedral.

Bus C4 connects the bus station at the Plaza de Armas to Pr. San Sebastián. To walk to El Centro from Pl. Armas (10min.), walk along the river (on your left) three blocks and make a right onto C. Alfonso XII. To walk to the cathedral (20min.), exit right onto Po. Cristóbal Colón along the river (on your right) and take the first left onto C. Adriano. This street leads to C. García Vinuesa, which ends at the cathedral.

Public Transportation: TUSSAM (☎ 900 71 01 71), the city bus network, is extensive and useful. Most lines run every 10min. (6am-11:15pm) and converge on Pl. Nueva, Pl. Encarnación, or in front of the cathedral on Av. Constitución. Limited night service departs from Pl. Nueva (every hr., midnight-2am). Fare 125ptas, *bonobús* (10 rides) 650ptas. Particularly useful are buses C3 and C4, which circle the center, and #34, which hits the youth hostel, university, cathedral, and Pl. Nueva.

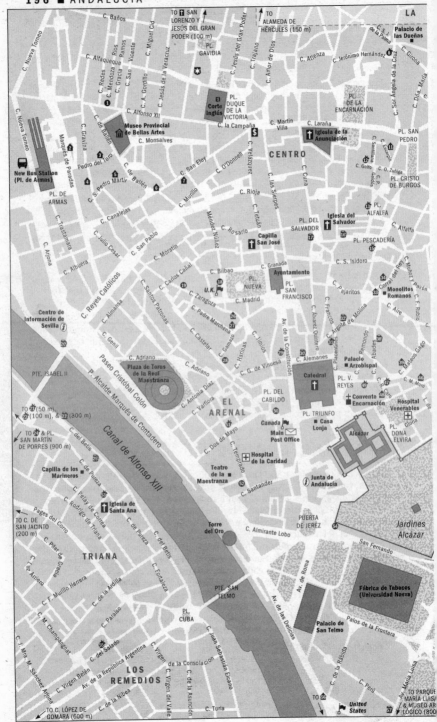

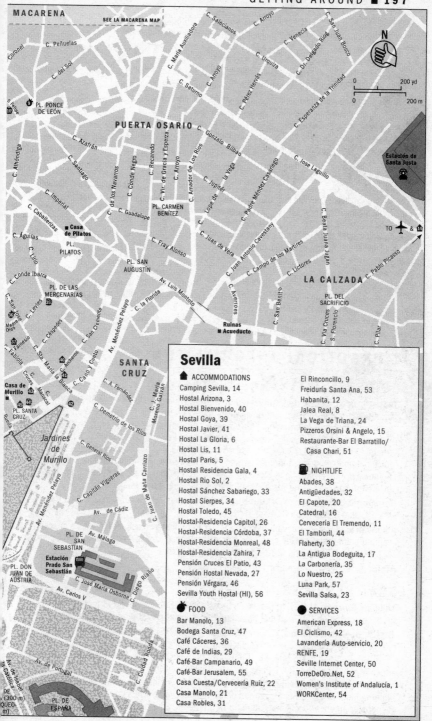

MACARENA

SEE LA MACARENA MAP

PUERTA OSARIO

LA CALZADA

SANTA CRUZ

Estación de Santa Justa

TO ✈ &

N

0   200 yd
0   200 m

Sevilla

🏠 ACCOMMODATIONS

Camping Sevilla, 14
Hostal Arizona, 3
Hostal Bienvenido, 40
Hostal Goya, 39
Hostal Javier, 41
Hostal La Gloria, 6
Hostal Lis, 11
Hostal Paris, 5
Hostal Residencia Gala, 4
Hostal Rio Sol, 2
Hostal Sánchez Sabariego, 33
Hostal Sierpes, 34
Hostal Toledo, 45
Hostal-Residencia Capitol, 26
Hostal-Residencia Córdoba, 37
Hostal-Residencia Monreal, 48
Hostal-Residencia Zahira, 7
Pensión Cruces El Patio, 43
Pensión Hostal Nevada, 27
Pensión Vérgara, 46
Sevilla Youth Hostal (HI), 56

🍴 FOOD

Bar Manolo, 13
Bodega Santa Cruz, 47
Café Cáceres, 36
Café de Indias, 29
Café-Bar Campanario, 49
Café-Bar Jerusalem, 55
Casa Cuesta/Cervecería Ruiz, 22
Casa Manolo, 21
Casa Robles, 31

El Rinconcillo, 9
Freiduría Santa Ana, 53
Habanita, 12
Jalea Real, 8
La Vega de Triana, 24
Pizzeros Orsini & Angelo, 15
Restaurante-Bar El Barratillo/
    Casa Chari, 51

🍷 NIGHTLIFE

Abades, 38
Antigüedades, 32
El Capote, 20
Catedral, 16
Cervecería El Tremendo, 11
El Tamboril, 44
Flaherty, 30
La Antigua Bodeguita, 17
La Carbonería, 35
Lo Nuestro, 25
Luna Park, 57
Sevilla Salsa, 23

● SERVICES

American Express, 18
El Ciclismo, 42
Lavandería Auto-servicio, 20
RENFE, 19
Seville Internet Center, 50
TorreDeOro.Net, 52
Women's Institute of Andalucía, 1
WORKCenter, 54

Taxis: TeleTaxi (☎ 954 62 22 22). **Radio Taxi** (☎ 954 58 00 00). Base rate 360ptas, Su 25% surcharge. Extra charge for luggage and night taxis as well.

Car Rental: Hertz, Av. República Argentina, 3 (☎ 954 27 88 87), and at the airport (☎ 954 51 47 20). Min. age 25. From 10,000ptas a day. Open M-F 9am-1:30pm and 4-7pm, Sa 9am-1pm. **Triana Rent A Car,** C. Almirante Lobo, 7 (☎ 954 56 44 39 or 954 33 68 97). Min. age 21, but they will negotiate. From 5100ptas a day.

Moped Rental: Alkimoto, C. Fernando Tirado, 5 (☎ 954 58 49 27), at Av. de Luis Montoto, near Est. Santa Justa. 3500ptas per day. Open M-F 9am-1:30pm and 5-8pm.

Bike Rental: El Ciclismo, Po. Catalina de Ribera, 2 (☎ 954 41 19 59), off Menéndez Pelayo, at the end of the Jardines de Murillo. 1500ptas per weekday, 2500ptas for the weekend. Open M-F 10am-1:30pm and 6-8pm, Sa 10am-1pm.

✠ ORIENTATION

Over the centuries, Sevilla has incorporated a number of neighboring villages, now distinct neighborhoods. The **Río Guadalquivir** flows roughly north to south through the city. Most of the touristed areas of Sevilla, including the alleyways of the old **Barrio de Santa Cruz** and **El Arenal,** are on the east bank. The historic and proud **Barrio de Triana,** the **Barrio de Santa Cecilia, Los Remedios,** and the Expo '92 fairgrounds occupy the west bank. The cathedral, next to Barrio de Santa Cruz, is Sevilla's centerpiece. If you're disoriented, look for the conspicuous Giralda (the minaret-turned-bell tower). **Avenida de la Constitución,** home of the regional tourist office, runs alongside the cathedral. **El Centro,** a busy commercial pedestrian zone, lies north of the cathedral, starting where Av. Constitución hits **Plaza Nueva,** site of the Ayuntamiento. **Calle Tetuan,** a popular street for shopping, takes off from Pl. Nueva and runs northward through El Centro.

⊠ PRACTICAL INFORMATION

TOURIST AND FINANCIAL SERVICES

Tourist Offices: Centro de Información de Sevilla, C. Arjona, 28 (☎ 954 50 56 00), at the Puente Isabel II. Worthy of being every tourist's first stop. Huge, new, and replete with city and events information. Free maps and monthly magazine for tourists. Open M-F 9am-9pm, Sa-Su 8:30am-2:30pm. **Another office** at Junta de Andalucía, Av. Constitución, 21B (☎ 954 22 14 04; fax 954 22 97 53), 1 block from the cathedral. Regional and city maps and info. English spoken. Always swamped, but most crowded before and after siesta. Open M-F 9am-7pm, Sa 10am-2pm and 3-7pm, Su 10am-2pm. **Info booths** in Est. Santa Justa and Pl. Nueva carry maps and bus guides.

Currency Exchange: Banco Central Hispano, C. Sierpes, 55 (☎ 954 56 26 84). Open M-F 8:30am-2:30pm, Sa 8:30am-1pm.

American Express: Pl. Nueva, 7 (☎ 954 21 16 17). Changes cash and traveler's checks without commission, holds mail, and offers emergency services for cardholders. Open M-F 9:30am-1:30pm and 4:30-7:30pm, Sa 10am-1pm.

ATMS: All along Av. Constitución and near Pl. Nueva.

LOCAL SERVICES

Luggage Storage: At Pr. San Sebastián bus station (250ptas; open 6:30am-10pm), Pl. Armas bus station (300ptas per day), and Santa Justa train station (300-500ptas).

English Bookstore: Vertice, C. San Fernando, 33 (☎ 954 21 16 54), near Pta. Jerez. Large and diverse collection of English-language texts (including *Let's Go*). Open M-F 9:30am-2pm and 5-8:30pm, Sa 10am-1:30pm. July closed Sa. **Librería Beta,** a chain with stores all over Sevilla, has an English-language section.

VIPS: C. República Argentina, 25 (☎ 954 27 93 97), 3 blocks from Pl. Cuba, in Triana. International newspapers, liquor, non-perishable groceries, and a restaurant that serves a popular American breakfast. Open Su-Th 8am-2am, F 8am-3am, Sa 9am-3am.

Women's Institute of Andalucía: C. Alfonso XII, 52 (☎ 955 03 49 53). Info on feminist and lesbian organizations, plus legal and psychological services for rape victims. Employment listings for women. Open M-Th 8am-8:30pm, F until 3pm.

Gay and Lesbian Services: COLEGA (Colectiva de Lesbianas y Gays de Andalucía), Cuesta del Rosario, 8 (☎ 954 18 65 10). Open M-F 10am-2pm.

Laundromat: Lavandería Auto-servicio, C. Castelar, 2 (☎ 954 21 05 35), From the cathedral, walk 2 blocks down G. Vinuesa and turn left. Wash and dry (1hr.) 1000ptas. Open M-F 9:30am-1:30pm and 3-8:30pm, Sa-Su 9am-2pm.

EMERGENCY AND COMMUNICATIONS

Emergency: ☎ 112. **Police:** Po. Delicias, 15 (☎ 954 61 54 50).

Late-Night Pharmacy: Check list posted at any pharmacy for those open 24hr.

Medical Assistance: Ambulatorio Esperanza Macarena (☎ 954 42 01 05). **Hospital Universitario Virgen Macarena** (☎ 954 24 81 81), Av. Dr. Fedriani. English spoken.

Internet Access: WORKcenter, C. San Fernando, 1 (☎ 954 21 20 74), at the Puerta de Jerez. 100ptas for 10min. Also has **fax** services. Open 24hr. **TorreDeOro.Net,** C. Núñez de Balboa, 3 (☎ 954 50 28 09), next to the Teatro Maestranza, at Po. Cristóbal Colón. Coin-operated computers. 300ptas per hr. Open daily 8:30am-1am. **Seville Internet Center,** C. Almirantazgo, 2, 2nd fl. (☎ 954 50 02 75), across from the Cathedral. 10ptas per min. Open M-F 9am-10pm, Sa-Su noon-10pm. **Cibercenter,** C. Julio Cesar, 8 (☎ 954 22 88 99), off C. Reyes Católicos. 200ptas for 10min, students 600ptas per hr. Open daily 8am-10pm.

Post Office: Av. Constitución, 32 (☎ 954 21 64 76), opposite the cathedral. **Lista de Correos** and **fax.** Open M-F 10am-8:30pm, Sa 9:30am-2pm. **Postal Code:** 41080.

■ ACCOMMODATIONS

During Semana Santa and Feria de Abril, rooms vanish and prices soar; it would be wise to make reservations months ahead. At other times, call a few days before arriving. The tourist office has lists of *casas particulares* that open on special occasions to accommodate the influx of visitors.

BARRIO DE SANTA CRUZ AND EL ARENAL

The narrow streets east of the cathedral around C. Santa María la Blanca are full of cheap hostels with virtually identical rooms. The neighborhood is overwhelmingly touristed, but its disorienting streets and shady plazas are all within a few minutes' walk of the cathedral, the Alcázar, and El Centro.

Hostal Sierpes, C. Corral del Rey, 22 (☎ 954 22 49 48; fax 954 21 21 07), on the continuation of C. Argote de Molina. A hopping hostel that takes Seville's festivals seriously. Simple rooms all have phones; some have A/C, the others fans. Parking 1500-2500ptas per day. Reservations recommended. Singles with shower 3000-4000ptas, with bath 4000-5000ptas; doubles with shower 4000-6000ptas, with bath 5500-10,000ptas; triples with shower 5500-8000ptas, with bath 7000-14,000ptas.

Pensión Vergara, C. Ximénez de Enciso, 11, 2nd fl. (☎ 954 21 56 68), at C. Mesón del Moro. This newly renovated 15th-century house is a bargain. Up to 4 people in a room. 2500ptas per person.

Hostal Sánchez Sabariego, C. Corral del Rey, 23 (☎ 954 21 44 70), on the continuation of C. Argote de Molina. A/C upstairs, fans all other rooms. Singles 4000ptas; doubles with bath 8000ptas; triples with bath 9000ptas.

Hostal-Residencia Córdoba, C. Farnesio, 12 (☎ 954 22 74 98), off C. Fabiola. Immaculate, with spacious rooms and a beautiful indoor patio. A/C. Singles 3500-5000ptas, with shower 4500-7000ptas; doubles 5500-8000ptas, with shower 7000-9500ptas.

Hostal-Residencia Monreal, C. Rodrigo Caro, 8 (☎ 954 21 41 66). From the cathedral, walk up C. Mateos Gago and take the 1st right. Lounge area and bar on the 1st floor. Singles 2675ptas; doubles 5350ptas, with bath 7500ptas; triples 10,500ptas. V, MC.

🌿 **Pensión Cruces El Patio,** C. Cruces, 10 (☎ 954 22 96 33 or 954 22 60 41). Gregarious owner oversees hostel and multiple bird cages in the patio. Fans on request. Up to 6 people in a room (1500-2000ptas per person). Laundry 1500ptas. Singles 2000ptas; doubles 4000-5000ptas, with bath 5000-6000ptas.

Hostal Bienvenido, C. Archeros, 14 (☎ 954 41 36 55). Roof terrace converted to outdoor lounge. All rooms have sinks. Up to 4 people per room. Singles 2000-2500ptas; doubles 4000-4600ptas; triples 2000-2300ptas per person.

🌿 **Hostal Goya,** C. Mateos Gago, 31 (☎ 954 21 11 70; fax 954 56 29 88), 3 blocks from the cathedral. Dark rooms with modern bathrooms cooled by fans. Lounge area with leather recliners. Doubles with shower 6400ptas, with bath 7300ptas; triples with shower 9000ptas, with bath 10,000ptas.

🌿 **Hostal-Residencia Capitol,** C. Zaragoza, 66 (☎ 954 21 24 41), near Pensión Hostal Nevada. Spacious rooms. Lounge with phone and TV. A/C. Singles 3210ptas; doubles with shower 5500ptas, with bath 6420ptas. V, MC, AmEx.

Hostal Toledo, C. Santa Teresa, 15 (☎ 954 21 53 35), off C. Ximénez de Enciso. Singles with shower 4000-8000ptas, with bath 3500-6000ptas; doubles 6000-12,000ptas; IVA not included.

🌿 **Pensión Hostal Nevada,** C. Gamazo, 28 (☎ 954 22 53 40). From Pl. Nueva, take C. Barcelona and turn right on C. Gamazo. Tapestry-laden lobby and hallways lead to cool courtyard. Some rooms with A/C. Parking 2000ptas per day. Singles 3000-3500ptas; doubles 5000-6000ptas, with bath 6000-6500ptas.

🌿 **Hostal Javier,** C. Archeros, 16 (☎ 954 41 23 25). Well-furnished, comfortable rooms with fans. Singles 3500-4000ptas, with bath 3500-4000ptas; doubles 4000-5000ptas, with bath 5000-6000ptas; triples 7500-9000ptas. V, MC.

EL CENTRO

El Centro, a mess of narrow streets radiating from Pl. Encarnación, is a bustling shopping district during the day, but most streets are deserted at night.

🔳 **Hostal Lis,** C. Escarpín, 10 (☎ 954 21 30 88), on an alley near Pl. Encarnación. Each room decorated with its own unique Sevillian tiles. All have fans. Up to 4 in a room. Singles 3000ptas; doubles 6000ptas, with bath 7000ptas; triples with bath 9000ptas.

Hostal La Gloria, C. San Eloy, 58, 2nd fl. (☎ 954 22 26 73), at the end of a lively shopping street. Tiled floors and a homely lounge with TV and sofa. Singles 2000-2500ptas; doubles 4000ptas, with bath 4500ptas; triples 6000ptas.

Hostal-Residencia Zahira, C. San Eloy, 43 (☎ 954 22 10 61; fax 954 21 30 48). Hotel-sized lobby masks smaller rooms. All rooms have bath and A/C. Lounge with TV. Singles 3500-4000ptas; doubles 6000-7000ptas. V, MC, AmEx.

NEAR ESTACIÓN PLAZA DE ARMAS

Most hostels near the Pl. Armas bus station center on C. Gravina, parallel to C. Marqués de las Paradas and two blocks from the station. These are the most convenient for El Centro and the lively C. Betis on the west bank of the river.

🔳 **Hostal Río Sol,** C. Márquez de Parada, 25 (☎ 954 22 90 38), 1 block from Plaza de Armas bus station. Extremely convenient location. Small rooms have newly renovated bathrooms and A/C. Singles with sink 2000ptas, with bath 3000-4000ptas; doubles with bath 6500ptas; triples with bath 9000ptas. V, MC.

Hostal Paris, C. San Pedro Mártir, 14 (☎ 954 22 98 61 or 954 21 96 45; fax 954 21 96 45), off C. Gravina. All rooms have baths, A/C, phones, and TVs. Singles 3500ptas; doubles 6000ptas; triples 9000ptas. Student discounts. V, MC, AmEx.

Hostal Residencia Gala, C. Gravina, 52 (☎ 954 21 45 03). Clean, simple rooms; some are windowless. Laundry 2000ptas per load. Singles 3000ptas, with bath 4000ptas; doubles 4500ptas, with bath 6000ptas; triples with bath 7500ptas.

Hostal Arizona, C. Pedro del Toro, 14 (☎ 954 21 60 42), off C. Gravina. Clean rooms with fans and tiled floors; some have balconies. Singles 2000-2500ptas; doubles 4500ptas, with bath 4500ptas; triples 5000-6000ptas.

ELSEWHERE AND CAMPING

Sevilla Youth Hostel (HI), C. Isaac Peral, 2 (☎ 954 61 31 50; fax 954 61 31 58). Take bus #34 from Pr. San Sebastían; it stops behind the hostel just after Po. Delicias. A bit out of the way. Bright, white, and disinfected. Up to 4 per room. Many private baths. Breakfast included. Dorms 1605ptas, over 26 2140ptas. Non-members can pay an additional 300ptas a night for 6 nights to become members.

Camping Sevilla, Ctra. Madrid-Cádiz, km 534 (☎ 954 51 43 79), near the airport. From Pr. San Sebastián, take bus #70 (stops 800m away at Parque Alcosa). Hot showers, supermarket, and pool. 475ptas per person, per car, and per tent, children 375ptas.

Club de Campo, Av. Libertad, 13, Ctra. Sevilla-Dos Hermanas (☎ 954 72 02 50), 8km out of town. Los Amarillos buses leave from C. Infante Carlos de Borbón, at the back of Pr. San Sebastián, to Dos Hermanas (every 45min., 140ptas). Lots of grass and a pool. 525ptas per person, per car, and per tent, children 425ptas.

ⓖ FOOD

Sevilla is a city of *tapas*; locals prepare and devour them with a vengeance. Other favorites include *caracoles* (snails), *cocido andaluz* (a thick soup of chick peas), *pisto* (tomato and egg-plant hash), *espinacas con garbanzos* (spinach with garbanzos), and all manner of fresh seafood. *Pescado frito*, lightly fried fish, is a particular specialty of Sevilla. Defying the need for hydration, locals imbibe Sevilla's Cruzcampo beer, a light, smooth pilsner. **Mercado del Arenal,** near the bullring on C. Pastor y Leandro, between C. Almansa and C. Arenal, has fresh meat and produce (open M-Sa 9am-2pm). For a supermarket, try **%Día,** C. San Juan de Ávila, near El Corte Inglés (open M-F 9:30am-2pm and 6:30-9pm, Sa 9am-1pm).

BARRIO DE SANTA CRUZ AND EL ARENAL

Restaurants near the cathedral cater almost exclusively to tourists. Beware the unexceptional, omnipresent *menús* featuring *gazpacho* and *paella* for 1000ptas. Food and prices improve in the backstreet establishments between the cathedral and the river in El Arenal, and along side streets in the Barrio Santa Cruz.

▨ Restaurante-Bar El Baratillo/Casa Chari, C. Pavia, 12 (☎ 954 22 96 51), on a tiny street off C. Dos de Mayo. Call or ask in advance for the tour-de-force: homemade *paella* with a jar of wine, beer, or *sangría* (2500ptas for 2). *Menú* 500ptas. Open M-F 9am-11pm, Sa noon-5pm.

Café-Bar Campanario, C. Mateos Gago, 8 (☎ 954 56 41 89), ½ block from the cathedral, on the right. Mixes the best jugs of *sangría* around (1200-1500ptas). *Tapas* 175-325ptas, *raciones* 650-1000. Open daily noon-midnight.

Café Cáceres, C. San José, 24. The closest thing to a buffet-style breakfast in Sevilla. Choose from spread of cheeses, jams, and countless other condiments. *Desayuno de la casa* (orange juice, coffee, ham, eggs, toast) 650ptas. Open daily 7:30am-8pm.

Bodega Santa Cruz, C. Rodrigo Caro, 1 (☎ 954 21 32 46). Take C. Mateos Gago from the fountain in front of the cathedral; it's on the 1st corner on the right. Casual and crowded at all hours. *Tapas* 175-200ptas. Open daily 8am-midnight.

Casa Robles, C. Placentines, 2 (☎ 954 21 31 62), 1 block from the cathedral. Hidden from tourists and deemed by locals as one of the best eateries in the neighborhood. *Tapas* 250ptas. Entrees 800-2200ptas. Open daily noon-1am. V, MC.

EL CENTRO

This area belongs to professionals and shoppers by day and young people at night. Inexpensive *tapas* bars can be found on the streets radiating from Plaza Alfalfa.

▨ Pizzeros Orsini & Angelo, C. Luchana, 2 (☎ 954 21 61 64), 2 blocks from Pl. del Salvador. The aroma filtering out of this tiny pizza joint can be picked up blocks away—their fresh-baked creations are served straight out of the oven. Pizzas 400-950ptas. Salads 400-700ptas. Open daily 1-4pm and 8pm-1am.

Jalea Real, Sor Ángela de la Cruz, 37 (☎ 954 21 61 03). From Pl. Encarnación, walk 150m on C. Laraña, then turn left at Iglesia de San Pedro. Fabulous vegetarian cuisine. Fresh, tasty salads 475-800ptas, *menú* 1250ptas. Open July-Aug. M-F 1:30-5 and 8:30-11:30pm, Sa 8:30-11:30pm; Sept.-June M-Sa 2-5 and 8:30-11:30pm.

Bar Manolo, Pl. de Alfalfa, 3 (☎ 954 21 41 76). One of the mainstays of the plaza; the outdoor seating area is always packed. The *tapas* here are fresh and filling. *Tapas* 200-425, *raciones* 1100ptas. Open daily 7am-12:30pm.

El Rinconcillo, C. Gerona, 40 or C. Alhóndiga, 2 (☎ 954 22 31 83). This *bodega*, founded in 1670, is a popular pit-stop with quite a history. Sip your drinks on top of authentic-looking wine barrels. *Tapas* 185-300ptas, *raciones* 225-1850ptas. V, MC.

TRIANA AND BARRIO DE SANTA CECILIA

This old maritime neighborhood, on the far side of the river, was once a separate village. Avoid overpriced C. Betis and plunge down less expensive sidestreets, where fresh seafood and *caracoles* abound. *Tapas* bars cluster around Pl. San Martín and along C. San Jacinto.

⊠ La Vega de Triana, C. Asturias at Pl. San Martín de Porres. A hectic atmosphere behind the bar and wine-barreled tables make for a lively meal like no other. *Tapas* 200-300ptas, *raciones* 1100-1300ptas. Open daily 11am-midnight.

Freiduría Santa Ana, C. Pureza, 61 (☎ 954 33 20 40), parallel to C. Betis, 1 block from the river. Both the fresh fried fish and the restaurant itself are local institutions. Free samples ease the wait. Seafood served by the kg. Open Sept.-July Tu-Su 7pm-midnight.

Casa Cuesta/Cervecería Ruiz, C. Castilla, 3-5 (☎ 954 33 33 37), 1 block from the Puente Isabel II. Enjoy your meal in the beautiful dining room in the back of the bar. Expensive, but worth it. *Raciones* 600-1500ptas, entrees 550-1700ptas. Restaurant open W-M 8:30am-12:30am; bar open 1:30-4:30pm and 9pm-midnight. V, AmEx.

Café-Bar Jerusalem, C. Salado, 6, at C. Virgen de las Huertas. Bar with an international crowd and creative *tapas*. Chicken, lamb, or pork and cheese *shwarmas* called a *bocadillo hebreo*—it's not kosher, but it sure is tasty (400-625ptas). Open daily 8pm-3am.

🎯 SIGHTS

Sevilla is full of sights, from the famous Alcázar and cathedral to the churches, monuments, and winding streets of the *casco viejo* and Barrio de Santa Cruz.

BARRIO DE SANTA CRUZ

▧ THE CATHEDRAL. Legend has it that the *reconquistadores* in 1401 wished to demonstrate their religious fervor by constructing a church so great, they said, that "those who come after us will take us for madmen." With 44 individual chapels, the cathedral is the third largest in the world, after St. Peter's Basilica in Rome and St. Paul's Cathedral in London, and it is the world's biggest Gothic edifice ever constructed. Not surprisingly, it took more than a century to build.

LOYALTY REMEMBERED During Spain's civil wars of the 1270s, King Alfonso X the Wise was betrayed by his own son Don Sancho, who wrested from his father all of Castile, León, Galicia, Extremadura and Andalucía—with the sole exception, that is, of Sevilla, whose people remained loyal to the old king. Alfonso is recorded as having sighed in gratitude "*No m'a dejado*" ("She has not forsaken me"). To remind generations to come of the city's loyalty, the king added a new logo to the city shield which has since become the emblem and motto of Sevilla: a NO and DO with a double knot in between, similar to "NO&DO." *Nodo* in Spanish means "knot," and *madeja* means "skein." The rebus reads *No m'a dejado* perfectly and is a particularly clever word play which proud Sevillians have emblazoned all over the city, from the sides of buses to government buildings.

In 1401, Christians destroyed the 12th-century Almohad mosque to clear space for a massive cathedral. All that remains of the former mosque is the **Patio de Los Naranjos,** where the faithful would wash before prayer, and the famed minaret **La Giralda,** built in 1198. The tower and its twins in Marrakesh and Rabat are the oldest and largest surviving Almohad minarets, with the lower walls standing 2.5m thick. Alterations to the belfry were made throughout the 16th century, including the addition of 25 bells. There are 35 ramps inside leading to the top of the tower; these once allowed the *muezzin* to climb up on his horse to call for prayer and are now used by tourists to see panoramic views of Sevilla.

The inside of the cathedral is disorienting; the points of interest listed here are in counter-clockwise order. In the middle of the cathedral, the **Capilla Real** (main chapel), built in Renaissance style, and its altar stand opposite the dark wooden **choirstalls** made of mahogany recylced from a 19th-century Austrian railway. The **retablo mayor** (altarpiece), one of the largest in the world, is a golden wall of intricately wrought figurines depicting 36 biblical scenes. Walking around the choirstalls leads to the **Sepulcro de Cristóbal Colón** (Columbus's tomb). The black and gold coffin-bearers represent the eternally grateful kings of Castilla, León, Aragón, and Navarra. There is considerable mystery surrounding the actual whereabouts of Columbus's remains, since there are currently four of his tombs throughout the world. The Sepulcro was inaugurated in 1902, 396 years after Columbus died; chances are this tomb isn't the jackpot.

Farther on and to the right stands the cathedral's precious museum, the **Sacristía Mayor,** which holds the gilded panels of Alfonso X "El Sabio", done by Juan de Arefe, as well as works by Ribera and Murillo and a glittering Corpus Christi icon, **La Custodia Processional.** A small, disembodied head of John the Baptist eyes visitors who enter the gift shop and overlooks two keys presented to the city of Sevilla by Jewish leaders after King Fernando III ousted the Muslims in 1248. The neighboring **Sacristía de los Cálices** (or **de los Pintores**) maintains a collection of minor canvases by Zurbarán and Goya. In the corner of the cathedral are the impressive **Sala de Las Columnas** and the perfectly oval **cabildo** (chapter house). (☎ 954 21 49 71. Open M-Sa 10:30am-5pm, Su 2-6pm. Tickets sold until 1hr. before closing. 700ptas, seniors and students 200ptas, under 12 free. Su free.)

■**ALCÁZAR.** If you can't make it to the Alhambra in Granada, at least come to Sevilla's Alcázar; the Moorish architecture and gardens are nothing short of magnificent. The imposing 9th-century walls of the palace stand next to Pl. Triunfo and face the cathedral, serving as a testament to the flow and exchange of cultures that Sevilla has experienced; it was once a Roman necropolis, a paleo-Christian basilica, and later Visigothic buildings, all before the Moors built the fortress and residences in the 7th century. It was later embellished by the Christians after the 13th century with Gothic, Renaissance, and Baroque elements and now serves as the residence of the King and Queen of Spain during their visits to Sevilla. Visitors enter through the **Patio de la Montería,** directly across from the intricate Almohad facade of the Moorish palace. Through the archway lies the Arabic residences, including the **Patio del Yeso** and the exquisitely carved **Patio de las Muñecas** (Patio of the Dolls), so named because of its miniature proportions. Of the Christian additions, the most notable is the **Patio de las Doncellas (Maids' Court).** Court life in the Alcázar revolved around this colonnaded quadrangle, which is encircled by archways adorned with glistening tilework. The astonishing golden-domed **Salón de los Embajadores** is allegedly the site where Fernando and Isabel welcomed Columbus back from America. Nearby, the **Corte de las Muñecas** contains the palace's private quarters, decorated with the building's most exquisite carvings. Stunning, peaceful **gardens** stretch from the residential quarters in all directions. (Pl. Triunfo, 7. ☎ 954 50 23 23. Open Tu-Sa 9:30am-7pm, Su 9:30am-6pm. 700ptas; students, disabled, over 65, and under 16 free. Audio guides in several languages give anecdotes, historical info, and a clearly marked route through the buildings and gardens; 400ptas.)

ANDALUCÍA

CASA LONJA. Between the cathedral and the Alcázar stands the 16th-century Casa Lonja, built by Felipe II as a *Casa de Contratación* (commercial exchange) for trade with the Americas. In 1785, Carlos III converted the building into the **Archivo General de las Indias (Archive of the Indies).** Today it contains a collection of over 44,000 documents relating to the discovery and conquest of the New World. Among its books is Juan Bautista Muñoz's "definitive" history of the conquest, commissioned by Carlos III. Other highlights of the collection include Juan de la Costa's wildly inaccurate *Mapa Mundi* and letters from Columbus to Fernando and Isabel, as well as a 1590 letter from Cervantes (pre-*Don Quijote*) requesting employment in America. (☎ 954 21 12 34. Exhibits open M-F 10am-1pm. Free. Full access to documents is restricted to scholars.)

BARRIO DE SANTA CRUZ

The tourist office has a detailed map of the winding alleys, wrought-iron gates, and courtyards of the Barrio de Santa Cruz. King Fernando III forced Jews in flight from Toledo to live in this former ghetto. Haloed with geraniums, jasmine, and ivy, every street corner in the neighborhood echoes with a legend. On **Calle Susona,** a glazed skull above a door recalls the beautiful Susona, a Jew who fell in love with a Christian knight. When Susona learned that her father and friends planned to kill several inquisitors, including her knight, she warned her lover. A bloody reprisal was unleashed on the Jewish ghetto, during which Susona's entire family was slaughtered. She requested that her skull be placed above the doorway in atonement for her betrayal, and the actual skull supposedly remained until the 18th century. C. Susona leads to **Plaza Doña Elvira,** where Sevillian Lope de Rueda's works, precursors to the dramas of Spain's Golden Age, were staged. A turn down C. Gloria leads to Pl. Venerables, site of the 17th-century **Hospital de los Venerables,** a hospital-church adorned with art from the Sevillian school, including Leal and Montañés. (☎ 954 56 26 96. Open daily for guided visits 10am-2pm and 4-8pm. 600ptas.)

Calle Lope de Rueda, off C. Ximénez de Enciso, is graced with two noble mansions, beyond which lies the charming and fragrant **Plaza de Santa Cruz.** South of the plaza are the **Jardines de Murillo,** a shady expanse of shrubbery and benches. **Convento de San José** cherishes a cloak and portrait of Santa Teresa of Ávila. (C. Santa Teresa, off Pl. Santa Cruz. Open daily 9-11am.) The church in Pl. Santa Cruz houses the grave of the artist Murillo, who died in what is now known as the **Casa Murillo** after falling from a scaffold while painting frescoes in Cádiz's Iglesia de los Capuchinos. The house has information on Murillo's life and work. (C. Santa Teresa, 8. ☎ 954 22 12 72. Open M-F 8am-3pm and 4-8pm. Free.) **Iglesia de Santa María la Blanca** was built in 1391 on the foundation of a synagogue. It features red marble columns, Baroque plasterwork, and Murillo's *Last Supper*. (C. Santa María la Blanca. Open M-Sa 10-11am and 6:30-8pm, Su 9:30am-2pm and 6:30-8pm.)

SIERPES AND THE ARISTOCRATIC QUARTER

Originating from the plaza, **Calle Sierpes** cuts through the Aristocratic Quarter. At the beginning of this pedestrian street lined with shoe stores, fan shops, and chic boutiques, a plaque marks the spot where the royal prison once loomed. Some scholars believe Cervantes began writing *Don Quijote* here.

CASA DE PILATOS. This semi-preserved private residence gives a fascinating glimpse into what being wealthy in 15th-century Sevilla might have been like. In a typically Andalucian mix of Medieval and Renaissance artistic elements, it houses Roman antiquities, Renaissance and baroque paintings, colorful tiled walls, several courtyards, and a pond. Use the bell if the gate is closed during visiting hours. (Pl. Pilatos. ☎ 954 22 52 98. Open daily 9am-7pm. 1000ptas)

IGLESIA DEL SALVADOR. Fronted by a Montañés sculpture, this 17th-century church is built on the foundations of what was once the city's main mosque. The courtyard and the belfry's base are remnants of the old mosque. As grandiose as a cathedral, it is adorned with outstanding baroque *retablos* (altarpieces), sculptures, and paintings, including Montañés's *Jesús de la pasión*. (Pl. Salvador, 1 block from C. Sierpes. Open daily 6:30-9pm.)

OTHER SIGHTS. A few blocks southeast of Pl. Salvador stand the excavated ruins of an old **Roman temple.** The remaining columns rise 15m from below street level and offer a glimpse of the literal depth of Sevilla's history; river sediment that accumulated after the construction of the temple caused the level of the land to increase. *(C. Mármoles.)* The **Ayuntamiento** has 16th-century Gothic and Renaissance interior halls, a richly decorated domed ceiling, and a Plateresque facade. *(It often displays art exhibitions; check with the tourist office for information. Pl. San Francisco. ☎ 954 59 01 01. Open Tu-Th 5:30-6:30pm, Sa-Su 11:30am-12:30pm.)* The interesting **Iglesia de la Anunciación** features a pantheon honoring illustrious *sevill-anos*, including poet Gustavo Adolfo Bécquer. *(Pl. Encarnación; enter on C. Laraña. Open daily 9am-1pm.)*

EL ARENAL, TRIANA, AND PASEO ALCALDE MARQUÉS DE CONTADERO

Immortalized by *Siglo de Oro* (Golden Age) writers Lope de Vega, Quevedo, and Cervantes, Triana was Sevilla's chaotic 16th- and 17th-century mariners' neighborhood. El Arenal was once a stretch of sand by the harbor on the opposite bank, exposed when the river was diverted to its present course. The inviting riverside esplanade Po. Marqués de Contadero stretches along the banks of the Guadalquivir from the base of the Torre del Oro. Bridge-heavy boat tours of Sevilla leave from in front of the tower (1hr., 700ptas).

⊠ MUSEO PROVINCIAL DE BELLAS ARTES. This museum contains Spain's finest collection of works by painters of the Sevilla school, most notably Murillo, Valdés Leal, and Zurbarán, as well as El Greco and Dutch master Jan Breughel. The building and gardens themselves are works of art. *(Pl. Museo, 9, off C. Alfonso XII. ☎ 954 22 07 90. Open Tu 3-8pm, W-Sa 9am-8pm, Su 9am-3pm. 250ptas, EU citizens free.)*

PLAZA DE TOROS DE LA REAL MAESTRANZA. The tiled boardwalk leads to Pl. Toros de la Real Maestranza, Spain's best and most beautiful bullring. Home to one of the two great bullfighting schools (the other is in Ronda), the plaza fills to capacity for the 13 *corridas* of the *Feria de Abril* as well as weekly fights. The museum inside displays costumes, paintings, and antique posters. *(☎ 954 22 45 77. Open on non-bullfight days 9:30am-2pm and 3-7pm, on bullfight days 9:30am-3pm. Tours every 30min., 500ptas. See La Corrida, p. 209, for tickets and other info.)*

HOSPITAL DE LA CARIDAD. A 17th-century complex of arcaded courtyards, this hospital was founded by Don Miguel de Marañe, who is believed to be the model for legendary Sevillian Don Juan. This playboy allegedly converted to a life of piety and charity after stumbling out of an orgy into a funeral cortège that he was told was his own. His body rests inside the crypt of the **Iglesia de San Jorge,** part of the hospital. The church's walls display paintings and frescoes by Valdés Leal and Murillo. Murillo supposedly couldn't refrain from holding his nose when he saw Leal's morbid *Finis Gloria Mundi*, which depicts corpses of a peasant, a bishop, and a king beneath a stylized rendition of Justice and the Seven Deadly Sins. *(Behind the Teatro de la Maestranza on C. Temprado. ☎ 954 22 32 32. Open M-Sa 9am-1:30pm and 3:30-6:30pm, Su 9am-1pm. 400ptas.)*

TORRE DEL ORO. The 12-sided Torre del Oro (Gold Tower), built by the Almohads in 1200, overlooks the river from Po. Cristóbal Colón. While a glaze of golden tile once sheathed its squat frame, today a tiny yellow dome is the only reminder of its original splendor. Inside is the **Museo Náutico,** with engravings and drawings of Sevilla's port in its heyday. *(☎ 954 22 24 19. Open Sept.-July Tu-F 10am-2pm, Sa-Su 11am-2pm. 100ptas. Tu free.)* On the far bank of the river, the **Torre de la Plata** (Silver Tower) used to be connected to the Torre de Oro by underwater chains designed to protect the city from river-borne trespassers. The Torre de la Plata has since been absorbed by a bank building, but one side is still visible near the corner of C. Santander and C. Temprado.

OTHER SIGHTS. The **Capilla de los Marineros** in Triana was constructed in the 18th century to worship the Esperanza de Triana, who, along with the Virgin Mary and the "Macarena", is one of the most adored figures of Sevilla. *(C. Pureza, 53.)* One block further inland, midway between Puente de Isabel II and Puente de San Telmo, stands the **Iglesia de Santa Ana,** Sevilla's oldest church and the focal point of the exuberant fiestas that take over the area in July. *(Open M and W 7:30-8:30pm.)* The terraced riverside promenade **Calle Betis** is an ideal spot from which to view Sevilla's skyline and sparkling nights.

🕮 LA MACARENA

"Ehh, Macarena, ¡ay!" When most people hear "Macarena," they think of the song and dance popular in the mid-1990s. But to natives of Sevilla, La Macarena is the Virgin of the city and namesake of an enchanting church and neighborhood northwest of El Centro.

CONVENTS. The founder of **Convento de Santa Inés,** as legend has it, was pursued so insistently by King Pedro the Cruel that she disfigured her face with boiling oil so that he would leave her alone. Cooking liquids are used more positively today—the cloistered nuns sell patented puff pastries and coffee cakes through the courtyard's revolving window. *(C. María Coronel.)* **Convento de Santa Paula** includes a church with Gothic, Mudéjar, and Renaissance elements, a magnificent ceiling, and sculptures by Montañés. *(Pl. Santa Paula. ☎ 954 53 63 30. Open Tu-Su 10:30am-12:30pm and 4:30-6:30pm.)* The **museum** next door has Ribera's *St. Jerome.* Nuns here peddle scrumptious homemade marmalades and angel-hair pastry. *(Pl. Santa Paula, 11. Open Tu-Su 11am-noon and 4:30-6:30pm.)*

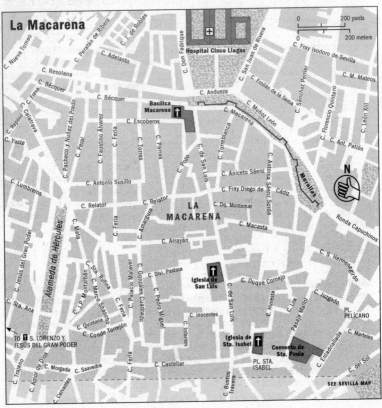

CHURCHES. Opposite the belfry of the Iglesia de San Marcos rises **Iglesia de Santa Isabel,** featuring an altarpiece by Montañés. Nearby stands the exuberantly Baroque **Iglesia de San Luis,** crowned by octagonal glazed-tile domes. The site of the church was the endpoint of a 12-step prayer route based on the ascent to Golgotha. More recently, it has been immortalized by the Cruzcampo beer logo. *(C. San Luis.* ☎ *954 55 02 07. Open W-Th 9am-2pm, F-Sa 9am-2pm and 5-8pm.)* A stretch of **murallas** (fortress walls), created in the 12th century, runs between the Pta. Macarena and Pta. Córdoba on the Ronda de Capuchinos road. Flanking the west end of the walls, the **Basílica Macarena** houses the venerated image of *La virgen de la Macarena,* which is hauled around town during *Semana Santa* processions. A **treasury** glitters with the virgin's jewels and other finery. *(Pl. San Gil.* ☎ *954 37 01 95. Basilica open daily 9:30am-1pm and 5-9pm. Free. Treasury open daily 9:30am-1pm and 5-8pm. 400ptas.)* Toward the river is **Iglesia de San Lorenzo y Jesús del Gran Poder,** with Montañés's remarkably lifelike sculpture *El cristo del gran poder.* Worshipers kiss Jesus' ankle through an opening in the bullet-proof glass for luck. *Semana Santa* culminates in a procession honoring his statue. *(Pl. San Lorenzo.* ☎ *954 38 45 58. Open Sa-Th 8am-1:45pm and 6-9pm, F 7:30-10pm. Free.)*

OTHER SIGHTS. A large garden beyond the *murallas* and the basilica leads to the **Hospital de las Cinco Llagas,** a spectacular Renaissance building recently renovated to host the Andalucian parliament. Toward the river is the **Alameda de Hércules,** a leafy promenade that hosts the tremendous Sunday morning *Rastro* (flea market) and by night fills with prostitutes and other shady types.

ELSEWHERE

◩**PARQUE DE MARÍA LUISA.** In 1929, Sevilla made elaborate plans for an Ibero-American world fair. Though plans for the fair were interrupted by the stock market crash, the lovely landscapes of the Parque de María Luisa remained, framed by Av. Borbolla and the river. Innumerable courtyards, turquoise-tiled benches, and tailored tropical gardens make for a perfect place to take a *siesta.* On the park's northeast edge, the twin spires of **Plaza de España** poke above the city skyline. The plaza is the perfect setting for a Sunday afternoon outing, evoking images of horse-drawn carriages, top hats, puffy dresses, and bottles of wine beside the fountain, but only **boat rides** along the narrow moat are real. Mosaics depicting every provincial capital in Spain line the decaying colonnade. The balconies above offer a beautiful view. *(Park open daily 8am-10pm. Boat rides 300ptas per hr.)*

OTHER SIGHTS. Sevilla's **Museo Arqueológico** shows off a small collection of pre-Roman and Roman artifacts excavated in the surrounding provinces. *(Pl. América, in the park.* ☎ *954 23 24 01. Open Tu 3-8pm, W-Sa 9am-8pm, Su 9am-2:30pm. 250ptas, EU citizens free.)* On C. San Fernando stands the 18th-century **Antigua Fábrica de Tabacos** (Old Tobacco Factory), setting of Bizet's *Carmen* and now part of the university. Near the river on Palos de la Frontera is the 17th-century **Palacio de San Telmo,** built as a sailor training school. Saint Telmo, patron saint of sailors, hovers over the door amid a maelstrom of marine monsters.

🌀 NIGHTLIFE

The tourist office and stores distribute *El Giraldillo,* a free monthly magazine with complete listings on music, art exhibits, theater, dance, fairs, and film. Sevilla's reputation for partying is tried and true. A typical Sevillian sampling of *la marcha* (going out) begins with visits to several bars for *tapas* and *copas,* continues with dancing at *discotecas,* and culminates with an early morning breakfast of *churros con chocolate.* Most clubs don't get crowded until well after midnight; the real fun often starts after 3am. Popular bars can be found around C. Mateos Gago near the cathedral, C. Adriano by the bullring, and C. Betis across the river in Triana. Sevilla is also famous for its *botellón,* the (mostly student) tradition of getting drunk in massive crowds in plazas or at bars along the river to start the night. In the winter, the most popular places to *botellón* are in Pl. Alfalfa and Pl. del Salvador. In summer, the crowds sweep toward the river in hopes of a breeze, and even on "slow" nights, most *terrazas* stay open until 4am. New locations open every summer; check with the Centro de Información de Sevilla for the latest info.

BARRIO DE SANTA CRUZ

🖾 **La Carbonería,** C. Levies, 18 (☎ 954 21 44 60), off C. Santa María La Blanca. Free live flamenco in an intimate, cave-like space. Includes a huge outdoor patio and bar (also with live music) hidden beyond the door at the far side of the cave. Beer 200-275ptas. Flamenco nightly at 10:30pm. Open M-Sa 8pm-3:30am, Su 8pm-2:30am.

El Tamboril, Pl. Santa Cruz (☎ 954 56 15 90). Put on your best and come see *sevillanas* and *rumbas* with well-to-do Spaniards.Music and dancing start after midnight. *Sangría* and beer 300ptas a glass. Open daily 10pm-dawn. V, MC.

Flaherty, C. Alemanes, 7 (☎ 954 21 04 51). Across from the entrance to the cathedral. Irish bartenders and English-speaking tourists keep this new and remarkably good restaurant and bar lively all night long. Pints of beer 600ptas. *Tapas* 350-375ptas. Entrees 750-950. Open Su-Th 11am-2am, F-Sa until 3am.

Luna Park, Av. de María Luisa at Av. del Perú, across from the Lope de Vega theater. With an ancient-rock motif resembling Stonehenge, this half-indoor, half-outdoor club has two floors for Latin and pop music, as well as a dance floor just for *sevillanas*. No cover. Open Th-Su 11pm-dawn.

Abades, C. Abades, 13 (☎ 954 22 56 22). This 18th-century palace is now a charming bar. Sip *agua de Sevilla* (500ptas) or non-alcoholic *Saufco* (700ptas) to the sounds of the gurgling fountain. Open daily 4pm-dawn. V, MC.

EL CENTRO

🖾 **El Capote,** at the Pte. Isabel II. Make your way through the throngs of young people who start the night at this hugely popular *terraza* bar for mixed drinks and beer. Live music performances, throughout the summer. Open nightly 11pm-3am.

La Antigua Bodeguita, Pl. del Salvador, 6 (☎ 954 56 18 33). The crowds just can't be contained at any hour of the day in this tiny bustling bar. Beer 125ptas, *tapas* 200ptas. Open daily 12:30-4pm and 8pm-midnight.

Cervecería El Tremendo, C. San Felipe, 15. So popular, locals crowd not only the bar, but the entire vicinity. Beer 100-150ptas. Open Th-Tu noon-4:30pm and 8pm-12:30am.

Catedral, Cuesta del Rosario, 12, 1 block from Pl. del Salvador. Underground disco whose metal, stone and wood decor feels straight out of New York City. No cover for women and those who arrive with coupons (available in stores, restaurants, and hostels). Tends to be an older crowd. Cover for men 1000ptas, includes 1 drink or 2 beers. Open Th-Tu midnight-8am, W midnight-6am.

ELSEWHERE

Lo Nuestro, C. Betis, 31A, in Triana. A local hangout in an area plagued by touristy bars. Images of bulls and matadors plaster the rust-colored walls. *Sevillanas* are spontaneous and frequent. Mixed drinks 300-900ptas. Open daily 10pm-dawn.

Sevilla Salsa, C. Castilla, 137 (☎ 954 34 22 04), 2 blocks from the Pte. del Cachorro. In Santa Cecilia. One floor of this small-scale club is dedicated to salsa and popular Latin music, while the other spins hip-hop, reggae, and house. It doesn't get lively until after 2am. No cover. Open Th-Sa 11pm-dawn.

🎵 ENTERTAINMENT

THEATERS

If a night at the movies is in order, **Cine Avenida**, C. Marqués de las Paradas, 15 (☎ 954 22 15 48) and **Cines Warner Lusomundo**, Co. Comercial, Pl. Legión (☎ 902 23 33 43) show predominantly American films dubbed in Spanish. **Corona Center**, Pagés del Corro y Paraíso, in the mall between C. Salado and C. Paraíso in Barrio de Triana, screens subtitled films, often in English. (☎ 954 27 80 64. M-F movies 450ptas, Sa-Su 550ptas.) For more information, check under "Cinema" in *El Giraldillo*.

SEVILLANAS When in Sevilla, do as the *sevillanos* do. *Sevillanas* is the widely popular folk form of flamenco. While elegant flamenco dancers must study technique for years, just about anyone can perform *sevillanas*. In little bars in Sevilla, yuppie couples, chic young women, and toothless old men take the dance floor side-by-side when the guitar begins to play its song. A partnered dance, *sevillanas* consist of four segments that act out a courting ritual. The basic step is easy to pick up; ask sweetly for an impromptu lesson, and before long you'll be twisting your wrists like a native. During the *Feria de Abril* the whole city takes to the streets, stomping their feet, flipping their skirts, and holding their heads high as they turn and sashay. If you can't catch the dancing live, check out Carlos Saura's movie *Sevillanas*.

Sevilla is a haven for the performing arts. The venerable **Teatro Lope de Vega** (☎ 954 59 08 53), near Parque María Luisa, has long been the city's leading stage. Ask about scheduled events at the tourist office or check the bulletin board in the university lobby on C. San Fernando. If you can't see a show, at least stop by for a drink at **Casino**, the popular *terraza* outside. **Sala La Herrería** and **Sala La Imperdible** put on avant-garde productions in Pl. San Antonio de Padua. (Both ☎ 954 38 82 19.) **Teatro de la Maestranza**, on the river next to Pl. Toros, is a splendid concert hall accommodating both orchestral performances and opera. (☎ 954 22 33 44. Box office open M-F 10am-2pm and 6-9pm.) On spring and summer evenings, *barrio* fairs are often accompanied by free **open-air concerts** in Santa Cruz and Triana.

FLAMENCO

The lightning-quick *zapateado* of Andalucía's flamenco dancers dazzle the eyes, while the wailing *cantaores* delight the ears. Three tourist-ridden venues feature comparably flashy shows, though a more affordable option would be to visit the more casual flamenco bars (see above). **Los Gallos**, Pl. Santa Cruz, 11, is small and intimate and probably the best tourist show in Sevilla. Buy tickets in advance at hostels or stores in Barrio Santa Cruz and arrive early. (☎ 954 21 69 81. Shows nightly 9 and 11:30pm. Cover 3500ptas, includes one drink.) **El Arenal** is similarly sized, but is a *tablao-restaurante*, so you can eat a meal while watching. (Shows nightly 9:30pm and 11:30pm. Cover 4300ptas, includes one drink.) **El Palacio Andaluz**, Av. María Auxiliadora, 18B, distinguishes itself with an immense performance theater. (☎ 954 53 47 20 or 954 42 56 02. Book ahead with hostels. Shows nightly at 7:30pm and 10pm. Cover 4000ptas, includes one drink.)

FÚTBOL

Sevilla has two wildly popular pro teams within its city limits. The pride of the Guadalquivir is **Betis**, which plays in Estadio Benito Villamarín (☎ 954 61 03 40), downstream on Av. Palmera. Team **Sevilla** has suffered from coaching changes and recently was demoted to second division, leaving followers humiliated. Sevilla plays in the Estadio Sámche Pizjuán (☎ 954 53 53 53), east of Av. Menéndez Pelayo on Av. Eduardo Dato. Tickets can be purchased at the respective stadiums; price and availability depend on the quality of the match-up. Even if you can't make it yourself, you'll know who's won by the colors worn by the crowds in the streets (Betis wears green and white, Sevilla white and red).

BULLFIGHTS

If you're going to see a bullfight somewhere in Spain, Sevilla is probably the best place to do it; the bullring here is generally considered to be the most beautiful in the country. The cheapest place to buy tickets is at the ring on Po. Marqués de Contadero. However, when there's a good *cartel* (line-up), the booths on C. Sierpes, C. Velázquez, and Pl. Toros might be the only source of advance tickets. Ticket prices, depending on the quality of both seat and matador, can run from 3000ptas for a *grada de sol* (nosebleed seat in the sun) to 13,000ptas for a *barrera de sombra* (front-row seat in the shade). Buying a ticket from a scalper usually adds 20% to the ticket price. *Corridas de toros* (bullfights) or *novilladas* (appren-

ANDALUCÍA

tice bullfighters and younger bulls) are held on the 13 days around the *Feria de Abril* and into May, every Sunday in June, more often during Corpus Christi in June and early July, and again during the *Feria de San Miguel* near the end of September. During July and August, they occur on occasional Thursdays. It's obvious when a top-notch *matador* is scheduled to fight: hours before the big event, the ring is surrounded by throngs of young female fans who don their most seductive dresses and alluring lipstick in hopes of catching the eye of their hero. Some of the most popular Sevillian bullfighters include the aging Curro Romero and Emilio Muñoz, known as "El Espártaco" (Spartacus). (For current info and **ticket sales,** call ☎ 954 22 35 06. For more info on **Bullfighting,** see p. 63.)

FESTIVALS

Sevilla swells with tourists during the *fiestas*, and with good reason—they are insanely fun. If you're in Spain during any of the major festivals, head straight to Sevilla. You won't regret it (if you can remember it, that is).

■ **SEMANA SANTA.** Sevilla's world-famous Semana Santa lasts from Palm Sunday to Good Friday. (Apr. 9-15 in 2001.) In each neighborhood of Sevilla, thousands of penitents in hooded cassocks guide *tronos*, stunning, extravagant floats, through the streets each day, illuminated by hundreds of candles. The climax is Good Friday, when the entire city turns out for the procession along the bridges and through the oldest neighborhoods. Book a room well in advance, and expect to pay triple the usual price. The tourist office has a helpful booklet with advice on where to eat and sleep during the week's festivities.

■ **FERIA DE ABRIL.** Two or three weeks after Semana Santa (Apr. 24-30 in 2001) the city rewards itself for its Lenten piety with the *Feria de Abril*. Begun as part of a 19th-century revolt against foreign influence, today circuses, bullfights, and flamenco shows roar into the night in a showcase of local customs and camaraderie. A spectacular array of flowers and lanterns decorates over 1000 kiosks, tents, and pavilions, collectively called *casetas*. Each has the elements necessary for a rollicking time: small kitchen, bar, and dance floor. Locals stroll from one to the next, sharing drinks and good food amidst the lively music and dance. *Casetas* are privately owned by families and businesses and the only way to get invited is by making friends with the locals. But never fear—people-watching from the sidelines can be almost as exciting, as costumed girls dance *sevillanas* and men parade on horse-back through the streets of Sevilla. The fairgrounds are on the southern end of Barrio Los Remedios.

ROMERÍA DEL ROCÍO. Folklore and religion unite in the *Romería del Rocío* which takes place 50 days after Easter on Pentecost and involves the veneration of the *Virgen del Rocío*. More than 70 brotherhoods of pilgrims from around the world make their way to the small town of Almonte, near Huelva, from all points in Spain. They arrive in flower-decorated carriages or on horses saddled in typical Andalucian style wearing traditional gypsy costumes. In the best Spanish fashion, the Romería is half penitence, half party. The solemnity of the days are broken with singing, dancing, and drinking around campfires from dusk until dawn.

🢒 DAYTRIPS FROM SEVILLA

OSUNA (1HR.)

Trains come from Sevilla (1hr., 8 per day 6:40am-9:40pm, 1000ptas). Empresa Dipasa/ Linesur (☎ 954 98 82 22) also runs buses to and from Sevilla (1½hr., 5-11 per day 6:15am-7:40pm, 830ptas one-way, 1300 round-trip, 50% discount for students).

Julius Caesar founded Osuna (pop. 17,500), naming it after the *osos* (bears) that once lumbered about the land. The peaceful stone mansions and April's World Motorcross Championships are a testimony to Osuna's more recent days as a cushy ducal seat. The **Colegiata de Santa María de la Asunción** (☎ 954 81 04 44), from

Pl. Mayor uphill along C. Farfana Boya, past the intersection and to the right of the bus station, was commissioned by the Dukes of Osuna in the Renaissance style and now houses the **Museo de Arte Sacro Panteón Ducal.** Goya's portrait of the Osuna family now hangs in the Museo del Prado in Madrid, but the Colegiata contains an impressive array of paintings, including religious artifacts and five Riberas. (Knock to enter. Open May-Sept. 10am-1:30pm and 4-7pm; Oct.-Apr. Tu-Su 10am-1:30pm and 3:30-6:30pm. 300ptas.) On the right side of the church sits the university and ◼**Monasterio de la Encarnación,** a Baroque church founded by the Duke of Osuna in the 17th century and lavishly decorated in the 18th. A resident nun will show you room upon room of polychromed wooden sculptures, silver crucifixes, painted tiles, and handmade Christ-doll clothes. Make sure to knock and wait until the previous tour group finishes. (☎ 954 81 11 21. Open Tu-Su 10am-1:30pm and 3:30-6:30pm. 250ptas.)

To reach Pl. Mayor from the **train station** (☎/fax 954 81 03 08; open 7am-8pm) walk up Av. Estación, curving right on C. Mancilla. At Pl. Salitre, turn left on C. Carmen and then right on C. Sevilla, which leads into the plaza. The **bus station** on Av. Constitución is a 10-minute walk from the center. (☎ 954 81 01 46. Open M-F 6:50-9am, 10:15am-2:30pm and 3:30-7:40pm; Sa 7:30-9am and 10:30am-2pm; Su 3:30-4:30 and 7-7:40pm). To get to Pl. Mayor from the bus station, walk downhill on C. Santa Ana past tiny Pl. Santa Rita; continue on Av. Arjona (don't be confused by signs directing you uphill) until you hit the plaza. Pick up a map at the **Oficina de Turismo,** in the Pl. Mayor (☎ 955 82 14 00. Open M-F 10am-1:30pm and 4-7pm, Sa 10am-2pm and 4-7pm, Su 10am-3pm). Although there is no reason to stay overnight, if needed, **Hostal Caballo Blanco,** C. Granada, 1, furnishes comfy rooms with bath and A/C. (☎ 954 81 01 84. Breakfast 350ptas. Parking 500ptas per day. Singles with bath 3500ptas; doubles with shower or bath 5800ptas.)

ITÁLICA (30MIN.)

Take Empresa Casal's bus (☎ 954 41 06 58) toward Santiponce from the Pl. Armas bus station. Tell the driver you're going to Itálica, and get off at the last stop (30min., every 30min. 6:30am-midnight, 125ptas).

Just 9km northwest of Sevilla and right outside the village of Santiponce (pop. 6200) lie the ruins of Itálica, the first important Roman settlement in Iberia. Itálica, constructed in 206 BC, was the birthplace of emperors Trajan (AD 53) and Hadrian (AD 76). After the later additions of the city wall and newer settlements during the apex of the city (AD 300 and 400), Itálica's power declined, and by the 5th century Sevilla had become the regional seat of power. Archaeological excavations began in the 18th century and continue today. The **Casa del Plantario** (The House of Planets), has preserved intricate **mosaic floors** depicting the seven gods that represent planets and whose names are given to the days of the week. There are also reconstructed patios and a bakery depicting life as it was during the decline of the city. The **anfiteatro,** among Spain's largest, seats 25,000. It was once used to stage fights between gladiators and lions; today it hosts more mellow classical music performances in the summer. (☎ 955 99 73 76. Open June-Aug. Tu-Sa 8:30am-8:30pm, Su 9am-3pm; Sept-May Tu-Sa 9am-5:30pm, Su 10am-4pm. 250ptas, EU citizens free.) For info on the annual **Festival Internacional de Itálica,** which brings dance, classical music, and theater to Itálica in July and August, check Sevilla's *El Giraldillo.*

CARMONA (1HR.)

Take the bus to Carmona from Sevilla (1hr., M-F 25 per day, Sa 10 per day, Su 7 per day, 7am-10pm, 295ptas) departing from Prado de San Sebastián station. In Carmona, buses return to Sevilla from the main square, along Av. Jorge Bonsor (23 per day, 6:15am-9pm).

Thirty-three kilometers east of Sevilla, ancient Carmona (pop. 25,000) dominates a tall hill overlooking the gold and green countryside. It was founded by the Carthaginians and due to its strategic position on the Vía Augusta, the main thoroughfare of Andalucía, it became an important trade city during Roman occupation in later centuries and a Moorish stronghold thereafter. Moorish palaces

ANDALUCÍA

mingle with Christian Renaissance mansions in a network of streets partially enclosed by fortified walls. The **Puerta de Sevilla,** a horseshoe-shaped passageway with both Roman and Arab architectural elements, and the Baroque **Puerta de Córdoba,** on the opposite end of town, once linked Carmona to the east and west. From the bus stop, walk directly away from the back end of the bus onto C. San Pedro. Cross the roundabout and walk through the Puerta de Sevilla noting on your way the **Iglesia de San Pedro,** whose Mudéjar tower is a scaled-down copy of Sevilla's Giralda. Enter the **Alcázar de la Puerta Sevilla** through the tourist office on your right. The Alcázar originally served as a Carthaginian fortification against Roman attack. During the reign of Augustus, the structure was expanded to its current size. (☎ 954 19 09 55. Open M-Sa 10am-6pm, Su 10am-3pm. 200ptas, students 150ptas, seniors and children under 12 100ptas. Tours M-Sa 11am, noon, 1, 4, and 5pm.) From the Alcázar, take C. Prim and then C. Martín to find Pl. Marqués de las Torres, where the late-Gothic **Iglesia de Santa María** (☎ 954 14 13 30) was built over an old mosque. The splendid **Patio de los Naranjos** remains from Moorish days. An even older Visigothic liturgical calendar graces one of the columns. (Open Tu-Sa 11am-2pm and 5-7pm. Mass Tu-Sa 9-11am and 7-9pm, Su 9am-12:30pm and 7-9pm.) The **Alcázar del Rey Don Pedro,** an old Almohad fortress and now a ritzy hotel, guards the eastern edge of town.

In the opposite direction from the bus stop, along C. Enmedio, lie the ruins of the **Necrópolis Romana,** Av. de Jorge Bonsor, 9 (☎ 954 14 08 11). Highlights include the **Tumba de Servilia** and **Tumba del Elefante,** where depictions of Mother Nature and Eastern divinities are overshadowed by the presence of a giant stone elephant. The **Museo Arqueológico** has remains from over a thousand tombs unearthed at the necropolis. (Both open June-Aug. Tu-F 9am-5pm, Sa-Su 10am-2pm; Sept.-May Tu-F 10am-2pm and 4-6pm, Sa-Su 10am-2pm. 250ptas, EU citizens free.)

The **tourist office,** on Arco de la Puerta de Sevilla, is located at the Puerta de Sevilla, down C. San Pedro from the bus stop (☎ 954 19 09 55; fax 954 19 00 80. Open M-Sa 10am-6pm, Su 10am-3pm). The **police** (☎ 954 14 00 08), are in Pl. San Fernando, and you can find **medical assistance** on C. Paseo de La Feria (☎ 954 14 09 97). If you need to spend the night, try **Casa Carmelo,** C. San Pedro, 15, toward the Alcázar from the bus stop. Don't miss the door hidden among shops. (☎ 954 14 05 72. Reservations recommended Apr.-July. Singles with toilet 2000ptas, with bath 2500ptas; doubles 3500, with bath 4000ptas. Su-Th curfew 1:30-2am.)

HUELVA

There is nothing particularly appealing about Huelva, a small town quite marked by industrialization—except perhaps the nearby beaches and especially friendly atmosphere. That said, however, travelers heading to or from Portugal shouldn't shy away from an opportunity to spend the night in a place truly free of tourism.

▐ TRANSPORTATION. RENFE trains (☎ 959 24 56 14), on Av. de Italia to: **Sevilla** (1½hr., 3 per day 7:15am-7:20pm, 995ptas); **Córdoba** (2¼hr., 4:55pm, 2700ptas); and **Madrid** (4¼hr., 4:55pm, 8300ptas). **Buses** depart from Av. Dr. Rubio (☎ 959 25 69 00) to: **Sevilla** (DAMAS: 1hr., 19-30per day 6am-8:30pm, 900ptas); **Faro, Portugal** (DAMAS: 2½hr., 2 per day 9am-6pm, 720ptas; ALCOTAN: 2½hr., 9:40am or 5:10pm, 1080ptas); **Cádiz** (DAMAS: 5hr., 10am, 2335ptas); **Madrid** (SOCIBUS: 6hr., 3 per day 9:45am-10:45pm, 3500ptas); **Lisbon** (AGOBE: 6½hr., M, W, and F 1:15pm, 3400ptas).

▐▐ ORIENTATION AND PRACTICAL INFORMATION. The central axis of the city is **Avenida Martín Alonso Pinzón** (a.k.a. Gran Vía). From the train station, go out the front door, cross the street, and go straight down the street directly in front of you (C. Alonso XII). At the third intersection turn either right or left. From the bus station, go out and cross Av. Alemania. Take C. Gravina, turn left onto C. M. Nuñez, then right onto C. Concepción and go straight for three blocks. This street now runs parallel to Av. Martín Alonso Pinzón, so turn left and cross over. There is a **tourist office** at Av. de Alemania, 12, across the street from the bus station and half a block to the right. (☎ 959 25 74 03. Open M-F 9am-7pm, Sa 10am-2pm.) The bus station has lockers for **luggage storage** (300ptas per day). **Police** are located on Av. Tomás Domínguez de Ortiz, 2 (☎ 959 24 93 50), and the **post office** is at Av. Tomás Domínguez de Ortiz, 1 (☎ 959 24 74 88). For **Internet access,** go to C. Vázquez López, Galería comercial 10-12, across from the Gran Teatro. (☎ 959 25 14 10. Open M-Sa 10am-10pm. 400ptas per hr.)

▐▝▛ ACCOMMODATIONS AND FOOD. Most of the accommodations in Huelva cluster between the train station and Av. Martín Alonso Pinzón. A decent option is **Hostal Virgen del Rocío,** C. Tendaleras, 18, a charmless but perfectly functional hostel. (☎ 959 28 17 16. 2am curfew on weeknights, none on weekends; singles with sink 3000ptas; doubles with bath 5000ptas; V, MC, AmEx.) Another choice is **Hostal Residencia Calvo,** C. Rascón, 31, a strangely spacious, small-scale hotel. (☎ 959 24 90 16. Singles 1100-1200ptas, doubles 2200-2400ptas, triples 3300-3600ptas; prices may go up in summer.) For fresh meats and veggies, try the **Mercado de Carmen,** the town's biggest market, at the intersection of C. Barcelona, C. Carmen, and C. Duque de la Victoria. **Restaurante Trattoria Camilo e Pepone,** Isaac Peral, 3, is *the* place to go for big portions. (☎ 959 24 13 63. Open June-Aug. F-Su, Sept.-May daily 12:30-5pm and 8:30pm-midnight.) For drinks, check out **Bar La Prensa,** Gran Vía, 15 (☎ 959 24 02 11), which vaguely resembles a Parisian hangout. **Helados La Ibense,** C. Concepción, 10, is the best *heladería* in Huelva (☎ 959 24 96 47; cones 90-340ptas, drinks 100-125ptas, *granizados* 135-275ptas). At night locals gather at the bars and cafes around Av. Pablo Rada.

CÓRDOBA

"Sevilla is a young girl, gay, laughing, provoking—but Córdoba...Córdoba is a dear old lady."

Nowhere else are the remnants of Spain's Islamic, Jewish, and Catholic heritages so visibly intermixed as in Córdoba (pop. 315,000). This Andalucian historical and cultural melange has left Córdoba a unique artistic and architectural legacy. Roman mosaics in the Alcázar are reminiscent of the playwright and philosopher Seneca, who settled here during the Roman occupation. The famous Mezquita testifies to Córdoba's political and intellectual reemergence under Islamic rule. The 14th-century Palacio del Marqués de Viana (14th century) anticipates Spain's Golden Age (16th-17th centuries), a time when literary luminaries such as poet Luís de Góngora resided here. Springtime festivals, flower-filled patios, and a busy nightlife make Córdoba one of Spain's most beloved cities. Both delicate and wise, Córdoba may be a "dear old lady," but she is far from tired.

ANDALUCÍA

█ TRANSPORTATION

Trains: (☎ 957 40 02 02), Plaza de las Tres Culturas, Av. América. To: **Sevilla** (AVE 45min., 18 per day 8:40am-11:40pm, 2300ptas); **Antequera** (1½hr., 3 per day, 1500ptas); **Madrid** (AVE 2hr., 18 per day 7:15am-10:45pm, 5100-6100ptas; regular 2-6hr., 14 per day 2am-11:15pm, 3700-6000ptas); **Málaga** (AVE 2¼hr., 5 per day, 2000-2200ptas; regular 3hr., 13 per day 5:40am-10:15pm, 1650-3000ptas); **Cádiz** (AVE 2¾hr., 2 per day 12:15am and 6pm, 3700ptas; regular 3-4hr., 5 per day 6am-8pm, 2370-3700ptas); **Granada** (4½hr., 3 per day, 2130-2785ptas); **Algeciras** (AVE 4hr., 1 per day 10:20am, 3400ptas; regular 5½hr., 2 per day 5am-10:15pm, 2800-3300ptas); **Barcelona** (10-11hr., 7 per day 9:45am-11pm, 6100-8400ptas). For international tickets, contact **RENFE,** Ronda de los Tejares, 10 (☎ 957 49 02 02).

Buses: Estación de Autobuses, Glorieta de las Tres Culturas (☎ 957 40 40 40; fax 957 40 44 15), across from the train station. **Alsina Graells Sur** (☎ 957 27 81 00) covers most of Andalucía. To: **Sevilla** (2hr., 10-13 per day 7am-10pm, 1200ptas, round-trip 1750ptas); **Antequera** (2½hr., 3 per day 9am-7pm, 1075ptas); **Granada** (3hr., 8 per day 8am-6:30pm, 1635-1810ptas, round-trip 3000ptas); **Málaga** (3-3½hr., 5 per day 8am-7pm, 1540ptas, round-trip 2575ptas); **Marbella** (4hr., 2 per day 8am-3:15pm, 2310ptas); **Cádiz** via Los Amarillos or Comes Sur (4-5hr., 1 per day 7am, 2120ptas); **Algeciras** (5hr., 2 per day, 2805ptas); **Almería** (5hr., 1 per day 8am, 2890ptas). **Bacoma** (☎ 957 45 65 14) goes to: Baeza, Ubeda, Valencia, and **Barcelona** (10hr., 1 per day 6:25pm, 8475ptas). **Secorbus** (☎ 902 22 92 92) provides exceptionally cheap service to **Madrid** (4½hr., 7 per day, 1600ptas, round-trip 2560), departing from Camino de los Sastres in front of Hotel Melia. **Transportes Ureña** (☎ 957 40 45 58) runs to **Jaén** (2hr., 7 per day 7:30am-8pm, 990ptas). **Eurobus** (☎ 902 11 96 99) runs to: **Sevilla** (2hr., 3 per day); **Bilbao** (10¼hr., 3 per day 12:10am-12:45pm, 4875ptas); **San Sebastián** (12hr., 3 per day 12:10am-12:45pm, 5560ptas). Intra-provincial buses depart from Av. República and Po. Victoria: **Autocares Priego** (☎ 957 40 44 79), **Empresa Carrera** (☎ 957 40 44 14), and **Empresa Rafael Ramírez** (☎ 957 42 21 77) runs buses to surrounding towns and camping sites.

Local Public Transportation: There are 12 bus lines (☎ 957 25 57 00) that run through the modern parts of the city and neighborhoods in the outskirts. Most buses run from the early morning until 11pm; check the tourist office for a listing of routes. Bus #3 makes a loop from the bus and train stations through Pl. Tendillas, along the river, and up C. Doctor Fleming. Bus #10 runs from the train station to Barrio Brillante. 115ptas.

Taxis: Radio Taxi (☎ 957 76 44 44) has stands at most busy intersections throughout the city. Be sure that the meter is turned on before you begin your journey. From the Judería to the bus and train stations about 500ptas; to Barrio Brillante about 600ptas.

Car Rental: Hertz (☎ 957 40 20 60), in the train station. Cheapest car 9200ptas per day. Min. age 25. Open M-F 8:30am-9pm, Sa 9am-1pm and 3:30-7pm, Su 9am-1pm.

Córdoba

♠ ACCOMMODATIONS

Camping Municipal, 1
Hostal Alcázar, 25
Hostal Almanzor, 12
Hostal Deanes, 19
Hostal El Portillo, 10
Hostal La Calleja, 11
Hostal La Fuente, 6
Hostal Los Arcos, 8
Hostal Maestre, 9
Hostal Perales, 3
Hostal-Residencia Boston, 4
Hostal-Residencia Séneca, 17
Hostal Rey Heredia, 13
Huéspedes Martínez Rücker, 15
Residencia Juvenil Córdoba (HI), 23

🍎 RESTAURANTS

Cafetín Halal, 14
Caroche Centro Cafetería, 5
El Churrasco, 22
El Picantón, 21
Mesón de la Luna, 24
Mesón San Basilio, 26
O Mamma Mía, 2
Píccolo Café, 18
Sociedad de Plateros, 7
Taberna Casa Salinas, 20
Taberna Santa Clara, 16

✴🔢 ORIENTATION AND PRACTICAL INFORMATION

Córdoba is split into two parts, the old city and the new city. The modern and commercial northern half extends from the train station on Av. América down to Plaza de las Tendillas, the center of the city. The old part in the south is a medieval maze known as the Judería (Jewish quarter). This tangle of beautiful and disorienting streets extends from Pl. Tendillas to the banks of the Río Guadalquivir, winding past the Mezquita and Alcázar. To get to the center of the city, exit left from the train station and make a right onto Av. de los Mozarabes. When you reach Gta. Sargentos Provisionales, cross the park on your left and make a right on Paseo de la Victoria. Turn left on C. Concepción and walk straight into Pl. Tendillas, or take bus #3 from the front of the bus station to Pl. Tendillas.

Tourist Offices: Oficina Municipal de Turismo y Congresos (☎ 957 20 05 22; fax 957 20 02 77), Pl. Judá Leví. Open M-F 8:30am-2:30pm. **Tourist Office of Andalucía**, C. Torrijos, 10 (☎ 957 47 12 35; fax 957 49 17 78), in the Junta de Andalucía, across from the Mezquita. From the train station, take bus #3 (bus stops on Av. América

Córdoba

TO BARRIO
EL BRILLANTE
AND ▲ (2 km)

C. Doña Berengueta

Paseo del Brillante

C. Haza Tranco
C. Molinos Alta

El Navegante

Acera Guerrita

C. de Azave

Alonso el Sabio

Av. de las Ollerías

Av. de los Agujones

Doce de Octubre

Av. de América

P

C. de Córdoba

Av. de Cervantes

TO ⊞ 🚌

Av. de los Mozárabes

C. de los Reyes Católicos

C. La Bodega

C. Ronda de los Tejares

El Corte Inglés

PLAZA DE COLON

C. Marroquíes

Mayor de Sta Marina

PL. CONDE DE RIEGO

C. M. de la Misericordia

C. Moriscos

PL. STA. MARINA

C. del Zarco

Cristo de los Faroles

PL. CAPUCHINAS

Cabrera

Isabel Losa

PL. D. GOME

Palacio del Marqués de Viana

C. Parras

R. Casas Deza

C. de los Indianos

Juan

Santa María

Conde de Arenal

C. Clotas

Pedro Fernández

Hijos Real

Av. del Gran Capitán

✉

C. Cruz Conde

C. del Osario

C. Conde de Torres

Obispo Fitero

C. Carbonell y Morand

C. Alfaros

C. San Pablo

Medical Assistance (Casa de Socorro)
⊞

PL. DE S. IGNACIO DE LOYOLA

C. Menéndez y Pelayo

C. Góngora

C. Morería

Concepción

C. de León

C. de Alfonso XIII

P

C. Conde de Gondomar

PL. TENDILLAS

C. Claudio Marcelo

Ayuntamiento

Av. de la República Argentina

Perez de Castro

C. Eduardo Dato

PL. SAN NICOLÁS

San Felipe

C. Sevilla

Málaga

C. Jesús María

Champion Supermarket

Diario Córdoba

C. Pedro López

Plaza de la Corredera

JARDINES DE LA VICTORIA

Paseo de la Victoria

Lope de Hoces

PL. R. Y CAJAL

PL. EMILIO LUQUE

P

R. Sánchez

J. de Mena

Reloj

Fernando Colón

P. Muñoz

PL. CAÑAS

C. Gutiérrez de los Ríos

Telón y Marín

C. de la Feria

Valladares

PL. TRINIDAD

PL. S. JUAN

Argote

R. Barroso

Juan Valera

C. Ambrosio de Morales

Maese Luis Tornillo

Sociobus Bus Stop

Puerta de Almodóvar

Statue of Maimonides

C. Almanzor

Romero

C. Fernández Ruano

C. Buen Pastor

Museo Arqueológico

M. del Villar

PL. J. PÁEZ

San Pedro del Real

C. de San Fernando

Julio Romero

Museo de Bellas Artes

PL. DEL Artes POTRO

Museo Julio Romero de Torres

C. Lineros

Calle Buen

Candelaria

Museo Taurino y de Arte Cordobés

C. Blanco Belmonte

Conde de Luque

Deanes

PL. BENAVENTE

Calleja de Flores

C. Cardenal Herrero

Encarnación

Calle de Osio

Sta. Clara

C. Cabezas

C. Lucano

S. Francisco

Barra

Posada del Potro

C. Caldereros

C. Card. González

Municipal Tourist Office ℹ

Tourist Office of Andalucía ℹ

PL. JUDA LEVÍ

C. Corregidor

M. Rueda

Mezquita

Luis de la Cerda

Po. de la Ribera

Río Guadalquivir

Palacio de Congresos

P

Ronda de Isasa

PL. CAMPO SANTO DE LOS MÁRTIRES

Amador de los Ríos

Puente Romano

Av. Conde Vallellano

Caballerizas Reales

Alcázar

N 👍

Museo Diocesano de Bellas Artes

Torre de la Calahorra

PLAZA STA. TERESA

C. del Santo Cristo

C. San Basilio

C. Enmedio

Av. del Corregidor

Av. de Alcázar

0   200 yards

0   200 meters

Av. de la Confederación

Av. de Cádiz

TO PUENTE SAN RAFAEL

ANDALUCÍA

between the train and bus stations) along the river until a stone arch appears on the right. Office is 1 block up C. Torrijos. General information on Andalucía. English-speaking staff with good free map of the monument section. Open May-Sept. M-F 9:30am-8pm, Sa 10am-7pm, Su 10am-2; Oct.-Apr. 9:30am-6pm, Su 10am-2pm.

Currency Exchange: Banco Central Hispano (☎ 957 47 42 67), Pl. Tendillas, charges no commission. Open June-Aug. M-F 8:30am-2:30pm; Sept.-May M-F 8:30am-2:30pm, Sa 9am-1pm. Banks and ATMs dot Pl. Tendillas.

Luggage Storage: Lockers at the train and bus stations (300-600ptas). Open 24hr. Also at **Champion** supermarket, C. Jesús María, between Pl. Tendillas and C. J. de Mena. Open M-Sa 9:15am-9:15pm.

El Corte Inglés: Av. Ronda de los Tejares, 30 (☎ 957 47 02 67), on the corner of Av. Gran Capitán. Supermarket (5th fl.) and a thorough map with traffic directions (575ptas). Open M-Sa 10am-9:30pm.

English Bookstore: Librería Luque, C. Cruz Conde, 19, off Pl. Tendillas. Actually a Spanish bookstore, but it carries English books.

Emergency: ☎ 112. **Police:** (☎ 957 47 75 00), Av. Medina Azahara.

Medical Assistance: Red Cross Hospital (☎ 957 42 06 66; emergency ☎ 957 22 22 22), Po. Victoria. English spoken. **Ambulance:** ☎ 29 55 70.

Late-Night Pharmacy: On a rotating basis. Refer to the list posted outside the pharmacy in Pl. Tendillas or the local newspaper.

Post Office: C. Cruz Conde, 15 (☎ 902 19 71 97), 2 blocks up from Pl. Tendillas. **Lista de Correos.** Open M-F 8:30am-8:30pm, Sa 9:30am-2pm. **Postal Code:** 14070.

Internet Access: El Navegante Café Internet, C. Llanos del Pretorio, 1 (☎ 957 49 75 36), at the intersection of Av. América and Paso del Brillante. A bar with a nouveau-nautical theme. 300ptas for 30min., 500 per hr. 300ptas minimum charge. Open daily 8am-4pm and 5pm-3am.

■ ACCOMMODATIONS

Hostels in Córdoba are on the whole quite impressive: charming, well-maintained, and affordable. Córdoba is especially crowded during Semana Santa (the week before Easter) and from May through September; you may have to call two to three months in advance for reservations. Prices are generally higher in summer.

IN AND AROUND THE JUDERÍA

The Judería's whitewashed walls, narrow, twisting streets, and proximity to major sights make it the nicest and most convenient area in which to stay. During the day, souvenir booths and cafes flood the streets and keep them lively; at night, the area seems desolate but is lit by streetlights. Take bus #3 from the train station to Pl. Tendillas and walk down C. Jesús María veering right as the streets curve. The white walls signal the Judería.

■ **Residencia Juvenil Córdoba (HI),** Pl. Juda Leví, (☎ 957 29 01 66; fax 957 29 05 00), next to the municipal tourist office and a 2min. walk from the Mezquita. Convenient and a bargain, this is definitely the place to stay in Córdoba. Huge, modern, and antiseptic, all rooms are doubles or quads with bath. Wheelchair accessible. A/C. Public telephones. Reservations recommended. Breakfast included, lunch and dinner 650ptas each. Towels 175ptas. 24hr. reception. 1605ptas per person; ages 26 and up 2140ptas. 300ptas extra per day for nonmembers for 6-night stay to gain membership.

■ **Hostal Deanes,** C. Deanes, 6 (☎ 957 29 37 44). From the top left corner of the Mezquita take C. Cardenal, then a sharp right onto C. Romero which becomes C. Deanes. The hostel will be on the left. Enormous traditional cordobés patio is shared with a popular restaurant and bar. Doubles 4000ptas, with bath 5000ptas.

Hostal-Residencia Séneca, C. Conde y Luque, 7 (☎ /fax 957 47 32 34). Follow C. Céspedes 2 blocks from the Mezquita. Impeccably maintained. Breakfast included. Reserve 1-2 months ahead. 1200ptas extra for A/C, all rooms have fans. Singles with sink 2300-2550ptas, with bath 4350-4750ptas; doubles with sink 4300-4700ptas, with bath 5400-5900ptas; triples with exterior bathroom 6150-6600ptas.

Hostal Alcázar, C. San Basilio, 2 (☎ 957 20 25 61), on an alley off the Jardines Santo Mártires, between C. Caballerizas Reales and C. Doctor Fleming. Furnishings reminiscent of a charmless motel. All rooms have fans. Breakfast 300ptas. Parking 700ptas per day. Reservations recommended. Singles with sink 2400ptas; doubles with sink 3200ptas, with bath 4200ptas. V, MC, AmEx.

BETWEEN THE MEZQUITA AND CALLE DE SAN FERNANDO

This quieter, more residential area of old Córdoba is still near the sights but a step away from the tourists. Some hostels are so nice you might want to stay a while. Buses stop along C. de San Fernando, the main corridor of the area.

Hostal La Fuente, C. San Fernando, 51 (☎ 957 48 78 27 or 957 48 14 78; fax 957 48 78 27), between C. San Francisco and C. Julio Romero. Relax in the traditional bar or beautiful courtyard. All rooms with bath, some with TV. Breakfast 275ptas. Parking 700ptas. Half of the building has A/C (at no extra charge). Singles 3000ptas; doubles 4000-5000ptas; 1800ptas per person for large groups. V, MC, AmEx.

Hostal Maestre, C. Romero Barros, 4-5 (☎ 957 47 53 95), off C. de San Fernando. All rooms have private bathrooms, some have TVs (no extra charge); for 500ptas you can make that fan an A/C. English spoken. Parking 900ptas per day. Singles 2500-2850ptas; doubles 4000-5000ptas; triples 5000-6500ptas. V, MC, AmEx.

Hostal La Calleja, Calleja de Rufino Blanco y Sánchez, 6 (☎/fax 957 48 66 06), at the intersection of C. Calereros and C. Cardenal Gonzalez. Only 3 years in the business and still in the works, but spacious rooms, bathrooms and private patios bode well. All rooms have TVs; some have A/C, others have fans for now. 24hr. reception. Singles 2700ptas; doubles 4200ptas, with bath 4800ptas, triple with bath 6000ptas. V, MC.

Huéspedes Martínez Rücker, Martínez Rücker, 14 (☎ 957 47 25 62). Take a right off the right side of the Mezquita. Rooms are clean and sparse. Modern common bathrooms. All rooms have fans. 1500-2000ptas per person; up to 4 in a room. V, MC.

Hostal Almanzor, C. Cardenal González, 10 (☎ /fax 957 48 54 00), 3 blocks from the Mezquita at the end of C. Rey Heredia closest to the river. Spotless rooms with balconies and TVs. All singles have king-sized beds. 24hr. reception. Parking included. Singles 1500-2000ptas; doubles with bath 3000-5000ptas. V, MC, AmEx.

Hostal El Portillo, C. Cabezas, 2 (☎ 957 47 20 91), off C. de San Fernando, between C. Caldereros and C. Julio Romero. Look for the sign that points up a steep driveway. Extremely modest rooms, quiet patio, and friendly owners. All have fans. Common bathrooms. Singles 2000ptas; doubles 3500ptas; triples 5000ptas.

Hostal Rey Heredia, C. Rey Heredia, 26 (☎/fax 957 47 41 82), on the long, narrow street parallel to the Mezquita. No A/C, but a good location. Some rooms have private baths. Singles 1500ptas; doubles 3000ptas; triples 4000ptas.

ELSEWHERE

Hotel Residencia Boston, C. Málaga, 2 (☎ 957 47 41 76; fax 957 47 85 23), on the corner of Pl. Tendillas, close to the modern part of town. Good price for the comforts: A/C, TV, phones, and baths. Breakfast 425ptas. Parking nearby. Singles with bath 3500-4100ptas; doubles with bath 5600-6700ptas; triples 1000-1500ptas. V, MC, AmEx.

Camping Municipal, Av. Brillante, 50 (☎ 957 28 21 65). From the train station, turn left on Av. América, left on Av. Brillante, and walk uphill for about 20min, or take bus #10 or 11 from Av. Cervantes near the station. Pool, currency exchange, supermarket, restaurant, free hot showers, laundry service. Camping equipment for rent. Wheelchair accessible. Individual tent 400ptas, family tent 560ptas; tax not included.

ANDALUCÍA

🗸 FOOD

The Mezquita area attracts nearly as many high-priced eateries as tourists to eat in them, but a five-minute walk in any direction yields local specialties at reasonable prices. In the evenings, locals converge at the outdoor *terrazas* between C. Severo Ochoa and C. Dr. Jiménez Díaz for drinks and *tapas* before dinner. Cheap eateries cluster farther away from the Judería in Barrio Cruz Conde, around Av. Menéndez Pidal and Pl. Tendillas. Regional specialties include *salmorejo* (a gazpacho-like cream soup topped with hard-boiled eggs and pieces of ham) and *rabo de toro* (bull's tail simmered in tomato sauce). **Supermarket Champion,** C. Jesús María, lies half a block from Pl. Tendillas (open M-Sa 9:15am-9:15pm).

El Picantón, C. F. Ruano, 19, 1 block from the Puerta de Almodóvar. From the top right corner of the Mezquita, walk up Romero and turn left. Take ordinary *tapas*, pour on a *salsa picante*, stick it in a roll, and voilà, you've got lunch (150-300ptas). Nothing else as cheap or as filling. No seats. Open daily 10am-3pm and 8pm-midnight.

Taberna Santa Clara, C. Osio, 2 (☎ 957 47 50 36). From the right side of the Mezquita, take C. Martínez Rücker and turn left. Spacious patio dining and exquisitely prepared meals. 2 pages of meat-free dishes. Fresh fish on Fridays. *Menú* 1300ptas. Entrees 800-1800ptas. Salads 650. Open Th-Tu noon-4pm and 7-11pm.

Sociedad de Plateros, C. San Francisco, 6 (☎ 957 47 00 42), between C. San Fernando and Pl. Potro. Patrons play dominoes on the weekends and tourists cool off in the shaded patio. A Córdoba mainstay since 1872. *Tapas* 200ptas. *Raciones* and *media-raciones* 400-1000ptas. Bar open Tu-Su 8am-4:30pm and 8pm-12:30am, restaurant 1-4pm and 8pm-midnight. Open M-Sa in summer, Tu-Su in winter. V, MC.

Taberna Casa Salinas, Puerto Almodóvar (☎ 957 29 08 46). A few blocks from the synagogue, up C. Judíos and to the left. Pepe Salinas has been running this place for over 40 years and its popularity shows. Stroll through the jam-packed bar to the outdoor patio to sample *raciones* (500-800ptas) and fine wines (100ptas). Open Sept.-July Th-Tu 11:30am-5pm and 8:30pm-12:30am.

Mesón San Basilio, C. San Basilio, 19 (☎ 957 29 70 07), to the left of the Alcázar, past Campo Santo de los Mártires. The locals love it, and so will you. The two-tiered dining room makes for a special and breezy atmosphere. *Menú del día* 1000ptas. *Raciones* 450-2000ptas. Meat and fish dishes 800-1750ptas. There is also a full bar with wine (75-225ptas) and beer (135ptas). Open daily 1-4pm and 8pm-midnight.

Caroche Centro Cafeteria, Garcia Lovera, 7 (☎ 957 49 25 71). From Pl. Tendillas, walk 1 block down C. Claudio Marcelo. A large-screen TV, video games, and extreme air-conditioning make this an ideal place to take a break from the heat. *Menú* 900ptas, *raciones* 300-600ptas. Open daily 7:30am-2:30am.

El Churrasco, C. Romero, 16. Straight from the top left corner of the Mezquita. Mainly a meat-lover's paradise, but even vegetarians will be happy. Pricey. Entrees 600-2800ptas. Glass of wine 375ptas. Open daily 1-4pm and 8pm-midnight. V, MC, AmEx.

🗿 SIGHTS

▧ LA MEZQUITA

☎ 957 47 05 12. Open daily Apr.-June 10am-7:30pm; July-Oct. 10am-7pm; Nov.-Mar. 10am-6pm. 900ptas, ages 8-13 450ptas. Same ticket valid for Museo Diocesano de Bellas Artes. Last ticket sold 30min. before closing. Opens M-Sa 8:30am for mass starting at 9:30am; Su mass 11am, noon, and 1pm.

Built in 784 on the site of a Visigoth Basilica, this breathtaking mosque is considered the most important Islamic monument in the Western world. Over the next two centuries, this architectural masterpiece was enlarged to cover an area the size of several city blocks with more than 850 columns, making it the largest mosque in the Islamic world at the time. Made of granite, jasper, and marble, the pillars, of differing heights, are capped by brick-and-stone arches, then an architectural innovation used to create the illusion of height and spaciousness.

Visitors enter through the **Patio de los Naranjos,** an arcaded courtyard featuring carefully spaced orange trees, palm trees, and fountains, where the dutiful would wash before prayer. The **Torre del Alminar** encloses remains of the minaret from where the *muezzin* would call for prayer.

The most elaborate additions, consisting of the dazzling **mihrab** (prayer niche) and the triple **maksourah** (caliph's niche) were created in the 10th century. The mihrab, whose prayer arch faces Mecca, formerly housed a gilt copy of the Koran; pilgrims circle it seven times on their knees, as evidenced by the worn stones. The intricate gold, pink, and blue marble Byzantine mosaics shimmering across its arches were given by the Emperor Constantine VII to the *cordobés* caliphs; his gift is estimated to weigh close to 35 tons.

At the far end of the Mezquita lies the **Capilla Villaviciosa,** where Caliphal vaulting, greatly influential in later Spanish architecture, appeared for the first time. It was the first Christian chapel to be built in the mosque, completed in 1371. Thus began the transition of the mosque to a place of Christian worship. The **Capilla Mayor (High Chapel)** was enlarged in 1384. In 1523, Bishop Alonso Manrique, an ally of Carlos V, proposed to build a Renaissance cathedral in the center of the mosque. The town rallied violently against the idea, promising painful death to any worker who helped tear down the Mezquita. Nevertheless, the Christians soon erected the towering **crucero** (transept) and **coro** (choir stalls), combining the Renaissance style of the epoch with the 16th- and 17th-century architecture. The townspeople were far from pleased, and even Carlos V lamented the changes to the Mezquita, griping, "You have destroyed something unique to create something commonplace." What remains, though, is far from commonplace.

IN AND AROUND THE JUDERÍA

A combined ticket for the Alcázar, Museo Taurino y de Arte Cordobés, and Museo Julio Romero (see Outside the Judería, below) is available at all three locations. 1075ptas, students 550ptas. Individually, admission to each sight costs 450ptas. F free.

⊞ALCÁZAR. Along the river on the left side of the Mezquita lies the Alcázar. Built in 1328 during the *Reconquista*, the building served as both a fortress and residence for Alfonso XI. Fernando and Isabel bade Columbus farewell here, and from 1490 to 1821, it served as a headquarters for the Inquisition. Its walls enclose a manicured garden with flower beds, terraced ponds, multiple fountains, and palm trees. Inside, the museum displays 1st-century Roman mosaics and a 3rd-century Roman marble sarcophagus. *(☎ 957 42 01 51. Open May-Sept. Tu-Sa 10am-2pm and 6-8pm, Su 9:30am-3pm; Oct.-Apr. Tu-Sa 10am-2pm and 4:30-6:30pm, Su 9:30am-3pm. Illuminated gardens open July-Aug. 8pm-midnight. Admission 300ptas, students 150ptas. F free.)*

SINAGOGA. Tucked away downhill from the Moorish arch. Built in 1315, the Sinagoga is a solemn reminder of the 1492 expulsion of the Jews. The only other Jewish temples remaining in Spain are in Toledo. Its walls are covered by Hebrew inscriptions of the psalms and are decorated with Mozarabic patterns. *(C. Judíos, 20. ☎ 957 20 29 28. Open Tu-Sa 10am-2pm and 3:30-5:30pm, Su 10am-1:30pm. Currently free because of restoration.)*

MUSEO TAURINO Y DE ARTE CORDOBÉS. The museum is dedicated to the history and lore of the bullfight. The main exhibit includes a replica of the tomb of Spain's most famous matador, Manolete, and the hide of the bull that killed him. *(Pl. Maimonides. ☎ 957 20 10 56. Open May-Sept. Tu-Sa 10am-2pm and 6-8pm, Su 9:30am-3pm; Oct.-Apr. M-Sa 10am-2pm and 5-7pm, Su 9:30am-3pm. 450ptas, students 225ptas, seniors free. F free.)*

MUSEO DIOCESANO DE BELLAS ARTES. The works of 13th-18th-century local artists are on display in this splendid 17th-century palace. *(C. Torrijos, across from the Mezquita in the Palacio de Congresos. ☎ 957 47 93 75. Open June-Sept. M-F 9:30am-3pm, Sa 9:30am-1:30pm; Oct.-Mar. M-F 9:30am-1:30pm and 3:30-5:30pm, Sa 9:30am-1:30pm. 150ptas, under 12 free, free with admission to Mezquita.)*

OTHER SIGHTS. Townspeople take great pride in their traditional **patios,** many dating from Roman times. These open-air courtyards—tranquil havens of orange and lemon trees, flowers, and fountains—flourish in the old quarter. Among the streets of exceptional beauty are **Calleja del Indiano,** off C. Fernández Ruano at Pl. Angel Torres, and the aptly named **Calleja de Flores,** off C. Blanco Belmonte where colorful geraniums in full bloom crowd the narrow white walls of the alley. In Pl. Tiberiades, rub the toes of the statue of **Maimonides** to gain his knowledge. The statue was used as the model for the face of the New Israeli Shekel.

OUTSIDE THE JUDERÍA

MUSEO DE BELLAS ARTES. This museum now occupies a building that served as a hospital during the reign of Fernando and Isabel. Its small collection displays works by Córdoban artists. Check out the sculptures by Mateo Inurria and Juan de Mesa on the ground floor. *(Pl. Potro, 5-10 min. from the Mezquita.* ☎ *957 47 33 45. Open Tu 3-8pm, W-Sa 9am-8pm, Su 9am-3pm. Enter 20min. before closing. 250ptas; EU citizens free.)*

MUSEO JULIO ROMERO DE TORRES. Located in the artist's home, it shares the courtyard with the Museo de Bellas Artes. Spice up your life with a visit to the exhibits of Romero's sensual portraits of Córdoban women. *(Pl. Potro, 5-10min. from the Mezquita.* ☎ *957 49 19 09. Open May-Sept. Tu-Sa 10am-2pm and 6-8pm, Su 9:30am-3pm; Oct.-Apr. Tu-Sa 10am-2pm and 5-7pm, Su 9:30am-3pm. Last entrance 30min. before closing. 450ptas, students 225ptas, seniors free. Part of the combined ticket listed above.)*

PALACIO DEL MARQUÉS DE VIANA. An elegant 14th-century mansion, the palace displays 12 quintessentially Córdoban patios complete with sprawling gardens and majestic fountains, as well as tapestries, furniture and porcelain. *(Pl. Don Gome, 2. A 20min. walk from the Mezquita.* ☎ *957 48 01 34. Open June 16-Sept M-Sa 9am-2pm; Oct. 1-May M-Sa 10am-1pm and 4-6pm; closed June 1-15. Patio only 200ptas. Guided tours every hr. 500ptas, children 200ptas.)*

MUSEO ARQUEOLÓGICO. Housed in a Renaissance mansion, the museum contains a chronological exhibit of tools, ceramics, coins, and sarcophagi from the Roman to the Renaissance periods. Particularly impressive are the Roman mosaics. *(Pl. Paez, several blocks from the Mezquita.* ☎ *957 47 40 11. Open Tu 3-8pm, W-Sa 9am-8pm, Su 9am-3pm. 250ptas, EU citizens free.)*

OTHER SIGHTS. Near the Palacio del Marqués de Viana, in Pl. Capuchinos (a.k.a. Pl. Dolores) and next to the monastery is the **Cristo de los Faroles** (Christ of the Lanterns). This is one of the most famous religious icons in Spain and is the site of frequent all-night vigils. The eight lanterns that are lit at night symbolize the eight provinces of Andalucía. Facing the Museo de Bellas Artes and the Museo Julio Romero de Torres is the **Posada del Potro,** a 14th-century inn mentioned in *Don Quijote.* Across the river from the Mezquita stands the **Torre de la Calahorra,** a Muslim military tower which was built in 1369 to protect the Roman bridge and now houses a museum that covers Cordoba's cultures during the Middle Ages.

🎵 ENTERTAINMENT

For the latest cultural events, pick up a free copy of the *Guía del Ocio* at the tourist office. Cheap flamenco isn't easy to come by in Córdoba. Tourists fill the Tablao Cardenal, C. Torrijos, 10, facing the Mezquita, where national prize-winning dancers perform passionate *flamenco puro.* Reserve seats at the Tablao or your hostel. ((☎ 957 48 33 20. Shows Tu-Sa 10:30pm. 2800ptas, includes 1 drink.) Another option is **La Bulería,** C. Pedro López, 3, which has shows every night at 10:30pm. (☎ 957 48 38 39. 1500ptas, includes 1 drink).

From the first weekend of June until the heat subsides, the cool Barrio Brillante, uphill from Av. América, is the place to be at night. Throngs of well-dressed, young *cordobeses* walk the streets, hopping from one packed outdoor bar to another until reaching a dance club. Bus #10 goes to Brillante from the train station until about 11pm; a taxi should cost 500-900ptas. If you're walking, head up Av. Brillante passing along the way **El Rocio, Pub BSO,** and **El Navegante** at C. Llanos de Pretorio. Right around the corner is **Brujas (Witches) Bar,** where every Tuesday and Thursday witches can tell your fortune. Once in Barrio Brillante, where C. Poeta Emilia Prados meets C. Poeta Juan Ramón Jiménez, go through **Cafetería Terra** to discover a massive open-air patio where the backs of nearly ten bars (**Havanna, Canaveral,** and **El Puerto** to name a few) converge. Across the street is **El Torre,** an outdoor nightclub that plays a mix of well-known Latin and Spanish music. From there, proceed down Av. Brillante toward the city center, passing the very popular nightclub **El Cachao,** as well as **Pub La Mondoa, Club Pon Luis, Club Kachomba,** and **Bar Chicote** along the way. Finish a packed night with some coffee and a late-night snack at **Cafeteria Aqua,** Av. Brillante, s/n (☎ 957 40 42 82), where a full bar complements desserts (300-500ptas) and ice cream (225-500ptas). To get home, catch a taxi at the corner of Av. Brillante and C. Las Acacias. During the cooler months of winter, nightlife tends to center around the Universidad de Córdoba, especially pubs on C. Antonio Maura and C. Camino de los Sastres. From there, the crowds move on to Av. Gran Capitán, Av. Ronda de los Tejares and C. Cruz Conde.

❋ FESTIVALS

The month of May is a never-ending party, beginning with the **Concurso de los Cruces** the first week in May. Organizations sponsor the decoration of crosses that go up for display around the city. During the **Festival de los Patios,** beginning the first weekend in May and lasting for two weeks, Córdoba is transformed into a lush garden, when more than 150 private patios are open to the public. The last week in May brings the riotous week-long **Feria de Nuestra Señora de la Salud** (commonly known as *La Feria*), for which thousands of Córdoban women don colorful, traditional apparel and bullfights are held daily. A carnival, dozens of stands, lively flamenco dancing, and nonstop drinking keep spirits high for the entire week. The **Concurso Nacional de Arte Flamenco** (National Flamenco Contest) is held every third year during May. The next one will be in 2001. The **Festival Internacional de la Guitarra** is held every year in mid-July when concerts, seminars, and courses abound. For info and tickets stop by F.P.M. Gran Teatro, Av. Gran Capitán, 3 (☎ 957 48 02 37). In early September, Córdoba celebrates its patroness with the **Feria de Nuestra Señora de la Fuensanta.**

🏛 DAYTRIP FROM CÓRDOBA

MEDINA AL-ZAHRA (1HR.)

Medina al-Zahra can be hard to reach. The O-1 bus (☎ 957 25 57 00, or see the list in the tourist office) leaves from Av. República Argentina in Córdoba for Cruce Medina Al-Zahra, 3km from the site (every hr., 115ptas). From the bus stop, it's about a 45min. walk (mostly uphill). On the way back, the bus stop is along the highway at the cross, on the opposite side of the street from the gas station. A taxi costs about 1600ptas.

Built in the **Sierra Morena,** Córdoba's mountain range, by Abderramán III for his favorite wife, Zahra, this 10th-century medina was considered one of the greatest palaces of its time. The site, long thought to be mythical, was discovered in the mid-19th century and excavated in the early 20th century. Today, it is one of Spain's most impressive archaeological finds. The Medina al-Zahra is divided into three terraces: one for the palace (*alcázar*), another for the servants' living quarters, and a third for an enclosed garden and almond grove. After moving from Granada, Zahra missed the Sierra Nevada; to appease her, Abderramán planted the white-blossoming almond groves as add substitute for her beloved snow. The Salón de Abd al-Rahman III, also known as the *salón rico,* on the lower terraces, is being restored to its original intricate and geometrical beauty.

A complete tour of the ruins takes between 20 and 45 minutes, depending on your level of interest. (☎ 957 32 91 30. Open May-Sept. Tu-Sa 10am-2pm and 6-8:30pm, Su 10am-2pm; Oct.-Apr. Tu-Sa 10am-2pm and 4-6:30pm, Su 10am-2pm. 250ptas, EU citizens free.) **Córdoba Visión** offers transportation and a 2½-hour guided visit to the sight in English, Spanish, or French. (☎ 957 23 17 34; fax 957 23 73 94. Tours May-Sept. Tu-Sa 10:30am-6pm, Su 10:30am; Oct.-Apr. Tu-Sa 10:30am-4pm, Su 10:30am. 2500ptas. Meets at Triunfo de San Rafael near the mosque.)

JEREZ DE LA FRONTERA

Though unremarkable in appearance, Jerez de la Frontera (pop. 200,000) is the cradle of three staples of Andalucian culture: flamenco, Carthusian horses, and, of course, *jerez* (sherry). It is the sheer quantity and quality of this third staple that draws in the tourists, most of whom are older, well-to-do Europeans. The city also makes a good departure point for the *ruta de los pueblos blancos* (see p. 228), but those not particularly interested in winery tours or horse shows would be better off spending their time elsewhere, as Jerez can be expensive.

▣ TRANSPORTATION

Flights: Airport (☎ 956 15 00 00), 7km from town on Ctra. Jerez-Sevilla. Taxi to the airport 1500-2000ptas. **Iberia** (☎ 956 18 43 94) and **British Airways** (☎ 956 15 00 93) both have their offices at the terminal. Flights operate regularly to and from Madrid and Barcelona, as well as other major European cities.

Trains: (☎ 956 34 23 19), Pl. Estación, at the end of C. Medina after it becomes C. Cartuja. **RENFE**, C. Larga, 34 (☎ 956 33 48 13). To: **Cádiz** (45min., every 30min. 6:40am-10:30pm, 430ptas); **Sevilla** (1¼hr., 12 per day 6:30am-8:30pm, 910ptas); **Madrid** (4½hr., 2 and 5pm, 7800-9100ptas); and **Barcelona** (12hr., 7:30pm, 8960ptas).

Buses: (☎ 956 34 52 07), on C. Cartuja, at the corner of C. Madre de Dios, 2 blocks from the train station. **Transportes Generales Comes** (☎ 956 21 17 63). To: **Puerto Santa María** (30min., 4 per day 7am-8:30pm, 155ptas); **Cádiz** (1hr., 19 per day 7am-9pm, 360ptas); **Vejer** (2hr., 6:45pm, 810ptas); and **Ronda** (2¾hr., 4 per day 7:45am-3:30pm, 1320ptas). **Los Amarillos** (☎ 956 32 93 47). To: **Arcos** (30min., 8-17 per day 7:15am-8:15pm, 300ptas) and **Córdoba** (4hr., 1 per day, 1925ptas). **Linesur** (☎ 956 34 10 63) to: **Sanlúcar** (30min., every hr. 7am-9pm, 215ptas); **Chipiona** (1hr., 12 per day 7am-9pm, 300ptas); **Sevilla** (1½hr., 7-13 per day 6:30am-11pm, 700ptas); and **Algeciras** (2hr., 7-13 per day 7:15am-10pm, 1090ptas). **Secorbus** (☎ 902 22 92 92) to **Madrid** (7hr., 6 per day 8:50am-11:50pm, 3005ptas).

City Buses: Each of the 12 lines runs every 15min., most passing through Pl. Arenal and by the bus station. One ride 110ptas. **Info office** (☎ 956 34 34 46) in Pl. Arenal.

Car Rental: Niza, C.N. IV Madrid-Cádiz, KM, 637; also Av. Alvaro Domecq (☎ 956 30 28 60). Starts at 8000ptas per day. Min. age 21. Open daily 8:30am-1pm and 4:30-8pm.

✳ ▣ ORIENTATION AND PRACTICAL INFORMATION

The labyrinthine streets of Jerez are difficult to navigate without a map. Get one free from the tourist office or buy one from any bookstore or newsstand (around 500ptas). To reach the town center from the **bus station,** exit left onto C. Cartuja, which becomes C. Medina, which leads into **Plaza Romero Martínez** (the city's commercial center). From here, walk left on C. Cerrón, which leads to C. Santa María and C. Lencería, heading into **Plaza del Arenal.** From the **train station,** exit to the right and take C. Cartuja to the bus station, then follow the directions above.

Tourist Office: C. Larga, 39 (☎ 956 33 11 50; fax 956 33 17 31). From Pl. Arenal, take C. Lencería to C. Larga. English-speaking staff has free maps and info on sherry production, *bodegas* tours, and horse shows. Open June-Aug. M-F 9am-7pm, Sa-Su 10am-2pm and 5-7pm; Sept.-May M-F 8am-3pm and 4-7pm, Sa-Su 10am-2pm and 5-7pm.

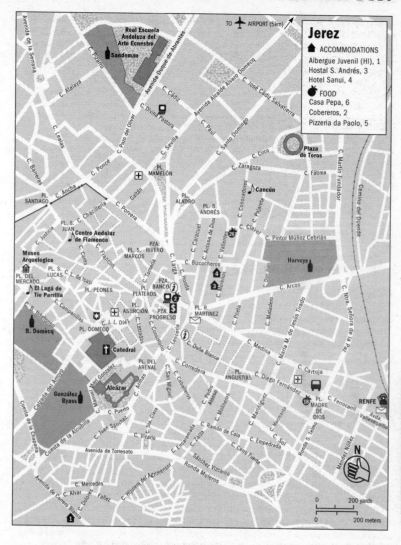

Jerez

⌂ ACCOMMODATIONS
Albergue Juvenil (HI), 1
Hostal S. Andrés, 3
Hotel Sanui, 4
🍎 FOOD
Casa Pepa, 6
Cobereros, 2
Pizzeria da Paolo, 5

ANDALUCÍA

Currency Exchange: Banco Central Hispano, C. Largo, 11 (☎ 902 24 24 24), charges no commission. Open M-F 8:30am-2:30pm.

Emergency: ☎ 112. **Police:** ☎ 091, 092, or 956 33 03 46.

Medical Assistance: Ambulatorio de la Seguridad Social (☎ 956 34 84 68), C. José Luis Díaz.

Post Office: Main Office, C. Cerrón, 2 (☎ 956 34 22 95), off Pl. Romero Martínez. **Lista de Correos.** Open M-F 8:30am-8:30pm, Sa 9am-2pm. **Postal Code:** 11480.

Internet Access: RJP Informática, C. Larga, 2nd fl. of the Centro Comercial (☎ 32 12 53). 400ptas per 30min., 700ptas per hr. Open M-F 9:30am-1:30pm and 5:30-9pm, Sa 10:30am-1:30pm. **Cybersur,** C. Divina Pastora, 48 (☎ 956 32 87 90). 500ptas per hr. Open M-F 10am-1:30pm and 5:30-8:30pm, Sa 10:30am-2pm.

▌ ACCOMMODATIONS

In Jerez, finding a place to crash is as easy as finding a cork to sniff. Look along C. Medina, near the bus station, and C. Arcos, which intersects C. Medina at Pl. Romero Martínez. The area may not be interesting to look at, but it's close to the fountains and *terrazas* of C. Larga. Prices increase during Jerez's festivals.

Hostal Sanvi, C. Morenos, 10 (☎ 956 34 56 24). Take C. Fontana (off C. Medina), for 1 block, then turn left; C. Morenos is the first right. Friendly management gives it that family-run feel. Quiet, newly renovated, impeccably clean rooms. Singles 2500ptas, with bath 3000ptas; doubles with bath 3750ptas; triples with bath 6000ptas.

Albergue Juvenil (HI), Av. Carrero Blanco, 30 (☎ 956 14 39 01; fax 956 14 32 63), in an ugly suburb, a 25min. walk or 10min. bus ride from downtown (bus L-8 from the bus station, bus L-1 from Pl. Arenal). One of Jerez's very few budget options. Clean and modern, with spacious doubles, a pool (open July-Aug.), tennis and basketball courts, small soccer field, library, TV/VCR room, and rooftop terrace. Laundry service available. Check-out 10am. Call ahead. Dorms 800-1300ptas, over 26 1100-1800ptas.

Hostal San Andrés, C. Morenos, 12 (☎ 956 34 09 83; fax 956 34 31 96). Follow direction for Hostal Sanvi. Two beautiful patios, one with stained glass, the other with hanging grapes. Rooms are basic. Singles 2400-2600ptas, with bath and TV 3000ptas; doubles 3600ptas, with bath and TV 4500ptas.

▐ FOOD

Tapas-hoppers bounce around Pl. Arenal, C. Larga and in the old town around Pl. del Banco. Supermarket **Cobreros** sells the basics on the second floor of the Centro Comercial, C. Larga, above McDonald's (open daily 9am-2pm and 5:30-9:30pm).

Casa Pepa, Pl. Madre de Dios, 14 (☎ 956 32 49 06), around the corner from the bus station, between 2 tall buildings. A local meeting place and landmark. *Menú* 850-1300ptas. Entrees 450-700ptas. Open daily 11am-4pm and 7-11pm.

Pizzeria da Paolo, C. Clavel at C. Valientes. Popular new pizzeria makes 'em fresh (700-900ptas) and serves up filling portions of pasta (750ptas and up). Open Tu-Su 1-4:45pm and 8:30pm-midnight.

▐ SHERRY BODEGAS

People come to Jerez for the *jerez*. Multilingual tour guides distill the sherry-making process for you, then let you sample for free. The best time to visit is early September during the harvest; the worst is August when many *bodegas* close down. *Bodegas* are plotted on any map, and the tourist office can help find the right one for you. Group reservations for hour-long tours must be made at least one week in advance; reservations for individuals are usually unnecessary. *Bodegas* open during specific hours, and all conduct tours in English. Call ahead for exact times.

González Byass, C. Manuel María González, 12 (☎ 956 35 70 16; fax 956 35 70 46). The tour of choice of visiting royalty and celebrities, with a motorized trolley, costumed guides, and trained mice that climb miniature ladders to sip the juice. English tours M-F at 10:30, 11:30am, 12:30, 1:30, 5:30, and 6:30pm. 1000ptas. V, MC.

B. Domecq, C. San Idelfonso, 3 (☎ 956 15 15 00). The oldest and largest in town. Tours M-F 9am and 1pm. 500ptas. Reservations required for groups.

Sandeman, C. Pizarro, 10 (☎ 956 30 11 00), next to the Royal Andalusian School of Equestrian Art. Large and conveniently located. Their labels sport the imposing Don, the man with the black cape. Tours M-F 10am-5pm. 400ptas. Sa-Su appt. only. 500ptas.

Harveys, C. Arcos, 54. (☎ 956 34 60 04; fax 956 33 86 74). Shows a videotape explaining the wine-making process. Open M-F 9am-1:30pm. Tours 450ptas. Reservations required for groups.

📷 SIGHTS

▨ALCÁZAR. Colorful gardens, cool *baños árabes* (Arab baths), and an 11th-century mosque once used for private worship lie within the walls of the fortress. The **Cámara Oscura** in the palace offers exhibits on Jerez as well as startling views of the city. (☎ 956 31 97 98. Open May-Sept. M-Sa 10am-8pm, Su 10am-3pm; Oct.-Apr. daily 10am-6pm. Alcázar 400ptas, students 100ptas. Alcázar and Cámara Oscura 500ptas.)

REAL ESCUELA ANDALUZA DE ARTE EQUESTRE. Jerez's love for wine is almost matched by its passion for horses. During the first or second week of May, the Real Escuela Andaluza de Arte Equestre (Royal Andalusian School of Equestrian Art), on Av. Duque de Abrantes, sponsors a **Feria del Caballo** (Horse Fair) with shows, carriage competitions, and races of Jerez-bred Carthusian horses. During the rest of the year, weekly shows feature a troupe of horses dancing in choreographed sequences. Dress rehearsals are almost as impressive. (☎ 956 31 80 08. Dress rehearsals M, W, and F 11am-1pm. 1000ptas. Shows June-Oct. Tu noon, Th 10am and noon; Nov.-May Th noon. 2000-3000ptas, children and students 40% off.)

CATEDRAL. Near the Alcázar is the huge, imposing Baroque cathedral, with a Mudéjar belfry, built on the site of another mosque. (☎ 956 34 84 82. Open daily June-Aug. 11am-8pm; Sept.-May 10am-6pm. Free.)

🎵🎭 ENTERTAINMENT AND NIGHTLIFE

FLAMENCO. Rare footage of Spain's most highly regarded flamenco singers, dancers, and guitarists is available for viewing at the **Centro Andaluz de Flamenco,** in Palacio Pemartín, on Pl. San Juan. (☎ 956 34 92 65; fax 956 32 11 27. Open M-F 9am-2pm. Audio-visuals every hr., 9:30am-1:30pm. Free.) Most *peñas* and *tablaos* (clubs and bars that host flamenco) hide in the old town and host special performances during July and August. Ask for details in the tourist office or look out for posters along the main streets. For more frequent (and more tourist-oriented) shows, make the trek to **El Lagá de Tío Parrilla**, Pl. Mercado. (☎/fax 956 33 83 34. Shows M-Sa 10:30pm. Cover 1200-1500ptas, includes 1 drink.) Most expensive restaurants also have shows on the weekends but require that you dine as well.

NIGHTLIFE. Visitors to Jerez tend to be on the older side; *tapas* bars are more popular than dance clubs here, although plenty of people go out on weekends. For bars and *terrazas*, look around the triangle formed by C. Santo Domingo, C. Salvatierra, and Av. Méjico and Pl. Canterbury, a mini-mall of nightspots located on C. Paul at C. Santo Domingo. **Cancún,** C. Pajarete, 18, a huge, trendy *bar-musical* off C. Zaragoza (a block from Pl. Canterbury), features Caribbean themes, but the usual techno-pop blasts from the speakers. (☎ 956 33 17 22. Couples, ladies, and "members" only. Free.)

FESTIVALS. Autumn, in addition to being grape harvest season, is festival season, when Jerez showcases its best equine and flamenco traditions. The **Fiesta de la Bulería** in September celebrates flamenco, as does the September **Festival de Teatro, Música, y Baile.** These festivals are collectively known as the **Fiestas de Otoño,** occurring from September 10 until October 13. The largest **horse parade** in the world, with races in Pl. Arenal, is the highlight of the final week. Ask for details at the tourist office; schedules are available in September for the upcoming year.

SANLÚCAR DE BARRAMEDA

Sanlúcar de Barrameda (pop. 62,000), at the mouth of the Río Guadalquivir, borders both the **Parque Nacional Coto de Doñana** (see **Mother Nature and Family,** p. 226) and some of Spain's most pristine beaches. Home to a handful of sherry *bodegas* and a few palaces, Sanlúcar is a cross between Spanish *pueblo blanco* and a European seaside resort. Its industrial outskirts are a bit of an eyesore, but it boasts superbly fine sands, forming the third corner of the illustrious "sherry triangle," along with Jerez and El Puerto de Santa María.

MOTHER NATURE AND FAMILY Bust out your binoculars—the 60,000 acre **Parque Nacional Coto de Doñana** on the Río Guadalquivir delta is home to flamingos, vultures, and thousands more of your feathered favorites, along with geese (and mongeese), wild boars, and lynx. Despite a huge mining spill on a tributary of the Guadalquivir River in April of 1998 that threatened to be one of Spain's biggest ecological disasters, the park has done surprisingly well, and tourist visits have continued relatively unaffected. If ornithological delights don't entice you, the salt marshes, sand dunes, wooded areas, and beach might. Nature purists beware, though, lest you stumble upon the lair of the dreaded species *turgrupus touristicus*—the park borders the town of Matalascañas, with a concrete shopping center and hotel complex.

Access to most of the park is restricted and back-country hiking and camping are prohibited. The western end of the park is accessible from Huelva and Matalascañas. Also, boat tours on **S.S. Real Fernando** depart from **Sanlúcar.** (☎ 956 36 38 13. 4hr; Apr.-Aug. Tu-Su 9:30am and 5pm; Sept.-Mar. Tu-Su 10am.) Call to make reservations or visit the office in the old ice factory by the dock on Av. Bajo de Guía. Those more interested in sand than life on the wild side can take the launch across the bay (8am-8pm, 400ptas) to one of the few *chiringuito* (refreshment stand)-free beaches in Spain. To get a taste of Doñana without leaving Sanlúcar, stop by the **Visitor Center,** also in the ice factory. (☎ 956 38 16 35. Open daily June-Aug. 9am-8pm; Sept.-May 9am-2:30pm and 4-7pm.)

⌐ TRANSPORTATION. Los Amarillos (☎ 956 38 50 60), on Pl. Pradillo at the end of C. San Juan, runs **buses** to: **Chipiona** (30min., every hr. 8am-9:45pm, 105ptas); **Cádiz** (1hr., 10 per day 6:15am-6:20pm, 380ptas); and **Sevilla** (2hr., 13 per day 6:45am-9:15pm, 915ptas). **Linesur La Valenciana** (☎ 956 34 10 63) is two blocks toward the beach from Pl. Cabildo, by the tourist office. Buses run to **Chipiona** (30min., every hr. 8am-9pm, 105ptas) and **Jerez** (45min., every hr. 7:20am-10:20pm, 220ptas). Buy tickets on the bus. For **taxis,** call ☎ 956 36 11 02 or 956 36 00 04.

⤷ PRACTICAL INFORMATION. The **tourist office** is on Calzada del Ejército, which runs perpendicular to the beach. English-speaking staff has info on the **Parque Nacional de Doñana.** (☎ 956 36 61 10; fax 956 36 61 32. Open June-Aug. M-F 9am-2pm and 6-8pm, Sa-Su 10am-2pm; Sept.-May M-F 10am-2pm and 5-7pm, Sa 10am-1pm.) Services include: **emergency** (☎ 112); **Ambulatorio de la S.S.** (☎ 956 36 71 65), Calzada del Ejército; **police** (☎ 956 38 80 11), Av. Constitución; and the **post office,** C. Correos and Av. Cerro Falcón, toward the beach from the tourist office. (☎ 956 36 09 37. Open M-F 8:30am-2:30pm, Sa 9am-1pm.) The **postal code** is 11540.

▣⌂ ACCOMMODATIONS AND FOOD. Few true bargains exist in Sanlúcar; it may be worth it to inquire at doorway signs reading "*se alquilan habitaciones*" (rooms for rent). **Hostal La Blanca Paloma,** Pl. San Roque, 15, keeps spacious, clean rooms, a few with balconies. (☎ 956 36 36 44. Singles 2200-2500ptas; doubles 3400-4230ptas.) **Pensión La Bohemia,** C. Don Claudio, 5, just off C. Santo Domingo, offers rooms with beige bedspreads, cold showers, and no frills. (☎ 956 36 95 99. Singles 2200ptas, with bath 3000ptas; doubles 4200ptas, with bath 5500ptas.) Sanlúcar is famous for its *langostinos* (king prawns). For a sit-down meal, head for the side streets off C. San Juan. *Terrazas* fill Pl. San Roque and Pl. Cabildo, its tree-lined neighbor. **Bar-Restaurante El Cura,** C. Amargura, 2, between the two plazas, serves up divine *paella* (500ptas), *tapas* (from 200ptas), and entrees (400-1300ptas) in a comfortable family atmosphere. (☎ 956 36 29 94. Open daily 7:30am-3am.)

◉⌂ SIGHTS AND ENTERTAINMENT. Most of the sights in town are best accessed via the tourist office. Two impressive palaces compete with the enormous 14th-century **Iglesia de Nuestra Señora de la O,** Pl. Paz, for the attention of sun-struck tourists. (church ☎ 956 36 05 55. Open 30min. before and after mass. Mass M-Sa 7:30pm, Su noon and 8pm. Free.) The **Palacio Medina Sidonia** is inhabited by the Duque de Medina Sidonia. (☎ 956 36 01 61. Call to arrange group visits on Sunday or Monday. Free.) The 19th-century **Palacio Infantes de Orleans** now houses the Ayuntamiento. (☎ 956 38 80 00. Open for guided visits Th-Tu 10am-2pm. 100ptas.) Several **bodegas** tower over Sanlúcar's small streets. Check at the tourist office for their revolving schedules. (Tours M-Sa 12:30pm, 300ptas.) For 500ptas per person, the tourist office organizes tours of the monuments and *bodegas*. Locals celebrate their sherry during the **Feria de la Manzanilla** (late May or early June). In August, **Carreras de Caballos** (horse races) thunder along the beach, and the **Festival de la Exaltación del Río Guadalquivir** (end of Aug.) brings poetry readings, a flamenco competition, dancing, and bullfights.

CHIPIONA

A quiet seaside village for most of the year, Chipiona (pop. 15,000) takes a summer-time somersault into domestic tourism. This phenomenon began 200 years ago, when Chipiona's salty and mineral-filled waters (the scent pervades the air) were reputed to have medicinal powers. A recuperative hospital was even opened along the beach to nurse ailing patients back to health. Today, the hospital has closed, but locals and day-trippers still descend in throngs upon the sandy beaches.

⑦ PRACTICAL INFORMATION. Los Amarillos buses (☎ 956 37 70 10), on Av. Regla at the top of C. Peral, run to: **Sanlúcar** (30min., 15 per day 6am-8pm, 105ptas); **Cádiz** (1½hr., 9 per day 6am-6:30pm, 480ptas); and **Sevilla** (2hr., 10 per day 6:30am-8pm, 1010ptas). **Linesur La Valenciana** buses (☎ 956 37 12 83) roll to **Jerez de la Frontera** (1hr., 14 per day 8am-10:20pm, 280ptas) from Pl. San Sebastián. Follow C. Larga to reach C. Isaac Peral. The **tourist office**, Plaza de Andalucía, dispenses a free map and beach information. To get there from the bus station, exit to the main intersection and take C. Victor Pradera to C. Peral, then turn at the pharmacy onto C. Larga. The office is up ahead on the left. (☎ 956 37 28 28. Open June-Aug. M-F 10am-1:30pm and 7-9pm, Sa 11am-1pm; Sept.-May M-F 9am-2pm and 5-7pm, Sa 11am-1:30pm.) Services include: **emergency** (☎ 112); **police** (☎ 956 37 10 88), C. Camacho Baños; and the **post office**, C. Padre Lerchundi, 15, near Pl. Pío XII. (☎ 956 37 14 19. Open M-F 8:30am-2:30pm, Sa 9am-1pm.) The **postal code** is 11550.

◢⦗⦘ ACCOMMODATIONS AND FOOD. Accommodations in Chipiona seem to have conspired against budget travelers; consider sleeping in Jerez and commuting to the beach. One luxurious option is **Hostal Gran Capitán**, C. Fray Baldomero, 3, off C. Isaac Peral, which sports a charming patio and large rooms with baths and TVs. (☎ 956 37 09 29; fax 956 37 43 35. Singles 3000-3500ptas; doubles 4000-6400ptas.) The municipal campground, **El Pinar de Chipiona**, on Ctra. Rota at 3km, 800m from the beach, has a supermarket on-site. (☎ 956 37 23 21. Electricity 450ptas; 555ptas per person and per tent, 480ptas per car.) C. Isaac Peral and the small streets nearby are dotted with bars and restaurants specializing in non-Spanish cuisine. Eateries also line Po. Cruz del Mar (at the end of C. Isaac Peral) and the area around Pl. Juan Carlos I and Pl. Pío XII. In the latter, try the scrumptious *pan montadito* (mini sandwiches on hot bread; 200ptas) at **El Rincón de Jabugo.** Another option is **Bar Toro,** Po. Marítimo Cruz del Mar, 24, along the beachfront, which serves *tapas* (250-300ptas) and entrees (750-1500ptas) both indoors and out. (☎ 956 37 03 04. Open daily 9am-12:30am.) The **market**, C. Victor Pradera, is on the left as you exit Los Amarillos bus station (open M-Sa 9am-2pm).

◉⛵ SIGHTS AND NIGHTLIFE. Iglesia de Nuestra Señora de la O, constructed in the 16th century, stands in the gorgeous Pl. Juan Carlos I (open M-F shortly before 8pm mass, Su before 9, 11am, noon, and 8:30pm mass). There are two things to do in Chipiona: sunbathe and party. **Bugui II** in Zona Central, **Picoco** on Po. Marítimo, and **Mohama Palladium** next to the lighthouse are the most popular discos (open summer weekends 10pm-8am). Bars cluster around these clubs, as well as opposite the tourist office on Pl. Andalucía. American-run **Generations Bar**, C. Larga, 38, has sports memorabilia on the walls and computers with **Internet** access. (☎ 956 37 20 87. Beer 125ptas. Internet 800ptas per hr. Open daily 5pm-3am.)

ARCOS DE LA FRONTERA

The Spanish novelist Azorín once described Arcos (pop. 33,000) by saying: "Imagine a long, narrow ridge, undulating; place on it little white houses, clustered among others more ancient; imagine that both sides of the mountain have been cut away, dropping downward sheer and straight; and at the foot of this wall a slow, silent river, its murky waters licking the yellowish stone, then going on its destructive course through the fields... and when you have imagined all this, you will have but a pale image of Arcos." The most popular of Spain's *pueblos blancos*, Arcos is a historic and romantic treasure. Unfortunately, mopeds have made their appearance since Azorín's day, and those in search of a truly peaceful escape may want to try some of the other stops on the *ruta* (see p. 228).

⌐ TRANSPORTATION

Buses: C. Corregidores. **Transportes Generales Comes** (☎ 956 70 20 15). To: **Jerez** (30min., 7 per day 7:20am-7:15pm, 200ptas); **Cádiz** (1½hr., 6 per day 7:20am-7:15pm, 675ptas); **Ronda** (1¾hr., 4 per day 8:20am-4pm, 950ptas); **Costa del Sol** (3-4hr., 4pm, 1535-2060ptas). **Los Amarillos** (☎ 956 70 02 57). To **Jerez** (15min., 8-18 per day 6:30am-7:15pm, 300ptas); **Sevilla** (2hr., 7am and 5pm, 905ptas).

Taxis: ☎ 956 70 13 55 or 956 70 00 66.

✴🛈 ORIENTATION AND PRACTICAL INFORMATION

To reach the town center from the **bus station,** exit left, turn left, then continue uphill for two blocks on. C. Josefa Moreno Seguro, turning right on C. Muñoz Vásquez. Walk for about 20 minutes; the street changes names more than an outlaw on the run (turning into C. Debajo del Corral, then C. Corredera, which then turns into Cuesta de Belén and finally C. Dean Espinosa, also known as Callejón de las Monjas before it reaches the old quarter). Luckily the road runs straight (albeit uphill) the whole time. Mini-buses run every 30 minutes from the bus station to C. Corredera (100ptas); a taxi costs 500ptas.

Tourist Office: (☎ 956 70 22 64; fax 956 70 22 66), on Pl. Cabildo. General info and free map of town. Open June-Aug. M-F 9am-2pm and 5:30-7:30pm, Sa 9am-2pm and 5-6:30pm, Su 10:30am-12:30pm; Sept.-May M-F 9am-2pm and 5-7pm, Sa 10am-2pm and 5-6:30pm. Also offers tours of the old city. M-F 10:30am, 12:30, 5, and 6:30pm; Sa 10:30am, 12:30, and 6:30pm; Su 12:30pm. 400ptas, children free.

Emergency: ☎ 112. **Police:** ☎ 091 or 092. (☎ 956 70 16 52), on C. Nueva.

Medical Emergency: ☎ 956 70 04 98.

Post Office: C. Murete, 24 (☎ 956 70 15 60), overlooking the cliffs and the river. Open M-F 8:30am-2:30pm, Sa 9:30am-1pm. **Postal Code:** 11630.

RUTA DE LOS PUEBLOS BLANCOS
If you've seen pictures of Spain, chances are you have seen shots of perfect little towns with white houses under cloudless blue skies. These villages dot the regions north of Cádiz and Granada and make up a popular hiking and touring circuit known as the *ruta de los pueblos blancos* (route of the white towns). While it is the brightly whitewashed houses that give the route its name, the towns are also characterized by labyrinths of narrow winding streets, medieval castles and churches, and an unhurried, tranquil way of life. The long history of the towns stretches back to before the Romans and Celts, but it was the Moors and their Arabic influence that gave them much of the character they still have today. Arcos de la Frontera, Vejer de la Frontera, and Ronda are probably the most popular pueblos blancos, but there are over 25 in all, divided into four distinct routes, and the lesser-known villages are often the more picturesque. The Spanish Tourist Office maintains a website with maps and information about the routes, as well as tips on finding accommodations (www.spa.es/turismo/spain/pblanco).

ACCOMMODATIONS

Arcos has only a few budget hostels; call ahead during *Semana Santa* and in the summer to be safe. As always, the tourist office has a list of accommodations.

Pensión El Patio, C. Dean Espinosa (a.k.a. Callejón de las Monjas), 4 (☎ 956 70 23 02), in old quarter behind Iglesia de Sta. María. Roomy, with fans or A/C; all have bath and TV. Upstairs rooms have terraces. Doubles 4000ptas, with bath 6000ptas. V, MC.

Hostal San Marcos, C. Marqués de Torresoto, 6 (☎ 956 70 07 21), past C. Dean Espinosa and Pl. Cabildo. Run by a friendly young owner and his family and crowned by a scenic rooftop terrace. Clean rooms with private baths. Call ahead for reservations. Singles 2500ptas; doubles 4500-5000ptas.

FOOD

Restaurants huddle at the bottom end of C. Corredera, while *tapas* heaven can be found uphill in the old quarter.

Bar Típico Alcaraván, C. Nueva, 1 (☎ 956 70 33 97), down from Pl. Cabildo. Popular hangout in a beautiful whitewashed 900-year-old cave draped with bougainvillea. *Tapas* 250-450ptas. Beer 125ptas. Mixed drinks 350-450ptas. Open daily 11:30am-4:30pm and 7:30pm-midnight.

Cafeteria Albeniz, C. Muñoz Vázquez, 10 (☎ 956 70 14 99). A good view of the valley and plenty of outdoor seating make this cafe an extremely popular rest-stop. Coffee 125-150ptas. Sandwiches 300-600ptas. Open M-Sa noon-3pm and 7-11pm.

Los Faraones, C. Debajo del Corral, 8 (☎ 956 70 06 12), downhill from C. Corredera. An Egyptian-Spanish couple serves Arab cuisine and Spanish staples (go for the Arab). Extensive vegetarian *menú* 800ptas. Huge *bocadillo de falafel* 400ptas (not on menu but available on request). A/C. Open Tu-Su 9am-midnight.

SIGHTS AND ENTERTAINMENT

The most beautiful sights in Arcos are the winding white alleys, Roman ruins, and hanging flowers of the old quarter, combined with the view from ☒**Plaza Cabildo.** The plazas earned the nickname *Balcón de Coño* because the view is so startling that people often exclaim *¡coño!* (*#%&*$!) out of disbelief. In this square stands the **Iglesia de Santa María,** a mix of Baroque, Renaissance, and Gothic styles, built between the 15th and 18th centuries. Its most impressive attribute is the well-preserved 14th-century wall-painting. A symbol of the Inquisition—a circular design within which exorcisms were once performed—is still etched into the ground on the church's left side. (Open M-F 10am-1pm and 3:30-6:30pm, Sa 10am-2pm. 150ptas.) The late-Gothic **Iglesia de San Pedro** was built on the site of an Arab fortress in the old quarter. An assortment of Murillos, Zurbaráns, and Riberas decorate the interior. (Open M-F 10am-1pm and 3:30-6:30pm, Sa 10am-2pm. 150ptas.)

An artificial **lake** made in 1960 laps at Arcos's feet, its gentle waters inviting overheated travelers to take a dip; most choose to swim near Porto Alegre, a beach-like strip on the lake. Urban buses descend to the beach, **Mesón de la Molinera** (4 per day, 9:15am-8:15pm, 100ptas). For further information on water sports at the lake, call the **Oficina de Deportes** (☎ 956 70 30 11).

Festivals in Arcos are highly spirited. A favorite is the **Toro de Aleluya,** held on the last Sunday of *Semana Santa.* Two bulls run rampant through the steep, cobbled streets as residents drink and dance flamenco.

CÁDIZ

Cádiz makes for an interesting sandwich, with a powerful ocean on one side, a placid bay on the other, and a whole lot of history in between. Founded by the Phoenicians in 1100 BC, Cádiz (pop. 155,000) is considered the oldest inhabited city in Europe. From the 16th to the 18th century, the Spanish colonial shipping industry transformed the port into one of the wealthiest in Europe. When the New World fervor subsided, liberal politics took over as the hallmark of Cadisian life. In 1808, the city's decisive resistance to Napoleon was crucial in preserving the Spanish nation. Residents subsequently designed the Constitución de Cádiz (1812), an assertion of democratic ideals that inspired a wave of Latin American nationalism. Sadly, it proved ineffectual in its own land. Cadisian liberalism was thwarted again during the Civil War when it fell quickly, and hard, to Franco's Nationalist army. As fitting retaliation, Cádiz continued to rekindle its immortal spirit once a year, celebrating its extravagant *Carnaval*, the only festival of its size and kind not suppressed by Franco's regime. Perhaps Spain's most dazzling party, *Carnaval* makes Cádiz an imperative destination on February itineraries. During the rest of the year, the city offers a little of everything to visitors—a metropolis trimmed by golden sand beaches that puts pebble-strewn eastern neighbors to shame.

Cádiz

🏠 ACCOMMODATIONS
Camas Cuatro Naciones, 8
Hostal Colón, 5
Hostel Imar, 9
Hostal San Francisco, 1
Quo Qádis, 3

🍎 FOOD
Bar-Restaurante Pasaje
 Andaluz, 6
Freiduría Sopranis, 7
Market, 4
Méson Churrasco, 2

▚ TRANSPORTATION

Trains: RENFE (☎ 956 25 43 01), Pl. Sevilla, off Av. Puerto. To: **Pto. de Sta. María** (30min., 35 per day 6am-10:10pm, 310ptas); **Jerez** (40min., 20-35 per day 6:40am-10:10pm, 380ptas); **Sevilla** (2hr., 12 per day 6:35am-9:30pm, 1290ptas); **Córdoba** (5hr., 10-12 per day 8am-6:45pm, 3900ptas); **Madrid** (5hr., 8am and 4:25pm, 9500ptas); **Granada** (6hr., 3 per day 6am-3:10pm, 3700ptas); and **Barcelona** (14hr., 8am and 6:45pm, 9200ptas). RENFE's **AVE** line runs to: **Sevilla** (1½hr., 8am and 4:25pm, 1600-2100ptas); **Córdoba** (2½hr., 8am and 4:25pm, 3700-3900ptas); and **Madrid** (4¾hr., 8am and 4:25pm, 8000-9600ptas.)

Buses: Transportes Generales Comes, Pl. Hispanidad, 1 (☎ 956 22 78 11). To: **Jerez de la Frontera** (1hr., 6-14 per day 7am-9pm, 340ptas); **Arcos de la Frontera** (1½hr., 6 per day 7am-6pm, 680ptas); **Vejer de la Frontera** (1½hr., 6-10 per day 9am-9pm, 570ptas); **Sevilla** (2hr., 11 per day 7am-9:30pm, 1385ptas); **Algeciras** (3hr., 10 per day 7am-8:30pm, 1260ptas); **La Línea** (3hr., 4 per day 8am-8:30pm, 1500ptas); **Málaga** (4hr.; 7, 9am, and 4pm; 2650ptas); **Córdoba** (5hr., 5pm, 2610ptas); **Granada** (6hr., 1:30 and 9pm, 3650ptas). **Transportes Los Amarillos** (☎ 956 28 58 52) leaves from beside the port, off Pl. San Juan de Dios, across from Po. Canalejas. Purchase tickets on the bus or at the office on nearby Av. Ramón de Carranza (open M-F 9:30am-1pm and 5-8:30pm, alternate Sa 10am-1pm). To: **Sanlúcar** (1hr., 5-11 per day 7:15am-9:30pm, 390ptas); **Chipiona** (1½hr., 5-11 per day 7:15am-9:30pm, 470ptas); and **Arcos** (1hr., 2-3 per day 12:30-7pm, 580ptas). Both companies reduce service on weekends. **Secorbus** (☎ 902 22 92 92) has service to **Madrid** (8hr., 6 per day 8:10am-11:10pm, 3075ptas). Buses leave from next to Estadio Ramón de Carranza, just past Pl. Glorieta Ingeniero, in new Cádiz.

Ferry: El Vapor (☎ 956 87 02 70) leaves from the port next to the Comes station and runs to **Pto. de Sta. María** (Tu-Su 45min., 4 per day 10am-6:30pm, 275ptas).

Catamaran: (☎ 670 69 79 05). Leaves the port for **Pto. de Sta. María** (25min., 5-8 per day 7:50am-9pm, 375ptas).

Municipal Buses: (☎ 956 26 28 06). Pick up a map/schedule and *bonobus* (discount packet of 10 tickets for 830ptas) at the kiosk across from the Comes bus station. Most lines run through Pl. España. Beach bums' favorite bus #1 (Cortadura) runs along the shore to new Cádiz (every 10min. 6:40am-1:10am, 115ptas). Bus #7 runs the same route, leaving from **Playa de la Caleta.**

Taxis: ☎ 956 21 21 21.

⚒🛈 ORIENTATION AND PRACTICAL INFORMATION

Cádiz's old town was built on the end of the peninsula, and the new town grew up behind it farther inland. The old town hosts most of the cheap hostels and historic sights (not to mention the bus and train stations), while the new town is home to high-rise hotels, numerous bars and restaurants, kilometers of lovely sand, and deep blue seas. To reach **Plaza San Juan de Dios** (the town center) from the **Comes bus station,** walk along Av. Puerto for about five minutes, keeping the port on the left; the plaza lies to the right, just after a park. From the **Los Amarillos bus stop,** walk inland about 100m. From the **train station,** walk past the fountain, keeping the port on the right, for about two blocks; Pl. San Juan de Dios is the first plaza on the left. The tangled *casco viejo* is pretty disorienting—a map is necessary. When you take the bus into new Cádiz (down the main avenue), hop off at the square with the McDonald's and the modern-looking Hotel Victoria. This square is called **Glorieta Ingeniero.**

Tourist Office: Municipal, Pl. San Juan de Dios, 11 (☎ 956 24 10 01), in the mauve Pozos de Miranda building at the end of the plaza. Bright yellow "i" marks the spot. Useful free map. English spoken. Open M-F 9am-2pm and 5-8pm. On weekends, a kiosk opens in front of the main office (open Sa-Su and holidays 10am-1pm and 5-7:30pm).

Junta de Andalucía, C. Calderón de la Barca, 1 (☎ 956 21 13 13). From the Comes bus station, cross over to Pl. España and walk uphill on C. Antonio López. Office is across Pl. Mina, on the corner of C. Calderón de la Barca and C. Zorrilla. Great staff and good regional and transport info. Free map. Open M and Sa 9am-2pm, Tu-F 9am-7pm.

Currency Exchange: Banco Central Hispano, C. Ancha, 29 (☎ 956 22 66 22). Open M-F 8:30am-2pm. On weekends, try major hotels or **Gades Tour,** Pl. España, 1 (☎ 956 22 46 08). Open M-F 10am-1pm and 5:30-8:30pm, Sa 9am-1:30pm.

Luggage Storage: Lockers at train station (400ptas), to the right on the way out to the platforms. Open daily 8am-11pm.

Emergency: ☎ 112. **Municipal police:** ☎ 091 or 092. In Campo del Sur in the new city.

Medical Assistance: Ambulatorio Vargas Ponce (☎ 062 or 956 28 38 55).

Post Office: (☎ 956 21 39 45), the red building in Pl. Flores, next to the market. Open M-F 8:30am-8:30pm, Sa 9:30am-2pm. **Postal Code:** 11070.

Internet Access: Ciber La Sal, C. Dr. Marañón, 14 (☎ 956 21 15 39). Enter on C. Felipe Abarzuza. Coin-operated computers 400ptas per hr. Open M-Sa 9am-10pm. **Informática Café Internet,** Pl. Glorieta Ingeniero, 1 (☎/fax 956 28 24 59), across from McDonald's, in front of Playa Victoria. 250ptas per 15min., 800ptas per hr. Open June-Aug. M-Sa 11am-2pm and 5-10pm, Su 5-10pm; Sept.-May M-Sa 10:30am-2pm and 5:30-10pm, Su 5:30-10pm.

▌ ACCOMMODATIONS

Most hostels huddle around the harbor, in Pl. San Juan de Dios, and just behind it on C. Marqués de Cádiz. Others are scattered throughout the old town. Singles and private bathrooms are scarce. Call months in advance to find a room during February's *Carnaval;* calling a few days in advance during the summer should be fine.

▨ **Hostal Colón,** C. Marqués de Cádiz, 6 (☎ 956 28 53 51), off Pl. San Juan de Dios. Spotless rooms with sinks and colorful tiles. All rooms have balconies, but the best view—the cathedral surrounded by hundreds of TV antennas—is from the terrace. 2 windowless singles 2000ptas; doubles 3500ptas; triples 4500ptas.

▨ **Quo Qádis,** C. Diego Arias, 1 (☎/fax 956 22 19 39), 1 block from Pl. Falla. Fun youth hostel with clean rooms, roof terrace, TV room, and laundry facilities. Offers flamenco classes, planned excursions, and vegetarian dinners. Breakfast included. Sheets 200ptas. Lockout 11am-5pm for dorms. Reservations wise. Dorms 1000ptas; singles 2100ptas; doubles 3200ptas; triples 4800ptas. 10% discount if you arrive by bike.

Hostal San Francisco, C. San Francisco, 12 (☎ 956 22 18 42), 2 blocks from Pl. España. Patience at the door pays off; spacious dainty rooms surround a Spanish patio with Japanese decor. Huge communal bathrooms. Singles 2400-2500ptas; doubles 3700-4250ptas, with bath and TV 4800-5850ptas. V, MC, AmEx.

Hostel Imar, Pl. Glorieta Ingeniero, 3 (☎ 956 26 05 00; fax 965 26 03 07), right on the main square in new Cádiz. The only semi-budget place next to Cádiz's best beach, Playa de la Victoria. Reservations a must. Doubles 5800ptas, with bath 7600ptas. Visa.

Camas Cuatro Naciones, C. Plocia, 3 (☎ 956 25 55 39), in a corner of Pl. San Juan de Dios. The cheapest place in Cádiz—welcome to the *budget* part of budget travel. Dark, dingy and full of backpackers counting their *pesetas.* Rooms facing the street get a lot of sunshine. Singles 1500ptas; doubles 3000ptas; triples 4000ptas.

▌ FOOD

Once you leave Pl. San Juan de Dios, finding eateries can be a trying experience. Opt for cafes and *heladerías* around Pl. Flores, near the post office and the municipal **market.** If you detest seafood, head to **Supermarket Champion,** next to the municipal market, off Pl. Flores (open M-Sa 9:15am-9:15pm).

Mesón Churrasco, C. San Francisco, 3 (☎ 956 22 72 81), 1 block from Pl. San Francisco. Hanging hams drip juice onto the bar, but the hearty *menú* (800ptas) is more than filling, and olives and bread are free. Crowded with locals. Open daily noon-11pm.

Freiduría Sopranis, C. Sopranis, 2 (☎ 956 25 64 31), off Pl. San Juan de Dios. Every type of seafood imaginable. Take-out only. 1200-2200ptas per kg (feeds 4). Open daily 11:30am-4pm and 7-11pm.

Bar-Restaurante Pasaje Andaluz, Pl. San Juan de Dios, 9 (☎ 956 28 52 54). Outdoor metal tables with plastic covers hardly spell "Ritz," but this casual place has a solid *menú* (900-1200ptas) and happy patrons. Open daily 12:30-4:30pm and 8-11:30pm.

SIGHTS AND ENTERTAINMENT

CATHEDRAL. This gold-domed 18th-century masterpiece is considered the last great cathedral built by colonial riches. Its treasury bulges with valuables—the *Custodia del Millón* is said to be set with a million precious stones. *(From Pl. San Juan de Dios, follow C. Pelota. ☎ 956 28 61 54. Museum open Tu-Sa 10am-1pm and 4-7pm, Sa 10am-1pm. 500ptas, children 200ptas. Cathedral open M-F 5:30-8pm. Mass Su at noon. Free.)*

PASEO. Cádiz's seaside *paseo* runs around the old city and along the Atlantic; walking the path is a good way to get a feel for the layout of the city. Stupendous views of ships leaving the harbor recall the golden age; at the end of the *paseo*, infinite rows of antennae rising from the rooftops recall the 1950s. Exotic trees, fanciful hedges, and a few chattering monkeys enliven the adjacent **Parque Genovés.** *(Paseo accessible via Pl. Argüelles or C. Fermín Salvochea, off Pl. España.)*

MUSEO DE CÁDIZ. Thanks to the fusion of a Fine Arts and Provincial Archaeological Museum, Murillo, Rubens, and Zurbarán live here in unholy union with Phoenician sarcophagi. *(Pl. Mina. ☎ 956 21 22 81. Open for guided tours Tu 9am-2:30pm; for public Tu 2:30-8pm, W-Sa 9am-8pm, Su 9:30am-2:30pm. 250ptas, EU citizens free.)*

MUSEO DE LAS CORTES DE CÁDIZ. This museum is home to an enormous, painstakingly wrought 18th-century ivory and mahogany model of the city upstairs, among other treasures. *(C. Santa Inés, 9. From Pl. Mina, follow C. Zorrilla inland 5 blocks. ☎ 956 22 17 88. Open June-Aug. Tu-F 9am-1pm and 4-7pm, Sa-Su 9am-1pm; Sept.-May Tu-F 9am-1pm and 4-7pm, Sa-Su 9am-1pm. Free.)*

BEACHES

Since Cádiz was built on a peninsula, the exhaust-spewing ships on one coast don't pollute the pristine beaches on the other. **Playa de la Caleta** is the beach most convenient to the old city. Better sand and more space can be found in the new city, serviced by bus #1, which leaves from Pl. España (115ptas). The first beach beyond the rocks is the unremarkable 400m long **Playa de Santa María del Mar.** Next to it, **Playa de la Victoria,** stretching 2500m, has earned the EU's *bandera azul* (blue flag) for cleanliness. Get off bus #1 at Pl. Glorieta Ingeniero in front of McDonald's. A more natural landscape, with fewer hotels and straw mats, belongs to **Playa de Cortadura** (5000m), where the coveted *bandera azul* also flaps proudly. Take bus #1 until it almost reaches the highway, where the bus turns around. The boardwalk ends here, and sunbather density falls steadily the farther one walks.

ENTERTAINMENT

For the cafe scene, try the area around **Plaza Mina,** which is especially lively on winter weekends. **Calle de Manuel Rances,** nearby off C. Antonio López, features some of the hippest bars in the old city. In the new city, C. General Muñoz Arenillas off Pl. Glorieta Ingeniero and the **Paseo Marítimo,** the main drag along Playa Victoria, have some of Cádiz's best bars. **La Jarra** (☎ 956 26 57 74), on C. José G. Agullo, is one such hotspot, blaring *música española* and American top-40 late into the night. Club-rats will prefer **Punto de San Felipe,** a strip of almost 10 bars and clubs, reached by walking north along the sea from Pl. España, just beyond the Comes station (take a right before the tunnel); these establishments don't get going until 4 or 5am. Look for signs on the boardwalk advertising theme parties.

   Carnaval insanity is legendary. The gray of winter gives way to dazzling color as the city hosts one of the most raucous *carnavales* in the world (Feb. 22-Mar. 4 in 2001). Costumed dancers, street singers, ebullient residents, and spectators from the world over take to the streets in a week-long frenzy that makes New Orleans' Mardi Gras look like Thursday night bingo.

ANDALUCÍA

🏠 DAYTRIP FROM CÁDIZ

EL PUERTO DE SANTA MARÍA (30MIN.)

El Puerto's bus stop is in front of Pl. Toros (right next to the bullring), but many buses passing through drop off and pick up passengers at the train station; ask at the tourist office for specific times and departure points. Buses connect El Puerto to: Sanlúcar and Chipiona (20min., 5-11per day 7:45am-9pm, 220-280ptas); Jerez (30min., 9-15 per day 7:20am-9:30pm, 150ptas); and Cádiz (40min., every 20min. 6:30am-10:30pm, 200-300ptas). Trains (☎ 956 54 25 85) depart to: Jerez (12min., 20 per day 7:10am-10:40pm, 215ptas); Cádiz (30min., 35 per day 7am-10:30pm, 380ptas); and Sevilla (1½hr., 12 per day 6:35am-9:30pm, 1100ptas). A Moto Nave ferry (☎ 956 87 02 70) leaves from the port for Cádiz (45min., 4 per day 9am-3:30pm, 275ptas), and a catamaran now also makes the trip. (25min., 5-8 per day 7:25am-8:30pm, 375ptas.)

El Puerto de Santa María (pop.75,000) is one of three cities (along with Jerez and Sanlúcar) that form the renowned "sherry triangle." Neither the beaches nor the *bodegas* are as good as Cádiz's, but people still escape here to sunbathe, and the town's history as a point of departure for exploration and conquest has resulted in a few noteworthy monuments. Columbus's second voyage to the New World was launched here (he even had a house in El Puerto), and as business in the Americas developed, prominent families built houses along the town's winding streets. Before the boom in the 13th century, Alfonso X El Sabio constructed the **Castillo de San Marcos.** Visitors can survey the city from the castle's tower. (Open Tu 10am-2pm, other days by appointment. 500ptas, children 300ptas.) **Iglesia Mayor Prioral** has a Baroque front topped with a one-armed nude and two sidekicks. (Open daily 8:30am-1pm and 6:30-8:30pm. Free.) Two of El Puerto's *bodegas* sponsor tours: **Bodega Terry** has standard tours. (☎ 956 54 36 90. M-F by appointment, Sa noon. 450-750ptas.) **Bodega Osborne,** original sponsor of those gigantic black, bull, signs that dot the countryside (see **Bullboards,** p. 188), has an amusing promotional film in addition to the basics. (☎ 956 85 52 11. Open M-F 10:30am-1pm, 10:30am tour in English. 300ptas.) But most people visit *bodegas* in Jerez and stick to the **beaches** in El Puerto de Santa María. The three options are **Playa La Puntilla** (accessible by city bus #8 or 26, 90ptas), **Playa Santa Catalina-Fuentebravía** (bus #35), and **Playa Valdelgrana** (also bus #35). The latter two lie west of the city and are less popular.

The **tourist office,** C. Luna, 22, is a few blocks up from Pl. Galeras Reales and the ferry stop. From the train station, take a left on Ctra. Madrid, then a right onto C. Pozas Dulces. Follow its right branch (C. Ribera del Río) through Pl. Herrería, then turn right on C. Luna. From the bus stop in front of Pl. Toros, follow C. Santa Lucía past Pl. España to Pl. Juan Gavala. Turn right on C. Luna; the tourist office is 3½ blocks down on your left. Staff has info on the province of Cádiz and everything you would ever want to know about El Puerto. (☎ 956 54 24 13; fax 956 54 22 46. Open daily June-Aug. 10am-2pm and 6-8pm; Sept.-May 10am-2pm and 5:30-7:30pm.) In an **emergency** call ☎ 091 or 092 or ☎ 956 54 18 63 for the **municipal police,** at Ronda de las Dunas. In a **medical emergency** dial ☎ 956 54 33 02 or 956 87 11 11. Find the **post office** at Pl. Polvorista, 3. (☎ 956 85 53 22. Open M-F 8:30am-8:30pm, Sa 9am-2pm.) The **postal code** is 11500.

If you must spend the night in El Puerto, the family-run **Pensión Santamaría,** C. Nevería/C. Pedro Muñoz Seca (*not* C. Dr. Muñoz Seca), 38, keeps 12 small, clean rooms around a relaxing patio. From the tourist office, head up C. Palacios toward Pl. España and take the fourth left. (☎ 956 85 36 31. Singles 1750ptas; doubles 3500ptas, with bath 4000ptas; triples with bath 6000ptas.) **Camping Playa Las Dunas** Po. Marítimo La Puntilla, is a 20-minute walk along the shore from the tourist office or a painless local bus ride (#26); a cafeteria, supermarket, and clean showers await. (☎ 956 87 22 10. 600ptas per adult and per tent, 500ptas per child, 500ptas per car.) Avoid overpriced restaurants near the water; instead, head down C. Misericordia near Parque Calderón. Try **La Tortillería,** C. Palacios, 5, a bar famous for its inventive *tortilla* sandwiches. (☎ 956 87 72 77. Open Tu-Th and Su noon-3:30pm and 8:30pm-1am, F-Sa noon-3:30pm and 8:30pm-2am.) Locals love the seafood at **La Nueva Portovense,** C. Palacio, 19. (Open daily noon-11pm.)

VEJER DE LA FRONTERA

Perched atop a hill of rippling wheat, beautiful Vejer (pop.13,000) is one of Andalucía's most enchanting *pueblos blancos*, with white-washed houses lining cobblestoned alleys and old men discussing politics and bullfights on street corners. The hike up to town is nothing short of painful, but pure relaxation in an unbelievably tranquil atmosphere awaits at the top. Because of its tiny size, Vejer makes the most sense as a daytrip from Cádiz or as a stop en route to Tarifa.

TRANSPORTATION. Getting to Vejer can be a pain. While some buses stop at the end of **Avenida de Los Remedios**, which leads uphill into La Plazuela (10min.), many just leave you by the highway at **La Barca de Vejer**, a small town at the base of the hill. Take one of the numerous taxis waiting by the bus stop (700ptas). The alternative, a steep 20-minute uphill walk is extremely difficult with a backpack. If you do make the trek, climb the cobbled track to the left of the restaurant. When you reach the top, keep walking straight; all roads lead to quiet **Plaza de España**, not to be confused with La Plazuela, which is a tiny intersection (where Av. Los Remedios and C. Juan Bueno meet).

For **bus** info, visit either the tourist office or the telephone kiosk just off La Plazuela toward Av. Los Remedios, where tickets are sold (☎ 956 44 71 46). Short-distance buses run from Av. Los Remedios to **Cádiz** (1½hr., 8 per day 6:15am-7:15pm, 570ptas) and **Sevilla** via **Jerez** (3½hr., 1 per day 6:45am, 1665ptas). For other destinations, descend the hill to La Barca de Vejer, with service to: **Tarifa** (1hr., 9 per day 8am-10pm, 470ptas); **Cádiz** (1½hr., 8 per day 8am-7:15pm, 570ptas); **Algeciras** (2hr., 9 per day 8am-10pm, 700ptas); **Sevilla** (3½hr., 5 per day 8:30am-5:45pm, 1575ptas); and **Málaga** (4hr., 3 per day 8am-5pm, 2045ptas). For a **taxi,** call ☎ 956 45 04 08.

PRACTICAL INFORMATION. The staff at the **tourist office**, C. Marqués de Tamarón, 10, speak some English. (☎ 956 45 01 91. Open June-Aug. M-F 10:30am-2pm and 6-9pm, Sa 10:30am-2pm; Sept.-May M-F 9am-2:30pm and 5-9:30pm.) **Exchange currency** at the **Banco Central Hispano**, C. Juan Bueno, 5, off La Plazuela (open M-F 8:30am-2:30pm). In a **medical emergency**, go to the **Centro de Salud** (☎ 956 44 76 25), Av. Andalucía, and for **police** call ☎ 956 45 04 00. Mail your letters at the **post office,** C. Juan Bueno, 22. (☎ 956 45 02 38. Open M-F 8:30am-2:30pm, Sa 9:30am-1pm.) The **postal code** is 11150.

ACCOMMODATIONS AND FOOD. The best places to stay in Vejer are in *casas particulares* (private houses). One of the best is run by James Stuart, a 12-year resident of Vejer and the owner of the Magnum Bike and Surf shop (see below). Called **Casa de los Pescaítos**, Pl. España, 17, it has one double and two elaborate apartment suites. (☎ 956 44 75 75; fax 956 44 75 77; info@discoverandalucía.com. Double 3500ptas; apartments 5500ptas.) Make sure to call or email in advance—James will probably be at the shop. There are two *casas particulares* on C. San Filmo, up a stone staircase from Av. Los Remedios. The friendly Sra. Rosa Romero owns **Casa Los Cántaros**, C. San Filmo, 14, a beautifully restored Andalucian home with a grape-vined patio. The spotless suites have sitting rooms, antique furniture, private bathrooms, and kitchen access. (☎ 956 44 75 92. Doubles 2500-3000ptas.) Sra. Luisa Doncel keeps tidy little rooms with common bathrooms in **Calle San Filmo, 12.** If Doña Luisa is not at #12, try #16. (☎ 956 45 02 46. Singles 2000ptas; doubles 2500-3500ptas.) Where you stay may depend on which woman you meet first. The cheapest eats are *tapas* or *raciones* at the bars around the Plazuela. At peaceful **Bar El Cura**, Po. Cobijadas, 1, at the bottom of C. Juan Bueno, locals place bets on who can make the solemn owner laugh (or at least crack a smile). Enjoy the gorgeous view around the corner while sipping *fino* (dry sherry) for a mere 50ptas. (☎ 956 45 07 76. Open daily 7am-3pm and 5:30pm-late.)

■ **SIGHTS.** The best way to enjoy Vejer is by wandering along the labyrinthine streets and cliffside *paseos*, stopping occasionally for drinks or *tapas*. As for monuments, the **Castillo Moro**, down C. Ramón y Cajal from the church, offers the usual assortment of battlements and crenelated walls. (Open July-Aug. M-Sa 11am-2pm and 6-9pm; Sept.-June M-Sa 10am-2pm. A Boy Scout troop leads the way around the ramparts. Donations accepted.) The oh-so-pretty **Iglesia del Divino Salvador**, behind the tourist office, is a choice blend of Romanesque, Mudéjar, and Gothic styles. (Open daily 11am-1pm and 7-9pm. Free.)

Ten kilometers from Vejer on the road to Los Caños lies **El Palmar**, 7km of fine white sand and clear waters easily accessible by car. Many beach-goers hitch rides at the bend of Av. Los Remedios or catch the bus to **Conil de la Frontera** and walk southeast along the beach for 3-4km. For information on the town and outdoor activities, consult **Magnum Bike and Surf Shop**, Av. Los Remedios, 44. (☎ 956 44 75 75. Bikes from 1500ptas per day. Surfboards from 1000ptas per day. Open M-F 10:30am-2pm and 6-9:30pm, Sa 10:30am-2pm. V, MC, AmEx.)

■ **ENTERTAINMENT.** Vejer's old quarter hops at night. Leave another little piece of your heart at **Bar Janis Joplin**, on C. Marqués de Tamarón. Sit on plush wicker chairs, enjoy an amazing view, and keep an eye out for Bobby McGee. (Open nightly 9:30pm-late.) Several other popular pubs lie downhill from the Plazuela on C. Sagasta and C. Santísimo. From July to August, everyone dances among the thatched huts at *discoteca* **La Carpa** in Parque de Los Remedios, behind the bus stop. Stupendous terrace views make **Café-Bar El Arriate**, C. Corredera, 55 (☎ 956 44 71 70 or 956 45 13 05), a good place for a *copa* and *tapas* anytime. The village throws brilliant *fiestas*. As soon as the **Corpus Christi** revelry ends in June, Vejer starts anew with the **Candelas de San Juan** (June 23), climaxing with the midnight release of the *toro de fuego* (bull of fire) at midnight. A local (obviously one with a death wish) dressed in an iron bull costume charges the crowd as a bevy of attached firecrackers fly off his body in all directions. The town demonstrates its creativity again during the delirious **Semana Santa** celebrations, when a *toro embolao* (sheathed bull), with wooden balls affixed to the tips of his horns, is set loose through the narrow streets of Vejer on the Sunday of the Resurrection. The good-natured **Feria de Primavera** (2 weeks after *Semana Santa*) is a bit tamer, with people dancing *sevillanas* and downing cupfuls of *fino* until sunrise.

TARIFA

When the wind picks up in Tarifa (pop. 15,000), the southernmost city in continental Europe, visitors can easily understand why it is known, even to locals, as the Hawaii of Spain. Shelter-seeking residents and tourists leave miles of white sandy beaches desolate but for the few, the proud—the windsurfers. You'll see more frame backpacks, stickered vans, Quicksilver attire, and Reefs than you could ever imagine. Still, there is more to Tarifa than just windsurfing—sandy beaches and an enchanting old city make for pleasant afternoon and evening walks.

■ **TRANSPORTATION. Transportes Generales Comes** buses roll in from C. Batalla del Salado, 19. (☎ 956 67 57 55. Window open M-F 7:30-11am and 2:30-7pm, Sa-Su 3-8pm.) **Buses** run to: **Algeciras** (30min., 7-12 per day 6:30am-10:15pm, 230ptas); **Cádiz** (2¼hr., 9 per day 7:25am-8:55pm, 1030ptas); and **Sevilla** (3hr., 3 per day 10:25am-5:10pm, 2075ptas). **Ferries** leave from the port for **Tangier** (40min.; M-Th and Sa-Su 9, 11am, and 5pm; F 9 and 11am; 3000ptas, children 1500ptas.) Prices and travel length for the return trip are the same, but running times are not (M-Th and Sa 10am, 4, and 6pm; F 10am, 4, and 7:45pm; Su 10am and 4pm).

■ **PRACTICAL INFORMATION.** The **tourist office**, Po. Alameda, has a basic plan of the city, a list of hostels, bus schedules, and good adventure sports information. From the bus station, exit toward the castle-shaped arch, follow C. Batalla del Salado for 2½ blocks, turn right before the arch on Av. Andalucía, then left after the park onto tree-lined Alameda. The tourist office is the small glass building under the stairwell. (☎ 956 68 09 93; fax 956 68 04 31. Open daily July 15-Aug. 10:30am-2pm and 6-8pm; Sept.-July 14 M-F 10am-2pm and 5-7pm.) In an **emergency** call ☎ 091 or 092. **Police** (☎ 956 68 41 86), are in Pl. Santa María, and the **Centro de Salud (health center)** can be reached at ☎ 956 68 15 15. Find **Internet access** at **Planet,** C. Santísima Trinidad, 20. (10ptas per min. Open M-Sa 11am-3pm and 5pm-midnight, Su 5pm-12am.) The **post office,** C. Colonel Moscardó, 9, is near Pl. San Maleo. (☎ 956 68 42 37. Open M-F 8:30am-2:30pm, Sa 9:30am-1pm.) The **postal code** is 11380.

▛▟ ACCOMMODATIONS AND FOOD. Affordable rooms line the main strip, C. Batalla del Salado. If you visit in August, call ahead or arrive early. Prices rise significantly in summer. Comfortable and clean **Hostal Villanueva,** Av. Andalucía, 11, features a rooftop terrace with an ocean view and friendly management. (☎ 956 68 41 49. Singles 2500ptas; doubles 4500ptas; triples 7000ptas.) The dining room downstairs serves specialty *paella* for 950ptas (open Tu-Su 1-4pm and 8-11pm). Uphill, where Av. Andalucía becomes C. Amador de los Ríos, **Hostal El Asturian** keeps brightly tiled rooms, all with full bath. Ask for the deluxe quad that is part of an Arab castle adjoining the hostel. (☎ 956 68 06 19. Doubles 4000ptas; triples 6000ptas; quads 8000ptas.) A number of official **campgrounds** lie a few kilometers to the west on the beach (600-700ptas per person); ask the bus driver to let you off. Eateries cluster in the streets through the arch and downhill in the old town. **Café-Bar Central,** on C. Sancho IV El Bravo, has one of the few wind-free *terrazas* in town. It serves a wide variety of *bocadillos* (400-500ptas) and specialty drinks to a chill crowd of locals and backpackers. (☎ 956 68 05 90. Open daily 9am-2am.) Up the street, **Ali-Baba,** C. Sancho IV El Bravo, 8, serves falafel (350ptas) and kebab (400ptas) to go (open daily 1:30-4pm and 7pm-1am).

▣▨▤ SIGHTS, BEACHES AND ENTERTAINMENT. Just outside the old town, next to the port, stand the ruins of the **Castillo de Guzmán el Bueno.** In the 13th century, the Moors kidnapped Guzmán's son and threatened to kill him if Guzmán didn't relinquish the castle. Surprisingly, the father did not surrender, even after they brutally sliced his son's throat right before his eyes. (Open Tu-Su 10am-2pm and 6-8pm. 200ptas, free Su afternoon.) Those with something more tranquil in mind can head 200m south to **Playa Lances** for 5km of the finest white sand on the Atlantic coast. Bathers should be aware of the occasional high winds and a strong undertow; **Playa Chica,** on the Mediterranean adjacent to Playa Lances, is smaller but more sheltered from the winds. **Tarifa Spin Out Surfbase** (☎ 956 23 63 52), 9km up the road toward Cádiz, rents windsurfing boards and instructs all levels, and many campgrounds and hotels along CN-340 between km 70 and km 80 provide instruction and gear for outdoor sports. Pick up a guide at the tourist office. At night, sunburned travelers mellow out in the old town's many bars, which range from jazz to psychedelic to Irish; follow the crowds as they bar-hop, or ask the young tourist office staff for tips on the latest *terrazas* and discos.

ALGECIRAS

Few visitors to Algeciras venture beyond the seedy, noisy port area. Moroccan migrant workers, Spanish army recruits, and an assortment of tourists, all in transit between North Africa and Spain, keep it busy day and night. Hidden in the city proper is the calmer, more attractive old neighborhood, a decent refuge from the chaotic port. Less harried travelers can escape to Tarifa's calming coastline only a short bus ride away (30min.) or saunter off to Gibraltar for the day.

▛ TRANSPORTATION

Trains: RENFE (☎ 902 24 02 02), Ctra. Cádiz, down C. Juan de la Cierva. To **Ronda** (1½hr., 4 per day 7am-7:10pm, 910-1500ptas) and **Granada** (4hr., 4 per day 7am-3:55pm, 2415-2665ptas). Also to **Bobadilla** (1455ptas) with connections to: **Córdoba** (5hr., 5 per day 7am-9:30pm, 2575-4500ptas); **Málaga** (3½hr., noon and 3:55pm, 2100ptas); **Sevilla** (6hr., 4 per day 7am-3:55pm, 3050-3200ptas); and **Madrid** (6hr., 5 per day 7-9:30pm, 5200-9100ptas).

ANDALUCÍA

Buses: Empresa Portillo, Av. Virgen del Carmen, 15 (☎ 956 65 10 55). To: **Marbella** (1hr., 5-7 per day 8am-10pm, 790ptas); **Málaga** (1¾-3hr., 10 per day 8am-10pm, 1390ptas); **Granada** (5hr., 10:30am and 4pm, 2595ptas); and **Córdoba** (6hr., 8am and 3pm, 2905ptas). **Linesur,** Av. Virgen del Carmen, 31 (☎956 66 76 49). To **Sevilla** (3hr., 8 per day 6:30am-9pm, 1985ptas). **Transportes Generales Comes,** C. San Bernardo, 1 (☎956 65 34 56), by Hotel Octavio. To: **Tarifa** (30min., 7-10 per day 7:05am-9pm, 230ptas); **La Línea,** for **Gibraltar** (45min., every 30min. 7am-9:30pm, 235ptas); and **Cádiz** (2½hr., 10 per day 7am-10:30pm, 1260ptas). **Empresa Bacoma,** Av. Marina, 8 (☎956 66 50 67), left of Banco Zaragozano. To **Barcelona** (19hr., 3 per day 10am-9pm, 9900ptas).

Ferries: To get to the ferries from the bus and train stations, walk to the end of C. Juan de la Cierva and turn left. The port entrance will be on the left. **Tickets** are the same price in any of the dozens of travel agencies in town as at the port. Purchase tickets at the port rather than the train station. Allow 30min. to clear customs and board, 90min. with a car. In summer to: **Ceuta** (*buque* ferry 1½hr., 6-10 per day 8am-8:30pm; 2890ptas per adult, 1975ptas per child, 8930ptas per car, 1870ptas per motorcycle; *embarcaciones rápidas* 45min., 18 per day 6:30am-10pm, 3095ptas, under 12 1550ptas) and **Tangier** (2½hr., 12 per day 6am-10pm; 3500ptas, under 12 1600ptas, car 9900ptas, motorcycle 3000ptas; 20% discount with Eurail pass available at some agencies). Service is limited in winter and is not offered during bad weather.

✦❼ ORIENTATION AND PRACTICAL INFORMATION

Stretching along the coast, **Avenida de la Marina,** which turns into Av. Virgen del Carmen north of the port, is lined with travel agencies, banks, and hotels. **C. Juan de la Cierva** runs perpendicular to the coast from the port, becoming **C. San Bernardo** as it nears the **train** and **bus** stations. To reach the **tourist office** from either one, follow C. San Bernardo/C. Juan de la Cierva along the abandoned tracks toward the port, past a parking lot on the left. From the **port,** take a left onto Av. Virgen del Carmen, then a quick right onto C. Juan de la Cierva; the office is on the left. All services necessary for transit to Morocco cluster around the port, accessible by a single gate and driveway. Be wary of imposters who peddle ferry tickets.

Tourist Office: (☎ 956 57 26 36; fax 956 57 04 75), C. Juan de la Cierva, in the tube-shaped, pink glass building. Provides sketch maps (free for Algeciras, 100ptas for maps of other cities). Some English spoken. Open M-F 9am-2pm.

Currency Exchange: Banco Central Hispano, Av. Virgen del Carmen, 9-11, changes traveler's checks without commission. Open June-Aug. M-F 8:30am-2:30pm; Sept.-May M-F 8:30am-2:30pm, Sa 9am-1pm. For a daytrip to Tangier, buying **dirhams** may not be necessary (many places accept *pesetas*), and you will not be able to convert them back to *pesetas*. For longer trips, convert money in Morocco.

Luggage Storage: At **Empresa Portillo bus terminal.** Lockers 400ptas per day. Open daily 7:40am-9:50pm. At **RENFE,** 400ptas per day. Open daily 5:30am-10:30pm. At the **port,** lockers 400ptas per day, **office** 150-500ptas. Open daily 7am-9:30pm.

Camping Gear: Adventura Sport, Ventura Morón, 5 (☎ 956 66 92 34), off Pl. Alta. Hiking boots, tents, sleeping bags, etc. Open June-Aug. M-F 10am-1:30pm and 5:30-9pm, Sa 10:30am-2pm; Sept.-May M-F 10am-1:30pm and 5:30-8:30pm, Sa 10:30am-2pm.

Emergency: ☎ 112. **Police: Local** (☎ 956 66 01 55), C. Ruiz Zorilla.

Medical Assistance: Ambulatorio Central, Pl. Menéndez Tolosa (☎ 956 66 19 56).

Women's Center: Instituto Andaluz de la Mujer (☎ 900 20 09 99).

Gay and Lesbian Services: Información Sexual Telefónica (☎ 901 10 00 68). Open M-Th 10am-2pm and 5-7:30pm, F 10am-2pm.

Post Office: Ruiz Zorilla, 42 (☎ 956 66 36 48). **Lista de Correos.** Open M-F 8:30am-2:30pm, Sa 9:30am-1pm. **Postal Code:** 11203.

ACCOMMODATIONS

Lots of convenient hostels bunch around C. José Santacana, parallel to Av. Marina and one block inland following the train tracks, and C. Duque de Almodóvar, two blocks farther from the water. Ask for a back room—local teenagers cruise the narrow streets on Vespas at ungodly hours.

Hostal Rif, C. Rafael de Muro, 11 (☎ 956 65 49 53). Follow C. José Santacana into the small market square, bear left around the large kiosk and continue up C. Rafael del Muro for 1 block. In a restored 18th-century inner building with a palm-studded inner courtyard, Rif is quiet, cool, and spotless. Management dispenses info on forays into Morocco. Communal showers with hot water. Singles 1200-1500ptas; doubles 2400ptas; quads 4800ptas.

Hostal Residencia González, C. José Santacana, 7 (☎ 956 65 28 43). A decent bargain close to the port. Lounge with TV and nice wood carving. Singles 1750-2000ptas, with shower 2000-2500ptas; doubles 4000-4500ptas, with shower 4500ptas; triples 4500ptas, with bath 6000-6500ptas; quads 6000ptas, with bath 7000ptas.

Hostal Residencia Versailles, C. Moutero Rios, 12 (☎/fax 956 65 42 11), off C. Cayetano del Toro. Close to transportation stations. Decently sized rooms have phones and TVs. Singles with shower 2500ptas; doubles with shower 3300-4000ptas, with bath 4500ptas; triples with bath 5500ptas.

FOOD

Many outdoor cafes line C. Regino Martínez, the main drag. Welcome yourself back from Morocco with *pollo asado* (baked chicken)—or relish your last taste of it—on your way south along Av. Virgen del Carmen, near the port, and on C. Juan de la Cierva. There is a **supermarket** on the corner of C. José Santacana and C. Maroto (open daily 9am-2pm and 5-8pm). Or try the outdoor **market** at Pl. Palma, one block from Av. Virgen del Carmen (open M-Sa 8:30am-2pm).

La Alegría, C. José Santacana, 6 (☎ 956 66 65 09). Whopping portions of Moroccan cooking. Entrees 700ptas. Open daily 9am-midnight.

La Buganvilla (☎ 930 55 05 25), C. García de la Torre. From the Banesto bank corner of Pl. Alta, head down C. Joaquín Costa and take an immediate left down an alley to the unmarked entrance at its end. Eclectic and mellow *tapas* bar draws a young crowd. Delicious *tapas* from 100ptas. Open M-Sa 11am-4pm and 7pm-1am.

Casa Blanca, C. Juan de la Cierva, 1 (☎ 956 57 18 89), the big green building near the tourist office. No-nonsense eatery frequented by port employees. Tortillas (400-500ptas) make a substantial meal. *Menú* 900ptas. Open Su-F noon-11pm.

GIBRALTAR

Anglophiles and homesick Brits will get jolly well excited over Gibraltar's fish 'n' chips, pints of bitter, and changing of the guard. Called "Gib" by locals, this colony takes its Britishness seriously. Citizens use both the Queen's English and Andalucian Spanish, but most look up to Britain and down on mainland Spain.

The ancients considered the Rock of Gibraltar one of the Pillars of Hercules, marking the end of the world. Supernatural connections aside, it remains one of history's most contested landmarks. After numerous squabbles between Moors and Spaniards, English troops stormed Gibraltar's shores during the War of Spanish Succession; the Treaty of Utrecht (1713) solidified Britain's hold on the enclave, now one of the last outposts of Britain's empire. When a 1969 vote showed that Gibraltar's populace overwhelmingly favored its British ties (12,138 to 44), Franco sealed off the border and forbade any contact between Spain and Gibraltar. After 16 years of isolation and a decade of negotiations, the border reopened on February 4, 1985. Tourists and residents now cross with ease, but Gibraltar remains culturally detached from Spain.

ANDALUCÍA

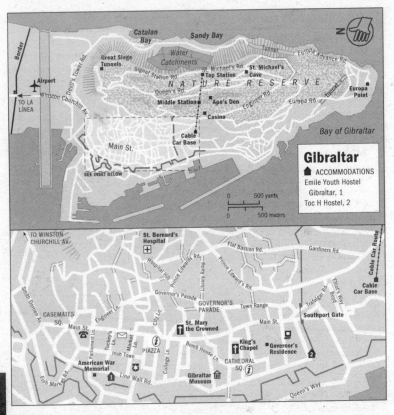

Gibraltar

▲ ACCOMMODATIONS
Emile Youth Hostel Gibraltar, 1
Toc H Hostel 2

Despite the peninsula's history and famed landmarks, it's a tourist trap. Go to Gibraltar to stand atop the imposing Rock, practice your neglected English, and stock up on duty-free liquor and tobacco (cigarettes are 90 pence a pack), then scurry back to the more picturesque Spanish coast.

 POUNDS OR PESETAS Although **pesetas** are accepted everywhere (except in pay phones), the **pound sterling (£)** is the preferred method of payment in Gibraltar. Merchants sometimes charge a higher price in *pesetas* than in the pound's exchange equivalent. Change is often given in English currency rather than Spanish. As of press date, **1£ = 272ptas = US$1.47.**

▐⁼ TRANSPORTATION

Flights: Airport (☎ 730 26). **British Airways** (☎ 793 00) flies to **London** (2½hr., £100-200).

Buses: From the closest Spanish town, La Línea, to: **Algeciras** (40min., every 30min. 7:45am-10:15pm, 235ptas); **Marbella** (1¾hr., 4 per day 7:15am-5pm, 695ptas); **Ronda** (2hr., 8:30am, 990ptas); **Cádiz** (3hr., 5 per day 6:30am-8pm, 1500ptas); **Málaga** (3¼hr., 4 per day 7:15am-5pm, 1270ptas); **Granada** (5-6hr., 7:15am and 2:15pm, 2475ptas); **Sevilla** (6hr., 3 per day 7am-4:15pm, 2640ptas); **Madrid** (7hr., 12:40 and 10:15pm, 3280ptas).

Ferries: Tourafrica Int. Ltd., 2a Main St. (☎ 776 66). To **Tangier** (M and W 8:15am, F 6:30pm; return Tu 3pm, F 9am, Su 3pm). One-way ticket £20, under 12 £10, car £40; round-trip £30, under 12 £15, car £80.

Public Transport: Most bus lines run from one end of the Rock to the other. Buses #9 and 10 go between the border and the Rock for 40 pence or 100ptas.

Taxis: ☎ 700 27.

✦? ORIENTATION AND PRACTICAL INFORMATION

Most buses from Spain terminate in the nearby town of **La Línea**. From the bus station, walk directly toward the Rock; the border is five minutes away. After bypassing the line of motorists, Spanish customs, and Gibraltar's passport control, catch bus #9 or 10 or walk across the airport tarmac (look both ways) and along the highway into town (20min.). Stay left on Av. Winston Churchill when the road forks with Corral Lane. Gibraltar's **Main Street,** a commercial strip lined with most services, begins at the far end of a square, past the Burger King on the left.

Tourist Office: (☎ 450 00; fax 749 43; email gib1@gibnet.gi), Duke of Kent House, Cathedral Square, across the park from Gibraltar Museum. Free street map. Open M-F 9am-5:30pm. **Info Centre** (☎ 749 82), Main St., The Piazza. Open M-F 9:30am-5:30pm, Sa-Su 10am-4pm. There is another office at the border.

American Express: Bland Travel (☎ 770 12), Irish Town St. Holds mail and sells and cashes traveler's checks. Open M-F 9am-6pm.

Luggage Storage: Lockers at the bus station (400ptas). Open daily 7am-10pm.

Emergency: ☎ 199. **Police:** 120 Irish Town St. (☎ 725 00).

Hospital: St. Bernard's Hospital (☎ 797 00), on Hospital Hill.

Internet Access: At the **John McIntosh Hall Library,** 308 Main St., 2nd fl. 75 pence per 30min. Open M-F 9:30am-11pm.

Post Office: 104 Main St. (☎ 756 62). Possibly the world's easiest **Poste Restante** address: Name, Poste Restante, Gibraltar (Main Post Office). Open June-Aug. M-F 9am-2:15pm, Sa 10am-1pm; Sept.-May M-F 9am-4:30pm, Sa 10am-1pm.

Telephone Code: From Britain **(00) 350**. From the US **(011) 350**. From Spain **9567**.

▮◖ ACCOMMODATIONS AND FOOD

The few affordable accommodations in the area are often full, especially from July to September, and camping is illegal. If worse comes to worst, crash in La Línea, a 20-minute trudge across the border. **Emile Youth Hostel Gibraltar,** Montague Boston, off Line Wall Rd., across from the square at the beginning of Main St., offers cramped bunkbeds but clean communal bathrooms. (☎ 511 06. Breakfast included. Lock-out 10:30am-4:30pm, but owner is friendly and flexible. Dorms £12; singles £15; doubles £26.) **Toc H Hostel,** Line Wall Rd., is a maze of plants, cats, and travelers. Walk toward the Rock on Main St., turn right just before the arch at Southport Gate, then left in front of Hambros Bank. (☎ 734 31. Warm showers during the day. Singles £6; doubles £10.) International restaurants in Gibraltar are the easiest to find, but you may choke on the prices. As a back-up, there's always the **Safeway** supermarket in the Europort commercial complex (open 8am-8pm).

♟ SIGHTS AND ENTERTAINMENT

THE ROCK OF GIBRALTAR

Top of the Rock and Nature Reserve are accessible by car or cable car. Cars depart every 10min. M-Sa 9:30am-6pm. £3.65, round-trip £4.90. You can buy a one-way ticket and walk down (1hr.). Tickets, sold until 5:15pm, include admission to St. Michael's Cave and Apes' Den. Nature Reserve. Tickets £5, in your own car £1.50. Castle open daily 9:30am-7pm.

About halfway up the rock is the infamous **Apes' Den,** where a colony of barbary monkeys cavorts on the sides of rocks, the tops of taxis, and tourists' heads. These tailless monkeys have inhabited the rock since before the Moorish invasion; when the ape population nearly went extinct in 1944, Churchill ordered reinforcements from North Africa and now they are proliferating so quickly that monkey population control has become something of an issue for Gibraltar. At the northern tip of the Rock, facing Spain, are the **Great Siege Tunnels**, built into the cliffside in the 1770s to defend against a Spanish assault and to allow for the mounting of the Koehler gun—the first able to fire downward. At the southern tip of Gibraltar, guarded by three machine guns and a lighthouse, **Europa Point** commands a seemingly endless view of the straits. *(Take bus #3 or 1B from Line Wall Rd., just off Main St., all the way to the end. Departs every 15min., £0.40.)* The spooky chambers of **St. Michael's Cave** were cut into the rock by thousands of years of water erosion.

Main St. and Irish Town host throngs of lively **pubs. Bourbon Street,** 150 Main St., has Cajun and English cookin', a pool table, darts, and live music every night. (☎437 65. Open M-Th 11am-midnight, F-Sa 11am-1am, Su 5:30pm-midnight.)

COSTA DEL SOL

The coast has sold its soul to the Devil and now he's starting to collect. Artifice covers its once-natural charms as chic promenades and swanky hotels come between small towns and the shoreline. The Costa del Sol officially extends from Tarifa in the southwest to Cabo de Gata, east of Almería; post-industrial Málaga lies smack in the middle. To the northeast, the hills dip straight into the ocean, where rocky beaches have helped to preserve some of the natural beauty. To the southwest, water seems to wash up on more concrete than sand. That said, nothing can take away from the coast's major attraction: eight months of spring and four months of summer. News of Costa del Sol's fantastic weather has spread far and wide, and July and August bring swarms of pale-skinned Brits and thick-walleted German tourists. Make reservations days in advance to avoid having to sleep on the beach (which is not advisable for solo travelers and women). Alternatively, ask around for *casas particulares.* June is the best time to visit, after summer has hit the beach but tourists haven't. Private bus lines offer connections along the coast itself; trains only go as far as Málaga and Fuengirola. Railpasses are not valid on the Costa del Sol, but train prices are reasonable.

MÁLAGA

Once celebrated by the likes of Hans Christian Andersen, Málaga (pop. 531,140) has since lost much of its charm. In the hundred years since Andersen and other Romantics discovered the city, 19th-century villas have been replaced by 70s highrises, and the beach is better known for its bars than untouched sand. The second-largest city in Andalucía and a critical transportation hub for the province, Málaga has all the requisite historical monuments—fortress, cathedral, bullring—but they are best seen in passing, en route to more enjoyable coastal stops.

▛ TRANSPORTATION

Flights: (☎ 952 04 88 04). From the airport, bus #19 (every 30min., 200ptas) runs from the City Bus sign and stops at the bus station and the corner of C. Molina Lario and Postigo de los Abades behind the cathedral. RENFE's train connecting the city and the airport is cheaper (135ptas) and quicker (12min.). **Iberia,** C. Molina Larios, 13 (☎ 952 13 61 66; 24hr. reservations ☎ 902 400 500).

Trains: Estación de Málaga (☎ 952 36 02 02), Esplanada de la Estación. Take bus #3 at Po. Parque or #4 at Pl. Marina to the station. Tickets and reservations also at the RENFE office, C. Strachan, 4 (☎ 902 24 02 02), off C. Molina Lario. To: **Torremolinos** (20min., every 30min. 5:45am-10:30pm, 160ptas); **Fuengirola** (30min., every 30min. 5:45am-10:30pm, 325ptas); **Córdoba** (2hr., 12 per day 6:45am-8:50pm, 2000-2800ptas); **Sevilla** (3hr., 5 per day 7:45am-7:45pm, 2130ptas); **Madrid** (7hr., 11:25am, 8000ptas); and **Barcelona** (13hr.; 7:15am, 7:40, and 8:05pm; 6700ptas).

ANDALUCÍA

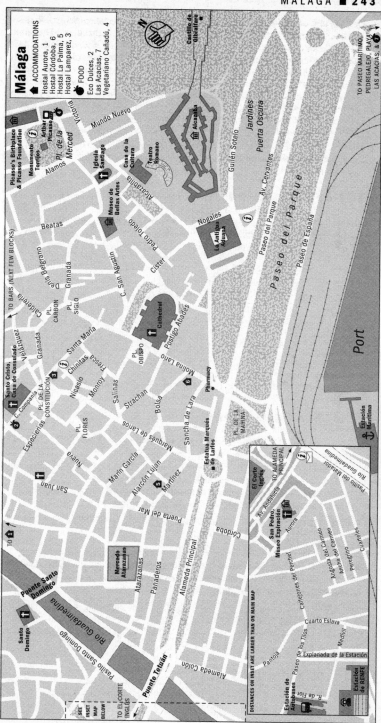

Málaga

ACCOMMODATIONS
Hostal Aurora, 1
Hostal Córdoba, 6
Hostal La Palma, 5
Hostal Lamparez, 3

FOOD
Eco Dulces, 2
Las Acacias, 7
Vegetariano Cañadú, 4

TO PASEO MARÍTIMO, PEDREGALEJO, PLAYA, LAS ACACIAS, &

Castillo de Gibralfaro

Picasso's Birthplace & Picasso Foundation

Artbar Picasso

Monumento Torrijos

Pl. de la Merced

Mundo Nuevo

Victoria

Alamos

Iglesia Santiago

Casa de la Cultura

Alcazabilla

Alcazaba

Teatro Romano

Jardines Puerta Oscura

Guillén Sotelo

Av. Cervantes

Museo de Bellas Artes

Beatas

Luis Belgrano

Granada

Pedro Toledo

Cister

Nogales

La Antigua Aduana

Paseo del Parque

Paseo de España

TO BARS (NEXT FEW BLOCKS)

Calderería

Pl. CARBON

Pl. SIGLO

C. San Agustín

Santa María

Cathedral

Postigo Abadés

Paseo del Parque

Port

Santo Cristo, Casa de Consulado

Granada

Velázquez

Nicasio

Chinitas

Fresca

Monroy

Salinas

Pl. OBISPO

Molina Lario

Pl. DE LA MARINA

Estación Marítima

C. Compañia

Pl. DE LA CONSTITUCIÓN

Espicerías

Pl. FLORES

Nueva

Strachan

Bolsa

Sancha de Lara

Pharmacy

San Juan

Marín García

Marqués de Larios

Estatua Marqués de Larios

Alarcón Luján

Martínez

Puerta del Mar

Córdoba

Mercado Atarazanas

Atarazanas

Panaderos

Alameda Principal

TO

Santo Domingo

Puente Santo Domingo

Pasillo Santo Domingo

Río Guadalmedina

Puente Tetuán

Alameda Colón

TO EL CORTE INGLÉS

SEE INSET MAP BELOW

INSET MAP
DISTANCES ON INSET ARE LARGER THAN ON MAIN MAP

El Corte Inglés

Av. Andalucía

San Pedro, Museo Explicación

Aurora

RIO ALAMEDA PRINCIPAL

Río Guadalmedina

Pasillo del Matadero

Agosta del Carmen

Ancha del Carmen

Peregrino

Cuarteles

Callejones del Perchel

Cuarto Eslava

Medina

Paseo de los Tilos

Pantoja

R. de Flor

Estación de Autobuses

Explanada de la Estación

Estación de RENFE

Buses: Po. Tilos (☎ 95 235 00 61), 1 block from the RENFE station along C. Roger de Flor. To: **Torremolinos** (20min., every 15min. 6:15am-1am, 145ptas); **Fuengirola** (30min., every 40min., 310ptas); **Nerja** (1hr., every hr. 7am-9:30pm, 465ptas); **Antequera** (1hr., 12-14 per day 7am-8:45pm, 525ptas); **Marbella** (1½hr., every hr. 7:45am-9:30pm, 615ptas); **Granada** (2hr., 17 per day 7am-10pm, 1205ptas); **Ronda** (3hr., 4 per day 8:15am-4:30pm, 1220ptas); **Algeciras** (3hr., 17 per day 5am-9:45pm, 1390ptas); **Córdoba** (3hr., 5 per day, 1500ptas); **Sevilla** (3hr., 6-10 per day 7am-3am, 1900ptas); **Cádiz** (5hr., 3 per day 7:30am-midnight, 2605ptas); **Madrid** (7hr., 10 per day, 2650ptas); **Murcia** (6hr., 5 per day 8:30am-midnight, 3890ptas); and **Alicante** (8hr., 5 per day 8:30am-midnight, 4500ptas). **La Línea** runs to **Gibraltar** (3hr., 1 per day, 1650ptas).

Taxis: Radio-Taxi (☎ 952 32 00 00 or 952 33 33 33). A taxi from the town center to the waterfront costs 850-950ptas, to the airport 1300ptas.

✴❷ ORIENTATION AND PRACTICAL INFORMATION

To get to the town center from the **bus station** (20min.), exit right onto C. Perchel, walk straight through the big intersection with Av. Aurora, take a right on Av. Andalucía, and cross the bridge, Puente Tetuán. From here, **Alameda Principal** leads into **Plaza de la Marina.** Or take bus #4 or #21 along the same route (115ptas). For public transportation, walk one block on C. Roger de Flor to the train station (5min.). From the **train station,** you can walk a block up Esplanada de la Estación, turn left toward the bus station, and follow the directions above, or take the C-1 local train (Centro-Alameda) to Puente Tetuán (135ptas). Even better, bus #3 goes directly to Pl. Marina (115ptas). From Pl. Marina, C. Molina Lario leads to the **cathedral** and the old town. C. Marqués de Larios connects Pl. Marina to **Plaza de la Constitución,** while Po. Parque leads past the **Alcazaba.** Farther on, seaside Po. Marítimo stretches toward the lively beachfront district **El Pedregalejo** (bus #11 or a 40min. walk). After dark, be wary of the neighborhoods of **Alameda de Colón, El Perchel** (toward the river from the train and bus stations), **Cruz del Molinillo** (near the market), and **La Esperanza/Santo Domingo** (up the river from El Corte Inglés).

Tourist Offices: Municipal, Av. Cervantes, 1 (☎ 952 60 44 10; fax 95 221 41 20), a little gray house along Po. Parque. Also has a kiosk in front of the post office on Av. Andalucía. Open M-F 8:15am-2:45pm and 4:30-7pm, Sa 9:30am-1:30pm. **Junta de Andalucía,** Pasaje de Chinitas, 4 (☎ 952 21 34 45), off Pl. Constitución at the corner of C. Nicasio. Enter the alley through the arch and take the 1st right. Open June-Sept. M-F 9am-7pm, Sa-Su 9am-1pm; Oct.-May M-F 9am-2pm, Sa 9am-1pm.

Currency Exchange: Banco Español de Crédito, Alameda Principal, 8 (☎ 952 21 15 41), at the intersection with Pta. Mar. Open M-F 8:30am-2pm.

Luggage Storage: Lockers at the **train station** (open daily 7am-10:45pm) and **bus station** (open daily 6:30am-11pm). Both 300-600ptas per day.

Emergency: ☎ 112. **Police:** ☎ 952 12 65 00.

Pharmacy: Farmacia y Laboratorio Laza, C. Molina Lario, 2 (☎ 952 22 75 97). Open M-F 9:30am-1:30pm and 5-8:30pm, Sa 10:30am-1:30pm.

Medical Services: ☎ 952 30 30 34.

Post Office: Av. Andalucía, 1 (☎ 952 35 90 08), just over the Puente Tetuán. **Lista de Correos.** Open M-F 8:30am-8:30pm, Sa 9:30am-2pm. **Postal Code:** 29080.

Internet Access: Artbar Picasso, Pl. de la Merced, 20 (☎ 952 22 62 41). 100ptas per 15min. Student discounts. Open daily 11am-4am.

▚ ACCOMMODATIONS

Most budget establishments are in the old town, between Pl. Marina and Pl. Constitución. Try bargaining if prices seem unreasonable (above 3000ptas for a single, 4700ptas for a double). Excluding August, the market is usually slow.

Hostal La Palma, C. Martínez, 7 (☎ 952 22 67 72), off C. Marqués de Larios. Spotless, with a great family atmosphere. Downstairs rooms share communal baths; upstairs doubles are brand new, with A/C, mini-terraces, and private baths. Singles 2000-3000ptas; doubles 3500-5000ptas; triples 3300-4500ptas; quads 4400-6000ptas.

Hostal Aurora, Muro de Puerta Nueva, 1 (☎ 95 222 40 04), 5min. from Pl. Constitución, away from the busiest areas. Rooms in this quiet home are cool, airy, and clean. Shared bath. Singles 2000-3000ptas; doubles 3200-4500ptas.

Hostal Córdoba, C. Bolsa, 11 (☎ 952 21 44 69), off C. Molina Lario. Neat, decently sized interior rooms with antique furniture. Spotless common bathrooms. Singles 1800ptas; doubles 3000ptas; triples 4500ptas.

Hostal Lamparez, C. Santa María, 6 (☎ 952 21 94 84), off Pl. Constitución, near C. Granada. Basic, clean rooms with floral patterns that match the landlady's dresses. Singles 1800ptas; doubles 2600-3000ptas; triples 4000ptas.

☕ FOOD

Along Po. Marítimo in **El Pedregalejo,** beachfront restaurants specialize in fresh seafood. For a cheap snack, grab some sardines roasted over an open flame (usually in old rowboats) on the beach. The eateries around C. Granada near Pl. Constitución specialize in land creatures. Fresh produce fills the **market** on C. Afaranzas (open daily 8am-2pm), and you can buy groceries at **El Corte Inglés.**

Vegetariano Cañadú, Pl. de la Merced, 21 (☎ 952 22 90 56). A huge variety of refreshingly healthy but hearty meatless. Entrees 700-1000ptas. Open Su-Th 1:30-4pm and 8:30-11:30pm, F-Sa 1:30-4pm and 8:30pm-midnight. V, MC, AmEx.

La Acacias (☎ 952 29 89 46), Playa Las Acacias, El Pedregalejo. Frantic waiters, cheap food, and gusty sea breezes make this one of the liveliest eateries on the waterfront. Entrees 600-1200ptas. Open daily 7pm-1am.

Eco Dulces (☎ 952 22 77 94), C. Compania. Super-cheap, fabulous bakery perfect for breakfast, picnics, afternoon snacks, midnight feasts, or just getting away from seafood. *Bocadillos* 175ptas. Desserts 70-130ptas. Open W-M noon-3pm and 6-9pm.

👁 SIGHTS

ALCAZABA. With 10 major towers inside concentric walls, the Alcazaba is Málaga's most impressive sight. Guarding the east end of Po. Parque, this 11th-century structure was originally built as a fortified palace for Moorish kings. It now houses the ruins of a Roman theater and a **museum** of Moroccan art, and there's an incredible view of the harbor from its ramparts. *(Open W-M 9:30am-7pm. Free.)*

PICASSO FOUNDATION. Picasso may have high-tailed it out of Málaga when he was quite young, but according to local officials, he always "felt himself to be a true *malagueño.*" The painter's birthplace now houses the Picasso Foundation, which organizes a series of exhibitions, concerts, and lectures every October and occasionally throughout the year. *(Pl. Merced. ☎ 952 21 50 05. Open M-Sa 11am-2pm and 5-8pm, Su 11am-2pm. Free.)*

CASTILLO DE GIBRALFARO. An Arab lighthouse was built in this Phoenician castle, which offers sweeping views of Málaga and the Mediterranean. Exploring the grounds alone can be dangerous. *(Buses to Castillo leave every hr. from the plaza below, otherwise it's an uphill hike. Open daily 9:30am-7pm.)*

CATHEDRAL. Málaga's cathedral is a blend of Gothic, Renaissance, and Baroque styles. The cathedral's second tower, which was under construction from the 16th to 19th century, was never completed—hence the cathedral's nickname *La Manquita* (One-Armed Lady). The organs date from 1781. *(C. Molina Larios. ☎ 952 21 59 17. Open M-Sa 9am-6:45pm. 300ptas.)*

MUSEO DE BELLAS ARTES. The Museo de Bellas Artes, soon to include a new Picasso museum, recently opened in the Palacio Buenavista. The hours are in flux; check at the tourist office for the latest info. *(C. San Agustín, 8. ☎ 952 21 83 82.)*

ANDALUCÍA

🎵 ENTERTAINMENT

In summer, young *malagueños* crowd the boardwalk bars in El Pedregalejo. The **Nocturno 1 bus** takes over the Pedragalejo line daily from 12:45 to 5:45am (every hr.). **La Tortuga,** El Pedregalejo, redefines "international relations" as Spanish-language students practice their lessons over mixed drinks and beer. (Drinks 400-1000ptas. Open daily 10pm.) A slightly older crowd drinks *copas* on C. Bolivia, parallel to and a few blocks up from the beach. Stop by the bar **Donde Bolivia 41,** C. Bolivia, 97, to mellow out among shrubbery, pillows, and a pool table. On weekends, crowds invade the bars in the area between C. Comedias and C. Granada, which leads out of Pl. Constitución. **O'Neill's,** C. Luis de Velázquez, 3 (☎ 952 60 14 60), has dark wooden decor, pints of Guinness (550ptas), Celtic music, and friendly bartenders imported from the Emerald Isle.

Málaga's **Semana Santa** celebrations are nearly as grandiose as those in rival Sevilla, and the **Feria de Agosto**—complete with bullfights, flamenco, and a *moraga* (sardine bake on the beach)—is among the most spectacular *fiestas* in all of Andalucía. The *Guía del Ocio* (200ptas), available at newsstands, lists special events, singles bars, and gay and lesbian entertainment.

📑 DAYTRIPS FROM MÁLAGA

GARGANTA DEL CHORRO (1HR.)

Trains leave Málaga and return from Estación del Chorro. Renting a car may be easiest.

Just 50km northwest of Málaga lies the Garganta del Chorro (a.k.a. El Chorro), one of Spain's premier natural wonders. The ravine's rocky terrain rises to 1190m, while the Río Guadalhorce, 180m below, splits the landscape in two. To truly experience El Chorro, walk the **Camino del Rey,** which leads to the bridge above the gorge, from the village of Álora.

TORREMOLINOS (30MIN.)

Portillo Buses (☎ 95 238 24 19) and C-1 local trains (☎ 95 238 57 64) connect Torremolinos to Málaga, Fuengirola, and other destinations.

Along the coast between Málaga and Marbella, Torremolinos offers the classic package-holiday trilogy: sun, sand, and beer. English is spoken, eaten, and drunk everywhere; the only trace of Spain is the pottery and lace that spill out of the souvenir shops. By day, visitors bask in the sun on the wide, sandy beach; by night they wander along **Avenida Palma de Mallorca,** the main thoroughfare, or join the hordes farther west at **La Carihuela,** a sandy expanse dotted with bars and shops. Exit the **train station,** and walk through the alleyway on the right to Av. Palma de Mallorca; turn right and the pedestrian C. San Miguel will be on the right. To reach the beach, turn left onto C. Danza Invisible (at the end of the pedestrian walkway) and turn left at the dead end. Follow Camino de la Playa on the right down the cliffs to the beach. From the **bus station,** exit to the right and follow C. Hoyo to Pl. Costa del Sol and Av. Palma de Mallorca; C. San Miguel is on the left. The **tourist office** is on Pl. Pablo Ruiz Picasso, uphill from Av. Palma de Mallorca. The staff speaks English, German, and French. (☎ 95 237 11 59. Open daily 9am-2pm.) Hostels in Torremolinos tend to get lost amid towering hotels and apartment complexes; look on Cuesta de Tajo and on streets off Pl. Costa del Sol. Prices surge in August. **Hostal La Palmera,** Av. Palma de Mallorca, 37, a few doors down from the post office (enter around the corner), rents airy rooms with big closets. A TV and bar spice up the reception room. (☎ 95 237 65 09. Breakfast 350ptas. Reservations suggested. Singles 2500-3000ptas; doubles 3500-5000ptas; triples 4800-7500ptas.)

FUENGIROLA (45MIN.)

The bus station (☎95 247 50 66), on C. Alfonso XIII, runs buses to: Marbella (30min., every 30min. 7am-10:30pm, 310ptas); Málaga (45min., every 30min. 6:15am-9:15pm, 310ptas); Ronda (2hr., 5 per day 8:55am-5:15pm, 910ptas); and Algeciras (2hr., 11 per day 5:30am-8pm, 1030ptas). Trains leave for Málaga (40min., 6:30am-11:15pm, 325ptas) from the RENFE station (☎902 24 02 02), on Av. Jesús Santos Reino. To get to Los Boliches, get off 1 stop early.

European visitors come to Fuengirola for the beach, though in August it becomes so crowded that there's barely room to open a blanket. Since temperatures on the coast can be as much as 15°F cooler than they are even three blocks inland, visitors crowd into bars on Po. Marítimo and on the beach in Los Boliches, the eastern part of town. The English-speaking staff at the **tourist office**, Av. Jesús Santo Reino, 6, provides free maps. (☎952 46 74 57. Open M-F 9:30am-2pm and 4:30-7pm, Sa 10am-1pm.) Reasonable hostels hide between Pl. Constitución and the beach. **Hostal Costabella**, Av. Boliches, 98, is only one block up from the beach and one block seaward from RENFE's **Los Boliches** stop. Some rooms have beach views; all have private baths. (☎952 47 46 31. Singles 2100-3700ptas; doubles 3200-5000ptas.)

MARBELLA

Like your vacation spots shaken, not shtirred? Scottish smoothie Sean Connery and a host of other international jet-setters choose five-star Marbella (pop. 100,000) to dock their yachts, park their weary jets, and live the glitzy, glamorous life. Surprisingly, though, it's still possible to have a good time on a budget in Marbella. The city's controversial mayor has "cleaned up" many of the "marginal" elements (drug dealers, prostitutes, dogs, fellow politicians, etc.) in town; best catch it now before he sets his sights on backpackers.

▅ TRANSPORTATION

Buses: Av. Trapiche, (☎95 276 44 00). To: **Fuengirola** (30min., every 35min. 7am-10:30pm, 310ptas); **Málaga** (1½hr., every 30min. 6:45am-9:45pm, 610ptas); **Ronda** (1½hr., 4 per day 9am-6pm, 610ptas); **Algeciras** (1½hr., 9 per day 6:10am-8:30pm, 770ptas); **Granada** (4hr., 4 per day 8:30am-5:25pm, 1820ptas); **Sevilla** (4hr., 3 per day 1975ptas); **Cádiz** (4hr., 4 per day, 2030ptas); **Madrid** (7½hr., 10 per day 7:30am-midnight, 3085ptas); **Barcelona** (16hr.; 12:05, 5:40, 10:35pm; 9365ptas).

Taxis: ☎95 277 44 88.

◤ ❷ ORIENTATION AND PRACTICAL INFORMATION

Marbella, 56km south of Málaga, can be reached only by bus. The **bus station** surveys the sea from atop Av. Trapiche. To reach the main strip, exit and walk left, make the first right onto Av. Trapiche, and turn right at the end of the road onto C. Salvador. Continue downhill on Av. del Mercado along the curve and turn left on C. Castillejos, which leads to the perpendicular Av. Ramón y Cajal. This becomes Av. Ricardo Soriano on the way to the super-swanky harbor of **Puerto Banús.** C. Peral curves up from Av. Ramón y Cajal around the **casco antiguo** (old town).

Tourist Office: In the old town (☎95 282 35 50), on Pl. Naranjos. From C. Castillejos, pass through Pl. Victoria and follow C. Estación into Pl. Naranjos. Another office (☎95 277 14 42), is located at C. Glorieta de la Fontanilla. Free maps. English spoken. Both open June-Aug. M-F 9.30am-9pm; Sept.-May M-F 9:30am-8pm, Sa 10am-2pm.

Currency Exchange: Banco Central Hispano, Av. Ramón y Cajal, 9 (☎ 95 277 08 92). Good exchange rates. Open June-Sept. M-F 8:30am-2:30pm; Oct.-May M-F 8:30am-2:30pm, Sa 8:30am-1pm. **ATMs** abound, especially near the *casco antiguo.*

Luggage Storage: At the **bus station** (400ptas). Open daily 6:30am-11:30pm.

Emergency: ☎ 112. **Police:** Pl. Naranjos, 1 (☎ 95 282 24 94).

Hospital: Comarcal, CN-340, km187 (☎ 95 286 27 48).

Post Office: C. Jacinto Benavente, 26 (☎ 95 277 28 98), uphill from C. Ricardo Soriano. Open M-F 8:30am-2:30pm, Sa 9:30am-1pm. **Postal Code:** 29600.

Internet Access: Cibercafé, C. Miguel Cano, 6, 2nd fl. (☎952 90 00 13). 850ptas per hr., students 700ptas per hr. Open daily 10am-midnight.

▌ ACCOMMODATIONS

If you are reservationless, especially from mid-June through mid-September, arrive early and pray for a miracle. The area in the *casco antiguo* around Pl. Naranjos is loaded with quick-filling hostels.

■ **Hostal del Pilar,** C. Mesoncillo, 4 (☎95 282 99 36), off C. Peral, an extension of C. Huerta Chica, or from the bus station off C. San Francisco. The bar downstairs is a great place to start the evening. Breakfast 700ptas. Rooms 1500-2500ptas per person, roof 1000-1500ptas per person.

■ **Albergue Juvenil (HI),** C. Trapiche, 2 (☎95 277 14 91; fax 95 286 32 27), downhill from the bus station. Like a proper hotel, only affordable. Facilities include a large pool, garden, TV room, and basketball court. Call before arriving. Dorms 800-1300ptas per person, over 26 1100-1800ptas. Tents outside 700ptas per person.

El Castillo, Pl. San Bernabé, 2 (☎95 277 17 39), in old town, a few blocks uphill from Pl. Naranjos. Older clientele enjoys the medieval decor in sunny, comfortable rooms with private bathrooms. Singles 2000-3000ptas; doubles 4000-5500ptas. V, MC.

Pensión Aduar, C. Aduar, 7 (☎95 277 35 78). The beautiful courtyard, overflowing with flowers and songbirds, gives a sunny glow to well-kept rooms. Balconies upstairs. Singles 1800-2500ptas; doubles 3000-3600ptas.

Camping Marbella Playa (☎95 277 83 91), 2km east on N-340, on the Marbella-Fuengirola bus line; ask the bus driver to stop at the campground. 325-585ptas per person, 530-980ptas per tent. Open year-round.

◖ FOOD

Terrazas fill Pl. Naranjos but are not particularly budget-friendly—the multilingual menu spells tourist trap. Restaurants farther uphill are less picturesque but easier on the wallet. Locals retreat to Av. Nabeul for deliciously cheap eats. Seaside Av. Miguel Cano and Av. Pta. Mar are both lined with lively and inexpensive bars and cafes. The municipal **market** is on Av. Mercado, uphill from C. Peral (open M-Sa 8am-2pm). A **24-hour minimarket** beckons through the night on the corner of C. Pablo Casals and Av. Fontanilla, which intersects with Av. Ricardo Soriano.

■ **La Casa del Té,** C. Ancha, 7 (☎ 63 916 79 18). Glass-canopied courtyard filled with cushions, paintings, and incense. Vegetarian sandwiches and crepes (275-325ptas), fruit juices (325ptas), and Indian yogurt drinks (300ptas). Open daily 5:30-11:30pm.

■ **Bar Avenida,** Av. Miguel Cano, 11 (☎952 86 23 73). A local dive with the freshest and tastiest seafood at market prices. *Raciones* 600-1200ptas. Open daily noon-midnight.

Pizzería Mama Rosa, Po. Marítimo (☎952 82 00 11), at Av. Miguel Cano. Take-out pizza at its beachfront best. Pizzas 650-1000ptas. Open daily noon-1am.

Picobello (☎952 86 19 93), C. Miguel Cano, 2 blocks from the beach. An elegant tea room with surprisingly affordable pastries, sandwiches, cheese, salads, and sundaes. Teas 200ptas. Coffee 140ptas. Open daily 8am-noon.

◑ ◖ SIGHTS AND BEACHES

Although most visitors come to Marbella for the 320 days of sunshine per year, no visit to the city would be complete without a stroll through the **casco antiguo**, a maze of cobbled streets and ancient whitewashed facades. The **Museo del Grabado Español Contemporáneo,** C. Hospital Bazán, in a restored hospital for the poor, is a treasure-trove of engravings by Miró, Picasso, Dalí, Goya, and contemporary artists. (Open M-F 10:15am-2pm and 5:30-8:30pm. 300ptas.) To the northeast is the **Parque Arroyo de la Represa**, site of the **Museo del Bonsai**. (☎ 95 286 29 26. Open daily 10am-1:30pm and 4-7:30pm. 500ptas, under 12 200ptas.)

City buses along Av. Richard Soriano (destination San Pedro or Hipercor, 135ptas) bring you to chic and trendy **Puerto Banús**, beautifully clean beaches buffered by imposing white yachts, and row upon row of boutiques and fancy restaurants. On exceptionally clear days, the Moroccan coast becomes visible. The port has been frequented by the likes of Sean Connery, King Fahd of Saudi Arabia (who built a huge palace modeled on the White House), Antonio Banderas, and even the late Princess Diana; throngs of Euro-chicks mill about the marina, in search of prospective husbands. With 22km of **beach**, Marbella offers a variety of sizzling settings, from its chic promenade to **Playa de las Chapas**, 10km east via the Fuengirola bus. **Funny Beach**, a 10-minute bus ride along the coast, is a paradise of beach games and sports, including jet-skiing and volleyball. Because of the towering mountains nearby, Marbella's winter temperatures tend to be 5-8°F warmer than Málaga's, and beach season lasts for at least 10 months.

🎵 ENTERTAINMENT

Nightlife in Marbella begins and ends late. The rowdiest corner of the *casco antiguo* is where C. Mesoncillo meets C. Peral. Loud music and cheery Spaniards spill out from **El Güerto**, C. Peral, 9, and **The Tavern**, C. Peral, 7. (Both open daily at 10pm.) A mellow ambiance suffuses the **Townhouse Bar**, C. Alamo, on an alley off C. Nueva, which leads downhill from Pl. Naranjos (opens daily at 10pm). A young international crowd socializes in **Kashmir**, C. Rafina, 8, off C. Aduar, whose smoky lounges might remind Amsterdam natives of home (open daily at 10pm). Between the beach and the *casco antiguo*, C. Puerta del Mar is home to several gay bars, including **Ojo**, C. Puerta del Mar, 9 (open daily at 11pm), and the younger **Bocaccio**, C. Puerta del Mar, 17 (opens at 10pm). On the way to the beach, **Bar Incognito**, Av. Miguel Cano, 15, serves divine cocktails at half-price (350ptas) from 9 to 11pm.

While the *casco antiguo* gets crowded on weekends, the Euro-elite scene at **Puerto Banús** is hopping all week long. Bars and clubs line the yacht port and the parallel C. Ribera, and are hard to miss. Buses run there on the hour all night along Av. Ricardo Soriano (destination San Pedro, 125ptas). Taxis from Marbella (1300ptas) will also stop near the port's most popular people-watching, celebrity-sighting hangout, **Sinatra Bar**. (Mixed drinks 700-1200ptas. Open daily at 11pm.) Around 4am, the action shifts to the clubs, where **Comedia**, (terrace-level, C. Ribera) draws in the younger crowds and **Flicks Bar**, further down C. Ribera rocks until dawn. (Cover for men 2000ptas.)

NERJA

Renowned for pristine beaches and remarkable caves, Nerja (pop. 15,000) offers the best and worst of a coastal resort town. Spectacular beaches are crowded with bikini-clad tourists and flip-flopped English-speakers. At Nerja's **Balcón de Europa**, they gather to catch a glimpse of the Costa del Sol's most stunning ocean view.

🚩 PRACTICAL INFORMATION. The **bus station**, C. San Miguel, 3 (☎ 95 252 15 04), sends buses to: **Almuñécar** (30min., 9 per day 4am-8:30pm, 300ptas); **Málaga** (1½hr., 17 per day 6:30am-9:45pm, 460ptas); **Granada** (2¼hr.; 6:30am, 4:45, 7:15pm; 1100ptas); **Almería** (4hr., 6 per day 8am-7:50pm, 1475ptas); **Sevilla** (4hr.; 2, 7:30am, 4:30pm; 2310-2695ptas). The multilingual **tourist office**, Pta. del Mar, 2, beside the Balcón de Europa, gives out a free map of central Nerja and sells a more detailed version for 100ptas. (☎ 95 252 15 31. Open June-Aug. M-F 10am-2pm and 5:30-8:30pm, Sa 10am-1pm; Sept.-May M-F 10am-2pm and 5-8pm, Sa 10am-1pm.) Services include: **emergency** (☎ 112); **police** (☎ 95 252 15 45), C. Virgen del Pilar; and the **post office**, C. Almirante Ferrándiz, 6. (☎ 95 252 17 49. Open M-F 8:30am-2:30pm, Sa 9am-1pm.) The **postal code** is 29780.

⛌⛌ ACCOMMODATIONS AND FOOD. It's worth breaking a sweat for ⬛**Hostal Estrella del Mar,** C. Bellavista, 5. From the bus station walk up the *carretera,* turn right toward "El Parador," turn left on C. General Asensio Cabanillas, and take the third right. An outdoor pool table and spacious rooms with baths and terraces, most with ocean views. (☎ 95 252 04 61. Breakfast 350ptas. Singles 3000-4000ptas; doubles 4000-5300ptas.) Otherwise, **Hostal Residencia Mena,** C. El Barrio, 15, conveniently located off the Balcón de Europa, has bare rooms. (☎ 95 252 05 41. July-Sept. singles 3200ptas; doubles 4500ptas. Oct.-June singles 2500ptas; doubles 3500ptas.) Overpriced restaurants near and along the Balcón de Europa tempt passersby with views. On Playa de Burriana, **Merendero Montemar** serves fresh fish, English breakfasts (350ptas), and *paella* (with salad, bread, and a drink 1000ptas). In the heart of town, **Coconuts,** C. Pintada, 11, has two-for-one happy hour drinks (daily 8-10pm). A **market** two blocks up C. San Miguel sells produce. (☎ 95 252 01 81. Open daily 8am-2pm.)

⛏ SIGHTS. To get to the ⬛**Balcón de Europa,** a promenade that overlooks Playa de la Caletilla, follow the highway uphill from the bus stop to C. Pintada, which then leads downhill to the *balcón.* Below the cliff are some exploring-worthy **caves,** best approached from the **Paseo de los Carabineros** (off the stairs to the right of the tourist office). The walkway winds along the rocky shore to the east, past **Playa de Calahonda, Playa Carabeo,** and **Playa Burriana.** To reach the sprawling **Playa de la Torrecilla** from the *balcón,* cut west through town to the Playa de la Torrecilla apartments and follow the shoreline from there (15min.). Much closer but more crowded is **Playa del Salón,** accessible through an alley off the *balcón,* to the right of Restaurante Marisal.

DAYTRIP FROM NERJA: LA CUEVA DE NERJA (10MIN.)

Buses run from Nerja (14 per day 8:30am-6:15pm, returns 8:45am-8:30pm; 100ptas).

One of Nerja's most popular attractions is just outside the city. **Cueva de Nerja,** just 5km east of Nerja, has piped-in music and photographers who try to sell tourists a picture of themselves in a cave-shaped frame. The caves consist of large chambers filled with rock formations formed over millions of years by calcium deposits and sea-borne erosion. Intrepid spelunkers have recently discovered a new section of caves, reportedly four times as large as the current attraction. *(Open daily July-Aug. 10am-2pm and 4-8pm; Sept.-June 10am-2pm and 4-6:30pm. 650ptas, children 6-12 350ptas.)* One cave is used as an amphitheater during the spectacular **Festival Cueva de Nerja,** held every July. Paths from **Maro,** a nearby speck of a village, lead to nearly empty, rocky beaches and coves. For local hikes, consult the Nerja tourist office.

ALMUÑÉCAR

In the 4th century BC, a booming fish-salting industry brought prosperity to this Phoenician port town. The Romans took over 100 years later, constructing temples and an aqueduct and naming the town **Sexi.** Though not quite as exciting as its Roman name promises, Almuñécar entices visitors with its seemingly endless boardwalks and alluring tropical environment.

⛏ PRACTICAL INFORMATION. Buses (☎ 950 63 01 40) run from the corner of Av. Fenicia and Av. Juan Carlos I to: **Nerja** (30min., 10 per day 7am-9:15pm, 305ptas); **Málaga** (1½hr., 8 per day 7am-9:15pm, 765ptas); **Granada** (1½hr., 10 per day 6:30am-9pm, 860ptas); and **Madrid** (7hr., 1 per day, 2300ptas). The **tourist office,** in a mauve mansion on Av. Europa, off Av. Costa del Sol, provides info and maps. From the bus station, exit right and follow Ctra. Concepción through the rotary to Av. Costa del Sol; turn left onto Av. Europa and walk past the park. The office is on the right. (☎ 958 63 11 25. Open daily 10am-2pm and 5-8pm.) **Store your luggage** at the bus station. 300ptas. Open daily 6:30am-9:30pm). Services include: **emergency** (☎ 112); **police** (☎ 958 83 86 14), at the Ayuntamiento in Pl. Constitución; and the **Centro de Salud** (☎ 958 63 20 63), Ctra. Málaga.

THE FIFTH BOMB In the 1960s, as Spain was debating whether to join NATO, a USAF B-52 bomber carrying five hydrogen bombs blew up during an in-flight refueling mishap over the village of Palomares, 20km north of Mojácar. Locals looked on as US personnel in radiation suits combed the town in search of the bombs. Four were recovered and identified; the fifth supposedly emerged wrapped in a plastic tarp and without a serial number (Spanish Greenpeace still doubts that it was ever found). Much of Spain boycotted the area's produce (primarily tomatoes), and anti-NATO sentiment reached new heights. To downplay the accident, the US Ambassador and Franco's Minister of the Interior staged a seaside photo-op, swimming in the water before a dozen CIA agents. To top it off, the US built a health clinic in the town. Palomares has since prospered, with copious harvests of tomatoes, leeks, and melons, but some locals still blame defects and illnesses on the mysterious fifth bomb.

ACCOMMODATIONS AND FOOD. Several convenient and reasonably priced hostels lie on Av. Europa. Situated near the tourist office and the beach along Av. Europa, **Hotel Goya**, Av. Europa, 31, has large, pristine rooms with bath, TV, phone, and heating. (☎ 958 63 05 50 or 958 63 11 92; fax 958 63 11 92. Singles 2000-3500ptas; doubles 3000-6000ptas. V, MC.) **Residencia Tropical**, Av. Europa, 39, a half-block from the beach, has a bar and spotless, well-furnished rooms with private bathrooms. (☎ 958 63 34 58. Singles 3500ptas; doubles 6200ptas. V, MC.) Plenty of beach-front *terrazas* line Po. Puerta del Mar and Po. San Cristóbal, providing the perfect place to savor the catch of the day. Locals frequent **Bar Avenida Lute y Jesús**, Av. Europa, 24, which specializes in *fritura de pescado* (fried fish) for 650-1000ptas. (☎ 958 63 42 76. *Menú* 800ptas. Open daily 8am-1:30am.)

SIGHTS AND BEACHES. Alumuñécar's historical protagonists, the Phoenicians, Romans, and Moors, fought over this subtropical paradise, and each left a distinct mark. The Moorish **Castillo de San Miguel** rests atop a massive hill at the front of Pl. Puerte del Mar. The 1900-year-old, 8km long **aqueduct**, 3km up the Río Seco from the tourist office, watered the ancient Roman town; parts of it are still in use. Almuñécar is also home to nearly 100 different species of birds, which nest in the **Parque Ornitológico Loro Sexi**, beside El Castillo de San Miguel, 100m from the beach. (Open daily June-Aug. 11am-2pm and 6-9pm; open Sept.-May 10am-2pm and 4-7pm. 450ptas.) Uphill from the tourist office, **Parque El Majuelo** has 400 varieties of imported plants and great views of Roman ruins (free).

Located on the **Costa Tropical**, Almuñécar is a beach-lover's paradise. The two main beaches are separated by the jutting **Peñón del Santo**. One beach, **Puerta del Mar**, is on the left (when facing the water); the other, **San Cristóbal**, is on the right. Most streets from the bus station terminate at the beach. The easiest way to get there is via Av. Europa (signs point to Playa San Cristóbal). Walk far beyond Puerta del Mar, past Apartamentos Las Goudolas, to beautiful **Playa de Velilla**. Buses to Málaga go through **La Herradura** (15min., 11 per day 7am-9:15pm, 105ptas) a suburb/beach frequented by windsurfers and scuba divers. The largest **nude beach** on the Costa Tropical is **Playa Cantarrijan**.

ALMERÍA

Once one of the poorer cities in Andalucía, Almería has been experiencing growing prosperity as new residents come for the city's temperate climate, flowery promenades, and granular beaches. A huge Moorish fortress presides over the city, but the best parts of Almería are the kilometers of sand stretching along the sea toward Cabo de Gata, at the eastern edge of the Costa del Sol.

TRANSPORTATION. The **airport** (☎ 950 21 37 00), 9km out of town, has daily flights to Madrid and Barcelona. **Trains** (☎ 950 25 11 35), Pl. Estación, run to: **Granada** (2hr., 4 per day, 1740ptas); **Sevilla** (6hr., 3 per day, 4180ptas); and **Madrid** (7hr., 3 per day, 4100ptas). **Buses** (☎ 902 42 22 42) leave from Pl. Estación to: **Mojácar**

(1½hr., 5 per day, 830ptas); **Granada** (2hr., 5 per day, 1300-1600ptas); **Murcia** (3hr., 5 per day, 2125ptas); **Málaga** (3½hr., 7 per day, 1915ptas); **Sevilla** (5½hr., 3 per day, 3800ptas); **Córdoba** (6hr., 1 per day, 2815ptas); **Madrid** (8hr., 3 per day, 3000ptas); **Barcelona** (14hr., 3 per day, 7045ptas); and **Valencia** (3 per day, 4070ptas).

🛈 PRACTICAL INFORMATION. The city revolves around **Puerta de Purchena,** a six-way intersection with a fountain, just down C. Tiendas from the old town. To reach Pta. Purchena from the **bus station** or the connected **train station** by Pl. Estación, follow Av. Estación, turn right onto Av. Federico García Lorca, then go left onto Rbla. Obispo Orbera. Po. Almería runs out of Pta. Purchena to the port; any services you need can be found on Po. Almería or just off it. The **tourist office,** Parque Nicolás Salmerón, distributes a map. Follow Po. Almería out of Pta. Purchena toward the port, and turn right onto Parque de Salmerón. (☎ 950 27 43 55. Open M-F 9am-7pm, Sa 10am-2pm.) Services include: **emergency** (☎ 112); **Hospital Torre Cardenas** (☎ 950 01 60 00); and the **post office,** on Pl. Juan Cassinello, down Po. Almería. (☎ 950 24 02 31. Open M-F 8:30am-8:30pm, Sa 9:30am-2pm.) The **postal code** is 04080. For **Internet access** go to the **Heladería La India II,** Carretera Granada, 304, 15min. from the center of town. (☎ 950 27 48 61. 8am-3pm 300ptas per hr.; 3pm-2am 600ptas per hr.).

🛏🍴 ACCOMMODATIONS AND FOOD. The tourist office provides a list of accommodations, most of which surround Pta. Purchena. There's an **Albergue Juvenil** far outside the town center (35min. walk) on C. Isla Fuerteventura. From Pl. Estación, take C. Ronda, then left onto Av. Cabo de Gata. Continue straight as it becomes C. Bilbao, turn left onto C. Vinaroz, then right on C. Úbeda; Fuerteventura is on the left. (☎ 950 26 97 88. 1300ptas per person, with 3 meals 2800ptas. V, MC.) **Hostal Bristol,** Pl. San Sebastián, 8, beside the church in Pta. Purchena, provides a TV and full bath in every room. (☎/fax 950 23 15 95. July-Aug. call a week in advance. July-Aug. singles 4000ptas; doubles 6000ptas. V, MC.) Cafes line Po. Almería. With ham chandeliers and over 70 types of *tapas* (all 100ptas), **Casa Puga,** C. Jovellanos, 7, in the old quarter, packs them in. (☎ 950 23 15 30. Open M-Sa 11am-4pm and 8pm-midnight. Visa.) For groceries, browse the aisles of supermarket **Champon,** Po. Almería. (☎ 950 23 28 00. Open M-Sa 9:15am-9:15pm.)

🏯📷 SIGHTS AND NIGHTLIFE. Built in 995 by order of Abderramán III of Córdoba, the **🏰Alcazaba,** a magnificent 14-acre Moorish fortress, spans two ridges overlooking the city and the sea. In its heyday, it was said to have housed 20,000 men and their ammunition. (From Pl. Carmen next to Pta. Purchena, follow C. Antonio Vico. ☎ 950 27 16 17. Open daily 9am-8:30pm. 250ptas, free with EU passport. Guided night-tours in Spanish Tu-Th 9:15, 9:30, and 9:45pm.) The **cathedral,** in the old town, looks like a fortress due to repeated raids by Berber pirates. While scabby on the outside, the inside is all Renaissance with a touch of Baroque on the altar. (☎ 609 57 58 02. Open M-F 10am-5pm, Sa 10am-1pm. 300ptas.)

Nightlife centers around the small streets behind the post office. A youthful crowd gathers in pub **Endanza,** while **Venue** (☎ 950 26 19 24) attracts booty-shakers with dance lessons Monday and Tuesday and occasional live music; both are on C. San Pedro off C. Padre Luque. At **Carpa,** a few miles east along the coastal road to Cabo de Gata, a half-dozen tented bars keep the beach party going all night long. Buses stop running around 11pm, but a taxi will go there for about 800ptas.

DAYTRIP FROM ALMERÍA: CABO DE GATA (1HR.)

Autocares Becerra (☎ 950 22 44 03) sends buses from Almería to San Miguel de Cabo de Gata (1hr., every hr. 7am-9pm, 275ptas); Autocares Bernardo (☎ 950 25 04 22) runs to San José (45min., 3 per day, 350ptas).

Thirty kilometers east of urban Almería lies pristine **🏞Parque Natural de Cabo de Gata-Níjar,** a 60km stretch of protected coast and inland environs. The near-desolate peninsula juxtaposes tropical and barren climates; flamingos flock to the area's salt marshes, while a desert and mountains farther inland have hosted a number of movie sets, including the *The Good, the Bad, and the Ugly* and *Lawrence of Arabia*. Many flock to Cabo de Gata to scuba dive by the **Mermaid's Reef**, or windsurf on the rippling waves of **Nijar**, whose nearby town houses a Moorish church and samplings from local crafts. **Grupo J. 126** (☎ 950 38 02 99) or **Ocio y Mar** (☎ 608 05 64 77) provide tourist information and guided tours of the park; contact them a day of two before arriving. Long, sandy shores await in the refreshingly low-key fishing town of **San Miguel de Cabo de Gata** (or simply **Cabo de Gata**). Farther south, the little resort of **San José** boasts one of the nicest beaches on the Spanish Mediterranean coast; it serves as a base for exploring the park.

MOJÁCAR

Mojácar is the ideal getaway—a white-stoned, picture-perfect hilltop village with 17km of smooth coastline and a jamming nightlife. Stunning sunsets sweep the countryside at twilight, when tourists and residents alike relax on the numerous outdoor terraces. During the day, the village clears out as everyone with a brain flocks downhill to the turquoise Mediterranean to escape the heat. The beachfront resorts fill up quickly in July and August, when hordes of international visitors join the large contingent of expats who have made Mojácar their home.

⁋ PRACTICAL INFORMATION. At the bus stop, wait for a yellow local **Transportes Urbanos** bus (2 per hr. 9:30am-midnight, 100ptas) to zip you up to the mountaintop village. Those staying at the beach can catch a yellow bus going in the other direction or just walk down the strip. The 30-minute hike up the mountain to Pl. Nueva, the town center, is not for the faint of heart. **Buses** leave for **Almería** (1½hr.; M-Sa 5 per day, Su 3 per day, 7:30am-10:45pm; 815ptas); **Murcia** (3hr.; M-Sa 3 per day, Su 2 per day; 1300ptas); **Madrid** (7hr., 2 per day, 4340ptas); and **Barcelona** (12hr., 2 per day, 6400ptas). For a **taxi**, call ☎ 630 09 66 09. The **tourist office, post office,** and **police** (☎ 950 47 20 00) are all in Pl. Nueva. (Tourist office ☎/fax 950 61 50 25. Open M-F 10am-2pm and 5-8pm, Sa 10am-1pm.) The **postal code** is 04638.

⚏ ACCOMMODATIONS AND FOOD. Finding a bed at the last minute in Mojácar can be difficult, as many are reserved months in advance. The five elegant bedrooms at **Pensión Torreón**, C. Jazmín, 4, dance in a sea of pastel-stained glass and magenta blossoms and open onto fantastic oceanfront views. From Pl. Nueva, follow C. Indalo out of Pl. Nueva, and take the second right on C. Enmedio, a left downhill along C. Unión, and a right at the end of the hill toward the hostel. (☎ 950 47 52 59. Doubles with shared bath 6000ptas.) To reach the intimate **Pensión La Luna**, C. Estación Nueva, 11, walk up three flights of stairs from Pl. Nueva, continue straight ahead, and turn left at the ceramics shop past the church. Rooms are complemented by spectacular views and woven tapestries. (☎ 950 47 80 32. Breakfast included. Doubles with full bath 6000ptas. Visa.) If all you want is a place to rest your head, **Hostal Esquinica**, C. Esquinica, has small, simple rooms. From Pl. Flores follow C. Arrabal to the right. (☎ 950 475 009. Singles 3000ptas; doubles 5000ptas.) For food, you'll find more variety and better value in the old or new town than at the beach or in Pl. Nueva. **L'arlecchino**, Pl. Flores, through the Moorish arch off C. Puntica, serves fresh Italian dishes on a scenic roof-top *terraza* (☎ 950 47 80 37. *Menú* 1000ptas.) Open daily 12:15-4pm and 7:30pm-12:30am).

⚏ BEACHES AND ENTERTAINMENT. Mojácar's winding streets and breathtaking *miradores* (plazas with picture-perfect views) make it well-suited to daydreaming and romantic strolling. Buses run twice an hour between the town and beach and along the shore (9:45am-1:45pm and 3:45-11:45pm; 100ptas). In town, buses leave from the stop below Pl. Nueva. From the beach, get on at one of the stops along Av. Mediterránea. Choose between a slew of beaches, from the crowded **Playa Del Cantal** and **Playa del Lobo** to the more sedate **Playa Piedra Villazar**.

ANDALUCÍA

Mojácar pulses with nightlife. **Budú Pub,** C. Estación Nueva, has a soaring rooftop terrace that may be the most romantic spot in Mojácar (open nightly 10pm-3:30am). Tented *chiringuitos* (beach bars) sprawl out along the water. Go by car if you can; buses stop running at 11pm, taxis disappear at sundown, and walking the highway is a poorly lit, dangerous alternative. Some of the best *chiringuitos* include **Tito's, Waikiki Pub,** and **Zic Zac Rock** (all on Po. Mediterráneo). Among the most popular discotecas is **Paschá,** on Po. Mediterráneo, where palm trees shade the bar. For a midnight dip, the pool at **Master Disco** (☎ 950 46 81 33), on the highway between the beach and town, is open until 5am. Back in town, expats run more laid-back watering holes. **Time and Place,** in Pl. Flores, serves soothing cocktails, while Gordon pours Guinness and cultivates an intellectual atmosphere at **La Sartén** (a.k.a. Gordon's), on C. Estación Nueva, behind the church. **El Lord Azul,** C. Fronton, 1, plays blues and classic rock for an international crowd well into every night. Pick up the free *Guía de Ocio* leaflet for more detailed info (available at all restaurants and bars). In the second week of June, Mojácar goes haywire with the **Festival de Moros y Cristianos,** a week filled with beautiful costumes, loud parades, and revelry. War and reconciliation are recreated as "hostile" troops surround the city, fire rockets, make speeches, and later join the night-long fiesta in peace.

RONDA

Most people's strongest impression of Ronda, the birthplace of bull fighting, is the stomach-churning ascent to get there. What lasts, however, is the love most come to have for this spectacular city (pop. 38,000). Divided in two by a 100m gorge, Ronda was referred to as Arunda ("surrounded by mountains") by Pliny, Ptolemy, and pfriends, and it was a pivotal commercial center for the Romans. In Moorish times, the Machiavellian Al Mutadid ibn Abbad annexed the town for Sevilla by asphyxiating the ruling lord in his bath. More recently, Ronda has attracted forlorn artistic types—German poet Rainer Maria Rilke wrote his *Spanish Elegies* here, and Orson Welles had his ashes buried on a bull farm outside of town. Only an hour and a half from the resorts of the Costa del Sol, Ronda draws streams of daytrippers to its famed bullring and Moorish monuments. It also makes a convenient base for exploring the *pueblos blancos* to the south.

■★❷ ORIENTATION AND PRACTICAL INFORMATION

The 18th-century **Puente Nuevo** (new bridge) connects the city's old and new areas. On the new side of the city, **Carrera Espinel** (the main street, including the pedestrian-only walkway known as **Calle la Bola**) runs perpendicular to C. Virgen de la Paz. The **train** and **bus stations** are in the new city three blocks away from each other on Av. Andalucía. To reach the tourist office and the town center from the **train station,** turn right on Av. Andalucía and follow it through Pl. Merced past the **bus station** (it becomes C. San José) until it ends. Take a left on C. Jerez, and follow it past lush **Alameda del Tajo** (city park) and the bullring to **Plaza de España** and the new bridge. Cra. Espinel intersects C. Virgen de la Paz between the bullring and Pl. España. From the bus station, turn right and follow the directions above (10min.).

Trains: (☎ 95 287 16 73), Av. Alférez Provisional, near Av. Andalucía. **Ticket office,** C. Infantes, 20 (☎ 95 287 16 62). Open M-F 10am-2pm and 6-8:30pm. To **Algeciras** (2hr., 6 per day, 910ptas). Change at Bobadilla for: **Málaga** (2hr., 6 per day, 1225ptas); **Granada** (3hr., 3 per day, 1800ptas); **Sevilla** (3hr., 2 per day, 2955ptas).

Buses: Pl. Concepción García Redondo, 2 (☎ 95 218 70 61 or 95 287 22 62), near Av. Andalucía. To: **Marbella** (1½hr., 8 per day 6:30am-8:30pm, 605ptas); **Málaga** (2½hr., 8 per day 6:30am-7:30pm, 1120ptas); **Cádiz** (4hr., 5 per day 7am-7pm, 1610ptas); and **Sevilla** (2½hr., 5 per day 7am-7pm, 1335ptas).

Taxis: (☎ 95 287 23 16). From the train station to the town center costs 350ptas.

Tourist Office: Pl. España, 1 (☎ 95 287 12 72). Info on Andalucía and a helpful city map. Open M-F 9am-2pm and 4-7pm, Sa-Su 10am-3pm.

Currency Exchange: Banco Central Hispano, Cra. Espinel, 17, near C. Remedios. Open June-Sept. M-F 8:30am-2:30pm; Oct.-May M-F 8:30am-2:30pm, Sa 9am-1:30pm.

Luggage Storage: At the **bus station** (400ptas per day). Open daily 8am-10pm.

Emergency: ☎ 112. **Police:** (☎ 95 287 13 69), Pl. Duquesa de Parcent.

Medical Services: Emergency Clinic: Notfall (☎ 95 287 58 52), C. Espinillo.

Post Office: C. Virgen de la Paz, 20 (☎ 95 287 25 57), across from Pl. Toros. **Lista de Correos.** Open M-F 8:30am-2:30pm, Sa 9:30am-1pm. **Postal Code:** 29400.

Internet Access: Zaidín Cervecería, C. Pozo, 11 (☎ 95 287 93 77), off Pl. Merced. Loud, lively bar. 300ptas per 30min., 400ptas per hr. Open daily 7am-midnight.

ACCOMMODATIONS AND FOOD

Most budget lodgings are concentrated in the new city near the bus station, along the streets perpendicular to Carrera Espinel—try C. Naranja and C. Lorenzo Borrego. Expect room shortages during the *Feria de Ronda* in the first week in September. The **Hostal Ronda Sol,** C. Almendra, 11, has a cool and leafy patio. (☎ 95 287 44 97. Singles 1700ptas; doubles 2800ptas; triples 4000ptas.) Pay a little extra at **Hotel Morales,** C. Sevilla, 51, and get brand new spacious rooms, all with bath and some with TV. (☎ 952 87 15 38. Singles 3000-3500ptas; doubles 5000-6000ptas. V, MC.) Ronda has a ton of restaurants and cafes, many of them on the streets around Pl. España and heading to Cra. Espinel. **Restaurante Royal,** C. Virgen de la Paz, 40, has large portions. (*Menú* 900ptas. Open daily noon-5pm and 7:30pm-midnight.)

SIGHTS AND ENTERTAINMENT

BRIDGES. Ronda's precipitous gorge, carved by the Río Guadalevín, dips 100m below the **Puente Nuevo,** across from Pl. España. During the Civil War, political prisoners were cast into the canyon's depths from the middle of the bridge. Two other structures bridge the unsettling gap: the innovative **Puente Viejo** was rebuilt in 1616 over an earlier Arab bridge, and the **Puente San Miguel** (a.k.a. **Puente Árabe**) is a prime Andalucian hybrid with a Roman base and Arab arches.

CASA DEL REY MORO. A colonnaded walkway leads to the Casa del Rey Moro (House of the Moorish King), which, despite its name and Moorish facade, dates from the 18th century. From the gardens in back, 365 zig-zagging steps descend to the spring, which once pumped in the town's water supply. Four hundred Christian prisoners were employed in the arduous task of drawing the water. *(C. Cuesta de Santo Domingo, 17. ☎ 952 18 72 00. Open daily 10am-8pm. 600ptas, children 300ptas.)*

ANDALUCÍA

A WHOLE LOT OF BULL
Bullfighting aficionados charge over to Ronda's **Plaza de Toros** (☎ 95 287 41 32), Spain's oldest bullring (est. 1785) and cradle of the modern *corrida*. The **Museo Taurino** inside tells the story of local hero Pedro Romero, the first matador to brave the beasts *a pie* (on foot), and to use the red cape. *(Open daily June-Sept. 10am-8pm; Oct.-May 10am-6pm. 500ptas.)* Romero killed his first bull at age 17 in 1771, the start of a glorious career: "From 1781-1799, it can be said that I killed in each year 200 bulls, whose sum totals 5600 bulls, yet I am persuaded that there may have been more." The museum displays heads of bulls, legendary for their ferocity, and bloodied matador shirts, including the shirt of Francisco Rivera ("Paquirri"), who was gored to death in 1984. Elaborate *trajes de luces,* the traditional costume of the bullfighter, are kept behind glass cases. An exhibit on 20th-century bullfighting showcases photos of Orson Welles, Ernest Hemingway, and their giddy fans. In early September, the Plaza de Toros hosts *corridas goyescas* (bullfights in traditional costumes) as part of the **Feria de Ronda.** The town fills to capacity, so book rooms months ahead.

PALACIO DEL MARQUÉS DE SALVATIERRA. Across the street from the Casa del Rey Moro, behind a forged iron balcony and a stone facade portraying four Peruvian Incas, stands the 18th-century Palacio del Marqués de Salvatierra. With spectacular antiques and gardens, it has belonged to the same family since 1485. (☎ 95 287 12 06. Open M-W and F-Sa 11am-2pm and 4-7pm, Th and Su 11am-2pm. 400ptas.)

IGLESIA DE SANTA MARÍA. The Iglesia de Santa María la Mayor is a large 16th-century church crowned by a Renaissance belfry in the heart of Ronda's old city. The small arch just inside the entrance and the verses from the Koran behind the sacristy are the only vestiges of the mosque that was once here. A faint sign announces *"Julius Divo, Municipe,"* revealing the church's original incarnation as a church consecrated for Caesar. (Off C. Marqués de Salvatierra. ☎ 95 287 22 46. Open daily 10am-7pm. 250ptas, groups 200ptas per person.)

OTHER SIGHTS. Facing east stands the **Minarete de San Sebastián,** part of a former mosque converted into a church after 1485, when Ronda was reconquered by the Christians. On the other side of the church lies the **Palacio de Mondragón,** once owned by Don Fernando Valenzuela, one of Carlos III's ministers. Its Baroque facade, bracketed by two Mudéjar towers, hides 15th-century Arab mosaics and displays about ancient life in Ronda. (☎ 95 287 84 50. Open M-F 10am-7pm, Sa-Su 10am-3pm. 250ptas, students and groups 150ptas per person, under 14 and disabled free.)

ENTERTAINMENT. At night, Ronda congregates in pubs and *discotecas* along C. Jerez and on the streets behind Pl. Socorro, including C. Pozo. **Disco-Bar Niágara,** C. Jerez, 17, blasts music in an aquatic atmosphere. (☎ 929 84 41 82. Open daily 4pm-late.) For a more tranquil evening, head to **Tetería Al-Zahra,** C. Tiendas, 19, where patrons sip tea from all over the world. The Islamic decor, floor pillows, and arched entryways invite long stays. (☎ 95 287 16 98. Open daily 4pm-late.)

◪ DAYTRIP FROM RONDA

CUEVAS DE LA PILETA (25MIN.)

By car, take highway C-339 north (Ctra. Sevilla from the new city). The turnoff to Benaoján and the caves is about 13km out, in front of an abandoned restaurant. Los Amarillos buses run from Ronda to Benaoján (22min.; 8:30am and 1pm, returns to Ronda 9am and 1pm; 195ptas). Plan your return trip ahead of time, as there are no accommodations. Caves open daily 10am-1pm and 4-6pm. Tours last 1¼hr. Groups up to 8 900ptas per person, 9 or more 800ptas per person.

Twenty-two kilometers west of Ronda along the road to Sevilla are the **Cuevas de la Pileta** (☎ 95 216 73 43 or 95 216 72 02), a subterranean museum of bones, stalactites, stalagmites, and paleolithic paintings. Over 22,000 years ago, inhabitants colored the walls with enormous paintings of human figures, animals, and cryptic symbols. Among the most notable are the *Yegua preñada* (pregnant mare) and *Pez* (fish). In order to preserve the climate of the cave, only 25 people are admitted at a time. Wear comfortable shoes and dress warmly. Upon arrival at the caves, climb to the mouth to see if the guide is inside. If no one is around, walk to the farm below and the owner will help you.

ANTEQUERA

Few sunsets rival those from atop the old Moorish fortress at the crossroads of Andalucía, with Antequera's (pop. 41,000) whitewashed houses spread out below. The Romans gave Antequera its name, but older civilizations preceded them—pre-Roman *dólmenes* (funerary chambers built from rock slabs, the oldest in Europe) lie on the outskirts of town. The alluring Sierra del Torcal, a Mars-like wasteland of eroded rock, also looms within 15km of Antequera. Wise travelers kick back here for a few days of inland visual splendor.

▐ TRANSPORTATION

Trains: (☎ 902 24 02 02), on Av. Estación. To: **Málaga** (1½hr., 3 per day, 615ptas); **Sevilla** (2½hr., 5 per day 8:30am-8:45pm, 1100-1600ptas) via **Bobadilla; Ronda** (1½hr., 3 per day 10:20am-7:15pm, 735ptas); **Granada** (2hr., 4 per day 8:35am-10pm, 1000ptas); and **Algeciras** (4hr., 3 per day 10:20am-7:15pm, 1610-1775ptas).

Buses: (☎ 95 284 13 65), on Po. García del Olmo, near the Parador Nacional. To: **Málaga** (45min., 3 per day 9:30am-7pm, 480ptas); **Granada** (2hr., 5 per day 6:30am-1am, 930ptas); **Córdoba** (2¼hr., 9:45am and 5:45pm, 1095ptas); **Sevilla** (2¼hr., 5 per day 4:10am-6:45pm, 1475ptas); **Jaén** (3hr., 3:45pm, 1465ptas); **Almería** (5hr., 2am and 9:30am, 2350ptas); and **Murcia** (5½hr., 1:20 and 9:45am, 3290ptas).

Taxis: (☎ 95 284 10 76 or 95 284 10 08). The center to either station costs 500ptas.

✦▐ ORIENTATION AND PRACTICAL INFORMATION

From the train station, it's a 10-minute hike up a shadeless hill (Av. Estación) to the town center. At the top, continue straight past the market, turn right on C. Encarnación, and go past the Museo Municipal to reach **Plaza San Sebastián.** The **bus station** perches atop a neighboring hill. To reach Pl. San Sebastián from the bus station, walk downhill (to the right as you exit), pass the bullring to the roundabout, and turn left onto Alameda de Andalucía. At the fork, follow C. Infante Don Fernando (the right branch) to the plaza. C. Encarnación connects Pl. San Sebastián to C. Calzada, which leads uphill to **Plaza San Francisco** and the market.

Tourist Office: Pl. San Sebastián, 7 (☎/fax 95 270 25 05). Super-helpful staff has free maps, transport schedules, and town info. Open June-Aug. M-Sa 10am-2pm and 5-8pm, Su 10am-2pm; Sept.-May M-Sa 9:30am-1:30pm and 4-7pm, Su 10am-2pm.

Banks: Banco Central Hispano, C. Infante Fernando, 51 (☎ 95 284 04 61). Open June-Aug. M-F 8:30am-2:30pm; Sept.-May M-F 8:30am-2:30pm, Sa 9am-1pm.

Emergency: ☎ 112. **Municipal Police:** (☎ 95 270 81 04), on Av. Legión.

Pharmacy: on C. Encarnación, near C. Calzada. Open M-F 9:30am-1:30pm and 5-8:30pm, Sa 10am-1:30pm.

Hospital: Hospital Comarcál, C. Polígono Industrial, 67 (☎ 95 284 62 63).

Post Office: (☎ 95 284 20 83), C. Nájera. **Lista de Correos.** Open M-F 8am-2pm, Sa 9:30am-1pm. **Postal Code:** 29200.

▐▐ ACCOMMODATIONS AND FOOD

Accommodations in Antequera are generally cheap and comfortable. Most establishments cluster near C. Infante Don Fernando.

Pensión Toril, C. Toril, 3-5 (☎/fax 95 284 31 84), off Pl. San Francisco. Grandfatherly owner offers clean, bright rooms and guests gather on patios to chat and play cards. The restaurant downstairs has whopping entrees for 500ptas, a *menú* for 800ptas, and generous drinks for 100ptas. Meals served daily 1-4pm and 7:30-9:30pm. Singles 1200ptas, with bath 2000ptas; doubles 2400ptas, with bath 4000ptas.

Pensión Madrona, C. Calzada, 25 (☎ 95 284 00 14), through Bar Madrona. Newly renovated, with A/C, hand-made quilts, and heating in every room. Restaurant/bar downstairs offers a tasty *menú* (900ptas). Singles 1600ptas, with bath 2600ptas; doubles with bath 3600ptas. V, MC.

Hotel/Pensión Colón, C. Infante Fernando, 29 (☎/fax 95 284 00 10). Spotless, classy joint with wood floors, simple furniture, and a labyrinth of hallways. Ritzy section has full baths, A/C, and TVs. Laundry service. Singles 1100-2200ptas, with bath 3200ptas; doubles 2200ptas, with bath 4000-6000ptas. V, MC, AmEx.

⚡ FOOD

Get fresh goods at the **market,** in Pl. San Francisco (open M-Sa 8am-3pm). Ten-aisle **Mercadona,** C. Calzada, 18, has all the basics. (Open M-Sa 9am-9pm. V, MC.)

La Espuelados, C. San Agustín, 1 (☎ 95 284 13 45), on a narrow street off C. Infante Fernando. Pizza 650-1200ptas. Pasta 700-950ptas. Veggie options 600-1000ptas. *Menú* 1000ptas. Open daily noon-4pm and 8-11:30pm. V, MC.

Manolo Bar, C. Calzada, 14 (☎ 95 284 10 15), downhill from the market. Filled with Wild West paraphernalia and good-humored patrons. Ultra-cheap *tapas* (100ptas) may cost more if the staff finds you impolite. Open Tu-Th 4:30-11:30pm, F-Sa 4:30pm-3am.

La Espuela (☎/fax 95 270 34 24), in Pl. Toros. The only restaurant in the world *inside* a bullring. Not surprisingly, the prize-winning kitchen's specialty is *rabo de toro* (bull's tail). *Menú* 2000-2400ptas, worth it if you have the cash. Open daily noon-midnight. V, MC.

👁 SIGHTS

■ **CUEVAS DE DÓLMENES.** Antequera's three ancient caves are the oldest in Europe. Giant rock slabs form the antechamber (storeroom for the dead's posses-sions) and burial chamber. Hefty ancients lugged the mammoth 200-ton roof of the **Cueva de Menga** (2500 BC) over five miles to the burial site. The four figures engraved on the chamber walls typify Mediterranean Stone Age art. The elongated **Cueva de Viera** (2000 BC), discovered in 1905, is also oversized and dark—bring a flashlight. Small, flat stones cement the circular interior walls and domed ceiling of **Cueva de Romeral,** dated from 1800 BC. *(To reach the Cuevas de Menga and Viera, fol-low the signs toward Granada from the town center (20min.) and watch for a small sign on C. Granada just past the gas station. To reach Cueva de Romeral from the other caves, con-tinue on the highway to Granada for another 3km. Just past Almacenes Gómez, one of the last warehouses after the flowered intersection, a gravel road cuts left and bumps into a nar-row path bordered by tall fir trees. Take this path across the train tracks to reach the cave. All three open Tu 9am-1:30pm, W-Sa 9am-6pm, Su 9am-3:30pm. Free.)*

OTHER SIGHTS. Back in town, all that remains of the **Alcazaba** are its two towers, the wall between them, and well-trimmed hedges. The view of the city is tremendous. *(Open Tu-F 10am-2pm. Free.)* Next to it, the towering **Colegiata de Santa María** was the first church in Andalucía to incorporate Renaissance style. *(Open Tu-Su 10am-2pm. Free.)* The plaza in front of the church offers views of the massive **Peña de los Enamorados (Lovers' Rock),** which looks exactly like the Sphinx lying down, if you tilt your head sideways. Legend has it that a Christian man and his Moorish girlfriend, fearing separation by invading soldiers, leaped to their deaths from atop the rock. Downhill, the **Museo Municipal** exhibits avant-garde 1970s paintings by native son Cristóbal Toral alongside dozens of Roman artifacts, including the graceful **Efebo,** a rare bronze statue of a Roman page; the postcards don't do him justice. *(☎ 95 270 40 21. Open Tu-Sa 10am-2pm, Su 10am-1pm. 200ptas.)* The new **Museo Conventual de las Descalzas** is housed in the Convento de las Carmelitas Descalzas and exhibits 16th- and 17th-century paintings, sculptures, and bronze works. *(Open Tu-Sa 9am-12:30pm, Su 10am-12:30pm. 300ptas.)*

🏃 DAYTRIP FROM ANTEQUERA

SIERRA DE TORCAL (15MIN.)

Two-thirds of the 13km to the Sierra de Torcal can be covered by bus; ask the driver to let you off at the turnoff for El Torcal. Casado buses (☎ 95 284 19 57) leave from Antequera (M-F 1pm, 170ptas); the return bus leaves from the turnoff (M-F 4:15pm). For more money, you can also take a taxi (the tourist office will call one for you) to the refugio (round-trip 2700ptas) and have the driver wait.

A garden of wind-sculpted boulders, the Sierra de Torcal glows like the surface of a barren and distant planet. The central peak **El Torcal** (1369m) takes up most of the horizon, but the surrounding clumps of eroded rocks are even more extraordinary. Several trails circle the summit. The green arrow path (1½km) takes about 45 minutes; the red arrow path (4½km) takes over two hours. All but the green path require a guided tour; call the **Centro de Información** for more details. (Open daily 10am-2pm and 4-6pm.) Each path begins and ends at the *refugio* (lodge) at the mountain base. Try to catch the sunset and the spectacular mountainous view from the ▓**Mirador de las Ventanillas;** if you get stranded, spend the night at **Camping el Torcal,** Cta. 331, 6km from Antequera. Expected to open in 2001, it will have a pool, supermarket, and laundry. Call ☎ 952 70 25 05 for up-to-date information.

GRANADA

When Moorish ruler Boabdil fled Granada, the last Muslim stronghold in Spain, his mother berated him for casting a longing look back at the Alhambra, saying, "Weep like a woman for what you could not defend like a man." The Alhambra, a spectacular palace-fortress complex, continues to inspire melancholy in those who must depart from its timeless beauty. The age-old saying holds true: *"Si has muerto sin ver la Alhambra no has vivido"* (If you have died without seeing the Alhambra, you have not lived).

Conquered by invading Muslim armies in 711, Granada eventually blossomed into one of Europe's wealthiest, most refined cities. As Christian armies turned back the tide of Moorish conquest in the 13th century, the city became the last Muslim outpost on the peninsula, surrounded by a unified Christian kingdom. In the latter decades of the 15th century, Fernando and Isabel's troops continually besieged the city. Meanwhile, ruling Sultan Moulay Abul Hassan, obsessing over one of his concubines, ignored his civic duties. When Queen Aïcha caught on, she drummed up local support, had her husband deposed, and thrust her young son Boabdil on the throne. Fernando and Isabel capitalized on the disarray by finally capturing Boabdil and the Alhambra on the momentous night of January 1, 1492. Although the Christians torched all the mosques and the lower city, embers of Granada's Arab essence still linger. The Albaícin, an enchanting maze of Moorish houses and twisting alleys, is Spain's best-preserved Arab settlement and the only part of the Muslim city to survive the *Reconquista* intact.

▐ TRANSPORTATION

Flights: Airport (☎ 958 24 52 37), 17km west of the city. A **Salidas** bus (☎ 958 13 13 09) runs from Gran Vía, in front of the cathedral (M-Sa 5 per day 8:15am-5:30pm, Su 5:30 and 7pm; 425ptas). A **taxi** to the airport costs 2000ptas. **Iberia** (☎ 902 40 05 00) flies to **Madrid** (45min., 2-3 per day) and **Barcelona** (1¼hr., 2-3 per day). Open M-F 9am-1:45pm and 4-7pm.

Trains: RENFE Station (☎ 902 24 02 02), Av. Andaluces. From Pl. Isabel la Católica, follow Gran Vía to the end, then bear left on Av. Constitución; or take bus #3, 4, 5, 6, 9, or 11 from Gran Vía to the stop marked Constitución 3. Turn left on Av. Andaluces; RENFE is at the end. To: **Antequera** (2hr., 5 per day 8:18am-5:26pm, 1000ptas); **Almería** (3hr., 4 per day 10:55am-8:15pm, 1775ptas); **Ronda** (3-4hr., 3 per day, 1510-1775ptas); **Sevilla** (4-5hr., 5 per day 8:18am-5:26pm, 2665ptas); **Madrid** (5-6hr., 3:40 and 11:30pm, 3800ptas); **Algeciras** (5-7hr., 3 per day, 2675ptas); and **Barcelona** (12-13hr., 8:10am and 10pm, 6500ptas).

Buses: All major bus routes originate from the new **bus station** on the outskirts of Granada on Ctra. Madrid, near C. Arzobispo Pedro de Castro.

Alsina Graells (☎ 958 18 54 80) to: **Jaén** (1½hr., 15 per day 7am-9:30pm, 930ptas); **Antequera** (2hr., 5 per day 4:30am-8:55pm, 310ptas); **Málaga** (2hr., 16 per day 7am-9pm, 1205ptas); **Almería** (2¼hr., 20 per day 6:45am-9:30pm, 1350ptas); **Córdoba** (3hr., 9 per day 7:30am-7:30pm, 1540ptas); **Sevilla** (3hr., 9 per day 8am-3am, 2380ptas); and **Cádiz** (4hr., noon and 3:30pm, 3765ptas). **La Línea** runs to **Gibraltar** (4½hr., 8am and 3pm, 2475ptas); **Algeciras** (5hr., 6 per day 9am-8pm, 2595ptas); **Madrid** (5hr., 14 per day 7am-1:30pm, 1980ptas); and the villages in **Las Alpujarras** (10:30am, noon, and 5:15pm; 1000-2000ptas).

Bacoma (☎ 958 15 75 57). To: **Alicante** (6hr., 5 per day, 3410ptas); **Valencia** (8hr., 4 per day, 4995ptas); and **Barcelona** (14hr., 3 per day, 8055ptas). All buses run 10:15am-1:45am.

Autocares Bonal (☎ 958 27 31 00) sends one bus per day to **Veleta** from Palacio de Congresos. Follow C. Acera de Darro from Pta. Real across the river to Po. Violón, or take bus #1 from Gran Vía to the last stop. Tickets sold daily 8:30-9am at Ventorillo Bar across from the palace. Bus departs from the bar at 9am, returns from Veleta at 5:30pm (45min., round-trip 700ptas).

Public Transportation: (☎ 958 81 37 11). Important buses include: "Bus Alhambra" from Pl. Nueva; #10 from the bus station to the youth hostel, Camino de Ronda, C. Recogidas, and C. Acera de Darro; and #3 from the bus station to Av. Constitución, Gran Vía, and Pl. Isabel la Católica. All buses 120ptas, bonobus (15 tickets) 1000ptas. Handy free map at the tourist office.

Taxis: (☎ 958 28 06 54 or 958 13 23 23). Taxis cluster at Pl. Nueva and Pl. Trinidad.

Car Rental: Atasa, Pl. Cuchilleros, 1 (☎ 958 22 40 04). Cheapest car 46,000ptas per week with unlimited mileage and insurance. Prices rise with shorter rentals. Min. age 20, and must have had a license for at least 1 year.

■■❷ ORIENTATION AND PRACTICAL INFORMATION

Municipal **buses** cover practically the entire city, but the best way to explore is on foot. The geographic center of Granada is the small **Plaza de Isabel la Católica,** the intersection of the city's two main arteries, **Calle de los Reyes Católicos** and **Gran Vía de Colón.** To reach Gran Vía from the **RENFE station,** walk 3 blocks up Av. Andaluces to Av. Constitución, and take bus #3, 4, 5, 6, 9, or 11. From the bus station, take bus #3. On Gran Vía, you'll find the **cathedral.** Two short blocks uphill on C. Reyes Católicos sits Pl. Nueva. Downhill, also along C. Reyes Católicos, lie Pl. Carmen, site of the **Ayuntamiento,** and Puerta Real, the six-way intersection of C. Reyes Católicos, C. Recogidos, C. Mesones, C. Acera de Darro, C. Angel Gavinet, and C. Acero del Casino. The **Alhambra** commands the steep hill up from Pl. Nueva.

Tourist Office: Oficina Provincial, Pl. Mariana Pineda, 10 (☎ 958 22 66 88; fax 958 22 89 16; email infotur@dipgra.es). From Pta. Real, turn right onto C. Angel Ganivet, then take a right 2 blocks later to reach the plaza. Possibly the most helpful office in Andalucía. Free maps, posters, and brochures. English spoken. Open M-F 9:30am-7pm, Sa 10am-2pm. **Junta de Andalucía** (☎ 958 22 10 22; fax 958 22 39 27), C. Mariana Pineda. From Pta. Real, take C. Reyes Católicos to Pl. Carmen; C. Mariana Pineda is the 1st left. Free maps, hotel guide (800ptas) and brochures on hiking, hunting, and golf (400ptas). Open M-Sa 9am-7pm, Su 10am-2pm.

Currency Exchange: Banco Central Hispano, Gran Vía, 3 (☎ 958 21 73 00), off Pl. Isabel la Católica. Exchanges money and AmEx traveler's checks without commission. Open May-Sept. M-F 9am-2pm; Oct.-Apr. M-Sa 9am-2pm.

American Express: C. Reyes Católicos, 31 (☎ 958 22 45 12), between Pl. Isabel la Católica and Pta. Real. Exchanges money, cashes checks, and holds mail for members. Open M-F 9am-1:30pm and 2-9pm, Sa 10am-2pm and 3-7pm.

Gay and Lesbian Organizations: Juvenós, C. Lavadero de las Tablas, 15, organizes weekly activities for gay youth. **Información Homosexual Hotline** ☎958 20 06 02.

Luggage Storage: At the **train** and **bus stations** (400ptas). Open daily 4-9pm.

El Corte Inglés: (☎ 958 22 32 40), C. Geril. Follow C. Acera del Casino from Pta. Real onto the tree-lined road. Good map for 475ptas. Open M-Sa 10am-10pm.

Foreign Language Bookstore: Metro, C. Gracia, 31 (☎ 958 26 15 65). Vast foreign language section. Open M-F 10am-9pm, Sa 10am-2pm. **Librería Flash** (☎ 958 52 11 90), Pl. Trinidad. Modest selection. Open M-F 10am-2pm and 5-9pm, Sa 10am-2pm.

Laundromat: C. La Paz, 19. From Pl. Trinidad, take C. Alhóndiga, turn right on C. La Paz, and walk 2 blocks. Wash 400ptas per load; dry 100ptas for 15min. Open M-F 9:30am-2pm and 4:30-8:30pm, Sa 9am-2pm.

Emergency: ☎ 112. **Police:** C. Duquesa, 21 (☎ 958 24 81 00). English spoken.

Pharmacy: Farmacia Gran Vía, Gran Vía, 6 (☎ 958 22 29 90). Open M-F 9:30am-2pm and 5-8:30pm.

Central Granada Overview

♦ ACCOMMODATIONS

Albergue Juvenile
Granada (HI), 1
Hostal Antares, 10
Hostal Sevilla, 2
Hostal Zurita, 3
Hospedaje Almohada, 4
Pensión Olympia, 6
Hostal-Residencia Londres, 5
Hostal-Residencia Zacatín, 8
Hostal Gran Vía, 7
Hostal-Residencia Lisboa, 9
Hostal Residencia Britz, 11
Hostal Venecia, 12
Hostal Gomérez, 13
Hostal Navarro-Ramos, 14

SEE ALHAMBRA MAP, p. 265

ALHAMBRA

Generalife

Puerta Carros

Palacio Carlos V

Puerta de la Justicia

Puerta de las Granadas

Alcázar

Río Darro

S. Ana

Real Cancillería

ALBAICÍN

Walls of the Albaicín

Walls of the Albaicín

Monasterio Santa Isabel la Real

PL. SAN MIGUEL BAJO

Puerta de Elvira

PL. TRIUNFO

PLAZA NUEVA

PL. S. ANA

PL. PADRE SUÁREZ

PL. DE ISABEL LA CATÓLICA

Catedral

Palacio de la Madraza

S. Domingo

PL. MARIANA PINEDA

Corral del Carbón

C. Reyes Católicos

Puerta Real

PL. BIB-RAMBLA

Gran Vía de Colón

Santos Justo y Pastor

PL. UNIVERSIDAD

PL. TRINIDAD

PL. LOBOS

C. Gran Capitán

Monasterio de S. Jerónimo

Basílica San Juan de Dios

Av. del Hospicio

C. Santa Bárbara

Av. Fuente Nueva

C. Madrid

CAMPUS UNIVERSITARIO

C. Doctor Severo Ochoa

PL. SAN ISIDRO

Av. de Murcia

Av. de Pulianas

Paseo de la Cartuja

RENFE

ANDALUCÍA

N

200 yards

200 meters

Medical Assistance: Clínica de San Cecilio, C. Dr. Oloriz, 16 (☎ 958 28 02 00 or 958 27 20 00), on the road to Jaén. **Ambulance:** ☎ 958 28 44 50.

Post Office: (☎ 958 22 48 35; fax 958 22 36 41), Pta. Real, on the corner of C. Acera de Darro and C. Angel Ganinet. **Lista de Correos** and **fax** service. Open M-F 8am-9pm, Sa 9:30am-2pm. Wires money M-F 8:30am-2:30pm. **Postal Code:** 18009.

Internet Access: Net (☎958 22 69 19) has 3 locations: C. Santa Escolástica, 13, up C. Pavaneras from Pl. Isabel la Católica; Pl. de los Girones, 3, 1 block away from first locale; C. Buensucesco, 22, 1 block from Pl. Trinidad. English spoken. 100ptas per hr. All open M-Sa 9am-1am, Su 3pm-1am.

◤ ACCOMMODATIONS

Cheap accommodations abound in Granada. Finding lodgings is a problem only during *Semana Santa* when reservations are highly advised.

NEAR PLAZA NUEVA

Hostels line Cuesta de Gomérez, the street leading uphill to the Alhambra, to the right of Pl. Nueva. Crashing in this area is wise for those planning to spend serious time at the Alhambra complex, but these spots tend to fill up the quickest.

▩ **Hostal Venecia,** Cuesta de Gomérez, 2, 3rd fl. (☎ 958 22 39 87). Wake up to a soothing cup of tea, candles, and a hint of incense. A hospitable French and Spanish couple have made this exceptionally clean and cozy abode the most appealing bargain in town. Singles 1800ptas; doubles 3500ptas; triples and quads 1700ptas per person.

▩ **Hostal Residencia Britz,** Cuesta de Gomérez, 1 (☎/fax 958 22 36 52), on the corner of Pl. Nueva. Large rooms with luxurious beds and green-tiled bathrooms. Laundry 600ptas. 24hr. reception. Singles 2500ptas, with bath 4000ptas; doubles 4100ptas, with bath 5700ptas. 6% discount with *Let's Go* (if you pay in cash). V, MC.

Hostal Gomérez, Cuesta de Gomérez, 10 (☎ 958 22 44 37). Clean rooms with firm beds. Multilingual owner will assist guests planning longer stays. Laundry 1000ptas per load. Singles 1700ptas; doubles 2800ptas; triple 3800ptas. 100-200pta *Let's Go* discount in the off season.

Hostal Navarro-Ramos, Cuesta de Gomérez, 21 (☎ 958 25 05 55). Comfortable and cool in the evening. Small balconies in some rooms. Showers 150ptas. Singles 1600ptas; doubles 2600ptas, with bath 4000ptas; triples with bath 5300ptas.

NEAR THE CATHEDRAL/UNIVERSITY

The area along C. Mesones and C. Alhóndiga is close to the cathedral, Pta. Real, and Pl. Isabel la Católica. Hostels cluster around Pl. Trinidad, a cozy square at the end of C. Mesones when coming from Pta. Real. Many *pensiones* around C. Mesones cater to students during the academic year but free up during the summer. The ones listed below are open year-round.

▩ **Hospedaje Almohada,** C. Postigo de Zarate, 4 (☎ 958 20 74 46). Walk 1 block from Pl. Trinidad along C. Duquesa; it's to the right down C. Málaga (no sign, but a big red door). A successful experiment in communal living: guests enjoy socializing in the courtyard, living room, and kitchen. Laundry 500ptas per load. Singles 2000ptas; doubles 3700ptas. Longer stays 33,000-36,000ptas per month.

Hostal-Residencia Lisboa, Pl. Carmen, 29 (☎ 958 22 14 13 or 958 22 14 14; fax 958 22 14 87). Take C. Reyes Católicos from Pl. Isabel la Católica; Pl. Carmen is on the left. Rooms have phones and fans. Singles 2700ptas, with bath 4000ptas; doubles 4000ptas, with bath 5800ptas; triples 5400ptas, with bath 7800ptas. V, MC.

Hostal Zurita, Pl. Trinidad, 7 (☎ 958 27 50 20). Beautiful rooms, high-quality beds, remote-controlled A/C, and 24hr. hot water. Double-paned balconies ward off outside noise, while the chirping of Zurita's many caged birds fills the house. Singles 2000ptas; doubles 4000ptas, with bath 5000ptas; triples 5000ptas, with bath 7000ptas.

Hostal Sevilla, C. Fábrica Vieja, 18 (☎ 958 27 85 13). From Pta. Real, follow C. Alhóndiga into C. Fábrica Vieja. Spotless, well-furnished, and cool rooms. Singles 2300ptas, with bath 3000ptas; doubles 3300ptas, with bath 4500ptas; triples 4800ptas.

Hostal-Residencia Zacatín, C. Ermita, 11 (☎ 958 22 11 55). Enter through the Alcaicería archway from C. Reyes Católicos; C. Ermita is on the left. Ideal location. Rooms are amply sized; baths are immense. Singles 1900ptas, with bath 2700ptas; doubles 3200ptas, with shower 3600ptas, with bath 4400ptas.

ALONG GRAN VÍA DE COLÓN

Hostels are sprinkled along Gran Vía. In all cases, rooms with balconies over the street are much noisier than those that open onto an inner patio.

◪ Hostal Antares, C. Cetti Meriém, 10 (☎ 958 22 83 13), on the corner of C. Elvira, 1 block from Gran Vía. Spotless and cheap in a great location, 1 block from the cathedral. All rooms have balconies and sinks, and there are plenty of shared bathrooms. Winter heating. Singles 2500ptas; doubles 3500ptas, with bath 5500ptas; triples 5250ptas.

Hostal Gran Vía, Gran Vía, 17 (☎ 958 27 92 12), about 4 blocks from Pl. Isabel la Católica. Clean rooms with fans. Singles 4500ptas; doubles 3000-3500ptas, with bath 4500ptas; triples with bath 5500ptas.

Hostal-Residencia Londres, Gran Vía, 29, 6th fl. (☎ 958 27 80 34). Pretty rooms and a big patio with views of the Alhambra. 1 large bathroom for every 2 bedrooms. Singles 2500ptas; doubles 3500ptas; 1500ptas per additional person.

Pensión Olympia, Alvaro de Bazán, 6 (☎ 958 27 82 38). From Pl. Isabel, walk 6 blocks down Gran Vía and turn right. A cheaper version of Hostal Gran Vía (same owner). Communal bathrooms. Singles 2000ptas; doubles 3000ptas, with bath 4000ptas. V, MC.

ELSEWHERE

Albergue Juvenil Granada (HI), Ramón y Cajal, 2 (☎ 958 00 29 00 or 958 00 29 01; fax 958 00 29 08). From the bus station take bus #10; from the train station #11; ask the driver to stop at "El Estadio de la Juventud." A peach building across the field on the left. Spacious rooms. 24hr. reception. Towels 175ptas. Dorms 1800ptas, over 26 2300ptas. Non-HI guests can join by paying an extra 300ptas per night for 6 nights.

CAMPING

Buses serve five campgrounds within 5km of Granada. Check the departure schedules at the tourist office, sit up front, and ask bus drivers to alert you to your stop.

Sierra Nevada, Av. Madrid, 107 (☎ 958 15 00 62, fax 958 15 09 54). Take bus #3 or 10. Lots of shady trees, modern facilities, and free hot showers. If you arrive when the town fair is here, stay elsewhere or you'll have clown nightmares. 560ptas per person, per tent, and per car. Children under 10 460ptas. Open Mar.-Oct.

María Eugenia, Ctra. Nacional, 342 (☎ 958 20 06 06), at km 436 on the road to Málaga. Take the Santa Fé or Chauchina bus from the train station (every 30min.). 425ptas per person, per tent, and per car. Children 325ptas. Open year-round.

Los Alamos (☎ 958 20 84 79), next door to María Eugenia. Showers 50ptas. 1300ptas per person, per tent, and per car. Children 300ptas. Open Apr.-Oct.

⧉ FOOD

Granada offers a variety of ethnic restaurants to emancipate your taste buds from the fried-fish-and-pig-products doldrums. Cheap and tasty North African cuisine can be found in and around the **Albaicín,** while more typical *menú* fare awaits in Pl. Nueva and Pl. Trinidad. The adventurous eat well in Granada—*tortilla sacromonte* (omelette with calf's brains, bull testicles, ham, shrimp, and veggies), *sesos a la romana* (batter-fried calf's brains), and *rabo de toro* (bull's tail) are common. Picnickers can gather fresh fruit and vegetables at the **market** on C. San Augustín. Get groceries at **Supermercado T. Mariscal,** C. Genil, next to El Corte Inglés (open M-F 9:30am-2pm and 5-9pm, Sa 9:30am-2pm).

ANDALUCÍA

NEAR PLAZA NUEVA

The places around Pl. Nueva are great stops on a *tapas* route. *Tapas* are **free** in Granada (with a drink).

La Nueva Bodega, C. Cetti Meriém, 9 (☎ 958 22 59 34), out of Pl. Nueva on a small side street off C. Elvira. Popular with locals and tourists. *Menús* 1000-1100ptas. *Bocadillos* 275ptas. Open daily noon-midnight.

Restaurante Boabdil (☎ 958 22 81 36), C. Elvira. Serves lunch and dinner in a little outdoor nook. A variety of entrees (725ptas) includes staples like *paella* and macaroni and cheese. Open F-W 1-5pm and 8pm-midnight, Th 8pm-midnight. V, MC.

Bodega Mancha, C. Joaquín Costa, 10, and **Bodega Castañeda,** C. Almireceros 1-3, are off C. Elvira leading from Pl. Nueva. Drink and eat with the local good old boys. *Bocadillos* (under 300ptas) and *tapas* are the preferred fare in these dens of Dionysus. The pork aroma unsettles the stomach more than the wine and sherry (175-200ptas). Both open daily 8am-4pm and 6pm-1am, Sa-Su noon-4pm and 6pm-3am.

THE ALBAICÍN

Wander the romantic, winding streets of the Albaicín and you'll discover a number of budget bars and restaurants on the slopes above Pl. Nueva. C. Calderería Nueva, off C. Elvira leading from the plaza, is crammed with teahouses and cafes.

■ **Naturi Albaicín,** C. Calderería Nueva, 10 (☎ 958 22 06 27). Excellent vegetarian cuisine. Tasty options include *berenjenas rellenas* (stuffed eggplant), quiche, and *kefir* (a yogurt drink). *Menús* 950-1150ptas. Open Sa-Th 1-4pm and 7-11pm, F 7-11pm.

El Ladrillo II (☎ 958 29 26 51), C. Panaderos, off Cuesta del Chapiz near the Iglesia El Salvador, high on the Albaicín. Consume immense portions of delicious, fresh seafood to the sound of *sevillanas*. A popular evening hangout. Open daily 12:30pm-1:30am.

Los Chirimías (☎ 619 96 28 79), Po. Padre Manjón, up C. Acera de Darro from Pl. Nueva. Spectacular view of the Alhambra from its base. Pizzas 550-775ptas, *menú* 775-2250ptas. Open daily 12:30pm-2am.

Medina-Zahara, C. Calderería Nueva, 12 (☎ 958 22 15 41). Mediterranean take-out joint makes delicious *samosas* (275-325ptas) and falafel (325ptas).

GRAN VÍA AND ELSEWHERE

Botánico Café, C. Málaga, 3 (☎ 958 27 15 98), 2 blocks from Pl. Trinidad. Manhattan minimalism meets Spanish modernity at this student hangout, where a fusion of cultural food traditions brings new life to Spanish favorites. Entrees 800-1500ptas. Open M-Th 10am-3am, Su noon-1am.

Restaurante Chino Estrella Oriental, C. Alvaro de Bazán, 9 (☎ 958 22 34 67), 5 blocks down Gran Vía from Pl. Isabel la Católica. Bright-red Pagoda facade welcomes all to cheap, tasty *menús* (650ptas). Free delivery with orders of 1500ptas or more. Open daily 12:30-4:30pm and 7:30pm-12:30am. V, MC.

👁 SIGHTS

THE ALHAMBRA

To get to the Alhambra, take C. Cuesta de Gomérez off Pl. Nueva, and be prepared to pant (20min.; no unauthorized cars 9am-9pm). Or take the cheap, quick Alhambra-Neptuno microbus (every 5min., 120ptas) from Pl. Nueva. ☎ 958 22 15 03. Open Apr.-Sept. daily 8:30am-8pm; Oct.-Mar. M-Sa 9am-5:45pm. Nighttime visits June-Sept. Tu, Th, and Sa 10-11:30pm; Oct.-May Sa 8-10pm. 1000ptas, free for the handicapped and children under 8. Limited to 7700 visitors per day June-Sept., 6300 Oct.-May, so get there early to stand in line. Enter the Palace of the Nazarites (Alcázar) during the time specified on your ticket, but stay as long as desired. It is possible to reserve tickets a few days in advance at banks, but this is only recommended mid-July to mid-Aug. and Semana Santa.)

From the streets of Granada, the Alhambra appears simple, blocky, faded—a child's toy castle planted in the foothills of the Sierra Nevada. Up close, however, you will discover an astoundingly elaborate and detailed piece of architecture; one that magically meshes water, light, carved wood, stucco, ceramics, and sheepskin paintings to create a fortress-palace of rich aesthetic and symbolic grandeur.

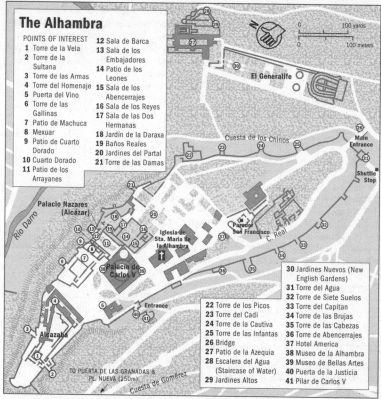

The Alhambra

POINTS OF INTEREST

1 Torre de la Vela
2 Torre de la Sultana
3 Torre de las Armas
4 Torre del Homenaje
5 Puerta del Vino
6 Torre de las Gallinas
7 Patio de Machuca
8 Mexuar
9 Patio de Cuarto Dorado
10 Cuarto Dorado
11 Patio de los Arrayanes
12 Sala de Barca
13 Sala de los Embajadores
14 Patio de los Leones
15 Sala de los Abencerrajes
16 Sala de los Reyes
17 Sala de las Dos Hermanas
18 Jardín de la Daraxa
19 Baños Reales
20 Jardines del Partal
21 Torre de las Damas

22 Torre de los Picos
23 Torre del Cadi
24 Torre de la Cautiva
25 Torre de las Infantas
26 Bridge
27 Patio de la Azequia
28 Escalera del Agua (Staircase of Water)
29 Jardines Altos
30 Jardines Nuevos (New English Gardens)
31 Torre del Agua
32 Torre de Siete Suelos
33 Torre del Capitan
34 Torre de las Brujas
35 Torre de las Cabezas
36 Torre de Abencerrajes
37 Hotel America
38 Museo de la Alhambra
39 Museo de Bellas Artes
40 Puerta de la Justicia
41 Pilar de Carlos V

El Generalife

Cuesta de los Chinos

Main Entrance

Shuttle Stop

Palacio Nazares (Alcázar)

Río Darro

Iglesia de Sta. María de la Alhambra

Parador San Francisco

C. Real

Palacio de Carlos V

Alcazaba

Entrance

TO PUERTA DE LAS GRANADAS & PL. NUEVA (250m)

Cuesta de Gomérez

THE ALCAZABA. The Christians drove the first Nazarite King Alhamar from the Albaicín to this more strategic hill, where he built the fortress Alcazaba, the section of the Alhambra with the oldest recorded history. A dark, spiraling staircase leads to the **Torre de la Vela** (watchtower), where visitors get a great 360° view of Granada and the surrounding mountains. The tower's bells were rung to warn of impending danger and to coordinate the Moorish irrigation system. During an annual festival, custom dictates that any local girl who scrambles up the tower and rings the bell by hand will receive a wedding proposal within a year. Exit through the **Puerta del Vino** (wine gate), the original entrance to the medina, where inhabitants of the Alhambra once bought tax-free wine (alas, no more).

THE ALCÁZAR. Follow signs to the *Palacio Nazaries* to see the Alcázar, a royal palace built for the Moorish rulers Yusuf I (1333-1354) and Muhammed V (1354-1391). Yusuf I was murdered in an isolated basement chamber of the Alcázar, and his son Muhammed V was left to complete the palace.

The entrance leads into the **Mexuar,** a great pillared council chamber. Note the glazed tile arrangements that reiterate the Nazarite mantra: "There is no victor but God." The Mexuar adjoins the **Patio del Cuarto Dorado (Patio of the Gilded Hall).** Off the far side of the patio, foliated horseshoe archways of diminishing width open onto the **Cuarto Dorado (Gilded Hall),** decorated by Muhammed V. Its painstakingly carved wooden ceiling, inlaid with ivory and mother-of-pearl, displays polygonal figures and colorful ceramic *dados*.

Next is the **Patio de los Arrayanes (Courtyard of Myrtles),** an expanse of emerald water filled with goldfish and bubbling fountains. Stand at the top of the patio for a glimpse of the 14th-century **Fachada de Serallo,** the palace's elaborately carved facade. The long and slender **Sala de la Barca (Boat Gallery),** with an inverted boat-hull ceiling, flanks the courtyard.

In the elaborate **Sala de los Embajadores (Hall of Ambassadors),** adjoining the Sala de la Barca to the north, Fernando and Columbus discussed finding a new route to India. Every surface of this magnificent square hall is intricately wrought with symbolic inscriptions and ornamental patterns. The dome, carved of more than 8000 pieces of wood and inlaid cedar, depicts the seven skies of paradise mentioned in the Koran (the ceiling style is called Mozarabic).

From the Patio de los Arrayanes, the Sala de los Mocárabes leads to the **Patio de los Leones (Courtyard of the Lions),** the grandest display of Nazarite art in the palace. The grandeur continues: a rhythmic arcade of arches and marble columns borders the courtyard, and a fountain supported by 12 marble lions babbles in the middle.

Moving counter-clockwise around the courtyard, the next room is the **Sala de los Abencerrajes.** Here, Sultan Abul Hassan piled the heads of his first wife's 16 sons so that Boabdil, son by his second wife, could inherit the throne. The rust-colored stains in the basin are said to mark the indelible traces of the butchering. Light bleeds into the room through the intricate domed ceiling, which features an eight-pointed star—a design said to represent terrestrial and heavenly harmony.

Through dripping stalactite archways, at the far end of the courtyard from the Patio de los Leones, lies the **Sala de los Reyes (Hall of Kings).** Fixed to the walls with bamboo pins, detailed sheepskin paintings depict important assemblies and hunts. On the remaining side of the courtyard, the resplendent **Sala de las Dos Hermanas (Chamber of the Two Sisters)** has a staggering honeycomb dome (Mozarabic style), comprised of thousands of tiny cells. From here a secluded portico, **Mirador de Daraxa (Eyes of the Sultana),** overlooks the Jardines de Daraxa.

Passing the room where American author Washington Irving resided in 1829, a balustraded courtyard leads to the 14th-century **Baños Reales (Royal Baths),** the center of court social life. Light shining through star-shaped holes in the ceiling once refracted through steam, creating indoor rainbows. *(Baths currently closed in summer for conservation studies and archaeological bubble baths.)*

TOWERS AND GARDENS. Just outside the east wall of the Alcázar in the **Jardines del Partal,** lily-studded pools flow beside terraces of roses. The **Torre de las Damas (Ladies' Tower)** soars above it all, a series of six towers traversing the area between the Alcazaba and El Generalife, one for captives, one for princesses, etc.

EL GENERALIFE. Over a bridge, across the **Callejón de los Cipreses** and the shady **Callejón de las Adelfas,** are the vibrant blossoms, towering cypresses, and streaming waterways of El Generalife, the sultan's vacation retreat. In 1313 Arab engineers changed the Darro's flow by 18km and employed dams and channels to prepare the soil for Aben Walid Ismail's design of El Generalife. Over the centuries, the estate passed through private hands until it was finally repatriated in 1931. The two buildings of El Generalife, the **Palacio** and the **Sala Regia,** connect across the **Patio de la Acequia (Courtyard of the Irrigation Channel),** embellished with a narrow pool fed by fountains that form an aquatic archway. Honeysuckle vines scale the back wall, and shady benches invite long rests.

PALACIO DE CARLOS V. After the *Reconquista* drove the Moors from Spain, Fernando and Isabel restored the Alcázar. Little did they know that two generations later Emperor Carlos V would demolish part of it to make way for his Palacio, a Renaissance masterpiece by Pedro Machuca (a disciple of Michelangelo). Although the building is glaringly incongruous amid all the Moorish splendor, scholars concede that the palace is one of the most beautiful Renaissance buildings in Spain. A square building with a circular inner courtyard wrapped in two stories of Doric colonnades, it is Machuca's only surviving effort. Inside, the **Museo de La Alhambra** contains the only original furnishings remaining from the Alhambra. (☎ 958 22 62 79. Open Tu-Sa 9am-2:30pm. 250ptas, free for EU citizens.) Upstairs, the **Museo de Bellas Artes** displays religious sculptures and paintings of the Granada School dating from the 16th century to the present. (☎ 958 22 48 43. Open June-Aug. Tu 2:30-6pm, W-Sa 9am-6pm; Sept.-May Tu 2:30-7:45pm, W-Sa 9am-7:45pm, Su 9am-2pm.)

IN THE CATHEDRAL QUARTER

■ **CAPILLA REAL.** Downhill from the Alhambra's Arab splendor, the Capilla Real (Royal Chapel), Fernando and Isabel's private chapel, exemplifies Christian Granada. During their prosperous reign, the king and queen funneled almost a quarter of the royal income into the chapel's construction (which lasted from 1504 to 1521) to produce a proper burial place. Their efforts did not go unrewarded; intricate Gothic carvings and meticulously rendered statues, as well as **La Reja,** the gilded iron grille of Master Bartolomé, now mark the resting place of the couple. Behind La Reja rest the elaborate, almost lifelike marble figures of the royals themselves. Fernando and Isabel's feet face visitors as they enter; beside them sleeps their daughter Juana la Loca (the Mad) and her husband Felipe el Hermoso (the Fair). To the horror of the rest of the royal family, Juana insisted on keeping the body of her husband with her for an unpleasantly long time after he died. The lead caskets, where all four monarchs were laid to rest, lie in the crypt directly below the marble statues, accessible by a small stairway on the left. The smaller, fifth coffin belongs to the hastily buried child-king of Portugal, Miguel, whose death allowed Carlos V to ascend the throne.

SACRISTY. Next door in the sacristy, Isabel's private **art collection,** the highlight of the chapel, favors Flemish and German artists of the 15th century. The glittering **royal jewels**—the queen's golden crown and scepter and the king's sword—shine in the middle of the sacristy. (☎ *958 22 92 39. Capilla Real and Sacristy both open Apr.-Sept. M-Sa 10:30am-1pm and 4-7pm; Oct.-Mar. M-Sa 10:30am-1pm and 3:30-6:30pm, Su 11am-1pm. 350ptas.)*

CATHEDRAL. The cathedral was built from 1523 to 1704 by Fernando and Isabel upon the foundation of the Arab mosque. The first purely Renaissance cathedral in Spain, its massive Corinthian pillars support an astonishingly high (45m) vaulted nave. (☎ *958 22 29 59. Open daily Apr.-Sept. 10:30am-1:30pm and 4-7pm; Oct.-Mar. M-Sa 10:30am-1:30pm and 3:30-6:30pm, Su 11am-1:30pm. Closed Su morning. 350ptas.)*

OTHER SIGHTS. The 16th-century **Hospital Real** is divided into four tiled courtyards. Above the landing of the main staircase, the Mudéjar-coffered ceiling echoes those of the Alhambra. (*C. San Juan de Dios. Open M-F 9am-2pm. Free.*) The 14th-century **Monasterio de San Jerónimo** is around the corner. Though badly damaged by Napoleon's troops, it was later restored. (☎ *958 27 93 37. Open Apr.-Sept. M-Sa 10am-1:30pm and 4:30-7:30pm, Su 11am-1:30pm; Oct.-Mar. M-Sa 10am-1pm and 3-6:30pm, Su 11am-1:30pm. 350ptas.)*

THE ALBAICÍN. The Albaicín is the fascinating old Arab quarter where the Moors built their first fortress. After the *Reconquista,* a small Moorish population clung to this hillside neighborhood until their expulsion in the 17th century. The abundance of North African cuisine and the recent construction of a mosque near Pl. San Nicolás attest to a continued Arab influence in Granada. A labyrinth of steep slopes and dark narrow alleys, the Albaicín warrants caution at night. (*Bus #12 runs from beside the cathedral to C. Pagés at the top of the Albaicín. There is another bus that departs from Pl. Nueva and weaves its way to the top. From here, walk down C. Agua through Pta. Arabe.*)

The best way to explore this maze is to proceed along C. Acera de Darro off Pl. Nueva, climb the Cuesta del Chapiz on the left, then wander aimlessly through Muslim ramparts, cisterns, and gates. On Pl. Nueva, the 16th-century **Real Cancillería** (or **Audencia**), with a beautiful arcaded patio and stalactite ceiling, was the Christians' Ayuntamiento. Farther uphill are the 11th-century **Arab baths.** (*C. Acera de Darro, 31.* ☎ *958 02 78 00. Open Tu-Sa 10am-2pm. Free.*) The **Museo Arqueológico** showcases funerary urns, Classical sculpture, Carthaginian vases, Muslim lamps, and ceramics. (*C. Acera de Darro, 41.* ☎ *958 22 56 40. Open Tu 3-8pm, W-Sa 9am-8pm, Su 9am-2:30pm. 250ptas, free for EU members.*) The terrace adjacent to **Iglesia de San Nicolás** affords the city's best view of the Alhambra, especially in winter when snow adorns the Sierra Nevada behind it.

ANDALUCÍA

🔲 🎵 NIGHTLIFE AND ENTERTAINMENT

Entertainment listings are near the back of the daily paper, the *Ideal* (120ptas), under *Cine y Espectáculos;* the Friday supplement lists bars and special events. The *Guía del Ocio,* sold at newsstands (100ptas), lists clubs, pubs, and cafes. The tourist office also distributes a monthly guide, *Cultura en Granada.*

FLAMENCO AND JAZZ

The most "authentic" flamenco performances, which change monthly, are advertised on posters around town. A list of the nightly *tablaos* is available at the tourist office. Tourists and locals alike flock to **Los Jardines Neptuno** (☎ 958 52 25 33), C. Arabial, near the Neptuno shopping center at the base of C. Recogidas. Rows of plastic chairs fill a huge, enclosed theater. (Cover 3800ptas, includes 1 drink and a bus ride to Albaicín). A smoky, intimate setting awaits at **Eshavira** (☎ 958 29 08 29), C. Postigo de la Cuna, in an alley off C. Azacayes, between C. Elvira and Gran Vía. This joint is *the* place to go for flamenco, jazz, or a fusion of the two. Photos of Nat King Cole and other jazz greats plaster the walls. (Min. 1 drink. Call for schedule.)

PUBS, BARS, AND CLUBS

Pubs and bars spread across several neighborhoods, genres, and energy levels. The most boisterous crowds hang out on C. Pedro Antonio de Alarcón, running from Pl. Albert Einstein to Ancha de Gracia, while hip new bars and clubs line C. Elvira from Cárcel to C. Cedrán. A few gay bars cluster around Carrera del Darro, while a more openly gay scene can be found at the Parque del Triunfo and the Paseo del Salón. A full list of gay establishments is available at the tourist office.

Sur, C. Reyes Católicos, 55, 2 blocks from Plaza Nueva. It may not have a sign, but Granada's student population clearly has no trouble finding this trendy new *bar-musical.* Mixed drinks 400-900ptas. Open daily 10pm-6am.

Vaticano, Camino del Sacromonte, 33, beyond the Albaicín. If you survive the uphill trek and all-night dancing in this cave bar, you'll be rewarded with a spectacular, if bleary-eyed, view of the Alhambra at dawn. Opens daily at 11pm.

Taberna El 22, Pl. Santa Gregorio, 5. Close to Pl. Nueva, at the top of C. Calderería Nueva. A young and mellow throng of vacationers lounge on the cobblestone patio. *Caña* 150ptas. Wine 175ptas. Open daily noon-3pm and 9pm-3am.

Kasbah, C. Calderería Nueva, 4 (☎ 958 52 31 73). With scented air, silky pillows, romantic nooks, and tasty Moroccan beverages (275ptas), Kasbah is perfect for a laid-back, shoeless Saturday night. Open daily 3pm-3am.

El Principa, Campo del Príncipe at Huerto San Cecilio. Well-to-do students dance the night away on an ample floor that resembles a throne room. Opens W-Sa at midnight.

Juaja, C. Cedrán at C. Sta Lucía, off C. Elvira. A bar jam-packed with rowdy, sweaty teens worshipping a disco ball. Opens Tu-Sa at 10pm.

Fondo Reservado, Cuesta de Sta. Inés, off Carrera del Darro. A popular gay bar with a fun, mixed crowd that parties hard. Opens daily at 11pm.

FESTIVALS

A number of festivals sweep Granada in summer. The **Corpus Christi** celebrations, processions, and bullfights here are famous (May or June). Every May, avant-garde theater groups from around the world make a pilgrimage to Granada for the **International Theater Festival** (☎ 958 22 93 44). The **Festival Internacional de Música y Danza** (mid-June to early July) sponsors open-air performances of classical music, ballet, and flamenco in the Alhambra's Palacio de Carlos V and other outdoor venues. (☎ 958 22 18 44. Tickets 1000-6000ptas, senior and youth discounts available.)

▶ DAYTRIPS FROM GRANADA

LA CARTUJA (5MIN.)

To get to the monastery, take bus #8 from the front of the Granada cathedral.

On the outskirts of Granada stands La Cartuja, a 16th-century Carthusian monastery and the pinnacle of Baroque artistry in Granada. Marble with rich brown tones and swirling forms (a stone unique to nearby Lanjarón) marks the sacristy of Saint Bruno. (☎ 958 16 19 32. Open Apr.-Sept. M-Sa 10am-1pm and 4-8pm, Su 10am-noon; Oct.-Mar. M-Sa 10am-1pm and 3:30-6pm, Su 10am-noon. 325ptas.)

FUENTE VAQUEROS (25MIN.)

Buses run hourly between the Granada train station and Fuente Vaqueros (25min.; 9am-9pm, returns 8am-8pm; 160ptas). From the bus stop in Fuente Vaqueros, turn right on Po. Prado and left on C. Poetra Lorca and follow signs for "Casa-Museo."

Poet and playwright Federico García Lorca, known for his works *Bodas de Sangre* and *Romancero Gitano*, was born outside the tiny town of Fuente Vaqueros and was killed by right-wing forces near Granada at the outbreak of the Civil War. The restored **Casa-Museo,** Lorca's house-turned-museum, has everything from the piano where the master played to the bed in which he was born. The upper level of the **granero** (granary) features photos of Lorca with Dalí and costumes from performances of his plays around the world. (☎ 958 51 64 53. Open Apr.-June Tu-Sa 10am-1pm and 5-8pm; July-Sept. Tu-Sa 10am-1pm and 6-8pm. Oct.-Mar. Tu-Sa 10am-1pm and 4-7pm. 200ptas. Tours every hr.)

VELETA (45MIN.)

The Autocares Bonal bus (☎ 958 27 31 00) from Granada to Veleta is a bargain (9am, returns 4:30pm from Albergue; round-trip 800ptas). Buy tickets in the bar El Ventorrillo, next to the bus stop (see Granada, p. 259).

Near the foot of the Alhambra, the highest road in Europe begins its long, gradual ascent to one of Europe's highest peaks, Veleta (3470m). The road begins in the arid countryside, then scales the daunting face of the Sierra. Due to snow, cars can cruise to the very top of Veleta only in August and September. Before you drive, check the road and snow conditions (☎ 958 24 91 19). Veleta has 39 slopes and 61 sq. km of skiing area, with a vertical drop of 1300m. Lift tickets cost 2325ptas in *temporada alta* (winter) and 2025ptas in *temporada baja* (off-season). **Ski rentals** are available in the Gondola Building and in Pl. Prado Llano (full equipment 2500ptas per day). This ski resort is the southernmost in Europe—wear sunscreen or suffer. The cheapest accommodation is the **Albergue Universitario** (☎ 958 48 01 22), the yellow building at the Veleta bus stop. (Breakfast included. Reserve early in winter. Singles 2200ptas; doubles 5200ptas.)

Ski season runs from December to April. The mountains are arguably less attractive in summer, with black slate slopes dotted by yellow-green moss, but tourists still go to paraglide, hike, and take jeep tours. Call **Cetursa** (☎ 958 24 91 11) for info on outdoor activities. If you plan to hike extensively, stop first at **Librería Flash** in Granada for their indispensable 800pta map of the Sierra (see p. 260).

LAS ALPUJARRAS

The secluded *pueblos blancos* (white villages) of Las Alpujarras are perched along the southern slopes of the Sierra Nevada. Although the roads are now paved and the towns well-traveled, a medieval Berber influence is still evident in the region's architecture; the low-slung houses rendered from earth and slate quite closely resemble those in Morocco's Atlas Mountains. The fall of Granada in 1492 is traditionally seen as the mark of the end of Moorish rule in Iberia, but the Berbers in fact relocated to Las Alpujarras and Christian-Muslim conflict continued until 1610, when John of Austria finally ousted the Moors. The legacy of Moorish defiance lives on every June during Trevélez's Fiestas de Moros y Cristianos, a dramatization of the Moorish-Christian conflict. Settlers from Galicia and Asturias made Las Alpujarras their home after the Moors were ousted, and they brought with them Celtic and Visigothic traditions found nowhere else in Andalucía.

Although tourists have recently discovered the beauty of these settlements and the surrounding region's numerous hiking trails, the Alpujarras remain one of Spain's poorest areas. Until the 1950s, travel was possible only by foot or mule, and the region still suffers from severe drought, unemployment, and low literacy rates. Nevertheless, the villages' slow-paced lifestyle, well-preserved beauty, and rooted cultural traditions make for a refreshing visit. For the more active tourist, the mountains themselves offer plenty of climbing and hiking opportunities.

Alsina Graells buses—the only available form of transportation—zoom from Granada to many of the high-altitude towns, including Lanjarón, Pampaneira, Bubión, Capileira, and Trevélez, and bus drivers will often stop to let travelers off at intermediate points. Some hard-core visitors hike from place to place, and the locals, well aware of the transportation problem, often sympathize with hitchers.

LANJARÓN

Lanjarón (pop. 4300) is Spain's version of Evian, France. Famed throughout the country for its mineral water, the tiny village attracted Spaniards in droves when good water was thought to have medicinal value. Lanjarón is only 45km from Granada, but it also offers plenty of its own accommodations. **Hostal Dólar,** Av. Andalucía, 5, has bright and clean rooms at a decent price. (☎ 958 77 01 83. Singles 1700ptas; doubles 3500ptas, with bath 3600ptas.)

PAMPANEIRA

As the road winds in serpentine curves up to Pampaneira, the lowest of the high Alpujarran villages (1059m), the landscape quickly becomes harsh. Probably the most tourist-accommodating town in Las Alpujarras, Pampaneira is the first in a trio of hamlets overlooking **Poqueira Gorge**, a massive ravine cut by the Río Poqueira; it makes a great springboard for climbing to **Bubión** (40min.) and **Capileira** (1¾hr.). For more info on the region's natural wonders, visit the local organization **Nevadensis** in Pampaneira's main square; they can arrange for rural accommodations, horseback riding, and other services. (☎ 958 76 31 27; fax 958 76 33 11. Open Tu-Sa 10am-2pm and 5-7pm, Su-M 10am-3pm.) **Hostal Pampaneira,** just off the highway in front of the bus stop, has large, comfortable rooms with polished chestnut furniture, all with private bath. (☎ 958 76 30 02. Singles 2000ptas; doubles 3500ptas; triples 4500ptas. V, MC.) The hostel **restaurant** serves a mean bowl of stew for 350ptas. (Entrees 650-1200ptas. V, MC.)

BUBIÓN

Bubión, a steep 3km (40min.) hike from Pampaneira, beams with Berber architecture, village charm, and three contemporary art galleries. For tourist info, stop by **Rustic Blue**, Barrio La Ermita. The helpful staff organizes excursions, cooking lessons with Irish mountaineer/chef Conor Clifford, and lodging. (☎ 958 76 33 81; fax 958 76 31 34. English spoken. Open M-F 10am-2pm and 5-8pm, Sa 11am-2pm.) **Las Terrazas,** Pta. Sol, has spotless rooms with tiled floors, Alpujarran bedspreads, and baths. (☎ 958 76 30 34. Singles 2750ptas; doubles 4000ptas.) Locals rave about the food at **Restaurante La Artesa,** on the main road in front of the bus stop. (*Menús* 1100-1500ptas. Open daily 1:30-4pm and 8-11pm.)

CAPILEIRA

Capileira (1436m), perched atop the Poqueira Gorge (2½hr. from Granada and a 1hr. hike from Bubión), makes a good base for exploring the neighboring villages and the back side of the Sierra Nevada. Cobblestone alleys wind up the slope while peaks loom above and the valley plummets below. Enjoy the vista from your bedroom window at **Mesón-Hostal Poqueira**, C. Dr. Castillo, 6. Rooms are pleasant, if small, and all have baths and central heating. (☎ 958 76 30 48. Singles 2100ptas; doubles 4000ptas; triples 4500ptas.) A scrumptious and filling 1200pta *menú* is served at the **restaurant** (open Tu-Su).

TREVÉLEZ

Rural isolation and lots of pork characterize Trevélez, continental Spain's highest community (1476m). Despite its secluded beauty and Alpujarran charm, the town is probably best known for its cured pork, whose special qualities will probably elude all but the true connoisseur. Ham gets its unique flavor from being cured in the cool, dry winter and sweated in the hot summer months. Steep roads weave through three distinct *barrios* and water rushes down Moorish irrigation systems still intact from 1000 years ago. (A few lucky Moors were once spared from the Inquisition because the Christians could not operate the channels without them.)

Trevélez is a logical base for the ascent to **Mulhacén.** Every August, throngs of locals climb to pay homage to the **Virgen de las Nieves (Virgin of the Snow),** whose shrine is at the peak. Summit-bound travelers should head north on the trail leaving the upper village; avoid the lower trail that follows the swampy Río Trevélez. Continue past the Cresta de los Postreros for a good 5½ hours and you will reach the **Cañada de Siete Lagunas** (the largest lake should be directly in front of you); go right to see a famous cave-refuge. To reach Mulhacén, go up the ridge south of the refuge. It is not advisable to hike Mulhacén the same day you visit the lake. Despite numerous signs near the bus stop advertising nearby *camas* (beds), the steep walk to **Hostal Fernando,** on C. Pista, 1km uphill on the left side of town from the bus stop, is well worth it. The friendly management keeps attractive, heated rooms with unbeatable views of the mountains from the terrace. (☎ 958 85 85 65. Singles 2500ptas; doubles 4000ptas.) They also rent apartments by the day for two (5000ptas) and four people (8000ptas). For food, try **La Fragua,** C. Carcel, which overlooks the town and valley. (☎ 958 85 85 73. *Menú* 750ptas.)

JAÉN

Olive trees and wheat fields, barely visible from the city's steep, crowded streets, streak Jaén's surrounding hills. Unfortunately, that is just about all Spain's bustling olive capital has to offer. Still, the city may be a necessary stopover—Baeza and Cazorla, two considerably more appealing destinations, lie only an hour away.

 TRANSPORTATION. Trains (☎ 902 24 02 02) leave from Po. Estación at the bottom of the slope and go to: **Córdoba** (1½hr., 8am, 1155ptas); **Sevilla** (3hr., 8am, 2210ptas); and **Madrid** (4-5hr., 3 per day 6am-5pm, 3000ptas). **Buses** (☎ 953 25 50 14), Pl. Coca de la Piñera, are much more efficient. They head to: **Úbeda** (30min., 12 per day 8:30am-8:45pm, 545ptas); **Baeza** (1hr., 12 per day 8:30am-8:45pm, 455ptas); **Granada** (1½hr., 14 per day 7:30am-9pm, 915ptas); **Cazorla** (2hr., noon and 4:30pm, 945ptas); and **Málaga** (3hr., 3 per day 7:30am-noon, 2040ptas).

 ORIENTATION AND PRACTICAL INFORMATION. Jaén centers around **Plaza de la Constitución,** roaring with autos and mopeds. C. Bernabé Soriano leads uphill from the plaza to the cathedral and the old section of town. C. Roldán y Marín and C. Virgen head downhill and become Po. Estación and Av. Madrid, respectively. To reach the town center from the bus station, exit from where the buses arrive and follow Av. Madrid uphill to Pl. Constitución (5min.). From the train station, turn right on Po. Estación, which becomes C. Roldán y Marín. If you're not up for the 25-minute walk, take the #1 bus along Po. Estación (90ptas).

The tiny **tourist office** can be found at C. Arquitecto Berges, 1, off C. Roldán y Marín, on the left when heading downhill. (☎/fax 953 22 27 37. Open M-F 9am-7pm, Sa 9am-1pm.) Change your money at **Banco Central Hispano,** in Pl. Constitución (open M-F 8:30am-2:30pm) and **store luggage** at the bus station (300ptas for 24hr.) In an emergency dial ☎ 112 or call the **police** at ☎ 953 26 18 50.

 ACCOMMODATIONS AND FOOD. Quality budget beds are scarce in Jaén. At the **Hostal La Española,** C. Bernardo López, 9, vines canopy the dining room and a staircase spirals its way upwards. Everything, including the sagging beds, exudes antiquity. To get to the hostel, follow C. Campanas up the side of the cathedral, turn right onto La Parra and turn left onto the alley Bernardo López. (☎ 953 23 02

ANDALUCÍA

54. Singles 1800ptas; doubles 3300ptas, with bath 4000-4500ptas.) **Hostal Carlos V,** Av. Madrid, 4, 3rd fl., downhill from Pl. Constitución, is more mainstream. (☎ 953 22 20 91. Singles 2500ptas; doubles 3700ptas.) C. Nueva, a pedestrian street down C. Roldán y Marín, offers several palatable restaurant options. **Yucatán,** C. Bernabé Soriano, 1, has tasty *bocadillos* (300-500ptas), burgers (300-350ptas), and entrees (900-1000ptas), served indoors or out. (☎ 953 24 17 28. Open daily 8am-2am.)

🏛🎶 **SIGHTS AND ENTERTAINMENT.** The Renaissance **Catedral de Santa María,** on C. Bernabé Soriano uphill from Pl. Constitución, was designed by Andrés de Valdelvira. (Open M-Sa 8:30am-1pm and 5-8pm, Su 8:30am-1pm and 6-8pm. Free.) The **Museo de la Catedral** displays sculptures by Martínez Montañés and canvases by Alonso Cano. (☎ 953 22 46 75. Open M-Sa 10am-1pm and 5-8pm, Su 10am-1pm. 200ptas.) Jaén's most imposing and least accessible sight is the **Castillo de Santa Catalina,** a 3km climb from the center of town. From the cathedral, take C. Maestra, which leads to C. Madre de Dios and continues to C. San Lorenzo. Turn left on Ctra. Circumvalación, which becomes Ctra. Neveral; this leads to the castle. Those who don't feel like walking can take a cab (900ptas) from the bus station to the castle. (☎ 953 21 91 16. Open Th-Tu 10am-2pm. Free.) The Renaissance **Palacio de Villadompardo,** in Pl. Santa Luisa Marillac, contains restored 11th-century baths, Spain's largest. Follow C. Maestra from the cathedral to C. Martínez Molina. (☎ 953 23 62 92. Open Tu-F 9am-8pm, Sa-Su 9:30am-2:30pm. Free.) Centuries-old **Peña Flamenca Jaén,** C. Maestra, 11 (☎ 953 23 17 10), uphill from the cathedral, serves up drinks and flamenco, indoors and out. **Del Posito,** a cafe bar tucked in a plaza below Yucatán, has the most popular outdoor tables in town.

BAEZA

A former Moorish capital and the first Andalucian town to fall during the *Reconquista*, Baeza (pop. 17,000) flaunts its Renaissance heyday with exceptionally well-preserved monuments on nearly every street. Thanks to the limited lodging options, the town remains uncorrupted by tourism, and those who spend the day here will satisfy their quest for a taste of quintessential old Spain. Antonio Machado, a poet who taught in Baeza, immortalized the village in his works when he wrote, *"Campo de Baeza, soñaré contigo cuando no te vea"* ("Countryside of Baeza, I shall dream of you when I see you no more").

🚆 **TRANSPORTATION. Trains** leave **Estación Linares-Baeza** (☎ 902 24 02 02), 13km from town on the road to Madrid, for **Madrid** (7 per day 7am-11:30pm, 2750ptas) and **Málaga** (3 per day 6:40am-5pm, 3000ptas). The **bus station** (☎ 953 74 04 68), at the top of Av. Alcalde Puche Pardo, which becomes C. Julio Barrel, offers service to: **Úbeda** (15min., 15 per day 8:20am-9pm, 105ptas); **Jaén** (1hr., 11 per day 7:10am-6:55pm, 455ptas); **Cazorla** (1½hr., 1 and 5:30pm, 500ptas); **Granada** (2-3hr., 7 per day 7:55am-6:55pm, 1335ptas); and **Málaga** (4hr., 8:10am, 2465ptas).

🛈 **PRACTICAL INFORMATION. Plaza de España,** which marks the center of town, leads downhill to Pl. Constitución. To get to Pl. España from the bus station, follow C. Julio Burrel to C. San Pablo (on the right), and continue to the plaza. The **tourist office,** Pl. Pópulo, offers free maps of Baeza and info on tours of Andalucía. (☎ 953 74 04 44. Open M-F 9am-2pm, Sa 10am-1pm.) Services include: **emergency** (☎ 112); **police,** C. Cardenal Benavides, 5 (☎ 953 74 06 59); **Centro de Salud Comarcal** (health center; ☎ 953 74 09 17), Av. Alcalde Puche Pardo; and the **post office,** C. Julio Burell, 19. (☎ 953 74 08 39. Open M-F 8:30am-2:30pm, Sa 9am-1pm.) The **postal code** is 23440. For **Internet access** try **Microware,** Po. Tundidores, 13, in Pl. Constitución. (☎ 953 74 70 10. 200ptas per hr. Open daily 11am-midnight.)

ACCOMMODATIONS AND FOOD. Hostels are scarce in Baeza—call ahead to ensure a room. **Hostal El Patio,** C. Romanones, 13, has a delightful lounge complete with plants and a mini-zoo. (☎ 953 74 02 00. Singles 1500ptas, with shower 2000ptas; doubles 3000ptas, with bath 4000ptas.) **Hotel El Alcázar,** Po. Arca del Agua, two long blocks from the bus station, has plain and simple rooms, all with bath. (☎953 74 00 28. Singles 3125ptas; doubles 5215ptas; triples 6500ptas.) A plethora of bars and restaurants line Pl. Constitución and neighboring streets. A popular choice with locals is the bar **Guadalquivir,** C. San Pablo, 44, where a family atmosphere entices passersby. (*Bocadillos* 275-350ptas, *raciones* 800-1000ptas. Open daily noon-4pm and 8:30pm-midnight.) **Helados Mercantil,** Portales Tundidores, 18, in Pl. Constitución, just might make the best ice cream in Spain. Cones go for 100-350ptas. (☎ 953 74 09 71. Open daily noon-2am.) **Supermarket,** Portales Carbonería, 15, sells groceries (open M-Sa 9am-2pm and 5-9pm, Su 10am-1pm).

SIGHTS. A stroll through the **Barrio Monumental** yields a sight on every corner. Follow C. Romanones up the stairs next to the tourist office before it opens onto Pl. Santa Cruz; the **Antigua Universidad** (founded in 1595) stands on the left. Ask someone to let you into the courtyard, where poet Antonio Machado used to teach French. (Open Tu-Su 10am-1pm and 4-6pm. Free.) Across from it sits the **Palacio de Jabalquinto,** featuring a gracefully decaying courtyard punctuated with ancient stonework and orange trees. (Open Tu-Su 10am-1pm and 4-6pm. Free.) To the right of the Antigua Universidad looms the 13th-century Romanesque **Iglesia de Santa Cruz,** Baeza's oldest church, with its frescoes of La Virgen, Santa Catalina, and the martyr San Sebastián (open M-Sa 11am-1pm and 4-6pm, Su noon-2pm). Adjacent to the *palacio*, the **seminario's** facade bears the names of some egotistical graduates and a caricature of an unpopular professor, rumored to be painted in bull's blood. Across the Pl. Santa María from the seminary towers, the **Santa Iglesia Catedral,** home to *La Custodia de Baeza*, Spain's second-most important (after Toledo's) Corpus Christi icon (open daily June-Aug. 10:30am-1pm and 5-7pm; Sept.-May 10:30am-1pm and 4:15-6pm). Fabulous views of the olive-carpeted Guadalquivir Valley, as well as Cazorla and Úbeda, unfold from the intersection of Po. Murallas and C. Argentina.

ÚBEDA

Fifteen minutes from Baeza and two hours from Granada and Córdoba, the cobbled streets of Úbeda's monument district dip between ivied medieval walls and old churches and palaces. A stop on the crucial 16th-century trade route linking Castilla to Andalucía, the town (pop. 35,000) prospered from American gold. The *barrio antiguo*, surrounded by friendly, newer neighborhoods, is one of the best-preserved gems of Spanish Renaissance architecture.

TRANSPORTATION. There's **no train service** to Úbeda; the nearest station is **Estación Linares-Baeza** (☎ 953 65 02 02), 40 minutes northwest by bus. **Buses** leave Úbeda from C. San José, 6 (☎ 953 75 21 57). **Alsina Graells** travels to: **Baeza** (15min., 17 per day 7am-7:30pm, 105ptas); **Estación Linares-Baeza** (30min., 8 per day, 260ptas); **Jaén** (1hr., 13 per day 7am-6:45pm, 555ptas); **Cazorla** (1hr., 4 per day 10am-6pm, 440ptas); and **Granada** (2-3hr., 7 per day 7:45am-6:45pm, 1445ptas). **Bacoma** goes to **Córdoba** (2½hr., 6 per day 5am-8:40pm, 1375ptas) and **Sevilla** (5hr., 6 per day 5am-8:40pm, 2660ptas).

ORIENTATION AND PRACTICAL INFORMATION. Úbeda centers around **Plaza de Andalucía.** From here, the **barrio antiguo** stretches downhill along C. Doctor Quesada (which leads to C. Real) and surrounding streets. To reach Pl. Andalucía from the **bus station,** go right from the front of the station, walk one block downhill, turn left on Av. Cristo Rey, which turns into C. Obispo Cobos and then C. Mesones, and continue to the plaza (5min.). The **tourist office** is in the **Palacio Marqués de Contadero,** C. Baja del Marqués, 4. From Pl. Andalucía follow C. Rastro, veering left onto C. Jurado Gómez and again onto C. Santo Domingo. Turn left on Corazón de Jesús and again at Baja del Marqués. (☎ 953 75 08 97; fax 953 79 26 70. Open M-Sa 8am-3pm.) **Banco Central Hispano**, Pl. Andalucía, 13, has an **ATM**. (☎ 953 75 04 43. Open May-Sept. M-F 8:30am-2pm; Oct.-Apr. M-F 8:30am-2pm, Sa 8:30am-1pm.) **Luggage storage** at the bus station (300ptas). Services include: **emergency** (☎ 112); **police** (☎ 953 75 00 23); **Centro de Salud** (health center; ☎ 953 75 11 03), C. Esplanada, off Av. Ramón y Cajal; and the **post office**, C. Trinidad, 4, along the Hospital de Santiago. (☎ 953 75 00 31. Open M-Sa 9am-2pm.) The **postal code** is 23400.

▓▐▌ ACCOMMODATIONS AND FOOD. Úbeda's best bargain is the **Hostal Castillo**, Av. Ramón y Cajal, 20, which offers comfy singles upstairs and a popular bar and affordable restaurant downstairs. (☎ 953 75 04 30 or 953 75 12 18. Singles 2200-2400ptas, with bath 2400-2700ptas; doubles 3400-3600ptas, with bath 4500-4800ptas; triples from 6300ptas.) The ritzier **Hostal Victoria**, C. Alaminos, 5, 2nd floor, offers glistening private bathrooms, color TVs, and air conditioning. From the bus station, walk down C. Mesones past Hospital de Santiago and turn right on C. Alaminos. (☎ 953 75 29 52. Singles 2400-2700ptas; doubles 4500-5000ptas.) For food, C. Rastro leading from Pl. Andalucía has many *terrazas* with combination platters under 1000ptas and entrees for around 600ptas. The **market** is down C. San Fernando from Pl. Andalucía (open M-Sa 7am-2:30pm).

▓ SIGHTS. A walk through historic Úbeda should begin with the **Hospital de Santiago**, right by the bus station. The building is a worthy sight in its own right. Inside, it houses a modern art museum, holds concerts, and has information on cultural events. (☎ 953 75 08 42. Open M-F 8am-3pm and 3:30-10pm, Sa 8am-3pm. 225ptas, children and seniors 75ptas.) From Pl. Andalucía, C. Real leads downhill to C. Juan Montilla, which continues to **Plaza de Vázquez de Molina**, the center of historic Úbeda. Two stone lions at the head of a garden-lined pathway guard the **Palacio de las Cadenas**, now the Ayuntamiento. Across the pathway is the Gothic **Colegiata de Santa María de los Reales Alcázares**, its side chapels embellished with wrought-iron grilles. Uphill from Pl. Vásquez de Molina along C. Juan Ruíz Gonzales is the pretty balcony-lined Pl. 1 de Mayo, in front of **Iglesia de San Pablo**. The **Museo Arqueológico**, C. Cervantes, 6, uphill from the church, narrates Úbeda's history through prehistoric, Roman, Moorish, and Castilian times. (☎ 953 75 37 02. Open Tu-Su 10am-2pm and 5-7pm. 250ptas, EU citizens free with passport.) A walk downhill leads to a stunning view of the olive-laden **Guadalquivir valley**.

CAZORLA

Nestled between foreboding cliffs and two ancient castles, Cazorla (pop. 9000) is one Andalucian *pueblo blanco* (white town) that should not be missed. Though most tourists pass through on their way to the **Parque Natural de las Sierras de Cazorla, Segura, y las Villas**, one of the largest national parks in Europe (1hr. away), a hike through the mountainous town itself provides exceptional views of the Guadalquivir valley. That said, the national park's 210,000 hectares of protected mountains and waterways offer some of the best hiking, mountain biking, and horseback riding in Andalucía, and possibly even Spain.

▓▐ ORIENTATION AND PRACTICAL INFORMATION. To reach **Plaza de Corredera** from the bus stop, face the peaks and walk down C. Dr. Muñoz to the right (5min.). Farther downhill is Pl. Santa María and the **barrio antiguo. Buses** (☎ 953 75 21 57) leave from Pl. Constitución to: **Granada** (4hr., 7am and 5:30pm); **Jaén** and **Úbeda** (2hr., 4 per day 7am-5:30pm, 960ptas and 440ptas); **Río Ebros** (5:45am and 3pm). Buy tickets in the unmarked booth next to the cafe in the plaza. The helpful **tourist office**, Po. Santo Cristo, 17, up a garden-lined walkway from Pl. Constitución, has free maps of Cazorla. (☎ 953 71 01 02; fax 953 72 00 60. Open M-F 10am-2pm and 5-9pm.) Services include: **emergency** (☎ 112); **police** (☎ 953 72 01 81), on Pl. Corredera; **Centro de Salud**, Av. Ximénez de Rada, 1 (☎ 953 72 10 61); and the **post office**, C. Mariano Extremera, 2, uphill from Pl. Corredera. (☎ 953 72 02 61. Open M-F 8:30am-2:30pm, Sa 9am-1pm.) The **postal code** is 23470.

◨◻ ACCOMMODATIONS AND FOOD. From the far end of Pl. Corredera, walk uphill on C. Carmen to reach the ◨**Albergue Juvenil Cazorla (HI),** Pl. Mauricio Martínez, 6. This sparkling clean hostel has a TV lounge, outdoor patios, and a heaven-sent poo. (☎ 953 72 03 29; fax 953 72 02 03. Sheets provided. HI members 1500ptas, over 26 2000ptas; nonmembers add 300ptas. Prices drop 500-700ptas Sept. 15-June 15.) **Hostal Betis,** Pl. Corredera, 19, has firm beds and great views of the valley. (☎ 953 72 05 40. Singles with bath 1300-1500ptas; doubles 2500-2800ptas, with bath 2700-3000ptas.) Open-air bar-restaurants serving traditional platters like *rin-ran* (a cold soup of potatoes, red peppers, olives, and fish) line Pl. Corredora and Pl. Santa María. Set in a 16th-century house on Pl. Santa María, **La Cueva** cooks veggies and roast rabbit in its ancient hearth. (☎ 953 72 12 25. *Menú* 1200ptas. Open daily noon-midnight. V, MC.) Cazorla's **market** is at Pl. Mercado, downstairs from C. Dr. Muñoz (open M-F 9am-noon). A **supermarket** sits in Pl. Corredera (open M-F 9am-noon and 6-9pm, Sa 9am-noon).

◧◪ SIGHTS AND HIKING. Cazorla offers many opportunities for scenic strolls. The **Castillo de la Yedra,** started by the Romans, provides a pretty view of Cazorla from its solitary peaks. (☎ 953 71 00 39. Open Tu 3-8pm, W-Sa 9am-8pm, Su 9am-3pm. 250ptas. EU citizens free.) For longer excursions, stop by **Quercus,** C. Juan Domingo, 2, where English-speaking tour operators provide info on the **Parque Natural de las Sierras de Cazorla, Segura, y las Villas.** (☎ 953 72 01 15. Open daily 9am-2pm and 5-9pm, holidays 10am-2pm and 6-9pm. Map 375ptas.) Buses run from Cazorla to the park (1hr.; June-Aug. 6:30am and 2:40pm, Sept.-May 5:45am and 3pm; 400ptas), but service is subject to change. Carecesa buses leave Pl. Constitución and go to the **Torre del Vinagre Visitor Center** (☎ 953 71 30 40), near the trailhead of the popular **Sendero Cerrada de Elias/Río Borosa,** which has 4- or 12km trails up a river canyon carved with natural pools. The center rents **horses** (1500ptas per hr., in groups of 4 or more) and **mountain bikes** (1200ptas per half-day, 2000ptas per day). The last bus back to Cazorla leaves Torre del Vinagre at 4:30pm. Tickets can be bought on the bus.

ANDALUCÍA

EAST COAST

VALENCIA

Valencia's rich soil has earned the region its nickname "Huerta de España" (Spain's Orchard). Spring and autumn river floods transport soil down the alluvial plain, nurturing Valencia's famous orange and vegetable groves, while irrigation networks designed by the Moors continue to nourish Valencia's farmlands. Dunes, sandbars, jagged promontories, and lagoons mark the grand coastline, and lovely fountains and pools grace the cities' carefully landscaped public gardens.

Valencia's past is a tangle of power struggles between the Phoenicians, Carthaginians, Greeks, Romans, and Moors. The region first fell under Castillian control when El Cid expelled the Moors in 1094; he ruled it in the name of Alfonso VI until his death five years later. Without El Cid's powerful influence, the city again fell to the Moors, remaining an Arab stronghold until 1238. In the 1930s, Valencia was again besieged, this time by Franco's troops. The *valencianos* resisted with characteristic strength; as a result Valencia was the last region incorporated into Franco's Spain. In 1977, with the reinstitution of the Bourbon monarchy, the region finally regained its autonomy.

Valenciano, the regional language spoken sparingly in the north and inland, is similar to Catalan. Although Valencia's regionalism is not as intense as Cataluña's, the Generalitat's recent mandate that all students enroll in one course of *valenciano* reflects a resurgence of regionalism. Valencia's festivals are some of the craziest in Spain (see below), and its culinary heritage has had a pronounced impact on Spanish cuisine. *Paella*, now considered a quintessential Spanish dish, was first concocted somewhere in the region's rice fields, and Valencian oranges are widely accepted as the best in the nation, if not the world.

HIGHLIGHTS OF VALENCIA

Valencia's festival of **Las Fallas**, a pyromaniac's dream (see p. 282).

Paella (and other rice-based specialties) straight from the source (see p. 281).

Nightlife in the capital city of **Valencia** (see p. 276) and **Alicante** (see p. 287).

The hilltop medieval fortress town of **Morella** (see p. 284)–if you can get there.

LOCAL FESTIVALS IN VALENCIA

Every March 12-19, **Valencia** celebrates the infamous *Las Fallas* with explosive effigy-burning, and the *Fira de Juliol* (July) turns a float parade into a flower-flinging fight. The tiny town of **Buñol,** near Valencia, hosts a town-wide tomato war (*La Tomatina*) every August. Locals in **Dénia** don't run with bulls, but they swim with them every July during the *Festa Major*. **Alicante** honors *Sant Joan* with fire displays and a ritual dousing of the entire town's youth by giant firehoses.

VALENCIA

Spain's third largest city is a stylish, cosmopolitan, and business-oriented nerve center that stands in striking contrast to the surrounding orchards and mountain ranges. Fountained parks and gardens soothe the city's congested environment, and soft-sanded beaches nearby complement its frenetic day and nightlife. An over-anxious government has been pouring money into making Valencia attractive to tourists, and the city now boasts some of Spain's most innovative architecture.

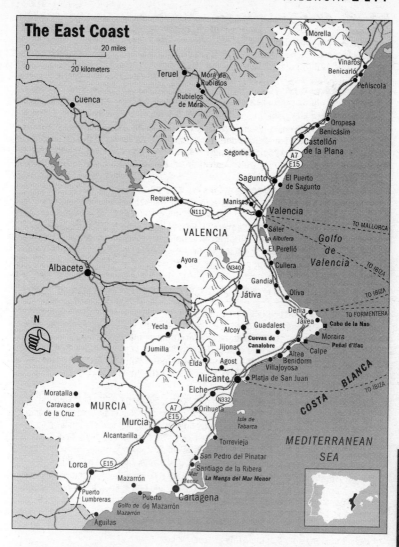

The East Coast

0   20 miles

0   20 kilometers

Morella

Teruel   Mora de Rubielos

Vinaros
Benicarló

Cuenca

Rubielos de Mora

Peñíscola

Oropesa
Benicásim
Castellón de la Plana

Segorbe

A7
E15

Sagunto   El Puerto de Sagunto

Requena   Manises

N111

Valencia

VALENCIA

Saler
La Albufera
El Perelló
Cullera

Golfo de Valencia

TO MALLORCA

Ayora

N340

TO IBIZA

Albacete

Gandía
Játiva

Oliva

TO IBIZA

Denia
Jávea   Cabo de la Nao

TO FORMENTERA

N

Yecla

Jumilla

Alcoy   Guadalest

Cuevas de Canalobre

Moraira

Jijona

Calpe   Peñal d'Ifac

Elda   Agost

Altea
Benidorm
Villajoyosa

Alicante   Platja de San Juan

Moratalla
Caravaca de la Cruz

MURCIA

Elche

N332

Orihuela

COSTA BLANCA

TO IBIZA

A7
E15

Murcia

Isla de Tabarca

MEDITERRANEAN SEA

Alcantarilla

Lorca   E15

Torrevieja

Mazarrón

San Pedro del Pinatar

Puerto Lumbreras

Santiago de la Ribera
La Manga del Mar Menor

Puerto de Mazarrón
Golfo de Mazarrón

Mar Menor

Cartagena

Aguilas

EAST COAST

TRANSPORTATION

Flights: Airport (☎ 96 159 85 15), 15km from the city. **Cercanías** trains run between the airport and train station (32min.; M-F every 30min., 150ptas; Sa-Su every hr., 170ptas). Domestic and international destinations. **Iberia,** C. La Paz, 14 (☎ 963 52 75 52; 24hr. info and reservation ☎ 902 400 500). Open M-F 9am-2pm and 4-7pm.

Trains: Estación del Nord, C. Xàtiva, 24. Ticket windows open 7:30am-9:30pm. **RENFE** (24hr. ☎ 902 24 02 02) to: **Alicante** (2hr., 15 per day, 3200-4300ptas); **Barcelona** (3hr., 18 per day 8am-10pm, 4500-5800ptas); **Madrid** (3½hr., 12 per day 8am-10:15pm, 5600-8500ptas); **Sevilla** (8½hr., 2 per day, 5300-5600ptas). **Cercanías** services Gandía, Játiva, Sagunto, Alicante, and the airport (prices range 135-550ptas).

Buses: Estación Terminal d'Autobuses, Av. Menéndez Pidal, 13 (☎ 96 349 72 22), across the river, a 25min. walk from the city center. Municipal bus #8 (125ptas) runs between Pl. Ayuntamiento and the train station. **Auto Res** (☎ 96 349 22 30) sends 3 regular and 12 express buses per day to **Madrid** (4hr., 7am-1am, 3175ptas). **Bacoma** (☎ 902 42 22 42) runs to: **Granada** (8hr., 6 per day, 4910ptas); **Málaga** (11hr., 5 per day, 6025ptas); **Sevilla** (11hr., 2 per day, 6380ptas). **Enatcar** (☎ 902 42 22 42) runs to **Barcelona** (4½hr., 10 per day 7am-1am, 2900ptas). **Ubesa** (☎ 902 42 22 42) stops along the Costa Blanca on its way to **Alicante** (2¼-3hr., 9 per day, 1980ptas). **Eurolines** (☎ 96 349 38 22) has international service.

Ferries: Trasmediterránea, Estació Marítima (☎ 902 45 46 45). Take bus #4 from Pl. Ayuntamiento or #1 or 2 from the bus station. Boats run to Mallorca and Ibiza (3920ptas slow, 11,325ptas fast). Buy tickets at a travel agency, or on the day of departure at the port. Ask a travel agent about **Balearia** (☎ 902 160 180) Denia-Eivissa service. See **By Boat,** p. 470.

Public Transportation: EMT Office, C. En Sanz, 4 (☎ 96 352 83 99). Bus map available at the tourist office and the EMT office. Open M-F 8am-2pm. EMT buses run out of Pl. Ayuntamiento. Bus #8 runs to the bus station. Bus #19 (in summer also #20, 21, 22) goes to Las Arenas and Malvarrosa. Buy tickets (125ptas) on board; 10-ride ticket (800ptas) or 1-day pass (500ptas) available at newsstands. Service stops at 10:30pm. Late-night buses go through Pl. Ayuntamiento (every 45min. 11pm-1:38am).

Taxis: ☎ 96 370 33 33 or 96 357 13 13.

ORIENTATION AND PRACTICAL INFORMATION

Since **Estación del Nord** is close to the city's center, Valencia is best approached by train. **Avenida Marquéz de Sotelo** runs from the train station to **Plaça del Ayuntamiento,** the center of town. Just about everything of interest, except for the university and beaches, is in the **casco antiguo** (old quarter), nestled in a bend of the Río Turia. Valencia's geographical sprawl will make you feel either lost or very closeted. To compensate, use the extensive bus system and explore the attractions outside of the main drag.

Tourist Office: Regional, Estación del Nord, C. Xàtiva, 24 (☎ 96 352 85 73), on the right of the train tracks (inside the station) as you disembark. Lots of pamphlets and maps. Open M-F 9am-6:30pm. The **main regional branch** with similar information is on C. Paz, 46-48 (☎ 96 398 64 22). Open M-F 10am-6pm, Sa 10am-2pm. **City office,** Pl. Ayuntamiento, 1 (☎96 351 04 17; tourist info ☎ 96 352 40 00), has Ajuntament-sponsored info. Open M-F 8:30am-2:15pm and 4:15-6:15pm, Sa 9am-12:45pm.

Budget Travel: IVAJ, C. Hospital, 11 (☎ 96 386 97 57). From the train station, head left on C. Xàtiva, which becomes C. Guillem de Castro, and turn right on C. Hospital. Several travel handbooks in English. Expect a line. ISIC 700ptas. HI cards 1800ptas. Open M-F June-Aug. 9am-2pm; Sept.-May 9am-2pm and 5-7pm.

Currency Exchange: Banco Central Hispano, C. Barcas, 8 (☎ 96 353 81 00), offers decent exchange rates. 24hr. **ATMs** are everywhere.

American Express: Duna Viajes, C. Cirilo Amorós, 88 (☎ 96 374 15 62; fax 96 334 57 00). From the tip of Pl. Ayuntamiento, take C. Barcas, which becomes C. Don Juan de Austria, then C. Sorní. When you reach Pl. América, take C. Cirilo Amorós on the right. No commission on AmEx traveler's checks. Accepts wired money. Will hold mail and provide fax service for cardholders. Open June-Aug. M-F 10am-2pm and 5-8pm, Sa 10am-1:30pm; Sept.-May M-F 9:30am-1:30pm and 4:30-7:30pm.

Luggage Storage: At the bus station, lockers 200-400ptas. At the train station, lockers 300-900ptas. Both open daily 7am-10pm.

Laundromat: Lavandería **El Mercat,** Pl. Mercado, 12 (☎ 96 391 20 10). Self-service wash and dry 1300ptas. Open M-Sa 10am-2pm and 5-8:30pm; closed Sa in Aug.

Emergency: ☎ 112. Ambulance: ☎ 085.

Late-Night Pharmacy: Check listing in the local paper *Levante* (125ptas) or check the *farmacias de guardia* schedule posted outside any pharmacy.

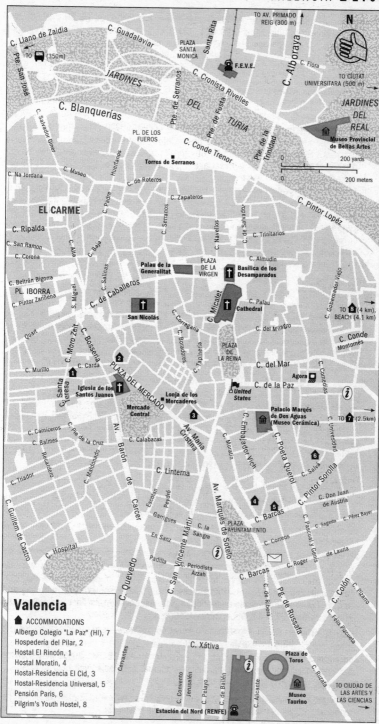

TO AV. PRIMADO REIG (300 m)

C. Llano de Zaidia
C. Guadalaviar
PLAZA SANTA MONICA
Santa Rita
C. Alboraya
C. Flora

Pte. San José
TO (350m)
JARDINES
C. Cronista Rivelles
F.E.V.E.

TO CIUTAT UNIVERSITARA (500 m)

C. Blanquerías
DEL
Pte. de Serranos
Pte. de Fusta
TURIA
Pte. de la Trinidad

JARDINES DEL REAL

C. Salvador Giner
PL. DE LOS FUEROS
C. Conde Trenor

Museo Provincial de Bellas Artes

C. Na Jordana
C. Museo
Torres de Serranos

0   200 yards
0   200 meters

C. Ripalda
Hüertanos
C. de Roteros
C. Zapateros
C. Pintor Lopéz

EL CARME

C. San Ramon
C. Padre
C. Serranos
C. Navellos
C. de Salvador
C. Trinitarios

C. Corona
C. Alta
C. Baja

C. Beltrán Bigorra
C. de Salinas
C. Almudin
C. Gobernador Viejo

PL. IBORRA
C. Pintor Zariñena
Palau de la Generalitat
PLAZA DE LA VIRGEN
Basílica de los Desamparados

C. de Caballeros
C. Micalet
Cathedral
C. Palau
TO (4 km), BEACH (4.1 km)

Quart
S. Miguel
San Nicolás
C. Coregaria
C. del Milagro
C. Conde Montornés

C. Moro Zeit
C. Bosseria
C. Boradores
PLAZA DE LA REINA

C. Murillo
C. Carda
2
C. Taplnería
C. del Mar
Agora

1
PLAZA DEL MERCADO
C. de la Paz
Comedias
i

C. Santa Teresa
Iglesia de los Santos Juanes
Lonja de los Mercaderes
United States
TO 7 (2.5km)

Mercado Central
3
Palacio Marqés de Dos Aguas (Museo Cerámica)

C. Carniceros
C. Pla de la Cruz
Av. Baron
Av. Maria Cristina
C. Embajador Vich
C. Poeta Querol
C. Pintor Sorolla
C. Universidad

C. Balmes
C. Calabazas
C. Moratin
6

C. Triador
C. Maldonado
C. Linterna
C. Don Juan de Austria

C. Guillem de Castro
de
Carcer
Av. Marqués de Sotelo
4
5
C. Barcas
C. Pascual y Genís
C. Sagasta
C. Pérez Bayer

Escolar
Peydró
Garrigues
En Sanz
Padilla
C. la Sangre
PLAZA DE AYUNTAMIENTO
C. Correos
C. Roger
de Lauria

C. Hospital
C. San Vicente Mártir
C. Periodista Azzah
i
C. Barcas
Pizarro

C. Quevedo
Cervantes
C. Convento Jerusalén
C. Pelayo
C. de Bailén
C. Alicante
C. de Ribera
Pd. de Russafa
C. Colón
C. Félix Pizcueta
C. Ruzafa

C. Xátiva

Plaza de Toros

i

Museo Taurino

TO CIUDAD DE LAS ARTES Y LAS CIENCIAS

Estación del Nord (RENFE)

Valencia

ACCOMMODATIONS

Albergo Colegio "La Paz" (HI), 7
Hospedería del Pilar, 2
Hostal El Rincón, 1
Hostal Moratin, 4
Hostal-Residencia El Cid, 3
Hostal-Residencia Universal, 5
Pensión Paris, 6
Pilgrim's Youth Hostel, 8

EAST COAST

N

Hospital: Hospital Clínico Universitario, Av. Blasco Ibañez, 17 (☎ 96 386 26 00), at the corner of C. Dr. Ferrer. Take bus #41, 71, or 81 from Pl. Ayuntamiento. An English-speaking doctor is often on duty.

Post Office: Pl. Ayuntamiento, 24 (☎ 96 351 67 50). Open M-F 8:30am-8:30pm, Sa 9:30am-2pm. **Postal Code:** 46080.

Internet Access: Agora Internet, C. Paz 33 (☎ 96 351 04 44). Speedy Internet connections are not Valencia's forte. 12 slow computers, but most convenient. 500ptas for 30min., students 400ptas. Open M-F 10am-2pm, 5-10:30pm. **Quisiera,** Dr. Vicente Zaragoza, 46 (☎ 902 14 71 47), between the Benimaclet and Zaragoza metro stops. 240ptas for 10min. Open M-Sa 9:30am-11:30pm, Su 4-11:30pm.

⌐ ACCOMMODATIONS

Since Valencia's accommodations are geared more toward businessmen than tourists, rooms are plentiful during the summer. During the *papier-mâché* orgy of *Las Fallas* (Mar. 12-19), reserve well in advance. The best deals cluster around **Plaza del Ayuntamiento** and **Plaza del Mercado.** For those willing to pay a little more, two-star hotels crowd **Paseo Neptuno** and **Paseo Maritimo** with double rooms for around 6000ptas. Last resort options are off C. Xátvia, near the train station. Avoid the areas by the *barrio chino* (red light district) around Pl. Pilar.

NEAR THE BEACH

▨ **Pilgrim's Youth Hostel,** Eugenia Vins St., 24 (☎ 96 356 42 88; fax 96 355 33 08; email albergue@ran.es). From Estació Nord, take Bus #32 until the last stop, cross the street and turn to the left. A/C, massages, TV, free load of laundry, kitchen access, free email, and Internet access (500ptas for 30min.). Free entrance to 2 summer nightclubs and the next door swimming pool. 24hr. reception. Check-out 11:30am. Quiet time 11pm. Dorms 1000ptas, over 26 1500ptas. V, MC for payments over 3000ptas.

Albergo Colegio "La Paz" (HI), Av. Puerto, 69 (☎ 96 369 01 52), nearly halfway between the city and the port. Take bus #19 from Pl. Ayuntamiento (next to Citibank) and get off at the 8th stop on Av. Puerto (20min. walk to the beach). Needs a visit from Mr. Clean. 2-4 people and a bathroom in every room. HI membership required. Breakfast included. Sheets 500ptas for 5 days. Lockout 10am-3pm. Curfew 2am. Reception daily 9am-2pm and 3pm-2am. Dorms 5400ptas, over 26 1900ptas. Open July-Sept. 15.

NEAR PLAZA DEL AYUNTAMIENTO

Hostal-Residencia El Cid, C. Cerrajeros, 13 (☎/fax 96 392 23 23). From the train station, pass Pl. Ayuntamiento and take the 2nd left off C. Vicente Mártir. Pay 1300ptas extra for TV and A/C. Singles 1700ptas; doubles 3200ptas, with shower 3500ptas, with bath 4500ptas.

Pensión Paris, C. Salvá, 12 (☎ 96 352 67 66). From Pl. Ayuntamiento, turn right at C. Barcas, left at C. Poeta Querol, and take the 2nd right onto C. Salvá. 13 spotless rooms complemented by lace curtains and balconies. Singles 2500ptas; doubles 3600ptas, with shower 4200ptas, with bath 4800ptas; triples 5400ptas.

Hostal-Residencia Universal, C. Barcas, 5 (☎ 96 351 53 84), off Pl. Ayuntamiento. Hallway showers require serious flip-flops. 24hr. access. Singles 2400ptas; doubles 3600ptas, with shower 4200ptas; triples 5100ptas.

Hostal Moratin, C. Moratin, 15 (☎/fax 96 352 12 20). From Pl. Ayuntamiento, take C. Barcas, and take the first left on C. Moratin. You get four walls, a bed, a rooftop terrace, and nothing more. Breakfast 300ptas. Keys distributed for 24hr. Singles with shower 2900ptas, with bath 3500ptas; doubles with shower 4500ptas, with bath 5500ptas; triples with shower 6750ptas, with bath 10,500ptas. V, MC, Maestro.

EAST COAST

NEAR PLAZA DEL MERCADO

Hostal El Rincón, C. Carda, 11 (☎ 96 391 79 98 or 96 391 60 83). From Pl. Ayuntamiento, Pl. Mercado extends past the market and continues as C. Carda. Singles 1500ptas, with bath 2000ptas; doubles 2800ptas, with bath 3600ptas.

Hospedería del Pilar, Pl. Mercado, 19 (☎ 96 391 66 00), past the market and Llonja, on the far right-hand side. Singles 1600ptas, with bath 2140ptas; doubles 2995ptas, with bath 3850ptas; triples 3900ptas, with bath 4815ptas.

◖ FOOD

Paella may be the most famous dish, but it is actually just one of 200 Valencian rice dishes. Other specialties include *arroz a banda* (rice and fish with garlic, onion, tomatoes, and saffron), *all i pebre* (eels fried in oil, paprika, and garlic), and *sepia con salsa verde* (cuttlefish with garlic and parsley). Valencia's restaurants are generally cheap, perfect for people on the run. Buckets of fresh fish, meat, and fruit are sold at the **Mercado Central,** on Pl. Mercado (open June-Aug. M-Th 7am-2:30pm, F-Sa 7am-3pm; Sept.-May M-Th 7am-2pm, F 7am-2pm and 5-8pm). For **groceries,** glide up to the fifth floor of **El Corte Inglés,** C. Pintor Sorolla, 26. (☎ 96 351 24 44; open M-Sa 10am-9:30pm.)

▨ Restaurante La Utielana, Pl. Picadero Dos Aguas, 3 (☎ 96 352 94 14). Take C. Barcelonina off the tapered end of Pl. Ayuntamiento, turn left at its end into and across Pl. Rodrigo Botet, turn right onto C. Procida, and duck into a little alley/plaza on the left (look for the La Utielana sign). Choose from a super scoop of scrumptious seafood paella (375ptas) or any of the other tasty meals (all under 825ptas). A/C. Open Sept.-July M-F 1:15-4pm and 9-11pm, Sa 1:15-4pm. Visa.

La Lluna (☎ 96 392 21 46), C. Sant Ramón, in El Carme district. From Pg. Guillem de Castro, take C. Corona, then the 1st left onto C. Beneficia; C. Sant Ramón is on the right. A veggie restaurant to moon over. Stuffed peppers and eggplant are the specialties. 4-course *menú* (served weekday afternoons) 900ptas. Entrees 400-650ptas. Open M-Sa 1:30-3:30pm and 8-11:15pm.

La Pappardella, C. Bordadores, 5 (☎ 96 391 89 15). Face the cathedral, and the restaurant is on the left. Packed daily with chic Italian-addicts enjoying the freshest pasta around (750-1100ptas). Outdoor tables and an upstairs veranda make for friendly get-togethers. *Menú* 1200pta. Open W-M 2-4:30pm and 9pm-midnight.

◉ SIGHTS

Touring Valencia on foot is complicated. Most of the sights line the Río Turia or cluster near Pl. Reina, which is linked to Pl. Ayuntamiento by C. San Vicente Mártir. EMT bus #5, dubbed the **Bus Turistic** (☎ 96 352 83 99), makes a loop around the old town sights (110ptas; 1-day pass 500ptas for all buses).

▨ CIUDAD DE LAS ARTES Y LAS CIENCIAS. In an effort to aid its weak tourism industry, Valencia has recently completed what the city calls "the largest urban complex under development in Europe." Built along the dried-up bed of the Río Turia, this mini-city has already become the fourth biggest tourist destination in Spain. The complex is divided into four large attractions, each with its own target audience. **L'Hemisfèric** wows the eyes with its IMAX theater and planetarium. **L'Oceanografic** is an underground water-world and recreation of diverse aquatic environments. The beautiful **Palau de les Arts** houses stages for opera, theater, and dance and the **Museu de Les Ciencies Principe Felipe** is an interactive playground for science and technology fiends. Designed by *valencianos* Santiago Calatrava and Félix Candela, the complex is finished but several of the exhibits have not officially opened. *(South along the riverbed off the highway to Salér.* ☎ *902 100 031. www.cac.es. IMAX shows 1000ptas, weekdays children and students 700ptas.)*

PYROMANIAC'S PARADISE Fire, fire! If you can choose any time of year to come to Valencia, make it March 12 to 19, when Valencia's most illustrious event, Las Fallas, grips the city. The city explodes with festivity, including parades, bullfights, fireworks, and street dancing. Neighborhoods compete to build the most elaborate and satirical *papier-mâché* effigy; over 300 such enormous *ninots* spring up in the streets. On the final day—*la nit del foc* (fire night)—Valencians burn all the *ninots* simultaneously in one last, clamorous inferno meant to bring luck for the agricultural season and to exorcise the social ills satirized by the *papier-mâché* giants.

■ **CATHEDRAL.** The cathedral was begun in the 13th century on the site of the desecrated Arab mosque, and was finished in 1482. The three different entrances display a melange of architectural styles, including Gothic, Baroque, and Romanesque. French novelist Victor Hugo once counted 300 bell towers in Valencia from atop the **Miguelete** (the cathedral tower); there are actually only about a hundred. The **Museo de la Catedral** squeezes a great many treasures into very little space. Check out the overwrought tabernacle made from 1200kg of gold, silver, platinum, emeralds, and sapphires, a Holy Grail, two Goyas, and the Crucifijo de Marfil (crucifix) statues depicting "man's passions." *(Pl. Reina. Cathedral ☎ 96 391 01 89. Open daily 8am-2pm and 5-8pm. Closes earlier in winter. Free. Tower open daily 10am-1pm and 4:30-7pm. 200ptas. Museum ☎ 96 391 81 27. Open Mar.-Nov. M-F 10am-1pm and 4:30-7pm, Sa 10am-1pm; Dec.-Feb. M-Sa 10am-1pm. 200ptas.)*

MUSEU PROVINCIAL DE BELLES ARTES. This compelling museum displays superb 14th- to 16th-century Valencian art and has been labeled one of Spain's premier art galleries. The collection also includes works by Spanish and foreign masters, including El Greco's *San Juan Bautista*, Velázquez's self-portrait, Ribera's Santa Teresa, and a slew of Goyas. Check out the sculpture pavilion. *(C. Sant Pius V, next to the Jardines del Reial. ☎ 96 360 57 93. Open Tu-Su 10am-2pm and 4-7:30pm. Free.)*

INSTITUTO VALÈNCIA DE ARTE MODERNO (IVAM). From classic avant-garde art between the world wars to the clash of the 1970s, this institute is home to a permanent collection of abstract works by 20th-century sculptor Julio González. *(C. Guillem de Castro, 118, west across the old river. ☎ 96 386 30 00. Open Tu-Su 10am-7pm. 350ptas, students 175ptas; Su free.)*

PARKS. Impressive parks lie on the outskirts of the historic district. Horticulturists will marvel at the **Jardín Botánico**, a university-maintained garden which cultivates 43,000 plants of 300 precisely labeled species from around the world. *(C. Beato Gaspar Bono, 6, on the western end of Río Turia. ☎ 96 391 16 57. Open Tu-Su 10am-9pm. 50ptas.)* One block farther, a series of manicured recreation areas marks the banks of the now diverted Río Turia. *(Open daily 10am-2pm and 5-9pm. Free.)*

OTHER SIGHTS. The elliptical **Basílica Virgen de los Desamparados** houses a resplendent golden altar. *(Behind the cathedral on Pl. Virgen. Open for mass M-F 7am-2pm and 5-9pm, Su 7:30am-2:30pm and 5-9:30pm. Free.)* The old **Lonja de la Seda (Silk Exchange)** is one of the foremost examples of Valencian Gothic architecture and a testament to Valencia's prominence in the medieval silk trade. *(Pl. Mercado. ☎ 96 352 54 78. Open Tu-Sa 9am-2pm and 5-9pm, Su 9am-1:30pm. Free.)*

◗ BEACHES

Sand-seekers can join the topless at the packed beaches on Valencia's coast. Sand and water quality is less than spectacular but the blistering heat converts all into sea-lovers. The most popular beaches are **Las Arenas** and **Malvarrosa**, connected by a bustling boardwalk and both on the Bus #19 route from Pl. Ayuntamiento (also #20, 21, and 22 in summer). Equally crowded but more attractive is **Salér**, a long, pine-bordered strand 14km from the city center straddled between lagoon and sea. Cafeterias and snack bars line the shore, and shower and bathroom facilities lie nearby. **Autobuses Buñol** buses (☎ 96 349 14 25) go to Salér (on the way to El Perello) from the intersection of Gran Vía Germanías and C. Sueca. To get to the bus stop, exit the train station, and take the street to the right (between the station and the bullfighting stadium) to Gran Vía Germanías. The bus stop is one block down (25min., every 30min., 160ptas).

🎭🎵 NIGHTLIFE AND ENTERTAINMENT

Use your siesta wisely—Valencia's nightlife will keep you drinking and dancing until sunrise. Bars and pubs around the **El Carme** district, just beyond the market, start hopping at 11:30pm. Follow Pl. Mercado and C. Bolsería (bearing right) to Pl. Tossal, where outdoor terraces, upbeat music, and *agua de Valencia* (orange juice, champagne, and vodka) entertain the masses.

Bar Sant Jaume and **Café Infanta**, both in Pl. Tossal, stay lively late into the night. American students and expats frequent two Irish pubs. One is **Finnegan's**, at Pl. Reina in front, and to the right, of the cathedral. The other is **The Black Sheep**, Pl. Porta de la Mar, 6, in the plaza on the old-city side of the huge bridge that looks like the dorsal fin of a fish; Wednesday is student night with pints of Guinness and Kilkenny for 350ptas. Both stay open until around 2am, when disco life begins.

Discos, which normally don't draw a crowd until at least 3am, dominate the university area, particularly on **Avenida Blasco Ibañez**. 20-somethings shake their bodies at the pubs off Av. Ibañez at Pl. Xúquer. In summer, however, the only places to be seen are the outdoor discos at Playa de Malvarrosa. **Caballito de Mar**, C. Eugenia Viñes, 22 (☎ 96 371 07 63), is the most popular and heats up with a psychedelic tunnel and huge outdoor deck. For more info, consult the *Qué y Dónde* weekly magazine, available at newsstands (150ptas), or the weekly entertainment supplement, *La Cartelera* (125ptas).

Valencia's most famous festival is **Las Fallas** (see **Pyromaniac's Paradise**, p. 282). During **Semana Santa**, the streets clog with lavishly attired monks enacting Biblical scenes and children performing the miracle plays of St. Vincent Ferrer. **Corpus Christi** follows soon after with its display of *rocas* or huge carriages symbolizing Biblical mysteries. The **Fira de Juliol** (July Fair) brings fireworks, cultural events, riverside concerts, bullfights, and a *batalla de flors*—a violent skirmish in which girls on passing floats throw flowers at the crowd, which in turn flings them back.

🔲 DAYTRIPS FROM VALENCIA

SAGUNTO (SAGUNT) (30MIN.)

Frequent RENFE Cercanías trains (☎ 96 266 07 28) from Valencia (the C-6 line) stop in Sagunto (30min.; every 30min. 8am-9pm, M-F 320ptas, Sa-Su 360ptas), as do Valldux- ense buses (☎ 96 466 18 50. 45min., every 30min., 275ptas).

The residents of Sagunto are thought to be the most courageous in Spain. Their reputation dates back to the 3rd century BC, when the citizens of Phoenician-con-trolled Sagunto (called Saguntum) held out for eight months against Hannibal's besieging Carthaginians. Some sources say that on the brink of annihilation, Sagunto's women, children, and elderly threw themselves into a burning furnace, while others insist that the residents chose starvation over defeat. Sagunto's monuments reflect the extensive list of those who have since conquered the region. By 1874, Sagunto had learned the hard way the art of surrendering; it became the first town to recognize Alfonso XII's restoration of the Bourbon monarchy.

The highlight of the old town is its refurbished **medieval castle**. (Open June-Sept. Tu-Sa 10am-8pm, Su 10am-2pm; Oct.-May Tu-Sa 10am-2pm and 4-6pm, Su 10am-2pm.) Along the way into town is the **Roman Theater,** which has survived a controversial restoration process to become an impressive modern performance stage, built entirely on the still-visible skeleton of the Roman structure. By the port (4km from the town center), **beaches** attract summer travelers. **Puerto de Sagunto** is the recent recipient of an EU beach award. **Buses** to the beaches leave from Av. Santos Patronos next to the tourist office (every 20min., 100ptas).

EAST COAST

MANISES (20MIN.)

Cercanías trains from Valencia along the C-4 line are a fast bet (20min.; every 30min.; M-F 155ptas, Sa-Su 175ptas) as are CVT buses (☎ 96 211 00 08), which depart from Valencia's bus station (30min., every 10min., 105ptas).

If you like ceramic artistry, you'll love the small town of Manises, famous for its hand-decorated ceramics. Venders push their colorful wares in the main square, and many houses in the town display the region's talents with hand-painted tiling.

CULLERA (35MIN.)

Cullera lies on the Cercanías train line between Valencia and Gandía (35min.; every hr.; M-F 320ptas, Sa-Su 360ptas). From the train station, take the bus into the city (105ptas); ask the bus driver to let you off near Pl. Virgen and point you toward Pl. Mercado. From Pl. Mercado go up the stairs in the back and continue up C. Calvari at the top. The road narrows as it climbs to the castle.

The rapidly growing town of Cullera stretches beneath the protective glare of its **13th-century castle,** recently reopened but still undergoing reconstruction. Those who complete the 15-minute zig-zag hike are rewarded with a 360-degree postcard-worthy view of the mountains, verdant rice paddies, the sea, the river, and the city beyond. Attached to the castle, the 19th-century **Santuari de la Verge** displays sundry religious treasures "collected" by castle residents over the years. (*Both castle and sanctuary open daily June-Aug. 10:30am-1:30pm and 5:30-8:15pm. Free.*)

L'ALBUFERA (40MIN.)

Autobuses Buñol buses (☎ 963 49 14 25) depart from the intersection of Gran Vía de Germanía and C. Sueca in Valencia and stop here en route to El Perello (40min., every 30min., 165ptas). To catch the return bus, walk with your back to the lagoon and cross the bridge on the right.

Spain's largest lagoon, L'Albufera, is 13km south of Valencia. L'Albufera is exactly what you'd expect from a nature enclave so close to business-minded Valencia—motorized boat tours weave around reeds while flying fish serenade cruisers.

MORELLA

The medieval fortress town of Morella looks like the scene of a Grimms' fairy-tale. Perched high on a mountain overlooking some of Cataluña's lushest countryside, Morella has seen its fair share of invaders trying to get their hands on the town's stunning **castle.** Celts, Romans, and Moors have all used Morella as a natural defense at different points in history, and they have left behind in their wake an interesting blend of cultures. The town itself is etched out of the mountainside. Most of its charming cobblestone streets climb the peak in spiraling switchbacks, but the tree-lined Cuesta de San Juan cuts vertically up the mountain with 200 stone steps bordered by small shops and delicious restaurants.

🚆 PRACTICAL INFORMATION. Morella is somewhat difficult to reach from Valencia. Visitors must pass through **Castelló,** which is on the **Cercanías train** line (1hr.; every 30min. 6:10am-10:20pm; M-F 495ptas, Sa 550ptas). From Barcelona, the **RENFE** Mediterranean line stops in Castelló (2½hr., 17 per day, 2065-2600ptas). From Castelló, **Autos Mediterráneo** (☎ 964 22 00 54 or 964 22 05 36) runs **buses** to Morella from their Pl. Fadrell office (2½hr.; from Castelló to Morella M-F 7:15am and 3:30pm, Sa 3:30pm; returns M-F 7:30am and 4pm, Sa 4pm; 1065ptas one-way). To get from the train station to the bus stop in Castelló, take a 525pta taxi or wait for one of the green buses to take you to Pl. Fadrell. The walk is long and tedious.

🏨🍴 ACCOMMODATIONS AND FOOD. Once you pass through the stone walls and Moorish archways of Morella into the town outskirts, you will never want to leave. Morella's nights are filled with cool breezes and glorious sunsets. For fantastic accommodations, try **Hostal El Cid,** Port Sant Mateu, 3, footsteps away from the bus station. Rooms are gigantic and come with all the luxuries of the nearest

Hilton, including TV, phone, bathtub, and balcony. (☎ 964 16 01 25. Singles 3200ptas; doubles 5200ptas.) Farther up the street is **Hostal La Muralla,** C. Muralla, 12, with perfume-scented rooms complete with private bath, striped comforters, and iron-wrought balconies. (☎ 964 16 02 43. Breakfast 400ptas. Singles 3000ptas; doubles 4000ptas. V, MC). The town's gourmet cuisine is filled with *rufas* (truffles) dug up from the local turf. Specialties include *paté de trufas* (truffle pâté) and *cordero relleno trufado* (lamb with truffle stuffing). The **Restaurante Casa Roque,** Cuesta de San Juan, 1, is the best truffle-joint in town. (☎ 964 16 03 36. Open Tu-Su 1-4pm and 8:30-11pm.) **Restaurante Cardenal Ram**, Cuesta Suner, 1 (☎ 964 1730 85), in the hotel and off C. Don Blasco de Alagon, offers beautiful views of the countryside. Hot rolls complement the delicious specialties, including hen, quail, rabbit, and lamb stuffed with truffles (1100-1600ptas). **Meson Del Pastor,** Cuesta Jovani, 5, serves delicious meals in an old-fashioned dining room. (☎ 964 16 02 99. Entrees 675-2200pta. Open daily noon-3:30pm, in summer also 9-11pm.)

🔘 **SIGHTS.** The ▨**Castell de Morella,** perched atop a massive rock, dazzles even the most seasoned of castle-goers. Celts, Romans, and Moors all chose Morella for its natural defenses. El Cid stormed the summit in 1084, and Don Blasco de Aragón took the town in the name of Jaume I in 1232. Civil wars in the 19th century and an internal explosion have damaged the castle, but the resulting craters only add to the castle's intrigue. The castle is surrounded by artillery walls with openings just wide enough for the arrows of fighting soldiers or the lens of your Olympus. Inspect the **Cadro guardhouse** or the **Catxo dungeon,** where the prince of Vienna spent his nights in the 15th century. (☎ 964 17 31 28. Entrance on C. Hospital, uphill from the basilica and through the Convent of St. Frances. Open daily 10:30am-7:30pm; in winter until 6:30pm. 300ptas, students 100ptas.) In Pl. Arciprestal, on the way to the castle, the Gothic **Basílica Santa María la Mayor** hovers over a windy stairwell, an overgrown organ and a ghostly statue of Nuestra Señora de la Asunción. The altar decked with gold chandeliers and balconies appears to tell its own story. (Open daily June-Aug. 11am-2pm and 4-7pm; Sept.-May noon-2pm and 4-6pm. Basilica free; museum inside costs 150ptas.) Exit the city from Puerta de San Miguel, turn left, and walk five minutes to the remnants of the 13th-century Gothic **aqueduct,** which has 16 towers and six gates. Morella's streets are just as charming as its sights. Cruise from pastry-shop to antique store on **Don Blasco de Alagon** and **Marquesa Segura Barreda** or walk up the 100 steps of the Cuesta de San Juan with its lovely stores and restaurants.

JÁTIVA (XÀTIVA)

Once the second most populated city in Valencia, Játiva, a place of palaces and churches, still retains traces of its opulent past. The birthplace of the Borgia Popes Calixtus III and Alexander VI and later home of the Baroque painter José Ribera, the town used to be prosperous and well-known. Unfortunately for Játiva, the last person of note to pass through was Felipe V, who burned it to the ground in the 18th century. Játiva is now a simple, pleasant city that snares few tourists and loses its locals to coastal neighbors during the hot summer months. **Alameda de Jaume I** divides the town into two parts: the new village and the old village, located at the foot of a hill topped by an awe-inspiring ▨**castle.** The castle has two sections: the **castell machor,** on the right as you enter, and the pre-Roman **castell chicotet.** The former, used from the 13th through the 16th century, bears the scars of many sieges and earthquakes. Its arched, stone **prison** has held some famous wrongdoers, including King Fernando el Católico and the Comte d'Urgell, would-be usurper of the Aragonese throne. Comte is now buried in its chapel. (Open Tu-Su 10am-7pm; in winter Tu-Su 10am-6pm. 300ptas, students and seniors 150ptas.) Exit the tourist office to the right, take the first right and ascend Portal de Lleo and C. Peris Urios to find **Colegiata de Santa María,** a giant church known as **La Seu.** Constructed from 1596 to 1920, the ornate *colegiata* now operates as a religious museum that features paintings and figurines. (Open daily 9:30am-1:30pm. Museum 100ptas.) Jativa's annual **Fira festival,** dating from 1250, storms the city with live music, bullfights, and pulling contests from August 15th to 20th.

EAST COAST

EL SEXENNI When the epidemic plague of the 1620s returned in 1672, the people of Morella faced extinction. After exhausting the scientific options, city leaders turned to religion for salvation. They asked for help from the Virgin of Vallivana, leading a prayer procession over 20km to the Sanctuary of Vallivana. When they returned the plague had left town, never to return. To thank the Virgin and remind future generations of the miracle, the town vowed to honor her every six years, beginning in 1678. The tradition continues today: Morella will celebrate its 52nd *Sexenni* in the year 2006, with nine days of festivities in the second half of August.

To reach the old village and the train station from the train station, walk straight up Baixada de L'Estació and turn left at its end. The **tourist office,** Alameda Jaume I, 50, across from the Ajuntament, has a map and restaurant guide. (☎ 96 227 33 46. English spoken. Open June 15-Sept. 15 Tu-F 10am-2:30pm and 5-7pm, Sa-Su 10am-2pm; Sept. 16-June 14 Tu-F 9am-2pm and 4-6pm, Sa-Su 10am-2pm.) In an emergency call ☎ 112 or the **Hospital Lluis Alcanyis** (emergency ☎ 96 228 95 21), Ctra. Alzira, 2km from the town center. The **post office** is on Av. Alameda Jaume I, 33 (open 8:30am-2:30pm, Sa 9:30am-1pm). The **postal code** is 46800. If you plan on staying the night, try **Margallonero,** Pl. Mercat, 42. From the train station, turn left on Alameda Jaume I, take the first right onto C. St. Francese, go straight up the ramp onto C. Alos, and take the first left on C. Botigues, which runs into Pl. Mercat. (☎ 96 227 66 77. 1400ptas per person.) Tuesday and Friday are **market** days in Pl. Mercat (open 8am-1pm) and the **Mercadona supermarket** is on Av. Abu Masaif, just off Baixada de L'Estació (open M-Sa 9am-9pm). **Trains** are the best way to get in and out of Játiva. **RENFE** (☎ 96 352 02 02) runs to: **Gandía** (45min., every 30min., 550ptas); **Valencia** (1hr., every 30min., 390-435ptas); **Madrid** (3hr., 2 per day, 5300ptas); **Barcelona** (4hr., 8 per day, 4800ptas); and **Granada** (2 per day, 5100ptas). **Chambitos** buses (☎ 96 219 20 36) go direct to **Gandía** (1¼hr., 1 per day, 400ptas).

GANDÍA

Centuries before the EU began blue-flagging the Mediterranean's best beaches, the powerful Borjas family—of Valencian lineage—had already discovered Gandía, transforming it into a center of noble activity. Five centuries later, the city still cashes in on agricultural products, but most of its income comes from the visitors seeking the simplicity and peace of a seaside vacation in Gandía; fine sands stretch for kilometers here, and there's little else to do but sunbathe. **La Marina buses,** Marqués de Campo, 14, next to the tourist office, run to the **beach** along Pg. Marítim (every 15min., last bus 1am in summer, 11:30pm in winter, 125ptas).

Everything you might need in Gandía is a stone's throw from the train station on **Marqués de Campo.** The **tourist office,** Marqués de Campo, across from the train station, offers a free detailed map (☎ 96 287 77 88. English spoken. Open June-Aug. M-F 10am-2pm and 4:30-7:30pm, Sa 10am-1pm; Sept.-May M-F 9:30am-1:30pm and 4-7pm, Sa 10am-1pm.) **Another branch** is at Pg. Marítim on the water. (☎ 96 284 24 07. Open Mar. 15-Oct. 15 M-Sa 10am-2pm and 5-8pm, Su 10am-1pm; Oct. 16-Mar. 14 Su 10am-1pm.) Services include: **emergency** (☎ 112); **police** (☎ 96 287 88 00); and the **post office,** Pl. Jaume I, 7, a few blocks behind the Ayuntamiento. (☎ 96 287 10 91. Open M-F 8:30am-2:30pm.) The **postal code** is 46700. **Email** your significant other at **Intern@ut@,** Magistrado Catala, 5. Walk through the cement park next to the tourist office and make a right. (☎ 96 964 960. 250ptas for 30min.)

Gandía is full of expensive hotels; if you want to stay here on the cheap, make reservations well in advance, especially in August and on weekends. **Hotel Europa,** C. Levante, 12-14, is the least expensive of the beachfront establishments and has some huge rooms with mountain views. From the tourist office, hop on the **La Marina** bus and ask to be let off at the C. Levante stop (135ptas), then walk down C. Ermita, which becomes C. Levante. (☎ 96 284 07 50. Breakfast 350ptas. Singles with bath 4000ptas; doubles with shower 5000ptas, with bath 6000ptas.) **Hotel La Alberca,** C. Cullera, 8, offers nicely decorated rooms with air conditioning and TVs. (☎ 96 284 51 63. Singles 4280ptas, doubles 7490ptas.) **El Nido,** C. Alcoy, 22, is right off the beach. (☎ 96 284 46 40. Doubles 7000ptas.) Stock up on groceries at **Supermarket Macedonia,** C. Perú, across from the La Amistad stop (open M-Sa 9am-9pm).

RENFE trains (☎ 902 24 02 02) run from Valencia to **Platja i Grau de Gandía**, Gandía's beach (3-4 per day, 495ptas). Trains also depart from Marqués de Campo to **Valencia** (1hr., every 30min 6am-10:20pm, 1600ptas) and **Játiva** (380ptas). **UBESA**, C. Magistrado Catalan, 3 (☎ 96 296 50 66; in Valencia ☎ 96 340 08 05) runs **buses** to: **Valencia** (1¼hr., 9-12 per day, 710ptas); **Alicante** (3hr., 9-12 per day, 1185ptas); and **Barcelona** (7-8hr., 1 per day, 3600ptas). Buses also stop in **Dénia** (320ptas), **Calpe** (540ptas), **Altea** (640ptas), and **Elche** (1280ptas). **Auto Res**, Marqués de Campo, 12 (☎ 96 287 10 64), across from the train station, runs buses to the beach at Pg. Marítim en route to **Madrid** (5½hr., 7 per day, 3300ptas).

NEAR GANDÍA: PLATJA DE PILES

Just 10km south and a short bus ride away from Gandía, Platja de Piles offers endless stretches of beach, plus a fantastic youth hostel. From Gandía, **La Amistad**, Av. Marqués de Campo, 9 (☎ 96 287 44 10), runs to and from Platja de Piles (10 per day 8:45am-8:30pm, 125ptas). Buses depart from outside the train station, across from the supermarket. While in Platja, spend the night at ◪**Alberg Mar i Vent (HI)** (☎ 96 283 17 48 or 283 17 25), on C. Dr. Fleming. Walk down the street from the bus stop, then follow the signs to the hostel. The beach is out the back door. **Bike rental** (1000ptas per day), **kayak rental,** and **windsurfing** lessons are also available. (No alcohol. Washing machine and library. 3-day max. stay, flexible if uncrowded. Curfew weeknights 2am, Sa 4am. Usually closed in Dec. and Jan. Call well in advance for reservations. Sheets 300ptas for entire stay. Dorms 800ptas, over 26 1100ptas.)

ALICANTE (ALACANT)

Alicante (pop. 285,000) is somehow both dutifully entertaining and quietly charming—the best type of resort town. While a multifaceted nightlife energizes the city, Alicante's famous, mosaic-lined waterside *explanada* relaxes it at sunset. The sizable Playa Postiguet sprawls a few feet from the town's center, where lanky palms line the avenues and fountained plazas. High above the rows of sun-darkened bodies, the ancient castle, spared by Franco, guards the wicked tangle of streets in the cobblestoned *casco antiguo*.

▐ TRANSPORTATION

Flights: Aeroport Internacional El Altet (☎ 96 691 90 00), 10km from town. **Alcoyana** (☎ 96 516 79 11) bus C-6 runs to the airport from Pl. Luceros (every 40min., 140ptas). **Iberia** (24hr. ☎ 902 40 05 00) and **Air Europa** (☎ 902 24 00 42).

Trains: RENFE, Estació Término (☎ 902 24 02 02), on Av. Salamanca, at the end of Av. Estación. Info open daily 7am-midnight. Many destinations require a transfer. Direct service to: **Elche** (30min., 240ptas); **Murcia** (1½hr., every hr. 6:05am-10:05pm, 570ptas); **Valencia** (1½hr., 12 per day, 2900-4700ptas); **Madrid** (4hr., 9 per day 4700-6900ptas); and **Barcelona** (4½-6hr., 9 per day, 6000-9900ptas). **Ferrocarriles de la Generalitat Valenciana,** Estació Marina, Av. Villajoyosa, 2 (☎ 96 526 27 31), on Explanada d'Espanya, by the beginning of the beach. Service along the Costa Blanca day and night (see **Costa Blanca: Getting There and Away,** p. 291). In summer the **Trensnochador** (night train; ☎ 96 526 27 31) runs to beaches near **Alicante** (F-Sa every hr., Su-Th 10:30pm-6am; round-trip 150-700ptas).

Buses: C. Portugal, 17 (☎ 96 513 07 00). To reach Explanada d'Espanya from the station, turn left on Carrer d'Italia and continue walking; the street will change to C. San Fernando. At Rambla Méndez Nuñez, make a right towards the waterfront. **UBESA** (☎ 96 513 01 43) runs to: **Altea** (550ptas); **Calpe** (650ptas); **Jávea** (895ptas); **Dénia** (1025ptas) and **Valencia** (1980ptas). **Mollá** (☎ 96 513 08 51) goes to **Elche** (M-Sa every hr., Su every other hr., 210ptas). **Enatcar** (☎ 96 513 06 73) runs to: **Granada** (6hr., 5 per day, 3375ptas); **Madrid** (6½hr., 7 per day, 3000ptas); **Málaga** (8hr., 5 per day, 4500ptas); **Barcelona** (8hr., 6 per day, 4700ptas) and **Sevilla** (10hr., 2 per day, 6000ptas). **Linebús** (☎ 96 522 95 04) to **Brussels** (7:30am, 13,000ptas); **Amsterdam** (7:30am, 14,000ptas); and **Paris** (11:30am, 15,675ptas).

Ferries: Flebasa lines leave from nearby Dénia (see p. 293).

EAST COAST

Taxis: ☎ 96 525 25 11.

Public Transportation: New since 1999: **TAM** (☎ 96 514 09 36). Buses #21 and 22 go from Alicante to Playa San Juan. For other routes, get a schedule at the tourist office.

⁑ 🛈 ORIENTATION AND PRACTICAL INFORMATION

Originating at the train station, **Avenida de la Estación** becomes **Avenida Alfonso X el Sabio** after passing through Pl. Luceros. **Explanada d'Espanya** stretches along the waterfront between Rbla. Méndez Núñez and Av. Federico Soto, which reach back up to Av. Alfonso X El Sabio. Together these form the grid of streets which constitutes the center of town.

Tourist Office: Main city office, C. Portugal, 17 (☎ 96 592 98 02), at the bus station. Open M-Sa June-Aug. 9am-2:30pm and 5-8pm; Sept.-May 9am-2:30pm. **2nd office** (☎ 96 520 03 77), on Playa Postiguet. English spoken. Open June-Aug. M-F 10am-8pm, Sa 10am-2pm; Sept.-May M-Sa 10am-2pm. **Regional office,** Explanada d'Espanya, 2 (☎ 96 520 00 00; fax 96 520 02 43). Info on the entire coast. English spoken. Open June-Aug. M-F 10am-8pm, Sa 10am-2pm and 3-8pm; Sept.-May M-F 10am-7pm, Sa 10am-2pm. Also an **airport branch** (☎ 96 691 91 00), a **branch** by the **Ayuntamiento** (☎ 900 21 10 27), and 1 by **Playa Postiguet** (☎ 96 520 03 77).

Budget Travel: TIVE, Pl. San Cristóbal, 8 (☎ 96 521 16 86). ISIC 700ptas. HI card 1800ptas. Open M-F 9am-1:30pm and 5-8pm.

Luggage Storage: At the **bus station** (200-500ptas per bag) and the **train station** (400ptas per bag). Both open M-Sa 8am-8:30pm, Su 10am-1pm and 3:45-7pm.

Emergency: ☎ 112. **Police:** Comisaría, C. Médico Pascual Pérez, 33 (☎ 96 510 7 200).

Hospital: Hospital General, C. Maestro Alonzo, 109 (☎ 96 593 83 00).

Post Office: Corner of C.Arzobispo Loaces and C. Alemania, near the bus station. (☎ 96 521 99 84). **Lista de Correos.** Open M-F 8:30am-8:30pm, Sa 9:30am-2pm. **2nd branch,** Bono Guarner, 2 (☎ 96 522 78 71), next to the RENFE Station. Same hours. **Postal Code:** 03070.

Internet Access: Yazzgo, Explanada, 3. next to Burger King. Open daily 8am-11:30pm. 250ptas for 30 min.

┏ ACCOMMODATIONS

Although there seem to be hostels on every corner, truly desirable rooms are rare. Good, cheap places require an early arrival or a reservation. In winter, prices drop significantly. If necessary, try the tourist office's accommodations list.

🏨 **Pensión Les Monges Palace,** C. Monjas, 2 (☎ 96 521 50 46), behind the Ayuntamiento. By far one of the most luxurious hostels in all of Spain. Rooms with satellite TVs, paintings, and A/C (700ptas per day). Winter heating. Parking 1000ptas per day. Singles 2200-2500ptas, with bath 3400ptas; doubles 4000ptas-4500ptas, with bath 5000ptas; triples 5300-5800ptas, with bath 6300ptas. V, MC.

Habitaciones México, C. General Primo de Rivera, 10 (☎ 96 520 93 07), off the end of Av. Alfonso X El Sabio.Internet 800ptas per hr. Laundry 1000ptas per load. A/C. Singles 1900ptas; doubles 3600ptas, with bath 4200ptas; triples with bath 6000ptas.

Residencia Universitaria (HI), Av. Orihuela, 59 (☎ 96 511 30 44). Take bus #03 (100ptas). Individual rooms with private bath and A/C, snack bar, big-screen TV, free laundry, pool table, and foosball. 3-day max. stay. Call well in advance. Dorms 800ptas, with breakfast 900ptas, with 3 meals 1900ptas; over 26 dorms 1100ptas, with breakfast 1400ptas, with 3 meals 2400ptas. Open July-Sept. only.

Hostal-Residencia Portugal, C. Portugal, 26 (☎ 96 592 92 44), across from the bus station. Very friendly atmosphere. The functional dining room/lounge has a color TV. Hospital-lit interior rooms have fans and good beds. Ask for a brighter room with windows to the street. TV 400ptas. Singles 2700ptas; doubles 4000ptas, with bath 4900ptas; triples 5400ptas, with bath 6600ptas.

Camping: Playa Mutxavista (☎ 96 565 45 26), 2nd-class site near the beach. Take bus #21. 520ptas per person and per tent. Open year-round.

Alicante

▲ ACCOMMODATIONS
Habitaciones México, 3
Hostal-Residencia Portugal, 2
Pensión Les Monges Palace, 4
Residencia Universitaria (HI), 1

Mediterranean Sea

N

C. Jovellanos

C. Virgen del Socorro

C. Vázquez de Mella

Castell de Santa Bárbara

Elevator to Castell

Iglesia de Sta. María

Museo de Arte del Siglo XX La Asegurada

PL. STA. MARIA

FGV

Platja de El Postiguet

TO NEW PORT

SAN ROQUE

SANTA CRUZ

C. la Fábrica

C. la Esperanza

C. Platos

Iglesia de Sta. Cruz

Monjas

PL. AYUNTAMIENTO

C. Altamira

Catedral

C. Gral. Primo de Rivera

C. San Vicente

Rambla de Méndez Núñez

Plaza de Toros

PLAZA ESPAÑA

C. Calderón de la Barca

C. El Pintor Velázquez

Av. Constitución

Mercado

C. Capitán Segura

C. Garcia Morato

C. Vasallo

C. Iglesias

Av. Alfonso X El Sabio

Av. Camelo Calvo

C. Belando

C. Segusa

Av. del General Marvá

C. Poeta Quintana

C. Médico Pascual Pérez

C. Álvarez Sereix

Supermarket

Av. Federico Soto

PL. DE LOS LUCEROS

C. Gral. O'Donnell

C. Poeta Vila y Blanco

Museu Arqueológico de la Diputación

C. San Juan Bosco

C. Benito

C. Tucumán

Av. La Estación

C. Cat. Ferré Vidiella

Cardenal Belluga

Av. Salamanca

Enriqueta Ortega

Paya

Cardenal

C. Pintor Gisbert

Av. Adolfo Muñoz Alonso

to (2 km)

C. Pardo Gimeno

C. Foglietti

C. Wenceslao Fernández Flórez

Castillo de San Fernando

C. Bazán

PL. DEL TEATRO

NUEVA

C. Colón

C. San Francisco

C. Chapaull

PL. BARÓN DE FINESTRAT

PL. GABRIEL MIRÓ

San Fernando

Explanada d'Espanya

Port

Av. Dr. Gadea

C. Alemania

C. Portugal

C. Gral. Lacy

El Corte Inglés

C. Serrano

Av. Maisonnave

C. Pintor Aparicio

C. Pintor Lorenzo Casanova

C. d'Italia

Av. Oscar Esplá

Av. Aguilera

0   200 yards
0   200 meters

EAST

Mayor

Soler

PL. DE CANALEJAS

PG. Canalejas

C. Arquitecto Morell

C. Gral. Soriano

FOOD

Most tourists refuel along the main pedestrian thoroughfares. The smaller, cheaper, family-run *bar-restaurantes* in the old city are less touristed. The most popular *terrazas* stuff C. San Francisco with cheap *menús* and *tapas;* locals and tourists devour *tapas* on C. Mayor. For pricier meals with lovely ambiance, head to the new port. The **market** is near Av. Alfonso X El Sabio (open M-Sa 8am-2pm). Buy basics at **Supermarket Mercadona,** C. Alvarez Sereix, 5, off Av. Federico Soto. (☎ 96 521 58 94. Open M-Sa 9am-9pm.)

Cafeteria Mediterráneo (☎ 96 514 08 40), C. Altamira, 8, 2 blocks from the Explanada. A low-key, bustling cafe bursting with locals. Chrome bar flaunts huge array of raw fish. 4-course *menú* 1000ptas. Open M-Sa 7am-4pm and 6-11pm.

La Venta del Lobo, C. San Fernando, 48 (☎ 96 514 09 85), 2 blocks toward the center from Av. Dr. Gadea. 6 different *menús* with regional specialties from all over Spain; 4-course seafood *menú* 1200ptas. Complement your courses with *sangría.* Entrees 400-1000ptas. Open Tu-Sa 1-4:30pm and 8:30pm-12:30am, Su 1-4pm.

El Sultan, C. San Fernando, 8 (☎ 965 21 02 47). Have your very own Arabian night with simmering kebabs, rice dishes, and hummus platters (375-950ptas). Music will leave you ready to jump off your flying carpet. Open daily 7:30pm-midnight, Sa-Su 1:30-4pm.

SIGHTS AND BEACHES

Complete with drawbridges, dark passageways, and hidden tunnels, the **Castell de Santa Bárbara** keeps silent guard over Alicante's beach. Built by the Carthaginians and recently renovated, the 200m high fortress has a dry moat, dungeon, and ammunition storeroom. The *Albacar Vell,* or lower zone, opened during the Middle Ages and is now home to a vast sculpture garden with exhibits from Spanish greats. Don't miss the view of Alicante from *Baluarte de la Mina.* A paved road from the old section of Alicante leads to the top although most people take the **elevator** from a hidden entrance on Av. Jovellanos, across the street from Playa Postiguet and near the white crosswalk. (☎ 96 526 31 31. Open Apr.-Sept. 10am-7:30pm; Oct.-Mar. 9am-6:30pm. Free. Elevator 400ptas.) The **Museu de Arte del Siglo XX La Asegurada** showcases Valencian modernist art pieces, along with a few Mirós, Picassos, Kandinskys, and Calders. (Pl. Santa María, 3, at the east end of C. Mayor. ☎ 96 514 07 68. Open May.-Sept. Tu-Sa 10:30am-1:30pm and 6-9pm, Su 10:30am-1pm; Oct.-Apr. Tu-Sa 10am-1pm and 5-8pm, Su 10am-1pm. Free.)

Alicante's **Playa del Postiguet** attracts intense beach volleyball players. Six-kilometer-long **Playa de San Juan** and **Playa del Mutxavista** are also popular options, and the regional tourist office has a listing of *bandera azul* beaches (an award for quality given by the EU) on the Alicante-Dénia rail line. (For San Juan, take TAM buses #21, 22, or 31. For Mutxavista, take #21. All depart every 15min., 105ptas. Or take the Alicante-Dénia train from the main station; 20min., every hr., 105ptas.)

ENTERTAINMENT

A good deal of Alicante's nightlife actually takes place outside of town. Most start their evening with *copas* and *chupitos* in the **pubs** and **tapas bars** of the *casco antiguo.* DJs spin from 7pm to 4am in Alicante's **new port;** learn to salsa and dance the merengue every night at 11pm at **Captain Haddocks.** Show off your moves at the crowded **Puerto Di Roma** or fight for seats at the classy, *Modernista*-style **Nelson Bar.** On the *explanada,* at Pl. Canelejas, **Petit Pachá** welcomes those who don't want to brave its bigger brother in Benidorm (cover 1000ptas and up). On Sundays, bands and orchestras line the *explanada. Bares-musicales* also line **Playa de San Juan.** A **taxi** for up to four people from Alicante to Playa San Juan costs about 1000ptas. The **Buhobus** also runs to Playa San Juan (TAM #21 and 21c, every 20min., 100ptas). In July and August, **Ferrocarriles de la Generalitat Valenciana** runs special **Trensnochador** night trains from Estació Marina to several points along the beach (see **Trains,** p. 288, for more info). Pick up a schedule, along with discounts on cover charges, at the tourist office.

During July and August, la Playa de San Juan also becomes a stage for early-evening **ballet and musical performances** as part of the *Plataforma Cultural* series; get schedules at the tourist office. The "Disco Benidorm" (round-trip 650ptas), in package-tour-crazy Benidorm, stops near hard-core *discotecas* like **Penélope, Pachá, KU, KM,** and **Insomnia.** (Open nightly until 9am. Cover from 1500ptas.)

❊ FESTIVALS

On January 17th, Alicante suburbs celebrate the **Porrat de Sant Antoni** with street parades, a pig raffle and offerings of sweets (called *pesas)* from boyfriends to their sweethearts. From June 20 to 29, hedonistic celebrations erupt for the **Festival de Sant Joan.** *Fogueres* (symbolic or satiric effigies) are paraded around the *casco antiguo,* then burned in a bonfire on the 24th. The revelry continues with breathtaking nightly fireworks and street decorations and ends with the *Banya,* or drenching of all the young people by firehoses. The **Verge del Remei** procession takes place on August 3; pilgrims trek to the monastery of Santa Faz the following Thursday. Alicante honors La Virgen del Demedio all summer with the **Fiestas del Verano,** when numerous concerts and theatrical performances are held in the new open-air theater on the port; inquire at the tourist office for a schedule.

▓ DAYTRIPS FROM ALICANTE

ISLA TABARCA (30MIN.)

This island, 15km south of Alicante, was once a lockup for Spanish exiles; today it is a natural reserve and a popular place for **scuba diving.** It also waves an EU blue flag for fabulous beaches. One of the most reliable scuba companies is **Cruceros Kon Tiki,** which leaves for Tabarca from the Explanada d'Espanya in Alicante. (☎ 96 521 63 96. 30min.; July-Aug. 4 per day 10:30am-3:30pm; Sept.-June 1 per day; round-trip 1700ptas.) For more information on the island, call ☎ 902 10 09 10.

COVAS DE CANALOBRE (30MIN.)

To get to the caves, rent a car in Alicante and drive to the tiny town of Busot.

These spectacular, stalagmited caves are situated 24km north of Alicante, above the tiny village of **Busot.** (☎ 96 569 92 50. Open daily June 21-Sept. 10:30am-7:50pm; Oct.-June 20 11am-5:50pm. 600ptas.)

COSTA BLANCA

You could while away a lifetime in the charming resort towns of the Costa Blanca. The "white coast" that extends from Dénia through Calpe, Alicante, and Elche derives its name from the fine, white sand of its shores. A varied terrain of hills blanketed with cherry blossoms, craggy mountains, lush pine-layered hillsides, and natural lagoons surrounds densely inhabited coastal towns. Altea, Calpe, Dénia, and especially Jávea offer relief from the disco-droves that energize Alicante and Benidorm, although even these towns are not tourist-free.

▐ TRANSPORTATION

UBESA (in Valencia ☎ 96 340 08 55; in Alicante ☎ 96 513 01 43) runs inexpensive **buses** between Alicante and Valencia (every hr., 6:30am-9pm). UBESA is the easiest and most cost-efficient way to get around the Costa Blanca. From **Valencia** buses run to: **Gandía** (1½hr., 12 per day); **Dénia** (2hr., 9 per day); **Jávea** (2hr., 5 per day); **Calpe** and **Altea** (3-3½hr., 10 per day); **Alicante** (4½hr., 13 per day 6:30am-6pm). From **Alicante** buses run to: **Altea** (1¼hr., 18 per day); **Calpe** (1½hr., 18 per day); **Jávea** (2½hr., 5 per day); and **Dénia** (2½hr., 14 per day). Only buses that

EAST COAST

leave before 6pm make it all the way to Valencia. **Ferrocarrils de la Generalitat Valenciana** (general info ☎ 96 592 02 02; in Alicante ☎ 96 526 27 31), with its Alicante-Dénia line, competes with UBESA and offers similar prices and frequencies, but adds stops at San Juan and El Campello, beaches near Alicante. Trains depart Alicante every hour on the hour from 6am to 9pm for **Altea** (1½hr.). Trains leaving on even-numbered hours continue to **Calpe** (1¾hr.) and **Dénia** (2¼hr.). From Dénia and Calpe, trains return to **Alicante** every two hours (6:25am-7:25pm), while from Altea trains depart every hour (6:24am-10:24pm). Railpasses are not valid on these trains. **Trensnochador** (☎ 96 526 22 33), the night train running out of Alicante, goes as far as Altea in the summer (F-Sa every hr., Su-Th every other hr. 10:20pm-6am).

ALTEA

Altea, perched atop a small hill, is a fabled land of stone and sun. On the planks of the narrow **Passeig Mediterrani,** the crests of furious waves jump from behind large boulders to drench passersby. With its proximity to Alicante, Altea can be either a pleasant daytrip or a relaxing getaway. From the beach, narrow cobblestone streets and steps wind up to **Plaza de la Iglesia.** Shaded by the cobalt dome of the church of the **Virgen del Consuelo,** the square commands breathtaking views of the turquoise Mediterranean. **Comte d' Altea** is the main drag and is filled with snack shops and beachware galore. During the last week of September the city erupts with music, gunpowder, and dance for the **Fiestas de Moros y Cristianos.**

Hostal Paco's air-conditioned rooms, Jaime I, 7-A, right off Comte d' Altea, have full baths and wide windows. (☎ 965 84 05 41. Singles 5000ptas; doubles 8000ptas.) Both trains and buses stop at the foot of the hill and along the coast on C. La Mar (coming out of the station, head left to go toward the center). If arriving by bus from Alicante, get off at the 1st stop; if arriving from Valencia, get off at the 2nd stop. The **tourist office** is on C. Sant Pere, 9, parallel to C. La Mar. From the train station or the bus stop, walk 50m toward the sea to C. Sant Pere. (☎ 96 584 41 14; fax 96 584 42 13. Open M-Sa 10am-2pm and 5-8pm.) Services include **emergency** (☎112) and **ambulance** (☎ 96 584 35 32). **Email** jealous *amigos* from **Red Attack,** C. Garganes, 9. (☎ 96 688 12 91. 200ptas for 30min.)

CALPE (CALP)

Stepping into Calpe is like stepping into a surreal Dalí landscape of dripping color and shocking contrast. Sixty-two kilometers northeast of Alicante, the sloping town sits diminutively beneath the **Peñó d'Ifach** (327m), a gargantuan, flat-topped rock protrusion whose precipitous face drops straight to the sea. Farther north are the cliffs and caves of the easterly **Cabo de la Nao,** from which, on clear days, you can see Ibiza. Around the bend from the *cabo,* a castle and watch-tower have protected the old fishing village of **Moraira** from pirates for centuries.

Commercialized Calpe attracts hordes of *madrileños* who stroll on the sand at dusk, enjoy summertime fireworks, and grab seaside seats at one of the many outdoor eateries. The main avenue, **Gabriel Miró,** descends to the blue-flagged (EU praised) **Platja Arena-Bol. Platja Levante,** beyond the Peñó, and the cove of **Calalga,** both bear the flapping *bandera azúl.* **UBESA buses** stop 2km from the beach at C. Capitán Pérez Jorda. To get to town, follow signs to the tourist office, across the intersection, and curve downhill to the left on Av. Masnou or take an **Autobuses Ifach bus** past the bus station and to the beach (1 per hr., 110ptas). The **tourist office,** Av. Ejércitos Españoles, 62, on the street that runs from the old town along the beach, has all the info you need on Costa Blanca beaches (open June-Aug. M-Sa 9am-9pm, Su 10:30am-2pm; Sept.-May hours vary). Get your web fix at **Internet Center Perlamar,** C. Benidorm, 1, right off Gabriel Miro, three blocks from the beach (200ptas per 30min). For a comfortable sleep, try the tiny English-run **Pensión Céntrica,** Pl. Ifach. (☎ 96 583 55 28. 1500ptas per person.) The most reasonably priced **restaurants** in Calpe line the incline toward the old town.

ELCHE (ELX)

An oasis-like city surrounded by one of Europe's only palm forests, Elche, 23km from Alicante, is a tropical paradise. Locals, however, have no time to lounge—they're busy supplying Spain with their highly regarded footwear. The **Dama de Elche**, Spain's finest example of pre-Roman sculpture, hails from here, although it now rests at the Museo Arqueológico Nacional in Madrid (see **Museums**, p. 111). At the corner of Av. Ferrocarril and Po. Estación begins the **Parque Municipal**, where doves and palm trees glide and sway above subtropical flora and imitation Arabic fountains (open daily June-Aug. 7am-midnight; Sept.-May 7am-9pm). Of Elche's parks and public gardens, the most beautiful is definitely the **Hort del Cura (Orchard of the Priest)**, where magnificent trees shade colorful flower beds. (Open June-Aug. 9am-9pm; Sept.-May 9am-6pm. 300ptas.)

Both the **train station, Estación Parque**, and the **bus station** (☎ 96 545 58 58), are on Av. Libertat. Buses serve **Alicante** and the private, quietly rolling sand dunes of **La Marina d'Elx** (M-Sa 6 per day, 210ptas), as well as other local routes. The best way to get to Elche from Alicante or Murcia is by **Cercanías train**, although buses also run (see **Getting There and Away**, p. 291). To get to the town center from the bus and train stations, go left leaving either station and left again on Po. Estación. The **tourist office** is on Pl. Parc, at the end of Po. Estación. (☎ 96 545 27 47. Open M-F 10am-7pm and 4:15-7:45pm, Sa-Su 10am-2pm.)

DÉNIA

Halfway between Valencia and Alicante on the promontory that forms the Golfo de Valencia, Dénia (named by the Greeks for Diana, goddess of the hunt, the moon, and purity) is an upscale family resort. Though the town has little to offer budget travelers in the way of bargains, its beautiful beaches, water-sports, and tasty restaurants are enough to make even the most thrifty splurge a little, and the harbor serves as an important ferry connection to the Balearic Islands. In the summer the town goes nuts with several wild festivals.

■ **ORIENTATION AND PRACTICAL INFORMATION.** The **train station** (☎ 96 578 04 45) is on C. Calderón. The **UBESA bus station** is on Pl. Arxiduc Carles. Local buses leave from the tourist office to nearby beaches (105ptas). To head toward the Balearics by sea, consult **Balearia Eurolinies Maritimes** (☎ 902 160 180). The same-day package for 7750ptas leaves from Dénia at 7:30am and returns at midnight from San Antonio. The disco-ferry package costs 10,000ptas and includes tickets to disco-giant, **Privilege**. For full transportation info, see **Getting There and Away**, p. 469. Most **tourist services**, including local **buses, trains, ferries**, the tourist office, and the **post office**, cluster on **Calle Patricio Fernández**, running straight to the port. Turn left out of the Enactean/UBESA bus office and turn left out of the plaza onto C. Patricio Fernandez to reach the center of town. The **tourist office**, C. Glorieta Oculista Baigues, 9, 30m inland from Estació Marítima, directs travelers to beach and accommodations. (☎ 96 642 23 67. Open July-Sept. daily 9:30am-2pm and 4:30-8pm; Oct.-June M-Sa 10am-2pm and 5-8pm, Su 10am-2pm.) Write your emails at **CiberDeni@**, C. Senija. Walk down C. Patricio Fernández from the bus station away from the port, make your third right on C. Sagunto, and your second right on C. Senjira. (☎ 96 643 14 81. 250ptas per 30min.)

▛▜ **ACCOMMODATIONS AND FOOD.** The tourist office has a list of accommodations; among the less expensive options is **Hostal Comercio**, C. de la Vía, 43, between the tourist office and the bus station. (☎/fax 96 578 00 71. Singles 5000ptas; doubles 7900ptas.) **Hotel Costa Blanca**, C. Pintor Llorens, 3, up the block from the tourist office heading away from the water. Cool down in the beautiful reception complex/bar/restaurant. (☎ 96 578 03 36. Singles 4500-4900ptas; doubles 7500-9500ptas.) Set up at camp at **Camping Las Marinas**, C. Les Bovetes Nord, 4, is a 3km bus ride (105ptas) from Platja Jorge Joan. (☎ 96 647 41 85 or 96 575 51 88. 500ptas per person and per tent. Open Nov.-Sept.) Restaurants cluster around C. Marqués de Campo. The best dining options are listed in the Dénia service guide from the tourist office. The **supermarket**, C. Carlos Senti, 7, is off C. Patricio Fernández. (☎ 96 578 22 61. Open M-Sa 9am-8:30pm.)

EAST COAST

⊡⛱ SIGHTS AND ENTERTAINMENT. An 18th-century **castle** sprawls across the hill overlooking the marina. The castle has symbolized Denian heritage from Roman times, through the Muslim and Christian eras to today. James II enforced the separation between the town below and the castle above in 1304 by moving all of Denia's inhabitants outside of the castle walls to the *villa vella*, the old quarter. (☎ 96 642 06 56. Open June-Sept. 10am-1:30pm and 4:30-8pm; Oct.-May 10am-1pm and 3-6:30pm; 300ptas.) A tourist train chugs to the castle from outside the tourist office (every 30min. 10am-1pm and 5-8pm; 500ptas includes ride and entrance to castle). Get yourself a tan on the 14km of Dénia **beach. Windsurfing** takes over the waves on **Playa Els Molins,** while **scuba** is the name of the game on **Las Playas Area Les Rotes.** For those who want to show the North Face who's boss, nearby **Montgo Natural Park** (☎ 96 642 32 05) has trails galore. Dénia holds a mini **Fallas festival** from March 16 to 20, burning effigies on the final midnight. During **Festa Major** (early July), locals prove they're just as gutsy as their countrymen in Pamplona—bulls and fans dive into a pool of water, a feat known as **Bous a la mar.** In mid-July, the **Fiestas de la Santísima Sangre (Holy Blood)** feature street dances, concerts, mock battles, and fireworks over the harbor. The parades and religious plays of the **Fiestas de Moros y Cristianos** celebration take place between August 14 and 17.

JÁVEA (XÀBIA)

Jávea's wide, sheltered position hides tranquil waters free from rambunctious tourists—for now, the town still lives up to its nickname as the "Jewel of the Costa Blanca." Although a municipal bus runs 2km inland to the port and then on to a larger beach, Jávea's hidden beauties—its coves, capes, and cliffs—are only accessible by bike, car, or foot. A number of secluded coves line the coast south of the port. The most populated beaches, **Playa La Granadella, Playa de Ambolo** (clothes optional), and **Playa La Barraca,** are serene and accessible. Jávea's **Moros y Cristianos festival** erupts the second half of July; fireworks jolt wide-eyed tourists roaming among costumed Moors and Christians.

Inconvenient transportation to Jávea has spared the town from being overtouristed. **UBESA buses** stop at C. Príncipe de Asturias but only arrive five times per day. To get to the port, take the **municipal bus** (☎ 96 642 14 08) from there (every 30min. 8am-2pm and 4-10pm; 110ptas). If you don't feel like waiting, continue walking down Av. Alicante, which runs directly to the port (20min.). In addition, **Autocarres Carrió** runs between Denia and Jávea (6 per day, 140ptas). The **tourist office,** Pl. Almirante Bastarreche, 11 (☎ 96 579 07 36; fax 96 579 60 57), is at the port. Jávea's remote location may necessitate spending the night. If so, **Pensión La Favorita,** C. Magallanes, 4, will be your favorite, with comfortable rooms near the port. (☎ 96 579 04 77. Singles 2800ptas; doubles 4500-6500ptas.) To get to the hostel, follow the signs near the tourist office. **Camping Jávea,** Partida Plà, 7 (☎ 96 579 10 70), is a second-class site between the town and the port. **Restaurants** with reasonable *menús* line C. Andrés Lambert, away from the port.

MURCIA

Four centuries ago, a bizarre wave of plagues, floods, and earthquakes wreaked havoc throughout Murcia. Along with their utter desecration of some areas, the earthquakes uncovered a rich supply of minerals and natural springs. Today, thermal spas, pottery factories, and paprika mills pepper the lively coastal towns, and orange and apricot orchards bolster Murcia's reputation as the "Huerta de Europa" (Europe's Orchard). With Valencia to the north, the Mediterranean to the east, and Andalucía to the west, Murcia is a mosaic of regional cultures. The diverse physical appearance of *murcianos* dates to the intermarriages of fair-haired Visigoths with Alfonso X El Sabio's dark-toned Castilian troops.

MURCIA

Residents of Murcia will tell you that their city is a pleasant place to visit in the fall, winter, and spring, when the city thrives on the energy of its university. In summer, from mid-July to mid-September, Murcia becomes a ghost town; even the most patriotic of residents flee from the oppressive heat of landlocked Murcia to the nearby Mediterranean.

HIGHLIGHTS OF MURCIA

Lorca's collage of **architecture** (see p. 296).
The glorious **beaches** of La Manga del Mar Menor (see p. 297).

TRANSPORTATION. Aeropuerto San Javier (☎ 968 17 20 00) has flights to Barcelona, Madrid, and London. **RENFE trains** (☎ 902 24 02 02), at Pl. Industria, head to: **Lorca** (1hr., every hr., 540ptas); **Alicante** (1½hr., 9-17 per day, 600ptas); **Valencia** (3½hr., 3 per day, 2000-3500ptas); **Madrid** (4-5hr., 3 per day, 5400ptas); and **Barcelona** (7-10hr., 2 per day, 6500ptas). **Buses** (☎ 968 29 22 11) leave from C. San Andrés, behind the Museo Salzillo. To: **Elche** (50min., 600ptas); **La Manga de Mar Menor** (1hr., every hr., 385ptas); **Lorca** (1½hr., 10 per day, 800ptas); **Alicante** (1½hr., 9-17 per day, 600ptas); **Valencia** (3¾hr., 3-7 per day, 1850ptas); **Almería** (4hr., 9 per day, 2250ptas); **Granada** (4-5hr., 6 per day, 2480ptas); **Sevilla** (7-9hr., 3 per day, 4900ptas); **Córdoba** (9hr., 1 per day, 4150ptas); **Madrid** (12 per day, 3285ptas); and **Barcelona** (7 per day, 5275ptas). Municipal buses (100ptas) cover the city and outskirts. Bus #9 runs a circular route past the train and bus stations.

ORIENTATION AND PRACTICAL INFORMATION. The **Río Segura** divides the city, with sights and services in the northern half and the train station in the south (take bus #9 or 11 between the two). The cathedral is in **Plaza Cardenal Belluga**, at C. Trapería's end, while the bus station is to the west of town (10min. walk). The **tourist office,** C. San Cristóbal, 6, is behind the casino. (☎ 968 36 61 00. Open Aug. M-F 9:30am-2:30pm; June-July M-F 9:30am-2:30pm and 5:30-7:30pm, Sa 11am-1:30pm; Sept.-May M-F 9am-2pm and 5-7pm, Sa 11am-1:30pm.) Services include: **emergency** (☎ 112); **police** (☎ 968 26 66 00), on Av. San Juan de la Cruz; **Hospital Morales Meseguer**, Av. Marqués de Vélez, 22 (☎ 968 36 09 00); and the **post office,** Pl. Circular, 8a, where Av. Primo de Ribera connects to the plaza. (☎968 24 10 37. Open M-F 8:30am-8:30pm, Sa 9:30am-2pm.) The **postal code** is 30008. For **Internet** access, try **Battlezone**, C. Albudeiteros, off Pl. de Romea. (400ptas per 30min. Open 11am-3pm and 4:30-10:30pm.)

ACCOMMODATIONS AND FOOD. When Murcia steams up and empties out in summer, finding a room is the only breeze in town; winter competition is a bit stiffer. A great option is **Hostal-Residencia Murcia,** C. Vinadel, 6, off Pl. Sta. Isabel; take bus #11 from the train station. TVs, phones and air-conditioning (500ptas extra) make for a pleasant stay. (☎ 968 21 99 63. Singles 3000ptas, with bath 3500ptas; doubles 6000ptas, with bath 7000ptas.) Or try **Hostal Legazpi**, Av. Miguel de Cervantes, 8. Take bus #9 or 11 from the train or bus station to the last Ronda Norte stop, and turn the corner to the right. The ample rooms have TVs and fans. (☎ 968 29 30 81; fax 968 29 91 27. Singles 2200ptas, with bath 3000ptas; doubles 4400ptas, with bath 4800ptas.) Sample the Murcian harvest at the **market** on C. Verónicas (open M-Sa 9am-1pm). For more veggies, head to **Tío Sentao,** C. La Manga, 12, hidden off Pl. Agustinas, one block from the Convento de Agustinas, where authentic Murcian fare is served up in a family atmosphere. From the bus station, take a right on C. Dr. Jesús Quesada, a left at Pl. San Agustín, and then a right on C. Sta. Cecilia. Turn right on C. Doctrinos, left on C. Baeza, and then left on C. La Manga. (☎ 968 29 10 13. *Menú* 1000ptas. Open daily 1-4pm and 8-11pm.)

◼⬛ SIGHTS AND ENTERTAINMENT. The palatial **Casino de Murcia** (Casino Cultural), C. Trapería, 18, began as a gentlemen's club for the town's 19th- and 20th-century bourgeoisie . Rooms inside were designed according to a particular theme, including the Versailles ballroom, English billiard room, Arabic patio, and Oxford library. (☎ 968 21 22 55. Open daily 10am-9pm. 100ptas.) The ◼**Museo de Arqueología de Murcia,** Gran Vía Alfonso X El Sabio, 9, one of the finest in Spain, chronicles provincial history from prehistoric times. (☎ 968 23 46 02. Open July-Aug. M-F 9am-2pm; Sept.-June M-F 9am-2pm and 4-8pm, Sa 10am-1:30pm. 75ptas.) The **Museo Taurino,** within the Jardín del Salitre between Pl. Circular and the bus station, displays bullfighting memorabilia, *matador* costumes, and mounted bulls' heads that pay homage to particularly valorous beasts. Of questionable taste is the enshrinement of José Manuel Calvo Benichon's shredded, bloody shirt, worn the day he was gored to death in Sevilla by his 598kg opponent. (☎ 968 28 59 76. Open June-Aug. M-F 10am-2pm and 5-8pm; Sept.-May 10am-2pm and 5-8pm, Su 11am-2pm. Free.) Just outside of Murcia, the Río España courses through rocky mountains dotted with the pines and sagebrush of the **Parque Natural Sierra Espuña** (highest elevation 1585m). The flowers explode into dazzling color in springtime, the best season to visit the park. On Thursday, Friday, and Saturday nights, local university students study the effects of alcohol at **tascas** near C. Saavedra Fajardo (near the main campus). On the day before Easter, the **Fiesta de Primavera** starts a week-long harvest celebration that brings jazz and theater to Murcia's streets.

DAYTRIP FROM MURCIA:◼ LORCA (1HR.)

RENFE Cercanías trains (☎ 902 24 02 02) run to Lorca Sutullena Station, Av. Estació, parallel to C. Juan Carlos I (1hr., every hr. 8:45am-9:45pm, 540-575ptas). Next door, the bus station (☎ 968 46 92 70) sends Trapemusa buses to Murcia (every hr., 625ptas), Barcelona, Granada, Alicante, Valencia, Almería, and Málaga.

A stroll through Lorca, from the colorful, modern train station to the crumbling medieval castle, leads you through centuries of aesthetic and economic variety. Medieval ghettos, Renaissance artistry, Baroque glory, post-Franco urban expansion, and contemporary elitism demarcate the town's neighborhoods.

Battles between Romans and Visigoths, and later Christians and Muslims, left Lorca without the orchards that extend through the rest of the region. Yet each conquering force left its own peculiar imprint on the **castillo** atop Lorca's central hill, a 20-minute walk from Pl. Espanya (stick to the main road when heading up; always open and free). The Moors built the **Torre Espolón** shortly before the city fell to Alfonso el Sabio of Castilla, who in self-adulation ordered the construction of the **Torre Alfonsín.** The ruins of Lorca's first church, the **Ermita de San Clemente,** deteriorate at the castle's eastern edge. When Granada fell in 1492, inhabitants left the fortresses and moved to the bottom of the slope, leaving in their wake three idyllic churches—**Santa María, San Juan,** and **San Pedro.** Starting anew, Lorcans erected six monasteries and the **Colegiata de San Particio.** One of many well-preserved private residences, **Casa de Guevarra,** a pharmacy in the 16th-century, has wreathed columns and intricate carvings (open M-F 11am-1pm and 5-7pm). The **tourist office** is just before the Casa de Guevarra on C. Lópes Gisbert. To get there from the train station, take the pedestrian path to C. Juan Carlos I, head down C. Juan Carlos I to the right, then left on C. E. García Navarro, and right onto C. Gisbert. (☎ 968 46 61 57. Open M-F 9am-2pm and 5-8pm, Sa 10:30am-1:30pm.) **Luggage storage** is available in the bus station (daily 6am-11pm, 400ptas).

DAYTRIP FROM MURCIA: ÁGUILAS (1½HR.)

Cercanías train line, 5 per day; 140ptas from Lorca, 740ptas from Murcia.

Tourists delight in the fortified medieval town of Águilas (**tourist office** ☎ 968 41 33 03), 45 minutes from Lorca and 1½ hours from Murcia. Tourists make the trip to see its 35 coves, picturesque beaches, pier on the Bay of Hornillo, and **Tower of Cope** (on the wonderfully named Cape of Cope).

LA MANGA DEL MAR MENOR

A geographic fluke created the popular vacation spot known as La Manga (the sleeve) of the Mar Menor. Centuries of marine deposits settled over a small volcanic ridge and then solidified into a 19km strip of land separating the Mar Menor from the Mediterranean. Windsurfers take advantage of the waveless sea, while beach-lovers relax in the white sands and crystal waters of the Mediterranean. La Manga has one main road, the **Gran Vía**, that runs its length. Addresses are indicated by km point (km 0 is at the mainland pole), plazas, and *urbanizaciones* (tourist complexes). Local **buses** zip back and forth along La Manga (every 20-30min., after 4am every hr., 150ptas). **Autobuses Gimenez Hermanos/Lycar** (☎ 968 29 22 11) runs to and from **Murcia** (5-6 per day, 690ptas) and makes several stops along the strip. **Autocares Costa Azul** (☎ 968 50 15 43) goes to **Alicante** (2½hr., 9:30am, 940ptas). **Autobuses Enatcar** cruises to **Madrid** (7hr., 4 per day, 3755ptas). The Enatcar office is next to Bar La Parada, across from the bus stop. The **tourist office,** Gran Vía, Salida 2, km 0 (☎ 968 56 33 55), has a map and accommodations list. **Serma, C.B.** (☎ 968 56 41 19), in Pl. Cavanna, rents **bikes** (1400ptas per day) and **scooters** (5000ptas per day; open daily 10am-2pm and 5-9pm). The **Escuela de Vela Pedruchillo,** km 8-9, sells water sports equipment. (☎ 968 14 04 12. Open daily 10am-2pm and 4-8pm.) The closest thing to a budget accommodation on La Manga is the **Albergue Juvenil Deportivo,** Urbanización Hawaii V, km 8-9 (☎ 968 14 07 42), in the Grimanga Club. Bunk beds, locker-room showers, and rambunctious summer campers are an unfortunate addition, but the front door opens onto one of the nicest beaches in Spain, **Playa de Pedrucho.** (Dorms 1700ptas, with 3 meals 3600ptas.)

EAST COAST

BARCELONA

Paris, London, and New York have been described as *noir* cities, best captured in black and white. Barcelona, on the other hand, must be seen in vivid colors—or better yet, experienced. There is a frenetic energy that rises from Barcelona's streets, a certain passion for life that has helped make it Europe's fastest growing center of tourism. Unforgettable Modernist architecture and the 1992 Summer Olympics have won Barcelona worldwide admiration. Even more interesting are its unique cultural tensions: fierce Catalan individualism resists mainstream Spanish culture, and trendy contemporary style pulls away from Old World quaintness.

Barceloneses have long been the privileged class of Spain. During the Middle Ages, the city was the commercial center of a vast Mediterranean empire. Barcelona suffered financial decline in the 15th century as both the "discovery" of America and Sevilla's trade monopoly shifted commercial routes away from the Mediterranean. The Industrial Revolution's textile mills, however, propelled a turn-of-the-century economic boom, and the aristocracy grew in status and power. As the twentieth century approached, Josep Batlló, Antoni Amatller, and their compatriots commissioned architects like Montaner, Cadafalch, and the legendary Antoni Gaudí to build private residences in L'Eixample, a spacious, gridded "upper" Barcelona district, higher in elevation and status than the tangled, lower-class Barri Gòtic. The result of these architectural pursuits was *Modernisme*, an artistic movement drawing its inspiration from nature. Even the suffocating years of Franco's Fascist regime could not dampen Barcelona's stature as the world's premier showcase of avant-garde architecture. Today, brilliantly daring buildings and parks stud the cityscape, battling for attention; only the people themselves, with their trend-setting fashion sense and dynamic lifestyle, offer any real competition.

HIGHLIGHTS OF BARCELONA

The fascinating contrast between gridded urban thoroughfares and curving Modernista architecture, especially Gaudí's **Sagrada Familia, Casa Mila,** and **Palau de la Musica Catalana** (see **Ruta de Modernisme,** p. 318).

Wandering amidst the maze of musicians, human statues, and magicians on **Las Ramblas,** Barcelona's most famous street (see p. 318).

The charm of **La Ribera's** winding streets, chic art galleries, eclectic shops, **Museu Picasso** (see p. 325), and statuesque **Esglesia Santa Maria Del Mar** (see p. 320).

Three breathtaking parks—**Parc Güell** (see p. 323), **Parc de la Ciutadella** (see p. 320), and **Vila Olímpica** (see p. 321).

Barcelona's never-ending, exhilarating **nightlife** (see p. 327).

The eerie rock formations at the mountaintop monastery of **Montserrat** (see p. 333).

◼ GETTING THERE AND AWAY

BY PLANE

All flights land at **El Prat de Llobregat** airport (☎ 93 298 38 38), 12km southwest of Barcelona. The **Aerobus** links the airport to Plaça de Catalunya, the center of town (40min.; every 15min.; to Pl. Catalunya M-F 6am-midnight, Sa-Su 6:30am-midnight; to the airport M-F 5:30am-11:15pm, Sa-Su 6am-11:20pm; 500ptas).

RENFE trains provide slightly cheaper transportation to and from the airport (20min.; every 30min.; 6:13am-10:40pm from airport, 5:40am-10:13pm from Pl. Catalunya; M-Sa 305ptas, Su 350ptas). The most useful stops are **Estació Barcelona-Sants** and **Plaça de Catalunya.** Tickets are sold at the red automatic machines. In Sants, buy tickets at the "Aeroport" window (open 5am-11pm). After 11pm, get them from the ticket machines or the Recorridos Cercanías window.

The city **bus** offers the only inexpensive late-night service. Take bus EN from the airport to Pl. Espanya (every hr.; airport to Pl. Espanya 6:20am-2:40am, Pl. Espanya to airport 7am-3:15am; 145ptas). The stop in Pl. Espanya is on the corner of Gran Vía de les Corts Catalanes and Av. Reina María Cristina. A **taxi** ride between Barcelona and the airport costs 3000-4500ptas.

Three **national airlines** serve all domestic and major international destinations. **Iberia/Aviaco**, C. Diputació, 258 (24hr. reservation and info ☎ 902 40 05 00), has the most extensive coverage. Iberia/Aviaco usually offers student discounts (except on already reduced fares). **Air Europa** (24hr. reservation and info ☎ 902 24 00 42) and **Spanair** (☎ 902 13 14 15) offer fares that are often cheaper.

All major **international airlines** serve Barcelona. **British Airways,** Pg. Gràcia, 85, 3rd fl. (☎ 93 215 69 00), **TWA,** Consell de Cent, 360, 5th fl. (☎ 93 215 81 88), and most other airlines have offices in Barcelona. For more information on international reservations, visit a travel agency in Barcelona (see p. 306).

BY TRAIN

Barcelona has three main train stations. When in doubt, go to Estació Barcelona-Sants; all domestic trains leaving França pass through here as well but not all trains leaving Barcelona-Sants necessarily pass through França. For general information about trains and train stations in Barcelona, call ☎ 90 224 4 02 02.

Estació Barcelona-Sants: (☎ 90 224 02 02), in Pl. Països Catalans. M: Sants-Estació. Barcelona-Sants is the main terminal for domestic and international traffic. For late arrivals, the N14 Nitbus shuttles to Pl. Catalunya (every hr., 11:30pm-4:30am, 160ptas). Currency exchange (open 8am-9:30pm), ATMs, pharmacy, tourist office. Lockers 600ptas for 24hrs. Station open daily 6am-11pm.

RENFE: (☎ 902 24 02 02; international ☎ 93 490 11 22; www.renfe.es). Open daily 7am-10pm. RENFE has extensive service in Spain and all of Europe. A few of the most popular connections include: **Valencia** (3hr., 15 per day 7am-8:30pm, 5000-7200ptas); **Montpellier, France** with connections to Geneva and Paris and the French Riviera (4½hr., 3 per day, 12,608-43,800ptas); **Madrid** (7-8hr., 6 per day, 6500-8400ptas); **Sevilla** (12hr., 3 per day, 10,000-27,700ptas); **Milan, Italy** (through Figueres or Montpelier; 13hr., 1 per day, 12,608-43,800ptas); and **San Sebastián** (8hr., 3 per day, 5000-10,000ptas). Student discounts available with a youth card.

Trenes Euromed: A subsidiary of RENFE offering high-speed service along Spain's Mediterranean coast. Trains leave from Barcelona-Sants for **Valencia** (3hr., 6 per day, 4900ptas) and **Alicante** (4¾hr., 3 per day, 6600ptas), stopping in smaller towns along the way.

Estació França: (☎ 902 24 02 02), on Av. Marqués de L'Argentera. M: Barceloneta. Services a few domestic and international destinations. Open daily 7am-10pm.

Ferrocarrils de la Generalitat de Catalunya (FFCC): (☎ 93 205 15 15; www.fgc.catalunya.net). Commuter trains with main stations at Pl. Catalunya and Pl. Espanya. Service to **Montserrat** (from Pl. Espanya). Symbols resembling two interlocking "V"s mark connections with the metro. The commuter line charges the same as the metro (150ptas) until Tibidabo. T1 passes valid on FFCC trains.

BY BUS

Most—but not all—buses arrive at the **Estació del Nord,** C. Ali-bei, 80 (☎ 93 265 65 08; info office open daily 7am-9pm). M: Arc de Triomf (exit to Nàpols). Others arrive at the Sants station. Buses are often cheaper and more direct than trains.

Enatcar, Estació del Nord (☎ 902 42 22 42; www.enatcar.es). Open daily 7am-1am. To: **Valencia** (4hr., 16 per day, 2690ptas); **Madrid** (8hr., 18 per day, 2690ptas); and **Alicante** (9hr., 5 per day, 4650ptas).

Sarfa, Estació del Nord (☎ 93 265 65 08 or 93 265 11 58). Sarfa buses stop at many beach towns along the Costa Brava, north of Barcelona. Open daily 8am-8:30pm. To **Tossa** (1½hr., 9 per day, 1070ptas) and **Cadaqués** (2½hr., 2 per day, 2205ptas).

Linebús, Estació del Nord (☎ 93 265 07 00). Open M-F 8am-2pm and 3-8pm, Sa 8:30am-1:30pm and 4:30-8pm. Discounts for travelers under 26. To **Paris** (15hr., 6 per week, 11,200-22,900ptas) and **London** (25hr., 3 per week, 14,650-26,375ptas). Also has daily service to southern France and Morocco.

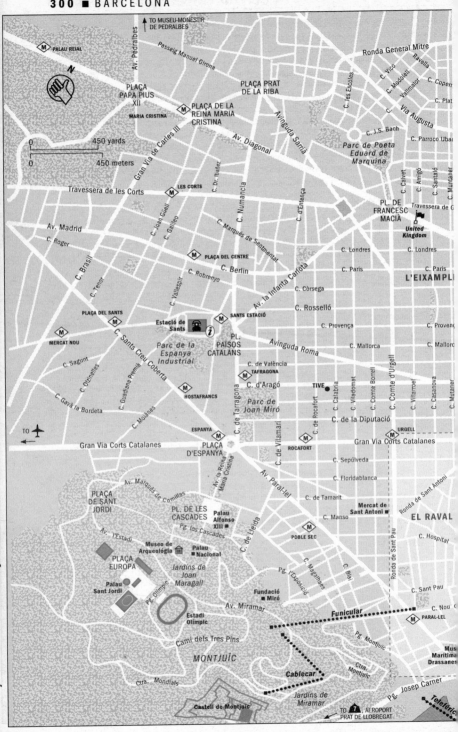

Barcelona

🏠 ACCOMMODATIONS

Albergue de Montserrat (HI), 1
Camping, 7
Hostal Bonavista, 3
Hostal de Joves Municipal, 6
Hostal Residencia Oliva, 5
Hostal Residencia Windsor, 4
Pensión San Medín, 2

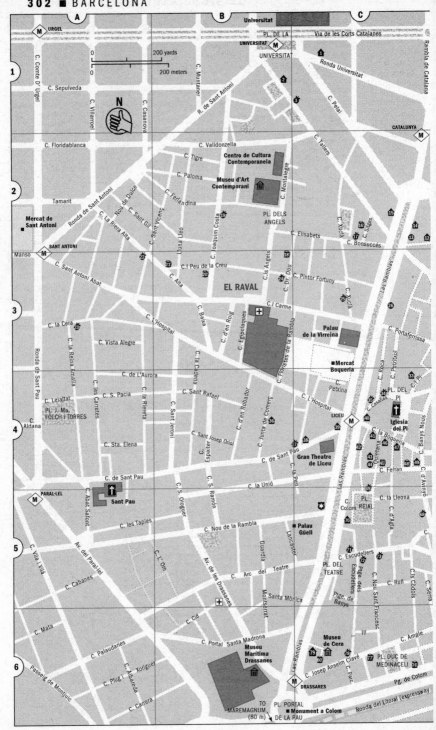

A   B   C

Universitat

Ⓜ URGEL

C. Comte D'Urgel

C. Sepulveda

PL. DE LA
UNIVERSITAT
Ⓜ
UNIVERSITAT

Via de les Corts Catalanes

Ronda Universitat

Rambla de Catalunya

0   200 yards
0   200 meters

C. Muntaner

C. Villarroel

C. Casanova

R. de Sant Antoni

C. Peral

N

C. Floridablanca

C. Validonzella

C. Tigre

Centro de Cultura
Contemporanela

C. Talers

CATALUNYA Ⓜ

Tamarit

Ronda de Sant Antoni

C. Paloma

C. Ferlandina

Museu d'Art
Contemporani

C. Montalegre

Mercat de
Sant Antoni ■

C. La Riera Alta

Nou d'Dulce

C. Sant Gil

C. Sant Vicenç

Junta Lleo

C. Joaquim Costa

PL. DELS
ANGELS

C. Elisabets

C. Xuclà

C. Lleas

Manso   Ⓜ SANT ANTONI

C. Sant Antoni Abat

C. Alta

C.I Peu de la Creu

C.ls Angels

C. Bonsuccés

Las Ramblas

C. Pintor Fortuny

EL RAVAL

C. la Cera

C. Vista Alegre

C. L'Hospital

C. d'en Roig

C. Espaciducs

C.l Carme

Palau
de la Virreina

C. Portaferrissa

Ronda de Sant Pau

C. la Reina Amalia

C. les Carretes

C. de L'Aurora

C. Cadena

C. la Riereta

C. Baixa

C. Florisles de la Rambla

Mercat
Boqueria ■

C. Roca

C. Petritxol

C. Leialtat

PL. J. Ma.
FÓLCH I TORRES

Ⓜ Aldana

C. S. Pacia

C. Sant Rafael

C. d'en Robador

C. Junta de Comerç

C. L'Hospital

C.
Petxina

LICEU Ⓜ

PL. DEL
PI

Iglesia
del Pi

C. Casanla

C. Sant Josep Oriol

C. Espalter

C. de Sant Pau

C. la Boqueria

C. Avinyó

C. Sta. Elena

C. Sant Jeroni

Gran Theatre
de Liceu

C. Ferran

C. de Sant Pau

Ⓜ PARAL·LEL

C. Abat Safont

Sant Pau ✝

C. S. Oleguer

C. S. Ramón

C. la Unió

PL.
REIAL

C. Colom

PL. la Lleona

C. d'Agla

C. les Taples

C. Nou de la Rambla

Palau
Güell ■

C. Vila i Vila

Av. del Parallel

C. l' Om

Guardia

Lancaster

C. Escudellers

PL. DEL
TEATRE

C. Ruff

C. Nou Sant Francesc

C.ls Códols

C. Serra

C. Cabanes

Arc del Teatre

Prge. dels Escudellers

C. Mata

C. Plug

C. Albarada

Santa Mònica

C. Cid

Museu
Marítima
Drassanes

C. Portal Santa Madrona

Museu
de Cera

C. Ample

PL. DUC DE
MEDINACELI

Passeig de Montjuïc

C. Carrera

C. Josep Anselm Clavé

C. Palc

Las Ramblas

Pg. de Colom

Ⓜ DRASSANES

TO
MAREMAGNUM
(80 m)

PL. PORTAL
DE LA PAU

■ Monument a Colom

Ronda del Litoral (expressway)

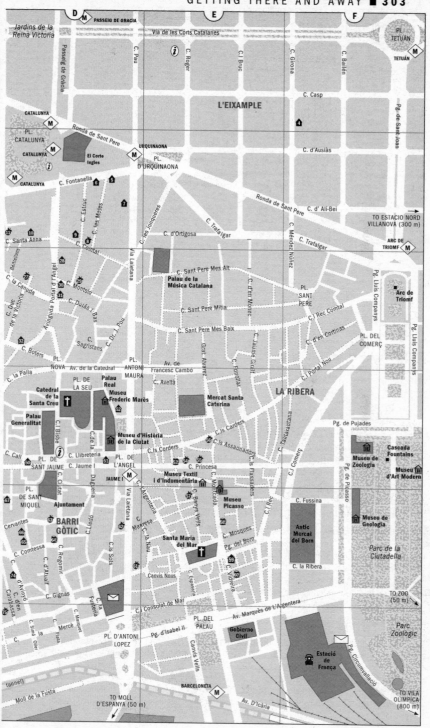

Central Barcelona

🛏 ACCOMMODATIONS

Albergue de Juventud Kabul, 70	C5
Albergue Juvenil Palau, 65	D5
Casa de Huéspedes Mari-Luz, 66	D5
H.-R. Europa, 46	C4
H.-R. Lausanne, 28	D3
H.-R. Rembrandt, 32	D3
Hostal Aviñyó, 74	D5
Hostal Fernando, 49	C4
Hostal Fontanella, 7	D2
Hostal Girona, 4	F1
Hostal Layetana, 52	D4
Hostal Levante, 67	D5
Hostal Malda, 33	C4
Hostal Marítima, 79	C6
Hostal Paris, 40	C4
Hostal Residencia Opera, 38	C4
Hostal Rey Don Jaume I, 51	D4
Hotel Call, 50	D4
Hotel Toledano & H.-R. Capitol, 14	C2
Mare Nostrum, 39	C4
Pensión Aris, 6	D2
Pensión Arosa, 31	D3
Pensión Bienestar, 43	C4
Pensión Dalí, 41	C4
Pensión Francia, 59	E5
Pensión Noya, 15	C2
Pensión Santa Anna, 12	C2
Residencia Victoria, 9	D2

🍴 FOOD

Bar Restaurante Los Tereros, 25	C3
Bar Restaurante Romesco, 37	C4
Buen Bocado, 71	C5
Can Maxim, 17	C2
Colibrí, 22	A3
El Cervol Roig, 8	D2
El Gallo Kiriko, 68	C5
Els Quatre Gats, 29	D3
Ikkiu, 54	E4
Il Mercante Di Venezia, 78	C6
Irati, 34	C4
Juicy Jones, 35	C4
La Fonda, 72	C5
La Habana Vieja, 57	E5
Las Caracoles, 73	C5
Le Quinze Nits, 69	C5
Lluna Plena, 56	E4
Nice-Café Milena, 61	D5
Peimong, 63	D5
Restaurante Bidasoa, 75	D6
Restaurante Biocenter, 24	B3
Restaurante Can Lluís, 23	A3
Restaurante Chino, 3	C1
Restaurante Riera, 19	B2
Restaurante Self Naturista, 11	D2
Terrablava, 62	D5
The Bagel Shop, 27	D3
Txirimira, 55	

🍸 NIGHTLIFE

Cafe d l'Opera, 42	C4
Cafe-Bar Vincent Van Gogh, 53	E4
Casa Almirall, 20	B3
Da-Da, 76	C6
El Cafe que pone Muebles Navarro, 21	B3
Harlem Jazz Club, 64	D5
La Oveja Negra, 16	C2
Les Bosq des Fades, 80	C6
Margarita Blue, 77	C6
Molly Malones, 45	C4
Mudanzas, 60	E5
Raval-Bar, 18	B3
Schilling, 48	C4
Xampanyet, 58	E5

⬤ SERVICES

Net Movil, 13	C2
Pharmacy, 26	C3
Tintorería Ferran, 44	C4

Alsa (☎ 902 42 22 42; www.alsa.es), a division of Enatcar. Trips to northwestern Spain. To **Zaragoza** (4½hr., 2 per day, 1655ptas) and **Gijon** (12hr., 1 per day, 4850ptas).

Julià Vía, Estación del Nord (☎ 93 232 10 92). To: **Marseille** (10hr., 5 per week, 7100ptas); **Paris** (15hr., 6 per week, 12,000ptas); and **Frankfurt** (19hr., 4 per week, 14,300ptas). Youth discounts available.

BY FERRY

For details on ferries to the Balearic Islands, see **Balearic Islands** (p. 469).

Transmediterránea, Estació Marítima-Moll Barcelona (☎ 902 45 46 45; fax 93 295 91 34), Moll de Sant Bertran. M: Drassanes. From the metro, head down Las Ramblas to the Columbus monument. Columbus points straight toward the Estació Marítima. Cross Ronda Litoral and pass the Aduana building on the left. During the summer, ferries to **Mallorca** (3hr.) leave 3 times a day; **Ibiza** ferries (9hr.) depart 5 times a week; and starting in mid-June ferries leave for **Menorca** daily. One-way trips start at about 10,350ptas. You can get tickets at any travel agency, but the main office is open M-F 8am-9pm.

BY THUMB

Hitchhikers to France often take the metro to Fabra i Puig and then walk along Av. Meridiana to highway A-7. Those en route to Tarragona and Valencia take bus #7 from Rambla Catalunya on the Gran Vía side—it's easy to access the *autopista* (toll road, marked by the letter A) from here. Hitchhiking on *autopistas* is illegal. Hitchhiking is permitted on national highways (marked by N). *Let's Go* does not recommend hitchhiking and urges its readers to consider all the risks involved.

⯐ GETTING AROUND

MAPS

El Corte Inglés's free map, distributed in their stores (see p. 307) and at mobile and stationary info centers, is accurate and highly informative. The Barcelona **tourist office** (in Pl. Catalunya or Pl. Sant Jaume) also has good maps of the city (100ptas) with the best enlarged inset of the streets of the Barri Gòtic you'll find anywhere.

METRO AND BUS

Barcelona's public transportation system (info ☎ 010, ☎ 93 318 70 74 for claims) is quick, cheap, and extensive. The useful *Guía d'Autobusos Urbans de Barcelona*, free at tourist offices and in metro stations, maps out all of the city's bus routes and the five metro lines. If you plan to use the metro and bus systems extensively, consider buying a **T1 Pass** or a **T-DIA Card**. The T1 Pass (795ptas), valid for 10 rides on the bus, metro, and most FFCC trains, is a great deal, especially since multiple people can share one pass. The T-DIA Card entitles you to unlimited bus and metro travel for one (625ptas) or three days (1600ptas); the one-day card is only worthwhile if you plan to take eight or more trips.

Metro: (☎ 93 486 07 52; www.tmb.net). Automatic vending machines and ticket windows sell metro passes. Hold on to your ticket or pass until you leave the metro—an official with a white-and-red pinstripe shirt may stop you and ask to see it. Riding without a ticket carries a hefty 5000pta fine. Trains run M-Th 5am-11pm, F-Sa 5am-2am, Su 6am-midnight. 150ptas.

Buses: Go just about anywhere, usually from 5am-10pm. 150ptas.

Nitbus: (☎ 93 395 31 11). Since both the regular bus system and metro close early, at night you'll have to ride the Nitbus. Open 10:30pm-4:30am. Stops in front of most of the club complexes. 160ptas.

Bus Turístic: The clearly marked Bus Turístic stops at 25 points of interest along 2 different routes (red for the northern, blue for the southern). You can get on and off both routes as often as you wish. The easiest place to hop on the Bus Turístic is Pl. Catalunya, in front of El Corte Inglés. Many of the museums and sights covered by the tour bus are closed on M. Buses run Mar. 28-Jan. 6 every 10-30min., 9am-9:30pm. Purchase tickets on the bus or at the Pl. Catalunya tourist office. 1-day pass 2000ptas, children ages 4-12 1200ptas; 2-day pass 2500ptas.

TAXIS

Taxis are everywhere in Barcelona but can be difficult to flag down. A *libre* sign in the windshield or a lit green light on the roof means they are vacant; yellow means they are occupied. Cabs can be summoned by phone (☎ 93 330 03 00 or 93 300 11 00; for disabled travelers ☎ 93 358 11 11 or 93 357 77 55). The first six minutes or 1.9km cost 300ptas; each additional kilometer is 110ptas .

CAR RENTAL

Docar, C. Montnegre, 18 (24hr. ☎ 93 439 81 19). Free delivery and pickup. From 4700ptas per day, 23ptas per km. Insurance included. Open M-F 8:30am-2pm and 3:30-8pm, Sa 9am-2pm.

Tot Car, C. Berlín, 97 (☎ 93 430 01 98). Free delivery and pickup. From 4500ptas per day, 21ptas per km. Insurance included. Open M-F 8am-2pm and 3-8pm, Sa 9am-1pm.

BICYCLE AND MOPED RENTAL

Everyone who's anyone in Barcelona has a motorcycle; it's probably the most popular method of transport. Be wary of speeding suits on motos.

Vanguard Rent a Car, C. Londres, 31 (☎ 93 439 38 80). Mopeds Tu-Th 4740ptas per day, F-M 7280ptas per day. Insurance, helmet, and IVA included.

Biciclot, C. Sant Joan de Malta, 1 (☎ 93 307 74 75). M: Clot. Leave through the Aragó-Meridiera exit, and turn 180 degrees at the top of the steps; take the 2nd right, the 2nd left (C. Verned), then the 2nd right onto C. Sant Joan de Malta. 10-speeds or mountain bikes 500ptas per hr., 2000ptas per day. Tandem 1000ptas per hr., 4000ptas per day. Multi-day and group rates available. Open M-F 9am-2pm and 5-8pm, Sa 10am-2pm.

Over-Rent S.A, Av. Josep Terradellas, 42 (☎ 93 405 26 60). Motorcycles for rent.

⊞ ORIENTATION

Barcelona's layout is quite simple. Imagine yourself perched atop Columbus's head at the **Monument a Colom** (on **Passeig de Colom,** which runs parallel to the shore), viewing the city with the Mediterranean at your back. From the harbor, the city slopes upward toward the mountains. Keep this in mind when you need to re-orient yourself. From the Columbus monument, the city's main thoroughfare, **Las Ramblas,** runs away from the harbor up to **Plaça de Catalunya,** the city's center.

To the east of Las Ramblas (to the right, with your back to the sea) spans the **Barri Gòtic,** enclosed on the other side by **Vía Laietana. Carrer de Ferran** bisects the Barri Gòtic into northern (upper) and southern (lower) halves. East of Vía Laiet-ana lies the maze-like neighborhood of **La Ribera,** which borders **Parc de la Ciuta-della** and the **Estació de França** train station. Beyond Parc de la Ciutadella (farther east) is the **Vila Olímpica,** with its twin towers (the tallest buildings in Barcelona) and a shiny assortment of malls, discos, and hotels.

On the west side (to the left, with your back to the sea) of Las Ramblas is **El Raval.** The southern half of El Raval comprises Barcelona's shrinking red-light district. In the background (farther west) rises **Montjuïc,** a picturesque hill crammed with gardens, museums (including the Fundació Miró), the 1992 Olympic grounds, the Montjuïc castle, and other tourist attractions.

Directly behind you as you sit atop the Monument a Colom is the **Port Vell** (Old Port) development, where a wavy bridge leads across to the ultra-modern shopping and entertainment complexes **Moll d'Espanya** and **Maremagnum.**

L'Eixample, the gridded neighborhood created during the urban expansion, fans outward from Pl. Catalunya toward the mountains. **Gran Vía de les Corts Catalanes** defines its lower edge and **Passeig de Gràcia,** L'Eixample's main commercial street, bisects the neighborhood. **Avinguda Diagonal** marks the upper limit of the grid-planned neighborhoods, separating L'Eixample from **Gràcia,** an older neighborhood in the foothills. The peak of **Tibidabo,** the northwest border of the city and the highest point in Barcelona, offers the most comprehensive view of the city.

> ! Barcelona is not a particularly dangerous city, but pickpocketing (and even mugging) is extremely prevalent. Try not to look too much like a tourist, secure your valuables and don't carry loose bills. Plaça Reial turns super-sketchy at night. Also be careful in the Barri Gòtic and along Las Ramblas and C. Escudellers, and don't wander too far into El Raval alone, especially after dark. Most areas with active nightlife (see p. 327) are well patrolled and well lit.

⊞ PRACTICAL INFORMATION

TOURIST AND FINANCIAL SERVICES

Tourist Info: (☎ 010, 906 30 12 82, or 93 304 34 21; www.barcelonaturisme.com). Barcelona has 4 main tourist offices and numerous mobile information stalls.

Informació Turística Plaça Catalunya, Pl. Catalunya, 17S, below Pl. Catalunya. M: Catalunya. The biggest, best, and busiest tourist office. Provides multilingual advice, maps, pamphlets, transportation passes, hotel information, currency exchange, telephone cards, email kiosks and souvenirs for purchase. Open daily 9am-9pm.

Informació Turística Plaça Sant Jaume, Pl. Sant Jaume, 1. M: Jaume I. Fewer services and more personal attention than its big sister in Pl. Catalunya. Open M-Sa 10am-8pm, Su 10am-2pm.

Estació de Barcelon-Sants, Pl. Paisos Catalans, in the Barcelona-Sants train station. M: Sants-Est-ació. Open June-Aug. M-F 8am-8pm; Sept.-May M-F 8am-8pm, Sa-Su 8am-2pm.

Aeroport El Prat de Llobregat (☎ 93 478 47 04), in the international terminal. Open M-Sa 9:30am-8:30pm, Su 9:30am-3pm.

Mobile information offices dot the city in the summer. Open Mar.-June 10am-8pm.

Tours: In addition to the Bus Turístic (see **Metro and Bus**, p. 305), Barcelona's tourist offices offer walking tours from Pl. Catalunya. Sa-Su at 10am (English) and noon (Spanish and Catalan). 950ptas, children ages 4-12 500ptas.

Budget Travel Offices: Most are located near the university.

Unlimited Student Travel (USIT), Rda. Universidad, 16 (☎ 90 232 52 75; www.unlimited.es), 1½ blocks from Pl. Catalunya. M: Catalunya. Also at C. Rocafort, 116-118, 2 blocks from the metro. M: Rocafort. Expect a long wait.Open M-F 10am-8pm, Sa 10am-1:30pm. Bring an ISIC card.

Centre d'Informació Assesorament per a Joves, C. Ferrán, 32 (☎ 93 402 78 00; www.bcn.es/ciaj.) More of a student assistance office than a travel agency. No tickets for sale, but plenty of free advice and a bulletin board with youth events. Excellent library of travel guides. Open M-F 10am-2pm and 4-8pm.

Currency Exchange: As always, **ATMs** give the best rates (with no commission). The next best rates are available at banks. General banking hours M-F 8:30am-2pm. **Banco de Espanya**, Pl. Catalunya, 17 (☎ 93 482 47 00) and the **American Express** office (see below) charge no commission on traveler's checks. Change US dollars at **Estació de Barcelona-Sants** (☎ 93 490 77 70) for no commission. Open daily 8am-10pm.

American Express: Pg. Gràcia, 101 (24hr. traveler's check info ☎ 90 099 44 26). M: Diagonal. The entrance is around the corner on C. Rosselló. Mail held free for cardholders. Open M-F 9:30am-6pm, Sa 10am-noon. Another office is located on Las Ramblas, 74, and is open daily 9am-midnight.

LOCAL SERVICES

Luggage Storage: Estació Barcelona-Sants. M: Sants-Estació. Small lockers 400ptas, large lockers 600ptas. Open 4am-midnight. **Estació França.** M: Barceloneta. Small lockers 400ptas, large lockers 600ptas. Open 6am-11pm. **Estació del Nord.** M: Arc de Triomf. Lockers 300-600ptas. Open 24hr.

El Corte Inglés: Pl. Catalunya, 14 (☎ 93 306 38 00), Av. Diagonal, 471-473, and Av. Diagonal, 617. Behemoth department store. Gives out a great map. Also has English books, haircutting parlor, rooftop cafeteria, supermarket, currency exchange, and telephones. Open M-Sa 10am-9:30pm.

English Bookstores: LAIE, Av. Pau Claris, 85 (☎ 93 318 17 39), 1 block from the Gran Vía. M: Urquinaona or Pl. Catalunya. Open M-F 10am-9pm, Sa 10:30am-9pm. **The Bookstore**, C. La Granja, 13 (☎ 93 237 95 19), in Gràcia off Travesera del Dalt. M: Lesseps. Best used bookstore around, run by an eccentric British expat. Trade-ins accepted. Open M-Sa 11am-1:30pm and 2:30-7pm.

Libraries: Biblioteca Sant Pau, C. Hospital, 56 (☎ 93 302 07 97). M: Liceu. Take C. Hospital off Las Ramblas and walk through the stone courtyard a few blocks down; the library is on the left. Do not confuse it with the Catalan library which you need permission to enter. Open M-F 10am-2pm and 3:30-8:30pm, Sa 10am-2pm. Closed for 3 weeks in Sept. **Institut d'Estudis Norteamericans**, Vía Augusta, 123 (☎ 93 240 51 10). Open Sept.-July M-F 9am-2pm and 4-7pm.

Religious Services: Comunidad Israelita de Barcelona (Jewish services), C. Avenir, 29 (☎ 93 200 33 75). **Comunidad Musulmana** (Muslim services), Mezquita Toarek Ben Ziad, C. Hospital, 91 (☎ 93 441 91 49). Services daily at prayer times.

Gay and Lesbian Services: Cómplices, C. Cervantes, 2 (☎ 93 412 72 83). M: Liceu. From C. Ferrán, take C. Avinyó and then the 2nd left. A gay and lesbian bookstore with publications in English and Spanish. Also provides a map of Barcelona's gay and lesbian bars and discos. Open M-F 10:30am-8:30pm, Sa noon-8:30pm.

Laundromats: Tintorería San Pablo, C. San Pau, 105 (☎ 93 329 42 49). M: Paralell. Wash, dry, and fold 1600ptas; do-it-yourself 1200ptas. Open M-F 9am-1:30pm and 4-8:30pm. **Tintorería Ferran**, C. Ferran, 11. M: Liceu. Ferran runs off Las Ramblas, just below Liceu. Full service 1500ptas. Open daily 8:30am-2pm and 4:30-7:30pm.

EMERGENCY AND COMMUNICATIONS

Emergency: ☎112. **National police** ☎ 091; **local police** ☎ 092; **medical** ☎ 061.

Police: Las Ramblas, 43 (☎ 93 344 13 00 or 93 301 90 60), across from Pl. Reial and next to C. Nou de La Rambla. M: Liceu. Multilingual officers. Open 7am-midnight. Local Barcelona police coordinate with national police in emergency situations.

Crisis Lines: Oficina Permanente de Atención Social (24hr. toll-free ☎ 93 319 00 42).

AIDS Information: Association Ciutadana Anti-SIDA de Catalunya, C. Tantarantana, 4 (☎ 93 317 05 05). Open M-F 10am-2pm and 4-7pm.

Late-Night Pharmacy: Pharmacies open 24hr. on a rotating basis. Check pharmacy windows for current listings.

Hospitals: Barcelona Centro Médico (BCM), Av. Diagonal, 612, 2nd fl., #14 (☎ 93 414 06 43), coordinates referrals, especially for foreigners. **Hospital Clínic,** Villarroel, 170 (☎ 93 454 60 00). M: Hospital Clínic. Main entrance at the intersection of C. Roselló and C. Casanova. **Hospital de la Santa Creu i Sant Pau** (☎ 93 291 90 00, emergency ☎ 93 291 91 91), at the intersection of C. Cartagena and C. Sant Antoni Moria Claret. M: Hospital de Sant Pau. **Hospital Vall d' Hebron** (☎ 93 374 60 00).

Post Office: (☎ 93 318 38 31), in Pl. Antoni López, at the end of Vía Laietana, portside. M: Jaume I or Barceloneta. **Fax** and **Lista de Correos.** Open M-F 8:30am-9:30pm. A little shop in the back of the post office building, across the street, wraps packages for mailing (about 300ptas). Open M-Sa 9am-2pm and 5-8pm. **Postal Code:** 08003.

Internet Access: The email-obsessed will rejoice at Barcelona's many Internet cafes. Surf the Web in almost any electronics store or in more posh locales where you can gnosh on *bocadillos* and drinks. These are great places to meet fellow travelers.

Travel Bar, C. Boqueria, 27 (☎ 93 342 52 52; www.barcelonatravelbar.com.) M: Liceu. This innovative joint is an everything-in-one tourist heaven: Internet access, bar, restaurant, tour information and travel library. 450ptas per 30min., 900ptas per hr. M-Su 9am-2am.

Café Interlight, Av. Pau Claris, 106 (☎ 93 301 11 80; interlight@bcn.servicom.es). M: Catalunya. From the metro, go up Pg. Gràcia, turn right onto Gran Vía des Corts Catalans, and take the first left onto Av. Pau Claris. Interlight is on the right, marked by a hanging "@" sign. Jarring aqua seat-compartments and silver piping make this cafe feel like a scene out of 2050. 450ptas per 30min., 700ptas per hr.; with student ID 600ptas per hr. Open June-Aug. M-Sa 9am-10pm; Sept-May M-Sa 11am-10pm, Su noon-10pm.

Net Movil, Las Ramblas, 130, (☎ 93 342 42 04; netmovil@yahoo.com.) M: Liceu. Brand-spanking new Internet cafe equipped with 50 high-speed computers, 20 of which can be used to play video games. Watch MTV in the lounge. 300ptas per 15min., each additional min. 10ptas; 10hr. pass for 4500ptas. Fax 25ptas per page; printer 25ptas per page; photocopies 15ptas per page.

El Café de Internet, Gran Vía de les Corts Catalanes, 656 (☎ 93 412 19 15; www.cafeinternet.es). M: Catalunya. From the metro, walk up Pg. Gràcia and turn right onto Gran Vía. The cafe is 1½ blocks down on the right. Dim lighting, a rainbow of colored chairs, and a free buffet make this a hotspot for email-checkers. With student ID 500ptas per 30min., 800ptas per hr. Monthly email packages also available. Daily *menú* 1200ptas. Open M-Sa 8am-midnight.

Internet Gallery Café, Barra de Ferro, 3 (☎ 93 268 15 07; www.benetcafe.com.), right down the street from the Picasso museum. M: Jaume I. This stone-and-marble cafe blends right in with its artsy surroundings. Grab some food and drink while you log on. 250ptas per 15min., 600ptas per hr.; 10hr. ticket available. Open W-Sa 10am-3am, Su-Tu 10am-1pm.

Telephones: Get phone cards at tobacco stores, tourist offices, post offices, and some newsstands on Las Ramblas. **Private phone service** (☎/fax 93 490 76 50), at Estació Barcelona-Sants. M: Sants-Estació. **Fax** also available (1st page 250ptas, each additional page 100ptas). Open M-Sa 8am-9:45pm. For **collect calls** dial ☎ 1009; for **information** dial ☎ 1003. For more on phones in Spain, see **Keeping in Touch,** p. 71.

▶ ACCOMMODATIONS

Ciutat Vella, the part of Barcelona between Pl. Catalunya and the water consisting of the **Barri Gòtic, Las Ramblas, El Raval,** and **La Ribera,** offers a wealth of budget accommodations, but visitors without reservations will still end up scrambling in summer, when tourists flood every corner of the city. Signs with a large "P" or "H" mark the location of hostels. *Albergues* (youth hostels), which offer basics at the lowest prices, are the best places to meet fellow backpackers. Prices listed are for summer unless noted otherwise. All hostels offer 24-hour access.

LOWER BARRI GÒTIC

The following hostels are centrally located in the areas of the Barri Gòtic south of C. Portaferrissa. Backpackers flock here to be close to the port and hip Las Ramblas; it is an ideal place to experience the city's heady, fast-paced atmosphere. But be careful at night, especially in the Plaça Reial and on C. Escudellers.

UNDER 2500PTAS FOR ONE PERSON

Hostal Avinyó, C. Avinyó, 42 (☎ 93 318 79 45; fax 93 318 68 93; www.barcelona-on-line.es/avinyo). M: Drassanes. With annual renovations, owners are on a mission to make Avinyó the most modern spot in the Gòtic. Classy bathrooms and bedrooms with couches, high ceilings, excellent fans, and stained glass windows. Rooms 1700-1900ptas per person, with bath 2300-2600ptas.

Hostal Maldà, C. Pí, 5 (☎ 93 317 30 02). M: Liceu. Turn onto C. Portaferrissa (on the right with your back to the sea) from Las Ramblas, take the 4th right onto C. Pí, and enter at the green "Galleries Maldo" sign. Clean, nicely furnished rooms make this one of the best deals in the Barri Gòtic, although better lighting might be in order. Relaxing dining room has a travel library. Singles 1500ptas; doubles 3000ptas, with bath 3500ptas; triples 4000ptas, with bath 4500ptas.

Albergue de Juventud Kabul, Pl. Reial, 17 (☎ 93 318 51 90; fax 93 301 40 34). M: Liceu. Head to the port on Las Ramblas, pass C. Ferran, and turn left onto C. Colon Pl. Reial; Kabul is on the near right corner of the *plaça*. This place is legendary among European backpackers. Co-ed barracks-style rooms are cramped, a who's who of the college frat-boy scene. The common area offers satellite TV, a breakfast/snack bar, email kiosks (100ptas per 10min.), a pool table, blaring pop music, and a 24hr. party. Be careful with your valuables. 130 beds. Sheets 200ptas. Laundry 800ptas. Free lockers (1000pta deposit). Dorms 2200ptas.

Casa de Huéspedes Mari-Luz, C. Palau, 4 (☎/fax. 93 317 34 63), next to Albergue Juvenil Palau. M: Liceu. Take C. Ciutat to C. Templaris, then take the 2nd left. With 25 years under their belt, Mari-Luz and husband Fernando know how to make their hostel feel like a home. Narrow hallways flanked by ultra-clean, barracks-style bedrooms for 4-6 people; comfortable doubles also. Ask for kitchen use. Lockers in rooms. Laundry 800ptas. Keys for 24hr. entry. Reservations accepted. Dorms 1900ptas. V, MC.

Albergue Juvenil Palau (HI), C. Palau, 6 (☎ 93 412 50 80). M: Liceu. From Las Ramblas, take C. Ferrán to C. Enseyança, which becomes C. Palau. A small, tranquil refuge in the heart of the Barri Gòtic for the young, lowest budget set. Use the kitchen and airy common room to swap stories with fellow backpackers or watch TV. Rooms are clean and staff helpful. 2-8 people per room; 40 beds total. Breakfast included. Showers available 8am-noon and 4-10pm. Sheets 200ptas. Reception 7am-3am. Curfew 3am. Kitchen closes at 10pm, common room at midnight. Dorms 1900ptas.

Hostal Marítima, Las Ramblas, 4 (☎ 93 302 31 52), down a tiny alley off the port end of Las Ramblas. M: Drassanes. Follow the signs to Museo de Cera, which is next door. Nothing to write home about, but the location is convenient and rooms are comfortable. Laundry 800ptas (no dryer). Singles 2000-2500ptas; doubles 4000-5000ptas.

Pensión Bienestar, C. Quintana, 3 (☎ 93 318 72 83). M: Liceu. From Las Ramblas (away from the port), turn right onto C. Ferrán and then left on C. Quintana. Brown is the hue of choice in these 30 dim and simple rooms. Mattresses could be firmer. Hot water 8am-midnight only. Singles 2000ptas; doubles 3500-3800ptas; triples 4500ptas.

Hostal-Residencia Europa, C. Boquería, 18 (☎/fax 93 318 76 20). M: Liceu. Despite its faded sheets and gloomy decor, tourists flock to Europa for its fabulous location, only a few feet off Las Ramblas. Rooms are basic, aside from the occasional bathtub. TV lounge. Singles 2000-2800ptas, with bath 5800ptas; doubles 4200-5200ptas, with bath 5400-6800ptas. Hot water 7:30am-12:30pm and 7:30pm-12:30am.

UNDER 5000PTAS FOR ONE PERSON

Hostal Fernando, C. Ferrán, 31 (☎/fax 93 301 79 93; www.barcelona-on-line.es/fernando.) M: Liceu. This hostel is a backpacker's dream. Charming and clean, it has become one of the most social lodgings in the area. Upbeat, multilingual staff, Internet kiosk (200ptas per 8min.), TV room, and good mattresses. Dorm beds 2100ptas; singles 2800ptas; doubles with bath 6500ptas; triples with bath 7500ptas. V, MC.

Hostal-Residencia Rembrandt, C. Portaferrisa, 23 (☎/fax 93 318 10 11). M: Liceu. From the port, walk up Las Ramblas and turn right onto C. Portaferrisa. Pastel-colored rooms have individual themes, ranging from "little kid" to "regal." Common spaces with comfy couches scattered throughout. Ask for a balcony. Breakfast 400ptas. Singles 3200ptas, with bath 4300ptas; doubles 5000ptas, with bath 6700ptas; triples 7000ptas. One 10,000pta suite with 2 balconies, gigantic marble tub and living room.

Hostal Levante, Baixada de San Miguel, 2 (☎ 93 317 95 65; fax 93 317 05 26). M: Liceu. Walk down C. Ferrán, turn right onto C. Avinyó, and take the 1st left onto Baixada de San Miguel. Large rooms with beautiful pink-stoned balconies. Light wood interiors, good ventilation, tiled bathrooms, and a good TV lounge. Safe available 7am-10pm. Reception 24hr. Singles 3500ptas; doubles 5500ptas, with bath 6500ptas. V, MC.

Hotel Call, Arco San Ramón del Call, 4 (☎ 93 302 11 23; fax 93 301 34 86). M: Liceu. From Las Ramblas, take C. Boqueria to its end, then veer left onto C. Call; the hotel is on the first corner on the left, under the neon "Hotel" sign. A quiet place with pleasant rooms, all equipped with phones, sparkling bathrooms, and firm beds. Ask for a room with a balcony, as many are windowless. Singles 4500ptas; doubles 6000ptas; triples 8000ptas; quads 7500ptas (tax not included). V, MC.

Hostal Layetana, Pl. Ramón Berenguer el Gran, 2 (☎/fax 93 319 20 12), less than a block from the metro, on the left as you walk away from the sea. M: Jaume I. Balconies open onto the cathedral or a fashionable plaza. Plush suede living room with terrace. Showers 200ptas. Singles 2700ptas; doubles 4700ptas, with bath 5900ptas; triples 6400ptas, with bath 8000ptas (tax not included). V, MC.

Hotel Rey Don Jaume I, C. Jaume I, 11 (☎/fax 93 310 62 08; email r.d.jaime@atriumhotels.com). M: Jaume I, in the heart of chic La Ribera. Bathroom and telephone in every room, double mattress on every bed. These people love to clean and it smells like it. Multilingual staff. Singles 5000ptas; doubles 7400ptas; triples 10,500ptas. V, MC, AmEx.

Hostal Paris, Cardenal Casañas, 4 (☎ 93 301 37 85; fax 93 412 70 96). Bright yellow sign is visible from Las Ramblas and right across from M: Liceu. Bland rooms have big bathrooms, A/C, and TVs. Great location. TV lounge. Singles 3000ptas, with bath 6500ptas; doubles 4800ptas, with bath 7500ptas; triple with bath 9700ptas. V, MC.

UPPER BARRI GÒTIC

This stunning section of the Barri Gòtic includes the area south of Pl. Catalunya, bounded by C. Fontanella to the north and C. Portaferrisa to the south. **Portal de L'Angel,** the better-behaved little brother of Las Ramblas, is a broad pedestrian thoroughfare avenue running through the middle, southward from Pl. Catalunya. Accommodations here are a bit pricier than those in the Lower Barri Gòtic but are just a few minutes from Las Ramblas and have a more serene ambiance. Reservations are almost obligatory in June, July, and August. The nearest metro stop is Pl. Catalunya, unless otherwise specified.

UNDER 3500PTAS FOR ONE PERSON

Hostal Residencia Opera, C. San Pablo, 20 (☎/fax 93 318 82 01). M: Liceu. From the metro, walk down las Ramblas toward the port and take the first right. The fantastic amenities here seem scripted: marble tables and chairs, huge bathrooms, phones, TVs, A/C, gorgeous decor, and a quiet TV salon. Singles 3000ptas, with bath 5000ptas; doubles with bath 7000ptas; triples with bath 9000ptas.

Pensión Dalí, C. Boqueria, 12 (☎ 93 318 55 90; fax 93 318 55 80; email pension-dali@wamadoo.es). Designed as a religious house by Luis Domenech i Montaner, the architect of the Palau de la Musica Catalana, Pensión Dalí still retains the stained glass and gaudy iron doors of its early years. Rooms are royal, with light wood floors, phones, TVs, gold sheets, and soundproof windows. A huge couch-filled common room keeps travelers entertained. Internet access 100ptas per 4min. Doubles 6000ptas, with bath 7000ptas; triples 9600ptas, with bath 12,000ptas. V, MC, AmEx.

Residencia Victoria, C. Comtal, 9 (☎ 93 317 45 97). From Pl. Catalunya, take the 1st left onto Av. Portal de L'Angel, then a left on C. Comtal. Cafeteria-style lounge, outdoor terrace, kitchen, TV, and small library. Rectangular rooms could be cleaner. Laundry 400ptas. Singles 3000-3500ptas; doubles 5000-5500ptas; triples 7000ptas.

Hostal-Residencia Lausanne, Av. Portal de L'Angel, 24 (☎ 93 302 11 39). Located on one of Barcelona's most happening streets, Lausanne is almost as grand as its imperial facade and entryway. All rooms have new wallpaper, renovated baths, sinks, and dressers. The living room is high-class, with satellite TV and Persian rugs. Ask for a room with a view. Doubles 5500ptas, with shower 6000ptas.

Pensión Santa Anna, C. Santa Anna, 23 (☎/fax 93 301 22 46), near Pensión Estal. M: Catalunya. This hostel is slowly undergoing a full-body transformation; the renovated 1st floor boasts colorful tiles, wooden mirrors, and sturdy furniture. The other floors suffer from a more dreary ambiance, but the friendly management and clean rooms make up for it. Singles 3000ptas; doubles 5000ptas, with bath 6000ptas; triples 7500ptas.

Pensión Arosa, Av. Portal de L'Angel, 14 (☎ 93 317 36 87; fax 93 301 30 38), next to Pensión Nevada. Enter by Andrew's tie shop. Definitely the pinkest *pensión* in town. Rooms are airy but small. 2500-3000ptas per person. V, MC, AmEx.

Pensión Noya, Las Ramblas, 133 (☎ 93 301 48 31), above the noisy Nuría restaurant. This 10-room hostel has time-warped back to the colors and styles of the 1950s. Bathrooms and hallways are cramped. No heat in winter. Hot water 8am-midnight. Singles 2300ptas; doubles 5000ptas; triples 6900ptas.

Pensión Aris, C. Fontanella, 14 (☎ 93 318 10 17), near Hostal Plaza. 13 huge, clean, and sparse rooms. Laundry 500-1000ptas. Singles 2500ptas; doubles 5000ptas, with bath 6000ptas; triples 6000ptas.

UNDER 7000PTAS FOR ONE PERSON

▨ **Hostal Fontanella,** Vía Laietana, 71 (☎/fax 93 317 59 43). M: Urquinaona. From the metro, head down Vía Laietana. Looks like a life-size dollhouse, with soft lights, floral bouquets, flowing curtains, and embroidered towels. Hotel-quality beds and baths. Singles 3000ptas, with bath 4000ptas; doubles 5000ptas, with bath 5800-6900ptas. Reservations with deposit. V, MC, AmEx.

▨ **Hotel Toledano/Hostal Residencia Capitol,** Las Ramblas, 138 (☎ 93 301 08 72; fax 93 412 31 42; email toledano@idgrup.ibernet.com), just off Pl. Catalunya. This family-owned, split-level hotel/hostel has been making tourists happy for almost 80 years. Rooms border on luxurious, with cable TV, phones, and some balconies. English-speaking owner. 4th-floor hotel: singles 3900ptas, with bath 4400ptas; doubles with bath 7600ptas; triples with bath 9500ptas; quads with bath 7400-10,600ptas. 5th-floor hostel: singles 3600ptas; doubles 5100ptas, with bath 5800ptas; triples 6500ptas, with bath 7200ptas. V, MC, AmEx.

Mare Nostrum, La Rambla, 67 (☎ 93 318 53 40; fax 93 412 30 69) M: Liceu. For those brought up with a silver spoon in their mouth (or those who wish they were). Mare Nostrum is like a modern resort. Chill in your air-conditioned palace, gaze onto Las Ramblas from your balcony, lie under your new comforter, watch your satellite TV, and love your life. Singles 5000ptas, with private bath 5800ptas; doubles 7500ptas, with private bath 8975ptas; triples 8975ptas, with bath 11,200ptas.

Hostal Plaza, C. Fontanella, 18 (☎/fax 93 301 01 39; email plazahostal@rete-mail.es). C. Fontanella stems right from Pl. Catalunya at El Corte Inglés. Every year this hostel flashes with new coats of colorful paint, bigger beds, and more modern amenities, all in Americana-style. The friendly Texan owners love students and the fantastic lounge offers all the comforts of home: phone, fax (300ptas), TV, Internet access (600ptas per 30min.), and a kitchen. Laundry 1500ptas for 5kg. Reception closed 2-5pm. Singles 6000ptas, with bath 7000ptas; doubles with bath 8000-9000ptas; triples 11,000ptas, with bath 12,000ptas. V, MC, AmEx. 1000ptas off if you pay in cash.

Hostal Palermo, C. Boqueria, 21 (☎/fax 93 302 40 02) M: Liceu. Large, party-conducive rooms make this hostel a favorite among backpackers. Walls are white-washed, bathrooms clean, and floors cold. The common room looks like an airport terminal but is a nice place to relax. Laundry 700ptas, safe 200ptas per day. Singles 4800ptas, with bath 6800ptas; doubles 7000ptas, with bath 8000ptas. V, MC.

Pensión Nevada, Av. Portal de L'Angel, 16 (☎ 93 302 31 01), just past Hostal Residencia Lausanne, under the "Raphael Roca Optico" sign. Great location. Bedrooms are just like grandma's house, complete with matching throw pillows, firm beds, coffee tables, balconies, and layers of linen. TV lounge. Singles 3800ptas; doubles 7000ptas.

Pensión Estal, C. Santa Anna, 27 (☎ 93 302 26 18). From the metro, take the Las Ramblas exit and then the 1st left onto C. Santa Anna. Some of these tiny, simple rooms offer views of Iglesia de Santa Anna. Space-age windows shut out all sound, ensuring a good night's sleep. Singles 3500ptas; doubles 5500ptas, with bath 6000ptas; triples 6000ptas, with bath 8000ptas.

EL RAVAL

Hostels in El Raval, the area west of Las Ramblas, are harder to come by and less-touristed; staying here will give you a better feel for *la vida catalana*.

■ **Pensión L'Isard,** C. Tallers, 82 (☎ 93 302 51 83; fax 93 302 01 17), near MACBA, the new contemporary art museum. M: Universitat. Take the C. Pelai exit from the metro, turn left at the end of the block, and then left again at the pharmacy. Simple, elegant and unbelievably clean—a great find. Bright rooms have enough closet space for even the worst over-packer. Ask for a room with a balcony. Singles 2400ptas; doubles 4400ptas, with bath 5000ptas; triples 6000ptas.

Residencia Australia, Ronda Universitat, 11 (☎ 93 317 41 77). M: Universitat. Guests are family at this hostel, and the rooms make you feel that way—all have embroidered sheets, curtains, balconies, artwork, and fans. Be prepared for the equally family-style quiet time, though, starting at 10pm. Curfew 4am. Singles 3000ptas; doubles 4800ptas, with bath 6000ptas. V, MC.

Hostal La Terrassa, Junta de Comerç, 11 (☎ 93 302 51 74; fax 93 301 21 88). M: Liceu. From the metro, take C. Hospital and turn left after Teatre Romea. A hostel experience for the minimalist, with 50 small, basic, clean rooms. The social courtyard is a rarity among non-youth hostels. Singles 2400ptas, with bath 3600ptas; doubles 3800ptas, with bath 4600ptas; triples with bath 6000ptas. V, MC.

L'EIXAMPLE

Barcelona's most beautiful accommodations lie along L'Eixample's wide, safe avenues—style is of the essence in this famously bourgeois neighborhood. Most hostels have colorfully tiled, carpeted interiors and Modernista elevators styled with wood and steel; most rooms have high ceilings and lots of light.

■ **Hostal Residencia Windsor,** Rambla Catalunya, 84 (☎ 93 215 11 98), near the intersection with C. Mallorca. M: Pg. Gràcia. With crimson carpets and palatial decor, this hostel lives up to its royal name. Rooms come equipped with comfy sleep sofas and gorgeous oval-shaped balconies. Singles 3900ptas, with bath 4900ptas; doubles 6500ptas, with bath 7900ptas (tax not included).

Hostal Residencia Oliva, Pg. Gràcia, 32, 4th fl. (☎ 93 488 01 62 or 93 488 17 89), at the intersection with C. Diputació. M: Pg. Gràcia. Elegant wood-worked bureaus, bed frames, and mirrors give this hostel a classy ambiance. Rooms have color TVs. Some windows overlook the *manzana de discòrdia* (see **Ruta del Modernisme,** p. 318). Reservations a must. Singles 3200ptas; doubles 6200ptas, with bath 7200ptas.

Hostal Girona, C. Girona, 24, 1st fl. (☎ 93 265 02 59; fax 93 265 85 32), between C. Casp and C. Ausias Marc. M: Urquinaona. Carpeted hallways, immense wooden doors, and room TVs come at a surprisingly small price. Singles 3000ptas, with bath 4500ptas; doubles 6000ptas, with bath 7500ptas. V, MC.

GRÀCIA

Locals outnumber travelers in Gràcia, a five- to 10-minute walk from M: Diagonal; Berlitz-Spanish won't help in this Catalan-dominated area. Its deceptively quiet atmosphere has earned it a reputation as Barcelona's "undiscovered" quarter, but native 20-somethings have most definitely discovered Gràcia's lively weekend nightlife. The accommodations listed here are small and well kept.

Hostal Bonavista, C. Bonavista, 21 (☎ 93 237 37 57). M: Diagonal. Head toward the fountain at the end of Pg. Gràcia and take the first right; the hostel is just off the traffic circle. Well-lit, clean, cared-for rooms with sinks. TV lounge. Showers 300ptas. No reservations. Singles 2500ptas; doubles 3800ptas, with bath 4800ptas (tax not included).

Pensión San Medín, C. Gran de Gràcia, 125 (☎ 93 217 30 68; fax 93 415 44 10). M: Fontana. Embroidered curtains and ornate tiling adorn this family-run pension; newly renovated rooms have nice furniture and phones. Common room with TV. Singles 3000ptas, with bath 4000ptas; doubles 6000ptas, with bath 7000ptas. V, MC.

ELSEWHERE

■ **Pensión Francia,** C. Rera Palau, 4 (☎ 93 319 03 76). M: Barceloneta. From Estació de França, turn left onto the main avenue (Av. Marquès de l'Argentera); C. Rera Palau is the 5th right. From the metro, head toward town, cross Pl. Palau, and turn right onto Av. Marquès de l'Argentera; C. Rera Palau is the 2nd left. Gorgeous balconies, gleaming furniture, and a friendly owner. Singles 2000ptas; doubles 4000ptas, with bath 5000-7000ptas; triples with bath 6500ptas; quads with bath 8000ptas. V, MC.

Albergue Mare de Déu de Montserrat (HI), Pg. Mare de Déu del Coll, 41-51 (☎ 93 210 51 51; fax 93 210 07 98), beyond Parc Güell (way out there). Bus #28 from Pl. Catalunya and Nitbus N-4 stops across the street from the hostel. Otherwise, from M: Vallcarca, walk up Av. República Argentina and cross the bridge at C. Viaducte de Vallcarca; signs point the way up the hill. This 180-bed government-sponsored hostel is nicer than most museums. Given the private woods, hilltop view of Barcelona, restaurant, Internet access, vending machines, and multiple common spaces, it is not surprising that travelers here are so friendly. HI members only. Breakfast included. Sheets 350ptas. Flexible 3-day max. stay. Reception 8am-11pm. Lockout 10am-2pm. Midnight curfew, but doors open every 30min. midnight-3am. Reservations accepted. Dorms 1900ptas, over 25 2500ptas. V, MC, AmEx.

Hostal de Joves Municipal (HI), Pg. Pujades, 29 (☎/fax 93 300 31 04). M: Arc de Triomf. From the metro, exit to C. Nápols, walk toward Parc de la Ciutadella, and turn left on Pg. Pujades. 68 beds and 6 bathrooms. No locks on doors. Breakfast included. Showers 7-9:30am and 3-10pm. Sheets 350ptas. Laundry 700ptas wash, 800ptas dry. 5-day max. stay. Reception 8-10am and 3pm-midnight. Lockout 10am-3pm. Curfew at midnight, but doors open briefly at 1 and 2am. Dorms 1500ptas.

CAMPING

Although there are no campsites within the city, intercity buses (200ptas) run to all the following locations in 20 to 45 minutes. For more info, contact the **Associació de Càmpings de Barcelona,** Gran Vía Corts Catalanes, 608 (☎ 93 412 59 55).

El Toro Bravo (☎ 93 637 34 62), 11km south of Barcelona, accessible by bus L95 from Pl. Catalunya. Laundry facilities, currency exchange, pool, and supermarket. Reception 8am-7pm. 1300ptas per person, 775ptas per tent (IVA not included). V, MC, AmEx.

Filipinas (☎ 93 658 28 95), 1km down the road from El Toro Bravo, accessible by bus L95. The same prices and services as El Toro Bravo. V, MC, AmEx.

La Ballena Alegre (☎ 93 658 05 04), 1km down the road from Filipines, 13km from Barcelona, accessible by bus L95. Same services as El Toro Bravo. 24hr. reception. 1300ptas per person, 1375ptas per tent. Open Feb. 16-Dec. 14. V, MC, AmEx.

⧉ FOOD

Drawing from both Spanish and Catalan culinary traditions, Barcelona's restaurants are a mix of authentic neighborhood haunts and stylish cosmopolitan hotspots. (See **Cataluña**, p. 337, for more information on typical Catalan food.) For the cheapest meals, 1000-1300ptas *menús* are posted in the restaurants on Barcelona's side streets. The crowded eateries on Las Ramblas and near the port are often great for ambiance but less worthy of their price than places in less-touristed areas like El Ravel, La Ribera, and Gràcia. Many of the best restaurants serve *cuisina del mercado*, menus created daily to match the best fresh market offerings. Traditional food shops, *colmados*, typically have hidden backroom tables for feasting. Marketplaces all have their own foodstands-turned-restaurants which may look grimy but are often delicious.

Consult the weekly *Guía del Ocio* (available at newsstands, 125ptas) for additional dining options; the *Guía* provides a laundry list of often overpriced specialty restaurants: *servicio a domicilio* (delivery), *para llevar* (take-out), *abiertos en domingo* (restaurants open Sundays), and *cenar de madrugada* (late-night dining). Be aware that food options shrink drastically in August, when restauranteurs and bar owners close up shop and take their vacations. Most untouristed places are closed Sundays.

BASICS

If you want to live on the cheap and do as the *barceloneses* do, buy your food fresh at a *mercat* (marketplace), hit up a grocery store for other essentials, and get hot bread and pastries at the city's *patisserías*. The marketplaces in particular are worth at least a visit. Urban planners in the late 1800s allotted space for one of them every ten blocks; today the city has more than 40 in all, barely enough to contain the bustling hordes of mothers, wives, and chefs.

Markets: La Boquería (Mercat de Sant Josep), off Las Ramblas, outside the Liceu metro station (Mercat exit). A wonderland of fresh food housed in an all-steel modernist structure. Wholesale prices for fruit, cheese and wine. **Mercat de la Concepi**, on C. Valencia between C. Bruc and C. Girona. M: Girona. A smaller version of La Boquería. **Mercat de Sant Antoni**, M: Sant Antoni. Barcelona's biggest flea market, with everything from antiques to anchovies. Visit M, W, F, or Sa for the best stuff. Book market Su mornings.

Supermarkets: Champion Supermarket, Las Ramblas, 113 (☎ 93 302 48 24). M: Liceu. From Liceu, walk up Las Ramblas and look to the left. Plenty of essentials, as well as an inexpensive *menú* and salad bar. Open M-Sa 9am-9pm. **Condis Supermercats**, Junta de Comercio, 19 (☎ 93 317 04 52). M: Liceu, in El Ravel.

LOWER BARRI GÒTIC

The further into the lower Barri Gòtic you trek, the more delicious the food. Great restaurants are scattered on C. Escudellers and C. Clave. Some of the liveliest between-meal hangouts surround Església Santa María del Pí—relax at the *terrazas* for drinks and ice cream. (From Las Ramblas, enter Llano de la Boquería, turn left at the Banco Central Hispano and follow C. Cardenal Casanyes into Pl. Pí.)

▨ **La Fonda**, C. Escudellers, 10 (☎ 93 301 75 15). M: Drassanes or Liceu. C. Escudellers branches off Las Ramblas between Liceu and Drassanes. Probably the most popular restaurant in all of Barcelona; definitely the classiest atmosphere for the lowest price. Be prepared to fight locals and tourists alike for a coveted table. Starters 275-700ptas. Entrees 500-1000ptas. Open daily 1-3:30pm and 8:30-11:30pm. V, MC, AmEx.

Irati, C. Cardenal Casañas, 17 (☎ 93 302 30 84). An excellent Basque restaurant that attracts droves of hungry *tapas*-seekers. Their creative twist on fresh fish and meat makes for delicious entrees. Bartenders pour *sidra* (cider) behind their backs—with the bottle high above your glass—and parade new platters of treats every 5min. All *tapas* 140ptas (they count the toothpicks to tally). Entrees around 2000ptas. Open Tu-Sa noon-midnight, Su noon-5pm. *Tapas* only noon-3pm and 7-11pm. V, MC.

Il Mercante Di Venezia, C. Jose Anselmo Clave, 11 (☎ 93 317 18 28). M: Drassanes. Gold drapes, dim lighting, and excellent Italian food make this perfect for a romantic meal. Enough pasta, meat, and fish choices to please even the pickiest eater. Appetizers 375-800ptas. Pasta under 1000ptas. Meat 1175-1800ptas. Open Tu-Su 1:30-3:30pm and 8:30pm-midnight.

Juicy Jones, Cardenal Casañas, 7 (☎ 93 302 43 30). M. Liceu. Head down Las Ramblas from the metro and take the 1st left (almost a U-turn) on Cardenal Casañas. Let the crazy flower-power of this psychedelic restaurant seep in as you enjoy some of the best vegan cuisine around. A refreshing, delicious combo of rice, veggies, fresh juices, beans, and sauces. Daily *menú* (after 1pm) 1100ptas. Open 10am-11:15pm.

Peimong, C. Templaris, 6-10 (☎ 93 318 28 73). M: Liceu. From Las Ramblas, take C. Ferrán. At Pl. Sant Jaume, veer right onto C. Ciutat and take the 2nd right on C. Templaris. Generous portions of hen, goat, veal, duck, and fish cooked Peruvian style (900ptas and under). Open Tu-Su 1-5pm and 8pm-midnight.

Las Caracoles, C. Escudellers, 14. (☎ 93 301 20 41). M: Drassanes. Mouth-watering decor: chicken breasts roasting in the window, walls and ceilings covered with oversized veggies and utensils, and your soup simmering in front of you in the open-view kitchen. Dishes taste as good as they look; specialties include the snails, suckled pig, lamb, and chicken. Meat 1100-2500ptas. Fish 1400-2800ptas. Open daily 1pm-midnight.

Buen Bocado, C. Escudellers, 31. (☎ 93 317 27 91). M: Drassanes. A little flavor of the Middle East for those midday or midnight munchies. Falafel 350ptas. Shawarma 425ptas. Sweets 125ptas. Open 1-3pm and 6pm-2:30am.

El Gallo Kiriko, C. Avinyó, 19 (☎ 93 412 48 38). M: Liceu. Walk down C. Ferrán from Las Ramblas; C. Avinyó is the 4th right. Take a break from Spanish food with Pakistani rice, Tandoori dishes, couscous, and fruit shakes. Veggie options. Most dishes under 700ptas. 5% discount with ISIC. Open daily noon-1am. V, MC (not with youth discount).

Restaurante Bidasoa, C. Serra, 21 (☎ 93 318 10 63). M: Drassanes. From the metro, follow C. J. A. Clavé, and take the 3rd left. 40 years of practice have produced delectable permutations of soup, salad, and meat and fish dishes (600ptas and under). Open Tu-Su 1:30-4pm and 8pm-midnight. Closed Aug.

UPPER BARRI GÒTIC

In the upper Barri Gòtic, the interiors of old buildings are continually being disemboweled to make room for classy cafes and restaurants. Thanks to free-market competition, the more cafes that pop up, the cheaper they get.

Els Quatre Gats, C. Montsió, 3 (☎ 93 302 41 40). M: Catalunya. From the metro, go down Av. Portal de L'Angel and take the 2nd left. Modernista hangout of Picasso's; he loved it so much he designed a personalized menu (on display at Museu Picasso; see p. 325). *Tapas* (150-650ptas) are the best way to go. Entrees around 2000ptas. Live music 9pm-1am. Open M-Sa 9am-2am, Su 5pm-2am. Closed Aug. V, MC, AmEx.

El Cervol Roig, C. Comtal, 19 (☎ 93 318 92 99). M: Urquinaona. A loud, animated gathering spot for locals escaping from the office—patrons manage to stuff huge platters of fish and meat into their mouths while rattling off stock quotes. *La comida* is a steal at 1195ptas. Starters 700ptas. Entrees 1300-2500ptas. Open daily 9am-9pm.

Terrablava, Vía Laietana, 55 (☎ 93 322 15 85). Cafeteria ease but much better taste. An all-you-can-eat buffet of fresh salads, veggies, pastas, pizza, meat dishes, and fruit. Lunchtime brings a circus of famished locals. 1095ptas. Open daily 1pm-1am.

BARCELONA

The Bagel Shop, C. Canuda, 25 (☎ 93 302 41 61). M: Catalunya. From the metro, walk down Las Ramblas and take the 1st left onto C. Canuda. Barcelona meets New York City. Monstrous bagel selection (100ptas each), sandwiches, varied spreads (350-550ptas), and a Su pancake brunch (Sept.-June). Open M-Sa 9:30am-11:30pm.

Restaurante Self Naturista, C. Santa Anna, 11-17 (☎ 93 318 26 84), off Las Ramblas. M: Catalunya. A self-service vegetarian cafeteria with enormous selection. Enough dessert options to fill a bakery. Portions tend to be small. Entrees under 500ptas. Lunch *menú* 965ptas. Open M-Sa 11:30am-10pm.

EL RAVAL

Students and blue-collar workers congregate in typical Catalan joints west of Las Ramblas. Restaurants line the streets and are fairly inexpensive. Most have simple decor, basic food, lots of noise, and unlimited bread and wine, although trendier gourmet places are starting to move into the area as well. Establishments off C. Lluna and Joaquín Costa often serve Galician fare.

▨ **Colibri** (93 443 23 06), Riera Alta. Take C. I. Carme and make your 6th right onto Riera Alta; Colibri is 2 blocks up on the left. With only a few months under her belt, Colibri's market cuisine brings a new level of freshness, flair, and service to eating-out in Barcelona. Impeccable wine selection and beautiful atmosphere. Dishes 1200-2500ptas.

▨ **Restaurante Can Lluís,** C. Cera, 49 (☎ 93 441 11 87). M: San Antoni. From the metro, head down Ronda S. Pau and take the 2nd left on C. Cera. For over 100 years, Can Lluís has been a defining force in Catalan cuisine. The menu overflows with hard-to-pronounce delicacies you've never tried before but should, among them *cabrit* (goat) and *conill* (rabbit). Daily *menú* 950ptas. Open M-Sa 1:30-4pm and 8:30-11:30pm. Visa.

Restaurante Chino, C. Tallers, 70 (☎ 93 317 49 30). M: Catalunya or Universitat. Take C. Tallers from Pl. Universitat or Las Ramblas. More pan-Asian than Chinese, this restaurant's varied, filling, and inexpensive menu won't disappoint. Dishes 595-900ptas. Open daily noon-4:30pm and 8pm-midnight.

Restaurante Riera, C. Joaquín Costa, 30 (☎ 93 443 32 93). M: Liceu or Universitat. Off C. Carme coming from Liceu; off Ronda de Sant Antoni from Universitat. The Riera family provides a feast fit for a very hungry king, complete with dessert and wine (900ptas). Open daily 1-4pm and 8-11:30pm.

Restaurante Biocenter, C. Pintor Fortuny, 25 (☎ 93 301 45 83), off Las Ramblas. M: Catalunya. Your ears will ring with Brazilian music and environmentalist propaganda but the enormous buffet will keep you silently content. *Menú* with unlimited soup and salad, vegetarian entree, and dessert 1150ptas. Open M-Sa 9am-noon and 1-5pm.

Bar Restaurante Los Toreros, C. Xuclá, 3-5 (☎ 93 318 23 25), on a narrow alley between C. Fortuny and C. Carme, both off Las Ramblas. M: Catalunya. Specializes in group meals—come with friends and order from one of the many *menús para grupos*. The solo lunch *menú* is cheap too (900ptas) and the nighttime *tapas* menu is extremely popular (2000ptas). Open Tu-Sa 9am-1am, Su 9am-1pm. Main *menú* available 1-4pm.

Bar Restaurante Romesco, C. Sant Pau, 28 (☎ 93 318 93 81). M: Liceu. From the metro, walk up Las Ramblas and turn left onto C. Sant Pau. Take the 1st right; Romesco is immediately on the left. This small diner serves simple, dirt-cheap food. *Frijoles* (beans) and *crema catalana* are their specialties; their fries are among the best in Barcelona. Fish, chicken, and meat dishes 375-800ptas. Open M-Sa 1pm-2am.

LA RIBERA

East of Vía Laietana, La Ribera is home to the Museu Picasso and numerous bars and small restaurants. Once a fisherman's enclave, the neighborhood is still far from touristed. Menus are available only in Spanish and Catalan, but if you guess right (hint: *sesos* means brains), you'll get one of the city's best bargains.

▨ **La Habana Vieja,** Carrer dels Banys Vells, 2 (☎ 93 268 25 04). C. Baños Viejos is parallel to C. Montcada. The pulsing Cuban music will tempt you to leave your seat to dance; the delicious food will convince you to stay put. Large portions are perfect for sharing among friends. Cuban rice 600-900ptas. Meat dishes 1600-2000ptas. Open M-Sa 8pm-1am, F-Sa 1pm-4pm. Visa.

Luna Plena, C. Montcada, 2 (☎ 93 310 54 29). M: Jaume I. From the metro, take C. Princesa; turn left onto C. Montcada. Smokehouse-like exterior belies a gleaming, sophisticated interior. Expensive Spanish dinner but well-priced lunch (1000ptas). Reservations accepted. Open Tu-Sa 1-4pm and 8-11:30pm, Su 1-4pm. Closed Aug. V, MC.

Ikkiu, C. Princesa, 11 (☎ 93 319 28 26). M: Jaume I. Cheap Japanese food, and lots of it. Daily 5-course lunch *menú* with tempura or sushi 975-1200ptas. Tu-Sa 1:30-3:30pm and 9-11:30pm.

Txirimira, C. Princesa, 11 (☎ 93 310 18 05). Enough *tapas* to feed a small village. (140ptas each). Sit at the long wooden bar and try *la gula,* a seafood and veggie specialty from northern Spain. Open Tu-Su noon-midnight. V, MC.

L'EIXAMPLE

When dining uptown, expect restaurants to be more expensive and the ambiance more elegant. L'Eixample also has its fair share of *tapas* bars on Passeig de Gracia. Small sidewalk cafes pop up everywhere.

🗑 **La Provenca,** C. Provenca, 242 (☎ 93 323 23 67). Enter through a hall of lanterns to a gourmet banquet of food that is anything but Spanish. La Provenca's food leans towards a Mediterranean influence. Specialties include carpaccio, fresh fish and vegetables. Entrees 1290-1700ptas. Dress well. Open daily 1:30-5:30pm and 9-11:30pm.

Saler, Consejo de Ciento, 316 (☎ 93 488 03 95). Quiet Saler has earned local acclaim for its excellent gazpacho and delicious Galician seafood specialties. Entrees 950-2300ptas. *Menú* 1075ptas. Open M-Sa 1-4pm and 8:30-11:30pm.

ba-ba-reeba, Pg. Gràcia, 28 (☎ 93 301 43 02). M: Pg. Gràcia. So many *tapas,* so little time (most under 500ptas). Good Catalan *pa* (bread) as well. Outdoor dining on the *passeig* recommended. Open daily 9am-2am.

GRÀCIA

You know you are in mellow Gràcia when you hear fellow diners speaking Catalan instead of Spanish, English, French, or German. The food is likewise authentic.

El Tastavins, C. Ramón y Cajal, 12 (☎ 93 213 60 31), near Pl. Sol. M: Joanic. A small offering of satisfying Catalan mainstays. No English menu (or speakers), but waiters become masters of charades impersonating the dishes they wish to explain. Try the bull. Entrees under 1250ptas. Open Tu-Su 1:30-4pm and 9pm-midnight.

Restaurant Illa de Gràcia, C. Sant Domenic, 19 (☎ 93 238 02 29). Satisfying vegetarian food picked at by stylish, young health-nuts. *Menú del día* 850ptas. Salads 500ptas. Entrees around 1000ptas. Open Tu-F 1-4pm and 8pm-midnight, Sa-Su 2-4pm and 8pm-midnight.

Xavi Petit, C. Bonavista, 2 (☎ 93 237 88 26), off C. Gran de Gràcia. M: Diagonal. Funky crêpes can be a filling meal or just dessert (550-750ptas). Crêpe-less afternoon *menú* 950ptas. *Tapas* 350-550ptas. Open M-Sa 8am-midnight.

XAMPANYERIES

For Barcelona natives, no dining-out experience is complete without a glass of *cava,* a Spanish wine similar to white sparkling champagne. *Xampanyeries* (champagne bars) fill the time between lengthy diners and late-night clubbing. Ordering full bottles of *cava* can get pricey, but a glass or two won't break the budget. Try **Xampu Xampany,** Gran Vía, 702 (☎93 265 04 83; open 6pm-2:30am), or **Barcelonin de Vins i Esperits,** C. Valencia, 304 (☎ 93 215 70 83; open 6pm-2am).

🔘 SIGHTS

Architecturally, Barcelona is defined by its unique Modernista treasures. Las Ramblas—a long bustling avenue smack in the city center—and the Barri Gòtic, Barcelona's "old city," are the traditional tourist areas. But don't neglect vibrant La Ribera and El Raval, the upscale avenues of L'Eixample, the panoramic city views from Montjuïc and Tibidabo, Gaudí's Parc Güell, and the harbor-side Port Olimpíc.

RUTA DEL MODERNISME

Ruta del Modernisme passes (600ptas, students 400ptas) are good for a month and give holders a 50% discount on entrance to Palau Güell, La Sagrada Familia, Casa Milà (La Pedrera), Palau de la Música, Casa-Museu Gaudí, Fundació Antoni Tàpies, and the Museu d'Art Modern. Purchase passes at Casa Lleó i Morera, on the corner of Pg. Grácia and C. Consedel (☎ 93 488 01 39; see p. 321).

In the late 19th and early 20th centuries, Barcelona's flourishing bourgeoisie commissioned a new class of architects to build their houses, reshaping the face of L'Eixample with Modernista architecture that employed revolutionary shapes, materials, and spaces to reflect nature and the signs and symbols of Cataluña. **Luis Domènech i Montaner** is known for his heavily decorated surfaces (see the Palau de la Musica Catalana and Casa Lleó i Morera), and **José Puig i Caldafach** developed an unique style uniting local and foreign traditions. Most famous of all Modernista architects, though, is **Antoni Gaudí**, with his serpentine rooftops, warrior-like chimneys, and fantastical facades. (See **Genius in Solitude**, below.)

Barcelona's hyper-organized tourist administration has designed a Gaudí-dominated route that covers prominent Modernista architecture all over the city. The best way to approach this macro-museum of Catalan architecture is with the *Ruta del Modernisme* booklet and pamphlet guides available at the tourist office. Barcelona's Modernista highlights include: **Palau Güell** (see p. 319); the fairy-tale **Parc Güell** (see p. 323); **Palau de la Música Catalana** (see p. 320); **Casa Calvet** (if you can peek in); the houses along the **Manzana de Discordia** (see p. 321); the amazing **Casa Milà** (**La Pedrera,** see p. 322); the **Templo Expliatorio de la Sagrada Familia** (see p. 321); **Els Quatre Gats** (see p. 315); **Casa Vicens** (see p. 324); and the **Museu d'Arte Modern** (see p. 326). As many of these sights have mandatory hour-long tours, visiting all of them on the same day is nearly impossible. During the summer, the easiest—and cheesiest—way to sight-see is to hop on the **Bus Turístic** (see p. 305).

LAS RAMBLAS

Las Ramblas's pedestrian-only median strip is a veritable urban carnival, where street performers dance, fortune-tellers survey palms, human statues shift poses, vendors sell birds, and artists sell caricatures—all, of course, for a small fee. The wide, tree-lined boulevard dubbed "Las Ramblas" actually comprises five distinct segments (Canaletes, Estudis, Sant Josep, Capuxtins, and Santa Monica) that together form one long boulevard. The sights below are arranged beginning with Pl. Catalunya in the north to the port in the south.

UPPER LAS RAMBLAS. A port-ward journey begins at the **Font de Canaletes** (more a pump than a fountain), where visitors who wish to eventually return to Barcelona are supposed to sample the water. The upper part of Las Ramblas has been dubbed "Rambla de las Flores" for the numerous flower vendors that inhabit it. Halfway down Las Ramblas by **La Boquería,** the traditional food market (see p. 314), **Joan Miró's** small pavement mosaic brightens up the street.

GENIUS IN SOLITUDE Though revered by many as the "father of Barcelona," architect Antoní Gaudí spent most of his life quite alone and far from the limelight. Born to a coppersmith in Reus, Spain in 1852, he read incessantly as a student, soaking up the theories which would come to influence his work. Religion and nature were his main inspirations, and he was known to sit in front of the sea for hours at a time, proclaiming that each wave was telling him something. He never married (though it is said he did have one great love) and agreed to pose for a photograph only once. The last 11 years of his life he lived in a makeshift house in the basement of La Sagrada Familia, hardly interacting with anyone, and in 1926 he was killed by a streetcar upon leaving the church. Taken to a pauper's morgue because of his poor clothing, he actually remained unidentified for weeks. Today, many believe that La Sagrada Familia should remain unfinished in honor of Gaudí's abruptly interrupted life. The Barcelona church has even approached the Vatican with a request to honor the architect as a Saint of Barcelona; the pope has yet to reply.

GRAN TEATRE DEL LICEU. The Gran Teatre del Liceu has been Barcelona's opera house for over a century. It was once one of Europe's leading stages, nurturing the likes of José Carreras. Ravaged by a fire in January 1994, it reopened for performances in 1999 (see **Music**, p. 330). It is adorned with palacial ornamentation, gold facades, sculptures, and grand circular side rooms—a Spanish hall of mirrors. *(Las Ramblas, on the corner of C. Sant Pau. Guided tours 800ptas, students 600ptas.)*

PALAU GÜELL. Antoni Gaudí's Palau Güell has one of Barcelona's most spectacular interiors, a cross between Modernista apartment building and haunted house. The rooftop chimneys display Gaudí's first use of the *trencadís*, or covering surfaces with irregular shards of ceramic or glass. *(C. Nou de la Rambla, 3-5, 2 blocks from the Teatre Liceu. ☎ 93 317 51 98. Open M-Sa 10am-1pm and 4-7pm. 400ptas, students 200ptas. Only a few tours per hr., so come early.)*

MONUMENT A COLOM. At the port end off Las Ramblas, the Monument a Colom towers above the city. When Renaixença enthusiasts "rediscovered" Spain's role in the discovery of the Americas, they convinced themselves that Christopher Columbus was really Catalan. The fact that the statue points proudly toward Libya, not the Americas, doesn't help their claim; historians now agree that Columbus was actually Genoese. At night, spotlights turn the statue into a firebrand. Take the elevator up to the top and get a stunning view of Barcelona. *(Portal de la Pau. June-Sept. 9am-8:30pm; Oct.-Mar. M-F 10am-1:30pm and 3:30-7:30pm, Sa-Su 10am-6:30pm; Apr.-May 10am-1:30pm and 3:30-7:30pm, Sa-Su 10am-7:30pm. 250ptas, children 150ptas.)*

AROUND THE PORT. Farther down Las Ramblas toward the port, Barcelona's drive to refurbish its seafront has resulted in the Vila Olímpica and the expansion of Port Vell, the port complex, and waterfront area near Monument a Colom. The port is picturesque day or night and clamors with the clink-clank of seaside eateries, loud discos, and overpriced shops. After moving the coastal road underground, the city opened **Moll de la Fusta**, a wide pedestrian zone that leads down to the docks past the **Museu d'Història de Catalunya** (see p. 326). The wavy, modern bridge **Rambla de Mar** links the cobblestone docks of the Moll de la Fusta with the bright **Maremagnum** mall (see p. 330).

L'AQUÀRIUM DE BARCELONA. Barcelona's new aquarium is state of the art, featuring an 80m-long glass tunnel and moving walkway through a tank of sharks and tropical fish. *(In Moll d'Espanya del Port Vell, next to Maremagnum and the cinema. M: Barceloneta. ☎ 93 221 74 74. Open July-Aug. 9:30am-11pm; Sept.-June 9:30am-9pm. 1450ptas per person, students 10% off. Admission up to 1hr. before closing.)*

BOAT TOURS. Tours sail from Portal de la Pau, in front of the Monument a Colom. **Las Golondrinas** (☎ 93 442 31 06) ferries steam around Montjuïc to **Rompeolas** and **Port Vell** (35min.; July-Aug. every 30min. noon-7:30pm; Sept.-June every hr. M-F noon-6pm, Sa-Su noon-7:30pm; 500ptas). A longer excursion includes a tour of **Port Olímpic** (1½hr.; July-Aug. every 30min. noon-7:30pm; Sept.-June 3 per day 11am-4:30pm; round-trip 1300ptas, students 900ptas).

BARRI GÒTIC

The weathered, narrow streets of the Barri Gòtic remain visibly distinct from the rest of Barcelona, and not without reason. In 1714, this neighborhood was home to proud Catalans who waged a (second) campaign for independence against King Felipe V. As punishment, Felipe V built walls around the Barri Gòtic, turning it into a Catalan ghetto. It was not until the cholera epidemic in the 1850s that the Spanish government permitted the walls to be torn down, and the slight cultural gap created by more than a century of separation has never quite faded.

PLAÇA DE SANT JAUME. Any tour of the "Old Quarter" should begin in the handsome Plaça de Sant Jaume, Barcelona's political center since Roman times. Two of Cataluña's most important buildings have dominated the square since 1823: the **Palau de la Generalitat**, the headquarters of Cataluña's autonomous government, and the **Ajuntament**, the Spanish government's seat of power. Fittingly, the two buildings face each other across the *plaça*. *(Palau de la Generalitat open the 2nd and 3rd Su of each month 10am-2pm. 30min. tours in English, French, Spanish, and Catalan. Ajuntament open Sa-Su 10am-2pm. Free.)*

BARCELONA

320 ■ BARCELONA

ESGLÉSIA CATEDRAL DE LA SANTA CREU. The jagged spires of the 14th-century Gothic Església Catedral de la Santa Creu are a sight in themselves. Construction on the church began in 1298, but the facade was not completed until the 1880s. Barcelona's patron saint and Christian martyr, Santa Euália, naps below the altar in the church **crypt.** The cathedral's lovely **cloister** has magnolias growing in the middle and geese waddling around the periphery. *(In Pl. Seu, past the Generalitat and up C. Bisbe. Cathedral open daily 8am-1:30pm and 4-7pm. Cloister open 9am-1:15pm and 4-7pm. Free. Elevator to the rooftop M-F 9:30am-12:30pm and 4-6:30pm, Sa-Su 9:30am-12:30pm; 200ptas. Entrance to 125ptas.)*

OTHER SIGHTS. Palaces and museums congregate on C. Comtes, on the opposite side of the Catedral. The former home of the royal family, the **Palau Reial** (Royal Palace), is the pearl of the plaça. Hidden inside are the **Museu d'Historia de la Ciutat** and **Museu Frederic Marès** (see p. 325). *(The royal palace can be visited with admission to the history museum.)* Also in the Barri Gòtic is the lively student hangout **Plaça del Pí** and the picturesque old **Església del Pí,** just off Las Ramblas. *(From Las Ramblas, follow C. Cardenal Casañas.)*

LA RIBERA

In the 18th century, Felipe V demolished much of La Ribera to make space for the Ciutadella. As the stomping ground of Barcelona's many fishermen and local merchants, La Ribera has always had a very plebian feel; in recent years, the neighborhood has evolved into Barcelona's bohemian nucleus, complete with art galleries, chic eateries, and exclusive bars.

■ **PALAU DE LA MÚSICA CATALANA.** In 1891, the growing Orfeo choir society commissioned Modernista architect Luis Domènech i Montaner to design this must-see palace. The music hall glows with tall, stained-glass windows, an ornate chandelier, marble reliefs, intricate woodwork, and ceramic mosaics. Debate continues over the political message of the inverted dome, which is painted with 40 women dressed as angels. Some believe that Montaner was implying that women sing like angels and should have been allowed in the choir (at that time it was exclusively male). Others think he was depicting women's fickleness by painting them with 40 different faces. The 2073-seat concert hall is also home to a 3000-pipe-tubed organ; concerts given at the Palau include all varieties of symphonic and choral music in addition to more modern forms of pop, rock, and jazz. *(C. Sant Francese de Paula, 2, off Vía Laietana near Pl. Urquinaona. Head up Vía Laietana to the intersection of C. Ionqueres. ☎ 93 268 10 00. Open M-Su 10am-9pm. Mandatory tours in Spanish, Catalan, and English every 30min. 10:30am-3pm. 700ptas, students 500ptas; 350ptas with Ruta del Modernisme pass. Concert tickets 1000-26,000ptas. Box office open M-Sa 10am-9pm, Su from 1hr. prior to the concert. No concerts in Aug.)*

SANTA MARÍA DEL MAR. La Ribera's streets converge at the foot of the Església Santa María del Mar's octagonal towers. Built in the 14th century in a quick 55-years, this church is a fascinating example of the limits of Gothic architecture—were it two feet higher it would collapse from structural instability. *(☎ 93 310 23 90. Open M-Sa 9am-1:30pm and 4:30-8pm, Su 9am-2pm and 5-8:30pm.)*

OTHER SIGHTS. Carrer de Montcada, beginning behind the church, validates Barcelona's local reputation as *"la ciudad del diseño"* (the city of design). Museums, art galleries, workshops, and Baroque palaces that once housed Barcelona's 16th-century bureaucrats are packed into just two blocks. The **Museu Picasso** (see p. 325) inhabits several such mansions, and the **Galeria Maeght** (#26), a prestigious art gallery on the block, was once a medieval aristocrat's manor (see **Art Galleries,** p. 327).

PARC DE LA CIUTADELLA AND VILA OLÍMPICA

PARC DE LA CUITADELLA. Barcelona's military resistance to the Bourbon monarchy in the early 18th century convinced Felipe V to quarantine Barcelona's influential citizens in the Ciutadella, a large citadel on what is now Pg. Picasso. The city razed the fortress in 1868 and replaced it with the peaceful promenades of Parc de la Ciutadella. Host of the 1888 Universal Exposition, the park now harbors several museums, well-labeled horticulture, the wacky **Cascada** fountains, a pond, and a zoo. Buildings of note include Domènech i Montaner's Modernista **Castell dels Tres Dragons** (now **Museu de Zoología**), the **geological museum** (a few buildings down Pg. Picasso from M. Zoología), and Josep Amergós's **Hivernacle**. Expo '88 also inspired the **Arc de Triomf**, just across Pg. Pujades from the park. Little Snowflake *(Copito de Nieve)*, the **world's only albino gorilla** behind bars, vegetates in the **Parc Zoològic**, on the end of the park closer to the sea. In the center of the park, on Pl. Armes, is the **Museu d'Art Modern** (see p. 326). *(M: Barceloneta or Arc de Triomf. Rowboat rental 10am-7pm; 250ptas per person for 30min. Parc Zoològic ☎ 93 221 25 06. Open June-Aug. Tu-W and F-Su 10am-2pm, Th 10am-6:30pm; Sept.-May 10am-5pm. 850ptas.)*

VILA OLÍMPICA. The Vila Olímpica, beyond the east side of the zoo, was built to house 15,000 athletes and entertain millions of tourists for the 1992 Summer Olympics. Today it is a dazzling yuppie village home to several public parks, a shopping center, and business offices. Toward the Mediterranean, **Port Olímpic** is an L-shaped complex flaunting twin towers, a huge metallic fish sculpture, a long pier of docked sailboats, and waves of upscale discos and restaurants, both indoors and out. In the area called **Barceloneta,** (see p. 332) mediocre beaches—good for little more than catching a tan or drooling over some sexy Spanish bodies—stretch out from the port. Barcelona's quaint old fishing quarter extends lazily along the waterfront, although pricey seafood restaurants are starting to move into the area. *(From M: Ciutadella/Vila Olímpica, walk along the waterfront on Ronda Litoral toward the 2 towers.)*

L'EIXAMPLE

The Catalan Renaissance and the growth of Barcelona during the 19th century pushed the city past its medieval walls and into ordered modernity. Ildefons Cerdà, a Catalan architect, drew up an aerial plan for a new neighborhood which called for a geometric grid of squares, softened by octagonal intersections with cropped corners. Cerdà envisioned both an escape from the stress that had festered in the overcrowded Barri Gòtic as well as a new city where people of all social classes could live side by side. (Or rather, floor above floor: he assumed that the poor would occupy the bottom floors of each building, reserving the upper floors for the rich.) He called each 10-block area a *massa (*neighborhood) and allotted each its own school, marketplace, and park. However, L'Eixample (pronounced luh-SHOMP-luh) did not thrive as a utopian community but rather as a playground for the rich bourgeois.

▨ **LA SAGRADA FAMILIA.** Only Gaudí's genius could draw thousands of tourists to a half-finished church. The architect himself estimated that the **Temple Expiadori de la Sagrada Familia** would take 200 years to complete. He gave 43 years of his own life to the task, living in the basement for the last decade before his death in 1926. Since then, construction has progressed erratically and controversially. Of the church's three proposed facades, only the first (one of the smaller ones), the nativity facade, was finished under Gaudí. A furor has arisen over recent additions, especially sculptor Josep Subirach's Cubist Passion Facade on C. Sardenya, the facade you see as you enter (see **Sex in the Sagrada,** below.) Elevators and a maze of staircases lead to the church's towers and bridges. The **museum** displays a model of the structure as it was meant to be completed, as well as artifacts relating to the building's construction. *(C. Marinara, between C. Mallorca and C. Provença. M: Sagrada Familia. ☎ 93 207 30 31. Open daily Apr.-Aug. 9am-8pm; Sept.-Oct. and Mar. 9am-7pm; Nov.-Feb. 9am-6pm. Tours daily Apr.-Oct. 11:30am, 1, 4, and 5:30pm; Nov.-Mar. 11:30am and 1pm. Church and museum 800ptas, students 600ptas. Elevator 200ptas.)*

▨ **MANZANA DE LA DISCÒRDIA.** A short walk from Pl. Catalunya, the odd-numbered side of Pg. Gràcia between C. Aragó and Consell de Cent is popularly known as *la manzana de la discòrdia* (block of discord), referring to the stylistic clashing of the three neighboring buildings. Regrettably, the bottom two floors of **Casa Lleó i Morera,** by Domènech i Montaner, were destroyed to make room for a fancy store, but you can buy the **Ruta del Modernisme pass** (see p. 318) there and take a tour of the upstairs, where sprouting flowers, stained glass, and legendary doorway sculptures adorn the interior. Puig i Cadafalch opted for a geometric, Moorish-influenced pattern on the facade of **Casa Amatller** at #41. Gaudí's balconies ripple like skulls, and tiles sparkle in blue-purple glory on **Casa Batlló**, #43. Experts and tourists alike debate the meaning of Battllo's forboding facade; the most popular theory is that the rooftop represents Cataluña's patron Sant Jordi slaying a dragon (the chimney plays the lance). Also of interest is **Fundació Antoni Tàpies** (see p. 326), designed by Domènech, around the corner from *la manzana*.

■ **CASA MILÀ (LA PEDRERA).** Modernisme buffs argue that the spectacular Casa Milà apartment building, an undulating mass of granite popularly known as *La Pedrera* (the Stone Quarry), is Gaudí's most refined work. Note the intricate ironwork around the balconies and the irregularity of the front gate's egg-shaped window panes. The roof sprouts chimneys that resemble armored soldiers, one of which is decorated with broken champagne bottles. Rooftop tours provide a closer look at the "Prussian helmets" (spiral chimneys inspired by the helmets worn in Wagner's operas). The winding brick attic (recently restored along with the rooftop in a multimillion-*peseta* project) has been transformed into the **Espai Gaudí**, a multimedia presentation of Gaudí's life and works. A refurnished and restored apartment awaits one floor below, as an example of the fine, captivating interior of Gaudí homes. *(Pg. Gràcia, 92. Enter around the corner on C. Provença. ☎ 93 484 59 95. Open daily 10am-8pm. Tour M-F at noon and 6pm, Sa-Su 11am. 600ptas, students 350ptas; with apartment 1000ptas.)*

MONTJUÏC. Throughout Barcelona's history, whoever controlled Montjuïc (Hill of the Jews) controlled the city. Dozens of despotic rulers have modified the **fortress**, built atop the ancient Jewish cemetery; Franco made it one of his "interrogation" headquarters. Somewhere deep in the recesses of the structure, his *beneméritos* ("honorable ones," a.k.a. the Guardia Civil) shot Cataluña's former president, Lluís Companys, in 1941. The fort was not available for recreational use until Franco rededicated it to the city in 1960. A huge stone monument expresses Barcelona's (forced) gratitude for the return of the fortress. The three statues in the monument symbolize the three seas surrounding Spain. Since reacquiring the mountain, Barcelona has made it a tourist attraction, and it was chosen as the site of the 1992 Olympics. To get to **Parc de Montjuïc**, take the metro to Pl. Espanya (M: Espanya) and catch bus #50 either at Av. Reina María Cristina (flanked by 2 large brick towers) or as it heads up the hill (every 10min.). Scenic outdoor escalators (installed for the Olympics) lead up to the Montjuïc from the Palau Nacional.

PALAU NACIONAL. The **Fonts Luminoses** (Illuminated Fountains), dominated by the huge central **Font Mágica** (Magic Fountain), are visible from Pl. Espanya, up Av. Reina María Cristina. During the summer, they are employed in a weekend music and laser show that illuminates the whole mountainside and the **Palau Nacional**, located directly behind the fountains *(Apr. 30-Oct. 3 Th-Su, every 30min., 9:30-11:30pm).* The palace was designed in what was considered the "international style" by German architect Pavelló Mies van der Rohe at his country's Expo pavilion in 1929. Now it houses the **Museu Nacional d'Art de Catalunya** (see p. 325), with its exquisite Romanesque and Gothic art collections. The view from the castle is one of the best in all of Barcelona. Just below the hillside to the left when facing the palace lies the **Museu del Arquelógica de Catalunya** (see p. 326).

OLYMPIC AREA. In 1929, Barcelona inaugurated the **Estadi Olímpic de Montjuïc** in its bid for the 1932 Olympic games. Over 50 years later, Catalan architects Federic Correa and Alfons Milà, who were also responsible for the overall design of the **Anella Olímpica** (Olympic Ring) esplanade, renovated the shell with the help of Italian architect Vittorio Gregotti. *(☎ 93 426 20 89. Open daily 10am-8pm. Free.)* Designed by Japanese architect Arata Isozaki, the **Palau d'Esports Sant Jordi** is the most technologically sophisticated of the Olympic structures. *(☎ 93 426 20 89. You must call in advance to visit.)* Test your swimming mettle in the **Olympic pools** (see **Recreational Sports**, p. 332) or visit the **Galeria Olímpica**, at the south end of the stadium. *(Galeria ☎ 93 426 06 60. Open Apr.-Sept. Tu-Sa 10am-2pm and 4-8pm, Su 10am-2pm; Oct.-Mar. Tu-F 10am-1pm and 4-6pm, Su 10am-2pm. 390ptas, students 340ptas.)* About 100m down the road from the stadiums is the **Fundació Miró** (see **Museums**, p. 322).

JESUS LOVES YOU If you are looking to pick a fight with any Catalan, just mention the name Josep Subirach. Subirach, renowned as a stonemason and sculptor, was chosen to create the passion facade of La Sagrada Familia. But he seems to have crafted one sculpture that is just having too much fun: the central figure of Jesus is argued by many to be sporting an erection. Dissenters insist that the firm abs of the Son of God make him look harder from afar than he actually is. Subirach, meanwhile, has been escaping the debate by following in Gaudí's footsteps, isolating himself from the public and living in the basement of the church.

CASTELL DE MONTJUÏC. At the top of Montjuïc mountain, this historically rich castle watches over the port. From the castle's exterior ramparts, gaze over the bay and the city. Inside, the **Museu Militar** has a large armaments display. From Barcelona, take the **funicular** to Av. Miramar. *(Pl. Raquel Meller. M: Parallel. ☎ 93 298 70 00. July 19-Sept. 23 every 10min. 10:45am-10pm; Sept. 24-July 18 10:45am-8pm; 225ptas, round-trip 375ptas.)* Take the **teleferic cable car** to the top. *(June 19-Nov. 1 M-F 11:15am-8pm, Sa-Su 11:15am-9:30pm; Nov. 2-June 18 M-F 11:15am-6:30pm, Sa-Su 11:15am-7:30pm.)*

POBLE ESPANYOL. This tourist-oriented "town" features replicas of famous buildings and sights from every region of Spain. While during daylight hours it is not much more than an artificial souvenir bazaar with several mediocre restaurants, at night the disco scene here (see p. 329) brings new meaning to the word "party." *(On Av. Marqués de Comillas, to the right when facing the Palau Nacional. ☎ 93 325 78 66. Open Su 9am-midnight, M 9am-8pm, Tu-Th 9am-2am, F-Sa 9am-4am. 950ptas, students with ID 760ptas. 1000pta cover at discos.)*

GRÀCIA

Just beyond L'Eixample, lovely, untouristed Gràcia is the real thing. The people here come from diverse backgrounds, and the neighborhood charms and confuses with its narrow alleys and numerous plazas.

⧉ PARC GÜELL. On a hill at the northern edge of Gràcia lies one of Barcelona's greatest treasures and the world's most enchanting public park. The park was designed entirely by Gaudí, and—in typical Gaudí fashion—was not completed until after his death. Gaudí intended Parc Güell (named after Eusebi Güell, its commissioner) to be a garden city, and its multicolored dwarfish buildings and sparkling ceramic-mosaic stairways to house the city's elite. But when only two aristocrats signed on, it became a park instead. The front entrance puts you face to face with a gaping, multicolored lizard. Some believe that the animal is a reference to the shield of the French city of Nîmes, the northern boundary of Old Cataluña. Two mosaic staircases flank the curious creature, leading to a towering Modernista pavilion that Gaudí originally designed as an open-air market for the park's would-be residents. The longest park bench in the world, a multicolored serpentine wonder made of tile shards, decorates the top of the pavilion. From here, sweeping paths supported by columns (meant to resemble palm trees) swerve through hedges and ascend to the park's summit, which commands tremendous views of the city. In the midst of the park is the **Casa-Museu Gaudí** (see p. 322). *(The easiest way to reach the park is by bus #24 from Pg. Gràcia, which stops at the upper park entrance. If a mild uphill hike does not disturb you, the most scenic way to enter the park is to take the metro to Vallarca, walk straight out of the metro down Av. L' Hospital Militar, turn left onto Baixada de la Gloria, and take the outdoor escalators uphill to the park's back entrance. Park ☎ 93 219 38 11. Open daily May-Aug. 10am-9pm; Apr. and Sept. 10am-8pm; Mar. and Oct. 10am-7pm; Nov.-Feb. 10am-6pm. Free.)*

PLAÇAS. Gràcia has several notable plaças. The first of these is **Plaça Rius i Taulet,** home to the **Torre del Reloj** (Clocktower), an emblem of the Revolution of 1868. **Plaça del Diamant,** on nearby C. Astúries, was made famous by Catalan author Mercè Rodoreda's novel. The most popular plaza is **Plaça del Sol,** skirted by cafes and bars and crowded with young locals at night. Here, activism is in the air: protest graffiti and banners fill the plaza, touching on everything from Catalan independence to the 1994 Zapatista uprising in Chiapas, Mexico.

BARCELONA

CASA VICENS. Modernisme brushed Gràcia in one of Gaudí's youthful experiments, Casa Vicens. The *casa* illustrates the colorful influence of Arabic architecture and a rigidness of angles that is uncharacteristic of Gaudí's later works. (*C. Carolines, 24-26. The interior is currently closed to the public.*)

SARRIÀ AND PEDRALBES

The northwestern neighborhood of Sarrià is home to Barcelona's old money—residents still talk about "going down to Barcelona." The last *barri* to lose its independence, Sarrià finally merged with Barcelona in 1921. A walk through the peaceful streets reveals elegant mansions, manicured gardens, exclusive private schools, and other signs of a privileged life.

MONESTIR DE PEDRALBES. The artistic high-water of this Gothic church and 14th-century cloister is in the **Capella Sant Miguel**, where murals by Ferrer Bassa depict the seven joys of Mary, as well as several of her sorrows. The monastery received a part of the Museo Thyssen-Bornemisza collection when the Madrid museum was purchased by Spain in 1993. (*Baixada del Monestir, 1. At the end of Pg. Reina Elisenda.* ☎ *93 280 14 34. Open Tu-Su 10am-2pm. 300ptas, students 175ptas.*)

TIBIDABO

This neighborhood's curious name comes from the Latin *tibi dabo* (meaning "I will give you"). The inspiration for the name is in the Gospel of St. Matthew when the devil tempts Jesus by saying, "All this I will give to you if you fall prostrate and worship me." The "all this" is undoubtedly in reference to the incredible view this area affords of Barcelona, the Pyrenees, the Mediterranean, and even, on clear days, Mallorca. The souvenir shop and telescopes tucked away in the spires of the huge **Temple del Sagrat Cor** (Church of the Sacred Heart) make its religious function appear an afterthought (round-trip elevator ride 75ptas). The adjacent **Parc d'Atraccions** is a favorite among Barcelona's youngsters. (☎ 93 211 79 42. Open June W-F 10am-6pm, Sa-Su noon-8pm; July-Aug. M-F noon-10pm, Sa-Su noon-1am. Unlimited use of 12 rides 1900ptas, no rides 700ptas.) Riding the elevator up the nearby **Torre de Collserola** communications tower (560m above sea level) can be almost as scary as the amusement park (500ptas).

There are several easy ways to get to Tibidabo. The Tibibús runs from Pl. Catalunya to the Torre de Collserola (June 9-Sept. 9 every 30min., from 30min. before park opening until 30min. after closing, Sept. 10-June 8 Sa-Su and holidays every hr., 270ptas.) An FFCC train from Pl. Catalunya runs to Av. Tibidabo (round-trip 1900ptas including funicular and park entrance fee.) To reach the mountaintop, take the city bus on weekdays (every 20min. starting at 7am) and take the Tramvia Blau (Blue Train) on weekends (runs same hours as amusement park). At the top of the street take the funicular (every 30min. during park hours, 200ptas).

🏛 MUSEUMS

> When I was a child, my mother said to me, "If you become a soldier, you'll be a general. If you become a monk, you'll end up as the Pope." Instead, I became a painter and wound up as Picasso.
> ——Pablo Picasso

In Barcelona, museums seem to spring up almost daily, providing an opportunity to explore the city's architectural feats, admire the works of accomplished Catalan artists, and delve into the world of modernism and contemporary art. Many museums offer **free admission** the first Sunday of each month; almost all close on Mondays. While this section includes all major museums, art-buffs should consult *Guía del Ocio* (125ptas at newsstands) or *Metropolitan* for additional listings.

■ MUSEU PICASSO. This truly incredible museum traces the development of Picasso as an artist, with a collection of his early works that weaves through five connected mansions once occupied by Barcelona's nobility. Although the museum offers little from Picasso's more well-known middle years, it boasts the world's best collection of work from his formative period in Barcelona. The collection also includes lithographs, ceramics, pencil sketches by an 11-year-old Picasso, and an excellent display of the artist's Cubist interpretations of Velázquez's *Las Meninas* (which hangs in the Prado in Madrid). The collection was started in 1968 with a donation from one of Picasso's friends; it was later expanded by Picasso himself and by relatives after his death. *(C. Montcada, 15-19. M: Jaume I. Walk down C. Princesa from the metro, and turn right on C. Montcada. ☎ 93 319 63 10. Open Tu-Sa 10am-8pm, Su 10am-3pm. 750ptas, students 400ptas, under 16 free. Free 1st Su of each month.)*

■ MUSEU D'ART CONTEMPORANI (MACBA). Inaugurated in 1995, the construction of the gleaming white MACBA was the final product of a collaboration between Barcelona's mayor and the Catalan government to improve the lives of the residents in El Raval by restoring the neighborhood as an artistic and cultural focalpoint. American architect Richard Meier was chosen to create a building whose sparse decor would allow the art to speak for itself, which it has—the MACBA has received world-wide acclaim for its focus on avant-garde art between the two world wars. Eclectic and often interactive exhibits focus on three-dimensional art, photography, video, and graphic work from the past 40 years. The MACBA also has excellent rotating exhibits. *(Pl. dels Angels, 1. M: Universitat or Catalunya. ☎ 93 412 08 10; www.macba.es. Open M and W-F 11am-8pm, Sa 10am-8pm, Su 10am-3pm. 775ptas, students 550ptas, 16 and under free. W 375ptas.)*

MUSEU D'HISTORIA DE LA CIUTAT. Exhibits in this museum display the history of Barcelona, from its Roman foundations in the first century BC through the sixth-century Visigoth takeover and medieval development to the modern day. The fantastic history of the city unfolds as you descend to the original Roman ruins in the basement and continue on toward former royal palaces. The upper floors are home to the **Capella de Santa Agueda,** which was built to store the king's holy relics. *(In Pl. del Rei. M: Jaume I. Walk up C. Jaume I and take the 1st right. Enter on C. Verguer. ☎ 93 315 11 11. Open June-Sept. Tu-Sa 10am-8pm, Su 10am-2pm; Oct.-May Tu-Sa 10am-2pm and 4-8pm, Su 10am-2pm. 1000ptas, students 700ptas. Free 1st Sa of each month 4-8pm.)*

FUNDACIÓ JOAN MIRÓ. Designed by Miró's friend Josep Luís Sert and tucked into the side of Montjuïc, the Fundació links interior and exterior spaces with massive windows and outdoor patios. Sky lights illuminate an extensive collection of statues, paintings, and tapestries from Miró's career, including the stunning *Barcelona Series*, which depicts Miró's personal reaction to the Spanish Civil War and several paintings from Miro's *Las Constelaciones* series, a reaction to Nazi invasion during World War II. His best-known pieces in the museum include *El Carnival de Arlequin, La Masia,* and *L'or de L'azuz*. Room 13 displays experimental work by young artists. The Fundació also sponsors music recitals and film festivals. *(In Parc de Montjuïc. Av. Miramar, 71-75, at Pl. Neptú. M: Espanya, then bus #50 from Pl. Espanya. ☎ 93 329 19 08. Open July-Sept. Tu-W and F-Sa 10am-8pm, Th 10am-9:30pm, Su 10am-2:30pm; Oct.-June Tu-W and F-Sa 10am-7pm, Th 10am-9:30pm, Su 10am-2:30pm. 800ptas, students and seniors 450ptas.)*

MUSEU NACIONAL D'ART DE CATALUNYA (MNAC). Besides housing the world's finest collection of Catalan Romanesque art, this museum also displays Gothic altarpieces and paintings of Cataluña's medieval churches, retrieved from museums around the world. The museum's Gothic art corridor displays murals from stately homes in Mallorca; paintings give a political history of the time. *(In Palau Nacional, Parc de Montjuïc. M: Espanya, then bus #50; or walk up Av. Reina M. Cristina and take the escalators. ☎ 93 423 71 99. Open Tu-W and F-Sa 10am-7pm, Th 10am-9pm, Su 10am-2:30pm. 800ptas, 900ptas with temporary exhibits. 50% off with youth card.)*

FUNDACIÓ ANTONI TÀPIES. Tàpies's bizarre wire sculpture atop Domènech's red brick building announces this collection of contemporary, abstract art. Tapies's art is characterized by his use of everyday materials like sand, glue, marble powder, and wire to show the eloquence inherent in simplicity. Most of his paintings include a "T" in some form. The symbolism of the "T" has been variously interpreted and misinterpreted as a religious cross, as sexual penetration, and as his own signature. The top floor is dedicated to famous Catalan artists. The other two floors feature special exhibits of other modern artists. *(C. Aragó, 255, around the corner from the Manzana de la Discordia and between Pg. Gràcia and Rbla. Catalunya. M: Pg. Gràcia. ☎ 93 487 03 15. Library upstairs open by appointment only. Open Tu-Su 10am-8pm. 700ptas, students 350ptas.)*

MUSEU D'ART MODERN. This museum, a part of MNAC, houses a potpourri of paintings and sculptures, all by 19th-century Catalan artists. Noteworthy works include Casas's *Plein Air*, Blay Fabregas's *Els Primers Freds*, Josep Llimona's *Desconsol*, and Isidre Nonell's paintings of Gypsy women. The museum also displays furniture designed by Gaudí. *(In Pl. Armes, in the Parc de la Ciutadella. M: Arc de Triomf. ☎ 93 319 57 28. Open Tu-Sa 10am-7pm, Su 10am-2:30pm. 500ptas, students 350ptas.)*

MUSEU DEL ARQUEOLÒGIA DE CATALUÑA. The exhibits cover prehistoric times up to the constitution of Cataluña. Several rooms feature a collection of Carthaginian art from Ibiza and excavated relics from the Greco-Roman city of Empúries (near Girona). *(Parc de Montjuïc, Pg. Santa Madrona, 39-41. Next to the Palau Nacional. M: Espanya, then bus #55. ☎ 93 424 61 77. Open Tu-Sa 9:30am-7pm, Su 10am-2:30pm. 400ptas, students 300ptas.)*

MUSEU D'HISTORIA DE CATALUNYA. This high-tech and hands-on museum guides visitors through Catalunya's history, from Roman times through the 20th century. Computer screens, original film clips, and music stations help narrate the region's tumultuous past. *(Pl. Pau Vila, 3. M: Barceloneta. ☎ 93 225 47 00. Open Tu-Th 10am-7pm, F-Sa 10am-8pm, Su 10am-2:30pm. 550ptas, students 350ptas.)*

MUSEU DE LA MÚSICA. An exhibit of antique instruments, including a particularly good guitar collection, guides the viewer through the development of music in Europe. *(In Casa Vidal-Quadras, Av. Diagonal, 373. M: Diagonal. ☎ 93 416 11 57. Open Tu-Su 10am-2pm. 400ptas. W afternoons and 1st Su of each month free.)*

PALAU DE LA VIRREINA. Once the residence of a Peruvian viceroy, this 18th-century palace displays temporary photography, music, and graphics exhibits. More importantly, it serves as information headquarters for Barcelona's festivals. *(Las Ramblas, 99, on the corner of C. Carme. M: Liceu. ☎ 93 301 77 75. Open Tu-Sa 11am-8:30pm, Su 11am-2:30pm. 500ptas, students 250ptas.)*

MUSEU FREDERIC MARÈS. Founded in 1946, this museum is home to the personal collection of the sculptor Marès. The first floor houses an almost overwhelming collection of crucifixes and other biblical motifs. The second and third floors contain an eclectic collection of commonplace 15th- to 20th-century objects, including canes, ashtrays, and pipes. *(Pl. Sant Lu, 5-6, in the Palau Reial. ☎ 93 310 58 00. M: Jaume I. Open Tu and Th 10am-5pm, W and F 10am-7pm, Su 10am-3pm. 300ptas, students 150ptas. W afternoon and 1st Su of the month free.)*

CENTRE DE CULTURA CONTEMPORÀNIA DE BARCELONA (CCCB). This cultural center investigates modern urban design and sponsors temporary exhibits, dance performances, concerts, workshops, and lectures. *(Casa de Caritat, C. Montalegre, 5. M: Catalunya or Universitat, next to the MACBA. ☎ 93 306 41 00. Open Tu-Sa 11am-8pm, Su 11am-7pm. 600ptas, students 400ptas, children under 16 free.)*

MUSEO DEL CALCAT. This hip new museum runs through time with its collection of shoes from the first to the 20th century. Adding just a pinch of Hollywood, the museum also displays a number of shoes that have covered celebrity feet. *(Pl. Sant Felip Neri, 5. M: Jaume I. ☎ 93 301 45 33. Open Tu-Su 11am-2pm. 200ptas.)*

ART GALLERIES

One of the capitals of cutting-edge art, Barcelona showcases many of the latest artistic trends. Many private showings display the works of both budding artists and renowned masters. Most of Barcelona's galleries are located in **La Ribera** around C. Montcada. Three of the best-known in the La Ribera area include: **Gallery Surrealista, Galeria Maeght,** and **Galeria Montcada**. For more in-depth gallery info check the *Guía del Ocio* (125ptas). The **Palau de la Virreina** also has information on cultural events. *(Las Ramblas, 99. Between La Boquería market and C. Carme. M: Liceu.* ☎ *93 301 77 75. Open M-F 10am-2pm and 4-8pm.)* **Centro de Información Cultural** distributes *Metropolitan*, Barcelona's only cultural magazine in English. *(Las Ramblas, 118.* ☎ *93 302 15 22, ext. 266; open M-F 11am-2pm and 4-8pm, Sa 10am-2pm.)*

◪ NIGHTLIFE

The whole world knows that Madrid sleeps less than any other city in Europe. Clearly, whoever's counting forgot to take their survey to Barcelona; as in Madrid, nightlife here begins with a 5pm stroll and doesn't wind down until nearly 14 hours later—if even then. Following the afternoon *siesta*, the masses stroll to their favorite *tapas* bars, crowded *plaças*, or outdoor cafes for drinks or a snack with friends. Most people dine between 9 and 11pm, the bar scene picks up around 10pm, and discos start to fill around 2am. Places on Las Ramblas tend to be tourist-dominated, as do the Maremagnum Mall and most portside establishments.

BARS AND DISCOS

The Barcelona evening can be divided into thirds, starting with the *bares-restaurantes* or *cervecerías*, moving to the *bares-musicales*, and finishing up with a bang at the *discotecas*. *Cervecerías* ranging from deli-like, *fútbol*-obsessed pubs to elegant lounges fill up on Las Ramblas and in the nearby Barri Gòtic and El Raval. As a general rule, the farther from Las Ramblas and the narrower the street, the less-touristed the bar. The trendiest *bares-musicales* are concentrated in Gràcia. Barcelona's *discotecas* don't heat up until around 2am and usually stay full until dawn, if not later. If you are planning on clubbing, dress the part: no backpacker attire allowed. Also expect to be overcharged for drinks (around 600ptas for a beer and 900ptas and up for mixed drinks). Listed below are some of Barcelona's best bars and discos, but keep in mind that what's popular changes on a daily basis—talk to locals for an up-to-the-minute report.

BARRI GÓTIC

Here, cookie-cutter *cervecerías* and *bares-restaurantes* can be found every five steps. Nightlife in the Barri Gótic is perfect for chit-chatting your night away, sipping *sangría*, or scoping out your next dance partner.

▧ **Les Bosq des Fades** (☎ 93 317 26 49), just off Las Ramblas near the water and next to the Museu de Cera. M: Drassanes. A fairy tale world, complete with gnarly trees, a small bridge, and plush side rooms. Open M-Th until 1:30am, F-Sa until 2:30am.

Schilling, C. Ferrán, 23 (☎ 93 317 67 87). M: Liceu. Though plush sofas, marble tables, and chandeliers cry out "exclusive," this chic bar is surprisingly diverse. Mixed gay and straight crowd. Excellent *sangría*. Mixed drinks 300ptas. Wine 200ptas. Open M-F 9am-2am, Sa-Su 11am-2am, Su noon-2:30am.

Da-Da, Pg. Colom, 17 (☎ 93 302 61 74). Cow decorations line the walls and hip patrons dressed for the discos drink specialty shots like "tampon," "climax," and "dracula." A fun mid-evening hotspot with few tourists. F-Sa 11pm-3am.

Margarita Blue, C. J. A. Clavé, 6 (☎ 93 317 71 76), off Las Ramblas, 1 block from the port. M: Drassanes. With blue margaritas and retro 80s pop tunes, this Mexican-themed bar draws a flamboyant 20- and 30-something crowd. Creative Mexican food (under 1000ptas) accompanies the tequila. Margaritas 350ptas before 10:30pm, 450ptas after. Open Su-W 11:30pm-2am, Th-F 11:30pm-3am, Sa-Su 7pm-3am.

Molly Malones, C. Ferran, 7 (☎ 93 342 40 26). Only 1 year old, this Irish bar is turning many a Spaniard into a Guinness lover. Every day is St. Patrick's day here, with blaring music, fast-flowing beer, and schmoozing patrons. Guiness on tap 650ptas. SoCo and RedBull 1350ptas. Open M-F 8pm-2:30am, Sa-Su 7pm-3am.

Harlem Jazz Club, C. Comtesa de Sobradiel, 8 (☎ 93 310 07 55), between Pl. Reial and Vía Laietana. M: Liceu. Not quite Louis Armstrong, but still pretty damn good. Live music every night, alternating between acoustic rock, folk, and jazz. Virtually empty before 1am. Su-Th free, Sa cover 500ptas, includes 1 drink. Open daily 10pm-4am.

Café d l'Opera, Las Ramblas, 74 (☎ 93 317 75 85 or 302 41 80). A drink at this Barcelona institution was once a post-opera tradition for bourgeois *barcelonenses*. Today, the cafe caters to a mostly middle-aged crowd of all types. Outdoor seating available. Liquid heaven hot chocolate 500ptas. *Bocadillos* 350-660ptas. 4-person *sangría* 2200ptas. Open M-Sa 9am-2:30am, Su 9am-3pm.

EL RAVAL

Though traditionally El Raval has been home to a local, unpretentious set of bars, this neighborhood to the west of Las Ramblas is rapidly becoming a hotspot for funky new lounge-style hangouts.

🏷 **El Café que pone Muebles Navarro,** Riera Alta 4-6, (☎ 907 18 80 96). Friends get friendlier as they snuggle on huge, comfy couches. Beer and wine 250ptas. Mixed drinks 500-700ptas. Snacks 225-600ptas. Open Tu-Th 5pm-1am, F-Sa 5pm-2:30am.

🏷 **La Oveja Negra,** C. Sitges, 5 (☎ 93 317 10 87). M: Catalunya. From Pl. Catalunya, go down Las Ramblas and take the 1st right onto C. Tallers; C. Sitges is the 1st left. The most touristed tavern in town. Gossip (in English) about your European backpacking romp over foosball and huge pitchers of *sangría*. Beer 325ptas. *Sangría* 1700ptas. Open M-Th 9am-2:30am, F 9am-3:30am, Sa-Su 5pm-3am.

Casa Almirall, C. Joaquim Costa, 33. A cavernous space with a decaying ceiling and weathered couches, Casa Almirall is Barcelona's oldest bar. Serves *absenta* (absinthe; 500ptas). See **Absinthe Abstinence,** below. Beer 250ptas. Open daily 7pm-3am.

Raval-Bar, C. Doctor Dou, 19 (☎ 93 902 41 33). No matter how tired or stressed, locals come here to sit with friends, listen to music, and waste their night away on huge U-shaped couches. Beer 350ptas. Wine 250ptas. Su-W 8pm-2:30am, F-Sa 8pm-3am.

LA RIBERA

In La Ribera, the name of the game is *tapas* bars, where mostly yuppie crowds gather to soak up the neighborhood's artsy flavor. La Ribera is more of a place to mingle than a meat-market—you may want to brush up on your Modernist art (not to mention your Spanish or Catalan) before giving one of these bars a try.

Xampanyet, C. Montcado, 2215. M: Jaume I. From the metro, cross Vía Laietana, walk down C. Princessa, and turn right on C. Montcado. Xampanyet is on the right after the Museu Picasso. Juan Carlos, the 3rd-generation proprietor, treats everyone like family. The house special—*cava* (Spanish champagne)—is served with anchovies at the colorful bar. Glasses 110ptas and up. Bottles 800ptas and up. Open Tu-Sa noon-4pm and 6:30-11:30pm, Su 6:30-11:30pm.

ABSINTHE ABSTINENCE Step inside the old-fashioned bars of Barcelona and you are likely to find dare-devils sipping *absenta*, the translucent turquoise firewater banned everywhere except Spain and the Czech Republic. This licorice-flavored alcohol comes from the ajenjo plant and is said to have hallucinogenic effects similar to peyote. Once France's national drink, 68-proof absinthe used to be all the rage among Impressionist painters and the Parisian bourgeoisie. According to Barcelona legend, in fact, it was the discovery of more than 200 bottles of the stuff under painter Paul Gaugin's bed (after his death) that finally put an end to the party and prompted France to call for absinthe abstinence. Spain chose not to follow suit, however, and the drink is still available at a safer 50-proof, although Spanish bartenders warn that even two absinthes may end your night early.

Mudanzas, C. Vidrieria, 15. Everything is black, even the suits. The only color comes from hundreds of illuminated bottles lining the wall behind the bar. A hip young professional crowd. Wide selection of rum, whiskey, and wines (300ptas). Open daily 9:30pm-2am.

Café-Bar Vincent Van Gogh, C. Princesa, 23 (☎ 93 319 89 18). An international joint for a young, chess- and pool-playing crowd. Van Gogh artwork stands out against all-black walls. Beer 300ptas. Cocktails 750ptas. Open M-F noon-3am, Sa-Su 10am-3am.

GRÀCIA

Nightlife in Gràcia is *la crème de la crème*, to borrow a phrase from Spain's northern neighbor. Most of Barcelona's funkiest *bares-musicales* are here, as are the most beautiful people.

▓ **Lizard,** Platon, 15 (☎ 93 414 00 32). Devil-red lighting, a central dance floor, and plenty of pool tables. DJs spin rap, hip-hop, and funk. Open Th-Sa 11:30pm-3am.

Mas i Mas, Maria Cubi, 199 (☎ 93 209 45 02). A small, crazy *bar-musical*. Spaniards cram themselves in to be part of the action. Open Th-Sa 11pm-3am.

Up and Down, Numancia, 179 (☎ 93 205 51 94). Go "down" to join the throngs of dancers; go "up" only if you are invited into the private room. Open daily 11pm-late.

MONTJUÏC

Lower Montjuïc is home to Barcelona's epic "disco theme park."

▓ **Poble Espanyol** (☎ 93 322 03 26), Av. Marqués de Comillas. M: Pl. Espanya. Take a cab from the metro and fall in lust with the craziest disco experience in all of Barcelona. This is where native Spaniards feel the heat. Dozens of restaurants, bars, and *bares-musicales* to choose from, but the discos are where it's happening. Some of the most popular (and surreal) include **La Terrrazza** (an outdoor mad house), **Torres de Avila** (with speedy glass elevators), and **Sixty-Nine** (no description needed). Dancing starts at around 1:30am and doesn't end until 9am. Most clubs have cover discounts. Open daily July-Aug.; Sept.-June Th-Sa.

PORT OLÍMPIC

Tracing the coast and marked by a gigantic metallic fish structure, the Olympic Village brims with glitzy restaurants and throngs of European dance fiends. Nearly 20 bars and clubs occupy the strip, and the dancing tends to jump onto elevated steps, chairs, platforms, and even the serving bars. Clubs distinguish themselves from their next-door neighbors by blaring different kinds of music (including salsa, rap, pop, hip-hop, and house) and hiring the most attractive, minimally clothed bouncers possible. If you don't like the music in one club, take five steps to the next. If dancing is not your thing, the port also provides a veritable festival of late-night eats and drinks. The action begins at midnight and winds down at 6am. From the metro stop Ciutadella-Vila Olímpica (L4), walk down C. Marina toward the twin towers. Bonus: there's **no cover anywhere.**

Just outside of the L-shaped olympic port but still considered part of the portvell complex are many other crazy late night haunts, including the following.

Luna Mora, C. Ramón Trias Fargas (Marina Village). Two levels, 7 bars—enough said. Latin music and house are the specialties. On Friday nights, they teach salsa to both locals and tourists. Open Th-Sa 11pm-5am, Su 7pm-1am.

Baja Beach Club, P. Maritim (Marina Village). Another disco, another crazy scene. Music is more mainstream. Open Th-Su until 5am.

El Gran Casino, C. de la Marina (Marina Village). Minimum bets are surprisingly low, given the super-glam atmosphere. Entrance fee 750ptas. Minimum bets for blackjack, American roulette, French roulette, craps, slots, and *punto banco* hover around 500ptas. No sneakers allowed. Passport ID required. Open daily 1pm-5am.

MAREMAGNUM

Like Dr. Jekyll, Barcelona's biggest mall has more than one personality. At the stroke of midnight, the complex turns into an overwhelming tri-level maze of dance clubs, complete with escalators to cut down on navigating effort. Each club plays its own music (expect to hear a lot of American pop) for crowds of international students, tourists, and the occasional Spaniard. This is not the most "authentic" experience to be had in Barcelona, but it certainly is an experience. No one charges cover; clubs make their money from exorbitant drink prices. (Beer 300-800ptas. Mixed drinks around 1000ptas.) Good luck catching a cab home.

ELSEWHERE

Most of the biggest and best *discotecas* are outside the tourist-heavy Ramblas area—these are where most natives do their dancing.

🔳 **Otto Zutz,** C. Lincoln, 15 (☎ 93 238 07 22), uptown near Pl. Molina where C. Balmes intersects Vía Augusta. M: FFCC Muntaner. The hippest club around. Ecstatic clubbers groove to house on the bottom floor while amazing DJs spin hip-hop and rap upstairs from a beat-up van. 23 floors, 6 bars. Live music on F midnight-2am. The beautiful people don't show up until after 3am. Dress to impress. Cover a negotiable 2000ptas, includes 1 drink. Open W-Sa midnight-5am.

Zeleste, C. Almogàvers, 122 (☎ 93 486 44 22), in an old warehouse. M: Marina. Walk 15min. from Pg. Lluís Companys, or take the Nitbus (11pm-4:30am). Live performances and occasional rooftop dancing for an additional charge. Cover 1000ptas, F-Sa 900ptas. Concert price varies. Open 1-5am.

KGB, C. Alegre de Dalt, 55 (☎ 93 210 59 06). M: Joanic. From the metro, walk along Pi i Maragall and take the 1st left. Loud rock and roll delivered to a mixed crowd of students and Soviet secret agents. No microfiche. Occasional live music. Cover 1000ptas, includes 1 drink. Open F-Su 1-8am.

Les Carpes del Cel, Castelldefels "Canal Olímpic," on Autovía A-16, Castelldefels Platja exit. Huge outdoor disco complex with 3 separate dance-floor tents, each pumping different types of music. 18 bars, plus other amusements. Cover 1000ptas, includes 1 drink. Open June 19-Sept. 19 10:30pm-5am.

La Boïte, Av. Diagonal, 477 (☎ 93 419 59 50). M: Hospital Clinic. More emphasis on dance than decor. Big names sometimes come to perform in the intimate disco setting. Live jazz, soul, and blues Tu, Th, and F. Open daily 11pm-5:30am.

🎵 ENTERTAINMENT

Barcelona offers a wide range of entertainment, from outdoor activities, sports, and bullfights to shopping, cinema, festivals, and performances of all sorts. Consult the *Guía del Ocio*, 125ptas at newsstands, for info on movies (*Cine*), live concerts, (*Música*), nightlife (*Tarde/Noche*), and cultural events.

MUSIC

The **Gran Teatre del Liceu,** Las Ramblas, 51-59 (☎ 93 485 99 00; www.liceubarcelona.com), founded in 1847, was one of the world's leading opera stages until its interior was destroyed by a fire in 1994. It recently reopened after extensive repairs (see p. 317). **Palau de la Música Catalana** stages choral and symphonic concerts throughout the year (see p. 317). **Concerts** are held in the main soccer stadium, the Olympic stadium, and in the sports palace Sant Jordi. Get tickets in the booth on Gran Vía at C. Aribau, next to the university (open M-Sa 10:30am-1pm and 4:30-7pm). Parks and museums (including Parc Güell, Parc de la Ciutadella, Fundació de Joan Miró, Fundació la Caixa, and the Centre de Cultura Contemporània) also host concerts and recitals. Consult the **Palau de la Virreina** office for further info (see **Art Galleries,** p. 327). Some concerts take place at other venues; contact the tourist office (see **Tourist and Financial Services,** p. 306), or check local periodicals (including the *Guía del Ocio*) for listings and ticket info.

THE SARDANA

The *sardana*, Catalunya's regional dance, is one of the highlights of any stint in Barcelona. It is a communal dance in which men and women join hands in a closed circle and perform a series of kicks and short steps to music; travelers are welcome to participate, as long as they observe the dance's solemn atmosphere. Dances take place Saturdays at 6:30pm and Sundays at noon in front of the cathedral, Pl. Sagrada Familia, or near Parc de la Ciutadella's fountains. Dances are also held in Pl. Sant Jaume on Sundays at 6:30pm, at Parc de l'Espanya Industrial on Fridays at 7:30pm, and elsewhere in the city on Tuesdays, Thursdays, and Fridays. Consult papers for current info.

THEATER

Barcelona offers many options for theater aficionados, although most performances are in Catalan (*Guía del Ocio* lists the language of the performance). Reserve tickets through **TelEntrada** (24hr. ☎ 902 10 12 12; www. telentrada.com) or any branch of **Caixa Catalunya** bank (open M-F 8am-2:30pm).

The **Grec-Barcelona** summer festival turns Barcelona into an international theater, music, and dance extravaganza from late June to mid-August (www.grecbcn.com). For information about the festival, ask at the tourist office or contact **Institut de Cultura de Barcelona (ICUB),** Palau de la Virreina, Ramblas 99. (☎ 93 301 77 75. Open M-F 10am-2pm and 4-8pm). Some of the major venues like the **Teatre Grec** and **Convent de Sant Augusti** are open-air theaters. Tickets can be purchased through TelEntrada, or at the Pl. Catalunya tourist office.

Major venues for theatrical performances include the **Teatre Nacional de Cataluya,** Pl. del Arts, 1, near the intersection of Av. Diagonal and Av. Meridiana (☎ 93 246 00 41; M: Monumental or Glòries i Marina); **Teatre de l'Eixample,** C. Arago, 140, which showcases flamenco (☎ 93 323 39 50 or 93 451 34 62; M: Urgell); and **Teatre Lliure,** C. Montseny, 47, in Gràcia, which features innovative contemporary productions (☎ 93 218 92 51; M: Fontana).

FILM

Most screens display the latest Hollywood features, some of which are in the original English. The *Cine* section in *Guía del Ocio* denotes these subtitled films with *V.O. subtitulada (version original);* other foreign films are dubbed, usually in Catalan. Many theaters have a bargain ticket day (usually Monday). **Filmoteca,** Av. Sarrià, 33, screens classic, cult, and otherwise exceptional films. (☎ 93 410 75 90. M: Hospital Clínic. 400ptas.) **Méliès Cinemas,** Villarroel, 102, shows classics. (☎ 93 451 00 51. M: Urgell. Tu-Su 600ptas, M 400ptas). For new releases, try **Maremagnum,** which has eight screens. (☎ 93 405 22 22. Tu and Th-Su 750ptas, W 600ptas.) **Icaria-Yelmo,** C. Salvador Espira, 61, in the Olympic Village, boasts 15 screens. (☎ 93 221 75 85. Tu-Su 750ptas, M 575ptas.) The new **IMAX Port Vell** on the Moll d'Espanya next to the aquarium and Maremagnum, has an IMAX screen, an Omnimax 30m in diameter, and 3-D projection. Get tickets at the door, through **ServiCaixa** automatic machines, or by phone. (☎ 93 225 11 11. Tickets 1000-1500ptas.)

FÚTBOL

For the record, the lunatics that run around the city covered head to toe in red and blue didn't just escape from a nearby asylum—they are **F.C. Barcelona** fans. Grab some face paint and head to the 110,000-seat **Nou Camp,** which has a box office on C. Aristedes Maillol, 12-18 (☎ 93 496 36 00). **R.C. Deportivo Espanyol,** a.k.a. *los periquitos* (parakeets), Barcelona's second professional soccer team, spreads its wings at **Estadi Olímpic,** Pg. Olímpic, 17-19 (info ☎ 93 405 02 97). Obtain tickets for both from Banca Catalana or by phoning TelEntrada (24hr. ☎ 902 10 12 12).

BULLFIGHTS

Although the best bullfighters rarely venture out of Madrid, Sevilla, and Málaga, Barcelona's **Plaça de Toros Monumental**, C. Castillejos, 248, is an excellent facility, complete with Moorish and Modernista influences. (Tickets ☎ 913 56 2200. M: Monumental.) Bullfights usually take place during the tourist season (June-Oct. Su at 7pm; doors open at 5:30pm). Tickets are available at local travel agencies or ServiCaixa ("la Caixa" banks; ☎ 902 33 22 11; 2400-12,500ptas). The box office also sells tickets just before the start of the *corrida*. Seats range from 2600 to 15,000ptas; the cheapest are in the Andanada section.

RECREATIONAL SPORTS

The tourist offices can provide info about swimming, cycling, tennis, squash, sailing, hiking, scuba diving, white-water rafting, kayaking, or just about any other sport. Info is available over the phone (☎ 93 402 30 00 or 93 402 30 40; no English). Though Barcelona tends to ignore its beaches, there's plenty of nearby sand.

Swimming Pools and Workout Facilities: Piscinas Bernat Picornell, Av. l'Estadi, 30-40 (☎ 93 423 40 41). M: Espanya, then bus #50 up Montjuïc. Not just Olympic-sized; this was the actual Olympic pool in 1992. Open M-F 7am-midnight, Sa 7am-9pm, Su 7:30am-8pm. A 1-day 1300pta pass gives access to all pools and workout facilities including a sauna, massage-parlor, and gym. **Club Sant Jordi**, C. París, 114 (☎ 93 410 92 61). M: Sants. Passes are available for other facilities, including the sauna, weights, and stairmaster. Bring your passport. Open M-F 7am-5pm, Sa 8am-6pm, Su and holidays 9am-2pm. Pool 500ptas per hr., closed Aug. 1-15.

Beaches: The entire strip between Vila Olímpica and the Maremagnum complex is a long public beach accessible from M: Ciutadella. The closest and most popular is **Platja Barceloneta**, off Pg. Marítim. **Sitges** (see p. 335) is a popular daytrip. **Castelldefels**, 20min. from Barcelona on the same train line as Sitges, is an enormous beach good for young children—the water takes its time to get deep. The L93 bus leaves Barcelona's Pl. Espanya for Castelldefels (180ptas).

SHOPPING

Many of Barcelona's stores are out of the budget range, but there's nothing wrong with window shopping. Expensive designer shops line **Passeig Gràcia, Rambla Catalunya,** and **Portal L'Angel**. For right off-the-runway style, Barcelona's signature stores include **Zara** (Pg. Gracia), **Mango** (Pg. Gracia), **Naf-Naf** (Carrer Portaferrissa), and **Blanco** (Ronda Universal). Fashion-snobs can be found roaming the avenues of **L'Eixample** while the fashion-smart go for some of the smaller boutiques hidden in side streets off **Las Ramblas**. Funky art, knick-knacks, and jewelry can be found all over **La Ribera**. Barcelona's most unique jewelry shop is probably **Carali** (on C. Cecila right near La Sagrada). Antiques get their 15 minutes of fame on **C. Rosa** and **C. Banys Nous** (off Pl. Pi). Flea markets are a mess of shopping options and are definitely the best places to find deals. Hold your wallets tightly in **Fira de Bellcaire** and visit **El mercado de Sant Antoni** (M,W, F, or Sa). For more of a mall-type experience, Pl. Catalunya hosts a number of places like **El Corte Inglés** and **VIPS. Maremagnum**, at Port Vell, has dozens of varied shops.

FESTIVALS

Fiestas abound in Barcelona. For more information on all festivals, call ☎ 93 301 77 75 (open M-F 10am-2pm and 4-8pm). Before Christmas, the **Feria de Santa Llúcia** fills Pl. Catedral and the area around the Pl. Sagrada Familia with stalls and booths. City residents celebrate **Carnaval** on February 7 to 13, but many head to even more raucous celebrations in Sitges and Vilanova i la Geltrù. Also in February is the **Festa de San Medir,** when neighbors gather at the base of Tibidabo mountain to be caught in a candy-shower orchestrated by men riding down the mountain on horses. Soon thereafter, the **Festa de Sant Jordi** (St. George), April 23, brings feasts in honor of Catalunya's patron saint. This is Barcelona's St. Valentine's Day; men give women roses, and women give men books. On May 11, the **Festa de Saint Ponç**, a traditional market of aromatic and medicinal herbs and honey, sets up in Carrer Hospital, close to Las Ramblas. Barcelona erupts on June 23, the night before **Día de Sant Joan**. Bonfires roar throughout the city, unsupervised children play with fireworks, and the fountains of Pl. Espanya and Palau Reial light up in anticipation of fireworks on Montjuïc. On August 15-21, city folk jam at Gràcia's **Fiesta Mayor**. Lights blaze in the plazas and streets, and rock bands play all night. On September 11, the **Fiesta Nacional de Catalunya** brings traditional costumes, dancing, and Catalan flags hanging from balconies. The **Feria de Cuina i Vins de Catalunya** draws wine and *butifarra* (sausage) producers to the Rbla. Catalunya. For one week you can sample fine food and drink for a small fee. On September 24, during the **Festa de la Verge de la Mercè**, fireworks light up the city while the traditional *correfocs* (parades of people dressed as devils) whirl pitchfork-shaped sparklers and the city's residents hurl buckets of water at the demons. The beginning of November marks the **Fiesta del Sant Çito**, when locals and tourists alike roll up their sleeves and party on Las Ramblas. Finally, from October through November, the **Festival Internacional de Jazz** hits the city's streets and clubs.

NEAR BARCELONA

MONTSERRAT

With its 1235m peak protruding from the flat Río Llobregat Valley and its colorful interplay of limestone, quartz, and slate stone, Montserrat (Sawed Mountain) has long inspired poets, artists, and travelers alike. Over a thousand years ago a mountaineer wandering the crags of Montserrat had a blinding vision of the Virgin Mary. His story spread, attracting pilgrims to the mountain in droves. In 1025 an opportunistic bishop-abbot named Oliba founded a monastery to worship the Virgin, who had become the spiritual patroness of Catalunya. Today 80 Benedictine monks tend the building, most of which dates from the 19th century (although two wings of the old Gothic cloister survive). During the Catalan *Renaixança* of the early 20th century, politicians and artists like poets Joan Maragall and Jacint Verdaguer turned to Montserrat as a source of Catalan legend and tradition. In the Franco era, it became a center for Catalan resistance—Bibles were printed here in Catalan, and nationalist demonstrations were held on the mountain. Today, the site attracts both devout worshippers and everyday tourists who come to see the Virgin of Montserrat, her ornate basilica, the accompanying art museum, and perhaps most of all, the panoramic views of the mountain's awesome rock formations.

⌨ TRANSPORTATION. FFCC trains (☎ 93 205 15 15) to Montserrat leave from M: Espanya in Barcelona (1hr.; every hr. 6:30am-11:30pm; one-way 1185ptas, same day round-trip including cable car pass 1905ptas); be sure to get off at Aeri de Montserrat, not Olesa de Montserrat. The train stops at the base of the mountain, where you can take the heartstopping **Aeri cable car** up to the monastery (every 15min. M-F 9:25am-1:45pm and 2:20-6:35pm, Sa-Su 2:20-6:35pm; price included in train fares or 950ptas round-trip by itself). Exit the upper cable car station, turn left and walk to Plaça Creu, Montserrat's commercial area.

🛈 PRACTICAL INFORMATION. The info booth in Plaça Creu provides maps, schedules of daily religious services, and advice on mountain navigation. (☎ 93 877 72 01. Open daily July-Sept. 10am-7pm; Oct.-June M-F 9am-6pm, Sa-Su 10am-7pm.) If you've got a few extra *pesetas*, pick up the *Official Guide to Montserrat* (825ptas). Other services in Pl. Creu include **currency exchange** with poor rates (open June-Sept. M-F 9:15am-2pm; Oct.-May M-F 9:15am-2pm, Sa 9:15am-1:30pm), **ATMs**, and a **post office** (open June-Sept. M-F 9am-12:45pm and 2-5:30pm, Sa 9-11:30am). For an **ambulance** or the **mountain rescue team**, call ☎ 93 877 77 77.

░░ ACCOMMODATIONS AND FOOD. For those who choose to spend the night, apartments for up to 10 people are available through **Administración de les Celles,** in the far plaza. (☎ 93 877 77 01; fax 93 877 77 24. Open daily 9am-1pm and 2-6pm; after 6pm, they're at the Hotel Abat Cisneros reception.) The office runs three *hostales* and a three-star hotel. **Abat Marcet,** the nicest of the three hostels, has rooms to accommodate one to four people; each comes with a private bath and a microwave. (Singles 1650-4680ptas; doubles 2700-4980ptas.) Rooms at **Abat Oliba,** all with bath, accommodate two to seven people but are closed during the low season (doubles 3680-4000ptas; quads 5780ptas-6300ptas).

Food options are less than thrilling. The prudent beat a path to the small excuse for a supermarket, on the right as you go up Pl. Creu. The more prudent pack food before coming to Montserrat. The **Forn Pastissería** sells meat, cheese, and baked goods to appreciate on the quiet mountain paths (open M-F 9am-6:45pm, Sa 9am-7:45pm, Su 9am-6:45pm), and the informal **Bar de la Plaça,** in the building past the info booth, serves up *bocadillos* (365-510ptas) and other basics. (Roast chicken 975ptas; hamburgers 445ptas. Open Su-F 9:30am-7:30pm, Sa 9:30am-8pm.)

▣ SIGHTS. Above Pl. Creu, the entrance to the **basilica** looks out onto Pl. Santa Noría. To the right of the main chapel, a special route through the side chapels leads to the glimmering 12th-century Romanesque **La Moreneta** (the black Virgin Mary), Montserrat's venerated icon of Mary and child. (Route open summer daily 8-10:30am, noon-6:30pm, and 7:30-8:30pm.) Legend has it that St. Peter hid the figure, which was carved by St. Luke, in Montserrat's caves. Removed from Montserrat after the Napoleonic Wars and the Spanish Civil War, the solemn little figure found its way back and is now showcased in an elaborate silver case. For good luck rub the orb in Mary's outstretched hand. Songs by the renowned **Escalonia** (a boys' choir) ring through the basilica, crescendoing to their rendition of Salve Regina. (Performances daily 1pm, except for July.) Also in Pl. Santa María, the **Museo de Montserrat** exhibits a variety of art, ranging from a mummified Egyptian woman to several Picassos, including *Sardana of Peace*, painted just for Montserrat, and *Old Fisherman*, completed when he was 14. The museum's Impressionist paintings are its highlights—look for works by Catalan artists like Joaquim Mir and Ramón Casas, whose famous *Madeline Absinthe* is one of many evocative portraits. The museum also holds an interesting collection of ancient Hebrew Torah scrolls, shofars, and mezuzzahs. (Open in summer daily 9am-6pm; winter 9:30am-6:30pm. 500ptas, students 300ptas.)

⚡ WALKS. A visit to Montserrat is not complete without a meditative walk along the "mountain of a hundred peaks." Some of the most beautiful areas of the mountain are accessible only on foot. To go down, the Santa Cova **funicular** descends from Pl. Creu to paths which wind along the sides of the mountain to ancient hermitages (every 20min.; summer daily 10am-1pm and 2-6pm, winter Sa-Su only; round-trip 360ptas). Take the St. Joan funicular up for more inspirational views of Montserrat (Mar.-Oct., every 20min. 10am-5:40pm, round-trip 895ptas). The dilapidated **St. Joan monastery** and **shrine** are only a 20-minute tromp from the highest station. But the real prize is **Sant Jerónim** (the area's highest peak at 1235m), with its mystical views of Montserrat's celebrated rock formations. The enormous domes and serrated outcroppings resemble a variety of human forms, including "The Bewitched Friars" and "The Mummy." The hike is about two hours from Pl. Creu or a one-hour trek from the terminus of the St. Joan funicular. The paths are long and winding but not all that difficult—after all, they were made for guys wearing long brown robes. En route, make sure you take a sharp left when, after about 45 minutes, you come to the little old chapel—otherwise, you're headed straight for a helicopter pad. On a clear day the hike offers spectacular views of Barcelona and surrounding areas. For guided visits and hikes call ☎ 93 877 77 01 in advance.

SITGES

Forty kilometers south of Barcelona, the resort town of Sitges has the craziest beach-oriented nightlife in mainland Spain, along with prime tanning grounds, lively cultural festivals, and a thriving gay community. Long considered a watered-down Eivissa (Ibiza City), Sitges has better beaches than the notorious Balearics hotspot, even though it may be a bit less picturesque and flamboyant. The town has also become something of a mecca for up-and-coming Spanish artists and designers and attracts its fair share of pro-soccer players and movie stars.

TRANSPORTATION. Cercanías Trains (☎ 93 490 02 02) run from Barcelona-Sants and M: Gràcia to Sitges (40min.; every 15min. 5:25am-11:00pm; M-F 310ptas, Sa-Su 355ptas) and continue on to **Vilanova** (7min.; every 15min. until 11:45pm; M-F 150ptas, Sa-Su 160ptas). The last train from Sitges back to Barcelona is at 10:25pm. To get to the beaches in between, rent a car at **Car Office,** Oasis Local, 14 (☎ 93 811 12 12), at the corner of C. Vilafranca and Vilanova, up C. Carbonell from the train station. For a **taxi** call ☎ 894 13 29.

PRACTICAL INFORMATION. For a good map and info on accommodations, stop by the **tourist office** on Pg. Vilafranca. From the station, turn right onto C. Carbonell and go downhill until you see the sign with the big "i." In summer, a smaller branch opens by the museums on C. Fohollar. (☎ 93 894 42 51. Open in summer 9am-9pm; in winter W-M 9am-2pm and 4-6:30pm.) Services include: **medical assistance** (☎ 93 894 64 26); **emergency** (☎ 93 894 39 49), way uptown on C. Samuel Barrachina; and the **post office,** in Pl. Espanya. (☎ 93 894 12 47. Open M-F 8:30am-2:30pm, Sa 9:30am-1pm. No packages Sa.) The **postal code** is 08870. **Internet access** and **fax** service are available at **PC Centre e-t@alleres,** C. Angel Vidal, 2. (☎ 93 811 10 46. 450ptas per 30min. Open M-Sa 9am-2pm and 5-10pm, Su 10am-2pm).

ACCOMMODATIONS AND FOOD. Accommodations are expensive and extremely difficult to find in high season, so consider daytripping to Sitges from Barcelona and reserve early if you plan to stay. **Hostal Parelladas,** C. Parellades, 11, one block from the beach, offers standard rooms and an airy terrace that are dirt cheap for Sitges. (☎ 93 894 08 01. Singles 2800ptas; doubles with bath 5800ptas). **Hostal Internacional,** C. Sant Francesc, 52, provides clean, bright rooms. (☎ 93 894 26 90. Doubles 5500ptas, with bath 6500ptas.) Chickens roasting on an open fire at **Restaurante La Oca,** C. Parellades, 41, attract long lines of hungry tourists. Try the succulent *half-pollo al ast* (roasted chicken) for 770ptas, or slosh one in sauce for 870ptas. (☎ 93 894 79 36. Open daily 1pm-midnight.) **Mont Roig Café,** C. Montroig, 11-13, just off Parellades, is an immensely popular people-watcher's paradise. Dine in the airy indoor lounge or shady outdoor patio. (Sandwiches 325-500ptas. Hamburgers 675-875ptas. Salads 600ptas. Open Su-F 9am-3am, Sa 9am-3:30am).

SIGHTS. Plenty of soothing sand pacifies vacationing families and 20-somethings. The **beach** is a 10-minute walk from the train station on any street. In summer, the main beaches can get crowded; a short walk leads to quieter areas.

Back in town, **Carrer Parellades,** with shopping, eating, and drinking galore, is the center of attention. Cultural activities seem to be as frightening as rain to some beachgoers, but Sitges has some can't-miss attractions, including Morell's whimsical **Modernista clock tower,** Pl. Cap de la Vila, 2, above Optica at the intersection of Parellades and Sant Francesc. Behind **Església del Evangelista** on C. Fonollar, the **Museu Cau Ferrat** hangs over the water's edge. Once home to Catalan modernist Santiago Rusinol and a rendezvous point for young Catalan artists Picasso and Ramón Casas, the building is a shrine to Modernista iron, glasswork, and painting (☎ 93 894 03 64). Next door, the **Museu Maricel del Mar** has a selective collection of Romanesque and Gothic painting and sculptures (☎ 93 894 03 64). The **Museu Romàntic,** C. Sant Gaudenci, 1, off C. Bonaire from the waterfront, is a 19th-century bourgeois house filled with period pieces like music boxes and 17th- to 19th-century dolls. (☎ 93 894 29 69. All 3 museums open June 15-Oct. 15 Tu-Su 9:30am-2pm and 5-9pm; Oct. 16-June 14 Tu-F 9:30am-2pm and 4-6pm, Sa 9:30am-7pm, Su 9:30am-3pm. Combo entrance 900ptas, students 500ptas; otherwise 500ptas per museum, students 250ptas.) Across the street from the museums the stately **Palau Maricel**, on C. Fonollar, built in 1910 for American millionaire Charles Deering, rivals Richie Rich's playpad. (☎ 93 894 03 64. Open in summer only, hours vary; occasional classical concerts July-Aug. 8pm; 800ptas, includes a glass of *cava*.)

🌙🎊 NIGHTLIFE AND FESTIVALS. The place to be at sundown is **Carrer Primer de Maig** (which runs directly from the beach) and its continuation, **Carrer Marques Montroig.** Even crazier is the "disco-beach" **Atlántida** (☎ 93 894 26 77), in Sector Terramar, and the legendary **Pachá** (☎ 93 894 22 98), on Pg. Sant Didac in nearby Vallpineda. Buses run all night to the two discos from C. Primer de Maig (midnight to 4am). Other popular digs include **Ricky's,** Sant Pau, 25 (☎ 93 894 96 81) and **Otto Zutz,** on Port d'Aiguadoc, to the left of the museums when facing the water. C. Boraire is also home to some pre-dawn action. **Road House 66,** C. Boraire, 12, has salsa on Saturday from 11:30pm to 3am.

Sitges celebrates holidays with all-out style. During the **Festa de Corpus Christi** on June 6, townspeople collaborate to create intricate fresh-flower carpets. For *papier-mâché* dragons, devils, and giants dancing in the streets, visit during the **Festa Major,** held August 23 to 25 in honor of the town's patron saint Bartolomé. Nothing compares to the **Carnaval,** on Sunday and Tuesday of the first week of Lent, when Spaniards crash the town for a frenzy of dancing, outrageous costumes, and vats of alcohol. On the first Sunday of March, a pistol shot starts the **Rallye de Coches de Epoca,** an antique car race from Barcelona to Sitges. June brings the **International Theater Festival** (1500-3500ptas per show), July and August the **International Jazz Festival** (1700ptas per concert), and mid-October the one- to two-week **Festival Internacional de Cine Fantástico de Sitges.** From September 15 to 17, competitors trod on fresh grapes on the beach for the annual **Grape Harvest.**

DAYTRIP FROM SITGES: VILANOVA I LA GELTRÙ(7MIN.)

Cercanías trains run from Vilanova to Sitges (7min.; every 15min.; M-F 150ptas, Sa-Su 160ptas), continuing to Barcelona (50min.; M-F 305ptas, Sa-Su 355ptas) and Tarragona (10 per day). Many also continue to Port Aventura (10min., 5-7 per day, 130ptas) and Valencia (30min.-2hr., delay due to necessary connection on 3-8pm trains, 330ptas). Mon Bus (☎ 93 893 70 60) also connects Vilanova to Sitges (185ptas), Vilafranca (255ptas), and Barcelona (450ptas, 800ptas roundtrip). The train station doubles as the bus station. A taxi ride between Vilanova and Sitges costs around 1500ptas.

Catalunya's most important port after Barcelona and Tarragona, **Vilanova i la Geltrù** is actually two cities in one: an industrial center and a well-groomed beach town. Since there's little in the dusty uptown areas except for a couple of old churches and stone facades, most visitors spend the day on the beach (10min. from the train station). In the evening, Vilanovans generally forgo late-night madness for beach volleyball or soccer at Parc de Ribes. To get to the **beaches,** exit the station, turn left on C. Forn de Vidre, take the third left onto the thoroughfare Rambla de la Pau, head under the overpass, and follow the *rambla* all the way to the port. The **tourist office** (☎ 93 815 45 17), with an excellent **map** and lodgings advice, is about 50m to the right, in a small park called **Parc de Ribes Roges.** (Open July-Aug. M-F 10am-8pm, Sa 10am-2pm; Sept.-June 10am-2pm and sometimes 4-7pm, unpredictably). To the right, past the tourist office, is **Platja de Ribes Roges;** to the left is the smaller **Platja del Far.** Expect fine sand, sun, and tons of company.

If you decide to stay in town, the popular **Can Gatell,** C. Puigcerdà, 6-16, has clean rooms. With your back to the station, head down C. Victor Balaguer, the leftward of the two parallel streets; at the end, turn right onto Rbla. Ventosa, and hang a quick left at the sign. (☎ 93 893 01 17. Singles 4500ptas; doubles 7000ptas; triples 9450ptas.) The hostel's four-course 1300pta *menú* (served M-F) is popular with locals. A less expensive alternative is **Supermarket Condis,** Av. Gairraf, 23, down the street from Can Gatell (open M-Sa 9am-9pm).

NORTHEASTERN SPAIN

CATALUÑA(CATALUNYA)

From rocky Costa Brava to smooth Costa Dorada, the lush Pyrenées to chic Barcelona, Cataluña is a vacation in itself. It has also been graced with many of the nation's richest resources, making it one of the most prosperous regions in Iberia. *Catalanes* are famous for their resourcefulness and work ethic. As the saying goes, *"El Català de les pedres fa pa"* (a Catalan can make bread out of stones).

HIGHLIGHTS OF CATALUÑA

The fascinating history and friendly people of seaside **Tossa de Mar** (see p. 341).
The jumbled streets of historic, charming, and under-touristed **Girona** (see p. 347).
Teatre Museu Dalí, Salvador Dalí's self-built monument (see p. 353).
The small yet bustling town of **Vielha** in the midst of the Pyrenees (see p. 362).

LOCAL FESTIVALS IN CATALUÑA

July and August bring rock, jazz, dance, and theater performances to **Tarragona** during the *Fiestal de Tarragona*. On even-numbered years the *Concurs de Castells* (1st Su in Oct.) features tall stacks of people called "human towers." In **Palafrugell,** the most intense party is the annual *Festa Major* (July 19-21). Flower exhibitions come to **Girona** during the second half of May, and the *Focs de Sant Joan* (June 24) feature fireworks and campfires. **Figueres** celebrates local wines and classical and jazz music each September.

Colonized first by the Greeks and the Carthaginians, Cataluña was later one of Rome's favored provinces. Only briefly subdued by the Moors, Cataluña's counts achieved independence in AD 874 and gained recognition as sovereign princes in 987. After nabbing the throne of Aragón in 1137, Cataluña became part of Spain, but Catalan legal codes remained in effect. King Felipe V was finally able to fully suppress Cataluña in the early 18th century when the Catalans sided against him in the War of Spanish Succession (1702-1714). In the late 18th century, the region's fortunes revived when it developed into one of Europe's premier textile manufacturers, opening trade with the Americas. Nineteenth-century industrial expansion nourished arts and sciences, ushering in an age known as the Catalan Renaixença (Renaissance). The 20th century gave birth to the Modernist movement and an all-star list of artists and architects, including Picasso, Miró, Dalí, Antoni Gaudí and Montener. Home to staunch opponents of the Fascists during Spain's Civil War, Cataluña lost its autonomy in 1939. During his regime, Franco suppressed Catalan language instruction (except in universities) and limited Catalan publications.

Since Cataluña regained autonomy in 1977, Catalan media and arts have flourished. Today, Catalan is once again the region's official language (though Cataluña is almost entirely bilingual). While some worry that the use of the regional dialect will discourage talented Spaniards from working or studying in Cataluña, effectively isolating the region, others argue that extensive regional autonomy has generally led to progressive ends. Cataluña's regional pride rivals that of the País

Cataluña

Vasco. Many *catalanes* will answer inquiring visitors in Catalan, even if asked in Castilian (the politically and technically correct name for "Spanish"). Lauded throughout Spain, Catalan cuisine boasts *pan con tomate*, bread smeared with olive oil, tomato, and garlic, and *ali-oli*, a garlic and olive oil sauce.

COSTA DORADA

TARRAGONA

Tarragona's strategic position made the city a provincial Roman capital under Augustus; today an amphitheater and other ruins pay homage to the city's imperial days. These vestiges of Tarragona's august past are the city's most compelling attractions, but plenty of visitors are satisfied with a sight-seeing-light and beach-heavy stay in Spain's second most important port city.

⊏ TRANSPORTATION

Trains: (☎ 977 24 02 02), on Pl. Pedrera by the water. Info open daily 6am-9pm. The best transportation option. To: **Barcelona** (1hr., 30-40 per day, 6000ptas); **Sitges** (45min., 23 per day); **Valencia** (2-3hr., 15 per day, 4200ptas); **Zaragoza** (3hr., 8 per day); **Alicante** (3hr., 7 per day, 4500ptas); **Madrid** (7hr., 4 per day, 5800ptas).

Buses: (☎ 977 22 91 26), Pl. Imperial Tarraco. **Transportes Bacoma** (☎977 22 20 72) serves most destinations. To: **Barcelona** (1½hr., 3 per day, 850ptas); **Valencia** (3½hr., 5 per day, 2300ptas); and **Alicante** (6hr., 5 per day, 3900ptas).

Public Transportation: EMT Buses (☎ 977 54 94 80) run all over Tarragona. Buses run daily 6am-11pm. 125ptas, 10-ride "bono" ticket 680ptas.

Taxi: Radio Taxi (☎ 977 22 14 14).

▟❷ ORIENTATION AND PRACTICAL INFORMATION

Most sights are clustered on a hill, surrounded by the remnants of Roman walls. At the foot of the hill, **Ramblas Vella** and **Nova** (parallel to one another) are the main thoroughfares of the new city. Rambla Nova runs from **Passeig de les Palmeres** (which overlooks the sea) to **Plaça Imperial Tarraco**, the monstrous rotunda and home of the bus station. To reach the center of the old quarter from the train station, turn right and walk 200m to the killer stairs parallel to the shore.

Tourist Office: C. Major, 39 (☎ 977 24 52 03; fax 977 24 55 07), below the cathedral steps. Crucial free map and a guide to Tarragona's Roman ruins. Open June-Sept. M-F 9:30am-8:30pm, Sa 9:30am-2pm and 4-8:30pm, Su 10am-2pm; Oct.-May M-F 10am-2pm and 4:30-7pm, Sa-Su 10am-2pm. **Information booths:** Pl. Imperial Terraco, at the bottom of Rambla Vella; another at the intersection of Av. Catalunya and Vía de L'Impera Romi; a 3rd at the corner of Vía Augusta and Pg. Sant Antoni. Open daily July-Oct. 10am-2pm and 4-8pm; Nov.-June Sa-Su 10am-2pm.

Luggage Storage: 24hr. at the train station. June-Aug. 400ptas; Sept.-May 600ptas.

Emergency: ☎ 112. **Police: Comisaría de Policía** (☎ 977 23 33 11), on Pl. Orleans. From Pl. Imperial Tarraco on the inland end of Rambla Nova, walk down Av. Pres. Lluis Companys, and take the 3rd left to the station.

Medical Assistance: Hospital de Sant Pau i Santa Tecla, Rambla Vella, 14 (☎ 977 25 99 00). Hospital Joan XXIII (☎ 977 29 58 00), on C. Dr. Mallafré Guasch.

Post Office: Pl. Corsini, 12 (☎ 977 24 01 49), below Rambla Nova off C. Canyelles. Open M-F 8:30am-8:30pm, Sa 9am-2pm. **Postal Code:** 43001.

Internet Access: Biblioteca Pública, C. Fortuny, 30 (☎ 977 24 05 44). Free use of the computers with passport.

▚ ACCOMMODATIONS AND CAMPING

Although Tarragona is not known for its abundance of cheap beds, shabby deals can be found near Pl. Pedrera (by the train station) and by Pl. Font, in the old quarter (parallel to Rambla Vella), a much cleaner option.

Pensión Noria, Plaça de la Font, 53 (☎ 977 23 87 17), in the heart of the historic town. Enter through the restaurant. Clean and bright rooms with pretty-in-pink bathrooms. Singles 2990ptas; doubles with bath 5140ptas.

Residencia Juvenil Sant Jordi (HI), C. Pres. Lluis Companys, 5 (☎ 977 24 01 95). Go left after leaving the train station, take the 1st right, and catch bus #2 in front of Bar Fa; it stops on C. Presidente Lluis Companys, 2 blocks from the bus station. Common room features TV and table tennis. Breakfast included. Laundry 300ptas; drying 200ptas. Sheets and towels 500ptas. July-Aug. singles 3500ptas; doubles 6000ptas.

Camping: Several sites line the road toward Barcelona (Vía Augusta or CN-340) along the beaches north of town. Take bus #9 (every 20min., 105ptas) from Pl. Imperial Tarraco. The closest is **Tarraco** (☎ 977 29 02 89), at Platja de l'Arrabassada. Well-maintained facilities near the beach. 24hr. reception. 555ptas per person and per car; 400ptas per tent. Open Apr.-Sept.

FOOD

Pl. Font and Ramblas Nova and Vella are full of cheap *menús* (800-1200ptas) and greasy *platos combinados*. Tarragona's indoor **Mercat de Sant Quadrat** takes place in Pl. Corsini next to the post office. (Open M-W and Sa 8am-2pm, Th-F 7am-2pm and 5:30-8:30pm. Flea market Tu and Th.) For **groceries**, head to **Simago**, C. Augusta at Comte de Rius, between Ramblas Nova and Vella (open M-Sa 9am-9pm). Try your food with Tarragona's typical *romesco* sauce, simmered from red peppers, toasted almonds, and hazelnuts. **El Serrallo**, the fisherman's quarter right next to the harbor, has the best seafood.

La Teula, C. Mercería, 16 (☎ 977 23 99 89), in the old city off Pl. Santiago Rusiñol. Great for salads (500-600ptas) and toasted sandwiches with interesting veggie/meat combos (675-1000ptas). Lunch *menú* 975ptas. Open M-Sa 1-4pm and 8pm-midnight.

Restaurant El Caserón, Trinquet Nou, 4 (☎ 977 23 93 28), parallel to Rambla Vella (off Pl. Font). Looks like a diner, serves food like mom's. Entrees 800-1400ptas. Nightly 3-course *menú* 1100ptas. Open M-Sa 1-4pm and 8:30-11pm, Su 1-3:30pm.

SIGHTS AND BEACHES

Tarragona's status as provincial capital transformed the small military enclosure into a glorious imperial port. Countless Roman ruins stand silently amid 20th-century hustle and bustle.

ROMAN RUINS. Below Pg. Palmeres and set amid gardens above El Mirade beach is the **Amfiteatre Romà**, where gladiators once killed wild animals and each other; this somewhat barbaric but highly popular activity dates to 218 BC when Publius Cornelius Scipio founded the city. Above the amphitheater, across Pg. Sant Antoni, is the entrance to the **Museu de la Romanitat,** which houses the **Pretori** and the **Circ Romans.** The Pretori was the governor's palace in the 1st century BC. Rumor has it that Pontius Pilate was born here. To see what remains of the 2nd-century BC walls, stroll through the **Passeig Arqueològic.** The walls originally stretched to the sea and fortified the entire city. The scattered **Fòrum Romà** with its ornate Corinthian columns lies near the post office on C. Lleida, clearly demonstrating how far the walls extended. (*All monuments and museums open June-Sept. Tu-Su 9am-9pm; Oct.-May Tu-Su 10am-1:30pm and 4-6:30pm. Joint ticket to Amfiteatre, Museu de la Romanitat, Pg. Arqueològic, and Forum 300ptas, students 100ptas, under 16 free.*)

MUSEUMS. The **Museu Nacional Arqueològic,** across Pl. Rei from the Pretori, displays ancient utensils, statues, and mosaics. (☎ 977 23 62 09. 400ptas, students 200ptas; includes admission to the Necropolis.) For a bit of the macabre, creep over to the **Museu i Necròpolis Paleocristians,** Av. Ramón y Cajal, 78, at Pg. Independència on the edge of town. The huge early Christian burial site has yielded a rich variety of urns, tombs, and sarcophagi, the best of which are in the museum. (☎ 977 21 11 75. 400ptas, students 200ptas; includes admission to Museu Arqueològic.) If you've had too much Roman roamin', descend the steps in front of the cathedral and take the 3rd right onto C. Cavellares to visit the **Casa-Museu Castellarnau.** It housed the Viscounts of Castellarnau, 18th-century nobles. (☎ 977 24 22 20. 300ptas.)

OTHER SIGHTS. The **Pont del Diable (Devil's Bridge)** is a well-preserved Roman aqueduct. (*Take municipal bus #5; every 20min., 105ptas) from the corner of C. Christò for Colom and Av. Prat de la Riba or from Pl. Imperial Tarraco.*) Lit by huge octagonal rose windows flanking both arms of the cross is the Romanesque-Gothic **cathedral.** The interior contains the tomb of Joan d'Arago, and the glass dates back to the 14th century. (*C. Major near Pl. Seu. Open June-Aug. M-Sa 10am-7pm; Sept.-May M-Sa 10am-12:30pm and 3-6pm. 300ptas, students 150ptas.*)

BEACHES. The hidden access to **Platja del Miracle,** the town's main beach, is along Baixada del Miracle, starting off Pl. Arce Ochotorena, beyond the Roman theater. A bit farther away are the larger beaches, **l'Arrabassada,** with dirt-like sand, and the windy **Llarga.** (*Take bus #1 or 9 from Pl. Imperial Tarraco or any of the other stops.*)

♫ ♪ NIGHTLIFE AND ENTERTAINMENT

Tarragona's nightlife is a smaller-scale version of Barcelona's. Between 5 and 9pm, Ramblas Nova and Vella (and the area in between) are packed with strolling families. Around 9pm, the bars liven up; around 10pm on Saturdays in summer, fireworks brighten the skies. **Puerto de Portivo** is the most popular spot. From Rambla Vella, take C. Sant Francese, which becomes C. Unío; bear left at Pl. General Prim and follow C. Apodaca to its end. Cross the tracks and keep walking. **Pau de Protectorat** is also a popular street. When these bars close around 2am, everyone heads to the new **Port Esportiu,** across the train tracks, for dancing at one of the shoulder-to-shoulder mini-discotecas.

July and August usher in the **Fiestal de Tarragona** (☎ 977 24 47 95; 24hr. tickets ☎ 902 33 22 11). The **Auditori Camp de Mart** near the cathedral holds film screenings and rock, jazz, dance, and theater performances. A booth on Av. Catalunya at Portal del Roser sells tickets until 9pm for the 10:30pm performances (1000-2500ptas). Arrive one hour before the performance. On even-numbered years, the first Sunday in October brings the **Concurs de Castells,** featuring tall stacks of people called "human towers." They also appear amid beasts and fireworks during the annual **Festa de Santa Tecla** (Sept. 23).

COSTA BRAVA

Tracing the Mediterranean Sea from Barcelona to the French border, the Costa Brava's jagged cliffs and pristine beaches draw throngs of European visitors, especially in July and August. Early June and late September can be remarkably peaceful; the water is still warm but the beaches are much less crowded. In the winter Costa Brava lives up to its name, as fierce winds sweep the coast, leaving behind tranquil, boarded-up and almost empty beach towns. Unlike its counterparts, Costa Blanca and Costa del Sol, Costa Brava offers more than just high-rises and touristy beaches. The rocky shores have traditionally attracted romantics and artists, like Marc Chagall and Salvador Dalí, a Costa Brava native. Dalí's house in Cadaqués and his museum in Figueres display the largest collections of his work in Europe.

⎡ TRANSPORTATION

Transportation on the Costa Brava is fickle, with frequent service during July and August, less service the rest of the tourist season (May-June and Sept.-Oct.), and little to no service in winter. **RENFE trains** (☎ 902 24 02 02; www.renfe.es) stop at Blanes, Figueres, and then farther north at Llançà and Portbou (near the French border). **Buses** are the preferred mode of transportation, often running along beautiful winding roads and connecting many major and less major towns with frequent and inexpensive service. **Sarfa** (☎ 932 65 65 08), **Pujol i Pujol** (☎ 972 36 42 36), and **Teisa** (☎ 972 20 02 75) are Costa Brava's principal carriers.

TOSSA DE MAR

Falling in love in (and with) Tossa is easy. In 1934, French artist Marc Chagall commenced a 40-year love affair with this seaside village, deeming it "Blue Paradise." When *The Flying Dutchman* was filmed here in 1951, Ava Gardner fell hard for Spanish bullfighter-turned-actor Mario Cabrera, much to the chagrin of Frank Sinatra, her husband at the time. Like many coastal cities, Tossa (pop. 4000) suffers from the usual tourist industry blemishes: souvenir shops, inflated prices, and crowded beaches. That said, it resists a generic beach town ambiance, drawing from its historical legacy and cliff-studded landscape to preserve a unique small-town feel. Raised in the 12th century as a fortified medieval village, the sun-baked walls of Vila Vella continue to overlook Tossa's blue Mediterranean waters.

┌─ TRANSPORTATION

Buses: Av. Pelegrí at Pl. Nacions Sense Estat. **Pujol i Pujol** (☎ 972 36 42 36) to **Lloret del Mar** (20min.; June-Aug. every 30min., Sept.-May every hr. 7:15am-8:45pm; 180ptas). **Sarfa** (☎ 972 34 09 03) to **Girona** (1hr.; in summer 2 per day, off-season 1 per day; 615ptas) and **Barcelona** (1¼hr.; M-F 9 per day 7:40am-6:40pm, Su 8 per day 6:10am-7:10pm; 1070ptas).

Ferries: Round-trip ferries are often more economical than the bus service. For a one-way trip, take the bus. **Crucetours** (☎ 972 36 60 37) runs from the main beach to **St. Feliu** (45min.; Apr.-Oct. 6 per day 9:35am-5:55pm; 950ptas, round-trip 1350ptas). Check with the booth near the Vila Vella end of the Platja Gran for info.

Car Rental: Viajes Tramontana, Av. Costa Brava, 23 (☎ 972 34 28 29; fax 972 34 13 20). **Avis** (☎ 902 13 55 31) and their affiliate, **Olimpia** (☎ 972 36 47 10), operate from the same storefront. Min. age 21. Expect to be asked for major credit card, driver's licence (international driver's licence required for longer rentals), and passport. One-day rentals start around 6700ptas.

Mountain Bike and Moped Rentals: Road Runner (☎ 972 34 05 03), Av. de la Palma. Bring passport and license (for moped). Mountain bike rental 600ptas per hr., moped rental 1950ptas for 2hr. Open Apr.-Oct. daily 9:30am-9pm.

┃✳ ORIENTATION AND PRACTICAL INFORMATION

Buses arrive at **Plaça de les Nacions Sense Estat** where **Avinguda del Pelegrí** and **Avinguda Ferrán Agulló** meet; the town slopes gently down from there to the waterfront. Walk away from the station down Av. Ferrán Agulló, turn right on Av. Costa Brava, and continue until your feet get wet (10min). **Passeig del Mar,** at the end of Av. Costa Brava, curves along the **Platja Gran** (Tossa's main beach) to the old quarter.

Tourist Office: Av. Pelegrí, 25 (☎ 972 34 01 08; fax 972 34 07 12), in the bus terminal at Av. Ferrán Agulló and Av. Pelegrí. Handy, thoroughly indexed map. English spoken. Open June 15-Sept. 15 M-Sa 9am-9pm, Su 10am-1pm; May and Oct. M-Sa 10am-1pm and 4-8pm; Sept. 16-June 14 M-F 10am-1pm and 4-7pm, Sa 10am-1pm.

Currency Exchange: Bancos Central Hispano, C. Ferrán Agulló, 2 (☎ 972 34 10 65). Open Apr.-Sept. M-F 8:30am-2:30pm; Oct.-Mar. M-F 8:30am-2:30pm, Sa 8:30am-1pm. **ATM.**

Police: Municipal police, C. Església, 4 (☎ 972 34 01 35), in the Ajuntament. English spoken. They'll escort you to the **24hr. pharmacy.**

Medical Services: Casa del Mar (☎ 972 34 18 28), Av. Catalunya. Primary health services and immediate attention. Nearest hospital is in Blanes.

Post Office: (☎ 972 34 04 57), C. Maria Auxiliadora, down Av. Pelegrí from tourist office. Open M-F 8:30am-2:30pm, Sa 9:30am-1pm. **Postal Code:** 17320.

Internet Access: Cyber-Café Bar La Playa, C. Socors, 6 (☎ 972 41 42 90), off the main beach. 300ptas per 15min., 500ptas per 30min. Open May-Oct. 15 M-Sa 10am-midnight. **La Luna** (☎ 972 34 30 27), Av. Sant Raimon de Penyafort. Before 8pm, 300ptas per 15min., 75ptas per each additional 5min; after 8pm, 400ptas per 15min., 100ptas per each additional 5min. Open daily May-Oct. 3pm-midnight.

┌ ACCOMMODATIONS

Tossa is a seasonal town, and therefore many hostels, restaurants, and bars open only from May to October. In the summer and during festivals, Tossa fills quickly. Make reservations in advance, as some establishments are booked solid in July and August. The **old quarter** hotels are the only ones worth considering.

▨ **Pensión Pepi,** C. Sant Miguel, 10 (☎ 972 34 05 26). Turn left off Av. de Pelegrí onto Maria Auxiliadora and veer to your immediate right through the Placa de L'Antic Hospital and onto Sant Miguel. This old, traditional house with its small courtyard has an authentic feel and good location. The high-ceilinged rooms, each with private bath, are somewhat beyond their prime. Breakfast 300ptas. June-Aug. singles 3000ptas; doubles 5000ptas. Sept.-June singles 2000ptas; doubles 4000ptas. V, MC.

■ **Fonda/Can Lluna,** C. Roqueta, 20 (☎ 972 34 03 65; fax 972 34 07 57). From Pg. del Mar turn right onto C. Peixeteras, veer left onto C. Estalt, walk up the hill until the dead-end, go left, and then head straight. Delightful family offers immaculate rooms, all with private baths. Breakfast included—eat on the rooftop terrace and enjoy a breathtaking view of the water. Washing machine 600ptas. A popular choice with Spanish tourists, rooms are booked months in advance July-Aug. Open Mar.-Oct. July-Aug. 2000ptas per person; Mar.-June and Sept. 1750ptas.

Pensión Moré, C. Sant Telmo, 9 (☎ 972 34 03 39). Downstairs, a dim and cozy sitting room with TV and couches. Upstairs, large doubles and triples with sinks and views of the old quarter. July-Aug. 1700ptas per person; Sept.-June 1500ptas per person.

Camping: Closest site is **Can Martí** (☎ 972 34 08 51; fax 972 34 24 61), at the end of Rambla Pau Casals, off Av. Ferrán Agulló, 15min. from the bus station. Hot-water showers, telephones. July-Aug. 825ptas per person, 850ptas per tent, 525ptas per car; May 15-June 30 and Sept. 1-15 675ptas per person, 725ptas per tent, 425ptas per car.

◖ FOOD

The old quarter has the best cuisine and ambiance in Tossa. Restaurants catering to tourists serve up *menús* at reasonable prices; most specialize in local seafood. If you need groceries, head to **Megatzems Palau,** C. Enric Granados, 4. (☎ 972 34 08 58. Open June-Sept. M-Sa 8am-2pm and 4pm-9pm, Su 8am-2pm.)

■ **Restaurant Marina,** C. Tarull, 6 (☎ 972 34 07 57). Faces the Església de Sant Vincenç and has outdoor seating for prime people-watching. A nice family restaurant. Multilingual menu features pizza, meat and fish dishes, and lots of *paella*. Entrees 800-1300ptas. *Menú* 1400ptas. Open *Semana Santa* to Oct. daily 11am-11pm. V, MC.

Pizzeria Anna, Pont Vell, 13 (☎ 972 34 28 51). Turn right on Pont Vell from Pg. Mar; it's the small restaurant on the left-hand corner. Though homesick Italians might be a little disappointed, the seafood-sick traveler will be in heaven. Seating inside and out. Pasta 700-900ptas, pizza 800-1000ptas. Open daily 11am-11pm. V, MC, AmEx.

La Taberna de Tossa, C. Sant Telm, 26 (☎ 972 34 14 47). In the heart of the old quarter, right off La Guardia. Serves up inexpensive house wine, traditional *tapas*, and provincial meat and fish specialities (entrees 700-1100ptas). Set *menús* 950-1200ptas. Popular among Spanish tourists. Open daily Apr.-Oct. 1-11pm.

◖ ♫ SIGHTS AND ENTERTAINMENT

Inside the walled fortress of the Vila Vella, a spiral of medieval alleys leads to tiny Pl. Pintor J. Roig y Soler, where the **Museu Municipal** has a nice collection of 20s and 30s art, including—because the artist had a house here—one of the few Chagall paintings still in Spain. Tossa's Roman mosaics, dating from the 4th to the 1st century BC, and other artifacts from the nearby Vila Romana are displayed in the museum, originally a 12th-century palace. (☎ 972 34 07 09. Open Tu-Su June-Sept. 10am-7pm; Oct.-May 10am-1pm and 3-6pm. 1000ptas.)

Tossa's main beach, **La Platja Gran,** nestles between surrounding cliffs and draws the majority of beach-goers. To escape the crowds, visit some of the neighboring *calas* (small coves) that are accessible by foot. Hiking and mountain-biking paths also criss-cross the area and offer impressive views of the coastline. The tourist office pamphlet provides lots of information. Several companies, like **Fonda Cristal** (☎ 972 34 22 29), send glass-bottom boats to nearby beaches and caves (1hr., 8 per day, 1000ptas per person). Tickets are available at booths on the Platja Gran. **Club Aire Libre,** on the highway to Lloret, organizes various excursions and rents equipment for water sports. (☎ 972 34 12 77. Canoeing, kayaking 2000ptas. Water skiing 4250ptas for 2 lessons. Scuba diving 44,000ptas for 5-day certification course. Sailing 1700ptas per hr. Windsurfing 1600ptas per hr.) Bars line the streets of the old quarter and offer live music from time to time. **Bar El Pirata,** C. Portal, 32, has outdoor tables overlooking the sea (☎ 972 34 14 43. Open Apr.-Oct. daily 10am-3am.)

PALAFRUGELL

Forty kilometers east of Girona, Palafrugell serves as the budget traveler's base for trips to nearby beach towns **Callela, Llafranc,** and **Tamariu,** which cater to wealthy Europeans whose idea of a budget accommodation is any hotel that doesn't leave mints on the pillow. To save some *pesetas*, stay in admittedly bland (and beachless) Palafrugell and daytrip to the beaches. Minuscule Tamariu is the most isolated is therefore likely to be the least crowded. Callela is the largest and liveliest of the three, and is connected to Llafranc by one of several **Caminos de Ronda,** a series of stone footpaths allowing exploration of the coast.

⌐ TRANSPORTATION

Buses: Sarfa, C. Torres Jonama, 67-79 (☎ 972 30 06 23). Prices rise on weekends. To: **Calella** and **Llafranc** (in summer 11-24 per day, in winter 4-5 per day, 145ptas); **Tamariu** (in summer 3-4 per day, 140ptas); **Sant Feliu** (45min., 16 per day, 260-320ptas); **Girona** (1hr., 15 per day, 515-560ptas); **Figueres** (1½hr., 3-4 per day, 760-900ptas); and **Barcelona** (2hr., 12 per day, 1500-1725ptas).

Taxis: Radio Taxi (☎ 972 61 00 00). 24hr. service throughout the area.

✳ 🛈 ORIENTATION AND PRACTICAL INFORMATION

To get from the bus station ticket office to the center of town, turn right and walk down C. Torres Jonama to Carrer de Pi i Maragall. Then turn right and walk past the Guardia Civil and the market until you hit **Plaça Nova.** Back up C. Pi. Maragall to your right lies the center of the city and **Plaça L'Església.** To get to the nearby beach towns, take a bus, spin away on moped or mountain bike, or take a pleasant, if lengthy, walk through the countryside (about 1hr. to each town).

Tourist Office: Can Rosés, Pl. L'Església (☎ 972 61 18 20; fax 972 61 17 56). First right off C. Cavallers walking away from Pl. Nova. The *Guía Municipal* is indispensable. A **larger branch** is at C. Carrilet, 2 (☎ 972 30 02 28; fax 972 61 12 61). From the bus station go left on C. Torres Jonama, left again at the traffic circle, and walk about 200m. In an inconvenient location, but lo.aded with info. Both open Apr.-Sept. M-Sa 10am-1pm and 5-8pm, Su 10am-1pm; Oct.-Mar. M-Sa 10am-1pm and 4-7pm, Su 10am-1pm; Carrilet branch open July-Aug. M-Sa 9am-9pm, Su 10am-1pm. **Branch** in **Llafranc** (☎ 972 30 50 08), C. Roger de Llúria. Open daily July-Aug. 10am-1pm and 5-9pm; Apr.-June and Sept. M-Sa 10am-1pm and 5-8pm. **Branch** at **Tamariu** (☎ 972 62 01 93), C. Riera. Open June-Sept. M-Sa 10am-1pm and 5-8pm, Su 10am-1pm.

Currency Exchange: Banco Central Hispano, the corner of C. Valls and Cavallers off Pl. Nova. **ATM.** Open M-F 8:30am-2:30pm; Oct.-Mar. also Sa 8:30am-1pm.

Luggage Storage: At the bus station for 200ptas per bag. Open daily 6:30am-8:30pm.

Emergency: ☎ 112. **Municipal police:** (☎ 972 61 31 01), Av. Josep Pla and C. Cervantes. Call them for **24hr. pharmacy** info.

Medical Services: Centro de Atención Primaria, C. d'Angel Guimerà, 6 (☎ 972 61 06 07). Open 24hr.

Post Office: C. Torres Jonama, 14 (☎ 972 30 06 07). **Lista de Correos.** Open M-F 8:30am-2:30pm, Sa 9:30am-1pm. **Postal Code:** 17200.

Internet Access: Internet Papereria Palé, C. Cavallers, 16 (☎ 972 30 12 48). 175ptas per 1st 15min., 550ptas per hr., 10hr. ticket for 5000ptas. Open Aug.-Sept. M 5-9pm, Tu-Sa 9am-1pm and 5-9pm, Su 9am-1pm; Oct.-July Tu-Sa 9am-1pm and 5-9pm, Su 9am-1pm. **La Muralla,** C. Valls, 11 (☎ 972 61 09 90), in the far corner of the parking lot, to the left when facing the church. 300ptas per 30min., 600ptas per hr. Open Tu-Sa 9:30am-11:30pm.

ACCOMMODATIONS

Though there are only three options, accommodation prices are reasonable and room quality high in Palafrugell. Be sure to call ahead on summer weekends.

Fonda L'Estrella, C. Quatres Cases, 13-17 (☎ 972 30 00 05), at the corner of C. La Caritat, a right off C. Torres Jonama. Lovely, high-ceilinged, well-lit rooms with sinks off a Moorish courtyard bursting with plant life. Common baths, but gorgeous 2nd-floor rooms have sinks. Singles 2600ptas (available only Apr.-May and Sept.-Oct.); doubles Apr.-May and Sept.-Oct. 4200ptas; June 4400ptas; July-Aug. 4800ptas.

Residencia Familiar, C. Sant Sebastià, 29 (☎ 689 269 538). C. Quatres Cases crosses Pl. Nova and turns into C. Sant Sebastià. Mattresses are on the saggy side but all rooms have sinks and some have high ceilings. Singles 2000ptas; doubles 4000ptas; less for longer stays and off-season. Open Apr.15-Oct.

Hostal Plaja, C. Sant Sebastià, 34 (☎ 972 30 05 26). Grand, frescoed foyer gives way to a broad courtyard surrounded by spotless rooms, all with balconies, clotheslines, new beds, and bathrooms. July-Aug. singles 3000ptas, with breakfast 3400ptas; doubles 5500ptas, with breakfast 6500ptas. Dec.-June singles 2800ptas, with breakfast 3200ptas; doubles 5000ptas, with breakfast 6000ptas. V, MC.

Camping: Camping Moby Dick, C. Costa Verda, 16-28 (☎ 972 61 43 07). Take the Sarfa bus to Callela and ask the driver to let you off. No white whale in sight, but it is close to the water (5min.). Plenty of shade from abundant pine trees. Nice showers. 530ptas per person, 540ptas per car and per tent. Open Apr. 15-Sept. 30.

FOOD

Restaurants near the beach are predictably expensive, making meals in Palafrugell proper a wiser option. Get **groceries** for daytrips at **MAXOR**, C. Torres Jonama, 33 (open M-Sa 9am-10pmn, Su 9am-2pm). **Vapor,** C. de Les Botines, 12, is a popular restaurant with unbelievable *tortilla española* and a fresh, exquisite *menú* for 1200ptas. (☎ 972 30 57 03. Pastas 900-1000ptas. Pizzas 750-900ptas. Regional entrees 950-1600ptas. Open Tu-Su 1-5pm and 8pm-1am.) **L'Arcobaleno,** C. Mayor 3, brings a touch of Tuscany to Catalan classics. The delicious lunchtime *menú* has everything from lasagna to roast chicken (1150ptas). (☎ 972 61 06 95. Open daily noon-4pm and 7pm-midnight. V, MC, AmEx, Maestro.)

SIGHTS AND ENTERTAINMENT

In addition to nearby beaches, Palafrugell boasts one of the world's few cork museums. The **Museu del Suro,** C. Tarongeta, 31, has everything you wanted to know (and more) about cork. From Plaça Nova, face C. Sant Sebastià, take a right onto C. Pi i Margall, and the first right onto C. Tarongeta; the museum is at the end of the block. (☎ 972 30 39 98. Open June 15-Sept. 15 daily 10am-2pm and 4-10m; Sept.16-June 14 Tu-Sa 5-8pm, Su 10:30am-1:30pm. 200ptas, students and seniors 100ptas. English explanations available.) For an outdoor adventure, take a 40-minute walk up the road from Llafranc to the **Ermita de San Sebastià.** Crowning the mountain of the same name (50m from the lighthouse), the hermitage offers views of the entire Palafrugell valley, beaches, and sea.

Palafrugell's Friday evening stroll ends up at the *plaça*, where young and old often dance the traditional Catalan *sardana* around 10:30pm in July and August. Don't be afraid to join in. For more familiar dancing, check out **Discoteca Xarai,** C. Barris i Buixo, 42. Dance the night away, but not in your Nikes: no athletic gear allowed. Take a right off C. Sant Sebastià onto C. Barris i Buixo and look for the lime-green and orange building. The tourist office prints a monthly bulletin of upcoming events; also check the *Guía Municipal.* The town's biggest party takes place July 19-21, when the dance-intensive **Festa Major** bursts into the streets. Callela honors **Sant Pere** on June 29 and Tamariu celebrates on August 15. The **festivals of the *hanaveres*** (Spanish-Cuban sea songs) come to town every July.

⚡ DAYTRIPS FROM PALAFRUGELL

CALLELA (15MIN.), LLAFRANC (35MIN.), TAMARIU (1HR.)

Take a Sarfa bus from Palafrugell to Callela (15min., several times a day, 150ptas.) From Callela follow the Camino de Ronda (see below) from in front of the tourist office and walk 20min. or so to Llafranc. Walk 30min. farther along the path to reach Tamariu.

The three beaches grow quieter the farther you walk from Callela; Tamariu is the most peaceful. In Callela, **Jardí Botànic de Cap Roig**, the botanical garden in front of Hotel Garbí, provides an excellent view of the coast. (☎ 972 61 53 45. Open daily June-Aug. 9am-8pm; Sept.-May 9am-6pm. 300ptas.) Russian Colonel Nicolas Voevodsky built the garden's **seaside castle** after fleeing the Bolshevik Revolution. He and his wife planted and pruned the splendid maze of paths and flower beds with their own hands. The first sign for the castle points to the right at the fork of Av. Costa Daurada and C. Consolat del Mar. The castle also hosts the **Festival de Jazz de la Costa Brava** in July and August. Callela's **tourist office,** C. Voltes, 6, provides maps of walking paths that criss-cross the area, including the **Camino de Ronda**, a beautiful, popular climbs along the coast from Callela to Llafranc. (☎ 972 61 44 75. Open daily July-Aug. 10am-1pm and 5-9pm; Apr-June and Sept. 10am-1pm and 5-8pm.) **Poseidón Nemrod Club,** Port Pelegri (☎ 972 61 53 45) offers **scuba diving** courses and rents equipment.

L'ESCALA

L'Escala (pop. 5000, in summer 75,000) is a good launching point for the numerous coves and beaches in the area. Once a fishing village that made it big with anchovies, L'Escala's old quarter has pleasant pedestrian paths and tree-lined promenades, and the beaches and ruins make the town a very worthwhile trip from Parafrugell. The beach crowd slims somewhat beyond the Greek and Roman ruins of **Empúries.**

🚌🛈 ORIENTATION AND PRACTICAL INFORMATION. Sarfa buses (☎ 972 77 02 18) stop in front of the tourist office. Tickets are available on the bus. To: **Palafrugell** (35min., 5 per day 7:10am-6:55pm, 365ptas); **Figueres** (55min., 5 per day 7:10am-7:05pm, 450ptas); and **Girona** (2hr., 7:30am and 2:30pm, 555ptas). With your back to the tourist office, the ruins are to the left (walk down Rda. del Pedró) and the heart of the town is straight ahead (down Av. Ave Maria). The youth hostel arranges **mountain bike rental** if you contact them in advance, and **Cicles JK,** Av. Ave Maria, 9, also rents bikes. (☎ 972 77 40 42. 450ptas per hr., 1700ptas per day. Open June-Sept. daily 9am-1pm and 4-9pm; Oct.-June Tu-Sa 9am-1pm and 4-9pm.) The **tourist office,** Pl. Escoles, 1, has a helpful map, tourist info, and **fax** service. (☎ 972 77 06 03; fax 972 77 33 85. Open June-Sept. M-Sa 9am-8:30pm, Su 10am-1pm; Oct.-May M-Sa 9am-1pm and 4-7pm, Su 10am-1pm.) The **Banco Central Hispano** at C. Maranges, 16 has an **ATM** (open Apr.-Oct. M-F 8:30am-2:30pm; Oct.-Mar. M-F 8:30am-2:30pm, Sa 8:30am-1pm). Services include: **medical emergencies** (☎ 908 09 43 33); **municipal police,** C. Pintor Joan Massanet, 24 (☎ 972 77 48 18); and the **post office** (☎ 972 77 16 51), next to the tourist office. (Open M-F 8:30am-2:30pm, Sa 9:30am-1pm.) The **postal code** is 17130.

🛏️🍴 ACCOMMODATIONS AND FOOD. Despite the abundance of options, finding a cheap room in L'Escala can be difficult. The **Alberg de Juventut,** Les Coves, 41, is a 15-minute walk from the Empúries ruins and three minutes from the beach in a grove of trees. Facing the tourist office, follow the road on the right toward the coast. When you get to the headless male statue, take a left down the small lane and into the wooded area; the hostel awaits about 5 minutes down the road. Friendly owners, English books, TV, and numerous beds make it worth the walk. (☎ 972 77 12 00. Apr.-Sept. dorms 2875ptas, over 25 3800ptas. Oct.-Mar. dorms 2450ptas, over 25 3300ptas. Breakfast included. HI members only; cards available at the hostel. To guarantee reservations, call Barcelona's youth office (☎ 93 483 83 63 1 month in advance). Another option is **Pensió Torrent,** Carrer Riera, 28. From Pl.

Escoles walk downhill one block on C. Pintor, turn left, and follow the street around the corner. The hostel has whitewashed rooms with bathrooms and tiled floors. (☎ 972 77 02 78. Doubles 4500ptas; off-season 4000ptas).

From May to September, the town **market** is held daily 7am to 2pm in **Plaça Victor Català** (Oct.-Apr. Tu, Th, Sa, Su 7am-2pm.) Alternatively, fill your basket at **MAXOR**, Pl. Escoles, 2, across the street from the tourist office (open M-Sa 8:30am-2pm and 4:30-9pm, Sa 8:30am-9pm, Su 9am-2pm). **Restaurante-Snack Galan**, C. d. L'Usach, 3 on a small street off C. de la Torre to the left, is a good place to try local dishes in a typical country-style setting. (☎ 972 77 30 54. *Menú* 1000ptas. Open daily 1-3:30pm and 7-10:30pm. Closed in Nov.) Vegetarians and those looking for a break from regional fare will rejoice over the Italian-Mediterranean fare at seaside **Pizzeria del Port**, C. de Port, 9. Pizzas are fresh and delicious. (☎ 972 77 03 34. Lunchtime *menú* 1500ptas. Pastas 750-1100ptas. Open daily Apr.-Sept. noon-11:45pm; Oct.-Mar. noon-3:45pm and 7-11:45pm.)

DAYTRIP FROM L'ESCALA: EMPÚRIES

To get to Empúries, walk 30min. north (ask for directions at the tourist office if confused) or take the little train, Carrilet (☎ 937 65 47 84), from La Punta in L'Escala (between the main beach and Port d'en Perris) to St. Martí d'Empúries and ask to get off at the ruins (June 15-Sept. 15 on the hr., every hr. 10am-9pm, 250ptas).

Just 1km north of L'Escala are the ruins of Empúries. In the 7th century BC, Greek traders landed on a small island on the northeast Iberian coast. As the settlement grew, it moved to the mainland and became the prosperous colony of Emporion (meaning "marketplace"); four centuries later it fell into Roman hands. Remnants of both Greek and Roman cities, including some gorgeous mosaic floors and a Visigothic basilica, fill Empúries's 40 hectares of ruins. Excavation of the ruins continues, backed by profits from the 1992 Olympic Games. (The Olympic torch first formally entered Spain through this ancient Greek port city.) The small but wealthy **Museu Monogràfic d'Empúries** showcases a large collection of ceramics and Etruscan wares. (☎ 972 77 02 08. Ruins and museum open daily June-Sept. 10am-8pm; Oct.-May 10am-6pm. 400ptas, students and seniors free. Audiovisual program screened every 30min. from 10:30am until closing, 300ptas. Audio tape 600ptas.) Explanatory signs through the ruins indicate the ancient urban plan without marring the aura of fountains, mosaics, and columns against a backdrop of cypress trees and the breezy Mediterranean. Half a kilometer north of the ruins is the entrance to the **Parc Natural dels Aiguamolls de l'Empordà**, a protected habitat with miles of marshland and lakes, filled with plant and animal species. For more details on the park, contact the information center, **El Cortalet** (☎ 972 25 42 22).

GIRONA

Girona (pop. 70,500) is a world-class city that the world has yet to really notice. First a Roman settlement and later an important medieval center, Girona was one of the few Spanish cities where Christians, Arabs, and Jews were able to peacefully coexist. This multiculturalism was a result of the city's geographical location, as Girona served as a gateway to the rest of Europe by land and to the Orient by sea. It was also the founding place of the renowned *cabalistas de Gerona*, a group of 12th-century rabbis who created an oral tradition called the *Kabbala* based on mystical and numerological readings of the Torah. Today Girona offers a taste of Catalan culture in a unique setting. The city is divided by the Riu Onyar, which separates the medieval alleys and Romanesque buildings of the old quarter from the Spanish dwellings of the new.

■ TRANSPORTATION

Trains: RENFE (☎ 972 24 02 02 for info and reservations; www.renfe.es), in Pl. Espanya. Info open daily 6:30am-10pm. To: **Figueres** (45min., 22 per day 6:15am-10:44pm, 325ptas); **Portbou** (1hr., 12 per day 6:15am-10:44pm, 250ptas); **Barcelona** (1¼hr., 21 per day 6:12am-9:29pm, 1265ptas); **Madrid** (9-10½hr., 1 per day, 9:05am, 6000-7500ptas); and **Paris** (11hr., 9:17pm, 16,900ptas).

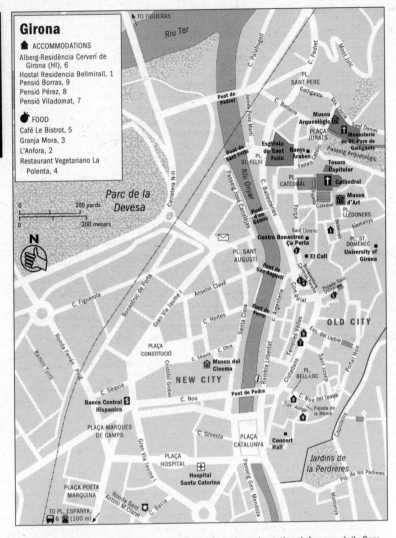

Girona

🏠 **ACCOMMODATIONS**

Alberg-Residència Cerverí de
  Girona (HI), 6
Hostal Residencia Bellmirall, 1
Pensió Borras, 9
Pensió Pérez, 8
Pensió Viladomat, 7

🍴 **FOOD**

Café Le Bistrot, 5
Granja Mora, 3
L'Anfora, 2
Restaurant Vegetariano La
  Polenta, 4

Buses: (☎ 972 21 23 19), around the corner from the train station. Info open daily 6am-10pm. **Sarfa** (☎ 972 20 17 96) runs to **Tossa de Mar** (1hr.; July-Aug. 2 per day, Sept.-June 1 per day; 625ptas) and **Palafrugell** (1hr., 12 per day, 525ptas), for connections to Begur, Llafranc, Callela, and Tamariu. **Teisa** (☎ 972 20 02 75) drives to: **St. Feliu** (45min., 9-15 per day, 435-500ptas); **Olot** (1¼hr., 6-16 per day, 625-725ptas); **Ripoll** (2hr., 3 per day, 1100-1400ptas); **Lerida** (3½hr., 2-4 per day, 2155ptas). **Barcelona Bus** (☎ 972 20 24 32) express to **Barcelona** (1½hr., 3-4 per day, 1100-1200ptas) and **Figueres** (1hr., 7 per day, 400-480ptas).

Taxis: (☎ 972 22 23 23 or 972 22 10 20). Try Pl. Independència and Pont de Pedra.

Car Rental: Most companies cluster around C. Barcelona, near the train station. Must be over 21 (for most) and have had a license for at least 1-2 years. **Hertz**, C. Bailen, 2 (☎ 902 42 24 05), walk through the parking lot away from the train station and you will see C. Bailen leading off diagonally to your left. Min. age 25. Rentals start at 5000ptas for 1 day with unlimited mileage. Open M-F 8am-1pm and 4-8pm, Sa 8am-1pm.

✴ ORIENTATION AND PRACTICAL INFORMATION

The **Riu Onyar** separates the new city from the old. The **Pont de Pedra** connects the two banks and leads directly into the old quarter by way of Carrers Ciutadans, Peralta, and Força, off of which are located the cathedral and **El Call,** the historic Jewish neighborhood. **RENFE** and **bus terminals** are situated off Carrer de Barcelona, in the modern neighborhood. To get to the old city from the stations, head straight out through the parking lot, turning left on C. Barcelona. Follow C. Barcelona for two blocks until it forks at the traffic island. Take the right fork via C. Santa Eugenia to Gran Vía de Jaume I, and continue straight across at the Banco Central Hispano to get on Carrer Nou, which runs directly to the Pont de Pedra.

Tourist Office: Rambla Llibertat, 1 (☎ 972 22 65 75; fax 972 22 66 12), in a yellow building directly on the left as you cross Pont de Pedra from the new town. Loads of info on the city and region. English spoken. Open M-F 9am-8pm, Sa 8am-2pm and 4-8pm, Su 9am-2pm. The **train station branch** (☎ 972 20 70 93) is to the right of the RENFE ticket counter. Open M-F 8:30am-1:30pm.

Currency Exchange: Banco Central Hispano, one on the corner of C. Nou and Gran Vía de Jaume I, and another on Pujada Pont de Pedra, on the right after crossing the bridge into the old city. **ATMs.** Open Oct.-Mar. M-F 8:30am-2:30pm, Sa 8:30am-1pm; Apr.-Sept. 30 M-F 8:30am-2:30pm.

Luggage Storage: Lockers in the train station for 600ptas. Open 24hr.

Hipercor (El Corté Inglés's Not-So-Chic Cousin): (☎ 972 24 44 44). On C. Barcelona; take a right out of the train station (15min.). Groceries, telephones, currency exchange, English books, and cafeteria. Open M-Sa 10am-10pm.

Travel Bookstore: Ulyssus, C. Ballesteries, 29 (☎/fax 972 21 17 73), on the left-hand side of the street as you walk up Ballesteries toward the Plaça Cathedral. Open M-Sa 10am-2pm and 4:30-8:30pm.

Emergency: ☎ 112. **Police: Policía Municipal,** C. Bacià, 4 (☎ 092). From Banco Central Hispano, turn right on the Gran Vía, then right on Bacià.

Hospital: Hospital Municipal de Santa Caterina, Pl. Hospital, 5 (☎ 972 18 26 00).

Post Office: Av. Ramón Folch, 2 (☎ 972 22 21 11), at the start of Gran Vía de Jaume I. Turn right on Gran Vía coming from the old city. **Second office,** Ronda Ferrán Puig, 17 (☎ 972 22 34 75). **Lista de Correos** only. Both open M-F 8:30am-8:30pm, Sa 9:30am-2pm. **Postal Code:** 17070.

⌐ ACCOMMODATIONS

Rooms are only hard to find in July and August. Most budget accommodations are sprinkled around the old quarter; they are both reasonably priced and well-kept.

Alberg-Residència Cerverí de Girona (HI), C. Ciutadans, 9 (☎ 972 21 80 03; fax 972 21 20 23). From the new city, cross Pont de Pedra, take a left on Ciutadans; it's about a block up on your left. A college dorm during the year. 8 beds available Oct.-June; 82 beds July-Sept. Sleek sitting rooms with TV/VCR; rooms of 3 and 8 beds with lockers. High-spirited staff, high-fashion sheets. Breakfast included. Other meals 850ptas. Sheets 350ptas. Laundry 500ptas. Members only, but HI cards for sale. Make reservations at the Barcelona office (☎ 93 483 83 63). Dorms 1900ptas, over 25 2500ptas.

Hostal Residencia Bellmirall, C. Bellmirall, 3 (☎ 972 20 40 09). With the cathedral directly behind you C. Bellmirall is straight ahead to the left; look for the blue hostel sign. Expensive, delightful stone rooms in a 14th-century house. Breakfast included and served in a cozy dining area or the garden. Make reservations. Mar.-Dec.15 singles 4990ptas, with bath 5280ptas; doubles 7920ptas, with bath 8580ptas. Cash only.

Pensió Viladomat, C. Ciutadans, 5 (☎ 972 20 31 76; fax 972 20 31 76), next door to the youth hostel. Clean, well-furnished rooms and bathrooms, some with balconies. Singles 2300ptas; doubles 4500ptas, with bath 6600ptas; triples 6500ptas. Cash only.

Pensió Pérez, Pl. Bell-lloc, 4 and **Pensió Borras,** Trav. Auriga, 6 (☎ 972 22 40 08). Continue straight after crossing Pont de Pedra into the old quarter onto C. Nou; Pl. Bell-lloc is on the right. To Pensió Borras from Pérez, take a right out the door and follow the street around the corner, making a left at its end. The Pensió is on the 2nd floor of the last building on your right. Both pensions, owned by the same woman, offer basic, inexpensive singles, doubles, and triples. Singles 1800ptas, with bath 2100; doubles 3000ptas, with bath 3500; triples 4000ptas. Cash only.

🍴 FOOD

Considered home to some of the best Catalan cuisine, Girona abounds with specialties to suit the tastes of traditionalists and adventurers alike. Some of the best cheap eats huddle near the cathedral and along Carrer Cort Reial. In the old quarter, numerous chic cafes cater to university students. In summer, an open **market** can be found near the Polideportivo in Parc de la Deversa (open Tu and Sa 8am-3pm). Get your **groceries** at **Caprabo,** C. Sequia, 10, a block from C. Nou off the Gran Vía. (☎ 972 21 45 16. Open M-Sa 9am-1:30pm and 5-8:30pm.)

Restaurant Vegetariano La Polenta, C. Corte Reial, 6 (☎ 972 20 93 74). Vegetarian fare with an international accent and innovative rice, tofu, and polenta dishes. Extensive daily lunch menu. The small, light restaurant fills up at lunchtime but maintains a quiet, pleasant atmosphere. *Menú* (lunch only) 1300ptas. Open M-F 1-3pm. Visa.

Café Le Bistrot, Pujada Sant Domènec, 4 (☎ 972 21 88 03), a right off C. Ciutadans. Excellent food and a sophisticated clientele are the hallmarks of this elegant cafe. Freshly made pizzas 575-675ptas. *Crêpes* 475-600ptas. Lunchtime *menú* 1400ptas, smaller version 1200ptas. Open M-Th 1-5pm and 7pm-1:30am, F-Sa 1-5pm and 7pm-1am. Closed some Mondays in winter. V, MC.

👁 SIGHTS

The narrow, winding streets of the medieval old city, interspersed with steep stairways and low arches, are ideal for wanderers. Start your self-guided historical tour at the **Pont de Pedra** and turn left at the tourist office down tree-lined **Rambla de la Llibertat.** Continue on C. Argenteria, bearing right across C. Cort Reial. Up the flight of stairs, C. Forçà begins on the left.

EL CALL. This was once the medieval Jewish neighborhood. ("Call" comes from *kahal,* "community" in Hebrew.) The site of the last synagogue in Girona now serves as a museum linking the baths, butcher shop, and synagogue, all of which surround a serene central patio. The center is named for Girona-born Rabbi Moshe ben Nahman (Nahmanides), best known for his studies of Jewish mysticism and the oral tradition known as the *Kabbala.* For details on El Call, see **Rebuilding Sepharad,** p. 351. *(El Call begins at C. Sant Llorenç and is centered on C. Forçà. The entrance to the Centre Bonastruc Ça Porta is off C. Sant Llorenç about halfway up the hill. ☎ 972 21 67 61. Open June-Oct. M-Sa 10am-8pm, Su 10am-2pm; Nov.-May M-Sa 10am-6pm, Su 10am-2pm. Free. The tourist office also offers guided tours of El Call in July and Aug. for 800ptas.)*

CATHEDRAL COMPLEX. Farther uphill on C. Forçà and around the corner to the right, Girona's imposing Gothic **cathedral** rises a record-breaking 90 steps (its Rococo stairway is the largest in Europe) from the plaza. The **Torre de Charlemany** and the cloister are the only structures left from the 11th century; the rest of the building dates from the 15th and 16th centuries. The most unique feature of the cathedral is its interior, where the three customary naves have been compressed into one, producing the world's widest Gothic **nave** (22m). A door on the left leads to the trapezoidal cloister and the **Tesoro Capitular,** home to some of Girona's most precious possessions. The *tesoro's* (and possibly Girona's) most famous piece is the **Tapis de la Creació,** a 15th-century tapestry depicting the creation story. *(Tesoro ☎ 972 21 44 26. Cathedral and Tesoro open July-Aug. Tu-Su 10am-2pm and 4-7pm; Sept.-June Tu-Sa 10am-2pm and 4-7pm, Su 10am-2pm. Tesoro and cloister 500ptas.)*

REBUILDING SEPHARAD Though Girona has a reputation for tolerance, the Jews of Girona were still victims of discrimination, ostracism, and eventual expulsion. Despite it all, they contributed ineradicably to the city's culture. The *aljama* (Jewish quarter) in Girona, once populated by 300 people, became a leading center for the study of the **Kabbala,** a mystical reading of the Torah in which number values are assigned to each Hebrew letter and numerical sums are interpreted to reveal spiritual meaning. Operating like a tiny, independent country within the city (inhabitants answered to their King, not the city government), El Call was protected by the crown of Cataluña in exchange for financial tribute. Until the 11th century, Christians and Jews coexisted peacefully, occasionally even intermarrying. Unfortunately, this did not last. Historical sources cite attacks and looting of the Jewish quarter in eight separate years, the first in 1276 and the last in 1418. Eventually, almost every entrance to El Call was blocked off. The reopening of the streets of El Call began only after Franco's death in 1975. In recent years, eight Spanish mayors have created a network called *Caminos de Sepharad,* an organization aimed at restoring Spain's Jewish quarters and fostering a broader understanding of the Sephardic legacy.

WALKS. Near the **University of Girona** is the start of the extremely beautiful **Passeig de la Muralla.** Railed steps lead onto the city walls for an impressive view of old Girona. The walk ends two blocks to the left of the Pont de Pedra. Another nice walk is the **Passeig Arqueològic,** partly lined with cypresses and flower beds, which skirts the medieval wall on the east side of the river and overlooks the city.

OTHER SIGHTS. The **Museu del Cinema** hides in Girona's commercial new city, along the river. The museum chronicles the invention of movies, from the rise of shadow theater to early special effects, in wacky interactive exhibits. *(Sèquia, 1. One block north of C. Nou off C. Santa Clara. ☎ 972 41 27 77; fax 972 41 30 47. Open Oct.-May Tu-F 10am-6pm, Sa 10am-8pm, Su 11am-3pm; May-Sept.30 Tu-Su 10am-8pm. 500ptas, students 250ptas.)* Inspired by Muslim bath houses, the graceful 12th-century **Banys Àrabs** once contained saunas and baths of varying temperatures. *(From the cathedral, with your back to the stairs, take a right on C. Ferran Catòlic. ☎ 972 21 32 62. Open Apr.-Sept. M-Sa 10am-7pm, Su 10am-2pm; Oct.-Mar. daily 10am-2pm. 200ptas, students 100ptas.)*

🎭 🌿 NIGHTLIFE AND FESTIVALS

The **Rambla** and **Plaça de Independencia** are the places to see and be seen in Girona. Locals usually end their days with a *passeig* (stroll), dinner, and then bar-hopping, which generally takes place in the new city. Bars near Pl. Ferrán Catòlic draw big crowds, but during the summer, **Parc de la Devesa,** across the river from the old town and several blocks to the left, has all the cachet and often live music as well. Of Girona's four discos, the most popular is **La Sala de Cel,** C. Pedret, 118, off Pl. Sant Pere in the north quarter of the city (☎ 972 21 46 64. Open Sept.-July Th-Su. Cover 2000ptas, includes 2 drinks). Artsy folk mill around the oh-so-cute bars and cafes in the old quarter. Enter on C. Ferreires Vellas, parallel to C. Ciutadans, to try the **Café del Liberia,** C. Ciutadans, 15, which serves cocktails, beers, and snacks to chic intellectual types. Small pizzas and sandwiches cost 600-850ptas. (☎ 972 20 48 18. Open M-Sa 8:30am-11pm, Su noon-midnight.) Low tables and cozy nooks fill the unmarked and decidedly hip **La Terra,** C. Ballesteries, 23. Try their flavored alcoholic slushies and 350pta fruit concoctions—everyone else does. (☎ 972 21 57 64. Open M-F 6pm-midnight, Sa-Su 6pm-1am, 2am in summer.)

During the second half of May, **flower exhibitions** spring up in the city, local monuments swim in blossoms, and the courtyards of Girona's fine old buildings open to the public. Some summer Fridays inspire spontaneous *sardanas,* traditional Catalan dances involving 10 to 12 musicians serenading a ring of dancers. Like the rest of northern Spain, Girona lights up for the **Focs de Sant Joan** on June 24, an outdoor party featuring fireworks and campfires.

FIGUERES (FIGUERAS)

In 1974, Salvador Dalí chose his native Figueres (pop. 35,000) as the site for a magnificent museum to house his works, instantly catapulting the city to international fame. Ever since, a multilingual parade of Surrealism fans has been awed and entranced by Dalí's bizarre perspectives and erotic visions. Though it is a beachless sprawl, Figueres hides other quality museums and some pleasant cafes. It is also a convenient base for visiting the Costa Brava.

◗ TRANSPORTATION

Trains: (☎ 972 20 70 93). To: **Girona** (30min., 21 per day 6:11am-8:58pm, 375ptas); **Portbou** (30min., 12 per day 6:42am-11:16pm, 250ptas); **Barcelona** (1½hr., 21 per day 6:11am-8:58pm, 1300ptas).

Buses: All lines leave from the **Estació Autobuses** (☎ 972 67 33 54), Pl. Estació. **Sarfa** (☎ 972 67 42 98) runs to **Llançà** (25min.; July-Aug. 4 per day, Sept.-June 2 per day; 300ptas) and **Cadaqués** (1¼hr.; July-Aug. 5 per day, Sept.-June 2-3 per day; 490ptas). **Barcelona Bus** (☎ 972 50 50 29) drives to **Girona** (1hr., 4-6 per day, 475ptas) and **Barcelona** (2¼hr., 4-6 per day, 1750ptas).

Taxis: (☎ 972 50 00 08). Taxis line up on the Rambla and outside the train station.

Car Rental: Hertz, Pl. Estació, 9 (☎ 902 40 24 65). Min. age 24. All-inclusive rental from 8900ptas per day.

✦ ORIENTATION AND PRACTICAL INFORMATION

Trains and buses arrive at **Plaça de Estació** on the edge of town. Cross the plaza and bear left on Carrer Sant Llàtzer, walk several blocks to Carrer Nou, and take a right to Figueres's tree-filled Rambla. To reach the **tourist office,** walk up the Rambla and continue on Carrer Lasauca straight out from the left corner. The blue all-knowing **"i"** beckons across the rather treacherous intersection with Ronda Frial.

Tourist Office: Main office (☎ 972 50 31 55), Pl. Sol. Good map and free list of accommodations. Open July-Aug. M-Sa 9am-9pm, Su 9am-3pm; Apr.-June and Oct. M-F 8:30am-3pm and 4:30-8pm, Sa 9:30am-1:30pm and 3:30-6:30pm; Sept. and Nov.-Apr. M-F 8:30am-3pm. Two **branch offices** in summer, one at Pl. Estació (open mid-July to mid-Sept. M-Sa 9:30am-1pm and 4-7pm), and the other in a yellow mobile home by the Dalí museum (open July-Sept. 15 M-Sa 10am-2:30pm and 4:30-7pm).

Currency Exchange: Banco Central Hispano, Rambla, 21. **ATM.** Open Apr.-Oct. M-F 8:30am-2pm; Nov.-Mar. M-F 8:30am-2pm, Sa 8:30am-1pm.

Luggage Storage: At the train station, large lockers 600ptas. At the bus station 300ptas. Both open daily 6am-10pm.

Emergency: ☎ 112. **Police: Mossos d'Esquadra** (☎ 972 67 50 89), on C. Ter.

Post Office: C. Santa Llogaia, 60-62 (☎ 972 50 54 31). Open M-F 8:30am-2:30pm, Sa 9:30am-1pm. **Postal Code:** 17600.

Internet Access: Bar-Arcadia, C. Sant Antoni, 7 (☎ 972 67 38 91). Follow C. Castello alongside the Pl. de Catalunya and toward C. Nou; take a left on C. Sant Antoni and look for the red "Estrella" beer sign on your left. 500ptas per 30min, 800ptas per hr. 15% discount with student ID. Open M-Sa 9am-10pm.

◤ ACCOMMODATIONS

Finding a place to sleep in Figueres can be a surreal experience, as affordable accommodations tend to hide in unlikely spots. Some cluster on C. Jonquera, around the Dali museum; others are located closer to La Rambla and C. Pep Ventura. The tourist office has an annually updated list of all pensions and hostels.

Alberg Tramuntana (HI), C. Anciet de Pagès, 2 (☎ 972 50 12 13; fax 972 67 38 08), 1 block behind the tourist office. The Alberg offers friendly hosts, fax service, VCR, library, board games, bike rentals, and laundry. Members only, but HI cards for sale (1000ptas). Breakfast included. Sheets 350ptas. Laundry service 500ptas. Reception daily 8:30am-1pm and 4-11pm. Lockout M-F 2-4pm, Sa-Su 1-7pm. Curfew midnight; in summer open for 10min. at 1, 2, 3, and 4am. Reserve 1 month in advance through the Barcelona office (☎ 93 483 83 63) or call the hostel 2-3 days prior to arrival. 4, 8 and 14-bunk dorms available. 1900ptas per bed, over 26, 2500ptas. V, MC, AmEx.

Hostal La Barretina, C. Lasauca, 13 (☎ 972 67 64 12). From the train station walk up the left side of La Rambla to its end and look for C. Lasauca directly ahead. A luxury experience–each room has TV, A/C, heat, and private bath. Reception is downstairs in the jointly-owned restaurant. Singles 3500ptas; doubles 6000ptas. V, MC, AmEx.

Pensión Mallol, C. Pep Ventura, 9 (☎ 972 50 22 83). Follow the Rambla toward the tourist office, turn right on Castell at its end, and take the 2nd left. Clean, simple rooms with shared bathrooms and firm mattresses. Singles 2000ptas; doubles 3450ptas.

🍴 FOOD

Restaurants near the Dalí museum serve overcooked *paella* to the masses; better choices surround the Rambla. The **market** is at Pl. Gra and near Pl. Catalunya (open Tu, Th, and Sa 5am-2pm). Buy your own mass-produced food at supermarket **MAXOR,** Pl. Sol, 5. (☎ 972 51 00 19. Open July-Sept. M-F 8am-9pm, Sa 9am-9pm; Oct.-June M-Sa 8am-8:30pm. V, MC.) Up the street from the youth hostel, **La Llesca,** C. Mestre Falla, 15, serves a delicious 1100pta *menú*. (☎ 972 67 58 26. Open M-F 7am-midnight, Sa-Su 7am-2am.) **Restaurante La Pansa,** C. l'Emporda, 8, a comfortable, modest restaurant, serves meat and fish dishes and a popular four-course *menú*. (☎ 972 50 10 72. *Menú* 1100ptas. Open M-Sa noon-4pm and 8-10pm. V, MC.

👁🎵 SIGHTS AND ENTERTAINMENT

▪ TEATRE-MUSEU DALÍ. Ever look at one of Dalí's paintings and ask yourself "Um, what was this guy *thinking*?" Welcome to the enchanting world of the Surrealist master. Despite his reputation as a fascist self-promoter, Dalí's personally designed theater/museum/monument-to-himself should be approached as a multimedia experience, an electrifying tangle of sculpture, painting, music, and architecture. It's all here: Dalí's naughty cartoons, his dramatically low-key tomb, and many paintings of Gala, his wife and muse, one of which, when viewed through a telescope (10ptas), transforms into a portrait of Abraham Lincoln. The treasure trove of paintings includes, among others, the remarkable *Self Portrait with a Slice of Bacon* and *Galatea of the Spheres*. While the museum is full of interesting art, not all the works are on the walls; look up as well. *(From the Rambla, take C. Girona from the end farthest from the tourist office, which goes past Pl. Ajuntament and becomes C. de la Jonquera. Steps by a Dalí statue lead to the museum. ☎ 972 51 18 00; fax 972 50 16 66. Open Tu-Su Oct.-June30 10:30am-5:15pm; July1-23 and Aug.30–Sept.29 9am-5:45pm; July 24-Aug.29 9am-5:45pm and 10pm-12:30am. 1000ptas, students and seniors 800ptas.)*

OTHER SIGHTS. Delight once again in the wonders of your favorite childhood toys at the **Museu del Joguet,** winner of Spain's 1999 National Prize of Popular Culture. A colorful collection of antique dolls, blocks, board games, comics, rocking horses, toys for the blind and more. *(Hotel Paris, Rambla 10. ☎ 972 50 45 85. Open July-Sept. M-Sa 10am-1pm and 4-7pm, Su 11am-1:30pm and 5-7:30pm; Oct.-June M, W-Sa 10am-1pm and 4-7pm, Su 11am-1:30pm. 750ptas, under 18 600ptas.)* Ten minutes from the Museu Dalí, the massive 18th-century **Castell de Sant Ferran** commands a spectacular view of the surrounding countryside and is the largest stone fortress in Europe at 12,000 square meters. *(Av. Castell de Sant Ferran. ☎ 972 50 60 94. Open July-Sept.15 daily 10:30am-8pm; Sept.16-June 30 Tu-Su 10:30am-2pm. 350ptas.)*

IS THAT A MELTING CANDLE IN YOUR POCKET, OR ARE YOU JUST A ROTTING DONKEY? From an early age, Salvador Dalí was plagued by nightmares and insecurities. By age 15, Dalí already had high hopes for himself: "I'll be a genius and the world will admire me." Although Dalí appeared to be confident in his talents, he was not equally confident in other aspects of his life. Sexually inexperienced until a late age, Dalí was sexually ambiguous and had a fear of sexual contact and impotence. This fear was one of the two central subjects of his work; the other, interestingly enough, was landscapes. Dalí was also influenced by Sigmund Freud, and sought to connect the unconscious with the conscious in his paintings. Surrealism itself attempted to explore the language of dreams in order to tap the unconscious. Although Dalí's paintings can be confusing at first, aspects of their symbol-language are consistent enough to be translated. Here a few examples:

Look carefully at Dalí's **women.** Those that are portrayed in a cubist style are that way because they pose no threat to Dalí.

Most of Dalí's **landscapes** are of the rocky shores of Cadaqués.

A rotting **donkey** or **fish** is Dalí's symbol of the bourgeoise.

The **crutches** propping up bits of soft flesh are symbols of masturbation.

The **grasshopper** is a symbol of terror, as Dalí had a great fear of the insect.

Staircases are a Freudian image, representing the fear of intercourse.

A **melting candle** is a symbol of impotence.

Lions represent animal aggression and **knifes** are meant to be phallic symbols.

A **fish hook** (found in Dalí's head) is a symbol of his entrapment.

When asked about the **clocks** he said, "the famous soft watches are nothing else than the tender, extravagant, solitary, paranoia-critical Camembert of time and space." (*Conquest of the Irrational,* 1969.)

FESTIVALS. In September, classical and jazz music come to Figueres during the **Festival Internacional de Música de l'Empordà.** *(Tickets available at Caixa de Catalunya. Call ☎ 972 10 12 12 or get a brochure at the tourist office.)* From September 9-12, the **Mostra del Vi de L'Alt Empordà,** a tribute to regional wines, brings a taste of the local vineyards to Figueres. Around May 3, the **Fires i Festes de la Santa Creu** sponsors cultural events, art and technology exhibitions, and parties, and merrymaking at the **Festa de Sant Pere,** held June 28-29, honors the town's patron saint.

NEAR FIGUERES

CADAQUÉS

The whitewashed houses and small bay of Cadaqués (pop. 2000) have attracted artists, writers, and musicians ever since Dalí built his summer home here in the 1930s. To preserve the town's authentic Mediterranean flavor, an affluent crowd of property owners and renters have kept at bay the commercial influx of sprawling condos, big hotels, and trains. The rocky beaches and dreamy landscape attract their share of tourists, but Cadaqués preserves a pleasantly laid-back atmosphere.

🔽 PRACTICAL INFORMATION. The bus to Cadaqués halts at a small stone tower beneath a miniature Statue of Liberty. With your back to the Sarfa office, walk right and downhill on Av. Caritat Serinyana to the waterfront square, **Plaça Frederic Rahola,** where a signboard map with indexed services and accommodations will orient you. Cadaqués has no train station, but Sarfa has **buses** (☎ 972 25 87 13) run to: **Figueres** (1hr., 3-5 per day, 500ptas); **Girona** (2hr., 1-2 per day, 940ptas); and **Barcelona** (2½hr., 2-5 per day, 2045ptas). **Escola de Vela Ones** sets up shop on the beach directly in front of the tourist office and rents **mountain bikes, kayaks,** and **wind-surfing** gear. (☎ 937 53 25 12. Bikes 900ptas per hr., 1900ptas per half-day, 2500ptas per day. Open daily July-Sept. 15 10am-8pm). Farther down the beach on Platja Es Poal, **Animal Area Cadaqués** also has rentals. (☎ 972 25 80 27. Kayaks 1200ptas per hr., 3000ptas per 4hr. Motorboats 8000ptas per 4hr., 15,000ptas per day. Scooters 3900ptas per 4hr., 5900ptas per day. The **tourist office,** C. Cotxe, 2, off Pl. Frederic Rahola opposite the *passeig,* has a helpful map of Cadaqués and the surrounding beaches. (☎ 972 25 83 15; fax 972 15 94 42. Open July-Aug. M-Sa 10am-2pm and 4-9pm, Su 10:30am-1pm; Sept.-June M-Sa 10am-2pm and 4-7pm.) **Banco Central Hispano** is on C. Caritat Serinyana, 4. (☎ 972 25 83 62. Open Oct.-Mar. M-F 8:30am-2:30pm; Apr.-Sept. M-F 8:30am-2:30pm, Sa 8:30am-1pm.) Services include: **local police** (☎ 972 15 93 43), Pl. Frederic Rahola, by the promenade; **medical assistance** (☎ 972 25 88 07); and the **post office,** Av. Rierassa off C. Caritat Serinyana. (☎ 972 25 87 98. Open M-F 9am-2pm, Sa 9:30am-1pm.) The **postal code** is 17488.

⌐⌐ ACCOMMODATIONS AND FOOD. Hostal Cristina, C. Riera, right on the water, has bright, newly renovated rooms. (☎ 972 25 81 38. Summer prices include breakfast. May-Sept. singles 3000ptas; doubles 5000ptas, with bath 6000ptas, with TV 8000ptas. Oct.-Apr. singles 3000ptas; doubles 4000ptas, with bath or terrace 5000ptas. V, MC.) **Hostal Marina,** C. Riera, 3, boasts clean, airy rooms, some with balconies. (☎ 972 25 81 99 or 15 90 91. Singles 3000ptas, with bath 4000ptas; doubles 5500ptas, with bath 8000ptas. Breakfast 550ptas. Open Apr.-Dec. V, MC.) **Camping Cadaqués,** Ctra. Portlligat, 17, is 100m from the beach on the left on the way to Dalí's house; follow the signs for Hotel Port Lligat. Amenities include a pool, supermarket, and bungalows. (☎ 972 25 81 26. 565ptas per person, 710ptas per tent, 565ptas per car; tax not included. Open late Mar.-Sept. 15.)

Cadaqués harbors the usual slew of overpriced, unexciting tourist **restaurants** on the waterfront; wander into the back streets for more interesting options. Heading uphill from the main beach on C. Vigilant stop by **Can Tito,** C. Vigilant, 8, on your left, for an exceptional historic and culinary experience. The stone archway at the entrance to this elegant restaurant is one of five portals dating back to 1100 AD when Cadaqués was still a fortified village, at the mercy of roving pirates. (☎ 972 25 90 70. Lunchtime *menú* 1600ptas plus tax. Fish and meat entrees 800-2000ptas. Open daily Mar.-Jan. 1-3:30pm and 7:30-11pm. V, MC.) Otherwise, pack a picnic from **Super Auvi,** C. Riera. (☎ 972 25 86 33. Open July 15-Aug. M-Sa 8:30am-1:30pm and 4:30-8:30, Su 8:30am-1pm; Sept.-July 14 M-Sa 8am-2pm and 4-9pm.)

⌐⌐ SIGHTS AND ENTERTAINMENT. The **Centre d'Art Perrot-Moore,** C. Vigilant, 1, near the town center, houses many Dalí masterpieces, including an erotic fantasy room (no children permitted) and mixed media from the Disney version of Dante's *Divine Comedy.* Also check out the impressive Picassos, backdrops for a 1953 García Lorca play, and his practice sketches for the phenomenal *Guernica.* (☎ 972 25 82 31. Open July-Aug. daily 10:30am-1:30pm and 4:30-8:30pm; Apr.-June and Sept.-Oct. M-Sa 10:30am-1:30pm and 4-8pm, Su 10:30am-1:30pm. 800ptas, students and children 500ptas.) The **Museu de Cadaqués,** C. Narcis Monturiol, has changing exhibits, often with a Dalí theme. (☎ 972 25 88 77. Open daily mid-June to Sept. 11am-1:30pm and 4-8:30pm. 800ptas, students and children 500ptas.) From there it is a pleasant walk (30min.) to ■**Casa-Museu Salvador Dalí,** in Port Lligat, the home where Dalí and his wife Gala lived until her death in 1982. Originally the modest house of a lone fisherman, the Casa de Dalí was transformed to meet the aesthetic and somewhat eccentric lifestyle led by Dalí and his treasured wife. The building flaunts Dalí's favorite lip-shaped sofa and more stuffed snakes and swans than you bargained for. Follow the signs to Port Lligat and take the right fork with your back to the statue of liberty; eventually Casa de Dalí signs appear. (☎ 972 25 10 15. Open June 15-Sept. 15 daily 10:30am-9pm; Mar. 15-June 14 and Sept. 16-Nov. Tu-Su 10:30am-6pm. Multilingual tours every 10min. Ticket office closes 45min. before closing. 1200ptas; students, seniors, and children 700ptas.)

THE LAST DAYS OF BENJAMIN Although Portbou may seem fairly insignificant on the cultural landscape, it gained notoriety in the 1940s as the site where the extremely influential literary and cultural critic Walter Benjamin died. Benjamin, a social theorist of the Frankfurt school and close friend of Bertold Brecht, left behind a profound legacy. A pessimistic Marxist, he elucidated the relationship between literature and social structures. Of German-Jewish descent, Benjamin was fleeing the Nazis in 1940 when he arrived at the border town of Portbou. Because of Spanish Fascist sympathy with the Nazi cause, Benjamin was detained there and not permitted to enter Spain. He retired to the Pensión at Restaurante Internacional (which can still be found at C. Del Mar, 5) and killed himself upstairs by overdosing on morphine. Local lore, however, claims that Benjamin was murdered by the Nazis. Perched above the water, a hauntingly poignant memorial commemorates Benjamin "and the memory of the nameless" who suffered under Nazi oppression. A five-minute walk from the town, the memorial and cemetery merit a visit. The **Civic Center**, Méndez Núñez, 2 (☎/fax 972 39 04 06), has a Walter Benjamin Documentation Center; which frequently holds exhibitions on the philosopher.

PORTBOU

Perched on the Spanish and French border, Portbou (pop. 1590) was a virtually non-existent fisherman's village until the Barcelona-Cerbère railroad was constructed in 1872, bringing life to the area. And while most visitors will see little more than the train station, the five-minute walk through the small town is worth the trek between connections. Nestled between two mountains, Portbou offers a magnificent view of the sea, a clean pebble beach, and tree-lined streets.

The train station lies above the town, and its only exit, down a set of stairs, leads onto C. Mercat. Go through Pg. Enric Granados and bear left; the tourist office and beach are straight ahead. **RENFE trains** (☎ 972 39 00 99) go to: **Figueres** (30min., 21 per day 5:47am-10:35pm, 250ptas); **Girona** (1hr., 21 per day 5:47am-10:35pm, 550ptas); and **Barcelona** (2¾hr., 12 per day 5:47am-10:35pm, 13000-2500ptas) via every town with a station in western Cataluña and Collioure, France. The **tourist office**, Paseo Lluís Companys, overlooks the beach. (☎ 972 12 51 61. Open Apr.-June 15 M-Sa 9:30am-1pm and 3-5pm, Su 9:30am-2pm; June 16-Sept. M-Sa 9:30am-2pm and 3-8pm, Su 9:30am-2pm). **Store luggage** at the train station for 600ptas. **Banco Central Hispano**, C. Mercal, 13, on the street from the train station, **exchanges currency** at somewhat unfavorable rates and has an **ATM**. (☎ 972 12 51 61. Open Oct.-Mar. M-F 8:30am-2:30pm, Sa 8:30am-1pm; Apr.-Sept.30 M-F 8:30am-2:30pm.) Other services include: **emergency** (☎ 629 43 52 23); **police** (☎ 972 39 00 44), in the town hall, at the end of Pg. Sardanes near the end of the beach, and the **post office**, Pg. Enric Granades, 10. (☎ 972 39 01 75. Open M-F 8am-2pm, Sa noon-1pm.) The **postal code** is 17497. **Hostal Juventus**, Av. Barcelona, 3, has simple rooms with sinks and recently-renovated shared bathrooms. From the train station, head straight down to the water, follow Pg. Sardana for one block, and take the last right. (☎ 972 39 02 41. Sept.-July singles 2000ptas; doubles 4000ptas; triples 6000ptas. Aug. 2500, 4500 and 6500ptas respectively.) Buy fresh fruits, vegetables, meat, and fish at **Mercat Municipal**, Passeig d'enric Granados, 1 (open daily 8am-1pm and 5pm-7pm).

CATALAN PYRENEES

While Barcelona and the Costa Brava attract beach-goers and city-dwellers in droves, Cataluña's portion of the Pyrenees draws a different kind of tourist. Hikers and high-brow skiers, most from Spain and France, come for the highly developed ski resorts and some of Spain's wildest mountain scenery, while history and architecture buffs eagerly explore the tranquil mountain towns and well-preserved Romanesque buildings. Early June to late September is the best time to visit the

Pyrenees for trekking; if earlier than that, avalanches are a potential danger; later, it can get prohibitively cold. Tourist offices distribute pamphlets with information on scenic areas and outdoor activities. Skiers will find the *Snow in Catalonia* or *Ski España* guides most useful, and the website www.pirineo.com is a fantastic general planning resource (for skiing and hiking both) for those who can speak Spanish. The Pyrenees are best explored with a car, as public transportation links are few and far between. Either way, entry from the east begins with Ripoll.

RIPOLL

Although the sleepy town of Ripoll (pop. 11,000) may be trapped in a permanent time-warp (don't expect to see too many up-and-coming commercial establishments) it continues to attract visitors in search of Spain's Romanesque architectural legacy; the elaborately carved portal of the **Monasterio de Santa María** is one of the most famous in all of Spain. Ripoll also serves as a convenient base for excursions to the nearby town of **Sant Joan de las Abadesses.**

🚆 **PRACTICAL INFORMATION. RENFE,** Pl. Mova, 1 (☎ 972 70 06 44), runs **trains** to **Puigcerdà** (1hr., 6 per day 8:56am-7:03pm, 400ptas) and **Barcelona** (1½hr., 5-12 per day 6:32am-8:04pm, 775ptas). The bus station next door sends **Teisa buses** (☎ 972 20 48 68) to: **Sant Joan de las Abadesses** (15min., 4 per day, 250ptas); **Barcelona** (4hr., 1 per day, 1700ptas); **Girona** (2hr., 6 per day, 1000ptas), via **Olat**. The **tourist office**, next to the monastery on Pl. Abat Oliba, gives out mediocre maps. (☎ 972 70 23 51. Open M-Su 9:30am-1:30pm and 4-7pm.) The **Banco Central Hispano** is on Pl. Sant Eudald, off Pl. Gran. (Open Oct.-Mar. M-F 8:30am-2:30pm and Sa 8:30am-1pm; Apr.-Sept. M-F 8:30am-2:30pm.) Other services include: **emergency** (☎ 112); **police,** Pl. Ajuntament, 3 (☎ 972 70 06 00); and the **post office,** C. d'Estacio, facing the tree-lined park. (☎ 972 70 07 60. Open M-F 8:30am-2:30pm, Sa 9:30am-1pm.) The **postal code** is 17500. Connect to the **Internet** at **Xarxtel,** Pl. d'Espanya, 10, a computer-electronics store that charges customers for use of their network connection. Alternatively, the **public library,** C. de les Vinyes, 6, offers free use of their computers. (Open M, Tu, Th, and F 4-8:30pm, W 9am-1:30pm, and Sa 10am-1:30pm.)

📷 **ACCOMMODATIONS AND FOOD.** For those in search of a place to sleep, the luxurious **Fonda La Paula,** C. Berenfuer, 4, on Pl. Abat Oliba alongside the tourist office, has big cream-colored rooms with comfortable beds, TVs, lots of light, and spacious, tiled bathrooms. (☎ 972 70 00 11. Singles 3100ptas; doubles 5000ptas. IVA not included. Visa.) Restaurants surround Pl. Gran. Follow C. Bisbe Morgades and take a right before the river on C. Mossen; the plaza is to the left. **Restaurante La Perla,** Pl. Gran, 4, serves regional meat and fish entrees (600-1400ptas) from a multilingual menu. (☎ 972 70 00 01. Open M-Sa 1-5pm and 8pm-midnight, Su 1-5pm. V, MC.) Stock up on **groceries** at the super-big supermarket, **Champion,** C. Progress, 33-37. (☎ 972 70 26 32. Open M-Th 8:30am-2pm and 4:30-9pm, F-Sa 8:30am-9:30pm, Su 10am-2pm. V, MC, AmEx.)

🏛 **SIGHTS.** Almost everyone who comes to Ripoll comes to see the incredibly intricate 11th-century portal of the ▣**Monasterio de Santa María.** To reach the monastery, take a left on C. Progrés from the train and bus stations, then follow it until it merges with C. Estació. Take the first left after the "metal dancers" (the colorful modern statues) onto Pont d'Olot, cross the river, and continue straight on C. Bisbe Morgades to the Pl. Ayuntament and Pl. Abat Oliba. Founded in AD 879 by Count Guifré el Pelú (Wilfred the Hairy), the Santa Maria monastery was once the most powerful in all of Cataluña. The curved doorway, nicknamed the "Stone Bible," depicts survival scenes from the Old and New Testaments as well as a hierarchy of the cosmos and a 12-month calendar. Explanatory panels (in Catalan) attempt to decode the doorway. Adjoining it is a beautiful two-story Romanesque and Gothic **cloister.** (Church open daily 8am-1pm and 3-8pm. Free. Cloister open 10am-1pm and 3-7pm. 100ptas.)

> **ISN'T IT ROMANESQUE?** Romanesque castles, churches, and monasteries are everywhere in the Pyrenees. The style appeared after the breakup of the Carolingian Empire in the late 10th century and dominated Europe until the end of the 13th century. Romanesque architecture mixes Roman building traditions (such as vaulted roofs) with newer techniques (such as massive masonry to uphold barrel vaults). The buildings are characterized by their rounded arched doors and windows coupled with modest (compared to Gothic) heights. Benedictine monks and the Knights Templar hired builders to spread Romanesque influence far and wide, making it the first truly pan-European architectural style. The increasing popularity of the Camino de Santiago contributed further to the propagation of the style.

DAYTRIP FROM RIPOLL: ST. JOAN DE LAS ABADESSES (15MIN.)

TEISA buses (☎ 972 74 02 95) connect Sant Joan to Ripoll (15min., 5-7 per day, 250ptas).

Wilfred the Hairy was nothing if not an equal-opportunity employer. After founding Ripoll's first monastery, he went on to endow a convent 10km away, to which he appointed his daughter Emma as the first abbess in 887. Sant Joan de las Abadesses (pop. 3700) developed around the nuns, but unfortunately some of The Hairy's successors were not so keen on female independence; their community was ousted in the 11th century and it took 100 years before anyone was allowed to move back. The Augustinians who eventually took over turned the convent into a monastery. Today it contains a Romanesque **church** with the **Santíssim Misteri,** a 13th-century seven-piece colored sculpture. One piece depicts Christ's removal from the cross; on Christ's forehead is a piece of Holy Bread that has been preserved for 700 years. (Open daily Mar.-Apr. and Oct. 10am-2pm and 4-6pm; May-June and Sept. 10am-2pm and 4-7pm; July-Aug. 10am-7pm; Nov.-Feb. M-Sa 10am-2pm, Su 10am-2pm and 4-6pm. 200ptas, includes the attached museum.) The **tourist office**, Pl. l'Abadia, 9, is next door to the monastery alongside a lovely 15th-century cloister. (☎ 972 72 05 99. Open M-F 10am-2pm and 4-7pm.)

NÚRIA

Núria, a family-oriented modern resort complex in a small valley near the French border, is best known for its vista-filled hiking trails. The surrounding mountains are inaccessible by train or car; for centuries, only the pious and infertile (see **Our Virgin of Fertility Drugs,** p. 360) made it through the high passes to the Santuario de Sant Gil. In 1931, however, the valley installed a second-hand cable car, the *Cremallera* (Zipper), to make Núria a major ski resort. As bigger, better ski stations appeared, the resort lost its popularity, but in recent years it has been revived, offering right-at-your-doorstep hiking, skiing, archery, horseback-riding, mini-golf, and even canoeing and boating on an artificial lake. The most popular **hikes** climb to the snow-capped peaks of **Puigmal** (2913m; 5-6hr.) and **Eina** (around 1000m; 3hr.). Less ambitious trekkers can follow the path to neighboring **Queralbs** (2-3hr.), which passes alongside waterfalls and gorges carpeted with wildflowers, but they should be warned that the way back up to Núria from Queralbs is significantly more challenging than the way down. In winter, 10 **ski trails** offer slopes ranging from *molt facil* (very easy) to *molt difícil* (very difficult or expert). Call ☎ 972 73 20 20 or go to www.valldenuria.com for further details on available activities.

To get to Núria and the surrounding slopes, take a train, bus, or car from Ripoll and stop in the tiny villages of **Ribes de Freser** or **Queralbs,** past which vehicles cannot continue. Catch the *Cremallara* for the final 1000m through virgin mountainpasses spotted with stubborn sheep, goats, and pine trees. (☎ 972 73 20 20. 45min. ride from Ribes de Freser, 20min. from Queralbs; 6-11 per day depending on the season; round-trip 1950ptas; closed Nov.) If you want to spend the night, a cable car (included in the price of a *Cremallera* ticket) whisks passengers straight to **Alberg de Joventut Pic de l'Aliga (HI),** a chalet-type hostel complete with roaming cows, a full-service bar, and maps of the surrounding peaks. The alternative route is an arduous 20-minute climb. (☎ 972 73 20 48, reservations ☎ 93 483 83 63. Breakfast included. Reservations recommended. Dorms 2250ptas, over 25 2800ptas.) The **Bar Finistrelles,** downstairs from the souvenir store in the main complex, sells sandwiches (500ptas) and entrees (1000ptas). The complex also offers other services, including **ski rentals, ATMS, telephones,** and **lockers** (300ptas).

If you find the shiny artificiality of Núria a little spooky, escape to the more honest mountain village of **Queralbs** (pop. 80 in winter, 500 in summer) for the sublime views from beside Queralbs' medieval rubble or the lovely 10th-century Romanesque church. There's one official *pensión* in town, and it's worth a visit. **Hostal L'Avet,** C. Mayor, 21, captures the warmth and simplicity of a rural lodge without skimping on the comfort. (☎ 972 72 73 77. Doubles with bath, breakfast and dinner 5000ptas.) **Cans Constans,** just off the main road at the entrance to Queralbs, rents four-person apartments with fireplaces. (☎ 972 72 70 13. 6000ptas.) The *Cremallera* stops in Queralbs on its way between Ribes and Núria.

PUIGCERDÀ

A challenge for foreign tongues, the town of Puigcerdà (pop. 7000; Pwee-chair-DAH) itself almost isn't worth the pronunciation effort. Its view of the valley is undeniably beautiful, however, and it can serve as a particularly cheap base for hiking, biking, or skiing the surrounding hillsides. Puigcerdà is perhaps best known for appearing in the 1993 *Guinness Book of World Records* for the world's longest *butifarra* (sausage), a Freudian nightmare measuring 5200m.

▣ TRANSPORTATION. RENFE trains (☎ 972 88 01 65) run to: **La Molina** (20min., 6 per day 6:33am-6:50pm, 350ptas); **Núria** (6 per day, round-trip train and *Cremallera* 2550ptas); **Ripoll** (1¼hr., 6 per day, 400ptas); **Barcelona** (3hr., 6 per day, 1100ptas). **Alsina Graells buses** (☎ 973 35 00 20) run to **La Seu d'Urgell** (1hr., 6 per day, 580ptas) and **Barcelona** (3hr., 1-4 per day, 1758ptas). From **La Seu** there is passage to **Andorra.** Buses depart in front of the train station and from Pl. Barcelona; purchase tickets on board. See the schedule in Bar Estació, to the right as soon as you walk into the train station. **Taxis** (☎ 972 88 00 11) wait on Pl. Cabrinetty. For **bike rental,** try **Top-Bikes,** Pl. d'Avenes, 21. (☎ 972 88 20 42. Bikes 800ptas per hr., 1500ptas per 4hr., 2500ptas per day. V, MC.)

◪◮ ORIENTATION AND PRACTICAL INFORMATION. Puigcerdà's center is at the top of a hill. **Plaça Ajuntament,** located off the main plaza, is nicknamed *el balcón de Cerdanya,* as it holds a commanding view of the valley and the less picturesque **train station** at the foot of the western slope. Buses stop at the train station and then Pl. Barcelona, where it's best to get off. To reach Pl. Ajuntament from the absolutely inconvenient train station, walk past the stairs in the station's *plaça* until you reach the first real flight of stairs (between 2 buildings). Walk up and turn right at the top; then look for the next set of stairs on your left, just before a sign for C. Hostal del Sol. Climb these to the top and turn left on C. Raval de les Monges, where the final set of stairs winds up to the right. From the *plaça* walk one block on Carrer Alfons I to **Carrer Major,** the principal commercial street. Turn left on C. Major to Pl. Santa María. From Pl. Santa Maria with your back to the bell tower, head out diagonally to the left to Pl. Barcelona.

The **tourist office,** C. Querol, 1, a right turn off Pl. Ajuntament with your back to the view, has friendly English-speaking staff that gives out good maps and helpful lodging, entertainment, and daytrip listings. (☎/fax 972 88 05 42. Open July-Sept. 15 M-Sa 9am-2pm and 3-8pm, Su 9am-2pm; Sept. 16-June Tu-F 10am-1pm and 4-7pm, Sa 10am-1:30pm and 4:30-8pm, Su 10am-2pm.) **Banco Central Hispano** is located on Pl. Cabrinetty. (Oct.-Mar. M-F 8:30am-2:30pm, Sa 8:30am-1pm; Apr.-Sept. M-F 8:30am-2:30pm.) Other services include: **emergency** (☎ 091 or 092); **municipal police,** Pl. Ajuntament, 1 (☎ 972 88 19 72); the **Centre Hospitalari** (☎ 972 88 01 50 or 972 88 01 54), in Pl. Santa María; and the **post office,** Av. Coronel Molera, 11, off Pl. Barcelona on the left after a block and a half. (☎ 972 88 08 14. Open M-F 8:30am-2:30pm, Sa 9:30am-1pm.) The **postal code** is 17520.

OUR VIRGIN OF FERTILITY DRUGS The Vall de Núria was just another remote mountain pass when recluse Gil of Nîmes settled here in 700. At some point he carved an elaborate statue of the Virgin and child. Almost 400 years later, that statue, along with Gil's bell and cooking pot, were discovered by a local shepherd, and the hermit's isolated sanctuary became a pilgrimage destination. In a twist of events on which it is best not to speculate, some daredevil pilgrim discovered that her fertility increased if she put her head in the pot while simultaneously ringing the bell. Ever since, barren women have been doing the same—one chime for each desired child. Visitors today can stick their own heads in the progeny-producing pot, but please do not hold *Let's Go* responsible for the consequences.

▟▛▙ ACCOMMODATIONS AND FOOD. Rooms in Puigcerdà come easily, if not cheaply. Most cheaper *pensiones* hole up off Pl. Santa María, in the old town. **Mare de Déu de les Neus (HI),** on Ctra. Font Canaleta, 500m from the La Molina RENFE station and 4km from the slopes, has modern facilities and a beautiful location. In winter a bus goes up to the slopes every 30 minutes. (☎ 972 89 20 12, reservations ☎ 93 483 83 63. Breakfast included. Sheets 350ptas. Reserve in high season. Jan.-Nov. dorms 1900ptas, over 25 2500ptas; Dec. dorms 2250ptas, over 25 2800ptas. V, MC, AmEx.) **Alfonso Habitaciones,** C. Espanya, 5, offers decent, dimly lit rooms with colorful bedspreads. Take a left off C. Alfons I when heading away from the church. (☎ 972 88 02 46. Singles 3000ptas, with bath 6000ptas; doubles with bath and breakfast 7000ptas). **Camping Stel,** 1km from Puigcerdà on the road to Llivia, offers full-service camping with the benefits of a chalet-style restaurant-bar and lounge. (☎ 972 88 23 61. Site with tent and car 2150ptas, 680ptas per person, 220V electricity for 480ptas. Open June 19-Sept. 29 and weekends in winter.)

The neighborhood off C. Alfons I is filled with markets and inexpensive restaurants. For fresh fruits and vegetables try the weekly **market** held on Sundays at both P. 10 d'Abril and the Pl. Cabrinetty. Get **groceries** at **Bonpreu,** C. Colonel Molera, 12, the small **supermarket** diagonally across from the post office. (Open M-Sa 9am-1pm and 5-9pm, Su 10am-2pm, V and MC.) At ▧**Cantina Restaurant Mexicà,** P. Cabrinetty, 9, you can kick back with a margarita and take in some excellent tacos, fajitas, and quesadillas. Friendly staff keep the vibrant, colorful restaurant squeaky clean. (☎ 972 88 16 58. Entrees 500-1300ptas. Open M-Tu and Th-F 7:30pm-midnight, Sa-Su 1-4pm and 7:30-midnight. V, MC, Maestro.)

▨◪ SIGHTS AND ENTERTAINMENT. Puigcerdà calls itself the "capital of snow." **Ski** in your country of choice (Spain, France, or Andorra) at one of 19 ski areas within a 50km radius. The closest and cheapest one on the Spanish side is **La Molina.** The Puigcerdà area is also popular for **biking;** the tourist office has a brochure with 17 potential routes mapped out. Between ski runs and two-wheeled exploration, dash over to the **campanario,** the octagonal bell tower in Pl. Santa María. This 42m high 12th-century tower is all that remains of the **Església de Santa María,** and it is an eerie reminder of the destruction wreaked by the 1936 Civil War. (Open daily July-Sept. 11am-2pm and 4-8pm; Oct.-June weekends only. Free.) **Església de Sant Domènec,** on Pg. 10 d'Abril, contains several Gothic paintings considered to be among the best of their genre (open 9:30am-8pm).

PARC NACIONAL D'AIGÜESTORTES

The full name of Cataluña's only national park is actually Parc Nacional d'Aigüestortes i Estany de Sant Maurici, a reference to the park's distinct halves. In the east lies the valley of the Riu Escrita, with the park's largest lake, the Estany de Sant Maurici; in the west, the wild tumbling of the Riu de Sant Nicolau through its own valley has earned it the nickname "Aigües Tortes" ("Twisted Waters"). On a sunny spring day, the park's snow-capped peaks, wildflower-dusted meadows, and ice-cold glacial lakes (more than 100 of them) are a sight to behold. With over 10,000 hectares to be explored, the park merits at least two days—if you rely on public transportation, it's hard to do it in fewer than three.

Don't rely on the free park maps from the tourist office; it's worth the extra cash to buy a better, more detailed map (1000ptas; also available in area stores). The red *Editorial Alpina* guides, one each for Montardo, Vall de Boí, and Sant Maurici, are also a useful option (800ptas at bookstores). One particularly popular hike to make is the east-west traverse through the park from Espot to Boí (see below for more on the towns themselves). From **Espot** to the **Estany de Sant Maurici** is about 8km (2hr.), and from the lake a path climbs 2½km to the **Portarró d'Espot,** the gateway between the park's two halves and a prime spot for viewing the scenery. From the pass it is nearly 2km to the **Estany Llong** and the **Aigüestortes** themselves (about 3½hr. from the Estany de Sant Maurici). Near the western tip of the Estany Llong lies the park's first *refugio,* also called **Estany Llong.** (☎ 973 69 61 07. Open mid-June to mid-Oct. and winter weekends. 1200ptas per person, under 18 800ptas.) Finally, to get to the western park entrance from the Estany Llong is 3.5km, and to **Boí** itself another 6½km, a total of three hours from the lake to town. The entire hike takes around nine hours but can be shortened by taking a jeep from Espot to the Sant Maurici lake or a taxi from the western entrance to Boí.

For more detailed hiking information, contact the park tourist offices (in Espot ☎ 973 62 40 36; in Boí ☎ 973 69 61 89; general info ☎ 973 69 40 00). The park's five *refugios* (about 2000ptas per person) and *Casas de Pagés* (lodging in private homes) are good accommodation options for those planning multi-day treks. The mountains are deceptively placid from afar, but the unpredictable weather can be dangerous, especially in winter. Also, though the main trails are clearly marked, it is easy to get lost should one stray into the wild mountainsides.

ESPOT AND ESTANY DE SANT MAURICI

The official gateway to the eastern half of the park, and the best way to enter if coming from the direction of Barcelona, is the quiet little town of **Espot.** Espot is actually a good 4.5km from the entrance proper, but the walk to the park entrance is quite scenic. Additionally, a **jeep service** runs from Espot to the **Estany Sant Maurici** (round-trip 600ptas) and to **Amitges** (round-trip 2200ptas) a northern point in the park close to the best and biggest **refugio.** (☎ 933 15 23 11 or 933 18 15 05. Open Feb. 13-28 and June 12-Sept. 26; call ahead.) Unfortunately for those relying on public transportation, the **Alsina Graells bus** (☎ 973 26 85 00 or 93 265 68 66) from Barcelona—the only mass transit in the area—only comes within 7km of Espot, on Highway C-147 at the La Torrassa crossing (3hr., M-Sa 1:30pm, 3000ptas). The jeep service covers the last stretch for a fee. (☎ 973 62 41 05. 1000ptas to Espot. Jeeps seat 7-8.) The **park information office,** on Espot's main road (on the right as you enter town), provides good brochures and advice. (☎ 973 62 40 36. Open daily 9am-1pm and 3:30-6:45pm.) In a **medical emergency** call ☎ 973 62 10 05.

Many local residences take in travelers; inquire at the tourist office. **Residència Felip** provides lovely rooms with lace curtains and private baths. Cross the main bridge, follow the road two blocks, and then turn left. (☎ 973 62 40 93. Breakfast 500ptas. Sept.-June singles 3000ptas; doubles 4000ptas. July-Aug. singles 4000ptas; doubles 5000ptas.) **Càmping la Mola** (☎ 973 62 40 24) and **Càmping Sol i Neu** (☎ 973 62 40 01), both on the way to Espot, have good facilities and pools. (Both open June-Sept. and *Semana Santa.* 625ptas per person, per tent, and per car.)

AIGÜESTORTES AND VALL DE BOÍ

The village of Boí is the best place from which to explore the western half of the park. Public transportation from the east to Boí is difficult but possible through Vielha, and from Boí's main *plaça* it is an easy taxi ride to the park. (☎ 973 69 60 36. 500ptas per person.) Boí's helpful **park information office** is near the bus stop on the *plaça.* (☎ 973 69 61 89. Open daily 9am-1pm and 3:30-6:45pm.) The **Guardia Civil** can be reached at ☎ 973 69 00 06. In an **emergency** call ☎ 973 69 11 59.

Despite the nearby ski resort in **Taüll,** Boí retains a pastoral feel. Low arches and cobblestone streets surround several family-run accommodations, including **Casa Guasch,** which lets simple rooms. Exit the plaza through the stone arch, turn right through the next arch, then bear left and turn left again where the street ends; the entrance is on the left. (☎ 973 69 60 42. Doubles 3000ptas. Open Dec.-Mar.)

NORTHEASTERN SPAIN

VAL D'ARAN

Some of the Catalan Pyrenees's most dazzling peaks cluster around green Val d'Aran, Cataluña's northernmost valley. Val d'Aran's main river flows into France and is hemmed in tightly by the highest peaks in the eastern range; consequently, the area's original native language is not Catalan but Aranese, a dialect close to *langue d'oc*, the medieval Romance language spoken in southern France. Today, modern transportation and the tourist industry have made substantial inroads into the valley's unique isolation, but it is still well worth exploring.

BAQUIERA-BERET

Baquiera-Beret is Spain's most chic ski resort; after all, the Spanish royal family's favorite slopes are here. Girls, it's probably as good a place as any to have a chance encounter with the very eligible Prince Felipe (see **SWM Seeking,** below). Currently, about 80 alpine trails and a few cross-country ones wind down the surrounding peaks. Although budget accommodations have disappeared at the ski station itself, the town of Salardú, a few kilometers away, has an enormous youth hostel, the **Albergue Era Garona (HI).** The hostel is accessible in the high season by shuttle bus from Vielha and offers dorms of four and six beds, as well as bike and ski rentals through the reception desk. (☎ 973 64 52 71, reservations ☎ 934 83 83 63. Breakfast included. Sheets 350ptas. July-Aug. and winter weekends dorms 1900ptas, over 25 2250ptas; rest of the year dorms 1775ptas, over 25 1900ptas.) The town of Vielha is only 12km from Bacquiera-Beret, and the two are connected by a shuttle bus in July and August. Check at the tourist office for schedules. For skiing information and reservations, contact the **Oficeria de Baquiera-Beret** (☎ 973 64 44 55; fax 973 64 44 88) or the tourist office in Vielha (☎ 973 64 01 10).

SWM SEEKING... Tall, dark, handsome, rich, famous, powerful, and searching for life partner. Enjoys water sports (competed on the Olympic sailing team). Educated at Georgetown. Looking for that special someone—attractive, charismatic, and preferably of noble lineage—to share interests and raise a family. His name is Felipe, the Prince of Asturias and heir to the Spanish throne. With his 30th birthday just behind him and his two elder sisters recently married, all eyes are on Felipe. Whom will he choose to be his queen when he takes over one of Europe's few powerful monarchies? The competition is fierce. Lovely ladies from wealthy families are stalking the streets of Madrid and the slopes of the Val d'Aran, but so far there are no front-runners. Cross your fingers and pack something nice—you could be the next queen of Spain.

VIELHA

The biggest town in the Val d'Aran, Vielha (pop. 3500) combines the charm of its small old quarter with the bustling activity of the main commercial thoroughfare. From its prime location, Vielha welcomes hikers and skiers to its lively streets with every sort of service the outdoorsy-type might desire.

🔁 **PRACTICAL INFORMATION. Alsina Graells** (☎ 639 38 03 73 or 973 26 85 00) runs buses from Vielha to **Barcelona** (5½hr., 2 per day, 3325ptas). For a **taxi** call ☎ 973 64 01 95. The **tourist office,** C. Sarriulèra, 6, is one block upriver from the *plaça;* the staff helps hikers, skiers, and Romanesque-seekers alike. (☎ 973 64 01 10; fax 973 64 05 37. Open July-Sept. 15 daily 10am-1pm and 4:30-7:30pm; Sept. 16-June M-Sa 10am-1pm and 4:30-7:30pm.) **ATMs** pepper Av. Castiéro, which intersects the river. Services include: **emergency** (☎ 091 or 092); the **Guardia Civil** (☎ 973 64 00 05); and the **post office,** C. Sarviulèra, 2, by the tourist office. (☎ 973 64 09 12. Open M-F 8:30am-2:30pm, Sa 9:30am-1pm.) The **postal code** is 25530. Go to **CCV Informática,** Edificio Val D'Aran, second floor, for **Internet access.** (☎ 973 64 12 88. 500ptas per 30min., 1000ptas per hr. Open M-Sa 9:30am-1:30pm and 4:30-8pm.)

⌐⌐ ACCOMMODATIONS AND FOOD. Several inexpensive *pensiones* fill the end of Camin Reiau, off Pg. Libertat (which intersects Av. Casteiro at Pl. Sant Antoni). The best of the bunch is **Casa Vicenta**, C. Reiau, 3, an up-scale place with cream-colored walls, great mattresses and modern furnishings. (☎ 973 64 08 19. Sept.-June singles 2500ptas; doubles 4000ptas. July-Aug. singles 3000ptas; doubles 4500ptas.) Enjoy every variety of tortilla under the sun at the warm and inviting **Restaurant Basteret,** C. Mayor 6B. Friendly staff and a well-priced daily *menú* (1300ptas) make this a great spot. (☎ 973 64 07 14. Open daily July-Sept. 1-3:30pm and 8-10:30pm; Oct.-June M-Sa 1-3:30pm and 8-10:30pm. V, MC.)

◉♪ SIGHTS AND ENTERTAINMENT. The **Iglesia de San Miguel**, a simple 12th-century Romanesque church, houses the intricate *Crist de Mijaran.* (Open daily 11am-8pm.) Also in Vielha is the **Museu de Val d'Aran,** on C. Mayor, with an ethno-graphic collection that attempts to shed light on Aranese culture. (☎ 973 64 18 15. Open Tu-F 5-8pm, Sa 10am-1pm and 5-8pm, Su 10am-1pm. 200ptas.) Vielha is also, and above all, a good base for all sorts of outdoor activities. **Camins,** Av. Pas d'Arro, 5, in the shopping gallery, is a good place to start planning. Staff there can answer questions, organize treks into the Aigüestortes National Park and the sur-rounding mountains (starting at 2500ptas), lead **rafting** and **horseback trips,** rent **mountain bikes** (half-day 2200ptas and full-day 2900ptas), and even teach you how to **snowboard,** in conjunction with the **Escola Snowboard Val d'Aran** (☎ 973 64 24 44).

ANDORRA

Welcome to Andorra, the forgotten European country. In this small Pyrenean nation the serenity of the stunning landscapes vie for attention with the energy of its neon-lit capital. Pragmatists say Andorra (pop. 65,000; 464 sq. km) offers the best of both worlds, though some may beg to differ. Known officially as Principat d'Andorra (Principality of Andorra), it is ruled by two co-princes—the French president and the Bishop of Urgell—and a popularly elected Consell General who represents the seven parishes and holds the bulk of the power.

According to legend, Charlemagne founded Andorra in 784 as a reward to the valley's inhabitants for having led his army against the Moors. For the next 12 centuries, Andorra played the rope in a game of tug-o'-war between the Spanish Counts of Urgell, the Church of Urgell, and the French King. Not until 1990 did Andorra create a commission to draft a democratic constitution, adopted on March 14, 1993. Andorra today is far less progressive than other western European nations. In the 1993 election, only the 10,000 native Andorrans (out of 65,000 total inhabitants) were granted the vote; women have had suffrage only since 1970.

Sandwiched between France and Spain, Andorra struggles to assert its identity. Its citizens are comfortably trilingual, although Catalan is the official language. The country has no currency of its own; all establishments are required to accept both *pesetas* and *francs*, although *pesetas* are more prevalent. In fact, currency seems to flow like water, as the absence of a sales tax (and the abundance of duty-free shops) draws consumers from all over Europe. With Andorran towns spaced mere minutes apart and an extensive local bus system, a single day can include wading through aisles of duty-free perfume, hiking through a pine-scented valley, eating in an informal country restaurant, and relaxing in a luxury spa.

⌨ TRANSPORTATION

The only way to get to Andorra is by car or bus, as the country has no airport or train station. Visitors must show a valid passport or EU identity card to enter the country. All traffic from France must come through the town of Pas de la Casa; the gateway to Spain is La Seu d'Urgell. **Andor-Inter/Samar buses** (in Madrid ☎ 91 468 41 90; in Toulouse ☎ 61 58 14 53; in Andorra ☎ 82 62 89) run to **Madrid** (9hr.; M, Th, and Su; 4900ptas). **Alsina Graells** (☎ 82 73 79) runs to **Barcelona** (4hr., 6-7 per day, 2800ptas), as does **Eurolines** (☎ 82 11 38; 3hr., 4 per day 6:15am-8:15pm, 2850ptas). All buses arrive at and depart from **Estació d'Autobusos**, on C. Bonaventura Riberaygua. To get to the station from Pl. Princep Benlloch, follow Av. Meritxell past the tourist office to the other side of the river. Make an immediate right after crossing the river and then an immediate left. Take the fourth right and go straight for four to five blocks (20min.). To go anywhere in Spain other than Madrid and Barcelona, you must first go to **La Seu d'Urgell** on **La Hispano-Andorra** buses (☎ 82 13 72; 30min.), 5-7 buses per day, 340ptas), which leave from Av. Meritxell, 11. From La Seu, Alsina Graells buses (☎ 82 73 79 in Andorra) continue into Spain via **Puigcerdà** (1hr., 2 per day, 570ptas) and **Lérida** (2½hr., 2 per day, 1650ptas).

Driving in Andorra la Vella is a nightmare. The main road turns into a parking lot, and drivers will find a map totally useless—it's best to follow signs and desert the car as soon as possible in one of the city's free parking lots. The first lot on the road from Spain is at the intersection of C. Moll and C. Prat de la Creu, across from the Holiday Inn. Efficient intercity buses connect the villages along the three major highways that converge in Andorra la Vella. The entire country is navigable in an hour or two via public transportation; most towns are only 10 minutes apart. Bus rides cost between 100 and 300ptas. All buses make every stop in the city, so don't worry about finding the right bus—just pay attention to the direction sign in the front window. The tourist office has schedules, and bus stops are easy to find.

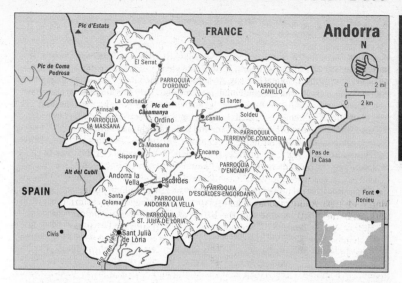

ANDORRA LA VELLA

Andorra la Vella (pop. 20,000), the country's capital, is little more than a narrow, cluttered road flanked by shop after duty-free shop and sprinkled with American fast-food chains. This city is anything but *vella* (old), as most of the old buildings have been upstaged by shiny new electronics and sporting goods stores. After doing a little shopping, you're best off escaping to the countryside.

ORIENTATION AND PRACTICAL INFORMATION. Avinguda Meritxell, the main artery, runs through the city, beginning at Pl. Princep Benlloch in the heart of the tiny **barri antic** (old quarter) and continuing across the Riu Valira to become the main highway to parishes northeast of the capital. West of Pl. Princep Benlloch (to the right when facing the Eglésia de Sant'Esteve) Av. Meritxell becomes **Avinguida Princep Belloch.** The **tourist office** is on Av. Doctor Villanova. From the bus stop on Av. Princep Benlloch, continue east (away from Spain) past the *plaça* on your left, and take C. Dr. Villanova, which curves to the right. The office is on the left before the hill. Multilingual staff has tons of brochures—the free *Sports Activities* and the *Hotels i Restaurants* guides are especially useful. (☎ 82 02 14; fax 82 58 23. Open July-Sept. M-F 9am-9pm, Sa 9am-1pm and 3-7pm and Su 10am-1pm; Oct.-June M-Sa 10am-1pm and 3-7pm, Su 10am-1pm.) Exchange currency at **Banc Internacional,** Av. Meritxell, 32. (☎ 88 47 05. 500ptas commission. 600ptas to exchange American traveler's checks. Open M-F 9am-1pm and 3-7pm, Sa 9am-noon.) In an **emergency** call ☎ 116 or 110 or the **police,** C. Prat de la Creu, 16 (☎ 87 20 00). For **weather and ski conditions** in Spanish, call ☎ 84 88 52. For a **taxi** call ☎ 86 10 05. To make a phone call, buy an STA *teletarjeta* (telecard) at the tourist office or post office (500ptas minimum); collect calls are not possible from Andorra. For directory assistance dial ☎ 111 or 119 (international). The **country code** is **376.** The **post office,** Carrer Joan Margell, 10, is across the river from Pl. Princep Benlloch. (☎ 82 02 57. **Lista de Correos** upstairs. Open M-F 8:30am-2:30pm, Sa 9:30am-1pm.) Check your **email** at **Baviera,** Pl. Rotunda, across from the tourist office. (☎ 81 26 12. 600ptas for 30min. 1100ptas per hr. Open daily 8:30am-1am.)

NORTHEASTERN SPAIN

⌂▢ ACCOMMODATIONS AND FOOD. Pensió La Rosa, Antic Carrer Major, 18, off Av. Princep Benlloch, has friendly owners and immaculate rooms. (☎ 82 18 10. Breakfast 400ptas. Singles 2000ptas; doubles 3500ptas.) **Hotel Andorra,** Av. Princep Benlloch, 24, offers well-furnished rooms, all with individual bath and good closet space. (☎ 82 09 97. Reception in downstairs cafe. Breakfast 350ptas. Singles 2500ptas; doubles 3500ptas. Closed mid-Jan. to mid-Feb.) **Camping Valira,** Av. Salou, behind the **Estadi Comunal d'Andorra la Vella,** boasts video games, hot showers, shade, and an indoor pool. (☎ 82 23 84. 575ptas per person, per tent, and per car. Call ahead.) Check out one of the amazing three-story supermarkets in nearby Santa Coloma (you can't miss them) or the **Grans Magatzems Pyrénées,** Av. Meritxell, 11, the country's biggest department store, which has an entire aisle dedicated to chocolate bars alone. (Open Sept.-July M-F 9:30am-8pm, Sa 9:30am-9pm, Su 9:30am-7pm; Aug. and holidays M-Sa 9:30am-9pm and Su 9:30am-7pm.)

▟ EXCURSIONS. The best thing to do in Andorra la Vella is drop your bags in a hostel and get out. The **Caldea-Spa,** in nearby **Escaldes-Engordany,** is the largest in all of Europe, with luxurious treatments and prices to match. (☎ 80 09 95. Open daily 10am-11pm. 2950ptas for 3hr., plus fees for each service.) The parish of **Ordino** bucks the Andorran trend toward "bigger is better" with its quirky, mega-small **▓Microminiature Museum,** Edifici Coma. Using intense yogic breathing, Nikolai Siadristy has created amazingly small objects, including the tiniest inscription ever made. (☎ 83 83 38. Open Tu-Sa 9:30am-1:30pm and 3:30-7pm, Su 9:30am-1:30pm. 300ptas.) The town of **Canillo** boasts the colossal **Palau de Gel D'Andorra,** an eclectic recreational complex almost as monumental as the mountains themselves. Available facilities include a swimming pool, ice-skating rink ("ice disco" at night), and squash courts, all open to the public and accessible with individual tickets. In winter, you can swim outdoors in the palace's heated pool while snow melts around its edges. (☎ 85 15 15. "Palace" open daily 10am-10pm; each facility has its own hours. 700ptas each or 1400ptas for all in one day. Equipment rental 400ptas.)

▟ HIKING AND THE OUTDOORS. An extensive network of hiking trails traverses Andorra, and like most everything else in the country, all the routes are close together. The free, multilingual, and extremely helpful tourist office brochure *Sports Activities* includes 52 suggested itineraries, potential routes, and bike rental locations, as well as cabin and refuge locations within the principality. The tourist office in Ordino also has area skiing and hiking brochures. (☎ 73 70 80. Open July-Aug. M-Sa 8am-7pm, Su 9am-5pm; Sept.-June M-Sa 9am-1pm and 3-7pm, Su 9am-1pm.) La Massana is home to Andorra's tallest peak, **Pic Alt de la Coma Pedrosa** (2946m). For organized hiking trips, try the **La Rabassa Sports and Nature Center** (☎ 84 43 45), in the parish of Sant Juliàde Lòria, in the southwest corner of Andorra. In addition to *refugio*-style accommodations, the center has mountain biking, guided hikes, horseback riding, archery, and other field sports.

▟ SKIING. In the winter, Andorra offers skiing opportunities galore. Four outstanding resorts within its boundaries all attract masses of skiers. **Pal** (☎ 73 70 00; fax 83 59 04), 10km from La Massana, is one of the biggest. Four buses leave for Pal from La Massana daily, the last returning at 5pm (255ptas). Seven buses run daily from La Massana to nearby **Arinsal** (☎ 83 58 22); the last one returns at 7:45pm (160ptas). On the French border, **Pas de la Casa Grau Roig** (☎ 85 69 92) boasts 600 hectares of skiable land, with 48 trails for all levels of ability. The resort has 27 lifts, lessons, two medical centers, and night skiing. **Soldeu-El Tarter** (☎ 89 05 01) occupies 840 hectares of skiable area between Andorra la Vella and Pas de la Casa. **Free buses** pick up skiers from their hotels in Canillo. Andorra's tourist office publishes a winter edition of *Andorra: The Pyrenean Country,* a guide to the ski resorts. **SKI Andorra** (☎ 86 43 89) or the tourist offices can also answer questions.

ARAGÓN

A striking collage of semi-deserts and lush mountain peaks, Aragón's landscape reflects the influence of both Mediterranean and Continental climates. In the south, a sun-baked assemblage of hardworking towns and flaxen plains, scattered with fine examples of ornate Mudéjar architecture, gives way to prosperous and industrious Zaragoza, Aragón's capital and the fifth largest city in Spain. In the north, the stunning snow-capped peaks of the Pyrenees peer down on tiny medieval towns and their remarkable Romanesque architecture. The country's biggest river, the Ebro, draws a watery dividing line between the vastly different terrains.

Aragón's harsh climate, coupled with the region's strategic location, has produced a predominantly martial culture. Established as a kingdom in 1035 and united with enterprising Cataluña in 1137, Aragón forged a far-flung Mediterranean empire that brought Roussillon, Valencia, Murcia, the Balearic Islands, Naples, Sicily, and even the Duchy of Athens under its sway. The region retained the privileges of internal government even after its union with Castilla in 1469, and it held those privileges until Felipe II marched into Zaragoza in 1591 and brought the region to its knees. Economic decline followed political humiliation; as eyes turned to the New World, people (and capital) moved to the coast in search of riches. Today, Aragón is back on its feet economically, while still remaining relatively tourist-free. Only some areas of the rural Pyrenees and the Parque Nacional Ordesa y Monte Perdido, with its dramatic peaks and copious hiking and skiing opportunities, attract many visitors, and even those are mostly urban Spaniards escaping the city heat during July and August.

Aragonese cuisine is as hearty as the people who make it. *Migas de pastor* (bread crumbs fried with ham) and lamb chops are ubiquitous; more surprising treats include *chilindrón* (lamb and chicken stewed with red peppers) and *melocotones al vino* (sweet native peaches steeped in wine). The *Guía de servicios turísticos de Aragón*, available at any tourist office in the province, makes roaming easy, with information on accommodations and tourist offices.

HIGHLIGHTS OF ARAGÓN

Zaragoza's breathtaking **Basílica de Nuestra Señora de Pilar** (see p. 372).

Exploring the **Castillo de Loarre** (see p. 379).

Hiking among the snow-covered peaks of **Parque Nacional de Ordesa** (see p. 381).

A summertime visit to the magical Pyrenean town of **Ansó**, with a warm bed and a hearty meal at a *casa rural* (see p. 381).

LOCAL FESTIVALS IN ARAGÓN

Every October 12, **Zaragoza** honors *La Virgen Santa del Pilar* with one of the biggest autumn festivals in Spain. The end of June brings the *Fiesta de Santa Gloria* to **Jaca,** and **Tarazona** kicks off the month-long *Foto Festival* in mid-July.

ZARAGOZA

The political and cultural nexus of Aragonese culture, Zaragoza (pop. 603,000) is one of Spain's lesser-known beauties. Firmly conscious of its rich historical and artistic heritages, yet a thoroughly modern city, Zaragoza has somehow achieved harmony between the old and new. Augustus founded the city in 14 BC as a retirement colony for Roman veterans, modestly naming it Caesaraugusta after himself. Eventually shortened to Zaragoza, the city gained everlasting fame years later when the Virgin Mary dropped in for a visit; it has been a pilgrimage site ever since. Centuries later, industrial, not spiritual, vibes drove General Motors to set up shop here, augmenting the already strong manufacturing sector. Zaragoza hums with prosperity, blessed by a beloved patron saint, *Nuestra Señora del Pilar*, and the convenience of low price tags.

⌐ TRANSPORTATION

Airplanes: Airport (☎ 976 34 90 50). Flights to major Spanish and European cities. **Iberia,** C. Canfranc, 22 (☎ 976 23 38 16; reservations ☎ 976 21 82 50). Open M-F 9:30am-2pm and 4-7pm, Sa 9:30am-1:30pm. **Ebrobus,** Pl. Aragón, 10 (☎ 976 32 40 09), off Pl. Paraíso at the beginning of Po. Independencia, runs to the airport (30-45min.; M-F 7-8 per day 6am-9:45pm, Sa 4 per day 6am-5:45pm, Su 5 per day noon-10:50pm; 200ptas). A taxi to the airport costs about 2000ptas.

Trains: Estación Portillo (24hr. ☎ 976 21 11 66), at Av. Anselmo Clavé. Taxi to Pl. Pilar (500ptas), or bus #21 from Po. María Agustín stops at Pl. España. Info booth open daily 8am-9pm. **RENFE office,** C. San Clemente, 11 (☎ 976 28 02 02). From Pl. Paraíso, follow Po. Independencia 4 blocks, then turn right. Open M-F 9am-1:30pm and 4:30-8pm, Sa 9:30am-1pm. To: **Tudela** (45min., 7-15 per day 6:30am-9:05pm, 515ptas); **Logroño** (2¼hr., 4 per day 6:30am-7:30pm, 1450ptas); **Pamplona** (2¼hr., 5 per day 6:30am-

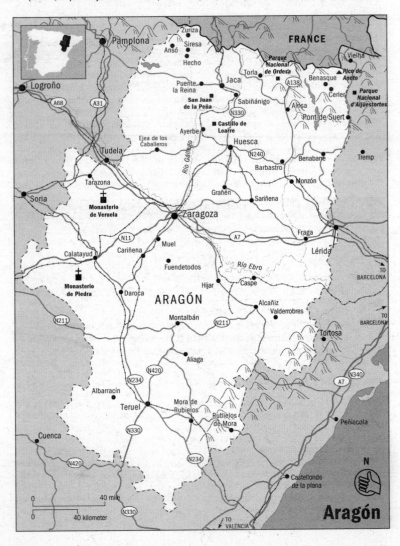

Aragón

Pack the Wallet Guide
and save 25% or more* on calls home to the U.S.

It's lightweight and carries heavy savings of 25% or more* over AT&T USA Direct and MCI WorldPhone rates. So take this YOU wallet guide and carry it wherever you go.

To save with YOU:
- Dial the access number of the country you're in (see reverse)
- Dial 04 or follow the English voice prompts
- Enter your credit card info for easy billing

Service provided by Sprint

Hmm, call home or eat lunch?
With  you can do both.

Nathan Lane for YOU[SM].

No doubt, traveling on a budget is tough. So tear out this wallet guide and keep it with you during your travels. With YOU, calling home from overseas is affordable and easy.

If the wallet guide is missing, call collect 913-624-5336 or visit www.youcallhome.com for YOU country numbers.

7:30pm, 1450ptas); **Jaca** (3hr., 7:15am and 3:20pm, 1405ptas); **Teruel** (3hr., 3 per day 8am-7:14pm, 1405ptas); **Madrid** (3hr., 8 per day 6am-3am 3300ptas); **San Sebastián** (4hr., 1:45pm and 5pm, 2900ptas); **Barcelona** (4hr., 12:20pm and 4:54pm, 3400ptas); and **Valencia** (6hr., 7:50am and 3:40pm, 2525ptas).

Buses: Various bus companies dot the city, each with private terminals.

Agreda Automóvil, Po. María Agustín, 7 (☎ 976 22 93 43). Bus #21 stops in front. From the station, turn right and follow Po. María Agustín to Pl. Paraíso. Info open daily 7:30am-9pm. To: **Soria** (2½hr.; M-Sa 5 per day 7:30am-4:30pm; Su 9am; 1230ptas); **Barcelona** (3½hr., 16-19 per day 1-10:30pm, 1655ptas); and **Madrid** (3½hr., 15-18 per day 1:15pm-10:30pm, 1750ptas). **Second Terminal,** Av. Valencia, 20 (☎ 976 55 45 88). Enter on C. Lérida (bus #38). To: **Daroca** (1½hr., 2-3 per day 7:15am-6:30pm, 720ptas).

La Oscense, Po. María Agustín, 7 (☎ 976 22 93 43). Shares terminal with Agreda Automóvil. To **Jaca** (2¼hr., 3-4 per day 10:55am-9:40pm, 1490ptas).

Therpasa, C. General Sueiro, 22 (☎ 976 22 57 23). From the station, turn left onto C. General Sueiro and follow for 1½ blocks, then turn left onto C. San Ignacio; after 2 blocks, turn right into Pl. Paraíso. To **Tarazona** (1½hr., 5-6 per day 8am-8:30pm, 765ptas).

CONDA, Av. Navarra, 81 (☎ 976 33 33 72). From the station, turn right and follow Av. Navarra, bearing left onto Av. Madrid. Cross the highway on the pedestrian bridge. After 2 blocks, turn right on Po. María Agustín and continue along Po. Pamplona to Pl. Paraíso. Or take bus #25 to Po. Pamplona. To: **Tudela** (1hr., 6 per day 7:15am-8:30pm, 700ptas); **Pamplona** (2hr., 7-8 per day 7:15am-8:30pm, 1660ptas); and **San Sebastián** (3¼hr., 4-5 per day 7:15am-7pm, 2350ptas).

Grupo Autobús Jimenez, C. San Juan Pablo Bonet, 13 (☎ 976 27 61 79). To get to the station, take bus #33 from Pl. España; find the road sign for C. San Juan Pablo Bonet after 2 stops on Po. Sagasta. To **Logroño** (2½hr., 3-7 per day 7am-10pm, 1430ptas) and **Teruel** (3hr., 6-7 per day 7am-10pm, 1340ptas).

Public Transportation: Red **TUZSA buses** (☎ 976 59 27 27; www.tuzsa.es) cover the city (85ptas, 10-ride pass 550ptas, tickets available at any kiosk). Tourist office has a free route map. Bus #21 runs from near the train station to Po. Pamplona, Pl. Paraíso, Pl. Aragón, Pl. España, Pl. Pilar, and up C. San Vincente de Paúl. Bus #33 is more central, going through Po. Sagasta, Pl. Paraíso, Po. Independencia, and Pl. España.

Taxis: Radio-Taxi Aragón (☎ 976 38 38 38). From train station to Pl. Pilar 500ptas.

Car Rental: Avis, Po. Fernando El Católico, 9 (☎ 976 55 50 94). From Pl. Paraíso, take Gran Vía, which becomes Po. Fernando El Católico. 12,686ptas per day. Min. age 23; must have credit card and valid license. Open M-F 8am-1pm and 4-8pm, Sa 8am-1pm.

✦🔢 ORIENTATION AND PRACTICAL INFORMATION

Bordered to the north by the Río Ebro, Zaragoza is laid out like a slightly damaged bicycle wheel. Five spokes radiate from the hub at **Plaza Basilio Paraíso.** Facing the center of the plaza with the IberCaja bank building at your back, the spokes going clockwise are: Po. Sagasta; Gran Vía, which turns into Po. Fernando el Católico; Po. Pamplona, which leads to Po. María Agustín and the **train station;** Po. Independencia, which ends at **Plaza de España** (the entrance to the *casco viejo*); and Po. Constitución. To get to Pl. Paraíso from the train station, start upstairs, bear right down the ramp, and walk across Av. Anselmo Clavé. Head one block down C. General Mayandía and turn right onto Po. María Agustín. Go seven blocks; the street becomes Po. Pamplona and ends at Pl. Paraíso.

The *casco viejo* lies at the end of Po. Independencia and stretches between Pl. España and **Plaza del Pilar,** along the river. Several key museums and sights frame Pl. Pilar, the most central being the grandiose **Basílica de Nuestra Señora del Pilar.** Its blue-and-yellow tiled domes make a good reference point. To reach Pl. Pilar from Pl. Paraíso, walk down Po. Independencia to Pl. España and continue onto C. Don Jaime I (a bit to the right), which runs to the plaza. The user-friendly bus system and city map blow-ups at major intersections make touring easy. The narrow streets to either side of C. Conde de Aranda may be unsafe at night.

Tourist Office: Main Branch (☎ 972 20 12 00 or 902 22 12 12; fax 972 20 06 35), Pl. Pilar, in the black glass cube across from the basílica. Multilingual staff. Request the tourist map, the guide Paseos del Color (thematically organized walking tours), and the *guía de TAPAS.* Open daily 10am-8pm. **Another branch** at the train station. Open M-Sa 11am-2:30pm and 4:30-8pm.

Currency Exchange: Banks line Po. Independencia; **ATMs** are everywhere. **Banco Central Hispano,** Pl. Aragón, 6, has good rates on traveler's checks.

American Express: Viajes Turopa, Po. Sagasta, 47 (☎ 976 38 39 11; fax 976 25 42 44). Enter around the corner , 6 blocks from Pl. Paraíso. Bus #33 from Pl. España stops nearby. Cardholder mail held. Open M-F 9am-1:30pm and 4-7:30pm.

El Corte Inglés: Po. Sagasta, 3 (☎ 976 21 11 21), and a smaller store at Po. Independencia, 11 (☎ 976 23 86 44). **Supermarket, telephones,** and a free map of the city. Open M-Sa 10am-10pm.

Luggage Storage: At the **train station** (small 300ptas, large 400ptas). Open 24hr. At **Agreda Automóvil** bus station, Po. María Agustín, 7 (200ptas). Open daily 8am-10pm. At the other **Agreda Automóvil,** Av. Valencia, 20 (100ptas per piece per day). Open M-F 10am-2:30pm and 4:30-8pm. At **Therpasa** bus station (100ptas). Open M-F 9am-1pm and 4:15-7:30pm, Sa 9am-12:45pm.

English Bookstore: Librería General, Po. Independencia, 22 (☎ 976 22 44 83; fax 976 22 89 48). The big store with the rainbow awning. Large selection of classics. Open June 15-Aug. M-F 9:30am-1:30pm and 4:30-8:30pm, Sa 10am-2pm; Sept.-June 14 M-Sa 9:30am-1:30pm and 4-8:30pm. V, MC, AmEx. Saucy romances and John Grisham novels can be found at **El Corte Inglés,** Po. Independencia, 11, 1st floor (see above).

Laundromat: Lavandería Rossell, C. San Vicente de Paul, 27 (☎ 976 29 90 34). From Pl. España, turn right on C. Coso, go 4 blocks, then head left 4½ blocks. Wash and dry 990ptas per load. Open M-F 8:30am-1:30pm and 5-8pm, Sa 8:30am-1:30pm.

Emergency: ☎ 112. **Police:** Domingo Miral (☎ 091 or 092).

Medical Services: Hospital Miguel Servet, Po. Isabel La Católica, 1 (☎ 976 35 57 00). **Emergency: Ambulatorio Ramón y Cajal,** Po. María Agustín, 12 (☎ 976 43 41 11).

Post Office: Po. Independencia, 33 (☎ 976 22 80 09 or 976 22 01 78), 1 block from Pl. Aragón on the right. **Fax** and **Lista de Correos** (downstairs at Window 26; open M-F 8:30am-2pm). Open M-F 8:30am-8:30pm, Sa 9:30am-2pm. **A branch** next to train station at C. Clavé. Open M-F 8:30am-8:30pm, Sa 9:30am-1pm. **Postal Code:** 50001.

Internet Access: Cybercentro Zaragoza (☎ 976 46 96 10), C. Ramón y Cajal, heading down Av. Cesar Augusto away from the river take a right on Ramón y Cajal and look for the yellow awning. 300ptas for 30min. Open daily 10am-1:30pm and 5-9pm. **El Corte Inglés,** Po. Independencia, 11 (☎ 976 23 86 44), first floor. 500ptas per hr., whether or not you use it all. Open M-Sa 9am-10pm. **Pub Via Sacra,** Arzobispo Domenech, 12 (☎ 976 22 04 73). From Pl. Paraíso, follow Gran Vía for 2 blocks, then a left on Arzobispo Domenech. 400ptas for 30min., 800ptas per hr. Open daily 6pm-3am.

ACCOMMODATIONS

Hostels and *pensiones* pepper the narrow streets of the *casco viejo*, especially within the rectangle bounded by C. Alfonso I, C. Don Jaime I, Pl. España, and Pl. Pilar, and in the area to the right of the train station exit. Be wary the week of October 12, when Zaragoza celebrates the *Fiesta de la Virgen del Pilar*. Make reservations as early as possible and expect to pay as much as double the rates listed below. *Ferias* (trade shows) are held from February through April (www.feriazaragoza.com). The biggest is the agricultural machinery show, FIMA, (Mar. 28-Apr. 1, 2001) when you may have to scour everything within a 100km radius to find a room.

Albergue-Residencia Juvenil Baltasar Gracián (HI), C. Franco y Lopez, 4 (☎ 976 55 15 04). Take bus #22 from the train station, or turn right out of the station onto Av. Clavé, take the 2nd right onto C. Burgos, walk 6 blocks, then turn right onto C. Franco y Lopez. Fifty beds in sparkling rooms of 2, 4, and 8. College dorm during the year. Must call ahead for reservations. HI members only. Breakfast during the school year, 250ptas. Sheets included. Midnight curfew. Dorms 1100ptas, over 25 1500ptas. Cash only.

Hostal Ambos Mundos, Pl. Pilar, 16 (☎ 976 29 97 04; fax 976 29 97 02), at C. Don Jaime I. Comfortable, high-ceilinged rooms with attractive bedspreads, showers, and sinks. French-speaking owner welcomes backpackers. Ask for a room with a balcony overlooking the plaza. Breakfast 350ptas; other meals 1200ptas. Singles 2700ptas; doubles 5000ptas. Cash only.

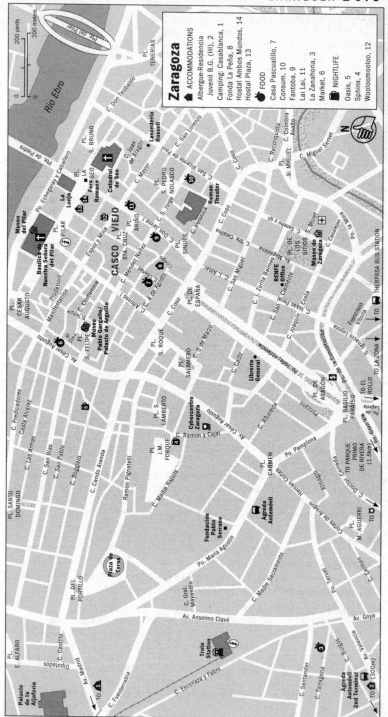

Zaragoza

▲ ACCOMMODATIONS
Albergue-Residencia
Juvenil B.G. (HI), 2
Camping: Casablanca, 1
Fonda La Peña, 8
Hostal Ambos Mundos, 14
Hostal Plaza, 13

🍴 FOOD
Casa Pascualillo, 7
Consum, 10
Fantoba, 9
Lai Lai, 11
La Zanahoria, 3
Market, 6

🎵 NIGHTLIFE
Oasis, 5
Sphinx, 4
Wooloomooloo, 12

Hostal Plaza, Pl. Pilar, 14 (☎ 976 29 48 30 or 976 28 48 39; fax 976 39 94 06). Snug, immaculate rooms are wonderfully decorated, quite comfortable, and have good mattresses. All rooms have a phone, some include TV. English and French spoken. Singles with shower and sink 3900ptas; doubles with bath 5900ptas. V, MC.

Fonda La Peña, C. Cinegio, 3 (☎ 976 29 90 89). Small but clean rooms with decent beds; some have sinks. Interior rooms are windowless. Two common baths for 9 rooms. Pleasant owners do not accept reservations. Singles 1500ptas; doubles 3000ptas.

Camping: Casablanca (☎ 976 75 38 70), Barrio Valdefierro, down Cra. Madrid. Bus #36 from Pl. Pilar or Pl. España to the suburb of Valdefierro. Ask the driver to let you off at the campsite, as it's notoriously difficult to find. By car, take the road to Madrid to the Valdefierro Exit (km 316, from there follow the signs). Picturesque spot and good facilities: bar, restaurant, laundry service, and pool open in summer. July-Aug. 625ptas per person, per tent, and per car; Sept-Oct. 15 and Apr.-June 575ptas each.

🍴 FOOD

Hungry budget travelers will love Zaragoza's *casco viejo*. *Tapas* bars, inexpensive restaurants, and *bocadillo* factories crowd the area known as **El Tubo** (C. Mártires, C. Cinegio, C. 4 de Agosto, and C. Estébanes). The tourist office gives out a *guía de tapas*, which lists *tapas* bars, many clustered around Pl. Santa Marta (to the right and behind the Catedral del Seo). The **market** thrives in the long green building on Av. César Augusto off Pl. Pilar. (Open M-F 9am-2pm and 5-8pm, Sa 9am-2pm.) Zaragoza's oldest candy store, **Fantoba,** C. Don Jaime, 21, has been around for 145 delectable years and continues to tempt with their *frutas de Aragon*, chocolate-dipped candied fruits in colorful wrappers. (☎ 976 29 85 24. 800ptas per half kilo. Open daily 10am-10pm). **Supermarket** shoppers can refuel at the **Consum,** C. San Jorge 22, the continuation of C. Merdeo Nuñez (open M-Sa 9am-9pm).

Casa Pascualillo, C. Libertad, 5 (☎ 976 39 72 03). In the El Tubo district, on a tiny street off C. Méndez Nuñez. Cheap, wholesome food in a simple, clean dining room. Fish, chicken, beef, egg and tortilla entrees (600-1300ptas) as well as an extensive menú (1000ptas). Open Tu-Sa 1-4pm and 8-11pm, Su 1-4pm. V, MC, AmEx.

La Zanahoria, C. Tarragona, 4 (☎ 976 35 87 94). From Pl. Paraíso, take Gran Vía, turn right on Av. Goya, then take the 1st left after crossing Av. Teruel/Valencia. Worth the trip. Young local crowd fills this small, cheerful and top-quality restaurant. Excellent salads and vegetable quiches. *Menú* 1100ptas, entrees 950ptas. Open daily 1:30-4pm and 9-11:30pm. V, MC.

Lai Lai, C. Don Jaime, 34 (☎ 976 20 06 51), a block away from the Pl. del Pilar. Behind the elaborate red facade you'll find a pleasant Chinese restaurant with good food at unbeatable prices. Rice and noodle entrees (595-695ptas). Daily *menú* 885ptas. Open daily noon-4pm and 7:30-midnight. V, MC.

👁 SIGHTS

PLAZA DEL PILAR

Pl. Pilar, a vast square surrounded by a unique combination of architectural styles, is Zaragoza at its best. It is also the perfect place to begin a tour of the old city.

■ **BASÍLICA DE NUESTRA SEÑORA DEL PILAR.** The Basílica de Nuestra Señora del Pilar, the patroness after whom millions of Spanish women are named, dominates Pl. Pilar. Its massive Baroque structure (begun in 1681) defines the skyline with brightly colored tiled domes, and the inside is even more incredible, with frescoes by Goya, González Velázquez, and Francisco Bayeau. Evidence of the miraculous abounds. Two bombs (now on display) were dropped on the basilica during the Civil War but failed to explode, purportedly due to the divine intervention of the Virgin. While the basilica's original pillar is encased in silver, a small piece of the underlying wood remains exposed. Along with Pope John Paul II (who visited in 1986), the faithful continue to line up to kiss the sacred relic, while proud little altar boys lead children to kiss the Virgin's embroidered cloak. The **Museo del Pilar** exhibits the glittering *joyero de la Virgen* (Virgin's jewels) and preliminary paintings of the ceiling frescoes. Don't leave without seeing the panoramic view of Zaragoza from one of the towers. The **elevator** is located in the corner, on the left when facing the Museo del Pilar. *(Basilica open daily 5:45am-9:30pm. Free. Museum ☎ 976 29 95 64. Open daily 9am-2pm and 4-6pm. 200ptas. Elevator open June-Aug. Sa-Th 9:30am-2pm and 4-7pm; Sept.-May Sa-Th 9:30am-2pm and 4-6pm. 200ptas.)*

OTHER SIGHTS. On the left as you exit the basilica is Zaragoza's **ayuntamiento**. Next door is the Renaissance **La Lonja**, which hosts occasional art exhibits and features an intricate vaulted ceiling that has been replicated in numerous tourist brochures *(☎ 976 39 72 39. Open Tu-Sa 10am-2pm and 5-9pm, Su 10am-2pm.)* In front of La Lonja is an outdoor **monument** where statues portray scenes from Goya's paintings. On the other side of C. Don Jaime I, a large glass-and-marble cube houses the entrance to the **Foro Romano,** one of three nearby museums dedicated to Zaragoza's classical past. Excavated ruins await underground, along with a 19-minute Spanish movie on the site's history. *(☎ 976 39 97 52. Open Tu-Sa 10am-2pm and 5-8pm, Su 10am-2pm. Prices include admission to the Public Baths Museum and the Caesaraugustus River Port Museum. Visits begin on the hr. 300ptas, students 200ptas, over 65 and under 8 free.)*

ELSEWHERE

▓ **PALACIO DE LA ALJAFERÍA.** Following the Muslim conquest of the Iberian Peninsula in the 8th century, a crisis over succession smashed the kingdom into petty tributary states called *taifas*. Renovations have somewhat encumbered the building's original grace, but its awesome stone exterior and exquisite interior still impress. The ground floor has a distinctly Moorish flavor that contrasts starkly with the Gothic second floor. The fortified tower imprisoned *el trovador* in García Gutierrez's drama of the same name, the inspiration for Verdi's opera *Il Trovatore*. *(C. Castillo. Take bus #21 and 33. Or head left on C. Coso from Pl. España; facing the casco viejo, continue onto Conde Aranda, make a right onto Pl. Maria Agustín and a left onto C. Aliaferia. ☎ 976 28 95 28. Open Apr. 15-Oct. 15. M-W and Sa 10am-2pm and 4:30-8pm, F 4:30-8pm, Su 10am-2pm; Oct. 16-Apr. 14 M-W 10am-2pm and 4-6:30pm, F 4-6:30pm, Su 10am-2pm. 300ptas, students and seniors 150ptas, under 12 free.)*

MUSEO DE ZARAGOZA. In addition to an extensive collection of medieval Aragonese paintings, the Fine Arts section headlines an impressive "Goya Room," with its selection of the painter's works, including an excellent collection of drawings. *(Pl. Los Sitios, 6. From Pl. España, follow Po. Independencia about 5 blocks, turn left and go 5 more blocks on C. Joaquín Costa. Turn left at Pl. Sitios; the museum is on the right. ☎ 976 22 21 81. Open Tu-Sa 9am-2pm, Su 10am-2pm; special exhibits 4-8pm. Free.)*

MUSEO PABLO GARGALLO. The Museo Pablo Gargallo, dedicated to one of the most innovative sculptors of the 1920s, houses a small but marvelous collection of his works in the graceful **Palacio de Arguillo,** which was built in 1670. *(Pl. San Felipe, 3. ☎ 976 39 20 58. From Pl. España, walk down C. Don Jaime I and turn left on C. Menéndez Nuñez. The museum is 5 blocks down in Pl. San Felipe. Open Tu-Sa 10am-2pm and 5-9pm, Su 10am-2pm. Free.)*

FUNDACIÓN PABLO SERRANO. This modern building houses bronze sculptures by the fascinating Pablo Serrano (1908-1985). Look for *Gran pan partido (Big Bread Parted)* and sculptural reinterpretations of works by Picasso, Velázquez, and Goya. *(Po. María Agustín, 20. ☎ 976 28 06 59. Open June-Aug. M and W-Sa 10am-2pm and 6-9pm, Su 10am-2pm; Sept.-May M and W-Sa 10am-2pm and 5-8pm, Su 10am-2pm. Free.)*

AND YOU THINK YOUR PACK IS HEAVY?

Although she is frequently overshadowed by the amazing deeds of her internationally-acclaimed son, the original Madonna had some adventures of her own. Sure, painters like to portray her meditating serenely, but there was a tough, rugged side to the Virgin Mary as well. One of history's most illustrious backpackers (much like yourself, perhaps), the blue-clad Virgin hiked it from Jerusalem to Spain, arriving in the Roman city of CaesarAugustus (present-day Zaragoza) on January 2, 40 AD. And she didn't pack light: Mary carried with her the sacred pillar that still stands, encased in silver, in Zaragoza's awe-inspiring cathedral. In honor of this journey and gift, the people of Aragón proudly sing that "she did not do anything like this with any other nation," reminding others that her visit was an actual "coming" rather than a mere spiritual apparition.

♫ ENTERTAINMENT

The Zaragozan nightlife scene begins in **La Zona**—the streets bounded by Po. Constitución, C. León XIII, Po. Damas, and Camino de las Torres. Gulping beer from *litros* (about 400ptas) is the primary sport around **El Rollo,** the zone bounded by C. Moncasi, C. Bonet, and C. Maestro Marquina at the southern end of Po. Sagasta. University students storm Po. Sagasta and its offshoot, C. Zumalacárregui. Around midnight, herds of *casco viejo*-goers move into the market area around Pl. San Felipe. Gay bars and discos center around the west side of the *casco viejo;* let loose on the small dance floor at **Sphinx,** C. Ramón y Caja, one block down from C. Conde Aranda. (Cover F-Su 2000ptas. Open daily 11pm-5am.) Hipsters of all nationalities party at the Australian bar/disco, **Wooloomooloo,** C. Espoz y Mina, 19, where midnight drink specials and popular tunes set the tone. (☎ 976 39 63 76. Open daily 6pm-4am.) **La Casa del Loco,** C. Mayor, 10-12, has frequent concerts and a range of music for its international, 20- to 30-year-old crowd. (No cover. Open 10pm-5am.) **Oasis,** C. Boggiero 28, may open its doors to people of all ages, but it also opens their wallets. (Cover 1100ptas for men, includes 1 drink; no cover for women. Open Th-Su 1pm-7am.) **Kitsch,** C. Fernando el Católico, fills with 20-somethings. Take Bus #35 from Pl. Espana to Pl. San Francisco (cover 1000-1500ptas).

The city erupts for a week of unbridled craziness around October 12 in honor of *La Virgen Santa del Pilar*, one of the few full-blown autumn *fiestas* in Spain. (For program details contact the tourist office.) You may not find lodging, but then again, you may not need it. City patrons **San Valero** and **San Jorge** are also celebrated on January 29 and April 23, respectively.

🏃 DAYTRIPS FROM ZARAGOZA

Ask at the Zaragoza tourist office for info on excursions like the *Ruta del Vino* (wine route) and the *Ruta de Goya.* Fans of all things Romanesque should inquire about visits to the **Cinco Villas** (five villages).

MONASTERIO DE PIEDRA (2HR.)

Aragón Tours buses, C. Almagro, 18 (☎ 976 21 93 20), leave from Zaragoza to the monastery (2hr.; July-Oct. 15 Tu, Th and Sa 9am; return same day 5pm; round-trip 2220ptas).

An oasis of waterfalls and trees springs out of the dry plain around the Monasterio de Piedra, about 110km southwest of Zaragoza. Founded in 1195 by an order of Cistercian monks from Tarragona, and abandoned under government orders in 1835, the monastery is now a three-star hotel. The 12th-century **Torre del Homenaje,** the only part of the existing building that hasn't been restored, towers over the valley. (☎ 976 84 90 11. Open daily 9am-9pm.) The main attraction is the surrounding park and the **Río Piedra,** which casts off waterfalls and lakes as it plunges down the valley. Follow the path leading through, under, and around this aquatic paradise. (Park open daily 9am-nightfall. 1000ptas for monastery and park.)

DAROCA (1HR.)

Buses to Zaragoza (1½hr., 3 per day 8am-4:30pm, 720ptas) and Teruel (M-Sa 4 per day, 8:15am-7:40pm) depart from Mesón Felix, C. Mayor, near Puerta Baja. Buses arriving in Daroca, the last stop on the Agreda Automóvil line, halt near Puerta Baja.

Burros and wagons still wander the streets of Daroca (pop. 2400). The town rests in a dramatic gorge; its burnt-sienna roofs match the surrounding cliffs. The main sight in town is the icon-filled museum of the **Colegiata de Santa María,** a 16th-century Renaissance church. To get there, take C. Juan de la Huerta from C. Mayor. (Open June-Aug. Tu-Sa 11am-1pm and 5:30-8pm, Su 1hr. before mass at 11:30am and 7pm; Sept.-May Tu-Sa noon-1pm and 5:30-7pm, Su 1hr. before mass at 11:30am and 6pm. Museum 300ptas. The tourist office arranges guided tours.) Little Daroca hosts some lively partying during its week-long **Fiesta de Corpus Christi,** held every year in late May or early June. The town also hosts the annual **International Program for Ancient Music** during the first two weeks of August. Musicians from the world over gather to teach, learn, and give free concerts.

The town's main artery, **Calle Mayor,** runs uphill from the **Puerta Baja** (lower gate) to the **Puerta Alta** (upper gate). Daroca's walls, 4 km in circumference, were started in the 9th century; at one time they were home to 114 towers. Dirt paths along the walls reward hikers with a sentry's-eye view of the town and surrounding valleys. **La Ruta de Castillo** reveals a spectacular view of Daroca and neighboring towns (45min.). **La Ruta de las Murallas** does the whole tour in two hours. Both routes start outside Puerta Alta; the tourist office has a map.

The **tourist office,** Pl. España, 7, sits opposite the Colegiata de Santa María. From Puerta Alta, walk down C. Mayor for four or five blocks and hang a right on C. San Juan de la Huerta. (☎ 976 80 01 29. Open June-Aug. daily 10am-2pm and 5-7pm; Sept.-May M-F 11am-2pm, Sa-Su 11am-2pm and 5-6pm.) Although Daroca works best as a daytrip, sleepy travelers can try the comfortable **Pensión El Ruejo,** C. Mayor, 88, with modern rooms, heating, A/C, a disco, and a flowering courtyard. Inquire at the bar downstairs after 9am. (☎ 976 80 09 62. Singles with sink 2000ptas; doubles with sink 3500ptas, with bath 4500ptas.) The **restaurant** on the first floor serves a satisfying 1100pta *menú.* Picnickers can stock up at **%Día,** the supermarket on C. Mayor (open M-Sa 9:30am-2pm and 5-8pm).

TERUEL

The small capital of southern Aragón, Teruel (29,300) invites visitors to step into a world of love, heartbreak, and cultural exchange (see **"Star-Crossed Lovers"**). Lively and welcoming, this little town's narrow streets and old plazas belie its cosmopolitan history. From the 12th to the 15th centuries, Muslims, Jews, and Christians lived here in cultural collusion. The resulting Mudéjar architecture blends Arab patterns with Gothic and Romanesque touches. An easy stopover between Valencia and Zaragoza, Teruel doesn't really reach its prime until July, when citizens celebrate the resilience of their *torico* (iron bull) in an 168-hour liquor fest.

▛ TRANSPORTATION. Trains leave from Camino de la Estación, 1 (☎ 978 61 02 02), down the stairs from Pl. Ovalo. To **Valencia** (2¾hr., 3 per day 7:40am-6:37pm, 1265ptas) and **Zaragoza** (3hr., 3 per day 6:45am-6:02pm, 1405ptas). **Buses** leave from the new **station** (☎ 978 61 07 89), Ronda de Ambeles, only a few blocks from the *casco viejo.* **La Rápida** (☎ 978 60 20 04) to **Barcelona** (5½-6½hr., M-Sa 12:30pm, 3210ptas) and **Cuenca** (3hr., M-Sa 11:45am, 1205ptas). **Samar** (☎ 978 60 34 50) to **Valencia** (2-2½hr.; 5-6 per day M-Sa 7:15am-7pm, Su 8am-7pm; 1160ptas) and **Madrid** (4½-5hr., 3 per day M-F 7:30am-5pm, 2415ptas). **Magallón** (☎ 976 41 72 52) and **Jiménez** (☎ 978 60 10 40) to **Zaragoza** (Magallón M-Sa 6:30am and 2:30pm, Su 3:30pm; Jiménez 4 per day 7am-7pm). To rent a car, call **BMW** (☎ 978 60 65 36).

STAR-CROSSED LOVERS The tombs of Diego de Marcilla and Isabel de Segura in the **Mausoleo de los Amantes**, next to Torre San Pedro, are the source of Teruel's nickname: *ciudad de los amantes* (city of lovers). The story began when Diego left Teruel to make his fortune and prove his worth to Isabel's affluent family. Five years later, he returned a rich man, just in time to watch Isabel marry his childhood rival. Diego begged for one last kiss but was refused; he immediately died of grief. At the funeral, Isabel kissed the corpse and, overcome with sorrow, died herself. The lovers are commemorated with life-size statues of the lovers, reaching out over to touch hands but not quite making it. For a peek at the lover's remains, duck down near their heads. (From Pl. Torico, take the alleyway to the left of the purple *modernista* house. Stairs lead directly to the mausoleum. Open M-Sa 10am-2pm and 5-7:30pm, Su 10:30am-2pm and 5-7:30pm. 50ptas.)

🚩 **ORIENTATION AND PRACTICAL INFORMATION.** Teruel's somewhat non-sensical layout can be confusing. The *casco viejo* perches on a hilltop, linked to modern Teruel by bridges. The center of the *casco* is **Plaza de Carlos Castell**, affectionately known as **Plaza del Torico**. To reach Pl. Torico from the **train station**, take the staircase from the park and follow signs to the *centro*. To get to Pl. Torico from the new **bus station**, get on C. Judería and make the second left onto C. Hartzembusch, which zigzags to the plaza.

The **tourist office** is at C. Tomás Nogues, 1. From Pl. Torico, follow C. Ramón y Cajal (C. San Juan) and take the first left; the office is one block away on the right, at the corner. (☎ 978 60 22 79. Open July-Sept. M 9am-2pm and 5-7:30pm, Tu-F 9am-2pm and 4:30-8pm, Sa 10am-1:30pm and 4:30-8pm, Su 10am-2pm; Oct.-June M 10am-1:30pm and 5-7:30pm, Tu-Sa 9am-2pm and 5-7:30pm.) **Luggage storage** is available at the train station (400ptas) or the bus station (100ptas per piece per day; both open daily 6:30am-10:30pm). The **Banco Central Hispano** is at Pl. Torico, 15. (☎ 978 60 11 35. Open M-F 8:30am-2:30pm; Oct.-May also Sa 8:30am-1pm.) Services include **emergency** (☎ 112) and the **post office**, C. Yagüe de Salas, 19, which can send **faxes**. (☎ 978 60 11 90 or 60 11 92. Open M-F 8:30am-8:30pm, Sa 9:30am-2pm). The **postal code** is 44001. For **Internet access**, try **Pub Lennon**, C. San Andres, 23 (☎ 978 60 19 70. 700ptas per hr. Open W-M June-Aug. 7pm-2am, Sept.-May 3pm-2am.)

📷🍴 **ACCOMMODATIONS AND FOOD.** Lodgings are scarce during August and *Semana Santa* and impossible during *fiesta*-time in early July. Thought to be the oldest hostel in all of Spain, **Fonda el Tozal**, C. Rincón, 5, promises the rustic charm and comfort of a "*casa rurale*" with several features of typical *mudejar* design, including stunning and spacious tiled bathrooms. Along with great beds, guests will enjoy the impressive stable-turned-bar that awaits downstairs. (☎ 978 60 10 22. Singles 1500-1800ptas; doubles 4500ptas; triples 6300-6600.) To get to **Hostal Aragón**, C. Santa María, 4, head in the direction the Torico faces, and take the first left as you leave Pl. Torico. Friendly owners keep airy rooms with colorful tiled floors and some with TV. (☎ 978 60 13 87. English spoken. Singles 2000ptas, with bath 3000ptas; doubles 3200ptas, with bath 4900ptas; triples with bath 7000ptas.)

Teruel is famous for its salty, flavorful cured ham, *jamón de Teruel*, featured in *tapas* bars in Pl. Torico. Restaurant standards and prices are high; the *casco viejo* is the place to look. **Restaurante La Parrilla**, C. Esteban, 2, two blocks uphill from the tourist office, specializes in regional dishes (1300-2000ptas) and has a magnificent 1300ptas *menú* with succulent meats grilled on a stone fireplace. (☎ 978 60 59 17. Open M-Sa 1-4pm and 8:30-11:30pm, Su noon-5pm. V, MC.) Lovers of all things Italian will appreciate the pastas and crisp specialty pizzas (850-1100ptas) served at **Los Caprichos**, C. Caracol 1, two blocks uphill from Pl. Torico. (☎ 978 60 03 30. Open Tu-Su 1:30-3:30pm and 8:30-11:30pm.) There is a **market** on Pl. Domingo Gascón; from Pl. Torico, take C. Joaquín Costa/Tozal (open Th 8am-1pm).

🔲 **SIGHTS.** The mother of all of Teruel's Mudéjar monuments is the 13th-century 🔲**Catedral de Santa María de Mediavilla.** The magnificently decorated brick tower is a mere preface to the 14th-century stylized *artesonado mudéjar* (Mudéjar coffered ceiling) roofing of the central nave. (All roads left of Pl. Torico lead one block away to Pl. Catedral. Open daily 11am-2pm and 4-8pm. 300ptas with mandatory guide.) Muslim artisans built the brick-and-glazed-tile **Torres Mudéjares** (Mudéjar Towers) between the 12th and 15th centuries, then Christian churches adapted the Almohad minarets to their own purposes. The most intricately designed of the three towers is the 13th-century **Torre de San Salvador,** on C. Salvador. Climb 123 steps through several chambers to the panoramic bell tower. (Open July-Sept. daily 11am-2pm and 5-8pm; Oct.-June Sa 11am-2pm and 5-7pm, Su 11am-2pm. 250ptas.) Behind the cathedral, the **Museo Provincial,** devoted mainly to archaeological and ethnographic pursuits, rests in the 16th-century porticoed Casa de la Comunidad, a leading example of the "Aragonese Renaissance Style." Don't miss the exquisite reproduction of an 18th century chemist's shop. (Pl. Fray Anselmo Polanco. ☎ 978 60 01 50. Open Tu-F 10am-2pm and 4-9pm, Sa-Su 10am-2pm. Free.)

DAYTRIPS FROM TERUEL

Protected by ancient walls, medieval townships in Teruel's countryside stand amid acres of wild land. Getting to these mystical hamlets is less of an ordeal than it once was, but unless you have a car—and there is only one rental agency in Teruel—you'll have to spend the night. The *Guía de servicios turísticos*, available at any Aragonese tourist office, has information on accommodations in the area.

ALBARRACÍN (30MIN.)

Autotransportes Teruel (☎ 978 60 26 80) runs a bus from Teruel to Albarracín (30min.; leaves daily 3:30pm, returns at 9am the next day; 380ptas). Ruelilla (☎ 978 60 57 01) also runs a bus from Teruel (45min., M-Sa 3:30pm).

Just west of Teruel, the former Moorish city of Albarracín (pop. under 1000) has a surprising history of autonomy: from 1009-1113 it was a small, independent Islamic state called Ibn Razin, and from 1170-1285 it was an independent Christian kingdom. Today, the small medina-like town lives off the fading grandeur of its stone houses, small churches, and dispersed towers. The **tourist office,** Pl. Mayor, 1, will direct you to tours of the *pinturas rupestres*, post-Paleolithic cave paintings dating from 5000 BC. (☎ 978 71 02 51. Open July-Sept. M-Sa 10am-2pm and 5-7:30pm, Su 10am-2pm. Free tours daily at 2:30 and 5:30pm. Oct.-June consult the **Ayuntamiento** at ☎ 978 71 02 51; open M-F 9am-3pm.)

RUBIELOS DE MORA (50MIN.)

Trains (☎ 978 61 02 02) come to Rubielos de Mora from Teruel (50min., 7:40am, 410ptas). Furio buses (☎ 964 60 01 00) also come from Teruel (1½hr., 2:30pm).

Local connoisseurs insist that the most exquisite of the medieval towns around Teruel is Rubielos de Mora (pop. 600), 15km east of Mora de Rubielos. Residents live in an unrestored architectural set-piece from medieval days, complete with city gates and a 16th-century town hall (with the usual courtyard and dungeon). The **tourist office** is in the Ayuntamiento, Pl. Hispano América, 1. (☎ 978 80 40 96. Open July-Aug. daily 10am-2pm and 5-7pm; Sept.-June M-F 10am-2pm.)

MORA DE RUBIELOS (1HR.)

Furio (☎ 964 60 01 00) buses run to Mora de Rubielos (1hr., 2:30pm) from Teruel. Trains also come from Teruel (45min., 3 per day 7:40am-6:37pm, 410ptas), but the closest train station to Mora de Rubielos is 14km away.

Forty-two km east of Teruel, Mora de Rubielos has the area's largest and best-preserved 15th-century castle. For centuries the castle and town were passed from one noble family to another until finally becoming part of Aragón in 1365. In the summer, a tourist office (☎ 978 80 00 00) sets up shop on C. Diputación.

ARAGONESE PYRENEES

Historians look at the Aragonese Pyrenees, note the infrequency with which northern enemies have invaded Spain, and say it all makes sense. Everyone else looks at the jagged cliff faces, deep gorges, icy rivers, and alpine meadows and can't say a word. The most popular launching point for the Aragonese Pyrenees is **Jaca**, from which most walkers head to the spectacular **Parque Nacional de Ordesa.** In the east, **Benasque** draws hard-core mountaineers with its access to the highest peaks in the Pyrenees, and the western valleys of **Ansó** and **Hecho** are ideal for less strenuous mountain rambling. The Aragonese mountains are less extensively developed than those of Cataluña, but there are still a number of resorts awaiting skiers, including Astún, Panticosa, Cerler, and Candanchú. For details on winter in Aragón, get the free tourist office pamphlets *Ski Aragón* or *El Turismo de Nieve en España.*

JACA

For centuries, pilgrims bound for Santiago would cross the Pyrenees into Spain, nest in Jaca (pop. 14,000) for the night, and be off by sunrise. They had the right idea. Although Jaca served a brief stint as capital of Aragón (1035-1095), there is little to do here but organize excursions into the Pyrenees and nearby ski resorts.

▛ TRANSPORTATION. RENFE trains (☎ 974 36 13 32; ticket booth open 10am-noon and 5-7pm) run to **Zaragoza** (3hr., 7:36am-6:12pm, 1325ptas) and **Madrid** (7hr., 3:30pm, 4200ptas). **Alosa** buses (☎ 974 35 50 60) go to: **Zaragoza** (2hr., 1 per day, 1460ptas); **Pamplona** (2hr., 4:30pm, 860ptas); and **Sabiñánigo** (20min., 11am, 185ptas), where **Empresa Hudebus** (☎ 974 21 32 77) connects to **Torla,** near Ordesa and Aínsa. **Josefa Escartín** (☎ 974 36 05 08) runs one bus (M-Sa 6:30pm) to: **Hecho** (55min., 400ptas); **Siresa** (1hr., 425ptas); and **Ansó** (1½hr., 500ptas). **Taxis** (☎ 974 36 28 48) line up at the intersection of C. Mayor, Av. Regimiento Galicia, and Av. Viernes de Mayo. For **car rental,** try **Avis** (☎/fax 941 20 23 54) in Logroño. You must be 21 and have had a license for at least one year.

▛▞ ORIENTATION AND PRACTICAL INFORMATION. Buses drop passengers on Av. Jacetania, at the edge of the city center. From the bus station on Av. Jacetania, walk through the plaza to C. Zocotin and go straight two blocks to reach the city's central artery **Calle Mayor.** The shuttle bus from the **train station** runs to the **Ayuntamiento,** in the middle of C. Mayor, or to the intersection of C. Mayor and Av. Regimiento de Galicia. Shuttle buses run from downtown to the **RENFE train station,** C. Estación, roughly 30 minutes before each train leaves. If you're walking to town from the station, take Av. Juan XXIII to its end, turn left on C. Francia, continue straight as it becomes C. Primer Viernes, then make a left onto C. Mayor.

The English-speaking staff at the **tourist office,** Av. Regimiento de Galicia, 2, off C. Mayor, offers useful maps and hiking advice. (☎ 974 36 00 98. Open July-Aug. M-F 9am-2pm and 4:30-8pm, Sa 10am-1:30pm and 5-8pm, Su 10am-1:30pm; Sept.-June M-F 9am-1:30pm and 4:30-7pm, Sa 10am-1pm and 5-7pm.) For **ski rental,** head to **Nieve Sport,** Av. Francia, 33 (☎ 974 36 35 72). For **adventure tourism,** try **Alcorce,** Av. Regimiento Galicia, 1, across from the tourist office, which organizes hiking, rock climbing, spelunking, and rafting trips. (☎/fax 974 36 08 90; email alcorce-pirineos@encomix.es. Guided hiking trips start at 5000ptas per person per day. Rafting starts at 5500ptas. Open M-Sa 10am-1:30pm and 4:30-8:30pm, later in July and Aug. V, MC.) For **ski conditions,** call **Teléfono Blanco** (☎ 976 20 11 12) or the resorts. Exchange currency at **Banco Central Hispano,** C. Primer Viernes de Mayo, at the corner of C. Mayor (open Apr.-Sept. M-F 8:30am-2pm; Oct.-Mar. M-F 8:30am-2pm, Sa 8:30am-1pm). Town services include: **police,** C. Mayor, 24 (☎ 091 or 092), in the Ayuntamiento; the **Centro de Salud (health center),** Po. Constitución, 6 (☎ 974 36 07 95); and the **post office,** C. Correos, 13, off Av. Regimiento de Galicia, across from the tourist office. (☎ 974 35 58 86. Open M-F 8:30am-2:30pm, Sa 9:30am-1pm.) The **postal code** is 22700. For **Internet access** go to **CIVA Informatica,** Pasaje del Carmen, 5, within the gallery. (☎ 974 35 67 75. 300ptas for 30min., 550ptas per hr. Open M-Th 11am-2pm and 5-10pm, F-Sa 11am-2pm and 5-11pm.)

⌐⌐ ACCOMMODATIONS AND FOOD. Jaca's hostels and *pensiones* cluster around C. Mayor and the cathedral. Lodgings are scarce only during the bi-annual *Festival Folklórico* in late July and early August. For Santiago-bound pilgrims, the **Albergue de Peregrinos** is on C. Hospital (☎ 974 35 51 16. 200ptas for towels. Reception open daily 9-10am and 6-11pm. 700ptas per person.) Other visitors might try to get to the **Albergue Juvenil de Escuelas Pias** (HI), Av. Perimetral, 6. From C. Mayor, turn left onto C. Regimiento de Galicia, and left again on Av. Perimetral. On the right side of the road after the long bend, then turn off on the unmarked dirt driveway immediately before the skating rink. The hostel has rows of red-shuttered bungalows, rooms with two to four beds and sinks, and clean common bathrooms. (☎ 974 36 05 36. Sheets and breakfast included. Midnight curfew. 2500ptas per person, over 26 3100ptas. Nonmembers pay 500ptas more.) For a unique experience check out the decidedly hip *casa rural* ◙**El Arco**, C. San Nicolas, 4, where each room has its own distinctive flavor. (☎ 974 36 44 48. Breakfast 300ptas. 1800ptas per bunk; 1, 2 and 3-person suites available from 3000-4000ptas.) **Habitaciones Martínez**, C. Mayor, 53, above a bar, has small neat rooms with cheesy pastoral wall-paintings and saggy beds. To avoid the smell of cigarettes, request a balcony. (☎ 974 36 33 74. Singles 1700ptas; doubles 3400ptas.) **Camping Peña Oroel**, 3½km down the road to Sabiñánigo, has wooded grounds along a riverbank, a market, and a swimming pool. (☎ 974 36 02 15; reservations 934 50 44 44. 650ptas per person, per tent, and per car. Open *Semana Santa* and mid-June to mid-Sept.)

Look for restaurants serving *menús* and *tapas* off C. Mayor; those lining Av. Primer Viernes de Mayo serve *bocadillos* and *platos combinados*. Buy **groceries** at **Supermercado ALDI**, C. Correos, 9, next to the post office. (Open M-Sa 9:30am-2pm and 5-8pm, Su 9:30am-2pm and 5-8pm. Visa.) **Restaurante Vegetariano El Arco**, C. San Nicolas, 4, off the bus station plaza, serves a daily changing, tasty vegetarian *menú*. (Entrees 1000ptas. Open M-Sa 12:30-3pm and 8:30-11:30pm.)

DAYTRIP FROM JACA: MONASTERIO DE SAN JUAN DE LA PEÑA

Viages Arán, C. Mayor, 46 (☎ 974 35 54 80), schedules bus trips to San Juan July 15-Aug., for 1300ptas, usually on Thursdays. Taxis (☎ 974 36 28 48) will also make the journey for 5000ptas, with a 1hr. wait at the monastery. If you are driving, park in the lot above the monastery; a shuttle bus picks up monastery visitors every 30min.

The spectacular **Monasterio de San Juan de la Peña** is difficult to reach—it was designed that way. Determined hermits hid the original monastery in a canyon 22km from Jaca and maintained such extreme privacy that invading Moors never discovered it or the Holy Grail (supposedly concealed here for three centuries). It's worth a visit, both for the 10th-century underground church carved directly into the rock and the 12th-century cloister dwarfed by a massive boulder. The stunning carved capitals of the cloister's columns are among the best preserved around. Don't confuse the monastery with the uninteresting 17th-century *monasterio nuevo* 1km uphill. (☎ 974 35 51 19 or 974 35 51 45; fax 974 35 50 89. Open daily Nov.1-Mar. 15 11am-2:30pm and 4-5:30pm; Mar. 16-May 31 10am-2:30pm and 4-7pm; June 1-Aug. 31 10am-2:30pm and 3:30-8pm; Sept. 1-Oct. 31 10am-2:30pm and 4-7pm. 400ptas, 600ptas including shuttle from parking lot.)

DAYTRIP FROM JACA: CASTILLO DE LOARRE

Reaching the castle requires a little ingenuity. Alosa sends one bus from Jaca to the town of Loarre, 5km from the castle; the return bus at 5pm stops only in Ayerbe, 7km away from Loarre. (☎ 974 35 50 60. 1hr., M-Sa 1 per day, 7:15am, 665ptas). Trains go only to Ayerbe. From there, you can request a taxi or trek the 2hr. to the town of Loarre.

The power and magnificence of ◙**El Castillo de Loarre** (5km from the town of Loarre and 70km from Jaca) is visible for kilometers in each direction. A maze of history sits above the fields, every inch of which is open to exploration. No tours or guides shuffle people through the castle; each visitor is free to investigate, meander, or just sit and ponder the wonder of it all. In the 11th century, King Sancho Ramírez built the marvelous structure in an effort to protect the Western Pyrenees from a Moorish invasion. He succeeded—sharp cliffs at its rear and

400m of thick walls to the east make the castle nearly impenetrable. The building's outer walls follow the turns and angles of the rock so closely that a nighttime attacker might have seen only the silhouette of the awesome stone monolith. A crypt, which opens to the right of the steep entrance staircase, holds the remains of Demetrius, the French saint who died in Loarre. You can go up to the battlements of both towers, but be careful when climbing the wobbly steel rungs to the roof or descending into the dark and doorless basement. (Open May-June Tu-Su 10am-1:30pm and 4-7pm; July-Aug. daily 10am-8pm; Sept.-Apr. W-Su 11am-2:30pm. Free.)

VALLE DE HECHO

The craggy Valle de Hecho and its picturesque hamlets, just 40km west of Jaca, are the hiking areas closest to the city. Under the humid influence of the Atlantic, these western slopes and their dense forests encourage a wide range of ecological diversity and are favored by hikers in search of moderate hiking. From early July to early August, area villages host the **Simposio de Escultura y Pintura Moderna.** Artists come from far and wide, turning the surrounding hills into a huge open-air museum. The valley is best visited during the summer, as it is extremely quiet during the rest of the year. A **Josefa Escartin** bus (☎ 974 36 05 08) leaves Jaca Monday through Saturday at 6:30pm, stopping at **Hecho** (7:25pm) and **Siresa** (7:40pm) and continuing to **Ansó** (8:10pm). Every morning except Sunday the bus returns from Ansó (6am) via Siresa (6:30am) and Hecho (6:45am) on its way to Jaca (7:40am).

HECHO (ECHO)

Hecho (pop. 670) is the valley's geographical and administrative center, a serious title that doesn't seem to suit the small and inviting town. The **Ayuntamiento** houses a small **tourist office** in the summer months; someone upstairs will happily answer questions during the rest of the year. (☎ 974 37 53 29. Open July-Sept. 15 M-Sa 10am-2pm and 5-7pm, Su 10am-2pm). A **bank** is behind Pl. Fuente—follow Traversia Muro and turn left. (☎ 974 37 52 11. Open Apr.-Sept. M-F 8:30am-2pm; Oct.-Mar. M-F 8:30am-2pm, Sa 8:30am-1pm.) The **post office** sits in the Plaza Alta, right off C. Mayor (open M-F 8:30am-2:30pm, Sa 9:30am-1pm). Get your **groceries** at **Supermercado Aldi,** on C. Mayor (open July-Sept. M-Sa 9:30am-2pm and 5-8pm, Su 10am-2pm; Oct.-June M-Sa 10am-2pm and 5-8pm). Ansó and nearby campgrounds provide cheaper **accommodations** options, but the best deal in Hecho itself is **Casa Blasquico,** Pl. Fuente, 1, a white house with balconies, wood panelling and flowers, right in the main square. Complete with love-seats, carved chests, spacious baths, and TVs, these rooms are worth the cash. The family's home-cooking verges on a local legend. (☎ 974 37 50 07. Breakfast 550ptas. *Menú* 1700ptas. Call ahead. Doubles 3500ptas, with bath 6000ptas. Visa.) **Camping Valle de Hecho,** at the entrance to Hecho coming from Jaca, has clean facilities in a lovely location. Bunks (1100ptas) are also available in the large *albergue* on the same site. The knowledgeable staff will help you to organize excursions. (☎/fax 974 37 53 61. 557ptas per person, per car, and per tent; 7% IVA not included. Visa.) The **Compania de Guías Valle de Echo** sets up shop from time to time in the town proper, but it is usually best to call. Helpful guides lead hiking trips and rent cross-country skis. (☎ 974 37 53 87 or 676 85 08 43. Skis 2000ptas per day. 7900ptas for a 2-day trip to the Selva de Oza.)

VALLE DE ANSÓ

Slightly farther down the road from Jaca, the little town of Ansó is set in one of the most appealing valleys in the Pyrenees, a lush growth of oak and pine trees. Like Hecho, this valley lives for July and August, when it receives the bulk of its visitors. The best treks leave from Zuriza, farther up the valley than Ansó.

ANSÓ

Tiny Ansó's (pop. 530) cobblestone streets and matching stone houses are peacefully removed from the rest of the world. Near inviting mountains and lakes, the town is well worth a stop. At the **Museo de Etnología** inside the **Iglesia de San Pedro,** mannequins model traditional dress next to spinning wheels and looms. (☎ 974 34 00 22. Open July-Aug. M-F 10:30am-1:30pm and 3:30-8pm; mid-Sept.-June daily 11am-12:30pm. For more info, talk to the priest in the stone house in front of the church. 250ptas.) For more information on transportation, local festivals, and nearby hikes, drop by the seasonal **tourist office** in Plaza Domingo Miral next to the post office (☎ 974 37 02 25. Open July-Aug. daily 10am-2pm and 5-8pm.)

The **Josefa Escartín bus** (☎ 974 36 05 08) from Jaca stops at C. Mayor, departing for Jaca again the next day (1½hr., M-Sa 6am, 475ptas). Travelers are in for a treat if they stay with the friendly owners of **Posada Magoria,** C. Milagro, 32, the corner house with scroll-work details right below the church. In a recent expansion the owners have restored a traditional stone house with wide-planked wood floors and antique-filled rooms. They make their own yogurt, bake bread, and grow vegetables, serving it all at family-style meals. (☎ 974 37 00 49. Breakfast 700ptas, dinner 1800ptas. Call ahead in July and Aug. 2400ptas per person.) Around the corner of the wide cobbled street (look for the sign) you'll find Persian rugs, lacy curtains, and the occasional balcony at **Posada Veral,** C. Cocorro, 6. Owners will prepare authentic Peruvian cuisine upon request. (☎ 974 37 01 19. Lunch and dinner *menú* 1500ptas for guests only. Breakfast 400ptas. Singles 2000ptas; doubles 4000ptas.)

ZURIZA AND ENVIRONS

Around Zuriza, in the northern part of the Valle de Hecho, the terrain alternates between the shallow **Agujero de Solana** (Hole of Solana) and the steep summit of **Escoueste.** Many hikers use the area as a base for the arduous trek to **Sima de San Martín,** a gorgeous trail on the French border. To get there, drive from Zuriza to the Isaba-Belagua crossroads and take the Belagua direction, heading north. For a lighter trek, walk 2km south of Ansó to the fork in the road. Just above the tunnel toward Hecho is the striking, weather-sculpted rock formation called **El Monje y la Monja (The Monk and the Nun).** Sweep all lurid thoughts from your mind and enjoy the view. Fifteen kilometers north of Ansó, **Camping Zuriza,** which lies on a mountain stream 2km away from the Río Veral, is great for fishing, rafting, or kayaking. The site also provides a **supermarket, hostel,** and **pub/restaurant** where you can find information on nearby trails. (☎ 974 37 01 96 or 974 37 00 77. Breakfast 375ptas. Dinner 8:30-11pm. Hot showers included. Campsite 475ptas per person, per tent and per car; IVA not included. Hostel doubles 4500ptas, with bath 6000ptas; bunk in *literas* 1000ptas. V, MC.) From the campground, it's a dayhike of medium difficulty (3½hr.) to the **Mesa de los Tres Reyes,** a series of peaks close to the borders of France, Navarra, and Aragón (hence "los tres reyes").

▓ PARQUE NACIONAL DE ORDESA

The beauty of Ordesa tends to reduce even seasoned travelers to stupefied monosyllables. Extremely well-maintained trails cut across idyllic forests, jagged rock faces, snow-covered peaks, rushing rivers, and magnificent waterfalls. Located just south of the French border, Ordesa includes the canyons of Ordesa, Añisclo, Escuaín, and Pineta. The park has trails for hikers of all levels of experience, and as a result attracts huge crowds in July and August. It is easiest to enter Ordesa through the village of **Torla.**

▐ TRANSPORTATION. La Oscense (☎ 974 35 50 60) sends a **bus** from Jaca to **Sabiñánigo** in July (30min., M-Sa 10:15am and 6:15pm, Su 10:15am, 110ptas). Sabiñánigo is also easily accessible by **train;** all trains on the Zaragoza-Huesca-Jaca line stop here. From there **Compañía Hudebus** (☎ 974 21 32 77) runs to **Torla** (55min.; Sept.-June 11am; July-Aug. 11am and 6pm; 355ptas). A bus shuttles between Torla and **Ordesa** during July and August (every 15min., round-trip 200ptas). In the off-season you'll have to either hike the 8km to the park entrance or get a **taxi** for 1500-2000ptas (☎ 974 48 61 53). To leave the park area, catch the bus as it passes through Torla at 3:30pm on its way back to Sabiñánigo.

⚡ PRACTICAL INFORMATION. The **visitors center** awaits beyond the Ordesa park entrance, and has maps (400ptas) and information about the park and its various hikes. (Open daily July-Aug. 9am-1pm and 3:30-7pm; Apr.-May 9am-2pm and 3:30-6pm; June 9am-1:30pm and 4-7pm.) In Torla, consider buying the indispensable *Editorial Alpina* guide (2000ptas). Across from Refugio L'Atalaya, **Compañia de Ordesa** rents mountain bikes and organizes excursions. (☎/fax 974 48 64 17; www.pirineo.com/guiasordesa. Rafting 7000ptas per person. Kayaks 8000ptas per person.) You can find the **police** at the **Guardia Civil** (☎ 974 48 61 60). The **post office** is on C. Francia at Pl. Ayuntamiento (open M-Sa 9-11am). The **postal code** is 22376.

▐▛▐ ACCOMMODATIONS AND FOOD. Within the park, many *refugios* (mountain huts with bunks and unreliable hot water, usually without facilities) allow overnight stays. The 120-bed **Refugio Góriz,** a four-hour walk from the Ordesa's parking lot, has winter heating and meager hot showers. (☎ 974 34 12 01. 1000ptas per person.) The town of Torla has a greater range of accommodations, but it tends to fill up fast in July and August—reserve ahead. In Torla, ascend cobblestoned C. Francia, and on the right after one block, you'll find **⧉Refugio L'Atalaya,** C. Francia, 45, under some wooden beams. Communal lofts, tapestry pillowcases and spotless wood planking make this a hippy-hiker haven. The kitchen and dining area are available for use, or sit back with a beer and enjoy the owner's own *menú* for 1400ptas. (☎ 974 48 60 22. Loft-mat 1000ptas per person.) Offering more privacy, the slightly more conservative **Refugio Briet,** across the street, has two rooms of stacked bunks and a snug dining area with wood tables and benches. (☎ 974 48 62 21. *Menú* 1400ptas. Lodging 1000ptas per person. V, MC.) **Camping Río Ara** (☎ 974 48 62 48) and **Camping San Anton** (☎ 974 48 60 63) both lie right outside Torla. (Both 550ptas per person, per tent, and per car. Open Apr.-Oct.) Midway between these two is the more upscale **Camping Ordesa,** complete with pool, supermarket, tennis court, and bar (☎ 974 48 61 25. Open Apr.-Oct. 645ptas per person, 675ptas per tent and per car. 30% off in low season.) Stock up on food essentials at **Supermercado Torla,** on C. Francia, a few buildings down from Refugio L'Atalaya (☎ 974 48 61 63. Open daily Feb.-Nov. 8am-2pm and 4-8pm; Dec.-Jan. 10am-2pm and 4-8pm.) **Restaurante Bar El Rebeco,** up C. Francia and right at the parking lot, serves a 1650pta *menú*, plenty of meat and fish entrees (900-1800ptas), and a wide variety of desserts. (☎ 974 48 60 68. Open June-Oct. 1-3:30pm and 8-10:30pm.)

FAR TREK On your way to Berlin? A *Gran Recorrido* (Great Hike) trail will get you there—eventually. One of the most beautiful and rugged stretches of the pan-European *Gran Recorrido* network treks east to west just below the French-Spanish border. Strung together by old mountain roads, animal tracks, and forest paths, the Aragonese portion of **GR-11** passes by clear mountain lakes and under, over, and through snow-covered peaks (the highest being Mt. Aneto, at 3404m). Though some parts of GR-11 are pretty gentle, the full trek across Aragon requires hiking experience, especially when snow cover is extensive. The border-to-border route takes eight to ten days. For detailed info on this and other GR trails, consult tourist offices in the area or the **Federación Aragonesa de Montañismo** at C. Albareda, 7 (☎ 976 22 79 71) in Zaragoza, or pick up a detailed and trail-specific *Topoguía* guide. The extremely useful *Editorial Alpina* also has a good map of the route.

△ HIKING. If you have only a day to spend in Ordesa, the **Soaso Circle** is the most practical hike, especially for inexperienced mountaineers. Frequent signposts along the wide trail clearly mark the five-hour journey, which traverses forests, cliffs, and plateaus, passing the **Gradas de Soaso** waterfall on the way to **Refugio Góriz.** Check weather forecasts before starting out; heavy snow can make the trail impassable, and it becomes quite slippery and dangerous in the rain. Less intrepid travelers may want to reduce the hike to two hours, although the views from **Cascada del Cueva** (Cave Falls) and especially **Cascada del Estrecho** (Wide Falls) are well worth the 10-minute hike past the *aparcamiento* sign. Whichever route you choose, try to arrive at the park early in the day during July and August because by noon the entire Soaso Circle can resemble Picadilly Circus.

AÍNSA (L'AINSA)

An irresistible, romantic village about an hour away from Ordesa, Aínsa offers an adventure in time-travel. From the friendly shops along its main intersection, Ainsa leads the visitor up a winding road to its perfectly preserved and enchanting medieval quarter, where flowers spill over stone walls into the narrow cobbled streets. A thousand years ago Aínsa was the capital of the Kingdom of Sobrarbe (incorporated into Aragón in the 11th century), and the ruins of its 11th-century **castle** on Pl. Mayor remind visitors of its history. In 1181, priests consecrated the **Iglesia de Santa María,** across the plaza from the castle, where you can climb the tower for 100ptas (not for the tall or claustrophobic).

Compañía Hudebus (☎ 974 21 32 77) runs buses from **Sabiñánigo** to Aínsa, stopping in **Torla** along the way (2hr., 11am, returning at 2:30pm, 730ptas). **Compañía Cortés** (☎ 974 31 15 52) sends a bus from Aínsa to **Barbastro** (1hr., 7am), where buses connect to **Benasque.** The **tourist office,** Av. Pirenáica, 1, at the highway crossroads, advises on transport, lodgings, and excursions. (☎ 974 50 07 67. Open July-Aug. 10am-2pm and 4:30-8:30pm; Sept.-June Tu-Sa 10am-2pm and 4:30-8:30pm, Su 10am-2pm.) Though Aínsa is not as well situated for hiking as Torla or Benasque, the companies in town can arrange countless outdoor activities.

A place like the ▨**Casa Rural El Hospital,** C. Sta. Cruz, 3, only comes along every so often. A converted stone house in the medieval quarter, this small *casa* invites you to soak in the luxury of exposed stone walls, wrought-iron bedposts and antique wood furnishings. Request room #7 for a picture-perfect view. (☎ 974 50 07 50. Doubles with bath, TV, and A/C 4000-4500ptas.) Other budget lodgings lie uphill from the bus station, and **Camping Aínsa,** Ctra. Aínsa-Campo, km 1.8, is just outside of town. (☎ 974 50 02 60. 600ptas per person and per car, 575ptas per tent.) The supermarket **Alimentación M. Cheliz,** on Av. Ordesa at the new town's main intersection, stocks essentials. (☎ 974 50 00 62. Open daily July-Sept. 9am-9pm; Oct.-June 9am-2pm and 4-8pm.) **Restaurante Brasería,** at the *castillo* end of Pl. Mayor, offers a range of *menús* (1800-2400ptas) with fish, game, beef and pasta entrees. (☎ 974 50 09 81. Open daily 10am-5pm and 7pm-midnight. V, MC.)

VALLE DE BENASQUE: BENASQUE

The Valle de Benasque is a haven for no-nonsense hikers, climbers, and skiers. Countless trails wind through the steep mountains, and the area teems with *refugios,* allowing for longer expeditions. Casual hikers are often scared away by the valley's reputation for serious mountaineering—the area has the Pyrenees' highest peaks—but there is something here for even the most mild adventurer. With its many excursion companies and nearby trailheads, the mellow, harmonious town of **Benasque** (pop. 1100) offers an excellent base for outdoor activities. Although the town is growing commercially, its few cobblestone streets remain quiet.

If you start early from Benasque, you can hike just over 8km down the valley road, cross the river on the camping area bridge, and climb up, up, and away, following the falls of the Río Cregüeña. Four sweaty hours later you'll reach **Lago de Cregüeña** (2657m), the largest and highest lake in the surrounding area. To scale

Mount Aneto (3404m), the highest of the Pyrenees, acquire some climbing skills and gear and then head out at 5am with the experts from the **Refugio de la Renclusa** (☎ 974 55 21 06. Open June 22-Sept. 24. 600ptas for a bunk and free kitchen access.) To reach the *refugio*, take the main road north for about 15km until the paved road ends; from there it's a 45-minute hike. Many companies in Benasque also organize trips. For less strenuous nature wandering, head downhill to the road and follow signs to **Forau de Aigualluts,** a lovely pond at the base of a waterfall (30min.).

Crash at night at the **Fonda Barrabés,** C. Mayor, 5, a left from the bus stop and straight ahead 200m. The rooms are clean and well-kept, with flimsy plaid bedspreads and a cold, functional ambiance. (☎ 974 55 16 54. Breakfast 350ptas. Bunks 900ptas; singles 1700ptas; doubles 3300ptas; triples 4500ptas. Visa.) **Camping Aneto,** 3km out of town up the hill past the Cerler turnoff, also offers small bungalows for winter visits. (☎ 974 55 11 41. 475ptas per person, per tent, and per car.) **Restaurante-Crêperie Les Arkades** shares a piece of town history, occupying an old stone building that was constructed in 1647. Visit the delicious *crêperie*/pub for an evening snack or walk through the sun-drenched courtyard to the restaurant. (☎ 974 55 12 02. *Menú* 1500ptas. *Crêperie* open daily July-Sept. and Dec.-Mar. after 5:30pm. Restaurant open daily 1-3:30pm and 8-10:30pm.)

La Alta Aragonesa (☎ 974 21 07 00) runs buses between Benasque and **Huesca** (3hr., 1-2 per day, 1300ptas). To get to the **tourist office** and its volumes of hiking info, face the Hotel Aragüells at the main highway intersection and go one block down the alley, angling to the right. (☎/fax 974 55 12 89. Open July-Aug. and *Semana Santa* daily 9am-2pm and 4-9pm; Sept.-June Tu-F 10am-2pm and 5-8pm, Sa 5-9pm, Su 9:30am-1:30pm.) For the **Guardia Civil** call ☎ 974 55 10 08. Find the **post office** in the **Ayuntamiento** building (☎ 974 55 20 71. Open M-F 9am-noon, Sa 10am-noon, only for stamps.) The **postal code** is 22440.

LA RIOJA AND NAVARRA

The spirit of the Navarrese emanates from the rustic Pyrenean *pueblos* on the French border, through bustling Pamplona, to the dusty villages in the south. Bordered by Basque Country to the west and Aragón to the east, La Rioja and Navarra's little-visited villages greet tourists with open arms and a toast of wine.

Navarra has long experienced the difficulties of Spain's on-again, off-again regionalism. It gained regional autonomy in 1512, only to see it revoked in 1833. To avoid another devastating loss, they sided with the "winners" in the 20th century, allying themselves with Franco's Nationalist forces, victors of the Spanish Civil War. Unfortunately, they found themselves under a regime with no tolerance of regional differences. Since Franco's death, the Navarrese have continued to support regionalist causes and the subsequent re-establishment of provincial autonomy in 1983. Many of the region's northern inhabitants identify themselves as Basque and some are concerned with their regional exclusion from the País Vasco and the Basque independence movement. For one week each July, Navarra becomes the most touristed region in Europe; the festival of *San Fermín* (The Running of the Bulls), which usually triples the population of Pamplona, supports the region's tourist industry for the rest of the year. An extensive network of government-approved *casas rurales* host tourists in lovely private homes that often serve home-cooked meals. The region's epicurean specialty is *trucha a la Navarra* (trout stuffed with ham).

HIGHLIGHTS OF LA RIOJA AND NAVARRA

The world-famous **San Fermines** (Running of the Bulls) in **Pamplona** (see p. 395).

The fantastic views of and from the **Palacio Real** in Olite (see p. 398).

Ochagavía, exactly what a mountain village should be (see p. 403).

The darling towns and prime skiing grounds of the **Valle del Roncal** (see p. 403).

LOCAL FESTIVALS IN LA RIOJA AND NAVARRA

Natives of La Rioja like their wine. **Logroño** celebrates the *Fiestas de la Vendimia* by making an offering of crushed grapes to the Virgin of Valvanera (Sept. 20-26). Residents of **Haro** spray wine at innocent bystanders during the *Batalla del Vino* (June 29). In Navarra, **Estella** kicks off August with the *Fiestas de la Virgen del Puy y San Andrés,* which features baby bull runs. And then, of course, there's always **Pamplona,** home to *the* festival in Spain... (see above).

Tucked under Navarra, La Rioja is famous for one thing: great wine. "Rioja" is an internationally acclaimed wine classification with an 800-year tradition; both the 1994 and 1995 grapes received the highest ratings possible. The name derives from the Ebro tributary Río Oja, whose waters trickle through the vineyards. When ordering wine, asking for *"vino"* will get you the wine of the year, ordering *"crianza"* delivers higher-quality wine at least three years old, while a request for *"gran reserva"* brings the *crème de la crème* (and you'll pay for it). Logroño, capital of La Rioja, lies in the region's center. The best *bodegas* (wine cellars) draw from the lands in western Rioja Alta, around Haro. The Camino de Santiago (see p. 453) passes through much of La Rioja, and tourist offices can provide useful information on the route. The mountainous Sierra region, with tranquil fields at the feet of towering peaks, lines La Rioja's southern border.

LOGROÑO

With characteristic hyperbole, the tourist office brochure proclaims that Logroño (pop. 135,000) feeds both the body and the soul. In reality, although the Camino de Santiago makes a stop here, your soul will find little but bustling commerce for spiritual nourishment. The body, however, will have something to write home about. Logroño, the best entry point into the vineyard towns of La Rioja, is full of bars serving the region's renowned wines and savory, inexpensive *tapas.*

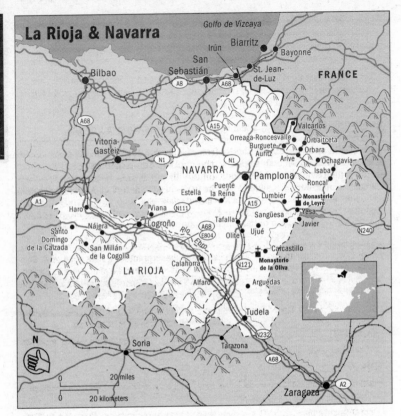

⌐ TRANSPORTATION

Trains: RENFE (☎ 941 24 02 02), Pl. Europa, off Av. España on the south side of town. Bus service is more frequent. Info open daily 7am-11pm. To: **Calahorra** (40min., 3-4 per day 7:30am-8:11pm, 455ptas); **Haro** (45min., 10:05am and 4:40pm, 395-1100ptas); **Burgos** (2hr., 2-3 per day 3:46-6:46pm, 1800ptas); **Zaragoza** (2-2½hr., 4-6 per day 7:30am-8:11pm, 1220-1800ptas); **Bilbao** (4hr.; M-Sa 3:46 and 6:55pm, Sa 3:50pm; 1800ptas); **Madrid** (5½hr., M-Sa 3:20pm, 4000ptas); and **Barcelona** (7hr., 3 per day 12:40-4:18pm, 4100-4200ptas).

Buses: (☎ 941 23 59 83), Av. España, on the corner of C. General Vara and Av. Pío XII. Several companies; check info board for the appropriate counter. Info open daily 6am-11pm. To: **Haro** (1hr., 3-6 per day 7:30am-9:30pm, 345ptas); **Santo Domingo de la Calzada** (1hr.; 3-9 per day, M-F 7:15am-8:30pm, Sa 8:30am-8pm; 11am-10:30pm; 365ptas); **Soria** (1½hr.; 4-5 per day, M-Sa 6:45am-7pm, Su 9:30am-10pm; 805ptas); **Bilbao** (2hr.; M-Sa 8:30am-7:30pm, Su 11am-9pm; 1475ptas); **Burgos** (2hr., 4-7 per day 10:20am-11:35pm, 850ptas); **Pamplona** (2hr., 3-5 per day 7am-7pm, 905ptas); **Vitoria-Gasteiz** (2hr.; 4-6 per day, M-F 7am-8pm, Sa 10:30am-8pm, Su 10:30am-8:45pm; 1005ptas); **Zaragoza** (2hr., 4-12 per day 7am-9pm, 1450ptas); **Madrid** (4hr., 5-8 per day 8am-9:30pm, 2525ptas); and **Barcelona** (6hr., 2-4 per day 1:30pm-1:14am, 3930ptas).

Public Transportation: All buses run to Gran Vía, 1 block from Parque Espolón; lines #1 and 3 pass the bus station. All rides 80ptas.

Taxis: (☎ 941 23 75 29). Stands at the bus station and the northwest corner of the park. **Radio Taxi** (☎ 941 50 50 50).

Car Rental: Avis, Gran Vía, 67 (☎ 941 20 23 54), left off C. General Vara. Min. age 23 and must have had a license for at least 1 year. Open M-F 9am-1:30pm and 4-7pm, Sa 10am-1:30pm. V, MC, AmEx.

■↗ ORIENTATION AND PRACTICAL INFORMATION

Both the old and new towns radiate from the **Parque del Espolón,** a tree-lined set of gravel paths with a fountain at the center. The **casco antiguo** stretches between the park and the Río Ebro, on the far north side of the city. To reach the park from the **train station,** cross the major traffic artery of **Avenida de Lobete** and angle left on Av. España. At the **bus station** (the next major intersection), turn right onto C. General Vara de Rey, which leads north to the park (8min.) and the *casco antiguo.*

Tourist Office: (☎ 941 26 06 65; fax 941 25 60 45; www.larioja.com/turismo), Po. Espolón, at the south end of Parque Espolón in the large rotunda. Take a left off C. General Vara coming from the bus and train stations. Maps and helpful advice in English. Open June 15.-Oct. M-F 10am-2pm and 5-8pm, Sa 10am-2:30pm and 5-8pm, Su 10am-2:30pm; Nov.-May M-Sa 10am-2pm and 4:30-7pm, Su 10am-2pm.

Currency Exchange: Banco Central Hispano, on C. General Vara at the corner of Parque Espolón. **ATM.** Open M-F 8:30am-2:30pm; Oct.-Apr. also Sa 8:30am-1pm.

Luggage Storage: At the **bus station** (200ptas). Open daily 6am-11pm. At the **train station** (400ptas). Open daily 7am-11pm.

Emergency: ☎ 112. **Police:** ☎ 091 or 092.

Medical Services: Hospital de la Rioja, Av. Viana, 1 (☎ 941 29 11 94), on the edge of town in the direction of Pamplona.

Post Office: (☎ 941 22 00 66), Pl. San Agustín, next to the museum. Open M-F 8:30am-8:30pm, Sa 9:30am-2pm. **Postal Code:** 26070.

Internet Access: Centro MAIL, Av. Dr. Mújica, 6 (☎ 941 20 78 33). 100ptas for 15min. Open M-Sa 10am-2pm and 5-9pm, Su noon-2pm and 5-9pm; July-Aug. closed Su.

▌ ACCOMMODATIONS

The *casco antiguo* brims with budget *pensiones* and hostels. Try C. San Juan, the second left past Parque Espolón from the stations, and C. San Agustín and C. Laurel, a little deeper into the old quarter past the far corner of the park. Reservations are crucial for the *fiesta* week around September 21.

Residencia Universitaria (HI), C. Caballero de la Rosa, 38 (☎ 941 29 11 45 or 941 26 14 22). From the stations, go right off C. General Vara onto Mura de Cervantes, which becomes Av. Paz. After 7 blocks, make a left on C. Caballero de la Rosa. Buses #1A and 4 stop nearby. 15-20min. walk from the *casco antiguo.* University dorms during the school year, also used by athletic teams in summer. Common room with TV. Clean doubles with bath. Breakfast 200ptas. Call ahead. HI card not required. Dorms 1000ptas, with sheets 1350ptas. Open July-Sept. with occasional rooms Oct.-June. Cash only.

Hostal Sebastián, C. San Juan, 21 (☎ 941 24 28 00). A central location in the *casco antiguo.* Spacious, clean, airy doubles have baby blue walls and minimal decoration. Good beds and small sinks. Doubles 3600ptas.

Fonda Bilbaína, C. Capitán Eduardo Gallarza, 10, 2nd fl. (☎ 941 25 42 26). Take C. Sagasta into the *casco antiguo*, turn left on C. Hermanos Moray and then right on C. Capitán Eduardo. Bright rooms with high ceilings, shiny floors, good beds, and sinks. Singles 1700ptas; doubles 3000ptas, with shower 3500ptas, with bath 4000ptas.

Camping La Playa, Av. Playa, 6 (☎ 941 25 22 53), off the main highway, across the river from the *casco antiguo*. Riverbank site with beach. Bungalows available. Free pool next door, open after July 15. Laundromat. Electricity 400ptas. Bungalows 5000ptas. 600ptas per person, per tent, per car. Open *Semana Santa* and June-Sept.

⬛ FOOD

Logroñeses take their grapes seriously. Wine is the beverage of choice; don't even try ordering anything else. Head to C. Laurel and C. San Juan, both of which brim with bars and cafes—many have little windows so passers-by can sample the goodies. The local market, **Mercado de San Blas,** is in a large concrete building on C. Capitán Eduardo Gallarza. Take a right off C. Mura de la Francisco de la Mata, along the park (open M-Sa 7:30am-1:30pm and 4-7:30pm). For groceries, head to supermarket **Champión,** Av. La Rioja, a left off C. Miguel Villanueva past the tourist office. (☎ 941 22 99 00. Open M-Sa 9:15am-9:15pm.)

🍴 **Bar Soriano,** Travesía de Laurel, 2 (☎ 941 22 88 07), where C. Laurel makes its 90° turn. Borders on the transcendent. Bartenders shovel shrimp and mushrooms out the window to eager crowds in the street. No indoor seating. The specialty *pintxo* is *champiñones con gambas* (mushrooms with shrimp; 1400ptas). Open daily 11am-3am.

La Taberna de Portales, C. Portales, 39 (☎ 941 25 40 55), across from the cathedral, has outside seating and a lovely view of the plaza. Stuffs just about anything between 2 slices of hot bread—try the *logroñesa* with tomato, bacon, and cheese (375ptas) or the *cordobés* with tomato and a skewer of spicy grilled beef (400ptas). Breakfast specials 275ptas. Lunch-time entrees 875ptas. Open Su-F 9am-midnight, Sa 9am-4am.

👁 🎵 SIGHTS AND ENTERTAINMENT

Housed in an old Baroque palace, the **Museo de la Rioja** has an interesting collection spanning the last eight centuries of art. Renaissance paintings and Impressionist works line the staircase, and most rooms are filled with religious sculptures and paintings. The collection originates from the 1835 state seizure of regional monasteries' and convents' artwork and wealth. (Pl. San Agustín, 23, along C. Portales and next to the post office. ☎ 941 29 12 59. Open Tu-Sa 10am-2pm and 4-9pm, Su 11:30am-2pm. Free.) The ornate Chirrugueresque towers of the **Catedral de Santa María de la Redonda** dominate the Pl. Mercado in the *casco antiguo*. (From C. General Vara turn left on C. Portales; the cathedral is 2 blocks away on the right. Open M-Sa 7:45am-1:15pm and 6:30-10pm, Su 8:15am-1:15pm and 6:30-9pm. Free.) The grassy knolls along the **Río Ebro** make for a nice walk; a pedestrian path and the bridges **Puente de Hierro** and **Puente de Piedra** cross the river.

Logroño **nightlife** begins in the *casco antiguo* along C. Laural and after midnight moves to C. Mayor along Pl. Mercado, C. Sagasta, and C. Carnicerías. The **Fiestas de San Bernabé** (June 11) bring dusk-to-dawn revelry to Logroño and finish with a fantastic fireworks display. But the biggest party in town takes place September 20-26, around the **Fiesta de San Mateo** (Sept. 21). During that same week, locals celebrate the grape harvest with the **Fiestas de la Vendimia,** in which they make a ceremonial offering of crushed grapes to the Virgin of Valvanera. Go to the Plaza de Espolón to see participants crush the grapes with their own bare feet.

THAT'S A WHOLE LOT OF EGGS A visit to one of the many *bodegas* in Haro will make any visitor appreciate the art of wine-making. After the grape juice has been gathered and put into 18,000-liter barrels, workers must ensure that all the grape leftovers are removed from the juice. Every morning, one man breaks between 1000 and 2000 eggs, separating the whites from the yolks. These egg yolks are then poured into the barrel (about 540 eggs per barrel), creating a thick film on the top. This film slowly begins to sink, and after 35 days it has removed any grape debris. The yolks are then donated to neighborhood bakeries to be used in cakes.

🚌 DAYTRIPS FROM LOGROÑO

HARO (1HR.)

RENFE trains (☎0 941 31 15 97) connect Haro to Logroño (35min., 5 per day 12:57-7:30pm, 455-900ptas). The bus station (☎ 941 31 15 43) also sends buses to Logroño (1hr.; 6-7 per day M-F 7:45am-8:30pm, Sa 8:45am-6pm, Su 8:45am-7pm; 345ptas).

The main attractions in Haro (pop. 10,000) are wine, wine, and more wine. With seventeen *bodegas*, the small town serves as the heart of La Rioja's wine industry. Most *bodegas* offer free tours of their facilities in English and Spanish between 9am and 2pm, although reservations are almost always required. Only **Bodegas Muga,** across the river and under the train tracks, can be visited without calling ahead. (☎ 941 31 04 98. Tours M-F June-Aug. 10, 11am (English), and noon; Sept.-May 11am and 4pm.) The tourist office has additional information on visiting *bodegas*. If you're interested in buying some of Haro's wine, try the **wine shops** on C. Santo Tomás. Most charge 200-500ptas per bottle, but some vintages can run up to 3500ptas. In the Estación Etnológica, the **Museo del Vino** has sleek exhibits in Spanish on everything you could ever want to know about wine. (☎ 941 31 05 47. Open M-Sa 10am-2pm and 4-8pm, Su 10am-2pm. 300ptas. W free.) Join the locals and *ir de vinos* ("go for wines") in the evening in **La Herradura,** the area around C. Santo Tomás, off Pl. Paz. Ask for *vino* and you'll get the vintage of the year (50-75ptas); for higher quality, order *crianza*, wine that is more than three years old (150ptas). Haro breaks out in festivities on June 24-29, culminating in the **Batalla del Vino** (June 29), when participants spray wine at innocent bystanders.

To reach Pl. Paz from the train station, take the road downhill, turn right and then left across the river, and follow C. Navarra uphill to the plaza (35min.). From the bus stop, follow signs to *centro ciudad* along C. Ventilla (on the right side of the station), continuing two blocks past the Consum supermarket. Head diagonally left across Pl. Cruz onto C. Araball, which leads straight into Pl. Paz. The bilingual staff at the **tourist office,** Pl. Monseñor Florentino Rodríguez, dispenses information and maps. With your back to the Ayuntamiento, take C. Vega from the far left corner of Pl. Paz. The office is in the plaza to the left around the bend. (☎ 941 30 33 66. Open June-Oct. 15 M-Sa 10am-2pm and 4-7pm, Su 10am-2pm; Oct. 15-May Tu-F 10am-2pm, Sa 10am-2pm and 4:30-7:30pm.) **Banco Central Hispano,** C. Vega, 20, offers **currency exchange** with no commission. (☎ 941 31 11 84. Open Apr.-Sept. M-F 8:30am-2pm; Oct.-Mar. M-F 8:30am-2pm and Sa 8:30am-1pm.)

If too much wine-sampling has left you sleepy, crash at the **Hostal Las Conchas,** C. Vega, 1, right on the main plaza; the rooms are cozy, with white bedspreads, flowered curtains, and TVs. (☎ 941 31 00 22. Singles 3000ptas, with bath 4500ptas; doubles 4500ptas, with bath 5500ptas; triples with bath 6000ptas.)

SANTO DOMINGO DE LA CALZADA (1HR.)

Buses connect Pl. Beato Hermosilla to Haro (20-30min., M-Sa 2-5 per day 8am-7:30pm, 160ptas) and Logroño (1hr.; M-Sa 9 per day, Su 3 per day; 360ptas).

A symbolically important stop along the Camino de Santiago, Santo Domingo de la Calzada (pop. 5800) was founded with the sole purpose of aiding pilgrims. Eleventh-century Saint Dominic retired to the woods southwest of Logroño in search of solitude. Yet day after day he witnessed the trials of pilgrims attempting to cross the river. Admiring their courage, he decided to do something to help. He built a bridge for them, created a road (*calzada*, or causeway) through the woods, and converted his hermitage into a hospice. Soon, business was booming and Santo Domingo became an important stop along the Camino.

King Alfonso VI noticed the work of the hermit and donated resources for the construction of the grand ■**Catedral de Santo Domingo,** even setting the first stone himself. The lavish *retablo* (altarpiece) was removed for restoration in 1994, and exquisite Romanesque pillars were discovered behind where the altarpiece had once stood. Consequently the *retablo* has been moved to a side chapel to preserve the stylistic cohesiveness of the Romanesque church. (☎ 941 34 00 33. Open M-Sa 10am-6:30pm. 300ptas, over 65 and pilgrims 150ptas, under 18 100ptas.) Not far from the cathedral, but over 100 steps up, awaits an outstanding view of the city from the **Tower of the Cathedral.** The present tower, finished in 1766, is actually the third to stand in its place; the first was destroyed by lightning and the second was considered unsafe. The present one (73m high) is supported by a base of limestone, wood, and cattle horns. (Open M-Sa 11am-2pm and 5-8pm. 125ptas.)

To reach the cathedral from the bus stop at Pl. Beato Hermosilla, cross Av. Juan Carlos I and follow C. Alcalde Rodolfo Varona. Take the next left (unmarked C. Pinar) for one block, then turn right on C. Hilario Pérez, which ends at Pl. Santo, bordered by the cathedral and pilgrim hospice-turned-parador. The town's **tourist office** sits in Casa de Trastámara, C. Mayor, 70. From Pl. Santo, face the cathedral, and go left onto C. Mayor. (☎ 941 34 33 34; fax 941 34 12 31. Open M-Sa 10am-2pm and 4:30-7:30pm, Su 10am-2pm.) Although Santo Domingo is best done as a daytrip, persistent non-pilgrims can try the recently renovated **Hostal Miguel,** C. Juan Carlos I, 23, a clean, comfy hostel with big windows. (☎ 941 34 32 52. Doubles 4000ptas, with bath 6000ptas.) **Restaurants** cluster near the cathedral on C. Mayor and adjoining plazas, luring hungry pilgrims with generous *menús*.

PAMPLONA (IRUÑA)

Long, long ago, Pamplona's fiesta in honor of its patron saint San Fermín was just another religious holiday. These days *San Fermines*, July 6-14, is Europe's premier festival and the most talked-about party on the European backpacker circuit. Ever since Nobel-prize-winning author Ernest Hemingway brought the city international attention with *The Sun Also Rises*, hordes of visitors from around the world have come to witness and experience the legendary running of the bulls. At the bullring, a statue of Hemingway welcomes fans to the eight-day extravaganza of dancing, dashing, and of course, drinking; no sleeping allowed.

Though *San Fermines* may be the city's only irresistible attraction, Pamplona (pop. 150,000) is a pleasant place to visit the other 357 days of the year as well. Lush parks, a lovely Gothic cathedral, a massive citadel, and the winding streets of the *casco antiguo* entertain those who show up in the "off season." Although Pamplona is the capital of the province of Navarra, its roots are truly Basque. The Basques had settled the area even before the Roman "founders," who named the city after Pompey the Great.

▐ TRANSPORTATION

Flights: Aeropuerto de Noaín (☎ 948 16 87 00), 6km away, accessible only by taxi (about 1200ptas). To **Barcelona** (30min., M-F 4 per day 7:35am-7:05pm) and **Madrid** (7 per day 6:30am-8:45pm).

Trains: Estación RENFE (☎ 948 13 02 02), off Av. San Jorge. Take bus #9 from Po. Sarasate (20min., 95ptas). Info open daily 6am-10pm. Another more accessible office, C. Estella, 8 (☎ 948 22 72 82), is located near the bus station but has limited hours during *San Fermines*. Exit the bus station and go around the right corner; the office is across the parking lot. Open M-F 9am-1:30pm and 4:30-7:30pm, Sa 9:30am-1pm.

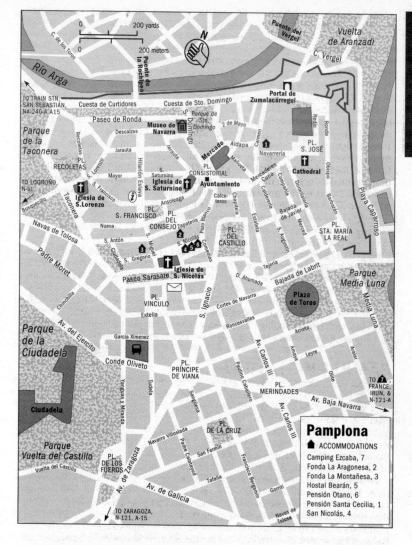

Pamplona
⛺ ACCOMMODATIONS

Camping Ezcaba, 7
Fonda La Aragonesa, 2
Fonda La Montañesa, 3
Hostal Bearán, 5
Pensión Otano, 6
Pensión Santa Cecilia, 1
San Nicolás, 4

Pamplona is miserably connected by rail; reservations are often mandatory on longer trains during *San Fermines,* and the bus is faster and easier. Trains run to: **Olite** (40min., 4 per day 7:58am-8:37pm, 380ptas); **Vitoria-Gasteiz** (1¼hr., 3 per day 8:40am-7:35pm, 585ptas); **Tudela** (1½hr., 4-5 per day 7:25am-6:50pm, 800-1300ptas); **Zaragoza** (2hr., 6 per day 7:25am-8:05pm, 1565-1900ptas); **San Sebastián** (2hr., 2 per day 5:40am-7:10pm, 1195-1500ptas); **Madrid** (5hr., 8 per day, 4200ptas); **Barcelona** (6-8hr.; M-Sa 3 per day, Su 2 per day 12:23-8:05pm; 4100-5300ptas); and **Paris** (13-15hr., 7 per day 9:30am-11:15pm, 11,500ptas).

Buses: Estación de Autobuses (☎ 948 22 38 54), at the corner of C. Conde Oliveto and C. Yanguas y Miranda. Info open daily 6am-10pm. Nearly 20 companies. **La Tafallesa** (☎ 948 22 28 86) to **Olite** (50min.; M-Sa 10 per day, Su 2 per day; 8:15am-8:30pm; 360-390ptas) and **Roncal** (2hr.; M-F 5pm, Sa 1 and 5pm; 990ptas). **La Ron-**

calesa (☎ 948 22 20 79) to **San Sebastián** (1hr., 9 per day 7am-10:45pm, 790ptas) and **Jaca** (1¾hr., 8:30am and 3:30pm, 855-875ptas). **Conda** (☎ 948 22 10 26) to: **Tudela** (1½hr., 7 per day 7:15am-8:45pm, 815-900ptas); and **Zaragoza** (2-3hr., 6-7 per day 7:15am-8:30pm, 1655ptas); and **Madrid** (5hr., 4-7 per day 7am-9:30pm, 3215ptas). **La Burundesa (ALSA)** (☎ 948 22 17 66) to **Vitoria-Gasteiz** (1½hr., 6-13 per day 7am-8:30pm, 900ptas) and **Bilbao** (2hr., 6-7 per day 10:30am-8pm, 1520-1500ptas). **Bilman** (☎ 948 22 09 97) to **Barcelona** (5½hr., 3-4 per day 8:45am-4:40pm, 2820ptas). **La Estellesa** (☎ 948 22 22 23) to **Logroño** (1hr., 4-12 per day 7:30am-7pm, 1000ptas).

Public Transportation: 14 buses cover the city. The tourist office has a list of routes. Bus #9 (orange line) runs from Po. Sarasate to the train station (20min., every 10-15min. 6:30am-10:30pm, 95ptas). During *San Fermines* buses run 24hr. (150ptas).

Taxis: (☎ 948 23 23 23), available at Pl. Castillo and Taconera.

Car Rental: Hertz (☎ 948 31 15 95) in Hotel Tres Reyes, on Jardines de la Taconera. Rentals start at 8000ptas per day, plus tax. Min. age 25. Open M-Sa 9am-1pm and 4-7pm. V, MC, AmEx. **Europcar,** Hotel Blanca Navarra, Av. Pío XII, 43 (☎ 948 17 60 02). Take bus #1, 2, or 4 and get off after the traffic circle on the way out of town. Min. age 21. 60,000ptas per week. Open M-F 9am-1pm and 4-7:30pm, Sa 9am-1pm.

■ ↗ ORIENTATION AND PRACTICAL INFORMATION

The **casco antiguo,** in the northeast quarter of the city, houses almost everything of interest in Pamplona. **Plaza del Castillo,** marked by a bandstand, is Pamplona's center. From the **bus station,** turn left onto Av. Conde Oliveto. At the traffic circle on Pl. Príncipe de Viana, take the second left onto Av. San Ignacio, follow it to the end of the pedestrian thoroughfare Po. Sarasate, and bear right. From the **train station,** take bus #9 (95ptas); disembark at the last stop, cut across Po. Sarasate, and walk diagonally left to Pl. Castillo. North of Pl. Castillo, the Baroque **Casa Consistorial (Ayuntamiento)** makes a handsome marker in the swirl of medieval streets.

Tourist Office: C. Hilarión Eslava, 1 (☎ 948 20 65 40; fax 948 20 70 34; www.pamplona.net). From Pl. Castillo, take C. San Nicolás, turn right on C. San Miguel, and walk straight through Pl. San Francisco. Map and minute-by-minute guides to the festivities. Also a map of Mt. Irati, the best hiking in Navarra (100ptas). English spoken. Info about currency exchange, public baths, and campsite buses is posted on a bulletin board outside. Will hold messages in envelopes for friends. Open during *San Fermines* daily 10am-5pm; July-Aug. M-Sa 10am-2pm and 4-7pm, Su 10am-2pm; Sept.-June M-F 10am-2pm and 4-7pm, Sa 10am-2pm.

Currency Exchange: Reception desk at **Hotel Tres Reyes** (☎ 948 22 66 00), Jardines de la Taconera, changes money 24hr. From the bus station, turn right, bear left at the second fork, and then left again; the hotel is to the left where the road forks. **Banco Central Hispano,** Pl. Castillo, 21 (☎ 948 20 86 00), and in Pl. Vinculo on the corner of C. Estella and C. Alhondiga, has **ATMs.** Open May-Sept. M-F 8:30am-2:30pm; Oct.-Apr. M-F 8:30am-2:30pm, Sa 8:30am-1pm; *San Fermines* 9:30am-12:30pm.

Luggage Storage: At the **bus station.** Bags 200ptas per day, large packs 300ptas per day. Open M-Sa 6:15am-9:30pm, Su 6:30am-1:30pm and 2-9:30pm. Closes for *San Fermines,* when the **Escuelas de San Francisco,** the big stone building at one end of Pl. San Francisco opens instead. Lines are long, and you must have a passport or ID. 300ptas each time you check on your luggage. Open 24hr. **RENFE** (☎ 948 13 02 02) also has lockers. 400ptas per day. Buy tokens at the ticket counter daily 7am-10pm.

Laundromat: Lavomatique, C. Descalzos, 28 (☎ 948 22 19 22). From Pl. San Francisco follow C. Hilarión Eslava to the end, then turn right. Wash, dry, and soap for 1000ptas. Open M-F 4:30-8:30pm; closed during *San Fermines.* **Lavandería Monasterio,** Monasterio de Urdax, 21 (☎ 948 17 50 48). From the bus station take C. Yanguas Y Miranda to the Pl. de Los Fueros, follow Vuelta de Castillo along the park, continue straight to pick up Monasterio de Urdax, and the laundromat is on the left. Wash and dry 1200ptas. Open M-F 8:30am-8pm, Sa 8:30am-2pm; July 8-14 9am-2pm.

Public Toilets and Baths: Squat **toilet booths** are set up for *San Fermines*, but the permanent bathrooms in the **Jardines de Taconera** are more comfortable. **Casa de Baño,** C. Hilarión Eslava, 2 (☎ 948 22 17 38), at the corner of C. Jarauta. Showers 110ptas, towel 40ptas, soap 40ptas. Open Tu-Sa 8am-8pm, Su 8am-2:30pm.

Emergency: ☎ 112. **Municipal Police** (☎ 092), C. Monasterio de Irache, 2.

Late-Night Pharmacy: Changes daily; all pharmacies post the phone number and address of that night's location; or call ☎ 948 22 21 11.

Medical Services: Hospital de Navarra (☎ 948 42 21 00), C. Irunlarrea. The **Red Cross** also sets up stands at the bus station and the *corrida* during *San Fermines*.

Post Office: Po. Sarasate, 9 (☎ 948 21 26 00). Open M-F 8:30am-8:30pm, Sa 9:30am-2pm; *San Fermines* M-Sa 8:30am-2pm. **Postal Code:** 31001.

Internet Access: IturNet Cibercafé, C. Iturrama, 1 (☎ 948 25 28 20; www.iturnet.es), on the corner of C. Abejeras. Bus #2 stops on C. Iturrama. From the bus station, take a left on C. Yanguas y Miranda, then head across Pl. Fueros to C. Abejeras. 500ptas per hr. Open M-Sa 10am-2pm and 4:30-10pm; *San Fermines* daily 9am-2pm. V, MC. **Netiruña,** C. Ezquiroz, 28 (☎ 948 26 01 51). From the bus station take C. Yanguas Y Miranda to Pl. de los Fueros and follow Av. Sancho El Fuerte to C. Ezquiroz. Turn left and go 3 blocks; it's on the right side, back entrance. 400ptas for 30min., 700ptas per hr. Open daily (including *San Fermines*) 10:30am-1:30pm and 3:30-10:30pm.

▌ ACCOMMODATIONS

If you are planning on finding a hotel room during *San Fermines*, good luck. If there was a lucky convergence of stars on the day of your birth and you have truckloads of cash, you *may* find a room during the first few days of the festival. Die-hard partiers book their rooms a year in advance, but most hostels and pensions don't start taking reservations until January. Expect to pay rates up to four times those normally listed (anywhere from 6000-9000ptas per person in most budget hotels). Early in the week, people accost visitors at the train and bus stations, offering couches and floor space in their homes. Be wary—accommodations and prices vary tremendously, and you might find yourself blowing your money for a blink of sleep on a dirty floor in a bad part of town. Check the newspaper *Diario de Navarra* for *casas particulares* and inquire at the tourist office about their extensive listings. Many who can't find rooms sleep outside on the lawns of the Ciudadela, Pl. Fueros, Pl. Castillo, and on the banks of the river. If you do this, store your luggage or sleep on top of it. Parking is free on most streets during *San Fermines*, and many who have cars sleep right in the back seat.

During the remainder of the year, finding a room in Pamplona is no problem. Accommodations that define the word "budget" line C. San Nicolás and C. San Gregorio off Pl. Castillo. Be aware that most hostel owners follow separate price schedules for *temporada alta (San Fermines)*, *temporada media* (summer), and *temporada baja* (rest of the year).

Pensión Santa Cecilia, C. Navarrería, 17 (☎ 948 22 22 30). From C. Chapitela (off Pl. Castillo), take the 1st right on C. Mercaderes, then turn left at a 45° angle; it's on the left. An impressive converted 18th-century mansion/palace. Comfortable rooms have high ceilings and winter heating. Laundry 500ptas. *San Fermines* 6000ptas per person. Rest of the year singles 2500ptas; doubles 4000-5000ptas; triples 6000ptas. V, MC.

Fonda La Aragonesa, C. San Nicolás, 22 (☎ 948 22 34 28). For the reception desk, walk across the street to Hostal Bearán. Simple, clean rooms, shiny hallways, and aromatic bathrooms. *San Fermines* doubles 9000ptas; July-Sept. doubles 3500ptas; Oct.-June doubles 3000ptas. V, MC, AmEx.

Hostal Bearán, C. San Nicolás, 25 (☎ 948 22 34 28). Squeaky-clean salmon-colored rooms, each with phone, TV, bath, safebox, and a whopping pricetag. *San Fermines* singles 13,000ptas; doubles 15,000ptas. July-Sept. singles 5500ptas; doubles 6500ptas. Oct.-June singles 4500ptas; doubles 5500ptas. V, MC, AmEx.

NORTHEASTERN SPAIN

Fonda La Montañesa, C. San Gregorio, 2 (☎ 948 22 43 80). You can't beat the price. No reservations are accepted during the festival, so show up early in the morning. No winter heating. *San Fermines* singles 6000ptas; doubles 12,000ptas. Rest of year singles 1800ptas; doubles 3500ptas. Owner may be flexible with how many to a room.

Pensión Otano, C. San Nicolás, 5 (☎ 948 27 85 08). A great place to eat and sleep. Classy, comfortable doubles have bath, TV, winter heating, and A/C. Several have balconies (good for watching the bulls run by). Breakfast 500ptas. *Menú* 1700ptas. *San Fermines* doubles 16,000ptas. Rest of the year 5500ptas.

San Nicolás, C. San Nicolás, 13 (☎ 948 22 13 19), next to the restaurant of the same name. Small but pleasant rooms, all with shared baths and decent beds. *San Fermines* doms 5000ptas. Rest of the year dorms 2000-2500ptas. V, MC, AmEx.

Camping Ezcaba (☎ 948 33 03 15), in Eusa, 7km away on the road to Irún. From Pl. Toros, La Montañesa bus runs to Eusa (4 per day 9:10am-8:30pm), or take the city bus, line 4-1 (every 20min., 95ptas). Get off at the gasoline station, the last stop. Capacity 714 campers; it fills fast during *San Fermines*. No reservations. *San Fermines* 1100ptas per person, per tent, and per car. Rest of the year 540ptas. Open June-Oct.

🍴 FOOD

While *San Fermines* draws street vendors selling everything from roast chicken to *churros*, the tiny neighborhoods of Pamplona advertise hearty *menús* throughout the year. Try the side streets near Pensión Santa Cecilia, the area above Pl. San Francisco, and C. Jarauta and C. Descalzos, near Po. Ronda. C. Navarrería and Po. Sarasate house numerous *bocadillo* bars. Bars in Pl. Castillo serve sandwiches and pizza, but service is horrendous during the festival. The *barracas políticas* (bars organized by political interest groups that don't expect any interest in their platforms), next to the amusement park in the Ciudadela, offer cheap drinks and equally cheap ideology. Many cafes and restaurants close for one to two weeks after *San Fermines* to recover. The **market,** C. Mercado, is to the right of Casa Consistorial's facade, down the stairs (open M-Sa 8am-2:30pm). For a **supermarket,** check out **Vendi** at the corner of C. Hilarión Eslava and C. Mayor. (Open M-F 9am-2pm and 5:30-7:30pm, Sa 9am-2pm; *San Fermines* M-Sa 9am-2pm. V, MC.)

🍴 **Restaurante Sarasate,** C. San Nicolás, 19-21 (☎ 948 22 57 27), above the seafood store. Delicious organic vegetarian cuisine awaits toxin-filled *Sanferministas* in a pleasant, spotless dining room. Rice, pasta, and vegetable dishes are specialties. Lunchtime *menú* 1500ptas. Open M-Th 1:15-4pm and 8:15-11pm, F-Sa 1:15-4pm and 9-11pm.

Bar-Restaurante Lanzale, C. San Lorenzo, 31 (☎ 948 22 10 71), between C. Mayor and C. Jarauta, above Pl. San Francisco. Cheery dining room is packed with hungry locals eager for the changing *menú* (1150ptas) and delicious desserts. Entrees 1000-1700ptas. Open M-Sa 1:30-3:30pm and 9-11pm. Bar open daily 10am-midnight with lots of *bocadillos* (500-700ptas). V, MC, AmEx.

Hong Kong, C. San Gregorio, 38 (☎ 948 22 66 35). Look for the red balcony. Ignore the cheesy Chinese pop music and fill up on the extensive, inexpensive choices. Come with friends and split a 2-, 3-, 4-, or 5-person *menú* (2700-6750ptas). Noodle and fried rice entrees 600-1000ptas. Open daily noon-4pm and 8pm-midnight. Visa.

🏛 SIGHTS

CATHEDRAL AND CHURCHES. Pamplona's rich architectural legacy is ample reason to visit all year long. The recently restored late 14th-century **Gothic cathedral** houses an ornate alabaster mausoleum where Carlos III and his wife Queen Leonor are entombed. Off the cloister is a five-chimneyed kitchen, one of four of its kind in all of Europe. (*At the end of C. Navarrería.* ☎ 948 21 08 27. *Open M-F 10am-1:30pm and 4-7pm, Sa 10am-1:30pm. Tours at 10:30, 11:30am, 12:30, and 5pm. 500ptas.*) Church lovers will also enjoy the Gothic 13th-century **Iglesia de San Saturnino,** near the Ayuntamiento, and **Iglesia de San Nicolás,** in Pl. San Nicolás. (*Both open daily 9am-12:30pm and 6-8:30pm. Free.*) For a peek at San Fermín himself, head to **Iglesia de San Lorenzo.** (*C. Mayor, 74. Open daily 8am-12:30pm and 6:30-8pm.*)

CIUDADELA. The pentagonal Ciudadela was built by Felipe II in an effort to secure the city's safety. Today it is part of a grassy park that hosts free exhibits and concerts in the summer. Its impressive walls even scared off Napoleon, who refused to launch a frontal attack and staged a trick snowball fight instead; when Spanish sentries joined in, the French entered the city through its gates. To get to the intimidating **walls** from the old quarter, pick up C. Redín at the far end of the cathedral plaza. A left turn follows the walls past the **Portal de Zumalacárregui** and along the Río Arga. Bear left through the gardens of **Parque de la Taconera**—where some random deer, swans, and peacocks hang out—until reaching the Ciudadela. (*Av. Ejercito.* ☎ *948 22 82 37. Open daily 7:30am-10pm; closed during San Fermines. Free.*)

MUSEO DE NAVARRA. The Museo de Navarra shelters beautifully preserved 4th- and 5th-century Roman mosaics, murals from all over the region, and a nice collection of 14th- to 20th-century paintings, including Goya's portrait of the Marqués de San Adrián. (*In the casco antiguo, up C. Santo Domingo from Casa Consistorial.* ☎ *948 42 64 92. Open Tu-Sa 10am-2pm and 5-7pm, Su 11am-2pm; San Fermines Tu-Su 11am-2pm. 300ptas, students 150ptas, Su and Sa afternoons free.*)

🎵 ENTERTAINMENT

Plaza de Castillo is the social heart of Pamplona throughout the year. Hemingway's favorite haunt was **Café-Bar Iruña,** the backdrop for much of *The Sun Also Rises.* Though the turn-of-the-century cafe maintains a timeless feel, its prices are very 21st century. (*Café con leche* 200ptas. Good *bocatas* 500ptas. Prices go up by 100ptas for outside tables. Open daily 5pm-2am; *San Fermines* 8am-4am).

The young and the restless booze up at bars in the *casco antiguo.* C. de Jarauta is a nighttime favorite, as well as C. San Nicolás and C. San Gregorio. **Bodegan La Ribera,** C. Navaria, 11, is a good place for cheap beers (175ptas) and poolside rock 'n' roll. Bars across the street draw an older but equally hip crowd. Claustrophobes escape the cramped streets of San Gregorio and San Nicolás to bars in Barrio San Juan, beyond Hotel Tres Reyes on Av. Bayona; many draw a gay clientele.

> Although Pamplona is usually a very safe city, crime skyrockets during *San Fermines,* when assaults and muggings do occur. Unfortunately, some come to the fiesta to take advantage of tourists. Do not roam alone at night, and be extremely cautious in the parks and shady streets of the *casco antiguo.* Enthused revelers who pass out in parks can say good-bye to their wallets and money belts.

📑 LOS SAN FERMINES (JULY 6-14)

"My gosh! I'm sleepy now, doesn't this thing ever stop?"
"Not for a week," was the seasoned response.
    — The Sun Also Rises

Visitors from the world over crowd Pamplona for the *Fiestas de San Fermín*—known to most as "The Running of the Bulls"—in search of Europe's greatest party. Pamplona delivers, with an eight-day frenzy of parades, bullfights, parties, dancing, fireworks, concerts, and wine. Pamplonese, uniformly clad in white garb with red sashes and bandanas, literally throw themselves into the merry-making, displaying obscene levels of physical stamina and alcohol tolerance.

Around 11am on July 6, the whole city crowds its way into the plaza around the Ayuntamiento. The mass sings and chants "*San Fermín!*" with *pañuelos* flying until the mayor appears at noon. He fires the first rocket (*chupinzao*), from the Ayuntamiento's balcony, and a barbaric howl explodes from the sea of expectant *sanferministas* in the plaza below. Champagne rains (be wary of flying corks) along with eggs, ketchup, wine, and flour. Within minutes the streets of the *casco antiguo* flood with improvised singing and dancing troupes. The *peñas*, societies more concerned with beer than bullfighting, lead the hysteria. At 5pm on the 6th and at 9 or 9:30am every other day, they are joined by the *Comparsa de Gigantes y Cabezudos*, a troupe of *gigantes* (giant wooden monarchs) and *zaldikos* (courtiers on horseback). *Kilikis* (swollen-headed buffoons) run around chasing little kids and hitting them with play clubs. These misfits, together with church and Ayuntamiento officials, escort San Fermín on his triumphant procession through the *casco antiguo*. The saint's 15th-century statue is brought from the Iglesia de San Lorenzo at 10am on July 7, the actual day of *San Fermín*. (Note: virtually everything closes on the 7th; hours listed for the festival refer only to the 6th and the 8th through 14th.)

THE RUNNING OF THE BULLS

The running of the bulls, called the *encierro*, is the focal point of *San Fermines*. The ritual dates back to the 14th century, when it served the practical function of getting the bulls from their corrals to the bullring. These days, the first *encierro* of the festival takes place at 8am on July 7 and is repeated at 8am every day for the following seven days. Hundreds of bleary-eyed, hung-over, hyper-adrenalized runners flee from very large bulls as bystanders cheer from barricades, windows, balconies, and doorways.

A rocket marks the release of the bulls onto the 825m course. One to three animals are released from their pens as runners scurry away. If you want to participate in the bullring excitement, you can line up by the Pl. Toros well before 7:30am and run in *before* the bulls are even in sight (though such a "cowardly" act will bring booing from the locals). You can then "play" with the bulls in a mass of 350 people or so. Three to six steers accompany the six to nine bulls—watch out, they have horns, too. Both the bulls and the mob are dangerous. Terrified runners, all convinced the bull is right behind them, flee for dear life and react without concern for those around them. Experienced runners, many of whom view the event as an athletic art form, try to get as dangerously close to the bull as possible. The course has three sharp turns which the fast-running bulls have difficulty cornering; when their legs slide out from under them, they falter, creating a pile of bull. One of the turns is often left unbarricaded—here, a human wall, held together by linked arms, is the sole reinforcement.

RUNNING SCARED So, you're going to run with the bulls. No one wants to see you end up on evening news programs around the world, so here are a few words of *San Fermines* wisdom:

■ Research the *encierro* before you run. The tourist office dispenses a pamphlet that outlines the exact route of the three-minute run and offers tips for inexperienced runners. You should also watch it once on TV to get a glimpse of what you're in for, and once in person to experience the crush and hysteria first-hand. Check out the tourist office for exhibitions on the event's tradition and history.

■ Do not stay up all night drinking and carousing. Not surprisingly, hung-over foreigners have the highest rate of injury. Experienced runners get lots of sleep the night before and arrive at the course no later than 7am. Many locals recommend arriving at 6am. Access to the course closes at 7:30am.

■ Wear proper clothing (nothing loose or baggy) and appropriate shoes. Do not carry anything with you (especially a backpack or video camera).

■ Give up on getting near the bulls and concentrate on getting to the bullring in one piece. Although some whack the bull with rolled newspapers, runners should never distract or touch the animals; anyone who does is likely to anger the bull and locals alike.

■ Try not to cower in a doorway; people have been trapped and killed this way.

■ Be particularly wary of isolated bulls—they seek company in the crowds.

■ If you fall, **stay down.** Curl up into a fetal position, lock your hands behind your head, and **do not get up** until the clatter of hooves has passed.

After cascading through a perilously narrow opening (where a large proportion of the injuries occur), the run pours into the bullring, amid shouts and cries from appreciative spectators. Hemingway had the right idea: don't run—watch the *encierro* from the bullring instead. Music, waves, chanting, and dancing pump up the spectators until the headline entertainment arrives. Bullring spectators should arrive around 6:45am. Tickets for the *Grada* section of the ring are available before 7am (M-F 450ptas, Sa-Su 600ptas). You can watch for free, but the free section is overcrowded, and it can be hard to see and breathe.

To watch one of the actual bullfights, you must wait in the line that forms at the bullring around 8pm every evening (tickets start at 2000ptas). As one bullfight ends, tickets go on sale for the next day. Though the *sol* section can get pretty damn hot, it is cheaper and generally more fun.

THE REST OF THE DAY

Once the running is over, the insanity spills into the streets, gathering steam until nightfall when it explodes with singing in the bars, dancing in the alleyways, spontaneous parades, and a no-holds-barred party in Pl. Castillo, which quickly becomes Europe's biggest open-air dance floor. The right attire for this dance-a-thon includes sturdy shoes (there's glass everywhere), a white t-shirt (that will soon be soaked with wine), a red *pañuelo* (bandana), and a cheap bottle of champagne (to spray, of course). English speakers often congregate where C. Estafeta hits Pl. Toros, an outdoor consortium of local *discotecas*. A word to the wise: avoid the fountain-jumping (you'll know it when you see it). It is *not* a traditional part of the festivities—it was inaugurated by Americans, Aussies, and Kiwis—and several people have died in recent years. The truly inspired partying takes place the first few days of *San Fermines*. After that, the crowds thin, and the atmosphere goes from dangerously crazed to mildly insane. The party begins (or ends) each day at 6am, when bands march down the streets, waking everyone for the running. In between, the city eases the transition with concerts, outdoor dances, and a host of other performances. The end of the festivities culminates at midnight of July 14 with the singing of *Pobre de mí* ("Poor Me"): *"Pobre de mí, pobre de mí, que se han acabao las Fiestas de San Fermín."*

Nearby towns sponsor *encierros* as well: **Tudela** holds its festival during the week of July 24, **Tafalla** during the week of August 15, and **Sangüesa** for a week beginning September 11. Many Pamplonese opt to take part in a festival less touristed than their own.

▐ DAYTRIPS FROM PAMPLONA

The following daytrips are actually closer to small towns in the Pyrenees, especially Sangüesa, but the only public transportation runs from Pamplona.

▧ GORGES (1HR.)

Rio Irati buses (☎ 948 22 24 70) run to Lumbier from Pamplona (1hr.; M-F 2 per day, Sa 1 per day; 365-410ptas). From Lumbier to Iso you have to walk, drive, or take a taxi.

Two fantastic gorges cut into the mountains near Pamplona. Outside the little town of Lumbier, the **Foz de Lumbier** (Lumbier Gorge) drops 50m to the Río Irati. A path alongside the gorge leads through old railway tunnels. 12km down the road, near the town of Iso, awaits an even more impressive gorge, the 6km **Foz de Arbayún.** A lookout affords gorgeous views and glimpses of swooping griffin vultures, and a small footpath follows the Río Salazar until it gets too narrow.

CASTILLO DE JAVIER (1HR.)

La Tafallesa (☎ 948 22 28 86) runs a bus from Pamplona to Javier (1hr.; M-F 5pm, Sa1:30pm; 500ptas). Buses return Monday through Saturday at 8am.

Near the entrance to the small village of Javier is the restored **Castillo de Javier,** the birthplace of San Francisco Xavier (Javier). On the border between Navarra and Aragón, this picture-perfect castle has changed hands numerous times over the last millennium, landing finally in the Jesuits' possession. Its **Chapel of the Holy Christ** houses a 14th-century effigy that is said to have suffered a spontaneous blood-sweating fit at the moment of San Francisco Xavier's death. (Open daily 9am-1pm and 4-7pm; last entrances at 12:40 and 6:40pm. Free, but donations requested. Occasional tours in Spanish.)

MONASTERIO DE LEYRE (1HR.)

The La Tafallesa (☎ 948 22 28 86) bus that runs from Pamplona to Javier (1hr.; M-F 5pm, Sa 1:30pm; 500ptas) continues to nearby Yesa for 10ptas more. Buses return M-Sa 8am. From Yesa, it's a 5km uphill walk to the monastery.

Windswept and austere, the Monasterio de Leyre silently surveys the foothills of the Pyrenees and the fabricated lake, Lago de Yesa. In the 12th century, Navarrese kings took up residence in the **monasterio medieval.** Because monks still live at Leyre, you can enter neither this part nor the 20th-century **monasterio nuevo,** but the dank, subterranean **cripta** eagerly welcomes visitors. The architectural highlight of the monastic complex itself is the ghoulish 12th-century **Portal de la Iglesia,** but perhaps more intriguing is the **Fuente de San Virila,** a fountain in the precise place where, according to legend, the abbot of San Virila fell into a 300-year trance induced by the singing of a nightingale. (☎ 948 88 41 50. Open Apr.-Oct. M-F 10:15am-2pm and 3:30-7pm, Sa 10:15am-2pm and 4-7pm; Nov.-Mar. M-Sa 10:15am-1:30pm and 3:30-6pm, Su 10:15am-1:30pm and 3:30-6pm. 250ptas, children 50ptas. Guided tours with 15 people. Gregorian mass M-Sa 9am and Su at noon.)

Connected to the monastery, the **Hospedería de Leyre** offers comfortable rooms that, with cozy beds, TVs, and private bathrooms, make the monks' original cells look like, well, monks' cells. (☎ 948 88 41 00; fax 948 88 41 37. Breakfast 775ptas. Lunch and dinner *menú* 1550ptas. July-Aug. and *Semana Santa* singles 4725ptas; doubles 9240ptas. Rest of the year singles 4350ptas; doubles 7625ptas. V, MC, AmEx). Cheaper shut-eye, a **supermarket,** and **banks** await downhill in Yesa.

OLITE

Olite (pop. 3000) was a city fit for kings in the early 15th century. Its proximity to Pamplona (35min.) and its Gothic, Baroque, and medieval architecture may make it fit for you too. The **Palacio Real,** former palace of the Navarrese kings, is Olite's crown jewel. In the early 15th century, Carlos III made this sumptuous palace the focus of Navarrese court life. Although the 1937 restoration was far from subtle, the palace's spiral staircases, lookout perches, and abundant towers are fun to explore. (☎ 948 74 00 35. Open daily July-Aug. 10am-2pm and 4-8pm; Apr.-June and Sept. 10am-2pm and 4-7pm; Oct.-Mar. 10am-2pm and 3-5:30pm. Closed Dec. 25 and Jan. 1. 400ptas, seniors and children 250ptas, under 6 free. Guided tours in Spanish every hr. on weekends.) Sandwiched between the Palacio Real and the **Palacio Viejo,** at the base of Plaza de Carlos III, is the **Iglesia de Santa María,** noted for its 14th-century Gothic facade and belfry. **Iglesia de San Pedro** is fitted with an octagonal tower; turn right on Rua Villavieja from the Palacio Real and follow it to its end. (Ask in the tourist office about guided visits.)

Trains (☎ 948 70 06 28) run to **Pamplona** (40min., 2 per day 7:50am-4:05pm, 410ptas), Tudela, and other points on the Vitoria-Gasteiz-Zaragoza line. To get from the **RENFE station** to Pl. Carlos III, take C. Estación to Bar Orly, walk through the archway, and follow Rua San Francisco past **Plaza Teobaldos** and through another arch to **Plaza Carlos III.** The bus is more convenient and cheaper. **Conda** (☎ 948 22 10 26) and **La Tafallesa** (☎ 948 22 28 86) run buses to **Pamplona** (35min., 6-12 per day 7am-8:30pm, 370ptas), and there are 4-7 buses per day from Pamplona to Olite (8:15am-7:30pm, 370ptas). Conda also runs to **Tudela** (5-7 per day, 460ptas). La Tafallesa stops at Bar Orly; to reach Pl. Carlos III, follow the instructions from the train station. Conda stops at the *Carretera;* to reach Pl. Carlos III, follow C. El Portillo for a block. The staircase leading underground from the middle of Pl. Carlos III goes to the **tourist office.** (☎/fax 948 74 17 03. Open Apr.-Sept. M-F 10am-2pm and 4-7pm, Sa-Su 10am-2pm; Oct.-Mar. daily 10am-2pm.) Services include: **emergency** (☎ 112); **banks** in Pl. Carlos III; and the **post office** on the far end of the plaza from the palace. (☎ 948 74 05 82. Open M-Sa 9-11:30am.) The **postal code** is 31390.

The luxurious air of the court lingers in many of Olite's restaurants and accommodations. **Fonda Gambarte,** Rua Seco, 13, 2nd fl., off Pl. Carlos III, has basic doubles for 3500ptas and a downstairs **restaurant** (☎ 948 74 01 39. 2-course *menú* 1400ptas. Open M-F 1-3:30pm and 8:30-10:30pm. Visa). A more expensive but newly renovated option is **Carlos III El Noble,** Rúa de Medíos, 1, right off Pl. Carlos III, near the tourist office. All doubles have TVs, fans, and clean bathrooms. (☎ 948 74 06 44. July-Aug. 8500ptas; off-season 6500ptas. IVA not included. V, MC.) **Camping Ciudad de Olite** (☎ 948 74 06 04; fax 948 74 10 14), 1km outside of town on C. de Sta. Brígida, provides decent accommodations at 425ptas per person and car and 475ptas per tent. There are **supermarkets** on C. Mayor, off Pl. Carlos III, and a **market** on Po. Doña Leonor and Pl. San Antón, at the end of R. Mayor (W 9am-1:30pm).

TUDELA

A major Muslim center until Christian King Sancho the Strong outmuscled the Moors in 1114, Tudela (pop. 26,000) hosted eminent Muslim and Jewish populations throughout the Middle Ages. The city is not worth going out of the way for, but it definitely makes a pleasant stop en route to Pamplona or Zaragoza. The airy Gothic ■**cathedral,** built on the site of the town's old mosque, rises from Pl. Vieja in the *casco antiguo,* across from the tourist office. An amalgam of styles from different periods, the cathedral features a Romanesque **cloister,** 15th-century Gothic *retablos* (altarpieces), and a chilling Last Judgment tympanum over the west portal. (Open Tu-Sa 9am-1pm and 4-7pm, Su 9am-1pm. M-Sa mass at 9:30 and 11am. Cloister 100ptas.) The ominous 12th-century **Iglesia de la Magdalena,** visible from the city entrance, stands out from Tudela's pleasant *casco antiguo.* An imposing 16th-century mansion, the **Palacio del Marqués de San Adrián,** is next to P. Judería, a left off Muro heading toward the train tracks and out of town.

Old town and new meet in the **Plaza de los Fueros.** To get to Pl. Fueros from the combined **bus and train station,** cross the plaza up Cuesta de la Estación, make the second right onto Av. Zaragoza, go straight for five blocks, and then turn left onto C. Gaztambide-Carrera, which leads to the plaza. The **Casa del Reloj,** with its ornate clock tower, presides over the city's west end. Right (north) of the plaza when facing the clock is the **casco antiguo,** overlooked by the **Castillo de Sancho el Fuerte** and the **Monumento al Corazón de Jesús,** which crown a hill at the edge of town. The **tourist office,** on Pl. Vieja alongside the cathedral, has a **fax** machine and a great map. To get there from Pl. Fueros, head sharply right when facing the clock tower onto C. Concarera. Cross Pl. San Jaime to the street in the far right corner, follow it around the corner, and look to your right. (☎ 948 84 80 58. Open Apr.-Oct. M-F 9am-3pm and 4-7pm, Sa-Su 10am-2pm; Nov.-Mar. M-F 9am-3pm, Sa 10am-2pm.)

Budget accommodations are not exactly abundant in Tudela. However, modern, hotel-quality accommodations at a reasonable price can be found at the perfectly situated **Hostal Remigio,** C. Gaztambide, 4, on the way from the train and bus station to Pl. Fueros. . (☎ 948 82 08 50. Breakfast 425ptas, *menú* 1500ptas. Singles 1900ptas, with bath 2800ptas; doubles 3800ptas, with bath 5100ptas. Higher rates July, Aug., and *Semana Santa.* V, MC, AmEx.) **Bar/Casa de Huéspedes Estrella,** C. Carnicerías, 14, off C. Yanguesa y Miranda from the northwest corner of Pl. Fueros, offers rooms overlooking a pleasant plaza. Ask in the bar about rooms. (☎ 948 41 04 42. Reception 9am-3pm and 6pm-midnight. Doubles 3200ptas.)

Two **RENFE** train lines (☎ 948 82 06 46) run through Tudela: one connects La Miranda to Zaragoza via Castejón de Ebro; the other connects Zaragoza to Vitoria-Gasteiz via Pamplona. Trains go to: **Zaragoza** (7 per day 6:40am-9:27pm, 1100ptas); **Miranda** (3:38pm, 1420ptas); **Pamplona** (5pm, 820ptas); and **Vitoria** (7:15am-8:29pm, 1420ptas). Conda **buses** (☎ 948 82 03 42) run to: **Pamplona** (1½hr., 6-9 per day 8am-9:30pm, 845ptas); **Olite** (1hr., 5 per day 8am-6pm, 475ptas); **Tarazona** (1hr., M-Sa 5 per day 10:15am-7:30pm, 220ptas); and **Madrid** (3-4 per day 7:30am-7pm, 2480ptas) via Soria, Zaragoza, and San Sebastián.

NEAR TUDELA: BARDENAS REALES

The awesome desert **Bardenas Reales,** with textured hills and cliffs wrought by erosion, covers over 400 sq. km near the beginning of the Tudela-Pamplona road. The vistas are best contemplated from a mountain bike or car. To rent a bike, take the bus from Tudela to Pamplona and ask to be let off in the unremarkable, sunblasted town of **Arguedas** (20min., 125ptas). There, **Ciclos Marton,** C. San Ignacio, 2, has mountain bikes for full-day rental. (☎ 948 83 15 77 or 948 83 00 85. 2000ptas for first day, 1000ptas each additional day.) Cyclists should remain on the official roads for safety's sake, and call ahead (☎ 948 84 80 58) about weather conditions, as the heat can sometimes be prohibitive. The tourist office in Tudela can provide tips and directions on visiting the Bardenas.

ESTELLA

Hiding between the robust cities of Logroño and Pamplona, charming Estella (pop. 13,000) snuggles into a bend in the Río Ega. What it lacks in size and glamor, it makes up for in hospitality toward the faithful. With tell-tale walking sticks in hand, pilgrims traversing the Camino de Santiago have been descending upon Estella since the town's founding for that exact purpose in 1090. Even non-religious visitors will find Estella enjoyable. With an appealing plaza, mellow cafes, and heaven-sent pastry shops on every corner, it is a perfect place to stay if you can't get Pamplona accommodations for *San Fermines*, or a nice stop-over en route to larger destinations.

■■ **ORIENTATION AND PRACTICAL INFORMATION.** Two streets form a cross through the heart of town, which in turn is bounded by the river. **Calle San Andrés/Calle Baja Navarra** runs north-south from the bus station on Pl. Coronación to the **Plaza de los Fueros. Paseo de la Inmaculada Concepción** runs east-west from C. Dr. Huarte to the **Puente (bridge) del Azucarero,** which spans the river and leads to the old town, where most sights and the tourist office await. To get to the *puente* from the bus station, go right and then follow the river road to the left.

La Estellesa buses (☎ 948 55 01 27) leave from the station on Pl. Coronación to: **Logroño** (50min., 9 per day 8:30am-8:30pm, 495ptas); **Pamplona** (1hr., 6-12 per day 6:50am-8pm, 430-510ptas); **San Sebastián** (1½-2hr., 5-6 per day 8:45am-7:45pm, 1210ptas); **Zaragoza** (2½hr., M-Sa 8:30am, 1640ptas). The **tourist office,** C. San Nicolás, 1 (☎/fax 948 55 63 01), is a straight shot from the bridge through Pl. San Martín, around the corner to the right. The staff has a map and info on the *camino* and surrounding areas. (Open June-Sept. M-Sa 10am-8pm, Su 10am-2pm; Oct.-May M-Sa 10am-5pm, Su 10am-2pm.) Town services include: **emergency** (☎ 112); **police,** Po. Inmaculada, 1 (☎ 948 54 82 00); and the **post office,** Po. Inmaculada, 5, which sells stamps and has **Lista de Correos.** (☎ 948 55 17 92. M-F 8:30am-2:30pm, Sa 9:30am-1pm.) The **postal code** is 31200.

▶ **ACCOMMODATIONS.** Near Pamplona, Estella is a good place to catch some shut-eye during *San Fermines*. Reservations are advisable during its own August *encierro* (running of the bulls). **Pensión San Andrés,** C. Mayor, 1, overlooks a pretty plaza; take the first left off C. Baja Navarra after crossing Po. Inmaculada, down C. Mayor. The friendly proprietess adorns her tidy rooms with TVs and woven bedspreads, and some have refrigerators. (☎ 948 55 41 58. Breakfast 350ptas. July-Aug. and *Semana Santa* singles 1800ptas, with bath 3500ptas; doubles 3500ptas, with bath 5000ptas. Sept.-June singles 1800ptas, with bath 3000ptas; doubles 3200ptas; with bath 4500ptas. IVA not included.) **Hostal Cristina,** C. Baja Navarro on the corner of Pl. de los Fueros, houses guests in spacious doubles, complete with large windows, private bathrooms and TV. (☎ 948 55 04 59; fax 948 55 07 72. July-Aug. and *Semana Santa* doubles 7000ptas; Sept.-June 6000ptas. IVA not included.) **Fonda Izarra,** C. Calderería, 20, off Pl. Fueros, offers simpler rooms with pretty comforters but sagging bed-springs. (☎ 948 55 06 78. Breakfast 250ptas. June-Aug. doubles 4000ptas; Oct.-May 3500ptas. Closed Sept. Visa). **Camping Lizarra** is on C. Ordoiz, left from the tourist office and and a 20min. walk (1km) down-river, past the factory. If you're taking the bus in from Pamplona, tell the driver you're going to the campsite and he'll save you 10-15 minutes by dropping you off at the turn-off. The grounds have a supermarket, pool, 18-bed hostel, and small restaurant-bar, and are divided into four- and two-spot (*parcela* and half-*parcela*) plots; a tent and a car each count as one spot. (☎ 948 55 17 33; fax 948 55 47 55. 725ptas per half-*parcela*, with tent, car, and electricity; 515ptas per extra adult; hostel bunks 950ptas.)

FOOD. Estella is known throughout the region for its *gorrín asado* (roast piglet, also called *gorrín de Estella*). Picnickers can stock up at **Supermarket Vendi,** C. Zapatería, at the corner of C. Navarrería and C. Mayor. To get there, take the first right off C. Baja Navarra after Po. Inmaculada Concepción, then go straight three blocks. (Open M-Sa 9am-2pm and 4:30-8pm, July-Sept. closed Sa afternoon.) To enjoy the regional cuisine at **Restaurante Casanova,** C. Fray Wenceslao de Oñate, 7, take the first left as you enter Pl. Fueros and look for the wood sign. A classy upstairs dining room awaits with overwhelming portions sure to slow any pilgrim's progress. (☎ 948 55 28 09. *Menú* M-F 1300ptas, Sa-Su 2200ptas. Fish and meat entrees 1400-2000ptas. Open in summer daily 1-3:30pm and 8-11pm; off-season M 1-3:30pm, Tu-Su 1-3:30pm and 8:30-11pm.)

SIGHTS AND ENTERTAINMENT. In the "modern" quarter, the 12th-century **Iglesia de San Miguel** commands a view of the town from the hilltop Pl. San Miguel. Its highlight is its ornately carved stone portal depicting St. Michael fighting dragons, weighing souls, and generally taking care of business. Up the stairs and opposite the tourist office, the **Iglesia de San Pedro de la Rúa** towers above **Calle de la Rúa,** the main street of the original mercantile center. The bulbous 12th- to 13th-century late Romanesque/early Gothic church has an unusual half-destroyed cloister. Left from the tourist office at the end of C. Rúa lurks the **Iglesia del Santo Sepulcro,** whose 14th-century facade features a monstrous Satan swallowing the damned by the mouthful. (Outside of mass hours, the San Miguel and San Pedro churches can be visited only by taking guided tours, offered in Spanish, English and French. Tours of all the monumental sites cost 550ptas and can be arranged at **Cultura 5,** C. San Nicolas, 3, ☎ 948 55 00 70.) Across from San Pedro and next to the tourist office, the oldest representation of Roland in the world jousts with Farragut the Moor on the columns of the 12th-century Romanesque **Palacio de los Reyes de Navarra,** now the **Museo Gustavo.** Inside are the impressive works of painter Gustavo de Maesta, who spent his last years in Estella. Changing temporary exhibits are held on the first floor. (☎ 948 54 60 37; fax 948 55 32 57. Open Tu-Sa 11am-1pm and 5-7pm, Su 11am-1pm. Free.) The week-long **Fiestas de la Virgen del Puy y San Andrés** kicks off the beginning of August. Estella has an *encierro* with baby bulls, smaller and less ferocious than Pamplona's. Kiddie entertainment, a fair, and Navarrese dancing and *gaitas* (bagpipes without the bags) round out the *fiestas.*

NAVARRESE PYRENEES

Navarra includes the most topographically diverse range of the Pyrenees. Forbidding peaks dominate the eastern Valle de Roncal, but the mountain slopes to the west are gentler, allowing easier access to the area's streams, waterfalls, and green meadows. Mist and fog obscure visibility at high altitudes, creating a dreamy atmosphere or nerve-racking driving conditions, depending on your point of view.

While most inhabitants log or raise cattle, tourism is also a booming business in the Navarrese Pyrenees. The French route of **El Camino de Santiago** (see **Pilgrim's Progress,** p. 453) crosses the border at Roncesvalles and winds down through Pamplona on the way to Santiago de Compostela in Galicia. Many free and cheap *refugios* cater to certified modern-day pilgrims along the way, and the area's *casa rurales* (rural lodging houses) are also particularly beautiful. We recommend picking up a copy of the useful *Guía de alojamientos de turismo rurales*, free in any of Navarra's tourist offices. As a rule, these homes are welcoming places to stay and great budget options; doubles usually run between 3200 and 4400ptas. For reservations, call the multilingual tourist office (☎ 948 20 65 40). **Pamplona** is a sensible exploration base for those dependent upon public transportation; you can head east toward **Valle de Roncal,** or north toward **Roncesvalles.** Buses are one-a-day affairs (if that) throughout most of the area.

RONCESVALLES AND AURITZ-BURGUETE

The first stop in Spain on the French Camino de Santiago path, **Roncesvalles'** mistenshrouded 10-odd buildings rest amid miles of thickly wooded mountains. This itty-bitty town (pop. 31), 48km from Pamplona, 20km from France, and eons from reality, lives off legends and the tourists who love them. Charlemagne's favorite soldier Roland was supposedly slain just up the hill in AD 778, at the hands of the ambushing Basque-Navarrese, who were furious that Charlemagne had razed the walls of Pamplona. **Puerto Ibañeta** (1057m), less than 2km up the main road from the monastery, supposedly marks the spot where Roland breathed his final breath. The heavily restored **Capilla de Sancti Spiritus** stands over the remains of the bone heap (courtesy of dead soldiers and pilgrims), where his tomb is thought to be. The tiny 12th-century **Capilla de Santiago** is next door to the left. (The chapels can only be visited by guided tours; see below.)

Inside the **Colegiata,** up the driveway from the *capilla*, the tombs of King Sancho El Fuerte (the Strong) and his bride rest in solitary splendor, lit by the huge stained-glass windows of the **Capilla de San Agustín.** (☎ 948 76 00 00. Chapel and cloister open Tu-F 10:30am-1:30pm, Sa-Su 10am-2pm and 4-7pm. 300ptas; students, seniors, and pilgrims 225ptas.) In the decisive battle of the Navas de Tolosa, Sancho reputedly broke the chains protecting the Arab king Miramomolin with his own hands, then promptly decapitated him. The heavy iron chains hanging from the walls of the chamber are represented in Navarra's flag. The monastery's lovely French Gothic **church,** endowed by Sancho and consecrated in 1219, is its main attraction. (Call ☎ 948 79 04 80 for more info. Open daily 8am-8pm. Free. Guided visits including all the monuments and the Roncesvalles museum, 500ptas; students, seniors, and pilgrims 375ptas.)

🚹 **PRACTICAL INFORMATION. La Montañesa buses** (☎ 948 22 15 84) run to and from **Pamplona** to Roncesvalles (1¼hr.; M-F 6pm, Sa 4pm; 555ptas; return bus leaves Roncevalles M-Sa 7am). The bus stops in **Burguete** each way. A **tourist office** in Roncesvalles, in the mill behind Casa Sabina Hostería, has maps and guides to the Camino de Santiago. (☎ 948 76 03 01. Open M-Sa 10am-2pm and 3-6pm, Su 10am-2pm.) For **Banco Central Hispano** (open Apr.-Sept. M-F 8:30am-2:30pm; Oct.-Mar. M-F 8:30am-2:30pm, Sa 8:30am-1pm) a **supermarket,** and **restaurants,** head to nearby Burguete (2km south); there is hardly any food for sale in Roncesvalles.

🚻 **ACCOMMODATIONS AND FOOD.** The **monastery** in Roncesvalles has free lodging for official pilgrims—enter the door to the right as you face the monastery. The attached **Oficina de Peregrinos** (☎ 948 76 00 00) gives out credentials. **Albergue Juvenil Roncesvalles (HI)** tucked to the right behind the monastery, is in a large and somber building that was a pilgrims' hospital in the 18th century. (☎/fax 948 76 03 02. Breakfast 300ptas. Members only. HI cards for sale. Call in winter, as the hostel sometimes closes. 4- to 8-bed dorms 1500ptas per person, with meals 3000ptas; over 26 1900ptas, with meals 3400ptas.)

In nearby **Burguete,** accommodations are plentiful, including several *casas rurales.* Those following the **Camino de Hemingway** can check out the **Hostal Burguete,** San Nikolas, 71. The big boy slept here and did some writing on his way back to Paris from *San Fermines.* The place hasn't changed much since then, with its high, springy beds in spacious, old-fashioned rooms. (☎ 948 76 00 05. Breakfast 450ptas. *Menú* 1350ptas. Sept.-July singles 2900ptas; doubles with bath 5600ptas. Aug. singles 3400ptas, with bath 6800ptas. Open Mar. 15-Dec. 10. V, MC, AmEx.) **Camping Urrobi,** 2½km downhill from Burguete in Espinal, has a **grocery store.** (☎ 948 76 02 00. Open Apr.-Oct. M-Sa 9am-2pm and 5:30-8:30pm, Su 9am-2pm. 500ptas per person, 475-525ptas per tent, and 475ptas per car.)

VALLE DE SALAZAR: OCHAGAVÍA

On the banks of the Río Andena, **Ochagavía** (pop. 600) is that perfect picturesque mountain village urbanites only dream about. Forty kilometers from Pamplona, the Valle de Salazar's biggest town spans both sides of a cheerful, gurgling river. Ochagavía's whitewashed houses and cobbled streets lead to forested mountains that make it a great base for hiking, trout fishing, and cross-country skiing. The charming 12th-century **Santuario de Muskilda,** the spiritual and cultural nexus of the town, is a two-hour hike away; follow the path from behind the church or, if you've got wheels, take the road toward the town of Izalzu and look for the stone cross. Local dances featuring elaborate costumes are performed at the sanctuary on September 8, the first day of Ochagavía's annual **festival.** (☎ 948 89 00 38. Open daily July 15-Sept. 15 11am-2pm and 4-7pm; Sept. 15-July 15 Sa-Su 11am-2pm and 4-6pm; the schedule may vary.) **Hikers** will find the climb up the **Pico de Orhy** (2021m) fairly easy. The trail leaves from the parking lot at **Puerto de Larrau,** 9km north of Ochagavía on the highway to France. The ascent from there takes about one hour. Another good hike (20km; 6hr. one-way) follows the Río Irati through the **Selva de Irati** to **Orbaitzeta;** to do this hike, leave your car at the **Ermita de las Nieves,** 24km from Ochagavía. **Cross country skiers** can also enjoy two circuit trails starting a little farther down the same highway.

Río Irati (☎ 948 22 14 70) runs **buses** to and from Pamplona (M-Sa 7am, 825ptas). The **tourist office,** on the main road, is in the same building as a nature center and offers the free and indispensible lodging guide, *Guía de Alojamientos Turísticos.* (☎/fax 948 89 06 41. Office open *Semana Santa* to Oct. M-Sa 10am-2pm and 4:30-7:30pm, Su 10am-2pm; Nov. to *Semana Santa* Sa-Su 10am-2pm and 4:30-7:30pm). Several **ATMs** are located on the main road. In an **emergency** call ☎ 112. The **pharmacy** can be found at C. Urrutia, 31 (☎ 948 89 05 06), and the **post office** is on C. Labaria, near the Ayuntamiento. (☎ 948 89 04 52. Open M-Sa 8:30-9:30am.)

A good lodging choice is ▧**Casa Ñavarro,** up the street from the bank and to the left. The large, immaculate rooms have balconies, couches, and loving attention to detail, and the owner is warm and welcoming. (☎ 948 89 03 35. Breakfast 350ptas. Reservations recommended. Doubles 3500ptas, with bath 4000ptas). **Hostal Orialde,** across the river from the main road on the edge of town, has attractive, spacious rooms. (☎ 948 89 00 27. Breakfast 400ptas, *Menú* 1600ptas. Singles 3100ptas; doubles 3900ptas, with bath 4900ptas; IVA not included.) Ask at the tourist office or look for the "CR" signs advertising one of the town's 25 *casas rurales.* **Camping Osate,** at the entrance to town, provides a modern campsite on the river with supermarket, bar, and **mountain bike** rentals. (☎ 948 89 01 84. Bikes 3000ptas per day. Camping 500ptas per person and per car, 450ptas per tent. V, MC.)

VALLE DE RONCAL

Carved by the Río Esca, Valle de Roncal is a particularly handsome valley stretching from the French border. With its darling towns, inviting *casas rurales*, prime **hiking** and **cross-country skiing** grounds, and overall laid-back air, Valle de Roncal is a showcase of the best the Navarrese Pyrenees have to offer.

RONCAL

Smack in the center of the Valle de Roncal, the diminutive town of **Roncal** (pop. 300) puffs up with pride over its famed *queso Roncal*, a sharp cheese made from sheep's milk, and its own Julián Gayarre (1844-1889), a "world-renowned" tenor. **Casa Museo Julián Gayarre**, on C. Arana, is a museum in the singer's birthplace, showcasing his personal belongings and assorted memorabilia. (☎ 948 47 51 80. Open Apr.-Sept. Tu-Su 11:30am-1:30pm and 5-7pm; Oct.-Mar. Sa-Su 11:30am-1:30pm and 4-6pm. 200ptas, seniors free). **La Tafallesa buses** (☎ 948 22 28 86) run from **Pamplona** (depart M-F 5pm, Sa 1pm), through Javier, and on to Roncal (2hr., 880ptas from Pamplona, arrive at 6:45pm). Buses also return to Pamplona and Javier from Roncal (depart M-F 7am). There is an extremely helpful **tourist office** on Roncal's main road. Ask about nearby hiking and *casas rurales*. (☎ 948 47 52 56; fax 948 47 53 16. Open June-Sept. M-Sa 10am-2pm and 4:30-7:30pm, Su 10am-2pm; May-June and Oct.-Dec. M-Sa 4:30-7:30pm, Su 10am-2pm.) Town services include: **emergency** (☎ 112); the **Guardia Civil** (☎ 948 47 50 05); a **pharmacy** next door to the tourist office (open M-F 10am-2pm and 5-8pm, Sa 10am-2pm); and a **Banco Central Hispano** across the street from the tourist office (open Apr.-Sept. M-F 8:30am-2:30pm; Oct.-Mar. M-F 8:30am-2:30pm, Sa 8:30am-1pm; no commission). **Supermarkets** and **telephones** cluster by the bridge at the base of the town. For a night's rest, try one of the splendid *casas rurales*. **Casa Villa Pepita**, Po. Julián Gayarre, 4, can be found across from a small playground before crossing the bridge from town. The friendly owners offer adorable rooms, flower-strewn balconies, and a familial atmosphere. (☎ 948 47 51 33. Breakfast 350ptas. Meals 1400ptas. Singles 2000ptas; doubles 3500ptas, with bath 4500ptas). If Pepita is full, the owner will gladly direct you to another *casa rural*.

ISABA AND ENVIRONS

North of Roncal, the more populous village of **Isaba** (pop. 542) draws numerous hikers and skiiers even though the town itself has little to offer. A standard yet stunning hike goes from Isaba to **Zuriza** in the Valle de Hecho (5-6hr.). Shorter, but steeper, are the ascents from Collado Argibiela to **Punta Abizondo** (1676m) and **Peña Ezkaurre** (2050m). Ask the tourist office for routes of differing durations and difficulty. Ski trails run north of Isaba, at the **Estación de Ski Larra-Belagna** (☎ 608 16 51 67 or 948 39 40 02). The **Escuela de Esquí Valle de Roncal**, with offices in Hotel Isaba, offers lessons and skis (☎ 948 89 32 66. Hour lessons 4000ptas for 1 person; 4500ptas for 2 people. Group lessons also available.) A village **festival** featuring a local rendition of polo and stone-throwing contests runs from July 25 to 28 in honor of San Santiago, and Isaba comes to life with dancing and general merriment on September 16, in honor of **San Cipriano.**

Isaba's **tourist office** is right off the main road. (☎ 948 89 32 51. Open in summer Tu-Sa 10am-2pm and 5-8pm, Su 10am-2pm; off-season Tu-Su 10am-2pm). Most **telephones** and **ATMs** can be found at the southern end of town. If you decide to stay the night, **Albergue Oxanea**, C. Bormapea, 47, has wooden bunks (8-14 to a room) and a TV/VCR room. (☎ 948 89 31 53. Breakfast 350ptas. Other meals 1400ptas. Hot showers included. 1200ptas per night, 1000ptas with own sleeping bag; IVA not included.) **Camping Asolaze**, 6km toward the French border, has a restaurant, store, and bunkbeds in addition to plots of ground. (☎ 948 89 30 34. Bunks 1200ptas per person. Sheets 200ptas. Camping 500ptas per person, per tent, and per car. V, MC, Maestro). Eight kilometers north of Isaba, the mountains open up into the idyllic **Valle de Belagua**, where **Refugio Angel Oloron** offers bunks year-round. The refuge is located at km 19 on the highway to France from Isaba. (☎/fax 948 39 40 02. Breakfast 300ptas, other meals 1500ptas. 1100ptas per person.)

PAÍS VASCO (EUSKADI)

As the Basque saying goes, "Before God was God and the rocks were rocks, the Basques were Basque." The País Vasco is officially composed of the provinces Guipuzcoa, Alava, and Vizcaya, but those who identify themselves as Basque are not restricted by boundaries. In fact, the Basque country is often thought to expand into Navarra and southwestern France. The varied landscape of the País Vasco resembles a nation complete unto itself, with cosmopolitan cities, verdant hills, industrial wastelands, and quaint fishing villages. The people are bound by their deep attachment to the land, an almost spiritual appreciation for fine food and drink, and immense cultural and national pride.

Many believe that the Basques are the native people of Iberia, as their culture and language are untraceable to any known source. Today's nationalistic sentiment stems from the 18th-century abolition of the Basque *fueros* (ancient rights of self-government), the Basques' military defeat in the late 19th-century Carlist wars, and Franco's heavy repression of Basque identity. The organization Euskadi ta Askatasuna ("Basque Country and Freedom"; ETA) began an anti-Spanish terrorist movement (aiming lately at politicians) that has lasted over 30 years, despite the fact that many Basque Nationalists are critical of the group and its affiliated political party, Euskal Herritarrok. The Spanish government and ETA agreed upon a truce in September 1998, but the cease-fire was broken after only 14 months and the violence continues anew.

Most Basques share a strong desire to preserve their cultural identity. Although Castilian Spanish is the predominant language, Basque *(euskera)* has enjoyed a resurgence of popularity since Franco's death. Other regional traditions like *cesta punta* or *pelota vasca* (known outside of Spain as *jai-alai*) continue to thrive. Basque cuisine is some of Iberia's finest, including *bacalao a la vizcaína* (salted cod in a tomato sauce), dishes *a la vasca* (in a delicate parsley-steeped white wine sauce), and *chipirones en su tinta* (baby squids in their own ink). *Tapas* in the País Vasco, considered regional specialties, are called *pintxos* (PEEN-chos); locals wash them down with *sidra* (cider) and the local white wine, *txakoli*.

HIGHLIGHTS OF THE PAÍS VASCO

Pintxos at **San Sebastián's** bars after a day at the beautiful beach (see p. 405).

A walk along the marina in refreshing seaside **Hondarribia** (see p. 414).

Frank O. Gehry's shiny new **Guggenheim Museum** in **Bilbao** (see p. 420).

The educational and powerful **Guernika Museum** (see p. 422).

LOCAL FESTIVALS IN THE PAÍS VASCO

The biggest annual events in **San Sebastián** are the *Festival Internacional de Danza* (May), the *Festival Internacional de Cine* (September), and the *Festival de Jazz* (late July), all three of them world-renowned. *Semana Grande* brings fireworks and concerts to town in late August. **Bilbao** also celebrates the *Semana Grande,* and **Vitoria-Gasteiz** holds its own *Festival de Jazz* in late July.

SAN SEBASTIÁN (DONOSTIA)

Glittering on the shores of the Cantabrian Sea, San Sebastián (pop. 180,000) is a cool, elegant city. By the beginning of the 19th century it had become one of Spain's great ports, but much of it was destroyed by Anglo-Portuguese troops during the Peninsular War (1813). The city's damaged walls were finally torn down in 1863 and construction of a new San Sebastián began, one that gained international fame when Queen Isabel II made it her summer residence. The city's popularity has been increasing ever since, particularly among land-locked Spaniards desperate to escape the heat of central Spain. Vacationers come for its world-famous beaches, *pintxos*, and bars, as well as its strong sense of regional culture.

⌐ TRANSPORTATION

Flights: Airport (☎ 943 66 85 00) in Hondarribia (Fuenterrabía), 20km east of the city. **Interurbanos buses** to Hondarribia pass by the airport (45min., every 15min. 7:45am-11pm, 200ptas). A **taxi** costs 3200ptas. Flights to **Madrid** (4 per day) and **Barcelona** (3 per day). **Iberia** (☎ 902 40 05 00) has an office at the airport.

Trains: San Sebastián has two train stations.

RENFE, Estación del Norte (☎ 943 28 30 89 or 943 28 35 99), on Po. Francia, on the east side of Puente María Cristina. Info open daily 7:15am-11:15pm. To: **Vitoria-Gasteiz** (1¾hr., 9 per day 6:57am-10:37pm, 1500-1600ptas); **Pamplona** (2hr., 2-12 per day 10:35am-10:59pm, 1500ptas; the bus costs half as much and takes half the time); **Burgos** (3½hr., 7-8 per day 6:57am-10:37pm, 2400-2600ptas); **Zaragoza** (4hr., 4 per day 10:35am-9:59pm, 2700-3900ptas); **Madrid** (8hr., 4 per day 8:32am-10:37pm, 4600-4800ptas); **Barcelona** (9hr., 2-3 per day 10:35am-10:59pm, 4700-4900ptas); and **Paris** (8-11hr., 3-4 per day 7am-9:10pm, 11,000ptas).

Estación de Amara (Euskotren) (☎ 943 45 01 31), Pl. Easo. From the bus station take Sancho el Sabio toward the center of the city and veer left on C. Easo when it forks. Commuter trains to **Irún** (30min., every 15min. 5:55am-2pm, 150ptas).

Buses: Several private companies run from different points in the city but most operate from the tiny "station," around the corner from the main concourse at Po. Vizcaya, 16. Buses drop off on Pl. Pío XII, a block from the river and 13 blocks south of Av. Libertad on Av. Sancho el Sabio; to get to the "station," face the river, turn left, and walk a few stores down. Public bus #28 goes to the city center from the bus station. Buy tickets at each company's office. **PESA**, Av. Sancho el Sabio, 33 (☎ 943 46 29 52), to **Bilbao** (1¼hr., every 30min. 6:30am-10pm, 1120ptas) and **Vitoria-Gasteiz** (2hr., 1-4 per day 8:15am-6pm, 1020ptas). **Continental Auto**, Av. Sancho el Sabio, 31 (☎ 943 46 90 74), to **Burgos** (3-3½hr., 8 per day 7:15am-12:30pm, 1855ptas) and **Madrid** (6hr., 9-12 per day, 3800ptas). **La Roncalesa**, Po. Vizcaya, 16 (☎ 943 46 10 64), to **Pamplona** (1hr., 9 per day 7am-9:15pm, 790ptas). **Vibasa**, Po. Vizcaya, 16 (☎ 902 10 13 63), to **Barcelona** (7hr., 3-5 per day 7:30am-11:20pm, 3350ptas). **Turytrans**, Po. Vizcaya, 16 (☎ 943 46 23 60), to **Paris** (11hr., 8:30pm, 9400ptas). **Interurbanos** (☎ 943 64 13 02) are the green buses that stop at Pl. Guipuzcoa (pay on board). To **Irún** (35min., every 15min., 175ptas) and **Hondarribia** (45min., every 15min., 210ptas).

Public Transportation: (☎ 943 28 71 00); tourist office has a list of 19 routes. Each trip 115ptas. Bus #16 goes from Alameda del Boulevard to the campground and beaches.

Taxis: Santa Clara (☎ 943 31 01 11) or **Donostia** (☎ 943 46 46 46). Taxis to **Pamplona** take about 45min., fit up to 4 people, and usually cost around 13,000ptas.

Car Rental: Europcar (☎ 943 32 23 04; fax 943 29 07 00), Estación de RENFE. Min. age 21. Must have a passport and driver's license. (International driver's license not required.) Open M-F 8am-1pm and 4-7:30pm, Sa 9am-1pm.

Mountain Bike Rental: Comet, Av. Libertad, 6 (☎ 943 42 66 37). Half-day 2500ptas, full-day 3000ptas, 2000ptas per additional day. Open M 4-8pm, Tu-F 10am-1pm and 4-8pm, Sa 10am-1:30pm and 4-7:30pm. V, MC, AmEx.

WHAT THE DEVIL ARE THEY TXPEAKING?

Linguists still cannot pinpoint the origin of *euskera*. Its commonalities with Caucasian and African dialects suggest that prehistoric Basques may have migrated from the Caucasus mountains through Africa. Referred to by other Spaniards as *la lengua del diablo* (the devil's tongue), *euskera* has come to symbolize cultural self-determination. Only half a million natives speak the language, chiefly in País Vasco and northern Navarra. During his regime, Franco banned *euskera* and forbade parents to give their children Basque names (like Iñaki or Estibaliz). Since his death, there has been a resurgence of everything from *euskera* TV shows to *ikastolas* (Basque schools), and the language is frequently used for street signs and menus in the País Vasco.

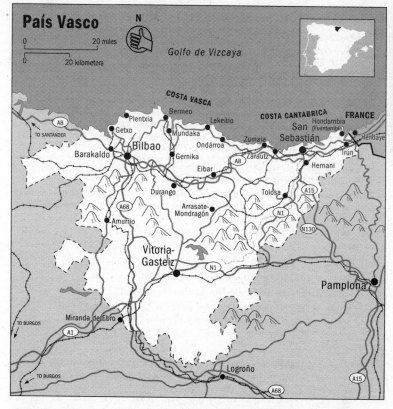

ORIENTATION AND PRACTICAL INFORMATION

Street and plaza signs are usually in both *castellano* and *euskera*. The street guide on the tourist office map gives both versions in its index, so don't despair if you see "kalea" and "tx" everywhere. The **Río Urumea** splits San Sebastián in two. The city center, most monuments, and the two most popular beaches are on the peninsula on the west side of the river. The tip of the peninsula is **Monte Urgulla**. Inland is the **parte vieja** (old city), where nightlife rages and budget accommodations and restaurants cluster. South of the *parte vieja*, at the base of the peninsula, is the commercial district. The **bus station** lies in the south of the city on Pl. Pío XII. Av. de Sancho el Sabio runs to the right (north) straight toward the cathedral, ocean, and old town. East of the river lie the **RENFE station, Barrio de Gros**, and **Playa de la Zurriola**. Both sides of the river are connected by three bridges: Puentes Zurriola, Santa Catalina, and María Cristina (listed from north to south). To get to the *parte vieja* from the train station, head straight to Puente María Cristina, cross the bridge, then turn right at the fountain, and walk four blocks north to Av. Libertad. Turn left and follow it to the port; the *parte vieja* fans out to the right, and Playa de la Concha to the left.

Tourist Office: Municipa, Centro de Atracción y Turismo (☎ 943 48 11 66; fax 943 48 11 72), C. Reina Regente, on the corner of the plaza right next to the river. From the train station, turn right immediately after crossing Puente María Cristina. Continue until reaching Puente Zurriola; C. Reina Regente will be on the left. From the bus station, go down Av. Sancho el Sabio. At Pl. Centenario, bear right on C. Prim and follow the river, passing two bridges. At the third bridge, Puente Zurriola, look to the plaza at your left;

the office is on the corner. English- and French-speaking staff, map, transit and accommodations info, and a bulletin board. Open June-Sept. M-Sa 8am-8pm, Su 10am-1pm; Oct.-May M-Sa 9am-2pm and 3:30-7pm, Su 10am-1pm. **Regional office,** Oficina de Turismo del Gobierno Vasco (☎ 943 02 31 50), Po. Fueros, down the river from the municipal office, near the train station. More of a focus on trips outside of San Sebastián. Open June-Aug. M-F 9am-1:30pm and 3-7pm, Sa-Su 9am-1pm and 3-7pm; Sept.-May M-F 9am-1:30pm and 3:30-6:30pm, Sa-Su 9am-1pm and 4-7pm.

Hiking Information: Club Vasco de Camping, San Marcial, 19 (☎/fax 943 42 84 79), 1 block south of Av. Libertad. Organizes excursions. Open M-F 6-8:30pm. **Izadi,** C. Usandizaga, 18 (☎ 943 29 35 20). Sells hiking guides and maps, some in English. Organizes tours and rents skis, wetsuits, and hiking equipment. Open M-F 10am-1pm and 4-8pm, Sa 10am-1:30pm and 4:30-8pm.

Luggage Storage: Train station. 400ptas per day; buy tokens at the ticket counter. Open daily 7am-11pm. **Bus station.** 300ptas per day. Open daily 7am-8:30pm.

English Bookstore: Donosti, Pl. Bilbo, 2 (☎ 943 42 21 38), 1 block west of Puente María Cristina on the circular plaza. Excellent selection of classic novels and travel literature. Open M-F 9am-1pm and 4:30-8pm, Sa 9am-1pm. V, MC, AmEx.

Laundromat: Lavomatique, C. Iñigo, 13 (☎ 943 42 38 71), off C. San Juan. Self-service. 575ptas wash (cold water only), 400ptas dry. Soap 60ptas. Ironing 75ptas for 15min. Open M-F 10am-1pm and 4-7pm, Sa-Su 10am-2pm.

Emergency: ☎ 112. **Police: Municipal** (☎ 943 45 00 00), on C. Easo.

Medical Services: Casa de Socorro, Bengoetxea, 4 (☎ 943 44 06 33).

Post Office: (☎ 943 46 34 17), C. Urdaneta, the street just south of the cathedral. Open M-F 8:30am-8:30pm, Sa 9:30am-2pm. **Lista de Correos** at window #11. **Address mail to be held:** PRICE, Alexandra; Lista de Correos; C. Urdaneta; 2080 San Sebastián. **Postal Code:** 20006.

Internet Access: Netline, C. Urdaneta, 8 (☎ 943 44 50 76). 8 computers; the wait is long. 200ptas for 20min., 300ptas for 30min., 600ptas per hr. 4500ptas for a 10hr. ticket. Open M-Sa 10am-10pm. **Donosti-Net,** C. Embletran, 2 (☎ 943 42 58 70), at the corner of C. Narrica. Has 8 speedy computers, **phone cards** for sale, and helpful English-speaking staff. 250ptas for 15min., 350ptas for 30min., 550ptas per hr. Open 9am-9pm. **Zarr@net,** C. San Lorenzo, 6 (☎ 943 43 33 81). Lots of quick computers in the center of old quarter. 250ptas for 15min., 350ptas for 30min., 550ptas per hr. Open June-Aug. M-Sa 10am-midnight, Su 4-10pm; Sept.-May M-Sa 10am-10pm.

▟ ACCOMMODATIONS

Desperate backpackers will have to scrounge for rooms in July and August—particularly during *San Fermines* (July 6-14) and *Semana Grande* (starts Su the week of Aug. 15); September's film festival is not much better. To make matters worse, many places don't take reservations in summer. Budget options center in the *parte vieja* and around the cathedral; there are often a few per entryway—look for signs in doorways. Solo travelers should be prepared to pay for a double, as single rooms are virtually impossible to come by, especially in summer. The tourist office has lists of budget accommodations, and most hostel owners know of *casas particulares*—don't be afraid to ask for help. Owners of *casas particulares* often solicit guests at the RENFE station. Be wary—this is illegal.

PARTE VIEJA

A bit of a hike from the bus and train stations, the *parte vieja* is brimming with reasonably priced *pensiones*. Its proximity to Playa de la Concha and the port makes this area a prime nightspot; scores of places offer a night's sleep above loud *pintxos (tapas)* bars. Call in advance for reservations.

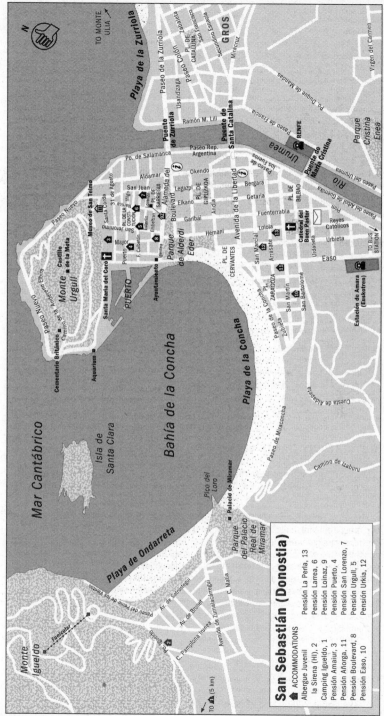

San Sebastián (Donostia)

♦ ACCOMMODATIONS

Albergue Juvenil
    la Sirena (HI), 2
Camping Igueldo, 1
Pensión Amaiur, 3
Pensión Añorga, 11
Pensión Boulevard, 8
Pensión Easo, 10

Pensión La Perla, 13
Pensión Larrea, 6
Pensión Loinaz, 9
Pensión Puerto, 4
Pensión San Lorenzo, 7
Pensión Urgull, 5
Pensión Urkia, 12

Pensión Amaiur, C. 31 de Agosto, 44, 2nd fl. (☎ 943 42 96 54). From Alameda del Boulevard, go up C. San Jerónimo to the end and turn left. Look for the flower-obscured facade. 10 pastel rooms (several with TV) have distinctive charm and the 5 common bathrooms are gorgeous. Delightful English- and French-speaking owner will make you feel at home. *Semana Santa* to Oct. 3000-38000ptas per person; Nov. to *Semana Santa* 1900-2500ptas per person. *Let's Go* discount 300ptas. V, MC.

Pensión San Lorenzo, C. San Lorenzo, 2 (☎ 943 42 55 16), off C. San Juan. Recently refurbished and now a San Sebastián gem. Cheerful, light yellow doubles have TV, radio, and small refrigerator. Immaculate modern bathrooms. Laundry 1000ptas. Internet access 100ptas for 12min. July-Sept. doubles 8000ptas, 7000ptas for foreigners; Oct.-June doubles 4000ptas. Singles sometimes available. *Let's Go* discount 500ptas.

Pensión Larrea, C. Narrica, 21, 1st fl. (☎ 943 42 26 94). Adorable and adoring owner has a reputation as the "best mom in town." Don't be surprised to find your clothes washed, your ego boosted, and your belly filled. Appealing rooms with sparkling bathrooms. July-Aug. singles 3000ptas; doubles 5000ptas; triples 6000ptas. Sept.-June singles 2500ptas; doubles 4000ptas; triples 5000ptas.

Pensión Loinaz, C. San Lorenzo, 17 (☎ 943 42 67 14), off C. San Juan. Friendly English-speaking owners offer bright rooms with big windows and high ceilings. Clean common bathrooms. Laundry 1000ptas. July-Aug. doubles 5500-6000ptas; triples 8500ptas. Apr.-June doubles 4000ptas; triples 6000ptas. Sept.-March doubles 3500ptas; triples 5000ptas. Singles sometimes available for 3000-3500ptas.

Pension Urgull, Esterlines, 10, 3rd fl. (☎ 943 43 00 47). Inexpensive, in a central loction. Attractive old rooms with tall windows, small balconies, and sinks. Nice common bathrooms. Prices are not set in stone. July-Aug. singles 3000ptas, doubles 5000-6000ptas; Sept.-June singles 2500ptas; doubles 3500ptas.

Pensión Boulevard, Alameda del Boulevard, 24 (☎ 943 42 94 05). Beautiful, spacious, modern rooms, all with radios, some with balconies. 2 large shared bathrooms for 8 rooms. July-Aug. doubles 6500ptas; triples 9000ptas. Sept.-June doubles 3500ptas; triples 4500ptas. Prices may drop "in between" seasons and on weekdays.

Pensión Puerto, C. Puerto, 19, 2nd fl. (☎ 943 43 21 40), off C. Mayor. Spotless and attractive doubles and singles with big closets, high ceilings, good beds, and the occasional balcony. 3000-4000ptas per person.

OUTSIDE THE PARTE VIEJA

Most of these hostels lie in the heart of the commercial zone, around the cathedral. They tend to be quieter than those elsewhere yet are still close to the port, beach, bus and train stations, and no more than five minutes from the old city. This area is also home to the city's most elegant boulevards and buildings .

Albergue Juvenil la Sirena (HI), Po. Igueldo, 25 (☎ 943 31 02 68; fax 943 21 40 90), a big, light-pink building 3min. from the beach at the far west end of the city. Bus #24 runs from the train and bus stations to Av. Zumalacárregui (the stop in front of the San Sebastián Hotel). Bus #5 drops you off 1 street away on C. Matia. From Av. Zumalacárregui, take the street that angles toward the mountain (Av. Brunet) and turn left at its end. Clean, modern, dorm-style rooms and multilingual staff. HI members and ISIC-carriers only. HI cards on sale. Breakfast included. Sheets 395ptas. Luggage storage, laundry facilities, and kitchen available 24hr. Best to arrive before 11am. Lockout 10am-3pm. Curfew June-Aug. daily 2am; Sept.-May Su-Th midnight, F-Sa 2am. June-Oct. 15 and *Semana Santa* 2100ptas, over 26 2555ptas; Oct. 15-May 1600ptas, over 26 2000ptas. July-Aug. 3-night max. stay. Visa.

Pensión Urkia, C. Urbieta, 12, 3rd fl. (☎ 943 42 44 36). C. Urbieta borders the cathedral on the west; the hostel is 1 block north at C. Arrasate. Polished knick-knacks and gilt mirrors in an elegant dark wood foyer. Rooms with lovely blue-and-white linens, firm beds, full bathrooms, and TVs. July-Sept. doubles 6000ptas; triples 9000ptas. Oct.-June singles 3000ptas; doubles 4000ptas; triples 6000ptas.

Pensión La Perla, C. Loiola, 10, 2nd fl. (☎ 943 42 81 23), on the street directly ahead of the cathedral. Friendly, English-speaking owner. Attractive, immaculate rooms with polished floors, private baths, TVs, and noise-proof windows. #7 is a gem. July-Sept. singles 4000ptas; doubles 6000ptas. Oct.-June singles 3500ptas; doubles 4500ptas.

Pensión Añorga, C. Easo, 12, 1st fl. (☎ 943 46 79 45), at C. San Martín. Shares entry-way with 2 other *pensiones*. Spacious rooms have shiny wood floors, large windows, and great beds. Possible wait for common bathrooms, and towels are provided only for the private ones. July-Aug. singles 4000ptas; doubles 5000ptas, with bath 6500ptas. Sept.-June singles 2000ptas; doubles 3000ptas, with bath 4000ptas.

Pension Easo, C. San Bartolomé, 24 (☎ 943 45 39 12). Head toward the beach on C. San Martín, turn left on C. Easo, and right on C. San Bartolomé. Huge windows, TVs, and attractive bedspreads. July-Sept. 15 singles 5200ptas, with bath 7200ptas; dou-bles 6500ptas, with bath 9000ptas; triples 9000ptas, with bath 12,000ptas. Sept. 16-June singles 3000ptas, with bath 5000ptas; doubles 4000ptas, with bath 6000ptas; triples 6000ptas, with bath 9000ptas.

Camping Igueldo (☎ 943 21 45 02), 5km west of town. The 268 spots fill in the blink of an eye. Bus #16 ("Barrio de Igueldo-Camping") runs between the site and Alameda del Boulevard (every 30min., 110ptas). Keep San Sebastián's quirky weather in mind. Reception June-Aug. 8am-midnight; Sept.-May 9am-1pm and 5-9pm. *Parcela* (including tent and up to 2 people) June-Aug. and *Semana Santa* 2889ptas, extra person 425ptas; Sept.-May 1386ptas, extra person 357ptas.

FOOD

Pintxos (tapas), chased down with the fizzy regional white wine *txacoli,* are a religion here; bars in the lively old city spread an array of enticing tidbits on tooth-picks or bread. *Pintxos* rarely cost more than 175ptas each, so eat up! In the har-bor, many small places serve tangy sardines with the strong, slightly bitter *sidra* (cider), another regional specialty. Custom demands pouring it with arm extended upward so the force of the stream hitting the glass releases the *sidra's* bouquet of flavor. From January through April, San Sebastián's gourmands turn their atten-tion to **sidrerías,** which are open to the public and provide the same, standard meal (cod, beef chop, and cheese) as an accompaniment to the *sidra.*

Restaurants and bars clamor for attention on C. Fermín Calbetón, in the old quarter. In fact, the entire *parte vieja* seems to exist for no other purpose than to feed. The majority of restaurants offer their best deals on lunchtime *menús.* The underground shopping center located between Alameda del Boulevard and C. San Juan houses the **Mercado de la Bretxa** (open M-Sa 9am-9pm). The local marketplace, **Mercado de San Martín,** on C. San Marcial between C. Loiola and C. Urbieta, sells fresh local meats, fish, and produce (open M-F 7:30am-2pm and 5-7:30pm, Sa 7:30am-2pm). For **groceries,** go to **Super Todo Todo,** Alameda del Boulevard, around the corner from the tourist office. (☎ 943 42 82 59. Open M-Su 8:30am-9pm.)

PARTE VIEJA

Bar La Cepa, C. 31 de Agosto, 7-9 (☎ 943 42 63 94). One of the best in San Sebastián, packed with locals. Authentic Basque flavor with a dark-wood bar and beef slabs hang-ing from the ceiling. *Pintxos* 160-325ptas. *Bocadillos* 450-475ptas. Weekday lunch *menú* 1700ptas. Open daily 1pm-midnight. V, MC, AmEx, Maestro.

Cantina Mariachi, C. Fermín Kableton, 45 (☎ 943 42 48 66). Hearty, cheap Mexican food in an environment that's warm, inviting, and decorated to the max. *Menú* 990ptas. Fajitas 1200ptas. Open M-Sa 1:15-3:45pm and 8-11:30pm, Su 1:15-3:45pm. V, MC.

Pizzeria Trattoria Capricciosa, C. Fermín Calbetón, 50 (☎ 943 43 20 48). A traditional, family-oriented Italian restaurant. Pastas 975-1200ptas. Pizzas 850-950ptas. Open M-F 1-3pm and 8:30-11pm, Sa-Su 1:30-3pm and 9:30-11:30pm. V, MC.

PARTE NUEVA

Tenis Ondarreta (☎ 943 31 11 50 or 943 31 41 18), on Po. Peine de los Vientos, along the *Playa de Ondarreta*. Escape the brouhaha of the *parte vieja* to mingle with San Sebastián's preppy blue-bloods; this is a whole different scene. Gourmet food, including Basque seafood dishes. Daily *menú* 1550ptas. Entrees 1700-2100ptas (IVA not included). Open M-Sa 1-4pm and 9-11pm, Su 1-4pm. V, MC, AmEx.

La Mamma Mia, C. San Bartolomé, 18 (☎ 943 46 52 93). Great ambiance and excellent, freshly made pastas. Scrumptious pizza (875-975ptas) and a wide range of tortellini, fettucine and lasagna dishes (895-995ptas). *Menú* 1200ptas plus IVA. Open daily 1:30-4pm and 8:30pm-12:30am. V, MC.

Caravanseri Café, C. San Bartolomé, 1 (☎ 943 47 54 78), alongside the cathedral. Trendy, chic, and artsy, without pretentious prices. So popular you'll probably have to wait. Fabulous vegetarian options include tofu and veggie burgers (400ptas). Entrees 800-950ptas. Open M-Th 8am-midnight, F-Sa 8am-1am, Su 10:30am-midnight.

🔍 SIGHTS

San Sebastián's most attractive sight is the city itself—green walks and parks, grandiose buildings, and attractive hillsides encircle a placid, fan-shaped bay and the pleasant island of Santa Clara.

■ MONTE IGUELDO. Although the views from both of San Sebastián's mountains are spectacular, those from Monte Igueldo are superior. By day the countryside meets the ocean in a line of white and blue; by night Isla Santa Clara, lit by floodlights, seems to float on a ring of light. The sidewalk toward the mountain ends just before the base of Monte Igueldo with Eduardo Chillida's sculpture *El peine de los vientos* (Wind's Comb). The walk up is not too strenuous, but the funicular is nice on hot days. A small amusement park at the top aims to please with bumper cars, water rides, and trampolines. (☎ 943 21 02 11. Open daily June-Sept. 11am-10pm and weekends in winter. 170ptas.)

■ MONTE URGULL. Across the bay from Monte Igueldo, the gravel paths on Monte Urgull wind through shady woods, monuments, love-struck teenagers, and stunning vistas. The overgrown **Castillo de Santa Cruz de la Mota** tops the summit with cannons, a chapel, and the statue of the Sagrado Corazón de Jesús that blesses the city. (Open daily June-Aug. 8am-8pm; Sept.-May 8am-6pm.)

MUSEO DE SAN TELMO. The Museo de San Telmo resides in a Dominican monastery. The serene, overgrown cloister is strewn with Basque funerary relics, and the main museum beyond the cloister displays a fascinating array of pre-historic Basque artifacts, a few dinosaur skeletons, and a piece of contemporary art. (Po. Nuevo. ☎ 943 42 49 70. Open Tu-Sa 10:30am-1:30pm and 4-8pm, Su 10:30am-2pm. Free.)

PALACES. As soon as Queen Isabel II started vacationing here in the mid-19th century, fancy buildings began to spring up like wildflowers. **El Palacio de Mirama** has passed through the hands of the Spanish court, Napoleon III, and Bismarck; today anyone can stroll through the "cottage-style" grounds and contemplate the picturesque views of the bay. (Between Playa de la Concha and Playa de Ondarreta. Open daily June-Aug. 9am-9pm; Sept.-May 10am-5pm.) The other royal residence, **Palacio de Ayete,** is closed to the public, but the surrounding trails are not. (Head up Cuesta de Aldapeta or take Bus #19. Grounds open June-Aug. 10am-8:30pm; Sept.-May 10am-5pm.)

■ PASAJES DE SAN JUAN. Thirty minutes from the town center, between a lush hill and a dark, gray-green bay, lies the town of Pasajes de San Juan. The charming fishing village's wood-balconied houses and small bay crowded with colorful *chalupas* (little boats) make an enchanting time warp. (A Herribus bus goes to Pasajes de San Juan every 20-30min. for 120ptas from Pl. Gipúzkoa.)

A STEP ABOVE SQUASH The Basque sport known as *cesta punta*, or *jai alai*, is the world's fastest ball game. In this unique form of handball, burly players fling balls at a walled court (called a *frontón*) at speeds up to 200km per hour. The traditional game is played with bare hands, but the faster version incorporates *txisteras*, hand-held baskets of sorts. Local teams often play in public *frontones*; watch for the trademark white uniforms with red or blue sashes. Spreading beyond its homeland, *jai alai* now exists in more than 20 variants, 14 of them at the world championship level. The sport has even caught on in such far-flung places as Cancún, Cuba, and Connecticut, but sorry ladies: so far only men have played.

OTHER SIGHTS. An **aquarium** lies on the edge of the port with fish and sea creatures from various aquatic habitats. Highlights include a small "petting pond" and a glass tunnel with stingrays, sharks and the occasional scuba-diver gliding past overhead. *(Po. Muelle, 34. ☎ 943 44 00 99. Open July-Aug. 10am-10pm; Sept.-June 10am-1:30pm and 3:30-7:30pm. 1100ptas, students 550ptas.)* Wandering through the *parte vieja* reveals **Plaza Constitución,** with the ornate portal of **Iglesia Santa María** and numbered balconies dating from the plaza's days as a bullring.

◙ BEACHES AND WATER SPORTS

The gorgeous **Playa de la Concha** curves from the port to the **Pico del Loro,** the beak-shaped promontory home to the Palacio de Miramar. The virtually flat beach disappears during high tide, and each year erosion narrows the sand space a little more. Sunbathing crowds jam onto the smaller and steeper **Playa de Ondarreta,** beyond Miramar, and surfers flock to **Playa de la Zurrida,** across the river from Mt. Urguel. Picnickers head for the alluring **Isla de Santa Clara** in the center of the bay, either by rented rowboat or public motorboat ferry (5min., June-Sept. round-trip 250ptas). Check at the portside kiosk for further information on both options.

Several sports-related groups offer a variety of activities and lessons. For **windsurfing** and **kayaking,** call the Real Club Náutico, C. Igentea, 9 (☎ 943 42 35 75. Classes 5000-8000ptas.) For **parachuting,** try Urruti Sport, C. José María Soroa, 20 (☎ 943 27 81 96). An afternoon with an instructor will cost you 8000ptas. **Surfers** can check out the Pukas Surf Club, C. Mayor, 5, for info on lessons and a huge variety of gear. (☎ 943 42 72 28; pukas@facilnet.es. Open 10am-1pm and 4-8pm.) Sub Centro de Buceo, C. Trinidad, 2 (☎ 943 13 24 72; email k-sub@euskalnet.net), rents **scuba-diving** equipment and offers classes. For general information on all sports, pick up a copy of the *UDA-Actividades deportivas* brochure at the tourist office.

◙ NIGHTLIFE

The *parte vieja* pulls out all the stops in July and August, particularly on C. Fermín Calbetón, three blocks in from Alameda del Boulevard. During the year, when students outnumber backpackers, nightlife tends to move beyond the *parte vieja.* Keep an eye out for discount coupons on the street, as covers can be exorbitant.

The World's End, Po. de Salamanca, 14 (☎/fax 943 42 62 53), 1 block outside of the *parte vieja* in the direction of the beach. Rapidly becoming a fixture on the backpacker circuit. Great pub-ambiance, plenty of space, and tasty snacks (500-700ptas), but not much Spanish spoken here. Open Su-Th 2pm-2:30am, F-Sa 2pm-3:30am.

Zibbibo, Pl. Sarriegi 8. This hip little club with a small dance floor and blend of big-hit and techno tunes has become a common backpacker stop en route from World's End to Tas-Tas. Popular "grande" *sangría* 650ptas. Open Su-Th 6pm-2am, F-Sa 6pm-3:30am.

Bar Tas-Tas, C. Fermín Calbetón, 35 (☎ 943 43 06 12), a notorious hotspot for international backpackers, particularly of the American and Australian variety. Drink to the tune of American pop hits during the happy hour, Su-Th 8-11:30pm. Open daily 3pm-3am.

Bars Sariketa, C. Fermín Calbetó, 23 (☎ 943 42 29 85), behind the red doors. A narrow, distinctive, darkly decorated joint with plaid walls, a long bar, and top-40 hits every night. A slightly older crowd than Tas-Tas. Open daily 5:30pm-3:30am.

Akerbeltz, C. Koruko Andra Mari, 10 (☎ 943 45 01 83). Face the cathedral, take a left, and it's right on the corner. A tiny, sleek, cave-like bar miles away from the teeming backpacker scene. Open M-Th 4pm-2:30am; F-Sa 4pm-3:30am.

Molly Malone, C. San Marín, 55 (☎ 943 46 98 22), right off the Po. de la Concha, outside of the *parte vieja*. A classic Irish pub with complete descriptions of the brew selections. Beer 400-600ptas. Open daily 3pm-3am.

❋ FESTIVALS

The tourist office has the *Guía del Ocio* as well as a tri-monthly booklet of events. The city runs a **marathon** in November, **El Día de San Sebastián** (Jan. 19-20) brings traditional parades, a **carnival** swings 40 days before *Semana Santa*, and the **Festival Internacional de Danza** (☎ 943 48 21 11) takes to the stage in May. San Sebastián's five-day **Festival de Jazz,** in mid- to late July, is one of Europe's most ambitious jazz venues; such giants as Art Blakey, Wynton Marsalis, and Dizzy Gillespie have played here. For info on the 2001 festival, contact the Oficina del Festival de Jazz (☎ 943 48 11 79; email jazzaldia_donostia@donostia.org; www.jazzaldia.com). Movie stars and directors own the streets for a week in September during the **Festival Internacional de Cine,** one of the four most important in the world (along with Venice, Cannes, and Berlin). For info about the 2001 film festival (Sept. 21-30), call the Victoria Eugenia Theater (☎ 943 48 12 12; fax 943 48 12 18). **Semana Grande,** the week of August 15, is ablaze with concerts, movies, and a fireworks festival. The **Fiestas de San Juan,** June 23-24, bring their own share of folklore performances, Basque sports competitions, and general revelry. **La Quincena Musical,** in the Victoria Eugenia Theater, C. Reina Regente, sponsors more than two weeks of classical music concerts in late August, most of them free.

NEAR SAN SEBASTIÁN

HONDARRIBIA

Less than an hour east of San Sebastián by bus, Hondarribia (pop. 14,000) is a European beach town designed the way European beach towns should be. Stretching along the Txingudi Bay, the town flaunts a silky-smooth beach and brightly painted houses with flower-filled balconies. Compared to chic San Sebastián, Hondarribia is refreshingly simple. In the peak days of summer, the beach can become ridiculously crowded with vacationers from Madrid and Barcelona, but it's usually pleasantly calm through June.

🚩 **PRACTICAL INFORMATION. Interurbanos buses** (☎ 943 64 13 02) leave for Hondarribia from San Sebastián's Pl. Guipuzcoa; pay on board (45min., every 15min. M-Sa 7:45am-10:45pm, Su 7:45am-9:45pm, 210ptas). Return buses pick up in front of the Hondarribia post office. **AUIF buses** (☎ 943 63 31 11) go to **Irún** (10min., every 15min. 10am-8pm, 150ptas). The **airport** (☎ 943 66 85 00) is within walking distance of the town center. The English-speaking staff at the **tourist office, Bidasoa Turismo,** C. Javier Ugarte, 6, right off Pl. San Cristóbal, has maps and lodging lists. (☎ 943 64 54 58. Open July-Aug. M-Sa 10am-2pm and 3-8pm; Sept.-June M-F 9am-1:30pm and 4-6:30pm, Sa 10am-2pm.) Services in town include: **emergency** (☎ 112); **police** (☎ 943 64 43 00); and the **post office,** Pl. San Cristóbal, 1. (☎ 943 64 12 04. Open M-F 8:30am-2:30pm and Sa 9:30am-1pm.) The **postal code** is 20280.

ACCOMMODATIONS. Reservations are key in the summer, so call ahead. The modern **Albergue Juan Sebastián Elcano (HI)**, Ctra. Faro, sits on a hillside with a spectacular view of the beach and mountains. From the bus stop, head to the beach on C. Itsasargi, bearing left at the coast, and continuing straight for several long blocks. At the traffic circle turn left and follow signs up the steep hill to the hostel. Two hundred beds and a TV room satisfy young budget travelers. Guests can also take advantage of a playground and tennis and basketball courts. (☎ 943 64 15 50; fax 943 64 00 28. Members only; HI cards 1000-1500ptas. Breakfast included. 3-night max. stay when full. Reception daily 9am-noon and 4-7pm. Curfew midnight, but doors open at 1 and 2am. Sheets 120ptas. Dorms 1325ptas, over 30 1975ptas. Visa.) In the other direction from Pl. San Cristóbal is the small and familial **Casa Hostal Txoko Goxoa**, C. Murrua, 22, in the old quarter. Head up C. Javier Ugarte from the tourist office, take the second right onto C. Juan Laborda, and follow the street down a steep hill until it ends. Look for the stairs on your left and hike up to the old city walls; the hostel is on the right. The cozy rooms with sinks and decent beds are immaculate. (☎/fax 943 64 46 58. Breakfast 500ptas. July-Sept. doubles 6500ptas; Oct.-June doubles 5750ptas; IVA not included. Discounts for longer stays. V, MC.) **Camping Jaizkibel** (☎ 943 64 16 79; fax 943 64 26 53) lies 2km from town, on Ctra. Guadelupe toward Monte Jaizkibel. Charming wood bungalows come complete with full bath and small kitchenette. Services include hot water showers, cafeteria, restaurant, and self-service laundry. (Reception daily 9am-11pm. 575ptas per person, per tent, and per car. Bungalows for 1-2 people 6000-9000ptas, for 3-4 8000-12000ptas.)

FOOD. Several **markets** spill onto C. San Pedro, three blocks inland from the port. Stock up on staples at **Charter**, C. Santiago 19. (Open M-F 8:30am-1:30pm and 5-8pm; Sa 8:30am-1:30pm. V, MC.) Beach bums refuel at **Gaxen**, C. Zuloaga, 8, the little green shop a block down from the post office, toward the beach. The friendly young staff cooks up take-out burgers and sandwiches (350-550ptas), smoothies, shakes, and fruit juices (200-300ptas) for locals and tourists alike. (☎ 943 61 14 62. Open M-Th 9am-11pm, F-Su 9am-midnight. Closes 1hr. earlier in winter.) The daily *menú* (1000ptas) at **Xaia Jatetxea**, Bernat Etxepare, 4, is delicious, fresh, and super-cheap. Look for the carved-wood storefront diagonally across from the post office. (☎ 943 64 52 57. Open M-Sa 1-3:30pm and 8-10pm. V, MC.)

SIGHTS AND EXCURSIONS. The gorgeous stone-and-timber **casco antiguo**, centered around Carlos V's imposing palace in Pl. Armas (now a *parador*—peek inside to catch a glimpse of the renovations), provides welcome relief from Coppertone fumes. The **Parroquía de Nuestra Señora de la Asunción**, also in Pl. Armas, is a lovely 15th-century Gothic church where Louis XIV of France married, by proxy, the Spanish Habsburg Infanta María Teresa. (Officially open only for Mass and tours; check at the desk in front. 400ptas.)

There are several possible excursions from Hondarribia. Six kilometers up Av. Monte Jaizkibel, **Monte Jaizkibel**, the highest mountain on the Costa Cantábrica, guards the **Santuario de Guadalupe**. Hiking the mountain affords incredible views of the coast; on a clear day you can see as far as Bayonne, France, 45km away. **Boats** (☎ 943 61 64 47) shuttle travelers 5km to **Hendaye**, a French town with a bigger beach. They leave from the pier at the end of C. Domingo Egia, off La Marina (every 15min. in summer, every 20min. in winter; 200ptas).

IRÚN

Visitors to Irún (pop 15,100) are usually in a hurry to get somewhere else, and with good reason—the city is little more than a transportation hub with services to Paris, Madrid, San Sebastián, and the French border. **RENFE trains** (☎ 943 61 67 08) fan out to all of Spain and connect frequently to **San Sebastián** (25min., every 40min. 5:23am-10:23pm, 150-175ptas). The train station has **currency exchange**, a **post office**, and **luggage storage** (400ptas, ask for token at the bar; open daily 6am-10:20pm). The **Ayuntamiento (SAC office)**, C. Juan de la Cruz, 2, on Pl. Zabaltza off

Po. Colón, dispenses maps and free pens. (☎ 943 64 92 00. Open M-F 8:30am-2pm and 4:30-7:30pm, Sa 9:30am-1pm. Closed afternoons in Aug.) Services include **emergency** (☎ 112) and **police** (☎ 092), in Pl. Ensanche. Most people who stay overnight in Irún arrived too late in the day to continue on to their final destinations. Affordable hostels line C. Estación in front of the station. **Hostal Residencia Lizaso,** C. Aduana, 5, has bare but very clean, well-lit rooms, all with TV. Follow C. Estación, bear right on Po. Colón, and take the first right. (☎ 943 61 16 00. Doubles with shower 5000ptas, with bath 5500-5700ptas; prices may fall during off-seasons. A few singles available. IVA not included.) **Bar Restaurant Las Ruedas,** C. Estación, 20, serves cheap, hearty meals in a small, pleasant dining room up the street from the RENFE station. (☎ 943 61 54 26. Open daily 9am-11pm. Daily *menú* 1000ptas.)

BILBAO (BILBO)

The economic engine of the Basque country, Bilbao (pop. 1,200,000), known affectionately as "Botxo" to its Basque inhabitants, has been making people wealthy since the 16th century, when its shipbuilding industries and coastal location made it a key trade link between Castile and Flanders. Today, thanks to decades of careful investment, the city is finally overcoming its reputation as a bourgeois, business-minded industrial center. Economic booms in the 19th century funded wide boulevards lined by grandiose buildings, and 20th-century success has showered the city with a new subway system, an overhauled international airport, a stunning new bridge, and a stylish riverwalk project, all designed by renowned international architects. It is the shining, curving Guggenheim museum, however, that has most powerfully fueled Bilbao's rise to international prominence.

▐ TRANSPORTATION

Flights: Airport (☎ 94 486 93 00), 10km from Bilbao in Sondica (Sondika). Take **Bizkai Bus** (☎ 94 454 05 44) A-3247 from C. Sendeja next to the Ayuntamiento, on the left after crossing Puente Arenal into the old town (40min., every 40min. 6am-10:30pm, 130ptas). Taxi 2500ptas. **Iberia,** C. Ercilla, 20 (☎ 94 471 12 10), C. Colón de Larreátegui. Open daily M-F 9:30am-1:30pm and 3-6pm.

Trains: Bilbao has 3 train stations.

    RENFE: Estación de Abando/del Norte, Pl. Circular, 2 (☎ 94 423 86 23). Info open 7am-9pm. To: **Salamanca** (5½-6½hr.; 9:25am and 2:05pm, 3500ptas); **Madrid** (5¾-9hr., 3 per day 9:50am-11:05pm, 4200-4400ptas); and **Barcelona** (9½-11hr., 10am and 10:45pm, 5100ptas). From Pl. Circular, head right around the station and cross the Puente del Arenal (bridge) to reach Pl. Arriage, the entrance to the *casco viejo.*

    FEVE: Estación de Santander, C. Bailén, 2 (☎ 94 423 22 66). From Pl. Circular, walk down C. Navarra toward the river and take a right before the bridge; it's the gilded building on the water. Info open M-F July-Aug. 9am-2pm and 4-7pm; Sept.-June 7-10pm. To **Santander** (2½hr., 3 per day 8:05am-6:55pm, 920ptas).

    Ferrocarriles Vascongados/Eusko Trenbideak (FV/ET): Atxuri Station, Cl. Atxuri, 6-8 (☎ 94 200 80 08). Follow the river south from Pl. Arriaga. To **Guernica** (1hr.; 17-20 per day M-F 6:18am-8:18pm, Sa 8:18am-8:18pm; 300ptas).

Buses: Most bus companies are based at the **Termibús terminal,** C. Gurtubay, 1 (☎ 94 439 52 05; M: San Mamés), on the west side of town. Tickets can be purchased here or at the individual bus company locations. To get to Pl. Arriaga from the Termibús station, take the metro to Casco Viejo, exiting at Pl. Unamuno. Take a right on C. Sombrería and the first right onto C. Correo. The tourist office can also help with bus info.

    ANSA (GETSA, Viacarsa): C. Autonomía, 17 (☎ 94 444 31 00). From Pl. Circular, go down C. Hurtado de Amézaga to Pl. Zabálburu, bearing right on C. Autonomía for 2 blocks; enter through Bar Ansa. To: **Burgos** (2hr., 4-5 per day 8:30am-9:30pm, 1435ptas); **Madrid** (4-5hr., 10-17 per day 7am-1:30am, 3270ptas); **Barcelona** (7hr.; M-F 4 per day 6:30am-11pm, Sa-Su 3 per day 10:30am-11pm; 4900ptas); and **León** (7hr., 8:45pm, 3200ptas).

    ENATCAR: Termibús terminal (☎ 94 439 50 48). To **Salamanca** (5hr.; M-Sa 8:30am and 8:45pm, Su 5:30pm; 3200ptas).

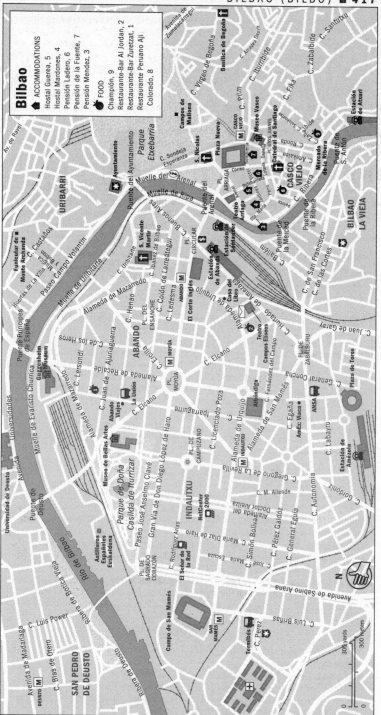

Bilbao

ACCOMMODATIONS
Hostal Guerra, 5
Hostal Mardones, 4
Pensión Ladero, 6
Pensión de la Fuente, 7
Pensión Mendez, 3

FOOD
Champión, 9
Restaurante-Bar Al Jordan, 2
Restaurante-Bar Zuretzat, 1
Restaurante Peruano Aji
Colorado, 8

PESA: Termibús terminal (☎ 94 424 88 99; info ☎ 902 10 12 10). To **San Sebastián** (1¼hr.; M-Sa every 30min. 6:30am-10pm, Su every hr. 9am-10pm; 1120ptas).

La Unión: C. Henao, 29 (☎ 94 439 50 77). From Pl. Circular, walk down Gran Vía to Pl. Federico de Moyúa, turn right on Alameda de Recalde, and go 2 blocks to C. Henao. To **Vitoria-Gasteiz** (1hr.; 14-22 per day M-F 6:45am-10pm, Sa 7:30am-10pm, Su 8:30am-9:30pm; 665ptas). **Leaving from Termibús** (☎ 94 439 50 77) to: **Haro** (1hr., 2-5 per day 8:30am-7:30pm, 1050ptas); **Logroño** (1¾hr., 3-6 per day 8:30am-7:30pm, 1475ptas); and **Pamplona** (2hr., 5-6 per day 7:30am-8pm, 1580ptas).

ALSA Grupo: Termibús terminal (☎ 94 441 99 22; info ☎ 902 42 22 42). To: **Santander** (3½hr., 3 per day 8am-1pm, 925ptas); **Zaragoza** (4hr., 9-10 per day 6:30am-8:45pm, 2430ptas); and **La Coruña** (5½hr., 4 per day 1:45pm-9pm, 5775ptas).

Public Transportation: Bilbao recently opened an attractive and user-friendly **metro** (☎ 94 425 40 25; www.metrobilbao.net) which has 1 line with terminal points in the suburbs. Look for 3 interlocking red circles to find entrances, and hang onto your ticket after entering—you'll need it again to exit. Travel within 1 zone 140ptas, 2 zones 165ptas, 3 zones 195ptas. 10-trip ticket within 1 zone 860ptas, 2 zones 1020ptas, 3 zones 1225ptas. Trains run Su-Th 6am-11pm, F-Sa 6am-11pm and every 30min. 11pm-6am. **Bilbobús** (☎ 94 448 40 80) runs 23 lines across the city (6am-11:30pm; M-F 125ptas, Sa-Su 140ptas, 10-ride ticket 715ptas). **Bizkai Bus** (☎ 94 454 05 44) connects Bilbao to suburbs and the airport in Sondica (Sondika).

Taxis: Teletaxi (☎ 94 410 21 21). **Radio Taxi Bilbao** (☎ 94 444 88 88).

Car Rental: Europcar, C. Licenciado Poza, 56 (☎ 94 442 22 26 or 94 471 01 33). Min. age 21 and must show passport and valid driver's license. 6000ptas per day. Open M-F 8am-1pm and 4-7:30pm, Sa 9am-1pm.

✴ 7 ORIENTATION AND PRACTICAL INFORMATION

It's wise to get a map, as Bilbao's sights are all over the place. The city's main artery, **Gran Vía,** leads east from the oval Pl. Federico Moyúa to **Plaza Circular** (sometimes referred to by its former name, Plaza Espana), the axis for many important stops and stations. Past Pl. Circular, you will cross Ría de Bilbao on Puente del Arenal, which deposits you on **Plaza de Arriaga,** the entrance to the *casco viejo* to the right of the tourist office.

Tourist Office: Oficina de Turismo de Bilbao (☎ 94 479 57 60; fax 94 479 57 61; www.bilbao.net), Pl. Arenal. Look for the big yellow "i" along the river. Gives out a good map and bimonthly bulletin of events. English spoken. Open M-F 9am-2pm and 4-7:30pm, Sa 9am-2pm, Su 10am-2pm.

Currency Exchange: Banco Central Hispano, Pl. Circular. Open June-Aug. M-F 9am-2pm; Sept.-May M-Th 9am-5:30pm, F-Sa 9am-2pm.

American Express: Viaca, Alameda de Recalde, 68 (☎ 94 444 48 62), off C. Autonomía. Open M-F 9am-1:30pm and 4:30-7:30pm, Sa 10am-1pm.

Luggage Storage: In **Estación de Abando,** lockers 400ptas. In **Termibús,** 100ptas a day. Both open daily 7:30am-11pm.

El Corte Inglés: Gran Vía, 7-9 (☎ 94 424 22 11), on the east side of Pl. Circular. Distributes maps. Also offers novels, guidebooks, haircuts, a supermarket, cafeteria, restaurant, and **currency exchange.** Open M-Sa 10am-9pm.

English Bookstores: Casa del Libro, C. Urkijo, 9 (☎ 94 415 32 00). A terrific selection. Open M-Sa 9:30am-9pm. V, MC.

Budget Travel: Abando Viajes, C. Henao, 31 (☎ 94 423 08 02; fax 94 424 29 45). Open M-F 9am-2pm and 5-7pm.

Emergency: ☎ 112. **Police: Municipal,** C. Luis Briñas, 14 (☎ 94 420 50 00 or 092).

Medical Services: Hospital Civil de Basurto, Av. Montevideo, 18 (☎ 94 400 60 00). **Ambulance:** ☎ 94 473 16 34.

Post Office: Main office, Alameda Urquijo, 19 (☎ 94 422 05 48; fax 94 443 00 24). Walk 1 block down Gran Vía from Pl. España and turn left after El Corte Inglés; it's on the corner of C. Bertendona. **Fax** and **Lista de Correos** (around the corner). Open M-F 8am-8:30pm, Sa 8am-2pm. **Postal Code:** 48005.

Internet Access: El Senor de la Red, C. Rodríguez Arias, 69 (☎ 944 277 773). Take Gran Vía from the *casco viejo*, turn left on C. María Díaz de Haro and take your 1st right. Caffeinate while you navigate. 200ptas per 30min., 350ptas per hr. Free coffee. Open every day 10am-10pm. **NetCenter 2000,** C. Doctor Areilza, 15, 2nd fl. (☎ 94 441 82 50 or 94 439 80 86). 250ptas per hr. Open M-F 9am-11pm and Sa 10am-1pm.

ACCOMMODATIONS

At any time other than during the August festival season (when rates can be higher than those listed below), it shouldn't be hard to find a reasonably priced room in Bilbao if you arrive before noon; rooms tend to fill up by late afternoon from July through September. Pl. Arriaga and C. Arenal have budget accommodations galore. Another option is the HI hostel **Albergue Bilbao Aterpetxez,** Ctra. Basurto-Kastrexana Errep., 70, on the bus #58 route from Pl. Circular. (☎ 94 427 00 54; fax 94 427 54 79. July-Sept. singles 2300ptas, over 25 2500ptas; Oct.-June 2100ptas, over 25 2300ptas. V, MC.)

Hostal Mardones, C. Jardines, 4, 3rd fl. (☎ 94 415 31 05). From the bridge, turn right onto C. Bidebarrieta and right again. Lovely rooms, some with balconies, all with polished floors, wood-frame beds, and marble sinks. Call ahead in summer. Singles 4000ptas, with bath 5000ptas; doubles 5600ptas, with bath 6600ptas; triples 8500ptas, with bath 10,500ptas.

Pensión Méndez, C. Santa María, 13, 4th fl. (☎ 94 416 03 64). From the bridge, turn right on C. Ribera; C. Santa María is on the left as the street curves. Insulated from the raging nightlife below. Airy, clean rooms have flowery bedspreads and tall windows. Most have balcony and sink. Singles 3000-4000ptas, with bath 6000ptas; doubles 5000ptas, with bath 8000ptas; triples 7500ptas, with bath 10,000ptas.

Hostal Gurea, C. Bidebarrieta, 14 (☎ 94 416 32 99). Young owners maintain fresh, airy rooms with sinks, firm beds, polished floors, and minimal decoration. Several have floor-to-ceiling windows or balconies. TV lounge. Singles 3600ptas, with bath 3900ptas; doubles 4000ptas, with bath 4800ptas. V, MC.

Pensión Ladero, C. Lotería, 1, 4th fl. (☎ 94 415 09 32). From Pl. Arriaga, take C. Bidebarrieta and turn left on C. Lotería. Rooms can be cramped and musty, but all have TVs, cheery blue bedspreads, and winter heating. Singles 3000ptas; doubles 4500ptas.

Pensión de la Fuente, C. Sombrería, 2 (☎ 94 416 99 89). From C. Arenal, turn right on C. Correo, follow it 2 blocks past Pl. Nueva, then turn left. A beautiful old building with pleasant rooms and high ceilings. Heating and TV extra (500ptas). Singles 2200-2500ptas; doubles 4000-4500ptas, with bath 5000-6000ptas. Cash only.

FOOD

Restaurants and bars in the *casco viejo* offer a wide selection of local dishes, as well as *pintxos* and *bocadillos* aplenty. For a sampling of a typical Basque dish try the cod cooked in a delicate green *pil-pil* sauce. The new city has more variety but less ambiance. **Mercado de la Ribera,** on the bank of the river heading left from the tourist office, is the biggest indoor **market** in Spain. It's worth a trip even if you're not eating (open daily 7am-noon). Pick up **groceries** at the massive **Champión,** Pl. Santos Juanes (open M-Sa 9am-9pm).

Restaurante Peruano Ají Colorado, C. Barrencalle, 5 (☎ 94 415 22 09), in the *casco viejo*. A unique, charming combination of Andean decorations and traditional Peruvian cuisine. Specializes in *ceviche* (marinated raw fish salad; 1400-1730ptas), *lomo saltado* (salted pork; 1800ptas), and potato dishes. M-F *menú* includes 2 courses, bread, wine, and dessert (2000ptas). Open M-Sa 1:30-3:30pm and 9-11:30pm. V, MC.

Restaurante Bar Zuretzat, C. Iparraguirre, 7 (☎ 94 424 85 05), near the Guggenheim. The classy, polished restaurant in back serves top-quality fish, shellfish, and meat entrees (1200-2000ptas). Don't miss the incredibly sweet pudding, included in the *menú* (1500ptas) or by itself (700ptas). Open daily 1-5pm. V, MC, AmEx.

Restaurante-Bar Al Jordan, C. Elcano, 26 (☎ 94 410 42 55), a side street near the train station. Excellent Middle Eastern food in an ornate, atmospheric dining room. Weekend *menú* includes appetizer, couscous entree, and wine (1500ptas). More extensive lunch *menú* served M-F (1500ptas). Open Su-Th 9am-1am, F-Sa 9am-3am. V, MC, AmEx.

👁 SIGHTS

■ **THE GUGGENHEIM.** Frank O. Gehry's Guggenheim Museum Bilbao can only be described as breathtaking. Lauded in the international press with every superlative imaginable, it has catapulted Bilbao straight into cultural stardom. Visitors are greeted by Jeff Koons's "Puppy," a dog composed of 60,000 plants and standing almost as tall as the actual museum. The main attraction is constructed mainly out of titanium, limestone, and glass in a series of interconnected pieces. The US$100 million building, with its undulating curves and multiple levels, is said to resemble an iridescent scaly fish or a blossoming flower. The amazingly light and airy interior features a towering atrium and a series of non-traditional exhibition spaces, including a gargantuan 130m by 30m hall. The museum currently hosts rotating exhibits drawn from the Guggenheim Foundation's collection but will gradually acquire its own international sampling of 20th-century works. Sleek black-and-red suited staff slap bracelets on the streams of visitors filing through the door—may you enjoy your stay. *(Av. Abandoibarra, 2. ☎ 94 435 90 00 or 94 435 90 59; www.guggenheim.bilbao.es. Open daily July-Aug. 9am-9pm; Sept.-June Tu-Su 10am-8pm. 1200ptas, students and seniors 600ptas, under 12 free. 1600ptas includes entrance to Guggenheim and Museo de Bellas Artes (see below). Audio tour 600ptas. Guided tours in English Tu-F 11am, 12:30, 4, and 6:30pm, Sa-Su 1 and 4pm. Sign up 30min. before tour at the info desk.)*

■ **MUSEO DE BELLAS ARTES.** Often overshadowed by its popular big sister, the Museo de Bellas Artes hoards aesthetic riches behind an unassuming facade. An impressive collection of 12th- to 20th-century art features excellent 15th- to 17th-century Flemish paintings, works by El Greco, Zurbarán, Goya, Gauguin, Francis Bacon, Velázquez, Picasso, and Mary Cassatt, as well as canvases by Basque painters. *(Pl. Museo, 2. Take C. Elcano to Pl. Museo, or take bus #10 from Puente del Arenal. ☎ 94 439 60 60. For guided visits call ☎ 94 459 61 41. Open Tu-Sa 10am-8pm, Su 10am-2pm. 600ptas, seniors and students 300ptas, under 12 free. W free.)*

MUSEO VASCO. Dip into Basque culture and history at the Museo Vasco, in the old city. Housed in a 17th-century building with a beautiful cloister, its exhibits cover a variety of topics, including weaving, blacksmiths, pastoral life, and the sea. *(C. Cruz, 4. Walk past Pensión de la Fuente away from C. Correo to Pl. Miguel de Unamuno, where C. Cruz appears. ☎ 94 415 54 23. Open Tu-Sa 10:30am-1:30pm and 4-6pm, Su 10:30am-1:30pm. 300ptas, students 150ptas, seniors and under 12 free. Th free.)*

OTHER SIGHTS. The best view of Bilbao's surrounding landscape and the perfect place for a picnic is at the top of **Monte Archanda,** north of the old town and equidistant from both the *casco viejo* and the Guggenheim. *(Funicular to the top every 15min., 110ptas. Turn left from Pl. Arenal with your back to the new town and follow the riverside road past the Ayuntamiento. On Po. Campo de Volantín, turn right on C. Mugica Y Butrón and continue until Pl. Funicular.)* A short Metro ride leads to **beaches** north of the city at **Plencia (Plentzia)** or **Sopelana** along the way. Along with Sopelana, **Getxo** attracts a surfer crowd and lies just a little nearer to the Cantabrian Sea; its illuminated **Puente Colgante** (suspension bridge) fords the river, leading to a plethora of all-night bars.

🎵 ENTERTAINMENT

Like most Spanish cities, Bilbao has a thriving after-dark bar scene, especially on the weekends. In the *casco viejo* revelers spill out into the streets to sip their *txikitos* (chee-KEE-tos; small glasses of beer or wine characteristic of the region), especially on C. Barrencalle (Barrenkale), one of the original "seven streets" from which the city of Bilbao has grown exponentially. Teenagers and 20-somethings also jam onto C. Licenciado Poza on the west side of town. For a mellower scene,

NO CAMP DAVID IN SIGHT

One of Europe's longest-running guerrilla rebellions—that of Basque terrorists against the Spanish government—shows no sign of ending anytime soon. Since 1968, the Basque separatist group ETA (Eskadi ta Askatasuna) has been blamed for more than 800 deaths, most of them among members of the Spanish government. A cease-fire was agreed upon in September 1998 (to negotiate bringing Basque prisoners closer to home), but ETA broke the truce in December 2000 and in the following eight months alone was pinned with nine terrorist murders. Most Spaniards are fed up with the violence. Vigils have been held nationwide, and more than half a million people marched in Madrid to protest ETA violence. Prime Minister José María Aznar has declared that he simply will not deal with terrorism. "They will not see us blink," he said at the funeral of former Basque governor Juan María Jauregui, a recent victim who had repeatedly pressed for peace talks. On the other side, Arnaldo Otegi, spokesman for Euskal Herritarok, the radical nationalists seen as ETA's political wing, has said that violence will not end until the Basques have an independent state. But by no means does the entire País Vasco support this stance. Surveys show that only about 30% of Basques hope for complete sovereignty, and fear is spreading tangibly in the region; a recent poll by a regional university showed that 70% of Basques are afraid to participate openly in politics, up 20% from three years ago. The future of Basque terrorism is uncertain at best. Jonan Fernández, coordinator of Elkarri, a nonprofit pro-separatist peace group, laments the lack of international help. "Why," he implored, "is there no Camp David for us?"

munch on *pintxos* (150-200ptas) and people-watch at Bilbao's oldest coffee shop (est. 1871), **Café Boulevard,** C. Arenal, 3. This art-deco cafe was once an important site for literary meetings and one of Miguel de Unamuno's favorite haunts. (☎ 94 415 31 28. Open M-Th 7:30am-midnight, F-Sa 8am-2am, Su 11am-midnight.)

The massive blow-out fiesta in honor of *Nuestra Señora de Begoña* takes place during **Semana Grande,** a nine-day party beginning the weekend after August 15 (August 17 in 2001; info ☎ 94 479 57 60). Documentary filmmakers from the world over gather from October to November for the **Festival Internacional de Cine Documental de Bilbao.** During the summer, there are free **concerts** every Sunday evening at the bandstand in the Parque Arena. For current goings-on, pick up *Bilbao Guide* from the tourist office.

GUERNICA (GERNIKA)

On April 26, 1937, the Nazi "Condor Legion" released an estimated 29,000kg of explosives on Guernica (pop. 15,600), obliterating 70% of the city in three hours. The tragedy marked the first mass civilian aerial bombing attack, and the nearly 2000 people who were killed have been immortalized in Pablo Picasso's stark masterpiece *Guernica*, which now hangs in Madrid's Reina Sofía gallery (see **The Tragedy of Guernica,** p. 422). The small, reconstructed city is not much of an attraction in itself, but for those interested in learning more about Basque history and the infamous event that occurred here, Guernica is a rewarding daytrip.

⁊ PRACTICAL INFORMATION. Trains (☎ 94 625 11 82) connect Guernica to **Bilbao** (45min., every 30min. 6:18am-9:18pm, 315ptas). **Bizkai Bus** (☎ 94 454 05 44) sends more convenient, and more frequent, **buses** between Guernica and **Bilbao's Estación Abando** (55min., every 15-30min. 6:15am-10pm, M-F 315ptas, Sa-Su 325ptas). Another pick-up point for the same line is right behind the Bilbao tourist office on Muelle de Sendeja. To reach Guernica's **tourist office,** C. Artekalea, 8, from the train station, walk three blocks up C. Adolfo Urioste and turn right on C. Artekalea. The entrance is around the corner on the right. (☎ 94 625 58 92; fax 94 625 32 12; www.gernika-lumo.net. Open July-Sept. M-Sa 10am-7:30pm, Su 10:30am-2:30pm; Oct.-June M-F 10am-1pm and 4-7:30pm, Sa-Su 10am-1pm.) The **post office,** C. Iparragirre, 26, is immediately to the left as you exit the train station. (☎ 94 625 03 87. Open M-F 8:30am-2:30pm, Sa 9:30am-1pm.). The **postal code** is 48300.

THE TRAGEDY OF GUERNICA Founded on April 28, 1366, Guernica was virtually erased from the map on April 26, 1937. It was a Monday market day when the church bell rang three times to warn the small town of an aerial invasion. The German Condor Legion began to bomb the small town at 4:30pm and didn't stop until 7:45pm. Heavy bombs and hand grenades were first dropped from small planes in order to create a panic and a stampede. Next, low-flying planes machine-gunned those running on foot or hiding in the fields. These planes forced the townspeople into buildings, which were then wrecked and burned by 12 bombers. The entire main city was effectively demolished. Strangely, the Casa de Juntos and the oak tree were untouched, as was Franco's war-material factory a few kilometers down the road. Guernica was far behind the lines; the destruction was fueled solely by a desire to rob the anti-fascist Basque people of their desire to fight.

Many pictures, sketches, and paintings have attempted to capture this day. In a painting now at the Gernika Museoa, Sofía Gandarias depicted clocks stopped at 4:30, women holding dead children, and the words *"y del cielo lloría sangre"* (and the sky cried blood). But it was Pablo Picasso who brought the town's tragedy to international fame. The still-republican Spanish government had commissioned the artist to paint a mural for the Universal Exhibition in Paris in 1937, and he used the bombing for inspiration. In ten days he had 25 sketches; he finished the painting—his largest work—in only one month. When asked about the symbolism, Picasso answered, "The bull represents brutality and the horse represents the people." However, in regard to the painting as a whole, Picasso replied, "Let them interpret as they wish." Picasso was even approached by a German ambassador who asked of the painting, "Did you do this?" Picasso answered, "No, you did."

🛏️🍴 ACCOMMODATIONS AND FOOD. Although Guernica's main attractions can be seen in a daytrip from Bilbao, clean, light rooms, all with TV, are available at **Pensión Iratxe,** C. Industria, 6. From the train station, go up C. Urioste and turn left on C. Pablo Picasso, which becomes C. Industria. If nobody's home, knock at Bar Frontón next door. (☎ 94 625 31 34. Singles 2500ptas, with bath 3000ptas; doubles 4000ptas, with bath 5000ptas; triples 6000ptas, with bath 6500ptas. Prices decrease for longer stays.) Popular family-run ⭐**Restaurante Zallo Barri,** C. Juan Calzada, 79, dishes out a tasty 1000pta *menú* with several fish, meat, and dessert choices. After exiting the train station, walk up C. Urioste and take the second left; the bright blue facade is several blocks down on the left. (☎ 94 625 18 00. Open daily 8:30am-11pm; *menú* offered 1-3:30pm only. V, MC, AmEx.)

🏛️ SIGHTS. The emotional focus of Guernica is **El Arbol.** Encased in stone columns, the 300-year-old "Old Tree" (an oak) marks the old political center of the País Vasco, the place where medieval Basques gathered to debate community issues and Castilian monarchs ritually swore their respect for the autonomy of the local governments and laws. Next to the oldest tree grows an oak that was planted in 1860, and next to that, a "sapling" only 20 years old. The **Casa de Juntos,** next to the trees, is the meeting place of the Vizkaya (Basque) General Assembly. (☎ 94 625 11 38. Open daily June-Sept. 10am-2pm and 4-7pm; Oct.-May 10am-7pm. Free.) There are two sights worth seeing in Guernica's **Parque de los Pueblos de Europa.** Eduardo Chillida's dramatic sculpture **Gure aitaren etxea** (Our Father's House), a peace monument, was commissioned for the 50th anniversary of the city's bombing, and it stands alongside Henry Moore's voluptuous 1986 **Large Figure in a Shelter,** which suggests a female form and symbolizes rebirth. To get to the park from the bus station, follow C. Adolfo Urioste as far as it goes. At the top, enter the park and cross the little wooden bridge to the right. (Open daily June-Aug. 10am-9pm; Sept.-May 10am-7pm. Free.) The modest ◧**Gernika Museoa,** Foru Plaza, 1, has an informative and moving exhibition chronicling the bombardment in several languages. (☎ 94 627 02 13. Guided tours in English. Open daily July-Aug. 10am-7pm; Sept.-June M-Sa 10am-2pm and 4-7pm, Su 10am-2pm. 300ptas, under 16 free.) Paintings and artifacts on display inside the **Museo de Euskal Herria,** C. Allende Salazar, 5, document Basque political and cultural history. (☎ 94 525 54 51. Guided tours in English, French, and Spanish. Open Tu-Sa 10am-2pm and 4-7pm, Su 10am-1:45pm. Free.) The city also holds a **fiesta** with crafts, music, and games on the first Saturday of every summer month. The tourist office has maps and pamphlets on the city's four **scenic walking itineraries;** it also offers a **historic tour** of the city's principal attractions; call to schedule one. (Tours Tu-Sa at 11am. 500ptas.)

VITORIA-GASTEIZ

Vitoria-Gasteiz (pop. 230,000) is an attractive, up-and-coming city. Packed with tree-canopied avenues and leafy parks, it has the highest ratio of greenery to people in all of Spain, as well as a certain old charm that belies its status as a sleek cosmopolitan center. The city's hyphenated name testifies to its regional loyalty: renamed Villa de Nueva Vitoria (from Gasteiz) by the King of Navarra in 1181, the Basques re-incorporated the city's original name upon recovering regional autonomy in 1979. Vitoria-Gasteiz should not be a priority destination, but it is a worthwhile place to visit for those spending some time in the País Vasco.

Vitoria-Gasteiz

⌂ ACCOMMODATIONS
Casa 400, 3
Hostal-Residencia Nuvilla, 1
Pensión Araba, 2

▛ TRANSPORTATION

Flights: Aeropuerto Vitoria-Foronda (☎ 945 16 35 00), 9km out of town. Accessible only by car or taxi (2000ptas). Info open 7:30am-10pm. **Iberia** (☎ 945 16 36 39 or 945 16 37 30). Info open 7am-11pm.

Trains: RENFE (☎ 941 23 02 02; fax 945 14 33 33), Pl. Estación, at the end of C. Eduardo Dato, south of the old city. Info open 7:30am-10:30pm. To: **Pamplona** (1hr., 2-3 per day 7:50am-7pm, 595ptas); **Burgos** (1½hr., 2-4 per day 7:30am-6:05pm, 1090ptas); **San Sebastián** (2hr., 3 per day 9:28am-6:50pm, 1175ptas); **Zaragoza** (3hr., 3 per day 7:50am-7pm, 2285ptas); **Madrid** (4½-7hr., 5-6 per day 7:30am-12:30am, 4200ptas); and **Barcelona** (6½hr., 4:15pm, 4500ptas).

Buses: C. Herrán, 50, on a traffic island east of the old city. General info (☎ 945 25 84 00) open M-F 8am-8pm, Sa-Su 9am-7pm. **ALSA** (☎ 945 25 55 09; www.alsa.es) to **Pamplona** (1½hr.; 3-11 per day M-Sa 7am-8:30pm, Su 9am-9pm; 890ptas) and **Zaragoza** (3hr., 3-8 per day 7:30am-9pm, 2020ptas). **La Unión** (☎ 945 26 46 26) to **Bilbao** (1hr.; 17-20 per day M-F 6:45am-9pm, Sa 7:30am-10pm, Su 8:30am-9:30pm; 665ptas). **Continental Auto** (☎/fax 945 28 64 66) to: **Burgos** (1½hr.; 8-9 per day M-Sa 6:45am-10:15pm, Su 10:45am-10pm; 950-1150ptas); **San Sebastián** (1½hr., 7-10 per day 5am-11:30pm, 935ptas); and **Madrid** (4½-5hr.; 9 per day M-Sa 6:45am-8:30pm, Su 8:45am-10pm; 2830-4390ptas). **Eurobus** (☎ 945 27 71 90) to **Barcelona** (6½-7hr.; 2-3 per day M-Th 8am-3:30pm, F 8am-11:15pm, Sa 10:45am-midnight, Su 10:45am-11:15pm; 4500ptas).

Public Transportation: (☎ 945 16 15 70). **Buses** cover the metropolitan area and suburbs (6:30am-11pm, 95ptas). The tourist office has a pamphlet with routes. Bus #2 goes from the bus station to C. Florida (home to many hostels).

Taxis: Radio-Taxi (☎ 945 27 35 00 or 945 25 30 33).

Car Rental: Avis, Av. Gasteiz, 53 (☎ 945 24 46 12), just past C. Adriano VI. From 10,000ptas per day (includes mileage, insurance, and tax). Min. age 25 and must have had a license for 1 year. Open M-F 9am-1:30pm and 4-7pm, Sa 9am-1:30pm.

▟ ▟ ORIENTATION AND PRACTICAL INFORMATION

The medieval **casco viejo** (old city) is the egg-shaped center of Vitoria-Gasteiz. At its base, **Plaza de la Virgen Blanca** marks the center of town. From the **train station,** follow C. Eduardo Dato to its end, turn left on C. Postas, and head straight to the plaza. Buses run from a glass building on C. Herrán, between C. Prudencio María Verástegui and C. Arana. To get to the center of town from the bus station, turn left on C. Herrán (with your back to the station), then make an immediate right onto C. Verástegui. Follow C. Verástegui to its end and turn left on C. Francia. Follow C. Francia for four blocks as it becomes C. Paz and turn right onto C. Postas, which leads straight to Pl. Virgen Blanca.

Tourist Office: (☎ 945 13 13 21; fax 945 13 02 93), Parque de la Florida. From the train station, follow C. Eduardo Dato (go straight exiting the station) and take the 2nd left onto C. Florida; follow it to the edge of the park. From the bus station, head toward Pl. Virgen Blanca, but follow C. Francia/Paz 2 blocks past C. Postas to C. Ortiz de Zárate on the right, which leads to C. Florida. Once in the park, follow the tree-lined path to the left; the tourist office is in a stone house on the corner. Trilingual staff gives out a great map, accommodations listings, and info on all of the País Vasco. Open daily Sept.-May 9am-1pm and 3-7pm; June-Aug. M-F 9am-7pm, Sa-Su 9am-1pm and 3-7pm.

Currency Exchange: Banco Central Hispano, C. Eduardo Dato, 26, at the intersection with C. San Prudencio. Open M-F 8:30am-2pm; Nov.-Feb. also Sa 8:30am-1pm.

Luggage storage: At the **train station** (400ptas). Buy tokens from the ticket counter 6am-1am. At the **bus station.** 105ptas the 1st day, 87ptas each additional day. Open M-Sa 8am-8pm, Su 9am-7pm.

El Corte Inglés: (☎ 945 26 63 33), on the corner of C. Paz and C. Independencia, 1 block past C. Postas coming from bus station. English books, supermarket, currency exchange, and helpful staff. Open M-Sa 10am-9:30pm.

English Bookstore: Axular, Pl. Arca, 11 (☎ 945 13 22 03). From Pl. de Espana, follow C. de Eduardo Dato away from the *casco viejo*. At C. de San Prudencio, take a left and then a right into the long, narrow Pl. Arca. Large 2-story bookstore has English novels and 5 computers with **Internet access** downstairs. 250ptas for 30min., 500ptas per hr. Open M-F 9:30am-1:30pm and 4:30-8pm, Sa 10am-1:30pm and 5-8pm.

Emergency: ☎ 112. **Police:** ☎ 091 or 092.

Medical Services: Hospital General de Santiago (☎ 945 26 40 40 or 945 27 29 52), C. Olaguíbel. From the bus station, go left 1 block after C. Francia becomes C. Paz.

Internet Access: Link Internet, C. San Antonio, 31 (☎ 945 13 04 84). Head down C. Florida toward the park and turn left on C. San Antonio. 8 computers in a comfortable space. 125ptas for 15min., 350ptas for 30min., 500ptas per hr.

Post Office: C. Postas, 9 (☎ 945 23 05 75; fax 945 23 37 80), on the pedestrian street leading to Pl. Virgen Blanca. Open M-F 8:30am-8:30pm, Sa 9:30am-2pm. For **Lista de Correos,** walk around the corner to the C. Nuestra Señora del Cabello side of the building. **Postal Code:** 01008.

▌ ACCOMMODATIONS

Vitoria-Gasteiz has only a handful of cheap hostels, although slightly more deluxe hostels abound. If you plan to drop in during the Jazz fest (third week of July) or the *Fiestas de la Virgen Blanca* (Aug. 4-9) try to make reservations at least a month in advance.

Pensión Araba (2), C. Florida, 25 (☎ 945 23 25 88). On the road to the tourist office from the bus station; from the train station, turn right onto C. Florida. Good value for the price. White walls, dark wood floors, and clean, tiled bathrooms. Attractive rooms have sinks, TV/VCRs, and radios. Elevator and parking garage. Doubles 4500ptas, with bath 5500ptas; triples 6600ptas, with bath 7100ptas.

Hostal-Residencia Nuvilla, C. Fueros, 29, 3rd fl. (☎ 945 25 91 51). From the bus station, follow directions to Pl. Virgen Blanca (see **Orientation,** p. 424) but take the 1st left off C. Postas. Kind owner keeps rooms comfortable, clean, quiet, and attractive. All have wrought-iron balconies and marble sinks. Rare singles 3000ptas; doubles 4200ptas; triples 5500-6000ptas.

Casa 400, C. Florida, 46, 3rd fl. (☎ 945 23 38 87), right off C. Eduardo Dato coming from the train station. Youthful atmosphere—it's a college dorm during the year. Breakfast 300ptas. Singles 2700ptas; doubles 5200ptas. Rooms available July-Sept.

Camping Ibaya (☎ 945 14 76 20), 3km from town toward Madrid. Follow Portal de Castilla west from the tourist office intersection. Supermarket, cafe/restaurant, hot showers. 550ptas per person, per tent, and per car. Open year-round.

▌ FOOD

You can't go wrong in the *casco viejo* and the surrounding streets. From the train station, take C. Eduardo Dato, turn right on C. Postas, then turn left past the post office and go uphill, where C. Cuchillería and other old town streets radiate from C. San Francisco. There are *pintxos* galore in the streets around Pl. España. Fresh produce and meat fill the two-level **Mercado de Abastos,** on Pl. Santa Bárbara off C. Paz (open M-Th 9am-2pm and 5-8pm, F 9am-2pm and 5-8:30pm, Sa 8am-3pm). Buy groceries at **Champión,** C. General Alava, 10, between C. Eduardo Dato and C. San Antonio (open M-Sa 9:15am-9:15pm).

Museo del Organo, C. Manuel Iradier, 80 (☎ 945 26 40 48). Take C. Florida east from the park to Pl. Toros, then turn right. A favorite among locals, with remarkably fresh, filling vegetarian cuisine at outstanding prices. M-F 4-course *menú* 1300ptas, Sa 1800ptas. Open M-Sa 1-3:30pm. Visa.

Restaurante Argentino La Yerra, C. Correria, 46 (☎ 945 26 57 59). Tucked away in the old quarter, this small treasure of a restaurant will exceed the expectations of meat connoisseurs and interior decorators alike. Exposed stone wall meets urban chic. Good beef and chicken entrees (1200-2000ptas) as well as pasta dishes (900-1300ptas). Open Su and Tu-W 1:30-4pm; Th-Sa 1:30-4pm and 9:30pm-midnight. V, MC.

◉ SIGHTS

The tree-lined pedestrian walkways of the new city and steep narrow streets of the *casco viejo* make for pleasant wanderings. **Plaza de la Virgen Blanca** is the focal point of the *casco viejo* and site of Vitoria-Gasteiz's *fiestas*. Beside Pl. Virgen Blanca is the broad, arcaded **Plaza de España,** marking the division of the old town from the new. **Los Arquillos,** a series of arches that rise above Pl. España, were designed by architects Sefurola and Olaguíbel in 1802 to connect the *casco viejo* with the rapidly growing new town below.

PALACIOS. Many of the old quarter's Renaissance *palacios* are open to the public as museums. The gorgeous ◪**Palacio Augustín** houses the **Museo de Bellas Artes,** with sculptures in the front garden and works by Ribera, Miró, El Greco, and Picasso inside. *(Po. Fray Francisco de Vitoria. Open Tu-F 10am-2pm and 4-6:30pm, Sa 10am-2pm, Su 11am-2pm. Free.)* The 15th-century **Casa del Cordón,** so-called because of the stone *cordón* (rope) that embellishes its central arch, is open to the public and hosts changing exhibitions, many featuring student art. *(C. Cuchillería, 24. ☎ 945 25 96 73. Open M-Sa 6:30-9pm, Su noon-2pm and 6:30-9pm. Free.)*

CATHEDRALS. Construction of the Gothic **Catedral de Santa María** (also known as the Catedral Vieja, or Old Cathedral), at the top of the *casco viejo*, began in the 14th century; today it flaunts two especially expressive doors. *(Closed for restoration; check with the tourist office for info.)* The 20th-century neo-Gothic **New Cathedral** is in the new town. Located in its sun-dappled apse is the **Diocesan Museum of Sacred Art,** a small collection from Basque churches, including a single canvas by El Greco. *(C. Monseñor Cadena y Eleta. Cathedral open M-Sa 11am-2pm. Free. Museum ☎ 945 15 06 31. Open Tu-F 10am-2pm and 4-6:30pm, Sa 10am-2pm, Su 11am-2pm.)*

♫ ENTERTAINMENT

After nightfall, the *casco viejo* is the place to be. Bars line C. Cuchillería ("La Cuchi"), C. Herrería, C. Zapatería, and C. San Francisco; check out **Bar Carajo** and **Gasteiz-bi,** C. Mateo Moraza, 9 and 23, off C. San Francisco. Dancing types can head to **Mana,** C. Florida, 39. Music starts thumping at 1am, and it's packed with 20-somethings until 6am (cover 900ptas, includes 1 drink). **Aural,** on Po. Fray Francisco near Parque Florida, also has a 20-something crowd and two floors of dancing in the dark. (Open 8pm-6am. Cover 1000ptas, includes 1 drink.) For more intimate socializing, **Sherezade,** C. Correría, 42, has created an atmospheric Moroccan tea room with small tables and embroidered cushions. Sip on a kiwi shake (300ptas) and let your creative juices flow—crayons and paper are provided. (☎ 945 25 58 68. Open 11:30am-midnight.)

For info on **theater** and special events, pick up the *Gaceta Municipal* at the tourist office or newsstands. World-class jazz grooves into Vitoria-Gasteiz in the third week of July for the week-long **Festival de Jazz de Vitoria-Gasteiz.** Tickets for big name performers cost 700-3000ptas, but there are plenty of free performances on the street. Call or visit the **Asociación Festival de Jazz de Vitoria,** C. Florida, 19, for specific concerts (☎ 945 14 19 19; www.jazzvitoria.com). On July 24-25, the "blue blouses" hold their own festival with wine, music, and games. The blue (or sometimes black) shirts represent the old shepherds that used to live in Vitoria. Rockets launch the **Fiesta de la Virgen Blanca** (Aug.4-9) in, you guessed it, Pl. Virgen Blanca.

NORTHWESTERN SPAIN

ASTURIAS AND CANTABRIA

Jagged cliffs and hell-reaching ravines lend an epic scope to the tiny lands of Asturias and Cantabria, tucked away between the País Vasco and Galicia. With the decline of Asturias's traditional crafts production and of the region's mining, steel, and shipping industries, the economic livelihood of Asturias and Cantabria has come to rely upon scientific research and green tourism. Now an extensive network of quaint tourist towns, cottages, and country inns in old *casas de indianos* (rambling Victorian mansions built by settlers who scored big in the Americas) provides the residents of Asturias and Cantabria a means to get rich off Spain's vacationing elite. Along with its industrial centers, the area is known for its prosperous dairy farms and its National Parks, especially the Picos de Europa.

Agricolar Moors had little use for the region's rough terrain, enabling the Christians to make the land their northern base. The *Reconquista* officially began in Asturias (in the small Picos town of Covadonga), and it was the only region never to fall to the Moors, which is why today Spain's heir to the throne is titled the Príncipe de Asturias. During the Civil War this historical defiance translated into a legendary, blue-collar resistance to the Fascists.

HIGHLIGHTS OF ASTURIAS AND CANTABRIA

Spelunking among 15,000 year-old paintings in **Cueva del Buxu** (see p. 434).
Bovine fraternizing beside the mesmerizing lakes of **Enol** and **Ercina** (see p. 436).
The sunset glow of the west face of the mythical **Naranjo de Bulnes** peak (p. 432).
A post-hike bowl of Asturian *fabada*, washed down with a tall glass of *sidra*.

LOCAL FESTIVALS IN ASTURIAS AND CANTABRIA

Every July 25, the entire town of **Cangas de Onís** hikes 12km up the mountain-side for the lakeside celebration aptly nicknamed *"Romería cerca del cielo"* ("Feast near the sky"). From July 15 to 17, **Comilla** lets loose with fireworks, pole-walking and goose-chasing. **San Vincente de la Barquera** has huge sardine cookouts during *Las Fiestas de la Virgen del Carmen* (July 14-16).

Because of the diverse terrain and unpredictable weather, public rail transportation in Asturias and Cantabria can be erratic; buses are the most reliable mode of transportation. But the roads are striking, winding through alpine forests and green valleys quilted with cornfields and pastures. Asturias is famous for its apples, cheeses, and wholesome fresh milk; the dairy desserts, especially *arroz con leche* (rice pudding), are also delectable. *Sidra* (cider) and *fabada asturiana*, a thick, hearty bean-and-sausage stew, grace menus everywhere, and true Asturians can be recognized by the way they drink their cider: it must be poured from several feet above the glass and downed immediately. Cantabrian cuisine draws from both the mountains and sea, with good dairy products and beef as well as delicious anchovies, tuna, and sardines. Local favorites include *cocido montañes* (bean stew) and *marmita* (tuna, potato, and green pepper stew).

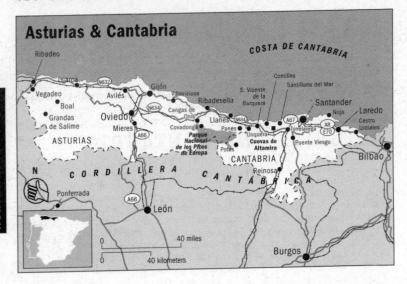

Asturias & Cantabria

ASTURIAS

OVIEDO

Oviedo's name comes from the Latin word for city *(ovetum)*, and for a few centuries, at least, it really was *the* city in Spain: one of the few places able to ward off Moorish attacks, it was made the capital of the Kingdom of Asturias as early as 810. It was not so lucky during Franco's regime, when the Nationalist army crushed a workers' uprising and nearly destroyed the city in the process. Most of the old quarter survived intact, though, and today Oviedo boasts immense public parks and stunning, well-preserved 19th-century buildings. It may not be the prettiest place in Spain, but Oviedo makes an excellent base for trips into the Picos.

⎗ TRANSPORTATION

Flights: Aeropuerto de Ranón/Aeropuerto Nacional de Asturias (☎ 985 12 75 00), in Avilés, northwest of Oviedo. **Prabus,** C. Marqués de Pidal, 20 (☎ 985 25 47 51), runs frequent buses from the ALSA station to the airport. **Aviaco** (☎ 985 12 76 03) and **Iberia** (☎ 985 12 76 07) fly to Madrid, Barcelona, and London.

Trains: Oviedo has 2 main train stations.

RENFE (☎ 985 24 33 64 or 985 25 24 02), C. Uría, at the junction with Av. Santander. Pay attention to the type of train; a slow local train through the mountains can double your travel time. Info daily 7:45am-11:15pm. V, MC, AmEx. To: **Gijón** (30min., every 30min. 300-350ptas); **León** (2-2½hr., 7 per day 7:37am-11pm, 945-2300ptas); **Madrid** (6-9hr.; 9:43am, 4:20pm, and 11pm; 5900ptas); and **Barcelona** (12-13½hr., 11am and 7:40pm, 6100-8000ptas).

FEVE (☎ 985 29 76 56 or 902 10 08 18), Av. Santander, above RENFE. Info open daily 9am-10pm or until last train. To: **Ribadeo** (4hr., 7:47am and 2:47pm, 1280ptas); **Llanes** (4½hr., 3 per day, 885ptas); **Santander** (4½hr., 9:08am and 3:48pm, 1685ptas); **Bilbao** (7hr., 9:08am, 2625ptas), via Santander; and **Ferrol** (6½hr., 7:47am and 2:47pm, 2470ptas).

Buses: There are 2 major bus companies: **Alsa** (national) and **Económicos** (regional).

ALSA, Pl. General Primo de Rivera, 1 (☎ 985 96 96 96 or 902 42 22 42), unmarked, on the lower level of a shopping arcade. To: **León** (2hr., 8 per day 7:30am-10:30pm, 1030ptas); **Santander** (3-4hr., 8-10 per day 7am-8:30pm, 1710-2800ptas); **Burgos** (4¼hr., 7:30am and 8pm, 1540ptas); **La Coruña** (4½-6¾hr., 5-6 per day 7am-7pm, 3165ptas); **Madrid** (5hr.; M-F 12 per day, Sa 10 per day, Su 15 per day, 6:30am-12:30am; 3825-6000ptas); **Santiago** (5½-7hr.; 3-4 per day 7am-4:30pm, Su until 7pm; 3740ptas); **Vigo** (7-9hr., 7am and 3pm, 4470ptas); and **Barcelona** (12hr., 7:30am and 8pm, 4715ptas).

Económicos (EASA), C. Jerónimo Ibrán, 1 (☎ 985 29 00 39). With your back to the ALSA bus station, walk up C. General Elorza and look immediately to the right for the EASA sign. To: **Cangas de Onís** (1-1½hr., 9-10 per day 8am-9:30pm, 700ptas); **Covadonga** (1¾hr.; M-F 4 per day 6:45am-5:30pm, Sa-Su 7 per day 9:30am-4:40pm; 805ptas); **Arenas de Cabrales** (2hr., 3-4 per day 9:30am-6pm, 995ptas); and **Llanes** (1½-2hr., 11 per day 6:45am-9:15pm, 1050ptas).

Public Transportation: TUA (☎ 985 22 24 22) runs **buses** 8am-10pm (110ptas). #4 goes to the bus, FEVE, and RENFE stations. #2 goes to the youth hostel and hospital. #2, 3, 5, and 7 run from the RENFE station to near the old city.

Taxis: Radio Taxi (☎ 985 25 00 00 or 985 25 25 00). There are taxi stands in front of the RENFE/FEVE station as well as on Pl. Primero de Rivera near the ALSA bus stop and on C. Mendizabal and Av. Fruela in the old sector of town.

Car Rental: Avis, C. Ventura Rodríguez, 12 (☎ 985 24 13 83). From 9600ptas per day. Weekend specials. Open M-F 9am-1pm and 4-7:30pm, Sa 9am-1pm.

✷💶 ORIENTATION AND PRACTICAL INFORMATION

The easiest way to navigate through Oviedo is to find **Calle de Uría,** which bisects the city and originates at the **RENFE station.** The **FEVE station** is located in a new building above the RENFE station. **ALSA buses** arrive in an unmarked station in the **Plaza General Primo de Rivera.** From there, take C. Fray Ceferino (on the other side of the plaza) straight to C. Uría. Walking down C. Uría with the RENFE station behind you, you'll pass the leafy Parque de San Francisco on the right; to the left is the old city, whose two main plazas are **Plaza Mayor** and **Plaza de Alfonso II,** known to locals as **Plaza de la Catedral** and to tourists as Plaza de la **Tourist Office.**

Tourist Office: (☎ 985 21 33 85), Pl. Alfonso II. Handy city guide (maps included) and advice on Picos treks. English spoken. Open M-F 9:30am-1:30pm and 4:30-6:30pm, Sa 9am-2pm. **Municipal Office** (☎/fax 985 22 75 86), off C. Uría, on the corner of Parque San Francisco. Open M-F 10:30am-2pm and 4:30-7:30pm, Sa-Su 11am-2pm.

Budget Travel: TIVE, C. Calvo Sotelo, 5 (☎ 985 23 60 58), past Campo San Francisco, up from C. Marqués de Santa Cruz. Hiking info. ISIC 750ptas. HI card 500ptas, over 26 1000ptas. Open M-F 8am-3pm. **Viajes Iberia,** C. Gil de Jaz, 9 (☎ 902 10 81 08).

Currency Exchange: Banco Central Hispano, one at Av. Galicia, 24 (☎ 985 23 67 81) and another at Av. Galicia, 8 (☎ 985 23 29 50). Open M-F June-Sept. 8:30am-2:30pm; Oct.-May 8:30am-4:30pm.

Luggage Storage: At the **RENFE station.** Lockers 300ptas. Open daily 7am-11pm. At **ALSA bus station.** Lockers 300ptas. Open daily 7am-11pm.

Emergency: ☎ 112. **Police: Policía Municipal** (☎ 985 21 80 29), C. Quintana.

Hospital: Hospital General de Asturias (☎ 985 10 61 00), C. J. Clavería.

Post Office: C. Alonso Quintanilla, 1 (☎ 985 21 41 86 or 902 19 71 97). From C. Uría, turn left onto C. Argüelles and then left again. Open for stamps and **Lista de Correos** M-F 8:30am-8:30pm, Sa 9:30am-2pm. **Postal Code:** 33060.

Internet Access: Laser Internet Center, C. San Francisco, 9 (☎ 985 20 00 66). 300ptas per 30min. Open 24hr. Another branch located on C. Fernando Vela, 10 (☎ 985 11 88 24). Open M-F 10am-11pm.

RESURRECTING THE TOWER OF BABLE
Galicians have Gallego, Catalans have Catalan, and Asturians have...Bable? It's not an official language, but the dialect has returned full-force with the sweeping post-Franco reassertion of regional tradition and is now taught to children in school. A codification of a hodgepodge of more than 10 distinct traditional dialects originating in different corners of Asturias, Bable's grammar borrows from many but belongs to none. As a result, almost no one is fluent in the tongue (you probably won't hear it on the street) and grandmothers tend to express bewilderment at their grandchildren's bable-ing.

ACCOMMODATIONS

Pensiones pack the new city. They cluster on C. Uría, C. Campoamor (with the RENFE station behind you, walk 1 block to the left), C. Nueve de Mayo (2 blocks off C. Manuel Pedregal), and C. Jovellanos (near the cathedral).

Residencia Juvenil Ramón Menéndez Pidal, C. Julián Clavería, 14 (☎ 985 23 20 54), just off Pl. Toros. Walk down C. Uría from the RENFE station, take a right on Conde de Toreno, walk through 2 plazas, past the Plaza de Toros, and turn left on C. J. Clavería (25min.). Or take bus #2 from C. Uría. TV room, library, and dining room. Rooms vary in size, but all have sinks. Only a few available in winter. Reservations recommended in summer. Curfew 1am. Dorms 780ptas, with breakfast 941ptas; over 26 1066ptas, with breakfast 1325ptas. V, MC, AmEx.

Pensión Pomar, C. Jovellanos, 7 (☎ 985 22 27 91). This spacious old building has 20 super-clean, airy rooms with big windows and high ceilings. Communal bathrooms. Lots of backpackers headed to the Picos. Breakfast 250ptas. Reserve a few days ahead. Singles 3000-4000ptas; doubles 4000-5000ptas; triples 4500-6000ptas. Cash only.

Pensión Martinez, C. Jovellanos, 5 (☎ 985 21 53 44). A modern apartment building with clean, spartan-looking rooms with sinks. Pristine communal bathrooms. Singles 1600ptas; doubles 3000ptas; triples 3000ptas. Cash only.

Pensión Riesgo, C. Nueve de Mayo, 16, 1st fl. (☎ 985 21 89 45). Clean, basic rooms. Singles 1800ptas; doubles 3600ptas, with shower 4000ptas. Cash only.

FOOD

Order *sidra* (cider) by the bottle (usually 250-600ptas)—it goes fast, and much of it ends up on the floor (due to the unconventional pouring method). For the best *sidra* experience, head to the wooden-beamed, ham-hung **sidrerías,** where waiters pour from above their heads and make you swallow it in one huge gulp. Cheap restaurants line C. Fray Ceferino, between the bus and train stations. The posh indoor **market** is on C. Fontán, off Pl. Mayor (open M-Sa 8am-8pm). For groceries, try **El Corte Inglés,** C. General Elorza, 75, opposite the ALSA station.

■ **Mesón Luferca,** a.k.a. **La Casa Real del Jamón,** C. Covadonga, 20 (☎ 985 21 78 02). You may think you've seen a lot of hanging hams, but nothing can prepare you for the sheer quantity of pig parts in this place. Feed the big bad wolf inside of you; huffing and puffing optional. *Tapas* 790-3500ptas. Artisan cheeses (manchego, de cabra, da Peral, Cabrales, etc.) 690-1590ptas. Don't miss the local favorites *fabada asturiana* (1400ptas) and *chorizo a la sidra* (300ptas). Open M-Sa 8:30am-midnight. V, MC.

Cervecería Gambrinus, Plaza de América, 3 (☎ 985 27 43 67) From C. Uría, go right onto C. Conde de Toreno and take it to the plaza in the middle of Av. de Galicia. Bright, popular pub-cafeteria. Sandwiches 400-750ptas. *Raciones* 300-9050ptas. *Platos combinados* 800-1300ptas. Long beer list. Open daily noon-4pm and 8pm-12:30am.

SIGHTS

CATHEDRAL. Built in 1388, Oviedo's cathedral has suffered much from pollution over the last 600 years, but recent renovation has been restoring its original beauty. The cathedral's saving graces are its two chapels and the brilliant blue ceiling above the altar. The **Capilla del Rey Casto,** which houses the royal pantheon, was chosen by Alfonso II El Casto in 802 to house the remains of Asturian monarchs and Christian relics rescued from the Moors. An intense metal relief sculpture in the unusual **Capilla de San Pedro** depicts Simon Magnus dropped from the sky by hideous demons. The cathedral complex also includes an 80m **tower** with great views of the city's rooftops, a *cámara santa* (holy chamber), a **cloister,** and a church **museum.** *(Pl. Alfonso II. ☎ 985 22 10 33. Cathedral open 10am-1pm and 4-7pm. Free. Cámara Santa 200ptas. Museum ☎ 985 20 31 17. Museum, chamber, and cloister open M-F 10am-8pm, Sa 10am-6:30pm. 400ptas, seniors 300ptas, children 150ptas. Th free.)*

OTHER SIGHTS. The two-building, three-story **Museo de Bellas Artes** in the **Palacio de Velarde** displays a wide range of Asturian art and a small collection of 16th- to 20th-century (predominately Spanish) art. *(C. Santa Ana, 1, and C. Rúa, 8, just up C. Santa Ana from Pl. Alfonso II. ☎ 985 21 30 61 or 985 21 20 57. Open M-F 11am-2:30pm and 5-9pm, Sa 11am-2:30pm.)* Behind the cathedral is the **Museo Arqueológico-Antiguo Monasterio de San Vicente** and the **Iglesia de San Vicente,** which was the original urban center of medieval Oviedo. *(C. San Vicente, 3. Museum ☎ 985 21 54 05. Open June-Sept M-F 10am-7:30pm, Sa-Su 10am-8pm; Oct.-May Tu-Sa 10am-1:30pm and 4-6pm, Su 11am-1pm. Church ☎ 985 21 18 70. Open M-F 11:30am-1pm, 4:30-7pm. Both free.)* For a change of pace, check out the temporary exhibits at the **Centro de Arte Moderno.** Asturian Pre-Romanesque was the first European attempt to blend architecture, sculpture (including human representations), and mural painting since the fall of the Roman Empire. The style was developed under Alfonso II (789-842) and refined under his son Ramiro I, for whom the *Ramirense* style is named. *(C. Alonso Quintanilla, 2, opposite the post office. Open M-Sa 5:30-9pm.)* Two beautiful examples of this style, **Santa María del Naranco** and **San Miguel de Lillo,** tower 4km outside Oviedo on **Monte Naranco.** *(Santa María del Naranco. ☎ 985 25 72 08. Both buildings open May-Sept. M-Sa 9:30am-1pm and 3-7pm, Su 9:30am-1pm; Oct.-Apr. Su-M 9:30am-1pm, Tu-Sa 9:30am-1pm and 3-7pm. 250ptas, children 125ptas. M free.)*

▨ HIKING

For a good **English guidebook** to the trails and towns near Oviedo, try Robin Walker's *Picos de Europa.* If you read Spanish, check out the many publications of Miguel Ángel Andrados. Helpful organizations and businesses are listed below, all based in Oviedo unless otherwise noted. Most towns in the Picos have excursion-organizers; check specific towns for listings. Oviedo is the place to buy all of your supplies—stores closer to the mountains get smaller and more expensive.

ICONA, C. Arquitecto Reguera, 13, 2nd fl. (☎ 985 24 14 12). Excursions, camping, and trail info, and a video on flora and fauna. Open M-F 8am-3pm and 5-7pm. The office in **Cangas de Onís,** Av. Covadonga, 35 (☎ 985 84 91 54), is the best place to get detailed (free) information on the Picos.

Federación Asturiana de Montaña (☎ 985 25 23 62), C. de Julián Clavería, near the bull ring, a 30min. walk from the city center (or take bus #2). If you walk, get the big map from the tourist office. Organizes excursions, has good trail maps, and provides mountain guides and info about weather conditions and the best hiking routes. Instructors for everything from paragliding to kayaking to spelunking. Open M-F 6-8pm.

Oxígeno (☎ 985 22 79 75), on C. Manuel Pedregal, a continuation of C. Nueve de Mayo. Pass C. Fray Ceferino and head toward the RENFE station. A hard core mountaineer shop with 2 walls of maps, guides, and hiking books. Staff of Picos veterans enthusiastically doles out advice. Open M-Sa 10am-1:30pm and 4:30-8:30pm. V, MC, AmEx.

Deportes Tuñón, C. Campoamor, 8, on the block between C. Dr. Casal and C. Fray Ceferino. Extensive selection of camping and rock-climbing gear, long underwear, and a few maps. Open M-Sa 10am-1:30pm and 4:30-8:30pm. V, MC, AmEx.

♫ ENTERTAINMENT

The streets south of the cathedral, around Pl. Riego, Pl. Fontán, and Pl. Paraguas, teem with noisy *sidrerías* and clubs. Stylish **Bar Riego,** on Pl. Riego, serves tasty *batidos* (milkshakes) on a breezy *terraza* (open M-Sa noon-4pm and 8pm-2am). Wine connoisseurs follow **la ruta de los vinos,** from *bodega* to *bodega* along C. Rosal (*copas* 300-600ptas). On C. Cuna, between Alcalde García Conde and C. Jovellanos, **Danny's Jazz Café,** C. La Luna, 11, offers jazz recordings and videos. (☎ 985 21 14 83. Beers 300ptas. Mixed drinks 600ptas. Open daily 8pm-4am.) The **Teatro Filarmónica,** C. Mendizábal, 3 (☎ 98 521 27 62), hosts dramatic productions in September and musical concerts the rest of the year. Oviedo celebrates its **patronal fiesta** in honor of San Mateo from September 19 to 21.

LLANES

Plunging eucalyptus forests to the west and rolling pastures to the east characterize the calm Asturian coast. The secluded, monument-speckled coves of Llanes are home to some of the most popular beaches and rocky bluffs on the Asturian coast. **Playa de Sablón** and **Playa Puerto Chico** host parties all summer long on their small, wavy shores, and more remote but much prettier **Playa de Toró** is just a few minutes away from Llanes, off Av. de Toró. **Paseo de San Pedro,** an elevated grassy path along a scenic bluff above Playa Sablón, is perfect for a quiet picnic or peaceful nap. Ask at the tourist office for directions to other spots, or wander on your own.

The **tourist office** hands out maps in a 13th-century tower on C. Alfonso IX, around the corner from the yellow Ayuntamiento. (☎ 985 40 01 64. Open July-Aug. M-Sa 10am-2pm and 5-9pm, Su 10am-3pm; Sept.-June M-F 10am-2pm and 4-6:30pm, Sa 10am-1:30pm and 4:30-6:30pm.) For adventure activities in the Picos area, stop by **Vindius Aventura,** Estación de FEVE (☎/fax 985 40 14 58). Services include: **emergency** (☎ 112); **municipal police,** C. Nemesio Sobrino (☎ 985 40 18 87); the **health center** (☎ 985 40 23 00 or 985 40 20 43), Av. de San Pedro; and the **post office** on C. Pidal. (☎ 985 40 11 14. Open M-F 8:30am-2:30pm, Sa 9:30am-1pm.) The **postal code** is 33500. For **Internet access,** try **CyberDream,** C. La Calzada, 1-A. (☎ 985 40 06 72. 600ptas per hr. Open M-F noon-2pm and 5-9pm, Sa-Su 5-9pm.)

Rooms fill early in summer. ▓**Hostería Los Barquitos,** C. Pidal, 26, is a beautifully restored cottage with gorgeous, spacious rooms, not 10 minutes from **Playa Puerto Chico.** (☎ 985 40 26 12. Breakfast 500ptas. Reserve a month ahead in summer. Doubles 5500ptas; master quad with bathroom 11000ptas. Cash only.) **Casa del Río,** Av. San Pedro, 3, has wonderful rooms near the beach, some with two balconies and all with a sink and large windows. To get there, face the Ayuntamiento and hang a left to the first real street, San Pedro. (Singles 2000-3000ptas; doubles 4000-6000ptas; triples 6000-7000ptas. Cash only.) **Pensión La Guía,** Pl. Parres Sobrino, 1, has spacious, bright rooms in the thick of the action. Watch out for pesky flies in the summertime. (☎ 98 540 25 77. Doubles 4500-7500ptas; triples 5500-7500ptas. Open *Semana Santa*-Oct. Cash only.) Camp at **Las Barcenas,** 200m past the bus station, toward Santander. The view of the Picos de Europa in the distance helps you forget that your neighbor is just four feet away. (☎ 985 40 15 70. Showers and currency exchange. Reception open daily 8am-11pm. July-Aug. 525ptas per person, 500ptas per car, 700ptas per tent.) For groceries, go to **El Arból,** at the intersection of C. Manuel Romano and C. Román Romano (open M-Sa 9am-9pm).

The bus and train stations are at opposite ends of town. **ALSA-Turytrans** runs **buses** to: **Cangas de Onís** (45min., 8:10am, 580ptas); **Santander** (2¼hr., 11 per day 8:45am-9:45pm, 825ptas); **Oviedo** (1½hr., 10 per day 8am-9:45pm, 1000-1050ptas); and **Madrid** (8hr., 1:45pm, 4290ptas). To reach the town center from the **bus station,** take a left down C. Cueto Bajo to the post office, then turn left; Castillo Mercaderes leads to the Ayuntamiento and tourist office. (☎ 985 40 24 84 or 985 40 24 85. Info open M-F 8:30am-7:30pm, Sa-Su 8:30am-2pm and 3:15-8pm.) **Trains** chug from the **FEVE** station (☎ 985 40 01 24), at the end of Av. Estación, to **Santander** (2hr., 11:27am and 6:13pm, 810ptas) and **Oviedo** (2½hr., 4 per day 8:05am-6:13pm, 885ptas). For a **taxi** call ☎ 985 40 11 77.

PICOS DE EUROPA

Three hundred million years ago, Mother Nature's mere flapping of her limestone bedsheet erected the Picos de Europa, a mountain range of curious variation and chaotic beauty. Today, myriad caves and caverns testify to centuries of glacial abuse, and restless rivers like the Sella, the Dobra, and the Cares thread through lush valleys, tumbling into fierce gorges and percolating into mountaintop springs. Herds of wild horses, boars, and *chamois* (a goat-type animal) roam through lands adorned with 800 species of plants, and the skies are spotted with long-eared owls, Egyptian vultures, songbirds, and eagles. Other European mountain ranges may stretch higher than the Picos (2600m), but few are as much of a rugged playpen for rock-climbers, spelunkers, trekkers, and nature-lovers. Other popular activities include mountain biking, whitewater rafting, kayaking, salmon and trout fishing, paragliding, and bungee jumping.

Picos de Europa

The rugged barrier created by the Picos is one of the main reasons that Asturias never fell under Moorish control. For centuries it remained wild and unclaimed, and in 1916 the area was finally turned into Spain's first national park, the Picos de Europa, split between Asturias, Cantabria, and León. Today it is continental Europe's largest national park and an increasingly popular vacation destination. Despite the crowds, the best time to head for the Picos is late summer. The region is cold and often stormy through May and even June, and the autumn weather is chilly and unpredictable.

✦ ORIENTATION

Spanning a region 64,660 hectares (160,000 acres) in area, the Picos de Europa consist of three mountainous massifs: the **Occidental** (Cornión), the **Central** (Urrieles), and the **Oriental** (Ándara), with the highest peak **Torrecerredo** (2646m) rising out of the Central massif. The **Garganta del Cares** (Cares Gorge), which marks the dramatic division between the Central and Oriental massifs, holds the park's most popular trails and most famous peaks: the life-claiming Peña Vieja and Pico Tesorero, the stark Llambrión, and the mythic **Naranjo de Bulnes** (Picu Urriellu; 2519m).

Getting to the Picos is relatively easy. **ALSA buses** link the main towns, and the highways are well maintained. Route **AS-114** runs along the north edge of the Picos from **Cangas de Onís** (10km north of **Covadonga**) through **Arenas de Cabrales,** and on to **Panes**, where it intersects Route **N-621**. (Maps often refer to these towns as "Arenas" and "Pan.") N-621 runs 50km south and west to **Potes**, where a branch leads to **Fuente Dé.** Arenas de Cabrales is a prime base for serious hiking. Larger Potes is a more expensive take-off point. Covadonga, Onis, Cabrales, and Fuente Dé all have excellent guided day hikes (free) of varying length and difficulty.

For a list of mountain **refugios** (usually cabins with bunks but not blankets) and general information on the park, contact the **Picos de Europa National Park Visitors' Center** (☎ 985 84 86 14). *Refugios* can generally only be contacted by phone or short-wave radio (the Guardia Civil can often help). Other lodging options include **albergues** (ancient, non-heated buildings with bunks and cold water) and **casas** (buildings with bunks, hot water, and wood stoves). In all cases you should bring a sleeping bag. Campsites sometimes have vacancies in July and August, but they often fill up as well. Call *hostales* or *pensiones* well ahead of time to make reservations. For those in a jam, tourist offices have lists of beds in private residences.

The key to hiking in the Picos is planning ahead. Water sources and campsites are rather hard to come by. Covadonga does not have an ATM or a supermarket, so stock up in Oviedo or Cangas de Onís. Having your own car is the best way to go. Those depending on public transportation must be patient and flexible; buses run infrequently on weekdays, and service is even more limited on weekends. Throughout this section, *Let's Go* provides numerous trail suggestions. Contact the park office for details on specific trails. For more general information on camping and hiking see **Camping and the Outdoors**, p. 26.

CANGAS DE ONÍS

Founded in 722 by the leader of the army that defeated the Moors at Covadonga, Cangas de Onís (pop. 6285) prides itself on being the first capital of the Asturian monarchy and a launch pad for the *Reconquista*. Just 25km from the Cantabric Sea and 10km from the park border, Cangas de Onís is now considered the gateway to the Picos. Though not the most central of the Picos towns, Cangas offers its own mini-hikes as well as great eats, sleeps, and groceries between excursions.

E TRANSPORTATION. ALSA (☎ 985 84 81 33), Av. Covadonga, across from the tourist office, runs buses to: **Arenas de Cabrales** (30min., 4 per day 11am-7:30pm, 295ptas); **Llanes** (40min., 1 per day, 500ptas); **Oviedo** (1½-2hr., 10 per day 6:15am-8:30pm, 700ptas); **Madrid** (7hr., 2:35pm, 3870ptas); **Panes** (1hr., 11am and 7:30pm, 515ptas); and **Covadonga** (30min., 8-10 per day 10am-5:30pm, 125ptas; returns to Cangas noon-6:30pm, 250ptas round-trip). For a **taxi** call **Radio Taxi** (24hr. ☎ 985 84 87 97 or 985 84 91 02) or wait in front of the Ayuntamiento, Av. Convadonga, 21.

⑦ PRACTICAL INFORMATION. The main street in Cangas de Onís is **Avenida Covadonga**. The **tourist office** is next to the Ayuntamiento, across from the bus stop behind Los Lagos Hotel. It offers maps, brochures, and a beautiful park video. (☎ 985 84 80 05. Open daily May-Sept. M-F 10am-2pm and 3-10pm, Sa 10am-1pm and 5-10pm, Su 10am-1pm and 4-9pm; Oct.-Apr. daily 10am-2pm and 4-7pm.) Not far to the left (with the tourist office behind you), the **Picos de Europa National Park Visitors' Center**, Av. Covadonga, 43, in the **Casa Dago**, has a list of mountain *refugios*, maps, a nature exhibit, and a fantastic, official three-dimensional model of the park. (☎/fax 985 84 86 14. Open daily June-Aug. 8am-9pm; Sept.-May 9am-2pm and 4-6:30pm.) **Exchange currency** at **Banco Central Hispano**, Av. Covadonga, 6. (☎ 985 84 87 84. Open M-F 8:30am-2:30pm, Sa 8:30am-1pm.) Services include: **emergency** (☎ 112); **municipal police** (☎ 985 84 85 58), in the Ayuntamiento; the **health center** (☎ 985 84 85 71), C. de la Cárcel down C. Emilio Laria; and the **post office** (☎ 985 84 81 86), Av. Constantino Gonzalez. The **postal code** is 33550. For **Internet access**, try **Ingapublic**, C. El Censo, 15 Bajo A. (☎ 985 84 94 27. 250ptas per hr.)

⬤ ACCOMMODATIONS AND FOOD. A few clean *pensiones* along Av. Covadonga will gladly accept your *pesetas*. **El Choffer,** C. Emilio Laria (ask in the restaurant), has clean rooms, firm beds, Oriental rugs, and hall baths. (☎ 985 84 83 05. Winter heating. Singles 2500-3000ptas; doubles 3000-4500ptas. Cash only.) **Hospedaje Principado,** Av. Covadonga, 16, 3rd fl., is a slightly nicer option, with color TV. (☎ 985 84 83 50 or 985 84 83 15. Singles 1500-2000ptas; doubles 3000-5000ptas. Triples and a quad 1500ptas per person. Special prices for large groups or long stays.) **Camping Covadonga**, Soto de Cangas, 4km up the road toward Arenas de Cabrales (5-7 buses per day), has a cafeteria, bar, supermarket, and showers. (☎ 98 594 00 97. 575ptas per person, 475ptas per car, 500ptas per tent. Open *Semana Santa* and June-Sept. 20.) Most restaurants on Av. Covadonga serve *menús* slightly over 1000ptas. For a do-it-yourself-meal try **Alimerka Supermercado** on Av. Covadonga (open Su-M 9am-2pm, Tu-Sa 9am-9pm).

SIGHTS AND EXCURSIONS. From the **Puente Romano,** a gorgeous medieval bridge with an ornate dangling cross, walk into Cangas, turn left opposite the park, and cross a modern bridge to **Capilla de Santa Cruz.** This Romanesque chapel sits atop the town's oldest monument, a Celtic *dolmen* (monolith). The cave underneath once shielded priests from invading Moors. Also of interest is **Cueva del Buxu** (BOO-shoo), whose walls are adorned by 15,000-year-old paintings. To reach the cave, follow the main road to Arenas de Cabrales for 3km until the sign for the *cueva* directs you left. From here, it's a gradual 1km climb past pastures and chicken coops to the easily missed sign to the caves, by Bar Cueva El Buxu. **Buses** to Covadonga, Llanes, and Arenas run near the cave; ask to be dropped off at the **Cruce de Susierra.** Come early, as only 25 people are allowed in each day. (☎ 608 17 54 67. Open June-Sept. W-Su 9:30am until full; Oct.-May W-Su 9am-1pm and 3pm-5:30pm unless the limit is reached earlier. 900ptas. W free.) Those with wheels will want to head south from Onís along Río Sella. This route winds through Santillan, Sames, and finally to the **Desfiladero de los Beyos,** a spectacular 11km gorge filled with jagged wet rocks and blossoming beech trees. If you're looking to party Picos-style check out the **Fiesta del Pastor** (July 25th) in Vega del Enol, near the glacial lakes of Ercina and Enol. Called the *Romería cerca del cielo* ("feast near the sky") for its mountainous location, the party starts at 8am, when most of the town starts the trek up to the lakes. Competitions like the **Escalada a la Porre de Enol** (a type of local alpinism race), the bareback horse race, and the town tug-of-war are serious affairs; the winners of the last 12 years are listed in local newspapers.

ADVENTURE TOURISM. Cangas de Onís is the perfect place to arrange outdoor activies, but it is imperative to reserve ahead of time, especially during the summer. **Aventura,** Av. Covadonga (☎ 985 84 92 61 or 985 84 85 76; fax 985 84 85 61), sets up various expeditions, including hiking (only in the low season), white-water rafting, spelunking *(espeología)*, *barranquismo* (canyoning, swimming, and spelunking), canoeing, horseback riding, 4-wheeling, and bungee jumping. Prices usually range 3000-5000ptas per person and include equipment, a guide, transportation to and from Cangas, and sometimes a bagged lunch. Discounts are offered for large groups and/or multiple activities. Call for departure times and destinations. Reservations are recommended, especially June through August. **Los Cauces,** Av. de Covadonga, 23, offers most of the same activities for similar prices. (☎ 985 94 73 18. Open daily 9:30am-9:30pm.) The tourist office can provide the names of other agencies offering adventure tourism as well.

COVADONGA

"This little mountain you see will be the salvation of Spain," prophesied Don Pelayo to his Christian army in 718, gesturing to the rocky promontory above what is now Covadonga. The mountain soon became the site of the first successful rebellion against the Moors, although legend claims that it was not geography but the intervention of the Virgin Mary that made victory possible. Don Pelayo became the first king of Asturias, and out of this battle grew the *Reconquista.* Today, visitors come to Covadonga to see the cliffside basilica, the cave where the Virgin is said to have appeared, and the town's incredible lakes.

ALSA buses (☎ 902 42 22 42) from **Oviedo** (1¾hr.; 7 per day M-F 6:45am-6:30pm, Sa-Su 7:45am-6:30pm; 785ptas) and **Cangas** (30min.; M-F 8:30am-7:40pm, Sa-Su 9:15am-7:40pm; 125ptas) grace Covadonga with two stops: one at the Hospedería and one uphill at the basilica. To reach Llanes or Arenas from Covadonga, you must backtrack to Cangas and catch a bus there. Head to Covadonga's **info office** for details on local accommodations and sights. (☎ 985 84 60 35. Open daily May-Oct. 10am-2pm and 3-7pm; Nov.-Apr. 11am-2pm and 3-5pm.) Those planning a serious hike should get trail info from the visitors center in Cangas. Cangas also offers cheaper accommodations, but it's hard to resist **Hospedería del Peregrino,** on the main highway. (☎ 985 84 60 47; fax 985 84 60 51. 1235-7350ptas, depending on room and season. V, MC, AmEx.) The only **groceries** in town arrive for Hospedería guests twice a week (W and Sa) by truck—buy them from the driver at the hostel.

Nearly 1300 years ago, Don Pelayo prayed to the Virgin from atop a gushing waterfall in the ■Santa Cueva (Holy Cave). Today, pilgrims and tourists crowd the quiet, candlelit sanctuary. (Open daily 9am-9pm; in winter 9am-7pm. Free.) The **Santuario de Covadonga,** a neo-Gothic basilica built in 1901, towers above the town. (Open daily 9am-9pm; in winter 9am-7pm. Free.) The **Museo del Tesoro,** across from the basilica, displays the *Corona de la Virgen*, a gold-and-silver crown studded with 1109 diamonds and 2000 sapphires; below it lies a sparkling crown crafted to honor Jesus. (Open daily 11am-2pm and 4-7:30pm. 200ptas, children 100ptas.)

LOS LAGOS DE ENOL Y ERCINA

Perhaps the most impressive site in the park, the ice-cold ■**Lagos de Enol y Ercina** sparkle silently among limestone slopes and open valleys. **Buses** run from Oviedo to Cangas and continue 12km higher, past Covadonga, to the lakes (July-Aug. 5 per day 10am-5:30pm, returning to Cangas 11:30am-6:30pm; Sept.-June 2 per day, 220ptas). Buses leave from the basilica at Covadonga and follow an absolutely frightening but spectacular road hemmed in by cliffs and precipitous pastures; sit on the right side of the bus on the way up for the best views. (It's not worth the trip on cloudy days.) Monday through Friday there are free guided hikes around the lakes (2½hr., 10:30am) leaving from the Enol parking lot. The office is open daily 9:30am to 5:30pm but has no telephone; call Cangas' Casa Dago (☎ 985 84 86 14). The **Refugio de Vega de Enol** sits just off the trails leading from the lakes, 300m past the intersection and behind the free campgrounds. The refuge has 30 spots year-round and provides meals and guides. To get there by car, follow highway C-6312 (the Cangas de Onís—Panes highway), take the *desvío hacia* (exit) for Covadongas y Lagos, go right at Lago Enol, and continue straight to the *refugio*. (☎ 985 84 85 76. Meals 650-1400ptas. No reservations accepted, but call the Cangas tourist office first to see if there's space. 500ptas per person. Cash only.)

Two especially good hikes from the lakes take travelers east to the **Vega de Ario,** which offers a panoramic view of the Urrieles mountains (8-9hr.), or south to the **Mirador de Ordiales,** a vantage point overlooking the Pico de las Vidriosas, Río Pomperi, and a frightening gorge (6-7hr.). Alternatively, head west (2km) to the **Mirador de Rey** lookout point, then wander among the beeches of the **Bosque de Pome** (4-5hr.). Both lookouts are accessible by car driving from Covadonga to Los Lagos.

ARENAS DE CABRALES

Some say the small town of Arenas de Cabrales (pop. 800) sits "as close to the sky as to the ground," and they are not all that far from the truth. The most mountainous community in the Asturias, Arenas draws outdoor enthusiasts eager to take advantage of the excellent hiking and climbing. It is also home to Cabrales' famous blue cheese made of cow, sheep and goat milk. **ALSA buses** (4 per day 7:25am-5:50pm) go west to **Cangas de Onís** (50min., 295ptas) and **Oviedo** (2½hr., 995ptas) and east to **Panes** (30min., 11:35am and 8:05pm, 220ptas) and on to **Santander** (1½hr., 650-700ptas). **Palomera** buses leave from Panes to **Potes** (2 per day, 45min., 220ptas). **Taxis** (☎ 985 84 50 96 or 985 84 66 81) gather near the tourist kiosk.

The **tourist office** is small but helpful. (☎ 985 84 64 84 or 985 84 52 84. Open July-Sept. 20 Tu-Su 10am-2pm and 4-8pm). **Pico Urrielly** (☎ 985 85 67 70), outside of town toward Panes, arranges hiking expeditions, spelunking, canoeing, and horseback-riding; prices range from 2000 to 8000ptas. For an incredibly knowledgeable English-speaking guide, call Emilio Fernandez Gavela (☎ 985 33 12 37). Services include: **emergency** (☎ 112); an **ATM** at **Caja de Asturias;** the **Guardia Civil** (☎ 985 84 50 04); the **Consultorio Médico** (☎ 985 84 55 04); the **farmacia** (☎ 985 84 50 16); and the **post office,** near the bus stop (open M-Sa 9am-11am). The **postal code** is 33554.

Since many of Arenas's visitors opt for camping, the town has few reasonably priced hotels. **El Castañeu,** near the tourist office, offers decent doubles and triples with breathtaking views of the Picos. To get there, cross and walk along the street opposite the bus stop and look left. (☎ 985 84 65 73. Make reservations 2 months ahead of time. Doubles 2500-4500ptas; triples 5000ptas. Cash only.) Family-style **Pensión Casa Fermín** (though it is now called Pensión Covadonga, the sign has yet to be changed), around the corner from the tourist office, is one of the oldest hostels in Arenas de Cabrales. Standard doubles open up to incredibly beautiful mountain views. (☎ 985 84 65 66. Make reservations 2 months early. 2500-3500ptas, with bath 3000-4500ptas. Occasional quad for 4500-7500ptas.) **Naranjo de Bulnes Camping,** 1km east on Crta. AS-14, has both a campsite and cabins, as well as a cozy TV room, cafeteria, bar, shower facilities, and tons of info on various mountain sports. (☎/fax 985 84 65 78. Camping 600ptas per person, 550ptas per car and per tent. Cabins 1-2 people 5500ptas; each additional person 1000ptas.) Spelunkers should ask about trips to **Cueva Jou de Alda,** a fascinating nearby cave. For a cozy after-dinner atmosphere, ⬛**Bar La Panera,** perched on a small hill to the left of Banco Bilbao Vizcaya and behind **La Jueya Restaurant** (with an incredible view of Arenas), has the look and the feel of an intimate alpine lodge, complete with a romantic balcony and outdoor terrace. (*Raciones* 375-1300ptas. Restaurant open daily noon-4pm and 8pm-midnight. Upstairs cafe open until 2am or later. V, MC, AmEx.) For a first-class budget meal try the **Alimentacion** store across the street from the tourist office (open daily 6:30am-7pm).

PONCEBOS

Arenas's hiking trails actually begin 6km away from town in **Poncebos. ALSA** buses run from Arenas de Cabrales (20min., M-F 6 per day 10:15am-7:15pm). To get there by car, travel along AS-114 to Las Arenas, then turn across the river to AS-264, which leads to the town (taxi 900ptas). The walk to the trailhead cruises through the roots of surrounding mountains; tight, winding roads make some corners dangerous. For those interested in spending the night, **Hostal Poncebos** (☎ 985 84 64 47) and **Hostal-Restaurante-Bar Garganta del Cares** (☎ 985 84 64 63), have comfortable rooms. (Singles in both 3000-4000ptas; doubles 6000ptas.) Check with the tourist office about **refugio** options.

Poncebos marks the start of one of the Picos's most famous trails, the 12km **Ruta del Cares.** Blasted out of the mountains, the gorges' vertical walls drop 200m down to the Río Cares below. The **Poncebos-Bulnes** route leads along the Río Tejo to Bulnes, a small village that is seemingly frozen in time. If Bulnes seduces you, consider tucking in at the **Albergue de Bulnes,** which has 20 beds in three rooms, a bar, library, games, showers, guides, and meals. (☎ 985 36 69 32. Reservations suggested. 1400ptas per person, with breakfast 2000ptas.) The ⬛**Poncebos-Invernales de Cabao-Naranjo de Bulnes** route, a killer 17km hike (10-12hr.), crawls first to Invernales de Cabao and then inches 9km farther to the Picos's most famous mountain, **Naranjo de Bulnes,** named for its unmistakable sunburnt orange face. From here you can see all the major *picos* in the area and the dancing blue waves of the Cantabrian Sea in the distance. Most climbers actually start the hike in Sortes and continue from there (9-10hr.). Don't miss one of the daily free **guided tours** from Poncebos. If the trail is offered, it's worth going beyond the **Poncebos-Camareña** path, up a rocky slope that requires use of all four limbs, to the **Puertos de Ondón,** where the view will take your breath away.

ASTURIANS CUT THE CHEESE It's an odd selling point, but somehow Cabrales has become famous by emphasizing the unbridled moldy funkiness of its blue cheese. To produce the cheese, locals arduously empty cow, goat, and ewe udders into large tin bins. After allowing the mix to "mature," cheese-makers drain extra liquid, add a pinch of cow afterbirth and a twist of lamb fetus, store the mush inside cabbage leaves, wooden bowls, or aluminum foil and let them stew in mountain caves in humid darkness. Half a year later, the Holey Cheese God shouts "Let there be light," and the speckled brown wheels rolls out onto the sidestreets of every tourist destination in Asturias. Brave tasters rave about the pungent flavor, the creamy texture, and the "knock you to the floor and have you begging for yo' *madre*" kick.

POTES

The Potes (pop. 2000) tourist brochure prophesies *"...Y Volverás"* (you'll return) and it's probably right; visitors tend to fall in love with this tiny, charming town nestled in the shadow of the mountains. Typical Asturian specialty shops crowd the town center, tempting visitors with overpriced walnut honey and do-it-yourself kits for making *fabada*.

TRANSPORTATION. Palomera buses (☎ 942 88 06 11 or 942 50 30 80) travel to and from **Fuente Dé** (45min.; M-F 8:15am, 1pm, and 8pm, Sa-Su 1pm; 185ptas) and **Santander** (3½hr.; M-F 7am, 9:45am, and 5:45pm, Sa-Su 10:30am and 5:45pm; 950ptas). Coming into town, Palomera buses stop twice—in front of Hotel Rubio and farther into town across from Pl. Jesús de Monasterio and the tourist office; they depart from the latter stop as well. For a **taxi** call ☎ 942 73 04 00 or 942 73 04 01; they usually cluster about Plaza de La Serna.

PRACTICAL INFORMATION. The **tourist office**, C. Independencia, 30, in the old church, has info about the region (though very little on Potes itself) and a list of suggested trails and *refugios* with contact info. (☎/fax 942 73 07 87. Open daily 10am-2pm and 4-8pm; less in winter.) **Aventura**, C. Cervantes, 3, at the end of C. Dr. Encinas toward Panes, organizes expeditions, including horseback-riding, mountain-biking, paragliding, and canyoning. (☎ 942 73 21 61; fax 985 73 21 45. Prices range 2500-8500ptas. Open daily 10am-2pm and 4:30-8:30pm. Closed Su Nov.-May. V, MC.) **Bustamante**, C. Dr. Encinas, 10, sells **maps** and guidebooks. Services include: the **Ayuntamiento** (☎ 942 73 00 06), inside La Torre del Infantado on C. de Independencia; the **Guardia Civil** (☎ 942 73 00 07) on C. Obispo off C. Doctor Encinas; and the **health center** (☎ 942 73 03 60) on C. Eduardo Garcí de Enterria, inside the **Cruz Roja** (Red Cross) building (☎ 942 73 01 02). The **Farmacia F. Soberón**, C. Doctor Encinas, has enough medicine to cure any hiker's ailment.

ACCOMMODATIONS AND FOOD. Several hostels line the main road. The cheapest rooms fill early in the day, so make reservations. **Hostal Lombraña**, C. el Sol, 2, through a passageway off the main road, offers spacious rooms. (☎ 942 73 05 19. Singles 2780ptas, with bath 3200ptas; doubles 3425ptas. IVA not included. Cash only.) At the ◪**Casa Cayo**, C. Cántabra, 6, on the right as you walk from the second bus stop to town, enjoy in-room TVs, phones, bathrooms, and a cozy lounge with an even bigger TV. (☎/fax 942 73 01 19. Singles 3000ptas; doubles 6000ptas; triples 7000ptas. V, MC.) Closer to Panes off C. Dr. Encinas, **Fogón de Cus**, C. Capital Palacios, 2, has sunny, ample rooms . (☎ 942 73 00 60. Singles 2000-2500ptas; doubles 3500-4000ptas.) There are also several *casas de labranza* (farm houses for rent) in the area; ask at the tourist office for details. There's no official camping in Potes proper. The closest site is first-class **Camping La Viorna**, about 1km up the road to Monasterio Santo Toribio, which helps organize excursions and has a restaurant, supermarket, and pool. (☎ 942 73 20 21 or 942 73 21 01. 475ptas per person, car, and tent. Open *Semana Santa*-Oct. 30.) The road through town brims with cafes and restaurants. Classy ◪**Restaurante El Fogón de Cus** is in a quiet corner below the *pensión;* the hearty local *menú* (1150ptas) will satisfy even the most famished of hikers. (☎ 942 73 00 60. Open daily 1:30-4pm and 8:30-11pm.) Another delicious dining option is riverside ◪**Restaurante La Caseta II** (☎/fax 942 73 07 13), C. Cántabra next door to Casa Cayo, where veal, lamb, and group menus are the specialties. Even Santiago himself would need divine help to finish the mammoth-sized *menú del peregrino* (1700ptas).

EXCURSIONS. Only 23km from Potes, the ◪**Teleférico de Fuente Dé** is well worth an excursion. Three **buses** per day connect Potes to the cable base, which includes a few restaurants, two pricey hotels, an ATM, and a daily "birds of prey" show. (1, 4, and 6:30pm. 600ptas.) The mind-blowing, cold-sweat-inducing *teleférico*, the third largest cable car in the world, jets 750m to the mountain top in fewer than four minutes. (☎ 942 31 89 50. Open daily July-Aug. 9am-8pm; Sept.-June 10am-6pm. 800ptas, round-trip 1300ptas; under 10 300ptas, round-trip 500ptas.) If cable cars aren't your thing, climb the zig-zagging trail just left of the cable (3hr.). At the top, there are many safe routes along four-wheel-drive tracks. If you're feeling ambitious, take the northern trail to **Sortes**. Another good, less demanding Fuente Dé trek starts and ends at the cable car's lower station (11½km; 4½hr.). The **Somo Waterfall Route** swings through the Berrugas cattle sheds, the soft Bustantivo meadows, and on to the Somo waterfall.

From the top of the *teleférico*, it's a 4km walk to **Refugio de Aliva** (1670m). Don't be fooled by the name—it's a quite expensive *parador* that offers complete baths in rooms, heat in winter, a cafe, and a restaurant. (☎/fax 942 73 07 13. Singles 5000ptas; doubles 7500ptas.) To return to road-level, retrace your steps to the *teleférico* or walk (3hr.) to **Espinama,** where **Habitaciones Sebrango** offers respite from the Picos. (☎ 942 73 66 15. Singles 3800ptas; doubles 4800ptas.) Behind the lower cable car station, you can follow signs to the decent Redondo **campground.**

Urdón, 15km north of Potes on the road to Panes, is the start of a challenging 6km (4hr.) hike to **Treviso,** a tiny town where chickens outnumber human inhabit-ants. Trail details are on posters all over Potes. Another option for outings from Potes is **Peña Sagra,** about 13km east (2hr.) of the towns of **Luriezo** or **Aniezo.** From the summit, you can survey the Picos and the sea, 51km away. On your way down, visit **Iglesia de Nuestra Señora de la Luz,** where the beautifully carved patron saint of Picos lives 364 days a year. The Virgin, known affectionately as *Santuca* (tiny saint), is removed from the church and honored on May 2.

CANTABRIA

Picturesque fishing villages, hopping beach towns, world-famous caves, and a crazy nightlife await visitors along the soft, sandy shores of Cantabria. The crash-ing waves of the Cantabric Sea have made the province an international surfing hotspot, and most of the coastal towns are within easy reach of Santander, the wealthy capital and transportation hub. Claiming to have the purest air in Spain, Cantabria is also known for its air sports like paragliding and bungee jumping.

SANTANDER

After an enormous fire gutted Santander (pop. 200,000) in 1941, local visionaries rebuilt the peninsular city with hopes of gaining high cosmopolitan standing. Today, with a slew of trendy beaches, the nationally renowned "El Sardinero" promenades, a swanky casino, and an upscale shopping district, Santander sur-passes their wildest commercial dreams. An active fisherman's wharf adds a touch of urban charm to the blandness of the city's more industrialized areas, and stu-dents from the university keep things lively in the off-season.

■ TRANSPORTATION

Flights: Aeropuerto de Santander (☎ 942 25 10 07; fax 942 25 10 04), 4km away. Daily flights to Madrid and Barcelona. Accessible by taxi only (1500ptas). **Iberia,** Po. Pereda, 18 (☎ 942 22 97 00). Open M-F 9am-1:30pm and 4-7pm.

Trains: Pl. Estaciones, on C. Rodríguez. **RENFE** (☎ 902 24 02 02). Info open 7:30am-11pm. To: **Palencia** (2¼hr., 5 per day 8:10am-11pm, 1545-3200ptas); **Valladolid** (5hr., 5 per day 8:10am-11pm, 1975-3700ptas); **Madrid** (7hr., 3-4 per day 8:10am-11pm, 4300-5700ptas). **RENFE ticket office,** Po. Pereda, 25 (☎ 942 21 23 87). Open M-F 9am-2pm and 5-7pm, Sa 9am-1:30pm. **FEVE** (☎ 942 21 16 87). Info open daily 7am-10pm, Sa-Su 9am-2pm and 4-7pm. To: **Bilbao** (2½hr.; 8:26am, 2:15pm and 6:55pm; 925ptas); **Oviedo** (4½hr., 9:15am and 4:15pm, 1685ptas); **Ribadeo** (7hr., 9:15am, 2940ptas); **Ferrol** (9hr., 9:15am, 4115ptas); **Viveiro** (8hr., 9:15am,

3485ptas); **Llanes** (1¾hr., 9:15am and 4:15pm, 410ptas); **Luarca** (7½hr., 9:15am, 2470ptas); and **Unquera,** which is the closest point to **Los Picos de Europa** (1¼hr., 9:15am and 4:15pm, 615ptas). Santander is the north terminus of one RENFE line. For service to points north, take FEVE to Bilbao and then pick up RENFE again.

Buses: (☎ 942 21 19 95), Pl. Estaciones, across C. Rodríguez from the train station. Info open M-Sa 8am-10pm, Su 9am-9pm. To: **Santillana del Mar** (45min., 4-7 per day 10:30am-7:15pm, 300ptas); **San Vicente** (1½hr., 4-7 per day 10:30am-7:15pm, 500ptas); **Llanes** (2¼hr., 10 per day 6:30am-7:30pm, 825ptas); **Luarca** (6¼hr., 3:30am and 11:45am, 2955ptas); **Bilbao** (1½hr., 30 per day, every 30min. 6am-11:30pm, 925ptas); **León** (3½hr., 1 per day, 2740ptas); **Oviedo** (3½hr.; M-F and Su 9 per day, Sa 7 per day, 6:30am-7:30pm; 1710ptas); **Madrid** (6hr., 6 per day 8:30am-1:30am, 3300-4550ptas); and **La Coruña** (12hr., 11:45am and 3:30pm, 4745ptas).

Ferries: Brittany Ferries, Muelle del Ferries (☎ 942 36 06 11; www.brittany-ferries.com), near the Jardines de Pereda. To **Plymouth, England** (2 per week, 13,400-36,400ptas, plus 900ptas for seat reservation). Get tickets at Modesto Piñeiro at the ferry station. Info open M-F 9am-3:30pm and 4:30-7:30pm. In summer reserve 2 weeks ahead. **Las Reginas** (☎ 942 21 66 19), Embarcadero, by the Jardines de Pereda, offers tours of the bay (1½hr., June-Aug. 3-6 per day, 625ptas).

Public Transportation: Municipal buses run frequently throughout the city (July-Aug. 6am-midnight, Sept.-June 6am-10:30pm, 100ptas). Buses #1, 3, 4, 5, 7, and 9 run between the city center and El Sardinero (every 15min., 110ptas).

Taxis: Radio Taxi (☎ 942 33 33 33). Taxis wait on C. Vargas and near the Ayuntamiento.

Car Rental: Avis, C. Nicolás Salmerón, 3 (☎ 942 22 70 25). Min. age 25, must have had driver's license for at least 1 year. From 9000ptas per day. Open M-F 8am-1pm and 4-7:30pm, Sa 9am-1pm.

✦🛈 ORIENTATION AND PRACTICAL INFORMATION

This slender, elongated city sits on the northwest side of a bay. The small **Plaza Porticada** is its heart. Av. Calvo Sotelo becomes Po. Pereda to the east and runs along the waterfront. Buses and trains arrive at Pl. Estaciones, six blocks west of Pl. Porticada. Beach activity centers in **El Sardinero,** a neighborhood in eastern Santander. South of El Sardinero is **La Península Magdalena** with its famous park and Palacio Real. The best way to navigate Santander's sprawling streets is to take the municipal bus; routes are posted at the bus stops.

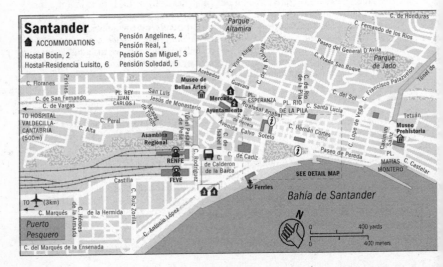

Tourist Office: (☎ 942 21 61 20 or 942 36 20 54; fax 942 36 20 78), Jardines de Pereda. From the stations, follow C. Calderón de la Barca into the park; the office is off Po. Pereda. Maps and info on Santander and Cantabria. Open July-Sept. daily 9am-9pm; Oct.-June M-F 9am-1:30pm and 4:30-7:30pm, Sa 9am-1:30pm. **Other offices** in the ferry station, off Pl. Porticada, and in El Sardinero across from Pl. Italia.

Budget Travel: TIVE, C. Canarias, 2 (☎ 942 33 22 15). Bus #5 just off Av. General Camilo Alonso Cela. ISIC 700ptas. HI card 1800ptas. Open M-F 9am-2pm.

Currency Exchange: Banco Central Hispano, across from the post office. Open May-Sept. M-F 8:30am-2:30pm; Oct.-Apr. M-F 8:30am-2:30pm, Sa 8:30am-1pm.

American Express: Viajes Altair, C. Calderón de la Barca, 11 (☎ 942 31 17 00; fax 942 22 57 21). Open M-F 9:30am-1:30pm and 4:30-8pm, Sa 10am-1:30pm.

Luggage Storage: At the **train station,** by the counter at the ticket window (400ptas). Open daily 7am-11pm. At the **bus station** (300ptas). Open daily 7:30am-10:30pm.

Laundromat: El Lavadero, C. Mies del Valle, 1 (☎ 942 23 06 07), just off C. Floranes, west of the train station. Wash 350ptas per 6kg load, dry 200ptas. Soap 50ptas. Open M-F 9:30am-1:30pm, Sa 5-8pm.

Emergency: ☎ 112. **Police:** (☎ 942 33 73 00 or 942 22 07 44), Pl. Verlade.

Hospital: Hospital Valdecilla-Cantabria (☎ 942 20 25 20), off Av. Valdecilla.

Post Office: (☎ 942 21 26 73; fax 942 31 02 99), Av. Alfonso XIII. **Lista de Correos** and **fax.** Open M-F 8:30am-8:30pm, Sa 9:30am-2pm. **Postal Code:** 39080.

ACCOMMODATIONS

Santander has limited accommodation options during July and August, especially during the July festivals. The highest hotel densities are near the market, across from the train station on C. Rodríguez, and along elegant Av. Castros in El Sardinero. Call ahead to avoid getting stuck without a room.

CITY CENTER

Though not the prettiest part of Santander, the center is full of restaurants and businesses. Calle Rodríguez, near the stations, offers several good hostels. From either station, cross the street and turn right to reach this backpacker haven.

Pensión Angelines, C. Rodríguez, 9, 1st fl. (☎ 942 31 25 84). High-tech motion detecting lights, strong showers, winter heating, and TV lounge. July-Aug. singles 3000ptas; doubles 4200ptas. Sept.-June singles 2000ptas; doubles 3000ptas (IVA not included).

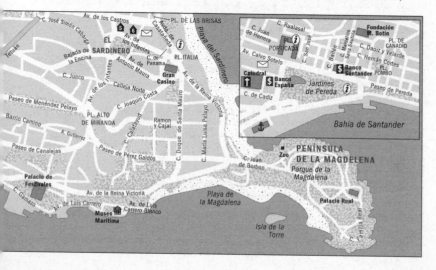

Pensión Real, Pl. Esperanza, 1, 3rd fl. (☎ 942 22 57 87), in the peach building at the end of C. Isabel II. Communal baths. Reservations accepted July-Aug. only with pre-pay. Singles 3500-5000ptas; doubles 4000-6000ptas; triples 5000-7000ptas.

Pensión San Miguel, C. Rodriguez, 9, 4th fl. (☎ 942 22 03 63). Located in the same building as Pensión Angelines, Pensión Miguel offers tidy rooms with firm beds. Clean communal showers. Breakfast 350ptas. Lunch and dinner 1500ptas each. Singles 2500-3500ptas; doubles 4000-5500ptas. Cash only.

Hostal Botín, C. Isabel II, 1, 1st fl. (☎ 942 21 00 94 or 630 49 26 06). Balconies overlook the bustling market. 25% discount on the public parking lot (100m away). Reservations accepted with pre-pay. Dorms 2000ptas; doubles 3400-5900ptas; triples 4600-8000ptas; quads 6000-10,000ptas.

EL SARDINERO

Both pensions are just a block from the beach. Take bus #7 to Hotel Colón (Pl. Brisas), then walk along El Sardinero's rose-colored sidewalks to the beach (3min.).

■ **Hostal-Residencia Luisito,** Av. Castros, 11 (☎ 942 27 19 71). Family-style atmosphere in a charmingly restored townhouse. Reservations accepted. Breakfast 200ptas. Singles 2400ptas; doubles 4200ptas (IVA not included). Open July-Sept. Cash only.

Pensión Soledad, Av. Castros, 17 (☎ 942 27 09 36), next door to Luisito. 16 large rooms with sinks and good views. Breakfast 200ptas. Reservations wise. Singles 2600-2700ptas; doubles 4400-4800ptas (IVA not included). Open July-Sept. Cash only.

Camping: Two sites lie on the scenic bluff of Cabo Mayor, 3km from Playa Magdalena. Take the Cueto-Santander bus (110ptas) from Jardines de Pereda. **Camping Bellavista** (☎ 942 39 15 30; fax 942 39 15 36) is a 1st-class site on the beach. Reception daily 8am-midnight. 600ptas per person and per car, 650ptas per tent. **Camping Cabo Mayor** (☎ 942 39 15 42), Av. del Faro. Pool and tennis courts. Reception daily 8am-11pm. 500ptas per person and per car, 550ptas per tent. Open July 15-Sept. 30.

◖ FOOD

Seafood restaurants crowd the **Puerto Pesquero** (fishing port), grilling up the day's catch on a small stretch at the end of C. Marqués de la Ensenada. From the train station, walk eight blocks down C. Castilla and turn left on C. Héroes de la Armada; cross the tracks and turn right after about 100m (20min.). Closer to the city center, reasonable *mesones* and bars line C. Hernán Cortés, C. Daóiz y Velarde, and Pl. Cañadío. Buy your own food at the **Mercado de Plaza Esperanza,** C. Isabel II near Pl. Generalísimo, or at the **Supermercado BM,** C. Calderón de la Barca, 12, only a block from the train and bus stations.

■ **Bar Restaurante La Gaviota** (☎ 942 22 11 32 or 942 22 10 06), C. Marqués de la Ensenada, at the corner of C. Mocejón in the *barrio pesquero* (fishermen's neighborhood). An elegant dining room hides behind the rough exterior. Specializes in seafood; try the fresh grilled sardines (12 for 600ptas). *Menú* 1200ptas. Open daily 11:30am-4:15pm and 7:30pm-midnight. V, MC.

La Cueva (☎ 942 22 20 87 or 942 36 27 06), C. Marqués de la Ensenada. The gigantic frying pan outside brims with steaming *paella* and lures many a hungry sailor. *Raciones* 650-1500ptas. Open daily noon-5pm and 7:30pm-midnight. V, MC.

◉ SIGHTS

Santander's sights scene is small on architecture and big on seaside beauty. The many free museums are an added benefit.

■ **PENÍNSULA DE LA MAGDALENA.** Jutting into the sea between El Sardinero and Playa Magdalena, the Península de la Magdalena is crowned by a fantastic early 20th-century, neo-Gothic *palacio*. Originally Alfonso XIII's summer home, the cliff-top palace now provides classrooms and dormspace for the university.

The peninsula itself is a **park** of beautiful lawns, hedges, and gardens overlooking the sea. *(Península de La Magdalena. ☎ 942 27 25 04. Park open daily June-Sept. 8am-10pm; Oct.-May 8am-8:30pm. The palace has no scheduled visiting hours.)*

CATEDRAL DE SANTANDER. Built in the Middle Ages, Santander's Gothic cathedral is often called the city's first monument. The heads of martyred Roman soldiers Emeterio and Celedonio are kept inside the ruins of an oven once used to heat Roman baths; every once in a while they are taken out for religious processions. Sent flying into the guillotine basket in 300 AD in Calahorra, La Rioja, they were brought to Santander for safekeeping during the 8th-century Moorish invasion. *(Pl. Obispo Eguino, near C. Lealtad off Av. Calvo Sotelo. ☎ 942 22 60 24. Open M-F 10am-1pm and 4-7:30pm, Sa 10am-1pm and 4:30-8:45pm, Su 8am-2pm and 4:30pm-9pm. Free.)*

MUSEO MARÍTIMO DEL CANTÁBRICO. The top floors of the Museo Marítimo chart regional fishing-boat evolution, while the bottom floor highlights the sea's living creatures. *(C. San Martín de Bajamar, beyond the Puerto Chico. ☎ 942 27 49 62. Open mid-June to mid-Sept. Tu-Sa 11am-1pm and 4-7pm, Su 11am-2pm; mid-Sept. to mid-June M-Sa 10am-1pm and 4-6pm, Su and holidays 11am-2pm. Free.)*

MUSEO DE PREHISTORIA Y ARQUEOLOGÍA. Paleolithic skulls and tools rattle around at the Museo de Prehistoria y Arqueología. Artifacts and photographs of the **Cuevas de Altamira** (see p. 444) are truly spectacular. *(C. Casimiro Sáinz, 4. ☎ 942 20 71 05. Open June 15-Sept. 15 Tu-Sa 10am-1pm and 4-7pm, Su 11am-2pm; Sept. 16-June 14 Tu-Sa 9am-1pm and 4-7pm, Su and holidays 11am-2pm. Free.)*

BEACHES. Santander's beaches are spectacular; **El Sardinero's** powdery sands stretch on forever. In July and August, unfortunately, every inch is covered by fluorescent tourist sardines marinating in cocoa butter. Less crowded beaches—**Playas Puntal, Somo,** and **Loredo**—line the other side of the bay. In summer, Las Reginas **boats** (☎ 942 21 66 19) run across to the beaches of Pedreña and offer 80-minute sailing tours around the bay (see **Ferries,** p. 440).

🖼️🎵 NIGHTLIFE AND ENTERTAINMENT

As night falls, Santander goes wild as students forget their studies, tourists forget their sunburns, and everyone heads for Pl. Cañadío, C. Pedrueca, and C. Daóiz y Velarde. In **El Sardinero,** tourists, students, and spirits mingle all night long. Pl. Italia and nearby C. Panamá are popular neighborhood hotspots. The **Gran Casino** on Pl. Italia brings out the card shark in everyone. Passport, proper dress (pants and shoes), and a minimum age (18 to gamble) are required. Start the evening on **C. Vargas.** Later in the evening, follow the street toward the city to Pl. Rey Juan Carlos and up to C. San Luis; among the many back-alley bars lies **Ojoncano,** a smoky local favorite. Around 2 or 3am, crowds flood **Río de la Pila** or **Casimiro Sainz.**

The August **Festival Internacional de Santander** brings hordes of people and myriad music and dance recitals to town, culminating in the **Concurso Internacional de Piano de Santander.** For more info, contact the **Oficina del Festival,** Palacio de Festivales de Cantabria (☎ 942 21 05 08 or 942 31 48 53), on C. Gamazo. The **Baños de Ola,** a famous turn-of-the-century style type of celebration on El Sardinero Beach, takes place in the third week of July, with contests and bathers clad in antique swimming suits. That same week, the *barrio pesquero* celebrates the patron of fishermen, **Santiago.** For the latest info about concerts, festivals, and movies, check the local paper *El Diario de las Montañas* (110ptas).

🏞️ DAYTRIP FROM SANTANDER

CUEVAS DEL CASTILLO (45MIN.)
Continental-Auto buses stop en route to Burgos (45min., 2 per day, 480ptas).

In the spacious and softly lit caves of Puente Viego's Cuevas de Castillo, sculpted stairs descend into carved caverns and jagged rocks hang from the ceiling. Remind yourself that you're not in some newfangled Madrid nightclub; this is the real thing—a Neanderthal living room—and those paintings are 3 million years old. Animal depictions and red dust handprints line the walls. (Open daily 10am-12:15pm and 3-7:15pm. 225ptas, EU citizens free.)

SANTILLANA DEL MAR

Known as the town of the three lies, Santillana del Mar (pop. 4000) is neither *Santa* (holy), *llana* (flat), nor *del mar* (of the sea). Its name actually derives from Santa Iuliana (Saint Juliana), an unlucky woman killed by her husband 1200 years ago for refusing to renounce her virginity and faith in God. The town is pretty and worth a stop, but it has become overwhelmingly commercialized and tourist-oriented. The **Colegiata de Santa Juliana,** a 12th-century Romanesque church (the largest on the Cantabric coast) occupies one end of C. Santo Domingo. The sepulchre guards the relics of Saint Juliana and the beautiful high altarpiece is a 15th-century Spanish-Flemish painting depicting the saint's martyrdom. (Open daily 9am-1pm and 4-7:30pm. 300ptas also gets you into the Museo Diocesano.) In a town that's a museum itself, the **Museo Diocesano** tries hard to pull its weight; religious art and artifacts fill the harmonious Romanesque cloister and corridors of the Monasterio Regina Coeli. (Open Tu-Su 10am-2pm and 4-8pm. 500ptas.) Peer into the dark side of Christianity at the **Museo Solar-Museo Inquisición,** down the street from La Colegiata. Inquisition instruments of punishment and torture like the Iron Maiden and a belly-turning needled interrogation chair will send you running back to La Colegiata to say your prayers. (☎ 942 84 02 73. Open daily 10am-9pm. 600ptas.)

Santillana is a short trip from Santander by **bus. La Cantábrica** (☎ 942 72 08 22) sends buses from Pl. Estaciones in Santander (45min.; M-F 7 per day 9am-9:30pm, Sa-Su 5 per day 10:30am-9:30pm; 270ptas). The **tourist office,** in **La Casa del Aguila y la Parra** in Pl. Mayor, supplies a bus schedule and map. (☎ 942 81 82 51. Open 9am-1pm and 4-7pm.) To get there from the bus stop, go to Hotel Santillana on the corner and head uphill. In a **medical emergency** call ☎ 942 82 06 94. The **post office** is to the left of the tourist office. (☎ 942 81 80 40. Open M-F 8:30am-2:30pm, Sa 9:30am-1pm.) Santillana's few budget rooms fill fast in July and August; many visitors choose to daytrip from Santander. **Pensión Angélica,** C. de los Hornos, 3, off Pl. Mayor next to the post office (look for the crescent *habitaciones* sign), is as beautiful inside as out. (☎ 942 81 82 38. Singles 2500-3000ptas; doubles 3500-4500ptas; triples 4500-5500ptas.) Outside the historic center of Santillana, in a more residential area near the parking lot, is **Posada Revolgo,** Campo de Revolgo. (☎ 942 81 83 41. Call ahead. Doubles 3500-6000ptas.) For **camping, Santillana,** Carreterra Comillas, km 9 (1km away), is on the road to Comillas; bear left at the fork. (☎ 942 81 82 50. Reception daily 9am-9pm. 675-725ptas per person, 600-700ptas per tent and per car. Bungalows 6900-13,400ptas.) Stock up on groceres at the **Lupa supermarket,** at Pl. Rey, near C. Jesús de Tagle heading away from Pl. Mayor. From the bus stop, walk down the street to the left, take the first left and walk through the parking lot (open daily 9am-4pm and 7-9pm). The **postal code** is 39330.

CUEVAS DE ALTAMIRA

Bison roam, horses graze, deer prance, and goats butt heads on the ceilings of the limestone ▨**Cuevas de Altamira,** dubbed the "Sistine Chapel of Paleolithic Art." The large-scale (over 2m in length) polychrome paintings are renowned for their scrupulous attention to naturalistic detail and resourceful use of the caves' natural texture; in 1985 the caves were declared a UN World Heritage site. Unfortunately, excessive tourism has caused substantial damage, and now only 20 people per day are allowed to visit. **To see the caves yourself, you must be at least 13 years old and must write to request permission at least one year in advance.** Rumor has it there's a three-year waiting list, but if you do write, include a photocopy of your passport and address the request to the **Centro de Investigación de Altamira,** Santillana del Mar, Cantabria, Spain 39330. (☎ 942 81 80 05; fax 942 84 01 57; email altamira@museo.mec.es). Otherwise, content yourself with photographed versions at the **Museum de Prehistoria y Arqueología** in Santander.

COMILLAS

Comillas (pop. 2500) is a picturesque, understated resort favored by Spain's few remaining noble families, who have retained their modest palaces along with their anachronistic titles. Comillas makes an excellent daytrip from Santillana del Mar or Santander, but beachside camping at the town's first-class site is also an appealing nighttime option. The broad **Playa Comillas,** adjacent to the port, or the longer, quieter beach of **Oyambre,** 4km away, are both part of a series of beaches in the **Parque Natural de Oyambre.** Many petite **palaces** and an enormous **Jesuit university** rise in Gothic splendor in Comillas, framed by the ocean and the Picos de Europa. The neo-Gothic **Palacio de Sobrellano,** on the outskirts of town, dominates a pretty park. Inside, the **Capilla-Pantheon** contains furniture designed by Gaudí. Between July 15 and 18, Comilla's **fiestas** go up in a blaze of fireworks, pole-walking, goose-chasing, and dancing in the plaza.

La Cantábrica buses (☎ 942 72 08 22 or 942 72 08 22) run to **Santander** and **San Vicente de la Barquera,** stopping at Comillas, and an equal number return (July-Aug. 5-7 per day, Sept.-June 3 per day; leave Santander 9am-9:30pm; return 7:15am-8pm; 425ptas, from San Vicente 105ptas). The **tourist office** is at C. Mariá del Piélago, 2. From the bus stop near the Palacio, continue on the main road past the turn-off for the beach, through the plaza, and then uphill one block, at which point a sign directs you to the office. If you got off the bus at the top of the hill, walk down 25m until you see the sign. (☎ 942 72 07 68. Open May-Sept. M-Sa 10am-1pm and 5-9pm, Su 11am-1pm and 4:30-7pm.) The **post office** resides at C. Antonio López, 6, on the main road uphill from the tourist office turn-off. (☎ 942 72 00 95. Open M-Sa mornings.) Comilla has few budget options, and they fill quickly in summer. Call ahead, especially if you're coming during the July *fiestas.* Floral **Pensión Bolingas,** C. Gonzalo de la Torre, is downhill from the tourist office. (☎ 942 72 08 41. Doubles 3000-3800ptas. Extra bed 2000ptas. Open June 15-Sept. 15.) **Pensión Villa,** Cuesta Carlos Díaz de la Campa, 21, offers clean rooms with splendid views of the university and surroundings. Rooms are plain, but pretty. (☎ 942 72 02 17 or 617 90 76 89. Singles 4000-5000ptas. IVA included. Cash only.) **Camping de Comillas** is on the water. *Parcela* prices include a tent and car; *media-parcelas* are just a tent. (☎ 942 72 00 74. 2425ptas per *parcela,* 1685ptas per *media-parcela.* Open *Semana Santa*-Oct.) While upscale restaurants dot the small streets of Comillas, less expensive bars and *cafeterías* jockey for business in Pl. Corro. **Supermercado Greyfuss,** at the turn-off to the beach, replenishes beachgoers with fluids and fruits (open M-Sa 9am-2pm and 4:30-8pm). The **postal code** is 39520.

SAN VICENTE DE LA BARQUERA

Spanish writer Camilo José Cela described San Vicente de La Barquera (pop. 5000) as "the villa of romantic ivy." Yet another town with a lovely beach and lovelier views, July andAugust bring an unending stream of camera-clicking tourists. While only the exterior of the 8th-century **castillo** above town can be seen, the 12th-century church-fortress **Santa María de los Angeles** shows off a handsome Romanesque portico (open daily 11am-2pm and 5:30-8:30pm). For bikinis galore, hit the sand at **Playa Merón** or **El Rosal.** From Merón, a 15-minute walk over the 15th-century stone **Puente de la Maza** leads to fabulous views of the Picos de Europa. After *Semana Santa,* San Vicente hosts a maritime procession called **La Folia.** Every September 7-9, the ancient feast of **La Barquera y El Mozucu** features free servings of *sorro-potún,* a typical Barquera tuna-based stew. From July 14-16, the town breaks out with dances and sardine cookouts during **Las Fiestas de la Virgen del Carmen.**

Reaching San Vicente is easy, but traffic can make it a slow process in summer. **ALSA-Turytrans buses** (☎ 942 21 56 50) run between **Llanes** and San Vicente (10 per day 7:30am-8:30pm, 295ptas). La Cantábrica buses (☎ 942 72 08 22) connect **Santander** and San Vicente (1½hr.; leaving for San Vicente July-Aug. 6-7 per day, Sept.-June 3 per day, 9am-9:30pm; returning to Santander 7am-7:45pm; 550ptas), stopping at **Comillas** (20min., 105ptas). The **bus station** (☎ 942 71 09 21) is open daily 7am to 8pm. The **tourist office**, on Av. Generalísimo, 20, can help with accommodations. (☎/fax 942 71 07 99. Open *Semana Santa* and July-Sept. M-F 9:30am-2pm and 4:30-9pm, Sa-Su 10:30am-2pm and 4:30-8pm; rest of the year W-Sa 9:30am-2pm and 4-9pm.) The **post office,** is located at Po. de La Barquera, 1. (☎ 942 71 16 33. Open M-F 8:30am-2:30pm, Sa 9:30am-1pm.) There are a only a few budget accommodations in San Vicente, so make reservations weeks ahead. The best place in town, **Hostal La Barquera,** is adjacent to the **Santuario de la Barquera,** where it is said the Virgin Mary once appeared. (☎ 942 71 00 75. Doubles 4500-4700ptas. Reception up the road at Hotel Miramar, Po. de la Barquera, 20.) **Hostería La Paz,** C. Mercado, has 16 rooms in an old hotel-looking house in the center of town. (Singles 2000-2900ptas; doubles 3400-4700ptas, with bath 4500-7500ptas; quads 5600-7600ptas, with bath 6500-8700ptas. IVA not included. V, MC.) **Camping El Rosal** is near the beach. From the bus stop, cross the bridge and keep going (20min.). (☎ 942 71 01 65; fax 942 71 00 11. Reception daily 10am-10pm. 615ptas per person, 550ptas per car and per tent. Open *Semana Santa*-Oct.) Most restaurants off C. Miramar and Av. Generalísimo serve 900-1000ptas *menús*. **Supermercado Greyfuss,** C. El Arenal, 9, off Av. Generalísimo, stocks the basics (open M-Sa 9am-2pm and 4:30pm-8:30pm). The **postal code** is 39540.

GALICIA (GALIZA)

If, as the old Galician saying goes, "rain is art," then there is no gallery more beautiful than the misty skies of northwestern Spain. Galicia looks and feels like no other region in the country. Often veiled in a silvery drizzle, it is a province of fern-laden eucalyptus woods, slate-roofed fishing villages, and seemingly endless white beaches. Rivers wind through hills and gradually widen into estuaries that empty into the Cantabric Sea and Atlantic Ocean.

A rest stop on the Celts' journey to Ireland around 900 BC, Galicia displays enduring Celtic influences. Ancient *castros* (fortress-villages), inscriptions, and bagpipes testify to this Celtiberian past, and lingering lore of witches, fairies, and buried treasures have earned Galicia a reputation as a land of magic. The rough terrain here has historically hampered trade, but ship-building, auto manufacturing, and even renowned fashion labels are contributing to the region's gradual modernization and development, and Galicia squirms beneath its stereotype as rural and old-fashioned. Tourists have started to permeate even the smallest of towns, and Santiago de Compostela, the terminus of the Camino de Santiago, continues to be one of the most popular backpacking destinations in the world.

Galicians speak *gallego*, a linguistic missing link of sorts between Castilian and Portuguese. While newspapers and street signs alternate between languages, most conversations are conducted in Spanish. Regional cuisine features *caldo gallego* (a vegetable broth), *vieiras* (scallops, the pilgrim's trophy), *empanadas* (turnovers stuffed with assorted fillings), and *pulpo a gallego* (boiled octopus). Regionalism in Galicia doesn't cause quite the stir it does in the País Vasco or Catalunya, but you still may see graffiti calling for *"liberdade."*

HIGHLIGHTS OF GALICIA (GALIZA)

Arriving amid mobs of pilgrims at **Santiago de Compostela's** cathedral (see below).

Camping on the idyllic, undeveloped **Islas Cíes** (see p. 458).

The enchanting Celtic **O Castro de Baroña** (see p. 454).

LOCAL FESTIVALS IN GALICIA

Not surprisingly, **Santiago's** biggest festival centers around the *Día de Santiago* (June 25). **Vigo** diverges from the norm with the mid-June **Expomagia**, a celebration of all things occult, and nearby **Catoira** reenacts the Viking landing every August. **La Coruña** honors its most famous citizen for a month during *Las Fiestas de María Pita*, and **Betanzos** launches the world's largest paper balloon every August 16. Towns near the northern mountains, including **Cedeira,** are best known for their centuries-old wild horse-shearing festival, *La Rapa Das Bestas.*

SANTIAGO DE COMPOSTELA

Ever since the remains of the Apostle St. James were discovered here in 813, Santiago has drawn a plethora of pilgrims, many having just completed the legendary Camino de Santiago. Built over the saint's alleged remains, the cathedral marks the end of the Camino, an 800-year-old, 900km pilgrimage believed to halve one's time in purgatory (see **Pilgrim's Progress,** p. 453). Today, sunburnt pilgrims, street musicians, and hordes of tourists fill the granite streets by the cathedral. In addition to the religious monuments, visitors enjoy the modern art gallery, the state-of-the-art concert hall, and an eclectic and lively nightlife.

Galicia

ATLANTIC OCEAN

Rías Altas

Cedeira · Ortigueira
Valdoviño · Vivero
El Ferrol · Foz · Ribadeo
La Coruña · Pontedeume · Mondoñedo · Castropol
Miño · Río Eume
Malpica · Betanzos · Villalba · Río Eo
Laxe · Corme · (NVI)
Camariñas · Carballo
Muxía · Vimianzo · (N550) · (A9) · Lugo · Fonsagrada
Corcubión · Cee
Cabo Finisterre · Ezaro · Santiago de Compostela · Arzúa · Melide · Palas de Rei
Louro · Muros · O Pedrouzo · Camino de Santiago · Portomarín
O Castro de Baroña · Noya · Padrón · Río Ulla · Monterroso · Sarría · (NV1) · O Cebreiro
Villanueva de Arousa · Vilagarcía de Arousa · Lalín · Río Miño · Somos
Cambados · Carballino
El Grove · Pontevedra · Monforte de Lemos
Sanjenjo · Carballino
Marín · Redondela · Río Sil · Ponferrada
Cangas · Mondariz · Orense · La Rúa de Valdeorras
Islas Cíes · Vigo · (A52) · Ribadavia · Puebla de Trives
Bayona · Túy · Celanova
La Guardia · Bande
Rías Bajas
Viana do Castelo · Braga · Verin · (A52) · Bragança

PORTUGAL

0 · 20 miles
0 · 20 kilometers

N

TRANSPORTATION

Flights: Aeropuerto Lavacolla (☎ 981 54 75 00), 10km away on the road to Lugo. A bus goes to Santiago, stopping at the bus and train stations and C. General Pardiñas, 26 (8 per day, 125ptas). Schedule in the daily *El Correo Gallego* (125ptas). **Iberia,** C. General Pardiñas, 36 (☎ 981 18 72 59). Open M-F 9:30am-2pm and 4-7:15pm.

Trains: (☎ 981 52 02 02 and 902 24 02 02) go from C. de Hórreo in the southern end of city to: **La Coruña** (1hr., 19 per day, 515-645ptas); **León** (6½hr., 2:50pm, 3500ptas); **Burgos** (8hr., 9am, 4600ptas); **Bilbao** (10¾hr., 9am, 5600ptas); **Hendaya** (12½hr., 9am, 5700ptas); and **Madrid** (8hr.; 9:52am, 1:47, and 10:25pm; 5700ptas). Schedule printed daily in *El Correo Gallego*.

Buses: Estación Central de Autobuses (☎ 981 58 77 00), C. San Cayetano, a 20min. walk from downtown. Bus #10 and bus C Circular leave from the R. Montero Ríos side of Pl. Galicia for the station (every 15-20min., 100ptas). Info open daily 6am-10pm. **ALSA** (☎ 981 58 61 33, reservations 902 42 22 42) open daily 7:30am-9:30pm. To: **San Sebastián** (13½hr., 8am and 4:30pm, 7150ptas); **Madrid** (8-9hr., 4 per day 8am-9:30pm, 5135ptas); **Bilbao** (11¼hr., 9am and 9:30pm, 6345ptas). **Castromil** (☎ 981 58 90 90). To: **Noya** (1hr., 15 per day 8am-9pm, 400ptas); **La Coruña** (1½hr., every hr. 6am-9pm, 825ptas); **Pontevedra** (1½hr., 15 per day 6:15am-9:15pm, 625ptas); **El Ferrol** (2hr., 4 per day 7:30am-8pm, 1000ptas); **Vigo** (2hr., 15 per day 6:15am-9:15pm, 925ptas). **Finisterre** (☎ 981 58 85 11) to **Camariñas** (2hr., 8am and 6:30pm, 1050ptas) and **Finisterre** (2½hr., 4-5 per day 8am-7:30pm, 1425ptas).

Public Transportation: (☎ 981 58 18 15). Bus #6 to the train station (open daily 10am-10:30pm), #9 to the campgrounds (10am-8pm), #10 to the bus station. All buses stop in Pl. Galicia—check the signs to see which side. Except for bus #6 and 9, buses run daily 7am-10:30pm (100ptas).

Taxis: (☎ 981 58 24 90 or 981 59 84 88, 24hr. ☎ 981 59 5 64). Taxis wait at the bus and train stations and Pl. Galicia. For late-night service, try near the clubs in Pl. Roxa.

Car Rental: Autotur, C. General Pardiñas, 3 (☎ 981 58 64 96), 2 blocks from Pl. Galicia. Min. age 21, must have had a license at least 1 year. Small cars with unlimited mileage from 8000ptas per day. Open M-F 9am-2pm and 4-8pm.

■ 🛈 ORIENTATION AND PRACTICAL INFORMATION

Street names in Santiago can be confusing, as languages do not always coordinate between street signs and maps: *calle* in Castilian becomes *rúa* in Galician, *del* becomes *do*, etc. The **cathedral** marks the center of the old city, which is above the new city. From the **train station** in the southern end of town, three main streets lead to the cathedral: **Rúa de Franco** (C. Franco), **Rúa de Vilar** (C. Vilar), and **Rúa Nova** (C. Nueva). From the station, cross the street, bear right at the top of the stairs, and take R. Hórreo (not Av. Lugo) to Pl. Galicia, then go one more block to C. Bautizatos, where the three cathedral-bound streets originate. From the **bus station,** take bus #10 or bus C Circular to Pl. Galicia (every 15-20min., 90ptas). On foot, exit the station onto R. Angel Castro and turn left onto R. Pastoriza; continue for 20 minutes as the street name changes. Turn right onto R. Atalia, then left after one block onto Pl. Pena. Follow this road through Pl. San Mariño to the cathedral.

Tourist Office: (☎ 981 58 40 81). 1 **branch** on R. Vilar in the old town under the arches of a colonnade. English spoken. Open M-F 10am-2pm and 4-7pm, Sa 11am-2pm and 5-7pm, Su and festivals 11am-2pm. Or try the **little Modernist structure** (☎ 981 55 51 29; fax 981 58 48 55), in the center of Pl. Galicia. Open daily 9am-9pm.

Budget Travel: TIVE (☎ 981 57 24 26), Pl. Matadero. Turn right up R. Fonte Santo Antonio from Pl. Galiza. Train, bus, and plane tickets for international destinations. ISIC 700ptas, HI card 500ptas. Open M-F 9am-2pm.

Currency Exchange: Banco Central Hispano, R. Vilar, 30 (☎ 981 58 16 12). Open May-Sept. M-F 8:30am-2:30pm; Oct.-Apr. M-F 8:30am-2:30pm, Sa 8:30am-1pm.

American Express: Ultratur Viajes, Av. Figueroa, 6 (☎ 981 58 70 00). Open M-F 9:30am-2pm and 4:30-7pm, Sa 10am-12:30pm.

Luggage Storage: At the **train station,** lockers 400ptas. Open daily 7:30am-11pm. At the **bus station,** 80ptas per bag. Open daily 6am-9:45pm.

Laundromat: Lavandería Lobato, C. Santiago de Chile, 7 (☎ 981 59 99 54), 1 block from Pl. Vigo in the new city. Self-service wash and dry 675ptas per 4kg load. Full service 800ptas per load. Open M-F 9:30am-2pm and 4-8:30pm, Sa 9am-2pm.

English Bookstore: Fallas Novas, R. Montevo Ríos, 50 (☎ 981 58 03 77 45). Walk 5-10min. along C. Montevo Ríos (just off Pl. Galicia).

Religious Services: Mass in the cathedral M-Sa 7:30, 8, 9, 9:30, 11, 11:15am (in Capilla Cortizela), noon (Misa del Peregrino), 6, and 7pm, Su 9, 10:30am, 1, 5, and 7pm. Most nights also offer a special **pilgrim's mass,** featuring the *botafumeiro* (a gigantic incense burner).

Emergency: ☎ 112. **Police: Guardia Civil** (☎ 981 58 16 11).

Medical Assistance: Hospital Xeral (☎ 981 54 00 00), on C. Galeras.

Post Office: (☎ 981 58 12 52; fax 981 56 32 88), Travesa de Fonseca, on the corner of R. Franco. **Lista de Correos** (around the corner, R. Franco, 6) and **fax** service. Open M-F 8:30am-8:30pm, Sa 9:30am-2pm. **Postal Code:** 15701.

Internet Access: Nova 50, R. Nova, 50 (☎ 981 56 01 00). 26 fast computers. 200ptas per hr. Open daily 9am-1am. **Corredoira Virtual,** R. Doutor Teixeiro, 20, 2nd fl. (☎ 981 55 24 41). Walk past Pl. Galicia with the info booth to the left. 200ptas per hr.

ACCOMMODATIONS

Hostels and *pensiones* cluster around R. Vilar and R. Raíña (between R. Vilar and R. Franco), and hand-drawn *habitaciones* signs are just about everywhere else. Call ahead in winter when university students occupy most rooms.

Hospedaje Ramos, C. Raíña, 18, 2nd fl. (☎ 981 58 18 59), above O Papa Una restaurant. Super-cozy beds and spacious, sparkling clean rooms, some with views of a cathedral tower. Pilgrim shell decor. Winter heating. Reservations recommended. Singles 1800ptas, with bath 2000ptas; doubles 3350ptas, with bath 3650ptas. Cash only.

Hospedaje Itatti, Pl. Mazarelos, 1 (☎ 981 56 01 11). From Pl. Galicia, take a right onto R. Fonte San Antonio, then the 1st left. Huge, sunny, recently renovated rooms with TVs, phones, bathrooms. Winter heating. June-Sept. singles 3000ptas; doubles 5000ptas. Oct.-May singles 2000ptas; doubles 3500ptas. V, MC.

Hospedaje Santa Cruz, R. Vilar, 42, 2nd fl. (☎ 981 58 28 15). Big windows in these large, simple rooms overlook the most popular street in Santiago. English spoken. Winter heating. Reserve ahead in summer. June-Sept. singles 3500ptas, doubles 4000ptas; Oct.-May singles 2000ptas, doubles 3500ptas.

Hospedaja Fonseca, R. Fonseca, 1, 2nd fl. (☎ 981 57 24 79) next to the cathedral. A university residence during the year. Clean rooms can be a bit cramped but the location can't be beat. Singles 2000ptas; doubles 4000ptas; triples 6000ptas; quads 8000ptas. Discounts for pilgrims, large groups, and long stays. Open July-Sept.

Hospedaje Sofía, C. Cardenal Paya, 16 (☎ 981 58 51 50), off Pl. Mazarelos. Enter the restaurant on the ground floor, but head directly upstairs. Clean, spacious rooms. Communal baths. Winter heating. Singles 2500-2700ptas; doubles 5000ptas.

Monte do Gozo (HI), C. Santiago-Aeropuerto, km 3 (☎981 55 89 42; fax 981 56 29 92). Take Bus #6 2km outside of town towards Lavacolla Airport. The complex is open all year, but beware the influx of pilgrims June-Aug. Cafe, soccer field, pool. Reservations required. Singles with HI card 7510ptas, over 26 1000ptas. V, MC, AmEx.

Camping As Cancelas, R. 25 de Xullo, 35 (☎ 981 58 02 66), 2km from the cathedral on the northern edge of town; take bus #6 or 9. Laundry, supermarket, and pool. Electricity 450ptas extra. 575ptas per person, 615ptas per car and per tent.

FOOD

Tapas-weary budget travelers will appreciate Santiago's selection of restaurants. Bars and cafeterias line the streets with a variety of remarkably inexpensive *menús;* most restaurants are on R. Vilar, R. Franco, and R. Raíña. In the new city, look near Pl. Roxa. End your meal with a *tarta de Santiago*, rich almond cake emblazoned with a sugary St. James cross. Santiago's **market**, between Pl. San Felix and Convento de San Augustín, is a sight in its own right (open M-Sa 7:30am-2pm). **Supermercado Lorenzo Froiz,** Pl. Toural, is one block into the old city from Pl. Galicia. (Open M-Sa 9am-3pm and 4:30-9pm, Sa 9am-3pm and 5-9pm. V, MC.)

O Cabaliño do Demo, R. Aller Ulloa, 7 (☎ 981 58 8146). Walk to A Porta Do Camino, where Rúa Cerca meets Rúa San Pedro. Chic vegetarian restaurant with creative, organic recipes and filling portions. Specialty salad 350ptas. *Menú* 1000ptas. Veggie lasagna 800ptas. Organic wines from 650ptas. Open daily 2-4pm and 9pm-midnight. Cafe downstairs open 8am-midnight. 5% discount with *Let's Go.*

Casa Manolo, R. Travesa, 27 (☎ 981 58 29 50). By the market and Pl. San Augustín. Cheap, well-known pilgrim hangout with great homestyle cooking but long waits to eat. *Menú* 750ptas. Open M-F 1-4pm and 8-11:30pm.

Pizzería Oasis, R. Nova de Abaixo, 3 (☎ 981 59 98 55). A plaque recognizes the restaurant as a Galician pizza champion. Pizzas 650-950ptas. Hearty calzones 750-900ptas. Open M noon-5pm, W-Su 1-4pm and 8pm-midnight. V, MC.

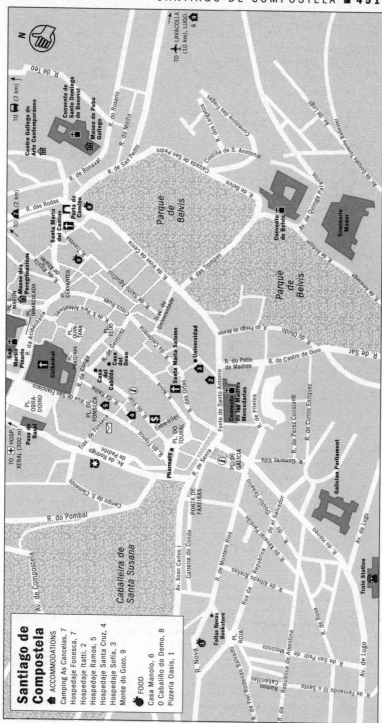

NORTHWESTERN SPAIN

Santiago de Compostela

▲ ACCOMMODATIONS
Camping As Cancelas, 7
Hospedaje Fonesca, 7
Hospedaje Itatti, 2
Hospedaje Ramos, 5
Hospedaje Santa Cruz, 4
Hospedaje Sofía, 3
Monte do Gozo, 9

🍴 FOOD
Casa Manolo, 6
O Cabaliño do Demo, 8
Pizzería Oasis, 1

SIGHTS

THE CATHEDRAL

Pl. Obradoiro. ☎ 981 58 35 48. Open daily 7am-9pm.

A cool, quiet sanctuary to priests, pilgrims, and tourists alike, Santiago's cathedral rises above the center of the lively old city. The nave comes to life during mass, when every candle burns and every pew buckles with traveling pilgrims.

Santiago's cathedral has four facades, each a masterpiece from a different time period, with entrances opening to four different plazas: Platerías, Quintana, Obradoiro, and Azabaxería. From the southern **Plaza de Platerías** (with the spitting sea horse), enter the cathedral through the Romanesque arched double doors. The **Torro de Reloxio** (clock tower), Pórtico Real, and Porta Santa face the **Plaza de Quintana**, to the west of the cathedral. To the north, a blend of Doric and Ionic columns grace the **Plaza de Azabaxeria** (also called Pl. Inmaculada), combining Romanesque and Neoclassical styles. Consecrated in 1211, the cathedral later acquired Gothic chapels in the apse and transept, a 15th-century dome, a 16th-century cloister, and the 18th-century Baroque **Obradoiro facade** with two towers that soar above the city. This facade faces the west and **Plaza de Obradoiro,** an immense plaza scattered with souvenir hawkers and *tunas* (young lute-strumming men in medieval garb).

Many consider the Maestro Mateo's **Pórtico de la Gloria,** encased in the Obradoiro facade, the crowning achievement of Spanish Romanesque sculpture. This unusual 12th-century amalgam of angels, prophets, saints, sinners, demons, and monsters forms a compendium of Christian theology. Unlike most rigid Romanesque statues, those in the *Pórtico* seem to smile, whisper, lean, and gab. Galician author Rosalía del Castro once remarked, "It looks as if their lips are moving… might they be alive?" The cathedral includes a bust of Mateo, which is unusual, as artists in the Middle Ages were rarely recognized in sculpture. Headstrong visitors knock their noggins three times against Mateo's head, hoping that some of his talent will rub off on them. The **revered remains of St. James** lie beneath the high altar in a silver coffer, while his bejeweled bust, polished by the embrace of thousands of pilgrims, rests above the altar. The **botafumeiro,** an enormous silver censer supposedly intended to overpower the stench of dirty pilgrims, swings from the transept during high mass and major liturgical ceremonies. Much older than the towers that house them, the **bells** of Santiago were stolen by Moorish invaders and transported to Córdoba on the backs of Christian slaves. Centuries later, when Spaniards conquered Córdoba, they took back their bells and completed their revenge by forcing some unlucky Moors to carry them.

MUSEUM AND CLOISTERS. Inside the museum are several gorgeous, intricate 16th-century tapestries and two poignant statues of the pregnant Virgin Mary. The museum also houses manuscripts from the *Códice Calixtino* and Romanesque remains from one of many archaeological excavations conducted in the cathedral. The 12th-century *Códice*, five volumes of manuscripts on the stories of the Apostles, includes travel information for early pilgrims. (☎ *981 58 11 55. Museum open June-Sept. M-Sa 10am-1:30pm and 4-7:30pm, Su and holidays 10am-1:30pm; Oct.-Feb. M-Sa 11am-1pm and 4-6pm, Su and holidays 11am-1pm; Mar.-June M-Sa 10:30am-1:30pm and 4-6:30pm, Su 10:30-1:30pm. Museum and cloisters 500ptas.*)

OTHER SIGHTS

■ **MUSEO DAS PEREGRINACIÓNS.** This three-story Gothic building is chock-full of creatively displayed historical info about the *Camino*, including exhibits on the rites and rituals of pilgrimage, the iconography of St. James, and statues of the Virgin as a baby-Jesus-toting pilgrim. (*Pl. San Miguel. ☎ 981 58 15 58. Open Tu-F 10am-8pm, Sa 10:30am-1:30pm and 5-8pm, Su 10:30am-1:30pm. 400ptas, students 200ptas.*)

HOSPITAL REAL. The 15th-century Renaissance Hospital Real, now a ritzy *parador*, upholds an ancient tradition of feeding 10 pilgrims per day. Try to catch one of three splendid art exhibitions given in the lobby; linger long enough and you may be let in to see the Hospital's four courtyards, chapel, and sculpture. (*Pl. Obradoiro. Open daily 10am-2pm and 4-7pm. Free.*)

PILGRIMS' PROGRESS One night in 813, a hermit trudged through the hills on the way to his hermitage. Suddenly, miraculously, bright visions flooded his senses, revealing the long-forgotten tomb of the Apostle James ("Santiago" in Spanish). Around this *campus stellae* (field of stars) the cathedral of Santiago de Compostela was built, and around this cathedral a world-famous pilgrimage was born.

Since the 12th century, thousands of pilgrims have traveled the **Camino de Santiago.** Many have made the pilgrimage in search of spiritual fulfillment, most as true believers, some to adhere to a stipulation of inheritance, a few as an alternative to prison, and at least one to find romance (the wife of Bath in Chaucer's *Canterbury Tales* sauntered to Santiago in bright red stockings to find herself a husband). Clever Benedictine monks built monasteries to host pilgrims along the *camino,* giving rise to the world's first large-scale international tourism and helping make Santiago's cathedral the most frequented Christian shrine in the world. In the 12th century, an enterprising French monk created *Codex Calixtus,* the first known travel guide, filled with information on the quality of water at various rest stops and descriptions of villages and monuments along *La Ruta Francesa* (beginning near the French border in Roncevalles, Navarra). The scallop-edged conch shell, used for dipping water from streams along the way, became a symbol of the Camino de Santiago.

Pilgrims are easily spotted by the crook-necked walking sticks, sunburnt faces, and shells tied onto weathered backpacks. True *peregrinos* (pilgrims) must cover 100km on foot or horse or 200km on bike to receive *La Compostela,* an official certificate of the pilgrimage issued by the cathedral. A network of *refugios* (refuges) and *albergues* (shelters) offer free lodging to pilgrims on the move and stamp the requisite "pilgrims' passports" to provide evidence of completion of the full distance. For more information and free guides to the Camino de Santiago, contact the **Oficina de Acogida del Peregrino,** R. Vilar, 1 (☎ 981 56 24 19), in the Casa del Deán. The best available guide is the *Guía práctica del peregrino,* published by Ediciones Everest in French and Spanish (2500ptas). At a rate of 30km per day, walking the entire *camino* (750-870km) takes about a month, and places you in the ranks of such illustrious pilgrims as royal couple Fernando and Isabel, St. Francis de Assisi, Pope John Paul II, and Shirley MacLaine.

PAZO DE RAXOI. The majestic facade of the former Pazo de Raxoi shines with gold-accented balconies and monumental Neoclassical columns. Once a royal palace, it now houses the Ayuntamiento and office of the president of the Xunta de Galicia. At night, floodlights illuminate the remarkable bas-relief of the Battle of Clavio. *(Across Pl. Obradoiro, facing the cathedral.)*

MONASTERIO DE SAN MARTÍN PINARIO. Once a religious center almost as powerful as the cathedral, the monastery is a mixture of Romanesque cloisters, Plateresque facades, and Baroque sculpture. This composite style is the most outstanding architecture of its type in Santiago. *(In Pl. San Martín, across from the cathedral in Pl. Inmaculada. Open Tu-Su 11:30am-1:30pm and 4:30-6:30pm. Free.)*

MUSEO DE POBO GALLEGO. Find out everything you have ever wanted to know about traditional Galician living. Documentary exhibits on shipbuilding, pottery, house construction, and bagpipe-making are the highlights, but the museum also includes several rooms dedicated to Galician painting. *(Just past the Porto de Camino, inside the Gothic Convento de Santo Domingo de Boneval. ☎ 981 58 36 20. Open June 7-Mar. 2 M-Sa 10am-1pm and 4-7pm. Mar. 3-June 6 M-Sa 10am-2pm and 4-7pm. Free.)*

CENTRO GALLEGO DE ARTE CONTEMPORÁNEO. The expansive galleries and rooftop *terraza* of the sparkling Centro Gallego de Arte Contemporáneo (CGAC) house bizarre, multi-media exhibitions of international modern art. *(Next door to the Museo de Pobo Gallego. ☎ 981 54 66 21. Open Tu-Su 11am-8pm. Free.)*

NIGHTLIFE AND ENTERTAINMENT

At night, crowds looking for post-pilgrimage consumption flood cellars throughout the city. To boogie with local students, hit the bars and dance joints off Pl. Roxa (take C. Montevo Ríos). Clubs open roughly from midnight to 6am. **Modus Vivendi** provided a clubhouse for revolutionary Galician youths in the 1970s and now serves as headquarters for Santiago's nightlife. Combining bagpipes, Aretha Franklin, and local art, Modus's intimate setting often features concerts or debates. The local newspaper *El Correo Gallego* (125ptas) and the free monthly *Compostela Capital* list art exhibits and concert information. Consult any of three local monthlies, *Santiago Dias Guía Imprescindible*, *Compostelán*, or *Modus Vivendi*, for updates on the live music scene. The city celebrates the **Día de Santiago** (July 25) for a full two weeks, from July 15 to 31, and on the night of the 24th, a Pontifical Mass with incense is held in the cathedral during **Las Visperas de Santiago.** Fireworks, concerts, and theater groups fill the city on the 24th as well.

■ **Casa das Crechas,** Vía Sacra, 3 (☎ 981 56 07 51), just off Pl. Quintana. A smoky stone-and-wood pub with a witchcraft theme. Park your broom for a Guinness and other magical brews. Beer 250-325ptas. Drinks 550ptas. Open M-F noon-2am, Sa-Su noon-4am.

■ **Moore's and Co.,** Av. Figueroa, 1 (☎ 981 55 73 11), on the corner of Rodrigo de Padrón. Large traditional Irish/Celtic pub with theme nights and a mostly tourist clientele. *Tapas* 200ptas. Mixed drinks 600ptas. *Mojito* (vodka, lemon, liqueur) 500ptas. Food served daily noon-8pm. Bar open M-F 8pm-3am, Sa-Su 8pm-4am. V, MC.

Cervecería Dakar, R. Franco, 13 (☎ 981 57 81 92). A good late evening stop. Serves rich *batidos* (milkshakes; 350-650ptas) and 4 delicious liqueurs, which will draw even the most dedicated of students away from their work. Open daily 7am-midnight.

Ultramarinos Pub, Casas Reais, 34-36 (☎ 981 58 24 18), on a street that feeds into Porta de Camino. The downstairs has drinking and dancing; upstairs is ideal for sipping and chatting. Beers 250-400ptas. Mixed drinks 600ptas. Open daily 11:30pm-4am.

Discoteca Liberti (☎ 981 59 91 81), Alfredo Branas, across from Casting Araguaney. Salsa and "Top 40" hits. Pool table. Beers 350ptas. Mixed drinks 500ptas. Cover 500ptas. Open daily midnight-6am.

DAYTRIPS FROM SANTIAGO DE COMPOSTELA

The northern parts of the Rías Bajas don't see too many tourists, but these small towns are an easy daytrip from Santiago and have some interesting granite architecture and nice beaches. The area's gem is the Celtic castle, **O Castro de Baroña.**

O CASTRO DE BAROÑA (1½HR.)

Hefsel buses run between Noya and Riveira, stopping in (but often passing—tell the driver where you are going) O Castro de Baroña in front of Café-Bar O Castro (30min.; M-F 14 per day 6:50am-9:30pm, Sa 7 per day 8am-9pm, Su 11 per day 8am-10pm; 205ptas). Catch the bus across the road on the way back.

Nineteen kilometers south of Noya lies Galicia's only populated coastal Celtic village, ■O Castro de Baroña. The seaside remains of a 5th-century Celtic **fortress** cover the neck of the isthmus, ascending to a rocky promontory above the sea and then descending to a crescent **beach** where clothing is notoriously optional. The mesmerizing natural beauty inspires many visitors to watch the sunset on one of the cliffside rocks and then pitch a tent at the free public campsite in the forest, just 300m from the shore. For those who need a shower, **Café-Bar O Castro,** Lugar Castro de Baroña, 18, in **Porto do Son** (the O Castro bus stop), offers spotless rooms upstairs. (☎ 981 76 74 30. Reservations recommended. Doubles 3500-4500ptas. Open June-Aug.) The **restaurant** downstairs has a *menú* for 1200ptas. The nearest town, **Baroña,** 1km north, has a supermarket, restaurant, and bus stop.

CABO FINISTERRE (2HR.)

Finisterre buses make daily trips from Santiago to Finisterre (2hr.; M-F 5 per day 8am-7:30pm, Sa-Su 8am and 6pm; 1425ptas) and back (M-F 4 per day, 7am-4pm).

Jutting out precariously from the infamously rocky Costa de Muerte ("Coast of Death"), Cabo Finisterre was once considered Europe's westernmost point, and for centuries it was a crucial port for all naval trade along the Atlantic. But the town's greater claim to fame has to do with the ancient belief that it was off these shores that the world ended, and it is here that the Camino de Santiago officially ends. (See **Pilgrim's Progress,** p. 453). To one side of town spreads the Ría de Corcubión and its attractive beaches, while on the other side jagged mountains meet the dark uncertainty of the open sea. On sunny days the port is full of activity, as colorful fishing boats move in and out of the harbor and fishermen line the length of the harborside cleaning and untangling their fishing nets.

Those who want to get close to the water themselves can take a **Pleasure Boat Tour** of the Ría de Corcubión. (☎ 981 74 03 75. Leaves from the harbor. 100ptas per person per hr.) For the land-inclined, the hike from the port to the **Monte San Guillermo** is long, but the traveler will be blessed with incredible views and Finisterre's famous, bed-shaped **fertility rocks.** Couples having problems conceiving are advised to make a go of it on the rocks under a full moon (harvest moons are even better). On the same mountain are **As Pedras Santas,** two fairly large rocks which cannot be lifted by themselves, but which slide effortlessly side-to-side if you press the right spot. Try it yourself—the contact point is well marked. Four kilometers out from town stands the **lighthouse** that has beckoned ships for years. The views from the tower are stunning, and its beaches have seduced such travelers as Camilo José Cela, Spain's Nobel Prize winning novelist. To reach the **beach,** climb uphill from the statue at the port past C. Carrasqueira, then turn right at the first dirt road. After 50m, turn left onto the seaward path at the white house.

For maps, brochures and tourist information, try the **Albergue de Peregrinos,** C. Real, 2. (☎ 981 74 07 81. Open M-F 9:30am-1pm and 7-11pm, Sa-Su noon-2pm and 7-11pm.) If you are forced to spend the night in Cabo Finisterre, the **Hospedaje López,** C. Carrasqueira, 4, has 18 cheap, immaculate, light-filled rooms (some with ocean views), and a touch of Disney cheer. To get there, take the stairs across the street from the tourist office onto C. Carrasquiera; signs point the way. (☎ 981 74 04 49. Singles 1500-2000ptas; doubles 3000-3500ptas; triples 4500ptas.)

RÍAS BAJAS (RÍAS BAIXAS)

According to Galician lore, the Rías Baixas (Low Estuaries) were formed by God's tremendous handprint, with each *ría* stretching like a finger through the land. The crystal sea-green pools, countless sandy coves, and breezy winds have lured vacationing Galicians for decades. Only recently have foreign tourists caught on to the area's unique charm, and they now arrive at the beaches in droves every summer. The countryside is equally appealing, with its Spanish-style chalets, colorful fishermen's shacks and traditional farmhouses. For summer travelers, the cool, misty mornings in the Rías Baixas are a refreshing break from the scorching heat of central and southern Spain.

VIGO

José María Alvarez once wrote that "Vigo does not end, it goes on into the sea." Often called Spain's door to the Atlantic, Vigo (pop. 300,000) began as a small, unobtrusive fishing port; with the arrival of the Citroen manufacturing factory, it exploded into the biggest city in Galicia. The noise and pollution can be a nuisance, but the nightlife and shopping are among the best in the region, and the city is a good base for visiting nearby daytrip villages and beaches.

NORTHWESTERN SPAIN

⌐ TRANSPORTATION

Flights: Aeropuerto de Vigo (☎ 986 26 82 00), on Av. Aeroporto, 15km from the center of Vigo, has daily flights to **Madrid, Barcelona, Bilbao,** and **Valencia.** The R9 bus runs regularly from R. Urzáiz near R. Colón to the airport (120ptas). **Iberia,** Marqués de Valladares, 13 (☎ 986 22 70 04).

Trains: RENFE (☎ 986 43 11 14), on Pr. Estación, downstairs from C. Lepanto, is open daily 7am-11pm and runs trains to: **Pontevedra** (20min., 18 per day, 255-345ptas); **Túy** (45min., 2 per day 8:25am and 2pm, 325ptas); **Santiago de Compostela** (2hr., 18 per day 5:55am-9:35pm, 790-960ptas); **La Coruña** (2½hr., 17 per day 5:55am-9:35pm, 1275-1500ptas); **Madrid** (8-9hr., Su-F 1:25 and 10:15pm, Sa 9:30am; 5900-9100ptas); and **Porto, Portugal** (2½hr., 2 per day 8:25am, 2pm, 1920ptas).

Buses: Estación de Autobuses (☎ 986 37 34 11) at Av. Madrid, on the corner with R. Alcalde Gregorio Espino. **Castromil** (☎ 986 27 81 12) buses run to: **Pontevedra** (45min., 31 per day 7am-8:30pm, 300ptas); **Santiago de Compostela** (1¼hr., 27 per day 7:30am-8:30pm, 925ptas); and **La Coruña** (2½hr., 10 per day 7am-8:30pm, 1750ptas). For **ATSA buses** (☎ 986 61 02 55), buy tickets upon boarding. To: **Túy** (45min.; M-F every 30min. 7:30am-9pm, Sa every hr. 8:30am-8:30pm; 325ptas); **Bayona** (50min., every 30min. M-Sa 7am-10pm, Su 8am-11pm; 245ptas); and **La Guardia** (1½hr., every 30min. 7:30am-9pm, 645ptas). **Auto Res, S.A.** (☎ 986 27 19 61) runs to **Madrid** (9hr., 6-7 per day 8:30am-11:30pm., 4255-4580ptas).

Ferries: Estación Ría (☎ 986 22 52 72), on Av. Avenidas past the nautical club, runs ferries to: **Cangas** (20min., every 30min. 6:30am-10:30pm, 225ptas); **Moaña** (30min., every hr. 6:30-10:30pm, round-trip 400ptas); and **Islas Cíes** (50min., 5 per day, round-trip 2000ptas).

Car Rental: Atesa, R. Urzáiz, 84 (☎ 986 41 80 76). Min. age 21. Must have had a license for at least 1 yr. Open M-F 8:30am-1:30pm and 4:30-7:30pm, Sa 9am-1pm.

▰▱ ORIENTATION AND PRACTICAL INFORMATION

The **Gran Vía** is Vigo's main thoroughfare, stretching south to north from Pr. América, through Pr. España, and ending at the perpendicular **Rúa Urzáiz.** A left turn (west) onto R. Urzáiz leads to Pta. do Sol and into the **casco antiguo.** As you exit the **train station** onto R. Urzáiz, go right two blocks to reach the central Gran Vía-Urzáiz. The city center is a 25-minute trek from the **bus station.** Exit right uphill along busy Av. Madrid. Eventually, a right on Gran Vía at Pr. España leads to the intersection with R. Urzáiz (marked by the sculpture of a naked man). The R4 bus from the bus station also goes to R. Urzáiz (120ptas).

Tourist Office: (☎ 986 43 05 77). Take R. Urzáiz to R. Colón, follow R. Colón to the water, and turn left onto R. Montero Ríos (the pedestrian street in front of the port lined with cafes). Walk past the nautical club toward the ferry station, pass the station, and head toward the large cement building (the only other one left on the dock). Walk inside the gates; the tourist office is immediately to your left. English-speaking staff hands out brochures and maps. Open M-F 9am-2pm and 4:30-6:30pm, Sa 10am-12:30pm.

Currency Exchange: Banco Central Hispano, R. Urzáiz, 20. Open M-F 8:30am-2:30pm.

Luggage Storage: 400ptas at the train station. Open daily 7am-9:45pm. 60ptas per bag at the bus station. Open M-F 9:30am-1:30pm and 3-7pm, Sa 9am-2pm.

Emergency: ☎ 112. **Police:** (☎ 986 43 22 11), Pr. do Rey.

Hospital: Hospital Municipal, C. Camelias, 109 (☎ 986 41 10 44).

Post Office: Pr. Compostela, 3 (☎ 986 43 81 44 or 986 43 90 06). Open for stamps and **Lista de Correos** M-F 8:30am-8:30pm, Sa 9:30am-2pm; for **fax** service M-Sa 9am-9pm. **Postal code:** 36201.

Internet Access: CiberStation, C. Príncipe, 22 (☎ 986 44 76 10), off R. Urzáiz. 300ptas per hr. Open 10am-3am or until the last person leaves.

ACCOMMODATIONS AND FOOD

Vigo's inexpensive rooms make the city a logical base for exploring surrounding areas. C. Alfonso XIII (to the right upon exiting the train station) is full of cheap sleeps, as are streets around the port like C. Carral, C. Urzáiz, and C. Lepanto. **Hostal Ría de Vigo,** C. Cervantes, 14, left off C. Alfonso XIII, has spacious and squeaky clean rooms, some with balconies and private bathrooms. (☎ 986 43 72 40. Singles 2500ptas; doubles 3500ptas. Prices drop up to 500ptas in off-season.) **Barcia Casa de Huéspedes,** C. Mexico, 2, offers comfy rooms with TVs, balconies, and huge hall bathrooms. Take a right off R. Urzáiz; it's about two minutes from the train station. (☎ 986 42 51 45. Singles 2000ptas; doubles 3200ptas.) The Gran Vía and C. Venezuela are brimming with bright *cafeterías* and *terrazas*. Streets leading away from the port hide seafood paradise. The red-wood paneling and stone-block interior at **Restaurante Curcuma Vegetariano,** C. Brasil, 4, could have been stolen from an Inca ruin. (☎ 986 41 11 27. Entrees 700-900ptas. Open M-Sa 1-4pm and 8pm-midnight.)

■ NIGHTLIFE

There isn't much to see or do in Vigo besides party. Starting in the late afternoon, students pack the *casco antiguo,* where cafes, bars, and discos abound just off the steep, mossy steps. **Rúa Real,** down by the water, has a few lively spots, as does C. Concepción Arenal. For some good music and funky atmosphere try the **El Arenal** building on Rua Real, a place jam-packed with discos, nightclubs, and bars. On weekends C. Churruca comes alive with students on their way to the street's notorious nightclubs, and the swanky *vinos barrio* are the place to down *chupitos.* **20th Century Rock,** El Arenal, 18, is Vigo's version of the Hard Rock Café, complete with an authentic jukebox, Cadillac, New Orleans trolley, and loud rock. (Beers 200-400ptas. Mixed drinks 600-800ptas. Open Su-Th 7pm-2am, F-Sa 7pm-3:30am. V, MC.) **Café Uf,** C. Placer, 19, is an artsy jazz/funk bar that serves specialty teas and coffees. Photographs of literati on the walls, a dixsplay of books-of-the-month, a small public library, and board games for the tongue-tied. **Negra Sombra,** the jazz club downstairs, occasionally has live shows. (Beers 275-500ptas. Mixed drinks 500-800ptas. Tea 250ptas. Coffee 300-450ptas. Open daily 7pm-2:30am.)

■ BEACHES AND FESTIVALS

If you're looking for **beaches,** it is best to take a daytrip to the Rías Baixas region (see below). However, Vigo and its immediate surroundings offer a few options. Either take the L10, L11, L15, L16, L27, or the LN to get to **Samil** (20-25min., 120ptas) or hop on the ferry and head to Cangas' **Praia do Rodeira.**

In honor of its notorious past as a haven for witches (both good and evil), Vigo hosts **Expomagia,** a celebration of all things occult, in mid-June. Watch for the magical **Fiesta de San Juan (Xuan)** on June 23rd, when neighborhoods light huge cauldrons of *aguardiente* (firewater) to make an infusion called *la queimada.* The potent potable consists of *aguardiente,* coffee, lemon, and sugar, and after careful brewing the sweet mixture is passed around in cups for all to drink and revel in traditional song and dance. A final summer festival, **Romería Vikinga,** in the seaside town of Catoira, sails into town the first week in August, when locals reenact the Viking landing, complete with period ships and costumes.

■ DAYTRIPS FROM VIGO

Ría de Vigo is home to several lively coastal towns. The Islas Cíes and Bayona are both easy daytrips from Vigo. Farther south but equally accessible, Túy and La Guardia lie along the Ría Miño, which borders Portugal.

NORTHWESTERN SPAIN

■ ISLAS CÍES (50MIN.)

June-Sept., 4 ferries per day make the trip to and from the island, sometimes more in nice weather. Though fairly expensive, the trip is worth every peseta (50min.; 4 per day 11am-7pm; 2000ptas round-trip per adult, 1000ptas per child)

The Romans called them the "Islands of the Gods," and one can hardly doubt that Jupiter had at least a villa in the Islas Cíes. Guarding the mouth of the Ría de Vigo and 14km from the city, the three islands—**Illa de Monte Agudo** o del Norte, **Illa do Medio** o del Faro, and **Illa do Sur** o de San Martiño—offer irresistible beaches and cliff-side hiking trails for travelers. The islands were declared a natural park in 1980; only 2200 people are allowed in per day, ensuring wide stretches of uncrowded beach. **Playa de Figueiras** and **Playa de Rodas** gleam with fine sand and sheltered turquoise waters. For smaller, wavier, and more secluded spots, walk along the trail beyond Playa de Figueiras, which leads to a plethora of coves and rocky lookouts. A 4km hike to the left of the dock on the main "road" leads to a bird conservatory, a lighthouse, and breathtaking views. Watch out for territorial seagulls that dive-bomb hikers walking too close to the birds' spotted chicks.

BAYONA (BAIONA) (1HR.)

Buses run to and from Vigo (1hr.; every 30min. M-F 7am-10pm, Sa 7:30am-10pm, Su 8am-11pm; 265ptas).

Twenty-one kilometers southwest of Vigo, in its own mini-estuary, Bayona (pop. 10,000) was the first European town to receive word from the New World when Columbus returned to port in March 1493. The town even boasts a reconstructed version of the famous globe-trotting ship **La Carabela Pinta** in the harbor. (Open W-M 8:30am-8:30pm. 125ptas.) However, Bayona's main attractions are its seductive **beaches** and the 16th-century **Fortress of Monte Real**, now a *parador nacional* (luxury hotel). A 2km *paseo peatonil* (foot path) loops around the grounds along the shore, passing the rocks of Playa Cuncheira and Playa de los Frailes—both beaches are perfect for picnics and sunbathing.

TÚY (TUI) (45MIN.)

An ATSA bus (☎ 986 61 02 55) from Vigo stops on C. Calvo Sotelo at Hostal Generosa and returns to Vigo from the other side of the street (45min., every 30min. M-F 5:45am-7pm, Sa 7am-8:30pm, Su 8:30am-9pm, 340ptas). Trains (☎ 986 60 08 13) run from Vigo to Túy, then on to Valença and Viana do Castelo, Portugal (2 per day 9:59am-10pm, 400ptas). They stop for 15min. on each side for customs and passport inspections. The train stations in each town are far from the border and the center of town; taking the bus or walking across makes more sense.

The charming border town of Túy (pop. 16,000) offers tourists the opportunity to walk into Portugal, but even more notable is the incredible scenery and views of the Río Miño. A 1km metal walkway over the Río Miño extends to Portugal's Valença do Minho. To get to the **tourist office** on Puente Tripe, follow Av. de Portugal from the International bridge until you approach the little wooden cottage on your left. (☎ 986 60 17 89. Open July-Sept. daily 9:30am-2pm, 4:30-8pm. The rest of the year open M-F 9:30am-1:30pm and 4-6pm.) Túy has a small but pretty **cathedral**; constructed in 1120, it is a mix of Gothic and Romanesque styles and home to the relics of San Telmo, patron saint of sailors. The cathedral's portico was the first piece of Gothic art to be created on the Iberian peninsula, and its organ is also impressive. One ticket gets you into the cathedral's **museum** and the **Museo Diocesano** as well. (Museo Diocesano ☎ 986 60 36 00. Both open daily July-Aug. 9:30am-9pm, museum closes at 8pm; Sept.-Dec. 9:30am-1:30pm and 4-8pm; Dec.-May 9:30am-1:30pm and 4-7pm. 300ptas.) For some good food and a spectacular view of Portugal while you're eating, try the 1200pta *menú* at **Le Boulevard**, C. Calvo Sotelo, 40. (☎ 986 60 12 09. Restaurant open only July and August.)

LA GUARDIA (A GUARDA) (1HR.)

Buses run to and from La Guardia from Vigo (1hr.; M-F every 30min., Sa every hr., 5:45am-7pm, Su 6 per day 8:30am-7pm; 645ptas).

Perched between the mouth of the Río Miño and the Atlantic Ocean, La Guardia (pop. 10,000) thrives on an active fishing industry and the 500,000 tourists who annually descend on its little beach and large mountain. The bus stops at the corner of C. Domínguez Fontela and C. Concepción Arenal. To reach the majestic **Monte Santa Tecla,** take C. Domínguez Fontela to reach C. José Antonio. From C. José Antonio, bear right onto C. Rosalía de Castro, which continues to the top (6km). Alternatively, hike five minutes up the road and look for the steps off to the left that mark the start of a shorter, steeper pathway through the woods (3km). Three-quarters of the way up lie the ruins of an old **Celtic village,** while near the peak is a **chapel** dedicated to Santa Tecla, the patron saint of headaches and heart disease. The wax body parts inside (hearts, heads, and feet) are gifts to Santa Tecla from cured worshippers. An extraordinary panoramic view of the ocean and valley greets tourists at the very top, along with booths of trinkets that will delight souvenir hunters but may disgust everyone else. La Guardia hosts a **lobster festival** the last Sunday in June, as well as the mysterious "Burial of the Swordfish" during **Carnaval** in March. Pilgrimages, *fútbol*, and folk festivals mark the **Feria de Monte de Santa Tecla** in the second week of August. During the summer, La Guardia's **tourist office** is at C. Rosalía de Castro, also called El Centro Cultural. (☎ 986 61 18 50. Open mid-June to mid-Sept. M-Sa 11am-2pm and 5-8pm.) The rest of the year it resides in the **Ayuntamiento** in Pr. España. (☎ 986 61 00 00. Open M-Sa 8am-3pm.)

PONTEVEDRA

According to legend, Pontevedra (pop. 74,000) was founded by the Greek archer Teucro as a place to convalesce after his Trojan War exploits. Its name comes from an old Roman bridge (Pontus Veteri), and since medieval times it has been an important stopover on the southern (Portuguese) Camino de Santiago. Today Pontevedra continues to be more of a transportation hub than a destination in itself, but it does have a wealth of beautiful parks and plazas and an interesting history.

▐ TRANSPORTATION

Trains: (☎ 902 24 02 02 or 986 85 76 02), Av. Calvo Sotelo. Info open daily 6am-11pm. To: **Vigo** (20min.; 22 per day 7:38am-10:58pm; 255ptas, express 345ptas); **Santiago** (1½hr.; 18 per day 6:25am-10:10pm.; 515ptas, express 645ptas); **La Coruña** (3hr.; 17 per day 6:25am-9:33pm; 1125ptas, express 1340ptas); and **Madrid** (11hr.; M-F 2 per day 12:40pm and 9:15pm, Sa 8:45am; 6000ptas).

Buses: (☎ 986 85 24 08), Av. Calvo Sotelo. Info open daily 9am-9:30pm. To: **Santiago** (1hr., every hr. 7am- 9pm, 625ptas); **Cambados** (1hr.; 12 per day M-F 7:55am-8:35pm, Sa 11:15am-8:35pm, Su 3 per day 12:30-8:35pm; 300ptas); **El Grove/La Toja** (1hr., every 30min. 7:45am-10pm, 445ptas); **La Coruña** (2½hr., 10 per day 7:30am-9pm, 1450ptas); and **Madrid** (8hr., 4 per day, 4255ptas).

Taxis: (☎ 986 85 12 85 or 986 85 12 00). 400ptas from the stations to downtown.

Car Rental: Avis, C. Peregrina, 49 (☎ 986 85 20 25). Rates vary with duration of rental. 1-day unlimited mileage 11,950ptas. Must be 23 and have had a license for at least 1 year. Open M-F 9:30am-1pm and 4-7pm, Sa 9am-12:30pm.

✳▐ ORIENTATION AND PRACTICAL INFORMATION

Six streets radiate out from the center of town, **Praza Peregrina.** The main streets are C. Oliva, C. Michelena, C. Benito Corbal, and C. Peregrina. **Praza Galiza** is a five-minute walk from Pr. Peregrina (with the stations vaguely behind you, walk down C. Peregrina until you are one block from Pr. Peregrina, and turn right onto C.

Andrés Mellado). The **train** and **bus stations,** located across from each other, are about 1km from town. To get to the city center, turn left after exiting the bus station. Continue on this street for 10-15 minutes as it changes from Av. Calvo Sotelo to Av. de Vigo to C. Peregrina, which deposits you in Pr. Peregrina.

Tourist Office: The **main office,** C. General Mola, 3 (☎/fax. 986 85 08 14), 1 block from Pr. Peregrina, left off C. Michelena (straight ahead with the monument to your right), offers tons of brochures and maps. English spoken. A **second office** opens in summer on Pl. de España. Both open Sept.-May M-F 9:30am-2pm and 4:30-6:30pm, Sa 11am-12:30pm. June-Aug. extended until 8pm, and also Su 10am-12:30pm.

Currency Exchange: Banco Central Hispano (☎ 986 84 48 64), Pl. Peregrina. No commission. Open M-F 8:30am-2:30pm, Sa 8:30am-1pm.

Luggage Storage: Lockers at the train station 400ptas; at the bus station 80ptas per item. Both open daily 8am-10pm.

Emergency: ☎ 112. **Police:** C. Joaquín Costa, 17 (☎ 986 85 38 00).

Hospital: Hospital Provincial, C. Doctor Loureiro Crespo, 2 (☎ 986 85 21 15). **Medical Emergencies:** ☎ 061.

Post Office: C. Oliva, 21 (☎ 986 84 48 64). Open M-F 8:30am-8:30pm, Sa 9am-2pm. **Postal Code:** 36001.

Internet Access: Cybercafé Gorgo, C. Javier Puig, 6 (☎ 986 85 00 21 or 986 86 62 93). Walking on C. Peregrina with the stations behind you, take a right onto C. Sagasta, then a right onto C. Benito Corbal, then a left onto C. Javier Puig. 10am-3pm 200ptas per hr.; 3-10pm 300ptas per hr. **Cyberteka** (☎ 986 86 63 25), just off Ruinas de Santo Domingo; enter the photocopy place and go up 1 floor. 200ptas per hr.

▌ ACCOMMODATIONS

C. Michelena, C. Peregrina, and Pr. Galiza are full of cheap accommodations.

Pensión Florida, (☎986 85 19 79), on C. García Camba. With the stations behind you, take a left before C. Peregrina becomes a plaza. Clean, modern rooms compensate for the long flights of stairs. Winter heating. Reservations accepted with pre-payment. Doubles 3000-3500ptas; triples 4000ptas; quads 5000ptas.

Pensión La Cueva, C. Andrés Mellado, 7 (☎ 986 85 12 71), in Pr. Galiza. With the stations behind you, take a left onto C. Mellado from C. Peregrina. The Cave is aptly named, with large, dim, but inexpensive rooms. Singles 1100ptas; doubles 2200ptas.

Hotel Madrid, C. Andrés Mellado, 5 (☎/fax. 986 85 10 06), next door to La Cueva. Spacious rooms with full baths. A great find for the price. Winter heating. Reservations wise. Singles 3600-4300ptas; doubles 6000-7500ptas. Extra bed 2000ptas. V, MC.

Casa Alicia, Av. de Santa María, 5, 1st floor (☎ 986 85 70 79) Small, comfortable doubles with lots of light. Winter heating. Doubles 3000-3500ptas; quads 4500ptas. Reservations recommended.

◖ FOOD

Like many towns in Galicia, Pontevedra prides itself on seafood. In the evenings, locals crowd tiny bars on C. Figueroa and C. San Sebastián to munch on a variety of fishy *tapas,* washed down with the local Albariño wine. Follow C. Soportales out of Pl. Peregrina. For land-based goods, there's **Supermercado Gadis** on C. Benito Corbal, 34, open M-Sa 9am-9pm.

▨ **Bodegón Micota,** C. Peregrina, 4 (☎ 986 85 59 17). Micota reinvents the term fast food, with speedy service and tasty, fun specialties like *revueltos* (750-885ptas), *venancias* (tortillas; 625-650), shishkabobs (1150-1850ptas), and *panchos* (large sandwiches; 585-885ptas). The best deal is the 950pta *menú del día.* Meat dishes 950-1785ptas. Salads 695-785ptas. Open daily noon-4:30pm and 8pm-1am.

✪ **O Merlos,** Av. de Santa María, 4 (☎ 986 84 43 43). From Pl. Peregrina, take C. Michelena with the flowered median to your left, take a right, and then a quick left before the building with large green windows. Tasty regional platters served in a unique atmosphere; thousands of key chains hang from the ceiling. Over 40 *tapas* (275-850). *Menú* 1000ptas. Seafood entrees 475-1600ptas. Open Tu-Su 10am-2am. V, MC, AmEx.

👁 🎵 SIGHTS AND ENTERTAINMENT

SIGHTS. Pontevedra proper's best sight is the extensive **Museo Provincial,** C. Pasantería, 10. Exhibits in the five-building collection cover a wide range of themes, including traditional Galician cooking, sacred and contemporary art, archaeology, and glasswork. The museum also includes the Gothic **Ruinas de Santo Domingo** in Pl. de España. (Museum open June-Sept. Tu-Sa 10am-2:15pm and 5-8:45pm, Su 11am-2pm; Oct.-May 10am-1:30pm and 4:30-8pm. 200ptas, EU members free. Ruins open June 1-Sept. 30 Tu-F 10am-2pm.) In the evening, the granite walls and arcades of Pontevedra's old town emit a luminescent glow. The 18th-century **Capilla de la Virgen Peregrina** is dedicated to Pontevedra's patron saint, a pilgrim version of the Virgin Mary, and is modeled after the scallop shell associated with Santiago. (☎ 986 85 13 75. Open daily 9am-9pm.) The **Basílica de Santa María a Maior** features a golden Plateresque door constructed in the 16th century that's illuminated by flood-lights at night. From Pl. España take Av. Santa María, on the left of the Ayuntamiento. (☎ 986 86 61 85. Open daily 10am-1pm and 5-9pm.)

BEACHES. Sunny days are sure to bring a crowd to the beaches of nearby **Marín.** A fleet of red APSA buses makes the journey from the outer corner of Pr. Galicia. (30min., every 15min., 115ptas.) You'll endure the horrid stench of a paper mill along the way, but the beaches are clean and inviting. From the bus stop in Marín, facing the water, head left on C. Angusto Miranda around the track and up the hill. To reach **Playa Porticelo,** turn right on C. Tiro Naval Janer, continue for 15 minutes, and bear right where the road splits. Another 10 minutes on foot brings you to the larger **Playa Mogor.** Both beaches come equipped with bar-cafes.

ENTERTAINMENT. For a glimpse of Pontevedra **nightlife,** check out the bars near the Basílica Menor de Santa María (especially along C. Isabel II) or on C. Cobián Roffignac. The festivals of **Santiago de Burgos** (July 25) and **La Peregrina** (2nd Sunday in August) bring city-wide celebration.

🚌 DAYTRIPS FROM PONTEVEDRA

The following towns are perfect daytrips from Pontevedra, as frequent bus service covers the area. The train from Santiago in the north swings toward the coast at Vilagarcía de Arousa, the commercial center of central Galicia.

I'M TOO SEXY FOR MY CLOAK
To the surprise of Spaniards everywhere, this culturally isolated region in northwestern Spain has recently received international recognition as a hub of modern fashion, catching the eyes of top French, Italian, and American designers. Leading this Galician fashion brigade are Antonio Pernas, Roberto Verino, and Zara (once a simple neighborhood store; now it produces over $1.19 billion in annual sales). Even more impressive than such booming success is the designers' stubborn and prideful insistence on keeping their companies rooted in Galician soil. So tourists looking for a genuine Galician souvenir can toss away that cumbersome *Tetilla* cheese block and head home wearing a flashy, newfangled Antonio Pernas designer suit. Perhaps, before too long, supermodels will be storming catwalks across the globe decked in the characteristic brown cloak and scallop shells of the Camino de Santiago Pilgrims. Or not.

NORTHWESTERN SPAIN

EL GROVE (O GROVE) AND LA TOJA (A TOXA) (1HR.)

All buses depart from the end of the waterfront, in front of the tourist office. Buses run from El Grove to Cambados on the way to Vilagarcía (30min., 4 per day, more in July-Aug., 240ptas) and to Pontevedra (1hr., 19 per day 7:30am-9pm, 445ptas). Schedules are posted inside and on the door of the bus office, 50m to the left.

Every July and August, affluent Europeans come in Land Rovers and BMWs to the seaside resort of El Grove (pop. 11,000) and its island partner, La Toja. Sea-saturated El Grove, on a tranquil strait west of Pontevedra, is lined with mussel farms, colorful boats, and clam-diggers. Restaurants line C. Beiramar with its paseo marítimo. La Toja, across the bridge, lures the wealthy (and the occasional desperate backpacker) with a casino, a decent beach, and aggressive vendors hoping to enchant with their "typical Galician dress." If nothing else, take a walk around the tiny island and ogle the incredible chalets that line its eastern end. Don't expect to find the La Toja Luxury Soap factory on this island, though. The soap company took its name from the thermal waters that were found on La Toja ages ago; the island remains a quiet hamlet for the wealthy. From July to mid-October the El Grove **tourist office,** Plaza do Corgo, 1, has an office in the square near the bus stop. (☎986 73 14 15. Open July-Oct. 15 M-Sa 10am-12:30pm and 4-9:30pm, Su 10am-12:30pm.) The rest of the year, brochures are dispensed on the second floor of the **Ayuntamiento.** (☎ 986 73 09 75. Open Oct. 16-June M-F 8am-3pm.) If you're in town between the 7th and the 15th of October, try not to miss the **Festa do Marisco** (seafood festival), which brings great regional seafood at unbelievably low prices.

LA LANZADA (1HR.)

To get to La Lanzada, take the bus from Pontevedra to El Grove/La Toja (1hr., every 30min. 9:20am-10pm, 435ptas) and tell the bus driver you are getting off at La Lanzada.

Five kilometers toward Pontevedra from El Grove, La Lanzada's beach—arguably the best in Galicia—lures topless bathers with its fine white sands and irresistible waves. Home to the pagan cult of the "Ninth Wave," this area's mysterious methods of aiding romance and fertility will either baffle or entice you. Two hundred meters past the end of La Lanzada sits **Restaurante La Lanzada,** Carretera San Vicente do Mar, accessible by beach or road—stay in a white *cabaña* with simple, spacious rooms 50m from the surf. (☎ 986 73 84 00 or 73 01 07. Doubles 4000ptas, with large bed and bath 5000ptas. Open July-Aug.).

CAMBADOS (1HR.)

Plus Ultra buses leave from the new bus station near Pr. Concello to Pontevedra (1hr., 9 per day, last at 7pm, 315ptas) and Santiago (M-F 8 per day 7am-7pm, Sa 3 per day 8am, 3, 7pm, Su 2 per day 9am and 7pm).

For a glimpse of small-town life and a glass of good wine, head to harborside Cambados (pop. 14,000), 26km northwest of Pontevedra. Lack of a beach has left Cambados out of the tourist loop—its taxi drivers play cards all afternoon. On a quiet hill 15 minutes from the center, the beautiful ruins of the **Iglesia Santa María** watch over the town's cemetery. For a lovely view of the town and the *ría*, climb the steps to the left of the ruins up to the small park. The **Pazo de Fefiñanes,** an attractive 16th-century palace-turned-*bodega*, brims with gigantic, sweet-smelling barrels of wine; venture over to the **Praza de Fefiñanes,** filled with bar-restaurants, and sip Cambados' prized beverage. The town throws a *fiesta* virtually every night in mid-summer, beginning with the July celebration of **Santa Mariña** and culminating the first weekend in August with an official tasting of the previous year's local Albariño, a light and fruity wine. A new **tourist office** (near the bus station) serves the town (open M-Sa 10am-1:30pm and 4:30-7pm).

RÍAS ALTAS

LA CORUÑA (A CORUÑA)

France has its City of Lights, and Spain has the Crystal City, La Coruña. A stroll down La Coruña's 8km of seaside promenades quickly reveals the origins of the city's name: sailors passing through the port used to be nearly blinded by the reflection of the setting sun on the harborside wall of windows created by closely constructed buildings. La Coruña's mythic lighthouse has been the subject of countless works of art and literature, and Picasso first learned to paint here. But perhaps most unique about La Coruña is its combination of modern infrastructure and nonstop nightlife with the charm of a fisherman's port and the mythical aura of the city's Celtic past. Santiago de Compostela may be the northwest's most touristed city, but La Coruña has been around longer, and proud *coruñeses* won't hesitate to claim that their city has always been the real Galicia.

▉ TRANSPORTATION

Flights: Aeropuerto de Alvedro (☎ 981 18 72 00), 9km south. Served only by **Aviaco** and **Air Europa,** with daily charters to Paris via Barcelona and Sa charters to London.

Trains: (☎ 981 15 02 02), in Pr. San Cristóbal. Info daily 7am-11pm. National **RENFE** number ☎ 902 24 02 02. To: **Santiago** (1hr., 20-23 per day 6:20am-10:25pm, 545-645ptas); **Pontevedra** (1½-2½hr., 19-23 per day 6:20am-8:10pm, 1125-1340ptas); **Vigo** (2-3hr., 20-23 per day 6:20am-10:25pm, 1265-1500ptas); **Madrid** (8½-11hr., 1-3 per day, 6200-17400ptas); and **Barcelona** (15-16hr., 2 per day, 6500-8000ptas).

Buses: (☎ 981 23 96 44 or 981 23 90 99), on C. Caballeros, across Av. Alcalde Molina from the train station. **ALSA-Intercar** (☎ 981 15 11 00). To: **Oviedo** (5hr., 4 per day 9am-5:45pm, 3175ptas); **Madrid** (8½hr., 5-6 per day 7:30am-10:30pm, 4955-6975ptas); **Santander** (9am and 5:45pm, 4880ptas); and **San Sebastián** (14hr., 9am and 5:45pm, 6575ptas). **Castromil** (☎ 981 24 91 92 or 981 23 92 41) to **Santiago** (50min.-1½hr., every hr. 7am-10pm, 825ptas). **IASA-Arriva** (☎ 981 23 90 01) to: **Betanzos** (40min.; M-F every 30min., Sa-Su every hr., 7am-10:30pm; 245ptas); and **Vivero,** with stops at O Barqueiro, Ortigueira, El Ferrol, Vicedo, and Betanzos (3½hr., 3-4 per day 6:30am-7:30pm, 1635ptas).

La Coruña

▲ ACCOMMODATIONS
Hospedaje María Pita, 1
Pensión la Alianza, 2

NORTHWESTERN SPAIN

Public Transportation: Red buses of the **Compañía de Tranvías de la Coruña** (☎ 981 25 01 00) run frequently (7am-11:30pm, 115ptas). Bus stops post full itineraries; buy tickets on board. City buses run M-F every 7-15min., weekends every 20-30min.

Taxis: Radio Taxi (☎ 981 24 33 33). **TeleTaxi** (☎ 981 28 77 77). With the tourist office and ocean to the right, walk along the sidewalk to the taxi stand. Also near Cuatro Caminos on C. Concepción Arenal, as well as the train and bus stations.

Car Rental: Autos Brea, Av. Fernández Latorre, 110 (☎ 981 23 86 45 or 689 53 94 86). Min. age 21; must have had license for at least 1yr. From 2075ptas per day with unlimited mileage. 3-day min. rental. Open M-F 9am-1pm and 4-7pm, Sa 9am-2pm. **Europcar,** Avda. de Arteixo, 21 (☎ 981 14 35 36). Min. age 21 and must have had a license for at least 1yr. From 5700ptas daily with unlimited mileage, insurance, and IVA. Open M-F 9:30am-1:30pm and 4pm-7:30pm, Sa 9am-1pm.

■■ 🛈 ORIENTATION AND PRACTICAL INFORMATION

La Coruña's new city stretches across the mainland; the isthmus and peninsula contain the *ciudad vieja* (old city). **Avenida de la Marina** leads past the tourist office and the obelisk to **Puerta Real,** which has an entryway into **Plaza de María Pita** in the *ciudad vieja.* Shaded streets fill the peninsula's southern tip overlooking the port. Surfboard havens **Praia del Orzán** and **Praia de Riazor** are 10-minute walks northwest from the tourist office, on the other side of the peninsula's neck. From the bus station, take bus #1 or 1A straight to the **tourist office** (115ptas). To get to the bus station from the train station, walk in the direction of El Corte Inglés and take the pedestrian overpass, which leads to the bus station (5min.). If you want to get to town on foot, head toward El Corte Inglés and down C. Fernández Latorre away from the bus station. Walk past **Plaza Cuatro Caminos** (recognizable by the large fountain in the middle) continuing on C. Fernández Latorre up to and then along the port; the main road tracing the coast will change names many times but will take you to the tourist office in Dársena de la Marina.

Tourist Office: (☎/fax 981 22 18 22), on Dársena de la Marina, right off Avda. de la Marina, connecting the peninsula and mainland. One of Spain's finest. Tips on daytrips and an accommodations guide. English spoken. Open M-F 9am-2pm and 4:30-6:30pm, Sa 10:30am-1:30pm; July 15-Sept. 15 Sa 10:30am-1pm and 5-7pm, Su 10am-2pm and 5-7pm. **Turismo Provincial A Coruña** (☎ 981 18 46 80), Pr. Luis Seoane, has more general info on Galicia. If the Dársena tourist office is completely full, try **Turismo A Coruña** (☎ 981 21 61 61), Edificio Atalaya, 1st fl., in Xardíns de Méndez Nuñez, 5min. from la Dársena. Open M-F 9am-2pm and 4-8pm.

Ayuntamiento: (☎ 981 18 42 00), Pl. de María Pita, 1.

Currency Exchange: Banco Central Hispano, Cantón Grano, 9-12 (☎ 981 22 25 83). No commission. Open M-F 8:30am-2pm. Another at Av. General Sanjurjo, 10 (☎ 981 28 90 23), near the bus station and El Corte Inglés. Open M-F 8:30am-2pm, Sa 8:30am-1pm. Apr. 1-Sept. 30 closed Sa.

American Express Travel: Viajes Amado, C. Compostela, 1 (☎ 981 22 99 72). Open M-F 9:30am-2pm and 4:30-8pm, Sa 10am-1pm.

Luggage Storage: At the **train station,** lockers 400ptas. Open daily 6:30am-1:30am. At the **bus station,** 75ptas per bag. Open daily 8am-10pm.

El Corte Inglés: C. Ramón y Cajal, 57-59 (☎ 981 29 00 11). A sharp right from the bus station exit. Currency exchange, maps, novels and guidebooks in English, haircutting, cafeteria, supermarket, restaurant, and telephones. Open M-Sa 10am-9:30pm.

Laundromat: Lavandería Glu Glu, C. Alcalde Marchesi, 4 (☎ 981 28 28 04), off Pr. Cuatro Caminos. Self-serve wash and dry 950ptas per 5kg load. Full service 1100ptas per load. Open M-F 9:30am-8:30pm, Sa 9:30am-6pm.

Late-Night Pharmacy: Telefarmacia (☎ 981 56 09 92 or 902 13 41 34). 24hr. service.

Emergency: ☎ 112. **Police: Municipal** (☎ 981 18 42 25), C. Miguel Servet.

Medical Services: Ambulancia San José (☎ 981 22 63 35), C. Comandante Fontanes.

Post Office: (☎ 981 22 51 75), C. Alcalde Manuel Casas, past Teatro Colón off Av. Marina. **Lista de Correos** and **fax** service. Open M-F 8:30am-8:30pm, Sa 9:30am-2pm. **Postal Code:** 15070.

Internet Access: Internet World, C. Juan Florez, 58 (☎ 981 14 38 12). From Pl. Pontevedra, with the beaches behind you, walk up C. Juan Florez for 2-3min.; it's on the right. Look for a large purple Gargoyle. 150ptas per hr. Open daily 4pm-4am. **Paixon E.D.,** C. San Nicolás, 37 (☎ 981 20 55 24), 1 block from C. Riegode Agua. 250ptas for 30min. Open daily 9am-1:30am, Sa-Su until 3:30am.

ACCOMMODATIONS

The most convenient area for lodgings is one block back from Av. Marina, near the tourist office. C. Riego de Agua and the surrounding area (from Pr. María Pita down to Pr. San Agustín) always have available rooms. There are many *pensiones* near the stations, but these are miles away from the *ciudad vieja*. Streets radiating south of Pl. Pontevedra are also full of cheap accommodations. HI hostels are quite inconveniently located; the cost of transportation to La Coruña proper and the burden of travel will most likely cancel out any price benefits.

Hospedaje María Pita, C. Riego de Agua, 38, 3rd fl. (☎ 981 22 11 87), above Hospedaje Morán (don't confuse them). White lace curtains, cheery rooms, pristine bathrooms (some in rooms, some not) and a homey feel. The owners are a friendly couple who will eagerly suggest places to go. Winter heat. Arrangements for singles possible. Great balcony views. Reservations wise in Aug. Doubles 2900-3500ptas. Cash only.

Pensión la Alianza, C. Riego de Agua, 8, 1st fl. (☎ 981 22 81 14). Dark wood and homemade oil paintings decorate quiet, simple rooms. Spotless gray-tiled bathroom down the hall. Reservations recommended. Check-out 1pm. Singles 1500-2200ptas; doubles 3000-3800ptas, depending on the season.

Marina Española (HI) (☎ 981 62 01 18 or 982 22 19 54; fax 981 22 13 36), in Sada, about 20km east of La Coruña. The Empresa Calpita bus (☎ 981 23 90 72) runs there (30min., 240ptas). Breakfast included. Heat in winter. 3-day max. stay. Call ahead, especially July-Aug. Dorms 750ptas, over 26 1100ptas.

FOOD

Cheap eats abound on C. Estrella, C. Franja, and nearby streets. For snazzier cafes and pizzerias, head for the ocean strips and the area around C. Rubine off Playa de Raizor. Buy fresh fruit and vegetables in the **market** in the oval building on Pr. San Agustín, near the old town (open M-Sa 8am-3pm). For groceries, head downstairs to **Supermercados Claudio** (open daily 9am-3pm and 5-9pm).

Restaurante Bania, C. Cordeleira, 7 (☎ 981 22 13 01). Friendly service, soothing, sunny environment, and great vegetarian cuisine. Salads (775-950ptas) are delicious, but not filling; order an appetizer. Open M-Sa 9:30am-1pm and 4pm-11:30pm.

Mesón Trotamundos, Pr. España, 9 (☎ 981 22 16 09). Sit under hunks of beef and hundreds of wine bottles and watch the staff make their famous *pulpo gallego* (Galician octopus). *Raciones* 250-1100ptas. *Menú* M-Sa 800ptas. Open daily 10am-2am.

SIGHTS

TORRE DE HÉRCULES. La Coruña's tourist magnet, the 2nd-century Torre de Hércules, towers over rusted ships at the peninsula's end. Legend has it that Hércules erected the tower, the world's oldest working lighthouse, upon the remains of his defeated enemy Gerión. Enter through the lower entrance to explore the original foundation, then climb a claustrophobic 239-step tunnel to the pinnacle for incredible views of La Coruña and its rivers. Weekends in July and August the lighthouse stays open until midnight and candles are distributed to light the ascent. *(Take the path from the Orzán and Riazor beaches, or bus #9 or 13 for 115ptas. Open Apr.-Sept. 10am-7pm; Oct.-Mar. 10am-6pm. 250ptas, seniors and children free.)*

■ **AQUARIUM FINISTERRAE.** Also known as **Casa de los Peces,** this new aquarium is La Coruña's homage to the sea. Huge underwater tanks, separated from the sea only by huge rocks, display 2000 species of ocean fish in their natural setting, including sharks, stingrays, and seals. The themed exhibitions are not to be missed; there's even a Beatles-inspired real live Octopus Garden. *(On the Po. Marítimo of Playa Orzán between Museo Domus and La Torre de Hércules.* ☎ *981 22 72 72; www.casaciencias.org. Open daily July-Aug. 11am-11pm; Sept. 10am-8pm; Oct.-June 10am-7pm. 1000ptas, children, seniors, and students 500ptas.)*

■ **MUSEO DOMUS.** The new Museo Domus (Museum of Man) houses three floors of interactive, high-tech exhibits on the human body. Watch "blood" spurt at 50kph from a model heart; hear "Hello, I love you" in over 30 languages (sadly, from a computer); and spend hours playing with microscopes, computers, and other fun gizmos. *(Santa Teresa, 1, on Po. Marítimo from Playa Orzán.* ☎ *981 21 70 00; www.casaciencias.org. Open July-Aug. daily 11am-9pm; Sept.-June Tu-Sa 10am-7pm, Su and festivals 300ptas, children, seniors, and students 100ptas.)*

■ **CASA DE LAS CIENCIAS AND PLANETARIUM.** The House of Sciences is an interactive museum designed to make science fun and exciting. Exhibits on computing, technology, nature, and the physical world fill the multilevel museum, and the planetarium down the hill in Parque Santa Margarita reproduces the night sky from any point on earth. *(Parque Santa Margarita. From the tourist office, take Avda. de la Marina, as it changes name, to Pr. de Orense. From there, follow C. Fernando Glez. Fontan as it becomes Avda. de Arteixo, which runs into the park.* ☎ *981 27 18 28; www.casaciencias.org. Museum 300ptas. Planetarium 200ptas, students, seniors, and children 100ptas.)*

MUSEO DE BELLAS ARTES. Housed in a renovated convent, this museum displays classic Spanish, French, Italian, and Flemish art as well as some local Gallego artists. Don't miss the Goya display. *(C. Zalaeta, 2. With the tourist office behind you, cross the street into the old sector and take C. Bailén until it becomes C. San Nicolás, which will run into C. Zalaeta and the museum.* ☎ *981 22 37 23. Open Tu-F 10am-8pm, Sa 10am-2pm and 4:30-8pm. Su 10am-2pm. Closed M 400ptas.)*

CASTILLO DE SAN ANTON. This 16th-century fort serves as La Coruña's archaeological museum, with displays of pieces from ancient Galician fortresses, as well as artifacts from the Roman, Bronze, and Megalithic Ages. *(Puerto Deportivo, on Po. Marítimo. From the tourist office follow Dársena de la Marina away from the port; once you reach the paseo, walk for 10min.; the fortress is on the thin peninsula.* ☎ *981 20 59 94. Open June-Sept. Tu-Sa 10am-9pm, Su 10am-2:30pm; Oct.-May Tu-Sa 10am-7pm, Su 10am-2:30pm. 300ptas.)*

REAL ACADEMIA GALLEGA. The Royal Galician Academy is housed in the former family seat of 19th-century novelist Condesa Emilia Pardo Bazán, and its library contains 25,000 volumes on Galician literature, history, and culture. The museum next door is dedicated to Bazán's work and exhibits of modern and 19th-century Galician art. *(C. Tabernas.* ☎ *981 20 73 08. Open M-F 9am-2pm and 4-7pm. Free.)*

◩ NIGHTLIFE

Summer nightlife in La Coruña reflects the upbeat nature of the peninsula's residents. Locals bar-hop around C. Franja, C. La Florida, C. San Juan and the surrounding side streets. When bars die down around 2am, **discos** pick up along the two beaches and on C. Juan Florez. **Sol. Pirámide,** C. Juan Florez, 50 (☎ 981 27 61 57), plays dance music loud enough to rouse the dead, while **Picasso** and **Lautrec,** opposite each other on C. Sol, attract the artistically inclined house-music lovers. (All open midnight-4am, on weekends till 5:30am or so.) Smoky **Café-Bar La Barra,** C. Riego de Agua, 33, offers innocent entertainment all day long. Students and old fogies gather to play cards, dominoes, and parcheesi. (☎ 981 22 73 82. Open daily 9am-2am.) **C. Santa Cristina** and

C. Humboldt on Playa Santa Cristina also host a nice stretch of bars and *pafs*. For something a little different, but lots of fun, try ■**Karaoke-Sitio Distinto,** on C. Santa Cristina, 12. This extremely popular joint offers daily karaoke and plenty of laughs. Waiting lists to sing are often an hour long. (☎ 981 63 60 53. Open daily 6pm to 4am.)

🌼 FESTIVALS

Although it is celebrated in many parts of Europe, La Coruña greets **La Noche de San Juan** (June 23) with particular fervor since it coincides with the opening of sardine season. Locals light the traditional *aguardiente* bonfires and spend the night leaping over the flames (contrary to what you might assume, the rite is actually supposed to ensure fertility) and gorging on sardine flesh. If you drop an egg white in a glass of water on this night, it will supposedly assume the form of your future spouse's occupation; many are led to believe they'll marry a cow. There is some sort of feast every weekend in La Coruña proper and its neighboring towns throughout the months of July and August, but the city's main festival is **Las Fiestas de María Pita** (Aug. 31). Party-hardy Coruñeses spend the entire month of August celebrating with various concerts, parades, and a mock naval battle to honor María Pita, the woman who single-handedly rallied a defense against the invading army of Sir Francis Drake (after the town's men had fled from the port in fear).

🎒 DAYTRIP FROM LA CORUÑA

BETANZOS (45MIN.)

IASA buses (☎ 981 23 90 01) run from La Coruña (45min.; M-F every 30min., Sa-Su every hr., 6:30am-10:30pm; 245ptas). Trains (☎ 981 77 24 02) stop in Betanzos on the way from La Coruña to El Ferrol (3:45 and 9:12pm; returns 7:28am and 3:28pm, Sa-Su 9pm also; 330ptas) and on the way from La Coruña to Monforte (8:35am and 6:42pm, returns 9:45am and 9:13pm). The train station sits across the river at the entrance to town in front of the high school.

A provincial capital of ancient Galicia, the modern-day city of **Betanzos** (pop. 12,000) assumes a low profile. Cafes line the central **Praza García Hermanos,** home to a statue of the brothers García, the city's great benefactors who made their fortune after emigrating to Argentina. **Igrexa de San Fransisco,** located several blocks down the hill from Pr. Hamanos, features the image of San Fransisco de Betanzos resting on the backs of a huge bear and a *jabalí*, or wild boar (symbol of the historically powerful Andrade House) and surrounded by his faithful puppies. Just outside Betanzos lies ■**Parque do Pasatiempo.** Built by the brothers García, this little known jewel features gardens, fountains, a small collection of animals, 41 international clocks, and man-made caves open for public exploration. (Park open daily 4-8pm. Caves open Sa-Su only. Tours available. Betanzos' great **festival** involves the launching of the world's largest paper balloon (about 25m high) on August 16, the night of San Roque. According to local residents, the balloon always flies toward the Betanzos cemetery where the originator of the tradition is buried. Betanzos also hosts a medieval fair on the second weekend of July.

Some think **Miño,** 12km north of Betanzos, has the nicest beach in the Rías Altas. **Camping Playa de Miño** in Miño, off the beach, is open from June to September. The place fills up pretty quickly in the summertime. (☎ 981 78 42 12. Electricity 450ptas. 475ptas per adult, 425ptas per tent, and 525ptas per car.) On Saturday afternoons in **Pontedeume,** a favorite fishing spot of Franco's 22km from Betanzos, workers at the town market cook *pulpo* (octopus) in huge copper urns and mock the citizens of Betanzos for making that ridiculously huge balloon. You can reach both towns on the bus lines heading to El Ferrol (every 30min., 280ptas).

LA RAPA DAS BESTAS

It is estimated that more than 100,000 wild horses roam the Galician hills, and records indicate that they have been there for nearly 4,000 years. No longer useful as cart-pullers, few of these animals are domesticated today, and the ancient branding rituals are still celebrated every July during *La Rapa das Bestas* ("Cropping of the Beasts").

"Here, we fight horses for tradition," says one rider, a sweaty, blood-speckled bandana across his hairline. The blood may not be his; for the past two hours he's straddled, head-locked, tail-pulled, herd-surfed, tackled, branded, been kicked and bitten by, and most importantly, sheared numerous feisty steeds. Consistent with one of the central themes of Spanish culture—man versus beast—*La Rapa* gives a new face to the traditional noble bull-gallant Matador dynamic. Before the festival begins, Spanish Marlboro men comb the mountains and valleys gathering herds of wild horses. The most exciting moment comes when the 400 unbridled horses thunder into the tight stone canal, enveloped in dust and panic. No one animal can be picked out of the writhing sea of horseflesh, but brave souls wielding scissors fight their way into the crowd, wrestle one horse at a time to submission, and send thick crops of shiny hair flying to the ground—to be collected later by children as souvenirs. By the end of the three-day festival, horses may be shaken by the unsolicited crew-cut, but unlike the unfortunate fallen bull, they will most definitely be ridden again.

THE NORTHERN COAST

The northern estuaries of Galicia are among the cleanest, loveliest and emptiest in all of Spain. To explore the Rías Altas often means spending hours on quiet coastal roads in the misty rain; if you want to escape the beaten path, coming here may be the answer. Public transportation is reliable, but renting a car is more convenient.

Cedeira, 84km northeast of La Coruña, has Spain's highest coastline and is home to pagan cults with thriving rituals involving worship of the *herba de enamorar* (love herb). It hosts the annual international **Pantín Classic** surfing competition at its famous **Playa de Pantín** and goes crazy for its annual horse-shearing festival (see **Las Rapas das Bestas,** above) every July. To reach the **tourist office,** C. Ezequiel López, 22, walk to the main street outside the bus station and take a right. Follow the street to the small river, cross the bridge, and turn left onto C. Ezequiel López. (☎ 981 48 21 87. Open Apr.-Sept. M-F 10:30am-1:30pm and 5-8pm, Sa 10am-2pm, Su and holidays noon-2pm.) **IASA buses** run to **El Ferrol** (1hr., 7 per day, 420ptas), where connections can be made to **La Coruña** and elsewhere.

Vivero, a tiny, beautiful old city poised between forest and sea, is known throughout Spain for its beaches, peaceful atmosphere, and July *fiestas,* especially **Las Rapas das Bestas.** Vivero's **tourist office,** on Av. Ramón Canosa and C. Carlos V (a wooden shack), hands outs maps and post information on accommodations. (☎ 982 56 08 79. Open daily June 15-Sept. 15 10am-2pm and 5:30-8:30pm; *Semana Santa* daily 11am-2pm and 4:30-8:30pm. **IASA buses** connect to **Ribadeo** (1½hr., 9:15am and 3:45pm, 625ptas); **El Ferrol** (2hr., 4-6 per day 6:30am-7:30pm, 985ptas); and **La Coruña** (4hr., 5 per day 6:30am-7:30pm, 1635ptas).

Ribadeo, official boundary between Galicia and Asturias, boasts one of the most beautiful beaches in Spain, the ⛱**Praia As Catedrais.** Natural rock archways curl into the sea, and low tide reveals caverns, coves, and warm lagoons perfect for exploring and swimming. The town itself has a quiet, almost ghostly, deserted air. The **tourist office** is in the Parque de San Francisco and can help with maps and accommodations. (☎ 982 12 86 89. Open M-F 10am-2:30pm and 4:40-8:30pm, Sa-Su 10am-8pm.) **IASA buses** run to **Vivero** (1½hr.; M-F 9am, 11:30am, and 6pm; Su 2:45 and 6pm; 625ptas); **La Coruña** (2½-3½hr.; M-Sa 7:15am, 8:45am, 1:30pm, and 6:15pm; 1610ptas); and **Santiago de Compostela** (3hr., 6:30am, 1885ptas).

BALEARIC ISLANDS

Dreaming perhaps of the vast fortunes to be made in the 20th-century tourist industry, nearly every culture with boats and colonists to spare has tried to conquer the Balearic islands (which have been Spanish since the 13th century). Foreign invasion continues today as two million of the trendiest and wealthiest European tourists flood the islands' discos and beaches each year.

While all four of the islands—Mallorca, Ibiza, Formentera, and Menorca—share fame for their gorgeous beaches and alluring topography, each has its own distinguishing characteristics. Mallorca, home to Palma, the islands' capital, absorbs the bulk of high-class invaders. With its museums, yacht-culture, and nightlife, Palma competes with Eivissa (Ibiza City) as the Balearics's cultural hub. Mallorca also harbors natural beauty, albeit in the shadows of urbanization. Condominiums loom over lazy bays that scoop into the coastline, while olive and orange orchards shade its fertile interior. Ibiza, a counter-culture haven since the 1960s, is the entertainment and style center of the islands and one of the trendiest spots on the globe. With its monstrous discos, famous DJs, and stronghold on the world's craziest and most beautiful party-goers, Ibiza offers what many consider the best nightlife in all of Europe. Ibiza's little sister, Formentera, is more peaceful, and unspoiled sands and unpaved roads abound. Wrapped in green fields and stone walls, Menorca leads a private life of empty white beaches, hidden coves, and mysterious Bronze Age megaliths.

Summers tend to be hot, dry, and crowded—but fun. Winters, especially on northern Mallorca and Menorca, are windy and chilly. Spring and autumn can be gorgeous, but the beaches remain a bit cool; the nightlife doesn't heat up—especially on Mallorca and Menorca—until early July. Most opening hours, schedules, and prices listed are for summer months only. Off-season prices at hotels can drop by up to 50%, and opening hours are often cut drastically.

HIGHLIGHTS OF THE BALEARIC ISLANDS

Need you ask? **Ibiza's** 24-hour party (see p. 491).

Formentera's eagle-eye views of the Mediterranean atop Formentera's seaside cliffs and lazy naps on sprawling expanses of untouched sands (see p. 493).

Menorca, the mysterious isle that's perfect for getting away from it all (see p. 480).

LOCAL FESTIVALS IN THE BALEARIC ISLANDS

Palma, Mallorca commemorates the *Día de Sant Joan* with singing, dancing, drinking, and fireworks every last Thursday in June. **Ciutadella, Menorca** celebrates the same holiday with even more gusto, running 250 wild horses through town on their hind legs. The *Verge del Carme* brings a colorfully trimmed armada into **Mahón, Menorca** on July 16, and the *Festa de Nostra Senyora de Gràcia*, a tribute to the city's patron saint, swings out in early September.

✈ GETTING THERE AND AWAY

Flying to the islands is fast and cheap—it makes a lot more sense than taking a ferry. Those under 26 can often receive discounts from **Iberia/Aviaco Airlines** (☎ 902 40 05 00 in Barcelona; www.iberia.com). **SOM** (Servicios de Ocio Marítimo; ☎ 971 31 03 99; email ibizasom@ctv.es) collaborates with bus companies, ferry lines, and *discotecas* on packages to Ibiza specially designed for disco fiends who seek transportation and an all-night party but have no particular use for lodging. The best way to book airline or ferry tickets is through a travel agency in Barcelona, Valencia, or on any of the islands.

BY PLANE

Scheduled flights are the easiest to book. Flights from Spain to any of the islands won't break the bank. Frequent flights soar from cities in Spain and throughout Europe (including Düsseldorf, Frankfurt, Hamburg, London, and Paris). On **Iberia** (24hr. info and reservation ☎ 902 40 05 00; www.iberia.com), many daily flights connect Palma de Mallorca and Ibiza to Madrid, Barcelona, and Valencia. Service from Alicante and Bilbao exists, but is less frequent.

Iberia offers student fares (must be 22 or under; with an ISIC 26 or under) on round-trip flights from Barcelona (40min., 10,000-20,000ptas) and Madrid (1hr., 25,000-30,000ptas). **Air Europa** (24hr. ☎ 902 24 00 42) and **Spanair** (☎ 902 13 14 15; www.spanair.com) also offer inexpensive flights to and from the islands. Schedules and prices change often, so contact a travel agent or the airlines themselves for details. Another option are **charter flights,** which can be the cheapest and quickest means of round-trip travel. Most deals entail a week's stay in a hotel, but some companies (called *mayoristas*) sell unoccupied seats on package-tour flights. The leftover spots, called "seat only" deals, can be found in newspaper ads or through travel agencies (check TIVE and other budget travel havens in any Spanish city). Prices during the summer and *Semana Santa* are often more than twice as much as in off-season (Oct.-May). Except in August, tickets are not hard to get a week or so before departure. Those planning to travel in July or August should reserve several months in advance.

BY BOAT

Ferry service is comparable in price to air service but longer in duration; the only reason to take a ferry is for the ride. On-board discos and small swimming pools on some boats help ease the longer passage. Ferries run from Barcelona and Valencia to Palma (on Mallorca) and Eivissa (on Ibiza); ferries also run from Dénia (in Alicante) to Ibiza. Though seats may be available up to an hour before departure, it's best to reserve all tickets a few days in advance.

Trasmediterránea (☎ 902 45 46 45; www.trasmediterranea.com) departs from Barcelona's Estació Marítima Moll and Valencia's Estació Marítima. Boats leave from both cities to Mallorca and Ibiza.

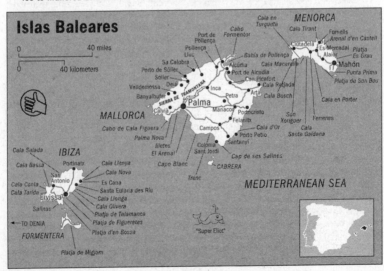

Flebasa Lines (☎ 902 16 01 80), which runs ferries out of Estació Marítima in Dénia (in the province of Alicante). The ferries make the short trip between Dénia and Ibiza (3-4½hr., 1 per day), continuing to Palma.

Pitra Car Ferries (Dénia ☎ 971 19 10 68), which run from Denía to Formentera via Eivissa and to San Antonio de Portmany (4hr., 2 per day; 5475ptas, children 2750ptas, cars 15,050ptas).

Buquebus (☎ 902 41 42 42 or 93 481 73 60) has super-fast catamaran service between Barcelona and Palma (4hr., 2 per day; one-way 8150ptas, cars 18,560).

▄ GETTING AROUND

Flying is the most efficient way to go from island to island. **Iberia** flies between Palma and Ibiza (35min., 4 per day, 8900ptas) and between Palma and Mahón, Menorca (35min., 4 per day, 8900ptas). **Air Europa** (☎ 902 24 00 42) and **Spanair** (☎ 902 13 14 15) also connect the islands at similar prices. Youth discounts are often available on round-trip flights.

A cheaper option is to take **ferries** between the islands. While they don't leave as regularly, ferries cost less than half as much as planes. Since prices and times are constantly changing, it is best to consult the tourist office or a travel agent for information. **Trasmediterránea** ferries (☎ 902 45 46 45) sail between Palma and Mahón (6½hr., 1 per week on Su, 3045ptas) and between Palma and Ibiza (fast 2½hr., 3 per week, 5210ptas; slow 4½hr., 3 per week, 3330ptas). There is no direct Mahón-Ibiza connection. **Trasmapi** (☎ 971 31 20 71) links Ibiza and Formentera (fast ferry 25min., 12 per day). Formentera-based **Inserco**, C. del Carmen, Formentera (☎ 971 32 22 10 or 902 45 46 45), also runs cheap Eivissa-Formentera boats (1hr., 6 per day 8:15am-10pm, round-trip 2000ptas). **Umafisa Lines** (☎ 971 31 45 13) runs car ferries on the same route (1hr.; M-F 6 per day, Sa 5 per day, Su 4 per day; 1350ptas, children 675ptas, cars 6000ptas). **Iscomar Ferries** (☎ 902 119 128) runs between Menorca's Port de Ciutadella and Mallorca's Port d'Alcudia for one-day trips (leaves 8:30am and returns 8pm, 4400ptas).

TRANSPORT WITHIN THE ISLANDS

All three major islands have extensive **bus** systems although Ibiza's is the only one that makes any sense. Mallorca has two narrow-gauge **train** systems (which unfortunately don't accept Eurailpasses). Intra-island travel is reasonably priced—bus fares between cities range from 200 to 800ptas each way. If you can, rent your own wheels for greater mobility and access to remote areas. On Mallorca and Menorca in particular, car rental is the only way to go. A day's rental of a tiny standard-transmission **car** usually costs around 4500ptas including insurance. **Mopeds** (2700ptas per day) and **bicycles** (1000ptas per day) are also available for rental.

MALLORCA

Mallorca, sought after since the days of the Romans, has a long history of popularity. It has continually attracted the rich and famous, whether as the site of the scandalous honeymoon of Polish pianist Fréderic Chopin and French novelist George Sand or as the vacation spot of choice for Spain's royal family. These days, ever larger numbers of European package tourists have converged on the island, in some areas virtually suffocating the coastline.

There are reasons for such Mallorca lust. To the northwest, white sand beaches, frothy water, lemon groves, and olive trees adorn the jagged Sierra de Tramontana. To the east, expansive beaches sink into calm bays, while to the southeast, a network of caves masks underground beauty. Inland, where many towns retain their unique history and culture, windmills drawing water for almond and fig trees power a thriving agricultural economy. Although the coastline has long been sacrificed to developers, even the most jaded of travelers sigh wistfully at the stunning expanses of sea, sand, and rock that sprawl across much of this island.

BALEARIC ISLANDS

PALMA

The capital of the Balearics, Palma (pop. 323,000) does not shy away from conspicuous consumption. Restaurants cater to expensive tastes and streets bustle with shoppers buying leather accessories, designer clothes, and jewelry. Even the city's namesake, the palm tree, has gone commercial: plastic palms in hotel lobbies almost outnumber the real thing. Though flooded by *pesetas* and nearly every other currency, Palma pleasantly surprises with its well-preserved old quarter, colonial architecture, and a noticeable local flavor.

▆ TRANSPORTATION

Flights: Aeroport Son San Juan (☎ 971 78 90 00), 8km from downtown Palma. Bus #17 goes to and from Pl. Espanya. **Iberia** (☎ 902 40 05 00), **Air Europa** (☎ 902 24 00 42), foreign carriers, and a host of charter operators all offer service to Palma. See **By Plane**, p. 470 or **Getting Around**, p. 471.

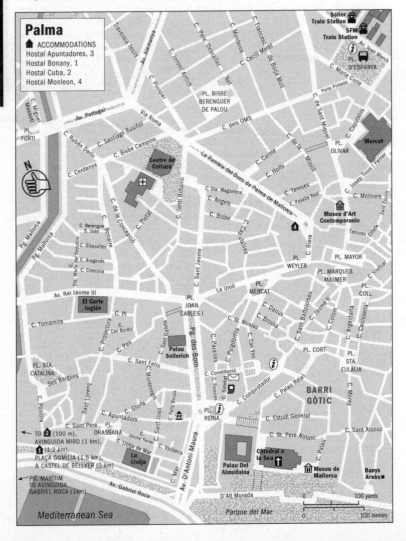

Palma

🏠 ACCOMMODATIONS
Hostal Apuntadores, 3
Hostal Bonany, 1
Hostal Cuba, 2
Hostal Monleon, 4

BALEARIC ISLANDS

Ferries: Trasmediterránea, Estació Marítim, 2 (☎ 902 45 46 45). Ferries dock at Moll Pelaires (south of the city). Bus #1 goes through Pg. Marítim. Tickets sold M-F 9am-1pm and 5-7pm, Sa 9am-noon. Tickets and info also available at travel agencies. Or try **Flebasa** (☎ 902 16 01 80). See **By Boat,** p. 470, or **Getting Around,** p. 471.

Trains: Ferrocarril de Sóller (☎ 971 75 20 51), Pl. Espanya. To **Sóller** (5 per day, 380ptas). Avoid the 10:40am "tourist train" when prices inflate to 735ptas for a 10min. stop in Mirador del Pujol d'en Banya. **Servicios Ferroviarios de Mallorca (SFM),** Pl. Espanya, 6 (☎ 971 75 20 51), to **Inca** (35min., every hr., 240ptas).

Buses: Bus travel to and from Palma is not too difficult, but travel between most other areas is inefficient and restrictive. The tourist office and the info kiosk in Pl. Espanya have a complete schedule that attempts to order the confusion; buy tickets aboard or in the kiosks in Pl. Espanya. The **tourist office** gives out an essential **blue packet** detailing the schedules of bus destinations to everywhere on the island. Most buses leave from Pl. Espanya and are run by a variety of companies serving different routes.

Public Transportation: Empresa Municipal de Transportes (EMT; ☎ 971 75 22 45). Pl. Espanya is the hub. Stops around town and as far as Palma Nova and Arenal. 175ptas, 10 tickets 1500ptas. Buy tickets aboard or in the kiosks in Pl. Espanya. Buses run approximately 6am-10pm. The airport bus, #17, runs until about 2am.

Taxis: (☎ 971 75 54 40, 971 40 14 14, or 971 72 80 81). Airport fare from the center of town is about 2000ptas—agree on the price before getting in.

Car Rental: Mascaro Crespi, Av. Joan Miró, 9 (☎ 971 73 61 03). 2000-3000ptas per day with insurance. Open M-Sa 8am-1pm and 3-8pm, Su 9am-1pm and 5-8pm. **Betacar/Europcar,** Pg. Marítim, 19 (☎ 971 45 51 11), is more reliable. 4000ptas per day with insurance. Open M-Sa 9am-1pm and 4-8pm, Su 9am-noon and 6-8pm.

Scooter Rental: RTR Bike Rental, Av. Joan Miró, 340 (☎ 971 40 25 85), near Pl. Gomila. Mopeds 2150ptas per day. Open M-Sa 9am-8pm, Su 9am-1pm.

ORIENTATION AND PRACTICAL INFORMATION

To get to the town center from the airport, take bus #17 to **Plaça d'Espanya** (15min., every 20min., 295ptas). From the dock, take Pg. Marítim (a.k.a. Av. Gabriel Roca) to Av. D'Antoni Maura, which leads to **Plaça de la Reina** and Pg. Born. Pg. Born leads away from the sea to **Plaça del Rei Joan Carles I,** the bustling center of the old town. **Avinguida Rei Jaume III,** the business artery, runs to the left. To the right, Carrer de la Unió leads (after some stairs) to **Plaça Major,** the center of Palma's pedestrian shopping district.

Tourist Offices: The **Palma branch,** C. Sant Dominic, 11 (☎ 971 71 15 27; turisme@palma.es), hands out bus and train schedules, a good free map of the city, and a monthly guide in Catalan. From Pl. Reina, take C. Conquistador until it turns into C. Sant Dominic; the office is at the bottom of a stairway, a level below the street above. Open M-F 9am-8pm, Sa 9am-1:30pm. An **info booth** sits in Pl. Espanya (same hours). The **island tourist office,** Pl. Reina, 2 (☎ 971 71 22 16), offers info on the other islands, a good city map, bus and train schedules, hiking info, and lists of all sporting and cultural events on Mallorca. Open M-F 9am-1pm and 5-8pm, Sa 9am-1:30pm.

Budget Travel: TIVE, C. Jeróni Antich, 5 (☎ 971 71 17 85), off Pl. Bisbe Berenguer de Palou. ISIC cards, HI cards, Interrail tickets, and mainland flights. Not for inter-island travel and charters. Free Internet access. Open M-F 9am-2pm and 5-7:30pm.

Currency Exchange: Seek out 24hr. **ATMs** (all around the center of town) for the best rates. **Banco Central Hispano,** Pg. Born, 17 (☎ 971 72 51 46), has good rates. Open May-Sept. M-F 8:30am-2:30pm; Oct.-Apr. M-F 8:30am-2:30pm, Sa 8:30am-1pm.

American Express: Av. Antonio Maura, 40 (☎ 971 72 23 44), downtown right next to C. Apuntadors, off Pl. Reina. Open M-F 9am-1pm and 2-8pm, Sa 10am-2pm.

Luggage Storage: SFM office, Pl. Espanya. Small lockers 300ptas; big lockers 500ptas. Open M-F 7am-8pm, Sa-Su 7am-2pm.

El Corte Inglés: Av. Rei Jaume III, 15 (☎ 971 77 01 77). **Fax,** photocopies, **phones,** a free map of town, and a supermarket. Open M-Sa 10am-10pm.

English Bookstore: Book Inn, C. Horts, 20 (☎ 971 71 38 98), right off La Rambla. An impressive selection of literature. Children's books too. Open M-F 10am-1:30pm and 5-8pm, Sa 10:30am-1:30pm. Hours change in Aug.

Women's Center: Centro de Derechos Mujeres, Galeria, 4 (☎ 971 72 25 51). Rape crisis assistance available. Open M-F 9am-2pm. 24hr. hotline ☎ 900 19 10 10.

Laundromat: Lavandería Fast, Joan Miró, 5 (☎ 971 45 46 14). 1500ptas for 5kg washed and dried. **Coronet Lavandería,** corner of C. Annibal and C. Argentina. A block from Hostal Cuba. 1300ptas for 5kg. Open M-Sa 8am-1pm and 4-8pm.

Emergency: ☎ 112. **Police:** ☎ 091 or 092, on Av. Sant Ferrá.

Late-Night Pharmacy: See listings in local paper, the *Diario de Mallorca* (125ptas).

Medical Services: Clínica Juaneda, C. Son Espanyolet, 55 (☎ 971 73 16 47), and **Femenía,** Av. Camilo José Cela, 20 (☎ 971 45 23 23). **Clínica Rotger,** Santiago Russinyol, 9 (☎ 971 71 66 00), is more centrally located. All open 24hr.

Post Office: C. Constitució, 5 (☎ 902 19 71 97), 1 block off Pl. Reina. Parcels upstairs. **Lista de Correos** downstairs at window #17. **Fax** service. Open M-F 8:30am-8:30pm, Sa 9:30am-2pm. **Postal Code:** 07080.

Internet Access: La Red, C. Concepció, 5 (☎ 971 71 35 74; www.laredcafe.com), next to the intersection with Av. San Martí. 500ptas per 30min. Drinks served. Open M-F 3pm-1am, Sa 4pm-2am, Su 4-11pm. **Cyber Central,** C. Soletat, 4 (☎ 971 71 29 27), in Pl. Reina. 1000ptas per hr.. Open M-Sa 9am-10pm, Su noon-8pm.

▐ ACCOMMODATIONS

Accommodations vary from beds-stuffed-in-a-closet to mini-villas; unfortunately, there are more of the former. Call in advance for any summer stay.

Hostal Cuba, C. San Magí, 1 (☎ 971 73 81 59), at C. Argentina, on the edge of the town center. From the port, go left along Av. Gabriel Roca and turn right onto C. Argentina. Look for the "Restaurant Cuba" sign. Rooms are the best Palma has to offer. Singles 2000ptas; doubles with bath 4000ptas; triples 5500ptas.

Hostal Bonany, C. Almirante Cervera, 5 (☎ 971 73 79 24), in a wealthy residential area 3km from the town center. Take bus #3, 20, 21, or 22 from Pl. Espanya to Av. Joan Miró and walk up C. Camilio José Cela. Take the 1st right, then the 1st left. Spacious doubles with bath and balcony overlook a small pool and patio. Smaller, hotter singles are more hit or miss. Light breakfast included. Singles 3600ptas; doubles 5800ptas.

Hostal Apuntadores, C. Apuntadores, 8 (☎ 971 71 34 91), less than a block from Pl. Reina. Rooms are uninspiring but clean; bathrooms could be more so. Great rooftop lounge and downstairs bar (happy hour 6:30-8:30pm). Breakfast available. Dorms 1800ptas per person; singles 2700ptas; doubles 4500ptas, with shower 4800ptas.

Alberg Platja de Palma (HI), C. Costa Brava, 13 (☎ 971 26 08 92), in the beach town El Arenal. Take bus #15 from Pl. Espanya (every 8min., 175ptas), and ask to get off at Hotel Acapulco. Lounge with big-screen TV. 4-person dorms, each with shower and balcony. HI card required. Breakfast included. Sheets 200ptas. Laundry service 1000ptas. Reception daily 8am-3am. Curfew Su-Th midnight, F-Sa 3am. 1700ptas per person.

Hostal Monleon, La Rambla, 3 (☎ 971 71 53 17). An old, vaguely spooky building with tall ceilings and big windows. Dimly lit, noisy rooms, but cheap for the area. Downstairs bar. Singles 2400ptas, with bath 3000ptas; doubles 4300ptas, with bath 5300ptas.

Camping: Platja Blava (☎ 971 53 78 63; fax 971 53 75 11), 8km out on the highway between Alcúdia and C'an Picafort. Take Autocares Mallorca from Pl. Espanya (2 per day 9am-7:30pm, 575ptas). 600ptas per person, 6-by-6 meter plot 1300-3000ptas.

⚫ FOOD

Palma's restaurants are paradise for the *tapas*-sick. Menus come in German, French, Swedish, Hittite, English, Spanish, and *mallorquín*, although the best international food is a blow to any budget. Mom-and-Pop operations serve tourists and locals along side streets, especially around **Passeig des Born,** and carbon-copy pizzerias and cafes crowd **Paseo Marítimo.** Make sure to try the *ensaimadas* (pastries smothered in powdered sugar) and the *sopas mallorquinas* (stewed vegetables over brown bread). Two **markets** vie for customers. One is in Pl. Olivar off C. Padre Atanasio; the other is across town at the corner of C. Pou and C. Dameto. For **groceries,** try **Servicio y Precios** on C. Felip Bauzà, near C. Apuntadores and Pl. Reina (open M-F 8:30am-8:30pm, Sa 9am-2pm).

Merendero Minyones, C. Minyones, 4, a teeny booth on a small street 1 block from C. Constitució. From Pg. Born, walk up C. Constitució, take your 1st left, and then the 1st right. As cheap as they come. Takeout only—they'll wrap up sandwiches (160-200ptas) for the beach. Open M-F 7:30am-7:30pm, Sa 8am-2pm.

Na Bauçano, Sta. Bárbara, 4 (☎ 971 72 18 86), off C. Brossa between Pl. Mercat and Pl. Cort. Global vegetarian cuisine with fresh, local ingredients. Popular with the foreign crowd. Try the homemade organic breads with curried vegetables and delicious soups. Afternoon *menú* 1450ptas. Open M-Sa 1-4pm.

Shogun, C. Camilo José Cela, 14. (☎ 971 735 748), right off Av. Joan Miró. Choose from a picture-filled menu of sushi (300-625ptas), fried noodles, soups, and huge meat and tempura combos (1200ptas). Food is a bit pricey but will leave you ready to brandish your sword. Open M-Sa 1-3:30pm and 8-11:30pm.

👁 SIGHTS

Palma's architecture is a medley of Arabic, Christian, and Modernist styles, a reflection of the island's multicultural past and present. Many of its landmarks are nestled amidst the narrow streets of the Barri Gòtic (medieval quarter).

▨ **CATEDRAL O LA SEA.** One of the world's largest cathedrals, this Gothic giant towers over Palma and its bay. The cathedral, dedicated to Palma's patron saint San Sebastián, was begun in the 1300s, finished in 1601, and then modified by Gaudí in Modernist fashion in 1909. Now the interior and the ceiling ornamentation blend smoothly with the stately exterior. *(Off Pl. Reina. ☎ 971 72 31 33. Cathedral and museum open Apr.-Oct. M-F 10am-6pm, Sa 10am-2pm; Nov.-Mar. M-F 10am-3pm. 500ptas.)*

▨ **PALAU DEL'ALMUDAINA.** Built by the Moors, this palace was later controlled by *Los Reyes Católicos,* Fernando and Isabel. Guided tours, which pass through the museum, are given in numerous languages, except when the king is here on business. *(Just off Pl. Reina. ☎ 971 72 71 45. Open M-F 10am-6:30pm, Sa 10am-2pm. 400ptas, students 225ptas. W EU members free.)*

COLLECCIÓ MARCH, MUSEO D'ART ESPANYOL CONTEMPORANI. The Collecció March houses one work each by a handful of different 20th-century Spanish artists, including Picasso, Dalí, Miró, Juan Gris, and Antoni Tàpies. *(C. Sant Miquel, 11. ☎ 971 71 35 15. Open M-F 10am-6:30pm, Sa 10am-1:30pm. 300ptas.)*

CASTELL DEL BELLVER. Overlooking the city and bay and set in a circular courtyard, Castell de Bellver served as a summer residence for 14th-century royalty. For centuries thereafter it housed Mallorca's most distinguished prisoners. The castle contains a municipal museum with several paintings and archaeological displays. *(Bus #3, 21, or 22 from Pl. Espanya. ☎ 971 73 06 57. Castle and museum open daily Apr.-Sept. 8am-8:20pm; Oct.-Mar. 8am-7:15pm. 265ptas, students 130ptas. Su free, but museum closed.)*

POBLE ESPANYOL. This Spanish village, filled with samples of Spanish architecture, is a replica of one in Barcelona. *(C. Poble Espanyol, 39. Buses #4 and 5 pass on C. Andrea Doria. ☎ 971 73 70 75. Open daily 9am-8pm; Dec.-Mar. 9am-6pm. 800ptas.)*

OTHER MUSEUMS. Palma is filled with museums. Inaugurated in December 1992, **Fundació Pilar i Joan Miró** displays the works found in Miró's Palma studio at the time of his death. *(C. Saridakis, 29. From Pl. Espanya, take buses #3, 21, and 22 to C. Joan Miró. ☎ 971 70 14 20. Open May 16-Sept. 14 Tu-Sa 10am-7pm, Su 10am-3pm; Sept. 15-May 15 Tu-Sa 10am-6pm, Su 10am-3pm. 675ptas.).* **Fundació "la Caixa"** hosts a permanent collection of paintings as well as other special exhibits in Domènech's Modernist Gran Hotel. *(Pl. Weyler, 3. ☎ 971 72 01 11. Open Tu-Sa 10am-9pm, Su 10am-2pm. Free.)* The **Casal Solleric** opens modern art exhibits to the public. *(Pg. Born, 27. Open Tu-Sa 10:30am-1:45pm, Su 10am-1:45pm. Free.)* **Centre de Cultura "Sa Nostra"** features rotating contemporary exhibits and sponsors cultural events such as lectures, concerts, and movies. *(C. Concepción, 12. ☎ 971 72 52 10. Open M-F 10:30am-9pm, Sa 10am-1:30pm.)* **Museu de Mallorca** is ideal for travelers interested in archaeology, medieval painting, or Moorish architecture. *(Cala Gran Christian. Open Apr.-Sept. Tu-Sa 10am-2pm and 5-8pm; Oct.-Mar. Tu-Sa 10am-1pm and 4-8pm, Su 10am-2pm.)*

BEACHES. Although other parts of Mallorca have better beaches, decent ones (complete with sand and snacks) are a mere bus ride from Palma. The huge beach at **El Arenal** *(Platja de Palma, bus #15)*, 11km to the southeast (toward the airport), is expansive and well-sanded but tends to be over-touristed. **Aquacity** *(☎ 971 44 00 00)*, a huge water park, resides next door. **Palma Nova** *(bus #21)*, 15km southwest, and **Illetes** *(bus #3)*, 9km southwest, are equally crowded. The tourist office distributes a list of over 40 nearby beaches—take your pick.

🎵🎭 NIGHTLIFE AND ENTERTAINMENT

Nightlife and entertainment *à la Mallorca* have a native Spanish flavor often missing in the other isles, but they are still well documented for visitors. The municipal tourist office keeps a comprehensive list of sporting activities, concerts, and exhibits. Every Friday, *El Día de Mundo* (125ptas) publishes an entertainment supplement with listings of bars and discos all over Mallorca, and *La Calle* offers a monthly review of Palma's hotspots.

The streets around Plaça Reina and La Llotja flow with bar-hoppers. **ABACO,** C. Sant Joan, 1, in the Barri Gòtic near the waterfront, may be the most perfect place on Earth for a cocktail. Sip drinks in the midst of a dreamy 19th-century courtyard, complete with elegant wicker and marble furniture, cooing doves, classical music, and a wide array of fresh fruit, flowers, and dripping candles. *(☎ 971 71 49 39. Fruit shakes 1100ptas. Cocktails 2200ptas. Open daily 9pm-12:30am.)*

You can't help but dance to the Cuban rhythms at **La Bodeguita del Medio,** C. Vallseca, 18, featuring Hemingway's favorite: *mojito* (500ptas), a drink with seltzer water, sugar, lemon juice, rum, and *hierbabuena*. The walls are covered with signatures of past visitors. *(☎ 971 71 49 39. Open Su-Th 9pm-3:30am, F-Sa 9pm-4am).* Follow the Aussie voices down C. Apuntadores to the popular **Bar Latitude 39,** C. Felip Bauza, 8. *(☎ 971 72 02 65. Beers 200ptas. Mixed drinks 500ptas. "Twofer nights"—two for the price of one—Tu and Th 9-10pm. Open M-Sa 7pm-3am.)* **Barcelona,** C. Apuntadores, 5, jams with live music nightly from midnight to 3am. *(☎ 971 71 35 57. Jazz M, Tu, and Th, salsa W. Open daily 11pm-4am).* Other nightlife spots include **Blues Ville,** Má Del Moro, 3 (from Pl. Reina, take a right off C. Apuntadores) and **La Longja Agua Bar,** C. Jaime Ferrer, 6 *(☎ 929 63 96 32).*

Palma's clubbers start their night in the *bares-musicales* lining the **Paseo Marítimo** strip. Though each mini-disco boasts different tunes, come 2am Spanish pop dominates. Some of the best places include **Mira Blau, Café Thalassa, Made in Brazil,** and **Aqua** (drinks all around 1000ptas). Other partiers head to the beaches and the nightclubs near **El Terreno**—a mother-load of clubs are centered on Pl. Gomilia and along C. Joan Miró. The bars and clubs around **El Arenal** are German-owned, German-filled, and German-centric. **Tito's Palace,** Paseo Marítimo, is Palma's hippest disco, with two floors of hard house in an indoor colosseum of mirrors and lights overlooking the water. (☎ 971 73 00 17. Cover 2000ptas. Open daily 11am-6am). **Plato,** across the street at Pl. Gomilia, 2, keeps a lower, more local profile. **Sa Finestra,** Av. Joan Miró, 90, features live music every night after 11:30pm. **Sombrero,** on Av. Joan Miró, 26 (☎ 971 73 16 00), is a lively gay bar, and the **Baccus,** around the corner on C. Lluis Fábregas, 2, draws lesbian and gay hedonists (open until 3am). Word is that **Pachá,** Av. Gabriel Roca, will found its own island by the year 2001; for now its owners will have to make do with a huge club. (Cover 2000-3000ptas and up; try for free tickets at bars in town. Open daily midnight-6am.)

Mallorcans use any and every occasion as an excuse to party. One of the more colorful bashes, **Día de Sant Joan** (June 24), brings singing, dancing, and drinking to Parc del Mar. The celebration begins with a fireworks display the night before.

WESTERN MALLORCA

The west coast of Mallorca is home to one of the most beautiful landscapes in the Mediterranean. It has attracted and inspired a range of creative minds, from Chopin and George Sand to Robert Graves and Michael Douglas. Ten minutes beyond the modern road and ever-spreading white highrises of Palma, the road enters a deep ravine (the island's first cave dwellers sheltered here) and begins to rise in tight, narrow curves. Taking the north road beyond Valldemossa, you find yourself traveling through olive groves pitching steeply toward the sea. Beyond is the northwestern cape of the island—wild, arid, volcanic, and totally uninhabited.

VALLDEMOSSA

Valldemossa's storybook colonial houses huddle against each other along cobblestone streets in the verdant slopes of the Sierra de Tramontana. Little in this tranquil village hints at the passion that shocked the townsfolk in the winter of 1838-39, when Frédèric Chopin and George Sand (her two children in tow) stayed in the picturesque and floral monastery called **Cartoixa Reial.** Chopin memorabilia includes the piano which he had to carry up the mountain in several pieces. Short piano recitals attempt to recapture the magic in the summer. (☎ 971 61 21 06. Recitals every hr. Open M-Sa 9:30am-6pm, Su 10am-1pm. 1300ptas, including visits to the Museu Municipal and the **Palau del Rei Sancho,** where folk dances take place M and Th 11-1:30pm.) **Hostal Ca'n Mario,** C. Vetam, 8, has rooms with showers and great views of town. (☎ 971 61 21 22; fax 971 61 60 29. Breakfast included. Singles 4000ptas; doubles 6600ptas. V, MC.) Several cafe-bars around the main square serve simple, cheap fare. The town goes to bed early, so don't expect much nightlife—enjoy the peace and quiet instead. **Nord Balear buses** (☎ 971 49 06 80) to **Valldemossa** leave Palma at C. Arxiduc Salvador, 1 (30min., 5 per day, 200ptas).

SÓLLER

Thirty kilometers up the coast from Valldemossa, cobblestoned Sóller basks in a valley that widens to a golden port. Every available plot of land is lined with either citrus groves or sunburned tourists. In August, the Ajuntament hosts an international **Festival of Folk Dancing,** with dancers from all over Europe and Asia. The old-fashioned Palma-Sóller **train,** run by Ferrocarril de Sóller, C. Castanyer, 7 (☎ 971 63 03 01, Palma ☎ 971 75 20 51), is a highlight in itself. Brave hearts ride between cars through olive orchards and scary tunnels (5 per day, 735ptas). Sóller's **tourist office,** Pl. Constitució, 1, has accommodation listings and maps, and the staff can suggest good hikes. (☎ 971 63 02 00. Open M-Sa 9:30am-1:30pm; info posted in front of the church near the entrance if the office is closed.) If you get hungry, try the *coca mallorquina,* a cold pizza-like snack (about 250ptas) in local bakeries.

PUERTO DE SÓLLER

From Sóller it is a pleasant half-hour walk (or a short ride on the Nord Balear bus) down the valley to Puerto de Sóller, which absorbs a large number of tourists. Trolleys also connect the two (every 30min., 115ptas). In Puerto de Sóller, a pebble-and-sand beach lines the small bay, where windsurfers zip back and forth. Numerous hotels lie on C. Marina along the water. **Hotel Miramar**, C. Marina, 12, provides spotless rooms and full baths. (☎ 971 63 13 50. Singles 4360ptas; doubles 5470ptas; triples 8060ptas.) Two **grocery stores** are located on C. Jaume Torrens, and numerous **restaurants** line the beach. **Restaurante Balear**, Santa Caterina d'Alexandria, 14, a few feet off the fork with C. Marina, is a budget godsend with its cheap *paella* (1275ptas) and *menú* for 950ptas. (Open Th-Tu 12:30-3:30pm and 7:30-10pm. Closed Jan.-Feb.) Exploring the rest of the coves on the coast is easiest by **boat. Tramontana** and **Barcos Azules**, on the port near the last trolley stop, sail to **Sa Calobra**, most people's final destination (May-Oct. 15, 3-5 per day, round-trip 1900ptas), and **Cala Deià** (June-Oct. 15, round-trip 1200ptas). Nord Balear **buses** link Puerto de Sóller to **Palma** (2hr., 5 per day, 450ptas), via **Valldemossa.**

SA CALOBRA

Much like an asphalt serpent, the road to Sa Calobra drops 1000m to the sea, writhing back underneath itself over 10 nail-biting kilometers. The boat from Puerto de Sóller is easier on the nerves (see above). **Torrent de Pareis**, toward the bottom of the road, is a popular photo opportunity (look for a landing packed with camera-toting tourists). Sa Calobra itself is a smooth pebble beach, bordered by ominous cliffs and the crystalline sea. Unfortunately, despite its beauty, the cove is quite infested with tourists, restaurants, and gift shops.

MONESTIR DE LLUC

Tucked away quietly in the mountains, the Monestir de Lluc is an inland enigma. Though there is little here of interest to the secular traveler, the monastery is perpetually filled with religious tourists and pilgrims. Twenty kilometers from the coast in Escorca, Lluc is the home of the 700-year-old wood-carved *La verge de Lluc (The Virgin of Lluc)*. Behind the monastery, the **Vía Crucis** winds around a hill over the valley's olive trees and jingling goats. Gaudí designed the path's Stations of the Cross. Monks, pilgrims, and a few guests stay at Lluc's **monastery.** (☎ 971 51 70 25. True pilgrims stay for a donation—others pay 3850ptas for doubles with bath; quads with bath 4350ptas.) The monastery's store sells groceries, and its restaurant-bar offers expensive food and drink. To reach the monastery, take **Autocares Alorda** direct from Palma (1hr.; M-Sa 2 per day, Su 1 per day; 555ptas); it is also possible to get there from Port Pollença, Alcúdia, Inca, or Sa Calobra.

NORTHERN MALLORCA

Known for their long beaches and fine sand, the northern gulfs of Mallorca have are popular among the older, package-tour crowd. The drive can be stunning, but those searching for secluded coves are best off exploring other parts of the island.

PUERTO DE ALCÚDIA

Puerto de Alcúdia is far from undiscovered. The hard-packed beaches stretching along the shallow-watered bay are packed with hotels, bars, and pizzerias outnumbering the boats in the marina. If you're looking for more than just another beach, visit Alcúdia's old Roman town with **14th-century ramparts, Roman remains** dating from 2 BC, and two sets of town walls from medieval times, when the town was constantly being conquered, destroyed, and rebuilt. (15min. walk; buses depart every 15min. from C. dels Mariners.) **Museu Pollentia** documents archaeological discoveries on Mallorca. (☎ 971 54 70 04. Open M-F 10am-2pm and 5-7pm, Sa-Su 10:30am-1pm. 200ptas.) **Parc Natural de L'Albufera** is one of the North's treasures, filled with marshes, flowers and pine-covered dunes. (Open daily 10am-7pm, in winter until 5pm. Free.) For active explorers, the tourist office hands out a brochure of 10 possible hiking and biking excursions in the area. One trek includes a trip through the mountains to the 16th-century La Victoria church. For mindless fun, use the **go-carts** and **trampolines** in the port, or head to **Hidropark** (☎ 971 89 16 72), a water park accessible by bus every 15 minutes from C. Mariners. For a **taxi**, call ☎ 971 54 98 70. **Vanrell Bicicletas**, Av. Reina Sofía, rents **bikes**. The multilingual **tourist office**, at the intersection of Av. Pere Mas Reus and Ctra. Arta, has maps. (☎ 971 89 26 15. Open May-Oct. M-Sa 9:30am-7pm.) Reach **police** at ☎ 971 54 50 78. **Buses** (☎ 971 54 56 96) leave for Alcúdia (570ptas) and Puerto de Alcúdia (590ptas) from Pl. Espanya in Palma (1hr.; M-Sa 17 per day, Su 5 per day). The bus to Port Pollença and Cap de Formentor leaves from C. dels Mariners.

   Hostal Puerto, C. Teodoro Canet, 29, on the road that leads up to Alcúdia, offers hotel-quality rooms with private baths. (☎ 971 54 54 47. Doubles with shower 3800ptas, with bath 4000ptas. Open May-Oct.). **Alberg Victoria (HI)**, Ctra. Cap Pinar, 4, lies 100m from an empty beach on the Bahía de Pollença. From the town center, signs lead east 4km to the hostel (1hr. walk or 1100pta taxi ride). Reserve at least six months in advance for July or August. (☎ 971 54 53 95. Members only. 2000ptas, with breakfast 2300ptas.)

PORT POLLENÇA (PUERTO POLLENSA)

Port Pollença features a stretch of sand which is slightly whiter, finer, and less crowded than its neighbors. It is particularly popular among Brits, which explains the number of pubs and English-named establishments in town. The area hosts a **Music Festival** from July to September. A complete schedule of events and list of ticket vendors are available at the **tourist office** (tickets 1000-5000ptas). **Rent March**, C. Joan XXIII, 89, rents bikes and mopeds (☎ 971 86 47 84. Open Apr.-Oct. M-Sa 9am-1pm and 3-8pm, Su 9am-1pm and 6-7:30pm. Bikes 600ptas per day. Mopeds 2500ptas per day). The helpful tourist office, C. Formentor, 31, across from Hotel Daina, can help plan excursions. (☎ 971 86 54 67; fundaciobocchoris@oninet.es. Open May-Oct. M-F 9am-1pm and 4-7pm, Sa 9am-1pm). Autocares Mallorca **buses** connect Alcúdia and Pollença (every 15min.).

CAP DE FORMENTOR

The end of Cap de Formentor, 15km northeast of Port Pollença, boasts views from spectacular seaside cliffs. Before the final twisting kilometer, the road drops to **Platja Formentor,** where a canopy of evergreens seems to sink into the water. These beaches are the best on the northern coast. **Autocares Villalonga,** San Isidro, 4 (☎ 971 53 00 57), sends **buses** from Palma (5 per day, 595ptas). **Autocares Mallorca** buses (☎ 971 5456 96) also leave from Port Pollença and Puerto de Alcúdia (every 30min.). Buses will drop you off at a narrow road 6km away from the stunning end of Cap de Formentor, where a lighthouse and a postcard-worthy view await. There's also a **boat** to **Formentor** from Port Pollença's Estació Marítima (6 per day; round-trip 825ptas to Platja Formentor, 1600ptas to Cabo Formentor).

SOUTHEAST MALLORCA

The signs along the highway of Mallorca's southeast coast might as well read "Welcome tourist hordes," as much of the area has been built up by major investors. On the coast, east of Cap de Salinas, Mallorca's southernmost point, scalloped fringes of bays and caves are the developers' most recent discovery. To their credit, builders have aspired to some architectural integrity.

◪ **CUEVAS DRACH.** The Cuevas Drach, near Porto Cristo, are among the most dramatic natural wonders in Mallorca's southeast, with their drooping, finger-like red and pink rock formations. A 30-minute walk into the depths of the cave, classical musicians give performances from illuminated rowboats on an underground lake; audience members can take free rides on the lake at concert's end. (*A bus runs from Palma to the caves, leaving from the corner of Costa i Llobera and Carrer Miquel Marques in Pl. Espanya. M-Sa 4 per day, last at 1:30pm, 1100ptas.*)

TRENC. West of Cap de Salinas and east of Cap Blanc sprawls one of Mallorca's best beaches, Trenc. To get to Trenc, take a **Dar Bus** from Palma's Pl. Espanya to Es Trenc. In most cases, a 1-2km walk is usually enough to put plenty of sand between you and the thickest crowds.

MENORCA

Menorca's (pop. 69,000) raw beaches, rustic landscape, and well-preserved ancient monuments draw ecologists, sun worshippers, and photographers alike. In 1993, UNESCO declared the entire island a biosphere reserve; since then, administrators have put great effort into preserving Menorca's natural harbors, pristine southern beaches, rocky northern coast, and latticed network of farmlands. The act has also encouraged protection, excavation, and study of Menorca's stone burial chambers and homestead complexes, remnants of a mysterious Talayotic stone-age culture dating from 1400 BC. Since its incorporation into the Catalan kingdom in 1287, Menorca has endured a succession of foreign invaders—Arab, Turkish, French, and British. After occupying the island several times during the 18th century, the Brits have returned to dominance as tourists, children and German neighbors in tow. Menorca has fewer tourists than the other Balearics, but it can be hard for the budget traveler to afford; it is mostly wealthy young families who have made the island their exclusive playpen. Menorca's main cities, Mahón and Ciutadella, serve as gateways to the island's real attractions.

MAHÓN (MAÓ)

Perched atop a steep bluff, Mahón's (pop. 23,300) white-splashed houses overlook a well-trafficked harbor. The British occupied the city for most of the 18th century, leaving Georgian doors, brass knockers, and wooden shutters in their wake. Gin distilleries, pubs, and British accents testify to a continuing British influence, as visitors here to spend money almost as old as the island. Those in search of a raging nightlife are better off on Ibiza; Mahón's residents value an early bedtime.

▐ TRANSPORTATION

Airplanes: Airport (☎ 971 15 70 00), 7km out of town (see **Orientation,** above.) Main office open daily 7:15am-midnight. **Iberia/Aviaco** (☎ 971 36 90 15); **Air Europa** (☎ 971 24 00 42 or 971 15 70 31); **SpanAir** (☎ 971 15 70 98). In summer advance booking is essential. See **By Plane,** p. 470, or **Getting Around,** p. 471.

Ferries: Estació Marítima, on Moll Andén de Ponent. Open M-F 8am-1pm and 5-7pm, Sa 8am-noon, Su 8am-noon and 3-4:30pm. **Trasmediterránea** (☎ 971 36 29 50). For fares and routes, see **By Boat,** p. 470, or **Getting Around,** p. 471.

Buses: Check the tourist office or the newspapers *Menorca Diario Insular* (125ptas) and *Menorca* for schedules. **Transportes Menorca (TMSA),** C. José M. Quadrado, 7 (☎ 971 36 03 61), off Pl. s'Esplanada. To: **Es Castell** (every 30min., 125ptas); **Alaior** (6 per day, 150ptas); **Platja Punta Prima** (9 per day on the hour starting at 8:30am, 225ptas); **Son Bou** (7 per day, 250ptas); **Es Mercadal** (6 per day, 250ptas); **Ferreries** (4 per day, 300ptas); and **Ciutadella** (55min., 6 per day, 550ptas). Some depart from Pl. s'Esplanada, some from nearby C. Quadrado; check signs at the bus stop. Buy tickets at the TMSA office, except for Punta Prima and Castell, which you buy on the bus. **Autobuses Fornells Roca Triay** (☎ 971 37 66 21) has buses that depart from C. Vassallo, off Pl. s'Esplanada. To: **Fornells** (3 per day); **Arenal d'en Castell** (3 per day); **Son Parc** (3 per day); and **Es Grau** (5 per day). Buy tickets on the buses.

Taxis: Main stop at Pl. s'Esplanada (☎ 971 36 12 83), or **Radio Taxi** from anywhere on the island (☎ 971 36 71 11). Flat rates for all routes. To: **Es Castell** (800ptas); the **airport** (1300ptas); **Cala Mesquida** (1300ptas); and **Cala'n Porter** (1865ptas).

BALEARIC ISLANDS

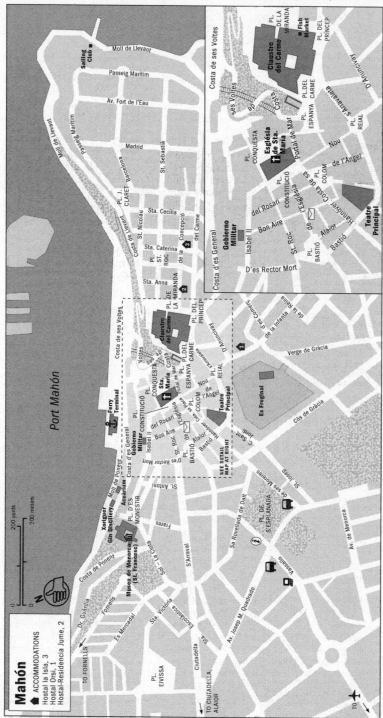

Mahón

■ ACCOMMODATIONS
Hostal la Isla, 3
Hostal Orsi, 1
Hostal-Residencia Jume, 2

Car Rental: English-speaking car rental at British **Jan Cars** (☎ 971 35 13 21, 24hr. ☎ 971 37 71 57), Pl. s'Esplanada. 4500ptas per day, 13,000ptas for 3 days. Tourist office has a list of all rental places on Menorca.

Bike and Scooter Rental: Motos Menorca, Anden de Levante, 35-36 (☎ 971 35 47 86), Puerto de Mahón. Bikes 1500ptas per day. Motorcycles 3500ptas per day. Deposit required. **Velo Rent Bike,** S'Arraval, 52 (☎ 971 353 798) rents bikes for 1350ptas for 1 day, 3700ptas for 3 days.

✴❷ ORIENTATION AND PRACTICAL INFORMATION

It is necessary to take a taxi (1300ptas) between the **airport** and downtown Mahón. To get to the heart of the city from the **ferry station,** walk to the left (with your back to the water) about 150m, then turn right at the steps that cut through the serpentine **Costa de ses Voltes.** The steps end between Pl. Conquesta and Pl. Espanya. To reach **Plaça de s'Esplanada,** the town center, from here, take Portal de Mar to Costa de Sa, which becomes C. Hanover and then C. Ses Moreres, and continue straight ahead to the plaça. To reach **Plaça de la Miranda,** walk through Pl. Espanya and Pl. Carme; when you reach Pl. Princep, turn left, and Pl. Miranda is about 100m ahead.

Tourist Office: Pl. s'Esplanada, 40 (☎ 971 36 37 90; fax 971 36 74 15; www.menorca.com), across the plaza from the taxi stand. Bus schedules and a fabulous free map. English spoken. Open M-F 8:30am-7:30pm, Sa 9am-2pm. Summer office at the airport (☎ 971 15 71 15) provides similar materials. Open daily Mar.-Oct. 8:30am-10:30pm. Free guided tours of Mahón leave from the town hall in Pl. Constitució every Th and F at 7pm.

American Express: Viajes Iberia, C. Nou, 35 (☎ 971 36 28 48), 2 doors from Pl. Reial. No commission on traveler's checks. Cardholder mail held. Open M-F 10am-2pm and 5-8pm, Sa 9:30am-1pm.

Currency Exchange: Banks with 24hr. **ATMs** line C. Hanover and C. Nou.

Emergency: ☎ 112. **Police: Municipal** (☎ 971 36 39 61), in Pl. Constitució.

Medical Assistance: Hospital Verge del Toro, C. Barcelona, 3 (☎ 971 15 77 00; emergency ☎ 971 36 77 26), near Pg. Marítim. English spoken. **Ambulance:** ☎ 061.

Post Office: C. Bonaire, 11-13 (☎ 971 36 38 92), at C. Església. From Pl. s'Esplanada, take C. Moreres until it turns into C. Hanover, then take the first left. Open M-F 8:30am-8:30pm, Sa 9:30am-2pm. **Postal Code:** 07703.

Internet Access: Bar & Café Telegraph, C. Sant Esteve, 8 (☎ 971 36 14 00), in Hotel Capri. From Pl. s'Esplanada, take C. Josep Maria Quadrado. 100ptas for 5min.

▰ ACCOMMODATIONS

Space is a problem only in August, but call a few days in advance. The tourist office keeps a complete listing. Prices listed below are for high season.

Hostal La Isla, C. Santa Catalina, 4 (☎ 971 36 64 92). Take C. Concepció from Pl. Miranda. Family-run hostel offers clean rooms and friendly service. All rooms with private bath and powerful, hot water pressure, but little ventilation. The restaurant downstairs (see **Food,** below) has a cheap, typical *menú*. Breakfast 300ptas, included with doubles. Singles 2200ptas; doubles 5200ptas. Visa.

Hostal Orsi, C. Infanta, 19 (☎ 971 36 47 51). From Pl. s'Esplanada, take C. Moreres as it becomes C. Hanover. Turn right at Pl. Constitució and follow C. Nou through Pl. Reial; Orsi is on the left. Super nice owners and clean, sunlit rooms. Breakfast included. Rooftop terrace has a great view. Laundry 1000ptas. Singles 2500ptas; doubles 4400ptas, with shower 5000ptas (IVA not included). V, MC.

Hostal-Residencia Jume, C. Concepció, 6 (☎ 971 36 32 66; fax 971 36 48 78), off Pl. Miranda. TV room downstairs, restaurant, and pool table. Nondescript rooms in tip-top shape, all with full baths. Ask for a room overlooking the street rather than the steamy indoor patio. Breakfast included. 2800ptas per person.

◖ FOOD

Bar-cafes around Pl. Constitució, Reial, and s'Esplanada serve filling *platos combinados* (450-850ptas) to sidewalks full of hungry customers. The myriad restaurants on the port offer scenic views and eye-sore prices. *Mahón-esa* (mayonnaise) was invented here and local chefs won't let you forget it. Regional specialties include *sobrasada* (soft chorizo spread), *crespells* (biscuits), and *rubiols* (turnovers filled with fish or vegetables). There is a fresh fruit and vegetable **market** in the cloister of the church in Pl. Espanya (open M-Sa 9am-2pm). **Groceries** are sold at **Miny Prix,** C. J.A. Clavé and Av. Menorca (open M-Sa 8am-2pm and 5-8:30pm). **Restaurante La Sirena,** Anden de Levante, 199, is considered by many the best restaurant in Mahón. German chefs prepare nutritionally balanced, delicious international cuisine for 900-1800ptas. (☎ 971 35 07 40. Open daily noon-3pm and 8pm-midnight.) **Llevant Restaurante Griego,** Moll de Llevant, 302, has excellent Greek meat and cheese dishes (955-1550ptas) and classic filo dough and honey desserts. (☎ 971 36 16 05. Open daily 1-4pm and 7:30pm-12am.)

◖ SIGHTS

The most awe-inspiring sights in Menorca lie outside of its cities, although Mahón does have a few attractions of its own. The **Museo de Menorca,** Av. Dr. Guàrdia, an old Franciscan monastery closed in 1835, displays excavated items and exhibits on Menorcan history dating back to Talayotic times. (☎ 971 35 09 55. Open Tu-Sa 10am-2pm and 5-8pm, Su 10am-2pm. 300ptas.) Founded in 1287 and rebuilt in 1772, the **Església de Santa María La Major** trembles from the 51 stops, four keyboards, and 3210 pipes of its disproportionately large organ, built by the Swiss Juan Kilburz in 1810. Mahón's **festival de música** in July and August showcases the immense instrument. (Pl. Constitució. Festival concerts M-Sa 11am. Seat "donation" 500ptas.) The **Arc de Sant Roc,** up C. Sant Roc from Pl. Constitució, the last fragment of the medieval wall built to defend the city from marauding Catalan pirates, straddles the streets of Mahón. Free liquor samples (15 brews) are available at the **Xoriguer Gin Distillery** on the port. Behind the store, visitors watch their drinks bubble and froth in large copper vats. (Open M-F 8am-7pm, Sa 9am-1pm.)

◖ NIGHTLIFE AND ENTERTAINMENT

Mahón is not known for its nightlife. Weekdays are quiet except in August, and dancing rarely picks up until 1 or 2am on weekends. A string of *bares-musicales* line the **Costa d'els Generals,** near the water. The most fashionable place on the strip is probably **Akelarre,** a dimly lit warehouse-turned-two-floor-bar. A mixed straight and gay crowd fills the dance floors upstairs. (☎ 971 36 85 20. Open daily June-Oct. 7:30pm-4am; Nov.-May 7pm-4am. Live music W-Th 11pm-2am). A few doors down, sultry hips shake at the oval-shaped **Salsa,** Anden de Poniente, 29. (Open daily 10pm-4am.) If dancing is not your thing, sip a *pomada* (Menorcan favorite combining gin and lemon) at the gold and shiny **Café Baixamar,** Moll de Ponent, 17. (☎ 971 36 58 96. Open daily 8am-3am.) Away from the port, **Discoteca Sí,** C. Virgen de Gràcia, 16, turns on the strobe only after midnight, while **Nou Bar,** C. Nou, 1, 2nd fl., serves drinks to a calm, older crowd, including Guinness on tap (600ptas per pint, 275ptas for other beers. Open daily noon-3pm and 7:30pm-3am).

From May to September, merchants sell shoes, clothes, and souvenirs in **mercadillos** held daily in various town squares (Tu and Sa Mahón; F and Sa Ciutadella; Th Alaior; Su Mercadal; Tu and F Ferrerias; M and W Es Castell). On July 16, Mahón's **Verge del Carme** celebration brings a colorfully trimmed armada into the harbor.

NEAR MAHÓN

■ **CAP DE FAVÀRTIX.** Almost eerily tranquil, the edge of this gray slate coast feels like the end of the earth. *(From Mahón, take a moped or car in the direction of Es Gran/Fornells, turn off the highway at Favàrtix (9km), pass through farmlands and lush greenery, then break off to the right from the bushy-edged roadway through an open gate. Enter the black rock cove and view the lighthouse there.)*

■ **PLATGES DE SON BOU.** This area is a gorgeous, 3km long string of beaches on the southern shore, complete with crystal waters and a blanket of tourists covering its soft, fine sand. There is a 5th-century Paleo-Christian **basilica** in the nearby tourist settlement of Son Bou, as well as a supermarket, water slides, and more. *(Transportes Menorca buses leave from Mahón to the beaches; 6 per day, 8:45am-7pm.)*

ARENAL D'EN CASTELL. This sandy, touristy ring around calm water lies on Menorca's northern shore, hidden behind a thin barrier of pine trees and coastal ravines. *(Autocares Fornells buses leave from C. Vasallo in Mahón; 6 per day, 10:30am-7pm.)*

CALAEN PORTER. Expansive and extremely touristy, Calean Porter greets thousands of visitors each summer with its gleaming whitewashed houses, orange stucco roofs, and red sidewalks. Here the **Covas d'en Xoroi,** spooky prehistoric dwellings, are inhabited by a network of bars during the day (open 11am-9pm; cover 500ptas, includes 1 soft drink). The disco inside the cave is hugely popular. *(TMSA buses run to Mahón; 6 per day, 9:30am-7:30pm.)*

MONTE EL TORO. The island's highest peak, Monte El Toro provides fantastic views of the Menorcan landscape, including farmland gridded with stone walls, abundant greenery, and scorched red earth. *(A road from Es Mercadel connects Mt. Toro to the main Mahón-Ciutadella highway, making the peak easily accessible by car.)*

ES GRAU. The center of the biosphere, Albufera Es Grau entices visitors with lagoons, pine woods, and farmland, as well as diverse flora and fauna. Recreational activities include hiking to coves across the bay or taking a nature walk through the protected lands. **Illa d'en Colom,** a tiny island with more beaches, is just a boat ride away. *(Autocares Fornells buses leave from C. Vasallo in Mahón; 3 per day.)*

TORRALBA D'EN SALORD. This Talayotic settlement may not be the best preserved overall, but it has one of the most perfectly preserved *taulas* on the island. It is also significant because of the bronze calf found here, now in the Museum of Menorca in Mahón. *(Halfway along the road connecting Alaior and Calean Porter.)*

TORRE D'EN GAUMÉS. A sparsely labeled but stunningly expansive Talayotic settlement dating to before 1500 BC. Includes a *taula* sanctuary, a filtration/storage system, and circular dwellings. *(Off the road from Alaior to Son Bou.)*

CIUTADELLA (CIUDADELA)

Ciutadella's (pop. 21,000) blue and red townhouses sink into serpentine streets. The colorful stucco architecture above meshes with dark cobblestone below, an unlikely but successful combination. There is a seductive charm in the city's ancient streets, broad *plaças*, and winding port. Though far more tranquil than Mahón, Ciutadella is quite expensive and out of reach for those on tight budgets.

▄ TRANSPORTATION

Buses: Transportes Menorca buses leave from C. Barcelona, 8 (☎ 971 38 03 93), and go to Mahón (6 per day, 550ptas). **Autocares Torres,** Poligona Industrial c/Sastres, 3 (☎ 971 38 64 61), offers daily service to surrounding beaches for less than 200ptas. To: **Cala Blanca** (14 per day); **Sa Caleta** and **Santandria** (14 per day); **Cala Blanes, Los Delfines,** and **Cala Forcat** (18 per day); and **Cala Bosch** and **Son Xoriguer** (18 per day). Torres' ticket booth and departure point are located in Pl. s'Esplanada.

Ferries: Balear de Ferrys (☎ 902 11 91 28) runs between Ciutadella and **Alcúdia, Mallorca** (2½hr.; 5 and 8:30pm; 4000ptas, students and seniors 3400ptas). **Cape Balear** (☎ 902 10 04 44) connects Ciutadella to **Cala Ratjada** (May-Oct. 1-2 per day).

Taxis: (☎ 971 38 28 96). Pl. s'Esplanada is a prime hailing spot.

Bike Rental: Bicicletas Tolo, C. Sant Isidor, 28-34 (☎ 971 38 15 76), across the street from Hostal Oasis. Supplies and repair services. Rental 600-800ptas per day, 3300-4600ptas per week. Open M-F 8:30am-1:30pm and 3:30-8pm, Sa 8:30am-1:30pm.

✳🛈 ORIENTATION AND PRACTICAL INFORMATION

To get from the **bus station** to **Plaça de la Catedral** and the tourist office, head left half a block, take a left on Camí de Maó, go straight through Pl. d'Alfons III, and continue along C. de Maó as it turns into Quadrado (Ses Voltes) after crossing Pl. Nova. To get from Pl. Catedral to **Plaça de s'Esplanada** (also called Pl. Pins), exit the plaza on C. Major d'es Born with the cathedral behind you and to the right, cross P. Born on its right side, and bear diagonally across to the left. The **port,** and its accompanying street, C. Marina, lie below the rest of the city and can be reached via a stone stairway just off the corner of Pl. Born.

Tourist Office: Pl. Catedral, 3 (☎ 971 38 26 93; www.infotelecom.es/ciutadella). Maps, beach info, Menorca guide. Open M-F 8am-3pm and 4:30-8pm, Sa 10am-2pm.

Banks: La Caixa, C. dés Seminari, 5, and **Central Hispano,** C. Negicle, 7.

Emergency: ☎ 112. **Police: Guardia Municipal** ☎ 971 38 07 87.

Medical Emergencies: Clínica Menorca (☎ 971 48 05 05), Canonge Moll. Open 24hr. **Ambulance:** ☎ 061.

Post Office: (☎ 971 38 00 81), Pl. des Born. **Lista de Correos.** Open M-F 8:30am-2:30pm, Sa 9:30am-1pm. **Postal Code:** 07760.

Internet Access: Accesso Directo, Pl. s'Esplanada, 37 (☎ 971 48 40 26). 360ptas per 30min. Open M-Sa 9am-9pm.

▮ ACCOMMODATIONS

Hostels are packed (and pricey) during peak season (June 15 to early Sept.). Ask about discounts in the off-season.

▧ **Hotel Geminis,** C. Josepa Rossinyol, 4 (☎ 971 38 58 96; fax 971 38 36 83). Take C. Sud off Av. Capital Negrete coming from Pl. s'Esplanada and turn left onto C. Josepa Rossinyol. Almost perfect. This family-run hotel has beautiful rooms with phones, baths, fans, and TVs. Outdoor terrace has small pool. Breakfast included. Reserve early for Aug. Singles 4500ptas; doubles 8000ptas.

Hostal Residencia Oasis, C. Sant Isidre, 33 (☎ 971 38 21 97). From Pl. s'Esplanada, take Av. Capitá Negrete to Pl. d'Artrutx and then C. Sant Isidre. A centrally located floral paradise with its own greenhouse. Breakfast included. Doubles with bath 6400ptas.

Pensió Bar Ses Persianes, Pl. Artruitx, 2 (☎ 971 38 14 45), off Av. Jaume I. Bright white walls enclose smallish rooms with new furniture. Air-conditioned bar below (also hotel reception) serves breakfast. All rooms are doubles with shared bath. Reservations recommended in Aug. 3500ptas per person, 4000ptas for 2 people. Closed Oct.-Mar.

◖ FOOD

Cruise C. Quadrado for *platos combinados* and *tapas.* Sandwich bars have infiltrated Pl. s'Esplanada. Shop at **Supermercado Diskont,** C. Purísima, 6 (☎ 971 38 32 68. Open M-Sa 8:30am-2pm and 4-9pm), or at the **market** on Pl. Llibertat.

La Guitarra, C. Dolores, 1 (☎ 971 38 13 55). Take C. Major d'es Born off Pl. Born, then turn right onto Carres del Roser, which leads to C. Dolores. The owners of this stone cave-turned restaurant challenge patrons to "try our meals the way we do them." Take their advice—this is Menorcan cuisine at its best. *Menú* 1000ptas. Entrees 1100-6000ptas. Open June-Sept. M-Sa noon-3:30pm and 7:30-11:30pm. V, MC.

Hostal Ciutadella Cafeteria, S. Eloy, 10 (☎ 971 38 34 62). From Pl. s'Esplanada, take Av. Capitá Negrete and continue onto Av. Jaume el Conqueridor to Pl. d'Alfons III. Take a left onto S. Eloy; the hostel is 1 block down on the right. Owner laughs that tourists won't try her rabbit or duck; prove her wrong. Generous *menú* 950ptas or 1250ptas. Open daily 8-10:30am, 1-3:30pm, and 8-10:30pm.

🎭 🎵 SIGHTS AND ENTERTAINMENT

An interesting complement to Menorca's beaches are the Bronze Age remnants at Menorca's archaeological sites. ◪**Naveta des Tudons,** one of the oldest structures in Europe (with some cosmetic restoration), sits 4km from the city. These ruins of community tombs are the island's best preserved. **Torretrencada** and **Torrellafuda** were rounded towers that overlooked the countryside. Both protect Stonehenge-like *taulas,* formations that have stood for over 3000 years. Buses don't come near these sights, so consider **hiking** (about 5km) along C. Cami Vell de Maó. The descriptive *Archeological Guide to Menorca* is available at the tourist office.

The Ciutadella community is one of early-to-bedders. **Asere,** C. de Curniola, 23, one block off Pl. Nova, spices things up a bit with a Cuban theme and mixed frozen drinks (600ptas and under; open F-Sa 8pm-midnight). From the first week in July to the end of August, Ciutadella hosts the **Festival de Música d'Estiu,** featuring some of the world's top classical musicians. Tickets (1600-3500ptas) are sold at Foto Born, C. Seminari (C. Bisbe Vila), 14 (☎ 971 38 17 54), and at the box office (open daily 9:30am-1:30pm and 5-8pm). On the 22nd of June, even veteran partiers of Palma and Ibiza join locals as they burn gallons of midnight oil during the **La Fiesta de San Juan,** Menorca's biggest *fiesta.* A week before the festivities, which include jousting and equestrian displays, a man clad in a sheepskin carries a decorated lamb on his shoulders through the city. (See **Hold Your Horses!,** below.)

🏖 BEACHES

The more popular (i.e., crowded) Menorcan beaches are accessible by bus from Mahón and Ciutadella. Most bus rides take around half an hour and cost between 50 and 200ptas. Many of the best beaches require a vehicle and some legwork, but they are worth the extra hassle. Northern beaches are rocky but less crowded; finer sands are hidden under hundreds of tourists on the southern coast. Don't limit yourself entirely to the beach scene, however—Menorca also offers a number of interesting natural and archaeological excursions.

NEAR CIUTADELLA

◪**NORTH SHORE.** The stretch east of Cala Morell is home to some of the most outstanding and pristine beaches on the island. **Platges d'Algaiarens** may be the superstar of the series, which also includes Cala en Carabó, Penyal de l'Anticrist, Sa Falconera, and the beautiful Cala del Pilar Ets Alocs. *(Cars can go only up to a few kilometers from these beaches; from there you must walk.)*

HOLD YOUR HORSES! (OR YOU JUST MIGHT KILL SOMEONE)
The mayor of Menorca, that is... Every last Thursday in June, Ciutadella celebrates *La Fiesta de San Juan,* a wild festival that rivals the infamous *San Fermines* in recklessness. The party begins with the arrival of the *fabioler* (herald of the ceremony) on a white horse. Playing a drum and flute, he gallops through town for four hours with crowds of drunken Menorcans following close behind. At 6pm sharp, village men ride 250 wild horses through town on their hind legs. Successfully bipedal horses are rewarded with cheers of *"Olé!"* and the rest charge into the crowd, often knocking over bystanders. In 1999, one particularly off-balance horse came crashing down on the mayor of Menorca, ending his term for good. *Note bene* for future office-holders: some P.R. opportunities just aren't worth it.

CALA MACARELLA. The 600pta toll for the private road to Macarella is well worth it. No tourist developments here, only crystal clear water lapping the shores of the cove. *Naturistas* (nudists) hang out on an even more secluded cove to the west. *(Access by bike, moped, or car off the country road to Sant Joan de Missa.)*

CALA BOSCH. Jagged cliffs plummet into clear pale-blue water. Crowded, but a fantastic backdrop for a refreshing dip in the Mediterranean. *(Accessible by Torres bus from Ciutadella; 18 per day, 8am-10:30pm.)*

SON XORIGUER. Located just down the road from Cala Bosch, on the same clear blue coastal water. It may be crowded, but it's only 20 minutes from Ciutadella. *(Accessible by a Torres bus from Ciutadella; 18 per day, 8am-10:30pm.)*

FORNELLS. A small fishing village known for its lobster farms, Fornells has only recently begun to attract tourists. Windsurfers zip around Fornells' long, shallow port, while beach gurus make excursions to **Cala Tirant** and **Binimella,** both a few kilometers west. Fornells also serves as a calm base from which to explore coves and jagged cliffs by car or bike, as bus service is very limited. *(Autobuses Roca Triay buses run to Fornells from C. Vassallo in Mahón; 30min., 5 per day.)*

CALA SANTA GALDANA. Though it lacks parking space, Galdana offers a pleasant, shallow cove filled with clear waters and white cliffs. *(7 buses per day from Ciutadella, 4 from Mahón; 8am-7pm, last bus back at 4pm.)*

IBIZA

Perhaps nowhere on Earth does style rule over substance more than on the island of Ibiza (pop. 84,000). Once a 1960s hippie enclave, Ibiza has long forgotten her roots in favor of a new-age decadence. Disco fiends, high-fashion gurus, movie stars, and the world's most beautiful people arrive in droves to showcase themselves and debauch in the island's outrageous, sex- and substance-driven summertime culture. A thriving gay community lends credence to Ibiza's image as a center of tolerance, but the island's high price tags preclude true diversity.

Amazingly enough, there is more to Ibiza than its famous nightlife; the beaches and mountains are some of the most spectacular in all the Balearics. The island also has places of historical interest, including several ancient castles. Since the Carthaginians retreated to Ibiza from the mainland in 656 BC, the island's list of conquerors reads like a "Who's Who of Ancient Western Civilization." Perhaps the most famous was the 1235 invasion by the Catalans, who brought Christianity and constructed the massive Renaissance walls that still fortify Eivissa (Ibiza City).

EIVISSA (IBIZA CITY)

Eivissa (pop. 35,000) is the world's biggest 24-hour party. During the day, when the sun blazes, the city resembles a ghost town, as most of its visitors are eagerly tanning or sleeping off hangovers. At sunset the show begins—grab a front-row seat at one of the outdoor bars to enjoy the action. Gorgeous club promoters smooth-talk their way into your wallet, drag queens in stilettos parade the streets brandishing whips, and tourists scope the scene for their next fling, all in a hard day's night. Eivissa is a place to see and be seen.

■ TRANSPORTATION

Flights: Airport (☎ 971 80 90 00), 7km south of the city. Buses (number #10) run between the airport and Av. Isidor Macabich, 20, in town (30min., every hr. 7:30am-10:30pm, 125ptas). Info booth open 24hr. for tickets and reservations. **Iberia,** Pg. Vara de Rey, 15 (☎ 902 40 05 00), at the end of the street, has flights to Palma, Barcelona, Madrid, Valencia, and Alicante. **Air Europa** and **Spanair** offer similar options. For routes and schedules, see **By Plane,** p. 470, or **Getting Around,** p. 471.

Ferries: Estació Marítima, at the end of Av. Bartolomé Rosselló. To get to the city center from the waterfront, take Av. Bartolomé Rosselló, which becomes Av. Isidor Macabich. **Trasmediterránea** (☎ 971 31 41 73) sells tickets at Estació Marítima and sends ferries to Palma, Barcelona, and Valencia. **Flebasa Lines** (☎ 971 31 40 05) runs daily to and from Dénia, near Alicante; a connection in Eivissa continues to and from Palma. For rates, fares, and schedules, see **By Boat,** p. 470, or **Getting Around,** p.470. For transport to the island of Formentera, see **Formentera: Getting There and Away,** p. 493.

Buses: The 3 main bus stops are Av. Isidor Macabich, 42, Av. Isidor Macabich, 20, and Av. Espanya (**Voramar** buses). For an exact schedule, check the tourist office or *El Diario.* Intercity buses are 250ptas or less and run from Av. Isidor Macabich, 42 (☎ 971 31 21 17) to **San Antonio** (M-Sa every 15min., Su every 30min.) and **Santa Eulalia** (M-F every 30min., Sa-Su every hr. 9:30am-10:30pm). Buses (☎ 971 34 03 82) to the beaches cost 125ptas and leave from Av. Isidor Macabich, 20, or Av. Espana to: **Salinas** (every hr. on the half-hour); **Platja d'en Bossa** (every 30min.); **Cap Martinet** (M-Sa 11 per day); and **Cala Tarida** (5 per day).

Taxis: ☎ 971 30 70 00 or 971 30 66 02.

Car and Motorbike Rental: Casa Valentín, Av. B.V. Ramón, 19 (☎ 971 31 08 22), the street parallel to Pg. Vara de Rey. Mopeds 1500-3500ptas per day. Cars 5000ptas and up per day. **Extra,** Av. Sta. Eulalia, 25 (☎ 971 19 17 17), near the Formentera ferries. Mopeds 2975ptas and up per day. Cars 6900ptas per day. Open M-Sa 8am-1:30pm and 4-8:30pm, Su 8am-noon and 5:30-7:30pm.

Jetski and Jetboat Rental: Jets Marivent Ibiza, (☎ 971 34 45 61). Full-day rental 35,000ptas. For 15min.-1hr. ride, check out the stands on Platja d'en Bossa, Cala Bassa, Cala Tarida, and Cala Vedella. 1 person 5000ptas; 2 people 6000ptas.

◀▪❷ ORIENTATION AND PRACTICAL INFORMATION

Three distinct sections make up the city. **Sa Penya,** in front of Estació Marítima, is mobbed with vendors, bars, and boutiques. Atop the hill behind Sa Penya, high walls circle **Dalt Vila,** the old city. **Sa Marina** and the commercial district occupy the gridded streets to the far right (with your back to the water) of the Estació.

The local paper *Diario de Ibiza* (www.diariodeibiza.es; 125ptas) has an *Agenda* page that lists essential information including the bus schedule for the whole island, the ferry schedule, the schedule of all domestic flights to and from Ibiza for the day, water and weather forecasts, info on the island's 24-hour pharmacies, a list of 24-hour gas stations, and important phone numbers.

Tourist Office: C. Antoni Riquer, 2 (☎ 971 30 19 00; www.ibizaonline.com), right on the water, across from where the ferries come in. Good maps, especially for hiking, excellent beach brochures, and a complete bus schedule. Open M-F 9:30am-1:30pm and 5-7pm, Sa 10:30am-1pm. Also a booth at the airport arrival terminal (☎ 971 80 91 18; fax 971 80 91 32). Open May-Oct. M-Sa 9am-2pm and 3-8pm, Su 9am-2pm.

Currency Exchange: La Caixa, Av. Isidor Macabich. Good exchange rates for cash and traveler's checks. **American Express** service at Viajes Iberia, C. Vicente Cuervo, 9 (☎ 971 31 11 11 or 971 30 43 64). Open M-F 9am-1pm and 4:30-7:45pm, Sa 9am-1pm.

Laundromat: Wash and Dry, Av. Espana, 53 (☎ 971 39 48 22). Do-it-yourself: wash 600ptas, dry 500ptas. **Internet access** for 900ptas per hr.

Emergency: ☎ 112. **Police:** (☎ 971 30 11 00), C. Madrid, by the post office.

Medical Assistance: Hospital (☎ 971 39 70 00), Barrio Can Misses, on the corner of Av. Espanya and C. Extremadura. **Ambulance:** ☎ 971 39 32 32. **Hospital Nuestra Senora** (☎ 971 39 70 21).

Post Office: C. Isidor Macabich (☎ 971 31 13 80). From the port, follow Av. Isidor Macabich to its end. **Lista de Correos.** Open M-F 8:30am-8:30pm, Sa 9:30am-2pm. **Postal Code:** 07800.

Internet Access: Centro Internet Eivissa, Av. Ignacio Wallis, 39 (☎ 971 31 81 61). 400ptas for 30min., 300ptas for each additional 30min. **Eurocentro,** C. Juan de Austria, 22 (☎ 971 31 09 09). 400ptas per 30min. Open 10am-1:30pm and 5-9pm.

BALEARIC ISLANDS

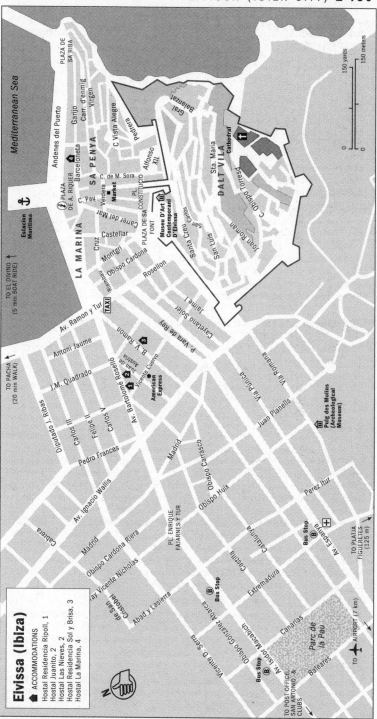

Mediterranean Sea

Elvissa (Ibiza)

ACCOMMODATIONS
Hostal Residencia Ripoll, 1
Hostal Juanito, 2
Hostal Las Nieves, 2
Hostal Residencia Sol y Brisa, 3
Hostal La Marina, 4

150 yards
150 meters

ACCOMMODATIONS

Decent, cheap hostals in town are rare, especially in the summer. The letters "CH" *(casa de huespedes)* mark many doorways, but the owner can often only be reached by the phone number on the door. In July and August, prices skyrocket, and you must make reservations two to three weeks in advance. Eivissa has a relatively safe and up-all-night lifestyle, and owners offer keys for 24-hour entry. All prices listed below are for high-season and can drop by as much as 1000ptas in the off-season. If you are willing to splurge an extra 2500-3000ptas per night, a small hotel may be worth it for the air-conditioning and private bathroom, amenities Ibiza's hostals tend to lack. Look for cheap hotels near Platja D'en Bossa.

Hostal Residencia Ripoll, C. Vicente Cuervo, 14 (☎ 971 31 42 75). Guaranteed cool with huge windows in doubles and triples and fans in interior rooms. July-Sept. singles 3500ptas; doubles 5500ptas; 3-person apartments 10,000ptas.

Hostal Residencia Sol y Brisa, Av. B. V. Ramón, 15 (☎ 971 31 08 18; fax 971 30 30 32), parallel to Pg. Vara de Rey. Upstairs from Pizzeria da Franco (signs point the way to the pizzeria). Clean and in a perfect port-side location, but rooms are sweltering hot in summer and communal bathrooms get dirty. Singles 3500ptas; doubles 6000ptas.

Hostal La Marina, Puerto de Ibiza, C. Barcelona, 7 (☎ 971 31 01 72; fax 971 314 894), across from Estació Marítima and right in the middle of the raucous bar scene. Room quality and price range from stark to plush, depending on the building. The best have TV, A/C, carpeting and balcony. At night, expect your room to shake from loud techno music. Singles 3250-7000ptas; doubles 5000-12000ptas.

Hostal Juanito and Hostal Las Nieves, C. Juan de Austria, 17-18 (☎ 971 19 03 19). Run by the same owner, both hostels offer cheap housing in a central area. Singles only available for longer stays. Singles 2000ptas; doubles 4000ptas, with bath 5000ptas.

Camping: Es Cana (☎ 971 33 21 17). 500ptas per person, 600ptas per site, 450ptas extra for a tent. Bungalow 2250ptas. Open daily 9am-1pm and 4:30-9:30pm. **Cala Nova** (☎ 971 33 17 74). 500ptas per person, 475ptas per tent. Both sites are close to Santa Eulalia del Río.

FOOD

Though the food is gourmet, few come to Ibiza to eat. Taut bodies are silent reminders that calories are always counted and dinnertime is for strategic people-watching. Inexpensive cuisine is hard to find; full meals rarely cost less than 1500ptas in the port and downtown areas, and **Sa Penya** and **Dalt Vila** offer exquisite fare in elegant settings for no less than 1800ptas per person. If you are willing to pay for the chaotic atmosphere, two of the best portside restaurants are **Restaurante Mexicano Trinidad,** C. Trinidad, 1, and **Restaurante Formentera,** C. Lluis Tur i Palau. For cheaper meals, try the more residential areas. Ibizan dishes worth hunting down are *sofrit pagès*, a deep-fried lamb and chicken dish; *flao*, a lush lemon- and mint-tinged cheesecake; and *graxonera*, cinnamon-dusted pudding made from eggs and bits of *ensaimada* (candied bread). The **market,** at C. Extremadura and C. Canarias, sells meat, fruits, and vegetables (open M-Sa 7am-1pm). For **groceries,** try **Comestibles Tony,** Carrer d'Enmig, 1 (open daily 9am-2pm and 5-8pm).

Casa Alfredo, Passeig Vara de Rey, 16 (☎ 971 31 12 74). Casa's reputation as the best restaurant in town is easy to explain; Ibizan specialties, fresh fish, an eclectic meat selection and heavenly desserts make this restaurant perfect for a date or some late-night indulgence. Open M-Sa noon-3pm, 8:30pm-midnight.

Comidas Bar San Juan, C. Montgrí, 8 (☎ 971 31 07 66). From Pg. Vara de Rey, take the 2nd right on the Puerto Moll. A tiny, old-style, family-run restaurant well-known for its refusal to go with the flow of rising prices and glam decor. Crowded with hungry locals, especially on weekend nights. Entrees 350-800ptas. Open M-Sa 1-3:30pm and 6-9pm.

SIGHTS AND BEACHES

SIGHTS. Wrapped in 16th-century walls, **Dalt Vila** (High Town) hosts 20th-century urban bustle in the city's oldest buildings. Its twisting, sloping streets lead up to the 14th-century **cathedral,** which offers superb views of the city, ocean, and beyond. (Open M-Sa 10:30am-1pm.) Next to the cathedral stands the **Museu Arqueològic D'Eivissa.** (Open Tu-Sa 10am-1pm and 5-10pm, Su 10am-2pm. 300ptas, students 150ptas.) Amid the weathered stone walls, the small **Museu D'Art Contemporani D'Eivissa** displays a wide range of current art exhibitions. (C. Sa Carrosa, on the left when entering through Dalt Vila's main entrance. ☎ 971 30 27 23. Open M-F 10am-1:30pm and 5-8pm, Sa 10am-1:30pm. 200ptas, students free.) The newly renovated archaeological museum, **Puig des Molins,** is on Vía Romana, which runs off the Portal Nou at the foot of the Dalt Vila. The museum displays Punic, Roman, and Iberian art, pottery, and metals. Adjoined to Puig is the 4th-century BC Punic-Roman **necropolis.** (Both open M-Sa 10am-2pm and 5-8pm. 150ptas.) Dalt Villa is prettiest at night just before sunset—window-shop at the art galleries and craft shops before heading to one of the many chill outdoor cafes. Plaça del Sol has a monopoly on good fruit shakes and other creative drinks.

BEACHES. The power of the rising sun draws thousands of topless solar zombies to nearby tanning grounds. **Platja Figueretes,** a thin stretch of sand in the shadow of tourists and large hotels, is a 10-minute bike ride from the port. Farther down, **Platja d'en Bossa** is an expansive tourist strip with waves just strong enough to bring bottle caps and other plastic goods ashore. **Platja des Duros** is tucked in across the port bay from Sa Penya and Sa Marina, just before the lighthouse. At **Platja de Talamanca,** the water is more of an enclosed bay than a sprawling sea. The most beautiful beach near Eivissa is probably **Playa de Las Salinas,** with its crystal-blue water and silky sand. More private coastal stretches lie in the northern part of the island and are accessible by car or scooter.

 NIGHTLIFE

The crowds return from the beaches by nightfall, when even the clothing stores (open until 1am) dazzle with throbbing techno and flashing lights. Ibizans are full of pomp: men masquerade as women and vamps stalk the portside walkways, vying for attention and turning the sidewalks into catwalks. Seaport cafes and bars crawl with club promoters who range from aggressive to super-aggressive. Flirt with a promoter for a cheap disco pass; most will bargain down to 3500ptas.

Bars in Eivissa are most popular between midnight and 3am and are virtually everyone's first stop before hitting the discos. The bar scene centers around **Calle Barcelona** and spins outward from there into a myriad of sidestreets. **Calle Virgen** is the center of gay nightlife and utterly outrageous fashion. While some joints try to snag tourists of specific nationalities, the place to be fluctuates nightly.

The island's ■**discos** (virtually all of which have a mixed gay-and-straight crowd) are world-famous and ever-changing—veterans claim that you will never again experience anything half as wild or fun. The best sources of information are regular disco-goers and the zillions of posters that plaster the stores and restaurants of Sa Marina and Sa Penya. There is something different going on each day of the week, and each club is known for its once-a-week theme party. For complete listings, check out *Ministry in Ibiza* or *Party Sun,* free at many hostels, bars, and restaurants. Better have some extra *pesetas* lying around—drinks at Ibiza's clubs cost about 1000ptas and covers start at 3500ptas. Generally, disco-goers pub-hop in Eivissa or San Antonio and jet off to clubs via bus or taxi (guess which is more chic) around 3am. The **Discobus** runs to and from all the major hotspots (midnight-6:30am, schedule at tourist office and hotels, 250ptas).

BALEARIC ISLANDS

■ **Privilege** (☎ 971 19 80 86), on the Discobus route to San Antonio or a 1500pta taxi ride from Eivissa. The wildest party ever. This mini-village/club packs in up to 30,000 bodies and has everything, including double-digit bars, garden terraces, and a stage set on a pool for bizarre acrobatics and fire shows. Best known for "manumission" parties on M that host kinky live sex shows. Cover 4000-12,000ptas, includes 1 drink. Open June-Sept. M and W-Sa midnight-7am. Visa.

Panchá: (☎ 971 31 09 59), 20min. from the port, 2min. in a cab. The most famous club chain in Spain, and the most elegant-looking of Ibiza's discos, with a rooftop terrace, hidden couch-filled side rooms, and wax candles. On F, Panchá hosts the Ministry of Sound, the best vocal house on the island; Th is "Circus Night." 5000ptas cover, includes 1 drink. Open daily 11:15pm-7:30am.

Space, Platja d'en Bossa (☎ 971 31 40 78 or 971 39 67 93). Feel your body take on extra-terrestrial form as you cruise Space's after-hours party. This club starts hopping around 8am and doesn't finish until the sun rises again at 6am the next day. The metallic get-up and feverish techno music is almost as hardcore as the dancers. Most popular Sa-Tu morning. Cover 4000ptas and up.

Amnesia, on the road to San Antonio; take the Discobus. Designed to mimic the London club scene, this converted warehouse with psychedelic lights and huge movie screens is essentially a British rave. Best known for Cream parties on Th, when London DJs play hard house or trippy trance. Cover 4000-7000ptas. Open daily midnight-6am.

El Divino (☎ 971 19 01 76), Puerto Ibiza Nueva. Terraced club right on the water overlooking Eivissa. Exotic dancers, strippers, and an S&M room make for a kinky experience. Outdoor tables cater to the non-tourist, well-connected crowd. El Divino fliers serve as free passes for the disco shuttle boat—otherwise, it costs 150ptas one-way. "MTV night" on Sa. Cover 5000ptas. Open mid-June to mid-Sept. nightly 1-6am.

Es Paradis Terrenal, C. Salvador Espiru, 20 (☎ 971 34 66 00), in San Antonio, portside. Looks can be deceiving, and at Es Paradis it's no different. A classy environment hosts some not-so-classy behavior at the water parties on Tu and Sa. Cover 4000ptas. Open midnight-6am.

Bora Bora, Platja de Bossa, across from Space. The place to be if you've got any energy left after a trip through Space. With its chill beach and disco scene, this club catches the crowd around 4pm.

NEAR EIVISSA

SAN ANTONIO DE PORTMANY

Every summer rowdy British hooligans storm San Antonio's huge crescent beach, harbor, and boozing 'n' bruising night scene, which has a rowdier, more down-to-earth flavor than Eivissa's. The town caters to the younger tourist, as restaurants are relatively cheap and beer flows like water.

To get to San Antonio from Eivissa, take the bus from Av. Isador Macabich (185ptas). Those headed for the mainland can contact **Pitra** car ferries (☎ 971 19 10 88) or **Flebasa,** both of which run to Dénia, near Alicante. The Pitra office in San Antonio de Portmany is on the **Muelle Comercial** (☎ 971 34 52 99), at the end of Pg. de la Mar. The tourist booth is in the stone hut at the top of Pg. Fonts. (☎ 971 34 33 63. Open Mar.-Oct. M-F 9:30am-8:30pm, Sa 9am-1pm, Su 9:30am-1:30pm; Nov.-Apr. M-Sa 9:30am-1pm). In an **emergency** call ☎ 091 or 092 or **municipal police,** Av. Portmany (☎ 971 34 08 30). For **medical assistance** (☎ 971 34 51 21), go to C. Alicant.

Many of Ibiza's sweetest beaches are just a stone's throw or boatride away from San Antonio. **Boats** and **buses** (180ptas) leave from Pg. Ses Fonts (before it becomes Pg. Mar) to **Cala Bassa** (700ptas), a gorgeous sandy beach on a thin strip filled with more nude Brits than even James Bond has seen; **Cala Conta** (700ptas), a slightly rocky beach; and the island of **Formentera** (2700ptas). Buses—the cheaper mode of transportation, also leave from Pg. Mar (before it intersects with C. Madrid) to **Cala Gració, Port des Turrent, Santa Eulalia,** and the protected inlet of **Cala Tarida** (140ptas). If you have wheels, explore **Cueva de Ses Fontanelles,** north of

Platja Cala Salada, where faint prehistoric paintings cover the walls. Or head north to **Cala Salada,** a tranquil cove that offers an escape from San Antonio's over-populated beaches. Consult the tourist office for **hiking** excursions around San Antonio. Walking routes pass sights like the **aquarium,** a small collection of fish displayed inside a cave. (Open daily 10am-10pm. 350ptas, children 150ptas.)

Hotels in San Antonio are a decent deal for the budget traveler who likes to party. Most run around 4000ptas per person per night (though prices rise in Aug.) and come with full bathrooms, telephones, A/C, a pool and a restaurant. Look on Av. Portus Magnus and C. Miramar. **Cala Bassa** offers camping on the bay, 6km west of San Antonio. (☎ 971 44 55 99. 500ptas per person, 475ptas per tent; 500ptas tent rental.) **Cafes** fill the waterfront area, as do bars and tattoo parlors. For inexpensive food in a loud, happening environment, check out **Terraza Kiwi Beach,** Av. Doctor Fleming, 2-4, by the beach and across from Es Pardis; look for the bright orange. Live music and waterfront location creates a funky atmosphere. (☎ 971 31 68 42. Entrees 350-600ptas. Alcoholic milkshakes 750ptas. Non-alcoholic shakes 350ptas. Open daily 10am-4am.)

FORMENTERA

The tiny island of Formentera is Spain's version of island paradise. Despite recent invasions by bourgeois, beach-hungry Germans and Italians, the 11mi. moat separating Formentera from Eivissa has deterred complete besiegement; the island's stunning white beaches maintain a heavy sense of hypnotic calm, at least for now. Join Formentera's "save our island" spirit by hiking or renting a bike—the tourist office offers a comprehensive list of "Green Tours" for hikers and cyclists.

▐ TRANSPORTATION. Several ferry lines at Estació Marítima in Eivissa provide the best alternative to swimming. **Pitra** car ferries (☎ 971 19 10 88), **Trasmapi-Balearia** (☎ 971 31 20 70), and **Umafisa** car ferries (☎ 971 31 45 13) all offer transportation to and from Formentera. Choose between **Linea Jet's** speedy ride (25min., 2085ptas) or ride with the trucks on the cheaper, slower mother ship (1hr., 1250ptas). For transport between Formentera and the mainland, see **By Boat,** p. 470. For transport from Eivissa to Formentera, see **Getting Around,** p. 471.

▐ PRACTICAL INFORMATION. Atop the northern side of the island is its main port, **La Savina.** The main artery runs from the port (km 0) to the eastern tip, **Punta D'Esfar** (km20). The island's "capital" **San Francisco,** which parts from the main artery at km 3.1, has the basics but little else. **Buses** run from La Savina to **Es Pujols** (8 per day), **Playa Illete** (2 per day), **Playa Migjorn** (10 per day), and to **San Francisco** (14 per day). For a **taxi,** call ☎ 971 32 80 16. **Car-scooter-bike rental booths** line the dock in La Savina. (Cars 5000ptas per day. Scooters 2500ptas. Bikes 500-1000ptas.) **La Savina Motos,** on the port, rents mopeds for 2500ptas a day. (☎ 971 32 22 75. Open 9am-1pm and 3-8:30pm. V, MC.) All the main roads have lanes for scooters to putter along freely with bicycles. The **tourist office,** Edificio Servicios La Savina, is at the port (☎ 971 32 20 57; fax 971 32 28 25; www.ifsystems.es/formentera. Open M-F 10am-2pm and 5-7pm, Su 10am-2pm). For **police** call ☎ 971 32 20 22; the **medical center** can be reached at ☎ 971 32 23 69.

▐▐ ACCOMMODATIONS AND FOOD. Formentera offers *la crème de la crème* of hostel-living. Almost all of the island's hostels are hotel-quality with attentive staff; the best of them are tucked away on their own stunning, deserted beaches. **Hostal Maysi,** Playa Arenal, km 11 is situated on some of the finest white sand on the island. Beautiful rooms with enormous seaview balconies were recently renovated, and the downstairs area has an airy bar and pool table. (☎ 971 328 547. Singles 6000ptas; doubles 8000ptas.) At **Hostal Costa Azul,** Playa de Migjorn, km 7, serene rooms are complemented by a quiet beach. (☎ 971 32 80 24. 3755ptas per person.) **Hostal Mayans** is in Formentera's best approximation of a beach "town," Es Pujols. The double rooms are spacious, with fridges, balconies, and large bathrooms. (☎ 971 328 724. Breakfast included. 5700ptas.)

When hunger strikes, try **El Mirador,** at km 14.3, for its equally satisfying ocean view and *paella* (1300ptas). From the restaurant, the narrow strip of the Formentera Island looks like the stem of a champagne glass that widens out to the northern port, La Savina. Others say it looks like a bull leering at the observer. (☎ 971 32 70 37. Open daily 12:30-4pm and 7-11pm). **Supermarkets** line all of the major roads in Formentera, as do various small restaurants (*menús* about 1100ptas).

📷 **BEACHES.** To bask on Formentera's best beaches, take Av. Mediterránea from the port, turn left at the sign pointing toward Es Pujols, and hop left onto the dirt road at the sign marking **Verede de Ses Salines.** Paths to the right lead to **Platja de Llevant,** a long strip of fine sand. Farther up the peninsula, roads to the left lead to **Platja de Ses Illetes,** with its more popular and rocky swimming holes. While the entire peninsula provides ample privacy, walking to the end (which requires wading through two shallow pools), will assure you of absolute solitude, though you might have to nestle between rocks to catch some rays. A tourist **boat** also runs to **Ses Illetes** and **Espalmador** from La Savina (leaves La Savina at 10:45, 11:45am, and 1:15pm; returns at 4:15, 5:30, and 6:45pm; 1200ptas). For **sailing, windsurfing, and parasailing** try **Wet 4 Fun** on Es Pujols beach. (Sailboats 4900ptas per hr. Windsurfing 2200ptas per hr. Parasailing 5900ptas.)

For stunning dry-land sightseeing, those with mopeds should drive through the mountainous regions of La Mola to **Punta de Sa Ruda** or cruise by the groves of bendy olive trees and wispy grass to **Cap de Barbaria.** Most beautiful of all are the rugged cliffs at Formentera's two southernmost tips. Cool air and the scent of pine trees mark the windy ascent to either of these breathtaking look-out points.

CANARY ISLANDS

From the snowy peak of Mount Teide to the fiery volcanos of Timanfaya, the Canary Islands have enchanted humanity since the beginning of time. Homer and Herodotus often referred to their gardens of great beauty, and the lost civilization of Atlantis was said to have left behind these seven islands when it sank into the ocean. Since then, the Canaries have been known as the "Fortunate Isles"—and with good reason. Constantly freshened by a gentle sea-breeze and blessed with perfect weather (a spring-like 20-24 °C year-round), they attract millions of European vacationers each year. But beyond the parties of Tenerife and Gran Canaria and the hotel-lined beaches of Fuerteventura, it is the natural beauty—the volcanic wastelands, the wind-swept dunes, the misty forests, and the palm-lush pockets in amber mountains—that gives the Canaries their magic.

The Canary Islands were once inhabited by Guanches, light-skinned and blond-haired hunters and gatherers, descendants of Berbers who migrated to the islands from North Africa. European conquests began when the Romans heard tales of the enchanting isles from the Mauritianians. The islands were later conquered by the Portuguese, French, and Spanish; in 1479 the Treaty of Alcáçovas declared the Canaries Spanish territory. By 1496, after nearly a century of battle with the Guanches, the Spaniards wrested control of the islands, later using them as stopovers en route to their colonies in the Americas. After the conquest, the Spaniards developed a booming plantation economy based on banana, sugar, and wine production; the islands still depend on such cash crops today.

Once a link between the Old and New Worlds, the islands' coastal towns are a tourist-oriented mix of craft stalls, surf shops, fruit stands, international restaurants and high-priced resorts, while their inland hamlets remain largely unchanged. The spoken Spanish here resembles that of Cuba and Puerto Rico more than that of the islands' Castilian conquerors, and typical Canarian fare is a mixture of Guanche, Spanish and Latin American cuisines. Remnants of Guanche culture—including *lucha canaria* (Canarian wrestling), *gofio* (a grain staple), delicious *plátano* (banana) dishes, and place names such as Tenerife, Timanfaya, and Doramas—still remain, especially in Lanzarote and the western islands.

HIGHLIGHTS OF CANARY ISLANDS

The peaks of Gomera's **Garajonay National Park,** where the last living example of a laurisilva forest offers views of three other islands above the clouds (see p. 518).

The rolling sand dunes of **Maspalomas** (see p. 502).

El Teide National Park, on the highest mountain in Spain (see p. 509).

Cesar Manrique's museums, home, and architectural impact on wonderfully undertouristed **Lanzarote** (see p. 513).

LOCAL FESTIVALS IN THE CANARY ISLANDS

Carnaval is the hair-down, beer-down party of the year in the Canaries—contests, competitions and debauchery take over the islands (particularly **Las Palmas**) for the three weeks preceeding *Semana Santa*. On the last night of the festival, black-clad weepers jokingly mourn the death of the party by burning and burying a a huge *papier-mâché* sardine on the beach. Around July 16, **Puerto de la Cruz** celebrates the *Fiestas de Julio* and **Corralejo** holds the *Fiestas del Carmen*.

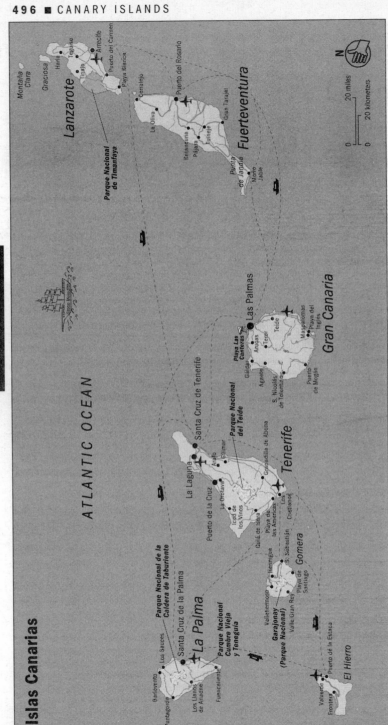

Islas Canarias

ATLANTIC OCEAN

Lanzarote

Montaña Clara
Graciosa
Haría
Teguise
Órzola
Tinajo
Arrecife
Puerto del Carmen
Playa Blanca

Parque Nacional de Timanfaya

Fuerteventura

Corralejo
La Oliva
Puerto del Rosario
Gran Tarajal
Betancuria
Pájara
Tuineje
Punta de Jandía
Morro Jable

N

20 miles
20 kilometers
0
0

Las Palmas

Gran Canaria

Playa Las Canteras
Gáldar
Teror
Teide
Arucas
Maspalomas
Playa del Inglés
Agaete
S. Nicolás de Tolentino
Puerto de Mogán

Santa Cruz de Tenerife

Parque Nacional del Teide

Tenerife

La Laguna
Tacoronte
Güímar
Puerto de la Cruz
La Orotava
Icod de los Vinos
Guía de Isora
Granadilla de Abona
Los Cristianos
Playa de las Américas

La Palma

Parque Nacional de la Caldera de Taburiente

Santa Cruz de la Palma

Barlovento
Puntagorda
Los Llanos de Aridane
Fuencaliente

Parque Nacional Cumbre Vieja y Teneguía

Gomera

Vallehermoso
Hermigua
S. Sebastián
Playa de Santiago
Valle Gran Rey

Garajonay (Parque Nacional)

El Hierro

Valverde
Puerto de la Estaca
Frontera

Call the USA

"feel free to call"

1-800-COLLECT

1 8 0 0

COLLECT

When in Ireland
Dial: 1-800-COLLECT (265 5328)

When in N. Ireland, UK & Europe
Dial: 00-800-COLLECT USA (265 5328 872)

Member of
Dublin Tourism

Australia	0011	800 265 5328 872
Finland	990	800 265 5328 872
Hong Kong	001	800 265 5328 872
Israel	014	800 265 5328 872
Japan	0061	800 265 5328 872
New Zealand	0011	800 265 5328 872

◪ GETTING THERE AND AWAY

Located off the western coast of Morocco, the Canaries make for a long haul by boat (2 days from Spain) but a relatively quick flight (2½-3½hr.) from the mainland. Competitive fares and quick flights make flying the best option. Many airlines fly direct from Spain, Portugal, Morocco, the US, and northern Europe. Flights from Madrid, which are the most frequent, are also the cheapest. European tourists, primarily Germans, flock to the islands in January and February; airfares during this time are the most expensive. As long as you plan ahead, getting to the Canary Islands does not have to be prohibitively expensive. Prices are the same whether you purchase your tickets in Spain or abroad.

Iberia/Aviaco (24hr. ☎ 902 400 500; www.iberia.com) flies from Madrid and Barcelona to the islands of Gran Canaria, Tenerife, and Lanzarote. A standard round-trip ticket costs between 70,000 and 80,000ptas.

Air Europa (24hr. ☎ 902 24 00 42) and **Spanair** (☎ 902 13 14 15; www.spanair.com) fly to the islands at cheaper rates (round-trip 35,000-60,000ptas).

Trasmediterránea (☎ 902 45 46 45; www.trasmediterranea.com) cruises from Cádiz, Spain to the islands of Gran Canaria, Tenerife, and La Palma (2 days; departs from Cádiz Sa, returns W; round-trip with dorm bed 58,500ptas).

◪ GETTING AROUND

Traveling between the islands by boat is the cheapest alternative. Boats come in two varieties, ferries and jetfoils, and both carry cars. For shorter trips ferries are the best option. Jetfoils, which are faster and more comfortable, also cost almost twice as much—consider taking them on the longer voyages. Prices for both ferries and jetfoils vary with accommodation; travelers can choose between a *butaca* (a seat like those on buses) and a *camarote a compartir* (a dorm bed).

Three major lines serve the five islands. The following chart lists the frequencies, durations, and one-way adult passenger fare for the most popular destinations. Students, children under 11, and seniors over 60 all receive discounts. Departure times and prices are subject to frequent change—be sure to call ahead and confirm. Arrive at least 30 minutes before departure to buy your ticket, and one hour early if you have a car.

Fred Olsen (☎ 922 62 82 00; www.fredolsen.es) runs jetfoils between islands. V, MC.

Trasmediterránea (24hr. ☎ 902 45 46 45; www.trasmediterranea.com). Ticket windows open 1hr. prior to departure. V, MC.

Naviera Armas (☎ 928 26 70 00). Often requires photocopies of student identification cards to grant the discount. V, MC.

Iberia/Aviaco (☎ 902 40 05 00) has daily flights between the islands. All prices listed are one-way. **Gran Canaria** to: **Tenerife,** north and south airports (30min., 10 per day, 6000ptas); **La Palma** (30min., 1 per day, 10,000ptas); **Fuerteventura;** and **Lanzarote. Spanair** (☎ 902 13 14 15) connects only Gran Canaria and Tenerife (5000ptas).

WHAT'S IN A NAME? Rumored by ancient writers to be the sight of divine afterlife, the Canary Islands have often been referred to as *Elysium*. The Spaniards called the islands *Islas Afortunadas* (Fortunate Islands) because of the wealth and opportunities they offered. However, there is still no definitive answer to the origin of the name "Canary Islands." Some link it to the particularly large yellow breed of *canus* special to the islands; others postulate that the islands were named after Cranus and Crana, mythical wanderers of the islands. Pliny the Elder believed that the name stemmed from the number of large *canes* (dogs) who inhabited the island. The most likely answer is that the name comes from the Guanche natives, descendants of the Moroccan Canarii tribe.

ORIGIN	DESTINATION	DUR.	FREQUENCY	TIME	PRICE
+Las Palmas	Morro Jable	4hr.	1 per day	7am	3010ptas
*Las Palmas (bus to Agate)	Santa Cruz, Tenerife	1hr.	6 per day	7:30am-8:30pm	3360ptas
+Las Palmas	Santa Cruz, Tenerife	6hr.	M-F 2 per day, Sa-Su 1 per day	7am and 3:15pm, Sa-Su 7am	
Las Palmas	Santa Cruz, Tenerife	6hr.	Th	10:30am	3005ptas
*Las Palmas	Puerto Rosario	6hr.	1 per day	5pm	3080ptas
Las Palmas	Puerto Rosario	8hr.	M,W,F,Sa	midnight	3985ptas
+Las Palmas	Puerto Rosario	8hr.	Tu, Th	11:50pm	
Las Palmas	Arrecife	8hr.	2-3 per week	2:30pm or midnight	3895ptas
+Las Palmas	Arrecife	10hr.	M, W, F	11:50pm	
Las Palmas	Santa Cruz, La Palma San Sebastián	9½hr.	W	10:30pm	5120ptas
*Los Cristianos	Corralejo	40min	7 per day	8am-8:30pm	2280-2760ptas
+Playa Blanca	Corralejo	45min	5 per day	7am-7pm	1700ptas
*Playa Blanca		45min	4-5 per day	8am-6pm	1850ptas
*Puerto del Rosario	Las Palmas	7hr.	1 per day	9am	3080ptas
Puerto del Rosario	Las Palmas	7hr.	M, W, F, Sa	M-F 1pm, Sa 3pm	3895ptas
+ Puerto del Rosario	Las Palmas	8hr.	W, F	1pm	1850ptas
*Puerto del Rosario	Arrecife	5hr.	1 per day	11:55pm	
Santa Cruz, La Palma	Los Cristianos	5hr.	M-Sa	1:45pm	2995ptas
Santa Cruz, La Palma	San Sebastián	3½hr.	M-Sa	1:45pm	2415ptas
Santa Cruz, La Palma	Valverde	9½hr.	M-Sa	1:45pm	2995ptas
San Sebastián	Los Cristianos	1½hr.	1 per day	5:15pm	2140ptas
*San Sebastián	Los Cristianos	40min.	6 per day	7:30am-6:30pm	2280-2760ptas
San Sebastián	Santa Cruz, La Palma	3½hr.	M-Sa	10:15am	2415ptas
*San Sebastián	Valverde	3hr.	1 per day	9:30am	2540ptas
San Sebastián	Valverde	3½hr.	1 per day	10:15am or 7:15pm	2615ptas
*Valverde	San Sebastián	2½hr.	1 per day	1:30pm	2540ptas
Valverde	Los Cristianos	8hr.	1 per day	11:45am or 2pm	2615ptas
Valverde	Santa Cruz, La Palma	14hr.	Sa-W	11:45pm	2995ptas
+Santa Cruz, Tenerife	Arrecife	20hr.	M, W, F	7:30pm	4740ptas
Santa Cruz, Tenerife	Las Palmas	3½hr.	Sa	9am	3005ptas
*Santa Cruz, Tenerife	Las Palmas	2hr.	6 per day	7:30am-8:30pm	3360-4070ptas
+Santa Cruz, Tenerife	Las Palmas	3½hr.	M-F 2 per day, Sa-Su 1 per day	11am and 7:30pm Sa-Su 7:45pm	
+Morro Jable	Las Palmas	4hr.	1 per day	7pm	6000ptas
*Arrecife	Puerto del Rosario	3hr.	5 per day	8am-6pm	4020ptas
+Arrecife	Las Palmas	8hr.	Tu, Th, Sa	1pm	
Arrecife	Las Palmas	8hr.	T, Th	noon	3895ptas
+Corralejo	Playa Blanca	45min.	5 per day	8am-8pm	1700ptas
*Corralejo	Playa Blanca	45min.	4-5 per day	9am-7pm	1850ptas

Unless otherwise noted, all ferries are run by Trasmediterránea. * denotes Fred Olsen jetfoils. + denotes Naviera Armas.

GRAN CANARIA

Often called the "miniature continent," Gran Canaria sports a wide range of climates, from the snow-covered Pico de las Nieves (1950m) to the rolling dune expanses at Maspalomas, the island's one worthwhile attraction. Although it is the least appealing of the islands, foreign visitors (mostly German) crowd Gran Canaria's eastern and southern beaches. The interior towns are less touristed, but Gran Canaria's parched mountains pale in comparison to the peaks and national parks of Tenerife and Lanzarote.

LAS PALMAS

The urban mecca of the Canaries, Las Palmas (pop. 350,000) moves to the rhythm of jackhammers by day and disco-bass by night. Residents of varied ethnic backgrounds mix with bronzed, fun-loving Europeans who are all cruising toward one inevitable destination—the beach. The city's dirty streets buzz with the frenzied commerce of a duty-free port where everything from cigarettes to sex is for sale. Unless you like sketchy clubs and Germans on your beach towel, your stay in Las Palmas need not extend past the wait for a transportation link to cleaner, less commercialized parts of the islands.

Las Palmas

■ ACCOMMODATIONS
Hotel Madrid, 3
Pensión Perojo, 2
Pensión Plaza, 1

CANARY ISLANDS

⌐ TRANSPORTATION

Flights: (24hr. ☎ 928 57 90 00). **Saccai buses** run between Parque Sta. Telmo and the airport (45min.; every 30min. 6:30am-9pm; every hr. 9pm-2am; 245ptas). **Iberia** (☎ 928 37 08 77). **Air Europa** (☎ 928 57 95 84). **Spanair** (☎ 928 57 94 07).

Buses: Estación de Guaguas (☎ 928 36 83 35, info ☎ 928 36 86 35), in front of Parque Sta. Telmo. Office open M-F 6:30am-8:30pm. Buses here are called *guaguas*. Two companies, under the umbrella company **Lineas Global,** connect Las Palmas to the rest of the island. A **bonobus** pass (2000ptas) is a good investment for those exploring the surroundings by bus as fares are 30% cheaper with the pass. Call for information on wheelchair accessible buses. See the bus listing in the city to which you would like to travel for more information.

  SALCAI (info ☎ 928 38 11 10; green *guaguas*) travels south. To: **Puerto Mogan** (#1, 30min., every 20min. 5:40am-7pm, 930ptas); **Maspalomas-Playa de Inglés** (#5 and 30, 30min., every 20min. 5:20am-9:20pm; Playa Ingles 595ptas, Maspalomas 630ptas); **Puerto Rico** (#31, 4 per day 6am-8:15pm, 805ptas). Buses also service Telde, La Garita, and Agumes.

  Utinsa (info ☎ 928 36 83 35; orange *guaguas*) travels west. To **Arucas** (#205, 209, 210, and 234; every 30min. 6am-11pm, 245ptas) and **Teror** (#216 and 218, every 30min. 7am-9:30pm, 245ptas). Buses also head to El Valle, Galdar, Moya, Casablanca, Lanzarote, Valsendero, Artenera, and Santa Brigida.

Ferries: Trasmediterránea (☎ 928 47 44 39; fax 928 26 30 77), **Fred Olson** (☎ 922 62 82 31 or 928 22 81 66), and **Naviera Armas** (☎ 928 26 70 00). Ferries depart from Muelle León y Castillo. Jetfoils depart from Muelle Santa Catalina. Fred Olson's jetfoil to Tenerife departs from the town of **Agate.** A free bus leaves Parque Santa Catalina 1hr. before the ferry leaves; you must have a ferry ticket to board the bus. Tickets sold at the docks or any travel agency. For destinations and times, see **Getting Around,** p. 500.

Public Transportation: Yellow **Guaguas Municipales** travel within the city. Bus #1 runs 24hr. from Puerto de la Luz-Teatro Pérez Galdós, passing Parque Sta. Catalina and Parque Sta. Telmo. Complete map of routes available at tourist offices. Individual ride 125ptas; 10-ride "bono" available at *estancos* (tobacco shops) for 745ptas.

Taxi: Radio Taxi (☎ 928 46 22 12). **Taxi Radio** (☎ 928 46 56 66).

Car Rental: Hertz, at the airport (☎ 928 57 95 77). Another branch in the Jetfoil office at Muelle de Sta. Catalina. Ford Fiesta 4703ptas per day, including tax, insurance, and unlimited mileage. Open M-Sa 8am-7:30pm. Cars can be taken to other islands.

✴🛈 ORIENTATION AND PRACTICAL INFORMATION

Las Palmas is not a compact city—to get around, you must use the bus system. The city is loosely divided into a series of districts, connected by the **Avenida del Marítima del Norte** running north to south along the east coast. **Santa Catalina,** framed by **Playa de Las Canteras** on the west and **Puerto de la Luz** on the east, is packed with accommodations, bars, discos, and sex shops—stay here for beach and bus access. Farther south through a series of residential neighborhoods lies **Triana,** a shopping district with the city's bus station, and **Vequeta,** home to most of the city's historical sights. Buses #1, 12, 13, 15, and 41 run between Parque Sta. Catalina, and Vegueta. Santa Catalina's **Parque Santa Catalina** houses the tourist office; all directions in Las Palmas are given from there.

  Tourist Offices: Main office (☎/fax 928 26 46 23), in front of Parque Sta. Catalina, in a colonial-style house. Staff speaks 6 languages, will point you in the right direction for anything. Open M-F 9am-2pm. The **kiosk** in the back left corner of Parque Sta. Catalina (with your back to the ocean) has good maps. Open M-F 10am-7:30pm, Sa 10am-3pm. The central **town-run office** is in the old Ayuntamiento, across Pl. Sta. Ana from the cathedral. Open M-F 10am-5:30pm. **Centro de Iniciaturas y Turismo** (☎ 928 24 35 93), in Pueblo Canario. Open M-F 10am-1pm and 5-8pm.

  Currency Exchange: Banco Central Hispano, C. Nicolás Estévanez, 5 (☎ 902 24 24 24). No commission. Open 8:30am-2pm. **ATMs** line Parque Sta. Catalina.

Laundromat: Lavesec, C. Joaquín Costa, 46 (☎ 928 27 46 17). Wash, dry, and iron (up to 7kg) 1000ptas. Open M-F 9am-1pm and 4-8pm, Sa 9am-3pm.

Emergency: ☎ 112. **Police: Policía Municipal** (☎ 928 26 05 51), in Parque Sta. Catalina. **Policía Nacional,** C. Dr. Miguel Rosa, 25 (☎ 928 26 16 71).

Hospital: Hospital Insular, Pl. Dr. Pasteur (☎ 928 44 40 00). **Ambulance:** ☎ 928 24 50 23. **Interclinic,** C. Sagasta, 62 (☎ 928 27 88 26 or 928 26 90 98). From Parque Sta. Catalina, turn left on C. Luis Morote, then right on C. Sagasta. A 24hr. emergency clinic geared towards tourists. English spoken.

Post Office: Main office, Av. Primero de Mayo, 62 (☎ 928 36 13 20). **Lista de Correos.** Open M-F 8:30am-8:30pm, Sa 9:30am-2:30pm. **Postal Code:** 35007.

Internet Access: Microtech, C. Luis Morote, 4 (☎ 928 49 31 95). 300ptas for 30min., 500ptas per hr. Open M-F 9:30am-1:30pm and 4-8:30pm, Sa 9:30am-1:30pm.

ACCOMMODATIONS

There are more beds than residents in Las Palmas, but apparently that's not enough. It's very difficult to find a place to stay without advance notice and nearly impossible during high season (Dec.-Feb., especially during *Carnaval*). If the places listed below are full, calling the **Reservations Center** (☎ 928 38 46 46 or 928 38 47 47; after hours fax 928 38 48 48) can save a lot of time; ask for Sr. Cabrera. Singles are limited, and solo travelers will often end up paying for a double. Las Palmas probably has the cheapest accommodations on the island, but since most of them are unimpressive, be sure to examine a room before committing to stay.

Hotel Madrid, Pl. Cairasco, 4 (☎ 928 36 06 64; fax 928 38 21 76), in the Triana-Vegueta district, inland from C. Mayor; enter through the cafe on the plaza. Excellent locatio. Franco stayed in room #3 the night before the Civil War began. Singles 3500ptas, with bath 4500ptas; doubles 4500ptas, with bath 5500ptas.

Pensión Plaza, C. Luis Morote, 16 (☎ 928 26 52 12), the red building facing Parque Sta. Catalina. The fantastic location near the ferry terminal makes up for old tile floors and negligible water pressure. 24hr. reception. Reservations recommended. Singles 2400ptas, with bath 2900ptas; doubles 3400ptas, with bath 3900ptas; doubles for 1 person 2900ptas, with bath 3400ptas. Extra beds 1000ptas.

Pensión Perojo, C. Perojo, 1 (☎ 928 37 13 87), at C. Bravo Murillo. Lots of street noise, but these simple, sparse rooms are close to the bus station for late-night arrivals, and a short walk from the old city. Reservations recommended; some rooms are given to quasi-permanent residents. Singles 2500ptas; doubles 3500ptas; triples 4500ptas.

Camping Guantánamo (☎ 928 56 02 07), in Mogán (a port town in the south). See **Buses** for transportation info. Ranked a 3rd-class site, near a eucalyptus forest and a hunting zone. Plenty of amenities, including a snack-bar, supermarket, restaurant, and pharmacy. 400ptas per person and per car, 450ptas per large tent.

FOOD

Las Palmas' cuisine is as international as its fluctuating population. A typical night might involve eating Indian *tapas* and swinging to Moroccan pop music in an Irish pub. Most restaurants cater to tourists, serving German *paella*, hamburgers, and pizza. For **groceries, Cruz Mayor** has a branch on C. Nicolás Estévanez, 38, in the new city, and C. Pérez Galdós, 17, in the Triana district (both open M-Sa 8:30am-8:30pm). **Mercado de Vegueta,** C. Mendizábal, a sensory parade of fruit, dairy, fish, and olive stands, is open daily. **Hipócrates,** C. Colón, 4 (☎ 928 22 64 15), across from Casa-Museo Colón in Vegueta, offers romantic vegetarian dining with a simple *menú* for 1300ptas. (Open Tu-Sa 1-4:30pm and 8:30pm-12:30am, Su 1-4:30pm, M 8:30pm-12:30am.) **Casa Montescdeoca,** C. Montesdecoa, down the street from Casa de Colon, serves delicious mains (650-2300ptas) in an garden that will erase memories of Las Palmas. (☎ 928 33 34 66. Open M-Sa 12:30-3:30pm, 8-11:30pm.)

🔊 🎵 SIGHTS AND ENTERTAINMENT

The easiest "sight" to see is Las Palmas' **historic neighborhood;** its colonial and neo-classical architecture and open markets make for a sweet respite from the new city's commercial buildings. For history buffs, the ■**Museo Canario,** C. Verneau, 2, off Dr. Chil, provides a comprehensive background on Guanche society. If the second floor's collection of Cro-Magnon skulls (the largest in the world) doesn't freak you out, inspect the mummies for more morbidity. (☎ 928 33 68 00. Open M-F 10am-8pm. Guided tours begin around 10am, 6, and 7pm. 500ptas, students 100ptas.) The city's new pride and joy, the **Museo Elder de la Ciencia y la Tecnología,** on the port side of Parque Santa Catalina, is a state-of-the-art exploration of state-of-the-art subjects, from energy and transport to a space station and a science workshop. (☎ 828 011 818. Open Tu-Su 10am-8pm.) In the white-washed **Pueblo Canario** (Canarian Village), built specifically for tourists, resides the ■**Museo Néstor,** a stunning collection of painter Néstor Marín-Fernández de la Torre's beautiful, pudgy figures. (In Dorames Park to the left when facing the hotel; between Parque Sta. Telmo and Parque Sta. Catalina. Take bus #1, 15, or 41. ☎ 928 24 51 25. Open Tu-F 10am-1pm and 4-8pm, Su 11am-2pm. 150ptas.) The 16th-century Gothic **Catedral de Santa Ana,** C. Espiritu Santo, 20, is an amalgam of architectural styles. From the bus stop, go left up C. Cavo Sotello and left on C. Obispo Cobina. José Lujan Pérez, the Canaries' favorite sculptor, designed the Neoclassical facade. (☎ 928 31 49 89. Open M-F 9am-1:30pm and 4-6:30pm, Sa 9am-2pm. 300ptas.) Columbus purportedly stayed several times in the old-style **Casa de Colón,** C. Colón, while fueling up for transatlantic voyages. (Follow C. Espiritu Santo from Pl. Santa Ana. Open Tu-Sa 10am-9pm. Free.)

The 3km **Playa de Las Canteras,** one of Europe's most famous beaches, is the only reason to stay in Las Palmas. Packed with largely local beach-goers who enjoy tanning, swimming, scuba diving, surfing, and windsurfing, the reef-sheltered lagoon is known as "the world's largest swimming pool." From Parque de Sta. Catalina, take a left on C. Luis Morote, and follow it to the end. **Medusa Sub,** Bernardo de La Torre, 33, specializes in diving, instructional courses, and equipment rental and sales. (☎ 928 26 27 86. Open M-F 11am-2pm and 5-9pm, Sa 11am-1pm and 6-8pm).

Nightlife in Las Palmas is nothing remarkable, with overpriced drinks (around 600ptas), flashing lights, and thumping bass. Most popular spots (including karaoke bars) are located around the Parque Sta. Catalina. Take advantage of year-round outdoor terraces on Pl. España and along Po. Canteras. A far cry from its Madrid namesake, **Kapital,** C. Luis Morote, 51, is your standard *discoteca,* while **Pequeña Habana** sizzles with salsa until 4am on weekend nights.

🏝 DAYTRIPS FROM LAS PALMAS

Las Palmas itself is no reason to come to the Isla de Gran Canaria. Use the cheap accommodations as a base for visiting more appealing parts of the islands, especially the sunny southern beaches and quaint interior villages.

MASPALOMAS (1HR.)

Buses run to and from: Las Palmas (#4, 5, 30, 61; 1hr., every 15min. 6:30am-9:30pm, 595-630ptas); Puerto Rico (#32, 39, 61; 30min., every 20min. 7am-8:30pm, 275ptas); Puerto Mogan (#32 and 61; 30min., every 20min. 7am-8:30pm, 415ptas); and the airport (#4, 5, 30, 61, 90; 40min., every 30min. 6:30am-9pm, 350ptas).

Located on the southern tip of Gran Canaria, the shores of Maspalomas are probably the best beaches in the Canary Islands. The famed **Playa del Inglés** offers parasailing, surfing (the current world-champion lives 5min. away), jet-skiing, scuba diving, and deep-sea fishing. The secret has long been out, and planeloads of European tourists swarm the coast every year. The crowds are worth putting up with, though, to see the awesome, wind-swept ■**Dunas de Maspalomas** beyond the beach; watch streaks of sand race and dart across the dune faces like startled schools of fish. (To get to the dunes from the beach, walk right, facing the water, down Playa del Inglés or from Pl. Fuerteventura, at the bottom of Av. Tirajana.)

Other good beaches include the flawless, quieter **Playa de Maspalomas** and the rocky **Playa de la Mujer** and **Playa de la Meloneras. Water Sport Center,** in the Kabash shopping center, rents jetskis (☎ 928 76 66 83; 5000-6000ptas for 20min.) and **Tortuga** (☎ 928 77 02 18), Edificio Habitat, offers wreck-diving trips. For exploring the dunes and surrounding areas, **Happy Biking,** Jumbo Center, rents bikes, equipment, guides, and picnic supplies. (☎ 928 76 82 98. 1500-4000ptas per day.)

The town of Playa del Inglés itself is little more than a cement wasteland, a sea of supermarkets and international restaurants catering to overnight guests. If you must stay here, **Residencia San Fernando,** C. La Palma, 16 (☎ 928 76 39 06 or 928 77 71 81), which goes by several other names, including "Casa de Huéspedes" and "Hotel," is the only budget accommodation in town. Follow Av. Tirajana uphill away from the beach; La Palma is the second right after the highway. Rooms are bare and clean, although bathrooms leave a little to be desired. Reservations are only accepted in person, but they'll tell you if there's anything available over the phone. The **tourist office** is on Av. España near C. Estados Unidos (☎ 928 77 15 50. Open in summer M-F 9am-2pm and 3-8pm, Sa 9am-1pm; in winter M-F 9am-9pm.) **Carnaval** hits Playa del Inglés with a vengeance, as it does every town in the Canaries (see **Carnaval!,** p. 495). The **Festival Atlántica,** a pop-music festival, features international stars for a long weekend in January.

ARUCAS (20MIN.)

Utinsa buses #205, 206, 209, 210, and 234 travel from the Las Palmas station to Arucas (every 30min. 6am-11pm, 245ptas).

Arucas, a delightful mountain town set on a dormant volcano, has a stunning neo-Gothic church and a genuine, relaxed atmosphere—for those who can tear themselves away from the beach, it makes a perfect daytrip from Las Palmas. Overlooking a set of gardens, the **Church of San Juan Bautista** is a magnificent structure almost wholly constructed by local stonemasons and artisans between 1909 and 1977. (Open daily 9am-1pm and 4-7pm. Free.) To get to the **tourist office** from the bus station, walk uphill to **Parque de La Paz,** and head left on C. León y Castillo to Pl. Constitución. (☎ 928 60 58 16. Open M-F 9am-2pm and 5-8pm, Sa 9am-1pm). There is one (and only one) place to stay in Arucas. A little *albergue* called **La Granja Escuela Anatol,** C. Ruz de Pineda, 5, provides a home for scholars—and you, too, if you reserve in advance. (☎/fax 928 60 55 44. 3200ptas per person.) A few cafes are scattered about Pl. San Juan, the square next to the church.

TEROR (20MIN.)

Ultinsa buses #216 and 218 run from Las Palmas to Teror (every 30min. 7am-9:30pm, 245ptas.) Bus #215 connects Arucas and Teror (every hr. 6am-9:55pm, 145ptas).

The quintessential Gran Canarian town, **Teror** is tucked away in the mountains. The town's church was built on the spot where 17th-century conquistador Don Juan de Frias saw a vision of the Virgin Mary. In the plaza facing the church is a small museum, **Casa de los Patrones de la Virgen,** built to resemble a 17th-century home.

THIS IS HAWK TO IBERIA, YOU'RE BIRDLESS FOR LANDING
The most important workers at Tenerife's airports wear their wings permanently: 21 intensively trained hawks patrol the skies above Los Rodeos and Reina Sofía, killing and scaring off seagulls and pigeons. The wayward gulls have caused near-wrecks in the past as they are sucked into plane engine turbines, and with an attractive landfill nearby, they flock in by the thousands. Fortunately, the hawks—especially the females—have carried out quite an effective anti-gull campaign. The best part? The search-and-destroy superstars only require wages of 120ptas a day in food. Handlers report that the hawks would never attack humans. As long as they're not flying, that is.

TENERIFE

Tenerife was aptly named from the Guanche words *tener*, meaning "snow," and *ife*, meaning "high mountain." In fact, Tenerife is home to the tallest mountain in Spain, El Teide (3718m). During Spanish conquest, the island was divided up into nine distinct *menceyatos*, and each developed its own architecture and culture. Although the island is now united, its broken landscape is indicative of its diverse rural populace; the northern half of the island is a verdant and hilly garden, while the south is an arid and endless black-sand beach. Tenerife's interior offers the Canaries' greatest hiking, a welcome escape from sun-scorched beaches, and sauerkraut *paella*. For those who long for still more seclusion, Santa Cruz and Los Cristianos provide transportation to the westernmost islands of El Hierro, La Palma, and La Gomera, not yet sacrificed to the lesser god of Tourism.

SANTA CRUZ DE TENERIFE

Before the Spanish Civil War, the government sent troublesome officers to out-of-the-way provinces. As a result, Franco became the General-in-Chief of the Canaries, scarring the port city of Santa Cruz (pop. 250,00) with the first shots of the Civil War. A somber cross commemorating the war-victims shadows the Plaza de España, but the city focuses on the future. With an expanding tourist industry, the port is a steel sea of ferries, jetfoils, and freighters, and the horizon is filled with cranes. Fortunately, although Santa Cruz rivals Las Palmas in commercialism, the city is comparatively scenic and pleasant and much more upbeat.

▐ TRANSPORTATION

Flights: See **Getting There and Away** and **Getting Around,** p. 500, for info on flights to, from, and around the islands. There are 2 airports on Tenerife. The majority of national flights head to the northern airport, **Los Rodeos,** while international flights dominate the south's larger **Reina Sofía** airport (☎ 922 75 92 00). Los Rodeos (☎ 922 63 59 98) is a few kilometers west of Santa Cruz. From Los Rodeos, buses #102, 107, and 108 run to town (20min., every 20min. 6am-midnight, 150ptas). From Reina Sofía (☎ 922 77 00 50), bus #341 heads to town (every hr. 5:30am-12:10am, 230ptas). **Iberia** (☎ 922 28 11 12). **Spanair** (☎ 922 63 58 13). **Air Europa** (☎ 922 75 92 94).

Buses: TITAS (☎ 922 21 56 99) serves all major towns from **Estación de Guaguas,** Av. Tres de Mayo, 47, down C. José Antonio Rivera from Pl. España. Some lines do not run during the summer, so call ahead for information. To **Puerto de la Cruz** (#102 has stops, #103 runs direct; 1hr., at least every 30min. 6:15am-9:40pm, then 11pm, 12:45, 3:15, 4:45am; 525ptas) and **Los Cristianos/Playa de América** (#110 and 111; 1hr., every 30min. 5:30am-11pm, 950ptas). Those planning to explore the island by bus should consider buying the **bonobus** ticket (2000ptas). The amount deducted from the card per ride is 30% less than the cost of individual tickets.

Ferries: Trasmediterránea (☎ 922 24 30 11). See **Getting Around,** p. 500.

Car Rental: Agencies are all over Santa Cruz, most around Pl. España. **Autos ADA,** C. Emilo Calzada, 10 (☎ 922 27 49 53). Cheapest car 4200ptas per day, including insurance and taxes. Open M-F 8am-1pm and 4-7pm, Sa 8am-2pm and 4-6pm, Su 9am-noon. **Avis** (☎ 903 135 531 or 913 480 348), in the airport. 4650ptas per day.

✳▐ ORIENTATION AND PRACTICAL INFORMATION

Despite its extensive bus system, Santa Cruz is easily navigable by foot. The port city expands from the **Plaza de España,** the center of tourist and local life. C. Castillo continues from the plaza into the commercial districts. Av. José Primo de Rivera and Av. Anaga, originating in Pl. España and running along the water, separate the port and the city. To get to Pl. España from the **ferry terminals,** turn left on Av. Francisco la Roche (with your back to the terminal), and follow it to the plaza (10min.). From the **bus station,** turn right on Av. Tres de Mayo, left on Av. de José Antonio Primo, and continue to the plaza (15min.).

Tourist Office: (☎ 922 23 95 92; fax 922 23 98 12; www.cabtge.es/puntoinfo), Pl. España. Facing the water, it's in the right corner nearest the water. Extremely helpful attendants. The free map, though lacking an index, is indispensable. Their website, updated monthly, is great. Open July-Sept. M-F 8am-5pm and Sa 9am-noon; Oct.-June M-F 8am-6pm, Sa 9am-1pm. The green **kiosk** in Pl. España (☎ 922 24 84 61) is less helpful than the office; an impractical aerial view map costs 200ptas.

Police: Av. Tres de Mayo, 72 (☎ 922 60 60 92).

Hospital: Hospital Militar, at C. Ramón y Cajal and C. Gral. Galcerán. From Pl. España, turn left on C. Murillo, right on C. Angel Guimera, and left on C. Gral. Galcerán.

Post Office: Pl. España, 2 (☎ 922 24 20 02). Open M-F 8:30am-8:30pm, Sa 9:30am-2pm. **Postal Code:** 38002.

Internet Access: Ciber Yakiciber, C. Ramón y Cajal, 23 (☎ 922 27 52 08). From Pl. España, turn left on C. Gen. Gutiérrez, right on C. Imeldo Seris, left on C. Valentín, and right onto C. Ramón y Cajal. Follow it past C. Iriarte and look left. 400ptas per hr. **El Navegante,** C. Combate, 12 (☎ 922 24 15 00). From Pl. España, take C. Béthencourt Alfonso and its continuations. Turn right on C. Combate; look on the right. A bar with a few computers in the corner. 200ptas for 15min., 400ptas for 30min., 800ptas per hr. Open M-F 7am-10:30pm, Sa 10:30am-11pm.

ACCOMMODATIONS

Unfortunately for budget travelers, hostels and *pensiones* in Santa Cruz are few and far between. What does exist fills up quickly, so reserve in advance. C. Castillo and C. Béthencourt Alfonso are scattered with one- and two-star hotels which are both luxurious and pricey. The tourist office has lists of accommodations, and their map marks hotels. Surprisingly, accommodations are even more difficult to come by on the rest of the island; consider reserving for a few days in Santa Cruz and exploring the rest of Tenerife on daytrips.

Hotel Horizonte, C. Sta. Rosa de Lima, 11 (☎ 922 27 19 36). From Pl. España take C. La Marina, a left onto C. Emilio Calzadilla, and a right onto C. Sta. Rosa de Lima. Simple rooms, all with bath. Singles 3500ptas; doubles 5225ptas; triples 6270ptas.

Pensión Mova, C. San Martín, 33 (☎ 922 28 32 61). From Pl. España, take C. Marina and turn left onto C. San Martín. Multiple floors of clean if charmless rooms. Singles 1700ptas; doubles 3200ptas, with bath 3700ptas.

Hotel Oceano, C. Castillo, 6 (☎ 922 27 08 00 or 922 27 08 04), off Pl. España. Each room has a mini-bar, TV, and phone. Breakfast included. Singles 4000ptas; doubles 6000ptas, with separate beds 7000ptas (tax not included). V, MC, AmEx.

Hotel Anago, C. Imeldo Serís, 19 (☎ 922 24 50 90). From the plaza, go left on C. General Gutiérrez and right on C. Imeldo Seris. Spacious and spartan rooms. Singles 3255ptas, with shower 3660ptas, with bath 4620ptas; doubles with shower 5995ptas, with bath 7650ptas. V, MC, AmEx.

FOOD

Santa Cruz's restaurants are the unfortunate result of the city's burgeoning international tourist industry; *casas de china*, waikiki bars, and German *paella* spots line the streets. Cafes, restaurants, and bars crowd Pl. España, but Av. Anaga has better deals (*menus* for 950ptas) and chic *terrazas*. The **Mercado de Nuestra Señora de Africa,** across the river and one block inland from the Museo de la Naturaleza y el Hombre (see **Sights,** below), sells meat and produce most mornings. **Restaurante Da Gigi,** Av. Anaga, 43, has a lively *terraza* overlooking the port. The food warrants passing other restaurants on Av. Anaga. (☎ 922 24 20 17. Delicious salads 850-950ptas. Pizza 850-1000ptas. Open daily 1-4:30pm and 8pm-1am. V, MC.)

📻 🎵 SIGHTS AND ENTERTAINMENT

Santa Cruz's museums and sights serve as little more than air-conditioned beach breaks for the city's sunburnt tourists. The **Museo de la Naturaleza y el Hombre,** C. San Sebastián across from the river bed, is devoted to the natural sciences and history of the Canaries and displays Guanche mummies. If you're going to visit a museum for island history, this is the best. Audio-visual volcano documentaries complement detailed exhibitions on the past of each island. (☎ 922 20 93 20. Open in summer daily 9am-8:30pm; in winter daily 9am-9pm. 400ptas, students 200ptas. 50% discount with *bonobus* pass. Su free.) Santa Cruz is also graced by two handsome churches, the 16th-century **Iglesia de la Concepción,** three blocks south of Pl. España (open M-F 6-7:30pm), and the 17th-century **Iglesia de San Francisco,** one block inland on C. Hervas Villalba. The **Parque García Sanabria** doubles as an impressive botanical garden and an open-air sculpture museum with avant-garde works by Pablo Serrano, Rafael Soto, and Gustavo Torner.

🏖 🎭 BEACHES AND NIGHTLIFE

As on Gran Canaria, the **beaches** are Tenerife's true attraction. The black sand of **Almáciga, Benijo,** and **Las Gaviotas,** and the golden sand of **Las Teresitas,** an artificial beach, lie near Santa Cruz; all are accessible by frequent buses departing from the central bus station. Santa Cruz's **nightlife** is much calmer than that of Las Palmas. Bars and *terrazas* line Av. Anaga and C. José Antonio Rivera along the waterfront. **Camel Bar,** Av. Anaga, 41, is a virtual shrine to the phallic-nosed mascot of the tobacco giant, sporting old posters and advertisements urging readers to smoke Camels. Trendy music and a long bar keep the local crowd dancing (open daily 9pm-5am.) The party at disco-bar **Noctua Anaga,** Av. Anaga, 35 (☎ 922 29 04 61), spills out to its streetside tables until dawn. Liquor companies often sponsor parties at nightspots on Av. Anaga, drawing big crowds. Drinks cost around 600ptas.

LOS CRISTIANOS AND PLAYA DE LAS AMÉRICAS

The white sand on man-made Playa de las Américas is no natural aberration; it was brought in from the Sahara desert to complement the nearby gray-sand Los Cristianos beach. Developed into full-fledged tourist resorts in the 1960s and 70s, these two adjacent towns probably have more five-star hotels than local residents. Their beaches are hardly the equals of Fuerteventura's, but they do boast better dining and nightlife than Tenerife's other tourist spots. Las Américas and Los Cristianos can serve as a base for exploring other shores in the south, including **Playa del Médano,** one of Tenerife's best and a windsurfing hot-spot. Los Cristianos also serves as the departure point for ferries to La Gomera.

◻ TRANSPORTATION. Although Playa de las Américas and Los Cristianos are actually two separate towns, they are considered one by tourists and tourist offices alike. **Paseo Marítima** connects Playa de las Américas to its southern neighbor Los Cristianos. Ferries leave from the port in Los Cristianos, connecting Tenerife to the western islands. **Fred Olson** (☎ 922 79 05 56) and **Trasmediterránea** (☎ 902 45 46 45) run ferries to **San Sebastián, Valverde** (on El Hierro) and **Santa Cruz** (on La Palma). For more info, see **Getting Around,** p. 500. The bus station (☎ 922 79 54 27) is on Ctra. General in Playa de las Américas. Buses run to **Santa Cruz** (#110, 111; every 30min. 6am-10pm, then 11:15pm, 12:30, and 4:30am; 950ptas), **Puerto de la Cruz** (#343, 4 per day 9am-5:45pm, 1475ptas), and the **Reina Sofía airport** (#487; every hr. 7:20am-9:20pm, 275ptas). Buses #110 and 111 link Playa de las Américas and Los Cristianos, stopping frequently along the shore.

⚡ ORIENTATION AND PRACTICAL INFORMATION. With your back to the bus station, take a left and then your first right and follow the shore to the **tourist office**, Av. Rafael Puig, 1, in Playa de las Américas. (☎ 922 75 06 33. Open M-F 9am-4pm.) **Police** (☎ 922 79 78 50), are on Av. Valle Menéndez, in Los Cristianos. From Av. Marítima, take C. General Franco, turn right on C. Barranquillo, and left on Av. Valle Menéndez. The **post office** is on C. Sabandenos. (Open M-F 8:30am-2:30pm, Sa 9:30am-1pm.) The **postal code** is 38650. For **Internet access**, try **Atlantis Net,** C. General Franco, 36. (☎ 922 75 37 17. 600ptas for 30min., 1000ptas per hr.

▟▛ ACCOMMODATIONS AND FOOD. Pl. Américas is full of resort hotels, so unless you're planning to splurge, stick to C. General Franco in Los Cristianos. Although there are quite a few *pensiones*, they are almost always full, so be sure to call ahead. **Pensión La Playa,** C. Paloma, 9, off Av. Marítima, across from the La Paloma restaurant, offers surprisingly quiet rooms. (☎ 922 79 22 64. Communal bathrooms. Singles 2500ptas; doubles 4000ptas.) **Pensión Corisa,** C. Antigua del General Franco, 18, connected to C. General Franco, a few blocks inland from Av. Marítima across from the gas station, has dark, small rooms and a boisterous restaurant below, but the price is right. (☎ 922 79 07 92. Singles 2500ptas; doubles 4000ptas.) **Food** in both towns caters to international taste buds and big budgets but is marginally better in Los Cristianos. **Supermercado Carolina,** C. General Franco, is a friend to the **grocery-shopping** budget traveler. (☎ 922 79 30 69. Open M-Sa 8am-2pm and 4-8:30pm. Visa.)

▟▛ BEACHES AND NIGHTLIFE. Playa de las Américas makes the most postcard appearances, but the beach in Los Cristianos is less crowded. Either way, you will tan. Information kiosks and parked info-vans line each beach, full of fliers for **water sports, fishing,** and **scuba diving. Naútica Eurocanaria** (☎ 922 71 26 45) offers parasailing (solo 4000ptas, tandem 7000ptas), and the **Yellow Boat** (☎ 922 75 24 16) leaves Los Cristianos three times a day for multilingual whale-watching. **Nightlife** in these towns is a collage of fluorescent lights, bikini contests, and imported beer averaging 400ptas. Both have plenty of two-story discos illuminated by flashing neon signs. Bars, which often host theme nights, also line the main drags.

PUERTO DE LA CRUZ

Filled with a wholesome energy, colorful streets, and two of the best restaurants in the Canaries, this port town (pop. 25,000) is one of the most enjoyable urban spots in the islands. Once a capital of the wine trade and an important 17th-century connection to the New World, Puerto de la Cruz draws an eclectic mix of sailors and visitors: the steep streets are filled with African vendors, Spanish fishermen, tanned Europeans, and some unusually large lizards.

⚡ ORIENTATION AND PRACTICAL INFORMATION. Buses, C. Pozo, 1 (☎ 922 38 18 07), leave Puerto de la Cruz for: **La Orotava** (#350, 101, 353; 30min.; every 30min. 6:30am-8:30pm, every hr. 9pm-1:10am; 145ptas); **Santa Cruz** (#101, 102, and 103; 1hr.; every 30min. 6:15am-9:40pm, then 11pm, 12:45am, 3:15am, and 4:45am; 525ptas); **Playa de las Américas** (#343; 1hr., 4 per day 9am-5:35pm, 1475ptas); and **El Teide** (#348; 1½hr., 9:15am, 1800ptas). Puerto de la Cruz wraps around a port, expanding from Playa San Telmo and the nerve-center, **Plaza del Charco.** To get to Pl. Charco from the **bus station,** turn right on C. Pozo (with your back to the station), continue as it turns into C. Dr. Ingram, and turn left on C. Blanc (10min.). Find help at the **tourist office** in Pl. Europa. From Pl. Charco, head toward the port on C. Blanco, and turn right on C. Santo Domingo; the office is across the plaza on the left. (☎ 922 38 60 00; fax 922 38 47 69. Open July-Sept. M-F 9am-7pm, Sa 9am-noon; Oct.-June M-F 9am-8pm, Sa 9am-1pm.) In an **emergency** dial ☎ 112; **police** (☎ 922 38 12 24), are in Pl. Europa. Mail your letters at the **post office,** C. Pozo, 14, across from the bus station. (☎ 922 38 58 02. Open M-F 8:30am-2:30pm, Sa 9:30am-1pm.) The **postal code** is 38400.

CANARY ISLANDS

⌐⌐ ACCOMMODATIONS AND FOOD. *Pensiones* are comfortable and plush in Puerta del Cruz—reserve in advance if you don't want to pay hotel prices. An excellent option is **Pensión los Geranios,** C. Lomo, 14. From Pl. Charco, turn left on C. Felipe, right on C. Pérez Zamora, and left on C. Lomo. (☎ 922 38 28 10. Doubles from 3800ptas.) Plain rooms overlook a stunning tropical garden at **Pensión la Platanera,** C. Blanco, 29, off Pl. Charco and toward the mountains. (☎ 922 38 41 57. Doubles 4900ptas.) A magical dinner awaits in the enchanting, candle-lit dining room of ⎧**El Mana,** C. Agustín de Béthencourt, 28, where a daytime tour guide serves up delicious vegetarian plates (1000ptas) from her tiny kitchen by night. (☎ 922 34 04 51. Open Th-Tu 7:30-11pm.) Equally delectable is ⎧**La Rosa de Bari,** C. Lomo, 23, a subtly elegant spot where a Bari native makes his own fresh pasta and Italian fare that puts imitators to shame. (☎ 922 36 85 23. Entrees 600-1500ptas. Open Tu-Su 12:30-3pm and 6:30-11pm.)

⎧⎧ SIGHTS AND ENTERTAIMENT. The parade of flowers, tourists, bathing suits and palm trees makes Puerta de la Cruz a sight in itself. A walking tour of the city, finishing on the water, is an afternoon well spent. Next to Pl. Europa, fishermen display their latest catches, and older women sell bunches of tropical plants. The **Museo Arqueológico,** C. Lomo, 9, exhibits replicate the processes and ceremonies used by the prehistoric natives to produce pots, urns, jewelry, and decorations. (☎ 922 37 14 65. Open Tu-Sa 10am-1pm and 5-8pm, Su 10am-1pm. 200ptas, students 100ptas.) Although beaches are lacking, the stunning **Lago Martiánez,** a nature-based water park of pools and fountains designed by César Manrique (see **César Manrique,** p. 515), fills the tanning and swimming voids. Nearby **Playa Martiánez** contains Guanche caves.

Party-primed locals and tourists mix in Puerto's virile **nightlife. Color Café,** building Rincon del Puerto 1st floor, Plaza de la Cruz, is a fantastic Cuban-themed bar with specialty drinks, cool jazz, and windows overlooking the plaza. (☎ 629 70 90 81. Drinks 400-600ptas.) Although high-season peaks in the winter months, tourists are also drawn to the **Fiestas de Julio,** two weeks of live performances and festive meals centered around the July 16th Fiesta del Virgen del Carmen, in which an image of the fisherman's saint is paraded through town and out into the ocean.

DAYTRIP FROM PUERTO DE LA CRUZ: LA OROTAVA (30MIN.)

Buses #350, 101, and 353 run from Puerto de la Cruz and stop here (30min., at least every 30min. 6:30am-8:30pm and every hr. 9pm-1:10am,145ptas).

Named after the lush valley that spreads out below its balconies, the small town of La Orotava warrants a daytrip from Puerto de la Cruz. Seventeenth- and 18th-century nobility resided here, leaving a number of elegant squares, streets, and churches renowned for their artistic balconies. If you intend to visit the sights, plan a weekday for the jaunt—most establishments here are closed on weekends. From the bus station, follow C. Calvario and its continuations to the **tourist office,** C. Carrera del Escultor Estévanez, 2. (☎ 922 27 85 10. Open M-F 10am-6pm).

The tourist office map cites over 15 houses and churches; though it would take forever to see them all, the following walking-tour should take two hours. From the tourist office, turn left down C. Tomás Zerolo to find **Iglesia de Santo Domingo,** whose chapel houses several notable paintings and a museum examining Spain's role in Latin America. (Church open during mass. Free. Museum open M-F 9am-6pm, Sa 9am-2pm. 250ptas.) **Iglesia de la Concepción,** off C. Cologon, is perhaps the Canaries' most graceful Baroque building. Rebuilt in the late 18th century after earthquakes ravaged it, the church has a marble dome over the altar and its myriad works. Especially delicate is Angelo Olivari's rendition of the Concepción. Check out the church's collection of jewels brought over from the Americas. (Open M-Sa 9am-1pm and 4-8pm. Free.) From the church, go uphill on C. Tomás Pérez and right on C. Carrera to see the neo-classical **Palacio Municipal** and the **Plaza del Ayuntamiento.** The cobblestones in the plaza are the result of regal egotism—Alfonso XIII ordered the streets paved before he visited. Just up C. Tomás Perez, the sensory explosion of **Hijuela del Botánico,** behind iron gates, offers celestial walkways through manicured displays of tropical flora. (Open M-F 8am-2pm. Free.)

EL TEIDE NATIONAL PARK

Towering 3178m over Tenerife, Spain's highest peak presides over a vast, unspoiled wilderness. El Teide itself forms the northern ridge of a much larger volcano that erupted millions of years ago; the remaining 16km wide crater only hints at the size of the explosion. Today the peak graces the Spanish 1000ptas note, and the Spanish park service likes to say that it allows us to ponder "our miserly insignificance." El Teide shadows peaceful fields of the most vibrant wildflower fields on earth, but the area's volcanic activity has not yet ceased. Slow sinking over centuries has produced the park's most unique features, including the crumbling **Caldera,** a crater with a diameter of 17km. In 1798, during the last major eruption, lava seeped down the slopes of **Pico Viejo** (3102m). **Las Canadas,** comprised of collapsed craters, is another evocative product of the sinking process. Watch out for the **Lagarto Tizón,** a rather large lizard lurking in the park.

The park is accessible by **bus** from Puerto de La Cruz. Bus #348 departs from the station at 9:15am and leaves El Teide at 4pm (1½hr., 1800ptas). Renting a **car** provides flexibility and allows exploration of the wildly different but equally beautiful views of the eastern (from Puerto de la Cruz) and western (from Los Cristianos) access roads. Bus #348 stops first at the **visitors center,** (☎ 922 29 01 29). The bus continues to the **cable car,** which climbs the final 1000m, ending next to Teide's peak (daily 9am-5pm; 3000ptas, children 1800ptas). It stops last at the **Parador,** which has free brochures, maps, and a restaurant but is less helpful than the visitors center. Several hiking trails start at the Parador.

By calling the national park information service (☎ 922 29 01 29 or 922 29 01 83; open M-F 9am-2pm) you can reserve a spot on one of the nine **free guided hikes** that depart daily, and inquire about the most scenic routes for the day. Eight **unguided hikes** allow for independent pacing and meandering. The Parador occupies an idyllic setting next to the emblematic **Roques de García** (2140m), rock chimneys and remnants of volcanic eruptions that face their creators, Mt. Teide and Pico Viejo. An enjoyable three-hour hike circles the huge formations and leaves plenty of time to spare for bus-riders. Hikes to the peak require two days; walkers spend the night at **Refugio Altavista,** past the Montana Blanca. To reserve a spot contact the office in Santa Cruz (☎ 922 23 98 11; open M-F 9am-2pm). The summit is difficult to reach in the winter, especially as the refuge is only open from March to October.

FUERTEVENTURA

Named Fuerteventura after the "strong winds" that whip along the western coast, this island is the second largest in the archipelago. Conqueror Jean de Béthencourt established a permanent base here in the 15th century, but Fuerteventura has had a relatively quiet history, save the occasional pirate raid. Today goat farms, fallen windmills, and whitewashed villages speckle the island's arid interior, while towering sand dunes and massive resorts line the exquisite beaches. Europeans fly in here by the jumbo-jet; those in search of touristless peace will have to escape to small towns in the mountains.

PUERTO DEL ROSARIO

Until 1957, Fuerteventura's whitewashed capital was known as Puerto de Cabras (Goats' Harbor) for the abundance of, you guessed it, goats. Although goats may still outnumber citizens, Puerto del Rosario (pop. 17,000) has continued to grow as an important port and fishing center since its founding in the 18th century. Lined with cement houses, the modest neighborhoods border on bleak, and most visitors do little more than pass through the city on their way to fairer sands.

CANARY ISLANDS

TRANSPORTATION. Transmediterránea and **Naviera Armas** run frequent ferries to and from Las Palmas; for more information, see **Getting Around**, p. 500. **Tiadhe buses** (☎ 928 85 21 66) stop at Av. Constitución and C. León y Castillo and run to: **Morro Jable** (#1, 2hr., M-Sa 8 per day 7am-7pm, 1055ptas); **Corralejo** (#6, 45min., every 30min. 7am-10pm, 360ptas); **Bentacuria** (#2, 45min., M-Sa 2 per day 11am and 2:30pm, 410ptas); and the **airport** (20min., 13 per day 7am-8pm, 130ptas). For a **taxi**, dial ☎ 928 85 00 59 or 928 85 02 16; they generally cost 800ptas from the airport to the town center. For **car rental, Orlando** has offices at the airport (☎ 928 86 90 18) and on C. Carrero Blanco in Corralejo (☎ 928 53 50 24). Cars cost 3400ptas per day, including insurance, and you must be 21 to rent.

■■ **ORIENTATION AND PRACTICAL INFORMATION.** Everything in Puerto del Rosario is within easy walking distance. **Calle León y Castillo** is the main thoroughfare, running downhill to the port and ferry station. **Av. Primero de Mayo,** which runs perpendicular to C. León y Castillo, is the town's commercial center. The **tourist office,** Av. Constitución, 5, down the street from the bus station and 2 blocks from Av. Primero de Mayo, has a handy map of Fuerteventura's major towns. (☎ 928 53 08 44. Open M-F 8am-2pm.) In an **emergency**, dial ☎ 112 or call the **police**, C. 23 de mayo, 16, at ☎ 928 85 05 03. Fuerteventura's main **hospital** is on Ctra. Aeropuerto, and the **post office** can be found at C. Primero de Mayo, 58. (☎ 928 85 04 12. Open M-F 8:30am-8:30pm, Sa 9:30am-1pm.) The **postal code** is 35600.

■■ **ACCOMMODATIONS AND FOOD.** Unprepared budget travelers might find themselves stuck in Puerto del Rosario for a night or two until accommodations in other, more scenic towns open up. The majority of the budget accommodations are near the port, around C. Almirante Lallermand. **Hostal Tamasite,** C. León y Castillo, 9, has clean, pretty rooms right on the waterfront, complete with new TVs and phones. (☎ 928 85 02 80. Singles 2800ptas; doubles for 1 person 4000ptas; doubles 5000ptas.) **Apartamentos Rubén Tinguaro,** C. Juan XXIII, 48, has comfortable rooms with TVs, although the neighborhood is a bit bleak and empty. From Av. Primero de Mayo, turn right on C. León y Castillo, follow its continuation C. Almirante Lallermand, and turn left on C. Juan XXIII. (☎ 928 85 10 88. Singles 3000ptas; doubles 4500ptas.) For modern, spartan rooms with communal bathrooms, try **Pensión Macario,** C. Juan de Austria, 24, off C. Juan XXIII. (☎ 928 85 11 97. Reserve well in advance. Singles 2500ptas; doubles 3000ptas.) Food in Puerto del Rosario is equally standard; *cafeterías* are scattered along Av. Primero de Mayo and C. León y Castillo. One good find is the ■**Getaria Taberna,** C. Guise, 3, on a small alley next to Hostal Tamasite. (Open M-Sa 10am-4pm and 7pm-1am.)

■■ **SIGHTS AND ENTERTAINMENT.** Although Puerto del Rosario is an island capital and important port, it offers few diversions. Locals will even tell you that the beaches are sandboxes compared to Corralejo's. The town's only museum, **Casa Museo de Unamuno,** C. Rosario 11, displays various furnishings and books used by the exiled philosopher Miguel de Unamuno. (Open M-F 9am-1pm, Sa 10am-1:30pm. Free.) Although the town houses the barracks of the Spanish Foreign Legion, the nightlife is limited to little more than a beer at an average bar. For discos and dancing, head to Corralejo.

CORRALEJO

Corralejo's center is a zoo of German and English families, car rental shops, and restaurants (replete with owners hustling amblers toward their tables). To the south, however, protected sand dunes unfold into the crystal ocean, where wind and sea are the only sounds. Daily jetfoils to Playa Blanca, Lanzarote, make the town a necessary stop en route to Lanzarote.

⊟ TRANSPORTATION. Fred Olsen and **Naviera Armas** run daily **jetfoils** to **Playa Blanca, Lanzarote** (see **Getting Around,** p. 500). To get to the **port** take Av. General Franco (beach on the right) until it ends. Turn left, then right on C. José Segura Torres, and then right on C. Gral. García Escamez (20min.). **Tiadhe** runs **buses** from the **station** (☎ 928 85 21 66), off C. Lepanto, to **Puerto del Rosario** (#6, 45min., every 30min. 7am-10pm, 360ptas). From the bus station, C. Lepanto (5min.) leads to Av. General Franco, which is lined with **car rental** shops. For a **taxi,** call ☎ 928 86 61 08.

◪ ORIENTATION AND PRACTICAL INFORMATION. All activity extends from **Avenida General Franco,** where sunburned tourists walk from the sand dunes in the south to their apartments in the north. The **tourist office** in Pl. Grande de Corralejo, left off the end of Av. General Franco nearest the port, offers a list of accommodations (☎ 928 86 82 35; fax 928 86 61 86. Open in summer M-F 9am-1pm and 5-7pm; in winter M-F 9am-1pm and 4-7pm, Sa 9am-noon). In an **emergency,** call ☎ 112 or contact the **police** (☎ 928 86 61 07), on Po. Atlántico, near the intersection with Av. General Franco. The **hospital, International Medical Center,** is at Av. General Franco, 13. (☎ 928 53 64 32. Open M-Sa 9am-8:30pm, Su 10am-1pm.) Mail your letters at the **post office,** C. Lepanto, 19. (☎ 928 53 50 55. Open M-F 8:30am-2:30pm, Sa 9:30am-1pm.) The **postal code** is 35660. **Internet access** is available at **Internet Saloon,** C. Juan Sebastián Elcano, 22, left off C. Lepanto, at the end of C. General Franco. (☎ 928 53 59 56. 500ptas per 30min., 1000ptas per hr. Open M-Sa 9am-1pm and 5-8pm.)

▛◪ ACCOMMODATIONS AND FOOD. Apartments and hotels line the beach, but budget accommodations are rare. Unless you reserve ahead, you might find yourself back in Puerto del Rosario for the night. The English-speaking crew at **Hostal Manhattan,** C. Gravina, 23, a left off Av. General Franco when heading toward the port, offers plain, cool rooms, all with bath. (☎ 928 86 66 43; fax 928 86 62 27. Singles 3500ptas; doubles 6000ptas.) Beachfront, and slightly quieter, **Hotel Corralejo** offers simple rooms with ocean views. (☎/fax 928 53 52 46. Singles 4180ptas; doubles 5225ptas; triples 6270ptas.) For the most private lodgings, try **Apartamentos Hoplaco,** Av. General Franco, 45, which has basic rooms surrounding a quiet and flowered courtyard. Access to a small beach sets it apart from the hundred other complexes in town. (☎ 928 86 60 40. Reception open daily 10am-2pm. Studios for 1-2 people 4700ptas; apartments for 1-2 people 5800ptas; triples 6700ptas; in off-season prices drop at least 500ptas.) Unfortunately, **food** in Corralejo is not much better than anywhere else on the islands. Restaurants line Av. General Franco, and breakfast deals abound. Food spots on the waterfront are the cheapest; keep an eye out for *menús del día.* For picnic supplies or cheap eats, try **Los Corales Supermarket,** Av. General Franco, 40 (☎ 928 86 70 43; open M-Sa 9am-9:30pm, Su 2-9pm) or the underground **Supermercado Mas y Mas,** C. Caballa, 10 (☎ 928 53 52 81), at Av. General Franco.

◪⊞ BEACHES AND ENTERTAINMENT. Like nearby Morro Jable, Corralejo offers little beyond the beach. The **Parque Natural de Corralejo y Lobos** contains 10km of protected and rugged sand dunes for walking or soaking up the sun's rays. Although nudists occupy the many rock structures, varying degrees of attire are welcome. Adventure companies compete for business along Av. General Franco, catering to all athletic tastes and abilities. **Dive Centre,** C. Nuestra Señora del Pino, 36, (☎ 928 53 59 06) offers dive trips, lessons, and equipment rental. **Celia Cruz** rigs daily trips on catamarans with glass bottoms for underwater viewing. (☎ 610 86 48 91. 1300-5000ptas per person.) **Ventura Surf,** in the Apartamentos Hoplaco complex on Av. General Franco, rents windsurfing equipment (3900ptas per day) and offers a three-hour (11,000ptas) beginner's course and an eight-hour (19,000ptas) course for those wanting extra assistance. (☎ 928 86 62 95. Open daily 10am-6pm.)

Nightlife in **Corralejo** is a spectacle of tipsy tourists and leering locals. Bars tend toward the cliché, with surf or pub themes; most of them can be found along Av. General Franco and in the connecting shopping centers. Closer to the port, several live music venues spill decent tunes and a more local crowd into the breezy night air. The **Fiestas del Carmen**, beginning every July 16 and lasting for two weeks, make for a particularly lively visit. During the festival, volleyball competitions, outdoor dances, and other activities celebrate the town's patron saint.

BETANCURIA

An escape from the touristed coast line, Fuerteventura's amber interior reveals rocky villages, fallen windmills, and small farms with goats as tough as their owners. Betancuria, named by the modest Jean de Béthencourt, has been carved out of the side of a dormant volcano; shady palms and pockets of lush vegetation rise out of the dry, rocky mountains like a Jericho of sorts. From the bus stop it's an easy walk to the central **Iglesia de Santa María.** Betancuria's tranquil state offers a restful night's stay (especially if you miss the only bus back to Puerto Rosario). **Vicente Ruiz Méndez,** Roberto Trondan, 2, just past the bus stop, on the opposite side from the Museo Arqueológico, is a sometimes-pension run by a charming civil war veteran, whose wife was the first female mayor of any town in Spain (☎ 928 97 80 95; 2000ptas). Only two **buses** (#2, 45min., 11am and 2:30pm, 410ptas) run M-Sa from Puerto del Rosario, and **only one bus runs back** (12:30pm) so plan your trip wisely.

MORRO JABLE

Although rumored to be the site of buried German treasure, the only foreign gold in Morro Jable (pop. 6500) dangles from the wrists of the peninsula's many tourists; heavenly white sand and turquoise water have turned this former fishing village into a choice destination for sun-starved Europeans. Unfortunately for tourist-a-phobes, Morro Jable is a necessary stop between the peninsula and northern towns.

⊏ TRANSPORTATION. Though there is no bus station in town, **Tiadhe** buses (☎ 928 85 21 66) stop at the Centro Commercial de Jandia, on C. Gambuesas (across from the post office), and throughout town. **Buses** run to **Costa Calma** (#5, 1hr., 11 per day 8:30am-9pm, 400-500ptas) and **Puerto del Rosario** (#1, 2hr., 8 per day 6am-7pm, 1055ptas). **Taxis** (☎ 928 54 12 57) stand at the port. A ride to town costs 300ptas and to the resorts 600ptas. **Orlando,** in Apartamentos El Matorral, rents cars; as the peninsula's rough dunes are only navigable with four-wheel-drive vehicles, consider spending those few extra *pesetas.* (☎ 928 54 03 09. Min. age 21. 3400-5500ptas per day. V, AmEx.)

⟦ ORIENTATION AND PRACTICAL INFORMATION. Morro Jable is unique among Spanish towns for its lack of a central square. Instead, it spreads along the beach, with local life to one side and resorts to the other. **Av. Jandia,** which becomes **Av. del Saladar,** connects the two. Centro Comercial de Jandia and most hotels and restaurants line these two streets. Most of the town's roads inevitably lead to the beach. The port is located about 1km out of town. Though the **tourist office**, Av. Saladar, in the Centro de Comercial de Jandia, is rather unhelpful, it does stock brochures for water sports and hotels. (☎ 928 54 07 76. Open M-F 9am-3:30pm.) In case of an **emergency**, dial ☎ 112 or the **police,** C. Hibisco, 1 (☎ 928 54 10 22). Medical assistance is available at the **hospital, Centro Médico Jandia,** at the Jandia Beach Center. (☎ 928 54 15 43 or 928 54 74 73. Open 24hr. V, MC, AmEx.) The **post office** is on Av. Jandia, near C. Nuestra Señora del Carmen. (☎ 902 19 71 97. Open M-F 8:30am-2:30pm, Sa 9:30am-1pm.) The **postal code** is 35625. For email, try **Infotex,** C. Semador Velázquez Cabrera, 35. (☎ 928 54 04 10. 1500ptas per hr. Open M-F 10am-1pm and 5-9pm.)

▋▋▌ ACCOMMODATIONS AND FOOD. Budget accommodations in Morro Jable cluster around C. Maxorata and C. Senador Velázquez Cabrera. It is imperative that you call ahead for reservations; many unprepared travelers find themselves catching a bus to Puerto del Rosario for the night. **Hostal Maxorata,** C. Maxorata, 31, has fresh and airy double rooms, some with views of the beach. (☎ 928 54 10 87. 3000ptas, with bath 4000ptas.) A reasonable second choice is **Hostal Omahy,** C. Maxorata, 47, which has plain but comfortable rooms, all with full baths and balconies (☎ 928 54 12 54. Singles 3000ptas; doubles 4000ptas). **Apartamentos Casa Hierro,** C. Senador Velázquez Cabrera, 16, one street from C. Maxorata,is a short walk to the beach. (☎ 928 54 11 13. Doubles 5500ptas.) Morro Jable's **restaurants** are full of international flair—the town's Italian bistros, seafood joints, and German *konfiterias* line the beach.

▋▋▌ BEACHES AND ENTERTAINMENT. Morro Jable's ▊beaches are lined with bodies (though not necessarily bathing suits) from early morning to late night. Blessed with some of the islands' calmest waters and lushest sea life, Morro Jable also offers excellent opportunities to practice **water sports.** Innumerable **windsurfing** schools set up camp on the beach (the coast hosts the world freestyle competition in July). **Barakuda Club,** Av. Saladar, offers **scuba diving** and equipment rental (☎ 928 54 14 18. Dives Su-F at 9:30am and 2:30pm. 5000ptas per dive; 4000ptas with your own equipment.) Several more secluded beaches flank Morro Jable, accessible by car and bike. **Playa de Barlovento de Jandia** to the west is a less-crowded, windy sandstorm of dunes and rough waters. With neither museums nor cultural centers, Morro Jable's only distraction from the beach is the **Centro Comercial de Jandia,** located on Av. Saladar; it is here that the town's sparse **nightlife** takes place, concentrated in a few raucous bars selling imported beers (450ptas).

LANZAROTE

Having avoided construction of the high-rises and resorts that litter its western neighbors, Lanzarote is only beginning to scar a landscape that has changed little over the last few decades. The Spanish called this isle the *"isla tranquila"* because of its peaceful nature, and even today the name still fits. Ferry companies make it rather difficult to access the island, but Lanzarote definitely merits a visit.

ARRECIFE

Meaning "rocky reef," Arrecife, Lanzarote's hamlet capital (pop. 30,000), resides on the island's eastern coast, fringed with blackened lava and yellow sands. Home to the archipelago's largest fishing fleet, the harbor is packed with peeling boats. Tourism remains relatively subdued here, and although the city has little to offer beyond a modern art museum, its surplus of accommodations provide an excellent base for exploration of the rest of Lanzarote.

▐ TRANSPORTATION. Guasimeta Airport serves other islands and mainland Spain. Bus #4 runs from the airport to Arrecife (20min., every 30min. 8:20am-7:20pm, 125ptas), stopping at the end of Av. Fred Olsen; follow it along the water to Av. Gen. Franco. **Iberia** (☎ 928 81 03 50) serves the island as well. The **bus station** (☎ 928 81 24 58), C. Vía Medular, is open daily 8am-10pm. To get from there to the center of town, turn left on C. Vía Medular and right on C. León y Castillo. A more accessible stop is in front of Playa Reducto on Av. Fred Olsen, a continuation of Av. Gen. Franco. Buses run to: **Costa Teguise** (#1, every 20min. 6:40am-11:40pm, 145ptas); **Puerto del Carmen** (#2, 40min., every 20min. 6:20am-11:20pm, 200ptas); **Playa Blanca** (#6, 6 per day 6am-8:15pm, 415ptas); **Maguez** (#7, 4 per day 11:45am-8pm, 330ptas); and **Teguise** (#7, 9, and 10; 6 per day 7:40am-8pm; 120ptas). **Naviera Armas** (☎ 928 82 49 30) and **Trasmediterránea** (☎ 928 81 10 19) run frequent **ferries** to **Las Palmas** (on Gran Canaria) and less-frequent service to **Santa Cruz de Tenerife.** Trips to **Puerto Rosario** (on Fuerteventura) depart from **Playa Blanca. Fred Olsen** runs a free bus there from Puerto del Carmen at 9am and 5pm. For more info, see **Getting Around,** p. 500. For **car rental,** try **Auto Timanfaya,** C. Luis Morote, 28. (☎ 928 81 39 23. 4000ptas per day. Open M-F 9am-2pm and 5-8pm, Sa 9am-1pm.) For a **taxi** call ☎ 928 80 31 04 or wait by C. León y Castillo and Av. Generalísimo Franco.

CANARY ISLANDS

🛈 ORIENTATION AND PRACTICAL INFORMATION. Arrecife is easy to navigate on foot. **Av. Generalísimo Franco** and its numerous continuations spread from the western coast, near the **port,** to the eastern folds of Playa Reducto. The **tourist office** sits on the avenue, near its intersection with **Calle León y Castillo,** the main pedestrian thoroughfare, which runs perpendicular to the ocean. Office staff have the only map available of Arrecife, a list of inexpensive accommodations, ferry schedules, and attraction descriptions. (☎/fax 928 81 18 60. Open M-F 9am-1pm and 5-7pm, Sa 9am-1pm.) **Banks** lining C. León y Castillo will **exchange currency.** In an **emergency,** call ☎ 112 or dial the **police,** Av. Coll, 5 (☎ 928 80 16 36). Mail your letters at the **post office,** Av. Generalísimo Franco, 8. (☎ 928 80 06 73. Open M-F 8:30am-8:30pm, Sa 9:30am-1pm.) The **postal code** is 35500. For **Internet access,** go to **Redes Servicios Informática,** C. Colonel Bens, 17, left off C. José Antonio, coming from C. León y Castillo. (☎ 928 81 22 09. 675ptas per hr., students 350ptas. Open M-F 9am-2pm and 5-8pm, Sa 9am-1pm.)

📷🍴 ACCOMMODATIONS AND FOOD. While the other towns in Lanzarote often have only one *pensión,* Arrecife overflows with cheap beds. A number of accommodations occupy the area around C. León y Castillo. The tourist office has a list of accommodations with phone numbers and addresses (but no prices). **▣Residencia Cardona,** C. 18 de Julio, 11, has an impressive lounge, monstrous rooms, and gleaming bathrooms. From the tourist office, turn left on Av. Generalísimo Franco and right on C. 18 de Julio. Make reservations well in advance. (☎ 928 81 10 08. Singles 3300ptas; doubles 4500ptas.) The friendly owners at **Hostal San Gines,** C. Molina, 9, offer clean, ample rooms complete with saggy beds and pink bedspreads. From the tourist office, walk down C. León y Castillo; when it curves right, take the first left. (☎ 928 81 23 5. Singles 1950ptas, with bath 2450; doubles 3100ptas.) **Hostal España,** C. Gran Canaria, 4, at the end of C. León y Castillo's pedestrian section, has small but cheap rooms. (☎ 928 81 11 90. Singles 1700ptas; doubles 2500ptas.) Unlike in the rest of the Canaries, finding an inexpensive, untouristed restaurant is not a problem in Arrecife. Pizzerias line the waterfront, and better eateries lie a few streets back on C. José Antonio de Ribera. The huge new supermarket, **Hiperdino,** is halfway down the pedestrian section of C. Leon y Castillo (open M-F 9am-1:30pm and 5-9pm, Sa 9am-1:30pm). **▣Castillo de San José Restaurante and Bar** beneath the modern art museum outside of town, is perhaps the loveliest restaurant in the Canaries; stop by, even if only for a drink. Blended into the castle, wrapped in glass, and overlooking the harbor, the dining room has a view well worth the price. (☎ 928 81 23 21. *Tapas* 600-1900ptas. Great desserts 500-1500ptas. Open daily 1-4pm and 8-11:30pm; bar open 11am-1am.)

📷🎵 SIGHTS AND ENTERTAINMENT. Arrecife is graced with the Canaries' best museum, the **▣Museo Internacional de Arte Contemporáneo,** to the west of town, off Av. Naos, a continuation of Av. Generalísimo Franco. The original building, an 18th-century fortress built by Carlos III, was intended to defend the island from pirate attacks. It was originally known as the "Fortress of Hunger," as its construction added to the famine plaguing Lanzarote. Two hundred years later, its simple stone walls epitomize **César Manrique's** revitalization of the island's history and architecture (see p. 515). Exhibits rotate frequently, but geometric, formal, and abstract works form part of the permanent collection, fitting into the grooves of the fort and hanging into the restaurant below. (A 40min. walk; taxis from town cost 300ptas, and are safer after dark. ☎ 928 84 00 57. Open daily 11am-9pm. Free.) On Av. Generalísimo Franco, next to the tourist office, the **Castillo de San Gabriel** houses the **Museo Arqueológico.** Pottery pieces and a few Guanche skeletons occupy the erstwhile fort. (Open M-Sa 11am-6pm. 300ptas.) C. José Antonio fills Arrecife's **nightlife** quota with small, rambunctious bars and restaurants. On weekends, this street is a sea of bar-hopping expats and young locals. There's nary a nun in the packed **El Convento,** C. José Antonio Ribera, 76, and just down the road, the recently opened **Goa Goa Bar** draws crowds of beautiful people.

CANARY VISIONARY It is virtually impossible to spend a day on Lanzarote without hearing the name **César Manrique.** Born in 1919 in Arrecife, Manrique, an artist and architect, sought to construct buildings as extended natural forms. After a brief service in Franco's army, he began painting abstract canvases; by 1964, his works made their way to New York's Guggenheim Museum. When he returned to Lanzarote, Manrique dedicated himself to creating "a paradise for those who have an eye for the special." He persuaded the government to ban billboards and halt skyscraper construction, leaving the capital city an unobtrusive maze of whitewashed houses. His individual projects, scattered throughout the island, incorporate natural surroundings and clean lines, aiming to coexist with nature, rather than against it. For the initial design of the **International Museum of Contemporary Art,** Manrique drew a small sketch on the earth with a piece of chalk. Near Guatiza and Mala resides Manrique's **Jardín de Cactus,** a decaying mill whimsically converted into a mammoth cactus garden. (☎ 928 52 93 97. Open daily 10am-5:45pm. 500ptas.) Accessible from Arrieta on the northern coast, **Los Jameos del Agua** is another of Manrique's magical designs, a natural saltwater lagoon connected to an underground volcano tube. Within the grotto's lava formations, Manrique incorporated a concert cave, a restaurant, and a bar. (☎ 928 84 80 20. Open daily 9:30am-6:45pm. Tu and F-Sa open for dancing 7pm-3am. Restaurant open 1-4pm and 8-11:30pm. 1000ptas., at night 1100ptas.)
In 1992, Manrique donated his home in Taro de Thiche to the citizens of Lanzarote. Now known as the **Fundación César Manrique,** it is integrated into the five volcanic bubbles below. The living room has been transformed into a gallery exhibiting his private collection of works. (Open M-Sa 10am-6pm.) Although tour companies organize buses to the sights, renting a car is the only way to see many of Manrique's creations.

PUERTO DEL CARMEN

Puerto del Carmen, Lanzarote's largest tourist resort, lacks both the beaches and the character of Lanzarote's small towns. Primarily British tourists flock to the hotels, packaged and lobster-tied by one of many tour companies. **Avenida de las Playas** squeezes in endless restaurants, bars, and bazaars, for sunburned ambling tourists. Aside from the strip, the yellow sands of **Playa Blanca** supply the only entertainment. Offshore reefs, however, offer some of the islands best **scuba diving.** For more information try the **Delfín Club,** Av. Playas, 38, in the Centro Aquarium, which runs four dives a day from 10am-3:30pm. (☎ 928 51 42 90. 4500ptas for a beginner's course; 4200ptas for certified dives with equipment; 3100ptas if you have your own. Open M-Sa 9am-6pm.)

Bus #2 runs between Arrecife and Puerto del Carmen and stops along Av. Playas (40min., every 20min. 6:20am-11:20pm, 200ptas). **Fred Olsen** (☎ 922 62 82 31) and **Naviera Armas** (☎ 928 51 79 12) also run buses to Playa Blanca to meet their ferry departures. The **tourist office** is on Av. Playas in a white kiosk near the beach, but it offers little more than a photocopied map. (☎ 928 51 53 37. Open M-F 9am-1pm and 5-7pm, Sa 9am-1pm.) To explore the island to its fullest, rent a car—there are a lot of good deals along Av. Playas. **Lanzauto,** Av. Playas, 19, rents for 4000ptas and up per day, insurance and unlimited mileage included. (☎ 928 51 06 18. Min. age 21. Open M-F 8:30am-1pm and 4-8pm, Sa-Su 8:30am-1pm and 6-8pm.)

PARQUE NACIONAL DE TIMANFAYA

Known as **Montañas de Fuegos** (Fire Mountains), the barren landscape of Lanzarote's national park erupts with evidence of the six-year explosion that began in 1730. Resembling the surface of the moon, copper *hornitos* (mud-volcanoes) and blackened folds of solidified lava carve their way into the loose soil; only lichen seems to survive in the scorching ground. The only way to view the volcanic route is by tour bus. The mandatory 30-minute tour is restrictive but extremely informative. (☎ 928 84 00 56. Park open daily 9am-5:45pm. 1000ptas. Tour leaves from the entrance booth.) The magic tricks of **Islote de Hilario's** geothermal heat are the tour's highlight. Legend has it that the hermit Hilario, who lived here with his lone camel, planted a fig tree whose fruit was consumed by the underground fires. Similar spectacles are performed by park employees to demonstrate the effects of the 400°C temperatures below—a piece of brush put into the earth bursts into a ball of flames, and water poured into a metal pipe turns into fountains of steam.

The **El Diablo** restaurant that now occupies the *islote* was designed by Cesar Manrique and constructed using only stone, metal, and glass (due to the high temperatures). Volcanic heat seeping from the earth powers the kitchen's grill. The panoramic view from the dining room is the best on the island, extending from the arid mountains to the azure sea. (☎ 928 84 00 57. Open daily noon-3:30pm.) Unfortunately, no buses run to the park; you'll need to rent a car.

TEGUISE

Brushing the side of the Guanapays mountains (452m), Teguise is hands-down Lanzarote's prettiest village. Frequent buses run daily from Arrecife to Teguise (#7, 9, and 10; 6 per day 7:40am-8pm, 120ptas), stopping in front of the Ayuntamiento. To get to the **Plaza de la Constitución,** the center of town, face the Ayuntamiento, turn right on C. Santo Domingo, right on C. Morales Lemes, then right into the plaza, the site of the **Sunday market.** Teguise is famous for its authentic Canary Islands cuisine, and food stands flood the town on market day. **Iglesia de la Virgen de Guadelupe** resides in the corner of the plaza. Decorated with understated religious icons, the church's simple exterior clashes with its modern interior.

Just off the plaza, Pl. San Miguel houses the **Casa Museo Palacio Spinola,** named after a wealthy local merchant. With old photos of festivals and Canarian customs, it is a worthwhile visit. (☎ 928 84 51 81. Open M-F 10am-5pm and Sa-Su 10am-4pm. 300ptas.) The 16th-century **Castillo Santa Bárbara,** an uphill walk out of town, offers one of the island's best views. Built by Sancho de Herrera on the side of the Guanay volcano, the castle has changed hands several times throughout the centuries. Today it houses the **Museo del Emigrante Canario,** detailing the toils of emigration to the new world. Its collection, however, barely rivals the castle itself, with its seaward views of the whitewashed town and lava landscape. (Exit Pl. Constitución on C. Marqués Herrera, following its continuations up the mountain to the castle. Open Tu-F 10am-4pm, Sa-Su 11am-3pm. 300ptas.)

GOMERA

Many believe the verdant island of Gomera, with its lush terraced gorges and steep mountain passes, to be the most blessed of all the Canaries. German fans and disco stars look elsewhere; La Gomera's relative isolation and small, stony beaches keep the droves of tourists at bay. Surrounded by bananas and avocado plantations, and freshened by a constant breeze, the island's main town, San Sebastián, is refreshingly provincial. Gomera's crown jewel, however, is the spectacular Garajonay National Park, the last refuge for a species of forest that died out elsewhere millions of years ago. In Gomera, even bus rides are awe-inspiring.

SAN SEBASTIÁN DE GOMERA

Heading off to find the mythical Middle Passage to India, Christopher Columbus dropped anchor here for a few days. He gathered water from the well, prayed at the church, and fell in love with a girl before "discovering" the Americas. May your stay be as storied. These days most explorers skip this charming town, opting for the sandy beaches to the south. Still, as a transportation hub littered with affordable accommodations, good restaurants, and wholesome local feel, San Sebastián makes an excellent base for discovering the rest of La Gomera.

◧ TRANSPORTATION

Buses: The main bus stop is next to the ferry station on the port. Three lines start in the port and branch out across the island. Line 1 to **Valle Gran Rey** with stops in the **Parque de Garonjay** (M-Sa 5, 7, 11:30am, 2, and 6:30pm, Su 8:30am and 3pm; 675ptas). Line 2 to **Playa de Santiago** and **Alajero** (M-F 11:30am, 3:30, 6:30, and 9:30pm, Su 11am and 6:30pm). Line 3 to **Hermigua, Agulo,** and **Vallehermoso** (M-F 11:30am, 3:30, 6:30, and 9:30pm, Su 11:30am and 6:30pm).

Ferries: Trasmediterránea (☎ 920 87 13 24 or 920 80 59 68) and **Fred Olson** run several daily ferries to **Los Cristianos.** See **Getting Around,** p. 500, for details.

Car Rental: In the port terminal. Or try **Hertz,** Av. Colón, 15 (☎ 922 87 00 28), right off C. Medio. Opel Corsa with insurance 4705ptas per day; cheaper weekly. Min. age 21. Open M-F 9am-1pm and 4-7pm, Sa 9am-1pm. V, MC, AmEx.

◪♄ ORIENTATION AND PRACTICAL INFORMATION

Navigating San Sebastián is a breeze. One road runs along the entire coast, intersected midway by **Calle del Medio,** the town's main drag, at Pl. Américas. To get to the plaza from the **port,** walk down the wharf and turn left on Av. Fred Olsen; the plaza is on the right (5min.). If you arrive after dark, consider taking a quick taxi into town (300ptas), as the streets aren't clearly named and are difficult to maneuver in the dark. A new **bus station** is under construction at the corner of Av. Colón and Vía de Ronda, but inter-city buses currently stop at the port, meeting most ferries (though they're quick to leave once the ferry has arrived). If you've rented a **car,** turn right on C. Vía de Ronda and left on C. Sur to head out of town toward Valle de Gran Rey. Use extreme caution driving the island; blind corners on narrow mountain passes and wide-turning buses can be treacherous—honk that horn.

Tourist Office: C. Medio, 4 (☎ 922 14 15 12; fax 922 14 01 51), behind Pl. Américas. Offers a map of La Gomera with detailed inserts for San Sebastián and Valle de Gran Rey, as well as long lists of water sports. Open M-Sa 9am-1:30pm and 3:30-6pm, Su 10am-1pm. For info on the park, head to **Park Service,** C. Sur, 6 (☎ 922 87 01 05). Open M-F 8am-2:30pm. Take a left onto Av. Colón from C. Medio, and follow it across the highway. Bear left and find the office on the right at the bend.

Currency Exchange: Banks line Pl. Américas. Open M-F 8:30am-2pm, Sa 8:30am-1pm.

Emergency: ☎ 112.

Hospital: Nuestra Sra. de Guadalupe (☎ 920 14 02 02). From Pl. Américas, go away from the port, turn right on C. Vía Ronda, left across the bridge, and take the 1st right.

Post Office: C. Medio, 60 (☎ 902 19 71 97). Open M-F 8:30am-2:30pm. **Code:** 38800.

Internet Access: Ditch the slow, pricey Internet cafe for the quick, numerous computers in the back room of **Pedalan Informática,** C. Medio, 79 (☎ 922 87 20 17). 750ptas per hr. Open M-F 9:30am-1pm and 4:30-8pm, Sa 9:30am-2pm.

◤ ACCOMMODATIONS

San Sebastián's budget accommodations are more budget and more accommodating than those elsewhere in the Canaries. *Hostal* and *pensión* signs hang out of windows on C. Medio. Pricier hotels reside one street over on C. Ruiz de Padrón.

Pensión Colón, C. Medio, 59 (☎/fax 922 87 02 35). Tiled floors and a quiet courtyard make this the best pick in town, though the windowless rooms can get stuffy. Singles 2500ptas, negotiate 2000ptas for several-day stays; doubles 3500ptas.

Apartamentos San Sebastián, C. Medio, 20 (☎ 922 87 13 54 or 649 49 80 27; fax 922 14 14 75). Breezy and newly furnished apartments with 2 twin beds, a kitchen, and living room. Reception is in the money exchange office to the right when facing the entrance. Open 8:30am-1pm and 4-8pm. July-Sept. several-day stays 2 people 5500ptas; 1 person 5000ptas. One-night stays 6000ptas. Cheaper Oct.-June.

Pensión Victor-Leralita, C. Medio, 23 (☎ 607 51 75 65 or 670 81 32 01). The rooms in this 250-year-old house are spacious, clean, and high-ceilinged, if a bit rickety. Ask for the room with the terrace. Noisy restaurant downstairs provides tasty sandwiches (200ptas) and cheap beer (150ptas). Singles 2500ptas; doubles 3000ptas.

FOOD

San Sebastián is filled with authentic Spanish restaurants and cheap *tapas* joints. Nicer options surround Pl. Constitución, and typical bars and *mesones* line C. Ruiz de Padrón and C. Medio. For a meal on the run, try **Super Mercado Brito,** Pl. Constitución. (☎ 922 14 18 18. Open M-Sa 9am-9pm. V, MC.) Wednesdays and Saturdays a **fruit and vegetable market** fills the plaza with great deals on fresh produce. **Bar-Restaurant Cubino,** C. Virgen de Guadalupe, 2, off Pl. Constitución, serves delicious seafood and meat dishes in healthy portions to a local crowd. (☎ 922 86 03 83. Entrees 600-1500ptas. Open W-M 9am-4pm and 7pm-midnight.) **Gomera Garden,** C. Medio, 12, is the perfect place for a date; carefully prepared local fare graces candlelit tables in a romantic interior garden. (☎ 922 14 12 63. Entrees 700-1400ptas. Open daily noon-4pm, 6:30-11pm.)

SIGHTS

The few sights in San Sebastián are centered on a foreigner: Columbus. On C. Medio (down the street from the Columbus Casino) is the **Iglesia de la Asunción,** where Columbus prayed before he left. The carved woodwork adorning the simple church is typical of Canarian architecture. Nearby, the **Casa de Colón,** C. Medio, 50, hosts a small and unimpressive exhibit on the explorer's life. Don't miss the religious icon made out of pure sugar. (Open M-F 4-7pm. Free.) The **Torre del Conde,** a small 15th-century fort, looms over the beach. In 1488, the wife of the murdered governor Hernán Peraza bolted herself inside as she watched the citizens take control of the port. (Open Tu-F 10am-1pm.) The tourist office is located inside **La Casa de la Aguada,** which features the well from which Columbus drew water to "baptize the Americas." Have a sip—maybe you'll get lucky too.

No Canarian city would be complete without a **beach.** Although there is a small patch of black sand in front of Pl. Américas, **Playa de la Cueva** has more sand, calmer waters, caved cliffs, and a view of Tenerife, if more wind. From Pl. Américas, follow Av. Fred Olsen toward the port and curve left away from the wharf. The tourist office has information on **diving, boating,** and **fishing** excursions.

GARAJONAY NATIONAL PARK

Blanketed in thick mist and fog that produces a "horizontal rain," the Garajonay National Park sustains the last **laurisilva forest** on earth. Once ubiquitous in the Mediterranean basin, these moss-filled forests fell victim to the Ice Age millions of years ago. Hikers in Garajonay wade through lush ferns, myriad streams, and dripping plants to reach a stunning mountaintop view of the other islands. The park maintains numerous trails and **three self-guided paths.** A **car** greatly facilitates exploration of the park, but several of the best trails are reachable via bus. Strangely, the **visitors center** (☎ 922 80 09 93) is in **Agulo,** 9km outside of the park (open daily 9:30am-4:30pm). To get to the visitors center take bus #3 from San Sebastián (45min., 4 per day 11am-9:30pm) and get off at the Las Rosas stop. The **Park Service,** Cta. General de Sur, 20, in San Sebastián, has the same info. (☎ 922 87 01 05. Open M-F 8am-2:30pm). Either office can make the reservations required for the free guided tours, and both carry the booklet whose descriptions corresponds to the numbered wooden signs on the park trails.

JUST GIVE A WHISTLE No, it's not the moped alarm and probably not that sleazy guy across the street; that piercing noise you just heard is a demonstration of **El Silbo**, the Guanche whistle language. This is not just your average whistle; "speakers" make full use of both hands to manipulate the sound. The language, which has a complete alphabet, developed in order to communicate over long distances over the island's rough terrain. During the Spanish conquest, El Silbo dwindled, and today it is only used to garner a few *pesetas* from amazed tourists.

VALLE GRAN REY

Green terrace farms slosh back from sandy beaches into the deep gorge of the "Valley of the Great King." The mellow shores keep a mostly tourist population content with sunbathing, cliff-exploring, and water sports, while farmers work the peaceful valley above. Because of its beaches, Valle Gran Rey is probably the nicest place to base a stay in La Gomera, but it can be slightly expensive.

The most popular beaches are **Playa de Aruga** and **Playa las Américas,** a short walk left (when facing the beach) of Vueltas. The sandy **Playa de Calera** and **Playa de Puntilla,** which stretch left from La Playa, have calm waters. **Playa del Inglés** features waves, nearby cliffs, and naked bodies, a 10-minute walk from La Playa. With your back to the tourist office turn right, take your first right, and follow the road, as it becomes dirt, to the beach. **Bus #1** runs from San Sebastián to the Valle Gran Rey's three small villages: **La Calera, La Playa,** and **Vueltas,** in that order. (2hr.; M-F 5 per day 5am-6:30pm, Su 8:30am and 3pm; 675ptas.) La Caleras sits up higher in the valley, while La Playa and Vueltas cover the shores below. The sides of the triangle they form are less than a kilometer long. Street signs are nonexistent, but the area is easy to navigate—for help, stop at the **tourist office** in La Playa on C. Noria, can help with lodging and info on **whale-watching, Internet access,** and **bike rental.** (☎/fax 922 80 54 58. Open in winter M-Sa 9am-1:30pm and 4-6:30pm, Su 10am-1pm; in summer M-Sa 9am-1pm and 4-6pm, Su 10am-1pm.) From the La Playa bus stop, face the beach, head right on the main road, and turn left on C. Noria.

Unfortunately, Valle Gran Rey's charm and scenery come at a price—expensive accommodations. The few *pensiones* only offer doubles. **Casa Bella Cabellos** on C. La Alameda in La Calera offers great views from modern, balconied apartments, as well as simple wooden doubles in an antique home. From the bus stop, follow the road up the valley, take the first left (almost an uphill U turn), follow the road past the San Sebastián bar, then bear right at the "do not enter sign," and follow the road up the hill until it flattens out. It's on the left. (10min.) Driving into town you'll see a "Centro de Salud" sign on your right. Turn and follow the road as it winds up to the Casa. (☎ 922 80 51 82. Modern apartments: double with fridge 3500ptas; 4-person with kitchen 6500ptas. House rooms: 2500ptas.) Also in La Calera, **Pension Parada** offers simple doubles (a bath for every 2 rooms) right next to the bus stop and a 10-minute walk from the beach. (☎ 922 80 50 52; fax 922 28 13 10. 3000ptas.) **Las Vueltas** has spartan doubles, just north of the island's best beaches. (☎ 922 80 52 16. Singles 5000ptas; doubles 5000ptas; cheaper for week-long stays.)

EL HIERRO

The smallest of the Canary Islands, El Hierro was thought by Ptolemy to be the edge of the world. Even now, few venture west to its scattered villages and jagged coastline. With a horizon free of high-rise resorts and neon signs and filled with jagged juniper trees, El Hierro offers visitors an opportunity to explore traditional interior towns and small fishing ports and to do some rewarding hiking. The island's most infamous celebration, **Bajada de los Virgen de dos Reyes,** starts every four years in **La Ermita de los Reyes.**

The port town and tourist center **La Restyinga** is renowned for its scuba diving. Farther north is **El Pinar**, a series of small villages encircled by dense pine forests. To the east emerges **Malpaso** peak (1501m), El Hierro's zenith. Unfortunately, beaches are scarce and inferior to the golden stretches on Gran Canaria and Fuerteventura. On the western coast, the sun-addicted can get their fix at **Playas del Verodal** and **Arenas Blancas.** To the northeast, the capital city of **Valverde** serves as little more than a bridge to the ferry stations and airport (see **Getting Around,** p. 500). The main **tourist office,** C. Licenciado Bueno, 1 (☎ 922 55 03 02 or 922 55 03 26; fax 922 55 10 52), is located here. El Hierro is most accessible by ferry from Los Cristianos de Tenerife. **Transmediterránea** comes from San Sebastián de Gomera (3½hr., 10:15am or 7:15pm, 2615ptas), as does **Fred Olsen** (3hr., 9:30am, 2540ptas).

LA PALMA

Painted green and lush by heavy rainfalls, it's easy to see the origins of La Palma's nickname, *"isla bonita."* It's also easy to see why Madonna used it as the subject of one of her songs. Although the island was an important transatlantic port during colonial days, today relatively few visitors sail into the capital of **Santa Cruz.** With colonial houses and carved-balconies lining the streets, the port city retains the old world charm of its glory days. Sharp coastlines and cliffs trace the island and dissuade sunbathers, but hikers will discover a mountainous paradise, as La Palma is the world's steepest island. A volcanic crater almost 10km wide, **La Caldera de Taburiente,** commands the center. Thick Canarian pines cover the rest of the national park, and a world-renowned observatory caps the **Roque de los Muchachos.** Although the northern town of **Los Llanos de Aridane** has a stunning **botanical garden** in the **Pueblo Parque La Palma,** the volcanos to the south offer more opportunities for hiking. The views from **Volcán Teneguía** and **San Antonio** stretch to the neighboring eastern islands. Contact the **tourist office** (☎ 922 41 21 06) for details on exploring the island. Ferry companies make it difficult to access La Palma, so be sure to plan ahead. **Trasmediterránea** (☎ 902 45 46 45) offers the most options, with ferries from **San Sebastián** (3½hr., M-Sa 10:15am, 2415ptas) and **Valverde** (14hr., Sa-W 11:45pm, 2995ptas).

PORTUGAL

LIFE AND TIMES

During the 14th and 15th centuries, Portugal was one of the most powerful nations in the world, ruling a wealthy empire that stretched from America to Asia. Although the country's international prestige declined by 1580, Portuguese pride did not. During the following centuries, Portugal struggled to assert its national identity (and its uniqueness from Spain). Modern Portugal, with its stable democracy and fast-growing economy, has proved the strength of its national character.

HISTORY AND POLITICS

EARLY HISTORY. Several tribes inhabited the Iberian Peninsula during the first millennium BC. The first clearly identifiable inhabitants were **Celts,** who began to settle in northern Portugal and Spanish Galicia in the 9th and 8th centuries BC, establishing small agricultural and herding societies throughout the countryside. Around the same time, **Phoenicians** founded several fishing villages along the Algarve and ventured as far north as modern-day Lisbon. The **Greeks** and **Carthaginians** followed them, settling the southern and western coasts. After their victory over Carthage in the Second Punic War (218-201 BC) and their defeat of the Celts in 140 BC, the **Romans** gained control of central and southern Portugal, integrating the region into their Iberian province of Lusitania. Six centuries of Roman rule, which introduced the *Pax Romana* and "latinized" Portugal's language and customs, also paved the way for Christianity.

VISIGOTHS AND ARABIAN KNIGHTS (469-1139). When the Roman Empire declined in the 3rd and 4th centuries AD, the Iberian Peninsula felt the effects. By AD 469, the **Visigoths,** a tribe of migrating Germanic people, had crossed the Pyrenees, and for the next two centuries they dominated the peninsula. In AD 711, however, the Muslims (also known as the **Moors**) invaded Iberia, toppling the Visigoth monarchy. Although these invaders centered their new kingdom of *al-Andalus* in Córdoba, smaller Muslim communities settled along Portugal's southern coast, an area they called the *al-Gharb* (now the Algarve), and after nearly four centuries of rule, the Muslims left a significant legacy of agricultural advances, architectural landmarks, and linguistic and cultural customs.

THE CHRISTIAN RECONQUISTA AND THE BIRTH OF PORTUGAL (1139-1415).
Though the *Reconquista* officially began in 718, it didn't pick up steam until the
11th century, when Fernando I united Castilla and León and provided a strong
base from which to reclaim territory. In 1139, **Afonso Henriques** (Afonso I), a noble
from the frontier territory of Portucale (a region centered around Porto), declared
independence from Castilla and León. Soon thereafter he named himself the first
King of Portugal, though the papacy did not officially recognize the title until 1179.

With the help of Christian military groups like the Knights Templar, the new
monarchy battled Muslim forces, capturing Lisbon in 1147. By 1249, the *Reconquista* defeated the last remnants of Muslim power with successful campaigns
in the Alentejo and the Algarve. The Christian kings, headlined by **Dinis I** (Dom
Dinis; 1279-1325), promoted use of the Portuguese language (instead of
Spanish) and with the **Treaty of Alcañices** (1297) settled border disputes with
neighboring Castilla and asserted Portugal's identity as the first unified,
independent nation in Europe.

THE AGE OF DISCOVERY (1415-1580). The reign of **João I** (1385-1433), the first
king of the House of Aviz, ushered in unity and prosperity never before seen in
Portugal. João increased the power of the crown and in so doing established a
strong base for future Portuguese expansion and economic success. The Anglo-
Portuguese alliance which he secured with the **Treaty of Windsor** (1386) would
come to influence Portugal's foreign policy well into the 19th century.

The 15th century was one of the greatest periods in the history of maritime
travel and naval advances. Under the leadership of João's son, **Prince Henry the Navigator,** Portugal established itself as a world leader in maritime science and exploration. Portuguese adventurers captured the Moroccan city of Ceuta in 1415,
discovered the Madeiras Islands in 1419, happened upon the uninhabited Azores in
1427, and began to exploit the African coast for slaves and riches a few years later.

Bartolomeu Dias changed the world forever when he rounded Africa's Cape of
Good Hope in 1488. Dias opened the route to the East and paved the way for Portuguese entrance into the spice trade. The Portuguese monarchs may have turned
down **Christopher Columbus,** but they funded a number of momentous voyages. In
1498, they supported **Vasco da Gama,** who led the first European naval expedition
to India; successive expeditions added numerous East African and Indian colonies
to Portugal's empire. Two years after da Gama's voyage, **Pedro Alvares Cabral**
claimed Brazil for Portugal, and Portugal established a far-flung empire.

Portugal's monarchy reached its peak with **Manuel I The Fortunate** (1495-1521) on
the throne. Known to foreigners as "the King of Gold," Manuel controlled a spectacular commercial empire. However, before the House of Aviz lost power in 1580,
signs of future decline were already becoming evident, and it was not long before
competition from other commercial powers took its toll.

IF GILLIGAN HAD BEEN SO LUCKY Paradise on
earth? Start with water, water, everywhere. Add some volcanic eruptions, for solidity's
sake. Mix in hearty, friendly, and pleasingly relaxed inhabitants. Pepper it with astounding beauty, alluring beaches, and filter out pollution, persecution, and stress. Voilà!—
you have Portugal's Atlantic islands, the Azores and Madeiras, considered by many to
be the world's most beautiful and most serene. While beyond the average *Let's Go*
budget, these isles are integral to the national landscape.

The **Madeiras**—Madeira, Porto Santo, and Desertas—rise abruptly from the ocean off
Africa's northwestern coast. Once an important stop-over for budding explorers, today
their climate, colorful fauna, tropical fruits, and luxurious hotels make them a strong
contender for the ideal resort spot. Immortalized in *Moby Dick,* the nine islands of the
Azores boast rolling hills, lush fauna, cavernous lakes, glimmering seas, and friendly
inhabitants. Tranquil and tempting, the Azores will leave the particularly melodramatic
to muse (as one brochure claims) "Is this the home of God?"

Portugal

N

ATLANTIC OCEAN

SPAIN

Valença
Vila Nova de Cerveira
Rio Minho
Caminha
MINHO
Parque Nacional da Peneda Gerês
Viana do Castelo
Serra do Gerês
Parque Natural de Montezinho
COSTA VERDE
Rio Cávado
Braga
Bragança
Barcelos
TRÁS-OS-MONTES
Guimarães
Amarante
Serra do Marão
Vila Real
Porto
DOURO LITORAL
DOURO ALTO
Espinho
Rio Douro
Ovar
BEIRA ALTA
Aveiro
BEIRA LITORAL
Viseu
Luso
Rio Mondego
COSTA DA PRATA
Buçaco
Guarda
Buarcos
Serra da Estrela
Figueira da Foz
Coimbra
Conimbriga
Serra da Gardunha
Rio Zêzere
Leiria
BEIRA BAIXA
Nazaré
Batalha
Fátima
Castelo Branco
São Martinho do Porto
Alcobaça
Tomar
ilhas Berlengas
Caldas da Rainha
Cabo Carvoeiro
Óbidos
Serra de Aire
Rio Tejo
Castelo de Vide
Peniche
Marvão
ESTREMADURA
Vila Franca de Xira
Santarém
Crato
Portalegre
Ericeira
RIBATEJO
Serra de São Mamede
Sintra
Mafra
Cascais
Queluz
Estremoz
Elvas
Estoril
Lisbon
ALTO ALENTEJO
Évora Monte
Parque Nacional de Arrábida
Setúbal
Tróia Peninsula
Évora
Cabo Espichel
Serra de Ossa
Sesimbra
COSTA AZUL
Santiago do Cacém
Rio Guadiana
Sines
Beja
BAIXO ALENTEJO
COSTA DOURADA
Rio Mira
Mértola
Serra de Monchique
Lagos
ALGARVE
Silves
Tavira
Cabo de São Vicente
Sagres
Portimão
Albufeira
Vila Real de Santo António
Faro
Olhão
Golfo de Cádiz

THE HOUSES OF HABSBURG AND BRAGANÇA (1580-1807). In 1580, Habsburg King of Spain **Felipe II** asserted his claim to the Portuguese throne, and the Iberian Peninsula was briefly ruled by one monarch. For 60 years the Habsburg family dragged Portugal into several ill-fated wars, including the Spanish-Portuguese Armada's crushing loss to England in 1588. Inattentive King Felipe did not even visit Portugal until 1619—his priorities were elsewhere—and by the end of Habsburg rule, Portugal had lost much of its once vast empire.

In 1640, during a rebellion against King Felipe IV, the **House of Bragança** engineered a nationalist rebellion. After a brief struggle they assumed control, once again asserting Portuguese independence from Spain. To secure its independence, the Bragança dynasty went to great lengths to reestablish ties with England. Nearly half a century later, **João V** (1706-1750) had restored a measure of prosperity, using newly discovered Brazilian gold and diamonds to finance massive building projects, including the construction of extravagant palaces.

The momentous **Earthquake of 1755** devastated Lisbon and southern Portugal, killing over 15,000 people. Despite the damage, dictatorial minister **Marquês de Pombal** was able to rebuild Lisbon while instituting national economic reform.

NAPOLEON'S CONQUEST AND ITS AFTERMATH (1807-1910). Napoleon took control of France in 1801 and set his sights on the rest of Europe. When he reached Portugal, his army encountered little resistance. Rather than risk death, the Portuguese royal family fled to Brazil. **Dom João VI** returned to Lisbon in 1821, only to face an extremely unstable political climate. Amidst turmoil within the royal family, João's son **Pedro** declared independence for Brazil the following year, becoming the country's first ruler. More problems developed when João died in 1826. The **Constitution of 1822,** drawn up during the royal family's absence, had severely limited the power of the monarchy, and after 1826, the **War of the Two Brothers** (1826-1834) between constitutionalists (supporting Pedro, the new king of Brazil) and monarchists (supporting Miguel, Pedro's brother) reverberated through Portugal. Eight gory years later, with Miguel in exile, Pedro's daughter **Maria II** (1834-1854) ascended to the throne at a mere 15 years old. The next 75 years brought continued tensions between liberals and monarchists.

FROM THE "FIRST REPUBLIC" TO SALAZAR (1910-1974). Portugal spent the first few years of the 20th century trying to recover from the political discord of the previous century. On October 5, 1910, 20-year-old King **Manuel II** fled to England. The new government, known as the **First Republic,** earned worldwide disapproval for its expulsion of the Jesuits and other religious orders, and the conflict between the government and labor movements heightened tensions at home. Portugal's decision to enter **World War I** (even though on the side of the victorious Allies) proved economically fatal and internally divisive. The weak republic wobbled and eventually fell in a 1926 military coup. General **António Carmona** took over as leader of the provisional military government, and in the face of financial crisis, he appointed **António de Oliveira Salazar,** a prominent economics professor, his minister of finance. In 1932 Salazar became prime minister, but he soon evolved into a dictator. His *Estado Novo* (New State) granted suffrage to women, but did little else to end the country's authoritarian tradition. While Portugal's international economic standing improved, the regime laid the cost of progress squarely on the shoulders of the working class, the peasantry, and colonial subjects in Africa. A terrifying secret police (PIDE) crushed all opposition to Salazar's rule, and African rebellions were quelled in bloody battles that drained the nation's economy.

REVOLUTION AND REFORM (1974-1999). The slightly more liberal **Marcelo Caetano** dragged on the increasingly unpopular African wars after Salazar's death in 1970. By the early 70s, international disapproval of Portuguese imperialism and the army's dissatisfaction with colonial entanglements had led General António de Spinola to call for decolonization. On April 25, 1974, a left-wing military coalition calling itself the Armed Forces Movement overthrew Caetano in a quick coup. The **Revolution of the Carnations** sent Portuguese dancing into the streets; today every town in Portugal has its own Rua 25 de Abril. The Marxist-dominated armed forces established a variety of civil and political liberties and withdrew Portuguese claims on African colonies by 1975.

The socialist government nationalized several industries and appropriated large estates in the face of substantial opposition. The country's first elections in 1976 put the charismatic socialist Prime Minister **Mario Soares** into power. When a severe economic crisis exploded and foreign debt, inflation, and unemployment skyrocketed, Soares instituted "100 measures in 100 days" to shock Portugal into economic shape. Through austere reforms, he helped stimulate industrial growth. The landmark year 1986 brought Portugal into the European Community (now the European Union), ending its age-old isolation from more affluent northern Europe. Despite challenges by the newly formed Social Democratic Party (PSD), Soares won the elections in 1986, becoming the nation's first civilian president in 60 years. Forced to step down because of constitutional limitations, Soares was replaced by the Socialist former mayor of Lisbon, **Jorge Sampaio,** in 1995. During the 1990s, the Portuguese government instituted a series of programs to prepare the country for economic integration with the rest of Europe.

CURRENT EVENTS. The European Union declared that Portugal qualified for inclusion in the EU Economic and Monetary Union (EMU) in 1998, and the nation continues in its quest to catch up economically with the rest of Western Europe. The EU summit on employment and economic reform was held in Lisbon in March 2000 and identified as target goals for Portugal improvements in budget imbalances, venture capital development, and the educational system.

On the international political front, Portugal and Indonesia have agreed to cooperate over the reconstruction of East Timor, an ex-Portuguese colony which Indonesia invaded 25 years ago. Prime Minister Guterres is eager to position Portugal as an interface between the European Union and Indonesia in their mutual efforts to promote stability and democracy in East Timor.

THE ARTS

PAINTING AND SCULPTURE

The Age of Discovery (1415-1580) was an era of vast cultural exchange with Renaissance Europe and beyond. Flemish masters such as **Jan van Eyck** brought their talent to Portugal, and many Portuguese artists polished their skills in Antwerp. King Manuel's favorite, High Renaissance artist **Jorge Afonso,** created realistic portrayals of human anatomy. Afonso's best works hang at the Convento de Cristo in Tomar and Convento da Madre de Deus in Lisbon. In the late 15th century, the talented **Nuno Gonçalves** led a revival of the primitivist school.

Portuguese Baroque art featured even more diverse styles and themes. Woodcarving became extremely popular in Portugal during the Baroque period. **Joachim Machado** carved elaborate crèches in the early 1700s. On canvas, portraiture was head and shoulders above other genres. The prolific 19th-century artist **Domingos António de Sequeira** depicted historical, religious, and allegorical subjects using a technique that would later inspire French Impressionists. Porto's **António Soares dos Reis** brought Romantic sensibility to 19th-century Portuguese sculpture.

In the 20th century, Cubism, Expressionism, and Futurism trickled into Portugal despite Salazar-inspired censorship. More recently, **Maria Helena Vieira da Silva** has won international recognition for her abstract works, and the master **Carlos Botelho** has become world-renowned for his wonderful vignettes of Lisbon life.

ARCHITECTURE

Portugal's signature **Manueline** style celebrates the prosperity and imperial expansion of King Manuel I's reign (see **The Age of Discovery,** p. 522). Manueline works routinely merge Christian images and maritime motifs. Their rich and lavish ornaments reflect a hybrid of Northern Gothic, Spanish Plateresque, and Moorish influences. The Manueline style found its most elaborate expression in the church and tower at **Belém,** built to honor Vasco da Gama. Close seconds are the **Mosteiro dos Jerónimos** in Belém and the **Abadia de Santa Maria de Vitória** in Batalha.

Though few actual Moorish structures survived the Christian *Reconquista*, their style influenced later Portuguese architecture. One of Portugal's most beautiful traditions is the colorfully painted ceramic tiles which grace many walls, ceilings, and thresholds. Carved in relief by the Moors, these ornate tiles later took on flat, glazed Italian and northern European designs. Despite the fact that many of these tiles are blue, their name does not come from *azul*, the Portuguese word for blue, but rather from the Arabic word *azulayj*, meaning little stone. Numerous museums showcase collections of *azulejos*, including Lisbon's Museu do Azulejo and Coimbra's Museu Machada do Castro.

LITERATURE

ORIGINS OF PORTUGUESE LITERATURE. Portugal's literary achievements, mostly lyric poetry and realist fiction, can be traced back to the 12th century, when the lyrical aspects of Portuguese were solidified by poet-king **Dinis I.** Dinis made Portuguese the region's official language (one of the first "official" non-Latin Romance vernaculars). **Gil Vicente** (1465-1537), court poet to Manuel I, is considered Portugal's equivalent to Shakespeare in style and importance. Vicente wrote dramas (tempered with comic relief) about peasants, nature, and religion. The witty realism of his *Barcas* trilogy (1517-1519) influenced contemporaries Shakespeare and Cervantes and earned him a distinguished place in literary ranks.

PORTUGUESE LITERARY RENAISSANCE. Portuguese literature blossomed during the Renaissance, most notably in the letters of **Francisco de Sá de Miranda** (1481-1558) and the lyrics of **António Ferreira** (1528-1569). During the Age of Discovery, conquest abroad inspired both historians and poets. An explorer himself, the humanist **João de Barros** (1496-1570) penned *Décadas da Ásia*, a history of Portuguese conquest in Goa. Influenced by the *Décadas*, the writer **Luís de Camões** (1524-1580) celebrated Vasco de Gama's sea voyages to India in Portugal's greatest epic, *Os Lusíadas* (*The Lusiads*, 1572), modeled on the Latin classic, the *Aeneid* (see **A Camões Cameo,** p. 553).

NINETEENTH CENTURY LITERARY MOVEMENTS. Spanish hegemony, intermittent warfare, and imperial decline conspired to make the literature of the 17th and 18th centuries somewhat less triumphant than that of past eras. The 19th century, however, saw a dramatic rebirth of Portuguese literature. Poet **João Baptista de Almeida Garrett** (1799-1854) and historian **Alexandre Herculano** (1810-1877), who were both exiled because of their liberal political views, integrated Portuguese literature with the Romantic school of fiction they encountered while in exile. A lyric poet, dramatist, politician, revolutionary, frequent exile, and legendary lover, Garrett is credited with reviving drama in Portugal. His most famous play is *Frei Luís de Sousa* (*Brother Luís de Sousa*, 1843).

Portuguese literature shifted from romantic to realist when political thinkers dominated the rise of the literary intelligentsia, the **Generation of 1870.** The most visible figure to influence this shift in the late 19th century was novelist and lifelong diplomat (residing almost always outside Iberia) **José Maria Eça de Queiroz.** He conceived of a distinctly Portuguese social realism, and he documented 19th-century Portuguese society, sometimes critical of its bourgeois elements. His best works were *O Crime do Padre Amaro* (*The Sin of Father Amaro)* and *Os Maias (The Mayas).*

CONTEMPORARY LITERATURE. Fernando Pessoa (1888-1935) was Portugal's most famed and creative writer of the late 19th and early 20th centuries. Pessoa wrote in English and Portuguese and developed four distinct styles under four different names: Pessoa, Alberto Caeiro, Ricardo Reis, and Alvaro de Campos. His semi-autobiography, *Livro do Desassossego (The Book of Disgust)* is his only prose work, posthumously compiled and today seen as a modernist classic. Other influential writers of the 20th century include **Aquilino Ribeiro,** author of *O Homem que Matou o Diabo (The Man Who Killed the Devil)*, and **José Maria Ferreira de Castro,** widely known for his realist fiction, especially his novel *A Selva (The Jungle).*

Contemporary writers, like **Miguel Torga,** have gained international fame for their wonderfully satirical novels. **José Saramago,** winner of the 1998 Nobel Prize for literature, is perhaps Portugal's most important living writer. His work, written in the realist style and laced with irony, has achieved new acclaim in the post-Salazar era. He is best known for *Baltasar and Blimunda*, the story of lovers who escape the Inquisition in a time machine, and *The Stone Raft*, a satire about Iberia's isolation from the rest of Europe.

The end of Salazar's reign brought literary liberation. Female writers, long discouraged or censored, have come out of the woodwork with a vengeance. In **Novas Cartas Portuguesas** *(New Portuguese Letters)*, the "Three Marias" (the authors) expose the mistreatment of women in a male-dominated society. Other acclaimed post-Salazar authors include **António Lobo Antunes** and **José Cardoso Pires.** Antunes has achieved the status of Saramago but with a dramatically different style, one known for its scattered form and psychoanalytic themes. Pires' works often comment on the repression of the Salazar regime, and his novel *Balada da Praia dos Cães (Ballad of Dog's Beach)* exposes the terror of Salazar's secret police.

MUSIC

The **fado** is said to cause the chords of the Portuguese soul to vibrate melancholically or passionately. Named after fate, *fado* is a musical tradition unique to Portugal, identified with a sense of *saudade* (yearning or longing) and characterized by tragic, romantic lyrics and mournful melodies. These solo ballads, accompanied by the acoustic *guitarra* (a flat-backed guitar, like a mandolin), appeal to the romantic side of Portuguese culture. **Amalia Rodrigues** (1920-1999) is often spoken of in association with the tradition; she has become, in her lifetime, an internationally known star as a singer of fado and Portuguese folk music. For more information on fado, see **Love Notes, p. 558**.

Apart from its folk tradition, the music of Portugal has yet to achieve international fame. Portuguese opera peaked with **António José da Silva** (1705-1739), a victim of the 1739 Inquisition. The Renaissance in Portugal led to the development of pieces geared for solo instrumentalists and vocals. Italian **Domenico Scarlatti** (1685-1757), brought to Lisbon by João V, composed brilliant keyboard pieces. His preeminent Portuguese contemporary, Coimbra's **Carlos Seixas,** thrilled 18th-century Lisbon with his genius and contributed to the development of the sonata form. **Domingos Bomtempo** (1775-1842) introduced symphonic innovations from abroad and helped establish the first Portuguese Sociedade Filarmónica, modeled after the London Philharmonic, in Lisbon in 1822.

Although the French invasion, Civil War, and decreased patronage somewhat stifled Portuguese music, folk music and dancing are still quite popular in rural areas. In the latter half of this century, Joly Braga Santo has led a modern revival of Portuguese classical music. The Calouste Gulbenkian Foundation in Lisbon has also kept Portuguese music alive, sponsoring a symphony orchestra since 1962, and hosting popular local folk singers (including Fausto and Sérgio Godinho), ballets, operas, and jazz festivals. The Teatro Nacional de São Carlos, which has its own orchestra and ballet company, has further benefitted Portuguese music. The Teatro has spawned a group of talented young composers, including Filipe Pires, A. Vitorino de Almeida, and Jorge Peixinho, all of whom have begun to make their mark in international competitions.

LANGUAGE

Thanks to the Romans who colonized Iberia in the late third century BC, practiced Romance speakers will find Portuguese an easy conquest (though pronunciation may be difficult). Although this softer sister of Spanish is closely related to the other Romance languages, modern Portuguese is an amalgam of diverse influences. A close listener will catch echoes of Italian, French, Spanish, Arabic, and even English and Slavic. Portugal's global escapades also spurred the spread of its language. Today, Portuguese (the world's fifth-most-spoken language) binds over 200 million people worldwide, most of them in Portugal, Brazil, Mozambique, and Angola. Prospective students of the language should note the differences between Brazilian and continental Portuguese, mainly in pronunciation and usage.

PORTUGAL

Some may be heartened to know that English, Spanish, and French are widely spoken throughout Portugal, especially in tourist-oriented locales. Look to the *Let's Go* glossary in the back of this book for terms (or their Castilian cousins) that are used in this guide (see **Glossary,** p. 730).

FOOD AND DRINK

TYPICAL FARE

The Portuguese season their dishes with olive oil, garlic, herbs, and sea salt but use relatively few spices, despite their historic role in bringing Eastern flavorings to Europe. The geography of Portugal means miles of coastlines; seafood forms the core of Portuguese cuisine and is usually prepared as simply as possible to emphasize freshness. Seafood lovers will enjoy *chocos grelhados* (grilled cuttlefish), *linguado grelhado* (grilled sole), and *peixe espada* (swordfish), to name a few. The more adventurous should try the *polvo* (boiled or grilled octopus), *mexilhões* (mussels), and *lulas grelhadas* (grilled squid). Meat is treated in the opposite manner from seafood; the taste is extensively embellished and even masked by heavy sauces in Portuguese cooking. Pork, chicken, and beef appear on most menus and are often combined as *cozida à portuguesa* (boiled beef, pork, sausage, and vegetables). True connoisseurs add a drop of *piri-piri* (mega-hot) sauce on the side. An expensive delicacy is freshly roasted *cabrito* (baby goat). No matter what you order, leave room for *batatas* (potatoes), prepared countless ways—including *batatas fritas* (french fries)—which accompany each meal.

The widespread availability of excellent produce means that **sopas** (soups) are usually made from local vegetables. As they can serve as a cheap alternative to a full meal, they are tasty and can often be substantial in consistency. Common soups are *caldo de ovos* (bean soup with hard-boiled eggs), *caldo de verdura* (vegetable soup), and the tasty *caldo verde* (a potato and kale mixture with a slice of sausage and olive oil). **Sandes** (sandwiches) such as the *bifana* or *prego no pão* (meat sandwich) may be no more than a hunk of meat on a roll. Cows, goats, and ewes please the palate by providing raw material for Portugal's renowned **queijos** (cheeses). Vegetarians should accustom themselves to the cheese sandwich and Portugal's delectable bread.

Portugal's favorite **dessert** is *pudim,* or *flan,* a rich, caramel custard similar to *crème bruleé.* For the sweet tooth in all of us, the almond groves of the Algarve produce their own version of marzipan. For something different, try *pêras* (pears) drenched in sweet port wine and served with raisins and hazelnuts on top. Most common are countless varieties of inexpensive, high-quality **sorvete** (ice cream)—look for vendors posting the colorful, ubiquitous "Olá" sign. *Pastelarías* (bakeries) are in most towns, and tasty **pastries** make for a cheap (80-180$) breakfast.

EATING OUT

Portuguese eat their hearty midday meal—*almoço* (lunch)—between noon and 2pm and *jantar* (dinner) between 9pm and midnight. Both meals entail at least three courses. There are no greasy lumberjack breakfasts to be found in Portugal—a pastry (80-180$) from a *pastelaría* (bakery) and coffee from a cafe suffices for *pequeno almoço* (breakfast). If you get the munchies between 4 and 7pm, snack bars sell **sandes** (sandwiches) and sweet cakes. It is advisable to make reservations when dining in some of the more upscale city restaurants.

A full meal costs 1000-2000$, depending on the restaurant's location and quality. **Meia dose** (half portions) cost more than half-price but are often more than adequate—a full portion may satisfy two. The ubiquitous **prato do dia** (special of the day) and **ementa** ("menu" in Portuguese) of appetizer, bread, entree, and dessert will stifle the loudest stomach growls. The **ementa turística** (tourist menu) is usually not a good deal—restaurants with menus translated into multiple languages are more likely to charge exorbitant prices. Standard pre-meal bread, butter, cheese, and pâté may be dished without your asking, but these pre-meal munchies are not free (300-500$ per person). You may appreciate them, however, since chefs only start cooking after your order; be prepared to wait. In restaurants (but not cafes), a service charge of 10% is usually included in the bill. When service is not included, it is customary to leave about 5 to 10% as a tip. Vegetarians may find themselves somewhat in the cold in Portugal, but given the availability and high quality of fresh fruits and vegetables, making special requests to chefs may prove fruitful. Smoking is still generally accepted in most establishments although there has been a recent move in Parliament to institute no smoking zones in some areas.

DRINKS

The exact date marking the birth of Portuguese wine is unknown, though 5000 B.C. is often used as an estimate. Though it does not quite rival the international renown of French and German wines, the quality and low cost of Portuguese *vinho* (wine) is truly astounding; the reds are perhaps the best known. The pinnacle, **vinho do porto** (port), pressed (by feet) from the red grapes of the Douro Valley and fermented with a touch of brandy, is a dessert in itself. Chilled, white port can be a snappy aperitif, while ruby or tawny port makes a classic after-dinner drink. A six-month-long heating process gives **Madeira** wines their unique "cooked" flavor. Try the dry Sercial and Verdelho before the main course, and the sweeter Bual and Malmsey after. Sparkling *vinho verde* is picked and drunk young; it comes in red and white versions. The red may be a bit strong but the white is brash and delicious by any standard; the latter is exported rather than consumed, and classifies as a semi-sparkling wine. The Adega Cooperatives of Ponte de Lima, Monção, and Amarante produce the best of this type. Excellent local table wines include Colares, Dão, Borba, Bairrada, Bucelas, and Periquita. If you can't decide, experiment with the **vinho de casa** (house wine); either the *tinto* (red) or the *branco* (white) is a reliable standby. Tangy **sangría** comes filled with fresh orange slices and makes even a budget meal festive at a minimal expense (usually around 500$ for a half-pitcher). Essential to your Portuguese drinking vocabulary should be the following terms: *adega*: a cellar or winery, *branco*: white wine, *claro*: new wine, *doce*: sweet wine, *espumante*: sparkling wine, *garrafa*: a bottle, *rosado*: a rosé wine, *seco*: dry wine, *vinho de mesa*: table wine, and *vinho verde:* a young wine.

Bottled Sagres and Super Bock are excellent beers. If you don't ask for it *fresco* (cool), it may come *natural* (room temperature). A tall, slim glass of draft beer is a **fino** or an **imperial,** while a larger stein is a **caneca.** To sober up and wake up, order a **bica** (cup of black espresso), a **galão** (coffee with milk, served in a glass), or a **café com leite** (coffee with milk, served in a cup).

MEDIA

Portugal's most widely read daily newspapers are *Público* (www.publico.pt), *Diário de Notícas* (www.dn.pt), and *Jornal de Notícas*. If you haven't yet mastered Portuguese, check out *The News*, Portugal's only online English language newspaper, at www.the-news.net. Those interested in international news stories can also pick up day-old foreign papers at larger newsstands.

Portuguese TV offers four main channels: the state-run Canal 1 and TV2 and the private SIC (Sociedade Independente de Communicação) and TVI (TV Independente). Couch potatoes can also enjoy numerous cable channels, most of which air Brazilian and Portuguese soap operas and subtitled foreign sitcoms.

SPORTS

Futebol (soccer to Americans) is the sport of choice for just about everyone. The country has shown signs of making it big—at the 1996 European Championships, the national team ousted Denmark en route to the semifinals—but has fallen short at crucial moments, such as the World Cup '98 qualification matches. Games create a crazed fervor throughout Portugal. Lisbon's club, **Benfica**, possesses some of the best players in the world. Native Portuguese have also made names for themselves in long-distance running, where marathon-queen **Rosa Mota** dominated her event for a number of years. For recreation other than jogging and pick-up soccer, native Portuguese often turn to the sea. **Windsurfers, body-surfers,** and **surfers** make waves along the north coast; **snorklers** and **scuba divers** set out on mini-explorations in the south and west.

RECOMMENDED READING

FICTION: PORTUGUESE AND FOREIGN. For the scoop on Portuguese classics in most every genre, check out **Literature** (p. 526). The more famous works have been translated into English; for additional options, consult your librarian. *Selected Letters and Journals*, by Lord Byron, narrates the days Byron spent in Portugal. The Portuguese classic *The Lusiads*, by Luís de Camões, chronicles Portuguese exploration during the Age of Discovery. *The Last Kabbalist of Lisbon*, by Richard Zimler, is a fantastic murder mystery exploring the world of Portugal's 16th-century Jewish mystics. To see why José Saramago won the 1998 Nobel Prize in Literature, read *Baltasar and Blimunda* or *The Stone Raft*.

HISTORY AND CULTURE. David Birmingham's *A Concise History of Portugal* (1991) packs it all in one handy volume. Elanea Brown's *Roads to Today's Portugal: Essays on Contemporary Portuguese Literature, Art, and Culture* (1983) provides a good introduction to 20th-century Portuguese culture. Though somewhat outdated, A.H. de Oliveira Marques's *History of Portugal* is among the most comprehensive Portuguese history texts available. *Modern Portugal* (1998), edited by António Costa Pinto, covers 20th-century Portuguese history from the rise of Salazar to the evolution of the nation's resilient democracy. *Europe's Best-Kept Secret: An Insider's View of Portugal* (1997), by Costa Matos, is a witty account of Portuguese culture and history, including amusing anecdotes about peculiar Portuguese personalities.

ESSENTIALS

The information in this section is mostly designed to help travelers get their bearings once they are in Portugal. For information about general **travel preparations** (including passports and permits, money, health, packing, international transportation, and more), consult the **Essentials** section at the beginning of this book (p. 8). That chapter also has important information about alternatives to tourism (**work** and **study** programs in Portugal, p. 46) and for those with specific concerns: **women travelers** (p. 42); **older travelers** (p. 43); **bisexual, gay, and lesbian travelers** (p. 43); **travelers with disabilities** (p. 44); **minority travelers** (p. 44); **travelers with children** (p. 45); and travelers with **dietary needs** (p. 45).

GETTING THERE AND AROUND

Portugal is easily accessible by plane from the US and Europe. Long-distance trains run from **Madrid** (p. 81) to Lisbon, and buses run from **Sevilla** (p. 192) to Lagos. Closer to the border, trains run from **Huelva** (easily accessible from Sevilla, p. 212) and **Cáceres** (p. 180) to Portugal. Trains and buses run from **Badajoz** (p. 189), only 6km from the border, to Elvas and elsewhere. **Ciudad Rodrigo** (p. 159) lies only 21km from the border. In the north, trains run from **Vigo** (p. 455) to Porto; from **Túy** (p. 458), you can walk across the Portuguese border to Valença do Minho.

BY PLANE

Most major international airlines serve Lisbon; some serve Porto, Faro, and the Madeiras. **TAP Air Portugal** (in US and Canada ☎ (800) 221 7370; in UK ☎ (171) 828 20 92; in Lisbon ☎ (21) 841 69 90; www.tap.pt) is Portugal's national airline, serving all domestic locations and many major international cities. **Portugália** (www.pga.pt) is a smaller Portuguese airline that flies between Porto, Faro, Lisbon, all major Spanish cities, and other Western European destinations. Its offices include Lisbon (☎ (21) 842 55 00) and Manchester, UK (☎ (161) 489 50 40).

BY TRAIN

Caminhos de Ferro Portugueses is Portugal's national railway, but for long-distance travel outside of the Braga-Porto-Coimbra-Lisbon line, the bus is much better. The exception is around Lisbon, where local trains and commuter rails are fast and efficient. Most trains have first- and second-class cabins, except for local and suburban routes. When you arrive in town, go to the station ticket booth to check the departure schedule; trains often run at irregular hours, and posted schedules (*horarios*) are not always accurate.

Unless you own a Eurailpass, the return on round-trip tickets must be used before 3am the following day. Anyone riding without a ticket is fined over 3500$. Children under four travel free; ages four to 11 pay half-price. **Youth discounts** are only available to Portuguese citizens. Though there is a Portugal Flexipass, it is not worth purchasing.

BY BUS

Buses are cheap, frequent, and connect just about every town in Portugal. **Rodoviária** (national info ☎ (21) 354 57 75), the national bus company, has recently been privatized. Each company name corresponds to a particular region of the country, such as Rodoviária Alentejo or Minho e Douro, with notable exceptions such as EVA in the Algarve. Private regional companies also operate, among them **Cabanelas, AVIC,** and **Mafrense.** Be wary of non-express buses in small regions like Estremadura and Alentejo, which stop every few minutes. Express coach service (*expressos*) between major cities is especially good; inexpensive city buses often run to nearby villages. Schedules (*horarios*) are usually printed and posted, but double-check with the ticket vendor to make sure they are accurate.

BY CAR AND THUMB

Portugal has the highest rate of automobile accidents, per capita, in Western Europe. The new highway system (IP) is quite good, but off the main arteries, the narrow, twisting roads prove difficult to negotiate. The locals' testy reputation is well deserved. Speed limits are effectively ignored, recklessness common, and lighting and road surfaces often inadequate. Buses and trucks are safer options. Moreover, parking space in cities borders on nonexistent. **Gas** comes in super (97 octane), normal (92 octane), and unleaded. Gas prices may be high by North American standards—130-200*escudos* (or US$0.58-0.88) per liter.

Portugal's national automobile association, the **Automóvel Clube de Portugal (ACP),** R. Rosa Araújo, 42, 1250 **Lisbon** (☎ (12) 318 01 00), provides **breakdown** and **towing service** (M-F 9am-5pm) and **first aid** (24hr.).

In Portugal, **hitchers** are rare. Beach-bound locals occasionally hitch in summer but otherwise stick to the inexpensive bus system. Rides are easiest to come by between smaller towns. Best results are reputedly at gas stations near highways and rest stops. *Let's Go* does not recommend hitchhiking (see p. 42).

MONEY

Official **banking hours** are Monday through Friday 8:30am to 3pm, but play it safe by giving yourself some extra time. For more information on money, see p. 13. **Taxes** are included in all prices in Portugal and are not redeemable like those in Spain and Morocco, even for EU citizens. **Tips** are customary only in fancy restaurants or hotels. Some cheaper restaurants include a 10% service charge; if they don't and you'd like to leave a tip, round up and leave the change. Taxi drivers do not expect a tip unless the trip was especially long. **Bargaining** is not customary in shops, but you can give it a shot at the local *mercado* (market) or when looking for a *quarto*.

SAFETY AND HEALTH

EMERGENCY ☎	Dial 112 for police, medical, or fire.

In Portugal, the highest rates of crime have been in the Lisbon area, especially on buses, trams, in train stations, and in airports. Exercise the most caution in the Alfama district, the Santa Apolonia and Rossio train stations, Castelo de São Jorge, and in Belém. The towns around Lisbon with the most reported crimes in recent years are Cascais, Sintra, and Fátima. Thieves sometimes try and distract people by staging loud arguments, passing a soccer ball back and forth on a crowded street, asking for directions, pretending to dance with their victim, or spilling something on their victim's clothing. Motorists should be wary of "Good Samaritans" who have been known to help ailing motorists by the side of the road and then steal their cars.

Like Spain, Portugal poses no particular health risks to travelers. For general **health** information, see p. 19. The public health system in Portugal is quite good, and many doctors speak English. A private clinic might be worth the money for convenience and quick service; most travel insurance will pick up the tab. For small medical concerns, Portuguese *farmacías* offer basic drugs and medical advice and are easy to find in most towns.

ACCOMMODATIONS

YOUTH HOSTELS

Movijovem, Av. Duque de Ávila, 137, 1050 Lisbon (☎ (21) 313 88 20; fax 352 14 66; email movijovem@mail.telepac.pt), the Portuguese Hostelling International affiliate, oversees the country's HI hostels. All bookings can be made through them. A bed in a *pousada da juventude* (not to be confused with plush *pousadas*) costs 2000-3000$ per night and slightly less in the off-season (breakfast and sheets included). Lunch or dinner usually costs 900$, snacks around 250$. Rates may be higher for guests 26 and older. Though often the cheapest option, hostels may lie far from the town center. Check-in hours are 9am to noon and 6pm to midnight. Some have lockouts 10:30am to 6pm, and curfews might cramp club-hoppers' style. The maximum stay is eight nights unless you get special permission.

To stay in an HI hostel an **HI card** (3000$) is usually mandatory. Although they are sold at Movijovem's Lisbon office, it is more convenient to get an HI membership before leaving home. To reserve a bed in the high season, obtain an **International Booking Voucher** from Movijovem (or your country's HI affiliate) and send it from home to the desired hostel four to eight weeks in advance. In the off-season (Oct.-Apr.), double-check to see if the hostel is open. Large groups should reserve through Movijovem at least 30 days in advance. For more info, see **Hostels**, p. 25.

PENSÕES AND HOTELS

Pensões, also called **residencias,** are a budget traveler's mainstay. They're far cheaper than hotels and only slightly more expensive (and much more common) than crowded youth hostels. Like hostels, *pensões* generally provide sheets and towels and have commons rooms. All are rated on a five-star scale and are required to visibly post their category and legal price limits. (If you don't see this information, ask for it.) During the high season, many *pensões* do not take reservations, but for those that do, booking a week ahead is advisable.

Hotels in Portugal tend to be pricey. Room prices typically include showers and breakfast, and most rooms without bath or shower have a sink. However, many force you out by noon. When business is weak, try bargaining down in advance— the "official price" is just the maximum allowed.

ALTERNATIVE ACCOMMODATIONS

Quartos are rooms in private residences, similar to *casas particulares* in Spain. These rooms may be your only option in less touristed, smaller towns (particularly in the south), or the cheapest one in bigger cities. The tourist office can usually help you find a *quarto*. When all else fails, ask at bars and restaurants for names and addresses, but you should try to verify the quality of the rooms. Prices are often flexible, and can drop as much as 500-1000$ with bargaining.

Pousadas, like Spanish *paradores,* outperform standard hotel expectations (and, unfortunately, rates). They are castles, palaces, or monasteries converted into luxurious, government-run hotels. "Historical" *pousadas* play up local crafts, customs, and cuisine and may cost as much as expensive hotels. Most require reservations. Priced less extravagantly are *regional pousadas,* situated in national parks and reserves. For info, contact ENATUR, Av. Santa Joana Princesa, 10, 1749 Lisbon (☎ (21) 844 20 00; fax 844 20 86).

CAMPING

In Portugal, over 150 **official campgrounds** *(parques de campismo)* feature tons of amenities and comforts. Most have a supermarket and cafes, and many are beach-accessible or near rivers or pools. Given the facilities' quality and popularity, happy campers are those who arrive early; urban and coastal parks may require reservations. Police have been cracking down on illegal camping, so don't try it. Tourist offices stock *Portugal: Camping and Caravan Sites,* a free guide to official campgrounds. Otherwise, write the **Federação Portuguesa de Campismo e Cara-vanismo,** Av. Coronal Eduardo Gallardo, 24D, 199-007 Lisbon (☎ (21) 812 69 00; open daily 9:30am-12:30pm and 1:30-6:30pm).

KEEPING IN TOUCH

Most useful communication information (including **international access codes, calling card numbers, country codes, operator** and **directory assistance,** and **emergency numbers**) is listed on the **inside back cover.**

PHONES. Portugal's national telephone company is **Portugal Telecom.** Phone offices exist in most cities, but there is little need to use them as all services are available in phone booths, located on the street and in post offices. Pay phones are either coin-operated or require a phone card; both are common. The country uses both the **Credifone** and **Portugal Telecom** systems. For both systems, the basic unit for all calls (and the price for local ones) is 18$. The Telecom phone cards, using "patch" (not strip) cards, are most common in Lisbon and Porto and increasingly elsewhere. Credifone cards, with magnetic strips, are sold at drugstores, post offices, and locations posted on phone booths, and are most useful outside these two big cities. Private calls from bars and cafes cost whatever the proprietor decides, typically 30-40$; a posted sign usually indicates the rates. City codes all have a two before them, and local calls do not require dialing the city code.

PORTUGAL

As of October 31, 1999, all of the city codes in Portugal changed. There is now a 2 before every old city code. (For example, Lisbon's code is now 21 as opposed to 01.) All numbers listed in *Let's Go* are updated to include the change.

Calling cards probably remain the best method of making international calls (see p. 28 for more details). The numbers to access major calling card services (including AT&T, MCI, Canada Direct, BT Direct, Ireland Direct, Telstra Australia, Optus Australia, Telecom New Zealand, and Telkom South Africa) are listed on the inside back cover. To **call home with a calling card,** contact the operator for your service provider in Portugal by dialing the appropriate toll-free access number (see p. 28).

MAIL. Mail in Portugal is somewhat inefficient—**Air mail** *(via aerea)* can take from one to two weeks (or longer) to reach the US or Canada. It is slightly quicker for destinations in Europe and longer for Australia, New Zealand, and South Africa. **Surface mail** *(superficie),* for packages only, takes up to two months. **Registered** or **blue mail** takes five to eight business days (for roughly 3 times the price of air mail). **EMS** or **Express Mail** will probably get there in three to four days for more than double the blue mail price. **Stamps** are available at post offices *(correios)* and automatic stamp machines are outside post offices and in central locations around cities. Also at post offices, **fax** machines are available for public use.

EMAIL. Email is both faster and more reliable than the standard mail system. Cybercafes are common in cities and most smaller towns, and are listed in the Practical Information section and in the index under Internet access. When in doubt, try the library; they often have at least one computer equipped for Internet access. For information on how to obtain a free email account, see p. 30.

EMBASSIES AND CONSULATES

Embassies and consulates are usually open Monday through Friday, mornings and late afternoons, with *siestas* in between—call for specific hours.

Australian Embassy: Refer to the Australian Embassy in Paris: 4, rue Jean Rey, 15th arrondisement Paris 75724 France (☎ (01) 40 59 33 00; fax (01) 40 59 33 10). An embassy in Lisbon is scheduled to open in summer/fall of 2000, but the embassy in Paris will still offer information and can redirect calls.

British Embassy: R. São Bernardo, 33, 1200 **Lisbon** (☎ (21) 392 40 00; fax 392 41 85; information.section@lisbon.mail.fco.gov.uk). **Consulates:** Av. Boavista, 3072, 4100 **Porto** (☎ (22) 618 47 89; fax 610 04 38); Largo Francisco A. Mauricio, 7-10, 8500 **Portimão** (☎ (28) 241 78 04; fax 241 78 06).

Canadian Embassy: Av. Liberdade, 196-200, 3rd fl., 1250 **Lisbon** (☎ (21) 316 46 00; fax 316 46 91). **Consulate:** R. Frei Laurenço do Santa Maria, 1, 1st fl., 8000 **Faro** (☎ (89) 80 37 57; fax 88 08 88).

Irish Embassy: R. Imprensa à Estrela, 4th fl., Ste. 1, 1200 **Lisbon** (☎ (21) 392 94 40; fax 397 73 63).

New Zealand Embassy: Refer to New Zealand Embassy in Italy: Via Zara, 28, **Rome** 00198 (☎ 396 441 71 71; fax 396 440 29 84; nzemb.rom@agora.stm.it). **Consulate:** Av. Antonio Agusto Aguiar, 122, 9th fl., 1050 **Lisbon** (☎ (21) 350 96 90; fax 347 20 04).

South African Embassy: Av. Luis Bivar, 10, 1097 **Lisbon** (☎ (1) 353 50 41; fax 353 57 13; email SAfrican.Embassy@individual.EUnet.pt).

US Embassy: Av. das Forças Armadas, 1600 **Lisbon** (☎ (21) 726 91 09; fax 727 91 09). **Consulate:** same address and ☎; fax (1) 727 23 54.

HOLIDAYS

As in Spain, festivals form a large part of local culture. Portugal hosts plenty of lively fairs and religious celebrations, some of which span weeks or months. The list below includes major Portuguese festivals for 2001. For more information on regional events consult the local tourist office.

DATE	FESTIVAL	LOCATION
January 1	New Year's Day	National
January 6	Epiphany	National
February 27	Carnival	National
April 9-15	Holy Week	National
April 12	*Senhor Ecce Homo* (Maundy Thursday)	National
April 13	Good Friday	National
April 15	Easter	National
April 25	Liberation Day	National
May 1	Labor Day	National
early May	*Queima das Fitas* (Burning of the Ribbons)	Coimbra (p. 620)
June	*Feira Internacional de Lisboa*	Lisbon (p. 536)
first week of June	*Feira Nacional de Agricultura (Feira do Ribatejo)*	Santarém (p. 598)
June 10	*Portugal Day*	National
mid-June	*Festa de Santo António*	Lisbon (p. 536)
June 14	Corpus Christi	National
first week of July	*Festas da Rainha Santa*	Coimbra (p. 620)
second week of July	*Feira Popular*	Coimbra (p. 620)
late July	*Festa do Sardinha*	Peniche (p. 602)
August 15	Feast of the Assumption	National
October 5	Republic Day	National
November 1	All Saints' Day	National
December 8	Feast of the Immaculate Conception	National
December 25	Christmas	National
December 31	New Year's Eve	National

PORTUGAL

LISBON
(LISBOA)

Over 400 years ago, Lisbon was the center of the world's richest and farthest-reaching empire. Though it was plagued by social and political problems in the last century, Lisbon has recently stepped back into the international spotlight. Today, it stands as one of Europe's grandest cities. Like Portugal itself, Lisbon has managed to preserve its traditions, continually renovating its historic monuments and meticulously maintaining its black-and-white mosaic sidewalks, pastel facades, and cobbled, medieval alleys.

Many ancient civilizations claim to have settled Lisbon, with one legend even crediting Odysseus as its founder. Officially, Lisbon is thought to have been inhabited over 3000 years ago by Phoenicians, Greeks, and Carthaginians in turn, until the Romans arrived in 205 BC. Under Julius Caesar's reign, Lisbon became the most important city in Lusitania; in 1255, it was made the capital of the kingdom of Portugal. City and empire reached their apex at the end of the 15th century when Portuguese navigators pioneered explorations of Asia, Africa, and South America. A huge earthquake on November 1, 1755, touched off the nation's fall from glory—close to one-fifth of the population died in the catastrophe, and two-thirds of Lisbon was reduced to a pile of smoldering rubble. Under the authoritarian leadership of Prime Minister Marquês de Pombal, the city recovered as magnificent new squares, palaces, and churches were built along the Cartesian guidelines of style and architecture in the heyday of the Enlightenment. Another wave of construction in the late 19th century extended the city to the north and west.

Lisbon has seen more than its share of changes over the course of the 20th century. During World War II, Lisbon's neutrality and Atlantic connections made the city a rendezvous for spies on both sides. In 1974, when Mozambique and Angola won independence, hundreds of thousands of refugees converged upon the Portuguese capital. Today, Portuguese of African, Asian, and European origin coexist in the capital city. In 1998, the World Expo descended upon Lisbon, providing the impetus for massive construction projects and a citywide face-lift while helping to renew Lisbon's seat at the forefront of European culture. Since then, the revival has continued, as more tourist hotspots and sites of cultural interest emerge.

HIGHLIGHTS OF LISBON AND NEAR LISBON

The **Alfama district,** especially the view from its castle (see p. 553).

The extravagant monastery complex at nearby **Belém** (see p. 555).

Lisbon's futuristic new **Parque de Nações,** in all its glory (see p. 556).

The magnificent palaces and castles at **Sintra,** less than an hour away (see p. 563).

⊠ GETTING THERE AND AWAY

BY PLANE

All flights land at **Aeroporto de Lisboa** (☎ 21 841 37 00), on the city's north edge. Walk out of the terminal, turn right, and follow the road around the curve to the bus stop. From here take **bus** #44 or 45 (20-40min., 165$; #44 runs to Pr. Restauradores on weekdays only) to Pr. Restauradores; the bus stops directly in front of the tourist office. Or take the express **AeroBus** to the same location (bus #91; 15min., every 20min., 7am-9pm, 460$); the bus, which leaves directly from the airport exit, is a better option during rush hour. A **taxi** from the airport downtown costs about 2000$, plus a 300$ luggage fee. Ask at the small tourist office located inside the airport about a taxi **voucher** program currently in the making, which will allow visitors to buy pre-paid vouchers for a cab rides from the airport to downtown, avoiding potential problems with fare dishonesty.

Major airlines have offices at Pr. Marquês de Pombal and along Av. Liberdade. Call for the current rates, as prices almost always fluctuate.

TAP Air Portugal, Aeroporto de Lisboa, Ed. 19 R/C, ground level (☎ 21 841 50 00; www.tap.pt). To Faro, Funchal (Madeira), Porto, Paris, London, Madrid, and Barcelona. Open M-F 9am-6pm.

Iberia, R. Barata Salgueiro, 28, 6th floor (☎ 21 355 81 19; www.iberia.com).

Portugália Airlines, Aeroporto de Lisboa, Ed. 70, Rua C (☎ 21 842 55 00; www.pga.pt). Serves major domestic destinations.

BY TRAIN

Train service in Lisbon is potentially confusing, as there are five main stations, each serving different destinations. Be aware that Portuguese trains are usually quite slow. For further info about Portugal's national railway system call **Caminhos de Ferro Portuguêses** (☎ 21 888 40 25 or 21 346 50 22; www.cp.pt).

Estação Rossio, between Pr. Restauradores and Pr. Dom Pedro IV (Rossio), up the stairs. Services points west. M: Rossio or Restauradores. Schedules and assistance available in info office on ground level (open daily 10am-1pm and 2-7pm). **Luggage storage** (550$ for 48hr.; not available in any other station). English spoken. Open daily 6:30am-1am. To **Sintra** (45min., every 10min. 6am-2am, 210$), via **Queluz** (140$).

Estação Santa Apolónia, Av. Infante Dom Henrique, east of the Alfama on the banks of the Rio Tejo, runs the international, northern, and eastern lines. All trains to Santa Apolónia also stop at the **Estação Oriente** (M: Oriente) by the Expo grounds. The international terminal, with **currency exchange** and an info desk (English spoken), is located off the right side of the main platform. To reach downtown from the station, take bus #9, 39, or 46 to Pr. Restauradores and Estação Rossio. To: **Coimbra** (2½hr., 7 per day 8:05am-8:05pm, 1510-2700$); **Aveiro** (3-3½hr., 4 per day 9:05am-8:05pm, 3240$); **Porto** (4½hr., 12 per day 7:55am-8:05pm, 2080-3700$); **Braga** (5hr., 2 per day 7:55am-5:55pm, 2800$); **Madrid** (10hr., 1 per day 10:05pm, 8200$); and **Paris** (21hr., 1 per day 6:05pm, 29,000$).

Estação Cais do Sodré, just beyond the end of R. Alecrim, to the right of Pr. Comércio when walking from Baixa. M: Cais do Sodré. Take the metro or bus #1, 44, or 45 from Pr. Restauradores or bus #28 from Estação Santa Apolónia. Trains to: the monastery in **Belém** (10min., every 15min. 5:30am-2:50am, 140$); the youth hostel in **Oeiras** (20min., every 15min., 170$); **Estoril** and **Cascais** (30min., every 20min., 210$). Consult the video monitors above each platform.

Estação Barreiro, across the Rio Tejo, serves southern destinations like the Costa Azul and the Algarve. Station accessible by ferries from the Terreiro do Paço dock off Pr. Comércio; be sure to distinguish the Estação from adjacent ferry docks. Ferries leave every 30min. and take 30min.; ferry ticket included in the price of connecting train ticket (otherwise 85$, 200$ round-trip). Trains to: **Setúbal** (1½hr., every hr. 7:55am-6:50pm, 210$); **Évora** (2½hr., 7 per day 6:50am-11:50pm, 1200$); and **Lagos** (5½hr., 5 per day 7:35am-7:45pm, 2800$).

BY BUS

Arco do Cego, Av. João Crisóstomo, around the block from M: Saldanha. Exit the metro onto Av. República and walk 1 block up from the *praça* (toward the McDonald's), then turn right onto Av. Duque d'Ávila, and right before the McDonald's. The bus station is a big beige building on the corner of Av. João Crisóstomo and Av. Defensores de Chaves. All "Saldanha" buses (#36, 44, 45) stop in the *praça* (165$). This is the terminal for virtually all buses. The terminal has fast **Rede Expressos** (☎ 21 354 54 39

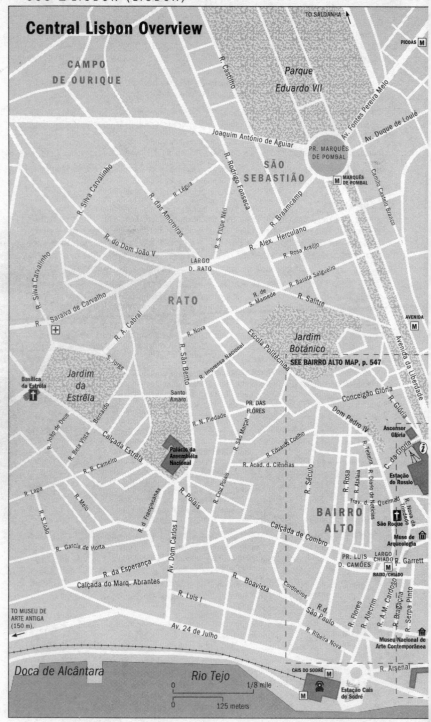

Central Lisbon Overview

TO SALDANHA

PICOAS M

CAMPO DE OURIQUE

R. Castilho

Parque Eduardo VII

Av. Fontes Pereira Melo

Av. Duque de Loulé

Joaquim António de Aguiar

PR. MARQUÊS DE POMBAL

SÃO SEBASTIÃO

R. das Amoreiras

R. Rodrigo Fonseca

R. Silva Carvalinho

R. Légua

R.S. Filpe Néri

R. Braamcamp

MARQUÊS DE POMBAL M

Camilo Castelo Branco

R. do Dom João V

R. Alex. Herculano

R. Rosa Araújo

R. Silva Carvalinho

LARGO D. RATO

R. Barata Salgueiro

R.

Saraiva de Carvalho

R. A. Cabral

RATO

R. de S. Mamede

R. Salitre

AVENIDA M

S. Jorge

R. Nova

R. São Bento

Escola Politécnica

Jardim Botânico

Avenida da Liberdade

Basílica da Estrêla

Jardim da Estrêla

R. Imprensa Nacional

SEE BAIRRO ALTO MAP, p. 547

Conceição Glória

R. Glória

R. João de Deus

Bernardo

Santo Amaro

R. Bela Vista

Calçada Estrêla

R. N. Piedade

PR. DAS FLÓRES

Dom Pedro IV

Ascensor Glória

C. da Glória

R. B. Carneiro

R. São Marçal

R. Eduardo Coelho

Estação do Rossio

Palácio da Assembléia Nacional

R. Acad. d. Ciências

R. Teixeira

São Roque

R. Lapa

R. Melo

R. Cruz Polais

R. Século

R. Rosa

R. Atalaia

R. Diário de Notícias

R. Nova do Trindade

R. S-João

R. d. Franciscanas

R. Polais

Trav. d. Queimau

Muse de Arqueologia

R. Garcia de Horta

Av. Dom Carlos I

Calçada de Combro

BAIRRO ALTO

LARGO CHIADO

R. Garrett

R. da Esperança

Calçada do Marq. Abrantes

R. Boavista

Cordoeiros

PR. LUIS D. CAMÕES

BAIXO/CHIADO M

R. Flores

R. Alecrim

R. A.M. Cardoso

R. Bragança

R. Serpa Pinto

TO MUSEU DE ARTE ANTIGA (150 m).

R. Luis I

R. d. São Paulo

Museu Nacional de Arte Contemporânea

Av. 24 de Julho

R. Ribeira Nova

CAIS DO SODRÉ M

R. Arsenal

Doca de Alcântara

Rio Tejo

0 — 1/8 mile

0 — 125 meters

Estação Cais do Sodré

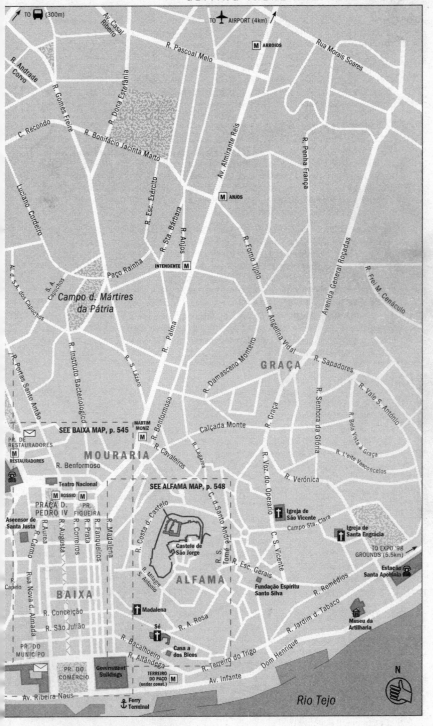

TO 🚌 (300m)

Av. Casal Ribeiro

TO ✈ AIRPORT (4km)

R. Pascoal Melo

R. Andrade Corvo

R. Gomes Freire

C. Recondo

M ARROIOS

Rua Morais Soares

R. Dona Estefânia

R. Bonifácio Jacinta Marto

Luciano Cordeiro

S. A. Capuchos

Al. d. S.A. dos Capuchos

R. Esc. Exército

R. Sta. Bárbara

R. Anjos

Av. Almirante Reis

R. Penha França

M ANJOS

R. Forno Tijolo

R. Frei M. Cenáculo

Paço Rainha

INTENDENTE M

Campo d. Mártires da Pátria

R. Portas Santo Antão

R. Instituto Bacteriológico

R. S. Lázaro

R. Palma

R. Damasceno Monteiro

Avenida General Roçadas

R. Angelina Vidal

GRAÇA

R. Sapadores

R. Vale S. António

R. Senhora da Glória

R. Bela Vista à Graça

R. L'eite Vasconcelos

R. Bentormoso

MARTIM MONIZ M

SEE BAIXA MAP, p. 545

PR. DE RESTAURADORES

M RESTAURADORES

MOURARIA

R. Benformoso

R. Cavaleiros

R. Lagares

Calçada Monte

R. Graça

R. Voz. do. Operário

R. Verónica

Teatro Nacional

M ROSSIO M

SEE ALFAMA MAP, p. 548

Ascensor de Santa Justa

PRAÇA D. PEDRO IV

PR. FIGUEIRA

R. Madalena

R. Costa d. Castelo

C. d. Santo André

Castelo de São Jorge

Igreja de São Vicente

Campo Sta. Clara

Igreja de Santa Engrácia

C. S. Vicente

TO EXPO '98 GROUNDS (5.5km)

R. Aurea

R. Carmo

R. Augusta

R. Prata

R. Correeiros

R. Fanqueiros

R. Milagre S. António

R. S. Tomé

R. Esc. Gerais

Estação Santa Apolónia

ALFAMA

Fundação Espírito Santo Silva

R. Remédios

BAIXA

R. Capelo

Rua Nova d. Almada

R. Conceição

R. São Julião

Madalena

Sé

R. A. Rosa

R. Jardim d. Tabaco

Museu da Artilharia

PR. DO MUNICÍPIO

R. Bacalhoeiro

R. Alfândega

Casa a dos Bicos

R. Terreiro do Trigo

Dom Henrique

PR. DO COMÉRCIO

Government Buildings

TERREIRO DO PAÇO (under const.) M

Av. Infante

Av. Ribeira Naus

Ferry Terminal

Rio Tejo

N

or 21 310 31 11; www.rede-expressos.pt) to many destinations. To: **Caldas da Rainha** (1¼hr., 10 per day 7am-11pm, 1000$); **Peniche** (2hr., 11 per day 7am-7:30pm, 1050$); **Coimbra** (2½hr., 16 per day 7am-12:15am, 1500$); **Évora** (2hr., 13 per day 7am-9:30pm, 1500$); **Portalegre** (4½hr., 8 per day 7:30am-9:55pm, 1700$); **Porto** (4hr., 7per day 7am-12:15am, 2300$), via Leiria; **Lagos** (5hr., 9 per day 5am-1am, 2500$); **Braga** (5hr., 6 per day 7am-12:15am, 2500$); **Tavira** (5hr., 5 per day 5am-1am, 2500$); and **Vila Real St. Antonio** (6hr., 7 per day 5am-1am, 2600$), via **Setúbal** (45min., 600$) and Faro.

▐ GETTING AROUND

Lisbon has an efficient system of buses, subways, trams, funiculars, and trains. Use them to full advantage—no suburb in or out of the city takes longer than 90 minutes to reach. If you don't speak Portuguese, taxi drivers and bus and train ticket booths may try to rip you off by charging an exorbitant fare or not returning all of your change. Make sure you know in advance what the fare should be, and don't hand the vendor more than 200$ for a local trip.

City Buses: CARRIS (☎ 21 361 30 00; www.carris.pt) runs the buses, trams, and funiculars in Lisbon. Fare 165$ within the city; pay on the bus. If you plan to stay for any length of time, consider investing in a *passe turístico* (tourist pass), good for unlimited travel on all CARRIS transports. 1-, 3-, 4-, and 7-day passes available (460$, 1080$, 1760$, 2490$). Passes sold in CARRIS booths located in most network train stations and the busier metro stations (e.g. Restauradores). Open daily 8am-8pm. You must show a passport to buy a tourist pass.

Subway: Metro (☎ 21 355 84 57; www.metrolisboa.pt) covers downtown and the modern business district in 4 color-coded lines. A red "M" marks Metro stops. *Let's Go* indicates a metro stop by writing "M:" followed by the name of the stop. Tickets 100$. Buy them at window or from vending machines. Book of 10 tickets 850$. Trains run daily 6am-1am, though some stations close earlier.

Trams (CARRIS): Everywhere 165$. They offer beautiful views of the harbor and older neighborhoods. Many date from before WWI. Line #28 is great for sight-seeing in the Alfama and Mouraria (stop in Pr. Comércio). Line #15 heads from Pr. Comércio or Pr. Figueira to Belém and the monastery complex.

Funiculars (CARRIS): Everywhere 165$. A cross between a tram and an elevator, funiculars link the lower city with the hilly residential area. A common one goes up Ascensor Glória from Pr. Restauradores to Bairro Alto.

Taxis: Rádio Táxis de Lisboa (☎ 21 811 90 00), **Autocoope** (☎ 21 793 27 56), and **Teletáxis** (☎ 21 811 11 00). Along Av. Liberdade and Rossio. Luggage 300$.

Car Rental: Pick up cars at the airport or in one of several locations downtown. Contact the agencies for pickup locations. **Budget,** R. Castilho, 167B (☎ 21 386 05 16; fax 21 383 09 78); **Hertz,** R. Castilho, 72A (☎ 21 381 24 30; fax 21 387 41 64); **Avis,** R. Castilho (☎ 21 356 11 76; fax 21 356 11 70); **Mundirent,** R. Conde Redondo, 38A (☎ 21 313 93 60; fax 21 313 93 69); **Solcar,** R. São Sebastião da Pedreira, 51D (☎ 21 313 90 70; fax 21 356 05 04); **Alô Car,** R. Quirino da Fonseca, 22B/C (☎ 21 843 88 50; fax 21 846 00 64). See **By Car,** p. 40, for toll-free numbers to get rates and other info from home. If you're just planning on visiting Lisbon, a car is not necessary. You won't want to be a part of the hair-raising traffic that defines Portugal's streets.

✳ ORIENTATION

According to legend, Lisbon, like Rome, was built on seven hills, though at times it might seem like many more. Navigating the maze of Lisbon's roller coaster streets requires patience and Stairmaster training. Thankfully for the not-so-hardcore, Lisbon also has an efficient system of public transportation made up of subways, buses, trams, and funiculars. The city center is made up of three main *bairros* (neighborhoods): the Baixa, (low district, resting in the valley), the Bairro Alto (high district), and the twisty-turny, topsy-turvy Alfama.

The **Baixa,** Lisbon's old business center, is the center of town, sandwiched between Bairro Alto and Alfama. Its grid of small, mostly pedestrian streets begins at the **Praça Dom Pedro IV** (better known as the **Rossio**) and ends at the **Praça do Comércio** on the **Rio Tejo** (or the **Tagus River,** though no self-respecting Portuguese will ever call it that). Once the site of the royal palace, Praça do Comércio was nicknamed **Terreiro do Paço** (the palace terrace) after it was destroyed in the 1755 earthquake. For tourists, Rossio is the center of the city. Adjacent to Rossio are two other important squares, **Praça dos Restauradores,** where buses from the airport stop and the tourist office is located, and **Praça da Figueira.** Pr. Restauradores lies just above the Baixa, and from it the sprawling **Avenida da Liberdade** runs uphill to the new business district centered around **Praça do Marquês de Pombal,** while Praça da Figueira extends towards the Alfama.

Facing Baixa with your back to the river, the **Ascensor de Santa Justa**—an elegant historic outdoor elevator that marks the left-hand border of the neighborhood—heads to the Bairro Alto's upscale shopping district, the **Chiado,** traversed by fashionable **Rua do Carmo** and **Rua Garrett.** The **Bairro Alto** is a mix of narrow streets, lush parks, and Baroque churches. Bairro Alto is also one of Lisbon's main party districts; the streets are crowded from noon until well past midnight. The other is the recently renovated **Docas de Santo Amaro** (docks), to the west of the Bairro Alto, where some of Lisbon's hottest nightlife is to be found.

On the other side of the Baixa (to the right with your back to the river), is the **Alfama,** Lisbon's famous medieval/Moorish neighborhood. Alfama, the lone survivor of the 1755 earthquake, is the city's oldest district. Alfama is made up of tiny whitewashed houses along a labyrinth of narrow alleys and stairways beneath the

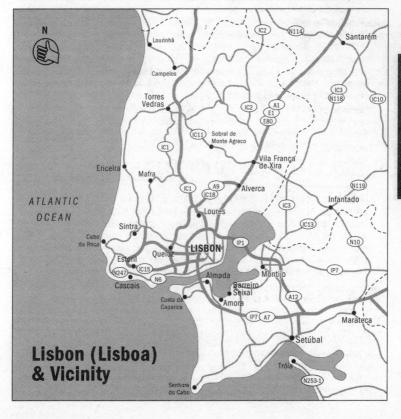

Lisbon (Lisboa)
& Vicinity

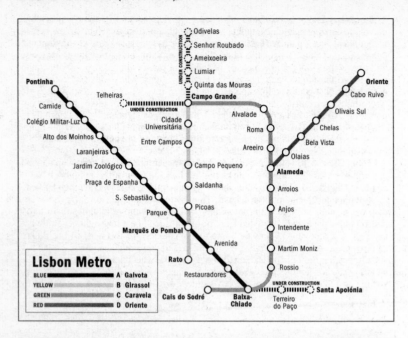

Odivelas
Senhor Roubado
Ameixoeira
UNDER CONSTRUCTION
Lumiar
Quinta das Mouras
Campo Grande
Pontinha
Telheiras
UNDER CONSTRUCTION
Oriente
Cabo Ruivo
Carnide
Alvalade
Olivais Sul
Colégio Militar-Luz
Cidade
Universitária
Roma
Chelas
Alto dos Moinhos
Entre Campos
Areeiro
Bela Vista
Laranjeiras
Olaias
Jardim Zoológico
Campo Pequeno
Alameda
Praça de Espanha
Saldanha
Arroios
S. Sebastião
Anjos
Parque
Picoas
Marquês de Pombal
Intendente
Avenida
Martim Moniz
Lisbon Metro
Rato
Rossio
BLUE ■■■■■ A Galvota
Restauradores
UNDER CONSTRUCTION
YELLOW ░░░░░ B Girassol
Santa Apolónia
GREEN ▒▒▒▒▒ C Caravela
Cais do Sodré
Baixa-
Chiado
Terreiro
do Paço
RED ■■■■■ D Oriente

Castelo de São Jorge. Expect to get lost. Without a detailed map expect to get twice as lost. The twisting streets either change names every three steps or include several different streets under the same name. Streets are labeled either *travessas* (side streets), *ruas* (streets), *calçadinhas* (walkways), or *escadinhas* (stairways). A street-indexed *GeoBloco* **Planta Turística de Lisboa** or the *Poseidon* **Planta de Lisboa** (with Sintra, Cascais, and Estoril on the back) are good maps and well worth the money (both sold in Estação Rossio and at most newsstands for 1200$).

Stretching along the river from the Baixa's waterfront are some of the fastest growing parts of Lisbon. The former Expo '98 grounds, now called the **Parque das Nações** (Park of Nations), welcomes visitors both day and night, while the **Alcântara** and the Docas do Santo Amaro show off Lisbon's most happening nightlife.

▊ PRACTICAL INFORMATION

TOURIST AND FINANCIAL SERVICES

Tourist Office: Palácio da Foz, Pr. Restauradores (☎ 21 346 63 07), M: Restauradores. Incredible staff provides bus schedules, accommodation listings, and a free map. English, French, Italian, and German spoken. Open daily 9am-8pm. Office at the **Aeroporto de Lisboa** (☎ 21 849 43 23), just outside the baggage claim area. English spoken. Open daily 6am-2am. Look for kiosks that read "Ask me about Lisboa" at Santa Apolónia, Rossio, Parque das Nações, and other locations around the city.

Budget Travel: Movijovem, Av. Duque d'Ávila, 137 (☎ 21 359 60 00; email movijovem@mail.telepac.pt), at the bus stop, in the alley, on the right. M: São Sebastião. Movijovem will make reservations at youth hostels throughout the country, though you have to pay in advance. Open daily 9am-7pm. Visa.

Embassies: see **Embassies and Consulates,** p. 534.

Currency Exchange: Banks are open M-F 8:30-3pm. For a low commission and decent rates, try **Cota Câmbio,** R. Áurea, 283 (☎ 21 342 52 32 or 21 347 00 73), 1 block off Pr. Dom Pedro IV in the Baixa. Open M-Sa 9am-8pm. The main post office, most banks, and travel agencies also change money. Ask about fees first—they can be exorbitant (1000$ or more).

American Express: Top Tours, Av. Duque de Loulé, 108 (☎ 21 319 42 90). M: Marquês de Pombal. Exit the metro stop and walk up Av. Liberdade toward the Marquês de Pombal statue, then turn right; the office is 2 blocks up on the left side of the street. The often-crowded Top Tours office handles all AmEx functions. English spoken. Open M-F 9:30am-1pm and 2:30-6:30pm.

LOCAL SERVICES

Luggage Storage: Estação Rossio. Lockers 550$ for 48hr. Open daily 8:30am-11:30pm.

English Bookstore: Livraria Británica, R. Luís Fernandes, 14-16 (☎ 21 342 84 72), in the Bairro Alto. Walk up R. São Pedro de Alcântara and keep going straight as it becomes R. Dom Pedro V and then R. Escola Politécnica. Turn left on R. São Marcal, then right after 2 blocks onto R. Luís Fernandes. Classics and best-sellers. Open M-F 9:30am-7pm. V, MC, AmEx.

Library: Biblioteca Municipal Central (☎ 21 797 38 62), Palácio Galveias. M: Campo Pequeno. Open M-Tu 10am-8pm, W-F 10am-7pm, Sa 10am-5pm.

Shopping Center: Amoreiras Shopping Center de Lisboa (☎ 21 381 02 00 or 21 381 02 40), on Av. Duarte Pacheco, near the intersection with R. Carlos Alberto da Mota Pinto. Take bus #11 from Restauradores. 383 shops including a huge **Pão de Açúcar** supermarket, English bookstores, and a 10-screen **cinema.** Open daily 10am-midnight. **Colombo,** Av. Lusiada (☎ 21 711 36 36), in front of Benfica stadium. M: Colégio Militar-Luz. Over 500 shops and a 10-screen cinema. **Centro Vasco de Gama,** Av. Dom João II (☎ 21 893 06 01). M: Oriente. Has it all. Open daily 10am-midnight.

Laundromat: Lavatax, R. Francisco Sanches, 65A (☎ 21 812 33 92). 1 block from M: Arroios. Wash, dry, and fold 1100$ per 5kg load. Open M-F 8:30am-1pm and 3-7pm, Sa 8:30am-1pm.

EMERGENCY AND COMMUNICATIONS

Emergency: ☎ 112. **Police:** R. Capelo, 3 (☎ 21 346 61 41). English spoken.

Late-Night Pharmacy: ☎ 118 (directory assistance). Posted on the door of every pharmacy is the address of the next night's neighborhood pharmacy to provide this service.

Drug Abuse Hotline: Centro das Taipas, R. das Taipas, 20 (☎ 21 347 41 15).

Medical Services: British Hospital, R. Saraiva de Carvalho, 49 (☎ 21 395 50 67). **Cruz Vermelha Portuguesa,** R. Duarte Galvão, 54 (hospital ☎ 21 771 40 00; **ambulance** ☎ 21 942 11 11).

Post Office: Marked by red *Correios* signs. **Main office** (☎ 21 346 32 31), Pr. Comércio. Telephone, **fax, Posta Restante,** and international express mail (EMS). Open M-F 8:30am-6:30pm. **Second office** (☎ 21 323 87 00) in Pr. Restauradores provides the same services with longer hours and a central location. Open M-F 8am-10pm, Sa-Su 9am-6pm. **Postal Code:** 1100 for central Lisbon.

Internet Access: Web Café, R. Diário de Notícias, 126 (☎ 21 342 11 81). 300$ for 15min., 500$ for 30min., 700$ for 45min., 800$ per hr. Open daily 4pm-2am. **Ciber Chiado,** Largo Picadeiro, 10 (☎ 21 346 67 22), just off Largo Chiado, up R. Paiva de Andrade. Take the last door on the left side of the square up to the 1st floor, then ring the bell. 350$ for 30min., 600$ per hr. Open M-F 4pm-midnight, Sa 8pm-midnight.

Telephones: Portugal Telecom, Pr. Dom Pedro IV, 68. M: Rossio. Has pay phones and booths for international calls. Pay the cashier after your call or use a phone card. **Phone cards** come in 50 units (650$), 100 units (1300$), or 150 units (1900$). Buy them here or at neighborhood bookstores and stationers. Local calls consume at least 1 unit (13$). Office open daily 8am-11pm. Visa.

▟ ACCOMMODATIONS

A price ceiling supposedly restricts the amount hostels can charge for particular types of rooms, so if the fee seems padded request the printed price list. During low- or mid-season, prices generally drop—try bargaining the price down at those times. Many establishments have rooms with only double beds and charge per person. Expect to pay from 3000 to 5000$ for a single and 5000 to 9000$ for a double, depending on amenities and location. If you're dissatisfied, ask the owner for a *livro de reclamações* (complaints book)—they are required to give these to the tourist bureau.

Most hotels are in the center of town on Av. Liberdade, while many convenient budget hostels are in the Baixa along the Rossio and on R. Prata, R. Correiros, and R. Ouro. Lodgings near the Castelo de São Jorge or in the Bairro Alto are quieter and closer to the sights. If central accommodations are full, head east to the hostels along Av. Almirante Reis. At night, be careful in the Baixa, the Bairro Alto, and especially the Alfama; many streets are isolated and poorly lit.

YOUTH HOSTELS

Pousada da Juventude de Lisboa (HI), R. Andrade Corvo, 46 (☎ 21 353 26 96; fax 21 353 75 41). M: Picoas. Exit the metro station, turn right, and walk 1 block; the hostel is on your left. This huge, ultra-clean youth haven has no curfew or lockout but does have an inconvenient location. English spoken. Breakfast included. Lockers 300$ per day. Reception 8am-midnight. Check out by 10:30am. HI card required. June-Sept. dorms 2900$; doubles with bath 6500$. Oct.-May dorms 2000$; doubles 5000$. V, MC.

Pousada da Juventude de Parque das Nações (HI), R. de Moscavide, lote 4-71-01 (☎ 21 892 08 90; fax 21 892 08 91). M: Oriente. Exit the station and go left on Av. Dom João II, walking past the Park of Nations until the street intersects with R. de Moscavide. The hostel is the striped building on the corner. Though a long way from downtown, this hostel is actually close to somewhere you want to be: the futuristic Park of Nations. Internet access 100$ for 15min., 150$ for 30min. English spoken. Breakfast included. Lunch and dinner 950$ each. Reception 8am-midnight. Midnight curfew, but no lockout. Wheelchair accessible. HI card required. Reserve 1 week ahead in the summer. June-Sept. dorms 2100$; doubles 5100$. Oct.-May dorms 1700$; doubles 4300$.

Pousada da Juventude de Catalazete (HI), Estrada Marginal (☎ 21 443 06 38), in the coastal town of Oeiras. Take a train from Estação Cais do Sodré to Oeiras (20min., every 15min. 5:30am-2:30am, 170$). Exit through the train station underpass, go right and cross the street. Go straight (following the signs to Lisbon) as the street curves under a bridge and through a residential district. Keep going as the street becomes R. São Pedro de Ariero and then R. Cidade do Mendelo. It will become a miniature highway; turn left under the bridge at the INATEL sign. Follow the signs into the INATEL complex, past the guard, past the apartments' reception building, continuing straight on the only road in the complex. Turn left at the sign for apartments 84-142; the hostel is the big yellow building. The hike will reward you with quiet rooms and beautiful ocean views from the patio. Breakfast included. Lunch and dinner 950$ each. Reception daily 8am-midnight. No curfew. Reserve 2 weeks ahead in the summer. HI card required. June-Sept. dorms 2000$; doubles with bath 5100$. Oct.-May 1700$; doubles 4300$.

BAIXA

Dozens of hostels surround the three connected *praças*, Pr. Restauradores, Pr. Dom Pedro IV, and Pr. Figueira, that form the heart of downtown Lisbon. Staying in this area is incredibly practical, as it makes a good base for visiting sights in and around the city. Although most hostels have fewer than 12 rooms, finding a vacancy shouldn't be difficult; still, reservations are recommended just about everywhere July-Sept. For a good night's sleep, look for a hostel along a pedestrian-only street. Some *casas de hospedes* may be brothels; though occasionally located beneath hostels, they are not desirable lodgings for most tourists.

Residencial Estrela do Mondego, Calçada do Carmo, 25, 2nd fl. (☎ 21 324 08 40), next to the Estação Rossio. Large, comfortable rooms, all with phones, cable TV, and A/C, in a great location. English spoken. Laundry 1500$ per load. Singles with bath 5000$; doubles 6000-6500$; triples with bath 7000$; quads with bath 8000$. V, MC.

TO PRAÇA MARQUÊS
DE POMBAL

■ Ascensor Glória

PRAÇA
DOS
RESTAURADORES

R. das Portas de Sº Antão

Cç. Nova do Colégio

Cç. de Santana

R. da Palma

R. Jardim do Regedor

R. Convento

Cç. Garcia

LARGO
MARTIM
MONIZ

R. do Arco da Graça

R. de Mouraria

Estação Rossio

Teatro Nacional
Dona Mario II

LARGO DE
S. DOMINGOS

R. Barros Queir

R. da Palma

R. Arco Marquês
do Alegrete

R. Marq.
Ponte Lima

LARGO
DUQUE
CADAVAL

R. do Duque

R. da Condessa

R. da Oliveira

PRAÇA DO
DOM PEDRO IV

Cç. do Carmo

R. 1º de Dezembro

PRAÇA DA
FIGUEIRA

Pr. do Borratém

R. do Regedor

LARGO DA
ACHADA

R. de Costa do Castelo

R. Betesga

Museu de
Arqueologia

R. da Trindade

LARGO DO
CARMO

Tv. do Carmo

Cç. Sacramento

R. do Carmo

Ascensor de
Santa Justa

R. de Sta. Justa

R. dos Dourados

R. da Prata

LARGO
ADELINO
A. DA COSTA

R. de S. Mamede

R. Garret

R. Ivens

R. Aurea (R. do Ouro)

R. de Assunção

R. Augusta

R. de Vitória

R. dos Correios

R. do Fanqueiros

R. da Madalena

Ruas das Pedras

R. Capelo

R. Nova do Almada

R. do Crucifixo

R. dos Sapateiros

R. São Nicolau

LARGO DA
MADALENA

Cç. Correio Velho

LARGO ACAD. NAC.
DE BELAS ARTES

Museu Nacional de
Arte Contemporânea

PRAÇA
MUNICIPIO

R. da Conceição

R. Aurea (R. do Ouro)

R. São Julião

R. da Prata

R. Augusta

R. do Comércio

R. de Padaria

R. Alfonso
de Albuquerque

R. dos Bacalhoeiros

R. do Arsenal

R. da Alfândega

N

Central
Post Office

PRAÇA DO
COMERCIO

0   100 yards
0   100 meters

Av. das Naus

Rio Tejo

LISBON

Baixa

ACCOMMODATIONS

Pensão Beira Minho, 5
Pensão Campos, 2
Pensão Moderna, 6
Pensão Prata, 8
Residencia do Sul, 3
Residencial Duas Nações, 7
Residencial Estrela do Mondego, 4
Residencial Florescente, 1

■ **Residencial Duas Nações,** R. Vitória, 41 (☎ 21 346 07 10; fax 21 347 02 06), on the corner of R. Augusta, 2 blocks up from M: Baixa-Chiado. Looks and feels just like a hotel, with one exception: you can afford it. 69 good-sized centrally-located rooms with phones (and some with patios) welcome weary travelers. Breakfast included. Laundry available. English spoken. Reserve a week ahead during the summer. Singles 3500$, with bath 6000$; double/twin 4500$, with bath 7500$; triples with bath 9000$. Show your copy of *Let's Go* to get these prices. V, MC, AmEx.

Pensão Campos, R. Jardim do Regedor, 24, 3rd fl. (☎ 21 346 28 64), between Pr. Restauradores and R. Portas de Santo Antão. M: Restauradores. Perfect location overlooking a lively pedestrian street near the Rossio run by friendly, helpful multilingual staff. Street-facing rooms can get a bit noisy at night, but back rooms provide quiet. Laundry 1500$ per load. Singles 4000$; doubles with shower 6000-7000$; triples 7000$.

Residencial Florescente, R. Portas de Santo Antão, 99 (☎ 21 342 66 09; fax 21 342 77 33), 1 block from Pr. Restauradores. M: Restauradores. The 72 spacious rooms, all with phone and TV, are luxurious by budget standards. Windowed rooms have incredible views of Pr. Figueira. Laundry available. Reserve 2 weeks ahead during the summer. Singles 5000$, with bath 7000$; doubles 6000$, with bath 8000$; triples 8000$, with bath 12,000$. Prices fall Oct.-May. V, AmEx, MC.

Pensão Beira Minho, Pr. Figueira, 6, 2nd fl. (☎ 21 346 18 46), beside the Rossio at the north end of the *praça*, through a flower shop. M: Rossio. 24 plain, well-lit rooms with phones, some with verandas overlooking the square. Breakfast included. English spoken. Reserve 1 week ahead during the summer. Singles 4000$, with bath 5000$; doubles 5000$, with bath 6000$; triples 7000$, with bath 8000$.

Pensão Moderna, R. Correeiros, 205, 4th fl. (☎ 21 346 08 18), 1 block from Pr. Figueira, toward the water. M: Rossio. Anything but modern, these comfortable, apartment-style rooms are filled with antiques, and have large windows and balconies. Great location. Singles 2500$; doubles 4000$; triples 6000$.

Pensão Prata, R. Prata, 71, 3rd fl. (☎ 21 346 89 08), 2 blocks from Pr. Comércio. M: Rossio. The entrance to a busy cafe obscures the staircase. 13 clean, peaceful rooms with tiny baths. Reserve 1 week ahead in the summer. Laundry 1500$ per load. Singles 5000$; doubles 6000-7000$. Prices fall Oct.-June.

Residência do Sul, Pr. Dom Pedro IV, 59, 2nd fl. (☎ 21 342 25 11), through the souvenir shop. M: Rossio. Somewhat dark but otherwise excellent rooms, all with TV and phone. Those opposite the square are quieter. English spoken. Singles 4500-7500$; doubles 6000-8000$; triples 10000$; quads 12500$.

IN AND AROUND THE BAIRRO ALTO

The quiet Bairro Alto has a communal feel that the town center lacks, but the uphill hike is inconvenient and daunting for luggage-bearers (try the Ascensor Glória from Pr. Restauradores). Blessed (and financially rewarded) are those who persevere; unto them shall be bestowed ample rooms of great value, enhanced by antiques and views of the castle. Most of Lisbon's nightlife is in Bairro Alto, but be cautious if you're out late alone.

■ **Casa de Hóspedes Globo,** R. Teixeira, 37 (☎/fax 21 346 22 79), on a small street across from the Parque São Pedro de Alcântara at the top of the funicular. From the park entrance, cross the street and turn right onto R. Teixeira. Convenient location. Refurbished, spacious rooms with sturdy furniture, cheerful bedspreads, and partitioned bathrooms. Reserve up to 1 week in advance. Laundry 1500$ per load. Singles 2500$, with bath 4500$; doubles/twins 6000$; triples 6500$.

Residencial Camões, Tr. Poço da Cidade, 38, 1st fl. (☎ 21 347 75 10; fax 21 346 40 48), off R. Misericórdia. From the top of Ascensor Glória, turn left onto R. São Pedro, which becomes R. Misericórdia; Tr. Poço da Cidade is the 5th right. A pristine set of rooms in the heart of the party district—it may get a bit noisy at night. TV lounge. English spoken. Breakfast included. Reserve 1 week ahead in summer. Singles 2500-3000$; doubles 5500-7500$, with bath 6500-8000$; triples with bath 8000-10,000$.

Jardim
Botánico

PRAÇA DA
ALEGRIA

Av. da Liberdade

R. da Alegria

Cç. Patriarcal

Tv. do Rosário

R. Sto. António da Glória

R. Conceição da Glória

R. da Glória

R. das Taipas

PRAÇA
PRÍNCIPE
REAL

Tv. do Fala Só

Bairro Alto

🏠 ACCOMMODATIONS

Casa de Hóspedes Globo, 2
Pensão Londres, 1
Residencial Camões, 3

R. Dom Pedro IV

R. Luisa Tod

PRAÇA DE SÃO
PEDRO DE
ALCANTARA

PRAÇA
DOS
RESTAURADORES

R. da Rosa

R. da Vinha

R. S. Boaventura

Cç. do Tijolo

R. Nova do Loureiro

Cç. Cabra

R. do Século

R. S. Pedro de Alcântara

Tv. da Boa Hora

Tv. da Aqua de Flor

Estação
Rossio

Tv. do Lusitano

LARGO
DUQUE
CADAVAL

R. João Pereira Rosa

Tv. dos Inglesinhos

Tv. da Queimada

Luz Soriano

Tv. dos Caetanos

Tv. das Noticias

R. das Gáveas

R. da Misericórdia

R. Nova da Trindade

R. Duque

R. Condessa

R. Oliveira

Ascensor de
Santa Justa

Tv. dos Fiéis de Deus

Tv. Poço Cidade

R. da Atalaia

R. da Barroca

R. do Diário de

R. do Norte

Igreja do Carmo

Tv. das Mercês

R. Dos Poiais
de S. Benito

Cç. do Combro

Tv. da R. Espera

R. da Trindade

Museu
Arqueológico

Cç. Sacramento

R. do Carmo

R. Aurea (R. do Ouro)

Museu de
São Roque

Cç. do Carmo

Igreja de
São Roque

R. do Loreto

PRAÇA CAMÕES

R. Garret

R. das Chagas

R. da Horta Seca

R. da Emenda

R. das Flores

R. do Alecrim

R. Ivens

R. Nova do Almada

R. do Crucifixo

Tv. do Cabral

Cç. da Bica

R. do Ataide

R. António Maria Cardoso

R. Capelo

R. de Bragança

R. Serpa Pinto

Museu de Chiado

Tv. Carvalho

R. de S. Paulo

R. Nova Carvalho

R. da Ribeira Nova

R. das Flores

Cç. S. Francisco

Av. 24 de Julho

R. Vitor Cordon

R. do Ferragial

PRAÇA DO
MUNICIPIO

Av. Das Naus

R. do Arsenal

0   100 yards

0   100 meters

N

LISBON

Pensão Londres, R. Dom Pedro V, 53, 2nd fl. (☎ 21 346 22 03; fax 21 346 56 82; www.desenvolve.com/plondres). Take the Ascensor Glória from Pr. Restauradores. Turn right and walk up R. São Pedro to R. Dom Pedro V; it's is on the left near the hilltop. Spacious, well-lit rooms have phones, and some TVs. All overlook the old town. Breakfast included. Laundry available. Reserve 1 month ahead in summer. Singles 5500-9000$; doubles 7700-12,200$; triples 12,800-15,200$, quads 17,200$. V, MC.

ALFAMA

Staying in the Alfama yields flowering balconies and amazing views. It also means steep streets, a long walk to the hostel, and potential danger at night. Yet rooms are cheap and surprisingly comfy, and the Alfama's narrow side streets and friendly *praças* are well worth exploring. Reservations are highly recommended.

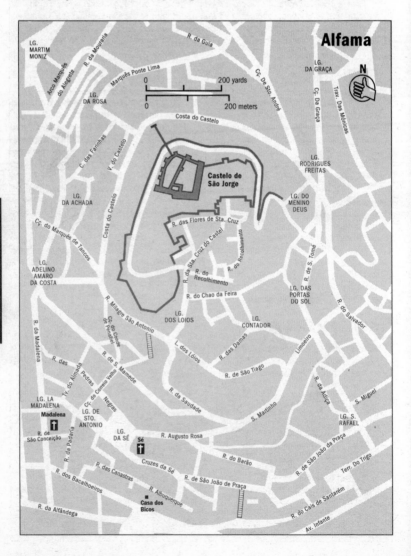

■ **Pensão Ninho das Águias,** R. Costa do Castelo, 74 (☎ 21 885 40 70), right behind the Castelo. From Pr. Figueira take R. Madalena to Largo Adelino Costa, then head uphill to R. Costa do Castelo. *The* place to stay if you want to stay in the Alfama. Spectacular views of Lisbon are well worth the long hike. A garden looks out over the old city. 16 cheerful rooms with phones. English spoken. Reserve at least 1 month ahead during the summer. Singles 5000$; doubles 7500$, with bath 8000$; triples 10,000$.

CAMPING

Although camping is popular in Portugal, campers are often prime targets for thieves. Info on campgrounds is available from the tourist office in the free booklet *Portugal: Camping and Caravan Sites.* There are 30 campgrounds within a 45-minute radius of the capital; listed below is the only one in Lisbon proper.

Parque de Campismo Municipal de Lisboa (☎ 21 760 96 20; fax 21 760 96 33), on the road to Benfica. Take bus #43 from the Rossio to the Parque Florestal Monsanto. Pool and supermarket. Reception daily 9am-9pm. July-Aug. 800$ per person and per tent, 500$ per car; June and Sept. 720$ per person and per tent, 450$ per car; Oct.-May 560$ per person and per tent, 350$ per car.

☐ FOOD

Lisbon has some of the least expensive restaurants and best wine of any European capital. A full dinner costs about 2000-2200$ per person and the *prato do dia* (special of the day) is often a great deal. One full meal will probably be enough to keep you full all day. Until then, just snack on surprisingly filling, incredibly cheap, and sinfully delicious Portuguese pastries; *pastelarias* (pastry shops) are everywhere. The sign of a good restaurant is a clientele made up of as many locals as tourists; the odd toddler running among tables adds to the authenticity. In Lisbon, the closer to the industrial waterfront, the cheaper the restaurant. The south end of the Baixa, near the port, and the area bordering the Alfama are particularly inexpensive. If you are searching for a bargain, avoid restaurants with menus translated into a Babel of different languages. Lisbon reels with seafood specialties such as *amêjoas à bulhão pato* (steamed clams), *creme de mariscos* (seafood chowder with tomatoes), and a local classic, *bacalhau cozido com grão e batatas* (cod with chick peas and boiled potatoes, doused in olive oil). Belém offers the world-famous, heavenly *pastéis de Belém,* ■**Pastéis de Belém,** R. Belém 84-92, established in 1837, serves every kind of Portuguese pastry imaginable (☎ 21 363 80 77. Open daily 8am-midnight. 130-250$.)

SUPERMARKETS

■ **Supermercado Celeiro,** R. 1 de Dezembro, 73 (☎ 21 342 74 95), 2 blocks from Estação Rossio. A centrally located, medium-sized market with a wide variety of fruit, meat, processed foods, fresh bread, and pastries. Open M-F 9am-8pm, Sa 9am-7pm.

SUPER COCK A few days in Portugal and you'll start to notice something of a national obsession with roosters. A very special rooster, that is—*o galo de Barcelos* (the cock of Barcelos). This particular animal, with flowers and hearts on its wings and tail, may seem like a psychedelic symbol of sorts, but it actually serves an altogether nobler cause. Once upon a time in the sleepy town of Barcelos, an innocent man was condemned to die for a crime he didn't commit. As his last wish he asked to have dinner with the judge so that he could try one last time to prove his innocence. The judge, who was having roast chicken for dinner that night, obliged. When the man saw the chicken at dinner, he blurted out that the cock would crow to prove his innocence. And sure enough the *galo* did—or so the story goes—forever securing itself a special place in Portuguese folklore as a symbol of truth, justice and faith. A superhero of sorts.

Mercado Ribeira (☎ 21 346 29 66), a vast market complex inside a warehouse on Av. 24 de Julho, just outside the Estação Cais do Sodré. Accessible by bus #40 or tram #15. Go early for the freshest selection. Open M-Sa 6am-2pm.

Supermercado Pão de Açúcar, Amoreiras Shopping Center de Lisboa, Av. Duarte Pacheco (☎ 21 382 66 80). Take bus #11 from Pr. Restauradores or Pr. Figueira. Open M-Sa 10am-8pm, Su 10am-6pm.

BAIXA

Although the Baixa is home to Lisbon's most tourist-oriented restaurants, it also has decent food at reasonable prices. Bargain eateries line R. Correeiros (parallel to R. Prata) and neighboring streets. One block from Pr. Restauradores on R. Portas de Santo Antão, several superb seafood restaurants stack the day's catch in their windows. The small streets north of Pr. Figueira are all packed with eateries.

◙ **Celeiro,** R. 1 de Dezembro, 51. Take the 1st right off Estação Rossio and go 2 blocks. This seatless restaurant will please vegetarians and meat-eaters alike with its creative and appetizing menu. Entrees 350-730$. Open M-F 9am-8pm, Sa 9am-6pm.

Lua de Mel, R. Prata, 242 (☎ 21 887 91 51), on the corner of R. Santa Justa. So sweet it'll make your teeth hurt. Caramelized everything draws crowds to this diner-style pastry shop. Pastries 110-160$. Open M-F 7am-9pm, Sa 7am-7pm.

Restaurante Bonjardim, Tr. Santo Antão, 11 (☎ 21 342 43 89), off Pr. Restauradores. The self-proclaimed *rei dos frangos* (king of chicken) legitimately rules the roost with its divine roast chicken (1400$). Entrees 980-2900$. Open daily noon-11:30pm. V, MC.

Churrascaria Gáucha, R. Bacalhoeiros, 26C-D (☎ 21 887 06 09), 1 block from the river towards the Alfama, near Pr. Comércio. Large, popular grill serves South American-style *churrasco* (roasted meat) dishes. Entrees 850-1700$; half-doses 900-1200$. *Pratos do dia* 1000-1700$. Open M-Sa 2pm-2am. V, MC, AmEx.

BAIRRO ALTO

Bairro is the place to be come dinner time. The neighborhood is home to a number of glamorous restaurants and an equal number of glamorous patrons. In addition, many inexpensive local haunts line Calçada do Combro, the neighborhood's main westward artery. R. Misericórdia's side streets offer cheaper restaurants for quiet dinners among an almost completely Portuguese crowd. Small culinary diamonds in the rough also pepper the area around Pr. Dom Pedro V.

◙ **Hell's Kitchen,** R. Atalaia, 176 (☎ 21 342 28 22). From the top of C. Glória (the steep hill from Pr. Restauradores), walk a few blocks into Bairro Alto and turn right on R. Atalaia; look for a small, black building. Small, but with an extensive selection of delicious entrees (1100-1650$), including vegetarian options. The hummus with pita (450$) and falafel with salad (1100$) are heavenly. Open Tu-Su 8pm-12:30am.

Casa da Té, R. Dom Pedro V, 63 (☎ 21 347 62 58), just past Parque de São Pedro de Alcântara, near the corner of R. da Rosa. Wood paneling and green iron chairs add pizzazz to this tiny budget goldmine. The entire menu changes daily. Take out also available, making it the natural choice for a picnic in the park. Entrees 750-900$. Open 8am-8pm.

Restaurante Calcuta, R. do Norte, 17 (☎ 21 342 82 95), near Lg. Camões. Fancy yet inexpensive Indian restaurant with wide selection of vegetarian options (a rarity in Portugal) is the perfect way to start a night out in the Bairro Alto. Pig out and then work it off at the neighborhood's plethora of nearby clubs. Vegetarian entrees 900-1000$. Meat entrees 1200-1600$. Open daily noon-3pm and 6:30-11pm.

Stravaganza, R. Grémio Lusitano, 18-26 (☎ 21 346 88 68), 1 block from the top of C. Glória, at R. Diário de Notícias. Italian food in an art-deco setting. Pastas and gourmet pizzas 900-1600$. Open M-F noon-3pm and 7pm-2am, Sa-Su 7pm-2am. V, MC, AmEx.

Cervejaria da Trindade, R. Nova Trindade, 20C (☎ 21 342 35 06), 2 blocks down a side street that begins in the square in front of the Igreja do São Roque and parallels R. Misericórdia. Excellent food in Portugal's oldest beerhouse. Elegant but noisy atmosphere draws tourists to the restaurant; locals prefer the bar. Entrees 790-2500$. *Sugestões do chefe* (chef's suggestions) 890$. Open daily noon-1:30am. V, MC, AmEx.

ALFAMA

The winding streets of the Alfama conceal a number of tiny, unpretentious restaurants, often packed with the neighbors and friends of the owners. Lively chatter echoes through the damp, narrow alleys. Watch the clock—the labyrinthine Alfama grows dangerously dark after nightfall.

> **Restaurante Arco do Castelo,** R. Chão de Feira, 25 (☎ 21 887 65 96), across from the gate to the Castelo de São Jorge. For a hearty, spicy meal, try one of their specialties from Goa, Portugal's former colony in India. Curry from 1300$. Other entrees 1080-1600$. Open M-Sa 12:30-4pm and 7pm-midnight.

> **Malmequer Bemmequer,** R. São Miguel, 23-25 (☎ 21 887 65 35). Follow Av. Infante Dom Henrique to Terreiro do Trigo; take the 1st left and climb the stairs to R. São Miguel. The name means "He loves me not, he loves me well." The breezy blue-and-yellow dining room is a great place to relax after hiking the hills of Alfama. Entrees 1380-1850$. Open daily noon-3:30pm and 7-10:30pm.

◨ SIGHTS

BAIXA

Although the Baixa features few historic sights, a lively atmosphere surrounding the neighborhood's three main *praças* make it a monument in its own right.

AROUND THE ROSSIO. The best place to embark upon your tour of Lisbon's 18th-century center is its heart—the **Rossio**. The **Praça Dom Pedro IV,** the city's main square, was once a cattle market and home to a public execution stage, bullfighting arena, and carnival ground. The *praça* is now the domain of drink-sipping tourists and ruthless local motorists circling the central statue of Dom Pedro IV. A statue of Gil Vicente—Portugal's first great dramatist (see **Literature,** p. 526)—peers down from the top of the **Teatro Nacional de Dona Maria II** (easily recognized by its large columns) at one end of the *praça*. Adjoining the Rossio is the elegant **Praça Figueira,** which lies on the border of the hilly streets of the Alfama district.

AROUND PRAÇA DOS RESTAURADORES. An obelisk and a bronze sculpture of the "Spirit of Independence" in the **Praça dos Restauradores,** just past the Rossio train station when walking from the Rossio itself, commemorate Portugal's independence from Spain (1640). The tourist office, post office, and numerous shops line the *praça* and C. Glória—the steep hill that leads to Bairro Alto. Pr. Restauradores is also the start of **Avenida da Liberdade,** Lisbon's most imposing boulevard and one of the city's most elegant promenades. Modeled after the wide boulevards of 19th-century Paris, this shady mile-long thoroughfare ends at **Praça do Marquês de Pombal;** from there an 18th-century statue of the Marquês overlooks the city.

AROUND PRAÇA DO COMÉRCIO. The grid of pedestrian streets on the other side of the Rossio from Pr. Restauradores caters to ice-cream eaters and window shoppers. After the earthquake of 1755, the Marquês de Pombal designed the streets to serve as a conduit for goods from the ports on the Rio Tejo to the city center. Built at the height of Enlightenment urban planning, each street was designated for a specific trade; *sapateiros* (shoemakers), *correeiros* (couriers), and *bacalhoeiros* (cod merchants) each had their own avenue. Two centuries later, the streets of the Baixa retain these names and their commercial nature. Pedestrians wander the wide mosaic sidewalks, cars race down the stately avenues, and affluent visitors swarm upscale shops along the side streets. From the streets of the Baixa, all roads lead to **Praça do Comércio** on the banks of the Tejo. Also known as **Terreiro do Paço** (the palace terrace) ever since the royal palace which stood there was destroyed in the Earthquake of 1755, Pr. Comércio lies before the towering statue of Dom João I, cast in 1755 from 9400 lbs. of bronze. The *praça* now serves as the headquarters of several Portuguese government ministries. Its center has been relegated to less dignified use as a fairgrounds for concerts and other events.

LISBON

BAIRRO ALTO

To reach Rua Garret and the heart of the chic Chiado neighborhood, turn left when exiting the elevator and walk 1 block; Rua Garret is on the right.

In the *Bairro* (the hip name for Chiado), pretentious intellectuals mix with insecure teens and idealistic university students. It's the only place in Lisbon that never sleeps; there is as much to do here at night as there is to see during the day. At the center of the neighborhood is **Praça Camões**, which adjoins **Largo Chiado** at the top of R. Garrett, a good place to rest and orient yourself while sightseeing.

AROUND THE ASCENSOR DE SANTA JUSTA. Although it's just as easy to get from the Baixa to the Bairro Alto by walking (with your back to the river, just walk up any side street on the left), be classy and take the **Ascensor de Santa Justa**, a historic elevator built in 1902 inside a Gothic wrought-iron tower. Tourists ride to admire the view from the upper levels, and locals use the elevator as transportation into the hilly Bairro Alto. From the upper terrace, a narrow **walkway** leads under a huge flying buttress to the 14th-century **Igreja do Carmo**. *(Elevator runs M-F 7am-11pm, Sa-Su 9am-11pm. 165$. Walkway open 7am-6pm. 100$. The walkway periodically closes; see if it's open before buying a ticket.)* The 1755 earthquake left the church roofless but its dramatic Gothic arches remain.

■ **MUSEU NACIONAL DE ARTE ANTIGA.** This museum hosts an interesting survey of European painting dating back as far as the 12th century and ranging from Gothic primitives to 18th-century French masterpieces. *(R. das Janelas Verdes, Jardim 9 Abril. 30min. down Av. Infante Santo from the Ascensor de Santa Justa. Buses #40 and 60 stop to the right of the museum exit and head back to the Baixa. ☎ 21 391 28 00. Open Tu 2-6pm, W-Su 10am-6pm. 600$, students 300$. Free Su before 2pm.)*

MUSEU DO CHIADO. An educational (and aesthetic) experience awaits in this museum, courtesy of Portugal's most famous post-1850 artists. Though the permanent collection is somewhat small, the Museu do Chiado is known for its incredible exhibits. *(R. Serpa Pinto, 4. From Pr. Camões, go through Largo Chiado and down R. Garrett, turn right onto R. Serpa Pinto, and walk 2 blocks downhill. ☎ 21 343 21 48. Open Tu 2-6pm, W-Su 10am-6pm. 600$, ages 14–25, seniors, and teachers 360$. Free Su before 2pm.)*

IGREJA DE SÃO ROQUE. This church is dedicated to the saint believed to have saved the Bairro Alto from the devastation of the great earthquake. Inside the church, the **Capela de São João Baptista** (4th from the left) is ablaze with precious gems and metals. The chapel caused a stir upon its installation in 1747 because it took three ships to bring it from Rome, where it was built. *(Largo Trinidade Coelho. From R. Carmo head uphill on R. Garret until R. Misericórdia. ☎ 21 323 53 83.)* Next door, the small but worthwhile **Museu de São Roque**, with its own share of gold and silver, features European religious art from the 16th to 18th centuries. There's also a helpful "Ask me about Lisboa" kiosk here. *(☎ 21 323 53 82. Open Tu-Su 10am-5pm. 200$, students and seniors free. Sunday free.)*

PARKS. For a perfect picnic, head to the mercifully shady ■**Parque de São Pedro de Alcântara.** The Castelo de São Jorge in the Alfama stares back from the cliff opposite the park; the city of Lisbon twinkles below. A mosaic points out the landmarks included in this vista. *(On the right off R. São Pedro de Alcântara—the continuation of R. Misericórdia. It's a 5-min. walk up R. Misericórdia from Pr. Camões; the park is right next to C. Glória.)* More greenery awaits uphill along R. Dom Pedro V at the majestic **Parque Príncipe Real**, which connects to Lisbon's extensive **Jardim Botánico**. Across from the church on Largo Estrela, the wide asphalt paths of the **Jardim da Estrêla** wind through flocks of pigeons and lush flora. Park walkways are popular for Sunday strolls, and the benches fill with smoochers. Behind the park tropical plants, cypress trees, and odd gravestones mark the **Cemitério dos Inglêses** (English Cemetery). Its musty Victorian chapel dates from 1885.

A CAMÕES CAMEO Pr. Camões, in the heart of the Bairro Alto off R. Garrett, is marked by a monument to Luís de Camões. Camões, whose 16th-century *Os Lusíadas* chronicled his nation's discoveries in lyric verse, is considered Portugal's greatest poet. Most likely born in Lisbon in 1524 (accounts of his life vary slightly), this swashbuckling stud had so many affairs with ladies of the court that he fled to North Africa to escape their vengeful husbands (official sources say his politics got him banished). Camões led an adventurous life for a poet, enlisting as a common soldier in the army in 1547. His service took him all over the globe, including the Arab and Indian coasts and numerous stops in Portugal's expanding empire; all the while he was working on his verses. By the time he made his way back to Lisbon in 1570, Camões had lost an eye in battle, been jailed and injured in a sword duel, and survived a shipwreck off the coast of Cambodia (clutching his precious poetry the whole time, of course). Two years later (1572) he published *Os Lusíadas;* despite its success he died in poverty somewhere in Asia in 1580. Portugal was never able to recover his body, but Camões is remembered with an honorary tomb just outside Lisbon in Belém's **Mosteiro dos Jerónimos** and on streets across the country which bear his name.

CHURCHES. For more neighborhood flavor, walk uphill through Pr. Camões and take R. Loreto, which turns into Calçada do Combro. Walk over the hill and down to where it levels out; from here turn right onto Tr. Convento de Jesús. Flowered balconies and hanging laundry frame the **Igreja das Mercês,** a handsome, 18th-century Travertine building on a small *praça.* Back on Calçada do Combro, a few hundred meters ahead, is Largo António Sousa de Maced and a fork in the road. Follow the right fork onto R. Poiais de São Bento, which becomes Calçada da Estrêla and leads to more churches, including the ornate **Basílica da Estrêla.** Built in 1796, the basilica's exquisitely shaped dome, poised behind a pair of tall belfries, steals the sky. Half-mad Maria I, desiring a male heir, made fervent religious vows promising God anything and everything if she were granted a son. When a baby boy was finally born, she built this church. Ask the sacristan to show you the gigantic 10th-century manger scene. *(On Pr. Estrela. Accessible by tram #28 from Pr. Comércio (165$).* ☎ *21 396 09 15. Open daily 8am-12:30pm and 3-7:30pm. Free.)*

ALFAMA

The Alfama, Lisbon's medieval quarter, was the lone neighborhood to survive the famous 1755 earthquake. The area slopes in tiers from the **Castelo de São Jorge** facing the Rio Tejo. Between the Alfama and the Baixa is the quarter known as the **Mouraria** (Moorish quarter), established, ironically, after Dom Afonso Henriques and the Crusaders expelled the Moors in 1147. Here, Portuguese grandmothers gossip and elementary school boys play soccer amidst camera-toting tourists, all enjoying the enchanting ambiance of Alfama's streets. Watch out for muggers, especially at night; visit by day without handbags, cameras, or snatchables. Though the constant hike that defines Alfama sightseeing is half the fun, the tired and lazy will want to hop on the scenic tram #28 from Pr. Comércio (165$), which winds up through the neighborhood past most of its sights.

THE LOWER ALFAMA. While any of the small uphill streets a few blocks east of the Baixa lead to the Alfama's maze of streets, the least confusing way to see the neighborhood is by climbing up R. Madalena, which begins two blocks away from Pr. Comércio (take R. Alfandega from the *praça*). Veer right when you see the **Igreja da Madalena** in the Largo Madalena on the right. Take R. Santo António da Sé and follow the tram tracks to the cleverly designed and richly ornamented **Igreja de Santo António da Sé,** built in 1812 over the saint's alleged birthplace. The construction was funded with money collected by the city's children, who fashioned miniature altars bearing images of the saint to place on doorsteps—a custom reenacted annually on June 13, the saint's feast day and Lisbon's largest holiday. *(*☎ *21 886 91*

45. Open daily 8am-7pm. Mass daily 11am, 5, and 7pm.) In the square beyond the church is the stolid 12th-century **Sé de Lisboa** (cathedral). Although the interior of the Sé is unremarkable, its sheer antiquity and relic-filled treasury make it an intriguing visit. As a sign outside reads, "The Sé is so old that no one really knows how old it is." *(☎ 21 887 72 44. Open M 10am-5pm, Tu-Su 10am-6pm. Treasury open 10am-5pm. 400$.)*

■**CASTELO DE SÃO JORGE.** Near the top of the Alfama lies the must-see **Castelo de São Jorge,** which offers spectacular views with Lisbon and the ocean. Built in the 5th century by the Visigoths and enlarged by 9th-century Moors, this castle was a playground for the royal family between the 14th and 16th centuries. Anyone can wander around the ruins, soak in the view of the cityscape below, explore the ponds, or gawk at the exotic bird population of the castle gardens. Nooks for sitting, relaxing, and enjoying the vista as well as stands selling well-merited ice cream, drinks, and *churros* await after the long climb up the hill. *(From the cathedral, follow the yellow signs for the castle on a winding uphill walk. Castle open daily Apr.-Sept. 9am-9pm; Oct.-Mar. 9am-7pm. Free.)*

MUSEU DAS ARTES DECORATIVAS. The impressive furnishings and decorations that fill this museum convey a good sense of 18th-century palatial luxury. It also features a tea room and bookstore with books in English on Portuguese art. *(Largo Portas do Sol, 2. To reach the museum, head up to the castle and turn right onto Largo Portas do Sol. ☎ 21 881 46 00. Open Tu-Su 10am-5pm. 500$, seniors and children under 12 250$.)*

ALONG TR. SÃO VICENTE. On the far side of the castle, follow the main tram tracks along Tr. São Tomé (which becomes R. São Vicente as it winds uphill) to Largo São Vicente and the **Igreja de São Vicente de Fora,** built between 1582 and 1629 and dedicated to Lisbon's patron saint. Ask to see the deathly still *sacristia*, with fabulous 18th-century walls inlaid with Sintra marble. *(From the bottom of R. Correeiros in the Baixa, take bus #12 or tram #28 (165$). Open Tu-Sa 9am-6pm, Su 9am-12:30pm and 3-5pm. Free. Chapel next door with scenic view 600$.)* At the **Feira da Ladra** (flea market) that takes place in the church's backyard, the din of a lively social scene drowns out cries of merchants hawking used goods. *(Tu and Sa 7am-3pm.)* The **Igreja de Santa Engrácia (National Pantheon)** is farther down toward the coast. This church, with its impressive dome, took almost 300 years to complete (1682-1966), inspiring the Portuguese expression, "endless like the building of Santa Engrácia." *(Walk along R. São Vicente and keep left as the road branches. Open Tu-Su 10am-5pm.)*

CONVENTO DA MADRE DE DEUS. This 16th-century convent complex houses the **Museu Nacional do Azulejo,** devoted to the classic Portuguese art of the *azulejo* tile, first introduced by the Moors (see **Architecture,** p. 525). On display are Portuguese, Spanish, and Dutch tiles from the last 500 years. The Baroque interior of the church, accessible through a fine Manueline doorway, is an explosion of oil paintings, *azulejos*, and gilded wood. The rapturous excess continues in the choir and the **Capela de Santo António,** where bright *azulejos* and paintings intoxicate the eye. *(R. Madre de Deus, 4. Follow Av. Infante Dom Henrique, which runs parallel to the Rio Tejo. The avenue leads to the Estação Santa Apolónia; from outside the station, take bus #13. ☎ 21 814 77 47. Open Tu 2-6pm, W-Su 10am-6pm. 400$, students 200$.)*

SALDANHA

Though most of Saldanha is dedicated to Lisbon's business affairs, this modern district does have two excellent museums, both owned by the Fundação Gulbenkian. These museums should factor into every Lisbon visit.

■**MUSEU CALOUSTE GULBENKIAN.** When oil tycoon Calouste Gubenkian died in 1955, he left his extensive art collection (some of it purchased from the Hermitage in St. Petersburg, Russia) to his beloved Portugal. Though the philanthropist was of Armenian descent and a British citizen, it was Portugal he chose to call home. (The Portuguese also gave him a substantial tax break.) The collection is divided into two sections, one of which is ancient art—Egyptian, Greek, Roman, Islamic, and Oriental—while the other is made up of European pieces from the 15th to 20th centuries. Highlights include the Egyptian room, Rembrants, Monets, Renoirs, and a Rodin. *(Av. Berna, 45. M: Palhavã or São Sebastião. Bus # 16, 31, 46. ☎ 21 782 30 00. Open Tu-Su 10am-5pm. 500$, free Su mornings for students and seniors.)*

MUSEU DO CENTRO DE ARTE MODERNA. Though not as famous as its neighbor, this museum is home to an extensive collection of modern art. Though most of the works are by Portuguese artists, the museum also houses pieces by other notable 20th-century artists. Make sure to spend some time in the gardens—the sculptures are incredible. *(R. Dr. Nicolau Bettencourt. M: São Sebastião. Bus #16, 31, 46. ☎ 21 795 02 41. Open Tu-Su 10am-5pm. 500$, free Su mornings for students and seniors.)*

BELÉM

To get to Belém, take tram #15 from Pr. Comércio (20min., 165$), bus #28 or 43 from Pr. Figueira (20min., 165$), or the train from Estação Cais do Sodré (10min., every 15min., 140$). From the train station, cross the tracks, then cross the street and go left. The Padrão dos Descobrimentos is by the water, across the highway on your left (use the underpass), while the Mosteiro dos Jerónimos is to the right, through the public gardens. From the bus station, follow the avenue straight ahead. All museums free Su before 2pm.

Belém is more of an outlying suburb than a neighborhood of Lisbon, but its high concentration of monuments and museums makes it a crucial stop in any comprehensive tour of the capital. Belém is imperial glory at the service of culture; here, a number of well-maintained museums and historical sites showcase the opulence and extravagance of the Portuguese empire. To visit Belém is to understand *saudade*, the "nostalgic yearning" expressed musically in *fado* (see **Fado**, p. 558).

▓MOSTEIRO DOS JERÓNIMOS. Established in 1502 to give thanks for the success of Vasco da Gama's expedition to India, the Mosteiro dos Jerónimos was granted UN World Heritage status in the 1980s. Today the Mosteiro rises from the banks of the Tejo behind a lush public garden. The country's most refined celebration of the Age of Discovery, it showcases Portugal's native Manueline style, combining Gothic forms with early Renaissance details. The main door of the church, to the right of the monastery entrance, is a sculpted anachronism; Prince Henry the Navigator mingles with the Twelve Apostles on both sides of the central column. The symbolic tombs of Luís de Camões (see **A Camões Cameo,** p. 553) and navigator Vasco da Gama lie in two opposing transepts. Inside the monastery, the octagonal cloisters of the courtyard drip with overdone stone carvings, a contrast to the simplicity of the rose gardens in the center. *(☎ 21 362 00 34. Open Tu-Su 10am-5pm. 600$, students 300$. Free Su 10am-2pm. Cloisters open Tu-Su 10am-5pm. Free.)*

▓TORRE DE BELÉM. One of two well-known towers on Belém's waterfront, the Torre de Belém rises from the north bank of the Tejo and is surrounded by the ocean on three sides. Built under Manuel I from 1515-1520 as a harbor fortress, it originally sat directly on the shoreline; today, due to the receding beach, it is only accessible by a small bridge. Nevertheless, this symbol of Portuguese grandeur and member of the UN's World Heritage list offers spectacular panoramic views of Belém, the Tejo, and the Atlantic beyond. *(A 10min. walk along the water from the monastery. Take the underpass by the gardens to cross the highway. ☎ 21 362 00 34. Open Tu-Su 10am-6pm. 600$, students and seniors 300$.)*

MONASTERY MUSEUMS. The intriguing **Museu da Marinha** displays the Portuguese prowess in the shipping business. Globes from the mid-18th century show the assumed boundaries of the continents with incredible accuracy. *(At the far end of the monastery complex. ☎ 21 362 00 19. Open Tu-Su June-Aug. 10am-6pm; Sept.-May 10am-5pm. 500$, students 200$. Free Su 10am-2pm.)* In the same complex is the **Museu Nacional de Arqueologia,** which uses artifacts of various media to depict Portugal's history. *(From the monastery, go right; while inside the monastery complex, the entrance is around the corner. Open Tu 2-6pm, W-Su 10am-6pm. 400$, students 200$. Free Su before 2pm.)*

CENTRO CULTURAL DE BELÉM. Contemporary art buffs will bask in the glow of the gigantic, luminous **Centro Cultural de Belém.** With four pavilions holding regular world-class exhibitions, several art galleries, and a huge auditorium for concerts and performances, the center provides slick entertainment amid a slew of imperial landmarks. *(Across the street from the monastery museums. ☎ 21 361 24 00; www.ccb.pt. Open daily 9am-10pm. Exhibitions 11am-7:15pm; prices vary.)*

PADRÃO DOS DESCOBRIMENTOS. Along the river is the Padrão dos Descobrimentos, built in 1960 to honor Prince Henry the Navigator. The view here is similar to that from the torre, but here an elevator (rather than stairs) transports visitors 50m up to a small terrace. Hold onto your hat; it can get windy at the top. The Padrão also hosts temporary exhibits. *(Across the highway from the monastery.* ☎ *21 303 19 50. Open Tu-Su 9am-5pm. 350$, students 175$.)*

PALÁCIO NACIONAL DE AJUDA. Back toward the center of Belém is the Palácio Nacional da Ajuda, on Largo Ajuda, a short bus ride away from the hills overlooking Belém. Constructed in 1802, the 54 chambers are a rather telling display of decadence. *(Take tram #18 (Ajuda), which stops behind the palace, or walk up Calçada de Ajuda (20min).* ☎ *21 363 70 95. Open Th-Tu 10am-4:30pm. 600$, students free. Free Su 10am-2pm.)*

▨ PARK OF NATIONS

The easiest way to reach the park from Lisbon is to take the metro to the end of the red line (Linha Oriente, 100$). The Oriente stop has escalators rising up to the park's main entrance at the Centro Vasco de Gama. Alternatively, city buses #5, 10, 19, 21, 25, 28, 44, 50, 68 and 114 all stop at the Oriente station (165$).

The **Parque das Nações** (Park of Nations; ☎ 21 891 93 33; www.parquedasnacoes.pt), at the former Expo '98 grounds 6km from downtown, is the newest addition to Lisbon's growing list of sights. In the mid-1990s, the area was a muddy wasteland along the banks of the Tejo; in just a few years the city transformed the land, preparing the grounds for the millennium's last World Exposition. After Expo '98 flopped, the government took a risk, pumping millions of dollars into the land and converting it into the Parque das Nações. Fortunately, the gamble has paid off. Today, the park is packed—day and night—with people enjoying its graceful, yet futuristic setting. If the proposed construction goes according to plan, the park will soon become a small city. The entrance to the park leads through the Centro Vasco de Gama **shopping mall** (☎ 21 893 06 01; open daily 10am-midnight) to the center of the grounds, where several information kiosks provide maps and offer free luggage storage (open 9:30am-8pm). For those who don't want to walk between attractions, a **teleférico** (gondola) connects one end of the park to the other (8min.; M-F 11am-8pm, Sa-Su 10am-9pm; 500$, under 18 or over 65 250$).

The biggest attraction is the **Pavilhão dos Oceanos,** the largest oceanarium in Europe. The enormous new aquarium has interactive sections showcasing the four major oceans (down to the sounds, smells, and climates). All of these connect to the main tank, which houses fish, sharks, and other sea creatures. *(Open daily Apr.-Sept. 10am-7pm, Oct.-Mar. 10am-6pm. 1700$, under 18 or over 65 900$.)* Another solid draw is the **Pavilhão do Conhecimento** (Knowledge Pavilion), an interactive science museum. *(*☎ *21 891 71 12. Open Tu-F 10am-5pm, Sa-Su 11am-6pm. 800$, under 18 or over 65 400$.)* Other **pavilions** scattered throughout the park, including the **International Fairgrounds,** accommodate rotating exhibits during the year. The **Atlantic Pavilion** (host to many of Lisbon's big concerts) and the 145m **Torre Vasco de Gama** (the city's tallest building) grab visitors' attention with their striking, 21st-century architecture. An elevator ascends 300 ft. to the observation tower, which offers spectacular views of the city. *(Open daily 10am-8pm. 500$, under 18 or over 65 250$.)*

▣ ENTERTAINMENT

Agenda Cultural and *Follow Me Lisboa*, free at kiosks in the Rossio, on R. Portas de Santo Antão, and at the tourist office, have information on concerts, movies, plays, and bullfights. They also have lists of museums, gardens, and libraries.

BARS AND CLUBS

Lisbon hardly suffers from a shortage of nightlife. The action is centered in the Bairro Alto, where a plethora of small bars and clubs invite exploration of the side streets. In particular, **R. Norte, R. Diário de Notícias,** and **R. Atalaia** have many small clubs packed into three short blocks, making club-hopping as easy as crossing the street. Most gay and lesbian clubs are found in the **Rato** area near the edge of Bairro Alto. The newest hotspot is the revamped **Docas de Santo Amaro,** a strip of waterfront bars, clubs, and restaurants. On the way to the Docas, look for additional party places along **Av. 24 de Julho.** While these places along the river are all within a mile-long stretch, it's best to play it safe late at night and take a cab between clubs as the walk can be desolate. A cab from Rossio (the only real choice for transportation to these locations) costs 800-1200$.

At clubs, decent clothes (pants and nicer shoes) are expected—some places have uptight fashion police at the door. Inside, beer ranges from 400-600$ and mixed drinks cost 900-1000$. Some clubs charge a cover (generally 1000-2000$); those that don't charge higher prices at the bar. As for timing, there's no reason to show up at a club before midnight; crowds flow in around 2am.

DOCAS DE SANTO AMARO

Havana, Doca de Santo Amaro, Armazem 5 (☎ 21 397 98 93). Crowded and popular. Plays salsa in addition to standard pop and dance tunes. The "New Havana" feel created by palm trees and ceiling fans helps keep things cool. Beer 400$, mixed drinks 900$. Restaurant open M-Sa noon-4am; disco open M-Sa 11pm-4am.

Cosmos, Doca de Santo Amaro, Armazem 243 (☎ 21 397 27 47). Restaurant (open daily 11am-midnight) gives way to a Eurotrash techno scene. Torches welcome the crowd of trendy 20-somethings out on the patio. Beer 400$, mixed drinks 900-1000$. Cover 2000$, includes 4 beers or 2 mixed drinks. Disco open midnight-6am.

Celtas & Iberos Irish Pub, Doca de Santo Amaro, Armazem 7 (☎ 21 397 60 37). Goes for that traditional pub feeling with its interior decorations and live music most nights (often Irish covers of pop songs). Upbeat atmosphere good for throwing back a few pints (700$). Smaller beer 400$, mixed drinks 900$. Open Tu-Su 12:30am-3am.

Salsa Latina, Gare Marítima de Alcântara (☎ 21 395 05 55), in its own building just across the parking lot from the cluster at Doca de Santo Amaro. Sophisticated crowds come for the live salsa (on the weekends after midnight). Minimum consumption 2000$. Beer 500$, mixed drinks 1000$. Open M-Th 8-11pm, F-Sa 8pm-1:30am.

Kremlin, Escandinhas da Praia, 5 (☎ 21 397 91 03), off Av. 24 de Julho. One of the top clubs in Lisbon with a young, fashionable crowd pulsating to house and dance music. Good-sized dance floor stays open past the time many people start work. Beer 600$, mixed drinks 1000-1200$. Cover 1000-2000$ on weekends. Open Tu-Sa midnight-9am. Next door also are equally trendy clubs **Kapital** and **Plateau.**

BAIRRO ALTO

Memorial, R. Gustavo de Matos Sequeira, 42A (☎ 21 396 88 91), 1 block from R. Escola Politécnica in the Bairro Alto. This lesbian-oriented disco-bar draws a refreshingly mixed crowd. Women and men, gay and straight, and young and old alike let loose to Euro-pop. Cover 100$, includes 2 beers or 1 mixed drink. Open Tu-Su 11pm-4am.

Divina Comida, Largo Santa Martinho, 6-7 (☎ 21 887 55 99), in the Alfama. The food's a bit pricey, but the bar here is divine. Try the killer Brazilian *caipirinha* (sugarcane alcohol, 1000$) or the dangerous *caipirosca* (with lime and vodka, 1000$). Open M-Th 12:30pm-2am, F-Sa 12:30pm-3am.

Trumps, R. Imprensa Nacional, 104B (☎ 21 397 10 59). Lisbon's biggest gay club features several bars in addition to a massive dance floor. Shirtless muscleboys bump and grind to mostly house and techno. Cover 1000$ (includes 1 drink), but minimum consumption of 2000$. Open Tu-Su 11:30pm-6am.

Solar do Vinho do Porto, R. São Pedro de Alcântara, 45 (☎ 21 347 57 07). Not a club and not a bar, but close enough—enjoy port in a sedate and mature setting. Start the night in style. Port 220-3810$. Open M-Sa 2pm-midnight.

LISBON

LOVE NOTES If the blues have a hold on your heart, then *fado* will capture your soul. The melodies and lyrics of *fado* drip with wrenching pain and passion of life and love. Although *fado* may have been rooted in African slave songs, the legendary *fadista* (*fado* singer) **Maria Severa** made *fado* quintessentially Portuguese. Although she lived a short life (1810-1836), Severa achieved mythical status because of her moving lyrics (through which she expressed her own real-life dramas). Severa's life and early death (due to excessive gastronomic consumption) were a turning point in the history of *fado*, providing the basis for the first Portuguese "talking picture" in 1931 and spawning many other poems, novels, and *fado* lyrics. Modern *fadistas*, including **Amália Rodrigues** and **Argentina Santos,** have helped spread *fado* throughout Portugal. *Fado* houses, including Adega Machado in Lisbon (p. 558), are the best places to enjoy a special *fado* moment and to celebrate the legend that Severa left behind. Coimbra is also home to many *fado* houses, though Coimbra *fado* differs significantly from the more urban, working-class-inspired Lisbon style Coimbra's has slower, more intellectual lyrics about romance and beautiful women and is often sung by male students from Coimbra's universities.

CAFES

Relaxing in cafes during the day and late into the night is a popular pastime in Lisbon. Look for outdoor seating, especially on summer evenings. There are several cafes in the Rossio area and on R. Augusta, the main pedestrian shopping street.

A Brasileira, R. Garrett, 120-122 (☎ 21 360 95 41). A famous 19th-century cafe in the Bairro Alto's stylish Chiado neighborhood. Considered by many to be "the best cafe in Portugal," it definitely has the best after-dinner scene. Look for the bust of poet and patron Fernando Pessoa outside. Members of the new literati gather here among the many mirrors and gold and green woodwork. Coffee 80-300$. Mixed drinks 650-900$. Open daily 8pm-2am.

Pastelaria Suiça (☎ 21 321 40 90), on the corner of Pr. Dom Pedro IV in the Baixa. A noisy gathering place that stays packed until midnight. Coffee 95-230$. Pastries 130-200$. More substantial fare (sandwiches 300-1000$) as well. Open 7am-10pm.

Costa do Castelo, Calçada Marquês de Tancos, 1-1B (☎ 21 888 46 36), just behind the Castelo in Alfama. Small, self-consciously trendy bar/cafe with outdoor patio. Sandwiches 250-400$. *Tapas* 400-500$. Drinks 300-700$. Open Tu-Su 12:30pm-2am.

Restaurante Passeio D'Avenida (☎ 21 342 37 55), Av. Liberdade, just up from Pr. Restauradores. This café occupies the little park in the middle of the busy avenue. You must be assertive to get the servers' attention. Outdoor seating for coffee (80-320$) and sandwiches (300-600$). Open daily 9am-2am.

FADO

Lisbon's trademark is the heart-wrenching *fado*, an expressive art that combines elements of singing and narrative poetry (see **Music,** p. 527). *Fadistas*, cloaked in black dresses and shawls, perform emotional tales of lost loves and faded glory. Their melancholy wailing is expressive of *saudade*, an emotion of nostalgia and yearning; listeners are supposed to feel the "knife turning in their hearts." On weekends, book in advance by calling the venues. The Bairro Alto has many *fado* joints off R. Misericórdia and on side streets radiating from the Museu de São Roque; it is the best place in the city for top-quality *fado*. However, many of the popular houses charge large covers or have "minimum consumption" requirements. To avoid these, try exploring nearby streets; various bars and other small venues often offer free performances. Call ahead to find out schedules and potential changes in performance times.

Adega Machado, R. Norte, 91 (☎ 21 322 46 40). Expensive, but the *fadistas* spotlighted here draw as many locals as they do tourists. Dinner 5000-6000$. Min. consumption 2900$. Open Tu-Su 8pm-3am; *fados* start after 9pm.

O Faia, R. Baroca, 54 (☎ 21 342 67 42), between R. Atalaia and R. Diário de Notícias. Elegant and expensive. Portuguese cuisine and some of Portugal's better known *fadistas*. Minimum consumption 3500$ includes 2 drinks. Open M-Sa 8pm-2am.

Sr. Vinho, R. Meio à Lapa, 18 (☎ 21 397 26 81), in the Madregoa district. Out of the way, but somehow hordes of tourists get there all the same. Take a taxi (about 7000$). Minimum consumption 3000$. Open M-Sa 9pm-3am.

FESTIVALS

The party-hearty will want to visit Lisbon in June. Open-air *feiras* (fairs)—smorgasbords of eating, drinking, live music, and dancing—fill the streets. After savoring *farturas* (Portuguese doughnuts) and Sagres beer, pick up your feet and join in traditional Portuguese dancing. On the night of June 12, the streets become a mega-dance floor for the huge **Festa de Santo António**—banners are strung between streetlights and confetti falls like snow during a costumed parade along Av. Liberdade. Commercial *feiras* combine shopping and cultural involvement. Bookworms burrow for three glorious weeks in the **Feira do Livro** (in the Baixa from late May to early June). The **Feira Internacional de Lisboa,** which has moved to the Park of Nations, occurs every few months, while in July and August the **Feira de Mar de Cascais** and the **Feira de Artesania de Estoril** take place near the casino. Year-round *feiras* include the **Feira de Oeiras** (Antiques) on the fourth Sunday of every month, and the **Feira de Carcanelos** for clothes (Th 8am-2pm). Packrats should catch the **Feira da Ladra** (flea market), held behind the Igreja de São Vicente de Fora in the Alfama neighborhood (Tu and Sa 7am-3pm). Take bus #12 or tram #28.

OTHER FUN THINGS TO DO

BULLFIGHTING

Portuguese bullfights (differing from the Spanish variety in that the bull is not killed) take place most Thursdays from the end of June to the end of September at **Praça de Touros de Lisboa** (☎ 21 793 21 43), Campo Pequeno (open 10pm-2am). The Praça de Touros is due to re-open in May after a series of renovations, but you'll want to call ahead or check at the tourist office to confirm that it's open before trekking out. Take the Metro to "Campo Grande" or bus #1, 44, 45, or 83 (165$).

BOAT CRUISES

To refresh your sea legs, try a two-hour cruise on the Tejo. Boats leave from the **Estação Fluvial do Terreiro do Paço** off Pr. Comércio. (☎ 21 882 03 48; fax 21 882 03 65. Boats run from Apr.-Oct. and leave at 3pm. 3000$, children 6-12 and students 26 and under 1500$.)

FUTEBOL

If sports are your thing, catch a *futebol* (soccer) match. Lisbon has two professional teams featuring some of the world's finest players: **Benfica** at the Stadium of Light (☎ 21 726 61 29. M: Colégio Militar Luz), and **Sporting** at Alvalade Stadium (☎ 21 756 79 14. M: Campo Grande). Check the APEB kiosk in Pr. Restauradores or the sports newspaper *A Bola.*

THEATER

The **Teatro Nacional de Dona Maria II,** Pr. Dom Pedro IV stages performances of classical Portuguese and foreign plays (☎ 21 347 22 26. 700-2000$, 50% student discount). At Lisbon's largest theater, the **Teatro Nacional de São Carlos,** R. Serpa Pinto, 9, near the Museu do Chiado in the Bairro Alto, opera reigns from late September through mid-June. (☎ 21 346 59 14. Open daily 1-7pm).

MOVIES

If all else fails, try the **São Jorge** theater (☎ 21 242 25 23), at the corner of Av. Liberdade and Av. Condes, directly across the square from the Pr. Restauradores tourist office. Huge 10-screen cinemas are also located in the **Amoreiras** and **Colombo** shopping centers and on the top floor of the **Centro Vasco de Gama** (M: Oriente). American movies are shown with Portuguese subtitles (Tu-Su 850-900$, M 550-900$).

LISBON

◪ DAYTRIPS FROM LISBON

The following coastal towns, many of them with beautiful beaches or sights, can be refreshing diversions from the city. Pay close attention to transportation links as you plan daytrips from Lisbon; many of these places lie en route to other destinations (including Sintra and Setúbal, see **Near Lisbon,** p. 563).

QUELUZ (25MIN.)

The best way to get to Queluz is by train. Take the Sintra line from Lisbon's Estação Rossio (M: Rossio) or Estação Sete Rios (M: Jardim Zoológico) and get off at the Queluz-Belas (not Queluz-Massomá) stop (25min., every 15min., 140$). To get to the palace, exit the train station through the ticket office and go left on Av. Antonio Ennes, continuing straight as the street becomes Av. República. Follow the signs until you see the expansive pink palace; the entrance is to the left of the statue of Dona Maria I.

Queluz itself is nothing too remarkable, but the **Palácio Nacional de Queluz** makes it a worthwhile stop on the way to Sintra. In the mid-18th century, Dom Pedro III turned an old hunting lodge into this summer residence with the help of Portuguese architect Mateus Vicente de Oliveira and French sculptor Jean-Baptiste Robillon. The well-ordered garden makes the palace feel like a miniature Versailles; don't miss the purely Portuguese *azulejo*-lined canal. Highlights inside include the **Sala dos Embaixadores,** with its gilded thrones, marble floors, and Chinese vases and the **Quarto Piquenique's** gilded beehive-style ceiling. Of historical interest is the oddly named **Quarto Don Quijote** where Dom Pedro I, the first emperor of Brazil, drew his first and last breaths. (Open W-M 10am-5pm. Closed major Catholic holidays. Palace 600$, seniors and students 300$. Garden 100$.)

ESTORIL (30MIN.)

Trains from Lisbon's Estação Cais do Sodré (M: Cais do Sodré) run to Estoril (30min., approximately every 20min. 5:30am-2:30am, 210$) continuing to Cascais (also a pleasant 20-min. seaside stroll from Estoril). Stagecoach bus #418 to Sintra departs Av. Marginal, down the street from the train station (40min., every hr. 6:50am-midnight, 440$).

Home to Europe's largest casino, Estoril's reputation is increasingly one of opulence. Yet Estoril's best assets, its stunning beaches, are free. One of the city's five beaches, **Praia Estoril Tamariz,** greets visitors upon arrival, and the palm-lined **Parque de Estoril** lies just across the street. Those bored of the beach can walk through the park to the **Casino Estoril** (☎ 21 466 77 00), if not to try their luck, then to marvel at the gaming palace itself. Over 25 million visitors frequent the sparkling game room, glitzy music hall, and 1000 slot machines each year. Never-ending renovations, both inside and out, continue to add to the modern feel of the bustling casino. (Open daily 3pm-3am. No swim-wear, jeans, or shorts. Slots 18+, game room 21+. Foreigners need passport.) A **music festival** also descends upon Estoril from mid-July to mid-August, bringing classical and jazz performances.

To get to the **tourist office** from the **train station,** cross Av. Marginal and look to the left of the Casino, on Arcadas do Parque. Be sure to grab a detailed free map of the entire Costa do Estoril (Estoril and neighboring Cascais) as well as event schedules from the helpful multilingual staff. (☎ 21 466 38 13; fax 21 467 22 80. Open M-Sa 9am-7pm, Su 10am-6pm). If you get lucky at the casino (or are stranded with no way back to Lisbon), cash in some chips and head over to the recently renovated **Residencial São Cristóvão,** Av. Marginal, 7079 (☎/fax 21 468 09 13). Facing the park, turn right off the train platform; about 2 blocks up the hill on the right are bright, airy rooms; continental breakfast included. (July-Sept. doubles 10,000$, with bath 12,500-15,000$; Sept.-May doubles 6000-7000$.) The best options for budget meals are the cafeteria-like stands and bars along the beach.

ALPS   ASPEN

AT&T Direct® Service

AT&T Direct Service access numbers are the easy way to call home from anywhere.

Global connection with the AT&T Network | **AT&T** direct service

www.att.com/traveler

AT&T Direct® Service

The easy way to call home from anywhere.

AT&T Access Numbers

Austria ● 0800-200-288	France 0800-99-00-11
Belarus ✕ ....8 ✦ 800-101	Gambia ● 00111
Belgium ● 0-800-100-10	Germany 0800-2255-288
Bosnia ▲ 00-800-0010	Ghana 0191
Bulgaria ▲ 00-800-0010	Gibraltar 8800
Cyprus ● 080-900-10	Greece ● 00-800-1311
Czech Rep. ▲00-42-000-101	Hungary ● 06-800-01111
Denmark 8001-0010	Iceland ● 800-9001
Egypt ●(Cairo)✝....510-0200	Ireland ✓......1-800-550-000
Finland ● 0800-110-015	Israel 1-800-94-94-949

AT&T Direct® Service

The easy way to call home from anywhere.

AT&T Access Numbers

Austria ● 0800-200-288	France 0800-99-00-11
Belarus ✕ ....8 ✦ 800-101	Gambia ● 00111
Belgium ● 0-800-100-10	Germany 0800-2255-288
Bosnia ▲ 00-800-0010	Ghana 0191
Bulgaria ▲ 00-800-0010	Gibraltar 8800
Cyprus ● 080-900-10	Greece ● 00-800-1311
Czech Rep. ▲00-42-000-101	Hungary ● 06-800-01111
Denmark 8001-0010	Iceland ● 800-9001
Egypt ●(Cairo)✝....510-0200	Ireland ✓......1-800-550-000
Finland ● 0800-110-015	Israel 1-800-94-94-949

The best way to keep in touch when you're traveling overseas is with **AT&T Direct**® Service. It's the easy way to call your loved ones back home from just about anywhere in the world. Just cut out the wallet guide below and use it wherever your travels take you.

For a list of AT&T Access Numbers, tear out the attached wallet guide.

AT&T

Italy ● 172-1011	Russia (Moscow) ▶▲●755-5042
Luxembourg + ..800-2-0111	(St. Petersbg.)▶▲● ..325-5042
Macedonia● ..99-800-4288	Slovakia ▲ ..00-42-100-101
Malta 0800-890-110	South Africa ..0800-99-0123
Monaco ● 800-90-288	Spain 900-99-00-11
Morocco 002-11-0011	Sweden 020-799-111
Netherlands ● ...0800-022-9111	Switzerland ● 0800-89-0011
Norway 800-190-11	Turkey ● 00-800-12277
Poland ▲● ..00-800-111-1111	Ukraine ▲ ....8◆100-11
Portugal ▲ 800-800-128	U.A. Emirates ● 800-121
Romania ●......01-800-4288	U.K..............0800-89-0011

FOR EASY CALLING WORLDWIDE

1. Just dial the AT&T Access Number for the country you are calling from.
2. Dial the phone number you're calling.   *3.* Dial your card number.

For access numbers not listed ask any operator for **AT&T Direct**® Service.
In the U.S. call 1-800-331-1140 for a wallet guide listing all worldwide AT&T Access Numbers.
Visit our Web site at: **www.att.com/traveler**
Bold-faced countries permit country-to-country calling outside the U.S.
- ● Public phones require coin or card deposit to place call.
- ▲ May not be available from every phone/payphone.
- ✚ Public phones and select hotels.
- ◆ Await second dial tone.
- ▶ Additional charges apply when calling from outside the city.
- † Outside of Cairo, dial "02" first.
- ✖ Not available from public phones or all areas.
- ✔ Use U.K. access number in N. Ireland.

When placing an international call *from* the U.S., dial 1 800 CALL ATT.

EMEA   © 8/00 AT&T

Italy ● 172-1011	Russia (Moscow) ▶▲●755-5042
Luxembourg + ..800-2-0111	(St. Petersbg.)▶▲● ..325-5042
Macedonia● ..99-800-4288	Slovakia ▲ ..00-42-100-101
Malta 0800-890-110	South Africa ..0800-99-0123
Monaco ● 800-90-288	Spain 900-99-00-11
Morocco 002-11-0011	Sweden 020-799-111
Netherlands ● ...0800-022-9111	Switzerland ● 0800-89-0011
Norway 800-190-11	Turkey ● 00-800-12277
Poland ▲● ..00-800-111-1111	Ukraine ▲ ....8◆100-11
Portugal ▲ 800-800-128	U.A. Emirates ● 800-121
Romania ●......01-800-4288	U.K..............0800-89-0011

FOR EASY CALLING WORLDWIDE

1. Just dial the AT&T Access Number for the country you are calling from.
2. Dial the phone number you're calling.   *3.* Dial your card number.

For access numbers not listed ask any operator for **AT&T Direct**® Service.
In the U.S. call 1-800-331-1140 for a wallet guide listing all worldwide AT&T Access Numbers.
Visit our Web site at: **www.att.com/traveler**
Bold-faced countries permit country-to-country calling outside the U.S.
- ● Public phones require coin or card deposit to place call.
- ▲ May not be available from every phone/payphone.
- ✚ Public phones and select hotels.
- ◆ Await second dial tone.
- ▶ Additional charges apply when calling from outside the city.
- † Outside of Cairo, dial "02" first.
- ✖ Not available from public phones or all areas.
- ✔ Use U.K. access number in N. Ireland.

When placing an international call *from* the U.S., dial 1 800 CALL ATT.

EMEA   © 8/00 AT&T

CASCAIS (30MIN.)

To get to Cascais from neighboring Estoril simply walk along the coast or Av. Marginal about 20min. Trains from Lisbon's Estação do Sodré head to Cascais (30min., approximately every 20min. 5:30am-2:30am, 210$), via Estoril. Stagecoach buses leave from outside the train station for Sintra (#417, 40min., every hr. 6:35am-7:08pm, 520$). Bus #403 also goes to Sintra (1hr., every 1-1½hr. 6:40am-7:45pm, 740$), via Cabo da Roca (30min., every 1½hr. 9:05am-6:35pm, 220$). Those taking the bus to several destinations might opt for the dayrover ticket (1250$) good for 1 day of unlimited use on stagecoach buses. Purchase tickets on the bus or at any Stagecoach office.

The only real reason to visit Cascais is its incredible coastline. Four popular beaches—all just minutes from the center of town—draw throngs of locals and tourists alike every day of the week. Once the summer vacation resort of the royal family, it still caters to the well-to-do. Cascais also has several historic sites and parks for the beach-weary, but don't expect to find an escape from fellow tourists. To reach the slightly overgrown **Parque de Gandainha**, take a left off Praia da Ribeira (facing Largo 5 de Outubro) and walk along the coast for 10 minutes on Av. Dom Carlos, which turns into Av. Rei Humberto de Itália. (Open daily 8:30am-7:45pm.) About 1km farther outside of Cascais (another 20min. walk up Av. Rei Humberto de Itália) lies the **Boca do Inferno** (Mouth of Hell), a huge cleft carved in the rock by the incessant Atlantic surf. While this sight fails to live up to its ominous name, the rocky turf makes a nice perch for sitting and sea-gazing.

Cascais is best done as a daytrip, but if you are too sunburned to move, your best bet is to bed down at **Residencial Parsi**, R. Afonso Sanches, 8, off the beachfront Lg. 5 do Outubro. The slightly pricey rooms all have baths and TVs; some provide stunning views of the ocean. (☎ 21 484 57 44. Breakfast included. In summer singles 5000$; doubles 9000$; prices fall during the low season. V, MC, AmEx.) Alternatively, ask at the **tourist office,** Av. Dos Combatentes da Grande Guerra, 25, for reliable *quarto* rooms (from 5000$, slightly higher in peak season). To get to the office from the train station, cross the square and take a right at the McDonald's onto Av. Valbom. At the intersection of Av. Valbom and Av. Combatantes, look for the big Turismo sign. (☎ 21 486 82 04. Open July-Sept. 15 M-Sa 9am-8pm, Su 10am-6pm; Sept. 16-June M-Sa 9am-7pm, Su 10am-6pm.)

ERICEIRA (1½HR.)

Green-and-white Mafrense buses (not to be confused with the green-and-white Rodoviária de Lisboa buses) run from Lisbon's Campo Grande to Ericeira (1¼-1½hr., every hr. 6:30am-11:20pm, 720$). Get off when you see the Centro Rodoviário Municipal (Ericeira's bus station). Buses leaving Ericeira depart from here and run to: Mafra (20min., every hr. 5:15am-9pm, 230$); Sintra (50min., every hr. 6:30am-8:30pm, 410$); and Lisbon (1¼hr., 12 per day 5:15am-9pm, 720$). Check at the tourist office for schedules.

Tourism is relatively new to Ericeira. Though it is becoming increasingly popular for its world-famous surfing waves and as a weekend hangout for young Lisbonites, the town still provides a taste of traditional Portugal, with its sandy coves, fishing harbor, and blue-and-white houses. Ericeira's two main beaches, **Praia do Sol** and **Praia do Norte**, crowd with happy beachgoers on summer weekends. If you're looking for something a little more secluded, stroll down the Largo de Feira toward Ribamar; soon you'll hit the unmistakable **Praia da Ribeira d'Ilhas**, known for its rolling surf, dramatic tides, stunning sand dunes, and impressive rock formations. The world surfing championships were held here in 1994, and surfers still come from around the world to test the waters. The local surf-shop **Utilmar** rents boards for 2000-25000$ per day. (☎ 261 86 23 71. R. 5 de Outubro, 25A.)

To get to the **tourist office**, R. Eduardo Burnay, 46, from the bus station, cross the road (EN 247-2), turn left, and walk uphill. Turn right onto Calçada do Rego when you see Estrada do Rego across the street on your left. Continue down R. Paroquial (to the right at the fork in the road), and turn left after three blocks onto R. 5 de Outubro, which runs straight to the small pedestrian square Pr. República. The tourist office is a white building with blue trim on the opposite end of the square;

enter on the right. Ask for a map and accommodations list. (☎ 261 86 31 22. Open M-Th 9:30am-8pm, F-Sa 9:30am-midnight, Su 9:30am-10pm; longer summer hours.) In an **emergency** call ☎ 112. **Police** (☎ 261 86 35 33) are at R. 5 de Outubro. If you choose to stay and party, you might have trouble finding a cheap room in summer; prices are lower from October to June. **Hotel Pedro O Pescador,** R. Dr. Eduardo Burnay, 22, up the street from the tourist office, has pleasant rooms with TVs, phones, and baths. (☎ 261 86 91 21. Breakfast included. Singles 9000$; doubles 12,000$; prices fall Oct.-June. V, MC, AmEx). Alternatively, ask for help at the tourist office.

MAFRA (1¼HR.)

Green-and-white Mafrense buses run from Lisbon's Campo Grande and stop in the square in front of the palace; don't confuse them with the also green-and-white Rodoviária de Lisboa buses. Be sure to ask the bus driver to let you know when you get there so you don't miss Mafra entirely. Mafrense buses serve Lisbon (1-1½hr., every hr. 5:30am-9pm, 540$) and Ericeira (20min., every hr. 7:30am-midnight, 230$). Do not take the train from Lisbon's Estação Santa. Apolónia unless you want to spend 2hr. walking to Mafra; the station is out in the countryside where cabs are few and far between.

The sleepy, otherwise unremarkable town of Mafra (north of Sintra) is home to one of Portugal's most impressive sights and one of Europe's largest historical buildings, the **Palácio Nacional de Mafra.** (☎ 261 81 75 50. Open W-M 10am-4:30pm. Closed on national holidays. 600$, students 300$.) Built by Dom João V in honor of the birth of his first child, the massive castle incorporates a cathedral-sized church, monastery, library, and palace. The monstrous 2000-room building, designed by architect Johann Friedrich Ludwig, took 50,000 workers 13 years (1717-1730) to complete. This Herculean task gave rise to a style of sculpture known as the Mafra School. The exterior of the magnificent Baroque church (☎ 261 81 53 79) gleams in recaptured glory after a series of restorations. Most renowned for its bell towers—two of the finest in Europe with 217 tons of bronze bells—the church also has a noteworthy dome which was lifted from Bernini's unexecuted plan for St. Peter's Cathedral in Rome. The richly decorated interior—with bas-reliefs and Carrara marble statues—is one of Portugal's hidden gems.

To access the building's seemingly interminable corridors and extravagant living quarters, go through the door to the right of the church exit. Although most of the original 16th-century furniture was taken by Dom João V to Brazil, the palace still makes a fascinating visit, if only to hear the guides' free tour. (45min. tours in Portuguese and English; tours daily in English at 11am and 2:30pm.) Of particular interest are the **Sala dos Trofeus** (Trophy Room), furnished with stag antlers, skins, chandeliers, and chairs, and the **biblioteca** (library), with 38,000 volumes printed in the 16th, 17th, and 18th centuries, displayed on 290 ft. of Rococo shelves.

To reach the **tourist office** on Av. 25 de Abril, take a right off the main steps of the palace and bear left—look for the blue Turismo sign. The office is on your right in a beige stucco building with a fountain in front. (☎ 261 81 20 23. Open M-F 9am-7pm, Sa-Su 9:30am-1pm and 2:30-6pm.)

SESIMBRA (1HR.)

Heavy traffic in the summer may lead you to take a ferry from Lisbon to Cacilhas (110$) from the Pr. Comércio station and catch a bus to Sesimbra (45min., 15 per day 6:40am-midnight, 450$). Regular Rodoviária buses leave for Sesimbra from Lisbon's Pr. de Espanha (M: Palhavã), (1hr., 7 per day 7am-7:30pm, 530$). Covas e Filhos and TST buses leave from the main bus station on Av. Liberdade to: Cacilhas (45min., 12 per day, 5:40am-11pm, 450$); Setúbal (45min., 9 per day 6:20am-6:50pm, 415$); and Lisbon (1hr., 8 per day 8am-6:10pm, 530$).

Nestled between unspoiled hillsides and the calm turquoise sea of the Costa Azul (Blue Coast), Sesimbra is a refreshingly traditional town. Still a pleasant fishing village, it has not been spoiled by recent influxes of beach-flocking tourists. Sesimbra will also appeal to the less aquatically inclined—a steep hour-long hike above town to the **Moorish castle** rewards with a Kodachrome view of the ocean and surrounding mountains. To reach the castle from the beach, follow the signs and take R. Gen. Humberto Delgado to the marked path. (Castle open 7am-7pm. Free.)

Buses to closer destinations leave from the corner of Av. 5 de Outubro and Av. Alexandro Hercularo, a block from the main bus station in Setúbal. Pick up maps, regional information, and accommodations information at the **tourist office**, Largo da Marinha, 27. (☎ 21 223 57 43. English spoken. Open daily June-Sept. 9am-8pm; Oct.-May 9am-12:30pm and 2-5:30pm.) In an **emergency** call ☎ 112; **police** (☎ 21 223 02 69) are located on Lg. Gago Coutinino. Inexpensive rooms are difficult to find, especially in the summer. The best option is to check with the tourist office for private rooms (doubles 4000$ and up). Otherwise, **Residencial Chic**, Trav. Xavier da Silva, 2-6 offers four breezy, decidedly un-chic doubles with common baths; breakfast included. (☎ 21 223 31 10. Singles 3500$; doubles 6000$).

NEAR LISBON

SINTRA

In the epic poem *Childe Harold*, British Romantic poet Lord Byron described Sintra as a "glorious Eden." His adulation made Sintra (pop. 20,000) a chic destination for 19th-century European aristocrats. These days, the town is more popular among foreign tour groups eager to experience its fairy-tale castles and incredible mountain vistas. They are rewarded by Sintra's enchanting gardens, villas, and its three castles, each from a different era; a walk through town presents a surreal mixture of history and fantasy.

▐ TRANSPORTATION

Trains run to Sintra from **Lisbon's** Estação Rossio and Estação Sete Rios (45min., every 15min. 6am-2am, 200$), after stopping in nearby **Queluz**. Stagecoach **buses** come from **Estoril** (#418, 40min., every hr. M-F 6:10am-11:40pm, Sa-Su 6:10am-9:50pm; 440$) and **Cascais** (#417, 40min., every hr. 6:35am-7:08pm, 520$; or #403, 1hr., every 1-1½hr. 6:40am-7:45pm, 740$). Mafrense buses come from **Ericeira** (50min., every hr. 6:30am-8:30pm, 410$).

Trains: Estação de Caminhos de Ferro, Av. Dr. Miguel Bombarda (☎ 21 923 26 05). To **Lisbon's** Estação Rossio and Estação Sete Rios (45min., every 15min. 6:07am-2:07am, 200$). No luggage storage available.

Buses: Stagecoach, on Av. Dr. Miguel Bombarda just outside the train station. To: **Estoril** (#418, 40min., every hr. 6:50am-midnight, 440$); **Cascais** (#417, 40min., every hr. 7:20am-8:30pm, 520$; or #403, 1hr., every 1-1½hr. 6:30am-7:55pm, 740$). **Mafrense**, just down the street from the Stagecoach buses. To: **Ericeira** (50min., every hr. 7:30am-9:30pm, 410$) with connections to points north. Fewer buses run on weekends and holidays.

✸❷ ORIENTATION AND PRACTICAL INFORMATION

Sintra is about 30km northwest of Lisbon and 10km north of Estoril. The town is split into three parts: a modern section around the train station, where most budget accommodations and banks are located; **Sintra-Vila**, where the historic sights perch on the mountainside; and **Portela de Sintra**, where shops and municipal offices cluster. To get to the old town from the train station (a 15min. walk), take a left out of the train station's ticket office, and turn right down the small hill at the next intersection. One block down the hill, turn left at the fountain in front of the castle-like **Câmara Municipal**, and follow the road as it curves past the **Parque da Liberdade**. From there, head up the hill to the **Praça da República**; the Palácio Nacional Desintra is the large white building (with 2 big chimneys) on the right.

Tourist Office: A small branch (☎ 21 924 16 23) is located at the train station. Grab a map as you walk through. Open June-Sept. M-Sa 9am-8pm; Oct.-May 9am-7pm. **Main office**, Sintra-Vila, Pr. República, 23 (☎ 21 923 11 57; fax 21 923 51 76). From the

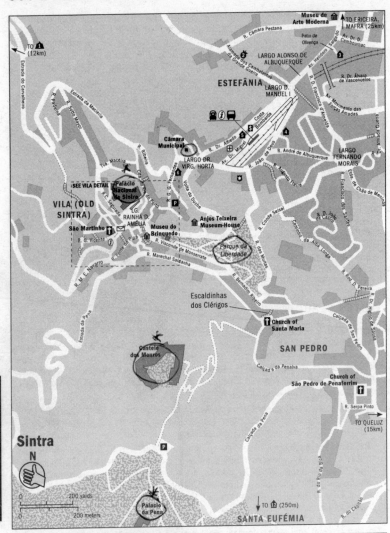

Sintra

N

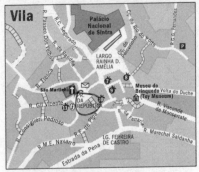

Vila

♦ FOOD

Cheap *pastelarias* (pastry shops) and restaurants crowd R. João de Deus (the street parallel to the train station on the other side of the tracks) and Av. Helidoro Salgado in modern Sintra. In the old town, narrow side streets off Pr. República, such as R. das Padárias near the Palácio Nacional, have a wide range of eateries. On the 2nd and 4th Sundays of every month, take bus #435 from the train station to the nearby town of São Pedro (15min., 220$) for a spectacular market.

🌋 Casa Piriquita, R. Padarias, 1 (☎ 21 923 06 26), just up a small side street off Pr. República. Inspiring bakery, snack bar, and candy counter flanked by a marble-floored coffee and tea room. Tiny pastries with cheese and cinnamon or egg filling are a welcome snack (90-200$ each). Open W-M 9am-10pm. A branch at R. Padarias, 18 (☎ 21 923 15 95), serves substantial sandwiches (200-300$). Open W-M 8:30am-10pm.

Artes & Tastes Galeria-Café, Alameda dos Combatentes da Grande Guerra, 12A-B (☎ 21 924 36 06). Exit the train station, turn right, walk 1 block, and turn left. This art gallery and cafe boasts art exhibits, inexpensive meals, and **Internet** access (400$ per 30min., 700$ per hr.). Pastries and crepes 350-400$. Entrees 890-1000$. Open M-F 9:30am-8:30pm, Sa-Su 10:30am-8:30pm; July-Aug. open until 10:30pm.

Alcobaça, R. Padarias, 9 (☎ 21 923 16 51), right off Pr. República, up the first side street on the left. Tourists and locals alike enjoy this elegant yet inexpensive restaurant. The *entradas* (appetizers, 120-900$) and *especialidades da casa* (house specials, 800-1800$) are budget finds. Open daily noon-11pm. Closed late Dec. V, MC, AmEx.

👁 SIGHTS

Except for the modern art museum, all of the sights in Sintra (including the two must-see palaces and the castle) are accessible from Sintra-Vila, the town's old quarter. From the train station, the road ambles and twists up the mountainside past the **Câmara Municipal** and its lush gardens before reaching the Paço Real.

🌋 PALÁCIO NACIONAL DE SINTRA. Also known as the Paço Real or Palácio da Vila, the palace, with its complex gardens and cone-shaped chimneys, sits prominently in Pr. República. Once the summer residence of Moorish sultans and their harems, the Paço Real and its gardens were built in two stages. During the early 15th century, Dom João I built the main structure; a century later, Dom Manuel I created the best collection of *azulejos* in the world. He added various wings to create a unique mix of Moorish, Gothic, and Manueline styles. More than 20 rooms run the gamut from the *azulejo*-covered **Sala dos Árabes** (Hall of the Arabs) to the gilded **Capela** (Chapel). Don't miss the **Sala dos Cisnes** (Hall of Swans), the **Sala Chinesa** (Chinese Hall), or the amazing **Sala dos Brasões** (Coat of Arms Room) with its breathtaking view of the gardens, town, and mountain. (☎ 21 910 68 40. Open Th-Tu 10am-5:30pm. Closed bank holidays. 600$, with student ID 300$. Buy tickets by 5pm.)

CASTELO DOS MOUROS. Perched on the boulder-studded peaks overlooking Sintra, this Moorish castle dates back to the 8th century. Stroll along the walls and clamber up the turrets for stunning views of the surrounding mountains and coast. The invigorating 3km ascent to the castle (and to the stunning Palácio Nacional da Pena farther up) climbs one of the highest peaks in the Sintra range. (Bus #434 runs to the top from outside the tourist office. 15min., every 30min. 10:20am-5:15pm, 600$ for all-day pass. Open daily 10am-6pm. Free. If you want to walk, start the steep, uphill hike (1-1½hr.) to the right of Pr. República and follow the blue signs up the mountain. Follow R. Visconde de Monserrate and continue straight as it becomes R. Bernardim Ribeiro, taking a right up the Escadinhas dos Clerigos. Turn left onto the Calçada da Santa Maria (towards the church), then right when you see a sign for Casa do Adro. Take another right at the first side street and follow it up the mountain to the Castelo. It is best to beware the escadinha (stair-alley) shortcut as many people get lost. If pressed for time, you can take a taxi directly from Sintra-Vila (one-way 2400$).

PALÁCIO NACIONAL DA PENA. Built in the 1840s by Prince Ferdinand of Bavaria, the husband of Queen Maria II, the fantastic Palácio looks like it belongs in Disney World. Nostalgic for his country, the prince rebuilt and embellished the ruined monastery with the assistance of a Prussian engineer, combining the artistic heritages of both Germany and Portugal. The result is a Bavarian castle decorated with Arabic minarets, Russian onion domes, Gothic turrets, Manueline windows, and a Renaissance dome. Interior highlights—decked out in regalia of Romantic Orientalism—include the chapel, the fully furnished kitchen, incredible views from the Queen's terrace, and **Her Majesty's Toilet**—crafted entirely with *azulejos*. *(1km farther uphill from the Castelo dos Mouros. July-Sept. Tu-Su 10am-6:30pm; Oct.-June Tu-Su 2-4:30pm. 600$, students 400$; Oct.-Apr. 200$.)*

OTHER SIGHTS. The **Sintra Museu de Arte Moderna** houses contemporary works by Andy Warhol, Francis Bacon, Morris Louis, and Gerhard Richter (among others) in a cheerful 19th-century building. *(Past the train station in modern Sintra, on Av. Heliodoro Salgado. ☎ 21 924 81 70. Open Tu-Su 10am-6pm. 600$, students 300$, children under 10 free; seniors and those 18 and under free on W.)* The **Anjos Teixeira Museum-House** displays sculptures by one of Portugal's most revered artists, Master Anjos Teixeira. His son, sculptor Pedro Anjos Teixeira, lives and works in the area and often greets visitors in person. *(Follow the signs into the park across the street from Parque da Liberdade on Volta do Duche, taking the stairs down with a pink building on your right; the entrance is at the bottom of the stairs. ☎ 21 923 88 27. Open Tu-F 9:30am-noon and 2-6pm, Sa-Su 2-6pm.)* For something very different, head to Sintra's **Museu do Brinquedo** (Toy Museum), which showcases traditional Portuguese toys and thousands of lead soldiers, dolls, puppets, and trains. *(On R. Visconde de Monserrate, up the block from Bristol Restaurante. ☎ 21 924 21 71. Open Tu-Su 10am-6pm. 500$, children under 13 and students 300$.)*

SETÚBAL

Setúbal's factories have created a noisy commercial center, surrounded on one side by sugar cane and cork tree plantations and on the other by a bustling port. Industry doesn't attract tourists, most of whom head straight for the Algarve. But wait—don't turn the page yet. Setúbal (pop. 120,000) was once home to an important Roman settlement. Today, the city's fine castle, some of Portugal's brightest *azulejo*-covered alleys, and the waters of the largely rural Costa Azul warrant at least a day's visit from Lisbon. Setúbal also makes a good base for daytrips to the beautiful beaches of Tróia and Figueirinha, the mountainous Serra da Arrábida, and the estuaries of the Rio Sado.

⌐ TRANSPORTATION

Trains run from **Lisbon's** Estação Barreiro (1½hr., every hr. 7:55am-6:50pm, 210$), accessible by ferry (85$, 200$ round-trip) from Terreiro do Paço off of Pr. Comércio. Get off at **Praça de Quebedo**, the city's center, instead of at the Setúbal stop. Buses make more sense from **Sesimbra** (45min., 9 per day 6:20am-6:50pm, 425$).

Trains: leave from either the central **Praça de Quebedo** or **Estação de Setúbal** (☎ 265 23 88 02), in Pr. Brasil. To: **Lisbon's** Estaçao Barreiro (1½hr., every hr. 5am-midnight, 210$) and **Faro** (4hr., 3 per day 9:20am-8:25pm, 1720$).

Buses: Setublanse, Av. 5 de Outubro, 44 (☎ 265 52 50 51). From the city tourist office, walk up to Av. 5 de Outubro and turn left; the station is about 2 blocks down on the right. To **Lisbon's** Praça de Espanha (45min., every 15-30min. 6am-10pm, 600$). **Covas & Filhos,** Av. Alexandre Herculano (☎ 21 223 31 03). Turn right 2 blocks past the Setubalanse station; the small office is on the left. To: **Sesimbra** (45min., 9 per day 7:20am-8pm, 425$).

Ferries: Transado, Doca do Comércio (☎ 265 52 01 52), off Av. Todi at the east end of the waterfront. Trips run back and forth from Setúbal to **Tróia** (15min.; every 15-45min. 7:15am-10pm.; 160$, children 80$, car with driver 750$).

Taxis: (☎ 265 23 33 34 or 265 23 14 13), along Av. Todi and by the bus station.

ORIENTATION AND PRACTICAL INFORMATION

Setúbal's main drag is **Avenida Luisa Todi,** a loud boulevard parallel to the **Rio Sado** with a nice park and cafes down its center. Inland from the river and Av. Todi lies a dense pedestrian district of shops and restaurants centered around **Praça de Bocage.** Pr. Bocage leads to another major thoroughfare, **Avenida 5 de Outubro.** To the right and down Av. 5 de Outubro is the bus station. **Avenida da Portela** is perpendicular to Av. 5 de Outubro and runs past the train station.

Tourist Office: Posto de Turismo Municipal (☎ 265 53 42 22), off Pr. Quebedo. From the bus station, turn left onto Av. 5 de Outubro; take 1st right and the office is on the left. From train station, take the 1st left onto Av. Portela, which leads into Pr. Quebedo. Open daily July-Aug. 9am-7pm; Sept.-June M-F 9am-12:30pm and 2-5:30pm.

Currency exchange: Banks line Av. Todi and are open M-F 8:30am-3:30pm. For after-hours banking, visit **Agência de Câmbios Central,** Av. Todi, 226 (☎ 265 53 43 36). Open M-Sa 9am-7:30pm.

Emergency: ☎ 112. **Police:** (☎ 265 53 52 31), on Av. Todi at Av. 22 de Dezembro.

Medical Services: Hospital (☎ 265 52 30 24), on R. Camilo Castelo Branco.

Post office: (☎ 265 52 27 78), on Av. Mariano de Carvalho at Av. 22 de Dezembro. Posta Restante and **telephones.** Open M-F 8:30am-6pm. **Branch office** in Pr. Bocage (☎ 265 23 55 55). Open M-F 9am-12:30pm and 2-6pm. **Postal code:** 2900.

Internet Access: Ciber Centro, Av. Bento Gonçalves, 21A (☎ 265 23 48 00). 6 computers. 500$ per 30min., 450$ with student ID. Open M-F 9am-11pm.

ACCOMMODATIONS

Many *pensões* line Av. Todi, but hours are erratic and summer prices can get a bit high. Check with the tourist office for a list of *quartos* (4000-9000$).

Pensão Bom Regresso, Pr. Bocage, 48 (☎ 265 22 98 12), an affordable, central location. Friendly owner offers 5 well-furnished, pristine rooms with communal bath, TVs and views of the *praça*. No reservations. Doubles 5000-8000$; triples 9000$.

Camping: Get-away-from-it-all types will want to escape to **Parque Natural da Arrábida** or one of the smaller locations near Setúbal in Azeitão or Sesimbra. If you must stay in Setúbal, try **Toca do Pai Lopes** (☎ 265 52 24 75), on the riverbank of R. Praia da Saúde, at the west end of Av. Todi on the road to Outão. Reception June-Sept. 8am-midnight; Oct.-May 9am-9pm. June-Aug. 320$ per person and per car, 280$ per tent. Sept.-May 200$ per person and per car, 140$ per tent.

FOOD

Hungry travelers will feel like they've hit the jackpot in old-town Setúbal. Inexpensive and untouristed restaurants line Pr. Bocage's side streets, especially **R. Álavro Castelões.** There's plenty of good seafood to be found at the end of **Av. Todi** just up the street from Doca do Comercío, where you can watch as they cut and fry your fish right in grills set up along the sidewalk. Get **groceries** and fresh baked goods at **Pingo Doce,** Av. Todi, 149. (☎ 265 52 61 05. Open daily 8am-10pm). Next door, on the corner of R. Ocidental do Mercado and Av. Todi, the **mercado municipal** sells groceries in open stands. (Open daily 7am-1pm.)

Jardim de Inverno, R. Álvaro Luz, 48-50 (☎ 265 23 93 73). From Pr. Bocage, walk 2 blocks past the post office on R. Álvaro Castelões, turning left onto this side street; its at the end on the right. Green walls and a garden brighten up this dirt cheap joint. Ask about festival specials—São João in late June brings fried pork, salad, fries, and *sangriá* for 650$. Entrees 750-1100$. *Menú* 900$. Open M-F 8am-8pm, Sa-Su 8am-3pm.

Casa de Santiago, Av. Todi, 92 (☎ 265 22 16 88). Known to locals as *choco frito,* after its most popular dish, this is one of the best seafood places in town. Try the house special, *choco frito* (fried cuttlefish, 1700$). Entrees 850-2200$. Open M-Sa 9am-10pm.

LISBON

👁🎵 SIGHTS AND ENTERTAINMENT

The most impressive sight in town is not really in town—the 16th-century **Castelo de São Filipe** perches on the top of a hill just outside the city. To reach the castle, take Av. Todi to its end (towards the beaches), turn right onto Escadinhas do Castelo, then ascend R. Estrada do Castelo about 600m. It's approximately a 40-minute walk from the town center. (Open daily 7am-midnight. Free.) Back in town, the **Igreja de Jesús**, begun in the 15th century, resides at Pr. Miguel Bombarda at the end of Av. 5 de Outubro (away from Pr. Quebedo). Maritime decorations and faux-rope pillars mark the beginnings of Manueline style. (☎ 265 52 47 72. Open daily 9am-12:30pm and 2-5:30pm. Free.) In the last week of July and first week of August, the industrial and agricultural extravaganza **Fiera de São João** brings a traveling amusement park, bullfighting, and folk dancing to Setúbal.

📷 DAYTRIPS FROM SETÚBAL

The most worthwhile sights around Setúbal are the natural ones. Outside of town are the stunning beaches of peninsular **Tróia**, a 15-minute ferry ride away from Doca do Comércio (every 15-45min. 7:15am-10pm, every hr. 10pm-3am; 160$, children 80$, cars with driver 750$). To the west of Setúbal is a large nature preserve, the **Parque Natural da Arrábida,** which includes a variety of nature trails and the pristine **Praia da Figueirinha,** 9km from Setúbal. Outdoor adventurers can contact **Mil Andanças,** Av. Todi, 121 (☎ 265 53 29 96), for somewhat pricey mountain biking, hiking, canoeing, and other nature trips.

ALGARVE

Behold the Algarve: a desert on the sea, an inexhaustible vacationland where happy campers from the world over bask in the sun. Nearly 3000 hours of sunshine per year have transformed this one-time fishermen's backwater into one of Europe's favorite vacation spots. In July and August, tourists mob the Algarve's resorts, packing the bars and discos from the 10pm sunset until way past the all-too-early sunrise. Still, not all is excess in the Algarve. In the off-season, the resorts become pleasantly de-populated, and the sun eases down a bit, presiding over tranquil grotto beaches at the base of rugged cliffs. The region between Olhão and the Spanish border remains particularly untouched, and to the west of Lagos, Luz, Burgau, Salema, and Sagres offer isolated beaches and steep cliffs. The west coast of the Algarve harbors a protected natural park, and Portugal's eastern border, near the town of Tavira, features floating flamingo wetlands.

Native culture in the Algarve is often ignored by the floods of international vacationers in search of wild parties and perfect tans, but the area actually has a long, varied history, dating back almost 3000 years to when the Phoenicians first landed. As in most of Portugal, Romans occupied the region for centuries; the cultural mark they left was not rivaled until the Moors arrived in the early 8th century and stayed for over 500 years. Within 200 years of their eventual expulsion in the 13th century, the Algarve became the most important area for Portugal's Age of Discovery. Prince Henry the Navigator built his famous navigational school and fortress in Sagres, once considered the end of the world. Ships launched out of Lagos reached Africa, Asia, and the "New World."

With nearly a hundred miles of coastline, the Algarve has perfected the art of delicious seafood; local favorites include *sardinhas assadas* (grilled sardines), and *caldeirada* (seafood chowder). Almonds and figs also make their way into most regional cooking, especially the tasty desserts.

HIGHLIGHTS OF THE ALGARVE

Lagos's nightlife—it doesn't get much nuttier than this (see p. 573).

The amazing coast, cliffs, and history of **Sagres** (see. p. 574).

Praia da Rocha, the best beach on the Algarve (see p. 574).

Tavira, a quiet town with excellent beaches and relatively few tourists (see p. 583).

LOCAL FESTIVAL IN THE ALGARVE
Southern Portugal may seem to spend more time sunbathing than partying, but the tiny town of **Silves** sets aside 10 days every year (mid-June) to pay homage to beer of all tastes and colors during the *Festa de Cerveja*.

LAGOS

As the town's countless international expats will attest, Lagos (pop. 22,000) is a black hole: come for two days and you'll be tempted to stay a month. The Algarve's capital for almost 200 years, Lagos launched and received many of the ships which brought Portugal wealth, power, and fame from the 15th through the 17th century. The 1755 earthquake destroyed most traces of the expeditions and naval battles fought off Lagos's coast, but no one's complaining; sun-worshipping Europeans, Australians, and North Americans swarm the town every summer not for its historical interest but for the beautiful beaches, crowded bars and infamously hedonistic backpacker lifestyle.

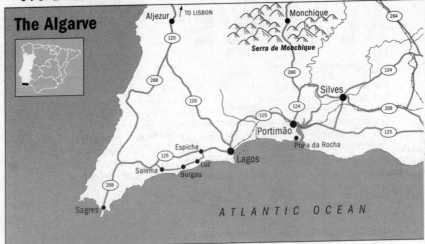

The Algarve

TO LISBON
Aljezur
120
268
120
125
Espiche
Salema
Burgau
Luz
Lagos
268
Sagres
Monchique
264
Serra de Monchique
266
124
Silves
124
269
125
Portimão
Praia da Rocha
125
125

ATLANTIC   OCEAN

◗ TRANSPORTATION

If you are trying to get to Lagos from northern Portugal, you must go through Lisbon; from the east you must transfer in Faro. Buses also come from Sevilla, Spain.

Trains: (☎ 282 76 29 87 or 282 79 23 61), across the river (over the metal drawbridge) from the main part of town. To: **Silves** (40min., 13 per day 5:55am-10:30pm, 260$); **Vila Real de Santo António** (4hr., 6 per day 6:55am-10:30pm, 1010$); **Faro** (1¾hr., 9 per day 5:55am-10:30pm, 750$); **Beja** (4hr., 2 per day 8:50am and 5pm, 1330$) via Faro; **Évora** (6hr., 2 per day 8:50am and 5pm, 1930$) via Faro; and **Lisbon** (4-4½hr., 6 per day 6:55am-10:30pm, 2110-2280$).

Buses: The **EVA** bus station (☎ 282 76 29 44), off Av. Descobrimentos, is just past the train station bridge (when walking out of town). To: **Portimão** (40min., 14 per day 7:15am-7:15pm, 360-450$); **Sagres** (1hr., 17 per day 7:15am-8:30pm, 470$); **Albufeira** (1¼hr., 12 per day 7am-6pm, 645-850$); **Faro** (2½hr., 7 per day 7am-8:20pm, 720-950$); **Lisbon** (5hr., 9 per day 7:30am-1:30am, 2500-2600$); **Sevilla, Spain** via **Albufeira** and **Huelva, Spain** (4¾hr., 2 per day 7:30am and 2pm, 3000$).

Taxis: ☎ 282 76 24 69 or 282 76 35 87.

Car Rental: Marina Rent A Car, Av. Descobrimentos, 43 (☎ 282 76 47 89). Min. age 21. June-Sept. cars start at 8700$ per day; May-June and Oct. 7500$; Nov.-Apr. 6500$; tax and insurance included. V, MC, AmEx. **Motoride,** R. José Afonso lote 23-C (☎ 282 76 17 20), rents bikes (1000$ per day) and scooters (4000-4800$ per day; min. age 16; must have license). Open daily 9am-7pm. **Hertz-Portuguesa,** Rossio de S. João Ed. Panorama, 3 (☎ 282 76 98 09), behind the bus station. Min. age 21. Cars start at 10,000$ per day, tax and insurance included.

✴ 🛈 ORIENTATION AND PRACTICAL INFORMATION

Running the length of the river, **Avenida dos Descobrimentos** is the main road that carries traffic in and out of Lagos. From the **train station,** exit to the left, go straight around the pinkish building, cross the river, and hang a left onto Av. Descobrimentos. Out of the **bus station,** turn right onto the main thoroughfare and follow it to R. Portas de Portugal, which leads into **Praça Gil Eanes,** the center of the old town. Most restaurants, accommodations, and services hover about this *praça* (also known as "statue square" after the Martian-like statue of Dom Sebastião that presides over it), the adjoining R. 25 de Abril, and the parallel R. Cândido dos Reis. Farther down Av. Descobrimentos, closer to the **fortaleza,** lies **Praça Infante Dom Henrique** (also known as **Praça República**).

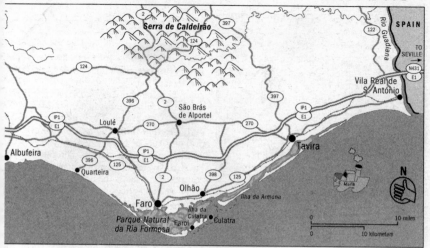

Tourist Office: (☎ 282 76 30 31), R. Vasco de Gama, an inconvenient 10min. walk past the bus station going out of town on R. Descobrimentos. Go through the traffic circle and pass the gas station; the office is on the left. Brochures, maps, transport info, and a list of *quartos.* English spoken. Open daily 9:30am-12:30pm and 2-5:30pm.

Currency Exchange: Cota Cambios, Pr. Gil Eanes, 11 (☎ 282 76 44 52), to the left of the statue. 500$ commission on currency; 750$ commission on traveler's checks. June-Sept. M-F 9am-10pm, Sa-Su 10am-8pm; Oct.-May M-F 9am-7pm, Sa-Su 10am-7pm.

English Bookstore: Loja do Livro, R. Dr. Joaquim Telo, 3 (☎ 282 76 73 47). Best-sellers, pulp romances, and travel guides. Open June-Aug. M-F 10am-1pm and 3-11pm, Sa 10am-1pm; Sept.-May M-F 10am-1pm and 3-7pm.

Laundromat: Lavandaria Miele, Av. Descubrimentos, 27 (☎ 282 76 39 69). Wash and dry 1250$ for 5kg, 10kg for 1900$. Open M-F 9am-1pm and 3-7pm, Sa 9am-1pm.

Scuba Diving: Blue Ocean Diving Center (☎/fax 282 78 27 18; www.blue-ocean-divers.de). Motel Ancora, Estrada de Porto de Mós. Medical license required for difficult dives. Lessons in English, French, German, and Portuguese. Half-day (in swimming pool) 4800$; full-day (in swimming pool and sea) 9000$.

Grotto Boat Tours: Companies offering tours of the coastal cliffs and grottoes set up shop on Av Descobrimentos. Ask for details at the tourist office. Most tours run about 45min. and start at 4000$ for 2 people (slightly less per person with a larger group). Smaller boats are preferable, as they can maneuver into rock caves and formations.

Emergency: ☎ 112. **Police:** (☎ 282 76 29 30), R. General Alberto Silva.

Medical Services: Hospital (☎ 282 76 30 34), R. Castelo dos Governadores.

Post Office: (☎ 282 77 02 50), R. Portas de Portugal, between Pr. Gil Eanes and the river. Open M-F 9am-6pm. For Posta Restante, label all letters "Estação Portas de Portugal" or they may arrive at the branch office. **Postal Code:** 8600.

Internet Access: The **youth hostel** has 1 computer and a wait that can be up to 2 days long. Sign up in advance or try to hop in if someone doesn't show up. 300$ for 30min., 500$ for 1hr. Open with hostel reception 9am-1am. **The Irish Rover,** R. de Ferrador, 9 (☎ 282 76 80 33). 4 computers. 300$ for 15min., 500$ for 30min., 900$ per hr. Beer 200-600$. Mixed drinks 550$. Happy "hour" 6-10pm. Open daily July-Sept. 2pm-2am; Oct.-June. 6pm-2am. **The Em@il Box (Ciaxa de Correieo),** R. Cândido dos Reis, 112 (☎ 282 76 89 50), has 4 computers. 350$ for 15min., 600$ for 30min., 1000$ per hr. Open June-Sept. M-F 9:30am-8pm, Sa 4-8pm, Su 11am-2pm; Oct.-May. M-F 9:30am-5:30pm. **Casa Rosa** (see **Food,** below) also offers Internet access. 300$ for 15min., 450$ for 30min., 900$ per hr.

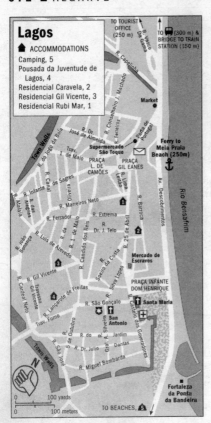

Lagos

♦ ACCOMMODATIONS
Camping, 5
Pousada da Juventude de Lagos, 4
Residencial Caravela, 2
Residencial Gil Vicente, 3
Residencial Rubi Mar, 1

ACCOMMODATIONS

In the summertime, *pensãoes* (and the youth hostel) fill up quickly; reserve rooms more than a week in advance. If full, the youth hostel will happily refer you to a *quarto* near the hostel (close to the nightlife) for about the same price. A mob of locals trying to rent rooms in their homes will probably be waiting to greet you at the bus or train station. Though these rooms are often inconveniently located, they can be the best deals in town at 2000-3000$ per person in summer. Try haggling with owners but shop before you decide, if possible, as room quality varies greatly.

▓ **Pousada da Juventude de Lagos (HI),** R. Lançarote de Freitas, 50 (☎ 282 76 19 70; fax 282 76 96 84). From the train and bus stations, head into town on Av. Descubrimentos, turn right into Pr. República, and take the small street in the back-center of the square 1 block; the hostel is on the right. Friendly staff and lodgers congregate in the central courtyard and TV room/bar. Free kitchen and Internet access. Free valuables storage. Breakfast included. Reception open daily 9am-1am. Check-out noon. In summer, book through the central **Movijovem** office (☎ 21 359 60 00; fax 21 359 60 01; email movijovem@mail.telepac.pt). July-Sept. dorms 2500$; doubles with bath 4300$. Oct.-June dorms 1700$; doubles with bath 3800$.

▓ **Residencial Rubi Mar,** R. Barroca, 70 (☎ 282 76 31 65, ask for David; fax 282 76 77 49; email rubimar01@hotmail.com), off Pr. Gil Eanes toward Pr. Infante Dom Henrique. Run by 2 friendly expats from London. Centrally located, quiet, and comfortable—a good deal if you grab one of their 8 rooms. Breakfast included and served in the room. Reserve 2 weeks ahead in summer. July-Oct. doubles 7000$, with bath 8500$; quads 15,000$. Nov.-June doubles 5500$, with bath 6500$; quads 10,000$.

Residencial Gil Vicente, R. Gil Vicente, 26, 2nd fl. (☎/fax 282 76 29 82; email ggh@clix.pt), behind the youth hostel. Business card says it's a "gay guest house," but it's open to anyone. Friendly owner has a wealth of information about the local and Lisbon gay scenes. Medium-sized rooms are somewhat stuffy but have high ceilings. Oct.-June reception open 8am-9pm; July-Aug. open 24hr. Breakfast included. Reserve a month ahead in the summer. Apr.-Oct. singles 5000$; doubles 6000-7000$. Nov.-Mar. singles 3000$; doubles 5000$. V, MC, AmEx.

Residencial Caravela, R. 25 de Abril, 8 (☎ 282 76 33 61), just up the street from Pr. Gil Eanes. 16 small but well-located rooms off a courtyard, some with balconies. Free valuables storage. English spoken. Breakfast included. Singles 4300$; doubles 6000$, with bath 6500$; triples 9000$.

Camping: The way most Europeans experience the Algarve; sites are crowded and expensive. **Camping Trindade** (☎ 282 76 38 93), just outside of town. Follow Av. Descubrimentos toward Sagres. 580$ per person, 630-735$ per tent, 620$ per car. **Camping Valverde** (☎ 282 78 92 11), on a beach 5km outside Lagos and 1.5km west of Praia da Luz). Free showers. 790$ per person, 650-790$ per tent, 680$ per car.

FOOD

Tourists can peruse multilingual menus around Pr. Gil Eanes and R. 25 de Abril, but a budget Portuguese meal is nearly impossible to find. The cheapest option is the morning **market,** on Av. Descobrimentos five minutes from the town center, or **Supermercado São Toque,** R. Portas de Portugal, 61. (☎ 282 76 28 55. Open July-Sept. M-F 9am-8pm, Sa 9am-7pm; Oct.-June M-F 9am-7:30pm, Sa 9am-7pm.) **Marrachinho,** Av. Descobrimentos, 15, also sells groceries. (☎ 282 76 97 28. Open daily July-Aug. 8am-midnight; June and Sept. 8am-10pm; Oct.-May 8am-8pm.)

Casa Rosa, R. Ferrador, 22 (cell ☎ 0936 511 10 52). A Lagos mainstay, for better or for worse. Enjoy cheap 650$ meal deals with backpacker hordes. M is all-you-can-eat spaghetti and garlic bread days (999$). Wide-ranging menu with many vegetarian options (650-1400$). Happy hour-and-a-half 10:30pm-midnight. Late breakfast served M-F noon-2:30pm. Internet access also available. Open daily 7pm-2am.

Snack-Bar Caravela, R. 25 de Abril, 14 (☎ 282 76 26 83), just off Pr. Gil Eanes. Well-touristed, but for good reason—the Italian food is incredible. Outdoor seating on a pedestrian street. Pizzas 750-1320$. Pastas 850-1175$. Open daily 9am-midnight.

A Vaca, R. Silva Lopes, 27 (☎ 282 76 44 31), a continuation of R. 25 de Abril. Once again, traditional Portuguese food is nonexistent; this restaurant serves traditional home-style Swiss dishes. Crepes 800-1100$. Entrees 950-1950$. Open daily Apr.-Oct. noon-2am; Nov.-Mar. M-F noon-2am.

SIGHTS AND BEACHES

SIGHTS. Although sunbathing and non-stop debauchery have long erased memories of Lagos's rugged, sea-faring past, most of the city is still surrounded by a nearly intact **16th-century wall.** The **Fortaleza da Ponta da Bandeira,** a 17th-century fortress holding maritime exhibitions, overlooks the Marina. (☎ 282 76 14 10. Open Tu-Sa 10am-1pm and 2-6pm, Su 10am-1pm. 330$, students 170$., children 13 and under free.) Also on the waterfront is the old **Mercado de Escravos** (slave market). Legend has it that the first sale of African slaves in Portugal took place here in 1441. Today the waterfront and marina offer jet-ski rentals, scuba diving lessons, sailboat trips, and motorboat tours of the coastal rocks and grottoes (see **Local Services,** p. 571).

BEACHES. Lagos's beaches are seductive any way you look at them. Flat, smooth, sunbathing sands (crowded during the summer, pristine in the off-season) line the 4km long **Meia Praia,** across the river from town. Hop on the 30-second ferry near Pr. República (70$ each way). For beautiful cliffs that hide smaller, less-crowded beaches and caves, keep the ocean on your left and follow Av. Descobrimentos toward Sagres (there are signs) to **Praia de Pinhão** (20min.). Five minutes farther down the coast lies **Praia Dona Ana,** with sculpted cliffs and grottoes that appear on at least half of all Algarve postcards.

NIGHTLIFE

You're tan, you're glam, now go find yourself a (wo)man. The streets of Lagos pick up as soon as the sun dips down, and by midnight the city's walls are shaking. The area between Pr. Gil Eanes and Pr. Luis de Camões is filled with cafes. R. Cândido dos Reis, R. do Ferrador, and the intersection of R. 25 de Abril, R. Silva Lopes, and R. Soeiro da Costa are packed with bars and clubs that rarely close until well past 5am. Staggered happy hours make drinking easy, even on the tightest of budgets.

Taverna Velha (The Old Tavern), R. Lançarote de Freitas, 34 (☎ 282 76 92 31), down the street from the youth hostel. The friendliest staff around. Nightly showings of classic American movies. Happy "hour" with 2-for-1 beers or cocktails 9pm-midnight. Beer 250-500$. Mixed drinks 500-700$. Open M-Sa 4pm-2am, Su 8pm-2am.

Phoenix Club, R. São Gonçalo, 29 (☎ 282 76 05 03), near the Old Tavern and the youth hostel. Rises from the nighttime ashes for some great after-hours dancing. Pop and dance music. Beer 600$. Cover 1000$, includes 2 beers or 1 mixed drink. Open nightly 1-6am, but the crowds don't arrive until 3:30am.

Whyte's Bar, R. Ferrador, 7. Live, request-taking DJ keeps it packed all night long. Opens a basement level during crowded summer months. Nightly happy hour. Beer 500$. Mixed drinks 500-700$. Open daily Oct.-June 8pm-2am; July-Sept. 7pm-2am.

The Lionheart, R. Castelo dos Governadores, 12 (☎ 282 76 22 46), off Pr. República. This bar, frequented mostly by locals, has a small dance floor as well as occasional karaoke (once a week July-Sept.). 2-for-1 happy hour 11pm-midnight. Beer 250-450$. Mixed drinks 450-600$. Open daily 5pm-4am.

✷ **Joe's Garage,** R. 1 de Maio, 78, across from Mullen's back door. The rowdiest, and possibly raunchiest, bar in town, but definitely a good time. Beer 350$. 2-for-1 beers or drinks 10pm-midnight. Open daily 10pm-2am.

DAYTRIPS FROM LAGOS

LUZ (10MIN.), BURGAU (20MIN.), SALEMA (40MIN.)

These towns are all accessible by the bus that runs from Lagos to Sagres (12 per day 7:15am-8:30pm). To reach Luz, get off at Espiche, 10min. away (170$); to Burgau ride 20min. (340$); and to Salema 40min. (310$). Another way to make the trip is by scooter (see Car Rental, p. 570). Make sure to check return bus schedules to avoid getting stuck.

These three small towns on the way to Sagres make perfect daytrips from Lagos. Less "discovered" than their larger neighbor and a bit more charming than wind-swept Sagres, they offer a quiet alternative to crowded Lagos. All three towns feature lovely beaches (although Salema's is less developed.) Try asking around for a *quarto* if you find yourself stranded at night. Fresh fruits, cheeses, and olives are sold by local farmers each morning at the main square in Salema, and decent bars and restaurants line the beachfront in all three towns.

PRAIA DA ROCHA (50MIN.)

To reach Praia da Rocha from Lagos, first take a bus to Portimão (40min., 14 per day 7:15am-7:15pm, 360-450$), then switch at the station to the Praia da Rocha bus (10min., every 30min. 7:30am-8:30pm, 220$).

A short jaunt from Lagos, this grand beach is perhaps the very best the Algarve has to offer. With vast expanses of sand, surfable waves, rocky red cliffs, and plenty of secluded coves, Praia da Rocha has a well-deserved reputation (and the crowds to match). The **tourist office,** at the end of R. Tomás Cabreina, offers maps and lists of accommodations and restaurants. (☎ 282 41 91 32. Open daily May-Sept. 9:30am-7pm; Oct.-Apr. M-F 9:30am-12:30pm and 2-5:30pm, Sa-Su 9:30am-12:30pm.)

SAGRES

Marooned atop a bleak, scrub-desert plateau in the barren southwestern-most corner of Europe, for centuries Sagres was considered the end of the world. The windswept, rugged cape leads to the Atlantic, where it plunges dramatically on three sides. Here, outward-looking Prince Henry founded his school of navigation, looking to inspire voyages to the far reaches of the globe. Sagres's dramatic, desolate location and relative lack of recreation discourages tour-groups and upscale vacationers; it is perfect for travelers interested in discovering uncharted beauty.

 PRACTICAL INFORMATION. EVA buses (☎ 282 76 29 44) run from **Lagos** (1hr., 17 per day 7:15am-8:30pm, 470$); check the schedule at the Sagres bus stop to avoid getting stranded. The friendly, English-speaking staff at the **tourist office** on R. Comandante Matoso, up the street from the bus stop, dispenses maps and information on Sagres's illustrious history. (☎ 282 62 48 73. Open Tu-Sa 9:30am-12:30pm and 2-5:30pm.) Privately run **Turinfo** in Pr. República is also a good source of info. The energetic, English-speaking staff recommends accommodations, rents **bikes** (1900$ per day, 1200$ per half-day), gives info on **jeep tours** of a nearby nature preserve (7000$, including lunch), and provides **scuba** advice. They'll even do your **laundry** (1300$ per load) and offer commission-free **currency exchange**. (☎ 282 62 00 03. Open daily 10am-1pm, 2-7pm.)

◪◩ ACCOMMODATIONS AND FOOD. Finding a bed in Sagres is not hard; windows everywhere display multilingual signs for rooms, many in boarding houses with guest kitchens. Prices range from 3000 to 5000$ for singles and doubles, 4000 to 7000$ for triples. Follow the main road toward the traffic circle and turn left after Supermarket Alisuper to reach **Atalaia Apartamentos;** the beautiful, fully-furnished apartments and rooms are a good deal. (☎ 282 62 44 87. Apartments for 2 July-Oct. 8000$; Nov.-Mar. 5000$; Apr.-June 6000$.) Open-air **camping** is strictly forbidden, so head to the **guarded ground** just off E.N. 268. (☎ 62 43 51; fax 62 44 45. June-Sept. 600-700$ per person, 500-850$ per tent, 350-450$ per car; Oct.-May 500$ per person, 400-600$ per tent, 250$ per car. Reception open daily June-Sept. 8am-11pm; Oct.-May 9am-7pm.) For groceries, try the **market,** on R. Mercado, which intersects R. Comandante Matoso not far from the tourist office (open M-Sa 8am-9pm), or **Supermarket Alisuper,** on R. Comandente Matoso (the main street), toward the port and Praia da Baleeira (☎ 282 62 44 87; open daily 9am-8pm). **O Dromedário Bistro,** on R. Comandante Matoso, whips up innovative pizzas (740-1180$) and vegetarian dishes (890-1310$). The bar is a Sagres hotspot by night. (☎ 282 62 42 19. Open daily 10am-midnight; bar open until 2am. Closed Jan.-Feb.)

◨◩ SIGHTS AND ENTERTAINMENT. Near town lurks the must-see **Fortaleza de Sagres,** the outpost where Prince Henry stroked his beard, decided to map the world, and founded his famous **school of navigation.** The pentagonal 15th-century fortress and the surrounding area yield vertigo-inducing views of the cliffs and sea. (Fortress open May-Sept. 10am-8:30pm; Oct.-Apr. 10am-6:30pm. 600$.) Six kilometers farther west lies the desolate **Cabo de São Vicente,** which features the second most powerful lighthouse in Europe, a towering structure that overlooks the southwest tip of the continent and shines over 100km out to sea. On weekdays, you can take the bus from the main road (10min.; 11:15am, 12:30, 4:15pm; 180$), but check schedules to avoid getting stuck there. On weekends, you're on your own—it's an hour on foot but is also accessible by bike (see **Turinfo,** above).

Several **beaches** fringe the peninsula, most notably **Mareta,** located at the bottom of the road from the town center. Rock formations jut into the ocean on both sides of this sandy crescent. Though not as picturesque or intimate as the coves of nearby **Salema** and **Luz,** Mareta is popular for its length and isolation. Just west of town, **Praia de Martinhal** and **Praia da Baleeira** have great **windsurfing.**

Although Sagres may seem dead upon arrival, it definitely develops a pulse at sundown. At night, the young crowd fills the lively bar **Rosa dos Ventos** in Pr. República. (☎ 282 62 44 80. Beer 150$. Mixed drinks 300$. Open daily 10am-2am.) Another hotspot is **Água Salgada,** on R. Comandante Matoso right next to another popular bar, **O Dromedário** (see **Accommodations and Food,** above), where trendy young locals let loose and a request-taking DJ keeps the party going (☎ 282 62 42 97. Beer 200$. Shots 350$. Mixed drinks 650-900$. Open daily 10am-2am.)

SILVES

Quiet Silves was once the Moorish capital of the Algarve; from the mid-11th to mid-13th centuries it was nearly as influential as Lisbon, with a population of 30,000 and a busy port. In 1189, however, the Moors were stripped of their possessions, tortured, and ousted by English crusaders who destroyed the town after a three-month siege of the castle. Although the Moors took back their town after a few years, the Christians gained a final foothold in 1249, and ever since Silves has been nothing but a remnant of its former self. Its castle has impressive views, however, and the town is a good place to relax away from over-touristed beach towns. Quirky attractions like the Cork Museum and annual Beer Festival draw visitors interested in an offbeat experience of the Algarve.

ALGARVE

☐ TRANSPORTATION. The train station is 1km out of town, so the best way to get to Silves is by **bus.** If you do take a train, catch the "Estação" bus (☎ 282 44 23 10) from the train station to town (10min., 6 per day 7:15am-7:40pm, 85$). **Trains** run to: **Lagos** (40min., 14 per day 5:55am-12:15am, 260$); **Portimão** (20min., 14 per day 5:55am-12:15am, 150$); **Faro** (1hr., 8 per day 6:30am-11pm, 520$); and **Lisbon** (4-5hr., 3 per day 9:25am-6:55pm, 1900-2280$), usually via Funcheira. **Buses** go to: **Albufeira** (40min., 7 per day 6:40am-6:50pm, 510$); **Portimão** (30min., 11 per day 7:15am-6:10pm, 340$); and **Lisbon** (4hr., 4 per day 8:20am-6:20pm, 2500$).

☑ PRACTICAL INFORMATION. The **EVA bus office,** on R. Francisco Pablos, is just next to the market (☎ 282 44 23 38; open M-F 8am-noon and 2-6pm), and buses stop on the main road, EN 124, which runs along the edge of town past the Largo António Enes, where the market is held. To get to the **tourist office,** R. 25 de Abril, 26-28, from Lg. António Enes, head straight up R. Francisco Pablos and continue up the steps; the office lies ahead. The English-speaking staff provides maps and can help with finding accommodations. (☎ 282 44 22 55. May-Sept. open daily 9:30am-1pm and 2-5:30pm; Oct.-Apr. M-F 9:30am-1pm and 2-5:30pm.) Just uphill from the tourist office is **Rua da Sé,** with its old cathedral and municipal museum, and **Rua do Castelo,** which curves past the castle. The **Centro de Saúde** (health center), is located just outside of town on R. Cruz de Portugal (☎ 282 44 00 20).

☐☐ ACCOMMODATIONS AND FOOD. Inexpensive places to stay are hard to come by in Silves. Ask at the tourist office or in any restaurant or bar for help in finding a private *quarto* (2000-5000$). *Pensãos* are few and far between. **Residencial Sousa,** R. Samora Barros, 17, just down the steps from the tourist office, offers small, simple, comfortable rooms. (☎ 282 44 25 02. July-Aug. singles 3000$; doubles 6000$; triples 7500$. Sept.-June singles 2000$; doubles 4000$; triples 5000$.) **Camping** is available in the neighboring town of Armação de Pera, accessible by bus (20-30min., 6 per day 7:50am-7:15pm, 340$). The **Armação de Pera** campsite is close to the beach (June-Sept. 650$ per person, 600-750$ per tent, 550$ per car; 50% discount Oct.-May), while **Caliço** is 2km inland (600$ per person, 600-700$ per tent, 500$ per car; 50% discount Oct.-May). For fresh fruits, vegetables, and fish, try the **mercado municipal** on Lg. António Enes (open M-Sa 8:30am-2pm). Restaurants line the pedestrian district, especially R. Policapo Dias.

☐☐ SIGHTS AND ENTERTAINMENT. Silves is home to the 13th-century Gothic Sé Velha (old cathedral), as well as a typical Portuguese *castelo*. Start your sight-seeing at the **Museu Municipal de Arqueologia,** R. das Portas de Loulé, built around a 12th-century Moorish well (open daily 10am-6pm; 300$). From there head up R. da Sé to the **Sé Velha.** The cathedral, thought to have been built in the 13th century on the site of a mosque, has undergone a series of renovations, most of them after the 1755 earthquake. (Open daily 8:30am-8:30pm. Mass M-F 9am, Su 8:30am, 10:15am and noon. Free.) The *caselo,* just up the hill from the cathedral, offers beautiful panoramic views of the town and surrounding valley. It also hosts art exhibits in a large 13th century Moorish well in the middle of the gardens. (☎ 282 44 56 24. July-Aug. open daily 9am-8pm; Apr.-June and Sept. 9am-7pm; Oct.-March 9am-5pm. 200$ for castle walls and garden. 650$ with art exhibit.) From the castle, turn left onto R. do Castelo and then right down R. Gregório Mascarenhas to get to the **Museu da Cortiça** (Cork Museum). Silves once served as the center of Portugal's cork industry, and this museum provides a fascinating look at both tradition and industrialization in Portugal, with photographs, machines, and plenty of cork in various processing stages. (☎ 282 44 04 80. Open daily June-Aug. 9:30am-12:45pm and 2-9:45pm; Sept.-May 9:30am-12:45pm and 2-7pm. 250$. Children 6-12 125$, under 6 free.) In the same complex as the cork museum (known as the Fábrica do Ingles), subdued Silves comes to life for 10 days in mid-June with the **Festival da Cerveja** (Beer Festival); locals crowd the old mill to swig beers of every kind and color. (☎ 282 44 04 40; www.fabrica-do-ingles.com. Starts the 3rd week in June, and is usually open 6pm-1am. Tickets 1300$, include 2 mugs of beer.)

ALBUFEIRA

Those who come to Albufeira, the largest seaside resort in the Algarve, are hell-bent on having a good time. Sun, surf, and beer keep the hordes of middle-aged British, German, and Scandinavian tourists satisfied; nary a Portuguese roams the cobblestone streets. The city also plays host to packaged tours, which fill the high-rise hotels with high-rolling guests. It may appear that there is little "authentic" Portuguese culture here, but a stroll through the old town or along the east edge of the beach hints at Albufeira's humble fishing origins. For those too jaded to care, the beaches are packed all day and the nightlife jumps from dusk till dawn.

E TRANSPORTATION. EVA buses connect the **train station** (☎ 289 57 16 16), 6km inland, to the town center (every hr. 7:05am-8:20pm, 200$). **Trains** run to: **Faro** (45min., 6 per day 5:15am-11:55pm, 300$); **Lagos** (1hr., 10 per day 7:45am-11:30pm, 520$); **Olhão** (1½hr., 6 per day 5:15am-11:55pm, 370$); **Tavira** (2hr., 6 per day 5:15am-11:55pm, 620$); **Vila Real de Santo António** (2¼hr., 6 per day 5:15am-11:55pm, 770$); and **Lisbon** (4-5½hr., 5 per day 7:45am-7:10pm, 2030$). The EVA **bus station** (☎ 289 58 97 55), on Av. Liberdade, is more conveniently located. **Buses** head to: **Faro** (1hr., 29 per day, every hr. 7:05am-7:30pm, 600$); **Lagos** (1½hr., 7 per day 8:40am-8:10pm, 645-850$); **Tavira** (1½hr., 4 per day 8:45am-11:15pm, 780$); and **Lisbon** (3½-4hr., 8 per day 6:35am-2:30am, 2600-2800$).

⊿ PRACTICAL INFORMATION. The English-speaking staff at the **tourist office**, R. 5 de Outubro, 8, offers maps, a list of rooms, and tons of brochures on water sports, including fishing and scuba diving. From the bus station, turn right and walk downhill into the main square, **Largo Eng. Duarte Pacheco** (also known as "Jardim Square") then turn right out of the square and left onto R. 5 de Outubro. (☎ 289 58 52 79. June-Sept. open daily 9:30am-7pm; Oct.-May 9:30am-5:30pm.) For a **taxi**, call ☎ 289 58 32 30. In an **emergency** dial ☎ 112; **police** (☎ 289 51 32 03), are on Av. 25 de Abril. The **post office** is next to the tourist office on R. 5 de Outubro. (☎ 289 58 08 70. Open M-F 9am-12:30pm, 2:30-6pm.) The **postal code** is 8200.

▼◫ ACCOMMODATIONS AND FOOD. Most lodgings in Albufeira are booked solid from late June through mid-September, and budget accommodations are scarce. Ask for *quartos* at the tourist office or any restaurant or bar. You will most likely be accosted by room renters at the bus and train stations as well. The modern **Pensão Albufeirense**, R. Liberdade, 16-18, a few blocks downhill from the bus station, has comfortable rooms and a TV lounge. (☎ 289 51 20 79. July-Aug. singles 4000$; doubles 6500$; triples 8600$. May-June and Sept. singles 3500$; doubles 5500$; triples 7500$. Closed Oct.-April.) Further up the street is **Residencial Limas**, R. Liberdade, 25-27, which offers comfortable medium-sized doubles on a pedestrian street near the town center. (☎ 289 51 40 25; fax 289 58 58 02. Doubles 5000-6000$, with bath 6000-8000$; discounts during the winter.) Open-air camping is illegal, but weary travelers can pay for the ritz and glitz of **Parque de Campismo de Albufeira,** a few kilometers outside town on the road to Ferreiras. It's more like a shopping mall than a campground, with four swimming pools, three restaurants, tennis courts, a supermarket, and a hefty price tag (☎ 289 58 76 29; fax 289 58 76 33. June-Sept. 850$ per person and per car, 795$ per tent; Oct.-May 50% discount.)

There is no shortage of cheap and varied eats in Albufeira. For fresh fruits and vegetables, check out the **mercado municipal** (open daily 8am-1:30pm; Thursdays offer the most variety). To get there, take the "Estação" bus from the EVA bus station on Av. Liberdade (every hr. 6:45am-8pm, 200$). Locals recommend **Tasca do Viegas**, R. Cais Herculano, 2, near the fisherman's beach. (☎ 289 51 40 87. Fish entrees 1200-2100$. Meat entrees 1000-2600$. Open daily noon-11pm.)

ALGARVE

⊞⊠ SIGHTS AND BEACHES. Once the last holdout of the Moors in southern Portugal, Albufeira preserves its graceful architectural heritage in its **old quarter,** off R. Miguel Bombarda and Pr. Miguel Bombarda. From the main square, take Tr. 5 de Outubro across R. 5 de Outubro and walk up R. Igreja Nova toward the beach. Tiny minarets pierce the small Byzantine dome of the **Santana** chapel, an exquisite filigree doorway heralds the **São Sebastião** church (open evenings in summer; free), an ancient Gothic portal fronts the **Misericórdia** (near Pr. República and the beach; closed to the public), and a barrel-vaulted interior receives worshippers into the **Matiz** (open W-Sa 2-6pm, Su 10am-1pm; free).

Albufeira's spectacular slate of **beaches** ranges from the popular **Galé** and **São Rafael** (4-8km toward Lagos), to the very chic **Falésia** (10km toward Faro). To get to the centrally-located beach **Inatel** from the main square (Lg. Eng. Duarte Pacheco), follow Av. 25 de Abril to its end and continue down R. Gago Coutinho until you hit the beach. The beautiful but packed **Praia de Albufeira** awaits through the gate to the tourist office. It pays to explore beyond these popular options as well; many small and relatively uncrowded beaches await discovery.

⊞ ENTERTAINMENT. Bars and restaurants line all the streets of Albufeira; clubs blast everything from salsa to techno to *fado* as soon as the sun sets—and continue until it rises. One prime spot is **Fastnet Bar,** R. Cândido dos Reis, 5, which is generally packed with northern Europeans. (☎ 289 58 91 16. Beer 300-500$. Mixed drinks 600$. Open daily noon-4am.) Down the street is **Classic Bar,** R. Cândido dos Reis, 10, with its Grecian decor and a gaggle of tourists grooving to everything from pop and rock to disco and house. (☎ 289 51 20 75. Beer 300-400$. Mixed drinks 850$. Open daily June-Sept. noon-4am; Oct.-May noon-midnight.) At **Café Latino,** on R. Latino Coelho in the old town, salsa tunes complement a stunning seaside view. (☎ 289 58 51 32. Beer 200-300$. Coffee 100-150$. Open daily 10am-2am.) The only thing strange about nearby **Bar Bizzaro,** R. Dr. Frutuoso Silva, 30, is that you might actually get a glimpse of locals (sometimes Albufeira makes you wonder if there's any such thing). This down-to-earth cafe-bar hosts live Brazilian music Tuesdays at 9pm. (☎ 289 51 28 24. Beer 250-400$. Open daily 9am-2am.) **7½ Disco** (☎ 289 51 33 06), on R. São Gonçalo de Lagos, is a popular beachside dance club. Many of the hottest new clubs are just outside of Albufeira (600-1200$ by taxi). Try **Reno's Bar, IRS Disco,** or **Kiss Disco** (all open daily 2am-6am).

FARO

Although many northern Europeans begin their holidays in Faro (pop. 55,000), the Algarve's capital and largest city, few bother to stay long enough to absorb its charm and local color. The city is divided into two parts, each with its own personality: a modern, commercial shopping district with a slick marina, and a quiet historical neighborhood, behind the walls of the perfectly preserved old town. The calm beaches of the estuary's islands satiate those seeking the sun.

▐ TRANSPORTATION

Flights: The international **Aeroporto de Faro** (☎ 289 80 08 00; flight info ☎ 289 80 08 01), 5km west of the city, has a police station, bank, post office, car rental companies, and tourist info booth. Open daily 10am-midnight. Buses #14 and 16 run from the street opposite the bus station to the airport (20min., every hr. 7:10am-8:40pm, 170$). From May 15-Oct. the **aerobus** runs from the big EVA Hotel on the main *praça* to the airport (15min., every hr. 8:15am-8:15pm, free with plane ticket). Taxis to the airport cost 1400-1600. **TAP Air Portugal** (☎ 289 80 02 00), R. Dr. Francisco Gomes. Open M-F 9am-5:30pm.

Trains: (☎ 289 80 17 26), Largo Estação. To: **Albufeira** (45min., 14 per day 7:20am-11pm, 300$); **Vila Real de Santo António** (1½hr., 12 per day 6:10am-12:10am, 520$); **Lagos** (2hr., 7 per day 7:20am-11pm, 750$); **Beja** (3hr., 2 per day 9:05am and 5:30pm, 1330$); **Évora** (5hr., 2 per day 9:05am and 5:30pm, 1650$); and **Lisbon** (5-6hr., 6 per day 7:20am-11pm, 2280$). Consult the schedule as departure times are often bunched together.

Buses: EVA (☎ 289 89 97 00), Av. República. To: **Olhão** (20min., every 20-40min. 7:15am-8:35pm, 210$); **Albufeira** (1hr., 14 per day 6:30am-7:30pm, 600$); **Vila Real de Santo António** (1½hr., 9 per day 7:15am-6:20pm, 625$); **Tavira** (1hr., 11 per day 7:15am-7:30pm, 435$); **Lagos** (2hr., 8 per day 7:30am-5:30pm, 720$); and **Beja** (3-3½hr., 7 per day 7:45am-4pm, 1550$). **Renex** (☎ 289 81 29 80), across the street, provides express long-distance service. To: **Lisbon** (4hr., 8 per day 5:15am-1:15am, 2500$); **Porto** (7½hr., 8 per day 5:15am-1:15am, 3500$) via Lisbon; and **Braga** (8½hr., 8 per day 5:15am-1:15am, 3600$) via Lisbon. **Intersul** (☎ 289 89 97 70) runs to **Sevilla, Spain** (2800$), with connecting buses to France and Germany.

Taxis: Táxis Rotáxi (☎ 289 89 57 95). **Táxis Auto Faro** (☎ 289 89 22 75). Taxis congregate near Jardim Manuel Bívar (by the tourist office) and at the bus and train stations.

✦💡 ORIENTATION AND PRACTICAL INFORMATION

Faro's ritzy center hugs the **Doca de Recreio,** a marina lined with yachts and bordered by the Jardim Manuel Bívar. The main road into town, **Avenida da República,** runs past the train station and bus depot along the harbor, spilling into a delta of smaller streets at **Praça Dr. Francisco Gomes** (the center of town), which borders the dock and garden. **Rua Dr. Francisco Gomes** and **Rua de Santo António** are the major pedestrian thoroughfares off Pr. Gomes. The old town begins at the **Avio da Vila,** a stone arch on the far side of the garden, next to the tourist office.

Tourist Office: R. Misericórdia, 8 (☎ 289 80 36 04), at the entrance to the old town. From the bus or train station, turn right down Av. República along the harbor, then turn left past the garden. From the main square, go past the garden; the office is to the left of the arch with the clock and bell tower. Helps find accommodations. English spoken. Open June-Aug. 9:30am-7pm; Sept.-May 9:30am-5:30pm. The **regional tourism office,** Av. 5 de Outubro, 18-20 (☎ 289 80 04 77) offers information about all of the Algarve. From the main square, follow R. Dr. Francisco Gomes as it becomes R. de Santo António and then Av. 5 de Outubro; the office is in a tall building on the right. Open June-Aug. 9:30am-7pm; Sept.-May 9:30am-5:30pm.

Currency Exchange: Cota Cambios, R. Dr. Francisco Gomes, 26 (☎ 289 82 57 35), off Pr. Gomes. No commission on currency exchange. Open June M-F 8:30am-9pm, Sa 10am-7pm, Su 10am-4pm; July-Sept. M-F 8:30am-9pm, Sa 10am-8pm, Su 10am-7pm; Oct.-May M-F 8:30am-7pm, Sa 10am-2pm.

Laundromat: Sólimpa, R. Batista Lopes, 30 (☎ 289 82 29 81), up R. 1 de Maio. Wash and dry 350$ per kg; with iron 400$. Open M-F 9am-1pm and 3-7pm, Sa 9am-1pm.

Emergency: ☎ 112. **Police:** (☎ 289 82 20 22), R. Polícia da Segurança Pública, across from the youth hostel.

Hospital: (☎ 289 89 11 00), R. Leão Pinedo, north of town.

Post Office: (☎ 289 86 03 82), Largo Carmo, across from the Igreja de Nossa Senhora do Carmo. Open M-F 8:30am-6:30pm, Sa 9am-12:30pm. **Postal Code:** 8000.

Internet Access: Free at the **Instituto Português de Juventude,** next to the youth hostel (open M-F 9am-7pm; 30min. limit). Also at the **Ciencia Viva** (Science Alive museum), on R. Comandante Francisco Manuel (☎ 289 89 09 20). From Pr. Gomes, walk through the gardens and turn right, heading toward the docks. Unlimited use 400$, students 200$. Wednesday 50% off. Open July-Sept. 15 Tu-Su 4-11pm; Sept. 16-June Tu-F 10am-5pm, Sa-Su 3-7pm.

🏠 ACCOMMODATIONS

Rooms are always available here, even during high season. Lodgings surround the bus and train stations. Most of the low-end budget *pensões* are plain but suffice. For something cheap and cheerful, try to scrape up a *quarto;* the tourist office maintains a top-20 list of possibilities.

Pensão-Residencial Central, Largo Terreiro Do Bispo, 12 (☎ 289 80 72 91), near the pedestrian area up R. 1 de Maio. Clean, bright, comfortable rooms, all with bath and TV, some with terraces. Reception 10am-1am. 3am curfew/lockout. June-Sept. singles 5000$; doubles 7000-7500$. Oct.-May singles 5000$; doubles 6500-700$.

Casa de Hóspedes Adelaide, R. Cruz das Mestras, 7-9 (☎ 289 80 23 83; fax 289 82 68 70). 12 rough, but clean rooms with kitchen access. The roof is a wonderful place to relax. Reception 10am-3am. Singles 3500$, with bath 5000$; doubles 5500$, with bath 7000$; quads 10,000$. 1000-4000$ discount in winter.

Pensão-Residencial Oceano, R. Ivens, 21, 2nd fl. (☎ 289 82 33 49). From Pr. Gomes, head up R. 1 de Maio; it's 1 block up on the right. 22 comfortable rooms with bath, phones, and TV. Breakfast 300$. July-Sept. singles 7000$; doubles 8000$; triples 10,500$. 500-1000$ discount Apr.-June and Oct. Nov.-Mar. singles 3000-4000$; doubles 4500-5000$; triples 6000$. V, MC, AmEx.

Pensão São Filipe, R. Infante Dom Henrique, 55, 2nd fl. (☎/fax 289 82 41 82). From the train station go up R. Ventura Coelho 3 blocks and turn right onto R. Infante Dom Henrique. A short walk from the center of town, these 10 rooms are quieter than others, comfortable, and close to the train and bus stations. Oct.-June singles 4500-5500$, doubles 6000-7000$; July-Sept. singles 7000$, doubles 8500$.

Pousada da Juventude (HI), R. Polícia de Segurança Pública (☎/fax 289 82 65 21), opposite the police station. Good value. Kitchen and TV room. Breakfast included. Reception 8am-noon and 6pm-midnight. Singles 1500-1900$; doubles 3500-4600$.

⬤ FOOD

Almonds and figs are native to the Algarve; local bakeries take good advantage of this and transform them into delicious marzipan and fig desserts. Faro has some of the Algarve's best cafes, many along R. Conselheiro Bívar, off Pr. Gomes. At the **market,** away from the center in Largo Dr. Francisco Sá Carneiro, locals barter fresh seafood (open daily 8am-1:30pm). Live the high life on R. Santo António, a pedestrian district where costly *marisqueiras* (seafood restaurants) and credit cards reign, or shop at **Supermercado Minipreço,** Largo Terreiro do Bispo, 8-10. (☎ 289 80 77 34. Open M-Sa 9am-8pm.)

Churrasqueira Fim do Mundo, R. Vasco da Gama, 53 (☎ 82 62 99). Go up R. 1 de Maio into the small square and turn right onto R. Vasco da Gama. It's the end of the world, and you'll feel fine with traditional Portuguese cuisine. Fish entrees 800-1300$. Meat entrees 650-1300$. Open M 11am-3pm, W-Su 11am-3pm and 6-10pm.

Pastelaria Chantilly, R. Vasco da Gama, 63A (☎ 289 82 07 80), next to Fim do Mundo. Indulge in delicious marzipan sweets and other homemade pastries (110-280$). Coffee 80-170$. Open daily June-Aug. 8am-midnight; Sept.-May M-Sa 8am-7pm.

⬤ ♪ SIGHTS AND ENTERTAINMENT

Faro's old town is a jewel—untouristed and traditional, it is a medley of ornate churches, museums, and shops selling local handicrafts. From Pr. Gomes, walk through the gardens to get to the entrance of the old town. Next to the tourist office, the early 19th-century **Arco da Vila** pierces the old city wall.

■ **CAPELA DOS OSSOS.** Step into **Igreja de Nossa Senhora do Carmo** to inspect the Capela dos Ossos (Chapel of Bones), a wall-to-wall macabre bonanza of crusty bones and fleshless skulls "borrowed" from the adjacent cemetery. Though not as spectacular as Évora's bone chapel, it's still worth a look. (*Lg. Carmo, in the city center.* ☎ 289 82 44 90. Open M-F 10am-1pm and 3-5pm, Sa 10am-1pm. Church free, chapel 120$.)

MUSEU DA MARINHA. The Museu da Marinha, near the marina and by the Hotel Eva, flaunts three notable and interesting boat models: the boat that took Vasco da Gama on his epic journey to India in 1497; the boat used by a group of imperialists on a ride up the Congo River in 1482; and a boat that out-classed the Turkish navy in 1717. (☎ 289 80 36 01. Open M-F 2-4:45pm. 100$.)

CATHEDRAL (SÉ). A narrow road leads through an Arab portico to the Renaissance cathedral, which stands in a deserted square. The **Capela do Rosário**, decorated with 17th-century *azulejos* and a red chinoiserie organ, interrupt the cathedral's understated Renaissance interior. Under the cathedral—a site once sacred to Romans, Visigoths, and Moors—lie traces of Neolithic civilization. The striking **cloister** is an ideal spot to relax with a book from the municipal library, housed in the same building. *(Open M-Sa 10am-6pm. 250$.)*

OTHER SIGHTS. The city's **Museu Regional do Algarve de Etnografia**, Pr. Liberdade, 2, introduces visitors to the folk life of the Algarve, with photos of the once-tranquil fishing villages of Lagos, Albufeira, and Faro. (☎ 289 82 76 10. Open M-F 9am-12:30pm and 2-5pm. 500$.) Behind the church, **Museu Municipal de Arqueológico e Lapidar** flashes assorted royal memorabilia, from diamond-studded hairpins to silver spurs and swords. (☎ 289 87 08 70. Open M-F 10am-6:30pm. 110$.)

ENTERTAINMENT. Sidewalk **cafes** crowd the pedestrian walkways off the garden in the center of town, and several **bars** populated by a young crowd liven R. Conselheiro Bívar and its side streets. One notable spot is **Upa Upa Café & Bar**, R. Conselheiro Bívar, 51, where the mixed crowd of locals and tourists spills out into the large patio. (☎ 289 80 78 32. Beer 300-500$. Mixed drinks 600-700$. Coffee 150-300$. Open daily 9pm-4am.) Faro's rock-free **beach** hides on an islet off the coast. Take bus #16 from the bus station or the stop in front of the tourist office, just across the garden from Pr. Gomes (5-10min., every hr. 7:10am-8:40pm, 170$).

OLHÃO

Olhão, 8km east of Faro, prefers fish to tourists. For hundreds of years, the few inhabitants of the area were fishermen, and modern locals have continued the tradition, helping to create one of Portugal's most productive fishing industries. Yet beyond this no-frills town, gorgeous beaches spread over the neighboring islands, easily accessible by ferry from Olhão's dock. Between the islands and Olhão's coast lies part of the **Parque Natural da Ria Formosa**, with its numerous species of exotic birds (including flamingos) and other water-based wildlife.

▊ TRANSPORTATION. The **train station** is on Av. Combatentes da Grande Guerra one block from Av. República. (☎ 289 70 53 78. Open daily 6:20-11am, 11:40am-7:30pm, 8:10-10:45pm.) **Trains** run to: **Faro** (10min., 17 per day 6:55am-10:45pm, 140$); **Tavira** (30min., 18 per day 6:20am-12:45am, 230$); and **Vila Real de Santo António** (1¼hr., 14 per day 6:20am-12:45am, 400$). The **bus station** is on R. General Humberto Delgado, one block from Av. República. (☎ 289 70 21 57. Open daily 7am-8pm.) **Eva buses** run to: **Faro** (20min., 11 per day 7:35am-7:50pm, 210$); **Tavira** (40min., 11 per day 7:35am-7:50pm, 330$); and **Vila Real de Santo António** (1½hr., 9 per day 7:35am-6:40pm, 570$).

▊▊ ORIENTATION AND PRACTICAL INFORMATION. To reach the **port** from Av. República, which cuts through the heart of town, turn down R. Diogo de Mendonça Corte Real or R. Leonardo (heading away from the bus and train stations) for a few blocks then turn right onto R. Gil Eanes, which becomes R. Conserveira as it nears the ferry dock. Alternatively, weave down to Av. 5 de Outubro, which runs parallel to the water, and turn left. The **tourist office** is on Lg. Sebastião Martins Mestre, an offshoot of R. Comércio. From the train station, head straight down R. 1 de Maio and left on R. General Humberto Delgado. Go right at the intersection with Av. República, and straight onto R. Comércio; the office is around the bend on the left. Its English-speaking staff has maps, ferry schedules, and sometimes free **luggage storage** during the day—ask nicely. (☎ 289 71 39 36. May-Sept. open Tu-Th 9:30am-7pm, F-M 9:30am-noon and 1-5:30pm; Oct.-Apr. open M-F 9:30am-noon and 1-5:30pm.) In an **emergency**, call ☎ 112. The **post office** is at Av. República, 17 (☎ 289 70 06 03; open M-F 8:30am-6pm) and the **postal code** is 8700.

A SLUG IN THE FACE Escargot? Well, not exactly. One of Portugal's favorite snack foods is the lowly *caracol* (snail). Unlike their classier French counterparts, *caracóis* are eaten in massive portions, boiled in shells with just a bit of salt and a sprig of fresh oregano. No forks here—pile a heap of the little creepies on your plate and skewer them with a toothpick. True connoisseurs use a needle-like spine carved out of palm leaves. If the dainty method doesn't suit you, crack the shell between your teeth. On a rainy day you might see folks prodding along the roadside in search of a snack; feel free to join in the fun. Alternatively, save your energy (the little fellas are surprisingly quick)—*caracóis* are served at restaurants across the country.

■□ ACCOMMODATIONS AND FOOD. Pensão Bela Vista, R. Teófilo Braga, 65-67, off a dusty side street around the corner from the tourist office, has nine cheerful, tiled rooms with TVs, some with baths. Exit the tourist office, turn left, take the first left and then the first right. (☎ 289 70 25 38. Singles 4000$; doubles 6000$.) **Pensão Boémia,** R. Cerca, 20, sits pretty with bright, clean rooms, all with bath, TV, and air conditioning. From the train or bus station, take Av. República and turn right on R. 18 de Junho. After four blocks on R. 18 de Junio, turn left again. (☎/fax 289 71 45 13. Breakfast included. Singles 5000-7000$; doubles 8000$. Discount in the winter. V, MC, AmEx.) Olhão's highly recommended year-round campground is the **Parque de Campismo dos Bancários do Sul e Ilhas.** It's off the highway outside of town and can be accessed by "Camara Municipal de Olhão" buses (9 per day 7:45am-7:15pm) which leave from in front of the gardens on R. 5 de Outubro. (☎ 289 70 03 00; fax 289 70 03 90. Showers included; July-Aug. 620$ per person, 440-1040$ per tent, 520$ per car; June and Sept. 520$ per person, 380-880$ per tent, 440$ per car; Oct.-May 310$ per person, 230-520$ per tent, 260$ per car).

Supermercado São Nicolau, R. General Humberto Delgado, 62, lies up the block from the bus station (open M-Sa 8am-8pm). The **market,** housed in two red brick buildings, is adjacent to the city gardens along the river, near Pr. Patrão J. Lopes (open M-Sa 8am-1:30pm). Many eateries on Av. 5 de Outubro grill the day's catch. At **Casa de Pasto O Bote,** Av. 5 de Outubro, 122, pick your slippery, silvery meal from the trays of fresh fish and watch it get charcoal-grilled right before your eyes. (☎ 289 72 11 83. Entrees 850-1400$. Open M-Sa 11am-3pm and 7-11pm).

▐▌ DAYTRIPS FROM OLHÃO

ARMONA (15MIN.), **CULATRA** (30MIN.), **FAROL** (45MIN.)

*Ferries go to **Armona** from Olhão's dock, near the intersection of R. Conserveira and R. 5 de Outubro; buy tickets from the stand (15min.; June M-F 9 per day 7:40am-7:30pm, Sa-Su 11 per day 8am-7:30pm; July-Aug. 13 per day 7:30am-8pm; Sept.-May 8:30am, noon, and 5pm; 170$; last return trip in June 8pm, July-Aug. 8:30pm). Another fleet serves **Culatra** (30min.; June-Aug. every 2hr. 7am-7:30pm; Sept.-May 4 per day 7am-6:30pm; 180$; last return trip June-Aug. 8pm) and **Farol** (45min.; June-Aug. every 2hr. 7am-7:30pm; Sept.-May 4 per day 7am-6:30pm; 230$; last return trip June-Aug. 8:20pm).*

Long expanses of uncrowded, sandy beach and deep blue sea surround **Ilhas Armona, Culatra,** and **Farol,** the three major islands off the coast of Olhão. Armona is the closest, followed by Culatra, and then Farol; all three are easy daytrips from Olhão. The farther away, the quieter the beaches become, although all of them have barely a fraction of the human traffic in more touristed parts of the Algarve. The islands and sandbars just offshore fence off the Atlantic, creating an important wetland habitat **(Parque Nacional da Ria Formosa)** for birds, fish, and other creatures. If you miss the last ride back from Armona, accommodations are available at Orbitur's **campsite** on the central path, five minutes from the dock. Twenty-nine bungalows, each of which house up to four people, require a minimum stay of two nights. At 9300$ per night from July to August, it's best not to find yourself stranded here. (☎ 289 71 41 73. Open May-Oct. Reception 9:30am-9:30pm.) Expect to pay a little more for snacks and meals on the islands than on the mainland. Several restaurant-bars vie for attention at the dock (entrees 1000-2000$).

TAVIRA

Farmers tease police by riding their motor scooters over the Roman pedestrian bridge, and that's about as eventful as Tavira gets. But for most visitors to this easy-going fishing port, that's just fine. White houses and palm trees fringe the river banks, and festive Baroque churches dot the hills above. Tavira has recently become a popular haven for travelers in search of relaxation on the peaceful beaches. But despite the influx of tourists, the town has kept its calm.

Most of Tavira's sights are scattered among the side streets off Pr. República. Steps off the *praça* lead past the tourist office to the **Igreja da Misericórdia,** whose superb Renaissance doorway has faces sprouting from twisting vines. (Open daily 9:30am-noon and 2:30-5pm. Free.) Just beyond, the remains of the city's **Castelo Mouro** (Moorish Castle) sit next to the church **Santa Maria do Castelo,** whose garden brims with flowers. (Castle and church open daily 9am-5pm. Free.) The seven-arched pedestrian-only **Ponte Romana** footbridge leads to the floral Pr. 5 de Outubro. From Pr. Padinha, head up R. Alvares Botelho to the **Igreja do Carmo.** The church's elaborately decorated chancel resembles a 19th-century opera set, with false perspectives giving the illusion of windows and niches supported by columns. (Open M-F 10am-1pm. Free.) Local beaches, including **Araial do Barril,** are accessible year-round by the bus to Pedras D'el Rei (10min., 8 per day 8:25am-6:10pm, 170$). To reach the excellent beach on **Ilha da Tavira,** an island 2km away, follow the directions to the island's campsite (below).

To get to the **tourist office, R. Galeria, 9,** up some steps off Pr. República, turn left from the bus station and follow the road to the *praça.* The English-speaking staff doles out maps and lodgings info. (☎ 281 32 25 11. Open daily M-Sa 9:30am-12:30pm and 2-5:30pm.) Rent **bikes** and **scooters** from **Loris Rent,** on R. Galeria next to the tourist office. (☎ 281 32 52 03. Mountain bikes 800-1000$ per day. Scooters 3000-4800$ per day.) In an **emergency** dial ☎ 112; for **police** call ☎ 281 32 20 22; the **Centro de Saúde (health center)** can be reached at ☎ 281 32 90 00. **Internet access** is available at **Snack-Bar Bela Fria** (see **Accommodations and Food,** below), but don't be fooled by the "free Internet" signs; you have to pay 200$ per 15min. The **post office,** R. Liberdade, 64, one block uphill from Pr. República, offers Posta Restante (open M-F 9am-6pm). The **postal code** is 8800.

There is no shortage of accommodations in Tavira. To find riverfront 🔆**Pensão Residencial Lagôas Bica,** R. Almirante Cândido dos Reis, 24, from Pr. República, cross the pedestrian bridge and continue straight down R. A. Cabreira; turn right and go down one block. This *pensaõ* has well-furnished rooms, an outdoor patio and rooftop picnic area, a sitting room, washing facilities, and a fridge for guest use. (☎ 281 32 22 52. July-Sept. singles 3500; doubles 5000$, with bath 7000$. 500$ cheaper in winter.) Back on the other side of the river, recently renovated **Pensão Residencial Castelo,** R. Liberdade, 22, features bright, spacious rooms and beautiful apartments, all with bath, phones, and TV. (☎ 281 32 07 90; fax 281 32 07 99. Breakfast included. Laundry 1000$ per load. Singles 6000-7000$; doubles 9000$; apartments 15,000$, 4-person max.) The privately run **Ilha de Tavira campground,** with its entourage of snack bars and restaurants, sprawls on the beach of an island 2km from Pr. República. (☎ 281 32 44 55; fax 281 32 17 16. Reception 8am-11pm. Showers 100$. 430$ per person, 700-800$ per tent. Open May-Oct. 15.) To get there, take the ferry from the "Quatro Águas" dock at the end of Estrada das 4 Aguas, a 2km walk downstream along the river, or catch the summer ferry from Lg. Dr. José Pires Padinha, just up R. Cais from Pr. República. (Sept. 16-June ferry 200$ round-trip. July-Sept. 15 ferry every 15min. 8:30am-midnight, 250$ round-trip.) Cafes and restaurants line Pr. República and opposite the garden on R. José Pires Padinha. On the other side of the river, across from the bus station, **Snack-Bar Bela Fria,** R. Pelames, 1, offers up lighter meals and Internet access. (☎ 281 32 53 75. Sandwiches 230-400$. Desserts 120-550$. Coffee 90-150$. Cocktails 850$).

Trains (☎ 281 32 23 54) leave Tavira for **Vila Real de Santo António** (30min., 14 per day 6:55am-1:10am, 260$); **Olhão** (30min., 17 per day 6:20am-10:10pm, 230$); and **Faro** (40min., 17 per day 6:20am-10:10pm, 300$). **EVA buses** (☎ 281 32 25 46) leave from the station upriver from Pr. República for **Olhão** (45min., 11 per day 6:50am-

7:10pm, 330$); **Vila Real de Santo António** (40min., 10 per day 6:55am-7:20pm, 405$); and **Faro** (1hr., 11 per day 6:50am-7:10pm, 435$). From the **train station** you can catch the local TUT bus to the town center (10min., every 30min. 8am-8pm, 100$) or call a taxi (☎ 281 32 15 44 or 281 32 67 88; about 650$).

VILA REAL DE SANTO ANTÓNIO

Located at the east end of the Algarve and at the mouth of the Rio Guadiana, Vila Real de Santo António is a common transfer point for travelers going to Spain. Before the construction of the highway bridge between the two countries was completed in 1992, the town got a lot more tourist traffic than it does today, as marooned Spain-bound travelers frequently spent the night. **Trains** (☎ 281 51 37 77) run to **Faro** (1hr., 13 per day 6am-9:45pm, 520$) and **Lagos** (3hr., 7 per day 6:35am-9:45pm, 1010$). To get to Spain, you can take the **ferry to Ayamonte, Spain** (every 30min. 8am-8pm; 180$ per person, 480$ per car) and from the main square catch a direct **bus** to **Huelva, Spain** (2hr., every hr., 540ptas). **Eva buses** (☎ 281 51 18 07) from Vila Real to the rest of the Algarve are more expensive, more reliable, and faster than trains. They service: **Tavira** (40min., 9 per day 7:05-6:30pm, 405$); and **Faro** (1½hr., 9 per day 7:05am-6:30pm, 625$). **Rede Expressos** buses go to **Lisbon** (6hr., 5 per day 6:30am-11:15pm, 2600$), leaving from the esplanade near the train station and the river. Buses to **Sevilla, Spain** (3hr., 2 per day 9:10am and 5:15pm, 1800$) eliminate the hassle of train-ferry-bus transfers. If stuck for a night in Vila Real de Santo António, try the **Pousada da Juventude (HI)**, R. D. Sousa Martins, 40, a white building on the fifth street from the river, two blocks to the left of R. Teófilo Braga. A living room, bar, kitchen, and washing facilities complement decent quarters. (☎/fax 281 54 45 65. Breakfast included. Reception daily 8am-noon. Lockout noon-6pm, but dropoff all day. Reserve at least 3 days in advance. June-Aug. dorms 1700$; doubles 3800$. Sept.-May dorms 1400$; doubles with bath 3200$.)

CENTRAL PORTUGAL

ALENTEJO

The Alentejo province covers almost one-third of Portugal, but with a population barely over half a million it remains the country's least populated and least touristed region. Its arid plains stretch to the horizon, punctuated only by olive and cork-oak trees. Endless wheat fields and the vineyards covering the rolling hills of northern Alentejo make the region a vast granary, though severe droughts have restricted its agricultural capacity. Évora, Elvas, and other medieval towns preserve their relatively pristine state in the Alentejo Alto (upper), while Beja remains the only major town on the seemingly endless Alentejo Baixo (lower) plain. The Alentejo is at its best in the spring; if you come in summer, be prepared for temperatures that can soar above 40°C (100°F).

HIGHLIGHTS OF THE ALENTEJO

The "museum city" of **Évora**, especially its fabulous **cathedral**—perhaps Portugal's finest—and its uniquely grotesque **Capela dos Ossos** (see p. 588).

The friendly, lively little town of **Elvas** (see p. 590).

LOCAL FESTIVAL IN ALENTEJO

The entire town of **Évora** turns out for the *Feira de São João*, a seven-day extravaganza starting the last Friday in June. Carnival rides, local dance troupes, bullfights and a circus abolish small-town "tranquility," at least for a week.

ÉVORA

Designated a World Heritage site by the United Nations, Évora (pop. 54,000) is known as the "Museum City," and rightly so. Considered Portugal's foremost showpiece of medieval architecture, the picture-perfect town boasts a Roman temple, an impressive cathedral, streets that wind past Moorish arches, and a 16th-century university, as well as several noteworthy churches. Elegant shops flash their wares in the windows, students chat on the streets, and a steady but not overwhelming stream of tourists flows in from Lisbon and the Algarve.

⌨ TRANSPORTATION

Trains: (☎ 266 70 21 25). On the Lisbon-Faro route. To: **Beja** (2hr., 4 per day 8:30am-12:40am, 770-1050$); **Lisbon** (3hr., 5 per day 5:15am-2:50am, 1075$); **Faro** (5hr., 7:15pm, 1720$); **Porto** (6½hr.; 3 per day 5:15am-2:15pm; 2650$) via Lisbon.

Buses: (☎ 266 76 94 10), on Av. Sebastião, just outside the town wall. Much more convenient than trains. To: **Beja** (1½hr., 6-8 per day 8:20am-8:20pm, 1200$); **Elvas** (1½-2hr., 3-5 per day 8am-9:05pm, 1300$); **Portalegre** (2hr., 4 per day 10:25am-5:40pm, 950-1350$); **Lisbon** (2-2½hr., 10 per day 6am-8pm, 1550$); **Faro** (5hr., 4 per day 8:45am-6pm, 1900$); **Vila Real de Santo António** (6hr., 2 per day 8:30am via Coimbra and 1:30pm via Viseu, 3100$); **Porto** (7hr., 5 per day 6am-8pm, 2700$); **Braga** (8½hr., 5 per day 6am-8pm, 3000$).

Taxis: (☎ 266 73 47 34 or 266 73 47 35). Taxis hang out 24hr. in Pr. Giraldo.

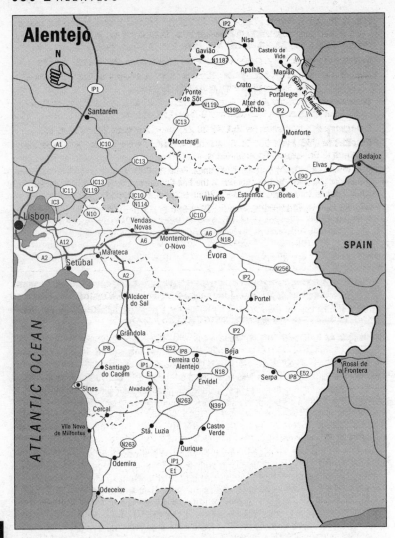

Alentejo

N

IP2
Nisa
Gavião
Castelo de Vide
N118
Apalhão
Marvão
IP1
Crato
Serra S. Mamede
Ponte de Sór
Portalegre
Santarém
N119
Alter do Chão
N369
IP2
IC13
Monforte
A1
IC10
Montargil
IC13
Badajoz
Elvas
A1
IC11
N119
IC13
Vimieiro
Estremoz
E90
IP7
Borba
IC3
IC10
Lisbon
N114
IC10
A6
N10
Vendas Novas
Évora
N18
A12
Montemor-O-Novo
A6
SPAIN
A2
Marateca
N256
Setúbal
A2
IP2
Alcácer do Sal
Portel
ATLANTIC OCEAN
Grândola
IP2
IP8
E52
IP8
Beja
IP1
Ferreira do Alentejo
Rosal de la Frontera
Santiago do Cacém
E1
N18
Serpa
IP8
E52
Sines
Alvadade
Ervidel
Cercal
N263
N391
Vila Nova de Milfontes
Stª. Luzia
Castro Verde
N263
Ourique
Odemira
IP1
E1
Odeceixe

CENTRAL PORTUGAL

✦ 🛈 ORIENTATION AND PRACTICAL INFORMATION

Évora is accessible by train from most major cities, including Lisbon, but buses are more convenient. No direct bus connects the **train station** to the center of town. To avoid hiking 20 minutes up R. Dr. Baronha from the station, hail a taxi (600$) or flag down bus #6 (130$), which halts a short way down the tracks. Near the edge of town, Av. Dr. Barahona turns into R. República, which leads to **Praça do Giraldo,** the town center and the location of most monuments and lodgings. From the bus station, turn right up Av São Sebastião, which turns into R. Serpa Pinto at the town wall and leads to Pr. Giraldo.

Tourist Office: Pr. Giraldo, 73 (☎ 266 70 26 71), to the left when facing the church. Helpful staff compensates for the illegible map. Open Apr.-Sept. M-F 9am-7pm, Sa-Su 9am-12:30pm and 2-5:30pm; Oct.-Mar. daily 9am-12:30pm and 2-5:30pm.

Currency Exchange: 24hr. machine outside the tourist office. Banks on Pr. Giraldo.

Luggage Storage: At the bus station. 150$ per bag. Open daily 8:30am-12:30pm and 2:30-5pm. Also available short term at the tourist office.

Laundromat: Lavandaria Ana, R. Aviz, 78 (☎ 266 70 73 88), up from Largo de Camões. 1000$ per kg. Open M-F 9am-1pm and 3-7pm, Sa 9am-1pm.

Emergency: ☎ 112. **Police:** (☎ 266 70 20 22), on R. Francisco Soares Lusitano.

Hospital: (☎ 266 74 01 00), Lg. Senhor da Pobreza, near the city wall and the intersection with R. Dr. Augusto Eduardo Nunes.

Post Office: (☎ 266 74 54 83), R. Olivença. From Pr. Giraldo, walk up R. João de Deus, take your first right (by the aqueduct), the first left uphill, then right at Pr. de Sertória. **Posta Restante** and **fax.** Open M-F 8:30am-6:30pm. **Postal Code:** 7000.

Internet Access: ▩ **Oficin@,** R. Moeda, 27 (☎266 70 73 12), off Pr. Giraldo. Also a lively bar with friendly, English-speaking staff. 100$ for 10min., 500$ per hr. Open daily Apr.-Sept. Tu-F 8pm-3am, Sa 9pm-3am; Oct.-Mar. Tu-F 8pm-2am, Sa 9pm-2am.

▟ ACCOMMODATIONS

Most hostels cluster on side streets around Pr. Giraldo. They are crowded in summer, especially during the late June mega-fest, Feira de São João, so reserve ahead. Prices drop 500 to 1000$ in winter. *Quartos*, from 4000 or 5000$ per double, are pleasant summer alternatives to crowded *pensões*.

▧ **Pousada da Juventude (HI),** R. Miguel Bombarda, 40 (☎ 266 74 48 48; fax 266 74 48 43). From the end of Pr. Giraldo opposite the church, walk down R. República a short distance and bear left on R. Miguel Bombarda; it's on the right. Recently converted from a hotel, this place is simply great. TV and entertainment rooms, bar, parking, and a friendly staff reward weary travelers. Breakfast included. Reception 8am-midnight. In summer, reserve through **Movijem** (☎ 21 359 60 00). June 16-Sept. 15 dorms 2500$; doubles with bath 6000$. Sept. 16-June 15 dorms 2000$; doubles 5000$.

▧ **Casa Palma,** R. Bernardo Mato, 29-A (☎ 266 70 35 60). From the tourist office, walk down the street and 3 blocks to the right. Pink bedspreads, a friendly owner, and a homey atmosphere make this place popular with backpackers. Bright doubles on the bottom floor, dimmer singles upstairs, all with TVs. Singles 2500-3000$, with bath 3500-4000$; doubles 5000-6000$, with bath 6500-7000$.

▧ **Pensão Giraldo,** R. Mercadores, 27 (☎ 266 70 58 33). From the tourist office, turn left, walk 2 blocks, and turn left again. Smallish singles and huge doubles, all with TVs and in a central location. Reserve a week ahead in summer. July-Sept. singles 6000$, with bath 7500$; doubles 6500$, with bath 8500$. Oct.-May singles 3000$, with bath 4500$; doubles 4000$, with bath 6000$. June singles 4000$, with bath 6500$; doubles 7500$, with bath 8000$. V, MC.

▧ **Pensão Os Manueis,** R. Raimundo, 35 (☎ 266 70 28 61), around the corner from the tourist office. A good deal. Ask for a room in the recently renovated section. Singles 2500-3500$, with bath 5000-6000$; doubles 4000-5000$, with bath 6000-7000$.

▧ **Orbitur's Parque de Campismo de Évora** (☎ 266 70 51 90; fax 70 98 30), a 3-star park on Estrada das Alcáçovas, which branches off at the bottom of R. Raimundo. A 30min. walk to town, but bus #14 (Malagueira) goes to the campsite and Pr. Giraldo (M-F 20 per day 7:35am-7:40pm, Sa 6 per day 7:50am-1:10pm). A taxi is 600$ or so. Washing machine and a market. Reception 8am-10pm. June-Sept. 640$ per person, 540-640$ per tent, 550$ per car; Oct.-Mar. 380$ per person, 300-380$ per tent, 330$ per car; Apr.-May 580$ per person, 450-580$ per tent, 500$ per car. V, MC, AmEx.

⬤ FOOD

Many budget restaurants are scattered near Pr. Giraldo, especially along R. Merca-dores. Setting up in the square in front of Igreja de São Francisco and the public gardens, the **market** sells produce, flowers, and a wild assortment of cheese (open Tu-Su 8am-1pm). For more processed food, try **Maxigrula**, R. João de Deus, 130. (☎ 266 70 22 62. Open M-Sa 9am-7pm.)

Restaurante A Choupana, R. Mercadores, 16-20 (☎ 266 70 44 27), off Pr. Giraldo, across from Pensão Giraldo. Snack bar on the left for a budget lunch, restaurant on the right for elegant Portuguese cuisine. Entrees 700-1800$. Half-portions 800-850$. *Pratos do dia* 1200-1300$. Half-portions 650-700$. Open M-Sa 10am-2am. V, MC, AmEx.

Pastelaria Bijou, R. da República, 15, off Pr. Giraldo. Popular pastry shop serves delicious snacks. Coffee 80-120$. Sweets 100-220$. Open daily 7am-7:30pm.

Restaurante A Gruta, Av. General Humberto Delgado, 2 (☎ 266 70 81 86). Exit Pr. Giraldo, follow R. República 15 toward the train station, and turn right at the end of the park; the restaurant is on the left. A Gruta is a crowded, casual, local hangout known for its lip-smacking *frango no churrasco* (barbecued chicken) buried under a heap of fries. Half-chicken 700$. Entrees 1050-1200$. Open Su-F noon-3pm and 5-10:30pm.

◉ SIGHTS

Streets brimming with architectural riches earned the "Museum City" its status as a UN World Heritage site.

▓**CAPELLA DE OSSOS.** One must-see is the truly bizarre Capella de Ossos (Chapel of Bones), attached to the pleasant **Igreja Real de São Francisco.** Above the door an irreverent sign taunts visitors: "*Nós ossos que aqui estamos, pelos vossos esperamos*" ("We bones lie here awaiting yours"). Don't let the seemingly normal exterior fool you; the interior is made entirely out of human bones. Three Franciscan monks took the remains of 5000 people (reportedly fellow monks) in order to construct this perverse chapel. Enormous femurs and baby tibias neatly panel every inch of wall, while rows of skulls and an occasional pelvis line the capitals and ceiling vaults. The three innovative founders grimace from stone sarcophagi to the right of the altar. *(Follow R. República from Pr. Giraldo; the church is on the right and the chapel is around back to the right of the main entrance. Open M-Sa 9am-1pm and 2:30-6pm. Closed Su. 100$, students and with photography permit 50$.)*

TEMPLE AND CHURCH. Évora's most famous monument is the 2nd-century **Roman temple,** which served for centuries as a slaughterhouse. Only a platform and 14 Corinthian columns remain today. Climbing up into the temple is a no-no. Immediately facing the temple is the town's best-kept secret, the **Igreja de São João Evangelista** (1485). The church is owned by the Cadaval family, who reside in their ancestors' ducal palace next door. The interior is covered with dazzling *azulejos*, but you must ask to be let into the church's hidden chambers. *(Largo do Vila Flor. Open Tu-Su 10am-12:30pm and 2-6pm. 500$ for church, 850$ for church and exhibition hall.)*

CATHEDRAL. The 12 Apostles adorning the doorway of this colossal 12th-century cathedral are masterpieces of medieval Portuguese sculpture. The **cloister** is designed in ponderous 14th-century Romanesque style, with staircases spiraling to its roof. The **Museu de Arte Sacra,** in a gallery above the nave, houses the cathedral's treasury and a 13th-century ivory *Virgem do paraíso*. *(From the center of Pr. Giraldo, head up R. 5 de Outubro. Cathedral open daily 9am-12:30pm and 2-5pm. Cloisters open daily 9am-noon and 2-4:30pm. Museum open Tu-Su 9am-noon and 2-4:30pm. Cloisters and museum 450$. Cathedral free.)*

MUSEU DE ÉVORA. Since the discovery of Roman, Visigoth, and Moorish ruins under its floor, archaeologists have sought to explore the basement of the building. Nowadays, both the museum's collection (ranging from Roman tombs to a 17th-century Virgin Mary) and the fascinating on-site digging capture the attention of visitors. *(Turn left at the top of R. 5 de Outubro when coming from Pr. Giraldo. Open W-Su 9am-12:30pm and 2-5:30pm, Tu 2-5pm. 300$, students 150$.)*

CENTRAL PORTUGAL

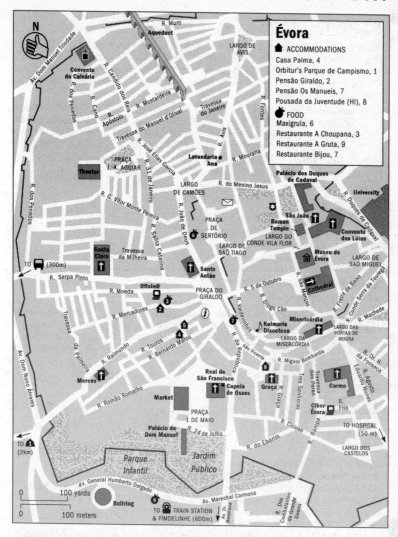

Évora

🏠 **ACCOMMODATIONS**
Casa Palma, 4
Orbitur's Parque de Campismo, 1
Pensão Giraldo, 2
Pensão Os Manueis, 7
Pousada da Juventude (HI), 8

🍴 **FOOD**
Maxigrula, 6
Restaurante A Choupana, 3
Restaurante A Gruta, 9
Restaurante Bijou, 7

🎭🎵 NIGHTLIFE AND ENTERTAINMENT

Although most of Évora turns in with the sun, **Kalmaria Discoteca**, R. Valdevinos, 21-A, the second right off R. 5 de Outubro when coming from Pr. Giraldo, draws a mixed local and tourist crowd that lets loose to standard pop and dance music. (☎ 266 70 75 05. Cover 1000$, includes two beers. Beer 200$. Open M-Sa 10pm-6am.) Another bigger, modern club, **Fimdelinha**, Av. Combatentes de Grande Guerra, 56, plays more techno and has live tunes on Fridays and Saturdays around 11:30pm. Take R. República outside the city walls and follow the street parallel to and one block left of its continuation. Fimedelhina waits near the end of the railroad line—hence the club's name, which means "end of the line." (Open W-Sa 11pm-4am; closed Aug. Beer 200-400$. Mixed drinks 500-700$. Cover 1000$ for men, 500$ for women.) The liveliest Évora gets, day or night, is during the **Feira de São João**, which starts the last Friday in June and lasts for seven nights. The entire town turns out for carnival rides, local dance troupes, a bullfight, and a circus.

BARE IT ALL? Proverbially speaking, the Alentejo is the land that knows no shade... or at least, so they (the humans) say. The sheep, however, know better. To avoid the blazing sun beating mercilessly down on the Alentejan plains, they retreat en masse into the few square meters of shadow provided by the mushroom-like trees that dot the landscape. If you look closely, you will notice that there is something unique about these trees (besides the clumps of fuzzy livestock cowering beneath them), something very shocking, indeed. Unabashedly stripped to the bone, they flaunt their unprotected under-layers to all. These *quercus subers*, otherwise known as cork oaks, have unusually thick bark (actually the cambium, outer layers composed of dead phloem cells) that is shaved off meticulously by hand once every nine years to obtain cork. The harvest of the area yields 160,000 tons of cork per year, which amounts to 60% of the world's output, and quite a lot of nekkidness.

ELVAS

Elvas is dead, you say? No, the town is just keeping a low profile. Perched on a steep hill amid arid fields 12km from the Spanish border, Elvas is the perfect place for a taste of small-town Alentejo life. Though it's often a necessary stopover to or from nearby Badajoz, Spain, Elvas merits a trip in itself. The quiet hamlet combines all things lovable in a Portuguese town: lively streets, friendly people, good food, few tourists, ruins, and great views.

▐ TRANSPORTATION. The nearest **train station** (☎ 268 62 28 16) is 3km away in the town of Fontainhas and has service to **Badajoz, Spain** (15min., 12:10pm, 180$). A **taxi** (☎ 268 62 22 87) is the only way to get from the train station to town. **Buses** are the best transportation option from Évora, with a convenient **station** (☎ 268 62 28 75) and go to: **Caia,** on the border (20min., 6:40am and 2pm, 230$); **Portalegre** (1½hr., 7am, 735$); **Évora** (1½hr., 3 per day 8:15am-5:20pm, 1300$); **Lisbon** (3½hr., 9 per day 5am-6:30pm, 1700$); **Beja** (3½hr., 6:40am, 1600$); **Albufeira** (5½hr., 6:40am, 2100$); and **Faro** (6½hr., 6:40am, 2300$).

▐▐ ORIENTATION AND PRACTICAL INFORMATION. Buses stop just outside of town. To get to the **tourist office** in Pr. República, exit the station to the right and follow it past the little square on your left. Cross the street, walk a block and turn left into the tunnel, which leads directly to Pr. República; the tourist office is on the right. The English-speaking staff gives out maps and can help with finding accommodations. (☎ 268 62 22 36. Open Apr.-Sept. M-F 9am-6pm, Sa-Su 9am-12:30pm and 2-5:30pm; Oct.-Mar. open daily 9am-5:30pm.) For **Internet access,** go to **O Livreiro de Elvas,** R de Olivença, 4-A. (☎ 268 62 08 82. 1 computer. 340$ for 30min. Open M-F 9:30am-1pm and 3:15-7:15pm, Sa 9:30am-1pm.) Services include: **emergency** ☎ 112; **police** (☎ 268 62 26 13), on R. André Gonçalves; and the **hospital** (☎ 268 62 22 25), just outside of town. The **post office** is one block behind the tourist office. (☎ 268 62 26 96. Open M-F 9am-6pm.) The **postal code** is 7350.

▐▐ ACCOMMODATIONS AND FOOD. The few *pensões* in Elvas are boarding houses for semi-permanent residents. Renting a room in a private home may be the most practical option; try to bargain the price of a single down to 2500-3000$ and a double to 4000-5000$, and confirm price and amenities in advance. ◀**António Mocissoe e Garcia Coelho,** R. Aires Varela, 15, has comfortable rooms with TVs, private baths, and a nice homey atmosphere. From the tourist office, take a right out of the *praça* and then your first left (at Banco Nacional Ultramarino). Go left at the end of the street and follow the signs to Elvas Cama (owned by the same friendly couple), where the reception is located. (☎ 268 62 21 26. Breakfast 500$. Reservations recommended in summer. Singles 3000$; doubles 5000$; quads

8000$.) Campers may try **Camping Torre Des Arcas,** in an orchard 4km from Elvas accessible via the bus to Varche (10min., 5 per day 6:20am-7:20pm), a 10-minute walk from the orchard. (Hot showers 500$. 5000$ per car, per tent, and per 4-person family.) For fresh fish, fruits, and veggies, try the **mercado municipal** on Av. São Domingos (open M-Sa 8am-1pm). Many restaurants line R. Cadeira and the two streets perpendicular to it, R. Carreira and R. Alcamim, just steps from Pr. República. Meat-eaters will love **Canal 7,** R. Sapateiros, 16, on the right side of Pr. República, which specializes in *frango assado* (roast chicken) and other Portuguese-style meat entrees. The whole roasted pigs make for a unique treat. (Half-portion chicken 650$, whole 1100$. Entrees 650-1200$.)

⬛ SIGHTS. Elvas's main spectacle, the ⬛**Aqueduto da Amoreira,** emerges from a hill at the entrance to the city. Begun in 1529 and finished almost a century later (1622), the colossal structure is Europe's largest aqueduct (its 843 arches span almost 8000m). Soak up the view from the **castelo** above Pr. República—rows of olive trees stretch to the horizon in every direction. To the right of the entrance, a stairwell leads up to the castle walls. Upon request, an attendant will unlock the museum upstairs and show you around. (Castle open 9am-6pm. Free.) At Pr. República, **Igreja de Nossa Senhora da Assunção** dominates the mosaic-covered main square. Abstract *azulejos* and a beautifully ribbed ceiling give splendor to the church's interior, which was rebuilt in a Manueline style. (Open M-F 9am-noon and 2-5pm. Mass at 6pm.) Behind the cathedral and uphill to the right is the **Igreja de Nossa Senhora da Consolação dos Aflitos,** also known as **Freiras.** Its octagonal interior has beautiful geometric tiles. (Open Tu-Su 9:30am-12:30pm and 2:30-5:30pm.) In the three-sided *praça* stands the 16th-century **pelourinho,** an octagonal pillory (originally a medieval whipping post) culminating in a pyramid.

CASTELO DE VIDE

Situated 600m above sea level on the edge of the Serra de São Mamede, the town of Castelo de Vide (pop. 4500) has maintained an age-old charm rooted in its picture-perfect whitewashed houses, cobblestone streets, and flowering fountains. The **medieval quarter** is Castelo de Vide's unique attraction. Located just below its castle, the old town consists of a series of impossibly steep and narrow cobblestone alleys overflowing with potted plants, roses, and sunflowers. Up above, the **castelo,** completed in 1280, offers stunning views of surrounding mountains. (Open daily July-Sept. 9am-6pm; Oct.-June 9am-5pm.) The town center surrounds the two 19th-century *praças*, evidence of Castelo's popularity as a spa resort over 100 years ago. On weekends, the only way to get to **Marvão** is by taxi (about 1600$). During the week, **buses** run from behind the tourist office to **Marvão** (25min., M-F 5:30pm, 170$) and **Portalegre** (30min.; M-F 4 per day 8:05am-4:50pm, Sa-Su 8:05am and 4:50pm; 310$), which offers frequent connections to larger cities. The **train station,** which lies 4km out of town, is accessible only by taxi (☎ 245 90 12 71; 750$). Trains run to **Lisbon** (3hr., 3 per day 6:15am-5:55pm, 2200$) and **Madrid.** The **tourist office,** in the wide space where the buses stop, offers maps, helps find accommodations, and **stores luggage** temporarily. (☎ 245 90 13 61. Open daily July-Sept. 9am-7pm; Oct.-June 9am-12:30pm and 2-5:30pm.) Services include: **emergency** (☎ 112); **police** (☎ 245 90 13 14), on Av. Anamenha; and the **Centro de Saúde** (health center; ☎ 245 90 11 05), in Pr. Dom Pedro V, behind the tourist office.

MARVÃO

The walled city of Marvão (pop. 185) is an unreal relic of a distant past. Lost as much in time as in the enveloping fog that descends nightly, the town perches atop a craggy mountain overlooking the **Parque Natural de São Mamede.** This national park covers over 31,000 hectares and surrounds Marvão with hillsides and flowering meadows. Almost all of the whitewashed houses of this ageless town still lie within the 17th-century walls. Marvão's virtually impenetrable 13th-century

castelo, at the west end of town, sits on top of the rocky ridge, guarding this town that hasn't been seized in 700 years. Prior to the castle's construction, however, Marvão passed through several different owners, among them the Romans, Visigoths, and Moors. Remnants of these early days await at the **Museu Municipal,** near the castle in the **Igreja de Santa Maria.** (Open daily 8am-10pm. 200$, students 150$.

Buses run to **Castelo de Vide** (25min., M-F 7:15am and 1:05pm, 170$) and **Portalegre** (50min., M-F 7:15am and 1:05pm, 330$). Ask at the tourist office about express buses to **Lisbon** (5½hr., 7:30am, 2100$); you must buy tickets one day in advance. To get to the **train station** (☎ 245 99 22 88), 9km north of town, where service to Lisbon and Madrid is available, you'll have to take a taxi (☎ 245 99 32 72). Taxis are also a valid option for getting to **Castelo de Vide** (about 1600$). If you arrive by bus, you will be dropped off just outside the town wall. Enter through one of the gates and proceed up R. Cima until you see the pillory (ancient stone whipping-post) in Pr. Pelourinho (also a parking area). From Pr. Pelourinho, R. Espíritu Santo leads toward the castelo and the **tourist office,** which can help you find accommodations and figure out transportation. (☎ 245 99 38 86. Open July-Sept. M-F 9am-6:30pm, Sa-Su 9am-12:30pm and 2-6:30pm; Oct.-June daily 9am-12:30pm and 2-5:30pm.) In an **emergency** dial ☎ 112.

BEJA

Tucked amid the vast, monotonous wheat fields of the southern Alentejo, Beja is a town of beautiful architecture and truly scorching temperatures. Its name, pronounced like the Portuguese word for "kiss" (*beija*), is a corruption of its original name, Pax Julia, given to Beja by the Romans in 48 BC to commemorate the peace with the Lusitanians. The present name is highly appropriate, however, for this town is steamy in more ways than one (see **Scandals? Nun Here,** p. 593). But more than just the perfect setting for romantic exploits (and a summertime oven), Beja is also a haven of traditional food, music, and handicrafts.

☐ TRANSPORTATION. Trains run from the station (☎ 284 32 61 35), about 1km outside of town, to: **Évora** (1½hr., 3 per day 12:30-8:40pm, 750$); **Lisbon** (2½-3hr., 4 per day 7:45am-2:30am, 1530$); and **Faro** (3½hr., 9:30am and 9:10pm, 1330$) via Funcheira. The **bus station** (☎ 284 31 36 20) is on R. Cidade de São Paulo, near the corner of Av. Brasil. Buses go to: **Évora** (1½hr., 7 per day, 1200$); **Lisbon** (3-3½hr., 6 per day 7:10am-7:20pm, 1550$); **Faro** (3-3½hr., 6 per day 8:20am-7:20am, 1550$); **Porto** (8½-10hr., 3 per day 11am-2:30pm, 3100$) usually via Lisbon; **Braga** (10-12hr. 3 per day 11am-2:30pm, 3200$) usually via Lisbon; and **Picalho,** a border town with connections to Spain (1hr., 6 per day 10:50am- 9:15pm, 1100$).

◪🖉 ORIENTATION AND PRACTICAL INFORMATION. Rua de Mértola and **Rua de Capitão João Francisco de Sousa** run through the center of town. The streets are unmarked and confusing, especially in the town center; the tourist office's free map is quite useful. To get to the center from the bus station, walk straight out of the terminal and through the traffic circle (past the statue). After one block, turn right onto R. Afonso de Albuquerque, go past the post office on the left, and continue up the curving street. At the intersection, take a left on R. Capitão J. F. de Sousa. Those with heavy bags might want to take a **taxi** (☎ 284 32 24 74; 500-600$) from the train station rather than walk uphill for 20 minutes. If you do decide to walk, exit the station and walk left to Lg. da Estação, turning left onto R. Pedro Victor. Follow this street as it curves around the old town, becoming R. Frei Manuel de Albuquerque and then R. D. Nuno Alvares Pereira, finally intersecting with R. Portas de Mertola (which is not R. Mertola). Turn right and walk a half block, then cross the street to R. Capitão J. F. de Sousa.

SCANDALS? NUN HERE Maria Alcoforado, the daughter of a nobleman, was born in 1640; she entered the convent of Nossa Senhora da Conceição in Beja at age 11. By the age of 16 she had taken her vows and was well on her way to a life of celibacy and utter devotion to God. But in 1666, about 10 years later, French troops were stationed near Beja while helping out in the War of Restoration. The French knight Chamilly was in charge of these troops, and before long Maria and Chamilly had fallen hopelessly in love—hopeless because she could only exchange words with her boyfriend through her barred convent window (which today is on display in the Museu Rainha Dona Leonor). The scandalous affair prompted a tell-all account, *Five Letters of a Portuguese Nun*, published in Paris in 1669 and widely considered one of the masterpieces of the time. The letters were so good, in fact, that they reportedly inspired poets, novelists and artists like Rilke and Matisse, and the town of Beja was vaulted forever into the annal of sexual impropriety.

The **tourist office,** R. Capitão J. F. de Sousa, 25, has an English-speaking staff that hands out incredibly helpful maps. (☎ 284 31 19 13. Open May-Sept. M-Sa 9am-8pm; Oct.-Apr. M-Sa 10am-1pm and 2-6pm.) **Luggage storage** is at the bus station (350$ per day). The town's **swimming pool,** on Av. Brasil near the bus station, is excellent. (☎ 284 31 19 14. Pool and adjacent park 280$; ages 10-12 140$. Open May-Sept. Tu-Su 9am-8pm.) In an **emergency,** call ☎ 112; the **police** (☎ 284 32 20 22) are on R. D. Nuno Álvares Pereira, one block downhill from the tourist office. The **post office,** on Largo do Correio, is down the street from the beginning of R. Capitão de Sousa. (☎ 284 31 12 70. Open M-F 9am-6pm.) The **postal code** is 7800.

⌨ ACCOMMODATIONS AND FOOD. Most rooms and *pensões* lie within a few blocks of the tourist office and the central pedestrian street. **Residencial Bejense,** R. Capitão J. F. de Sousa, 57, down the street from the tourist office, has beautiful rooms with tiled floors, ruffled bedspreads, TVs, phones, private baths, and air conditioning, as well as a TV lounge with a small bar. (☎ 284 32 50 01; fax 284 32 50 02. Breakfast included. Singles 5000-6000$; doubles 8000-8500$. V, MC, AmEx.) **Pensão Santa Bárbara,** R. Mertola, 56, around the corner from Residencial Bejense, has comfortable rooms with bath, phone, TV, and air conditioning, some with balconies. (☎ 284 32 20 28. Breakfast included. Singles 5500$; doubles 7000-8000$. V, MC, AmEx). For those who want to camp, **Parque de Campismo Municipal,** easily accessible at the end of Av. Vasco da Gama, lies past the stadium on the southwest side of town. From the bus terminal, go straight one block and take a left. The campsite is small, shady, and clean. (☎ 284 31 19 11. Free showers. May-Sept. 340$ per person, 250-500$ per tent, 250$ per car; 50% discount Oct.-Apr.)

Beja is one of the best places to taste authentic (and affordable) Portuguese cuisine. The municipal **market** sets up in a building one block up and one block to the right from the bus station (open M-Sa 6am-1:30pm). **Restaurante Alentejano,** Largo dos Duques de Beja, down the steps near the museum, serves unpretentious regional cuisine. (☎ 284 32 38 49. Entrees 800-1200$; *pratos do dia* 850-1000$. Open Sa-Th noon-3pm and 7-10pm.)

◨ SIGHTS. Beja's historical sites are scattered, but the outstanding **Museu Rainha Dona Leonor** makes an excellent starting point. Take a right from the tourist office and walk into the Pr. Diogo Fernandes de Beja. Go right on R. Dr. Brito Camacho, and through Lg. de São João to Lg. da Conceiçao; the museum is on your right. Built on the site of Sister Mariana Alcoforado's famed indiscretion with a French officer, the museum features a replica of the cell window through which the lovers exchanged secret passionate vows. Inside, the gilded church's 18th-century *azulejo* panels depict the lives of Mary and St. John the Baptist. Nearby are *intaglio* marble altars and panels of *talha dourada* (gilded carvings). The *azulejos* and Persian-style ceiling make the chapter house look like a mini-mosque. (Open Tu-Su 9:45am-12:30pm and 2-5:15pm. 100$. Su free. Ticket also good for the Museu Visigótico behind the castle.)

One block downhill from the Museu Rainha Dona Leonor is the 13th-century, adobe-like **Igreja de Santa María da Feira,** transformed into a mosque during the Moorish invasion and back into a church when the city reverted to Portuguese control. A miniature bull on its corner column symbolizes the city's spirit. (Church open daily 10am-1pm and 3-7pm. Free.) From here, R. Aresta Branco leads past handsome old houses to the city's massive **castelo,** built around 1300 on the remnants of a Roman fortress. (Open May-Sept. Tu-Su 10am-1pm and 2-6pm; Oct.-Apr. 9am-noon and 1-4pm. Free.) It still flaunts an enormous crenellated marble keep, vaulted chambers, stones covered with cryptic symbols, and walls covered with ivy. The castle's **Torre de Menagem** provides an impressive view of the vast Alentejan plains (100$). Between the police station and the center of town lies the convent-turned-luxury-*pousada* on R. Dr. Nuno Alvares Pereira. You can look around the lobby and the cloister of the **Convento de São Francisco** here, but do check in with the reception desk (between 10am-7pm) and be respectful of paying guests.

RIBATEJO AND ESTREMADURA

Jagged cliffs and whitewashed fishing villages line Estremadura's Costa de Prata (Silver Coast), with beaches that rival even those in the Algarve. Throngs of tourists and summer residents populate seafront Nazaré and Peniche. Smaller, less touristed towns with equally fantastic beaches line the coast, and the rugged and beautiful Ilhas Berlingas lie offshore. Nearby, the fertile region of the Ribatejo ("banks of the Tejo") is perhaps the gentlest and greenest in Portugal. Known as the "Heart of Portugal," it is famous for the rich pastures that border the arid Alentejan plain and Estremaduran wetlands. Its character is closely tied to the Rio Tejo and to two of the area's renowned inhabitants: the horse and the bull. It is also home to some of the country's finest sights, from the ornate monasteries in Alcobaça and Batalha, to the mysterious Knights Templar complex above Tomar and the medieval town of Óbidos. In this region just north of Lisbon, history and sights are packed into towns not yet overtaken by commercial tourism. Despite a few industrial blemishes, these towns remain the rule, rather than the exception.

HIGHLIGHTS OF RIBATEJO AND ESTREMADURA

Relaxing in peaceful **Santarém,** only an hour from Lisbon (see below).

Óbidos, a charming medieval town with a magnificent **castle** (see p. 598).

The incredible monasteries at **Alcobaça** (see p. 605) and **Batalha** (see p. 608).

LOCAL FESTIVALS IN RIBATEJO AND ESTREMADURA

Tens of thousands of people flock to **Santarém** the first Friday of every June for the *Feira Nacional de Agricultura,* which brings 10 days of bullfighting and horse-racing. **Peniche** celebrates the *Festa de Nossa Senhora da Boa Viagem* (Festival of Our Lady of the Good Voyage) with wine, seafood, and music every first weekend of August. Mid-September brings Peniche the *Sabores de Mar,* a fishing-focused dancing, eating, and musical extravaganza.

SANTARÉM

Perhaps the most charming of Ribatejo's cities, Santarém (pop. 30,000) presides from atop a rocky mound over the calm Rio Tejo and the soft green pastures. Once a ruling city in the ancient Roman province of Lusitania, and later a flourishing medieval center, Santarém has a long history of prosperity. It was also the capital of Portuguese Gothic style; its many appealing churches today display a mind-boggling range of architectural trends.

◰ TRANSPORTATION

Trains: Station (☎ 243 32 11 99), 2km outside town. **Bus** service to and from the bus station (10min., every 30min.-1hr., 210$). Otherwise take a taxi (600$); the walk is steep and dangerous. To: **Tomar** (1hr., every hr. 6:20am-1:25am, 520$); **Lisbon** (1hr., 37 per day 4:40am-3:55am, 670-1050$); **Coimbra** (2hr., 11 per day 6:25am-1:10am, 1020-1400$); **Portalegre** (3hr., 4 per day 8:50am-9pm, 1120$); **Porto** (4hr., 4 per day 9:55am-8:55pm, 1720-2100$); and **Faro** (4hr., 6 per day, 1700$), via Lisbon.

Buses: Rodoviária Tejo (☎ 243 33 32 00), on Av. Brasil, not far from the main *praça.* **Luggage storage** open 8:30am-7pm. To: **Lisbon** (1-1½hr., 20 per day 7:45am-9:30pm, 850-950$); **Peniche** (1¼hr., 4 per day 7:20am-2:45pm, 850$); **Caldas da Rainha** (1½hr., 5 per day 7:20am-6:15pm, 710$); **Leiria** (1½hr., 5 per day 8:15am-6:45pm, 900-1350$); **Nazaré** (1½hr., 7:30am and 5:30pm, 850$); **Coimbra** (2hr., 10:45am and 6:45pm, 1600$); **Porto** (4hr., 10:45am and 6:45pm, 2100$); **Braga** (5hr., 10:45am and 6:45pm, 2200$); and **Faro** (7hr., 5 per day 10:30am-4:30pm, 2600$).

Taxis: Scaltaxis (☎ 243 33 29 19) has a stand across from the bus station.

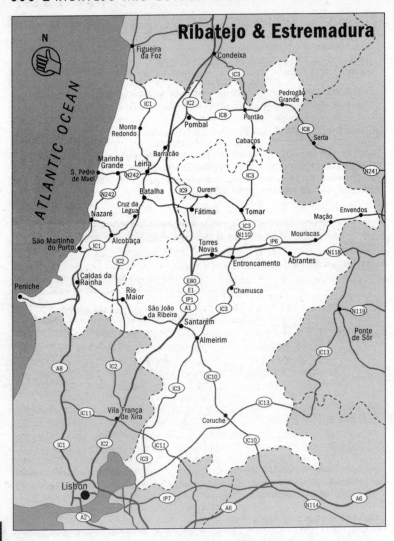

ORIENTATION AND PRACTICAL INFORMATION

The densely packed streets between **Praça Sá da Bandeira** (the main square) and the park **Portas do Sol** (above the Tejo) form the core of Santarém. **Rua Capelo Ivêns,** which begins at the *praça*, houses the tourist office and many hostels.

Tourist Office: R. Capelo Ivêns, 63 (☎ 243 30 44 37), down from the main *praça*. Maps and info on festivals, accommodations, and transportation. English spoken. Open Tu-F 9am-7pm, Sa-M 10am-12:30pm and 2:30-5:30pm.

Currency Exchange: Banco Nacional Ultramarino (☎ 243 33 00 07), at R. Dr. Texeira Guedes and R. Capelo Ivêns. 1000$ commission. Open M-F 8:30am-3pm.

Luggage Storage: At the bus station. 100$ per bag. Open 8:30am-7pm.

Emergency: ☎ 112. **Police:** (☎ 243 32 20 22), Av. Brasil, near the bus station.

Hospital: (☎ 243 30 02 00), Av. Bernardo Santareno. From Pr. Sá da Bandeira, walk up R. Cidade da Covilhã, which first becomes R. Alexandre Herculano and then Av. Bernardo Santareno. English spoken.

Internet Access: Free at the **youth hostel** M-F 9am-8pm (30min. limit). **Baku's Bar** (see **Entertainment**) also has 2 computers. 250$ for 30min.

Post Office: (☎ 243 32 05 77), on the corner of Largo Cândido and R. Dr. Texeira Guedes. Open M-F 8:30am-6:30pm, Sa 9am-12:30pm. **Postal Code:** 2000.

▌ ACCOMMODATIONS

You stay, you pay. Prices are fairly high year-round, but during the Ribatejo Fair (10 days starting the first F in June), they increase 10-40%. The tourist office can usually help you find a room in a private house (June-Aug. 3000-4000$; Sept.-May around 2500$). Be sure to negotiate the price.

Residencial Abidis, R. Guilherme de Azevedo, 4 (☎ 243 32 20 17 or 243 32 20 18), around the corner from the tourist office. Although the hallways are a bit dreary, the 27 recently renovated rooms have a homey feeling and a central location. Singles 4000$, with bath 5500$; doubles 4500$, with bath 7000$.

Residencial Beirante, R. Alexandre Herculano, 5 (☎ 243 32 25 47), on the extension of R. Cidade da Covilhã off Pr. Sá da Bandeira. Elevator leads to comfortable rooms, all with TVs, fans, phones, and private baths. Breakfast included. Singles 4500-6000$; doubles 7500-8500$; triples 8500-10,000$.

Pousada da Juventude de Santarém (HI), Av. Grp. Forçados Amadores de Santarém, 1 (☎/fax 243 39 19 14), near the bullring. From the bus station, turn right onto Av. Brasil, walk 4 blocks, and turn right onto Lg. Cândido dos Reis. Follow it as it becomes Av. Dom Afonso Henriques and then curves past the bullring; the hostel is on the left. Inconveniently located, but the rooms are clean and comfortable. Breakfast included. Reception 8am-noon and 6pm-midnight. Free Internet. June 16-Sept. 15 dorms 1900$; doubles with bath 4600$. Sept. 16-June 15 dorms 1500$; doubles with bath 3800$.

Residencial Muralha, R. Pedro Canavarro, 12 (☎ 243 32 23 99), next to the medieval wall. Basic rooms with TV and private bath; nothing special, but fine. Doubles 6500$.

◗ FOOD

Eateries cluster around the parallel R. Capelo Ivêns and R. Serpa Pinto. The **municipal market,** in the colorful pagoda on Lg. Infante Santo near the Jardim da República, sells fresh produce (open M-Sa 8am-2pm). **Supermercado Minipreço,** R. Pedro Canavarro, 31, is on the street leading from the bus station to R. Capelo Ivêns (open M-Sa 9am-8pm). If you're in the mood for home-style cooking, **Casa d'Avó,** R. Serpa Pinto, 62, serves Portuguese dishes (950$) as well as sandwiches (200-350$) and sweets (110-350$) on petite tables surrounded by cast-iron garden chairs. (☎ 243 32 69 16. Open M-F 9am-7pm, Sa 9am-2pm. Closed Aug.).

SCARY CHERRY Óbidos's castle has occupied its strategic position atop a steep hill since the Celts constructed it in 308 BC; in the Middle Ages, the Moors occupied the castle. From the height of the formidable walls, you'll see why Portugal's first king, Dom Afonso Henriques, was thwarted in several attempts to capture the town. But on January 11, 1148, forces at the back of the castle diverted the guards' attention, while men disguised as cherry trees tiptoed up to a small door on the other side (now known as the Door of Betrayal). Noticing the advancing trees, an astute Moorish princess asked her father if trees walked. The distracted king paid her no heed, and by the time he realized what was happening, Afonso's men had broken through the castle door. Today, January 11 is a holiday in Óbidos.

🏛 SIGHTS

■ **PRAÇA VISCONDE DE SERRA PILAR.** Centuries ago, Christians, Moors, and Jews gathered for social and business affairs in this *praça*. *(Take R. Serpa Pinto from Pr. Sá da Bandeira.)* The 12th-century **Igreja de Marvilha**, off the *praça*, has a 16th-century Manueline portal and a 17th-century *azulejo* interior. *(Open Tu-Su 9:30am-12:30pm and 2-5:30pm. Free.)* The early Gothic purity of nearby **Igreja da Graça** contrasts sharply with Marvilha's overflowing exuberance. Within Graça's chapel lies Pedro Alvares Cabral, the explorer who "discovered" Brazil and one of the few explorers to live long enough to return to his homeland. *(Church and chapel open Tu-Su 9:30am-12:30pm and 2-5:30pm. Free.)*

IGREJA DO SEMINÁRIO DOS JESUÍTAS. The austere facade of the Igreja do Seminário dos Jesuítas dominates Pr. Sá da Bandeira, Santarém's main square. Stone friezes carved like ropes separate the three stories and Latin biblical mottos embellish every lintel and doorway. *(Open Tu-Su 9:30am-12:30pm and 2-5:30pm. Free. If it is closed, enter the door to the right of the entrance and ask Sr. Domingos to unlock it.)*

TORRE DAS CABAÇAS. The medieval **Torre das Cabaças** (Tower of the Gourds) was named after the eight earthen bowls installed in the 16th century to amplify the bell's ring. Inside the tower is the **Museu de Tempo** (Time Museum), with clocks, clocks, and more clocks. *(Take R. São Martinho from Pr. Visconde de Serra Pilar. Open Tu-Su 9:30am-12:30pm and 2-5:30pm. 200$ for each, 250$ for both.)*

GARDENS. Portas do Sol, a paradise of flowers and fountains surrounded by Moorish walls, looks best on a clear day, when the walls offer a lovely view of the plains and the Tejo flowing by on its way to Lisbon. *(Take R. Serpa Pinto from Pr. Sá da Bandeira to Pr. Visconde de Serra Pilar, then continue on R. Cons. Figueiredo Leal, which becomes Av. 5 de Outubro and heads straight into the Portas do Sol. Open daily 8am-11pm. Free.)*

🎭 ENTERTAINMENT

Relieve your sightseeing boredom at ■**Baku's Bar,** R. Luís Matoso, 10, off Lg. Cândido dos Reis. From the bus station turn right onto Av. Brasil and follow it to Lg. Cândido dos Reis, taking the first right onto R. Luís Matoso. There you can chill with local high school kids in the back lounge, shoot darts in the small game room, enjoy a drink in the cafe-bar up front, or check your email. (☎ 243 32 13 90. Coffee 80-120$. Beer 120-180$. Mixed drinks 150-300$. Open M-Sa 9am-2am.) Next door is **Knockout,** a huge game room with arcade games and a pool table (open M-Sa 9am-midnight). For a slightly more sedate setting, head to a pub. **Cervejão,** Av. António Maria Baptista, 10, around the corner and two blocks down from the bus station, whose name means "big ol' beer," has got a lot of, well, beer, for 250$. (☎ 243 26 43 33. Cocktails 500$. Open M-Sa 4pm-midnight.)

For unrestrained daytime partying, simply wait for a festival. The largest is the **Feira Nacional de Agricultura** (also known as the Feira do Ribatejo), a national agricultural exhibition. Tens of thousands of people come for the six- to 10-day bullfighting and horse-racing orgy, usually starting the first Friday in June. (Contact the tourist office for dates.) Smack your lips at the **Festival e Seminário Nacional de Gastronomia** (the last half of October), when each region of Portugal has one day to prepare a typical local feast, complete with entertainment.

ÓBIDOS

Walking through the formidable stone gate to Óbidos (pop. 200 inside the walls) is like stepping into the Middle Ages; it is almost more a showpiece than a town, especially with the silence, stars, and mesmerizing views of nightfall. The tiny village sits atop a hill dominated by a 12th-century fortress (now a luxury inn), and the narrow streets and stunning views are just as romantic as they were in 1282, when King Dinis gave the entire town to Queen Isabel as a wedding gift.

IF I CAN'T HAVE NUN, YOU CAN'T
EITHER. The story of Santarém's founding could have been a Disney movie.
All the elements are there: beautiful young girl, frustrated love, bitter jealousy, a little bit of magic, and no sex whatsoever. All over town, parents tell their children the story, but one must wonder what exactly the moral is. Listen: The daughter of two 7th-century nobles, Iria was sent to a convent at an early age to live a life of purity and utter devotion to God. Soon Iria blossomed into a beautiful young woman and fell in love with a noble named Britaldo. The two contented themselves with innocent hand-holding (her being a nun-in-training and all) and tried to live happily ever after. Enter Remígio, a former teacher of Iria's, now madly in love with her as well. Cue the jealous rage. Remígio decides if he can't have Iria, no one can, and slips a potion into her soup that makes her look pregnant. Needless to say, sex is a convent no-no, and so the townspeople cast Iria into the river. Her nun friends (where is good ol' Britaldo now?) form a search party and eventually find her body washed up on the shore. Her body is in a coffin when they find it (strange since the mob hadn't placed her in one). Before anyone can give her a proper burial, the river rises, condemning the girl to a watery grave. Santarém was founded on this tragic site, "Santarém" being derived from "Santa Iria." Today a statue of her by the river just across from the train station marks the spot where Iria is said to lie still.

The **castelo** on the coast, a Moorish fortress rebuilt in the 12th century, gradually lost its strategic importance as the ocean receded. Although the castle itself, now a luxury *pousada*, opens only to guests, 1.5km of its walls are open to all; simply follow the signs showing stairs. The 17th-century *azulejo*-filled **Igreja de Santa Maria**, to the right of the post office in the central *praça*, displays Nun Josefa de Óbidos's vivid canvases off the main altar; it was also the site of the 1441 wedding of 10-year-old King Afonso V to his 8-year-old cousin, Isabel. *(Open daily Apr.-Sept. 9:30am-12:30pm and 2:30-7pm; Oct.-March 9:30am-12:30pm and 2:30-5pm. Free.)*

The **tourist office** is on R. Direita (different from the regional bureau on the same street). From the main gate to the town, take the high road to the left and walk 200m; the office is on the left just before Pr. Santa Maria. English-speaking staff has maps, bus info, and luggage storage. (☎ 262 95 92 31. Open daily May-Sept. 9:30am-7pm; Oct.-Apr. 9:30am-6pm.) In an **emergency** dial ☎ 112; **police** can be reached at ☎ 262 95 91 49. Private rooms for rent are everywhere in Óbidos; look for signs or ask in restaurants. **Agostinho Pereira**, R. Direita, 40, rents four homey rooms, some of which have window seats perfect for enjoying the view of the nearby church. (☎ 262 95 91 88. Reserve a week ahead during the summer. Singles 4000$; doubles 5000-6000$; triples 6000$.) "Typical" **restaurants** (with tourist prices) and several **markets** flesh out R. Direita. Eat light and save your *escudos* for Óbidos's signature *ginja* (wild cherry liqueur), even sweeter and more syrupy than the national norm. Stores on R. Direita sell small bottles for 300-350$.

While Óbidos is an easy **train** ride from Lisbon's Estação Rossio, the uphill walk to town from the station can be daunting. Take a commuter train to Cacém, then change trains for Óbidos (3hr., 10 per day 4:40am-10pm, 930$). Buy tickets aboard the train. Trains drop off passengers 10 minutes outside town; cross the tracks and climb the stairs to get to the town center. **Buses,** which stop just outside the town gate, are more convenient. Frequent connections go to: **Caldas da Rainha** (20min., 18 per day 7:35am-8:10pm, 170$); **Peniche** (40min.; M-F 10 per day 8:10am-7:40pm, Sa-Su 5 per day 8:10am-7:40pm, 385$); and **Lisbon** (1½hr., M-F 3 per day 7am-4:10pm, 1000$). On weekends you must stop in Caldas da Rainha to go to Lisbon (1½hr., 7 per day 7am-9pm, 1000$). Buses stop a few stairs down from the main gate. No bus schedules are posted here, so ask at the tourist office.

PENICHE

Many travelers overlook Peniche, a seaport town 22km west of Óbidos en route to the Ilhas Berlengas. What they miss is a lively city close to good beaches and hiking. Home to Portugal's second largest fishing fleet, Peniche is so obsessed with seafood that it used to dedicate an entire festival to the sardine; only recently it expanded the revelry to fishing and seafood in general.

◨ TRANSPORTATION

Buses: (☎ 262 78 21 33), R. Dr. Emesto Moureira, on an isthmus outside the town walls. To: **Caldas da Rainha** (1hr., 8 per day 8am-7:30pm, 435-850$); **Nazaré** (1½hr., 4 per day 10:45am-6pm, 730-1100$); **Santarém** (1½hr., 3 per day 7am-5:10pm, 850$), via Caldas da Rainha; **Alcobaça** (1¾hr., 3 per day 10:45am-5:10pm, 1150$), via Caldas da Rainha; **Leiria** (2hr., 3 per day 10:45am-5:10pm, 1400$), via Caldas da Rainha; **Lisbon** (2hr., 12 per day 6am-8:45pm, 1050$); and **Porto** (6½hr., 3 per day 7am-6pm, 2100$). Peniche is only accessible by bus.

Taxis: (☎ 262 78 44 24 or 262 78 29 10), in Pr. Jacob Pereira and Lg. Bispo Mariana.

◧✦ ❷ ORIENTATION AND PRACTICAL INFORMATION

Most of Peniche's points of interest are situated in or around the grid of streets between **Largo Bispo Mariana** and the **fortaleza** on the coast. **Praça Jacob Rodrigues Pereira** is the center of town, near the tourist office and the start of **Avenida do Mar,** which runs along the river to the docks and fishing port.

Tourist Office: (☎ 262 78 95 71), R. Alexandre Herculano. From the bus station, cross the river on Ponte Velha, turn left on R. Alexandre Herculano, and walk alongside the public garden, following signs to the office. English-speaking staff assists with accommodations and provides maps and info on trips to the islands. Open daily June-Sept. 9am-8pm; Oct.-May 10am-1pm and 2-5pm.

Emergency: ☎ 112. **Police:** (☎ 262 78 95 55), R. Herois Ultramar.

Hospital: (☎ 262 78 17 00), on R. Gen. Humberto Delgado.

Post Office: (☎ 262 78 00 60), R. Arquitecto Paulino Montez. From the tourist office, turn right on R. Alexandre Herculano, left on R. Arquitecto Paulino Montez, and walk 3 blocks. **Posta Restante** and **fax.** Open M-F 9am-6pm. **Postal Code:** 2520.

Internet Access: The **municipal library**, R. Luís de Camões, 2E (☎ 262 78 01 22), offers free access to its computers. Open M and W-F 9:30am-12:30pm and 2-7pm, Tu 10am-noon and 2-7pm. **On Line Cyber Café**, R. António Cervantes, 5 (☎ 96 685 77 49), near the fortaleza, has 2 computers. 120$ for 15min., 100$ for 15min. after the first hr. Coffee 80-120$. Beer 150$. Mixed drinks 500$. Open daily Sept.-June 2pm-2am; July-Aug. 11am-2am.

◤ ACCOMMODATIONS

Hostels fill quickly in July and August; try to arrive early in the day. Look for signs on Av. Mar. Hostesses also roam the streets advertising **beds** in their homes. Rooms in private houses may be good budget options, but insist on seeing them first and inquire about hot water and amenities. In summer, expect to pay 2500$ or so for a single and 4500$ for a double. Bargain—there are more beds than visitors.

▨ **Hospedaria Marítimo,** R. António Cervantes, 14 (☎ 262 78 28 50), off the *praça* in front of the fortress. Newly decorated rooms with comfy beds, bright pine furnishings, wicker lamp shades, and private baths. Breakfast included. Check-out 10:30am. Singles 3000-3500$; doubles 5000-7500$.

Residencial Maciel, R. José Estevão, 38 (☎ 262 78 46 85), on the corner of R. Elias Garcia, 3 blocks from Pr. Jacob Pereira. Spoil yourself with these gorgeous rooms, all with private bath, cable TV, and fans. Ask to be put in the R. Garcia annex; the rooms in the main building are a bit pricier. Reserve a week ahead in the summer. June-July and Sept. singles 5000$; doubles 6000$; triples 8000$. Aug. singles 7000$; doubles 8000$; triples 10,000$. Oct.-May singles 4000$; doubles 5000$; triples 7000$. V, MC, AmEx.

Residencial Mira Mar, Av. Mar, 40-44 (☎ 262 78 16 66), near the docks and above a seafood restaurant of the same name. Orange shag rug, oak furniture, great views, private baths, and TVs. Reception noon-midnight (inside the restaurant). Singles 2500-3000$; doubles 3500-4000$. V, MC, AmEx.

Hospedaria Cristal, R. Marechal Gomes Freitas de Andrade, 14-16 (☎ 262 78 27 24), 3 blocks up R. Latino Coelho from Pr. Jacob Pereira. Plain rooms with TVs and phones, some with balconies and private baths. Reception 8am-midnight. Singles 3000-3500$; doubles 4000-5000$; triples 5000-6000$; quads 6000-7000$.

Municipal Campground (☎ 262 78 95 29; fax 262 78 96 96), 3km outside of town, at least a 30min. walk from downtown. From the bus station, turn left onto Av. Porto de Pesca to reach EN 114 and follow it through the traffic circle and past the waterpark; the campsite is on the left. Or take a taxi (about 500$ from downtown). Free hot showers. 380$ per person, 310-420$ per tent, and 310$ per car. Open year-round.

⑂ FOOD

Peniche's seafood is as fresh as it gets. The real stuff sizzles in whale-sized portions on outdoor grills along Av. Mar. Peniche's *sardinhas* (sardines) are exceptional, as are the seafood *espetadas* (skewered aquatic treats served with a tub of melted butter). The outdoor cafes on Pr. Jacob Rodrigues Pereira are lively, particularly on Sundays, when the rest of town is virtually comatose. The **market,** R. António da Conceição Bento, has fresh produce (open Tu-Su 7am-1pm).

Restaurante Beiramar, Av. Mar, 106-108 (☎ 262 78 24 09). Delectable grilled fare served on wood tables in a stone-walled room, upstairs on the balcony, or on the patio out front. *Sardinhas grelhadas* (grilled sardines) 950$. Entrees 750-1500$. Open daily noon-3pm and 7pm-midnight. Visa.

Restaurante Chinês Leaõ de Ouro, Av. Mar, 30-32 (☎ 262 78 72 60), hidden among the dozens of seafood places. A nice good change of pace from seafood, with good vegetarian options (210-790$). Entrees 660-920$. Special plates 940-1250$. Open daily 11am-3pm and 6-11pm.

Café Oceano, Pr. Jacob Pereira, 12-13 (☎ 262 78 23 15), just up from the tourist office. Popular cafe in the main square, perfect for people watching. Sandwiches 350-1100$. Coffee 120-200$. Gourmet ice cream 150-800$. Open daily 8am-midnight.

👁 SIGHTS

FORTALEZA. António Salazar, Portugal's longtime dictator, chose Peniche's formidable 16th-century fortress for one of his four high-security political prisons. Its high walls and bastions later became a camp for Angolan refugees. It now houses the **Museu de Peniche,** highlighted by a small but fascinating anti-Fascist exhibition. Photos and text trace the dictatorship and underground resistance from the seizure of power in 1926 to the coup that toppled the regime on April 25, 1974. *(R. José Estevão, near the dock where boats leave for the Ilhas Berlengas. Fortaleza open Tu-Su 10:30am-noon and 2-5:30pm. Free. Museum ☎ 262 78 01 16. Open Tu-Su 10:30am-noon and 2-5:30pm. 130$, under 16 free.)*

BEACHES. For sun and surf, head to any of the town's three beaches. The beautiful but windy **Praia de Peniche de Cima,** along the north crescent, has the warmest water. It merges with another beach at **Baleal,** a small fishing village popular with tourists. The southern **Praia do Molho Leste,** known to many as "super-tubos" because of its big surf, is a bit cooler. Beyond it is the crowded **Praia da Consolação.** The strange humidity at this beach supposedly cures bone diseases. Unfortunately, on windless days, it also traps the stench of nearby sewers. *(Buses 7am-7pm, 160$. Check with the tourist office for changes.)*

♪ ENTERTAINMENT

At night in Peniche, two popular bars host plenty of locals and tourists. **Adega do Becas**, R. José Estevão, 91, attracts a fun crowd of young hipsters with electronic and acid jazz. (Beer 200-300$. Mixed drinks 500-600$. Open M-Sa 2pm-2am, Su 9pm-2am.) Nearby is **Bar No. 1**, R. Dr. Francisco Seia, close to the intersection with R. José Estevão, a slightly milder (but no less crowded) bar popular with locals and tourists alike. (Beer 150-300$. Mixed drinks 600$. Open daily noon-2am.) You'll need a taxi (800$) to get to the popular beachside club **Voila**, several kilometers from downtown Peniche in Baleal (open until 3am).

Peniche's biggest festival takes place on the first weekend of August, when boats—decked in wreaths of flags and flowers—file into the harbor in the procession that launches the two-day **Festa de Nossa Senhora da Boa Viagem,** celebrating the protector of sailors and fisherman. The whole town lets loose with carnival rides, live entertainment, and of course, wine and seafood. (Boat parade takes place Sa night around 10pm.) Mid-September brings the **Sabores do Mar** festival, focused on fishing and, well, fish. This massive seafood-devouring, wine-chugging party at the fishing port also features *fado* and folklore dancing.

☾ EXCURSIONS

To truly enjoy the ocean air, hike around the peninsula (8km). Start at **Papôa,** just north of Peniche. From Pr. Jacob Pereira, take R. Alexandre Herculano and then Av. 25 de Abril and follow the signs along the coast. Then stroll out to the tip, where orange cliffs rise from a swirling blue sea. Nearby lie the ruins of an old fortress, **Forte da Luz.** The endpoint of the peninsula, **Cabo Carvoeiro,** is the most popular and dramatic of Peniche's natural sights. The fortress's **farol** (lighthouse) punctuates the extreme west end of the peninsula. Nearby is a convenient snack bar where you can watch the waves crashing below as you relish *ginja* (Óbidos's cherry liqueur). The **Nau dos Corvos** (Crow's Ship), an odd rock formation and a popular bird roost, promises a seagull's-eye perspective.

⚐ DAYTRIPS FROM PENICHE

ILHAS BERLENGAS (1HR.)

From Peniche's public dock, the Viamar ferry zips to the island (1hr.; July-Aug. 3 per day 9:30, 11:30am, and 5:30pm, return trips at 10:30am, 4:30, and 6:30pm; May 15-June and Sept. 1-15, 10am, returns 4:30pm). In late July and Aug. the ferry gets so crowded that people begin to line up 2½hr. early; at other times, 1hr. in advance will suffice. A same-day round-trip ticket (3000$) for the 9:30am ferry means you'll return at 4:30pm; those who go at 11:30am return at 6:30pm. To stay overnight, buy a 1500$ one-way ticket for the 5:30pm boat and pay return fare on board the 10:30am boat back. Crossing can be rough—the vomit bags are all-too frequently appreciated. Alternatively, cruise around in a motorboat. Berlenga Turpesca, with an office on the docks at Largo Ribeira, 2, goes to the islands and tours underwater caves and other wonders in and around Peniche. (☎ 262 78 99 60. 3000-6000$; 6-person min., 10-person max.)

The rugged, terrifyingly beautiful Ilhas Berlengas (Berlenga Islands) rise out of the Atlantic Ocean, 12km northwest of Peniche. One minuscule main island, numerous reefs, and isolated rocks form an archipelago that's home to thousands of screeching seagulls (attracted to the protected **Reserva Natural da Berlenga**), wild black rabbits, and a very small fishing community. Deep gorges, natural tunnels, and rocky caves ravage the main island. Although it is fringed with several protected beaches, the only one accessible by foot lies in a small cove by the landing dock. For beach-goers willing to brave the cold, dips in the calm water bring instant respite from the heat. For hikers, the tiring trek to the island's highest point yields a gorgeous view of the 17th-century **Forte de São João Batista,** now a hostel.

This is a natural park, so if you're going to spend the night, be prepared to rough it. The **hostel** in the old fortress looks spectacular, but lacks facilities. Bring a sleeping bag and flashlight: the steep, rocky 30-minute walk from the boat landing to the hostel is lit only by periodic flashes from the lighthouse. The hostel has a kitchen, and the canteen and snack bar stock basic food. (☎ 262 75 02 44. Reception M-F 10am-11pm. Reservations through the Peniche tourist office required. Dorm beds 1500$. Open June-Sept.) There is also a small **campground** on a series of rocky terraces above the ferry landing. If you want to sleep there, make reservations in person at the Peniche tourist office, and be prepared to be shat upon by scores of seagulls. (7-day max. stay. 2-person tent 1000$ per night; 3-person tent 1500$; 4-person tent 2000$. Open June to mid-Sept.)

NAZARÉ

It's hard to tell where authenticity stops and tourism starts in Nazaré. Fishermen clad in traditional garb go barefoot and women typically don seven petticoats, thick shawls, and large gold earrings. The day's catch dries in the hot sun, locals string their nets along the shoreline esplanade, and streetside entrepreneurs sell everything from seashell necklaces to fishing nets to dried fruit. "Traditional" lifestyle has become the basis of Nazaré's most thriving business: tourism. But if Nazaré is part theater, at least it puts on a good show, and everyone gets front row seats on the stunning beach. August is not the time to drop anchor here, though; prices usually double and sunbathers jostle for tiny spots on the sand.

▐ TRANSPORTATION

Buses: (☎ 262 55 11 72), Av. Vieira Guimarães, perpendicular to Av. República. More convenient than taking the train (6km away). To: **Alcobaça** (30min., 14 per day 7:10am-8pm, 230$); **Batalha** (50min., 5 per day 7:10am-6:45pm, 470$); **Caldas da Rainha** (1¼hr., 11 per day 6:30am-7:15pm, 435$); **São Martinho do Porto** (20min., 11 per day 6:50am-8pm, 250$); **Leiria** (1¼hr., 10 per day 6:45am-7:10pm, 470-570$); **Fátima** (1½hr., 3 per day 7:10am-5pm, 570$); **Tomar** (1½hr., 3 per day 7:10am-5pm, 850$); **Peniche** (1½hr., 6 per day 8:35am-6pm, 740$); **Lisbon** (2hr., 8 per day 6:50am-8pm, 1250$); **Coimbra** (2hr., 5 per day 6:25am-7:25pm, 1400$); and **Porto** (3½hr., 5 per day 6:25am-7:25pm, 1800$).

Taxi: ☎ 262 55 31 25.

✦ ▐ ORIENTATION AND PRACTICAL INFORMATION

Practically all of the action in Nazaré—beaches, nightlife, and most restaurants—takes place in the **new town** along the beach. Its two main squares, **Praça Sousa Oliveira** and **Praça Dr. Manuel de Arriaga,** are near the cliffside, away from the fishing port. Either the cliffside funicular or a winding road leads up to the **Sítio,** the old town, which preserves a sense of calm and tradition less prevalent in the crowded resort below. To get to the tourist office from the bus station, go toward the beach and then right onto Av. República. The office is a five-minute walk along the beach, between the two major *praças*.

Tourist Office: (☎ 262 56 11 94), beachside on Av. República. Maps and entertainment and transportation info. English spoken. Open daily July-Aug. 10am-10pm; Sept. 10am-8pm; Oct.-March 9:30am-1pm and 2:30-6pm; Apr.-June 10am-1pm and 3-7pm.

Luggage Storage: In the bus station. 100$ per bag per day. Open daily 9am-7pm.

Emergency: ☎ 112. **Police:** (☎ 262 55 12 68), 1 block from the bus station at Av. Vieira Guimarães and R. Sub-Vila.

Hospital: Hospital da Confraria da Nossa Senhora de Nazaré (☎ 262 56 11 16), in the Sítio district on the cliffs above the town center. **Centro de Saúde** (☎ 262 55 11 82), in the new part of town.

Post Office: Av. Independência Nacional, 2 (☎ 262 56 16 04). From Pr. Souza Oliveira, walk up R. Mouzinho de Albuquerque, which veers to the right. It's 1 block past Pensão Central. Open M-F 9:30am-12:30pm and 2:30-6pm. **Postal Code:** 2450.

Internet Access: The **municipal library,** Av. Manuel Remigio (the continuation of Av. República in the direction of the port), offers free use. Open M-F 10am-1pm and 3-7pm.

▐ ACCOMMODATIONS

Nazaré is home to the most—and most aggressive—room-renters in Portugal; insistent old ladies wait at the bus station and on most street corners offering rooms in their houses. Be sure to check that they are authorized by the tourist office (they should have an authorization card from the city or the tourist board). Bargain down to 3500$ for singles and 4500$ for doubles, but insist on seeing the room (and feeling the hot water) before settling the deal. For rooms in hostels, look above the restaurants on Pr. Dr. Manuel de Arriaga and Pr. Sousa Oliveira.

Vila Turística Conde Fidalgo, Av. da Independencia Nacional, 21-A (☎/fax 262 55 23 61), 3 blocks uphill from Pr. Sousa Oliveira. Clean, comfortable rooms and apartments, all with private baths, surround a central courtyard. Reception 9am-1am. Reservations recommended in the summer and require 50% pre-payment. Oct.-June doubles 3000$; 2-person apt. with kitchen 4000$. July and Sept. doubles 4000$; 2-person apts. 6000$; 3-person apt. 10,000$. Aug. doubles 6000-7000$; 2-person apt. 8000-9000$; 3-person apt. 12,000$.

Hospedaria Ideal, R. Adrião Batalha, 98 (☎ 262 55 13 79), between the two main *praças*. Plain rooms are not exactly ideal, but at least the beds are comfy and the common baths are clean. July-Aug. breakfast included. Reception 10am-10pm in the restaurant downstairs. Doubles 6000-7000$; triples 7000-8000$; quads 8000-9000$. Discounts during the low season.

Residencal Marina, R. Mouzinho de Albuquerque, 6A, 3rd and 4th fl. (☎ 262 55 15 41), off Pr. Sousa Oliveira. Bright, carpeted rooms, some with baths, close to the beach. Reserve a week ahead in the summer. Reception 9am-11pm. Doubles 4000$.

Camping: Vale Paraíso, on Estrada Nacional 242 (☎ 262 56 18 00; fax 262 56 19 00), 2½km out of town. Take the bus to Alcobaça or Leiria (15min., 8 per day 7am-7pm). Swimming pools, a restaurant-bar, a supermarket, and occasional Internet access. Free showers. Laundry. Pool access 300$ in summer. Reception daily 8am-10pm. June-Sept. 630$ per person, 510-720$ per tent, 515$ per car; Apr.-May and Oct. 520$ per person, 435-600$ per tent, 435$ per car; Nov.-Mar. 390$ per person, 335-460$ per tent, 335$ per car. V, MC, AmEx.

▐ FOOD

For fruit and veggies, check out the **market** across from the bus station (open daily July-Sept. 8am-1pm; Oct.-June Tu-Su 8am-1pm). **Supermarkets** line R. Sub-Vila, parallel to Av. República and Pr. Dr. Manuel de Arriaga (open June-Aug. 9am-10pm; Sept.-May 9am-8pm).

A Tasquinha, R. Adrião Batalha, 54 (☎ 262 55 19 45), 1 block left of Pr. Dr. Manuel de Arriaga. Locals jostle for a seat at the family-style picnic tables. Perhaps the only restaurant in Nazaré with a Portuguese-only menu. *Sardinhas assadas* (fried sardines) 800$. Entrees 700-1400$. Open Tu-Su noon-3pm and 7pm-1am. V, MC, AmEx.

Charcutaria O Frango Assado, Pr. Dr. Manuel de Arriaga, 20 (☎ 262 55 18 42), facing the beach, at the far end of the square. Although there's only one dish on the menu (*frango assado*, roasted chicken), this take-out-only joint keeps locals coming back for more. Perfect for a picnic on the beach. Half-chicken with *piri-piri* (a tabasco-esque sauce) 500$. Open daily 9am-1pm and 3:30-8pm.

Da Vinci, Av. Nazaré, 43 (☎ 262 56 14 04), away from town, off Av. Manuel Remigio as it runs along the beach towards the port. Da Vinci's divine pizzas (650-1250$) and pastas (950-1250$) are good vegetarian options. Open M-F noon-3pm and 6-11pm, Sa noon-3m and 6pm-midnight, Su open 11am-11pm.

CLIFF HANGERS One-hundred and ten meters above the sea, the tiny, whitewashed **Ermida da Memória** stands in a corner of the square diagonally opposite the Sítio's church. Perched on the edge of the precipice, the chapel was built in 1182 by the lucky nobleman Dom Fuas Roupinho. Out on a hunting expedition, Dom Fuas was chasing a deer that just kept running until it fell off the cliff. Dom Fuas pulled hard on the reins and his horse stopped with two legs on *terra firme* and two over the side. In a split second, Our Lady of Nazaré appeared and pulled the horse (and Dom Fuas) to safety. Out of this event, the little chapel and the town of Nazaré were born.

♫ ENTERTAINMENT

Why are you staring at that church? Go to the **beach,** which runs alongside the main road. If you've been there and done that, take the **funicular** (every 15min. 7pm-1am, 105$), which runs from R. Elevador off Av. República to the **Sítio,** a cliff-top area of Nazaré that makes a perfect evening excursion with its uneven cobbled streets, weathered buildings, and wonderful views of the town and ocean. Around 6pm, fishing boats return to the **port** beyond the far left end (facing the ocean) of the beach; watch fishermen at work and eavesdrop as local restaurateurs spiritedly bid for the most promising catches at the **fish auction** (M-F 6-10pm).

Cafes in Pr. Sousa Oliveira teem with people past midnight. The intimate café-bar **TaBarEs,** on R. Mouzinho Albuquerque off Pr. Dr. Manuel de Arriaga, is a mellow haven from the sun by day but livens up at night, with live Brazilian and Portuguese music most summer evenings. (☎ 262 55 33 53. Coffee 100$. Beer 150-400$. Mixed drinks 600$. Open daily July-Sept. noon-4am; Oct.-June 2pm-4am.) During the summer, look out for late-night **folk music** gatherings on the beach. **Bullfights** are also popular; Nazaré is on the schedule that brings *corridas* to a different city in the province each summer weekend (usually Sa 10pm; tickets start at 2500$).

▌ DAYTRIPS FROM NAZARÉ

ALCOBAÇA (20MIN.)

With the nearest train station 5km away in Valado dos Frades, buses are the best way to get to Alcobaça. The bus station (☎ 262 58 22 21), on Av. Manuel da Silva Carolino, offers service to: Nazaré (20min., 15 per day 7:30am-8:20pm, 230$); Batalha (30min., 8 per day 7:30am-7:10 pm, 385$); Leiria (1hr., 6 per day 7:30am-7:10pm, 470$); Coimbra (2hr., 4:25pm, 1325$); Porto (3½hr., 4:25pm, 1650$); and Lisbon (2hr.; M-F 5 per day, Sa-Su 3 per day 6:30am-6pm; 1300$).

A sleepy town in the hills not too far from the coast, Alcobaça welcomes thousands of visitors each year for one reason: it is home to the impressive ▓**Mosteiro de Santa Maria de Alcobaça,** the oldest church in Portugal. The town was founded in 1153, following King Afonso Henriques's expulsion of the Moors, as a grant from the king to Cistercian monks. Afonso was attempting to secure Christianity in the region, and the monks responded; construction of their new monastery began in 1178, and additions continued over the course of several centuries. Today it is the largest building of the Cistercian order in all of Europe and was recently granted UN World Heritage status. In the smaller naves adjacent to the towering central one, the **tombs** of King Pedro I and his wife Inês de Castro flaunt sophisticated carvings and immortalize one of Portugal's great love stories (see **Eat your heart out, Don Juan,** p. 625). Surrounding the monastery's lovely cloisters are numerous Gothic and Manueline style rooms, most notably the immense **kitchen** and **refectory** (the monks could roast more than 6 oxen at a time), the **Sala dos Monges** (Monk's Hall), and the **Sala dos Reis** (Hall of Kings). (Monastery open daily Apr.-Sept. 9am-7pm; Oct.-Mar. 9am-5pm. Cloisters open daily Apr.-Sept. 9am-6:30pm; Oct.-Mar. 9am-4:30pm. 600$, students 300$.) If you have time left over after seeing the monastery, the **Museu da Vinha e do Vinho** (Museum of Wine and Winemaking), is five minutes from the bus station on R. Leiria, which branches off R. dos Combatentes on the way out of town. The exhibition about the history and methods of Portugal's wine industry is bound to be less crowded than the tourist-laden monastery. (☎ 262 58 22 22. May-Sept. open Tu-F 9am-12:30pm and 2-5:30pm, Sa-Su 10am-12:30pm and 2-6pm; Oct.-Apr. M-F 9am-12:30pm and 2-5:30pm. Free.)

To get to the center of town, **Praça 25 de Abril**, from the station, turn right out of the bus station's garage and then right again onto Av. Dos Combatentes. Follow it over the small river and into Pr. Afonso Henriques, which sits to the right side of the monastery. Keep walking; the town center is in the *praça* in front of the monastery and the **tourist office** is straight ahead (across from the post office). The **tourist office** doles out maps, lists of accommodations, and regional information. (☎ 262 58 23 77. Open daily May-Sept. 10am-1pm and 3-7pm; Oct.-Apr. 10am-1pm and 2-6pm.) **Luggage storage** is next to the ticket office. (100$ per bag per day. Open 8:30am-12:30pm and 2-6pm.) In an **emergency** call ☎ 112; the **police** can be reached at ☎ 262 58 33 88, on R. Olivença; and the **hospital** (☎ 262 59 74 16) is on R. Afonso de Albuquerque. The **post office,** Pr. 25 de Abril, is across the street from the tourist office. (☎ 262 59 71 87. Open M-F 8:30am- 6pm). The **postal code** is 2460.

Should you decide to spend the night, **Pensão Corações Unidos,** R. Frei António Brandão, 39, off Pr. 25 de Abril, offers 30 rooms, some with full bath and TV, around a small central courtyard. (☎/fax 262 58 21 42. Breakfast included. Reception 8am-midnight in the restaurant of the same name. Singles 2500-3500$; doubles 5500-7000$. V, MC, AmEx.) Restaurants and *pastelarias* line the two *praças* surrounding the monastery. **Restaurante Trindade,** Pr. Afonso Henriques, 22, with its slick mahogany and mirror interior, is a popular spot to dine on Portuguese cuisine or just take a break with drinks. (☎ 262 58 23 97. Entrees 950-2000$. Open daily July-Sept. 9am-midnight; Oct.-June Tu-Su 9am-midnight.)

SÃO MARTINHO DO PORTO (20MIN.)

Trains run from the station (☎ 262 98 94 85) to Leiria (1½hr., 5 per day 9:50am-8:10pm, 400$) and other points north and south, but buses are faster and more convenient, running to Nazaré (20min., 7 per day 9:30am-7:30pm, 225$) and other towns. Both train and bus schedules are posted in the tourist office. The bus stops on the main road leading into town.

The result of countless ages of surf smashing against, and finally through, the coastal cliffs, the bay of São Martinho do Porto is nearly enclosed on all sides. The town lies clustered at the base of the inlet, while the windless, swimmer-friendly **beach** sweeps 3km along and around the bay, forming an almost perfect circle. With its red-roofed houses crowding down a palm-studded hillside to a small and colorful fishing harbor, São Martinho do Porto has an almost Mediterranean charm that makes the town an ideal escape from crowded Peniche and Nazaré.

Although São Martinho do Porto is best done as a daytrip, the **tourist office,** on Lg. Frederico Ulrich at the end of Av. 25 de Abril, has a list of private rooms should you decide to spend the night. (☎ 262 98 91 10. Singles 3000-3500$; doubles 4500-5000$. Open June-Sept. Tu-Su 10am-1pm and 3-7pm; Oct.-May Tu-Su 10am-1pm and 2-6pm.) Services include the **health center,** R. Conde Avela, 29-B (☎ 262 98 93 90); the **police,** R. Conde Avelar, 6 (☎ 262 98 91 90); and for **emergencies** ☎ 112.

LEIRIA

Capital of the surrounding district and an important transport hub, prosperous, industrial Leiria fans out from a fertile valley, 22km from the coast. An impressive ancient castle peers over the city, gazing down upon countless shops, a shady park, and at the moment, a lot of construction; chosen to host the Euro 2002 soccer finals, Leiria is busy preparing itself for the crowds that will flood the city. While not the most exciting destination in Portugal, Leiria makes a practical base for exploring the nearby region. Buses heading away from the city run frequently enough to satisfy both culture-vultures aching to get to surrounding historic towns and beach-leeches set on the gorgeous sands of the Costa da Prata.

⌐ TRANSPORTATION

Trains: Station (☎ 244 88 20 27), 3km outside town. Buses run between the station and the tourist office (15min., every hr. 7:05am-7:20pm, 150$). To: **Figueira da Foz** (1¼hr., 6 per day 6:55am-8:50pm, 530$); **Coimbra** (1½hr., 7 per day 6:55am-8:50pm, 770$); and **Lisbon** (3½hr., 8 per day 8am-8:30pm, 1220$), via Cacém and sometimes Caldas da Rainha.

Buses: (☎ 244 81 15 07), just off Pr. Paulo VI, next to the town garden and close to the tourist office. They are the easiest way to leave Leiria. To: **Batalha** (20min., 9 per day 7:15am-7:10pm, 210$); **Alcobaça** (50min., 6 per day 7:15am-7:10pm, 470$); **Fátima** (1hr., 6 per day 7:15am-7:05pm, 380-405$); **Nazaré** (1hr., 6-9 per day 7:50am-7:10pm, 470$); **Coimbra** (1hr., 11 per day 7:15am-2am, 1050$); **Santarém** (2hr., 5 per day 7:15am-7:05pm, 900-1350$); **Figueira da Foz** (1½hr., M-F 8 per day 7:55am-6:35pm, 670$); **Tomar** (1½hr.; M-F 2 per day 7:15am and 5:45pm, Sa 6:15pm; 570$); **Lisbon** (2hr., 11 per day 7:15am-11pm, 1250$); and **Porto** (3½hr., 10 per day 7:15am-2am, 1600$).

Taxis: ☎ 244 81 59 00 or 244 74 18 60. Taxis gather at the Jardim Luís de Camões.

◼✳❼ ORIENTATION AND PRACTICAL INFORMATION

Most commerce centers around the streets leading from the **Jardim Luís de Camões,** where the tourist office and bus station are, so don't expect to wander far.

Tourist Office: (☎ 244 82 37 73), across the park from the bus station. English-speaking staff has schedules for beach-bound buses, maps, and temporary **luggage storage.** Open daily May-Sept. 10am-1pm and 3-7pm; Oct.-Apr. 10am-1pm and 2-6pm.

Emergencies: ☎ 112. **Police:** Largo Artilharia, 4 (☎ 244 81 37 99).

Hospital: (☎ 244 81 70 00), on R. Olhalvas along the road to Fátima.

Post Office: (☎ 244 81 29 40), in Largo Santana on Av. Combatentes da Grande Guerra, between the tourist office and the youth hostel. Label **Posta Restante** mail "Estação Santana." Open M-F 8:30am-6pm. **Main office,** Av. Herois de Angola, 99 (☎ 244 82 92 20), a bit farther away, past the bus station towards the mall. Open M-F 8:30am-6:30pm, Sa 9am-12:30pm. **Postal Code:** 2400.

Internet Access: The **library,** Largo Cândido dos Reis, 6 (☎ 244 82 08 5), a few doors down from the HI hostel, offers free access (1hr., twice a week); sign up in advance. Open M 1-5:45pm, Tu-F 10am-12:30pm and 1-5:45pm; Oct.-May also Sa 3-6:30pm.

⌐ ACCOMMODATIONS

Most accommodations in Leiria will not take your breath away. Cheap rooms are hard to find and most hostels have seen better days.

▨ Residencial Dom Dinis, Tr. Tomar, 2 (☎ 244 81 53 42). Turn left after exiting the tourist office, cross the bridge over Rio Lis, walk 2 blocks, and turn left again; the hostel is on the right. 28 bright, comfortable rooms with baths, telephones, and satellite TVs. Breakfast included. Singles 4000$; doubles 6000$; triples 7000-8500$. V, MC, AmEx.

Pousada da Juventude de Leiria (HI), Largo Cândido dos Reis, 9 (☎ 244 83 18 68). From the bus station, walk to the cathedral and exit Lg. Sé (next to Lg. Cónego Maia) on R. Barão de Viamonte, a narrow street lined with shops. Lg. Cândido dos Reis is 6 blocks ahead; the hostel is on the left. Clean, comfortable rooms. Breakfast included. Kitchen, bar/game room, shaded central courtyard. Reception open daily 8am-noon and 6pm-midnight. Lockout noon-6pm (bag drop-off still available). June 16-Sept. 15 dorms 1900$; doubles 4200$. Sept. 16-June 15 dorms 1500$; doubles 3500$.

Camping: Orbitur (☎ 244 59 91 68), 22km away in São Pedro de Muel. Take the bus from the station (45min.; M-F 8 per day 7:55am-6:30pm, Sa 7 per day 6:55am-5:30pm, Su 7 per day 7:55am-5:30pm; 150$). Reception daily 10am-8pm. June-Sept. 660$ per person, 510$ per tent, 570$ per car. Apr.-May 590$ per person, 460$ per tent, 520$ per car. Mar. and Oct. 390$ per person, 300$ per tent, 340$ per car. Open Mar.-Oct.

◢ FOOD

The **market** on Av. Cidade de Maringá, on the far side of the castle from the bus station, has fresh fruits and veggies (open M-F 8am-4pm, Sa 8am-1pm). Groceries and fresh baked bread can be purchased at **Supermercado Ulmar,** Av. Heróis de Angola, 56, just past the bus station. (☎ 244 83 30 42. Open M-Sa 8am-9pm, Su 10am-1pm and 3-8pm.) Leiria is not exactly a tourist hotspot, so inexpensive food is still easy to find here. Budget eateries line the side streets between the park and the castle. **Restaurante Aquário,** Mouzinho de Albuquerque, 17, serves regional specialties at for 900-1500$. (☎ 244 82 27 20. Open F-W 9am-10pm.)

◢ ♫ SIGHTS AND ENTERTAINMENT

SIGHTS. From the main square, follow the signs past the austere **sé** (cathedral) to the city's most significant monument, the **castelo.** This granite fort, built by Dom Afonso Henriques after he snatched the town from the Moors, presides atop the crest of a volcanic hill on the north edge of town. Left to crumble for hundreds of years, the castle retains only the **torre de menagem** (homage tower) and the **sala dos namorados** (lovers' hall). The terrace opens onto a panoramic view of town and the river. *(Castle open Apr.-Sept. M-F 9am-6:30pm, Sa-Su 10am-6:30pm; Oct.-Mar. M-F 9am-5:30pm, Sa-Su 10am-5:30pm. 150$.)* Nearby sits the roofless shell of the 14th-century **Igreja da Nossa Senhora da Penha.**

BEACHES AND ENTERTAINMENT. Nearby beaches, including **Vieira, Pedrógão,** and **São Pedro de Muel,** are all easily accessible via buses from the station. July-Sept. 14 buses run to: **Praia de Viera** (45min., 9 per day 7am-6:35pm, 150$; last return bus 7:25pm); **Praia Pedrógão** (1hr., 6 per day 8:25am-6:35pm, 170$; last return bus 6:15pm); and **São Pedro de Muel** (45min.; M-F 8 per day 7:55am-6:30pm, Sa 7 per day 6:55am-5:30pm, Su 7 per day 7:55am-5:30pm; 150$; last daily return bus 7:15pm). Check at the bus station or the tourist office for up-to-date schedules. **Bars** along Largo Cândido dos Reis near the youth hostel come alive after 10pm. The **Teatro José Lúcio da Silva,** on the corner of Av. Heróis de Angola behind the bus station, features films. *(☎ 244 82 36 00. Ticket office open daily 7-10pm. 600-700$. The tourist office has schedules of current features.)*

BATALHA

The only reason (but a good one) to visit Batalha (pop. 6000) is the gigantic **Mosteiro de Santa Maria da Vitória,** which rivals Belém's Mosteiro dos Jerónimos in monastic splendor. Built by Dom João I in 1385 to commemorate his victory over the Spanish, the complex of cloisters and chapels remains one of Portugal's greatest monuments. To get to the monastery, enter through the church.

▐ TRANSPORTATION. The **bus** stops in a small square (Lg. 14 de Agosto de 1385) across the street from the monastery. Inquire at the tourist office for info or call the bus station in Leiria (☎ 244 81 15 07). Buses run to: **Leiria** (20min., 10 per day 7:50am-8:25pm, 210$); **Fátima** (40min., 3 per day 8:05am-6pm, 280$); **Alcobaça** (45min., 13 per day 7:35am-6:50pm, 385$); **Nazaré** (1hr., 13 per day 7:35am-6:50pm, 520$), via Alcobaça; **Tomar** (1½hr., 3 per day 8:05am-6pm, 520$); and **Lisbon** (2hr., 6 per day 7:25am-6:50pm, 1200$).

◢ ▌ ORIENTATION AND PRACTICAL INFORMATION. The **tourist office,** on Pr. Mouzinho de Albuquerque along R. Nossa Senhora do Caminho, just across from the monastery, has maps and bus information. (☎ 244 76 51 80. Open daily May-Sept. 10am-1pm and 3-7pm; Oct.-Apr. 10am-1pm and 2-6pm.) In case of **emergency** call ☎ 112 or ring the **police** at ☎ 244 76 51 34, on Av. dos Descobrimentos, near the bus stop. The **post office** is in Lg. Papa Paulo VI, near the freeway entrance. (☎ 244 76 51 11. Open M-F 9:30am-1pm and 2:30-6:30pm.) The **postal code** is 2440.

▓▓ ACCOMMODATIONS AND FOOD. Batalha, devoid of cheap beds or even a campground, is best visited as a daytrip. If you do get stuck here, **Pensão Residencial Gladius,** in Pr. Mouzinho de Albuquerque, has bright, comfortable rooms overlooking the *praça* and monastery, all with TVs and either shower or full bath. (☎ 244 76 57 60. Reception 9am-1pm and 2:30-10pm. May-Sept. singles 5000$; doubles 6000$; triples 8000$. Oct.-Apr. singles 4000$; doubles 5000$; triples 6500$.) The cheapest beds are at **Pensão Vitória,** on Lg. Misericórdia next to the bus stop. Its six dim doubles (all with 1 queen-sized bed) are, well, monastic. (☎ 244 76 56 78. Reception 9am-midnight. Rooms 3500$.) The restaurant below does wonders with *pudim* (pudding). Several inexpensive *churrasquería* (barbecue houses) and **cafes** line the squares flanking the monastery.

▓ SIGHTS. Batalha's ▓**monastery complex** has been granted UN World Heritage status. Its flamboyant facade soars upward in a heavy Gothic and Manueline style, opulently decorated and topped off by dozens of spires. Napoleon's troops sacreligiously turned the nave into a brothel. The **Capela do Fundador,** immediately to the right of the church, shelters the elaborate sarcophagi of Dom João I, his English-born queen Philippa of Lancaster, and their son Prince Henry the Navigator. The rest of the complex is accessible via a door in the nave of the church. Enter through the broad Gothic arches of the **Claustro de Dom João I,** the delicate columns which initiated the Manueline style. Adjacent to the cloister lies the **Tomb of the Unknown Soldier.** Through the **Claustro de Dom Afonso V,** out the door and to the right are the impressive **Capelas Imperfeitas** (Imperfect Chapels), with massive buttresses designed to support a large dome that was never actually constructed; the project was dropped when Manuel I ordered his workers to build the monastery in Belém instead. (Open daily Apr.-Sept. 9am-6pm; Oct.-Mar. 9am-5pm. 600$, under 25 300$. Free Su before 2pm. Church free.)

Twenty minutes out of town, nature is at its most psychedelic in a spectacular series of underground *grutas* (caves) in Estremadura's natural park between Batalha and Fátima. The **Grutas de Mira de Aire** are the deepest; though **Grutas de Santo António** and **Alvados** are a bit more difficult to reach, they are equally impressive. Most of the caves have been "enhanced" with background music and strategically placed colored spotlights. The tourist offices in both Batalha and Fátima have further information. From Batalha, take a bus to Torre Novas (20min., 6 per day 7:35am-7:40pm, 350$; last bus back to Batalha 6:30pm). Ask the driver to stop at the *grutas.* (Caves open daily Oct.-Mar. 9:30am-5:30pm; Apr.-May 9:30am-6pm; June and Sept. 9:30am-7pm; July-Aug. 9:30am-8:30pm. 700$, students 500$.)

FÁTIMA

Fátima used to be a sheep pasture; now the once-quiet town has become a religious center, and total immersion in holy fervor awaits visitors. Only Lourdes rivals this site in popularity with Christian pilgrims, as the miracles believed to have occurred here are modern-day phenomena, well documented and witnessed by thousands. The plaza in front of the church, larger than St. Peter's Square in the Vatican, floods with pilgrims on the 12th and 13th of each month.

▐ TRANSPORTATION

Trains: The **Caxias** station (☎ 249 57 43 50), 10km out of town, is more (though still not quite) convenient than the Fátima station (☎ 249 56 61 22), 22km away. From Caxias to: **Coimbra** (1hr., 14 per day 5:25am-1:55am, 680$); **Porto** (4hr., 12 per day 5:25am-1:55am, 1330$); **Santarém** (1½hr., 10 per day 6:50am-9:35pm, 620$); and **Lisbon** (2½hr., 9 per day 6:50am-11:30pm, 1040$). **Buses** run between Caxias and the bus station (30min., 7 per day 7:50am-7:50pm, 360$) as well as the Fátima train and bus stations (45min., 5 per day 6:10am-6:35pm, 405$).

Buses: (☎ 249 53 16 11), Av. Dr. José Alves Correia da Silva. On bus schedules Fátima is often referred to as **Cova da Iria**. To: **Batalha** (45min., 3 per day 9am-6:35pm, 260$); **Leiria** (1hr., 15 per day 7:55am-8pm, 490-800$); **Santarém** (1hr., 3 per day 7:30am-3:15pm, 1100$); **Tomar** (1¼hr., 5 per day 8:30am-8:15pm, 470$); **Nazaré** (1½hr., 3 per day 9am-6:25pm, 590$); **Lisbon** (2½hr., 11-17 per day 7am-6:30pm, 1250$); **Porto** (3½hr., 5 per day 1:30-9:30pm, 1700$); and **Coimbra** (1½hr., 3 per day 2:30-6pm, 1350$).

Taxis: ☎ 249 52 14 62.

✦🛈 ORIENTATION AND PRACTICAL INFORMATION

Activity in Fátima centers around the basilica complex. The **Santuário de Fátima** is the huge, open *praça* that fills with visitors on special occasions and the 12th and 13th of each month. The bus station and tourist office are on **Avenida Dr. José Alves Correia da Silva**, which runs just south of the hubbub. A right turn and 10-minute walk from the bus station leads to the tourist office at the plaza off the basilica.

Tourist Office: (☎ 249 53 11 39), Av. Dr. José Alves Correia da Silva, to the right when exiting the bus station, just past the Santuário (on your left, through the trees). English-speaking staff provides maps, lists of accommodations, and temporary **luggage storage.** Open daily July-Sept. 10am-1pm and 3-7pm; Oct.-May 10am-1pm and 2-6pm.

Emergency: ☎ 112. **Police:** (☎ 249 53 11 05), Av. Dr. José Alves Correia de Silva.

Medical Services: Centro de Saúde (☎ 249 53 18 36), on R. Jacinta Marto.

Post Office: (☎ 249 53 18 10), R. Cónego Formagião. Open M-F 8:30am-6pm. **Postal Code:** 2495.

▮🍴 ACCOMMODATIONS AND FOOD

Scores of hostels inundate both sides of the basilica complex. Credit cards are almost universally accepted, and lodging prices vary little. The town fills during the grand pilgrimages on the 12th and 13th of each month; both hostel and hotel prices tend to increase 500 to 2000$ during these days. **Residencial São Francisco,** R. Francisco Marto, 100, just off the Santuário, has plain but comfortable rooms, all with TVs, phones, and private baths, some with balconies. (☎ 249 53 30 17; fax 249 53 20 28. Reception 7:30am-midnight. Singles 3000$; doubles 5000$; triples 7000$.) **Pensão Dona Maria,** Av. Dr. José Alves Correira da Silva, 122, between the bus station and tourist office, offers rooms with bath off *azulejo*-covered halls. (☎ 249 53 12 12. Breakfast included. Reception 8am-11:30pm. Lockout 11:30pm. June-Aug. singles 5000$; doubles 10,000$. Oct.-May singles 3500$; doubles 8750$.)

R. Francisco Marto, R. Santa Isabela, and R. Jacinta Marto have similar, touristy restaurants. **Adega Funda,** R. Francisco Marto, 103, serves hearty Portuguese dishes in its large wooden dining room. (☎ 249 53 13 72. Entrees 950-1600$. Open M-Sa 10am-3:30pm and 6:30-10pm, Su 10am-4pm. V, MC, AmEx.) **Snack Bar A Louca**, R. Jacinta Marto in the mini-mall-esque Pope John Paul II building, is one of the better budget options for lunch, with light fare including omelettes (650-900$) and *pratos do dia* for 850$. (☎ 249 53 16 21. Open daily 11am-midnight.)

👁 SIGHTS

Tall leafy trees shield the sanctuary from the commercial area, where religious memorabilia is sold for sacreligious prices.

▮**BASÍLICA DO ROSÁRIO.** At the end of the plaza rises the Basílica do Rosário (erected in 1928), featuring a crystal cruciform beacon perched atop the tower's seven-ton bronze crown. Many of the devout come to the basilica, traveling the length of the plaza on their knees praying for sick loved ones. While there is no longer a dress code, do be respectful, especially to those praying on the grounds. *(Open daily 7:30am-7:30pm. Mass at 7:30, 9, 11am, noon, 3, 4:30, and 6:30pm.)*

MARY AND THE THREE SHEPHERDS On May 13,
1917, Mary appeared before three shepherd children—Lucía, Francisco, and Jacinta—and issued a call for the end of World War I. Our Lady of Fátima returned to speak to the children on the 13th of each month, promising a miracle for her final appearance in October. Despite the skepticism of clergy and attacks from the press, the children remained steadfast in their belief that the Virgin had spoken to them. On that morning, 70,000 believers gathered under a torrential rain storm. At noon, the sun is said to have spun around in a furious light spectacle, appearing to sink to the earth. When the light returned to normal, no evidence remained of the morning's rain. Convinced by the "fiery signature of God," the townspeople built a chapel at the site to honor Mary. The three shepherd children were recently beatified during Pope John Paul II's visit to Fátima in May 2000. (Meaning they were given the title "Blessed" and a certain amount of public religious honor for having witnessed God in person.)

CAPELINHA DAS APARIÇÕES. Sheltered beneath a metal and glass canopy, the Capelinha das Aparições (Little Chapel of the Apparitions), built in 1919, holds masses in six languages all mornings and some evenings. The chapel is beside the same **oak tree** under which the children spoke to the Virgin (see **Mary and the Three Shepherds,** below).

MUSEUMS. Near the basilica are various museums commemorating the miraculous vision of Mary. To the right facing the basilica, the **Museu de Arte Sacra e Etnologia** exhibits Catholic icons from various centuries. *(R. Francisco Marto, 5, 3 blocks from the basilica. ☎ 249 53 94 70. Open Tu-Su Apr.-Oct. 10am-7pm, Nov.-Mar. noon-5pm. 400$, seniors and students 200$.)* To the left of the basilica, through the park, and in the complex beneath the Hotel Fátima, the **Museu Fátima 1917 Aparições** uses light, sound (in various languages), and special effects to re-create the apparition. This is as close to kitsch as Catholicism gets in Portugal. *(R. Jacinta Marto. ☎ 249 53 28 58. Open daily Apr.-Oct. 9am-7pm; Nov.-Mar. 9am-6pm. 400$, children under 12 200$.)*

TOMAR
The arcane Knights Templar—part monks, part warriors—plotted crusades from Tomar (pop. 22,000) for centuries. A celebrated convent-fortress perched high above the old town served as the Knights' powerful and mysterious headquarters. Known as the Convento de Cristo, the complex beautifully combines architectural styles from the 12th to 17th centuries. Today, Tomar rests peacefully in the shade of the eucalyptus and sycamore trees that line the banks of the Rio Nabão.

▮ TRANSPORTATION

Trains: (☎ 249 31 28 15), Av. Combatentes da Grande Guerra, at the southern edge of town. Tomar is the northern end of a minor line, so most destinations require a transfer at Entrocamento that can be purchased here. Ticket office open M-F 5am-8:30pm and 9:30-10:30pm; Sa 5:30-8:30am, 9:30am-6:30pm, and 7:30-10:30pm; Su 6:30am-10:30pm. To: **Santarém** (1hr., 18 per day 5:05am-10:05pm, 520-840$); **Lisbon** (2hr., 18 per day 5:05am-10:05pm, 1010-2040$); **Coimbra** (2½hr., 6 per day 6:05am-6:05pm, 960-1200$); and **Porto** (4½hr., 7 per day 8:05am-8:05pm, 1510-2210$).

Buses: Rodoviária Tejo (☎ 249 31 27 38), Av. Combatentes Grande Guerra, next to the train station. To: **Nazaré** (1½hr., 3 per day 7:50am-5:20pm, 850$); **Fátima** (30min., 3 per day 7:50am-5:20pm, 470$); **Leiria** (1hr., M-F 2 per day 7:15am and 5:45pm, Sa 7am, 570$); **Santarém** (1hr., 9:15am and 6pm, 1150$); **Lisbon** (2hr., 4 per day 9:15am-6pm, 1150$); **Coimbra** (2½hr., 7am, 1450$); **Porto** (4hr., 7am, 1900$); and **Lagos** (9hr.; M-Sa 9:15am via Santarém and Évora, 10:15am via Lisbon, Su 10:15am via Lisbon; 2900$).

Taxis: (☎ 249 31 37 16 or 249 31 23 73). Cabs congregate near the bus and train stations as well as on R. Santa Iria, across the river.

⟥⟤ ORIENTATION AND PRACTICAL INFORMATION

The **Rio Nabão** divides Tomar. Almost everything travelers need—the train and bus stations, accommodations, and sights—lies on the west bank. The lush **Parque Mouchão** straddles the two banks, while the ancient but fully functional **Ponte Velha** (old bridge) connects the two. The bus and train stations sit next to each other on **Av. Combatentes da Grande Guerra,** near the outskirts of town. The pedestrian-only **Rua Serpa Pinto** cuts across the town from river to castle and connects the Ponte Velha to the main square, **Praça da República.**

Tourist Office: (☎ 249 32 24 27), Av. Dr. Cândido Madureira, facing Parque Mata Nacional dos Sete Montes. From the bus or train station, walk through the small square onto Av. General Bernardo Faria. Continue 4 blocks and go left onto Av. Dr. Cândido Madureira; the office is at the end of the street on the right. Map, hostel list, and maybe **luggage storage** (ask nicely). Open daily June-Sept. 10am-8pm; Oct.-May 10am-6pm.

Emergency: ☎ 112. **Police:** (☎ 249 31 34 44), on R. Dr. Sousa.

Hospital: (☎ 249 32 11 00), on Av. Cândido Madureira, down from the tourist office.

Post Office: (☎ 249 31 04 00), on Av. Marquês de Tomar, across from Parque Mouchão. Open M-F 8:30am-6pm, Sa 9am-12:30pm. **Postal Code:** 2300.

Internet Access: INCA, R. João dos Santos Simões, 60 (☎ 249 32 16 06), over the bridge, off R. Marqués Pombal. 375$ for 30min. Open M-F 9:30am-1pm and 3-7pm, Sa 10am-1pm.

▌ ACCOMMODATIONS

Finding a place to stay is only a problem during the Festival dos Tabuleiros, which takes place once every four years (the next is in 2003). Tomar is a buyer's market—practice bargaining. Prices generally drop in the off-season.

▨ Residencial União, R. Serpa Pinto, 94 (☎ 249 32 31 61; fax 249 32 12 99), halfway between Pr. República and the bridge. Look for the oversized *azulejos* outside. 28 bright, plush rooms, all with TVs, phones, baths, and a well-stocked bar to welcome weary travelers. Breakfast included. Reception 8am-midnight. Reservations recommended for July and Aug. Singles 4000$; doubles 6500-7000$; triples 7500-8000$.

Residencial Luz, R. Serpa Pinto, 144 (☎ 249 31 23 17), down the street from Residencial União. Clean, comfortable, centrally located rooms, all with shower or full bath, some with TVs and phones. Swank TV room with leather couches. Reception 8am-midnight. July-Sept. singles 3700$; doubles 6000-6500$; triples 8000$; quads 12,000$. Oct.-June singles 3500$; doubles 4500-5000$; triples 7000$; quads 10,000$.

Camping: Parque Municipal de Campismo (☎ 249 32 98 24; fax 249 32 26 08), on the river, across Ponte Velha and to the left, near the stadium and swimming pool. Thickly forested campground with a pool. Showers free. Reception daily June-Aug. 8am-8pm; Sept.-May 8am-5pm. Jan.-June 420$ per person, 240$ per tent, 380$ per car; July-Dec. 440$ per person, 200$ per tent, 400$ per car.

◖ FOOD

Tomar is the perfect place for a **picnic;** a section of lush Parque Mouchão is set aside just for that purpose. The **market,** on the corner of Av. Norton de Matos and R. Santa Iria across the river, provides all the fixings (open Tu and Th-F 8am-2pm; the market on F is larger and has a flea market portion as well). Several inexpensive **mini-markets** line the side streets between the tourist office and Pr. República.

Pizzeria Bella Itaia, R. Everaro, 91 (☎ 249 32 29 96), near the river, between the 2 main bridges. Friendly family serves delicious pastas (800-1400$) and pizzas (800-1450$). Open daily noon-3pm and 7-11pm.

Restaurante Chinês China Town, R. Dr. Joaquim Jacinto, 31 (☎ 249 31 47 43), 1 block from the river and down from the synagogue. Look for the red doors with bright pine woodwork in the windows. Tasty Chinese food in a casual setting. Rice and noodles 190-895$. Meat entrees 765-970$. Open daily noon-3pm and 7-11pm. V, MC.

CENTRAL PORTUGAL

◉ SIGHTS

▨ CONVENTO DE CRISTO. It's worth trekking from the far corners of the earth to explore the mysterious grounds of the Convento de Cristo. The first structure was built by the Knights Templar in 1160, but various cloisters, convents, and buildings were added in successive centuries. An ornate octagonal canopy protects the high altar of the **Templo dos Templares,** modeled after the Holy Sepulchre in Jerusalem. A 16th-century courtyard is encrusted with the rich seafaring symbolism of the Manueline style: seaweed, coral, anchors, rope, and even artichokes, which mariners ate to prevent scurvy. Below stands the **Janela da Capítula** (chapter window), an exuberant tribute to the Age of Discovery. One of Europe's masterpieces of Renaissance architecture, the **Claustro dos Felipes** honors King Felipe II of Castile, who was crowned here as Felipe I of Portugal during Iberia's unification (1580-1640). Tucked behind the Palladian main cloister and the nave is the **Claustro da Santa Bárbara,** where grotesque gargoyle rain-spouts writhe in pain as they cough up a fountain. On the northeast side of the church is the Gothic **Claustro do Cemitério.** *(Walk out of the tourist office and take the 2nd right; bear left at the fork. Pedestrians can take the steeper dirt path a bit after the fork on the left or follow the cars up the paved road. From Pr. República, walk behind the praça and pick up the path. ☎ 249 31 34 81. Open daily June-Sept. 9am-6pm; Oct.-May 9am-5pm. 600$, under 25 300$.)*

SINAGOGA DO ARCO. This 15th-century synagogue, Portugal's most significant reminder of its once vibrant Jewish community, houses the **Museu Luso-Hebraico.** The museum keeps a collection of old tombstones, inscriptions, and donated pieces from around the world. A recent excavation of the adjacent building unearthed a sacred purification bath *(mikvah),* used only briefly by Jews for ritual purposes. *(R. Dr. Joaquim Jaquinto, 73. Open daily 10am-1pm and 2-6pm. Free.)*

OTHER SIGHTS. Pyromaniacs love the **Museu dos Fósforos** (match museum), which exhibits Europe's largest matchbox collection. *(In the Convento de São Francisco, just across from the train and bus stations. Open daily 10-noon and 3-5pm. Free.)* Nature lovers can take a hike on the trails leading away from the **Parque da Mata Nacional dos Sete Montes,** right across from the tourist office. *(Park open daily 10am-6pm. Free.)*

♫ ENTERTAINMENT

For a week near the end of June, handicrafts, folklore, *fado,* and theater storm the city during the **Feira Nacional de Artesanato,** but the biggest party in Tomar is the **Festa dos Tabuleiros,** which only takes place once every four years (the next will occur in 2003). Women construct 3 ft. decorative hats with bread, cardboard, and flowers made of colored paper and parade through town for days, accompanied by costumed children, bulls, and horses. Even though you'll be missing the party yourself, some of the costumes are on display on mannequins in the tourist office. Tomar also hosts three or four summer **bullfights;** look for big posters advertising the *corridas.*

THE THREE BEIRAS

The Three Beiras region offers a sampling of the best of Portugal: the exquisite beaches of the coast, the plush greenery of the interior and the rugged peaks of the Serra de Estrela. The fertile soil in this region yields some of Portugal's best farmland, and the countryside is dotted with red-roofed farmhouses and endless expanses of corn, sunflower, and wheat fields. The **Beira Litoral** (Coastal Region) encompasses the virtually unspoiled Costa da Prata (Silver Coast) beginning at the resort town of Figueira da Foz and passing through up-and-coming Aveiro on the way to Porto. Coimbra, a vibrant university city, overlooks the region from its perch above the Rio Mondego. Unlike more progressive towns to the west, the mountainous **Beira Alta** (High Region) and the **Beira Baixa** (Low Region) have been slow to develop and remain economically impoverished yet rich in tradition.

HIGHLIGHTS OF THE THREE BEIRAS

Partying and people-watching in the vibrant university town of **Coimbra** (see below).

The Sahara-like sun and sand of the beach at **Figueira da Foz** (see p. 621).

LOCAL FESTIVALS IN THE THREE BEIRAS

Students in **Coimbra** celebrate their graduation every May with the infamous *Queima das Fitas* (Burning of the Ribbons), a week of city-wide carousing initiated by graduates burning the ribbons they were given as first-year students. Choral music fills the street during July's *Festas da Rainha Santa*. **Figueira de Foz** lets loose with the month-long *Festa de São João* in late June and hosts the *Festival de Cinema da Figueira de Foz* in September. Every July, **Aveiro** takes a month to celebrate its long seafaring history with the *Festa de Ria*, during which locals race beautifully decorated traditional boats down the city canals.

COIMBRA

The country's only university city from the mid-16th to the early 20th century, Coimbra is a mecca for the country's youth and backpackers alike. A slew of cheap cafes and bars coupled with an energetic student body keep Coimbra swinging from September through May. The city, beautifully situated on the Rio Mondego, has long since blotted out Coimbra's infamous roles as center of the Portuguese Inquisition and educator of one-time economics professor Antònio Salazar, the former dictator of Portugal. Now the city's vivacious atmosphere keeps visitors from Lisbon and Porto coming year-round.

▐ TRANSPORTATION

Trains: (info ☎ 239 83 49 98). **Estação Coimbra-A (Nova)** is 2 blocks from the lower town center; **Estação Coimbra-B (Velha)** is 3km northwest of town. Trains to and from cities outside the region stop in Coimbra-B only. Regional trains stop first at Coimbra-B, then at Coimbra-A; they depart in the reverse order. If your train stops only at Coimbra-B, it is easiest to take a connecting train to Coimbra-A (5min., every 10min., 140$). Trains go to: **Aveiro** (45min., 22 per day 5:10am-3:10am, 520$); **Figueira da Foz** (1¼hr., 26 per day 5:15am-12:20am, 290$); **Ovar** (1½hr., 21 per day 5:10am-3:10am, 770$); **Porto** (2hr., 21 per day 5:10am-3:10am, 1040$); **Braga** (3hr., 9:55am and 7:55pm, 1220$); **Lisbon** (3hr., 23 per day 5:35am-2:20am, 1540-2700$); and **Paris** (19hr., 8:20pm, 23,550$).

Buses: Most buses leave from the **RBL station** (☎ 239 82 70 81), near the end of Av. Fernão Magalhães, on the university side of the river about 10min. out of town, past Coimbra-A. To: **Luso** and **Buçaco** (35-45min.; M-F 7 per day 7:35am-7:20pm, Sa 9am and 12:45pm, Su 10:15 and 5:30pm; 450-480$); **Porto** (1½hr., 10 per day 8:30am-9:30pm, 1400$); **Figueira da Foz** (1½hr., 9 per day 7:20am-6:35pm, 570$); **Lisbon** (2½hr., 17 per day 7:30am-2:15am, 1550$); **Évora** (4hr., 9:30am and 4:15pm, 2000$); and **Faro** (8hr., 3 per day 9:25am-2:10am, 3000$). **International service** (☎ 239 82 75 88) to **Paris** (24hr., M-Sa 11am, 15,300$) and other locations. The **AVIC station**, R. João de Ruão, 18 (☎ 239 82 01 41), between R. Sofia and Av. Fernão Magalhães, next door to Viagem Mondego, serves **Condeixa** (25min., 14 per day 7:35am-7:35pm, 250$) and **Conímbriga** (30min., 9:35am, 280$; return bus 6pm).

Public Transportation: SMTUC buses and street cars. Round-trip ticket 155$. Book of 10 740$; 3-day tourist pass 1100$. Tickets sold at vending machines at Lg. Portagem, Pr. República, and throughout the city. Main lines: #1 (Lg. Portagem-University-Estádio); #2 (Pr. República-Fornos); #3 (Coimbra A-Pr. República-Santo António dos Olivais); #5 (Coimbra A-Pr. República-São José); #7 (Lg. Portagem-Palácio da Justiça-Pr. República-Tovim); #29 (Coimbra A-Pr. República-Hospital); #46 (Cruz de Celas-Pr. República-Lg. Portagem-Santa Clara).

Taxis: Politaxis (☎ 239 48 40 45). Many wait outside Coimbra-A and the bus station.

Car Rental: Avis (☎/fax 239 83 47 86), in Coimbra-A, just outside the platform door in a tiny corner office. Min. age 21. Open M-F 8:30am-12:30pm and 3-7pm. Cars start at 14,500$ per day.

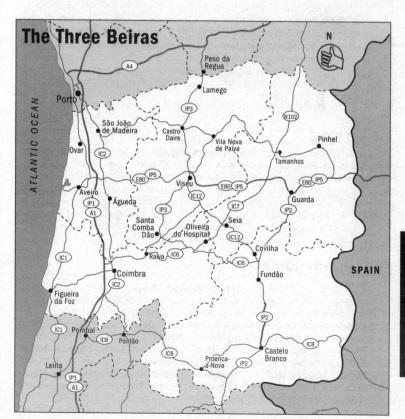

The Three Beiras

CENTRAL PORTUGAL

✦ 🗷 ORIENTATION AND PRACTICAL INFORMATION

Coimbra's steep streets rise in tiers above the **Rio Mondego**. There are three major parts of town, all on the same side of the river. The most central is the **lower town** (site of the **tourist office** and Coimbra-A **train station**), in the triangle formed by the river, **Largo da Portagem**, and **Praça 8 de Maio**. Coimbra's ancient **university district** is atop the steep hill overlooking the lower town. On the other side of the university, **Praça da República** plays host to cafes, a shopping district, and the youth hostel. The tourist office map is very helpful in sorting it all out.

Tourist Office: (☎ 239 85 59 30; fax 239 82 55 76), off Lg. Portagem, in a yellow building 2 blocks up the river from Coimbra-A. From the bus station, turn right, follow the avenue to Coimbra-A, then walk to Lg. Portagem (15min.). Open M-F 9am-7pm, Sa-Su 10am-1pm and 2:30-5:30pm. **University branch office** (☎ 239 83 25 91), in Pr. Dom Dinis. Open M-F 9am-6pm, Sa-Su 9am-12:30pm and 2:30-5:30pm. Another **branch office** (☎ 239 83 32 02) in Pr. República. Open M-F 10am-6:30pm.

Budget Travel: Tagus (☎ 239 83 49 99; fax 239 83 49 16), R. Padre António Vieira. Handles student and youth budget travel. Open M-F 9:30am-6pm.

Currency Exchange: Montepio Geral (☎ 239 85 17 00), Lg. Portagem, near the tourist office. 1000$ commission for amounts above 10,000$. Open M-F 8:30am-3pm.

Luggage Storage: Café Cristal, Av. Fernão Magalhães (☎ 239 82 39 44), across the street and to the left of Coimbra-A. 250$ per bag for 4hr. Open daily 5:30am-10pm.

Laundromat: Lavandaria Lucira, R. Sá da Bandeira, 86 (☎ 239 82 57 01). Wash and dry 1100$ per load. Open M-F 9am-1pm and 3-7pm, Sa 9am-1pm.

Emergency: ☎ 112. **Police:** Special division for foreigners (Serviço de Estrangeiros), R. Venâncio Rodrigues, 25 (☎ 239 82 40 45).

Hospital: Hospital da Universidade de Coimbra (☎ 239 40 04 00 or 239 40 05 00), Lg. Professor Mota Pinto. Take the #7 or 29 bus to the Hospital stop.

Post Office: Central office (☎ 239 85 07 00), in the pink powder-puff structure on Av. Fernão de Magalhães. Open M-F 8:30am-6:30pm. More convenient **mercado office** (☎ 239 82 50 51), on R. Olímpio Nicolau Rui Fernandes, across from the market. Label **Posta Restante** "Estação Mercado." **Telephones** and **fax** services available. Open M-F 8:30am-6:30pm, Sa 9am-12:30pm. **Branch office** (☎ 239 85 07 00), Pr. República, between the youth hostel and the university. Label Posta Restante "Estação Santa Cruz." Open M-F 9am-6pm. **Postal Code:** 3000 for central Coimbra.

Internet Access: Museu Sandwich Bar, R. da Matemática, 46 (☎ 239 82 75 66), off R. São João near the university. 600$ per hr., includes a drink. Open M-F 4-7pm and 10pm-3am, Sa 10pm-3am. **Post Net,** R. Antero de Quental, 73 (☎ 239 84 10 25), between Pr. República and the youth hostel. 150$ for 15min., 500$ per hr. Open M-F 10am-midnight, Sa 2pm-midnight, Su 7pm-midnight.

🗡 ACCOMMODATIONS

Decent hostels, most on side streets off Av. Fernão Magalhães, start at 5000$ for doubles; prices drop in winter.

▨ **Pousada da Juventude de Coimbra (HI),** R. Henrique Seco, 14 (☎ 239 82 29 55; fax 239 82 17 30). From either Coimbra-A or Lg. Portagem, walk 20min. uphill along R. Olímpio Nicolau Rui Fernandes to Pr. República, then up R. Lourenço Azevedo (to the left of the park). Take the 2nd right; the hostel is on the right. Alternatively, take bus #2, 7, 8, 29, or 46 to Pr. República and walk the rest of the way (5min.). Hot, high-pressure showers, TV room, and kitchen. Breakfast included. Laundry 1000$ per machine. Reception daily 8am-noon and 6pm-midnight. Lockout all other times. Bag drop-off still available except M-F 1-2pm and Sa-Su noon-6pm. June 16-Sept. 15 dorms 1900$; doubles with bath 4600$. Sept. 16-June 15 dorms 1700$; doubles with bath 4300$.

Coimbra

ACCOMMODATIONS
Municipal Campground, 5
Pensão Santa Cruz, 1
Pousada da Juventude de
 Coimbra (HI), 4
Residência Lusa Atenas, 2
Residêncial Moderna, 3

N

Parque de
Santa Cruz

TO 4 (500m)
& HOSPITAL (600 m)

R. Lourenço Azevedo

R. de Almeida Garrett

Rodrigues

R. de Tomar

Estação
de Sta. Cruz

PRAÇA DA
REPÚBLICA

R. Alexandre Herculano

Arcos do Jardim

TO 5

Al. Júlio
Henriques

BOTANICAL
GARDEN

Aqueducto de São Sebastião

Branch
Tourist
Office

R. Tenente Valadim

R.D. Manuel Pina
Correia Bastos
R. Tenente
Campos Rego

R. Eço de Queiróz

R. Antero de Quental

Avs. Sá da Bandeira

Avs. Sá da Bandeira

R. Dr. António de Vasconcelos

R. de Saragoça

R. Manutenção Militar

Rua Padre António Vieira

R. Inácio Duarte

R. de Montarroio

R. de Oliveira Matos

R. Venâncio

R. Castro Matoso

Municipal
Office

PRAÇA
DOM DINIS

160 yards

100 meters

PRAÇA
MARQUÊS
DE POMBAL

R. dos Estudos

Sé Nova

LARGO DA
SÉ NOVA

Medical
School

R. de São João

PRAÇA DA
PORTA
FÉRREA

King
John V
Library

R. S. Pedro

R. José Falção

Tv.
Trinidade

Couraça dos Apóstolos

R. da Matemátic

LG. DE
SÃO
SALVADOR

R. de S. Salvador

R. das
Condeixinhas

R. Borges Carneiro

University
of Coimbra

Biblioteca
Joanina

Market

Espaço
Mercado

R. do Colégio Novo

R. do Loureiro

B. da
Anarda

R. do Cabido

R. do Norte

Capela de
São Miguel

Sé Velha

R. Dr. Guilherme Moreira

R. de Lisboa

Couraça de Lisboa

R. Olímpio Rui Fernandes

Santa Cruz

R. Martins de Carvalho

R. do Corpo de Deus

R. Bordalo

R. dos Coutinhos

R. Sub Ripas

R. António António de Aguiar

R. da Ilha

Tv. Conde
de Lisboa

R. dos Esteiros

R. da Alegria

PR. 8
DE MAIO

R. Visconde da Luz

Arco de Almedina

R. Fernandes Tomáz

R. Ferreira Borges

Main
Tourist
Office

LARGO DA
PORTAGEM

TO STA. CLARA
CONVENTS (500m)
& PORTUGAL DOS
PEQUENINOS

Ponte de
Sta. Clara

R. da Sofia

R. Moreno

Arco de
S. Tiago

R. Nova

R. Direita

R. da Moeda

LG. DO
POÇO

R. do Corvo

R. E. Coelho

PRAÇA
DO
COMÉRCIO

R.
Almostré

Tv. A. Vega

R. da Louça

LG. DA
MARACHA

R. de Eanes
R. de Évora
R. Simão do Loja

R. das Padeiras

R. Adelino Veiga

LG. DO
ROMAL

R. das Azeiteiras

Rua do Poço da Cadeia

R. dos Gatos

R. Esteireiros

R. das Sota

R. da Sota

R. do Mol

Av. Emídio Navarro

Arco Bus
Station

R. Simões de Castro

TO MAIN BUS
STATION (500m),
COIMBRA B
TRAIN STATION
(2.5km)

R. João Cabreira

LARGO DA
OLARIAS

R. do Gingueira
R. da Figueira

Av. Fernão de Magalhães

R. António Granjo

R. António Granjo

Coimbra A
Station

R. dos
Oleiros

Arcomena do Anateia

Rio Mondego

▨ **Pensão Santa Cruz,** Pr. 8 de Maio, 21, 3rd fl. (☎/fax 239 82 61 97), directly across from the Igreja da Santa Cruz. From Lg. Portagem, follow R. Ferreira Borges as it becomes R. Visconde da Luz and leads to the *praça*. Comfortable rooms, all with cable TV, some with bath. Singles 4000$; doubles 6000$; triples 7500$.

Residência Moderna, R. Adelino Veiga, 49 (☎ 239 82 54 13). F17 bright, comfortable rooms all with private bath, phone, A/C, and cable TV; many with terrace. Breakfast included. June-Oct. singles 5000$; doubles 7500$; triples 9500$. Nov.-May singles 4000$; doubles 6000$; triples 7500$.

Residência Lusa Atenas, Av. Fernão Magalhães, 68 (☎ 239 82 64 12; fax 239 82 01 33), between Coimbra-A and the bus station, next to Pensão Avis (look for their neon sign). Private baths, phones, A/C, and cable TVs in ritzy rooms. Breakfast included. Reception 8am-midnight. July-Aug. singles 5000$; doubles 7000$; triples 9000$; quads 10,000$. June and Sept. singles 4000$; doubles 6000$; triples 7500$; quads 9000$. Oct.-May singles 3500$; doubles 5000$; triples 6000$; quads 8000$.

Municipal Campground (☎ 239 70 14 97; fax 239 70 24 96), in the recreation complex with the swimming pool and surrounded by noisy streets. The entrance is at the arch off Pr. 25 de Abril. Showers free. Reception May.-Sept. 9am-10pm; Oct.-Apr. 9am-6pm. May-Sept. 474$ per person, 312$ per tent, 602$ per car; Oct.-Apr. 237$ per person, 156$ per tent, 301$ per car.

◖ FOOD

The best cooks in Coimbra work in the area around R. Direita running off Pr. 8 de Maio, on the side streets between the river and Largo Portagem, and near the university district around Pr. República. Restaurants in these areas serve up steamy portions of *arroz de lampreia* (rice cooked with lamprey meat—it does not taste like chicken). The cheapest meal around is at **UC Cantina,** the university's student cafeteria, on the right side of R. Oliveiro Matos, about half a block downhill from the steps leading to Pr. República. A mere 300$ buys an entire meal (soup, salad, dessert, and beverage). An international student ID is (theoretically) mandatory. (Open M-F noon-2:15pm and 7-9:15pm.) Or grab a raw meal at the **mercado** in the huge green warehouse on the right just past the post office, uphill on R. Olímpio Nicolau Rui Fernandes (open M-Sa 8am-1pm). **Supermercado Minipreço,** R. António Granjo, 6C, is in the lower town center; turn left leaving Coimbra-A and take another left. (☎ 239 82 77 57. Open M-Sa 8:30am-8pm, Su 9am-1pm and 3-7pm.)

▨ **Café Santa Cruz,** Pr. 8 de Maio, 5 (☎ 239 83 36 17), right next to the church. From the tourist office, walk down R. Ferreira Borges to Pr. 8 de Maio. Formerly part of the cathedral (it still has a vaulted ceiling and stained-glass windows), this is the city's most famous cafe and a popular place to get wired on coffee (100-200$) and people-watch. Sandwiches 230-400$. Open May-Sept. M-Sa 7am-2am, Oct.-Apr. M-Sa 7am-midnight.

Porta Romana, R. Martins de Carvalho, 10 (☎ 239 82 84 58), just up from the Igreja da Santa Cruz in Pr. 8 de Maio. Delicious Italian dishes. Pizzas 750-1200$. Pastas 950-1200$. Open M-Sa 7am-midnight.

Restaurante Esplendoroso, R. Sota, 29 (☎ 239 83 57 11), up a side street opposite Coimbra-A. The real steals are the weekday lunch *combinados,* which include an egg roll, entree, and rice (780-850$). Open daily noon-3pm and 7-11pm. V, MC.

◉ SIGHTS

OLD TOWN. The best way to take in Coimbra's old town sights is to make the arduous climb from the river up to the university. Begin the ascent at the ancient **Arco de Almedina,** a remnant of the Moorish town wall, one block uphill from Largo Portagem, next to the Banco Pinto e Sotto Mayor on R. Ferreira Borges. The gate leads to a stepped street aptly named R. Quebra-Costas (Back-Breaker Street). Up a narrow stone stairway looms the 12th-century Romanesque **Sé Velha** (Old Cathedral). Don't miss the cool, peaceful cloister upstairs from the main nave. *(Open M-Th*

10am-noon and 2-7:30pm, F-Su 10am-1pm. Cathedral free. Cloisters 150$, students 100$.) Jump ahead a few centuries and follow the signs to nearby **Sé Nova** (New Cathedral), built for the Jesuits in the late 16th century by different architects. The result is an unbelievably elaborate exterior. *(Open Tu-Sa 9am-noon and 2-6:30pm. Free.)*

THE UNIVERSITY. From the new cathedral the 16th-century University of Coimbra campus is but a few glorious blocks uphill. From Pr. República, take R. Oliveira Matos to the big staircase; this leads to the university. Although many of the buildings were built in a functional-but-ugly 1950s concrete style, the law school gets an "A" in architecture. Enter the center of the old university through the **Porta Férrea** (Iron Gate), off R. São Pedro. *(Open daily 9:30am-12:30pm and 2-5:30pm. 250$.)* The staircase at the right leads up to the **Sala dos Capelos** (Graduate's Hall), where portraits of Portugal's kings (6 of whom were born in Coimbra) hang below a beautiful 17th-century ceiling. *(Open daily 9:30am-12:30pm and 2-5pm. 250$.)* The **university chapel** and mind-boggling, entirely gilded 18th-century **Biblioteca Joanina** (the university library) lie past the Baroque clock tower. *(☎ 239 85 98 41. Open daily 9:30am-noon and 2-4:30pm. 250$, teachers and students free. A package of tickets for all university sights can be purchased for 500$ from the office in the main quad.)*

ACROSS THE RIVER. Cross the bridge in front of Largo Portagem to the other side of the river to find the 14th-century **Convento de Santa Clara-a-Velha.** Far-sighted contractors built it on top of a swamp, and consequently it sinks a little more each year; today more than half of it lies underground and is closed indefinitely. The convent was abandoned in 1687 but was recently renovated to reveal an ancient church founded in 1330 by Queen Isabel, wife of Dom Dinis. The Queen's Gothic tomb was moved uphill to the **Convento de Santa Clara-a-Nova** (1649-1677) when Coimbra's citizenry realized what was going down. *(Open daily 8:30am-6pm. Church free. Cloisters 100$.)*

OTHER SIGHTS. For some green, walk downhill from the university alongside the Aqueducto de São Sebastião to admire the sculpture and fountains of the **Jardim Botânico** public gardens. *(☎ 239 82 28 97. Open daily June-Sept. 9am-7pm, Oct.-May 9am-5:30pm. Gardens free. Greenhouses 250$, students and over 65 150$.)* If you descend the large staircase and pass through Pr. República into the lush **Santa Cruz Park,** also known as the Jardim da Sereia (Mermaid's Garden), you'll encounter a beautiful moss-covered fountain. Back in the lower town at Pr. 8 de Maio, at the far end of R. Ferreira Borges, the **Igreja de Santa Cruz** (Church of the Holy Cross) sits in somber, 12th-century beauty. *(☎ 239 82 29 41. Church open M-Sa 9am-noon and 2-5:45pm. Cloisters and sacristy 200$.)*

◪ NIGHTLIFE

Nightlife gets high honors in Coimbra. After dinner, outdoor cafes around Pr. República buzz from midnight to 4am, and a young crowd fills the nightclubs.

Café-Bar Cartola (☎ 239 83 62 36), Pr. República. This packed cafe-bar is a good spot to people-watch and a popular choice for starting the night out. Sandwiches 170-400$. Coffee 80-170$. Beer 150-300$. Open M-Sa 8am-2am, Su 9am-1am.

Via Latina, R. Almeida Garrett, 1 (☎ 239 83 30 34), around the corner and uphill from Pr. República. Hot in all senses of the word–a young crowd lets loose and dances to salsa at this popular bar. Open F-Sa midnight-8am.

Bar 1910, above a gymnasium on R. Simões Castro. Enjoy free-form *fado* until the wee hours of the morning in this mellow bar and lounge. Beer 300$. Open 11pm-4am.

Diligência Bar, R. Nova, 30 (☎ 239 82 76 67), off R. Sofia. This popular bar is a student hotspot during the year and a tourist favorite in the summer; it is known for its *fado.* Open M-Sa 10pm-2am, Su 9pm-2am.

❊ FESTIVALS

Students rampage day and night during Coimbra's infamous week-long festival, the **Queima das Fitas** (Burning of the Ribbons), in the first or second week of May. The festivities begin when graduating students burn the narrow ribbons they received as first-years and get wide, ornamental ones in return. Live choral music echoes in festooned streets during the **Festas da Rainha Santa,** held the first week of July. In even-numbered years, the festivities more obviously reflect their religious roots with two processions (one at the beginning, one at the end) of a statue of the Rainha Santa, in addition to the standard street party fare. The firework-punctuated **Feira Popular** in the second week of July offers carnival rides and games across the river, as well as traditional Portuguese dancing exhibitions.

🎒 DAYTRIPS FROM COIMBRA

CONÍMBRIGA (30MIN.)

One AVIC bus runs from Coimbra to the ruins (30min., 9:35am, 280$; return bus 6pm); be sure to inquire at the Coimbra tourist office for up-to-date schedules to avoid getting stranded. Buses from Coimbra run more frequently to sleepy Condeixa, 2km away from Conímbriga. If you're done early and want to get back to Coimbra, walk 30min. through the olives groves or take a taxi (☎ 239 94 12 43) to Condeixa and catch a return bus to Coimbra there (25min., 6 per day 7:05am-6:05pm, 250$).

Thirteen kilometers south of Coimbra, Conímbriga is home to the **Ruínas de Conímbriga,** Portugal's largest Roman settlement. First founded by the Celts and later inhabited by the Romans, today it is a favorite stomping ground for local children. Highlights include a 3rd-century town wall, an ancient but luxurious villa, and baths complete with sauna and furnace room. Most amazing of all are the well-preserved mosaics under the shelter of a glass canopy. (Open daily Mar. 16-Sept. 15 9am-10pm; Sept. 16-Mar. 15 9am-6pm. Buy tickets at least 30min. before closing. 350$, students 175$. Price includes the Museu Monográfico de Conímbriga.) The nearby **Museu Monográfico de Conímbriga** displays artifacts unearthed in the area. (☎ 239 94 11 77. Same schedule as the ruins, but closed M.) If you do get stuck in Coimbra, inquire at restaurants about *quartos*. There is a small **tourism bureau** in the Condeixa Town Hall (☎ 239 94 11 14; fax 239 92 27 11) that can usually help with finding a place to spend the night.

BUÇACO FOREST AND LUSO (45MIN.)

Buses run from Coimbra to Buçaco (45min.; M-F 7 per day 7:35am-7:20pm, Sa 9am and 12:45pm, Su 10:15am and 5:30pm; 480$) and continue on to Viseu. Buses leave from Buçaco's station on Av. Fernão de Magalhães, near the palace and a 15min. walk from downtown (last bus returns to Coimbra daily at 6:25pm). Schedules change frequently; confirm departing times at the tourist office in Coimbra so you don't get stuck, as the hotel/palace is out of your budget. Buses back to Coimbra leave a couple of blocks from the tourist office, across from the natural springs (35min.; M-F 6 per day 7:35am-6:35pm, Sa 10:35am and 6:35pm, Su 9am and 4:35pm; 450$).

Buçaco (also spelled Bussaco), home to Portugal's most revered forest, has drawn wanderers trying to escape the city for centuries. In the 6th century, Benedictine monks settled in the Buçaco Forest, established a monastery, and remained in control until the 1834 disestablishment of all religious orders. The forest owes its fame, however, to another group monks, the Carmelites, who arrived here nearly 400 years ago. Selecting the forest for their *desertos* (isolated dwellings for penitence), the Carmelites planted over 700 types of trees and plants brought from around the world by missionaries.

In the center of the forest, adjoining the old Carmelite convent, is Dom Manuel II's exuberant **Palácio de Buçaco.** Now a luxury hotel, the building is a flamboyant display of neo-Manueline architecture. The *azulejos* on the outer walls depict scenes from

Os Lusíadas, the great Portuguese epic about the Age of Discovery (see **Literature**, p. 526). In the forest itself, landmarks include the **Fonte Fria** (Cold Fountain), the **Vale dos Fetos** (Fern Valley), and the **Porta de Rainha** (Queen's Gate). Hardcore hikers can trek one hour along the Via Sacra to a sweeping panorama of the countryside from the **Cruz Alta** viewpoint. The 17th-century chapels there represent stations of the cross.

After romping around the woods, the tiny town of **Luso**, a 3km walk downhill from Buçaco, makes a sweet stopover (provided you still have energy) before catching a bus back to Coimbra. Home to the crisp, cold spring **Fonte de São João**, Luso is the source of much of Portugal's bottled water. Be sure to get directions or a map from the hotel/palace (ask nicely) in Buçaco before attempting the long stroll. Once there, enjoy the free water—you've earned it. Luso's **tourist office**, R. Emídio Navarro, 136, in the center of town, provides a list of hostels. (☎ 231 93 91 33; fax 231 93 91 33. Open July-Sept. M-F 9:30am-1pm and 2-7pm, Sa-Su 10am-1pm and 3-5pm; Oct.-June M-F 9:30am-12:30pm and 2:30-6pm, Sa 10am-1pm).

FIGUEIRA DA FOZ

Figueira da Foz's best feature is undoubtedly its giant beach, 3 sq. km of Sahara-like sand. Figueira da Foz is also one of the biggest party towns in Portugal; pleasure-seekers who don't mind the proliferation of ugly concrete buildings come to pay homage to the sun and the neon sign. At night, tanned couples and rowdy youths crowd the numerous bars and discos and press their luck at the infamous casino. For those who seek a bit more relaxation, the little fishing town of **Buarcos**, on the northern end of the beach, replaces mindless entertainment with a badly needed breath of serenity.

▐ TRANSPORTATION

Trains: (☎ 233 42 83 16), on Lg. Estação, off Av. de Saraiva de Carvalho, near the bridge. Trains are the best way to reach Coimbra and Porto. The station is an easy walk to the tourist office and beach (25min.). With the river to the left, Av. Saraiva de Carvalho becomes R. 5 de Outubro at the fountain and then curves into Av. 25 de Abril. To: **Coimbra** (1hr., 27 per day 5:20am-12:20am, 290$); **Aveiro** (1½hr., 7 per day 8:50am-8:50pm, 850$), via Coimbra; **Leiria** (1½hr., 5 per day 9:10am-5:35pm, 530$); **Porto** (2¼hr., 8 per day 8:50am-8:50pm, 1120$), via Coimbra; and **Lisbon** (3½hr., 9 per day 9:25am-7:50pm, 1510$).

Buses: Terminal Rodoviário (☎ 233 42 67 03), in the center of town, 15min. from the tourist office. Confusing multiple ticket offices make trains the better option. To: **Coimbra** (1½hr., 9 per day 7:15am-8:05pm, 570$); **Leiria** (1½hr.; M-F 7 per day 9:20am-8pm, Sa-Su 3 per day 9:45am-7:15pm; 670$); **Aveiro** (1½hr., M-F 7 per day 7am-6:45pm, Sa-Su 5 per day 7:45am-6:45pm; 690-1150$); **Alcobaça** (1½hr., 8:45am, 1300$) via Leiria; **Fátima** (1½hr., 8:45am, 1200$) via Leiria; **Lisbon** (3hr., 4 per day 6:50am-6:15pm, 1550$); and **Faro** (12hr., 8:45am and 6:15pm, 3100$) via Lisbon.

Taxis: (☎ 233 42 08 80 or 233 42 35 00). Taxis congregate near Pr. 8 de Maio.

✳▐ ORIENTATION AND PRACTICAL INFORMATION

Packed with hotels, beachfront **Avenida 25 de Abril** is the town's lifeline; after the fortress, it turns into **Rua 5 de Outubro** and then again into **Avenida de Saraiva de Carvalho**, which leads toward the train station. Four blocks inland and parallel to the Av. 25 de Abril, **Rua Bernardo Lopes** harbors semi-affordable hostels and restaurants, as well as the casino-cinema-disco complex, center of the city's nightlife.

Tourist Office: (☎ 233 40 28 27; fax 233 40 28 20), Av. 25 de Abril, down the street from the casino, next to the Aparthotel Atlântico. From the bus station, turn right (facing the church) onto R. Dr. Santos Rocha, walk until you hit the waterfront, and turn right onto R. 5 de Outubro, which curves into Av. 25 de Abril. English-speaking staff provides a useful map and temporary **luggage storage.** Open June-Sept. daily 9am-midnight; Oct.-May M-F 9am-5:30pm, Sa-Su 10am-12:30pm and 2:30-6:30pm.

Emergency: ☎ 112. **Police:** (☎ 233 42 88 81), R. Joaquim Carvalho, by the bus station.

Hospital: (☎ 233 40 20 00), across the river in the Gala district. Take the "Gala" or "Hospital" bus from in front of the market on R. 5 de Outubro, or take a cab.

Post Office: Estação Jardim, Passeio Infante Dom Henrique, 41 (☎ 233 40 26 00), off the public gardens on R. 5 de Outubro. Label **Posta Restante** mail "Estação Jardim" or mail might go to the inconvenient Bairro da Estação branch, by the train station. Open M-F 8:30am-6:30pm, Sa 9am-12:30pm. **Bairro Novo branch,** R. Miguel Bombarda, 76 (☎ 233 40 23 30). Open M-F 9am-12:30pm and 2:30-6pm. **Postal Code:** 3080.

Internet Access: Café Nicola (☎ 233 40 84 00), R. Bernando Lopes, across from the casino. 500$ per hr. for the first 2hr.; 400$ per hr. afterwards. Open daily July-Sept. 8:30am-2am; Oct.-June Su-Th 8:30am-midnight, F 8:30am-1am, Su 8:30-2am.

ACCOMMODATIONS

Scour R. Bernardo Lopes and side streets for reasonable hostels. Proprietors may demand ridiculous prices for rooms, especially in summer. Arrive early in the day to secure a room; some *pensões* will not reserve by phone in summer and those that do accept reservations may require partial pre-payment.

Pensão Central, R. Bernardo Lopes, 36, 2nd fl. (☎ 233 42 23 08). Centrally located, next to Supermercado Ovo, and down the street from the casino complex. Breakfast included. June-Sept. singles 5000$, with bath 6000$; doubles 8000$; triples 9000$. Oct.-Apr. singles 3000$, with bath 4000$; doubles 6000$; triples 6000$.

Pensão Residencial Bela Figueira, R. Miguel Bombarda, 13 (☎ 233 42 27 28; fax 233 42 99 60), 2 blocks from the tourist office above an Indian restaurant of the same name. Clean rooms close to the beach, most with TVs. Breakfast included in the summer. June-Sept. singles 2650$, with bath 3600$; doubles 3850-6500$, with bath 4900-8500$; triples 4350-7500$, with bath 5450-9500$. Oct.-May singles 2650$, with bath 3500$; doubles 3650$, with bath 4500$; triples 4300$, with bath 5500$. Cheaper, smaller, dimmer rooms in the basement. V, MC, AmEx.

■ **Camping: Parque Municipal de Campismo da Figueira da Foz Municipal** (☎ 233 40 28 18), on Estrada Buarcos. With the beach on the left, walk up Av. 25 de Abril and turn right at the roundabout on R. Alexandre Herculano, then turn left at Parque Santa Catarina. Or take a taxi from the bus or train station (600$). Excellent site complete with an Olympic-size pool, tennis courts, market, and currency exchange. Showers 100$. 2-person min. per party. Reception daily June-Sept. 8am-8pm; Oct.-May 8am-7pm. Quiet hours midnight-7am. 400$ per person, 300-400$ per tent, 300$ per car.

FOOD

Restaurants in Figueira da Foz are more expensive than average. Thankfully, hope (and good food) comes in the form of R. Bernardo Lopes. The truly lazy can frequent any of the numerous eateries right on the beach. A local **market** sets up beside the municipal garden on R. 5 de Outubro (open daily June-Aug. 6am-7pm; Sept.-May M-F 6am-5pm, Sa 6am-1pm). For groceries, check out **Supermercado Ovo,** on the corner of R. Francisco António Dinis and R. Bernardo Lopes. (☎ 233 42 00 52. Open M-Sa 8am-8pm, Su 9am-2pm.)

Restaurante Bela Figueira, R. Miguel Bombardo, 13 (☎ 233 42 27 28), under the hostel of the same name. Tasty Indian and local cuisine, including many veggie options. Entrees 950-1500$. Open daily noon-3:30pm and 6pm-midnight. V, MC, AmEx.

Café Nicola (☎ 233 40 84 00), R. Bernando Lopes, across from the casino. Popular cafe makes for cheap eats and good people-watching. Coffee 80-160$. Sandwiches 150-450$. Pizzas 750-850$. *Prato do dia* 850$. Open daily July-Sept. 8:30am-2am; Oct.-June Su-Th 8:30am-midnight, F 8:30am-1am, Su 8:30-2am.

Restaurante Rancho, R. Miguel Bombarda, 40-44 (☎ 233 42 20 19), 2 blocks from the tourist office. Packed with locals enjoying hearty Portuguese meals in a dim and comfortable bar setting. Entrees 550-1200$. Open M-Sa noon-3pm and 7-10pm.

☞♪ SIGHTS AND ENTERTAINMENT

Figueira da Foz's only real sight is the **Palácio Sotto Mayor,** on R. Joaquim Sotto Mayor, the continuation of R. da Liberdade which runs parallel to the beach, whose modest exterior conceals the shameless extravagance inside. Lavish green marble columns line the main hallway and gold leaf covers the ceiling. (☎ 233 42 20 41. Open Tu-Su 2-6pm. 200$.) The **Museu Municipal do Doutor Santos Rocha,** in Parque Abadias, just up from the public gardens on R. 5 de Outubro, re-awakens the intellect with displays of ancient coins and the fashions of Portuguese nobility. (R. Caloust Gulbenkian. ☎ 233 40 28 40. Open Tu-Su 9:30am-5:15pm. Free.) If you tire of sunbathing, head to the neighboring town of **Buarcos**.

Nightlife in Figueira de Foz takes off between 10pm and 2am and continues until dawn. Bars and clubs line Av. 25 de Abril, next to and above the tourist office. **Rolls Bar,** on R. Poeta Acácio Antunes, 1E, is popular with just about everyone. (Beer 200-400$. Mixed drinks 500-800$. Open M-Sa 5pm-6am.) Most popular of all is the **casino complex,** on R. Dr. Calado, at the corner of R. Bernardo Lopes. This crowd-pleaser includes a nightclub, cinema, and arcade. (Nightclub ☎ 233 40 84 00. Cover 1000$, includes 2 beers. Beer 300-400$. Mixed drinks 600-800$. Open daily July-Sept. 12:30-6am; Oct.-June Th-Sa 12:30-6am. Cinema tickets Tu-Su 650$, M 500$. Casino open daily 3pm-3am. Entry to slot machines and bingo free. Age 18 and over with ID needed to gamble.)

Figueira's partying lifestyle shifts from high gear to warp speed during the month-long **Festa de São João,** usually starting the second week of June and continuing through the first week of July. Around 5am on Dia de São João (June 23) and again on June 24, a huge rowdy procession heads for the beach at nearby Buarcos, where all involved take a *banho santo* (holy bath) in the ocean. The **Festival de Cinema da Figueira da Foz** screens international flicks in September.

AVEIRO

The old center of Aveiro is graced with a network of canals along which traditional *gonalas* (seaweed-coated fishing boats reminiscent of Venice's gondolas) drift out to sea. This storied maritime town has inspired an amalgam of historical anecdotes and houses the convent where canonized princess Santa Joana once lived (see p. 625). But Aveiro is perhaps best known for its numerous beaches, all of which are easily accessible by ferries from town.

⌐ TRANSPORTATION

Trains: (☎ 234 42 44 85), Lg. Estação, at the end of Av. Dr. Lourenço Peixinho. To: **Porto** (45min., 21 per day 4:35am-1:10am, 330$); **Ovar** (20min., 21 per day 4:35am-1:10am, 290$); **Coimbra** (1hr., 19 per day, every hr. 6:10am-1:10am, 520$); **Braga** (2hr., 10:35am and 8:35pm, 960$); and **Lisbon** (5hr., 14 per day 6:45am-8:50pm, 1720-3250$).

Ferries: TransRia (☎ 234 33 10 95) ferries leave from **Forte da Barra;** buses go from R. Clube dos Galitos, across the canal from the tourist office, to Forte da Barra (30min.; M-F 10 per day 7:15am-6:40pm, Sa-Su 5 per day 10am-6pm; 250$). Ferries run daily to the beach at **São Jacinto** (15min.; 8-10 per day 7:10am-7:05pm, more in July and Aug.; 250$). The last ferry back from Forte da Barra is at 6:15pm, and the last bus to Aveiro is at M-F 6:55pm (Sa-Su 5:30pm). To avoid the hassle of a bus-ferry transfer, you can walk to the Vera Cruz docks (where the old fish auction is) to catch a **direct ferry** to São Jacinto (9 per day 7:05am-12:25am; last return ferry at midnight; 250$). From the tourist office follow R. João Mendonça as it winds around the park, turn left on R. João Afonso, and then right on R. B. Machado; the ferry dock is on a continuation of this street, past the small highway. Check at the tourist office for up-to-date schedules.

Taxis: (☎ 234 42 29 43 or 234 42 37 66). Taxis surround the train station on Av. Lourenço Peixinho and along the canal in Pr. Humberto Delgado.

✦🛈 ORIENTATION AND PRACTICAL INFORMATION

Aveiro is split by the central canal and a parallel street, **Avenida Dr. Lourenço Peix-inho,** which runs from the train station to **Praça Humberto Delgado.** The fishermen's quarter, **Beira Mar,** lies north of the central canal (the side with the train station). In the south end of the city lies the residential district and all of Aveiro's historical monuments. To reach the **tourist office** from the **train station,** walk straight up Av. Dr. Lourenço Peixinho (the left-most street) until you reach the bridge (about 15min.); the office is on the right on the next block.

Tourist Office: R. João Mendonça, 8 (☎ 234 42 36 80; fax 234 42 83 26), off Pr. Humberto Delgado, on the street to the right of the canal facing the ocean. Maps, bus and ferry schedules. English spoken. Temporary **luggage storage.** Open daily July-Sept. 9am-8pm; Oct.-June M-F 9am-7pm, Sa 9am-1pm and 2:30-5:30pm.

Currency Exchange: Banks line Av. Dr. Lourenço Peixinho and are open M-F 8:30am-3pm. **ATMs** also line Av. Dr. Lourenço Peixinho, as well as Pr. Humberto Delgado and Pr. Marquês de Pombal.

Emergency: ☎ 112. **Police:** (☎ 234 42 20 22), Pr. Marquês de Pombal.

Hospital: (☎ 234 37 83 00), Av. Dr. Artur Ravara, near the park across the canal.

Post Office: Main office (☎ 234 38 12 86), Pr. Marquês de Pombal, across the canal and up R. Coimbra. Open M-F 8:30am-6:30pm, Sa 9am-12:30pm. **Branch office,** Av. Dr. Lourenço Peixinho, 169B (☎ 234 42 01 95), 2 blocks from the train station. Open M-F 8:30am-6:30pm. **Postal Code:** 3800 for north of the canal, 3810 for south.

Internet Access: Byblos.arte@net, R. Cais do Alboi, 5 (☎ 234 37 84 60), across the river from the tourist office, to the right; an extension of R. Clube dos Gailitos. 400$ for 30min., 300$ with student ID. Open M-F 10am-1pm and 2:30-7:15pm, Sa 10am-1pm.

▌ ACCOMMODATIONS

The hostels lining Av. Dr. Lourenço Peixinho and across the river on the streets around Pr. Marquês de Pombal in the old city are a little expensive, but are good backups. Scour the streets of the old town (north of Pr. Humberto Delgado, on the side of the canal with the tourist office) for a *quarto*, or consider camping at São Jacinto. Hostel prices generally fall during the winter.

▨ Pensão Beira, R. José Estêvão, 18 (☎ 234 42 42 7), off Pr. Humberto Delgado. Friendly owner and big rooms, all with TVs, most with private baths. Breakfast included. Apr.-Sept. singles 4000-5000$; doubles 6000-8000$; triples 7500-9000$; quads 10,000-12,000$. Oct.-Mar. singles 3500$; doubles 5000$; triples 6000$; quads 8000$.

Residencial Santa Joana, Av. Dr. Lourenço Peixinho, 227, 2nd fl. (☎ 234 42 86 04), 1 block from the train station on the left. 5 floors stack 16 plain, spacious rooms with phones, TVs, and private baths. Singles 4500$; doubles 7500$; triples 9500$.

Residencial Estrela, R. José Estêvão, 4 (☎ 234 42 38 18). Aristocratic rooms on the 1st fl.; servant-sized quarters higher up. All with baths, TVs, and gilded ceilings. Friendly, English-speaking owner. Breakfast included. Singles 3000-4000$, with bath 4500$; doubles 5500$, with bath 6000$; triples 7000-8000$. Sizable discount in the winter.

Camping: Orbitur's Parque de Campismo de São Jacinto (☎ 234 83 82 84; fax 234 83 81 22). See **Ferries,** p. 623, for directions to São Jacinto. From there, hike 5km or take a bus (150$) to the campsite. Sometimes crowded. Free hot showers. Reception daily 8am-10pm. June-Sept. 590$ per person, 470$ per tent, 500$ per car; Apr.-May 530$ per person, 430$ per tent, 450$ per car; Feb.-Mar. and Oct.-Nov. 350$ per person, 290$ per tent, 300$ per car. Open Feb.-Nov.

EAT YOUR HEART OUT, DON JUAN There's love, and then there's *love*. Dom Pedro I was in the latter. While a prince, he fell head-over-heels for Inês de Castro, the daughter of a Spanish nobleman and lady-in-waiting to his first wife. Pedro's father, Afonso IV, objected to the romance, fearing that such an alliance would open the Portuguese throne to Spanish domination. Despite his father's opposition to the marriage, Pedro fled with Inês to Bragança, where the couple secretly wed. Soon thereafter, the disgruntled Afonso had Inês killed. Upon rising to the throne two years later, Pedro personally ripped out the hearts of the men who had slit his young wife's throat and proceeded to eat them. Henceforth, the hardy king became known as Pedro the Cruel. In a disheartening ceremony, he had Inês's body exhumed, dressed her meticulously in royal robes, set her on the throne, and officially deemed her his queen; he even, according to legend, made his court kiss her rotting hand. She was eventually reinterred in an exquisitely carved tomb in the king's favorite monastery, the Mosteiro de Santa Maria de Alcobaça. The king later joined her. The inscription on their tombs reads, *"Até ao fim do mundo"* (until the end of the world).

FOOD

Seafood restaurants are common in Aveiro, but prices will make you want to catch your own fish. Cast your nets off Av. Dr. Lourenço Peixinho and R. José Estêvão. Aveiro's specialty, a dessert pastry called *ovos moles* (sweetened egg yolks), can be found at most of the *pastelarias* (pastry shops) which line Av. Dr. Lourenço Peixinho. For groceries try **Supermercado Pingo Doce**, R. Batalhão Caçadores, 10, across the canal from the tourist office. (☎ 234 38 60 42. Open daily 9am-10pm.)

Restaurante Zico, R. José Estêvão, 52 (☎ 234 42 96 49), off Pr. Humberto Delgado. This diner-style restaurant is packed with locals pigging out on delicious Portuguese cuisine. Entrees 850-1550$. Half-portions 800-1000$. Open M-Sa 8am-2am.

Sonatura Restaurante Self-Service Naturista, R. Clube dos Galitos, 6 (☎ 234 42 44 74), directly across the canal from the tourist office. Vegetarian-macrobiotic-dietetic-foodstore-restaurant serves 2 daily menus (650-900$) that include soup, organic bread, and an entree, as well as delicious yet somehow healthy deserts (150-400$). Open M-F 8am-7pm, Sa 9am-4:30pm.

Restaurante Salimar, R. Luís Cipriano, 21, 2nd fl. (☎ 234 42 27 54), across the river and a block uphill from the tourist office. Ocean decor for ocean-fresh dishes. Their specialty is *arroz de marisco*, a bubbling, orange-red broth swimming with rice and seafood (1100$; 2000$ for 2). Entrees 850-1500$. Open Su-F 8am-10pm.

SIGHTS

Simple but strikingly blue *azulejos* make up the walls of the **Igreja da Misericórdia**, in Pr. República, across the canal and a block uphill from the tourist office. (☎ 234 42 67 32. Open M-F 10am-12:30pm and 2:30-5pm.) In the same square, the regal **Praça do Município** (town hall) flaunts its French design and bell tower. The old town's main attraction is the **Museu de Aveiro**, R. Sta. Joana Princesa. It was here that King Afonso and his daughter Infanta Joana, wished to become a nun despite her father's objections, fought it out in 1472. Luckily for the sick and poor of Aveiro, she won. Beneath *azulejo* panels depicting the story of her life is Santa Joana's Renaissance tomb, supported by the heads of four angels; it is one of the most famous works of art in Portugal. (☎ 234 42 32 97. Open Tu-Su 10am-5:30pm. 250$, seniors and students 125$. Su before 2pm free.)

◀♫ BEACHES AND ENTERTAINMENT

Some of the beach towns near Aveiro have beautiful sand dunes well worth a day-trip from Aveiro. Like the natural reserve at the **Dunas de São Jacinto** (10km away), most of them are easily accessible by ferry (see **Ferries,** p. 623). Closer to Aveiro, the beaches **Barra** and **Costa Nova** can be reached by bus from the *canal central* or train station stops (15min.; 12 per day 7:10am-8:45pm, last bus back 8:15pm; 250$).

At night, tap into the watering-holes along R. Canal de São Roque (on the side of the canal with the tourist office, along the waterfront perpendicular to the *canal central)*. Strut your stuff at **Salpoente,** on Cais de São Roque, or neighboring **Estrondo Bar** and **Urgência,** on R. São Roque. For a more casual setting, try the bars around **Pr. Peixe.** For four weeks starting in mid-July, the city shakes for the **Festa da Ria,** which celebrates Aveiro's long boating tradition. During the festivities, locals race traditional *moliceiros* (beautifully carved and decorated boats).

◢ DAYTRIP FROM AVEIRO

OVAR (20MIN.)

Buses to the beach, the hostel, and the campgrounds stop in front of the train station, just past the tourist office, to the right of the garden (M-F 21 per day 7:10am-8:10pm, Sa 11 per day 7:10am-7:10pm, Su 5 per day 9:30am-8:10pm; last return bus M-F 7:20pm, Sa-Su 6pm; 140$). The train station (☎ 256 58 59 76), on Lg. Serpa Pinto, off R. António Coentro Pinho, has service to Aveiro (20min., 19 per day 5:45am-12:45am, 260$).

This *azulejo*-filled town hemmed in on two sides by pine forest and on one side by an isolated beach, is a relaxing stopover on the way to Porto. While there's not much to do here except lounge on the virtually untouristed beach, **Praia do Furadouro,** no one seems to mind. The **tourist office,** on R. Elias Garcia, has maps and transportation info. From the train station, head straight up the street, through the traffic circle on Pr. São Cristóvão, and take Av. Bom Reitor (the 2nd left; not the sharp left, but the one across the rotary), following it as it becomes R. Elias Garcia. (☎ 256 57 22 15. Open July-Aug. M-F 9am-7pm, Sa-Su 10am-1pm and 3-6pm; Sept.-June M-Sa 10am-noon and 2-5:30pm.) Put your feet up at the brand-new ▧**Pousada da Juventude de Ovar (HI),** Av. Dom Manuel I (EN 327). Take the bus to the beach and get off at the stop just before the traffic circle. Turn right onto Av. Dom Manuel I (follow the signs to Porto), and walk for about 10 minutes. Pristine rooms, a bar with billiards and satellite TV, a swimming pool, and home-cooked meals (lunch or dinner 950$) make this modern hostel a prime rest-stop. **Bike rental** available for 200$ per hr. or 1000$ per day. (☎/fax 256 59 18 32. Reception 8am-midnight. Call ahead. June 16-Sept. 15 dorms 1900$; doubles with bath 4600$. Sept. 16-June 15 dorms 1500$; doubles with bath 3800$.) For food, shop at the **mercado municipal** (open Th and Sa 8am-5pm) on R. Gomes Freire.

NORTHERN PORTUGAL

DOURO AND MINHO

Although their landscapes and Celtic history invite comparison with the northwest of Spain, the Douro and Minho regions of northern Portugal are more populated, developed, and wealthier than Spanish Galicia. Thanks to the area's mineral richness, these regions have had a prosperous history. The evidence is everywhere from the abundance of luxurious villas to the traditional female dress, which includes layers of gold necklaces encrusted with charms. This affluence has a long legacy: the Kingdom of Portugal originated here in 1143 when Afonso Henriques defeated the Moors in Guimarães.

Ultimately, though, wealth and history take a backseat to the region's spectacular greenery. Douro and Minho are a haven for nature lovers: hundreds of trellised vineyards that grow grapes for *porto* and *vinho verde* wines beckon connoisseurs, and houses tiled in brilliant *azulejos* draw visitors to peaceful streets. The region's mild coastal climate is too cool to attract the beach crowd until July, and only a few ambitious travelers ever make it past Porto and the Douro Valley to the greens and blues of the Alto Minho, which hugs the Spanish border. Happily untouristed, the cities of Vila Nova de Cerveira, Braga, Viana do Castelo, and Guimarães will reward the intrepid traveler.

> **HIGHLIGHTS OF DOURO AND MINHO**
>
> **Porto,** with its dramatic **gorge** and world-famous **wine lodges** (see below).
> **Parque Nacional da Peneda-Gerês,** Portugal's finest nature reserve (see p. 641).
> **Viano do Castelo**'s marvelous **Praça da República** (see p. 644).

> **LOCAL FESTIVALS IN DOURO AND MINHO**
> The biggest bash in the area is undeniably the *Festa de São João* (June 23-24). The celebration in **Porto** is probably the most extravagant, but the residents of **Braga** give it a unique twist with their tradition of hitting each other on the head with toy hammers. Porto also honors Spanish and Portuguese theater with the *Festival Internacional de Teatro Expressão Ibérica* in early June.

PORTO (OPORTO)

Porto is one of Portugal's most sophisticated and modern cities. Although it is a center for all sorts of arts and commerce, the source of its greatest fame (and its name) is its sugary-sweet port wine. Founded by English merchants in the early 18th century, the port industry is at the root of the city's successful economy and provides good enough reason in itself to come visit. But there's more to Porto than just port. Magnificently situated on a gorge cut by the Douro River, just 6km from the sea, Portugal's second-largest city is marked by an elegance reminiscent of Paris or Prague, and it often seems more vibrant than Lisbon. Granite church towers pierce the skyline, closely packed orange-tiled houses huddle along the river, and three of Europe's most graceful bridges span the gorge above. All this has earned Porto the honor of being one of two European cities (Rotterdam is the other) designated as Cultural Capitals of Europe for 2001. The declaration has not only spawned a large "urban regeneration" project, but also focused new attention on the city's rich culture.

TRANSPORTATION

Flights: Aeroporto Francisco de Sá Carneiro (☎ 22 941 32 60), 20km from downtown Porto. The city bus (#56) to the airport from Pr. Lisbon can be very slow. The **aerobus,** which leaves from Av. dos Aliados near Pr. Liberdade, is more efficient (40min., every 30min. 7am-6:30pm, 500$). Buy tickets on board, at an **STCP** window, or at a participating hotel. Even quicker is a **taxi** (20-30min., about 2500-3000$). **TAP Air Portugal,** Pr. Mouzinho de Albuquerque, 105 (☎ 22 608 02 00), flies to major European cities.

Trains: Estação Campanhã (☎ 22 536 41 41). All trains pass through Porto's main station, east of the center. Trains run from Campanhã to: **Aveiro** (1¼hr., 30 per day 5:05am-11:15pm, 330$); **Viana do Castelo** (2hr., 11 per day 5:35am-12:35am, 770$); **Braga** (2hr., 21 per day 6am-11:20pm, 330-530$); **Coimbra** (1½hr., 17 per day every hr. 5:05am-10:05pm, 1010-1040$); **Lisbon** (4½hr., 14 per day 6am-8:05pm, 2080-3700$); **Faro** (9hr.; Tu, Th and Su 10:10pm; 3090$); **Madrid** (13-14hr., 6:10pm, 9030-9655$); and **Vigo, Spain** (2½hr., 7:40am and 6:55pm, 2225$). **Estação São Bento** (☎ 22 200 27 22), centrally located 1 block off Pr. Liberdade, is the terminus for trains with mostly local and regional routes. If your train stops at Estação de Campanhã, it is usually best to take a connecting train to São Bento. Frequent connections to **Estação São Bento** (5min., every 20-30min. 5:05am-11:15pm, 140$). Buses #34 and 35 also connect Campanhã to downtown (every 30min., 180$).

Buses: There is no central bus station; over 20 different companies operate out of garages all over the downtown area. **Garagem Atlântico,** R. Alexandre Herculano, 366 (☎ 22 205 24 59) has Rede Expressos to: **Braga** (1¼hr., 8 per day 9:25am-12:15am, 870$); **Bragança** (5hr., 7 per day 7:15am-8:15pm, 1500$); **Coimbra** (1½hr., 11 per day 7:15am-12:45am, 1410$); **Viana do Castelo** (1¾hr., 2 per day 10:55am and 6:40pm, 1500$); **Lisbon** (4hr., 12 per day 7:15am-12:45am, 2300$). **Rodoviaria Entre Douro e Minho** (☎ 22 200 31 52), 2 blocks from Pr. República, has buses to **Braga** (1hr.; M-F 26 per day 6:45am-8pm, Sa-Su 9-12 per day 7:15am-8pm; 680$). **Rodonorte** (☎ 22 200 56 37), R. Atenou Comercial do Porto, 1 block from R. Sá da Bandeira, goes to **Vila Real** (2hr.; M-F 16 per day 6:50am-10:30pm, Sa-Su 6 per day 6:50am-7:30pm; 1000$) and **Amarante** (1hr.; M-F 16 per day 6:50am-10:30pm, Sa-Su 6 per day 6:50am-7:30pm; 800$). **Renex,** R. Carmelitas, 32 (☎ 22 200 33 95), has express service via Lisbon to **Lagos** (9½hr., 8 per day 5:30am-1:15am, 3500$) and **Vila Real de São António** (9½hr., 5 per day 9am-4pm, 3500$). **Internorte,** Pr. Galiza, 96 (☎ 22 605 24 20) has international service to: **Madrid** (10½hr.; Tu, Th, and

Sa-Su 9am; 5470$); **Paris** (27hr., Tu-Sa 8am, 9000$); **Brussels** (28hr., Tu and F 9:30am, 19,745$); **Geneva** (30hr.; Tu, Th, and Sa 9:30am; 16,930$); and **Berlin** (39hr., Tu and F 9:30am, 25,930$). Booking tickets 3 days in advance is strongly recommended. Office open M-F 9am-12:30pm and 2-6:30pm, Sa 9am-12:30pm and 2-4pm, Su 9am-12:30pm and 2-5:30pm.

Public Transportation: New **tram** lines are springing up throughout the city (single ticket 85$), but **buses** are farther reaching. Buy tickets ahead of time (90$) from small kiosks around the city, or at the **STCP** office, Pr. Almeida Garrett, 27, half a block downhill and across the street from Estação São Bento. Tickets purchased on the bus cost twice as much (180$). One-day unlimited tickets (400$) are also a good deal (buy these on the bus). STCP office open M-F 8am-7:30pm, Sa 8am-1pm.

Taxis: Raditáxis, R. Alegria, 1802 (☎ 22 507 39 00). Taxis hang out on Av. dos Aliados and along the river in the Ribeira district.

✴🛈 ORIENTATION AND PRACTICAL INFORMATION

Do yourself a favor: pick up a free map at the tourist office. Constant traffic and a chaotic maze of one-way streets fluster even the most well-oriented of travelers. The city center is easy enough to navigate, where hillside **Praça da Liberdade** is joined to **Praça General Humberto Delgado** by **Avenida dos Aliados.** One of Porto's two train stations, **Estação São Bento,** lies just off Pr. Liberdade. The other, **Estação de Campanhã,** is 2km from the city center along the river. Between the Rio Douro and the city center lies the **Ribeira** district, where much of Porto's sights and nightlife are located on steep and narrow sidestreets that twist, turn, and confuse. Directly across from the Ribeira, **Ponte Dom Luís I** spans the river to **Vila Nova de Gaia,** where port wine ferments in 20-odd lodges. Back on the other side of the river, further to the west, is the **Foz** district, where beaches and bars are the main attraction.

Tourist Office: R. Clube dos Fenianos, 25 (☎ 22 339 34 72), off Pr. Liberdade. From the train station, take a left and cross the street to get to Pr. Liberdade; the tourist office is on the right side of the street further up, at the end of the square. Knowledgeable multilingual staff doles out maps and brochures. Open July-Sept. M-F 9am-7pm; Oct.-June M-F 9am-5:30pm. Smaller **branch**, R. Infante Dom Henrique, 63 (☎ 22 200 97 70), in the Ribeira district, offers service on the weekends. Open July-Sept. M-F 9am-7pm, Sa-Su 9:30am-4:30pm; Oct.-June M-F 9am-5:30pm, Sa-Su 9:30am-4:30pm. **ICEP (national tourism) office,** Pr. Dom João I, 43 (☎ 22 205 75 14), 1 block from Av. dos Aliados between Pr. Gen. Humberto Delgado and Pr. Liberdade, has info on all of Portugal, as well as the best free map of the downtown area in town. Open July-Aug. M-F 9am-7:30pm, Sa-Su 9:30am-7:30pm; Sept.-June M-F 9am-7pm, Sa-Su 9:30am-3:30pm. **ICEP airport branch** (☎ 22 941 25 34) open daily 8am-11:30pm. There are also 24hr. multilingual **computer info stands** in the main shopping centers and the larger squares; one sits in front of the McDonald's in Pr. Liberdade.

Budget Travel: Tagus, R. Campo Alegre, 261 (☎ 22 609 41 46). English-speaking staff; advice and student rates. Open M-F 9am-6pm, Sa 10am-1pm.

Currency Exchange: Portocâmbios, R. Rodrigues Sampaio, 193 (☎ 22 200 02 38), off Pr. Gen. Humberto Delgado, just across from the tourist office. No commission. Open M-F 9am-6pm, Sa 9am-1pm.

American Express: Top Tours, R. Alferes Malheiro, 96 (☎ 22 208 27 85). Facing the town hall at the top of Pr. Liberdade, take Av. dos Aliados 1 block past the tourist office (stay on the left side of the street) and turn left onto R. Alferes Malheiro. Handles all AmEx functions. Open M-F 9:30am-1:30pm and 2:30-6:30pm.

Luggage Storage: Free in **tourist office** during the day. At **Estação São Bento** in lockers to the right as you enter the platform. 2100$ for 48hr. Open daily 5:15am-midnight.

Laundromat: Lavanderia Tropical, R. Bragas, 329 (☎ 22 205 13 97), off R. Mártires da Liberdade. Wash and dry 500$ per kg. Open M-F 8am-12:30pm and 2-7pm, Sa 9:30am-1pm.

THAT TOOK GUTS Porto's history is the stuff from which nationalism is made. When native son Henry the Navigator geared up to conquer Cueta (a soon-to-be Christian base in Morocco) in the early 15th century, Porto's residents slaughtered their cattle, gave all of the meat to Prince Henry's fleet, and kept only the entrails for themselves. This dramatic generosity came at a time when much of Europe was suffering in the wake of the Plague and food supplies were extremely important. The tasty dish *tripàs a moda do Porto* commemorates the culinary self-sacrifice; to this day, the people of Porto are known as *tripeiros* (tripe-eaters). The sacrifice paid off. Henry's decisive victory at Ceuta made possible the spreading of the Portuguese Empire to Africa and eventually India and the Far East. If you're feeling adventurous you can try some of the tripe dishes, which locals—and few others—consider quite a delicacy.

Emergency: ☎ 112. **Police:** Multilingual **tourist station**, R. Clube dos Fenianos, 25 (☎ 22 208 18 33), right next to the main tourist office on the *praça*.

Late-Night Pharmacy: ☎ 118 (directory assistance). Posted on the door of every pharmacy is the address of the next night's neighborhood pharmacy to provide this service.

Hospital: Hospital de Santo António (☎ 22 207 75 00), R. Alberto Aires Gouveia, downtown between the Estação São Bento and the Palácio de Cristal.

Post Office: (☎ 22 340 02 00), Pr. Gen. Humberto Delgado. **Fax, phones, Posta Restante.** Open M-F 8:30am-9pm, Sa-Su 9am-6pm. **Postal Code:** 4000 for central Porto.

Internet Access: Get your fix at **Portweb**, Pr. Gen. Humberto Delgado, 291 (☎ 22 200 59 22), a few doors down from the tourist office. Before 4pm, 100$ per hr. After 4pm, 240$ per hr. Open M-Sa 9am-2am, Su 3pm-2am. **Rivoli Teatro Municipal,** Pr. Dom João I, 2nd fl. (☎ 22 339 22 00), across from the ICEP tourist office, has 2 computers. 200$ per hr. Open M-F 10am-6pm.

█ ACCOMMODATIONS

Rates for singles are higher than the norm, and the city's only youth hostel is somewhat small. For better deals, look west of Av. dos Aliados, or on R. Fernandes Tomás and R. Formosa, perpendicular to Av. dos Aliados. Prices usually dip in the off season, though Porto will likely see its fair share of tourists throughout 2001, given its status as Cultural Capital. Reservations are wise mostly everywhere.

■ **Residencial Paris,** R. Fábrica, 27-29 (☎ 22 207 31 40; fax 22 207 31 49). From the train station, cross the street and turn right into Pr. Liberdade and then left onto R. Dr. Artur de Magalhães Basto, which turns into R. Fábrica. English-speaking manager is a wealth of information. Large rooms, TV room, and lush gardens. Breakfast included. May 15-Sept. singles 3450$, with bath 5300$; doubles 5100$, with bath 7250$; triples 6600$, with bath 9450$. Prices fall Oct.-May 14.

Pensão Porto Rico, R. Almada, 237, 2nd fl. (☎ 22 339 46 90), 1 block over from Av. dos Aliados (to the left when facing city hall). Small but clean rooms with phones, satellite TVs, and radios; some with terraces and baths. Breakfast 350$. Reserve a few days ahead in summer. Singles 4500$; doubles 7500$; triples 9000$. V, MC, AmEx.

Pensão São Marino, Pr. Carlos Alberto, 59 (☎ 22 332 54 99). Facing the town hall, go up Av. dos Aliados on the left side of the street, take the 1st left onto R. Dr. Ricardo Jorge, which becomes R. Conceição, turn left on R. Oliveiras, and make a quick right on Pr. Carlos Alberto. 16 small, bright rooms, all with shower or full bath, phones, TV, and winter heat. Ask for a room overlooking the *praça*. May-Sept. singles 5000$; doubles 6500$; triples 6500-7500$. Oct.-Apr. singles 4000$; doubles 5500$; triples 6000$.

Pousada da Juventude do Porto (HI), R. Paulo da Gama, 551 (☎ 22 617 72 57; fax 22 617 72 47), 3km from town center in the Foz district. Bus #35 from Estação Campanha or #36 from Boavista stop in front of the hostel; #37 from Pr. Liberdade stops a block away on R. Diogo Botelho. In a somewhat dodgy neighborhood; women should be cautious walking around at night. The vending machine makes for a lively social scene. Reception daily 9-11am and 6pm-midnight. June-Sept. dorms 2500$; doubles with bath 6000$. Oct.-May dorms 2000$; doubles with bath 5000$.

NORTHERN PORTUGAL

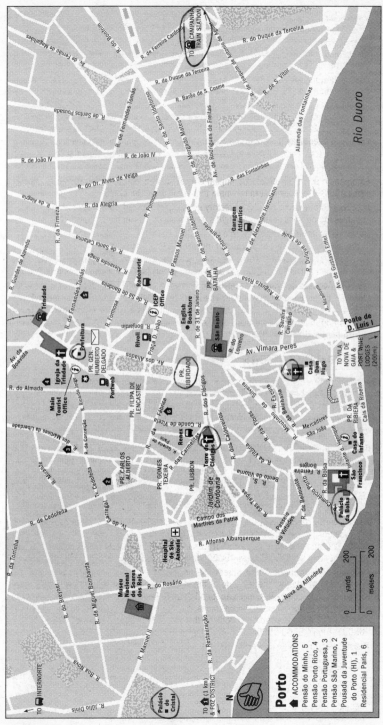

Porto

▲ ACCOMMODATIONS
Pensão do Minho, 5
Pensão Porto Rico, 4
Pensão Portuguesa, 3
Pensão São Marino, 2
Pousada da Juventude
  do Porto (HI), 1
Residencial Paris, 6

Rio Duoro

TO VILA
NOVA DE
GAIA &
PORT WINE
LODGES
(200m)

Ponte de
D. Luís I

TO INTERNORTE

TO (1 km)
& FOZ DISTRICT

N

yards   200
meters   200
0   0

R. Nova da Alfândega

Hospital
de Sto.
António

Museu
Nacional
de Soares
dos Reis

Palácio
do
Cristal

TO CAMPANHÃ
TRAIN STATION

Garagem
Atlântico

Trindade

Igreja da
Trindade

Main
Tourist
Office

Prefeitura

PR. GEN.
HUMBERTO
DELGADO

Penweb

Rodonorte

iCEP
Office

English
Bookstore

Rivoli

PR. DA
BATALHA

São Bento

Sé

Casa
Dom
Hugo

PR.
LIBERDADE

Av. Vímara Peres

Fábrica

Renex

Torre dos
Clérigos

Jardim de
Cordaria

Campo dos
Martíres da Patria

PR. CARLOS
ALBERTO

PR. GOMES
TEIXEIRA

PR. LISBON

São
Francisco

Palácio
da Bolsa

Casa do
Infante

PR. DA
RIBEIRA

Cais da Ribeira

Av. da Boavista

Pensão do Minho, R. Fernandes Tomás, 926 (☎ 22 205 12 72). Walk up Av. dos Aliados, keeping on the right side of the street, until you pass the post office. Take a right onto R. Fernandes Tomás. Small yet functional rooms near the train station, tourist office, and city center. Showers flood the bathroom floor: use the common bath. Mid-sized rooms with double bed (for 1 or 2 people). July-Sept. 3000$; Oct.-June 2500$.

Pensão Portuguesa, Tr. Coronel Pacheco, 11 (☎ 22 200 41 74), off R. Mártires da Liberdade, off Pr. Carlos Alberto. Very cheap, but consider a room with bath–the common bath is a bit dingy. Breakfast included. July-Aug. singles 2000$, with bath 3000$; doubles 3000$, with bath 4000$; triples with bath 4500$. Sept.-June singles 1500$, with bath 2500$; doubles 2500$, with bath 3000$; triples with bath 3500$.

Camping: Prelada (☎ 22 831 26 16), on R. Monte dos Burgos, in Quinta da Prelada, 2km from the town center and 5km from the beach. Take bus #6 from Pr. Liberdade or #54 at night. Reception 8am-1am. 620$ per person, 520$ per tent and per car. **Salgueiros** (☎ 22 781 05 00), near Praia Salgueiros in Vila Nova de Gaia, is less accessible and less equipped, but also less expensive and closer to the beach. 300$ per person, 100$ per tent, 150$ per car.

◘ FOOD

Eating out costs more in Porto than in any other Portuguese city. If you are on a tight budget, pick up fresh produce at one of the outdoor **markets** on Cais Ribeira (open daily 8am-8pm), or at the **Mercado de Bolhão,** on the corner of R. Formosa and R. Sá de Bandeira (open M-F 8am-5pm, Sa 8am-1pm). Doling out a few hundred more *escudos,* however, will land you some tasty dishes. The more touristy (and expensive) restaurants border the river in the Ribeira district, particularly on C. Ribeira, R. Reboleira, and R. Cima do Muro. Budget fare and rowdier environments prevail near Pr. Batalha on R. Cimo de Vila and R. Cativo. Even cheaper eateries lie around the Hospital de Santo António and Pr. Gomes Teixeira, a few blocks west of Pr. Liberdade. Adventurous eaters savor the city's specialty, *tripas à moda do Porto* (tripe and beans; see **That Took Guts,** p. 630).

Majestic Café, R. Santa Catarina, 112 (☎ 22 200 38 87). Touts itself as "the joy of the city of Porto" and some even call it the "second best cafe in Portugal." Chandeliers hang over marble-topped tables and wooden chairs. Treat yourself. Sandwiches 500-950$. Coffee 200-350$. Some of the fanciest (and sweetest) pastries in town 90-200$. Open M-Sa 9:30am-midnight.

Café Guarany, Av. dos Aliados, 85, just up from Pr. Liberdade. Mirror-covered walls and waiters with bow-ties add to this place's pizzaz, making it a popular spot to grab lunch. Usually quieter at dinner, when everyone's in the Ribeira. *Prato do dia* 700$. Sandwiches 200-900$. Pizzas 750-1200$. Entrees 650-1700$. Open daily 8am-11pm.

Restaurante Chinês, Av. Vímara Peres, 38 (☎ 22 200 89 15), on the left just before you cross the top level of the main bridge (Ponte Dom Luís I). Tasty and cheap Chinese food. Rice and noodles 280-950$. Meat entrees 880-1150$. Open Su-Th noon-3pm and 7:30-11pm; F-Sa noon-3pm and 7:30pm-1am. V, MC, AmEx.

SIGHTS

Your first brush with Porto's rich stock of fine artwork may be in, of all places, the **São Bento train station,** home to a celebrated collection of *azulejos.* Outside the station and at the top of adjacent **Praça da Liberdade,** the formidable **Prefeitura** (City Hall) is a monument to Porto's late 19th-century greatness.

CATHEDRAL. Fortified on the hilltop slightly south of the train station is Porto's pride and joy, the Romanesque *sé.* Built in the 12th and 13th centuries, the Gothic, *azulejo*-covered cloister was added later in the 14th century. The **Capela do Santíssimo Sacramento,** to the left of the high altar, shines with solid silver and plated gold. During the Napoleonic invasion, crafty townspeople whitewashed the altar to protect it from vandalism. Climb the staircase to the **Renaissance chapter house** for a splendid view of the old quarter. (*Terreiro da Sé.* ☎ 22 205 90 28. From Pr. Liberdade, walk past Estação São Bento and uphill on Av. Afonso Henriques; the cathedral is on the right. Open M-Sa 9am-12:30pm and 2:30-6pm, Su 2:30-6pm. Cloister 250$.)

■ PALÁCIO DA BOLSA. Cash acquires cachet at the Palácio da Bolsa (Stock Exchange), the epitome of 19th-century elegance. The ornate courtyard ceiling gives a hint of the carefully created opulence inside. It took a zealous artisan three years to carve the exquisite wooden table in the portrait room; the ornate **Sala Árabe** (Arabic Hall) took 18 years to decorate. Modeled after Granada's Alhambra, its gold and silver walls are covered with plaques bearing the oddly juxtaposed inscriptions "Glory to Allah" and "Glory to Queen Maria II." *(R. Ferreira Borges. ☎ 22 339 90 00. From the town center, walk past Estação São Bento and downhill on R. Mouzinho da Silveira to the square; signs lead the way. Open daily 9am-7pm. Multilingual tours every 30min. 800$. Main courtyard free.)*

MUSEU DE ARTE CONTEMPORÂNEA. This museum rotates temporary exhibits of contemporary Portuguese art and architectural design. Ask to see an English video on the artists—all descriptions in the museum are in Portuguese. The building crowns an impressive 44 acres of sculpted gardens, fountains, and old farmland all tumbling down toward the Douro River. *(R. de Serralves, 947-999. ☎ 22 618 00 57. Several kilometers out of town, on the way to the beach. Bus #78 leave from Pr. Dom João I; ask the driver to stop at the museum (30min., return buses run until midnight). Museum open Tu-W and F-Su 10am-7pm, Th 10am-10pm. Park closes at sundown. 800$. Free Su before 2pm.)*

TORRE DOS CLÉRIGOS. Torre dos Clérigos (Tower of Clerics) rises 76m above the adjoining **Igreja dos Clérigos.** Built in the mid-18th century, the granite bell tower, the city's tallest landmark, glimmers like a processional candle. Climb the 200 steps for spectacular views of Porto and the Rio Douro Valley. *(R. dos Clérigos. ☎ 22 200 17 29. Tower open daily June-July 10am-12:30pm and 2-5:30pm. Church open M-Th and Sa 10am-noon and 2-5pm, Su 10am-1pm and 8-10:30pm. Tower 200$; church free.)*

MUSEU NACIONAL DE SOARES DOS REIS. A former royal residence, this 18th-century museum houses an exhaustive collection of 19th-century Portuguese painting and sculpture, much of it by Soares dos Reis, often called Portugal's Michelangelo. *(R. Dom Manuel II, 44. ☎ 22 339 37 70. From the town center, walk down R. Clérigos and R. Restauração, then take R. Dom Manuel II past the churches and forested park (10min.). Open Tu-Su 10am-5:30pm. 350$, seniors and students 175$.)*

IGREJA DE SÃO FRANCISCO. The Gothic Igreja de São Francisco glitters with one of the most elaborately gilded wooden interiors in Portugal. Under the floor, thousands of human bones are stored in preparation for Judgment Day. *(R. Infante Dom Henrique. ☎ 22 206 21 00. From Pr. Liberade, follow the directions to the Palácio da Bolsa; the church is next door. Open M-Sa 9am-6pm. 500$, students 250$.)*

JARDIM DO PALÁCIO DE CRISTAL. A beautiful park lies outside the Palácio de Cristal (Glass Palace), near the hospital. Geese, swans, ducks, peacocks, fountains, and the best-kept garden in Portugal welcome those in search of a good reading spot. *(Exit Pr. Liberdade on R. Clérigos and follow the road around the hospital (right on R. Alberto Gouveia) before taking a left on R. Dom Manuel II. The park and palace are on the left, after the Museu Nacional de Soares dos Reis (10-15min.). Park open daily until dark.)*

THE STUFF THAT PORT IS MADE OF
Port wine is unusually sweet not just because of the grapes it is made from, but because 170-proof brandy is added to the fermenting juice only 2 days after harvesting (in a ratio of 80% grape juice to 20% brandy). The hard alcohol stops the fermentation process, leaving nearly half the natural grape sugar in the wine. Equally important to the making of good port, however, is the immense amount of human labor it requires. Because of the harsh, unpredictable weather in the area, the harvest must be timed precisely (usually mid-Sept. to mid-Oct.) and finished quickly. Mountain villagers flood in and work 12-hour days until the crop is completed. Until 20 years ago, the men spent their evenings crushing grapes by foot in huge concrete troughs, arms linked, and legs purple to their thighs; only recently was this intense labor of love replaced by machines.

BEACH AND ESPLANADE. Porto's rocky beach, in the ritzy **Foz** district in the west end of the city, is a popular destination despite pollution. Beyond the Foz district, on the city's western coastline are the beaches of **Matosinhos.** *(Bus #1 from the São Bento train station heads to both Foz and Matosinhos.)* Between Foz and downtown, at the bottom of the hill on R. Alfândega, past a marvelous dock filled with shops and restaurants, runs the esplanade in **Ribeira.** *(Tram #1 from the Igreja de São Francisco.)*

 # NIGHTLIFE

The place to party on weekend nights is the tirelessly fun **Ribeira**, where bars vibrate with the rhythms of Brazilian and Latin tunes. Pr. Ribeira, M. Bacalhoeiros, and R. Alfândega harbor most of the bars and pubs. Most clubs line the river in the **Foz** district. Bus #1 runs all night from Pr. Liberdade to the beach at Matosinhos, passing Foz along the way. A taxi to Foz from downtown costs about 700$.

Pub O Muro, Muro dos Bacalhoeiros, 87-88 (☎ 22 208 34 26), on a pedestrian street above the river in the Ribeira district. Barefoot bartender and picnic tables with benches give this place the feel of a neighborhood bar. A good place to start the night with a few drinks. Open daily noon-2am.

Discoteca Swing, Praceta Engenheiro Amaro Costa, 766 (☎ 22 609 00 19), near R. Júlio Dinis. Swinging action for a mixed gay-straight crowd grooving to alt-rock, new wave, and pop. Cover 1000$. Open daily 11pm-4am, but the fun starts around 1am.

Twins, R. Passeio Alegre, 994 (☎ 22 618 57 40), on the river in the Foz district. Trendy, international, jet-setting crowd throbs with all their might to blaring dance and house music. Cover 1000$. Open Tu-Sa midnight-4am.

❋ FESTIVALS

For two weeks in February, Porto hosts the **Fantasporto Film Festival,** screening international fantasy, sci-fi, and horror flicks for mobs of tourists. Early June brings the **Festival Internacional de Teatro de Expressão Ibérica,** which showcases Portuguese and Spanish theater, including pieces from the nations' former colonies. Free performances followed by street parties make this a favorite with theater buffs. Porto's biggest party, however, is a lot less cerebral. On the nights of June 23-24, the city lets loose with the street parties of the **Festa de São João,** when locals storm the streets for free concerts, folklore, *fado*, and of course wine. Ask at the tourist office for info about the plethora of events going down in Porto in 2001 to celebrate its status as a Cultural Capital of Europe.

 # PORT LODGES

Now for the reason you came to Porto. You can enjoy the warm glow of port wine by embarking on a "wine connoisseurship" cruise down the Douro River—grab a pamphlet at the tourist office, or just go to the docks off Pr. Ribeira. Wine lodges, however, are the best way to sample local port; most offer free tours and tastings. All of the lodges are across the river in **Vila Nova da Gaia**—walk down to the Ribeira district and cross the lower level of the large bridge (Ponte Dom Luís I).

▨ **Taylor's,** R. do Choupelo, 250 (☎ 22 371 99 99), in the center, up a huge hill. From Av. Diogo Leite (the main street), take a left on R. de França, which turns into R. do Choupelo. Follow it uphill as it curves; Taylor's is on the right. Winner of the highly unscientific *Let's Go* poll for best port lodge in Porto. Ask for your wine on their terrace, which has an amazing view of the city and the Rio Douro. Free tours (every 20-30min.) and tasting. Open July-Aug. M-Sa 10am-6pm; Sept.-June M-F 10am-6pm.

Sandeman, Lg. Miguel Bombarda, 3 (☎ 22 374 05 33), just off Av. Diogo Leite. Costumed guides and high-quality port make this a popular starter. Tours (every 15min.) last about 30min. 500$ entrance, under 16 free. Your ticket is good for a 500$ discount if you buy a bottle of port at the end of the tour. Open Apr.-Sept. daily 10am-12:30pm and 2-6pm; Oct.-Mar. M-F 9:30am-12:30pm and 2-5:30pm.

Cálem, Av. Diogo Leite, 25 (☎ 22 374 66 60), right on the main street along the river, to the right when crossing the bridge from Porto. A less stilted tour than Sandeman, and the port is almost as good. Free tours (every 10-15min.) and tasting. Open July-Sept. daily 10am-6:15pm; Oct.-June M-Sa 10am-5:15pm.

Quinta do Noval, Av. Diogo Leite, 256 (☎ 22 377 02 82), on the main street. No tours, but plenty of free tasting in this breezy bar. Tables and chairs look like wine casks and have a view of the river. Open daily June-Sept. 10am-8pm; Oct.-May M-F 8am-5pm.

Solar do Vinho do Porto, R. Entre Quintas (☎ 22 609 47 49), off R. Dom Manuel II, by the Palácio de Cristal. Take the 1st left after the palace park, which winds downhill and forks; go left into the park, right at the fountain, and down some stairs. A good choice if you're still not tired of tasting port once all the lodges have closed. Once a manor house, this upscale bar/lounge has a terrace with a gorgeous river view. "Glasses of port" start at 300$. Open M-Sa 2pm-midnight.

⌖ DAYTRIP FROM PORTO

AMARANTE (1½HR.)

Rodonorte buses stop at the station (☎ 255 42 21 94) in Largo Conselheiro António Cândido, just across the river from the sights and the tourist office. Buses zip to: Vila Real (45min.; M-F 16 per day 7:50am-11:30pm, Sa 7 per day 7:50am-8:30pm, Su 7 per day 7:50am-11:30pm; 800$); Guimarães (1hr., M-F 10:40am and 6pm, 510-800$); Porto (1½hr.; M-F 10 per day 7:05am-9pm, Sa 5 per day 10:10am-4:40pm, Su 7 per day 10:10am-11:10pm; 800$); and Bragança (2hr., 5 per day 8:30am-6pm, 1500$).

Porto quenches thirst, but Amarante (pop. 5600) feeds the soul, or at least lets it take a rest after sinful city escapades. Mass tourism has yet to rear its ugly head in this emerald green valley sprinkled with whitewashed houses. Amarante's two halves greet each other across the lazy Rio Tâmega, both lined with shady weeping willows. History buffs will want to cross the **Ponte de São Gonçalo,** once a Portuguese stronghold against Napoleonic troops. This historic bridge leads into **Praça da República,** where the lacy facade of Amarante's gem, the Romanesque **Igreja de São Gonçalo,** hides the resting place of the town's patron saint, São Gonçalo, whose tomb lies in the gilded chapel beside the altar. (Open daily 8am-7pm. Free). The **Museu Municipal Amadeo Souza Cardoso** is in the same complex. (Open Tu-F 9am-noon and 2-5pm, Sa-Su 10am-noon and 2-5pm. Closed holidays. 200$, students 100$). The short trek up R. 5 de Outubro offers a view of the ghostly remains of the **Solar dos Magalhães,** a burned-out manor which serves as a sordid but hauntingly beautiful reminder of Napoleon's pyromaniacal legacy.

To get to the **tourist office** from the bus station, cross the street, turn right, and follow R. 31 de Janeiro until the bridge. Cross the bridge onto Pr. República; the office is to the right in the same building as the museum entrance, on Alameda Teixeira de Pascoães. The staff there hands out good maps. (☎ 255 43 22 59. Open July-Aug. M-F 9am-7pm, Sa-Su 10am-7pm; Sept.-June M-F 9am-12:30pm and 2-5:30pm, Sa-Su 10am-12:30pm and 2-5:30pm.) After exploring a bit, pick a riverside terrace, drink in the sun, and gorge on Amarante's culinary specialties: sweets, sweets, and more sweets. Delicious regional *ovos moles* (egg pastries) and traditional cakes proliferate, particularly during the Festa de **São Gonçalo,** on the first weekend in June.

BRAGA

Braga (pop. 160,000) originally served as the capital of a district founded by Celtic tribes in 300 BC. In 27 BC it became "Bracara Augusta," a Roman administrative center; today's residents still consider their city's beautiful gardens, plazas, museums, and markets worthy of the nickname "Portuguese Rome." By outsiders, Braga is considered by some as the most extravagant, by others the most fanatic, and by all the most politically conservative city in Portugal. Not surprisingly, the 1926 coup that paved Salazar's path to power was launched from here (see **History,** p. 530). Yet in spite of Braga's austere reputation and large number of Gothic churches, hedonism—manifested in bars and discos—marches cheerfully onward. During Holy Week, religious processions cross the flower-carpeted streets and at night somber devotion explodes into fireworks and dancing. Lively pedestrian thoroughfares and fairy-tale plazas make Braga feel like a miniature Lisbon, but it wouldn't be wise to say so to the locals; they like to claim that their city, their food, and their hospitality far surpass that of the Portuguese capital.

☐ TRANSPORTATION

Trains: (☎ 253 26 21 66), on Largo Estação. It is easier to get to Braga by bus. Trains run to: **Porto** (1½hr., 10 per day 6:20am-9:20pm, 330$); **Coimbra** (4hr., 2 per day 7:50am and 6:50pm, 1150$); and **Lisbon** via Porto (2 per day 7:50am-6:50pm, 2800$). To get to **Viana do Castelo, Vila Nova de Cerveira,** and **Valença,** make a connection at **Nine** (20min., 14 per day 5:20am-10:05pm, 170$).

Buses: (☎ 253 61 60 80 or 253 68 31 33), Central de Camionagem, a few blocks north of the city center. **Rodoviária** runs to: **Guimarães** (1hr., every 30min. 7am-8pm, 385$); **Porto** (1½hr., every 45min. 6:45am-8pm, 680$); **Coimbra** (3hr.; M-F 6-9 per day, Sa-Su 7 per day, 6am-11:30pm; 1600$); **Lisbon** (5¼hr., 8-9 per day 9:30am-11:30pm, 2300$); **Faro** (12-15hr., 9 per day 6am-11:30pm, 3400$). **Hostelería do Gerês** runs to **Caldas de Gerês** (1½hr., 17-18 per day 6am-11:30pm, 1500$).

Taxis: ☎ 253 61 40 19.

✳☑ ORIENTATION AND PRACTICAL INFORMATION

Braga's focal point is the **Praça da República,** a spirited square bordered by gardens and filled with cafes and playful fountains. **Avenida Liberdade** stems out from the square. **Rua do Souto,** a pedestrian thoroughfare lined with shops, runs from the tourist office corner of Pr. República. R. Souto becomes R. Dom Diogo de Sousa and then R. Andrade de Corvo, which leads straight to the **train station.** To get to Pr. República from the **bus station,** stand with your back to the entrance, take a left, and then turn right up the commercial street. Go straight under the concrete building onto Pr. Alexandre Herculana. Take R. dos Cháos (the road ahead) into the square.

Tourist Office: Av. Central, 1 (☎ 253 26 25 50; fax 253 61 33 87), on the corner of Pr. República, across from the bank. Maps and info on rustic excursions. Train schedules and bus info. Temporary free **luggage storage.** Open July-Sept. M-F 9am-6pm, Sa-Su 9am-12:30pm, also Sa 2-5pm; Oct.-June M-F 9am-7pm, Sa 9am-12:30pm and 2-5pm.

Budget Travel: Tagus Youth Travel, Pr. Município, 7 (☎ 253 21 51 44). Student flights and other services. Open June-Sept. M-F 9am-6pm, Sa 9am-1pm; Oct.-May M-F 9am-1pm and 2:30-6pm. V, MC, AmEx.

Currency Exchange: Caixa Geral de Depósitos (☎ 253 60 01 00), on Pr. República, across from the tourist office. Open M-F 8:30am-3pm. **Mercâmbios—Agência de Câmbios,** Av. Liberdade, 728 (☎ 253 61 34 63), just down the block from the tourist office, does not charge commission. Open M-F 8:30am-3pm.

English Bookstore: Livraria Central, Av. Liberdade, 726, next to Residência Avenida.

Emergency: ☎ 112. **Police:** R. dos Falcões, 12 (☎ 253 20 04 20).

Late-Night Pharmacy: Farmácia Martins, (☎ 253 26 73 71), Av. Central, next to the tourist office. **Farmácia Brito,** Av. Liberdade, 77 (☎ 253 26 26 85), by the post office.

Hospital: Hospital de São Marcos (☎ 253 61 38 00), Lg. Carlos Amarante.

Post Office: (☎ 253 20 03 64), Av. Liberdade, 2 blocks downhill from the tourist office. For **Posta Restante,** indicate "Estação Avenida" in the address. **Telephones, fax,** and other services. Open M-F 8:30am-6pm. **Postal Code:** 4700.

Internet Access: Instituto Português da Juventude, R. de Santa Margarida, 6 (☎ 253 20 42 50). Free. Open M-F 9am-7:30pm. **Videotech Municipal,** R. do Raio, 2 (☎ 253 26 77 93). Free. Open M-Sa 10am-12:30pm and 2-6:30pm.

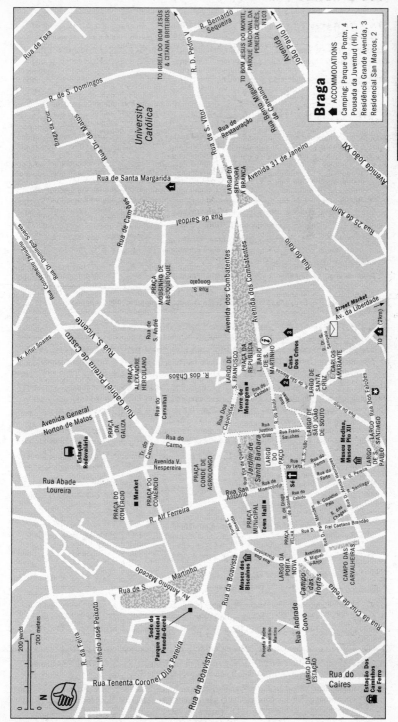

Braga

▲ ACCOMMODATIONS
Camping: Parque da Ponte, 4
Pousada da Juventud (HI), 1
Residência Grande Avenida, 3
Residencial San Marcos, 2

ACCOMMODATIONS

Braga is full of *pensões*, although few are truly budget. The cheapest cluster around the Hospital de São Marcos and the more expensive around Av. Central.

Pousada da Juventude de Braga (HI), R. Santa Margarida, 6 (☎/fax 253 61 61 63). From the tourist office entrance, take a right and follow Av. Combatentes. Turn left at the intersection with R. Santa Margarida. 15min. from the bus station and 35min. from the train station. A taxi from the train station costs 800$. Relaxing, but not intimate—4 beds fill each large room. Breakfast included. Reception 9am-noon and 6pm-midnight. July-Aug. reservations recommended. June-Sept. dorms 1700$; doubles 4000$. Oct.-May dorms 1500$; doubles 3500$. V, MC.

Residência Grande Avenida, Av. Liberdade, 738, 2nd fl. (☎ 253 60 90 20; fax 253 60 90 28), around the corner from the tourist office. 23 rooms with elegant mirrors, plush furniture, alarm clocks, and fans; some with TV, phone, and heat. Victorian sitting room. Breakfast included. June-Aug. make reservations. June-Sept. singles 3000-4000$, with bath 4500$; doubles 5000$, with bath 6000$. Oct.-May singles 3000$, with bath 4000$; doubles 4500$, with bath 5500$. V, MC.

Residencial San Marcos, R. de São Marcos, 80 (☎ 253 27 71 77; fax 253 27 71 87), just off the Pr. República. Elegant but pricey double rooms all have TV, A/C, heat, phones, and bath. July-Aug. 8000$; Sept.-June 7000$. V, MC, AmEx.

Camping: Parque da Ponte (☎ 253 27 33 55), 2km down Av. Liberdade from the center, next to the stadium and the municipal pool. Buses stop every 30min. Market and laundry facilities. 340$ per person, 260$ per tent, 280$ per car.

FOOD

Braga has many cafes and several superb restaurants, but little in between. A colorful **market** sets up in Pr. Comércio, two blocks from the bus station (open M-Sa 7am-3pm). Numerous restaurants in this *praça* serve the Minho's typically heavy dishes. For groceries, stop and shop at **Supercompra,** Av. Liberdade, 24, a few blocks down from the tourist office (open M-Sa 9am-8pm). For fast food, a mall atmosphere, and a movie theater, hit **Braga Shopping,** a commercial center facing the *praça* (☎ 253 20 80 10).

Churrasqueira da Sé, R. Dom Paio Mendes, 25 (☎ 253 26 33 87). This "cathedral barbecue" has pork chops, barbecued chicken, veal, and omelettes fit for His Excellence himself. Half-portions (680-980$) could feed the whole clergy. The super-cheap *prato do dia* (750$) is divine. Open Th-Tu 9:30am-3pm and 6:30-9:30pm.

Café Vianna, Pr. República, 87 (☎ 253 26 23 36), behind the fountain. A snappy, if somewhat tacky, pink marble cafe. At night it's a popular hangout, sometimes with live music. Full breakfasts (300-750$), light lunches, and dinner (sandwiches and *pratos combinados* 350-1180$). Open daily 8am-2am.

Brasileira Café, on the corner of R. Sousa and São Marcos. Perfect for a light lunch, a good cup of coffee, or just people-watching. Coffee 95-100$. Sandwiches 200-300$. Beers 200-300$. Open M-Th 7:30am-midnight, F-Sa 7:30am-1am.

SIGHTS

CATHEDRAL (SÉ). Braga's *sé*, Portugal's oldest cathedral, has undergone a series of renovations since its construction in the 11th and 12th centuries. Guided tours (in Portuguese) of its treasury, choir, and chapels run often during visiting hours. The treasury showcases the archdiocese's most precious paintings and relics. On display is the *Cruzeiro do Brasil*, a plain iron cross from the ship Pedro Álvares Cabral commanded when he "discovered" Brazil on April 22, 1500. Perhaps most interesting are the cathedral's collection of *cofres cranianos* (brain boxes), one of which contains the 6th-century cortex of São Martinho Dume, Braga's first bishop. Near a Renaissance cloister lie the cathedral's two historic chapels. The more notable, **Capela dos Reis** (Kings' Chapel), guards the 12th-century stone sarcophagi of Dom Afonso Henriques's parents as well as the mummy remains of a 14th-century archbishop. Also of interest is the choir—its organ has 2424 fully functional pipes elaborately decorated in gold. *(Cathedral and treasury open daily June-Aug. 8:30am-6:30pm; Sept.-May 8:30am-5:30pm. Cathedral free. Treasury 300$.)*

■ **IGREJA DO BOM JESÚS.** Braga's most famous landmark, Igreja do Bom Jesús, is actually 5km outside of town on a hillside carpeted in greenery. Built in an effort to re-create Jerusalem in Braga, this 18th-century church was to provide Iberian Christians with a pilgrimage sight closer to home. To visit Bom Jesús, either take the 285m ride on the antique funicular built in 1882 (8am-8pm, 120$) or take the long walk (25-30min.) up the granite-paved pathway that forks into two zig-zagging 565-step stairways. On the way up, check out the **staircase** depicting, among other things, the five senses (the "smell" fountain spouts water through a boy's nose), the virtues, and the prophets. The church, Braga's most elite resorts, and some small cafes are at the top. The view of the city is beautiful, especially at sunset. *(Buses labeled "#02 Bom Jesús" depart at 10min. and 40min. past the hour from Largo Carlos Amarante in front of Hospital de São Marcos or from Av. Liberdade in front of Farmàcia Cristal. Buses drop off at the bottom of the stairway; the last one leaves around 8:30pm. 195$.)*

🍷 🌸 NIGHTLIFE AND FESTIVALS

Braga comes alive at night, especially in the cafe-lined Pr. República. **Café Astoria,** next door to Café Vianna (see **Food,** above), has opened a newly renovated two-floor bar upstairs; the atmosphere is exaggeratedly chic and the music good (open M-Th 10pm-2am, F-Sa 10pm-6am). For action outside Pr. República, head down Av. Liberdade to Pr. João XXI and dance at **Club 84. Praça Mayor,** R. Gonçalo Sampaio, is a popular bar in the *barrio antiguo.* If you are in Braga on the 23rd of June, don't miss the **Festa da Sao João.** The biggest bash is supposedly in Porto, but the *bracarenses* don't fall too far behind; traditional folk music and dance, good food, concerts and general revelry take over the Pr. República, and don't be surprised to see locals running around beating each other on the head with toy hammers. Few locals seem to remember the origin of this bizarre ritual, but the older folk will tell you that it's a tribute to Sao João, Protector of the Head.

📸 DAYTRIPS FROM BRAGA

■ MOSTEIRO DE TIBÃES (25MIN.)
A city bus labeled "Sarrido" heads 6km from Braga to the monastery. Buses leave from Pr. Conde de Agrolongo, 1 block up R. Capelistas from Pr. República. The stop is in front of the "Arca-Lar" store, which also posts a schedule (25min., every 2hr.).

Nestled in an unspoiled forest, this beautiful, peaceful 11th-century Benedictine monastery has suffered from centuries of neglect. Stone tombs rattle eerily underfoot in the weathered cloister. Adjoining the cloister, however, is an exceptionally preserved church. (Open Tu-Su 9am-noon and 2-7pm. Tour free.)

GUIMARÃES (40MIN.)
Trains (☎ 253 41 23 51) connect Guimarães to Braga (40min; M-F 19 per day 6:30am-8:30pm, Sa-Su 13 per day 6:55am-8:30pm; 385$).

The road to Guimarães (pop. 170,000) is a delightful romp through small Portuguese towns full of colorful rainbow-tiled houses and orange trees. The cluster of houses and buildings that rises out of the verdant hills announces your arrival to the town. Although modernization and commercialism have made a place for themselves in Guimarães, the castle-dominated town center still retains a rustic air that attracts history buffs. It was here, in 1128, that Dom Alfonso Henriques defeated the troops of the King of Castilla y León to become the first king of Portugal. To honor the town he made it the jewel of his kingdom. Ever since then, Guimarães has been called the "cradle of the nation," as the huge *"Aqui nasceu Portugal"* ("Here Portugal was born") sign in Pr. Toural proclaims.

The Galician countess Mumadona established a Benedictine monastery here in the 10th century, and the founding of the city came a few years later. Though Mumadona's monastery no longer stands, her influence over the city is still evident in the **castelo,** which she also sponsored to protect the religious from Moorish invasions. Though it was nearly stripped to pave the city's roads, the huge granite structure, perched on a hill near the town center, remains one of Portugal's foremost national symbols. It was there that the first king of Portugal was born (old windows remain to point out the exact room) and baptized (in the São Miguel chapel at the foot of the castle). The castle was also the site of the **Battle of Mumadona,** Portugal's first bid for independence from Spanish Castilla. (Open daily July-Aug. 9:30am-6:30pm; Sept.-June 9:30am-5:30pm. Tower access 250$, 125$ for students. Best seen on a sunny day.) The Dukes of Bragança, however, apparently considered it too stuffy a place to live, and between 1420 and 1422, Dom Afonso, the bastard son of King Dom João I and future king of Bragança, had a versatile, spacious royal residence built on Holy Hill for his wife Dona Constança de Noronha. The ■**Ducal Palace** is located next door to the castle but is drastically different in style, as it is modeled after the manor houses of northern Europe. A museum inside includes furniture, silverware, tapestries, and weapons once used at the palace. In the banquet hall, tables that once seated 15th-century nobles now serve presidents of Portugal. At dinnertime, at least a quarter of the 39 fireplaces burn in an attempt to heat the building. Don't miss the elaborate Pastrana tapestries in the Hall of Lost Footsteps or the interesting display of archaic weaponry in the Arms room. (Downhill from the castle. Open daily July-Aug. 9am-7pm; Sept.-June 9:30am-5:45pm. 500$, seniors and students 300$. Su mornings free.)

The Guimarães **tourist office** is on Alameda de São Dámaso, facing Pr. Toural. From the bus station, take Av. Conde Margaride—the busy commercial road—to the right, walk uphill, and turn right at the fork; the tourist office is on the far corner of Pr. Toural. Maps are free, and an electronic sign outside displays opening hours for all sights. (☎ 253 41 24 50. Open M-F 9:30am-12:30pm and 2-6:30pm). A **branch office,** Pr. Santiago, 37, in the old city, has the same info and more helpful staff (☎ 253 51 87 90. Open M-Sa 9:30am-6:30pm, Su 10am-1pm). The **train station,** is a 10-minute walk down Av. Afonso Henriques from the tourist office. The **bus station** (☎ 253 51 65 29), which offers free **luggage storage,** is in the immense Guimarães shopping complex, which includes the supermarket **El Continente.** To get there, follow Av. Conde Margaride downhill. In an **emergency** call ☎ 112; for **police,** on Alameda Alfredo Pimenta, dial ☎ 253 51 33 34. The **hospital** (☎ 253 51 26 12), is on R. dos Cutileiros, near Matadouros. While restaurants in the old city are generally very expensive, it may be worth splurging a bit at ■**Restaurante Valdonas,** on R. Val de Donas, 4. Recently renovated, the restaurant occupies the first floor of a house originally constructed in 1620. Ask to eat in the patio with the fountain in the front, or in the serene, romantic garden in the back. The tourist-aimed but delicious *menú* costs 2500$. (☎ 253 51 14 11; fax 253 51 13 30. Open Th-Su June-Sept. noon-2am. Closed Oct.-May. V, MC.)

CALDAS DE GERÊS

Ten months of the year, the main pastimes in green, hilly Caldas de Gerês are crossword puzzles and knitting; the town is characterized above all by its renowned therapeutic spa and elderly population. But every year in July and August Caldas is overrun by tourists visiting nearby Parque Nacional de Peneda-Gerês or looking to have a soak in the famed mineral waters. Even those who don't plan on having water therapy might need it after the bus ride into town; the precarious, winding mountain roads, while beautiful, are not for the faint of heart.

Caldas' main attraction, the **Spa Caldas de Gerês,** is open from May 31 until October 31. The spa first became fashionable during the 19th century and run-down Victorian hotels still line Av. Manuel Francisco da Costa. The spa complex includes a pool, tennis, horseback riding, hiking services, canoeing, and nautical sports along with its famed waters. It also owns the next-door **Parque de Terma** (enter by the tourist office). According to locals, the flourine mineral waters here can only be found in Portugal and Germany. (170$, children under 12 80$. After June 1 access to the pool M-F 700$, Sa-Su 1100$; under 7 M-F 400$, Sa-Su 650$.)

Empresa Hoteleira Do Gerês (☎ 253 61 58 96) runs **buses** from Caldas to **Braga** (1½hr.; M-F 17 per day, Sa 10 per day, Su 7 per day, 6:30am-9pm; 570$). Caldas's **spa** dominates the center of town, about 50m above where the buses stop. Restaurants, cafes, *pensões*, and the tourist office lie along Av. Manuel Francisco da Costa, up around the corner from the bus stop. To get to the **tourist office** from the bus stop, walk uphill along Av. Manuel Francisco da Costa until you see the office surrounded by a semicircle of shops. (☎ 253 39 11 33; fax 253 39 12 82. English spoken. Open M-Sa 9am-12:30pm and 2:30-6pm.) The **police** (☎ 253 39 11 37) are one block from the tourist office, just off Av. Manuel Francisco da Costa. Find the **post office** off the rotary that leads uphill into the center. (☎ 253 39 11 11; fax 253 39 00 16. Open M-F 9am-12:30pm and 2-5:30pm.) There are so many *pensões* in Caldas that the traveler has the upper hand. Weekday and off-season prices are rarely fixed—try bargaining. One option is **Casa de Ponte**, on Av. Manuel Francisco da Costa. From the bus stop, head downhill until you see the hostel on the left corner where the road splits, next to the Escola Primaria. Spacious rooms have lots of light, elevated TVs, and low beds, and most have porches overlooking the garden. The owner speaks English. (☎ 253 39 11 25. Midnight curfew. Singles 4000-6000$; doubles 5000-8500$ depending on the season. V, MC.) For pleasant **camping**, try **Camping Vidoeiro** (☎ 253 39 12 89), by the river, 1km outside of town. Facing the tourist office, take the uphill road to the left to get to the site. Meals in Caldas de Gerês are available at the *pensões* throughout the town (as always, be aware that you must pay extra for bread, butter, or olives). The **supermarket** in the center of town is the best bet for saving money (open daily 8am-1pm and 2:30-7pm).

PARQUE NACIONAL DE PENEDA-GERÊS

Just an hour and half away from Caldas de Gerês, Parque Nacional de Peneda-Gerês has been called Portugal's finest natural reserve. Each year it attracts swarms of nature lovers, all looking to escape city smog for an invigorating breadth of flora and fauna. The second-largest protected area in the country, the crescent-shaped reserve is sandwiched along the Spanish border. It is believed that the region was first populated in the 3rd or 4th century BC; cemeteries in **Dolmens** and **Mamoas** date from this period. The 1st century brought Roman occupation to the assortment of Iron Age civilizations in the area; **Geira**, in the Gerês mountain range, deserves special attention for its remains of Roman roads.

In 1971, the park became Portugal's first protected area. Its 72,000 hectares can be divided into the southern **Serra do Gerês** and the northern **Serra da Peneda**. More casual hikers tend to stay south, where the few roads provide scenic and manageable journeys, while hard-core mountaineers usually head to the uncharted and often treacherous trails of the north. In both areas numerous hamlets and villages offer accommodations, campsites, and food. Hikers can attempt the 10- to 12-hour trek along an ancient Roman road beginning in Braga and passing through Rome to Byzantium. The route runs along the **Vilarinho das Furnas** reservoir, an optimal place for swimming and camping. In the height of the summer, one might be able to catch a view of the village that was submerged when the reservoir was dammed. Another possible hike follows the road toward **Portela do Homem**, a small town on the Portuguese-Spanish border with a river pool at the bottom of the **Minas dos Carris** valley. Southeast of Gerês is **Miradouro do Gerês**, a popular site overlooking the **Caniçada** reservoir—beware the en masse migration of weekend picnickers. The village of **Rio Caldo** at the base of the Caniçada reservoir is just 8km south of Gerês and offers **windsurfing** and **waterskiing**.

The **Park Information Office** (☎ 253 39 01 10) in Caldas de Gerês is uphill to the right of the tourist office (with the entrance behind you). English-speaking staff can help with maps and hike-planning.

VIANA DO CASTELO

Viana do Castelo (pop. 20,000) is an elegant and immaculate beach town—rampant commercialism has yet to rear its ugly head in this beautiful stop-over between Porto and Galicia, Spain. Viana boasts some intriguing architecture, including its main *plaça* and a bridge designed by Gustave Eiffel, as well as a superb beach just a ferry ride away. Even when the main beach fills in summer, empty and enticing expanses of sand can always be found a quick train ride away.

⊏ TRANSPORTATION

Trains: (☎ 258 82 22 96 or 258 82 13 15), at the north end of Av. Combatentes da Grande Guerra, under Santa Luzia hill. From the bus station, go left on Av. Capitão Gaspar de Castro through a pedestrian underpass (15min.), or take the bus (110$). Trains to: **Caminha** (40min., 8 per day 8:04am-8:22pm, 230$); **Vila Nova de Cerveira** (1hr., 8 per day 8:04am-8:22pm, 300$); **Porto** (2½hr., 13-14 per day 5:05am-10pm, 750$); and **Vigo, Spain** (2½hr., 2 per day 9:18am and 8:22pm, 1490$).

Buses: Rodoviária goes from **Central de Camionagem,** on the eastern edge of town, to **Braga** (1½hr., 10-12 per day 7am-7:05pm, 580$). **AVIC** (☎ 258 82 97 05) and **Auto-Viação do Minho** (☎ 258 80 03 41) go to **Porto** (1½hr., 8-10 per day 6:15am-7:30pm; 750$, express 1050$) and **Lisbon** (6hr., 5 per day 8am-7pm, 2300$).

Taxi: Táxis de Viana ☎ 258 82 23 22 or 258 82 20 61, or try Av. Combatentes.

▟❼ ORIENTATION AND PRACTICAL INFORMATION

Avenida dos Combatentes da Grande Guerra, the main drag along the Rio Lima, glitters from the **train station** south to the **port.** Most accommodations and restaurants are located on or just off the Avenida. The **old town** stretches east of the Avenida, while the fortress and sea lie to the west.

Tourist Office: (☎ 258 82 26 20 or 258 82 49 71; fax 258 82 78 73), Pr. Erva, 1 block east of Av. Combatentes. From the train station, take the 4th left at the sharp corner, then a quick right. Office is at the corner of the courtyard with the solitary tree. Maps and lists of lodgings available. English spoken. Open M-Sa 9am-12:30pm and 2:30-6pm, Su 9:30am-12:30pm.

Currency Exchange: Montepio Geral, Av. Combatentes, 332 (☎ 258 82 88 97), near the train station. Open M-F 8:30am-3pm. Also has a 24hr. **ATM.**

Emergency: ☎ 112. **Police:** (☎ 258 82 20 22), on R. Aveiro.

Hospital: Hospital de Santa Luzia, Av. Abril, 25 (☎ 258 82 90 81).

Post Office: (☎ 258 81 12 28), Av. Combatentes across from the train station. Open M-F 8:30am-6:30pm. **Postal Code:** 4900.

Internet Access: Public library (☎ 258 80 93 02), R. Cândido dos Reis. **Instituto de Juventude** (☎ 258 80 88 00), on R. Poço. Open daily 9am-12:30pm and 2-5:30pm.

▛ ACCOMMODATIONS

Except in mid-August, accommodations in Viana do Castelo are easy to find, although they are not particularly cheap. *Quartos* or *habitaciones* (private rooms) are the best option. Small, informal *pensões* (usually above family restaurants) are slightly cheaper but lower in quality. Check the tourist office's list of accommodations or hunt on side streets off Av. Combatentes. Listed prices can drop by as much as 500$ in the off season.

Pousada da Juventude de Viana do Castelo (Azenhas D. Prior), R. da Argaçosa (☎ 258 80 02 60; fax 258 82 08 70). Youth hostel right on the marina, off Pr. de Galiza. Great views. Kitchen, laundry, lounge, restaurant. Sept. 16-June 15 singles 2000$; doubles 2500$. June 16-Sept. 15 singles 2500$; doubles 6000$. V, MC, AmEx.

Pensão Guerreiro, R. Grande, 14 (☎ 258 82 20 99; fax 258 82 04 02), at the corner of Av. Combatentes. Bright rooms with high ceilings and big windows. Ask for a view of the port. Reservations recommended. June-Sept. singles 2500$; doubles 5000$; triples 6000$. Oct.-May singles 1500$; doubles 3500$; triples 5000$. V, MC, AmEx.

Residencial Viana Mar, Av. Combatentes, 215 (☎/fax 258 82 89 62). Large, luxurious rooms, all with phones. Breakfast included. Singles 3000$, with bath and TV 4500$; doubles 6000$, with bath and TV 6500$; triples with bath and TV 7500$. V, MC, AmEx.

Residencial Magalhães, R. Manuel Espregueira, 62 (☎ 258 82 32 93). From the tourist office, turn left onto Pr. República, then left again, and cross Av. Combatentes onto R. Manuel Espregueira. A quiet, homey, traditional establishment. Breakfast included. Singles 4500-7500$; doubles 5000-8500$; triples 6000-11,000$. Apartments with TV available for 2-4 people 6500-14,000$. V, MC, AmEx.

Camping: Orbitur (☎ 258 32 21 67; fax 258 14 80 45), near the Praia do Cabadelo. Open Jan. 16-Nov. 15. Catch a "Cabedelo" bus (100$) from the bus station or from behind the train station (near the funicular stop) or take the ferry from the end of Av. Combatentes (120$), and hike 1km from the 1st stop; signs point the way. Well-equipped, with showers included. 640$ per person and per tent, 550$ per car.

◖ FOOD

The bloodthirsty will drool over the local specialty *arroz de sarabulho* (rice cooked in blood and served with sausages and potatoes). Most budget restaurants lie on the small streets off Av. Combatentes. The large municipal **market** is in Pr. Dona Maria II, several blocks from Av. Combatentes. (☎ 258 82 26 57. Open M-Sa 8am-3pm.) For groceries, try **Pomar Bolama** on R. Grande. (☎ 258 82 30 37. Open M-Sa 9am-1:30pm and 2-7pm, Su 9:30am-noon.)

▨ **Maria de Perre,** R. de Viana, 118 (☎ 258 82 24 10), the last side street on the left off Av. Combatentes heading toward the water. Delicious meals (especially the regional dishes) are complemented by beautiful decorations, good Portuguese wines, and occasional live music. Dress well. Soup 200$. Entrees 900-2100$. V, MC, AmEx.

Restaurante Dolce Vita, R. Poço, 44 (☎ 258 82 48 60), across the square from the tourist office. Wonderful Italian cuisine. Pizza 750-925$. Portuguese dishes 1200-2000$. Open daily noon-3pm and 7:30-10:30pm. V, MC, AmEx.

FROM WHENCE COMES A NAME There is more than a castle alone behind Viana do Castelo's name, which translates in English to "Viana of the Castle." According to local legend, the name actually commemorates two star-crossed lovers. Supposedly, when the Moors still occupied Viana, the Moorish king and his beautiful, lonely daughter Ana lived alone in the town castle. Ana's only consolation was watching the seashore, and one day she met eyes with a young fisherman with whom she instantly fell in love. When the king found out about their mutual obsession, he became furious and locked Ana in the tower. The lovers, unable to communicate, died of lovesickness. But villagers swear that on clear nights, one can catch a glimpse of Ana's ghost through the tower window, waiting for her lover to arrive. The local saying *"Vi a Ana nel castelo"* ("I saw Ana in the castle") eventually became Viana do Castelo.

◉ SIGHTS

Contrary to popular belief, there is more to Viana do Castelo than just sand. Even in a country famed for its impressive squares, Viana do Castelo's ■**Praça da República** is remarkable. Its centerpiece is a 16th-century fountain encrusted with sculptures and crowned with a sphere bearing a cross of the Order of Christ. The small **Paço do Conselho** (1502), formerly the town hall, seals the square to the east. Diagonally across the plaza, granite columns support the playful and flowery facade of the **Igreja da Misericórdia** (1598, rebuilt in 1714). An intriguing *azulejo* interior lies within. The cliff-like ■**Colina de Santa Luzia,** north of the city, is crowned by magnificent Celtic ruins (100-250$) and an early 20th-century neo-Byzantine church. The view of Viana is fantastic. To reach the hilltop, head 200m behind the train station and take the long stairway. Otherwise take the **funicular.** (Daily, every hr. in the morning, every 30min. in the afternoon, 9am-7pm, 120$.) For great views of the harbor and ocean, visit the **Castelo de São Tiago da Barra,** built in 1589 by Felipe I of Spain. (From the train station, take the 2nd right off Av. Combatentes (R. General Luís do Rego) and walk 5 blocks.)

◐ BEACHES

Anyone who loves the **beach** will love Viana do Castelo. The recently renovated beach on **Rio Lima,** a short ferry ride across the harbor, has beautiful gardens and play areas for children. You can also head directly for the ■**Praia do Cabedelo** beach via the ferry behind the parking lot at the end of Av. Combatentes. (Daily every 30min.; July-Sept. 8:45am-midnight, May-June and Oct.-Dec. 8:45am-10pm, Jan.-Apr. 8:45am-5pm; 120$.) Those in search of a pristine beach experience abandon Viana and head north to some of the cleanest and least crowded beaches in Portugal. **Vila Praia de Âncora,** a 15-minute train ride north of Viana, is the largest and most popular. **Moledo** and **Caminha,** farther north, are equally gorgeous. But Viana is still the best place to spend the night—plan your return trip ahead of time.

▐ DAYTRIPS FROM VIANA DO CASTELO

The Alto Minho, Portugal's most northwestern corner, which is set apart from Spain only by the crystal clear Rio Minho, could have inspired Henry David Thoreau to pen a second *Walden*. Rocky mountains rise between unspoiled small towns and wildflowers spring from riverbanks, interrupted only by cottage gardens and eucalyptus outcroppings. Intrepid travelers jump the train at stops between towns and camp in the farmers' fields (with permission, of course).

CAMINHA (30MIN.)

One day Jesus and Peter were passing through these parts...
St. Peter: My Lord, what should this place be called?
Jesus: *Caminha, Caminha* (keep walking) we're in a hurry.
　　—an age-old Caminha legend

Caminha makes a good daytrip from Viana do Castelo, as accommodations are generally expensive and difficult to come by. The train station (☎ 258 92 29 25), on Av. Saraira de Carvalho, runs trains to and from Viana do Castelo (30min., 9 per day 5:55am-9:31pm, 240$) and Vila Nova de Cerveira (10min., 8 per day 8:50am-8:39pm, 260$).

While everyone else keeps on going, slip off the train into Caminha (pop. 20,000) and enjoy the entrancing green hills, wide beaches, and peaceful medieval square. The village is slightly larger than its cousin five stops down the line, Vila Nova de Cerveira. The latter may have a youth hostel, but Caminha has a **beach.** Put on your bathing suit, turn left on the riverside road, and keep going along the river about 1.5km to bask under the sun or get whipped by the wind (on breezy days). The zealous will hop on the bus (10min.) or trek 3km to the wide, pristine **Praia de Moledo,** where the Rio Minho rushes into the Atlantic. Caminha's **tourist office** is on R. Ricardo Joaquim Sousa. From the train station, walk straight ahead on Av. Manuel Xavier to the traffic circle, go down Tr. São João (diagonally to the left), and take the first left. (☎ 258 92 19 52. Open M-Sa 9:30am-12:30pm and 2:30-6pm.)

VILA NOVA DE CERVEIRA (40MIN.)

Trains (☎ 251 79 62 65) run to and from: Viana do Castelo (40min., 9 per day 5:43am-9:21pm, 300$); Valença do Minho (20min., 8 per day 9:07am-8:49pm, 190$); and Porto (2hr., 6 per day 8:37am-9:21pm, 1100$). Three bus companies take the same route as the train—upstream to Valença and down the coast to Porto. AVIC and A.V. Minho depart from the Centro de Camionagem between town and the train station on R. de Santo António (☎ 251 79 62 65) to: Valença do Minho (15min., 10 per day 7am-6:45pm, 205$); Porto (2¼hr., 5 per day, 1050$); and Lisbon (4½hr., 4-5 per day, 2400$).

Just 100m from Spain (close enough to hear Galicians partying at night), Vila Nova de Cerveira (pop. 11,000) is a sleepy town with lush mountain scenery, a historic town center, and a great youth hostel. The only thing to see in the town itself is the 14th-century **castle,** now the luxurious **Pousada Dom Dinis**—walks atop its walls offer great views of the countryside. Hardy travelers can hike up the winding road, through heath and rocky outcrops, to the deer statue (4km). From the main road just to the east of town, turn right and start climbing at the "Lovelhe Igreja" sign.

Vila Nova de Cerveira's **tourist office,** on R. António Douro in Pr. Muntápio, is diagonally across from Igreja de São Roque. From the train station, which is half a kilometer east of town, turn left, go up the road for about five minutes and look for the first yellow building on the right. (☎ 251 70 80 23. Open M-Sa 9:30am-12:30pm and 2-6pm.) In an **emergency** call ☎ 112; **police** are at R. do Forte (☎ 251 79 51 13). Should you decide to spend the night, sleep in the ⬛**Pousada da Juventude de Vila Nova de Cerveira (HI),** Largo 16 de Fevereiro, 21. Head to the left from the train station, then right at the fork, then left again at the Fonseca Porto mini-market (15min., signs lead the way). Guests enjoy large rooms, a grassy patio with a great view, TV with VCR, and a kitchen. Although there's usually plenty of space, the hostel hosts a summer camp and often fills to the brim with Portuguese youngsters. (☎/fax 251 79 61 13. Breakfast included. English spoken. Reception 8am-noon and 6pm-midnight. Call ahead. June-Aug. dorms 1700$; doubles 3800$, with bath 4100$. Sept.-May dorms 1400$; doubles 3200$, with bath 3500$.) Restaurants can be expensive, as there are only seven of them. At **Café-Restaurante A Forja,** however, upstairs at R. 25 de Abril, 63, you can feast on *arroz de mariscos* (shellfish and rice; huge portions 600$) and cheap local specialties. (☎ 251 79 53 11. Soups 150$. Meat dishes 500-1000$. Open Tu-Su 8am-midnight.) If you'd rather eat in the plaza, check out the tiny, hidden **Café-Restaurante Cova da Moura,** in Lg. do Torreiro. A sign in the plaza points to the stairs which lead to an underground, cave-like space. (☎ 251 79 41 43. Open daily 9am-2am.)

AN ARMY OF DEER Vila Nova de Cerveira gets its name from the old Portuguese-Galician word for deer, an animal that turned out to be the town's unlikely war hero. Back in the days before Spain and Portugal were EU buddies, the Rio Minho frontier hosted countless skirmishes. At one point when the Spanish invaded the town, fleet-footed locals ran into the hills surrounding Vila Nova and tied torches to the horns of all the deer they could catch. When the Spaniards saw the hills filled with the torches of what they presumed to be a massive army, they gave up and fled. To this day, Vila de Cerveira rests quietly under the gaze of a huge metal deer sculpture, visible on the summit of the mountain behind town.

VALENÇA DO MINHO (1HR.)

Valença do Minho is a stop on the Porto-Vigo train line with connections to: Vila Nova de Cerveira (15min., 9 per day 5:30am-9:10pm, 190$); Viana do Castelo (1hr., 9 per day 5:30am-9:10pm, 400$); Porto (4hr., 7 per day 8:25am-9:10pm, 1040$); and Vigo, Spain via Redondela, Spain (1hr., 2 per day 9:59am and 9pm, 1355$). From Redondela you can connect to Spanish RENFE trains serving points north.

Within easy reach of Vila Nova de Cerveira, Valença do Minho salutes Spanish Túy from the entrance to northern Portugal. A 17th-century **fortaleza** (fortress) protects the town's historic section. Valença's stone arches and cannon portals frame stunning views of rolling hills and the Rio Minho. Some of the most historically rich aspects of Valença have sadly fallen victim to commercial tackiness, but the impressive stone walls still yield spectacular views of both Spain and Portugal. A road winds 4km up to the breathtaking summit of **Monte do Faro,** overlooking the coastline, the Vale do Minho, and the Galician mountains. The **tourist office** is on Av. Espanha in a log cabin-like building; upon exiting the train station, walk through the rotary and turn right on the main drag; keep walking until you reach the grassy hill of the fortress. The office has maps and helpful brochures on both sides of the Alto Minho region. (☎ 251 82 33 74. Open daily 9:30am-12:30pm and 2:30-6pm; Sept.-May 9:30am-12:30pm and 2-5:30pm).

TRÁS-OS-MONTES

The country's roughest, rainiest, and most isolated region, Trás-Os-Montes ("behind the mountains") is light years off the beaten path. Although almost twice the size of its neighbor Minho, it has only a fraction of the population. Getting there epitomizes the Trás-Os-Montes experience. Train service (where it exists at all) is slow and rickety, and buses, especially from Spain, are few and far between. The weather is extreme as well: transmontinos like to describe their seasons as "nine months of winter and three months of hell." But the landscapes of Trás-Os-Montes—considered the last untouched region of Western Europe—are some of the most incredible in all of Iberia. Hikers will delight in the isolation of unspoiled natural reserves and ancient villages in the **Parque Natural de Montesinho,** one of the largest protected areas in all of Portugal.

Trás-Os-Montes has long been home to Portugal's political and religious exiles. Dom Sancho I practically had to beg people to settle here after he incorporated it into Portugal in the 11th century. And it was here that the Jews chose to hide during the Inquisition. Today, it is the region's isolation, combined with its beauty and tranquility, that is its biggest draw. With its conical stacks of hand-cut hay, old stone houses, and centuries-old festivals, it is one of the last outposts of traditional Portugal. The gastronomic specialities devoured by locals hint at the region's rustic character: cozido à portuguesa is made from sausages, pig parts, carrots, and turnips, and it takes some serious hikes to burn off the hearty feijoada à trasmontana (bean stew). But the most prized dish is probably posta a mirandesa, locally bred beef which trasmontinos claim is the most tender in the world.

HIGHLIGHTS OF TRÁS-OS-MONTES

Parque Natural de Montesinho, utterly wild and wonderfully timeless (see p. 649).

BRAGANÇA

Wedged in a narrow valley between two steep slopes, Bragança (pop. 40,000), the capital of Trás-Os-Montes, is a proud and steadfast wilderness outpost. While most visitors come for the clean air, blue skies, and olive-covered hillsides—or perhaps the massive 13th-century castle—it is the people of Bragança that really make it unique; its substantial distance from the rest of Portugal seems to have preserved in local residents an almost archaic sense of hospitality and festivity. Bragança is also the perfect base for exploring the starkly beautiful terrain of the **Parque Natural de Montesinho,** which extends north into Spain.

▐ TRANSPORTATION

Trains: No train service. The Portuguese rail system does, however, organize a somewhat awkward combination bus-train route between **Porto** and **Bragança** (3 connections required). Eurail passes can be used to pay for this combo. You can catch a train in **Mirandela,** the nearest station (accessible by bus).

Buses: Three companies offer expresses to Porto and Lisbon. **Rodonorte** (☎ 273 30 01 83) buses leave from Av. João da Cruz to **Porto** (5hr., 4-6 per day 6am-5pm, 1440$) via **Mirandela** and **Vila Real,** and **Lisbon** (8hr., 3 per day 6-11am, 2680$). **Rede Expressos** (☎ 21 310 31 11; www.rede-expressos.pt) buses leave from the same stop. Office open erratically, though always pre-departure. To: **Vila Real** (2hr.; M-F 6 per day, Sa-Su 3 per day 2-7pm; 1250$); **Porto** (5hr.; M-F 8 per day, Sa-Su 6 per day 6am-11pm; 1500$); **Coimbra** (6hr.; M-F 6 per day, Sa 5 per day 6am-9:30pm; 1800$); and **Lisbon** (8hr.; M-F 8 per day, Sa-Su 6 per day 6am-9:30pm; 2600$). **Internorte** runs to **Zamora, Spain** (2½hr.; M-Sa 2pm, Su 5:45pm; 2050$) and **Braga** (5hr., 2 per day 4:15pm and 1:15am, 1600$).

Taxis: (☎ 273 32 21 38). Cabs congregate near the post office and old train station.

✦❼ ORIENTATION AND PRACTICAL INFORMATION

Buses let you out on the modern square fronted by the cafe-lined **Avenida João da Cruz** (to your right when standing with your back to the bus station's front entrance). Downward-sloping R. Almirante Reis leads to budget pensões and the **Praça da Sé** at the heart of the old town. **Avenida Sá Carneiro** leads to the university and is lined with bars and tascas, traditional Portuguese eateries. To reach the **fortress,** situated on a hill west of Pr. Sé, take **Rua Combatentes da Grande Guerra** from Pr. Sé, walk uphill, and enter through the opening in the stone walls.

Tourist Office: (☎ 273 38 12 73), Av. Cidade de Zamora. With your back to the bus station front entrance, cross the street, take a right, and walk 1 block (with the grass to your right). Take the 1st left up the street. Continue to the top of the hill, keeping the cement house with a cross to the right, and walk down the hill (with multicolored garages on the left and a cemetery on the right). The office is at the bottom of the hill on the right (10min.). Maps, free daytime **luggage storage,** and help finding accommodations. English spoken. Open M-F 9am-12:30pm and 2pm-5pm, Sa 10am-12:30pm.

Currency Exchange: Banco Nacional Ultramarino, Av. João da Cruz, 2-6 (☎ 273 33 16 45), next to the post office, has **ATMs.** Open M-F 8:30am-3pm, after July, Sa 8:30am-3pm. A better and more convenient choice would be the bus station, where **San Vitur** will do the exchange for no commission (☎ 34 915 27 62 79).

English Bookstore: Livraría Miguel Péricles, R. Combatentes G. Guerra, 180 (☎ 273 32 25 49) A few doors down from **Restaurante Poças.** A small selection of classic and contemporary texts in English.

Emergency: ☎ 112. **Police:** (☎ 273 30 34 00), by the town hall on Av. Xavier Teixeira.

Hospital: Hospital Distrital de Bragança (☎ 273 33 12 33), Av. Abade de Baçal, before the stadium on the road to **Vinhais**.

Post Office: (☎ 273 30 03 50), at the end of Av. João da Cruz. **Posta Restante, fax,** and **telephones.** Open M-F 9am-5pm. **Postal Code:** 5300.

▛ ACCOMMODATIONS

Plenty of cheap pensões and residenciales line Pr. Sé and R. Almirante Reis.

Pousada de Juventude—Bragança, Forte de Sào Joào de Deus (☎ 273 30 46 00; fax 273 32 61 36). This renovated youth hostal is a bit removed from the center of town but is well worth the trek (10min. taxi ride). The 64 beds almost ensure availability, but it is still recommended to call ahead. Kitchen, playroom, and sitting room. Laundry. Sept. 16-June 15 singles 2000$; doubles with bath 5000$. June 16-Sept. 15 singles 2500$; doubles with bath 6000$. HI card required. V, MC.

Pensão Rucha, R. Almirante Reis, 42 (☎ 273 33 16 72). Follow the directions to Poças; Rucha is on the right just past the "Correio" building. The sign is inside the doors. Clean, nicely decorated lodgings with communal baths. Large elegant sitting room with TV. Breakfast included. No heat. Singles 2500$; doubles 4500$.

Pensão Poças, R. Combatentes da Grande Guerra, 206 (☎ 273 33 12 16). With your back to the bus station entrance, cross the street, take a right, and walk until the major intersection. Pass the gray building that says "Correio" on the left. Continue through the plaza with the tall cross and veer right down the street. The hostel will be on the left. Rooms are spartan and unattractive but also large, airy and clean. Breakfast included. Singles 2000$, with bath 2500$; doubles 4000$, with bath 5000$. Visa.

Camping: Parque de Campismo Municipal do Sabor (☎ 273 33 15 35), 6km from town on the edge of the Montesinho park. From the Caixa Geral de Depósitos on the corner of Av. João da Cruz, yellow-and-blue #7 STUB buses head to the campground (10min., M-F 3 per day, 130$). If you choose to hike, be careful—roads are narrow and corners sharp. Open May-Sept. Electricity 100$. 400$ per person and per car, 300$ per tent.
Parque de Campismo Cêpo Verde (☎ 273 99 93 71), 8km out on the road to Vinhais. Swimming pool. Open June-Sept. 500$ per person, 200-400$ per tent and per car.

◯ FOOD

Restaurants in the center of Bragança tend to be pricey but good. The region is celebrated for presunto (cured ham) and salsichão (sausages), as well as the local delicacy, alheiradas, sausages made out of tripe. You can find at least the first two at **Supermercado Bem Servir,** R. Abílio Beça, 120, below Pr. Sé (open M-Sa 9am-1pm and 2-7pm). **Restaurante Poças,** R. Combatantes da Grande Guerra, 200, off Pr. Sé, next to the pensão of the same name, serves large portions of regional specialties in a no-frills setting. The house specialty is posta a mirandeza, an enormous locally bred beefsteak. (☎ 273 33 14 28. Open daily 8am-midnight. Entrees 1000-1600$. V, MC.) An easy place to grab a meal is **Dom Fernando Restaurante,** inside the castle yard. (Entrees 900-1400$. Salads 400-800$. Menú 1500$. Open daily 8am-11pm.) For mammoth portions at inexpensive prices check out the dim tascas on **Av. Sá Carneiro.** Dim, bodega-like **Tasca Alcateia** on R. Alexandre Herculiano has a menú choice of either veal or rice with octopus (500$), and is always full of friendly locals and lively conversation.

◉ ♫ SIGHTS AND ENTERTAINMENT

A steep uphill battle from Praça Sé sits the historic old town and its brooding **castelo,** built in the 12th century when the area was a feudal land. The area around the castle proper is encircled by massive walls that provide incredible views of the Bragança and Spain. Don't be too fascinated by the architectural superiority of the walls, however; Bragança's best-kept secret is that the ramparts surrounding the castle are a 20th-century addition constructed to make the castle more "authentic" and aesthetically pleasing. Inside the walls, the castle's **Museu Militar** has a wide range of eccentric military paraphernalia, from medieval swords to a World War I machine gun to African art collected by Portuguese soldiers. (Open daily 9-11:45am and 2-4:45pm. 250$. Free Su mornings.) The venerable **pelourinho** (pillory) in the square behind the castle bears the coat of arms of the House of Bragança. At the base of the whipping post is a granite pig, a vestige of pagan ideology and the place where sinners and criminals were bound during the Iron Age. The **Domus Municipalis,** behind the church across the square from the castle, once served as the city's municipal meeting house. Today, it is the only existing example of 12th-century Roman civil architecture on the Iberian Peninsula.

While Bragança's sights are interesting, the town's real charm and popularity spring from the people's warm hospitality and their unique, timeless culture, best exhibited in local feasts. During the **Fiesta del Estudiante,** the town tuna gathers here to play for the entire town. The **Festa da Sào Joào,** June 23-24 is the town's principal celebration. If you're looking for a club-style atmosphere, head down Av. Sé Carneiro toward the university—the street is lined with bars and clubs.

◪ DAYTRIP FROM BRAGANÇA

PARQUE NATURAL DE MONTESINHO (15MIN.)

For directions, maps, brochures and advice on visiting the park, inquire at the information office in Bragança, Bo. Salvador Nunes Teixeira, lote 5. Walk downhill from the tourist office, take the first left on a paved street and the first left again. Park trails are unmarked, but the office has military maps and can help plan hikes. (☎ 273 38 14 44; fax 073 38 11 79. Open M-W and F-Sa 9am-12:30pm and 2-5:30pm.) There is no camping allowed in the park, but the info office rents Casas Abrigos (traditional houses) for reasonable prices. (☎ 273 38 12 34 or 273 38 14 44). Doubles 5000-7500$; quads 10,000$; 21-person rooms 50,000$.) The Serra de Montesinho portion of the park is just north of Bragança; the Parque Natural de Alvào portion is most accessible from Vila Real.

The Parque Natural de Montesinho is more than just a daytrip from Bragança—it is one of the main reasons visitors come to the town at all. One of the largest protected areas in Portugal, this reserve is proof that parts of Western Europe are still untouched by tourism. Some 9000 inhabitants, divided among 92 villages, continue to live much as they have since the land was first settled in the 8th century. Rich with tradition, these villages preserve age-old communal customs and enact rituals dating from past days of pagan worship, from the carving of the porcas, or pigs, to lively festivals such as the December 25th La Festa dos Rapaces, or "Young Men's Rite." Young men, adorned with shaggy suits and painted masks, skip throughout their villages in a tribute to Saturn—woe to the unfortunate, unsupervised rapaza (young girl) who crosses their path! Towns that predate the Roman conquest of the peninsula still preserve their Germanic names: Quirás, Fresulfe, Serrande, Guadramil. Some of the villages can be reached in a day's hike or bike ride, but hard-core visitors often design multi-day hikes linking together some of the most untouched locations.

Trekking on the old mountain paths linking the park's villages not only makes for a fascinating cultural experience; it also affords ample opportunity to linger among the park's flora (oak, chestnut, pine, and cherry trees) and less frequently sighted fauna (the endangered Iberian wolf, royal eagle, and black stork, among others). The area's rivers are also replete with fish; trout fishing is one of the main local livelihoods and is nearly as popular among park visitors as are hiking and horseback riding. Pombales, pigeon coops, dot the landscape of the Parque de Montesinho, and the rivers Onor and Sabor are idyllic spots for picnicking and swimming. The peaceful Onor, about 25km from Bragança, outlines the Spanish border and seems to exemplify the symbiotic relationship that has existed for years between Portuguese and Spaniards living on the frontier; they even speak their own dialect, rionores, a linguistic hybrid between Spanish and Portuguese.

VILA REAL

Vila Real (pop. 25,000) teeters over the edge of the gorges of the Corgo and Cabril Rivers in the foothills of the Serra do Marão. The wonderfully untouristed old town center is surrounded by new neighborhoods reaching into the hills, a lively main street, and a few hopping cafes. As the principal commercial center for the southern farms and villages of Trás-Os-Montes, Vila Real is a good point of departure for excursions into the fertile fields and rocky slopes of the Serra do Alvão and Serra do Marão.

▐▀ TRANSPORTATION

Trains: (☎ 259 32 21 93), Av. 5 de Outubro. To get to Vila Real's center, walk up Av. 5 de Outubro over the iron bridge onto R. Miguel Bombarda and turn left on R. Roque da Silveira. Continue to bear left until Av. 1 de Maio. Trains take longer than buses and require transfers at Régua. To **Porto** (4½hr., 5 per day 7:20am-7:45pm, 1010$).

Buses: Rodonorte (☎ 259 34 07 10), R. D. Pedro de Castro, on the square directly uphill from the tourist office. To: **Porto** (2hr.; M-F 13 per day 6:25am-8:20pm, Sa 7 per day 8am-7pm, Su 7 per day 9:30am-10:30pm; 1000$); **Amarante** (45min.; M-F 10 per day 6:25am-8:20pm, Sa 5 per day 8am-7pm, Su 6 per day 9:30am-10:30pm; 800$); **Guimarães** (3hr., 2-5 per day 10am-5:20pm, 1050$); **Bragança** (2hr.; M-F 6 per day, Sa-Su 3 per day; 8:45am-8pm; 1350$); **Lisbon** (7½hr.; M-F 2 per day 8am and 1:10pm, Sa 3 per day 9:30am-5:20pm, Su 4 per day 9:30am-8:20pm; 2500$). **Ruicar**, R. Gonçalo Cristóvão, 16 (☎ 259 32 47 61), up the street on the right across from Rodonorte, sells tickets for **Rede Expressos,** which stop in front of Rodonorte. To: **Bragança** (4hr., 2:15 and 8:50pm, 1350$); **Braga** (4½hr.; M-F 5 per day 7:55am-9pm, Sa 9pm, Su 3 per day 6-9:45pm; 1000$); **Coimbra** (4½hr.; M-F 6 per day 7:15am-9pm, Sa 3 per day 7:15am-9pm, Su 5 per day 7:15am-9:45pm; 1600$) and **Lisbon** (7½hr.; M-F 8 per day 7:15am-9pm, Sa 3 per day 7:15am-9pm, Su 5 per day 7:15am-9:45pm; 2500$).

Taxis: Radiotáxis (☎ 259 37 31 38). Cabs cluster along Av. Carvalho Araújo.

✴🛈 ORIENTATION AND PRACTICAL INFORMATION

Vila Real's old neighborhood is centered around **Avenida Carvalho Araújo,** a broad tree-lined avenue that runs downhill from the bus station to the Câmara Municipal. Most of the town's cafes, shops and hostels are here. The bus stops at Rodonorte Station on **Rua Don Pedro de Castro;** go right upon exiting to get to the main drag.

Tourist Office: Av. Carvalho Araújo, 94 (☎ 259 32 28 19; fax 259 32 17 12), to the right and downhill from the bus station, across the street. Info on **Parque Natural do Alvão** and other excursions, transportation schedules, and a map. Temporary **luggage storage.** English spoken. Open M-F 9:30am-7pm, Sa 9:30am-12:30pm and 2-6pm.

Currency Exchange: Realvitur, Largo Pioledo, 2 (☎ 259 32 18 00), 4 blocks uphill from the tourist office and to the right. Open M-F 9am-7pm, Sa 9am-1pm. **ATM,** Av. Carvalho Araújo, 84, at Banco Pinto and Sotto Mayor, next to the tourist office.

Emergency: ☎ 112. **Police:** (☎ 259 33 02 40), Lg. Condes de Amarante, 1 block over from Av. Carvalho Araújo.

Medical Services: Hospital: Distrital de Vila Real (☎ 259 30 05 00), north of town in Lordelo. More convenient is the **Centro de Saúde** (☎ 259 32 40 95), on R. Dr. Manuel Cardona, by the youth hostel.

Post Office: (☎ 259 32 28 19), Av. Carvalho Araújo, across the street and to the right of the tourist office. **Posta Restante, telephones,** and **fax.** Open M-F 8:30am-6pm, Sa 9am-12:30pm. **Postal Code:** 5000.

▌ ACCOMMODATIONS

Most accommodations are in the town center. Several cafes along Av. Carvalho Araújo advertise rooms upstairs.

Pousada da Juventude da Vila Real, R. Dr. Manuel Cardona (☎ 259 37 31 93; fax 259 37 47 44), just across the river from the town center. From the bus station, cross the street and follow the street to the right 2 blocks to Lg. Pioledo. Take a right onto Rampa do Calvario and then a left on Av. Almeida Lucena, which becomes R. Dr. Manuel Cardona after the intersection with the large avenue. The youth hostel is on the left; head down the driveway, around to the back, and up the stairs. Somewhat small, bright, disinfected rooms, all with terraces. TV room, patio, and kitchen. Breakfast included. Reception 8am-noon and 6pm-midnight. June 16-Sept. 15 dorms 1900$; doubles with bath 4600$. Sept. 16-June 15 dorms 1500$; doubles with bath 3800$.

Residencial da Sé, Trav. São Domingos, 19-23 (☎ 259 32 45 75), on a sleepy side street off Av. Carvalho Araújo, to the right next to the cathedral. 10 homey rooms with clean baths, TVs, phones, and winter heat. Breakfast included. Singles 3500-4000$; doubles 6000-7000$; triples 7000-8000$. Try negotiating the price, especially in the off-season. V, MC, AmEx.

Camping: Parque de Campismo Municipal de Vila Real (☎ 259 32 47 24), R. Dr. Manuel Cardona, across the river, past the youth hostel. From the bus station, cross the street and follow the street to the right 2 blocks to Lg. Pioledo. Go right onto Rampa do Calvario and then left onto Av. Almeida Lucena, which becomes R. Dr. Manuel Cardona after the intersection with the large avenue. Campgrounds are at the end of the street on the right. 500$ per person, 320$ per tent, and per car. Free showers. Free swimming pool. Reception daily June-Aug. 8am-11pm; Sept.-May 8am-12:30pm and 2-6pm.

🍴 FOOD

Restaurants and cafes around Av. António de Azevedo and Av. Primeiro de Maio cook affordable meals. For fresh produce and fish, hit the **Mercado da Praça,** R. D. Maria das Chaves, 75 (open Tu and F 8am-noon). **Restaurante Nova Pompeia,** R. Carvalho Araújo, 82, on the main drag, next to the tourist office, has low prices and high A/C. (☎ 259 33 80 80. Prato do dia 850$. Entrees 650-1200$. Open M-Sa 8am-midnight.) Pig out on pig at **Restaurante Museu dos Presuntos,** Av. Cidade de Orense, 43, at R. D. Afonso III and R. Morgado de Mateus. This self-proclaimed "ham museum" serves numerous presunto (ham) combinations. Walk uphill from the tourist office, up Av. Carvalho Araújo as it becomes R. D. Margarida Chaves. Take the right fork onto Av. D. Dinis, and turn left on R. Morgado de Mateus. (☎ 259 32 60 17. Entrees 900-1600$. Open M-Sa noon-3pm and 7-10pm.)

👁 🔼 SIGHTS AND EXCURSIONS

Most of Vila Real's sights lie outside of the city proper, but camera-toters still dote on three churches in town. The stodgy 15th-century **sé** (cathedral), with its simple interior divided by thick, arched columns, looms at the lower end of Av. Carvalho Araújo. (Opens only for mass M-F 7:30am and 6:30pm, Sa-Su 9am, noon, and 6pm.) Two blocks east of the cathedral, at the end of R. Central, the **Capela Nova** (New Chapel) blushes behind a floral facade. (Open daily 8:30am-6pm. Free.) One block up R. 31 de Janeiro, in Largo São Pedro, the **Igreja de São Pedro** is resplendent with 17th-century azulejos. (Open daily 9am-5pm. Free.)

Hard-core travelers who want to get out of town head to the **Parque Natural do Alvão,** a protected area reaching to the edge of the mountainous Serra country 15km north of Vila Real. For maps and hiking info, visit the **park information office,** Praçeta do Tronco, 17, in Vila Real. From the tourist office, go uphill and take the right fork onto R. Dr. Margarida Chaves. Keep straight on Av. D. Dinis, walk past Pr. Diogo Cão, and then go left on Cruz de Almas. The office is on the corner with R. Stuart Carvalhais. (☎ 259 32 41 38. Open M-F 9am-12:30pm and 2-5:30pm.)

MOROCCO المغرب

 Country Code: 212. **International dialing prefix:** 00.

LIFE AND TIMES

Morocco has carved its identity out of a host of different influences. At the cross-roads of Africa, Europe, and the Middle East, it boasts Arab culture and religion, African history and landscape, European influences and ties, and languages from all three. At the same time, the country teeters between the past and present as both an ancient civilization descended from nomadic tribes and a modern nation that has struggled against imperial powers for its sovereignty.

HISTORY AND POLITICS

PRE-ISLAMIC. Archaeological evidence along Morocco's Atlantic coast suggests that regions of the country have been settled for anywhere from 100,000 to 1,000,000 years. The **Berber** people arrived between 4000 and 2000 BC; evidence of the use of early Berber tools can still be found in rock carvings scattered throughout the High Atlas Mountains. Though the **Phoenicians** began to explore the area in the 12th century BC and developed small colonies along the coast, they exerted little control or influence over the area. The **Romans** sacked Carthage, near modern Tunis in Tunisia, and in 146 BC brought about a major change in the history of Morocco. Rome became dependent on North Africa's agricultural supply and, as a result, the Romans created the province of Mauritania Tingitana, a client-state with a somewhat independent status, in what is now Morocco. But when the *Pax Romana* deteriorated in the 4th century AD, the Romans abandoned Morocco. By 420 the country was ruled by the Vandals, followed by a period of brief **Byzantine** rule. Each of these civilizations faced similar problems—that it seemed nearly impossible to exert any control over the land without a reliable overland route. As a result, the majority of the country remained unexplored for centuries.

THE RISE AND FALL OF ISLAM (669-1554 AD). Morocco achieved stability in the late 7th and early 8th century when Muslim armies invaded North Africa. In 669 AD, **Uqba bin Nafi al-Fihri** spread the religion of the prophet Muhammad to Morocco. The Berbers could not hold off the Muslim troops, so instead of fighting they made peace with the leader Musa ibn Nusayr and many converted to Islam. This set the stage for the Arab invasion of Spain less than 50 years later.

MOROCCO

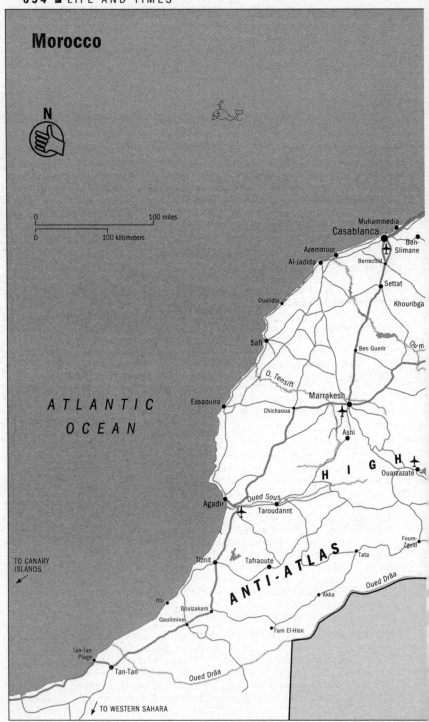

Morocco

N

0   100 miles

0   100 kilometers

ATLANTIC

OCEAN

TO CANARY
ISLANDS

Mohammedia
Casablanca
Ben-
Slimane
Azemmiour
Berrechid
Al-Jadida
Settat
Khouribga
Oualidia
Oum
Safi
Ben Guerir
O. Tensift
Marrakesh
Essaouira
Chichaoua
Ashi
H I G H
Ouarzazate
Oued Sous
Agadir
Taroudannt
Foum-
Zguid
Tiznit
Tafraoute
Tata
A N T I - A T L A S
Ifni
Akka
Oued Drâa
Bouizakarn
Gouliminei
Fam El-Hisn
Tan-Tan
Plage
Tan-Tan
Oued Drâa
↓ TO WESTERN SAHARA

MOROCCO

Arab rule was short-lived in Morocco, ending in 740 AD. Although Arabs remained in the Maghreb, they would not regain power until the 20th century. Instead, a series of local Muslim dynasties rose up to take control of the area, most of their rulers (including the current king), claiming descent from the prophet Muhammad to legitimize their rule. **Idris ibn Abdullah,** after fleeing Arabia, founded the first truly Moroccan state in 789 AD. When Idris was poisoned in 791 AD, his son moved the capital to Fez, but his kingdom did not last. Over the next few hundred years, Morocco was conquered by one minor dynasty after another, the most important of which was the **Almoravid Dynasty** from the Western Sahara, that founded Marrakesh in 1062, and the **Almohad Dynasty,** that conquered it in 1160.

A golden age during the reign of the **Marinid** (a Berber dynasty that ruled from the 13th to 15th centuries) and then **Wattasid** rule (1244-1554) promoted a cultural and intellectual boom and tied Morocco to Spain. As Muslim influence in Christian Iberia waned, however, the Spanish became aggressive. During the Spanish Inquisition in 1492, a wave of Jewish immigrants from Spain fled to Morocco when forced to choose between conversion or death. By the early 1500s, the Iberians had established control over Moroccan ports and a number of inland territories.

THE EUROPEAN CONTENDERS (1415-1912). The **Saadis** drove out the foreign influences and reunited Morocco. Under **Ahmed al-Mansour**—a.k.a. Ahmed the Gilded—Morocco expanded its trade in slaves and gold in Timbuktu and parts of the Sudan. When the **Alawite dynasty** overthrew the Saadis in 1659, they took over Marrakesh and the area around Fez. The Alawite dynasty rules to this day.

Morocco was one of the first African countries to be colonized by European armies. In 1415, Portugal seized Sebta (Ceuta) and began erecting forts along the Moroccan coast. Spain took possession of Melilla in 1497; it is still a Spanish enclave today. The Saadians were able to push the Iberians back for several centuries, ruling the rest of the country from Marrakesh and remaining in power until the 17th century. England took possession of Tangier in 1662 and Spain began controlling the northern coast. France invaded North Africa after winning the battle of Isly in 1844; but their major stroke of luck did not come until the death of Sultan Hassan of Rabat in 1893 and the ascension of his 13-year-old son Abd al-Aziz to the throne. Morocco, as the last independent state in North Africa, retained its independence until colonialism prevailed around the turn of the century. Under the Treaty of Fez (March 30th, 1912) Morocco became a protectorate of France. The northernmost part of the country fell to the Spanish, while Tangier was governed by a European council.

STRUGGLE FOR INDEPENDENCE (1921-1977). In 1921, **Abd al-Krim,** now considered the founder of modern Morocco, organized a rebel army that fought Spain over control of the Rif Country. Rifian tribes managed to get as far as Fez before a combined French and Spanish army drove them out in 1927.

Morocco's nationalist movement began in 1944 with the founding of the Independence Party, Istiqlal; by 1947 it had gained the support of the Moroccan Sultan, Moulay Muhammad V. The French deported nationalist leaders and exiled Muhammad in 1953. The ensuing popular unrest, combined with revolt in Algeria, forced the French to abandon their hard line. Muhammad was returned to the throne on November 18, 1955 and signed a treaty of independence for French Morocco on March 2, 1956. The independence of most of Spanish Morocco followed one month later.

Muhammad V's successor, King Hassan II, came to the throne in 1961 and introduced a constitution favoring monarchists. This was heavily protested by the opposition party UNFP; in 1963, ten of UNFP's leaders, including **Ben Barka,** were implicated in a plot to overthrow the monarchy and sentenced to death. In 1965, King Hassan declared a national **state of emergency,** snagging direct control of executive and legislative powers. Hassan's 1970 constitution ended the emergency and restored limited parliamentary government, but two military coups and governmental divisions delayed democratic parliamentary elections until 1977.

WORLDWIDE CALLING MADE EASY

The MCI WorldCom Card, designed specifically to keep you in touch with the people that matter the most to you.

MCI WORLDCOM   WORLDPHONE.

1·800·888·8000

J. L. SMITH

www.wcom.com/worldphone

Please tear off this card and keep it in your wallet as a reference guide for convenient U.S. and worldwide calling with the MCI WorldCom Card.

HOW TO MAKE CALLS USING YOUR MCI WORLDCOM CARD

> **When calling from the U.S., Puerto Rico, the U.S. Virgin Islands or Canada** to virtually anywhere in the world:
1. Dial 1-800-888-8000
2. Enter your card number + PIN, listen for the dial tone
3. Dial the number you are calling :
   Domestic Calls: Area Code + Phone number
   International Calls:
   011+ Country Code + City Code + Phone Number

> **When calling from outside the U.S.,** use WorldPhone from over 125 countries and places worldwide:
1. Dial the WorldPhone toll-free access number of the country you are calling from.
2. Follow the voice instructions or hold for a WorldPhone operator to complete the call.

> **For calls from your hotel:**
1. Obtain an outside line.
2. Follow the instructions above on how to place a call.
   Note: If your hotel blocks the use of your MCI WorldCom Card, you may have to use an alternative location to place your call.

RECEIVING INTERNATIONAL COLLECT CALLS*

Have family and friends call you collect at home using WorldPhone Service and pay the same low rate as if you called them.
1. Provide them with the WorldPhone access number for the country they are calling from (In the U.S., 1-800-888-8000; for international access numbers see reverse side).
2. Have them dial that access number, wait for an operator, and ask to call you collect at your home number.

* For U.S. based customers only.

START USING YOUR MCI WORLDCOM CARD TODAY. MCI WORLDCOM STEPSAVERS℠

Get the same low rate per country as on calls from home, when you:

1. **Receive international collect calls to your home** using WorldPhone access numbers

2. **Make international calls with your MCI WorldCom Card** from the U.S.*

3. **Call back to anywhere in the U.S. from Abroad** using your MCI WorldCom Card and WorldPhone access numbers.

* An additional charge applies to calls from U.S. pay phones.

WorldPhone Overseas Laptop Connection Tips —
Visit our website, www.wcom.com/worldphone, to learn how to access the Internet and email via your laptop when traveling abroad using the MCI WorldCom Card and WorldPhone access numbers.

Travelers Assist® — When you are overseas, get emergency interpretation assistance and local medical, legal, and entertainment referrals. Simply dial the country's toll-free access number.

Planning a Trip?—Call the WorldPhone customer service hotline at 1-800-736-1828 for new and updated country access availability or visit our website:

www.wcom.com/worldphone

MCI WorldCom Worldphone Access Numbers

Easy Worldwide Calling

MCI WORLDCOM.

The MCI WorldCom Card.
The easy way to call when traveling worldwide.

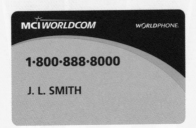

MCI WORLDCOM   *WORLDPHONE.*

1·800·888·8000

J. L. SMITH

The MCI WorldCom Card gives you...

- Access to the US and other countries worldwide.
- Customer Service 24 hours a day
- Operators who speak your language
- Great MCI WorldCom rates and no sign-up fees

For more information or to apply for a Card call:
1-800-955-0925

Outside the U.S., call MCI WorldCom collect (reverse charge) at:
1-712-943-6839

COUNTRY	WORLDPHONE TOLL-FREE ACCESS #
Argentina (CC)	
Using Telefonica	0800-222-6249
Using Telecom	0800-555-1002
Australia (CC) ♦	
Using OPTUS	1-800-551-111
Using TELSTRA	1-800-881-100
Austria (CC) ♦	0800-200-235
Bahamas (CC) +	1-800-888-8000
Belgium (CC) ♦	0800-10012
Bermuda (CC) +	1-800-888-8000
Bolivia (CC) ♦	0-800-2222
Brazil (CC)	000-8012
British Virgin Islands +	1-800-888-8000
Canada (CC)	1-800-888-8000
Cayman Islands +	1-800-888-8000
Chile (CC)	
Using CTC	800-207-300
Using ENTEL	800-360-180
China ♦	108-12
Mandarin Speaking Operator	108-17
Colombia (CC) ♦	980-9-16-0001
Collect Access in Spanish	980-9-16-1111
Costa Rica ♦	0800-012-2222
Czech Republic (CC) ♦	00-42-000112
Denmark (CC) ♦	8001-0022
Dominica+	1-800-888-8000
Dominican Republic (CC) +	
Collect Access	1-800-888-8000
Collect Access in Spanish	1121

COUNTRY	ACCESS #
Ecuador (CC) +	999-170
El Salvador (CC)	800-1767
Finland (CC) ♦	08001-102-80
France (CC) ♦	0-800-99-0019
French Guiana (CC)	0-800-99-0019
Germany (CC)	0800-888-8000
Greece (CC) ♦	00-800-1211
Guam (CC) +	1-800-888-8000
Guatemala (CC) ♦	99-99-189
Haiti +	
Collect Access	193
Collect access in Creole	190
Honduras +	8000-122
Hong Kong (CC)	800-96-1121
Hungary (CC) ♦	06*-800-01411
India (CC)	000-127
Collect access	000-126
Ireland (CC)	1-800-55-1001
Israel (CC)	1-800-920-2727
Italy (CC) ♦	172-1022
Jamaica +	
Collect Access	1-800-888-8000
From pay phones	#2
Japan (CC) ♦	
Using KDD	00539-121 ♦
Using IDC	0066-55-121
Using JT	0044-11-121

COUNTRY	ACCESS #
Korea (CC)	
To call using KT	00729-14
Using DACOM	00309-12
Phone Booths +	
Press red button ,03,then*	
Military Bases	550-2255
Luxembourg (CC)	8002-0112
Malaysia (CC) ♦	1-800-80-0012
Mexico (CC)	01-800-021-8000
Monaco (CC) ♦	800-90-019
Netherlands (CC) ♦	0800-022-91-22
New Zealand (CC)	000-912
Nicaragua (CC)	166
Norway (CC) ♦	800-19912
Panama	00800-001-0108
Philippines (CC)	
Using PLDT	105-14
Filipino speaking operator	105-15
Using Bayantel	1237-14
Using Bayantel (Filipino)	1237-77
Using ETPI (English)	1066-14
Poland (CC) +	800-111-21-22
Portugal (CC) ♦	800-800-123
Romania (CC) +	01-800-1800
Russia (CC) + ♦	
Russian speaking operator	747-3320
	747-3322
Using Rostelcom	747-3322
Using Sovintel	960-2222
Saudi Arabia (CC)	1-800-11

COUNTRY	WORLDPHONE TOLL-FREE ACCESS #
Singapore (CC)	8000-112-112
Slovak Republic (CC)	08000-00112
South Africa (CC)	0800-99-0011
Spain (CC)	900-99-0014
St. Lucia +	1-800-888-8000
Sweden (CC) ♦	020-795-922
Switzerland (CC) ♦	0800-89-0222
Taiwan (CC) ♦	0080-13-4567
Thailand (CC)	001-999-1-2001
Turkey (CC) ♦	00-8001-1177
United Kingdom (CC)	
Using BT	0800-89-0222
Using C&W	0500-89-0222
Venezuela (CC) + ♦	800-1114-0
Vietnam + ●	1201-1022

KEY

Note: Automation available from most locations. Countries where automation is not yet available are shown in *Italic*

(CC) Country-to-country calling available.

+ Limited availability.

★ Not available from public pay phones.

● Public phones may require deposit of coin or phone card for dial tone.

● Local service fee in U.S. currency required to complete call.

▶ Regulation does not permit Intra-Japan Calls.

* Wait for second dial tone.

● Local surcharge may apply.

Hint: For Puerto Rico and Caribbean Islands not listed above, you can use 1-800-888-8000 as the WorldPhone access number.

FOLD

Perhaps the most significant of Hassan's political triumphs was the **Green March** in 1975. The Spanish, who had long since controlled the Spanish Sahara, were confronted with a Saharan rebel group—the **Polisario Front**—precisely as General Franco (see p. 54) lay dying. Hassan capitalized on Spanish weakness, marching his troops into the Sahara. Because the Polisario Front was disorganized and the Spanish were preoccupied, Hassan was successful. Unfortunately, peace did not come easily or immediately. The Polisario Front gained support from the Algerians, but they were at war in the Sahara until the UN declared a cease-fire in 1989.

MODERN MOROCCO (1977-1999). Today Morocco is nominally a **constitutional monarchy:** though assisted by a parliament and Chamber of Representatives, the king can dissolve parliament and easily manipulate the country's political parties. Under Hassan, censorship ruled out opposition from such groups as trade union activists and university radicals. A drought further sapped monarchist support, but after sluggish industrial growth, riots, and the drain of war in the Western Sahara, Morocco began to recover in the 90s. Islamist movements throughout North Africa have kept Morocco cautious, though King Hassan's regime was stable in comparison to those in neighboring countries. Morocco's relations with neighbors are strained, particularly with Algeria, where illegal arms shuttling resulted in the closing of the Morocco-Algeria border in 1994. Southern Europe, also aligned against Islamist infiltration, has been taking a greater interest in Morocco, and has advocated tighter border controls.

In June 1999, President Mubarak of Egypt and King Hassan II met and established a trade agreement between Morocco and Egypt. They signed nine accords, one of which established the Egyptian-Moroccan Company for International Trade. The leaders also discussed other issues relating to the Middle East. Both countries agreed that it is essential that Israel carry out all agreements it has made toward the peace process, and noted that the United States and Europe need to continue to contribute as well. Morocco remains in opposition to Israeli occupation of Jerusalem and what they consider to be Palestine. Despite all the advances the country has made, Morocco remains a nation where almost half of the population lives below the poverty line, sometimes on less than a dollar a day. The country faces a 55% illiteracy rate.

CURRENT EVENTS. This past year has been one of readjustment and drastic change for Morocco. In July 1999, King Hassan, who had ruled the country as an autocratic leader since 1968, died of a heart attack, leaving his then 36-year-old son to govern. Over the past year, King Muhammad VI, the new king who is widely respected both by his people and the international community, has taken steps to reverse many of his father's restrictive policies in efforts to liberalize the political situation and to improve Morocco's human rights record. One of the most important reforms Muhammad has instituted has been the removal of restrictions on the practice of Islam. During the previous decade, other countries in the region had seen a massive revival of Islam, but Morocco, due to strict limitations imposed by the government, was resistant to it. Under Mohammed, however, new mosques have been sprouting up across the country. He released Islamic fundamentalist leader Sheikh Abd al-Salam Yassine, who had been under house arrest for 10 years by the government, and launched the Hassan II Foundation to combat poverty.

Among the more pressing issues currently facing Morocco is what to do with the **Western Sahara.** In the summer of 1999 the UN named a special representative to oversee the referendum on independence for Western Sahara, which was annexed by Morocco in 1975 (see above). The date of the referendum has been pushed back yet again and at press time is set for October 31, 2000. At this point, the UN will determine if Western Sahara should be a part of Morocco or if the Polisario Front will be granted independence as a state. The decision is a contentious and deeply rooted issue, tearing families and neighbors apart. To complicate matters, hundreds of thousands of Moroccans have recently been lured to the Western Sahara through tax breaks, subsidies, and public works projects.

MOROCCO

LANGUAGE

Morocco is a paradise for polyglots. Though Classical Arabic (*al-Fusha*) is the official language of the country, it is rarely spoken and has become almost exclusively a written language. Most people speak a modern Moroccan dialect called *Darija*, as well as at least some French. In certain northern towns, Spanish is also common. Many Moroccans also speak English, but while they can bargain with you, their conversational ability is sometimes limited. In this book, **city names** appear first in English, then in Arabic. (Fez is not written as Fès, the French spelling, nor Faas, the Arabic spelling.) Also, a massive shift from European street names is underway, so some of the streets mentioned in this book may go by a different title (here they are listed in both French and Arabic when necessary). *Rues* and *calles* (streets and roads) may revolt and become *zanqats*, *derbs*, or *sharias*.

RELIGION

The religion of Islam was founded by the Arab prophet Muhammad in 622 AD. Informed of his prophetic calling by the angel Gabriel, Muhammad is believed by Muslims to be the "seal of the prophets" and the end of a long chain of visionaries that includes Abraham, Moses, Elijah, and Jesus. Muhammad led his followers until his death in 632, during which time his words and deeds were recorded in *hadiths* (sayings) that comprise the *Sunna*, or exemplary practice of Muhammad. Following his death, the issue of who would rule divided Muslims into two branches, the Sunni and the Shi'a. The Sunni wanted Muhammad's successor chosen from a community of men; they believe strongly in God's will and predestination, while the Shi'ites believe in free will and insist on his successor being a blood relative of their prophet. More than 99% of Moroccans are Sunni Muslim, though Morocco also has a small Jewish minority and an even smaller Christian one. Islam is the official state religion.

At the heart of the Islamic faith is the Arabic word *islam*, meaning submission. The believer, or *Muslim*, accepts complete submission to the will of God *(Allah)* as embodied in the sacred scriptures of Islam and the Qu'ran (book of recitation). This Arabic text is considered by Muslims to be a miracle—perfect, immutable, and untranslatable; it replaces all earlier revealed books and is the final definitive form of God's word. Unlike the Christian conception of Jesus, the Islamic view considers Muhammad a human messenger of God. All practicing Muslims must adhere to the five pillars of Islam: the formal profession of faith, prayer toward Mecca five times daily, alms-giving, fasting during the month of Ramadan, and, if possible, a pilgrimage to Mecca.

UNDERSTANDING RAMADAN It is believed that Muhammad received the Qur'an during the month of **Ramadan.** Fasting during this holy month is the fourth pillar of Islam. Between dawn and sunset, Muslims are not permitted to smoke, have sexual intercourse, or let any food or water pass their lips; exceptions are made for pregnant or menstruating women, the sick, and travelers (though all must make up the fast at a later date). Fasting is meant to teach Muslims to resist temptation and thereby control all their unchaste urges. Ideally, Muslims read the Qur'an during the daylight hours. By experiencing hunger they are meant to better understand the plight of the poor and to be more thankful for the food which God has provided them. It is insensitive to eat in public during Ramadan. Finally, Ramadan inspires a sense of community. As soon as the sun sets, they break the fast and begin a night of feasting, visits to friends and relatives, and revelry, only to begin fasting again at dawn.

Moroccan Islam is somewhat unique. While there is the inevitable difference between popular and orthodox Islam in Morocco, there is less of a gap between the religious intellectuals and the general public than in other Arab countries. An additional Muslim category is Sufism, a mystical twist to Islam that is based on the belief that Muslims will find the truth of God's love and knowledge through a personal experience with God. Sufis were once quite politically influential; they are still a large presence, but their influence in politics has faded. Morocco has had its share of Islamic fundamentalist movements, but they have been substantially weaker than those in other North African countries, due to the popular belief that the king is a religious as well as political leader.

THE ARTS

ART AND ARCHITECTURE

Diverse architectural forms define Moroccan landscapes and cityscapes. An intense climate, combined with Berber austerity and Islamic privacy give **Berber architecture** an enclosed and stark nature. Kasbahs, the monumental houses of the Berbers, feature central courtyards, dark and narrow passageways, animal shelters, simple high slope-walled towers, thick walls, and plain facades. *Qsour* (plural of *qsar*; or fortified Berber villages) house densely packed "apartments." Both are made with *pisé* (packed earth), but are unfortunately gradually turning to ruins, unable to withstand wind and sand storms.

In the 10th century, Fez residents built the first Moroccan **mosques** (sometimes called *djemmas* or *masajid*), al-Andalus and the Qairaouine. The *qibla* (wall) contains the *mihrab* (prayer niche), which faces Mecca. There are two basic designs for mosques: Arab-style, based on Muhammad's house with a pillared cloister around a courtyard, and Persian-style with a vaulted arch on each side. Attached to most mosques, Qur'anic schools *(madrasas)* have classrooms, libraries, and a prayer hall around a central courtyard and fountain.

In order to avoid idolatry, Muslim artists are forbidden from portraying figures of people, animals, or even plants. The result is a style of incredibly ingenious geometric and calligraphic decorations. Colorful patterns swirl across tiles, woodwork, stone, and ceramic. In less doctrinaire times, Almoravid artists slipped in designs that vaguely resemble leaves and flowers. **Calligraphy,** particularly elegant renderings and illuminations of the Qur'an, became another outlet for creativity as well as religious devotion. Sultans reserved their most dazzling designs for **imperial palaces,** with long, symmetrical reception and dwelling rooms studded with decorative gates, hidden gardens, and tiny pools and fountains.

Non-Muslims are usually prohibited from entering Moroccan mosques, but tourists can gawk at the splendor through doorways. Out of respect, visitors should stay away during services (five times daily; Fridays at midday).

CRAFTS

Of Moroccan handicrafts, **carpets** are the most popular with tourists. There are two types of carpets: rugs and *kilims*. Rugs have a shag ruffle; *kilims* do not and they are woven, not knotted. The most expensive carpets will be old, with very detailed embroidery, with vegetable dyes instead of chemical dyes, and made of wool or linen, not cotton. Carpets from the Rif or Middle and High Atlas mountains are filled with a wide variety of colorful markings. Those from Rabat and other coastal cities are modeled on the famed Turkish carpets.

Fez has been the center of a renowned **leather** industry since the 15th century. High-quality Moroccan leather can be purchased where it's made for a fraction of its international price. Fez is also the center for Moroccan **pottery** and is famous for its classic blue-and-white designs. Saharan and Berber **terra-cotta** ware and roof tiles are also common, and the South is known for distinctive and chunky **silver jewelry,** often inlaid with colorful stones or plastic. Moroccan woodwork is amazing; craftsmen seem to effortlessly turn blocks of cedar wood into intricate pieces

All these handicrafts are sold in **souqs** (markets). *Souq*s in more touristy areas target visitors for the sale of craftwork; it is wiser to go to local *souqs* to do your real purchasing. Bargaining is key in buying anything. In general, the final price should be about 50% of the seller's starting price. To avoid getting hassled, declare that you've done your shopping already or claim student status. If you're interested in something but can't get the right price, try walking out the door and down the block: the owner is likely to chase after you with a better price; even if he doesn't, you'll find the same thing two stores down. (Also see p. 678.)

FOOD AND DRINK

Moroccan chefs lavish aromatic and colorful spices on their dishes—pepper, ginger, cumin, saffron, honey, and sugar are culinary staples. The notably Moroccan taste comes from a unique mixture of spices, known as *ras al-hanut*, making bland food a rarity. However, no matter how delicious everything may seem, be prepared to get sick at least once, as Morocco is full of germs and parasites to which tourists are not immune. Still, taking extra precautions may help. Bottled mineral water is the way to go, as is peeling all fruits and vegetables. The truly cautious may want to avoid salads as well, or at least be sure they are washed in purified water. Most food sold on the street, especially meat dishes, can be quite dangerous. The meat grinders are rarely cleaned, providing an ideal breeding ground for *E coli* and other bacteria. In general, beware of anything sold on the street.

TYPICAL FARE

Moroccan cuisine consists mainly of couscous, *tajine*, and soups. **Tajine** is a stew steamed in an oven in a cone-shaped clay dish. It usually consists of some kind of meat, chicken, lamb, or pigeon along with an assortment of vegetables, olives, and prunes. Vegetarian forms of *tajine* are common as well. **Couscous** is a seminola-grain pasta about the size of sesame seeds, and is also served with meat or vegetables. The most popular of the Moroccan soups is **harira,** a salty chick-pea soup, sometimes containing meat (it is served every day during Ramadan). **Baguettes** and **honey-soaked pastries** are everywhere, as are delicious Moroccan breads.

Other common dishes include **poulet** (chicken), which can be prepared either *rôti* (roasted on a spit with olives) or *limon* (with lemon). Pricier and harder-to-find specialties include **mechoui,** whole lamb spitted over an open fire, and **pastilla,** a combination of pigeon or chicken, onions, almonds, eggs, butter, cinnamon, and sugar under a pastry shell. For a lighter treat, slurp sweet natural yogurt with mounds of peaches, nectarines, or strawberries, or try an oily Moroccan salad with finely chopped tomatoes, cucumbers, and onions. Snackers munch briny olives (1dh per scoop), roasted almonds, dried chick-peas, and cactus buds (1dh per bud). Oranges abound as the cheapest, sweetest, safest fruit in the country.

EATING OUT

The restaurant scene in Morocco depends on whether you're in a big city or small town. Because eating out isn't that common a practice for locals, eateries in large, modern cities cater mainly toward tourists, featuring comprehensive menus with either typical Moroccan or French cuisine, with the occasional Chinese, Middle Eastern, or fast food restaurants scattered in between. The most authentic regional food in larger cities is found at small and often indistinguishable local restaurants in the medina. In less-populated villages, restaurants tend to have more limited menus of typical Moroccan food. A complete meal includes a choice of entree (*tajine*, couscous, or perhaps a third option), salad or *harira*, a side of vegetables, and yogurt or an orange for dessert. Almost every Moroccan main course includes meat; *couscous aux légumes* (couscous with vegetables) probably has the least meat. For vegetarians, the best bet is to cook with produce from the market, or to request an omelette at restaurants. Less expensive *tajine* is made with *kefta* (a ground beef cooked in an array of herbs and spices) and often served on a baguette, as is *merguez* (a spicy beef or lamb sausage). Lunchtime runs from noon to 2pm, dinner 7 to 9pm. Still, many restaurants will serve food at any time. If a service charge isn't automatically included, a 10% **tip** will suffice.

DRINKING

Although tap water is drinkable in most parts of the country, bottled, purified water by **Sidi Ali** and **Sidi Harazem** is a safer bet for tourists. If you get a bottle that isn't completely sealed, return it—chances are the bottle has been filled with tap water. Orange juice and other fruit drinks are popular, but make sure that they are diluted with purified water and not tap water.

Despite Islam's prohibition of alcohol, Morocco is a wine-lover's paradise. The local wines are excellent and have won international recognition. While the two best local wines are the Cabernet Medallion and Beauvillion (about 80dh a piece), the less expensive Vabernet du President, Amazir, and Guerraine Rouge are also quite good (all about 35dh). Moroccan, French, and Spanish **wines** are available in most supermarkets and some restaurants (but not in the medina). Watery local **beer,** usually Stork or Flag Speciale, is cheap but not particularly good. Moroccan **bars** are entirely male and focus on heavy drinking rather than socializing; otherwise, they are pricey, tourist-oriented, and tend to attract sleazy types. More pleasant are the many Moroccan coffee houses where you can get inexpensive Moroccan **coffee** and **tea.** Espresso is widespread and popular, as is coffee, which is almost always sweetened with sugar and diluted with varying degrees of milk. Green tea, the national drink, is sipped with fresh mint leaves and lots of sugar, and seems to be almost a staple of the Moroccan diet.

SPORTS

Moroccans are deeply passionate about soccer, and there are intense rivalries between competing clubs. Their national team was undefeated in qualifying matches for the 1998 World Cup, and only narrowly missed advancing to the second round. Basketball runs a distant second to soccer, but is still popular. Team sports remain fairly limited to men, although other participatory sports abound. Skiing is common in the High Atlas Mountains (late December to early March) and is possible in the Middle Atlas Mountains as well, hiking is available everywhere, water sports are popular on the Atlantic coast, and biking takes place nationwide.

CULT FICTION   Paul Bowles has become somewhat of a cult figure in Morocco and is considered one of America's best expatriate writers. He initially gained fame through his involvement in radical politics, but Bowles turned from politics to travel after marrying Jane Auer in 1938, and he ultimately settled in Morocco on the advice of Gertrude Stein. It was there that he began to use Moroccan drugs to enhance his creativity (don't get any ideas) and started writing fiction. His first and most famous novel, *The Sheltering Sky* (1949), details the lives of an American couple and their struggle with Moroccan culture and themselves. Many reviewers likened the novel to the works of Poe (who happened to be Bowles's childhood idol) and Hemingway. From that point on, most of Bowles's fiction was set in Morocco, though his only other piece to gain much fame was *The Spider's House* (1955). When Jane died in 1973, Bowles's work showed signs of a loss of hope. His career, however, received a boost in the early 1990s when Bernardo Berotolucci made a movie of *The Sheltering Sky*, starring Deborah Winger and John Malkovich. He died in Tangier in November 1999.

RECOMMENDED READING

LITERATURE ABOUT MOROCCO

In Morocco, by Edith Wharton. Episodic descriptions of Rabat, Salé, Fez, and Meknes.

Morocco That Was, by Walter Harris. A turn-of-the-century journalist's diary, featuring a wry account of a Brit's kidnapping by the international bandit Raissouli.

The Voices of Marrakech, by Bulgarian Nobel Prize recipient Elias Canetti. Eloquently records a European Jew's encounter with Moroccan Jews.

The House of Si Abd Allah, edited by noted scholar Henry Munson. An oral history of a Moroccan family which provides insight into the country's social history.

The Sheltering Sky, The Spider's House, Days: Tangier Journal, by Paul Bowles. Numbingly gorgeous introductions to the country and to Bowles (see **Cult Fiction,** p. 661).

MOROCCAN LITERATURE IN ENGLISH

Love With a Few Hairs, The Lemon, and **M'hashis,** by Muhammad Mrabet. Bits of contemporary Moroccan life, translated by Paul Bowles.

The Battle of Three Kings, by Youssef Necrouf. An entertaining account of medieval violence and intrigue under the Saadian dynasty.

Dreams of Trespass (Tales of a Moroccan Girlhood), by Fatima Mernissa. The author's story of growing up in Fez in the 1950s.

ESSENTIALS

The information in this section is mostly designed to help travelers get their bearings once they are in Morocco. For information about general **travel preparations** (including passports and permits, money, health, packing, international transportation, and more), consult the **Essentials** section at the beginning of this book. Essentials also has important information about alternatives to tourism (**work** and **study** programs in Spain; see p. 48) and for those with specific concerns: **women travelers** (p. 42); **older travelers** (p. 43); **bisexual, gay, and lesbian travelers** (p. 43); **travelers with disabilities** (p. 44); **minority travelers** (p. 44); **travelers with children** (p. 45); and travelers with **dietary concerns** (p. 45).

GETTING THERE AND AROUND

BY PLANE

Royal Air Maroc (in Casablanca ☎ (2) 31 41 41 (or airport ☎ (2) 33 90 00); in US ☎ (800) 344-6726; in UK ☎ (171) 439 43 61), Morocco's national airline, flies to most major cities in Europe, including Madrid and Lisbon. Domestically, a network of flights radiates from the Mohammed V Airport outside Casablanca. Planes fly daily to Marrakesh, Agadir, Tangier, and Fez and occasionally to Ouarzazate as well.

If you hope to see a lot of Morocco in a short time, flying can be both a convenient and affordable option; you don't have to commit to a flight until the day before, and the price of the ticket always remains the same, whether you buy it three months, three weeks, or three days beforehand. Royal Air Maroc (RAM) and its competitor, **Regional Airlines,** fly to all major domestic cities. RAM offers the best deals for students and the under-26 crowd, though Regional Airlines often flies more frequently within the country.

BY TRAIN

Where possible, trains are the best way to travel. They are faster than buses, more comfortable, and fairly reliable and prompt. Second-class tickets on trains are slightly more expensive than corresponding CTM bus fares; first-class tickets cost around 20% more than second-class ones.

The main line runs from Tangier via Rabat and Casablanca to Marrakesh. A spur connects Fez, Meknes, and points east with the main line at Sidi Kasem, near Meknes. There is one nightly *couchette* train between Fez and Marrakesh. Air-conditioning and "non-smoking" cars are usually available. Tickets bought on board cost at least 10% more and may cause you all kinds of trouble with the conductor. No student fares are available. Be wary of old schedules that show times for the Atlantic coast, south of Casablanca—this route has been out of service for a few years now. InterRail (see p. 37) *is* valid in Morocco, but Eurail is not. Fares are so low, however, that InterRail is not worth using in Morocco.

BY BUS

In Morocco, bus travel is less frequent and less reliable than in Spain or Portugal. Plan well ahead if you are thinking of using buses as your method of transport. They're not all that fast and they're not very comfortable, but they're extremely cheap and travel to nearly every corner of the country. **Compagnie de Transports du Maroc (CTM),** the state-owned line, has the fastest, most luxurious, most reliable, and generally most expensive buses (though "expensive" here means just a few more dirhams). In many cities, CTM has a station separate from other lines; reservations are usually not necessary. *Let's Go* lists CTM stations in each city. Several dozen other private companies operate as well. Though they may offer more frequent departures, the comfort level is so low, you'll probably wish you had waited for the next CTM. Other private companies, called **cars publiques** (a.k.a. *souq* buses), have far more departures and are generally slower, less comfortable, and cheaper. In the bus stations, each bus company has its own info window; window-hop for information on destinations and schedules.

The **baggage check** at CTM bus depots is usually safe. Your bags, however, may not be accepted for storage if you don't have padlocks on the zippers. Private bus companies also have baggage checkrooms; they're generally trustworthy and accept any kind of bag.

BY TAXI

Two separate hordes of taxis prowl Moroccan streets: intra-urban *petit taxis* and inter-urban *grand taxis*, both dirt cheap by European standards. *Petit taxis*, small Renaults or Fiats that can each hold a strict maximum of three passengers, are all painted in one color depending on the municipality (red in Fez, blue in Meknes, etc.) and can't leave the city or take you to the airport. Make sure the driver turns the meter on; they are required to do so by law. If the driver won't turn it on, take another cab; at the very least, agree on the price before you go (around 50% of what the driver asks is fair). There is a 50% surcharge after 8pm. Don't be surprised if the driver stops for other passengers or picks you up with other passengers in the car, but if you are picked up after the meter has been started, note the initial price.

Grand taxis, typically beige or dark-blue Mercedes sedans, are the most expensive way to travel, but do go just about everywhere. Unlike their *petit* cousins, they don't usually cruise for passengers, congregating instead at a central area in town. They hold up to six passengers (four in the back, two in the front), but if you plan on taking a long ride, you might buy two spaces to allow for extra room. A taxi won't go until it is filled with passengers going in the same direction. Ask other passengers what they are paying to avoid being ripped off.

BY CAR AND BY THUMB

There are two reasons to rent a car in Morocco: large group travel, or travel to areas not reached by Morocco's public transportation system. Otherwise, car rental is unnecessary. Moroccan roads can be very dangerous; reckless passing maneuvers, excessive speed, shoddy maintenance, and poorly equipped vehicles are all par for the course.

Hertz, Avis, and **Europcar** all rent cars; expect to pay about 400dh per day for an economy car, including taxes and insurance. Large local firms such as **Afric Car, Moroloc,** and **Locoto** offer cars for considerably less money but are also less reliable. Both international and local firms are easy to find in all major cities.

Once in your car, you face a myriad of complications, the most serious being police **security checks.** Virtually any trip you take will bring you to at least one checkpoint. Expect to be pulled over and asked to produce your passport and proof of rental. One tactic if pulled over is to immediately ask for directions, either in French or Arabic. You also may be stopped for **traffic violations,** real or not. The fine is payable on the spot in dirhams and may be negotiable; asking for a receipt could be construed as provocative. Whatever you do, do not travel with drugs (which are illegal) in your car.

Routes goudronées (principal roads), marked "P," are paved and connect most cities. **Pistes** (secondary roads), designated "S," are less smooth. If traveling in the **desert,** be sure to bring at least 10 liters of bottled water for each person and for the radiator. Move rapidly over sand; if you start to bog down, put the car in low gear and step on the gas. If you come to a stop in soft sand, push rather than sink. **Gas** costs about 10dh per liter.

Driving in Morocco without the **Michelin map** of Morocco all but ensures that you will get lost. Fortunately it is available both abroad and in Morocco. Even with the map, you still should inquire about specific road conditions. One place to make such inquiries is the automobile association, **Touring Club du Maroc,** 3 av. F.A.R., Casablanca (☎ (2) 20 30 64).

Almost no one in Morocco **hitches,** although flagging down buses and trains can feel like hitchhiking. Transportation is dirt cheap by European and North American standards. If Moroccans do pick up a foreigner, they will most likely expect payment for the ride. Hitching is more frequent in the south and in the mountains, where transportation is irregular. *Let's Go* does not recommend hitchhiking.

MONEY

In Morocco, **banking hours** are Monday through Friday 8:30 to 11:30am and 2:30 to 4:30pm, during Ramadan from 9:30am to 2pm. In the summer, certain banks close at 1pm and do not re-open in the afternoon. Do not try the **black market** for currency exchange—you'll probably be swindled.

Taxes are generally included in the price of purchases, though in malls and *grandes surfaces* (supermarkets and larger superstores) you will find a 7% Value-Added Tax on food and a 22% tax on luxury goods.

Tipping a small amount after restaurant meals, while certainly not necessary, is a nice gesture given the extreme degree of poverty of many Moroccan citizens.

Bargaining is definitely a legitimate part of the Moroccan shopping experience—it is most commonly accepted in outdoor markets. There are some guidelines to consider when bargaining. Tailor your bargaining to the situation—offering 40% of the asking price may be too much or too little, depending on where the seller has started. Pretend you know what the item is worth. Do not appear overly eager, point out imperfections in the item or mention that you saw the item elsewhere at a lower price, naming that price. Begin to walk away when the seller has quoted a "minimum" price. Do not try to bargain in supermarkets or established stores.

SAFETY AND SECURITY

EMERGENCY ☎	Police: 19. **Highway services:** 177.

Unfortunately, Morocco has received a bad rap among European travelers. While the **crime rate** is higher than in Spain or Portugal, there is more to Morocco than just hustlers, prostitutes, and drugs. However, visitors should be suspicious of people offering free food, drinks, or cigarettes, as they have been known to be drugged. Large cities like Tangier and Fez are filled with fake guides (see below) offering a tour of the city for a small price; they should be avoided, as there is a reason these people aren't employed by hotels and tour agencies.

Debates between the Moroccan government and the Algerian-based Polisario Front over possession of the Western Sahara resulted in a guerrilla war until the late 1980s. The UN called a cease-fire in 1991, but there are still a number of unexploded **landmines** in the area. Travel to Western Sahara is difficult and not recommended. Those interested in traveling there can obtain clearance information from the Moroccan embassy.

Women travelers will probably have extra difficulties traveling through Morocco without a male companion. At the very least, they should never travel alone. Visitors will feel safer and more comfortable (and will avoid offending local sensibilities) by not wearing short skirts, sleeveless tops, and shorts; moreover, females should always wear bras. Regardless, non-Moroccan women may be gawked at, commented upon, approached by hustlers, followed in a crowd, or even groped on the street. Moroccan women may "hiss" at indecently clad female travelers. The best response may be silence, but yelling *"shuma"* (meaning shame) may well embarrass harassers, especially in the presence of onlookers. If an uncomfortable situation persists, look out for a policeman or other respectable figures.

HEALTH

All travelers in Morocco face a different set of health issues than in Spain and Portugal; food and waterborne diseases in particular are a common cause of illness. The CDC recommends that travelers drink only bottled or boiled water, avoiding tap water, fountain drinks, and ice cubes. It is also advisable to only eat fruit and vegetables that are cooked and that you have peeled yourself. Stay away from food sold by street vendors, and check to make sure that dairy products have been pasteurized. There is only a slight malaria risk in Morocco, but it would still be wise to take extra precaution against insect bites and consider getting a vaccine before leaving. For further information on protection against insects and recommended vaccinations before entering Morocco, see **Health** on p. 23.

While there is a public health system in Morocco, travelers should seek out a private clinic, as these offer the best, most dependable, and affordable care. There are few English speaking doctors, though French is widespread; try to learn a few basic words of medical vocabulary in French in case of an emergency. Private clinics are to be found in large cities and university towns with medical schools, such as Casablanca and Rabat. Travelers with significant medical problems that might need sudden and immediate attention are advised to stay in the larger cities for reasons of accessibility. Abortion is not legal in Morocco, and is not available in public clinics, though one can find private clinics that will perform them.

ACCOMMODATIONS

YOUTH HOSTELS

The **Federation Royale des Auberges de Jeunesse (FRMAJ)** is the Moroccan Hosteling International (HI) affiliate. Beds cost 20-40dh per night, and there is a surcharge for non-members everywhere but in Casablanca. Some hostels sell HI memberships on the spot. Call ahead for reservations as beds can be popular. To reserve beds in high season, get an International Booking Voucher from FRMAJ (or your nearby HI affiliate) and send it to the hostel four to eight weeks in advance. You'll probably need to bring your own sleepsack and towel, and there are usually curfew and lock-out times. For hostel addresses, write to FRMAJ, Parc de la Ligue Arabe, B.P. 15998, Casa Principale, Casablanca 21000 (☎ (2) 47 09 52; fax 22 76 77). For info on your national youth hostel association and other general info, see **Accommodations**, p. 25.

HOTELS

Although there is an official star system for rating hotels in Morocco, the number of stars reflects little more than price. Hotels that are not part of the system are not necessarily worse—their standards vary greatly—but are usually cheaper. Rooms can vary widely even within a particular hotel, so ask to see another room if you don't like the first, or find another hotel, often next door. Cheap hotels in Morocco are really cheap—as little as 40dh per night. Listings are generally divided between medina and *ville nouvelle* establishments. Medina hotels are usually cheaper than their *ville nouvelle* counterparts, but less comfortable and with fewer amenities. Hot showers, when available, may cost extra (usually less than 10dh). Cold showers are usually free. Many hotels do offer laundry service.

CAMPING

Camping is popular and cheap (about 10dh per person), especially in the desert, mountains, and beaches. Like hotels, conditions vary widely. You can usually expect to find restrooms, but electricity is not as readily available. Use caution if camping unofficially, especially on the beaches, as theft is a problem.

KEEPING IN TOUCH

Most useful communication information (including international access codes, calling card numbers, country codes, operator and directory assistance, and emergency numbers) is listed on the inside back cover of this book.

TELEPHONES

Morocco has recently invested hundreds of millions of dollars into modernizing its telephone system, resulting in markedly improved services. Pay phones accept either coins (2dh will cover most local calls) or Moroccan phone cards. The rates for the two types of phones are the same. Available at post offices, phone cards are usually in denominations too large to be practical. Entrepreneurial Moroccans hang around phone banks (found near all post offices) and let you use their phone cards. You pay them only for the units used—typically 2dh per unit, a rate not much worse than doing it yourself. To use the card, insert and dial 00. Once the dial tone turns into a catchy tune, dial the number.

Phone offices *(téléboutiques)* are located in most cities. If you can't find one, head to the post office—they always have at least one phone for international calls. To make a collect call, ask the desk attendant at the local telephone office to place a call *en P.C.V.* ("ahn PAY-SAY-VAY"). Write down your name and the country, state, city, and telephone number you want to call. Collect calls can also be made from payphones; simply dial 12 and ask to call *en P.C.V.* Remember that the initial zero (0) in **city codes** is dialed only when calling from another area within Morocco; from outside of Morocco the number is omitted. Local calls do not require dialing any portion of the city code.

The best way to make international calls is with a **calling card.** See page 28 for more details; numbers for obtaining major international calling cards (AT&T, MCI, Canada Direct, BT Direct, Ireland Direct) are listed there. To **call home with a calling card,** contact the operator for your service provider in Morocco by dialing the appropriate toll-free access number (see page 28).

MAIL

Sending something **Air mail** *(par avion)* can take a week to a month to reach the US or Canada (about 10dh for a slim letter, postcards 4-7dh). Less reliable **surface mail** *(par terre)* takes up to two months. **Express mail** *(recommandé* or *exprès postaux),* slightly faster than regular air mail, is also more reliable. Post offices, shops, and some *tabacs* sell postcards and **stamps.** For very fast service (2 days to the US), your best bet is DHL (www.dhl.com), which has drop-off locations in most major cities.

EMAIL

Yes, email has reached Morocco. Cyber-cafes aren't everywhere, but they can be found at least in most major cities, as well as in the more touristed towns. *Let's Go* lists Internet access and rates whenever applicable.

EMBASSIES AND CONSULATES

In Morocco, most embassies and consulates are open Monday through Friday from around 8am to noon; some reopen after lunch until 6pm.

Algerian Embassy: 46-48 rue Tarek Ibr Ziad, B.P. 448, **Rabat** (☎ (7) 76 55 91; fax 76 22 37).

British Embassy: 17 bd. Latourhassan, B.P. 45, **Rabat** (☎ (7) 72 96 96 or 72 09 06; fax 70 45 31). **Consulates:** 43 bd. d'Anfa, B.P. 13, #762, **Casablanca** (☎ (2) 20 33 16 or 22 33 19 or 22 33 76; fax 20 74 34; 41); bd. Mohammed V, B.P. 2122, **Tangiers** (☎ (9) 94 15 57; fax 94 22 84).

Canadian Embassy: 13 Bis, Jaafar Assadik, B.P. 709, Agdal, **Rabat** (☎ (7) 67 28 80; fax 68 74 30).

Irish Embassy: Refer to the Irish Embassy in Lisbon (p. 534). In case of emergency, contact any Commonwealth embassy.

Australian Embassy: Refer to the Canadian Embassy in Rabat (above). In case of emergency, contact any Commonwealth embassy.

New Zealand Embassy: Refer to the New Zealand Embassy in Spain (p. 73). In case of emergency, contact any Commonwealth embassy.

South African Embassy: 34 Seediens, **Rabat** (☎ (7) 70 67 60; fax 70 67 56; email sugas@mail.sis.ne.ma), opposite the mausoleum.

US Embassy: 2 av. Marrakesh, **Rabat** (☎ (7) 76 22 65, 24hr. ☎ 76 96 39; fax 76 56 61). **Consulate:** 8 bd. Moulay Youssef, **Casablanca** (☎ (2) 26 45 50; fax 20 41 27).

HOLIDAYS

Moroccans celebrate several secular and Islamic holidays. The dates of all Muslim holidays, which begin at sundown before the day listed, are based on the lunar calendar and are valid for 2001 only. Be aware that many establishments are closed during most holidays, particularly the religious ones (and if the holidays fall near a weekend, places are likely to remain closed for an extended period.)

DATE	FESTIVAL	LOCATION
January 1	New Year's Day	National
January 11	Independence Manifesto	National
March 3	National Day	National
March 6	'Eid al-Adha	National
March 26	Islamic New Year	National
May 1	Labor Day	National
May 23	National Day	National
July 30	Ras al-Sana	National
August 14	Reunification Day	National
August 20	Anniversary of the King's and People's Revolution	National
August 21	Young People's Day	National
November 6	Anniversary of the Green March	National
November 18	Independence Day	National
Nov. 17 to Dec. 16	Ramadan	National
December 16	'Eid al-Fitr	National

EXPLORING MOROCCO

Morocco offers an enticing medley of sights, sounds, and smells. Despite its proximity to Europe, Morocco is no more "European" than any other Arab country and provides an excellent introduction to the Arab World. The country is blessed with a huge variety of climates and cultures in a relatively compact area (though short distances do not necessarily imply ease of travel). Many visitors who are limited to visiting only a few cities can hardly believe that they haven't crossed any international borders during their trip, so contrasting are the local atmospheres.

HIGHLIGHTS OF MOROCCO

Fez, with its 9000-street **medina** and exquisite **Bou Inania Madrasa** (see p. 683).

Rabat's eerily incomplete **Hassan Tower** and **Mohammed V Mausoleum** (see p. 694).

Castles in the sand at Jimi Hendrix's old hangout, **Essaouira** (see p. 704).

Marrakesh, especially its otherworldly bazaar, **Djema'a al-Fna** (see p. 709).

THE MEDITERRANEAN COAST

Northern Morocco comprises Mediterranean ports and beaches and the jagged Rif Mountains. The most accessible region from Spain, the Mediterranean coast is a common point of entry into the country; precisely because of its proximity to Europe and the prevalence of European influence throughout its history, the area is rarely considered "real Morocco." The Mediterranean cities provide a taste of the country, but they may not leave visitors with the most favorable impression. Those interested in observing true Moroccan culture should keep pushing south.

TANGIER طنجة ☎ 09

For travelers venturing out of Europe for the first time, disembarking in Tangier (pop. 700,000) can be a distressing experience. Even so, Tangier's peculiar, complex history continues to attract visitors. For centuries the region bounced from one imperial power to the next (Phoenicians, Romans, Portuguese, British, and Spaniards, to name a few), culminating in 1923 with the declaration of Tangier as an "international zone" loosely governed by the US and eight European powers. Law enforcement dwindled, and the city began to attract rich heiresses, drug users, spies, and Beat Generation poets. When Morocco declared its independence in 1956, the new government attempted to change Tangier's image, closing down most of the brothels and increasing police presence. But the city's days as an international zone have left behind a continued legacy. The Café de Paris—*the* cafe of WWII secret agents—still churns out lattes, the Anglican church still conducts mass, and a gay community remains surprisingly visible. On the underside, goods still trade on the black market, hashish still flows from the Rif, and hotels still rent by the hour. Nevertheless, rising tourism (thanks to expanded ferry service into the new port facilities) has propelled Tangier forward. Now most locals insist that Tangier is a thriving city with an unfortunate and undeserved bad reputation.

▣ TRANSPORTATION

Flights: Royal Air Maroc (☎ 93 55 01), pl. France. To Marrakesh, Casablanca, Gibraltar, Barcelona, Madrid, and London. **British Airways,** 83 rue de la Liberté (☎ 93 52 11 or 93 58 77), off of pl. France, flies to **London** (W and Sa 9:55am). A taxi to the **airport,** 16km from Tangier, costs 70dh for up to 6 people.

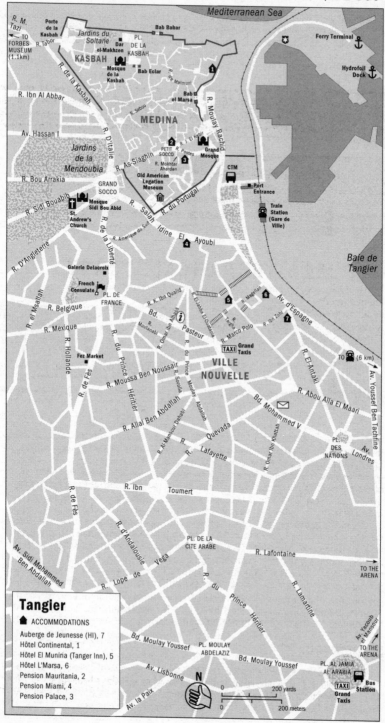

Mediterranean Sea

R. M. Tazi
← TO FORBES MUSEUM (1.1km)

Porte de la Kasbah
R. Tahor
Jardins du Soltane
Dar el-Makhzen
PL. DE LA KASBAH
Bab Bahar

KASBAH

Mosque de la Kasbah
Bab Eclar

R. de Maimuni

Ferry Terminal ⚓

Hydrofoil Dock ⚓

R. Ibn Al Abbar

R. de la Kasbah

R. Sebou

Bab el Marsa

R. Moulay Rachid

Av. Hassan 1

R. D'Italie

MEDINA

Jardins de la Mendoubia

R. As-Siaghin

R. J. El Kebir
PETIT SOCCO
R. des Postes

Grand Mosque

R. Mokhtar Ahardan

CTM

Port Entrance

R. Bou Arrakia

R. Sidi Bouabb

GRAND SOCCO

Mosque Sidi Bou Abid

St. Andrew's Church

Old American Legation Museum

R. du Portugal

Train Station (Gare de Ville)

R. Salah Idine El Ayoubi

R. de la Liberté

R. Amerique du Sud

Baie de Tangier

R. D'Angleterre

Galerie Delacroix

French Consulate

PL. DE FRANCE

R. el Msallah

R. Belgique

R. Mexique

R. Hollande

Fez Market

R. de Fès

R. K. Ibn Quald

Bd. Moutaabbi

R. Omar Ibn Abiabi

R. Pasteur

El Jabha El Ouataina

R. Tarifa

R. Marco Polo

R. Magellan

Av. d'Espagne

R. Ibn Zahr

R. El-Antaki

TO ☎ (6 km)

Av. Youssef Ben Tachine

R. du Prince

R. Moussa Ben Noussair

Héritier

R. Allal Ben Abdallah

R. Al-Mansour Dahabi

R. Seruia

Moulay Abdallah

Quevada

R. Lafayette

VILLE NOUVELLE

TAXI Grand Taxis

Bd. Mohammed V

R. Abou Alla El Maari

R. Omar Ibn Khattab

PL. DES NATIONS

Av. Londres

R. Ibn Toumert

R. de Fès

R. d'Andalousie

Vega

R. Lope de

R. du Prince Héritier

PL. DE LA CITE ARABE

R. Lafontaine

R. Lamartine

TO THE ARENA

Av. Sidi Mohammed Ben Abdallah

Tangier

♠ ACCOMMODATIONS

Auberge de Jeunesse (HI), 7
Hôtel Continental, 1
Hôtel El Muniria (Tanger Inn), 5
Hôtel L'Marsa, 6
Pension Mauritania, 2
Pension Miami, 4
Pension Palace, 3

Bd. Moulay Youssef

PL. MOULAY ABDELAZIZ

Av. Lisbonne

Av. la Paix

N

Bd. Moulay Youssef

Av. Yacoub el Mansour

TO THE ARENA

PL. AL JAMIA AL ARABIA

TAXI Grand Taxis

🚌 Bus Station

0 — 200 yards
0 — 200 meters

MOROCCO

Trains: Trains leave from **Mghagha Station** (☎ 21 09 98), 6km from the port (not the old station on av. d'Espagne). A **petit taxi** to the train station costs around 15dh. 2nd-class to: **Asilah** (1hr., 3 per day 7am-10:15pm, 13dh); **Meknes** (5hr., 3 per day 7am-10:15pm, 77dh); **Rabat** (5½hr., 3 per day 7am-10:15pm, 87dh); **Fez** (5½hr., 3 per day 7am-10:15pm, 93dh); and **Casablanca** (6hr., 3 per day 7am-10:15pm, 114dh).

Buses: **Non-CTM buses** leave from av. Yacoub al-Mansour at pl. Jamia al-Arabia, 2km from the port entrance. Ask blue-coated personnel or check the boards for ticket info. The standard price for luggage is 5dh. To: **Ceuta** (40min., 7 per day 6:15am-2:45pm, 10dh); **Tetouan** (1hr., 10 per day 7am-10pm, 14dh); **Rabat** (5hr., 15 per day 5am-11:15pm, 57dh); **Casablanca** (6hr., 15 per day 5am-11:15pm, 69dh); **Fez** (6hr., 10 per day 8:40am-9:30pm, 63dh); **Meknes** (5hr., 10 per day 6am-2:15pm, 57dh); and **Marrakesh** (10hr., 5 per day 6:45am-8:30pm, 115dh). The **CTM Station** (☎ 93 24 15 or 93 11 72) near the port entrance offers pricier and more posh bus service. A *petit taxi* from the port to the terminal costs 12dh.

Ferries: **Voyages Hispamaroc** (☎ 93 31 13; fax 94 40 31), on bd. Pasteur, below Hôtel Rembrandt. Open daily 8am-12:30pm and 3-7pm. To reach the ferry companies directly, call **Trasmediterránea**, 31 av. de la Résistance (☎ 93 48 83); **Limadet Ferry,** 13 av. Prince Moulay Abdallah (☎ 93 39 14); **Comanau,** 43 rue Abou Ala al-Maari (☎ 93 26 49); or **Transtour,** 4 rue al-Jabha Ouatania (☎ 93 40 04). The cheapest option is to buy a ticket at the port. You'll need a boarding pass (available at any ticket desk) and a customs form (ask uniformed agents). Near the terminal, pushy men with ID cards will try to arrange your ticket and fill out your customs card for 10dh. Just do it yourself. To: **Tarifa** (1½hr.; Sa-Th 3pm, F 7pm; 210dh); **Algeciras** (2½hr., every hr. 7am-9pm, Class B 2960ptas or 210dh); **Gibraltar** (2½hr.; Tu, F, and Su 4pm; 250dh).

Grand Taxis: Quick transport to nearby locations (Tetouan, Ceuta, Asilah). Prices subject to bargaining, but a fair price is 20dh per person when taxis are full (6 passengers). They can be found everywhere, but they congregate by the main bus stop, the Grand Socco, and the intersection of bd. Pasteur and bd. Mohammed V.

Car Rental: Avis, 54 bd. Pasteur. Open daily 8am-noon and 2-7pm. **Hertz,** 36 av. Mohammed V (☎ 93 30 31). Open M-Sa 8:30am-noon and 2-6:30pm, Su 9am-noon. Both agencies charge 500dh and a 20% tax for a Fiat Palio. Min. age 21 for small cars, 25 for four-wheel-drive vehicles.

✴ ORIENTATION

Compared to other Moroccan cities, Tangier is quite navigable. From the ferry terminal, you can take a blue *petit taxi* or walk to the center of town. If you take a **taxi**—which is advisable—either agree on the fare in advance (about 5dh to the center of town) or make sure the driver uses the meter. If you **walk**, leave the ferry terminal along the main road running through the port compound; it will lead you through the large double arches onto the **avenue d'Espagne.** On the right is a **CTM bus station;** the **train station** is 6km, left, down the same road.

The sprawling **ville nouvelle** (new town) surrounds the port in all directions and houses most of the city's businesses. The town's central road is the **boulevard Pasteur.** To find this road, follow av. d'Espagne away from the Medina and take a right on the narrow rue Ibn Zohr after the Hotel Marco Polo. Follow this street up as it bends to the right and changes into rue Marco Polo (straight through an intersection). After one more block, you will run into the intersection of bd. Pasteur to your right and bd. Mohammed V to your left. Turn right onto bd. Pasteur toward **place de France,** the heart of Tangier's *ville nouvelle.* A right turn at pl. France onto rue de la Liberté and a short walk down a winding hill leads to the **Grand Socco,** which is Tangier's largest square and sits outside the west wall of the **medina.** The **Petit Socco** can be reached by crossing the Grand Socco and entering the medina on rue al-Siaghin. For an alternate route to the medina and the Petit Socco from the port, take a sharp right and climb the steep road to the medina entrance. The Petit Socco is a short walk up av. Mokhtar Ahardan. When you get to the sign that reads "Hotel Continental 100m," turn left and walk for two blocks.

🛈 PRACTICAL INFORMATION

Tourist Office: 29 bd. Pasteur (☎ 94 80 50). Some English, French, and Spanish spoken. Tons of brochures but no map. Open M-F 8:30am-noon and 2:30-6:30pm.

Currency Exchange: There is a branch of **BMCE** on most ferries and one in the port complex, although these only change cash. BMCE's **main office** in Tangier is located at 21 bd. Pasteur (☎ 93 11 25). No commission here, but other Moroccan banks charge fees for exchanging traveler's checks. Open M-F 9am-12:45pm and 3-6:45pm. There is an **ATM** on bd. Pasteur. Travel agencies near the port are required to change money at official rates. Major banks line bd. Pasteur and bd. Mohammed V.

Luggage Storage: At the **train station** for 5dh per bag. Open 24hr. Also at the **bus station** for 4dh per bag. Open daily 5:30am-12:30am.

English Bookstore: Librairie des Colonnes, 54 bd. Pasteur (☎ 93 69 55), near pl. France. English classics, popular French and Spanish fiction, and novels, books, and magazines on Moroccan culture. Open M-F 9:30am-1pm and 4-7pm, Sa 9:30am-1pm.

Police: (☎ 19), at the port and main train station.

Late-Night Pharmacy: 22 rue de Fez (☎ 94 21 85), 2 blocks from bd. Pasteur at pl. France across from Cinema Le Paris. They dispense medicine through tiny windows in the green wall on the left side of the entrance. Open M-Th 9am-1pm and 4-8pm, F 9am-12:30pm and 4-8:30pm, Sa 9am-1pm, Su 9am-8pm. Call in an emergency.

Medical Services: Red Cross, 6 rue al-Monoui Dahbi (☎ 94 25 17), runs a 24hr. English-speaking medical service. **Ambulance:** ☎ 93 33 00.

Telephones: 33 bd. Mohammed V, to the right and around the corner from the post office. Open 24hr. There are dozens of teleboutiques around town as well.

Post Office: 33 bd. Mohammed V (☎ 93 25 18 or 93 21 25), the downhill continuation of bd. Pasteur. **Poste Restante** and **telephones.** Open M-Th 8:30am-6:30pm, Sa 8:30am-12:15pm.

Internet Access: PC Halle, halfway down bd. Pasteur. 15dh per hr. Open 9am-midnight.

🛏 ACCOMMODATIONS

If you're unfazed by the frenzy that is Tangier, pick from a number of hostels in the medina; if you're overwhelmed by it all, stay in the *ville nouvelle.* Expect to pay around 50-60dh for a single and 80-100dh for a double, though rates may decrease by as much as 10dh in the winter. Reservations are usually required in August.

MEDINA

The most convenient hostels cluster near **rue Mokhtar Ahardan** (formerly rue des Postes), off the Petit Socco. From the Grand Socco (see **Orientation,** above), take the first right down rue al-Siaghin to the Petit Socco. Rue Mokhtar Ahardan begins at the end of the Petit Socco closest to the port. At night the smaller streets off the medina can be unsafe.

Pension Mauritania (☎ 93 46 77), rue des Almohades at the Petit Socco. A backpacker's mecca. Shared toilets, free cold showers, and clean rooms. Great views of the medina and port from some rooms. 45dh per person.

Pension Palace, 2 rue Mokhtar Ahardan (☎ 93 61 28). Downhill, on the alley exiting the Petit Socco to the right. Stark but soothing rooms, inhabited mainly by students. Clean communal bathrooms. The courtyard was featured in Bertolucci's film adaptation of *The Sheltering Sky.* Singles 40-50dh; doubles 80-90dh, with bath 120dh; triples 120-140dh, with bath 160-170dh; quads 160-180dh, with bath 200-220dh.

Hôtel Continental, 36 Dar Baroud (☎ 93 10 24; fax 93 11 43). From the Petit Socco, follow the signs; take rue Jema'a al-Kebir (formerly rue de la Marine) downhill toward the port until you hit Continental's blue gate. Veer left at the raised overlook. A truly grand hotel furnished with a fusion of Moroccan and art deco. Home to first-time visitors and aging hippies. Breakfast included. Showers are hot only in the mornings. Reservations recommended. Singles 257dh; doubles 326dh; triples 424dh.

VILLE NOUVELLE

Hotels line av. d'Espagne as it heads away from the port. The best values lie a few blocks uphill toward bd. Pasteur and bd. Mohammed V.

 Auberge de Jeunesse (HI), 8 rue al-Antaki (☎ 94 61 27), down av. d'Espagne away from the port and half a block up the road to the right, after Hôtel Marco Polo. A backpacker hotspot; the common room is a good place to find new traveling companions. New, firm dormitory beds. Showers 5dh. Office open M-Sa 8-10am, noon-3pm, and 6-10:30pm, Su 8-10am and 6pm-midnight. Closes at 10:30pm in winter, though there is some flexibility. HI members 25dh; non-members 30dh.

Hôtel El Muniria (Tanger Inn) (☎ 93 53 37), rue Magellan. Take the 1st right after Hôtel Biarritz on av. d'Espagne, walking away from the medina, and follow as it winds uphill. William Burroughs wrote *Naked Lunch* in room #9 (unfortunately now the owner's room). Ask for room #4, where Jack Kerouac and Allen Ginsberg stayed. A great deal for Tangier, with spacious rooms, hot showers, and towels. Singles 100dh; doubles 130dh.

Pension Miami, 126 rue Salah Eddine al-Ayoubi (☎ 93 29 00), off av. d'Espagne. 45 frayed turquoise and magenta rooms, handsomely carved high ceilings, and a balcony on each floor. Basic communal bathroom. Hot showers 10dh. Singles 50dh; doubles 80dh; triples 120dh; quads 160dh.

Hôtel L'Marsa, 92 av. d'Espagne (☎ 93 23 39), away from the port on the main drag; you can't miss its restaurant (see **Food,** below), which juts out onto the sidewalk. Clean rooms with closets and mirrors. A good deal for the location. Hot showers 7dh. Laundry 5dh per piece. Singles 80dh; doubles 120dh; quads 200dh. V, MC.

◪ FOOD

MEDINA

The medina dining experience begins at the **Grand Socco,** where you can stall-hop while feasting upon Moroccan treats (goat cheese, nougat, and other delicacies usually only available during Ramadan). On the corner near the pl. France sprawls a huge vegetable and meat **market.** The best pastries in town can be found at **Café Patisserie Charaf,** 28 rue Smarine. Head from the Grand Socco in the direction of the Petit Socco and you will find a slew of inexpensive local eateries.

Restaurant Hammadi, 2 rue de la Kasbah (☎ 93 45 14), the continuation of rue d'Italie just outside the medina walls. The only Moroccans here are the waiters and serenading musicians. Avoid lunchtime, when tour groups fill every seat. Specialties are *tajine* (40dh) and couscous (45dh). Beer and wine served. Entrees 40-60dh. A 20% tax is added to each meal. Open daily 11am-3pm and 7pm-midnight. V, MC, Eurocard.

VILLE NOUVELLE

International cuisine is available throughout the *ville nouvelle.* The restaurants along av. d'Espagne tout unspectacular and overpriced *menus touristiques* for 50dh and up. Beachfront restaurants run by the high-end hotels are just what you'd expect—expensive and boring. You're better off starting at pl. France and scouting from there. For hot sandwiches, try the storefronts off bd. Pasteur.

Restaurant Africa, 83 rue Salah Eddine al-Ayoubi (☎ 93 54 36), just off av. d'Espagne near Pension Miami, opposite Hôtel Valencia. The name seems to indicate a sure-fire tourist trap, but the food and prices prove otherwise. Beer served. Big 4-course *menu du jour* 50dh. Entrees 25-80dh. Open daily 9am-12:30am.

L'Marsa, 92 av. d'Espagne (☎ 93 19 28). This popular restaurant and cafe has outdoor dining and a mixed Italian and Moroccan menu. Praiseworthy pizzas (23-35dh) and 10 flavors of Italian ice cream (12-25dh). Women traveling alone should avoid the rooftop terrace; the low table-to-chair ratio makes this a choice pick-up spot for Moroccan men. Entrees 25-70dh. Open daily June-Aug. 5am-3am; Sept.-May 5am-midnight. V, MC.

Star of India, av. des Far (☎ 94 48 66) across from the Hôtel Solazure. An exotic alternative along the beachfront strip. Surprisingly authentic Indian entrees (40-80dh). Vegetarian friendly. Open daily noon-3pm and 7pm-midnight. V, MC.

SIGHTS

IN AND NEAR THE MEDINA

DAR AL-MAKHZEN. An opulent palace with handwoven tapestries, inlaid ceilings, and foliated archways, the Dar al-Makhzen was once home to the ruling pasha of Tangier and is now a **Museum of Moroccan Art.** The collection includes intriguing exhibits of ceramics, carpets, silver jewelry, weapons, and musical instruments, with plaques in French and English. *(From the Petit Socco, head left past the Pension Mauritania on rue des Almohades. When it ends, bear left again uphill to rue Ben Raissouli. At the intersection, head right and uphill again through the Bab al-Assa. The entrance to the palace is on the left. ☎ 93 20 97. Open W-M 9am-12:30pm and 3-5:30pm. 10dh.)*

MARKETS. The medina's commercial center is the **Grand Socco.** This busy square and traffic circle is cluttered with fruit vendors, parsley stands, and *kebab* and fish stalls. Up and over the hill of the *ville nouvelle,* in the colorful **Fez Market,** local merchants cater to Tangier's European community. *(Uphill on rue de la Liberté, across pl. France, and 2 blocks down rue de Fez on the right.)* Berbers from the Rif come to the **Dradeb district** (west of the Grand Socco along rue Bou Arrakia and northwest on rue de la Montagne) every Thursday and Sunday to vend pottery, olives, mint, and fresh fruit. Unless Tangier is your only stop, it is best to wait until elsewhere to buy crafts and souvenirs. Tangier's markets cater mainly to hungry locals, and visitors will have to push their way into the bustle to get anything.

OLD AMERICAN LEGATION. In contrast to the frenzy of Tangier's medina goings-on, the Old American Legation is austere and refined. In 1820 this former home of the US ambassador became the first foreign property acquired by the United States. The museum contains many documents relating to Tangier's international past, including correspondence between George Washington and his "great and magnanimous friend," Sultan Moulay ben Abdallah. The ever-changing selection of art ranges from 16th-century maps to photographs of the 1943 Casablanca conference. The friendly curators will give excellent tours on request, but calling first is recommended. *(8 rue d'America. In the far corner of the medina, at the farthest point from the water. ☎ 93 53 17. Look for the yellow archway emblazoned with the US seal. Open M-F 10am-1pm and 3-5pm. Free, but donations are appreciated.)*

OTHER SIGHTS. Rue Riad Sultan runs alongside the **Jardins du Soltane,** where artisans weave carpets, and continues to **place de la Kasbah,** a sunny courtyard and adjacent promontory offering a view of Spain and the Atlantic Ocean. With your back to the water, walk straight ahead toward the far right corner of the plaza, where just around the corner to the right the sharp **Mosque de la Kasbah** rears its octagonal minaret. Just outside of the medina, 17th- and 18th-century bronze cannons hide in the **Jardins de la Mendoubia,** a peaceful park that seems far away from the excitement of the Soccos. *(Opposite rue de la Liberté, where rue Bou Arrakia joins the Grand Socco through the big white gate marked #50.)*

VILLE NOUVELLE

ST. ANDREW'S CHURCH. British expats congregate in and around St. Andrew's Church, designed by the British to look like a mosque; even the Lord's Prayer is carved in decorative Arabic. Surrounding gardens and benches offer respite from the medina. Mustafa, the caretaker of 32 years, leads informal tours. *(Rue Amengnedu Sud. Take a left as you enter the Grand Socco from rue de la Liberté and then a quick left onto rue Amengnedu Sud. Tours daily 9:30am-12:30pm and 2:30-6pm. A tip of a few dirhams is appreciated. Su communion 8:30am, morning service 11am.)*

OTHER SIGHTS. Though run by the French Cultural Center, the **Galerie Delacroix** also displays works by Moroccan and foreign artists. All works either depict Tangier or were painted in the city. The museum closed for repairs as of June 2000. *(Rue de la Liberté, heading toward the medina. Open Tu-Su 11am-1pm and 4-8pm. Free.)* The city's most recent monumental construction is the towering **New Mosque,** an ochre-and-white structure on pl. al-Koweit. *(Southwest of the Grand Socco along rue Sidi Bouabib. Visits by non-Muslims are prohibited.)*

MOROCCO

🎵 ENTERTAINMENT

Pl. France has hosted Tangier's social activity since the city's heyday. The most popular evening activity is sipping mint tea and people-watching from a cafe on bd. Pasteur. The **Café de Paris,** 1 pl. de France, more elegant than its neighbors, hosted countless rendezvous between secret agents during WWII. Coming from the Grand Socco, look to the left. (☎ 93 84 44. Tea and coffee 5-6dh. Open daily 5:30am-11pm.) Inside the medina, another pleasant option is **Café Central,** a favorite of William S. Burroughs (off the Petit Socco; same hours and prices). Cafes tend to attract a male crowd, but female tourists should not be afraid to grab a table and an orange juice—it's perfectly acceptable.

The best place for a beer with little hassle is the pub-like **Tanger Inn,** rue Magellan (open 9pm-late). Those in search of a quiet drink can try the relaxed **Negresco,** 20 rue Mexique, off the pl. France. The city's longest-running bar, Negresco regularly attracts resident expats and backpackers. (☎ 93 80 97. Beer 15-18dh. Mixed drinks 30-35dh. Open daily 10am-1am.) Boisterous and seedy affairs run their shady course at many of the discos along rue al-Moutanabi, parallel to bd. Pasteur near pl. France. Try **Morocco Palace,** 11 av. Moulay Abdallah, or **Borsalino,** 30 av. Moulay Abdallah, (☎ 94 41 63). Both are open from 11pm to 3am. Bear in mind that Moroccan discos are not safe for solo travelers but can be fun for groups.

CEUTA سبتة   ☎09

Those interested in avoiding the craze of Tangier may opt to enter Morocco through Ceuta, a Spanish sovereign enclave (over half of which is owned by the military). Ceuta, however, is less convenient for train travel to the Atlantic coast or Marrakesh. Most visitors don't stay long, opting instead to go on to Tetouan or Chefchaouen for their first night.

Public **buses** and **taxis** ply the route between downtown Ceuta, a couple of blocks from the port, and the border crossing into Morocco, 3km away. Bus #47 runs from pl. Constitución (100ptas); taxis are 400ptas. Once at the Moroccan border, you must cross on foot and find a **grand taxi,** in the big parking lot, to Tetouan. They won't leave until full; don't pay more than 15dh. There are eight **ferry** departures daily to and from Spain (1½hr., 6:30am-10pm, 1801ptas), with more during the high season. There are also eight **fast-ferry** departures (35min., 6:30am-10pm, 2945ptas). It is safer to buy your tickets at the port itself. There is a small **tourist office** on the way out of the port that can help with lodging or transportation details. (☎ 956 50 1410; fax 956 52 82 48. Open daily 8am-8pm.)

TETOUAN تطوان   ☎09

Odds are that most travelers in Tetouan either just crossed into Morocco via Ceuta or are about to leave from there. For new arrivals, Tetouan can be very intimidating because of hustlers and guides. As long as you stick to the popular areas, the two main plazas connected by Calle Mohammed V, Tetouan can be an enjoyable experience. The *ville nouvelle* centers around **place Moulay al-Mehdi,** with the medina and the spacious pl. Hassan II to the east, a few blocks down av. Mohammed V. The **bus station** is two blocks downhill from pl. Moulay al-Mehdi. Take the street to the left of the bank BCME. **CTM buses** (☎ 31 20 61) run to: **Tangier** (1½hr., 5:30am and 4pm, 15dh); **Chefchaouen** (1½hr., 4 per day 5am-8pm, 25dh); **Rabat** (6hr., 3 per day 6:30am-11pm, 100dh); **Casablanca** (7hr., 3 per day 6:30am-11pm, 120dh); and **Fez** (5hr., 11:30am and 1:45pm, 60dh). **Grand taxis** (15dh) to Ceuta leave from the bus station. Taxis to Chefchaouen (25dh) run from a stand several blocks away; walk from pl. Moulay al-Mehdi away from the bus station along rue Achra Mai and bear left onto rue al-Jazair. The **tourist office** is a half block down av. Mohammed V toward the medina, and has a map and info on guides. (Open M-F 8:30am-noon and 2:30-6:30pm.) The **post office, telephone office,** and banks with **ATMs** and currency exchange are in pl. Moulay al-Mehdi. Reach **police** at ☎ 19.

For accommodations, the best option in town is ▓**Pension Iberia**, pl. Moulay al-Mehdi, on the third floor above BMCE. Clean, breezy rooms make up for the long walk upstairs. (☎ 96 20 93. Hot showers 5dh. Singles 40dh; doubles 70dh; triples 105dh.) Another option is **Hotel Príncipe**, 20 rue Youssef. Archaically furnished rooms all have bath and toilet. (☎ 96 27 95. Singles 70dh; doubles 100dh.) The pocket-sized *pastillas* (6dh) at ▓**Café-Patisserie Smir** make a perfect budget lunch-on-the-go, though there is also a balcony on which to enjoy the variety of breads and pastries (1-5dh). A popular place among Moroccan families, the cafe is good for women travelers. (Open daily 6am-9pm.)

CHEFCHAOUEN (CHAOUEN) شفشاون ☎09

A whitewashed town high in the Rif Mountains, Chefchaouen is no longer the complete escape from hustlers it once was, but its relaxed atmosphere and cool mountain air still refresh even the weariest of travelers. Tourists are attracted by both its manageable, Mediterranean medina and the proximity to *kif* (hashish) farms, which have dominated the hills for centuries. This mellow town is a good place to spend your first few days in Morocco or your last night before departing.

▐ **TRANSPORTATION.** The bus station is downhill from town. **Buses** heading south fill up, so get tickets early. **CTM** goes to: **Tetouan** (1½hr., 4 per day noon-7pm, 16-18dh); **Ouazzene,** the best bet for connections (1hr.; 7am, 1:15pm, and 3:30pm; 18dh); **Tangier** (3pm, 33dh); and **Fez** (4hr., 1:15 and 3pm, 52dh). Private companies also have daily buses to Ceuta, Tangier, Fez, and Meknes. **Grand taxis** are probably the easiest way to get to **Tetouan** (24dh) and **Ceuta,** although they often take a while to fill. Taxis leave a block downhill from pl. Mohammed V.

▐ **PRACTICAL INFORMATION.** From the **bus station,** head up the steep hill and turn right after several blocks onto the large road, which leads to the tree-filled, circular pl. Mohammed V; it's about a 20-minute walk to the center of town (or a few dirhams for a cab). Cross the plaza and continue east on **avenue Hassan II,** the *ville nouvelle's* main road. Av. Hassan II ends at the **Bab al-Ain,** the main gate into the medina. From Bab al-Ain, the main, twisting street uphill leads to **place Uta al-Hammam,** the large plaza at the heart of the medina. Chefchaouen has no tourist office. For **currency exchange** go to **BMCE,** av. Hassan II (open M-F 8:15am-2:15pm). The **Hospital Mohammed V** is a block west from pl. Mohammed V, and police can be reached at ☎ 19. The **post office** is on av. Hassan II and has **telephones** (open M-F 8:30am-12:15pm and 2:30-6:30pm). Surf the web at **Internet a Chefchaouen,** 44 Ghazouat Badr, in front of the Mobile station, one block from pl. Mohammed V away from the medina. (☎ 98 89 30. 30dh per hr. Open daily 8:30am-1pm and 3-10pm.)

▐▐ **ACCOMMODATIONS AND FOOD.** Chefchaouen has a slew of colorful budget hotels. In the medina, head uphill from Bab al-Ain; hotels are clustered all along this street and around pl. Uta al-Hammam. Outside, follow av. Hassan II toward Hotel Rif and beyond. ▓**Hotel Andalus,** 1 rue Sidi Salem, directly behind Credit Agricola on pl. Uta al-Hammam, is extremely backpacker-friendly, with a book exchange, large common room, and inviting atmosphere. It also has possibly the cheapest rooms in all of Morocco. (☎ 98 60 34. Hot showers 5dh. Singles 25dh; doubles 50dh; triples 75dh; quads 100dh; lovely terrace 15dh.) Tucked in the corner of whitewashed walls and next to a *hammam,* ▓**Pension la Castel-lana,** 4 Sidi Ahmad Bouhali, caters almost exclusively to backpackers and encourages long stays. Walk to the end of pl. Uta al-Hammam to get there. (☎ 98 62 95. Communal kitchen and common room with stereo. Free hot showers. Singles 30dh; doubles 60dh; triples 90dh; quads 120dh; terrace 15dh.) **Hotel Rif,** just outside the medina walls, has clean, comfy rooms, great views, a TV lounge, and terraces decorated in a combination 16th-century Moroccan and 1970s

Americana motif; they also can help with mountain hikes. Follow av. Hassan II to the right around the medina; it's on the left after a few blocks. (☎/fax 98 69 82. Singles 50dh, with shower 90dh; doubles 80dh, with shower 120dh; triples 120dh, with shower 160dh. V, MC.) **Food** is remarkable easy to find in Chefchaouen. Restaurants and cafes are ubiquitous, even inescapable. Outdoor seating is available in pl. Uta al-Hammam; classier joints are along av. Hassan II. **Chez Aziz**, just outside Bab al-Ain, has cheap, tasty sandwiches. (Shrimp 15dh. Sandwiches 10-15dh. Open daily noon-midnight.)

🔲 **SIGHTS.** Chefchaouen's steep ▨**medina** is one of Morocco's best. Enter through Bab al-Ain and walk uphill toward pl. Uta al-Hammam, the center of the medina. In the *place* are several outdoor cafes, the 16th-century **Grand Mosque** with its red-and-gold minaret, and a kasbah built in the 17th century by Moulay Ismail, Morocco's most famous rogue. Inside the kasbah stands the 15th-century **Tower of Homage.** (Open daily 9am-1pm and 3-6:30pm. 10dh.) Chefchaouen's **souq** operates Mondays and Thursdays in the square beside the Hotel Magou. Berbers come from all over the Rif to sell fresh veggies and not-so-fresh clothes. (Down the stairs from av. Hassan II.)

🏔 **HIKING.** Chefchaouen is a good place to hike. Follow the **Ouad Laou River** upstream into the hills for just a few kilometers for spectacular results. Another good hike begins above the medina behind the Hotel Asmaq (follow signs for the *ville nouvelle*), winds up the peak to the left, and then runs down into the valley. You might try reaching the "Spanish mosque," about halfway up the peak to the right of the medina, or the spectacular rocky arch known as the **Pont de Dieu.** Most of the hikes are quick one-hour round-trip affairs, though it takes a full day to reach the Pont de Dieu. The Hotel Rif (see above) has maps and info about guides.

THE MIDDLE ATLAS الاطلس المتوسط

The cities and towns that lie among the peaks of the Middle Atlas mountains form Morocco's heartland. Home to the imperial cities of Fez and Meknes, the nation's agricultural bread basket, the Roman ruins of Volubilis, and the spiritual center of Moulay Idriss, this region embodies the true spirit of Morocco.

MEKNES مكناس ☎ 05

Meknes lies amid a gray-green agricultural checkerboard, an hour west of Fez and three hours east of Rabat. Named for the Berber tribe Meknassa, this provincial town has the largest Berber population in Morocco. Because Meknes is less arresting than Morocco's other imperial cities, its atmosphere is less touristy and its *souqs* a bit tamer. Nevertheless, the monuments left by Sultan Moulay Ismail, the famous Moroccan rogue, remain impressive. Ismail chose Meknes as his seat of power in 1672 and used notoriously brutal tactics to try and turn this relative backwater into a capital to rival Versailles. The city peaked during Ismail's reign and has never regained its former glory. Still, with the world-renowned ruins of Volubilis nearby, Meknes is worth a visit.

▣ TRANSPORTATION

Trains: Meknes has 2 stations. Use the **Meknes al-Amir Abdelkader Station** (☎ 52 10 60), on rue d'Alger, 2 blocks from av. Mohammed V. The misnamed **Meknes Main Station** is far from the center of town. Both have identical service. To: **Fez** (50min., 10 per day 9:57am-2:05am, 15dh); **Rabat** (2½hr., 8 per day 8:04am-3:35am, 45dh); **Casablanca** (3¾hr., 8 per day 8:04am-3:35am, 70dh); and **Tangier** (5hr., 10 per day 9:57am-2:05am, 60dh).

MOROCCO

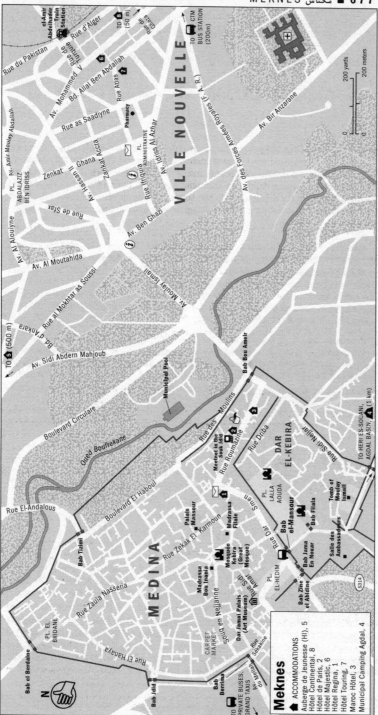

N

Meknes

ACCOMMODATIONS
Auberge de Jeunesse (HI), 5
Hôtel Continental, 8
Hôtel de Paris, 2
Hôtel Majestic, 6
Hôtel Regina, 1
Hôtel Touring, 7
Maroc Hôtel, 3
Municipal Camping Agdal, 4

VILLE NOUVELLE

MEDINA

DAR EL-KEBIRA

el-Amir Abdelhader Train Station
Rue d'Alger
Rue du Pakistan
Av. Amir Moulay Abdallah
Av. Mohammed V
Bd. Allal Ben Abdallah
Rue Atlas
Rue as Saadiyne
Pharmacy
Zankat Accra
Zankat II Ghana
Rue Iriquia
Av. Hassan II
PL. ABDALAZIZ BEN IDRISS
Rue de Sfax
Av. Al Alouiyne
Av. Al Moutahida
Rue al Mokhtai as Soussi
Av. Ben Ghazi
Av. Moulay Ismail
Bd. d'Ankara
Av. Sidi Abdern Mahjoub
Boulevard Circulaire
Oued Boufrekane
Municipal Pool
Rue des Moulins
Rue Dríba
Bab Bou Ameir
PL. ADMINISTRATIVE
Av. Idriss Al Azhar
Av. des Forces Armees Royeaes (F. A. R.)
Av. Bir Anzarane
TO CTM BUS STATION (200m)
Rue Roumaténe
Meknet in the Souk Idid
PL. LALLA AOUDA
Tomb of Moulay Ismail
Bab Filala
Bab el-Mansour
Salle des Ambassadeurs
Rue Sidi Nejjar
TO HERI ES-SOUANI, AGDAL BASIN (1 km)
Rue Dar Smen
PL. EL-HEDIM
Bab Jama En Nouar
Bab Zine el Abidine
Palais Mansour
Madrassa Filale
Mosquée Kebira (Great Mosque)
Rue Zekak El Karmoun
Madrassa Bou Inania
Rue Zauia Nasseria
Souq en Nejjarine
Dar Jamai Palais (Art Museum)
CARPET MARKET
Rue El Hanaya
Bab el Berdaine
Bab Idid
Bab Berrima
TO PRIVATE BUSES, GRAND TAXIS
Rue El-Andalous
Boulevard El Haboul
Bab Tizimi
PL. EL BRIDANE

200 yards
200 meters

Buses: CTM (☎ 51 47 59), on av. des F.A.R., a new station about 5 blocks from av. Mohammed V (take a left when exiting the station). To: **Fez** (1½hr., 8 per day 11am-11pm, 18dh); **Rabat** (3hr., 8 per day 5am-2am, 38dh); **Casablanca** (4hr., 8 per day 5am-2am, 63dh); **Tangier** (5hr., 3 per day 1pm-2:30am, 70dh); **al-Rachidia** (6hr., 10pm, 80dh) via Fez; and **Marrakesh** (8hr., 7pm, 132dh). **Private companies** depart from a station on av. Mellah just outside Bab al-Khemis, outside the medina opposite the *ville nouvelle*. Prices and departures vary.

Taxis: *Grand taxis* cluster next to the private bus station and outside the al-Amir Abdelkader train station. To **Fez** (17dh) and **Rabat** (40dh).

◢ 7 ORIENTATION AND PRACTICAL INFORMATION

The river **Oued Boufrekane** divides Meknes into three "boroughs": the **medina** and the **imperial city** to the west and the modern **ville nouvelle** to the east. The train and CTM buses deposit passengers in the *ville nouvelle*. Tree-lined **avenue Mohammed V,** the new city's main drag, intersects with av. Hassan II north of the large square, pl. Administrative, west of both the train (straight from the exit), and CTM (to the left upon exiting) stations. From the intersection, follow av. Hassan II, which turns into av. Moulay Ismail, to approach the medina via Bab Bou Amir. To reach the colossal **Bab al-Mansour** (the entrance to the imperial complex) and **Plaza al-Khedim** (the medina's main square), head up the hill from Bab Bou-Amir, take a right on rue Roumazine and then a left on rue Dar Smen. Local buses #5, 7, and 9 (1.50-2.30dh) shuttle between the CTM bus station in the *ville nouvelle* and Bab al-Mansour (a 20min. walk); a *petit taxi* should cost no more than 10dh.

Tourist Office: 27 pl. Administrative (☎ 52 44 26; fax 516 046). From the Abdelkader train station, go straight 2 blocks, turn left on av. Mohammed V, and make an immediate right. Cross rue Allal ben Abdallah, continue toward the Hôtel de Ville, and veer right. The tourist office is on the right just after the post office. Friendly staff with limited English. Official but unnecessary guides: half-day 120dh, full-day 150dh. July-Sept. open M-F 7am-6:30pm; Oct.-June M-F 8:30am-noon and 2:30-6:30pm. **Syndicat d'Initiative** (☎ 52 01 91), on Esplanade de la Foire, off av. Moulay Ismail and inside the yellow gate. Open M-F 8:30am-noon and 2:30-6:30pm.

BARGAINING 101 You'll have to do it for everything from taxi rides to camel treks, carpets to ice cream cones, so you might as well do it right. You'll get the best deals if you try to bargain in Arabic; key phrases include *sh-HAL ta-MAN* (how much does it cost) and *GHEH-lee bez-ZAF* (too expensive). You'll be expected to make a counter-offer to the initial asking price; don't be intimidated by the shopkeeper's enthusiasm, intensity, or claim that he's "making you a good price." Decide what you want to ultimately pay (probably half to one-third of the initial price) then offer one-third to half of *that*. The shopkeeper may respond harshly, by laughing or calling you a Berber (the true skinflints), at which point you may choose to politely but firmly walk out. (Generally speaking, you should leave at least once when haggling over a big purchase.) Invariably, you will be dragged back in. You can gauge the seller's willingness to negotiate by how quickly (and by how much) he drops his price.

If you're at a standstill, you can try any of the following: 1) You've seen the same thing elsewhere for X (lower) price. 2) You like it but it is flawed; point out inconsistencies, blemishes, etc. 3) You are a student/budget traveler (sellers scale their prices to what they think you can pay, so carrying expensive cameras or shopping with a group can make bargaining difficult). 4) Tell them you have made your final offer. In Arabic, that's *A-khir TA-man d-YA-li HU-wa HA-da*."

Currency Exchange: BMCE, 98 av. des F.A.R. (☎ 52 03 52). Exchange window open daily 10am-2pm and 4-8pm. **ATM** accepts V and MC. **Hôtel Rif,** on Zenkat Accra, around the corner from the tourist office, cashes traveler's checks.

Late-Night Pharmacy: Red Cross Emergency Pharmacy (☎ 52 33 75), in pl. Administrative. Open daily 8:30am-8:30pm.

Hospitals: Hôpital Moulay Ismail, (☎ 52 28 05 or 52 28 06) on av. des F.A.R., near av. Moulay Youssef.

Telephones: Available at the post office daily 8:30am-9pm. Use the side entrance if the post office is closed.

Post Office: pl. Administrative. Open M-Sa 8:30am-12:15pm and 2:30-6:45pm. **Branch office** on rue Dar Smen, near the medina.

Internet Access: Maison de Culture, 14 av. Hassan II. 8dh per hr. Open daily 9:30am-11pm. In the medina, **Meetnet in the Souk Jdid,** 38 rue Roumazine. 10dh per hr. Open daily 9:30am-10:30pm.

ACCOMMODATIONS

MEDINA

Rue Roumazine and Rue Dar Smen house most of the medina's budget hotels, although even backpackers opt for plusher accommodations in the *ville nouvelle*.

Maroc Hôtel, 7 rue Roumazine (☎ 53 00 75), off rue Roumazine. Mellow owner offers a collection of clean, small rooms situated around a leafy courtyard. Cold showers and squat toilets. Breakfast 20dh. Hot showers 10dh. 60dh per person.

Hôtel de Paris, 58 rue Roumazine, opposite a dentist's office. Look for the sign that says "Hôtel." Basic and clean, with textured walls and mattresses. Shower and hammam available next door, both 6dh. Singles 35dh; doubles and triples 70dh; terrace 20dh.

Hôtel Regina, 19 rue Dar Smen (☎ 53 02 80). Slightly seedy medina hotel, but large; they'll have rooms when the others are full. Request a room away from the street. Hot showers 5dh. Singles 60dh; doubles 90dh; triples 120dh; quads 150dh.

■ **Municipal Camping Agdal** (☎ 55 53 96), on the ramparts of the medina. Follow the signs from either Bab Mansour or Bab Bou Amir. Outdoes any option in the hotel scene. Crowds gather in the beautiful, wooded park with amenities including hot showers (7dh) and kitchen. Restaurant's 3-course *menu* 45dh. Reception daily 8am-1pm and 4-8pm. 17dh per adult, 12dh per child, 10dh per tent, 17dh per car.

VILLE NOUVELLE

The *ville nouvelle* offers greater comfort, easier access to banks, CTM buses, and trains, but prices are higher than in the medina. Most of the cheapest hotels lie around av. Mohammed V and rue Allal ben Abdallah.

Auberge de Jeunesse (HI), (☎ 52 46 98; fax 45 27 32), on av. Oqba ben Nafil, near the stadium. Head toward the medina on av. Hassan II; follow the arrows toward Hôtel Transatlantique. A 20min. walk or 5dh taxi ride from Abdelkader station. Clean mattresses, TV room, and a grassy courtyard. Cold showers free, hot showers 5dh (7-8pm only). Reception summer 8-9am, noon-4pm, and 7pm-midnight; in winter 8-10am, noon-3pm, and 6-10pm. Closed Su and holidays 10am-6pm. Swimming at 5-star Transatlantique Hotel next door 100dh. Dorms 27dh.

Hôtel Majestic, 19 av. Mohammed V (☎ 52 20 35; fax 45 27 32), near the train station. The backpacker meeting zone of the *ville nouvelle*. Comfortable rooms, a newly renovated courtyard, modern bathrooms, and hot showers. Breakfast included. Singles 112-189dh; doubles 150-225dh; triples 217-292dh. Prices depend on bathroom options.

Hôtel Continental, 92 av. des F.A.R. (☎ 52 54 71), opposite the Hôtel Volubilis. Coming from the train station, head down av. Mohammed V to the left and take a left at the junction with av. des F.A.R. Spacious rooms decorated with a surplus of red velvet. Singles 70-133dh; doubles 95-154dh. Prices depend on bathroom options.

Hôtel Touring, 34 rue Allal ben Abdallah (☎ 52 23 51), 1 block from av. Mohammed V when heading away from the train and CTM stations. One of the cheapest places in the *ville nouvelle*, this hotel is dark and without character, but clean and spacious. Singles 70dh, with shower 106dh; doubles 95dh, with shower 134dh.

▓ FOOD

MEDINA

Vendors in the **place al-Khedim** hawk *merguez* (spicy moroccan sausage) sandwiches, freshly made potato chips, and corn on the cob roasted over open coals. Other inexpensive fare sizzles in the one-man *brochetteries* on **rue Dar Smen.** Few places have menus, let alone copies in English or French—most have their options on display. The daily **vegetable market** sprouts beside Bab Mansour.

Restaurant Economique, 123 rue Dar Smen. Friendly manager serves staples at reasonable prices. Couscous or *tajine* 25dh. 4-course *menu* 40dh. Open daily 7am-10pm.

VILLE NOUVELLE

Restaurant Marhaba, 23 av. Mohammed V (☎ 52 16 32). Head away from the train station and pass Hôtel Majestic. Local diner-like atmosphere serves up the best bargain in the Middle Atlas—bread, eggs, corn fritters, and harira for 3.60dh. No vegetarian options. Entrees 18-30dh. Open daily 11am-11pm.

Pizzeria le Four, av. Zenkat Atlas (☎ 52 08 57), off av. Mohammed V near the train station. Tasty Italian cuisine. Popular with hip locals and traveling families with kids; this pizza joint also has a rare liquor license. The air-conditioned cavern is a good place for women traveling alone. Entrees 20-70dh. Open daily noon-3pm and 7pm-midnight.

New Mex Snack Grille, 20 rue de Paris. The hangout for locals who wish they weren't. The only tacos and burritos for miles (35-45dh). Open daily 11:30am-11pm.

◉ SIGHTS

Meknes's best sights cluster around the magnificent **Bab al-Mansour,** which has become a national symbol. Through the gate lie the remainders of Meknes's imperial past, and around it thrive the present-day medina and the lively pl. al-Khedim.

IMPERIAL MEKNES

Weakened by war, weather, and the Great Earthquake of 1755, the ramparts of the **Dar al-Kebira** (Imperial City) testify to Meknes's former glory. Sultan Moulay Ismail personally supervised the building of over 25km of protective **walls** for his city within a city. Strolling about the site with a pick-ax and whip in hand, the sultan criticized and occasionally decapitated workers who displeased him. Plundering materials from sights all over Morocco, including Roman marble from the ruins at Volubilis, Moulay Ismail created a radiant city. Ismail razed part of the medina to create **place al-Khedim** (plaza of destruction), an approach to **Bab al-Mansour,** Morocco's finest gate. Today, only the walls and several large monuments remain.

TOMB OF MOULAY ISMAIL. The tomb, along with its accompanying **mosque,** is one of only two Moroccan religious buildings open to non-Muslims. Part of the building remains off-limits, but anyone may peer in. Walk through the bright yellow rooms to reach the tomb, flanked by two functioning grandfather clocks. These clocks are a consolation prize from Louis XIV, who sent them after refusing Moulay Ismail's proposal to his daughter. *(Through the 2 blue arches, on the left. Open daily 9am-noon and 3-6pm. Free, but donations accepted.)*

SALLE DES AMBASSADEURS. Standing by itself in an open court is the green-tiled roof of the recently restored Salle des Ambassadeurs, where Ismail conducted affairs of state. Ask the guard to unlock the doors to the so-called **"Christian Dungeon,"** a 6 sq. km. underground storehouse and granary for the Sultan, his entourage, and their horses. This storehouse is said to have once housed some 50 to 100,000 Christian prisoners. Since the "dungeon" remains a cool 15°C even in summer, it is the perfect place to avoid the midday sun. *(From pl. al-Khedim, go through Bab al-Mansour or 1 of the nearby smaller gates, walk straight, and follow the wall on the right around the bend. Open June-Aug. Sa-Th 9am-noon and 3-6:30pm; Sept.-May Sa-Th 9am-noon and 3-6pm. 10dh.)*

OTHER SIGHTS. A short trek from Moulay Ismail's tomb is the **Heri al-Souani** (storehouse), a cool granary with immense cisterns designed to withstand prolonged sieges. Trees and birds have invaded, giving it a jungle-like feel. *(Open daily 9am-noon and 3-6pm. 10dh.)* Below lies the **Agdal Basin,** once Moulay Ismail's private country club and his reservoir in case of siege. His wives (more than 300 of them) and their 800 kids were said to swim there to escape the stifling summer heat. *(To get to the Heri al-Souani and Agdal Basin from Bab al-Mansour, follow the signs for camping and continue straight past the campsite for 20min., or take a petit taxi for 7dh. Free.)*

MEDINA

Meknes's medina is more pleasant, tranquil, and compact than those of the other imperial cities. Facing the Dar Jamaï Museum of Moroccan Art, take the alley to the left of the entrance. Push straight ahead to **Souq al-Nejjarine,** a major street. Heading left here brings you first to the **textile souq,** the **carpenters' souq,** and the **carpet market.** The rest of the medina is best explored like any other: wander until you get lost, then try to find your way out.

GREAT MOSQUE AND ▧MADRASA BOU INANIA. While everything except the green-glazed minaret of the Great Mosque *(al-masjid al-kebira)* is off-limits to non-Muslims, the breathtaking 14th-century Madrasa Bou Inania, across from it, is not. A college of theology and Muslim law, this *madrasa* typifies traditional Merenid architecture—the courtyard combines cedar, stucco, and mosaics with characteristic flair. Upstairs are a number of cells, each of which snugly hosted at least two students. The roof, which you may have to unlock yourself, offers a splendid view of the minaret of the Great Mosque and the rooftops of Meknes. *(Face Dar Jamaï in pl. al-Khedim, turn right onto rue Sidi Amar, and enter the medina. Follow the alley as it turns left, then fork right. Madrasa open Sa-Th 8:30am-12:30pm and 2:30-6pm, F 8:30-11:30am and 2:30-6pm. 10dh.)*

DAR JAMAÏ PALACE. Built in the 19th century by one of Sultan Moulay Hassan I's powerful government ministers, the Dar Jamaï Palace now houses a **Museum of Moroccan Art** which flaunts one of Morocco's best craft collections. Most pieces are contextualized in restored versions of the rooms where they were originally displayed. Check out the carpets and the master bedroom, stuffed with embroidered divans and topped by a magnificent cupola. *(At the far end of pl. al-Khedim. ☎ 53 08 63. Closed indefinitely for renovations as of July 2000. Call for updates. 10dh.)*

▓ DAYTRIPS FROM MEKNES

VOLUBILIS ولوبيلى (20MIN.)

Buses going from Meknes to Ouezzare (every hr. 7am-7pm, 10dh) will drop you off near the ruins. You can also hire a grand taxi near the private bus station in Meknes, although you need a 6-person party to get the cheapest fare; taking a taxi alone will cost 120dh. You can also take a grand taxi to Moulay Idriss (10dh) and walk the rest of the way (about 3km; follow signs straight from the junction).

Thirty-three kilometers from Meknes lie the ruins of Volubilis, the best-preserved Roman site in Morocco and perhaps all of North Africa. An extensive collection of **Roman mosaics** has earned these ruins must-see status on any traveler's itinerary. Once a major center for the olive oil trade, the city flourished under Roman rule, reaching its zenith in the 2nd and 3rd centuries AD when it became the capital of the kingdom of Mauritania. The Romans, who viewed their North African posses-ssions as a bread basket for their European citizens, ordered the deforestation of the area to make room for grain crops; from that point on local resources dwin-dled and the city began to decline in importance. When Moulay Idriss took control of the city in the 18th century, he siphoned off much of the residential population to Fez and Meknes, and claimed many of the city's pillars and stones for his own palace in Meknes. The Lisbon Earthquake of 1755, which wreaked devastation all along the Atlantic seaboard, finally sealed the city's fate.

When US General George C. Patton visited the ruins, he declined an offer of a guided tour—he believed he had been stationed here as a Roman centurion in his previous life and thus knew his way around. If you've been equally lucky, stop reading here. Otherwise, head past the ticket office and over a bridge, take a left and work your way up the hill, where among the ruins of a housing and industrial area are several **olive presses**. Walk down the main path to the **House of Orpheus** to view its **dolphin mosaic**. Continue through the ruins of **public baths** to the **Forum**,

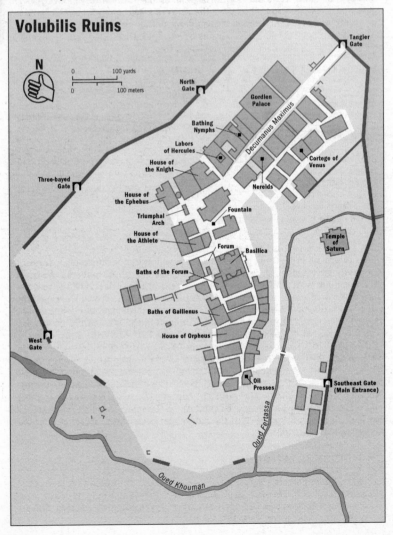

Volubilis Ruins

with the columned **capitol** and **basilica** on the right. The basilica, despite its name, served as the courthouse during Roman times. Follow the path to the **House of the Athlete** on the left, named for its mosaic depicting the victor of a *desultor* race (which involved mounting a moving horse). In the middle of town looms the **Triumphal Arch,** built in AD 217 to celebrate Emperor Caracalla and his scheming mother Julia Domna. Julia assured her son's power by helping him murder his rival Gota in AD 212. The gate marks the beginning of the town's main street, **Decumanus Maximus.** The houses along the street, including the **House of the Ephebus** and the **House of the Knight,** have impressive mosaics of Dionysus, Hercules, Orpheus, and other mythical figures. From the top of the hill is an amazing panoramic view of Volubilis. The **Tangier Gate,** with the **Gordien Palace** just before it, is atop the hill. Walk down the hill and head toward the only tree in front. Under it is the **Cortege of Venus,** which holds several mosaics including *Chariot Race, Bacchus Surrounded by the Four Seasons, Diana Bathing,* and the *Abduction of Hylas by Nymphs,* all dating as far back as the late 2nd or early 3rd century AD. Cross the stream back to the ticket gate to see the ruins of a **Temple** dedicated to Jupiter, Juno, and Minerva. (The ruins are open daily sunrise to sunset. They are more peaceful and scenic in the early morning or late afternoon (20dh). Unfortunately, there are no tourist booklets, maps, or signs on-site.)

MOULAY IDRISS سقتس عوالو، (30MIN.)

Take a bus (30min., every hr. 7am-7pm, 10dh; same schedule back to Meknes) or grand taxi (10dh) from the private bus station in Meknes.

Five kilometers before Volubilis, the road from Meknes passes through Moulay Idriss, a pilgrimage site named after the man who spread Islam through Morocco. A third-generation descendant of Mohammed, Idriss united the Berber tribes and founded the country's first dynasty. Non-Muslims cannot spend the night or visit the mosques or shrines; but Moulay Idriss is an easy stop on the way to Volubilis and is refreshingly tourist-free. Young locals can point out a magnificent view of the sacred **Mausoleum of Moulay Idriss** and the only **cylindrical minaret** in Morocco.

FEZ فاس ☎ 05

Fez's bustling, colorful medina epitomizes Morocco—no visit to the country is complete without seeing it. Artisans bang out sheets of brass, donkeys strain under crates of Coca-Cola, prayer callers wail, and children balance trays of dough on their heads. Along narrow streets, the scent of *brochettes* on open grills combine with whiffs of hash, the sweet aroma of cedar shavings, and the stench of the open sewer. Since UNESCO designated Fez a World Heritage Site, the city's walls have been largely restored, and fresh plaster and cobblestones make the medina even more fantastic. Founded in the 8th century by Moulay Idriss I, Fez rose to prominence with the construction of the Qairaouine, a university-mosque complex, which was one of the world's first universities. With such a wealth of resources, Fez emerged as the most prominent city in the Maghreb, nurturing (or destroying) political dynasties and handing down legal rulings to the rest of the region. Today, post-independence Fez has been somewhat eclipsed by Rabat (the political capital), Casablanca (the economic capital), and Marrakesh (the tourist capital). All the same, the city remains at the intellectual and spiritual helm of the nation and is central to many Moroccans' senses of national pride.

▐▀ TRANSPORTATION

Flights: Aérodrome de Fès-Saïs (☎ 62 47 12), 12km out of town on the road to Immouzzèr. Bus #16 leaves from pl. Mohammed V (3dh). *Grand taxis* (120dh) also run there. **Royal Air Maroc** (☎ 62 04 56), av. Hassan II, flies daily to **Casablanca**. Also services Tangier, Marrakesh, Marseilles, and Paris.

MOROCCO

Trains: (☎ 62 50 01), av. Almohades, at rue Chenguit. 2nd-class trains are comfier than buses, and only cost a few dirhams more. To: **Meknes** (1hr., 9 per day 7:15am-2:40am, 22dh); **Rabat** (3½hr., 8 per day 7:15am-2:40am, 50dh); **Casablanca** (5hr., 8 per day 7:15am-2:40am, 70dh); **Tangier** (5½hr., 4 per day 7:15am-2:40am, 72dh); and **Marrakesh** (9hr., 6 per day 7:15am-2:40am, 130dh).

Buses: CTM (☎ 73 29 84) stops near pl. d'Atlas, at the far end of the *ville nouvelle.* From pl. Florence, walk down bd. Mohammed V and turn left onto av. Youssef ben Tachfine. At pl. d'Atlas, take the 1st right. To: **Meknes** (1hr., 9 per day 6am-1am, 18dh); **Rabat** (3hr., 4 per day 6am-1am, 55dh); **Chefchaouen** (4hr., 3 per day 8am-11:45pm, 40dh); **Casablanca** (5hr., 9 per day 6am-1am, 80dh); **Tangier** (6hr., 5 per day 11am-1:30am, 85dh); and **Marrakesh** (8hr., 3 per day 6am-1am, 130dh).

Public Transportation: Pl. Mohammed V and pl. Résistance are the major hubs for city buses. Important routes include: bus #9 and 11 from the Syndicat d'Initiative to **Bab Boujeloud** and **Dar Batha;** #3 from the train station and pl. Mohammed V to **Bab Ftouh;** #4 from pl. Résistance to **Bab Smarine** in Fez al-Jdid. They cost 2.2dh; fares increase 20% July-Sept. 15 after 8:30pm, Sept. 16-June after 8pm.

Taxis: Stands at the post office, Syndicat d'Initiative, Bab Boujeloud, and Bab Guissa. Fares increase 50% July-Sept. 15 after 8:30pm, Sept. 16-June after 8pm. Staff at the Syndicat d'Initiative will help you into the correct *grand taxi.*

Car Rental: Avis, 50 bd. Chefchaouni (☎ 62 67 46). **Hertz,** 1 Kissauiat de la Foire (☎ 62 28 12). Fiat Unos 500dh per day.

■◄ 🛂 ORIENTATION AND PRACTICAL INFORMATION

Fez is three cities in one: the French-built **ville nouvelle,** and the Arab **Fez al-Jdid** ("New Fez") and **Fez al-Bali** ("Old Fez"). The *ville nouvelle's* two central streets are the divided **avenue Hassan II** and **boulevard Mohammed V,** which intersect at **plaza Florence,** the center of activity. Walking down av. Moulay Youssef from the *ville nouvelle* brings you to pl. Alaouites in Fez al-Jdid, directly in front of the king's palace, **Dar al-Makhzen.** After passing through Bab Smarine on the left, rue Fez al-Jdid takes you the length of the palace. At the end, a right through Bab Dakakeen leads to Fez al-Bali and its main gate **Bab Boujeloud.** The two main streets of Fez al-Bali, the **Tala'a Kebira** and **Tala'a Seghira,** are the most exciting, although they are barely wide enough for its shops, a donkey, and your backpack.

Tourist Office: Syndicat d'Initiative (☎ 62 34 60), pl. Mohammed V, on the way to the CTM bus station from av. Hassan II. Helpful *Fassi* (citizens of Fez) answer almost any question. Same meager maps as the Moroccan National Tourism Office. Hire official guides here for 120dh for half-day or 150dh for full-day. Open M-F 8:30am-noon and 2:30-6:30pm, Sa 8:30am-noon.

Currency Exchange: BMCE, pl. Mohammed V, opposite the Syndicat d'Initiative, to the right of the main bank entrance. Handles V/MC transactions and traveler's checks, and has **ATMs.** Open M-F 8:15-11:30am and 2:15-4pm. **Sheraton Fez Hôtel,** at the end of av. Hassan II, 4 blocks from the post office, has after-hours exchange.

Luggage Storage: At the train station. 2.5dh per bag per day. Open 24hr.

Police: ☎ 19.

Late-Night Pharmacy: Municipalité de Fès (☎ 62 33 80), av. Moulay Youssef off Pl. Résistance, 5min. uphill from the royal palace. Open daily 8pm-8am.

Hospital: Ghastani (☎ 62 27 76), at the end of av. Hassan II away from the medina.

Telephones: In the **main post office.** Enter from bd. Mohammed V, to the right of the main entrance. Open daily 8:30am-9pm. The **branch office** in the medina also has international phones. Open daily 8:30am-9pm.

Post Office: At the corner of av. Hassan II and bd. Mohammed V in the *ville nouvelle.* **Branch offices** at pl. d'Atlas and in the medina at pl. Batha. All open July-Sept. 15 M-F 8am-3pm; Sept. 16-June M-F 8:30am-6:45pm.

Internet Access: Sibed (☎ 94 13 83), av. Ahmed Loukili. Follow signs from the pl. Florence. 8dh per hr. Open 24hr.

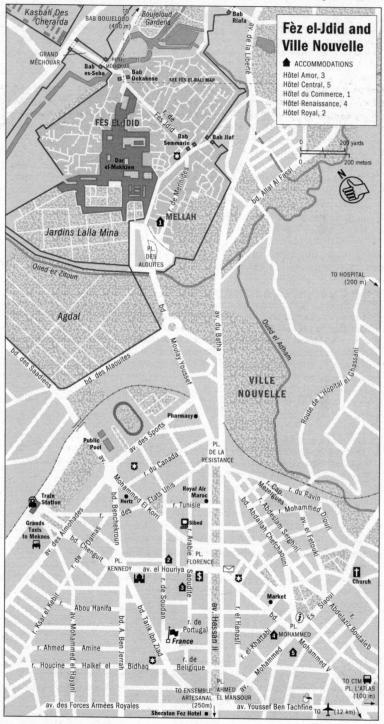

Kasbah Des
Cherarda

TO
BAB BOUJELOUD Boujeloud
(400 m) Gardens

Bab
Riafa

GRAND
MÉCHOUAR

PETIT
MÉCHOUAR

Bab
es-Seba

Bab
Dekakene

SEE FÈS EL-BALI MAP

FÈS EL-JDID

Dar
el-Makhzen

Bab
Semmarin

Bab Jiaf

r. de Merinides

MELLAH

1

Jardins Lalla Mina

PL.
DES
ALAOUITES

Oued ez Zitoun

Agdal

bd. des Saadiens

bd. des Alaouites

Moulay Youssef

av. du Batha

VILLE
NOUVELLE

Oued el Adham

Route de L'Hopital el Ghassani

TO HOSPITAL
(200 m)

Pharmacy

av. des Sports

Public
Pool

r. du Canada

PL.
DE LA
RESISTANCE

Train
Station

r. du Canada

Royal Air
Maroc

Herz

r. Cap.
Mezergues

r. du Ravin

Grands
Taxis
to Meknes

av. des Almohades

bd. Benchekroun

Mohammed El Korri

r. Tunisie

Sibed

r. Arabie

av. el Fetouki

av. Mohammed Diouri

bd. Abdeslam Serghini

bd. Abdallah Chefchaouni

r. de
C'Domas

bd. C'Domas

PL.
KENNEDY

2

av. el Houriya

Saoudite

PL.
FLORENCE

r. de Chenguit

r. de Soudan

3

Market

Abou Hanifa

r. Ksar el Kebir

av. Mohammed el Hayani

r. de
Portugal

France

r. de
Beligique

r. Ahmed Amine

r. Houcine el Haïkel el Bidhaq

bd. A. Ben Jerrah

bd. Tarik Ibn Ziad

r. el Hanasli

r. el-Khattabi

av. Hassan II

Slaoui Abdelaziz Bouialeb

PL.
MOHAMMED

4

Mohammed V

5

Church

TO ENSEMBLE
ARTESANAL
(250m)

av. des Forces Armées Royales

PL.
AHMED
EL MANSOUR

av. Youssef Ben Tachfine

Sheraton Fez Hotel ■

TO
EL MANSOUR

TO CTM
PL. L'ATLAS
(100 m)

TO ✈ (12 km)

**Fèz el-Jdid and
Ville Nouvelle**

🏠 ACCOMMODATIONS

Hôtel Amor, 3
Hôtel Central, 5
Hôtel du Commerce, 1
Hôtel Renaissance, 4
Hôtel Royal, 2

0   200 yards
0   200 meters

N

MOROCCO

⬛ ACCOMMODATIONS

VILLE NOUVELLE

Rooms here are hustler-free and more comfortable than those in the medina. The cheapest lodgings clump on or just off bd. Mohammed V, between av. Mohammed al-Slaoui near the bus station and av. Hassan II near the post office.

Hôtel Renaissance, 29 rue Abd al-Krim al-Khattabi (☎ 62 21 93), 1 block toward the medina from pl. Mohammed V. The cheapest of the *ville nouvelle* hotels, it combines the amenities of the new city with the prices of the medina. Don't be deterred by the gloomy entrance—the rooms are spacious and bright. Hot showers 5dh. Singles 40dh; doubles 70dh; triples 90dh; quads 120dh.

Hôtel Central, 50 rue Brahim Roudani (☎ 62 23 33), 1 block away from the medina and to the left of pl. Mohammed V. Springy beds and surplus chairs in plain but spotless rooms. Hot water in room sinks. Singles 59dh, with shower 89dh; doubles 89dh, with shower 119dh; triples 129dh, with shower 159dh.

Hôtel Amor, 31 rue Arabie Saoudite (☎ 62 27 24). From the post office, cross the street toward Bauk al-Maghrib and turn left (look for the sign). Classy almoravid decor, and prices to match. All rooms have private bath. Singles 160dh; doubles 190dh.

Hôtel Royal, 36 rue de Soudan (☎ 62 46 56). From the post office, walk past Bauk al-Maghrib and turn right. Near the train station. Very plain rooms, but all of them have showers. Singles 96dh, with toilet 120dh; doubles 132dh, with toilet 150dh.

FEZ AL-JDID

Fez al-Jdid has only one hotel of note, but the location is perfect—close to the medina without the annoyance of hustlers.

■ **Hôtel du Commerce** (☎ 62 22 31), pl. Alaouites. That this place is always packed is a testament to the friendly owners, comfortable rooms, and affordable prices. Cold showers. No reservations—arrive early. 40dh per person.

FEZ AL-BALI

Bab Boujeloud is the place to go for budget rooms. Although they're less pleasant than those in the *ville nouvelle*, and hustlers may seem to have tourist-radar, they're still economical and perfect for that 24-hour medina experience.

■ **Hôtel Cascade,** 26 Serrajine Boujeloud (☎ 63 84 42), just inside Bab Boujeloud and to the right. A popular place with backpackers and families. Sanitary and spacious rooms. The terrace and some rooms have a bird's-eye view of the medina. Squat toilets. Hot showers 5dh. 40dh per person; terrace 20dh.

Hôtel Lamrani (☎ 63 44 11), Tala'a Seghira. Enter Bab Boujeloud; take the 1st right, then a left and through the arch. Unusually clean, with in-room sinks. Backpackers head here when the Cascade is full. Nearby *hammam* 6dh. Singles 40-50dh; doubles 80-100dh; triples 120-150dh.

Hôtel du Jardin Public, 153 Kasbah Boujeloud (☎ 63 30 86), a small alley across from the Bab Boujeloud parking area. Relatively clean rooms, some with views. Singles 45dh; doubles 65dh; triples 80dh; quads 105dh. Oct.-Apr. 5dh less.

Hotel Batha (☎ 63 48 60; fax 74 10 78), pl. Batha, next to the Dar Batha Museum off the pl. Batha. A 3-star resort at the entrance to the medina with surprisingly low rates. Classy rooms have towels, soap, and toilet paper, and guests have free access to a swimming pool. Singles 198dh; doubles 253dh.

◖ FOOD

VILLE NOUVELLE

Cheap food huts line the streets on either side of bd. Mohammed V. Poke through stalls of fresh food at the **central market** on bd. Mohammed V, two blocks up from pl. Mohammed V. (Open daily 7am-1pm.)

La Mamia, 43 Imh Urbain (☎ 62 31 64), pl. Florence. Popular joint with tacky decor sells delectable pizzas and good burgers. Entrees 12-40dh. Open daily noon-midnight.

Restaurant Fish Friture, 138 bd. Mohammed V. (☎ 94 06 99). Fish are all over, on the walls as well as your plate; they also serve other Moroccan standards. A relatively comfortable environment for women traveling alone. Entrees 35-50dh. Open M-Sa 10am-3pm and 6:30pm-midnight. V, MC.

FEZ AL-BALI

Food stalls line Tala'a Kebira and Tala'a Seghira, near the Bab Boujeloud entrance to Fez al-Bali. A feast of *harira*, roasted peppers and eggplant, potato fritters, and bread will only set you back 10dh at the stalls inside, while a good *kefta* (ground meat) sandwich goes for 15dh. Go left from Tala'a Kebira at Madrasa al-Atarrine (see p. 689), and head deeper in the medina toward pl. Achabine for some of the cheapest eateries in Morocco.

MOROCCO

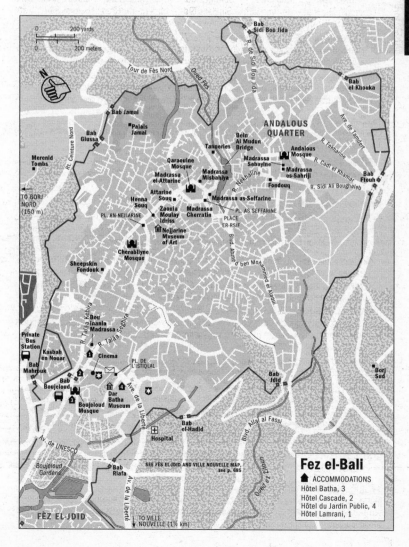

Fez el-Bali
▲ ACCOMMODATIONS
Hôtel Batha, 3
Hôtel Cascade, 2
Hôtel du Jardin Public, 4
Hôtel Lamrani, 1

Restaurant des Jeunes, 16 rue Serrajine (☎ 63 49 75), on the right as you enter the *bab*. Friendly staff serves regional favorites. Entrees 20-30dh. Open daily 6am-midnight.

Restaurant Bouayad, 26 rue Serrajine (☎ 63 62 78). Locals eat around satellite TV. *Menu* 40dh—don't pay the tourist rate (60dh). Open 24hr.

👁 SIGHTS

FEZ AL-BALI

With over 9000 streets, Fez's medina is possibly the most difficult to navigate in all Morocco. There are three ways to approach it. The first is simple and expensive: hire a guide. **Official guides** are available at the Syndicat d'Initiative. (Ask for a local guide; they know Fez better and are cheaper. Prices for local guides are 120dh for a half-day or 150dh per day.) Though much cheaper, **unofficial guides** are illegal, often lack historical knowledge, and usually take travelers only to shops from which they will get a 25% commission. If you do hire one, nail down an itinerary beforehand and establish your aversion to shopping. A second option is to follow the route below, which hits the major "sights." The final option is simply to get lost in the magnificent atmosphere that is Fez's medina. When it's time to tear yourself away, ask merchants or women how to get to Tala'a Kebira and follow it back uphill to Bab Boujeloud. Just remember: walking downhill will take you farther into the medina, while trekking uphill will lead you out (to Bab Boujeloud).

To see the medina at its liveliest, avoid the hours between noon and 3pm, when most shops and sights close, and Friday, the Muslim day of prayer. Although faux guides will probably follow you for a while, ignoring them or repeating *"Non, merci"* or *"La shukran"* should keep them at bay (see **Hustlers and Guides,** p. 664). The best way to see the main monuments in the medina is to head to Bab Boujeloud and then wander down Tala'a Kebira from there.

TALA'A KEBIRA. Virtually all of the sights in Fez's medina lie along the Tala'a Kebira (a.k.a. the Grand Tala'a), old Fez's main street and an essential reference point for anyone attempting to navigate the medina. The Tala'a Kebira heads downhill from Bab Boujeloud to the Qairaouine Mosque area. The Bab Boujeloud is the main entrance to the medina; faux guides tend to gather here. Once you pass the gate, however, they will tend to leave you alone. Built in 1912 by the Frenchman Maréchal Lauyote to gain the confidence of the locals, the *bab* is tiled in blue on one side (the color of Fez) and green on the other (the favorite color of Mohammed and consequently the color most identified with Islam). The square just inside the *bab* is where the Moroccan revolution against the French occupation began. Down to the right is the **Tala'a Seghira,** Fez's other main street, lined mostly by shops catering to locals (i.e., the famed underwear *souq*).

🖾 BOU INANIA MADRASA. To the right after a food *souq* is the spectacular Bou Inania Madrasa and mosque, a school built in 1326 for teaching the Qur'an and other Islamic sciences. The intricacy of the cedar and stucco work make this arguably the best *madrasa* in Morocco and perhaps even the world—not bad for a college dorm. Classes were held in the courtyard and the adjacent salons, and the students lived three or four to a two-by-two-meter cell on the upper floor. It's no surprise that this building came at a ridiculous cost. When the Merenid Sultan Abou Inan was presented with the totals for the construction, he simply threw them into the canal separating the mosque from the *madrasa*, exclaiming that no price tag could be placed on beauty. *(Open Sa-Th 9am-7pm. 10dh.)*

FUNDUQS. Plunging ahead down the road, you'll notice a series of *funduqs* (old inns now used as factories) on the left side. First is the drum *funduq*, where skins are stretched and thinned to produce the right tone. Next is the *funduq* for honey, olive oil, and butter, which was formerly a mental hospital. Lastly, you'll sniff the (almost) cured products of the **sheepskin funduq,** just after the entrance to a parking lot on the left. Beware the cries of *"Batica!"* (watch out) from the drivers of heavily laden donkeys.

SEEING RED One may see the hands, feet, and hair of Moroccan women decorated with the original temporary tattoo, *henna*. Stemming from the Arabic words meaning "tenderness" and "good luck," henna is made from the leaf of the *tafilat* plant, ground into a powder and mixed with warm water or tea to make a paste. The dye comes in different colors, including red, black, and green, and it has three main uses: as a medicine; for pregnant women in their seventh month; and for marriage ceremonies and the "Festival of the Girls" on the 27th day of Ramadan. The application of the design to the skin, which can take hours, is both an art and a ceremony unto itself. The intricate motifs are painted on freehand or using a pattern and are left to sit anywhere from a couple of hours to an entire day or overnight before being rubbed off. The resulting decorations may last on the skin for weeks.

NEJJARINE MUSEUM OF ART. To get to the **place Nejjarine,** with its tiled fountain, step off the Tala'a Kebira and turn right onto the only main street in the leather *souq;* go down the ramp, turn left again, and continue about 25m. The museum contents—tools, musical instruments, and decorated doors—are nothing unusual, but they are particularly nicely displayed. A luxury inn until the end of the 18th century, the building was later used by the French as a police station. Today, its rooftop **salon de thé** (tea room) offers a tranquil escape from the rushing traffic of peddlers and tourists. *(Open daily 10am-5pm. 10dh.)*

SPICE SOUQ TO ZAOUIA MOULAY IDRISS II. Back on the Tala'a Kebira, the **Attarine ("Spice") Souq,** perhaps the most exotic market, awaits about 200m down. When spices were a more prestigious commodity, its vendors got the privileged spot near the mosque. Off to the right at the beginning of the spice *souq* is the **Henna Souq,** which sells the plant used to temporarily tattoo women at weddings (see **Seeing Red,** above). At the far end is the **Maristan Sidi Frej,** which was built in 1286 and was the model for psychiatric hospitals in the West. Toward the end of the Attarine Souq are several turn-offs into a **cloth market,** selling slippers and *djellabas* (robes), and a **dried fruit market.** The fruit market in turn leads to **Zaouia Moulay Idriss II,** the resting place of the Islamic saint credited with founding Fez. Pilgrims touch the tomb through a slot in a brass star. Wooden barriers on the streets leading to the tomb delineate a sacred zone and were built to prevent donkeys from entering holy ground. As usual, non-Muslims are not allowed to enter but can peer through the doors.

MADRASA AL-ATTARINE. The Tala'a Kebira ends at Madrasa al-Attarine, which dates from 1324. Though often overlooked by visitors, this could be the most peaceful place in the old city. Built by Abou Siad, a Merenid, it is one of the smallest *madrasas* in Morocco, but is notable for its details and mosaics. The intricacies of the carvings are spectacular—they rival the Bou Inania's both in beauty and in style. *(Open daily June-Aug. 9am-6pm; Sept.-May 9am-5pm. 10dh.)*

QAIRAOUINE MOSQUE. Exiting the *madrasa,* turn left, and then left again; a few meters down is a little opening into the Qairaouine mosque. Founded in 857 by Fatima al-Fihri, a woman, the mosque is one of the oldest universities in the world. It trained students in logic, math, rhetoric, and the Qur'an while Europe stumbled through the Dark Ages. You can thank (or curse) the mosque for educating Pope Sylvester II, who introduced algebra and the modern number system. Non-Muslims can take pictures through the portals but may not enter. Its library, off-limits to tourists, holds what some think is the first manuscript of the Qur'an.

METAL SOUQ AND TANNERIES. Keeping the mosque on the right, you'll eventually come to pl. Seffarine, known for its **metal souq,** which deafens travelers with incessant cauldron-pounding. There are several potential routes from here. To reach the **tanneries,** turn sharply left and continue to bear left (follow the worn, six-sided cobblestones). Once the smell becomes intense, head right down a microscopic alley (a tannery *"guardien"* has probably grabbed you by now; 10dh is the basic fee). From a balcony above, you may view skins being soaked in green liquid, rinsed in a washing machine/cement-mixer hybrid, dunked in diluted pigeon excrement or water-logged wheat husks (for suppleness), and saturated in dye. Beware—the pervasive odor of the tanneries is not for the faint of stomach and can be overpowering on the hottest days. To exit the medina or reach Bab al-Rcif, a major bus and cab hub, follow the street heading away from the mosque to its end, turn left, and then right.

■ **THE DAR BATHA MUSEUM.** The beautiful Dar Batha Museum, with its well-kept garden, makes an excellent diversion for those tired of the endless, winding medina streets. The building itself, a 19th-century palace, may be the highlight of the museum. The spacious Andalucian mansion headquartered Sultan Hassan I and his playboy son, Moulay Abd al-Aziz, during the last years of decadence before the French occupation. The museum, which hosts Moroccan music concerts in September, chronicles Fez's artistic and intellectual history. The keynote is the display of ceramics with the signature "Fez blue" (derived from cobalt) on a white enamel background. *(Start at Bab Boujeloud, head straight down the Tala'a Seghira, take the 1st right past the movie theater, then turn right again at pl. I'lstiqlal, home to the museum. Open W-Th and Sa-M 8:30am-noon and 2:30-6pm, F 8:30-11:30am and 3-6pm. 10dh.)*

ANDALOUS QUARTER. The Andalous Quarter and its less-crowded streets are across the Oued Fez (Fez River) from the heart of Fez al-Bali. Many of the Moors who fled from Muslim Spain to Morocco during the 15th-century *Reconquista* settled around the grand Almohad house of worship in Fez, the **Andalous Mosque.** Its main attraction is the grandiose 13th-century doorway. *(To find the mosque, cross pl. Rcif, go through a small arched gate, turn right, and follow the wall on the right. From Fez al-Bali, cross the river at Port Bein al-Mudun near the tanneries and head straight down rue Seffrah.)*

FEZ AL-JDID

Christians, Jews, and Muslims once coexisted in Fez al-Jdid, which was built by the Merenids in the 13th century. King Mohammed VI's sprawling modern palace, the **Dar al-Makhzen** (off-limits to non-royals), borders pl. Alaouites. Diagonally off the plaza, grande rue des Merinides runs up to Bab Smarine and its seven bronze gates installed by King Hassan II in 1968. Just before the beginning of the main street is a peaceful, 17th-century **Jewish cemetery,** which provides the resting place for over 12,000 people (open daily dawn-dusk; 10dh). Off this boulevard, the meter-wide streets open into miniature underground tailors' shops, half-timbered houses, and covert alleyways. The **jewelers' souq** glitters at the top of grande rue des Merinides. Cackling chickens, salty fish, and dried okra vie for attention in the **covered market,** inside Bab Smarine at the entrance to Fez al-Jdid proper.

Bear left at the end of rue des Fez al-Jdid into the **Petit Méchouar;** on the left is **Bab Dakakeen,** the back entrance to the Dar al-Makhzen. **Bab al-Seba,** an imperial gate, opens onto the **Grand Méchouar,** a roomy plaza lined with street lamps. From here it's an easy walk to Bab Boujeloud—turn through the opening to the right of Bab al-Seba, continue straight for 250m, veer to the right, and pass through a large arch at the end of the road. The entrance to the refreshing **Boujeloud Gardens,** a refuge from the midday sun, is on the right. (Open Tu-Su. Free.) Inside is the delightful **Café Restaurant Noria,** a pleasant place for female travelers (as well as male) to relax under the grape-leaf arbor. (Coffee 5dh. Couscous 35dh.) **Bab Boujeloud** lies another 300m down the same road.

OUTSIDE THE MEDINA

In addition to the medina, a set of tombs and an odd museum are of interest. To reach the tombs and museum, exit the medina through a small gate to the right on pl. Baghdadi when walking from Bab Boujeloud toward Fez al-Jdid. Turn right on the main road, walk past the bus station 200m, then take a small path that winds its way up the hillside; the tombs are to the right and the museum to the left.

MERENID TOMBS. To the north of the old city lie the Merenid Tombs. The Palais des Merenides, a five-star hotel, overlooks the tombs from one of the most picturesque hill-sides in the Maghreb. From here, the medina unfolds with the same poetry that inspired Paul Bowles and countless other Orientalist writers. The panorama is particularly impressive in the half-light of dawn or dusk; during calls to prayer, when over a hundred *muezzin* simultaneously summon the faithful, the experience is almost mystical.

THE ATLANTIC COAST

The towns along Morocco's Atlantic coast, connected by the country's only extensive railway line, are undoubtedly more liberal, laid-back, and open than their conservative cousins in the interior. Men and women alike go to the beach regularly to sunbathe, swim, surf, and windsurf, usually among European tourists. The west coast contains Morocco's industrial boom towns—Casablanca, the country's commercial center, and Rabat, its most westernized city—which are best avoided by those with limited time in Morocco. If you're headed to the coast, your best bets are the peaceful and tranquil smaller cities like Essaouira and Asilah.

ASILAH أصيلة ☎09

Just a short trip from Tangier, Asilah's sandy shores, quiet streets, and brilliant white medina offer respite from the usual tensions of Moroccan tourism. Over the last 1000 years, every European power from the Vikings to the French have sent flotillas, armies, and even a crusade to wrench tiny Asilah from Moroccan hands. Rarely did Europeans last more than a generation or two before being sent packing from this fabled port city. Except for a few weeks in August when a large art and horse festival is held, Asilah remains a peaceful spot for kicking back and soaking up the sun on Atlantic beaches.

TRANSPORTATION. Trains run to: **Tangier** (1hr., 4 per day 5am-11pm, 15dh); **Rabat** (5hr., 3 per day 7:45am-11pm, 75dh); **Casablanca** (6hr., 3 per day 7:45am-11pm, 95dh); **Marrakesh** (9hr., 11pm, 130dh). **CTM** and **private bus companies** vend tickets together in the same stall off av. Prince Heritier Sidi Mohammed. Take the first right leaving pl. Mohammed V away from the medina; the station is in the lot on the left. **Buses** go to: **Tangier** (1hr., every 30min. 7:45am-5:15pm, 13dh); **Larache** (45min., 14 per day 11:45am-5:15pm, 10dh); **Fez** (3½hr., 4 per day 9:45am-11pm, 55dh); **Rabat** (4hr., 14 per day 5:45am-11:15pm, 50dh); **Meknes** (4hr., 8 per day 10am-11pm, 50dh); **Casablanca** (4½-5½hr., 14 per day 5:45am-10:15pm, 60dh); **Marrakesh** (9hr., 5:15pm, 80dh). Many buses arrive full, so get to the station early, especially during the summer. **Grand taxis** cluster in pl. Mohammed V, by the bus station, and head to Tangier (12dh).

PRACTICAL INFORMATION. The main street heading into town is bd. Mohammed V, which ends at the town's center, **place Mohammed V** (a traffic circle). The **train station** (☎ 41 73 27) is a 20-minute walk from town on the Asilah-Tangier highway, near a strip of campgrounds. To get to town, follow the road by the beach, keeping the sea to the right. A taxi to or from town costs about 10dh. A minibus connects the station to town; it leaves from the front of the station just after the train arrives (10dh; you may have to bargain). To get to the **post office** from pl. Mohammed V, take bd. Mohammed V and turn right onto pl. Nations Unies, keeping the park on the right. The post office is 20m up on the left. (☎ 41 72 00. Open M-F 8am-noon and 2:30-6:30pm.)

ACCOMMODATIONS AND FOOD. Most hotels cluster around pl. Mohammed V and the end of av. Hassan II away from pl. Mohammed V. In the months of July and August, they brim with French and Spanish beachgoers; call at least a day in advance to reserve a room. **Hôtel Marhaba**, 9 rue Zallakah, on the right as you approach the medina from pl. Mohammed V, fills up quickly in the summer. A constant flow of patrons has taken a toll on the mattresses, but the location is ideal and there's a great view of the town from the roof. (☎ 41 71 44. Free hot showers. Singles 80dh; doubles 100dh. In winter 10dh less.) **Hôtel Sahara**, 9 rue Tarfaya, a block inland from av. Mohammed V and two blocks before pl. Mohammed V, has immaculate rooms maintained by a Spanish-speaking staff. (☎ 41 71 85. Hot showers 5dh. Singles 98dh; doubles 126dh; triples 186dh; quads 252dh.) **Hôtel Belle Vue,** rue Hassan ben Tabit, offers warm rooms with dressers, couches, and murals of sunbathers on the walls. Budget-bus tours like to stop here; most visitors are over 50. From the top of av. Hassan II, take a left on av. Imam Asili and then the next right; there is a sign on av. Hassan II. (☎/fax 41 77 47. July-Aug. singles 100dh; doubles 200dh; triples 300dh; quads 400dh. Sept.-June singles 50dh; doubles 120dh; triples 180dh; quads 250dh. V, MC.) **Camping Echrigui,** 700m from the train station in the direction of town, where the new port finally ends, has a lounge with billiards and a restaurant. Bug repellent will come in handy here. (☎ 41 71 82. Hot showers 5dh. 10dh per person, per tent, and per car. Straw roofed bungalows that can fit 3 people 80dh; a large one for 3-4 with showers and a kitchen 150dh.)

Most hustlers spend their endless energy inviting tourists into the string of restaurants facing the ramparts along Hussan II. Luckily, neither the prices nor the menu differs too much between choices.) The restaurants facing the ramparts along av. Hassan II specialize in seafood and serve good meals for around 35dh. **La al-Kasabah,** rue Zallakah, toward the ocean and past Hôtel Marhaba, is definitely the best restaurant in town. Patrons dine on seafood and pasta from a terrace overlooking the street and port. (☎ 41 70 12. Entrees 25-70dh. Open daily 9am-2am, closes earlier in winter. V, MC.) The town **market** takes place on av. Hassan II.

🔲 **SIGHTS.** Asilah's stunning 🔲medina is bounded by heavily fortified 15th-century Portuguese walls. The Bab Kasaba, the gate off rue Zallakah, leads past the **Grand Mosque.** Right across from the mosque is the **Centre Hassan II des Rencontres Internationales,** a new building which houses a collection of art created during the great **International Festival.** (☎ 41 70 65. Open 9am-12:30pm and 3-7pm. Free.) During the festival (held in Aug.) artists from all over the Arab and African worlds flock to Asilah, but the city glows with artistic flair year-round; walls are covered with murals, music fills the air, and locals seem to be constantly dancing on the beaches. The most popular coastal stretches are those toward the train station and farthest from the medina, and Asilah's nicest is the enclosed **Paradise Beach,** an hour's walk from the medina. Those with extra cash can take a horse-drawn wagon for around 200dh round-trip. Some men might jeer at the sight of foreign women swimming; if you feel uncomfortable, just walk to a less-crowded area.

LARACHE الاعرا ايش ☎09

In the summer, when tourists and faux guides descend upon nearby Asilah, Larache compensates with quiet relief—this relaxing town along the Atlantic coast has no touristy veneer. A former colony of Spain (with the Spanish-style architecture to prove it), Larache's greatest attractions are its inexpensive accommodations and fresh seafood. Its whitewashed medina is also more manageable than those in most Moroccan cities, and the city makes a good base for exploring the Roman ruins at Lixus.

📶 **TRANSPORTATION. CTM buses** go to and from: **Asilah** (50min., 4 per day 11:15am-10:45pm, 13dh); **Tangier** (2hr., 4 per day 11:15am-10:45pm, 29dh); **Rabat** (4hr., 3 per day 8:15am-6pm, 56dh); **Casablanca** (5hr., 3 per day 8:15am-6pm, 82dh); **Meknes** (5hr., 3 per day 4:30-10:15pm, 46dh); **Fez** (6½hr., 3 per day 4:30-10:15pm, 61dh); **Marrakesh** (8hr., 6pm, 143dh). **Private buses** leave from the same station and send packed buses to the same locations at cheaper prices. **Taxis** park outside the bus station. **Local buses** (2.5dh) depart Kasbah de la Cigogne off av. Mohammed V, traveling to **Lixus** (buses #4 and 5) and the **beaches** (bus #4).

📌 **PRACTICAL INFORMATION.** Buses to Larache drop off passengers five blocks from **place de la Libération,** the center of activity. From the station, exit from where the buses enter, turn right, and head down **av. Mohammed ben Abdallah,** which runs into pl. Libération (about 8min.). Branching off pl. Libération to the right is the main artery, **bd. Mohammed V.** Also off pl. Libération, **Bab al-Khemis** (also called Bab Medina) leads to the **medina** and the **Zoco de la Alcaicería** (a.k.a. Zoko Chico). Larache's **beach,** beyond the medina and across the Loukkos estuary, is accessible by bus (2.50dh) or boat (2dh over, 4dh back). To reach the **bus station** from pl. Libération, turn right onto av. Mohammed ben Abdallah and continue past Pensión Salama; take the first left and go straight. **Banks,** across from the post office on bd. Mohammed V heading away from pl. Libération, exchange money and have **ATMs.** Contact the **police** at ☎ 19. International **telephones** are located in and around the **post office.** (Open M-F 8:30am-noon and 2:30-6:30pm. Phones inside available M-Sa 8:30am-noon and 2:30-6:30pm.) Access the **Internet** at **Marnet,** 4 rue Mouatamid ben Abbad (☎ 91 68 84. 15dh per hr. Open daily 9:30am-midnight.)

⌐⌐ ACCOMMODATIONS AND FOOD. While there are extremely basic hotels on the medina, many nicer budget options can be found on av. Mohammed ben Abdallah and off pl. Libération. The best bargain is **Pensión Amal,** 10 av. Abdallah ben Yassine. Head up av. Mohammed ben Abdallah for five blocks and then turn left and follow the sign. (☎ 91 27 88. Hot showers 6dh; cold showers 2dh. Singles 40dh; doubles 70-80dh; triples 90dh; quads 115dh.) **Hôtel España,** pl. Libération, is part of the family of once-grand hotels that are worth the extra cash; the large rooms have TVs and bathrooms are modern. (☎ 91 31 95. Singles 110dh, with bath 204dh; doubles 162dh, with bath 243dh; triples 200dh, with bath 313dh; quads with bath and TV 350dh.) Cheap **restaurants** line pl. Libération and the Zoko. **Restaurant Commerciale,** on pl. Libération away from the ocean, serves some of the cheapest fresh seafood, chicken, and *paella* in town. (☎ 91 02 60. Entrees 15-25dh.)

◉ SIGHTS. Though most tourists come to Larache to visit the Roman ruins of Lixus, Larache itself can make for pleasant wandering. From pl. Libération head into the Moorish area (Bab al-Khemis) and turn right into **Zoco de la Alcaicería,** a Spanish-built, 17th-century courtyard, now a bustling *souq.* The Zoco leads to **Kasbah de la Cigogne** (the Stork's Kasbah), located near the tall minaret of the mosque. Built by Felipe III, it is Larache's only intact 17th-century fortification. Unfortunately it's not open to visitors. Around the corner next to the citadel sits the tiny **archaeological museum,** which contains a small assortment of Roman and Phoenician artifacts. (☎ 91 20 91. Open M-Sa 9am-noon and 3-6pm. 10dh.) The old city walls and a ruined **kasbah** built by the Portuguese in the 16th century are visible from the walkway just off pl. Libération. You can climb among the fallen turrets, but beware of loose footholds. Farther downhill on the walkway, where couples and families stroll at sunset, to the **beach** across the **Loukkos estuary.** Entrepreneurial boatmen ferry passengers over for 2dh (4dh back) from dawn to dusk.

DAYTRIP FROM LARACHE: LIXUS

To get to Lixus, hop on bus #4 or 5 from the stop near Kasbah de la Cigogne in Larache (2.5dh) and tell the ticket collector you want to go to Lixus. Unfortunately buses going toward Larache don't stop here. To get back, walk along the highway (45min.) or flag down one of the rare taxis. Let's Go does not recommend hitchhiking, although tired travelers have reported it as a useful option.

The Roman ruins of Lixus are located 5km north of Larache on the highway to Tangier. Though not as impressive as Volubilis (see p. 681), Lixus is one of the Atlantic Coast's most interesting sights. It figured prominently in Greco-Roman mythology as the place where Hercules completed his 11th labor: collecting the golden apples from Mount Atlas. In real life, it was settled by an ancient sun-worshipping cult and became a highly successful **Phoenician settlement** around 1000 BC. As did all things Phoenician, the area fell to the Romans around 140 BC, and within a few years it had become a rich trading city occupying an important place in the Roman Empire. Unfortunately, the city lost prominence with the Empire's fall, and by the 5th century it was totally abandoned.

Visitors to the unrestored, unguarded, unmarked, and often entirely empty ruins often feel as though they are discovering them for the first time. From the main road between Larache and Asilah, follow the path that leads past the port silo and **factory** where *garum,* Lixus's famous fish-intestine paste, was made and stored for shipment. Farther along lie the ruins of a Greco-Roman **theater** with what was once one of the ancient world's largest orchestra pits; it was later converted to an **amphitheater** and, during Spanish occupation, a bullring. Located near the theater are the relatively famous **Mosaic of the Sea God** and the **Roman baths.** Follow the fork uphill and to the left to temples, villas, churches, and a view of the entire site.

RABAT الرباط ☎07

Stolen treasure and merciless pirates are a very real part of Rabat's past, just as many authors (like Daniel Defoe in *Robinson Crusoe*) have made them out to be. The Mediterranean and Atlantic were the pirates' oysters until the Alawites subdued them around 1700. Not until 1912 did Rabat return to prominence, when the French selected it as the seat of government. Today, the city is one of Morocco's safest, and boasts a healthy, thriving economy and a growing tourist industry.

King Muhammad VI resides here and his personal guards have kept hustlers off the main streets. As a political and business capital, Rabat has a fleet of public employees, a swelling upper-middle class, and a flourishing Mercedes-Benz trade. Admittedly, today's Rabat lacks the tradition of Fez, the color of Marrakesh, and the money of Casablanca, but don't be tempted to skip out. Not only can its moderation be a treat in and of itself, but calm and order, Western facilities, and several important sights all weigh heavily in this capital city's favor.

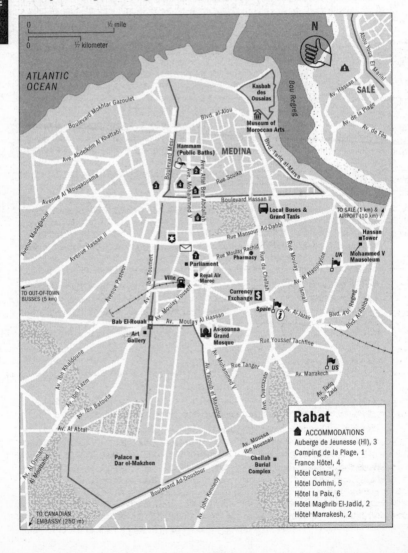

Rabat

🏠 ACCOMMODATIONS
Auberge de Jeunesse (HI), 3
Camping de la Plage, 1
France Hôtel, 4
Hôtel Central, 7
Hôtel Dorhmi, 5
Hôtel la Paix, 6
Hôtel Maghrib El-Jadid, 2
Hôtel Marrakesh, 2

▛ TRANSPORTATION

Flights: Rabat is served by its own airport, as well as the larger Mohammed V in Casablanca. **Royal Air Maroc** (☎ 70 97 66), on av. Mohammed V across from the Rabat Ville train station. Open M-Sa 8:30am-12:15pm and 2:30-7pm. **Air France,** 281 av. Mohammed V (☎ 70 77 28). Open M-Th 8:30am-12:15pm and 2:30-6:30pm, F 8:30am-12:15pm and 3:30-6:30pm, Sa 9am-12:15pm.

Trains: Rabat Ville Station, (☎ 70 14 69) av. Mohammed V, at av. Moulay Youssef. To: **Casablanca Port** (1hr., 19 per day 6:15am-9:30pm, 27dh); **Casablanca Voyageurs** (1 hr., 17 per day 4am-11:30pm, 25dh); **Meknes** (3hr., 8 per day 7:15am-11:45pm, 53dh); **Fez** (4hr., 8 per day 7:15am-11:45pm, 69dh); **Marrakesh** (5hr., 7 per day 4am-11:30pm, 99dh); and **Tangier** (5½hr., 4 per day 8am-1am, 87dh).

Buses: All companies operate from an enormous station (☎ 28 02 62), on the road to Casablanca, at pl. Mohammed Zerktouni. It's several kilometers from the town center, so take a *petit taxi* (12dh) or bus #30 from av. Hassan, near rue Mohammed V (2.50dh). **CTM** tickets at windows #14 and 15; other windows are private companies. CTM to: **Casablanca** (1hr., 6 per day 3:20am-10:30pm, 27dh); **Meknes** (2½hr., 8 per day 8am-9:30pm, 40dh); **Fez** (3½hr., 8 per day 8am-midnight, 57dh); **Tangier** (5hr., 5 per day 7:30am-1am, 80dh); and **Chefchaouen** (6hr., 10am, 65dh).

Taxis: Stands can be found at the train station, in front of the bus station along av. Hassan II, and at the entrance to the medina by the corner of av. Hassan II and av. Mohammed V. Expect to pay about 18dh from the bus station to the center of town and about 6dh from the train station (plus a surcharge of 5dh at night).

Car Rental: Hertz, 467 av. Mohammed V (☎/fax 70 92 27). **Budget** (☎ 70 57 89), headquartered in the train station. Both rent the Fiat Uno starting at 450dh per day, plus 2.5dh per km. Both open M-Sa 8am-noon and 2-7pm, Su 8:30am-6:30pm. Min. age 21 for most cars.

▚▜ ORIENTATION AND PRACTICAL INFORMATION

Rabat could not be easier to navigate. **Av. Mohammed V** runs north to south from the **medina,** past the post office and train station, to the **Great Mosque (al-Sounna).** Exiting the train station (the Rabat Ville stop), turn left up av. Mohammed V to reach most budget hotels and **bd. Hassan II,** which runs perpendicular to av. Mohammed V along the medina's walls, the center of town, as well as most budget hotels. When facing the medina, you will see Rabat's sister city **Salé** over the river to the right; the bus station on rte. de Casablanca is a good distance to the left.

Tourist Office: Municipal, 22 rue al-Jazair (☎ 73 05 62). Way out there. Turn right out of the train station, walk up av. Mohammed V to the Grand al-Sounna Mosque, turn left on av. Moulay Hassan, and after four blocks bear right onto rue al-Jazair. Not-so-fabulous maps of Rabat and other large cities. Some English and Spanish spoken. Open June 16 to mid-Sept. M-F 8am-2pm; mid-Sept. to June 15 M-F 8am-noon and 12:30-5:30pm; during Ramadan M-F 9am-3pm.

Currency Exchange: Banks and **ATMs** are located on av. Mohammed V and av. Allal ben Abdallah. **BMCE** is located at 260 av. Mohammed V and at the train station. Open M-F 8am-noon and 3-6pm, Sa-Su 10am-2pm and 4-8pm.

Luggage Storage: At the train station (2.50dh per bag, must be locked, locks for sale in station). At the bus station (3dh per day). Both open daily 4am-midnight.

English Bookstores: American Bookstore, 4 Zankat Tanja (☎ 76 87 17). Take av. Mohammed V past the Grand Mosque and turn left 3 blocks later. Great paperbacks. Open M-F 9:30am-12:30pm and 2:30-7:30pm, Sa 10am-12:30pm and 1:30-5:30pm.

Laundromat: (☎ 72 64 85), on rue Istanbul. Hotels charge 20-30dh per load.

Police: (☎ 19) rue Soekarno, 2 blocks from the post office off av. Mohammed V.

Late-Night Pharmacy: Pharmacie de Préfecture (☎ 70 70 72), av. Moulay Rachid. From post office, cross av. Mohammed V and veer right onto rue al-Qahira. On your right a few blocks down and across from Theatre Mohammed V. Open nightly 8:30pm-8am.

Medical Assistance: Hôpital Avicenne (☎ 67 28 71), av. Ibn Sina, at the end of bd. d'Argonne away from the medina. Free emergency medical care. US citizens can also go to the **US Embassy** (see p. 667) for medical assistance.

Telephones: Rue Soekarno, facing the post office. International phones and collect calls. Open 24hr. **Poste Restante** is also located in this building.

Post Office: (☎ 72 21 80), av. Mohammed V at rue Soekarno, to the left when leaving the train station. Open M-Th 8:30am-12:15pm and 2:30-6:45pm, F 11:30am-3pm.

Internet Access: I.N.T. Plus, 379 av. Mohammed V (☎ 20 43 88), ½block toward the train station from the medina, up 3 flights of stairs. 15dh per hr. Open daily 9am-10pm.

ACCOMMODATIONS

Medina hotels tend to be cheaper (and often less appealing) than those in the *ville nouvelle*. Cushier hotels line **av. Mohammed V** and **av. Allal ben Abdallah.** From the train station, turn left onto av. Mohammed V and walk toward the medina; av. Allal ben Abdallah runs parallel, one block to the right.

VILLE NOUVELLE

Auberge de Jeunesse (HI), 43 rue Marassa (☎ 72 57 69), 2 blocks along the medina walls on the road perpendicular to av. Hassan II. An old mansion with a once-beautiful courtyard that has recently passed its peak. Separate dorms for men and women, complete with cold showers and European-style toilets. Breakfast 8dh. Reception open 8-10am, noon-3pm, and 6:30-10:30pm. Dorms 33dh, members 29dh.

Hôtel Central, 2 rue al-Basra (☎ 70 73 56). From the train station, cross av. Mohammed V, walk 2 blocks toward the medina, and turn right; it's on the corner of rue al-Basra and rue Dimach. Big, clean rooms with high ceilings, sinks, and firm beds. Hot showers 10dh. Singles 80dh, with shower 100dh; doubles 110dh, with shower 136dh; triples 140dh, with shower 172dh; quads 170dh, with shower 208dh.

Hôtel de la Paix, 2 rue Ghazza (☎ 73 20 31 or 72 29 26), on the corner of av. Allal ben Abdallah and rue Ghazza, about 10min. from the train station and 2 blocks before the medina. Super-friendly management offers spotless, airy rooms with full baths, some with tables, chairs, and telephones. Ask for a balcony. Singles 157dh; doubles 183dh.

Camping de la Plage (☎ 78 23 68), far away on the beach in Salé. Take a *grand taxi* (10dh), or grab a bus from the av. Hassan II station (see map) and ask to be dropped off at Bab Mrisa, then follow the river towards the ocean. Running water, toilets, and a store/restaurant. Reception 24hr. Water and electricity both available for 12dh. 15dh per person. Cars and tents both 12dh; slightly more for larger vehicles and lodgings.

MEDINA

Hôtel Dohrmi, 313 av. Mohammed V (☎ 72 38 98), 1½ blocks inside the medina walls, on the right. Female management makes women feel at home. Rooms, some with toilets, surround a pleasant courtyard. Get here early in summer, as the hotel fills up quickly. Hot showers 7dh. Singles 80dh; doubles 100dh; triples 150dh; quads 200dh.

Hôtel Maghrib El-Jadid, 2 rue Sebbahi (☎ 73 22 07), at av. Mohammed V, a few blocks past Hôtel Dohrmi on the right. Spotless rooms with small beds complemented by a rooftop terrace. English spoken. Cold showers 4dh; hot showers 10dh. Singles 50dh; doubles 80dh; triples 120dh; quads 150dh. Additional bed 40dh. If it is full, try its sister **Hôtel Marrakesh,** 10 rue Sebbahi (☎ 72 77 03), down the block. Same prices.

France Hôtel, 46 rue Sout Sewara (☎ 72 34 57), off av. Mohammed V. One of the cheapest, but most basic, hotels around. No showers, but a *hammam* (5-10dh) nearby; ask at the desk. Singles 30-35dh; doubles 50dh; triples 60dh.

⬛ FOOD

Along with scores of traditional restaurants, Rabat is filled with mediocre international food options. Some might enjoy **Hong Kong**, a Chinese/Vietnamese restaurant on av. Mohammed V one block towards the train station from av. Hassan II, or **Taki Fried Chicken** (☎ 20 28 83), Rabat's original fast food, in a small arcade across from the Parliament. A **food market** sits at the entrance to the **medina** at av. Mohammed V, and there are *brochetteries* and sandwich shops within the medina walls.

  Café Restaurant Taghazout (☎ 72 40 61), across from Hotel Maghrib El-Jadid. Generally considered one of the best and cheapest restaurants in the medina. Entrees 23-36dh. Open daily 7:30am-11pm.

  Snack Bar Balima, under the Balima Hotel a block north of the train station on av. Mohammed V. Serves Western-style fast food for those craving their burgers and fries. Entrees 18-90dh. Open daily 7am-11pm.

👁 SIGHTS

⬛ **THE HASSAN TOWER.** Across town, along av. Abi Regreg (near the Moulay Hassan bridge to Salé), towers the famous minaret of the **Hassan Mosque,** a testament to the ambition of Sultan Yacoub al-Mansour. The mosque was to be al-Mansour's greatest achievement, to be built in the same style as the Giralda of Sevilla and the Koutoubia of Marrakesh—historians conjecture that he had caliphal ambition. The huge courtyard was once the prayer hall of what was to be the largest mosque in the Muslim world, begun in 1195 to commemorate a victory in Spain but abandoned shortly thereafter upon the sultan's death. All that remains are the 44m minaret (meant to reach a staggering 60m) and stubby reconstructions of the support pillars (which were originally destroyed by an 18th-century earthquake). Several have been fitted with benches— great places for a picnic or to read a book. *(Follow bd. Hassan II to the right when facing the medina; after a 15min. walk, the tower will be on the right. Open daily, sunrise to sunset. Free.)*

MOHAMMED V MAUSOLEUM. In the structure to the left when facing the Hassan Mosque is the Mausoleum of King Mohammed V, a tribute to the king who led Morocco's independence movement and lent his name to seemingly every third street in the country. Non-Muslims can enter the lower room of the incredible, traditional-style building, where spectacularly clad guards keep company with Mohammed V himself in his marble sarcophagus. *(Open daily sunrise to sunset. Free.)*

⬛ **THE CHELLAH.** Beyond the city walls at the end of av. Yacoub al-Mansour loom the deteriorating but impressive ruins of the Chellah, a former Roman city. In the 14th century the ruling Merenids encircled the city with walls and converted it into a royal necropolis. Because of its tranquil aura and spectacular views, the Chellah is often called one of the most romantic sites in Morocco. From the gate, descend through the overgrown gardens to reach the necropolis and its ruined mosque. Step inside to see the 13th-century tombs of Sultan Abu Yacoub Youssef and the adjacent stork-filled minaret. On the way back, a path to the right circles the Roman ruins, once the sight of a military camp and the first occupied territory in the region, and now a popular local picnic spot. *(Follow av. Mohammed V to the al-Sounna Mosque (see below) and keep going, keeping the wall on the right. At the end of the road, the Chellah is diagonally across the square to the left. Open daily, sunrise to sunset. 10dh.)*

AL-SOUNNA MOSQUE AND ARCHAEOLOGICAL MUSEUM. Rabat's principal place of worship, the splendid al-Sounna Mosque towers above the *ville nouvelle.* Although non-Muslims cannot enter, they may peek in. Near the mosque, the archaeological museum, often considered the best of Morocco's less-than-stellar museums, has an impressive collection of Hellenistic bronze works, all cast before 25 BC. *(Walk down av. Mohammed V away from the medina and turn left onto Abd al-Aziz at the Grand Mosque; the museum is on the next street off Abd al-Aziz to the right, near the Hôtel Chellah. Open W-M 9-11:30am and 2:30-5:30pm. 10dh.)*

BAB AL-ROUAH AND ART GALLERY. The salmon-pink Bab al-Rouah (Gate of Winds) is a massive four-arched gate, one of the most decorated and impressive in all of Morocco. The nearby art gallery houses an often-changing collection of paintings and sculpture. *(Facing the Grand Mosque with the train station at your back, follow av. Moulay Hassan to the right for 10min. Open daily 8:30am-noon and 2:30-8pm. Free.)*

OTHER SIGHTS. Compared to Fez or Marrakesh, there is little of interest to travelers in the medina. The **Kasbah des Oudaias,** however, just outside the medina, is impressive. It used to be a pirate stronghold until Moulay Idriss sent Saharan mercenaries to oversee the buccaneers' tributes of gold and slaves. Exiting the kasbah through Bab Oudaia and heading through the keyhole-shaped gate down the stairs leads to the sublime **Andalucian gardens,** of medieval Islamic-Spanish design and French construction. *(On your right after you enter the gate.)* The **Museum of Moroccan Arts,** next to the gardens, was the 17th-century hideaway of the infamous Moulay Ismail. The excellent ethnographic collection shows off the sultan's private apartment, signature Rabat-style carpets, traditional local costumes, and musical instruments. A charming cafe lies on the opposite side of the garden. *(Follow av. Mohammed V. through the medina and take a right on bd. al-Alou to its end, a 15min. walk. The kasbah is just to the left and gardens and museum just to the right. Museum and gardens open 8am-noon and 2-7:30pm. Museum entrance 10dh.)*

🎵 ENTERTAINMENT

Visitors to Rabat have a rare opportunity to sample Moroccan and Arab cinema at the **Royal Movie Theater,** on av. Allal ben Abdallah, a few blocks off the medina (Sa 10:30am, 20dh, in French or with French subtitles). The rest of the week the movie house screens foreign flicks. Locals who can afford it head to pricey, pseudo-European discos such as **Amnesia,** 18 rue Monastir near the **Cinema Royale** (☎ 70 18 60; weekends and W are crowded). **Café Balima** (see **Food,** p. 697) has a disco downstairs, sometimes with live music. (Open 10pm-3am; cover and a drink Su-Th 70dh, F-Sa 100dh.) For something more sophisticated, call the palatial **Tour Hassan Hôtel,** 22 av. Chellah (☎ 72 14 91), to sit in on a performance or concert.

▶ DAYTRIP FROM RABAT

SALÉ ۹ (15MIN.)

*The easiest way to get to Salé is via a **grand taxi** (2dh) or by **bus** #6 or 12 (2.5dh). Both leave from bd. Hassan II in Rabat and drop passengers off at Bab Mrisa, at the corner of the city. If you decide to take the bus, make sure to let the driver know where you want to get off. If you choose to walk from Rabat, head east on av. Hassan II and cross the bridge to Salé (30min. from av. Mohammed V) and then take a boat ride back (5dh per person). Catch the boat at the base of the bridge.*

Across the Bou Regreg from Rabat sits Salé, an ancient trading city that has recently come to be considered a suburb of the ever-expanding Rabat. This virtually tourist-free "White City" makes for an intriguing half-day trip from Rabat. The medina in Salé has three main attractions: the **souqs** along the **rue Grande Mosquée,** those along **rue Kechachine,** and the **Grand Mosque** and accompanying 14th-century *madrasa* (college of theology, literature, and law). The best way to see these sights is by walking along the walls perpendicular to the river and entering the medina through the towering **Bab Mrisa** (just on the right if walking or where the taxis/buses will drop you off). Follow the inside wall on the left until you get to a square. Since there are few tourists, the *souqs* in Salé are more traditional, lacking the high-tech or mass-produced goods often found in the medinas of large cities.

The two main streets from the Bab Mrisa lead to the **Grand Mosque,** which dates from the Almohad era. You'll know you're close when the path and walls suddenly become shiny white and clean. As usual, the mosque is closed to non-Muslims. The nearby ■**Madrasa,** however, lets visitors gaze at its architectural riches. Completed in 1333, this school once instructed students in the Qur'an and Islamic sciences. Today Moroccan architects consider the building the model to which all universities should conform. The school is paved with an intricate mosaic and decorated with elegant cedar carvings. Up a little flight of stairs, students' rooms are open for viewing. The rooftop affords a splendid panorama of Salé and Rabat. (Entrance to the *madrasa* 10dh, English-speaking guide.)

CASABLANCA الدارالبيضه ☎02

As time goes by, Casablanca (known as "Casa") continues to expand under the Maghreb sun. Already the largest city in Morocco, with nearly 4 million inhabitants (up from a mere 20,000 in 1900), Casablanca continues to attract rural Moroccans seeking urban prosperity. Here in the country's financial capital and Africa's largest port, Western dress predominates, and women participate actively in city life. With the construction of the gargantuan Hassan II Mosque, Casablanca established itself as a major religious center as well. Although the mosque is indeed spectacular, foreign backpackers generally view Casa as little more than a transport hub—and not without reason. Unfortunately there is no Rick's Café Américain in the kasbah and no one looking at you, kid, except the hustlers who prowl the port and medina. The movie *Casablanca* was based more on Tangier anyway.

MOROCCO

▄ TRANSPORTATION

The train and bus stations are in seedy parts of town; know where you're going before you get off.

Flights: Aéroport Mohammed V (☎ 33 90 40) handles international and domestic flights. Trains run between the airport terminal and the Casa Port train station (55min., every hr., 24dh), some stopping at Casa Voyageurs en route; some trains head to Rabat. **Royal Air Maroc** (☎ 31 11 22 or 31 41 41), at the airport and 44 av. des Forces Armées Royales, sells tickets for international and domestic (Agadir, Marrakesh) flights. For more information see **Getting Around,** p. 662.

Trains: Casa Port (☎ 27 18 37), Port de Casablanca. Mainly northbound service. To: **Rabat** (1hr., 17 per day 6:45am-8:45pm, 27dh); **Fez** (4½hr., 8am and 8:45pm, 100dh); **Tangier** (6hr., 6:45am and 5:50pm, 120dh); and **Marrakesh** (3½hr., 7:15am, 50dh). **Casa Voyageurs** (☎ 24 58 01), bd. Ba Hammed, away from the city center. Mainly southbound service but extensive connections. To: **Marrakesh** (3½hr., 8 per day, 70dh); **Meknes** (4½hr., 7 per day, 90dh.) and on to **Fez** (5¼hr., 7 per day, 110dh); and **Tangier** (6hr., 3 per day, 120dh; possible transfer at Sidi Kacem).

Buses: CTM, 23 rue Léon L'Africain (☎ 44 81 27), off rue Chaouia. To: **Rabat** (1½hr., 18 per day 6am-11:30pm, 30dh); **al-Jadida** (1½hr., 6 per day 5:30am-3pm, 25dh); **Marrakesh** (4hr., 6 per day 7:30am-11:30pm, 65dh); **Meknes** (5hr., 9 per day 6:30am-11:30pm, 63dh); **Essaouira** (5½hr., 3 per day 5:30am-5pm, 100dh); **Fez** (6hr., 8 per day 6:30am-11:30pm, 80dh); **Tangier** (6½hr., 6 per day 6am-11:30pm, 100dh); and **Agadir** (10hr., 6 per day 5:30am-5pm, 140dh).

Car Rental: Casa has dozens of companies. For rates and more detailed info about renting a car in Morocco, see **By Car,** p. 663. **Europcar,** 44 av. des F.A.R. (☎ 31 37 37) and **Avis,** 19 av. des F.A.R. (☎ 31 24 24) both have similar rates. Min. age 21.

▄ ORIENTATION AND PRACTICAL INFORMATION

Casa is Morocco's transportation hub for planes, trains, and buses. The **Casa Port train station** is near the youth hostel and the city center; the **Casa Voyageurs train station** is near nothing, a 50-minute walk from Casa Port or a 30dh *petit taxi* ride. To get from Casa Port to the **CTM bus station,** conveniently located downtown, cross the street, follow bd. Felix Houphëit-Boigny to pl. Nations Unies, turn left on av. Armée Royale, and watch for Hôtel Safir on the right; the station is behind and to the right of the hotel. The city has two main squares, **place Nations Unies,** below the landmark clock tower, and **place Mohammed V.** Pl. Nations Unies spreads out in front of the Hyatt Regency at the intersection of bd. Mohammed V, av. Hassan II, and av. Forces Armées Royales (F.A.R.). Pl. Mohammed V lies six blocks away from the port along av. Hassan II.

Tourist Office: Syndicat d'Initiative et de Tourisme, 98 bd. Mohammed V (☎ 22 15 24 or 27 05 38), at rue Chaouia, about 4 blocks down from pl. Nations Unies. English spoken. Open M-Sa 8:30am-noon and 2:30-6:30pm, Su 9am-noon. The **Office de Tourisme,** 55 rue Omar Slaoui (☎ 27 95 33 or 27 11 77; fax 20 59 29), has similar services. From pl. Mohammed V, take av. Hassan II, turn left on rue Reitzer, and then right on rue Omar Slaoui. Open M-F 8:30am-noon and 2:30-6:30pm, Su 9am-noon.

Currency Exchange: When the **banks** in the city are closed, try the airport and larger hotels, which change money at Morocco's official, uniform rates. The **Hyatt Regency, Hôtel Suisse,** and **Hôtel Safir** near the bus station and the other big hotels near pl. Nations Unies are all safe bets. **ATMs** are everywhere.

American Express: Voyages Schwartz, 112 av. du Prince Moulay Abdallah (☎ 22 29 47). They offer standard services but won't receive wired money. Open M-F 8:30am-noon and 2:30-6:30pm, Sa 8:30am-noon.

English Bookstore: American Language Center Bookstore (☎ 27 95 59), bd. Moulay Youssef at pl. Unité Africaine. Vast array of novels and reference books. Open M-F 9:30am-12:30pm and 3:30-6:30pm, Sa 9:30am-noon.

Emergency: Police (☎ 19), bd. Brahim Roudani.

Late-Night Pharmacy: Pharmacie de Nuit (☎ 26 94 91), pl. Nations Unies. Open nightly 8pm-8am. Other pharmacies are found on almost any city block.

Medical Assistance: Croix-Rouge Marocaine, 19 bd. al-Massira al-Khadra (☎ 25 25 21). **S.O.S. Medicins,** 81 av. F.A.R. (☎ 44 44 44).

Post Office: Bd. Paris, at av. Hassan II. **Poste Restante** and telephones. M-Th 8:30am-12:15pm and 2:30-6:30pm, F 8:30-11:30am and 3-6:30pm.

Internet Access: EuroNet, 51 rue Tata. 15dh per hr. Open daily 9am-11pm.

▮ ACCOMMODATIONS

For budget deals look along **rue Chaouia,** as well as **av. des Forces Armées Royales** (F.A.R.) and side streets. Avoid the overpriced medina.

Auberge de Jeunesse (HI), 6 pl. Amiral Philibert (☎ 22 05 51). From Casa Port, head right along bd. Almohades, walk along the medina walls, and go left up a small ramp-like street. Blue signs point the way. The biggest hostel in Morocco, with a pleasant courtyard and communal kitchen. Breakfast included. Reception open daily 8-9:30am and noon-11pm. HI card required. Dorms 45dh; doubles 120dh.

Hôtel Rialto (☎ 27 51 22), av. Mohammed al-Qorri. From pl. Nations Unies, take bd. Mohammed V, then the 3rd right off it, and then the first left. These clean, airy rooms are about as quiet as Casa gets. The owner just added a TV room. All rooms have showers (hot in the mornings). Singles 84dh; doubles 120dh.

Hôtel de Foucauld, 52 rue Arabi Jilali (☎ 22 26 66). From bd. Felix Houphëit-Boigny, take a left on av. des F.A.R., then the 1st right; it's adjacent to Hôtel Perigord. Whether or not you can fill the Foucauld's huge wardrobes, you're bound to appreciate its cozy, tidy (dimly lit) rooms. Singles 75dh, with bath 120dh; doubles 120dh, with bath 150dh; triples with bath 180dh.

Hôtel Kon-Tiki, 88 rue Allal ben Abdallah (☎ 31 49 27). Rooms are clean—all with sinks, some with terraces. Hot showers 5dh. Singles 62dh; doubles 76dh; triples 110dh.

Hôtel Excelsior, 2 rue al-Amraoui Brahim (☎ 20 02 63 or 20 00 48). Just opposite the clock tower and across pl. des Nations Unies. A once-great hotel that has lost its clientele to the glitz of big-name American chains but maintains its luxurious rooms, complete with full baths. Breakfast included. Singles 259dh; doubles 333dh; triples 446dh.

MOROCCO

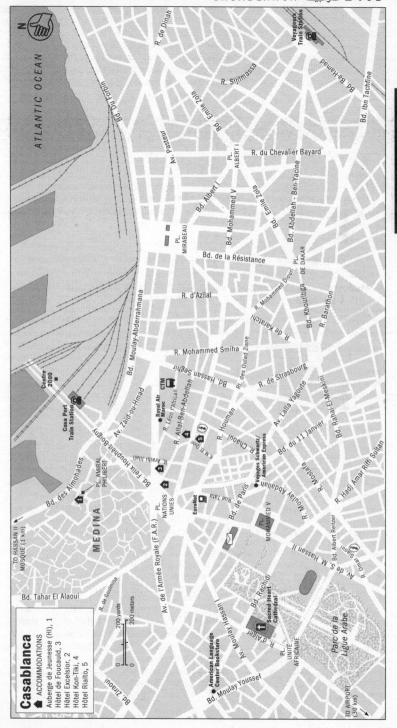

N

ATLANTIC OCEAN

R. de Dinah

Voyageurs
Train Station

R. Sijilmassa

Bd. Ba-Hamad

Bd. Ibn Tachfine

Bd. Du Fortin

Av. Pasteur

Bd. Emile Zola

PL.
ALBERT I

R. du Chevalier Bayard

Bd. Albert I

Bd. Mohammed V

Emile Zola

Bd. Abdellah — Ben-Yacine

PL.
MIRABEAU

Bd. de la Résistance

PL.
DE DAKAR

Bd. Khouribga

Bd. Barathon

R. d'Azilal

R. Mohammed Douri

R. de Karatchi

Bd. Moulay-Abderrahmana

R. Mohammed Smiha

Rt. des Oulad Ziane

R. de Strasbourg

Centre
2000

Bd. Hassan Seghir

CTM

Av. Lalla Yagoute

Casa Port
Train Station

Av. Zaïd-ou-Hmad

Royal Air
Maroc

R. Léon l'Africain

R. Allal-Ben-Abdellah

R. Houman

Av. du 11 Janvier

R. Chaoui

R. Rahal-El-Meskini

Bd. Félix Houphoüet-Boigny

R. Arabi Jilali

3

4

5

R. M.R Oum

Voyages Schwartz/
American Express

R. Hadj Amar Riffi Sultan

R. Mostafa

R. de Paris

Bd. des Almohades

PL. AMIRAL
PHILIBERT

2

EuroNet

R. Moulay Abdallah

Bd. du 11 Janvier

MEDINA

PL.
NATIONS
UNIES

R. Tata

MOHAMMED V

Bd. Albert Reitzer

TO HASSAN II
MOSQUE (1 km)

Av. de l'Armée Royale (F.A.R.)

Av. de S. M. Hassan II

R. Omar Slaoui

R. de Goulimina

R. Rachidi

Bd. Tahar El Alaoui

Sacred Heart
Cathedral

Parc de
la Ligue Arabe

Casablanca

▲ ACCOMMODATIONS
Auberge de Jeunesse (HI), 1
Hôtel de Foucauld, 3
Hôtel Excelsior, 2
Hôtel Kon-Tiki, 4
Hôtel Rialto, 5

0   200 yards
0   200 meters

R. d'Alger

PL.
UNITÉ
AFRICAINE

American Language
Center Bookstore

Av. Moulay Hassan

Bd. Ziraoui

Bd. Moulay Youssef

TO AIRPORT
(30 km)

MOROCCO

FOOD

While it's true that cosmopolitan Casablanca offers everything from French *haute cuisine* to Korean food to McDonald's, most restaurants are geared towards the city's wealthy business clientele. *Kebab* eateries line **rue Chaouia** in the *ville nouvelle*. Good values are also available near pl. Nations Unies and in the medina, though prices there are a bit higher. For fresh meats and produce, try haggling at the **central market,** 7 rue Chaouia (open daily 8am-1pm). And two blocks away from the center at 132 Hassan II is **L'Oliveri,** perhaps the best **ice cream shop** around.

Restaurant Snack Bar California, 19 rue Tata, midway down the street. Welcoming atmosphere for women traveling alone. Along with traditional food, features spectacular vegetarian dishes, a rarity in Casa. Entrees 20-50dh. Open daily 10am-11pm.

Taverne au Dauphin, 75 bd. Felix Houphëit-Boigny (☎ 22 12 00), up the road from the port. Tuxedoed waiters serve sizzling seafood to Casablancan professionals. House specialties include *crevettes grillées* (grilled shrimp, 55dh) and *filet de lotte* (filet o' fish, 70dh). Entrees 45-100dh. Beer 15dh. Open M-Sa noon-4pm and 7-11pm. V, MC.

SIGHTS

HASSAN II MOSQUE. The biggest sight in Casa, literally, is the fabulous new Hassan II Mosque, the third-largest mosque in existence. It's very easy to find: from anywhere in Casa, look toward the sea and spot the shiny minaret (200m high, the tallest minaret in the world). Begun in 1980 and inaugurated in 1994, this massive structure carried a price tag of over one billion US dollars (much of it collected from the Moroccan people through "universal voluntary conscription"). Though designed by a Frenchman, the mosque was constructed by 3300 Moroccan craftsmen. The prayer hall, much larger than St. Peter's in Rome, combines glass, marble, and precious wood in a space that holds over 25,000 worshippers. The courtyard accommodates another 80,000. Here, technology galvanizes religious devotion: the floor is heated for bare feet, the hall boasts a huge retractable roof, and a 20 mi. long laser beam shoots from the minaret toward Mecca. Non-believers are actually allowed inside, if you don't mind shelling out the cash. *(Walk past the medina along the coastal road (about 15min.), or take a petit taxi (no more than 10dh). Tours given Sa-Th 9, 10, 11am, and 2pm. Tours in English, French, and Arabic 100dh, students 50dh. Elevator up the side of the minaret 10dh.)*

OTHER SIGHTS AND ENTERTAINMENT. The Hassan II Mosque aside, Casa is too preoccupied with commerce to maintain a romantic veneer. A decaying **medina** disappoints veterans of Fez and Marrakesh, and the portside **Centre 2000,** meant to be a tourist draw, is just a collection of unexciting western cafes and restaurants. Government buildings, relics of the French occupation, surround the green **place Mohammed V.** Two blocks farther south along av. Hassan II sprawls the **Parc de la Ligue Arabe,** the grandest of Casa's parks. In the northwest corner you can enjoy a nice **picnic** in the shadows of the old **Sacred Heart Cathedral,** built in 1930. Since the local bars often attract a raucous clientele, the best bet for nighttime activities are the big hotel bars, like those at **Hôtel Safir** on av. des F.A.R.

AL-JADIDA الجديدة ☎ 03

Al-Jadida, a two-hour bus ride from Casablanca, is one of Morocco's largest Atlantic beach towns. With a quiet medina, historic battlements, palmy boulevards, and some of the country's most pleasant beaches, it's a welcome relief from the hustle and bustle of Casa and Marrakesh. The city's European feel comes courtesy of the Portuguese—al-Jadida (formerly known as Mazagan) was their first Moroccan foothold and last Moroccan stronghold. Once Morocco won independence, the city was renamed al-Jadida ("The New One") and became a retreat for Marrakesh's affluent families. Today, it serves as a prime destination for foreign and domestic tourists alike, attracting large crowds in July and August.

TRANSPORTATION

From al-Jadida, **CTM,** on bd. Mohammed V., sends **buses** to **Casablanca** (2hr., 3 per day, 24dh); and **Essaouira** (3hr., 7:15am and 3:15pm, 45dh). Buses to Essaouira begin in Casablanca and often have few seats left by the time they arrive in al-Jadida; purchase a ticket in advance. For connections to Rabat, Fez, and other major cities, transfer in Casablanca.

ORIENTATION AND PRACTICAL INFORMATION

Situated on a well-protected harbor, the northeast side of al-Jadida faces the Atlantic. From the **bus station,** exit left on bd. Mohammed V and continue up toward the city center (10min.). First you'll pass **place Mohammed V,** the center of town, which joins bd. Mohammed V at the post office, then **place al-Hansali** (a pleasant pedestrian square), and finally **place Mohammed ben Abdallah,** which connects bd. Suez to the old Portuguese **medina.**

Tourist Office: In pl. Mohammed V, next to Bata Shoes. Some English spoken. Open daily 9am-12:30pm and 3-7pm.

Currency Exchange: BMCE, 1 block from pl. Mohammed V along av. Mohammed Errafil, changes money and has an ATM. Open M-F 8:15am-2:15pm. **The Bank of Morocco,** pl. Mohammed V on the side toward the bus station.

Police: ☎ 19. At the bus station, at the beach, and on av. al-Jamia al-Arabi.

Late-Night Pharmacy: Av. Ligue Arabe off pl. Mohammed V. Look for the plaque next door to the Croissant Rouge Marocain (Red Cross). Open nightly 9pm-8am.

Medical Assistance: Hospital (☎ 34 20 04 or 34 20 05), rue Roux, near rue Boucharette in the south of town. **Ambulance:** ☎ 34 37 30.

Post Office: Pl. Mohammed V. **Poste Restante** and **telephones.** Open M-F 8:30am-noon and 2:30-6:30pm.

ACCOMMODATIONS

For a resort town, al-Jadida has a surprisingly large number of budget hotels. Most cluster around **place Mohammed V,** a few blocks from the ocean. Ask to see a room before you commit; rooms vary in quality even within a hotel. Reservations are a good idea in July and August, when the town fills up and prices skyrocket.

Hôtel Bourdeaux, 47 rue Moulay Ahmed Tahiri (☎ 37 39 21). A few narrow streets away from pl. al-Hansali; follow signs at the end of the pl. al-Hansali toward the medina (about 100m). Carpeted, bright, modern rooms at low prices. Rooftop lounge. Hot shower 5dh. Singles 41dh; doubles 57dh; triples 78dh.

Hôtel Maghreb/Hôtel de France, 16 rue Lescould (☎ 34 21 81), just off pl. al-Hansali. Spacious rooms with high ceilings, most with sinks and bidets, and some with excellent views of the water. Hot showers 5dh. Singles 41dh; doubles 57dh. Extra bed 21dh.

Hôtel de Provence, 42 rue Fquih Mohammed Errafil (☎34 23 47; fax 35 21 15). From the bus station, turn left off av. Mohammed V (away from the beach) at the post office. The "in" hotel for English speakers, with all the amenities (toilet paper, towels, nice sheets, and currency exchange). Continental breakfast (22dh) at the excellent French/Moroccan restaurant. Singles 174dh; doubles 218dh; triples 388dh. V, MC.

Camping Caravaning International (☎ 34 27 55), av. al-Oman al-Mouttahida. From pl. Mohammed V, go toward the beach, then right on av. al-Jamia al-Arabi. Take the 6th right (20min.). Large site with electricity, showers, and bungalows (160dh). 12dh per adult, 6.5dh per car, 10dh per tent plus 4dh *emplacement* and 14% TVA.

▐ FOOD

Cheap eateries serve *brochettes* along **place Mohammed V.** Most restaurants cluster in and around **place al-Hansali,** and numerous cafes dot the waterfront. On Sundays, a weekly **souq** that sells everything from fruit to cow lungs is held by the lighthouse around rue Zerktouni. *The* place to be is **Restaurant Tchikito,** 7 rue Moulay Ahmed Tahiri, a few meters off pl. al-Hansali on the street to Hôtel Bordeaux. Tchikito draws crowds of locals with its huge plates of fried fresh fish. (☎ 37 18 19. 25-30dh per plate. Open daily noon-10pm.)

▐ SIGHTS

Al-Jadida's main attractions are its **Cité Portugaise,** at the end of av. Mohammed V, and its **beaches,** on the east side of town, to the right when going toward the Cité.

CITÉ PORTUGAISE. The heart of al-Jadida is its lovely ramparted **Cité Portugaise,** completed in 1502 by Portuguese traders. In 1769, Moroccan forces finally sent them packing, but not before the retreating Portuguese blasted the old town walls to bits. After a sultan renovated the ramparts in the 19th century, the city was rebuilt as a Jewish settlement *(mellah)* mostly populated by merchants. *(Enter through the first fortified gate off pl. Mohammed ben Abdallah at the top of bd. Suez.)*

Up rue Mohammed Hachemi Bahbai on the left, a yellow plaque marks the entrance to the famed **Portuguese Cistern,** a Gothic structure lucky enough to have survived the Portuguese bombardment. It was designed in 1514 as an arsenal and later converted into a cistern. The water, illuminated by a shaft of light from the roof, reflects the cistern's columns and arches. The riot scene in Orson Welles's *Othello* was filmed here. *(☎ 34 30 64. Open Oct.-Apr. 9am-1pm and 3-7pm; May-Sept. 9am-7:30pm. Guided tour available.)* To join the locals promenading along the city's **ramparts,** either continue along and up a ramp or head back to the southwest corner of the medina (down the street to the right as you enter the medina), where there's a rickety staircase. Guards let you in and out for a tip of a few dirhams.

BEACHES. The town beach is popular among football-playing and sun-bathing locals and stretches a good distance to the south, ideal for long walks. For more peaceful beaches, head north of town beyond the Cité Portugaise. **Sidi Bouzid,** a beach 5km to the south, is sprawling and chic. Take a *grand taxi* (5dh per person) or the orange #2 bus (2.50dh) from near the Cité Portugaise.

ESSAOUIRA الصويرة　　　　　　　☎04

Essaouira is one of Morocco's most enchanting communities. Piracy boosted this port in the 18th century, when Sultan Muhammad ben Abdallah leveled the Portuguese city of Mogador and constructed the town fortifications to protect his band of pirates. In the late 1960s, the arrival of Jimi Hendrix and Cat Stevens triggered a mass hippie migration, and over the next decade Essaouira achieved international fame as an expat enclave. Though most of the hash smoke has cleared, Essaouira remains Morocco's most laid-back city. The miles of beautiful beaches are often too windy for sunbathing, but the tranquil fortified medina and splendid scenery provide ample diversion. In early June, acclaimed jazz musicians descend on the town for the Festival of Essaouira, a celebration of local and international jazz. Essaouira is a popular destination for many European tourists, and the high percentage of foreigners means that women travelers might feel more comfortable.

▐ TRANSPORTATION

Buses: Buses leave across the square from Bab Marrakesh, at **Agence Supratours** (☎ 47 53 17), where tickets are sold. To: **Agadir** (2½hr., 33 per day 5:30am-3:30pm, 37dh); **Marrakesh** (2½hr., 10 per day 4am-5pm, 40dh); **al-Jadida** (3hr., 5 per day 8:30am-12:30am, 54dh); and **Casablanca** (5hr., 26 per day 5am-12:30am, 75dh; midnight express 100dh). The fastest and most luxurious bus to **Marrakesh** (2½hr., 5pm, 40dh) is run by a train company, **ONCF.**

✦🛈 ORIENTATION AND PRACTICAL INFORMATION

Buses arrive at the **bus station,** about 1km northeast of the medina along bd. Industrie. Exit the rear of the station (where the buses park) and walk to the right, passing two *souqs* (or deserted wastelands, depending on the hour), to reach the medina gate, **Bab Doukkala** (10min.). The gate opens onto **av. Mohammed Zerktouni,** one of two main arteries; the other is the parallel street of **rue Mohammed ben Abdallah.** To reach the city center from Bab Doukkala, continue on av. Mohammed Zerktouni as it becomes av. l'Istiqlal (at an intersection surrounded by *souqs* and a mosque). Walk until you see a clock tower on the right. Go through the gate underneath the tower, pass through the square, and follow the road as it zig-zags to **place Moulay Hassan,** the heart of Essaouira.

Tourist Office: Syndicat d'Initiative du Tourism (☎ 47 50 80), on rue de Caine. From the top of pl. Hassan (away from the port), take a right and follow the road as it zig-zags out a gate. Continue 1 more block. Open M-F 9am-noon and 2:30-6:30pm.

Currency Exchange: Banks cluster around pl. Moulay Hassan. **Bank Credit du Maroc** (☎ 47 58 19), in pl. Moulay Hassan, cashes traveler's checks and has an **ATM.** Open M-F 8-11:30am and 2:15-3:30pm. Higher rates at **Hôtel Beau Rivage.** Open 24hr.

Luggage Storage: Available 24hr. at the bus station (5dh per bag).

Police: (☎ 19), in the *ville nouvelle* near the tourist office.

Hospital: (☎ 47 27 16), on av. al-Moquamah next to the post office.

Post Office: av. al-Moqamah at Lalla Aicha, the first left after Hôtel les Isles when walking away from the medina by the shore. Near the radio tower. **Poste Restante** and telephones. Open June-Sept. M-F 8am-3pm; Oct.-May 8:30am-noon and 2:30-6:30pm.

Internet Access: Several teleboutiques offer Internet access, but the cheapest is at **Mogador Informatique** (☎ 47 50 65), on Av. Oqba ben Nafil, two blocks away from the post, on the left (3rd floor). 10dh per hr. They claim to be open 24hrs., 7 days a week, but 9am-midnight is more accurate.

🭬 ACCOMMODATIONS

Though once Morocco's best kept secret, Essaouira has lost its anonymity; reservations may be necessary in summer. There are a number of nice, cheap hotels.

▨ Hôtel Smara, 26 rue Skala (☎ 47 56 55). From the top of pl. Moulay Hassan, head toward the port and take a right. Follow this street as it follows the ramparts (3min.). The beds are a bit worn, but rooms are clean and many have great views. Arrive early—this is the most popular hotel among backpackers. Laundry around 2dh per piece. Breakfast 10dh. No reservations. Some English spoken. Singles 62dh; doubles 84dh, with ocean view 104dh; triples 126dh; quads 158dh.

Hôtel Majestic, 40 rue Derb Laalouj (☎ 47 49 09). From pl. Moulay Hassan, head away from the port down the street to the right; take a quick left and then another. Clean, newly renovated rooms maintained by a friendly owner. The terrace—and a few toilets—have an ocean view. Hot showers 5dh. Singles 50dh; doubles 90dh.

Hôtel Tafraout, 7 rue Marrakesh (☎ 47 62 76). From the top of pl. Hassan, take a right and then a quick left onto the busy rue Sidi Mohammed ben Abdallah. Look for the sign a few blocks up. Newly renovated rooms and courtyard shine. Hot showers 6dh. Singles 100dh, with shower 150dh; doubles 150dh, with shower 250dh. Extra bed 50dh.

Hôtel Beau Rivage (☎/fax 47 29 25), pl. Moulay Hassan. Large, old hotel located above the main square's cafes. Bright, clean rooms, many with balconies, and a pleasant terrace. Singles 60dh; doubles 100dh, with shower 200dh; triples 150dh, with shower 220dh; quads with shower 240dh. Extra bed 50dh.

MOROCCO

 FOOD

Informal dining, mostly geared toward tourists, is common near the port and **place Moulay Hassan.** At the ▤**port fish grilles,** fried sardines (with fish, bread, and tomatoes; 20dh) and grilled shrimp (25dh) are sure bets. The so-called **Berber cafes,** near Porte Portugaise and off av. l'Istiqlal, have low tables, straw mats, and fresh fish *tajine* and couscous (20dh). Establish prices before biting in.

▤ **Restaurant Laayoure** (☎ 47 46 43). From the top of pl. Hassan (away from the port), take a right and continue past rue Sidi ben Mohammed Abdallah. Follow the road as it turns right and then left; the restaurant is up ahead on the left. The best Moroccan food in town, at reasonable prices, served in a beautiful, well-decorated setting. Banana and chocolate crepes 12dh. Entrees 38-50dh. Open daily 10am-midnight, later in summer.

Chez Sam (☎ 47 65 13), at the end of the harbor. Pricey and touristy, with warped ceilings and walls plastered with Hollywood movie stars, but has a nice ocean view and the town's only liquor license. Steaming heap of mussels 25dh. Fish dishes 40-70dh. *Menu* 70dh. Open daily noon-3pm and 7:30-10:30pm. V, MC, AmEx.

Dar Baba Restaurant, 2 rue Marrakesh, near the Hôtel Tafraout. Home of the city's only Italian cuisine, including their famous lasagna (38dh). Entrees 28-38dh. Open daily noon-2:30pm and 6:30-10pm. V, MC.

▤ **SIGHTS**

While many flock to Essaouira to simply sit back, relax, and do nothing at all, the ramparts, port, shops, museums, and the beaches can distract for hours on end.

RAMPARTS AND PORT. The view of the medina from the coastal walls provides the backdrop for one of the nicest walks in Morocco. Two *skalas* (forts) scowl atop the fortifications. Dotted by formidable ramparts, dramatic, sea-sprayed **Skala de la Ville,** up the street from Hôtel Smara, is the nicer of the two (it's also free). Visitors can go up the large turret and artillery-lined wall to where the cannons, gifts to the sultan from European merchants, face the sea and the medina. The other fort, **Skala de Port,** is near the port and less interesting *(10dh).*

MEDINA SHOPS AND MUSEUMS. Follow the sound of pounding hammers and the scent of *thuya* wood to the **carpenters' district,** comprised of cell-like niches set in the **Skala Stata de la Ville.** The craftsmen here inlay cedar and *thuya* wood with lemonwood and ebony to create some of the best woodwork in Morocco. On sale are unique masks and statues, as well as the more typical boxes, chess sets, dice, and desk tools. For a quality overview of Essaouira's goods and prices, go to **Afalkai Art** (pl. Moulay Hassan) and browse the many shops lining **rue Abd al-Aziz al-Fechtaly** (off rue Sidi ben Abdallah). At the carpenters' workshops themselves, prices are the cheapest and the marketing the least aggressive. For silver jewelry, head to the silver *souq,* located just outside the medina walls on Av. Oqba ben Nafil. Look for the sign that says "bijoux" above the entrance on the right, about a block away from rue de Caire on the right. The local **museum,** near the Hôtel Majestic on rue Derb Laalouj, is located in the former residence of a *pasha.* It features antique woodwork and important manuscripts, including a 13th-century Qur'an. (☎47 23 00. *Open W-M 9am-noon and 3-6:30pm. 10dh.*) Numerous galleries dot the medina—the best one, **Galerie d'Art Exposition,** near the clock tower, displays modern art crafted by local artists. *(Open 10am-1pm and 3-7pm. Free.)*

> ## PURPLE ISLES HAZE
> While certain stimulants are still available (especially for foreigners), Essaouira's heyday of "good times" was in the early 1970s when Jimi Hendrix and fellow hippies took over the isles. The fort **Burj al-Berad** at the far end of the beach and the ruins farther inland supposedly served as an inspiration to Hendrix's song *Castles Made of Sand*. When he tried to buy the nearby Berber village-turned-hippie-colony of **Diabat,** the Moroccan government decided that it had had enough of Hendrix and his expat friends, and swept the area clean of most non-Moroccans. Today, the village residents have almost forgotten their raucous past; the Purple (Isles) Haze has burned away.

BEACHES. To get to the beach, face the port and take a left. Strong winds can be painful for sunbathers—go in the morning when the winds are less fierce. Windsurfing clubs farther down rent boards by the hour. Try **Fanatic Fun Center** for good deals on rentals. (☎ *34 70 13. Windsurfing boards with harness and wet-suit 100dh per hr. or 300dh for a half day; body boards 20dh per hr. or 150dh per day; jet-skis 60dh for 15min.)* **Sidi Kaoki** (below) is *the* place for true windsurfing enthusiasts, but the wind might be a little much for beginners.

PURPLE ISLES. At the famed Purple Isles, just off-shore from Essaouira, the rare Eleanora's falcons hang out and breed. A Berber king from Mauritania, Juba II, set up dye factories on the islands around 100 BC, producing the purple dye used to color Julius Caesar's cape, among other things. In 1506, the Portuguese, under King Manuel, contributed a fortress and Moulay Hassan added a prison. Recently, the islands, including **Isle of Mogador,** have become a nature reserve. Though you can't visit the islands, you may be able to see the reserve's birds from the beach.

☒ DAYTRIP FROM ESSAOUIRA

SIDI KAOUKI (20MIN.)

> Take bus #5 (6dh), from the southwest corner of the medina (outside the gates).

Many Europeans consider **Sidi Kaouki,** located 25km south of Essaouira, to be the best windsurfing beach in the world. A blue sign on the main road points the way to the beach, where "Wind City" bumper stickers crowd the parking lot. A constant wind blows spurts of stinging sand down a shore filled only with windsurfers. There are no lifeguards, and you must BYOB (bring your own board).

AGADIR اكادير ☎08

Backpackers who come to Agadir may feel somewhat betrayed. At the juncture of the routes to the western Sahara, Agadir stands in stark contrast to the rugged High Atlas and Anti-Atlas mountains that surround it. Devastated by an earthquake in 1960, the town was redesigned as a European-style beach resort, and serves that purpose ably; grassy parks, clean beaches and a multitude of hotels, discos, and cafes lure Northern European tourists, driving prices up considerably. All the same, Agadir can be affordably managed by the budget traveler who needs respite from traditional Morocco or wants to spend some time on the Atlantic coast.

▛ TRANSPORTATION. Flights leave from **Airport al-Massira** (☎ 83 91 22), 25km out of town. The **Royal Air Morocco** office is on av. du General Kettani. (☎ 84 07 93. Open M-F 8:30am-12:15pm and 4:30-7pm, Sa 8:30am-noon and 3-6pm.) **Bus stations** are scattered along bd. Mohammed Cheikh Saadi. **CTM** (☎ 82 20 77) runs buses to: **Taroudannt** (2hr., 9:30am, 29dh); **Essaouira** (3hr., 2 per day 7:30am and 7pm, 45dh);

Marrakesh (4hr., 2 per day, 3 and 6pm, 75dh); **Ouarzazate** (5hr., 9:30am, 60dh); and **Rabat** (10:15pm). There are many options for **car rental** on bd. Mohammed V, including **Avis** (☎ 84 17 55), **Hertz** (☎ 84 04 39), and **Budget.** Their rates are indistinguishable (650dh per day for a Fiat Uno) and at least one will be open 8am-7pm. Local companies may have cars for less, but examine the car before you commit.

■▪ **ORIENTATION AND PRACTICAL INFORMATION.** Buses arrive and depart along bd. Mohammed Cheikh Saadi, where most budget hotels and eateries cluster. Going downhill toward the beach, you'll cross av. Prince Moulay Abdallah, av. Hassan II, and bd. Mohammed V, finally coming to the esplanade.

One **tourist office** can be found on pl. l'Esperance. From the CTM station, take a left when facing the beach onto av. du 29 Fevrier, walk for six blocks, then take a right on av. Prince Moulay Abdallah and a left on av. Prince Sidi Mohammed. There is also the **Syndicat d'Initiative et Tourisme** (☎ 84 06 95), av. Mohammed V, which offers a free map and bus schedule; some English is spoken. (Both open M-Sa 8:30am-noon and 2:30-6:30pm.) **Luggage storage** is available at the CTM station. **Police** are at rue 18 Novembre (emergency ☎ 19), at Hôtel de Police. **Hospital Hassan II** (☎ 84 14 77) is on Route de Marrakesh. The **post office** sits on av. Sidi Mohammed, near the tourist office on the corner of av. Prince Moulay Abdallah. (Open M-Th 8:30am-12:15pm and 2:30-6:30pm, F 8:30-11am and 3-6:30pm.) Check your **email** at **Agadia Net,** 33-34 av. Hassan II, 4th fl. (☎ 82 11 80). **Telephones** are next to the post office. (20dh per hr. Open daily 9am-10pm.)

▪▪ **ACCOMMODATIONS AND FOOD.** Budget hotels congregate around the bus stations. **Hôtel Paris,** av. Président Kennedy, is nicer than its competitors and the prices reflect it. Rooms are arranged around a central courtyard. (☎ 82 26 94. Breakfast 20dh. Singles 90dh, with shower 140dh; doubles 130dh, with shower 170dh.) **Hotel el Bahia,** rue al-Mehdi Ibn Toumert, a block toward the beach from the CTM station, is the cheapest of the hotels, with rooms that try hard to imitate European decor with full baths. (☎ 82 39 54 or 82 45 15; fax 82 45 15. Singles 188dh; doubles 223dh; triples 280dh.) There is a **campground** on bd. Mohammed V on the western edge of town, with gravelly plots surrounded by trees that are lush by Moroccan campground standards (which isn't saying much). (☎84 66 83. 2dh for water, 7.50dh for showers; 10dh per person, 15dh per tent; 14% tax not included). Affordable eateries also cluster around the bus stations. Boardwalk cafes offer more expensive, non-Moroccan cuisine. Four comparable restaurants behind the CTM station all have similar menus and outdoor tables (*menus* 35dh; open daily 8am-11pm). For something different, try the upscale Chinese restaurant **La Tonkinoise,** on av. du Prince Sidi Mohammed between the beach and the post office. (☎34 25 27. Entrees 20-85dh. Open daily 10am-noon and 6pm-midnight.)

▪▪ **SIGHTS AND ENTERTAINMENT.** For the budget traveler not willing to shell out the dirhams for excursions to harbor villages, kasbahs, and "natural spectacles" offered by large hotels, the **beach** is the main attraction in Agadir. Take the 15-minute walk down and enjoy one of the cleanest beaches in Morocco, with good swimming and surfing. Perched atop a hill overlooking the port is the partially restored **kasbah.** Up to 1000 troops—alternately Portuguese, French, and Moroccan—have been garrisoned here at various points in history. (*Petit taxi* 50dh.) The **Musée Municipal,** bd. Mohammed V, shows a decent collection of Southern Moroccan folk art, although with few explanations in any language. (☎84 07 84. M-Sa 9am-1pm and 2:30-6pm. 10dh.) The **Palace d'Esperance,** with its beaches and wide slate ground, makes an excellent spot to overlook the greenery of the **Vallée des Oiseaux** below. As for **nightlife,** head toward the beach and any one of a number of resort-type bars. For dancing, try **Club Almoggarb** on bd. Mohammed V near the campsite. There is even a casino, **Shem's,** also on bd. Mohammed V, which has blackjack, slot machines, and roulette.

THE HIGH ATLAS الاطلس الاعلى

Hollywood has anointed southern Morocco one of the most beautiful regions in the world, as evidenced by the numerous movies which have been filmed here over the last fifty years. Most visitors to the region would agree. Dunes, valleys, and mountains do eventually give way to sizable cities, but not without much protest and occasional sandstorms. With its unique architecture and exotic bazaar, Marrakesh vies with the natural scenery for a traveler's attention.

Falling southeast from the Atlas ranges and stretching through Ouarzazate to the sand-dune seas of the Sahara is Morocco's desert. Mountainous and desolate, its deep reds and oranges are softened only by the rare green veins of oases that creep through the valley floors. Set into this landscape are fantastic Berber towns and kasbahs, where *pizid* (mud and straw) castles tower over the road. Even though excursions are possible by local transportation, a rental car is useful for exploring this southeasternmost part of Morocco.

MARRAKESH مراكش ☎04

An oasis at the foot of the High Atlas mountains, Marrakesh is both a remote desert enclave and Morocco's most important imperial city. The Almoravid dynasty founded the city in 1062, elevating an infamous highwaymen's outpost to the status of cultural capital and infusing it with Andalucian influences from their empire in southern Spain. As it has for centuries, Marrakesh exerts an unshakable grip on the traveler. Tourists are still a minority at the Djema'a al-Fna, the medina's main square, where lively crowds of snake charmers, musicians, boxers, acrobats, mystics, dentists, scribes, and storytellers practice their crafts. The old city is huge, labyrinthine, and definitely worth a visit; the invasive hustlers and faux guides are part of the experience. Marrakesh also serves as a base for expeditions into the surrounding Atlas Mountains or the Sahara to the south.

⊏ TRANSPORTATION

Flights: Aéroport de Marrakesh Menara (☎ 44 78 65), 5km south of town. Taxi from town 50dh. Bus #11 from the Koutoubia Mosque to the airport (about 7am-10pm, 3dh). Domestic and international flights on **Royal Air Maroc** (☎ 44 64 44), Av. Mohammed V. Open M-F 8:30am-12:15pm and 2:30-7pm.

Trains: (☎ 44 77 68 or 44 77 63), av. Hassan II. Going away from the medina on av. Mohammed V, turn left on av. Hassan II and walk 5min. To: **Casablanca** (4hr., 8 per day 6:30am-8:30pm, 73dh); **Rabat** (5hr., 7 per day 6:30am-8:30pm, 95dh); **Meknes** (7hr., 6 per day 6:30am-7pm, 150dh); **Tangier** (8hr., 5 per day 6:30am-8:30pm, 140dh); and **Fez** (8hr., 2 per day 6:30am-7pm, 169dh).

Buses: (☎ 43 39 33), outside the medina walls by Bab Doukkala. To get there, walk out of the medina on av. Mohammed V, pass through Bab Larissa, and then turn right, continuing along the walls to Bab Doukkala. The station is to the left. Arrive 30min.-1hr. early, as seats fill quickly. CTM is window #10. To: **Essaouira** (3hr., 8 per day 6am-5pm, 30dh); **Agadir** (4hr., 6 per day 4:45am-6:30pm, 61dh); **Casablanca** (4hr., 10 per day 4am-8pm, 40dh); **Ouarzazate** (4½hr., 12 per day 5am-5:15pm, 65dh); **Zagora** (4-5hr., 4 per day 10am-10pm, 79dh); **Rabat** (5hr., 10 per day 5am-9pm, 55dh); **Taroudannt** (6hr., 4:30 and 6pm, 83dh) via Agadir; **Meknes** (8-9hr., 5 per day 6:30am-9pm, 115dh); and **Fez** (10hr., 5 per day 6:30am-9pm, 130dh). Private buses leave from Bab al-Rob, just south of Djema'a al-Fna, to locations in the High Atlas including **Asni** (every 30min., 10dh) and **Setti Fatma** (every 30min., 13dh).

Grand Taxis: It's best to start from Bab al-Rob, where you can share a taxi to Asni or Setti Fatma. 15dh per person for 6 passengers; slightly more for smaller groups.

Car Rental: Avis, 137 bd. Mohammed V (☎ 43 37 27), and **Hertz,** 154 bd. Mohammed V (☎ 43 99 84). Both rent Fiat Palios for 250dh per day plus 2.5dh per km or around 500dh per day for unlimited mileage. Min. age 21 for small cars, 25 for all others. Many hotels (like Hôtel Ali) arrange rentals for a discount. Open M-F 10am-noon and 2-7pm.

✴ 🛈 ORIENTATION AND PRACTICAL INFORMATION

Most of the excitement, as well as budget food and accommodations, centers on the **Djema'a al-Fna** and surrounding **medina**. The **bus** and **train stations**, administrative buildings, and luxury hotels are in the **Guéliz** *(ville nouvelle)* down av. Mohammed V; from the Djema'a al-Fna, walk to the towering Koutoubia Minaret and turn right. Also in the Guéliz are most of the car rentals, newsstands, banks, and travel agencies. Bus #1 runs between the minaret and the heart of the Guéliz (1.50dh). Or take one of the many *petits taxis* or horse-drawn carriages (15dh, sometimes more at night).

Tourist Office: Office National Marocain du Tourisme (ONMT) (☎ 43 61 79), av. Mohammed V, at pl. Abdel Moumen ben Ali, about a 35min. walk from Djema'a al-Fna. The office offers a mediocre map and access to **official guides** (half-day 120dh, full day 150dh). Office open daily 8:30am-noon and 2:30-6:30pm; Ramadan daily 9am-3pm.

Currency Exchange: Banks line av. Mohammed V and av. Hassan II in the Guéliz and cluster in the medina around the post office. Most touristy hotels will change money 24hr. Try Hôtel Ali or Hôtel Essaouira.

American Express: Voyages Schwartz, rue Mauritania, 2nd fl. (☎ 43 33 21 or 43 06 44), off av. Mohammed V, 2nd left after the post office. Open daily 6am-11pm.

Police: (☎ 19), south of the Djema'a al-Fna.

Late-Night Pharmacy: (☎ 44 54 26), off Djema'a al-Fna, on the way to av. Mohammed V, on the right. Open Tu-Su 9pm-6am.

Medical Emergency: Doctor on call until 10pm at the late-night pharmacy. It's best to avoid the government-run *polyclinique;* ask your consulate to recommend a private physician. See **Embassies and Consulates,** p. 667.

Post Office: pl. 16 Novembre (☎ 43 09 77), off av. Mohammed V. Unreliable **Poste Restante;** it's a madhouse. Open M-F 8am-noon and 4-7pm, Sa 8:30-11:30am. **Branch office** (☎ 44 09 77) in the Djema'a al-Fna. Open M-F 8:30am-noon and 2:30-6:45pm.

Internet Access: Reliably at the **Hôtel Ali** for 30dh per hr. Several **Internet cafes** have also recently sprung up on rue Bani Marine, the walking street parallel to rue Moulay Ismail in the medina. 15dh per hr. is the typical rate.

🏠 ACCOMMODATIONS

All of Marrakesh's cheap accommodations are within a stone's throw of the Djema'a al-Fna. Many places allow you to sleep on the roof for about 20dh.

🏨 **Hôtel Essaouira,** 3 Derb Sidi Bouloukat (☎ 44 38 05). From Djema'a al-Fna, facing the post office, head down the road in the left corner, through an archway. Take the first right after the Hôtel de France and look for the signs. A colorful, stylish hostel with the best terrace in town, a cafe, laundry basins, and an artist-in-residence. Hot showers 5dh. Luggage storage 5dh per day. 40dh per person, but there are few singles; don't pay more than 60dh for a bed in a double room.

Hôtel Medina, 1 Derb Sidi Bouloukat (☎ 44 29 97), beside the Hôtel Essaouira (and run by its manager's cousin). Spotless beds and a colorful courtyard adorned with traditional mosaic patterns. Laundry basins and a cafe. Breakfast 9dh. Hot showers 5dh. 40dh per person, students 35dh.

Hôtel Ali (☎ 44 49 79; fax 44 05 22), on rue Moulay Ismail past the post office in the Djema'a al-Fna. Tourist-central. Good suites with soap, towels, usually A/C, and toilet paper. English spoken. Also has a complete restaurant (see **Food,** below) and Internet cafe and organizes good expeditions into the High Atlas for around 300dh per day (food, lodging, guide, and transport included). If it's full, don't agree to go to Hôtel Farouk—it is far from the Djema'a and is no better than other budget hotels near Hôtel Ali. Dorms 25dh, includes breakfast. Singles with fan and shower 85dh; doubles with A/C and shower 120dh; triples with A/C 170dh.

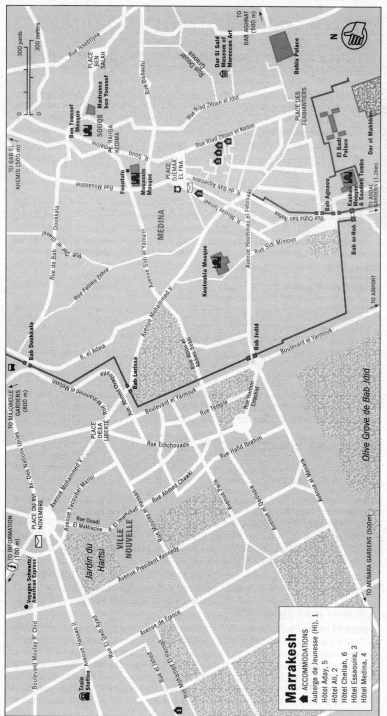

MOROCCO

Marrakesh

▲ ACCOMMODATIONS

Auberge de Jeunesse (HI), 1
Hôtel Aday, 5
Hôtel Ali, 2
Hôtel Chellah, 6
Hôtel Essaouira, 3
Hôtel Medina, 4

Hôtel Chellah, 14 riad Zitoun Qedim (☎ 44 29 77). From Djema'a al-Fna, walk down the same street as to Essaouira, but take the next right. Less stylish than its neighbors, but rooms are terrific. Hot showers 10dh, cold showers 2.5dh. 40dh per person.

Hôtel Aday, 11 Derb Sidi Bouloukat (☎ 44 19 20), across the street from the Hôtel Medina. The new hotel on the block. Clean and still growing. Hot showers 5dh, cold showers 3dh. 40dh per person.

Auberge de Jeunesse (HI) (☎ 44 77 13), on rue al-Jahed. 5min. from the train station in a dreamy part of the *ville nouvelle*, but a 30min. walk from the Djema'a al-Fna. Exit the train station and turn left on av. Hassan II. Take the 1st right at the traffic circle onto av. France. Take the 2nd right, continue for 2 blocks, then take a left and the 1st right. The hostel is at the end of the street. Cold showers. Reception daily 8-9am, noon-2pm, and 6-10pm. Some rules—such as lockout, 10pm curfew, and membership requirement—*may* be flexible. Dorms 25dh.

FOOD

Two **markets** peddle fresh produce along the fortifications surrounding the city, far from pl. Djema'a al-Fna. A closer daily fruit and vegetable market lies just outside Bab Aghmat. Bab al-Kemis hosts a lively Thursday market. For delicious bargains, head for the **food stalls** in pl. Djema'a al-Fna. Food vendors contribute to the square's madness—dozens of stalls deal from late afternoon until after midnight. Follow the crowds to the best *harira* (spicy bean soup; 2dh), *kebab* (skewered meat; 2dh), and fresh-squeezed orange juice (2.5dh).

Hôtel Ali (see **Accommodations,** above). An all-you-can-eat Moroccan buffet dinner situated 4 floors above the bustle of the pl. Djema'a al-Fna on the rooftop of the Hôtel Ali. A good place for women traveling alone. 50dh for Ali guests, 60dh for all others.

Pizzeria Venezia (☎ 44 00 81), on the roof of the Hotel Islanc, on Mohammed V across the street from the Koutoubia Mosque. Brick oven pizza (40dh), a bit of class, and a nice view of the mosque across the street. A refreshing escape from typical Moroccan fare. Serves alcohol, and good for women traveling alone. Open daily 7am-midnight.

SIGHTS

DJEMA'A AL-FNA. Welcome to the Djema'a al-Fna (Assembly of the Dead), one of the world's most frantically exotic squares, where sultans once beheaded criminals and displayed the remains (hence the name). Crowds of thousands participate in the bizarre bazaar that picks up in the afternoon and peters out after midnight. While snake-charmers and water-sellers pose to entice tourists, the vast majority of the audience are townspeople and Berbers from outlying villages. Solitary figures consult with potion dealers and fortune tellers; crowds congregate around the preachers, storytellers, and musicians; women have their children blessed by mystics; and promoters encourage bets on boxing matches between young boys (and girls). People come back night after night for the wonderful food and the chance to watch something spectacular.

MEDINA AND SOUQS. A worthwhile survey of the medina (primetime 5-8pm) begins at the *souqs*. Although dazzling and intimidating, the maze of streets doesn't necessitate a guide. If you do get lost, ask a merchant for directions, or a child will lead you out for a few dirhams.

From the Djema'a al-Fna, enter the medina on the pathway directly across from the Café-Restaurant-Hôtel de France. This path runs through the medina's main thoroughfare, turns past the enormous **souq smarine,** and takes a turn at the **pottery souq.** Berber blankets and cards of yarn pile the alleyways of the **fabric souq.** Head through the first major orange gateway and make a quick right to the Zahba Qedima, a small plaza containing the **spice souq,** complete with massive sacks of saffron, cumin, ginger, and orange flower, as well as the apothecaries' more unusual wares—goat hoof for hair treatment, ground-up ferrets for depression, and live chameleons for sexual frustration. Nearby is **La Criée Berbère** (the Berber Auction), once a slave-trading center. Nowadays it hosts aggressive carpet merchants. Farther on are the bubbling vats of the **dye souq.** Fragrant whiffs of cedar signal the nearby **carpentry souq,** where workers carve chess pieces with astounding speed. Go left through these stalls to see the 16th-century **Mouassin Fountain** bathe its colorful carvings, which are covered by an outer layer of grime. On the road going right where the **souq attarine** (perfume) forks, an endless selection of colorful leather footwear glows at the **babouche souq** (untinted yellow is traditional for men; women wear the fancier models). The right fork at the end of the street leads to the **cherratine souq,** which connects the *babouche souq* to the **souq al-kebir,** the leather *souq*. Those with strong stomachs can visit the **tanneries;** continue through the *souqs* and take a right after the Madrasa ben Youssef.

▨AL-BAHIA. The ruthless late-19th-century vizier Si Ahmad Ibn Musa, also known as Ba Ahmed, constructed this palace, naming it al-Bahia (The Brilliance). Serving as the de facto seat of government for the man who ruled in the sultan's stead, al-Bahia was built in an effort to assert Morocco's historical and cultural significance and thus stave off European domination. Today, it is beautifully preserved and makes for a wonderful stroll, although little artwork or furniture adorn its halls. Occasionally it serves as a gallery for modern art exhibits. *(From the Djema'a al-Fna, walk down rue Riad Zitoun al-Kedim to its end at pl. Ferbiantiers, then turn left; on the right, a red archway opens onto a long, tree-lined avenue that leads to the palace door. Open Sa-Th 8:30-11:45am and 2:30-5:45pm, F 8:30-11:30am and 3-5:45pm. 10dh.)*

KOUTOUBIA MOSQUE. Almost every tour of Marrakesh begins at the 12th-century Koutoubia Mosque, whose magnificent ▨**minaret** presides over the Djema'a al-Fna. Crowned by a lantern of three golden spheres, the minaret is the oldest (and best) surviving example of the art of the Almohads, who made Marrakesh their capital (1130-1213) and at their peak ruled the region from Spain to present-day Tunisia. In 1157, Abd al-Mumin acquired one of four editions of the Qur'an authorized by the Caliph Uthman and used it as inspiration for the design of the second Koutoubia Mosque. Possession of this holy book turned Marrakesh into a center of religious study. In fact, the name Koutoubia comes from the Arabic *koutoubiyyin* ("of the books"). Art historians revere the minaret, which has influenced eight centuries of Islamic architecture. *(Entrance is forbidden to non-Muslims.)*

MADRASA BEN YOUSSEF. In 1565, Sultan Moulay Abdallah al-Ghalib raised the Madrasa ben Youssef in the center of the medina. It reigned as the largest Qur'anic school in the Maghreb until closing in 1956. The Andalucian style includes the requisite calligraphy and intricate floral designs. Visitors can roam the students' cells and appreciate the size of their hostel rooms. *(Walk down the main souq street (rue Souq Smarine) and bear right onto rue Souq al-Kebir; follow it to its end. Open June-Aug. Tu-Su 8am-noon and 3-7pm; Sept.-May Tu-Su 8am-noon and 2-6pm. 10dh.)*

KOUBBA AL-BA'ADIYN MONUMENT. Beside the Madrasa protrudes the unpainted cupola of 12th-century Koubba al-Ba'adiyn, the oldest monument in town, the only relic of the Almoravid dynasty and the original from which all other Moroccan buildings have borrowed their unique style. Though excavated around the middle of the 20th century, much remains hidden either underground or by other structures. If you've had enough of keyhole arches, pine cone and palm motifs, and intricate dome carvings, ask the guard to open an ancient wooden door to the subterranean cisterns. *(Walk down the main souq street (rue Souq Smarine), bear right onto rue Souq al-Kebir, and turn left at the Madrasa. Open daily 8:30am-noon and 2:30-6pm. Bang on the door if it's closed. 10dh, plus 5-10dh tip for the custodian-guide.)*

SAADIEN TOMBS. Modeled after the interior of the Alhambra in Granada, the Saadien Tombs are Morocco's most lavish mausoleum. The tombs served as the royal Saadien necropolis during the 16th and 17th centuries, until Moulay Ismail walled them off to efface the memory of his predecessors. In 1912 the burial complex was rediscovered during a French aerial survey. One **mausoleum,** the tomb of Sultan Yacoub al-Mansour (the Victorious), brims with illuminated mosaic tilework. A second was built for his mother. Both date from the late 16th century. In the neighboring **Hall of the Twelve Columns,** trapezoidal tombs rise from a pool of polished marble. The sultan's four wives, 23 concubines, and the most favored of his hundreds of children are buried nearby; the unmarked tombs belong to the women. The minaret of the Mosque of the Kasbah, al-Mansour's personal mosque, towers above the complex. *(From Djema'a al-Fna, walk away from the souqs to the walkway left of Banque de Maghreb and walk for 5min. to Bab al-Rob. Take a left through Bab Agnaou and follow the signs. Multilingual tours. Open daily 8:30-11:30am and 2:30-5:45pm. 10dh.)*

DAR SI SAID. This 19th-century palace was built by Si Said, brother of Grand Vizier Ba Ahmed and chamberlain of Sultan Moulay al-Hassan. Although not as architecturally intricate as al-Bahia, it houses the **Museum of Moroccan Art,** which features splendid Berber carpets, pottery, jewelry, Essaouiran ebony, and Saadien woodcarving. One of the best classical Moroccan art museums in the country, it is well worth a visit (although the plaques are in French only). *(Go toward al-Bahia, and continue on rue Zitoun al-Jadid, taking the 2nd right heading toward the Djema'a al-Fna and then the first left onto the alley where the museum resides. Open W-Th and Sa-M 9-11:45am and 2:30-5:45pm, F 9-11:30am and 3-5:45pm. 10dh.)*

GARDENS. The midday sun in Marrakesh can be cruel; since the 12th century, rulers have dealt with it by constructing massive irrigated gardens. The most extravagant of these are the **Majorelle Gardens,** designed by French painter Jacques Majorelle in the 1920s. The gardens are owned and maintained by fashion designer Yves Saint-Laurent (who occasionally zips around the Djema'a al-Fna on his moped), and the exquisitely engineered explosions of colorful flowers rival his wildest collections—the gardens' small admission fee is clearly put to good use. *(From Djema'a al-Fna, walk toward Koutoubia Mosque and take a right on av. Mohammed V. After exiting the medina, take a right and follow the walls to the bus station. Bear left onto bd. Safi and turn right onto av. Yacoub al-Mansour; the gardens are on the left. Open daily June-Aug. 8am-noon and 3-7pm; Sept.-May 8am-noon and 2-5pm. 15dh.)* The largest, and one of the oldest, of Marrekesh's gardens is the **Jardin Agdal,** a 3km enclosure accessible via a roofed portal overlooking the Grand Méchouar. While olive trees predominate, the garden contains a variety of fruit-bearing trees that shade the avenues and large pools. *(From Bab al-Rob, walk left along the medina walls until you reach Bab Ahmar. Walk down rue Bab Ahmar for 5min.; the garden is on the right. Free. Closed only when the king is in residence.)* Also dating back centuries are the **Menara Gardens,** a vast enclave of olive groves around an enormous cold green reservoir (800m by 1200m) carved out during the Almohad era. To the left of the water lies the expansive olive grove of Bab al-Jadid, a continuation of the gardens. *(Head through Bab al-Jadid and straight down av. Menara, the wide boulevard that resembles an airport runway. Free.)*

GATES. The imperial city had considerable military importance (many sultans' campaigns to quell the tribes of the Atlas were launched from here), as evidenced by 2km of pink-tinged fortifications. The walls are punctuated by numerous gates. The **Bab Agnaou,** three blocks from the Koutoubia mosque away from Djema'a al-Fna, was formerly a portal to the Kasbah of Yacoub al-Mansour and is the most dazzling gate. Built in the 12th century, it often displayed trophies of war—mutilated corpses and heads of slain enemies. **Bab al-Rob,** next to Bab Agnaou, was once the southern doorway to the city. The Saadien tombs are just inside; *grand taxis* and buses wait outside. **Bab al-Khemis,** the site of a lively Thursday market, sits in the corner of Marrakesh, beyond the *souqs* if coming from Djema'a al-Fna. The bastion was reputedly designed and built by Andalucian architects and artisans. *(Head around the corner of the Madrasa ben Youssef and take the first major left.)*

🎵 ENTERTAINMENT

Most travelers hang around the Djema'a al-Fna or in one of the terrace cafes that overlooks it for most of the night. If you'd rather take part in the more international pastime of beer sipping, try the **bars** at the **Tazi** (☎ 44 27 87) and **Foucauld** (☎ 44 54 99) hotels, where locals and tourists mix with the help of 15dh Flag *spéciales*.(Both bars open at 9pm. Cover 50dh.) To find the Tazi, head away from the Djema'a al-Fna 200m down the street to the left of the Banque du Maroc. For the Foucauld, turn right by the Tazi onto the road that becomes av. Mohammed V and walk two blocks. For a change of scene, try the **Diamant Noir,** a nightclub on Mohammed V in Guéliz.

🏛 DAYTRIPS FROM MARRAKESH

CASCADES D'OUZOUD (3HR.)

A car is the easiest, fastest way to visit the Cascades (3hr., 167km northeast on S508). If you come by bus, you may end up spending the night. Buses leave from window #18 of the main station in Marrakesh (3½hr., 2 per day 8:30am-2pm, 40dh). Ask to be dropped off at the Cascades and then join a grand taxi (10dh) for the rest of the way; ask to be let out at the first cluster of hotels, closest to the steps down to the falls. If you miss the 2 buses back, organize a group to share a grand taxi back to Marrakesh (400dh).

The Moroccan tourist board clearly believes the Cascades D'Ouzoud to be one of the country's most beautiful natural landmarks; posters of the thundering falls are ubiquitous. Not surprisingly, the site is extremely over-touristed, but if you go, a perfect Kodak moment awaits on the cliff facing the falls. You can also descend the 300 or so steps to the pools, admiring the velocity of the falling water as you go. If you do end up spending the night, most cafes along the trail will let you camp for a nominal fee (5-10dh), and the **Hotel Restaurant Café Camping Dar Essalam** (☎ 45 96 57) offers bare, somewhat dilapidated rooms for 70dh apiece.

SETTI FATMA (2HR.)

To get to Setti Fatma, take a bus from Marrakesh's Bab al-Rob station (1½hr., 6am-noon, 10dh); the same ones run back 4-7pm. Grand taxis also make frequent runs (15dh). If you have a car, go 57km south on S513; ignore the first "P" (for parking) sign in Asgaour, even if men try to tell you can't drive further. You can in fact drive right to Setti Fatma and park near the taxi stand for free.

The **Ourika Valley,** just south of Marrakesh, is a popular vacation destination for city residents; with its grassy farmlands, lush greenery, and hillside roses, it makes for a refreshing break from Marrakesh. Particularly popular is Setti Fatma, a collection of seven small waterfalls and cool pools. Getting to the falls from the town requires a fair amount of hiking. Start by crossing the river near the farthest cluster of hotels and cafes and clamber up to the first, most popular cascade. Climbing farther up yields a much more isolated and tranquil waterfall and pool, perfect for a lounging afternoon. Crowd-lovers will want to go to Setti Fatma during the **moussem** (festival) in mid-August, when hundreds of Moroccans descend upon the tiny town. If you want to spend the night, try the **Café-Restaurant Asgaour** near the bridge (singles 50dh; doubles 70dh; triples 100dh) or the authentically decorated **Auberge Tafoukt,** a bit farther from the center of town and perched above the river (singles or doubles 100dh). Both places serve food (entrees 30-80dh).

HIGH ATLAS MOUNTAINS الأطلس الاعلى

Trekking in the Atlas Mountains can be a wonderful addition to your stories to tell your grandchildren. Unlike its European counterparts, the range's trails have yet to be fitted for tourists, and the valleys below remain green, unspoiled, and very accessible. Even travelers with limited funds, time, and skills can huff to the summit of **Djebel Toubkal,** North Africa's highest peak (4167m), in only two days—little more than a sleeping bag, food, water, and sturdy shoes is neces-

MOROCCO

sary. Treks of up to two weeks are also plausible, but for long trips, unless one is skilled and equipped with a full outfit of backpacking equipment (i.e., stove, tent, water purification system, compass, maps, etc.), the services of a guide and/or mule and muleteer are rather essential, as there are numerous unmarked trails. **Official guides** (ask to see their papers) or **mules** can be hired in **Imlil** for 250dh per day and 75dh per day respectively (not including tip). Alternatively, treks can be organized in Marrakesh at **Hôtel Ali** (see p. 712), where the owner knows several experienced guides. From Hôtel Ali, prices are about 300dh per day per person, with everything from food-and-shelter deals to guide-and-mule setups. During the **winter,** snow covers Toubkal and the upper valleys and full alpine gear and an experienced guide are completely necessary. No matter what time of year, **altitude sickness** is a potential risk, as the altitude change from Marrakesh is drastic.

The ascent of Toubkal, through the towns of **Asni** and **Imlil,** is outlined here; for longer treks, such as a three-day trek from Asni to Setti Fatma or an eight-day trek of the whole area, refer to guides, other trekkers, and detailed books (*The Atlas Mountains, Morocco* by Robin G. Collomb is a renowned source).

ASNI   ☎04

The first step up the mountain is a trip to the village of Asni, 1150m up the mountain. Try not to organize a trek here, as there is a greater chance of getting scammed. Most people move on to Imlil for the first night, but if you get stuck, there is a bare-bones **youth hostel** at the far end of town (turn left before the abandoned Hôtel du Toubkal), which has free showers and cooking facilities (20dh per bed; camping 20dh). To get to Asni from Marrakesh, take one of the **buses** that leave often (dawn to dusk, 10dh) or a shared *grand taxi* (about 15dh).

IMLIL   ☎04

The tiny village of Imlil is the ideal base for trekking Toubkal. There are plenty of places to stay, eat, and stock up on supplies, and the crisp mountain air and constant sound of running water soothe tired climbers and invigorate future ones. Martin Scorcese used this village as the setting for his film *Kundun,* which told the story of the Dalai Lama, substituting the Atlas Mountains for the Himalayas and the village mosque for a Buddhist temple. In the center of town, next to the CAF refuge, is the **official bureau of guides** (☎ 48 56 26). Ask questions and pick a personal guide from the photos on the wall, although if you're only aiming to top Toubkal, no guide is necessary (see **The Toubkal Trek,** below). To get to Imlil from Asni, hop on the first truck up, crowding in with the produce and poultry (10-15dh). The ride is an experience in itself; stand in the back and don't let anyone try to charge you more or take you to any shops.

There are a bunch of high-quality hotels that will provide meals (with a few hours notice) and store luggage as you trek. **Hôtel El'Aine,** at the start of town on the right, boasts a lovely courtyard, garden, terrace, and even a library of old French mountain books. The owners are extremely helpful with any trekking info you might need. (☎ 48 56 25. Hot showers included. 60dh per person.) The **Café Soleil** has clean rooms with futons on the floor, although showers are cold. (☎/fax 48 56 22. 40dh per person.) Café Soleil also serves decent food (entrees 25-35dh) and rents hiking gear (crampons 30dh; axes 25dh; boots 30dh). The **Shopping Centre** across the street also rents boots (20dh per day) and skis (100dh per day). The **Club Alpine Français (CAF)** refuge is worth it for members. (Cooking gas 6dh per hr. Dorms 26dh with CAF membership, 39dh with another ski club membership, 52dh without. Camping outside 10dh per tent, 5dh per person.)

THE TOUBKAL TREK

The trickiest part of the trek is finding the trailhead, which is about an hour's walk from Imlil. Walk uphill on the village's only road, taking a sharp right when you see a large boulder. Then veer onto a smaller path to the left (look for the sign for the Toubkal Kasbah on a building). Follow this path up past the kasbah for about 15 minutes until it joins a dirt road, weaving to the left. After five or 10 minutes you'll see the village of **Armoumd** on the opposite bank of the river. Continue on until you descend into a broad valley; the trailhead is on the opposite side (through a small village—look for the sign). This path is very clear the entire way up the mountain. At about the two- to 2½-hour mark you'll reach the tiny outpost of **Sidi Chamarouch,** home to a fiercely guarded **marabout** shrine and expensive beverages. A room here costs 50dh and *tajine* is 100dh (talk about a cornered market). The village marks the spring snow line, so be prepared for icy conditions through late April. Another three hours gets you to the newly expanded **Toubkal** (or **Neltner**) **Refuge,** where hikers from all over the world trade stories at night (32dh with CAF card, 48dh with other club cards, 64dh without). It gets mighty cold during all parts of the year at this altitude, so most hikers choose to spend the night here and ascend to the summit (3-4hr.) early the next morning. (Ask for the best route at the refuge.) This strategy also allows for the best view, as clouds tend to move in during the afternoon. After reaching the summit, most people descend on the same day.

TIZI-N-TEST

The direct route between Marrakesh and Taroudannt, the **Tizi-n-Test** is one of the most entertaining drives in the country. Built by the French in the 1920s and 30s, the road is still deemed so laborious and time-consuming that most buses prefer to take a longer, roundabout path. There is sometimes a bus that runs from Marrakesh to Taroudannt (6am), but the return trip is even less frequent; Tizi-n-Test is best explored with a car. Along the way, **Ijoukak** can be a good base for trekking, although it is not as established as other parts of the High Atlas. Several kasbahs established by the Goundafi family can be explored (or at least spotted from a zooming bus). The **Tin Mal Mosque,** an excellently preserved specimen of 12th-century Almohad architecture, offers a rare chance for non-Muslims to peek at a part of life usually kept secret from visitors. The mosque is unique in that the minaret is on the eastern side and the *mihrab* does not point toward Mecca.

TAROUDANNT تارودانت ☎08

The long, winding descent of the Tizi-n-Test through the High Atlas ends at Taroudannt's red earth walls. The northern gateway to the Anti-Atlas mountains, its bastions have controlled traffic through the mountains for centuries. Once known as "Little Marrakesh," Taroudannt was a frequent target for symbolic attacks in the 15th and 16th centuries. The result, an enormous rectangle of fortifications enclosing the town, makes Taroudannt one of Morocco's best-preserved walled cities, free of any *villes nouvelles*. Taroudannt has great *souqs* and comparatively few tourists (with only the occasional tour bus); it serves primarily as a quiet stop for those waiting to cross into the mountains or head down to the coast.

TRANSPORTATION. Buses are infrequent, inconvenient, and confusing. It's best to ask around at different companies, as routes change frequently. **SATAS** and **CTM** offices are found in pl. al-Alaouyine, while most private buses have their offices in pl. al-Nasr. SATAS buses go to **Agadir** (2hr., 3:30pm, 15dh) and **Ouarzazate** (5hr., 12:30pm, 50dh). CTM runs to **Ouarzazate** (5hr., 1 per day, 69dh) and **Marrakesh** (6hr., 9am, 91dh) via Agadir. Once in a while, a bus runs to Marrakesh via Tizi-n-Test from Pl. al-Nasr (55dh), but there is no set schedule.

40 KILOMETERS AND A MULE

40 KILOMETERS AND A MULE Ever wonder how wilderness guides get away with being the most expensive things you'll ever have to pay for in Morocco? Well, there are only 44 of them (licensed, that is) and they go through a hell of a lot to get where they are. Every year, the Club Alpine Français sends delegates to Casablanca to administer a three-day test. For the first two days, would-be guides are given a practical exam in Arabic and French on topics ranging from Berber history to wilderness survival. On the third day, applicants are sent to the backcountry, where they must hike 40km in under six hours. Understandably, not everyone makes the cut. Those who do are each required to take the Club Alpine representatives on a guided hike. The delegates can ask any question they can think of, from the height of the summit to the length of the hike to what to do with toilet paper in the woods. If applicants answer satisfactorily, they are granted status as certified guides and are legally required to collect 250dh per day (as opposed to the unlicensed 100dh).

🛈 🖪 ORIENTATION AND PRACTICAL INFORMATION. Most buses drop passengers off outside the city walls at **Bab Zorgane.** To get to the center of town, go through the gate, turn left when the road terminates, and follow this road as it weaves through the town, past a mosque, through pl. al-Nasr, and finally to **place al-Alaouyine,** where banks and several budget hotels are located. **Banks** that change traveler's checks are in pl. al-Alaouyine; after hours, Hôtel Palais Salam, set in the eastern wall of the kasbah, changes small amounts of traveler's checks or cash (around US$50). **Police** (☎ 19) are outside Bab al-Kasbah in the basement of the Public Works building, along the city walls to the right of the bus station (10min.). **Hôpital Mokhtar Soussi** (☎ 85 30 80) is inside the town walls through the Bab al-Kasbah. The **post office** is in Bab al-Kasbah, beyond the police station and in front of the mosque (open M-F 8:30am-12:15pm and 2:30-6:30pm, Sa 8-11am).

🛏🍴 ACCOMMODATIONS AND FOOD. Both of the following hotels are in pl. al-Alaouyine. **Hôtel Taroudannt,** on the right as you enter the plaza from the bus stop, spices up its clean rooms with a pleasant bar, a courtyard jungle, and a rooftop terrace. (☎ 85 24 16. Singles 55dh, with shower 80dh; doubles 70dh, with shower 100dh; triples with shower 140dh.) Its **restaurant,** complete with white tablecloths, serves excellent French dishes and wine. (Menu 70-90dh. Open daily noon-2:30pm and 7-10pm.) **Hôtel Roudani,** next to the CTM office, is the best of the budget hotels. (☎ 85 22 19. Small rooms for 1 or 2 people 40dh; larger rooms 70dh; showers included.) Its **restaurant** serves Moroccan specialties at tables on the square. (Menu 40dh. Open daily 8am-10pm.) **Suak al-Baraka,** 70 bd. Prince Sidi Mohammed, is between the two main squares and serves tasty and cheap chicken, *brochettes,* and *kefta* for 20-25dh. (☎ 85 03 31. Open daily 10am-3pm and 6-10pm.)

📷 SIGHTS. Taroudannt's monumental **fortified walls** and **kasbah** have been knocked down and reconstructed numerous times. The oldest ramparts date from the 16th century, when the town was an important military center; much of what stands today is left over from the 18th century. To fully enjoy the grandeur of the walls as you circumnavigate the town, walk or rent a bike (try a small shop next to a dentist's office across from the Hotel Taroudannt; 5dh per hr.). The **souqs** around the two squares are also worth a brief stop. Although their wares pale in comparison with those at the *souqs* of Fez or Marrakesh, Taroudannt is one of Morocco's silver-working centers. (Note that real silver bears a government stamp on the back—don't believe merchants who will try to convince you otherwise.) From pl. al-Alaouyine facing pl. al-Nasr, the **Arab souq** is on your left, while the **Berber souq** is to your right, just below pl. al-Nasr. Continuing past the two main squares on av. Mohammed V and out Bab Targhount are Taroudannt's **tanneries.**

TIZI-N-TICHKA

The route from Marrakesh to Ouarzazate, known as the Tizi-n-Tichka, will entertain passengers and drivers alike. While not as breathtaking as its western cousin Tizi-n-Test, the diverse landscape is eye-catching. As you wind south from Marrakesh, the land becomes more and more arid; geology lovers will delight in the numerous folded and tilted outcroppings. **Buses** run quite often (see the Marrakesh and Ouarzazate sections), as do *grand taxis*. However, renting a car from Marrakesh with a drop-off later in Ouarzazate might be worth the expense.

About two hours south of Marrakesh by car is the town of **Telouet,** 21km from the main road (P31) and home to a **Glaoui Kasbah.** Inhabited by the powerful Glaoui family up until the middle of this century, its red sandstone walls continue to crumble. Ask the caretaker to let you in (tip about 10dh) and he'll explain in French how the one well-preserved part of the kasbah was used for parties and feasts. Of particular note are the skylights and extensive mosaics. Transport to Telouet is difficult and expensive, even with a car, so it's better done as a short excursion rather than a daytrip or destination.

THE SOUTHERN DESERTS

OUARZAZATE ورزازات ☎04

After the scenic Tizi-n-Tichka, Ouarzazate is somewhat anticlimactic. Although once envisioned by the Moroccan government as a tourist mecca (they built a four-lane highway and erected five-star hotels), this French-built administrative center never lived up to expectations. Although there is little but the Taourirt Kasbah to see in town, the town does make a convenient spot to rent a car for exploring nearby towns, deserts, and valleys.

E TRANSPORTATION. The **CTM station** (☎ 88 24 27) is located in the center of town, one block from the main street. **Buses** go to: **Marrakesh** (4hr., 5 per day 8:30am-9pm, 65-80dh); **al-Rachidia** (8hr., 10:30am, 57dh) via Skoura, Boumalne du Dadès, and Tinerhir; **Agadir** (6hr., noon, 100dh); **M'Hamid** (6½hr., 12:30pm, 54dh) via Agdz and Zagora; and **Casablanca** (8hr., 2 per day 10am-9:45pm, 125-130dh). **Grand taxis** line up by the bus station and run fairly often to nearby destinations such as **Skoura** (45min., 13dh), **Zagora** (3hr., 45dh), and **Marrakesh** (4hr., 80dh). If the taxis are not full (fewer than 6 people crammed in), be prepared to pay extra. There are several **rental car** agencies in Ouarzazate, including Hertz, Avis, Eurocar, and Budget, all on av. Mohammed V. Larger companies charge about 500dh per day for a Fiat Uno (unlimited mileage); local companies offer fewer services but charge half that. Check out your car before making any payments. Hôtel Royal rents **mopeds** (150dh per half-day; 250dh per day; haggling acceptable).

⊠ ORIENTATION AND PRACTICAL INFORMATION. The main street in Ouarzazate is **avenue Mohammed V,** home to most administrative buildings, budget hotels, and restaurants. The helpful **tourist office,** on av. Mohammed V, where the road forks to follow the Oued Dra'a and the Oued Dadès, offers bus info and a directory of hotels in the Dra'a and Dadès Valleys. (☎ 88 24 85. Open M-Th 8:30am-noon and 2:30-6:30pm, F 8:30-11:30am and 3-6:30pm.) **Exchange currency** at the banks on av. Mohammed V; four- and five-star hotels will only exchange cash. The **post office,** with **telephones,** is on av. Mohammed V by the tourist office. (Open July-Aug. M-Sa 8am-noon and 2:30-6:45pm; Sept.-June M-Sa 8am-noon and 2:30-6pm.) Hook up to the **Internet** at **Info-Ouar,** around the corner from Café-Restaurant Essalam on rue de Marché. (☎ 88 45 60. 20dh per hr. Open daily 10am-midnight.)

MOROCCO

⛺🍴 ACCOMMODATIONS AND FOOD. For inexpensive lodging, try av. Mohammed V or parallel streets. **Hôtel Royal,** 24 av. Mohammed V next to Chez Dimitri, has welcoming, if simple rooms. Peace Corps volunteers are housed here during their orientation to Moroccan deserts. (☎ 88 22 58. Cold showers 3dh. Warm showers 10dh. Singles 36dh, with shower 80dh; doubles 72dh, with shower 92dh; triples 73dh, with shower 93dh; quads with shower 134dh.) The **Hôtel Bab Es Sahara,** on the corner of pl. Mouhadine where buses arrive, has big, cheap rooms. It also has a restaurant and currency exchange and accepts credit cards. (☎ 88 47 22; fax 88 44 65. Singles 50dh, with bath 70dh; doubles 80dh, with bath 120dh; triples 120dh, with shower 150dh.) The **supermarket** on av. Mohammed V across the street from Hôtel Royal, has an unrivaled selection of cured meats, canned goods, chocolate, wine, cold beer, and European goods. The best restaurant value in town is the **Café-Restaurant Essalem,** av. Prince Héritier Sidi Mohammed, just off av. Mohammed V. The *tajine* or couscous *menu* is 55dh; big parties can order a pigeon *pastilla* for a negotiable 200dh. (☎ 88 23 76. Open daily 7am-11pm.)

🔲 SIGHTS. The nearest example of desert architecture is the **Taourirt Kasbah,** once a Glaoui stronghold. The kasbah, 1½km east of town, was built in the mid-18th century and occupied until 1956. Recently restored, its interior is an entertaining maze of winding streets, stairways, and balconies. Tall visitors beware: low ceilings can make exploration painful. Its massive Krupp cannon, given by Moulay Hassan, could easily level any neighboring village. To get there, walk down av. Mohammed V, bear left at the tourist office, and head toward Club Med; it's right before the blue-awninged Café de la Kasbah. To enter, step onto the bamboo floors that are through the doorway just to the left of the kasbah as you face it from the street. (Open daily 8:30-6:30pm. 10dh.)

NEAR OUARZAZATE
The area to the north of Ouarzazate is a hot and dusty palette of desert browns and greens, periodically interrupted by small Berber **kasbahs.** Perhaps the most spectacular of these is in the village ◪**Aït Benhaddou,** 21km on the road toward Marrakesh. Built in the 17th century and last inhabited by the Glaoui family in 1955, the kasbah has been designated a UNESCO World Heritage site but is still home to a Berber family and several nests of storks. A member of the family will show you around for a 10dh tip. Some rooms still have intricate stone carvings and vegetable-dyed cedar wood ceilings. The terrace has a great view of the surrounding mountains. Movie buffs may recognize the forest of tapered turrets and backdrop—they're the region's film stars, featured in *Lawrence of Arabia* and *Jesus of Nazareth.* The best way to get here is to take a *grand taxi* from Ouarzazate (about 250dh round-trip; the driver will wait, but don't pay him until the journey is complete). It's also a beautiful ride on a rented moped, as long as the gas tank is full. From Marrakesh, take the second signed road (the paved one) to Aït Benhaddou and drive until restaurants appear on the right (10km). Park in front, and walk toward the kasbah in the distance (5min.). You'll have to cross a riverbed to get to the entrance; look for a bridge or just jump.

THE DRA'A VALLEY وادي دراع
South of Ouarzazate, passing through Agdz and Zagora and ending in M'Hamid, is the narrow Dra'a Valley, along which stretches a continuous grove of palm trees strewn with kasbahs and *qsours* (fortified strongholds). The route is best toured by rental car, although people also hop from village to village by bus, taxi, or thumb (hitchhiking is common in the south). Expeditions by camel or 4x4 vehicles are best taken from M'Hamid. Temperatures can peak at 67°C during July and August, but are tolerable the rest of the year; nights are always much cooler.

NORTHERN DRA'A TO ZAGORA

The route south from Ouarzazate (P31) is unexciting for the first 15km, although the lunar landscape continues in all directions. Volcanic rock soon gives way to an oasis of sorts; a small road to the left leads to the **al-Mansour al-Dahbi reservoir,** formed by heavy rains in 1989. **Ait Saour** is the first *qsour* along the way and marks the beginning of a steep ascent over the **Tizi-n-Tinifift,** which ultimately reaches an altitude of 1660m. On the way back down, the road passes by several kilometers of layered rock until the start of the Dra'a's main oases. The first city to take advantage of the waters is **Agdz,** 67km south of Ouarzazate. Set below **Djebel Kissane,** an imposing peak of the Djebel Sharo to the east, the town mainly functions as a resting point before continuing south; buses stop for 30 minutes to allow passengers to grab a drink. If you have time and your own vehicle, there is a palmery to the left when approaching from Ouarzazate, with a few small kasbahs within.

Just a few kilometers south of Agdz, the real *qsours* begin. The road intersects the Dra'a River, at which point it seems to become one long town, conforming to the snake-like river. The layout of the seemingly unending villages is remarkable: each community is divided into several clusters surrounding an oasis, with smaller homes adjoining central, fortified kasbahs. Many of the *qsours* are quite similar; the most notable is the first, **Tamnougalt,** 6km south of Agdz. Each building seems to exhibit its own towers, a tribute to its history as the area's capital. The next *qsour* is **Timiderte,** which boasts another Glaoui Kasbah worth investigating only if you have not yet seen one. Blending in next is **Tangihlit** and its explosion of palm trees; its neighbor **Tamezmoute** has another large kasbah. Just 37km north of Zagora is the somewhat larger **Tinezouline,** which has a kasbah and a lively Monday *souq.* The **Azlag Pass** just before Zagora opens the valley to a vast ocean of palms.

 HUSTLERS AND HITCHERS Many hustlers pose as hitchhikers or victims of auto breakdowns along the Ouarzazate to Zagora road. They invite anyone who picks them up back to their place in "gratitude" for the ride, and once there, try to get the driver to take a camel trek, buy jewelry, etc. A good way to avoid this is to pile your bags on the seats and say there is no space. Better yet, don't stop at all; just smile and wave as you go by.

ZAGORA اكورة ☎04

Stiflingly hot, tourist-trodden, and hustler-ridden, Zagora is the traditional jumping-off point for treks and excursions into the valley or desert. It is perhaps most famous for the fading, half-serious sign at the lower end of town: "To Tombouktou 52 *jours*—by camel." Zagora itself is not a very appealing place, and for those who wish to take a camel trek, M'Hamid offers a more authentic experience. The only time worth spending in Zagora is during the Mouloud, when the city celebrates the **Moussem of Moulay Abdelkader Jilali.**

All **buses** stop on av. Mohammed V, the road that the highway turns into, although **CTM** (☎ 84 73 27) stops on the far side of town while other private companies stop on the near side, along with **grand taxis.** CTM buses run to: **Ouarzazate** (2hr., 7am and 7pm, 36-45dh); **M'Hamid** (2hr., 4pm, 18dh); **Marrakesh** (6hr., 7am, 82-110dh); and **Casablanca** (12hr., 7pm, 170dh). The best way to get to M'Hamid is by *grand taxi* (25dh). Every sort of tourist and financial service is along av. Mohammed V, including **banks,** the **post office,** the **souq,** and most hotels and restaurants. The best-priced accommodation is the **Hôtel des Amis** in the middle of av. Mohammed V, with slightly dingy but decent rooms. (☎ 84 79 24. Singles with shower 30dh; doubles 50dh, with shower 60dh; triples with shower 75dh; 15dh to sleep on the roof. V, MC.) Signs indicate the way to **Camping Sindibad,** av. Hassan II, just off av. Mohammed V. Spots are shaded by rare trees and covered with grass; there is also a pool at no extra charge. (☎ 84 75 53. Hot showers 5dh. 10dh per person, 5dh per car, 10dh per caravan.) Both accommodations have restaurants; another option is the **Café-Restaurant Tombouktou** (☎ 84 71 27), on av. Mohammed V. The *menu* (48dh) and entrees (15-23dh) are both good bargains.

ROCK THE KASBAH Most of the ruined structures you'll pass while traveling in Morocco are **kasbahs**, four-towered fortified structures built for one family and its livestock. **Qsours**, while not necessarily larger, are fortified villages with any number of towers, designed for any number of families. Either of these (or a section of a city) may be referred to as a **mellah**, which means it was once inhabited by Jews. The structures were almost all built with **pizid**, a mixture of straw and mud that needs to be reapplied every year; that is why there are so many ruined kasbahs that date back only 40 or 50 years. The first floor of each is generally used for animals, the second for dining and the kitchen, and the third for living and sleeping. The prefixes **Ben** and **Aït** modify the family name: Ben means "son of," while Aït refers to the entire family.

Numerous **trek agencies** line av. Mohammed V, with the best and cheapest deals at the hotels or campgrounds (**Hôtel des Amis** and **Camping Sindibad** are good bets). Expect to pay around 200-250dh per person per day for trips around Zagora and 300-400dh per person per day to trek near M'Hamid (transportation included). The more people trekking, the cheaper the price per person.

SOUTHERN DRA'A

To cross the Dra'a at the southern edge of Zagora, travel out of town (away from Ouarzazate) for 3km and watch for a dirt road on the left (at the sign for Camping de la Montagne de Zagora). This rough track trundles its way to **Djebel Zagora**, a lone volcanic outcrop overlooking the fertile Dra'a. The best time to visit the mountain is at sunset, when the peaks shimmer in the dying light. Just south of Tamegroute (see below), the **Dunes of Tinfou** rise from the valley floor in smooth golden mounds. They are rare in that they can be easily reached by foot or any kind of car from the main road. Just watch for a well-marked dirt turn-off on the left as you come from Zagora. The dunes are visible from the road.

TAMEGROUTE

Just off the main highway is the town of Tamegroute, an oasis of date palms and *qsours*. Here, in what seems to be the middle of nowhere, is Morocco's best historical resource, Tamegroute's **library,** containing 4000 Moroccan manuscripts dating from the 11th to the 18th centuries. The collection includes a history of Fez, a copy of Bukhari's *Hadish*, poetry of al-Andalusi, countless astronomical algebraic charts, Muhammad's family tree, and a history of Egypt. The library's most treasured document is a history of Islam written on gazelle skin in 1063 by the great legal authority Iman Malik. To get to the library, ignore the painted *bibliothèque* signs (a scam) and turn left (coming from Zagora) down the only paved road in town. Just after the pavement ends, walk straight for a block and look for a large brown gate on the right; this leads to the library courtyard. (Open daily 9am-noon and 3-6pm. Free, but tip the multilingual caretaker around 5dh.)

M'HAMID   ☎04

M'Hamid is literally the end of the road. Forty-five kilometers from the Algerian border and 97km from Zagora, it stands as a lone outpost at the edge of the great deserts. M'Hamid lacks all but the most basic facilities; electricity made its debut a few years back. (As did Hilary and Chelsea Clinton on their tour of Africa.) This is the best place for guided **camel treks** into the Sahara, which range from 300 to 400dh per person per day, with meals included. **Four-by-four trips,** and even trips with your own car, can be arranged as well. One of the best centers from which to plan a trip is **Hôtel-Restaurant Sahara** (☎/fax 84 80 09; talk to Habi or M'Barek Naamani). Slightly more expensive is **L'Hôtel Iriqui,** which accepts Visa, MC and traveler's checks, unlike the Hôtel Sahara. (☎ 84 80 23; www.iriqui.com; booking in Ourzazate ☎ 88 57 99.) If you start here in M'Hamid instead of in Zagora, you can reach endless seas of sand dunes and isolated oases with a five- or six-day voyage, and very impressive landscapes on only a one- or two-day trip. The best times to go are November or December, when temperatures are least extreme. One **CTM bus** leaves each day for **Marrakesh** via Ouarzazate and Zagora (11hr., 5am, 100dh), as well as one private-owned bus (11hr., 7am or 2pm, 90dh). **Taxis** and trucks are more frequent. There are no banks and only a tiny **post office.** Spend the night at the newly expanded **Hôtel-Restaurant Sahara,** which offers rooms with free hot showers. (Singles 40dh; doubles 75dh; triples 105dh; sleeping in a Berber tent 10dh.) The hotel also serves food, including camel meat (entrees 15-5dh).

THE DADÈS VALLEY

Broader, drier, and more scenic than the Draa Valley, the Dadès Valley stretches eastward from Ouarzazate. Other than the kasbahs and palmeries along the way, the valley's main attractions are the **Dadès Gorge** and the **Todra Gorge,** extending north into the dry escarpment of the High Atlas, although the oasis of **Skoura** is an interesting stop as well. It is possible to get from one valley to the other across the **Djebel Sharo,** but a four-wheel-drive vehicle is required. If you are planning to venture off the roads and into the mountains, you are best off hiring a guide or making arrangements with an expedition company.

SKOURA   ☎04

Forty-two kilometers east of Ouarzazate is the kasbah-filled oasis of Skoura, surrounded by fields of grain and roses. Turn left off the highway to reach the first kasbah, **Ben Moro.** Recently restored and converted into a hotel, it was previously owned by five generations of Moros; the first Moro built it in the 17th century. The hill and horse decorations above the doorways indicate that the Moro family was once a nomadic Berber tribe. From the roof you can see the **Amridil Ksar** in the palms. An old Glaoui home, it gained fame with its appearance on the 50-dirham bill. Now inhabited by the Nassar family, it is only accessible when they are away (knock to find out). Nearby is the **mellah** Kasbah Aït Sidi Maocti, with its intricate exterior carvings. The owner of the Ben Moro Kasbah, Mohammed Sibir, is happy to show anyone around (tip 10-20dh). Skoura itself has little to offer, so plan to move on once you've seen the kasbahs. **Buses** may stop on the Ouarzazate to al-Rachidia route, but a *grand taxi* from Ouarzazate should cost no more than 20dh.

BOUMALNE DU DADÈS   ☎04

At a key junction between the Dadès Gorge and the Djebel Sharo, Boumalne du Dadès has succeeded where its neighbors have failed: not a single faux guide bothers visitors to this tourist-friendly, attractive town. Its vantage point from a steep cliff over the Dadès River has made sunset-watching a popular local pastime. The highway turns into the main road (P32) and goes through town and up the cliff to reach the plateau above. **Buses** arrive on the lower part of this street. The **CTM** office is farther downtown. Buses run to **al-Rachidia** (4hr., 12:30pm, 42dh) and **Marrakesh** via Ouarzazate (7hr., 9am, 70dh). Non-CTM buses go to **Agadir** (8hr., 8:30pm, 130dh) and **Rabat** (12hr., 7:30pm, 160dh). **Grand taxis** leave from near the bus station for Ouarzazate and Tinerhir, while minibuses and lorries (pickup trucks) will carry you up the Dadès Gorge for around 15-20dh. The **post office,** with several **téléboutiques,** is on top of the hill (a left at the Shell gas station; a 20min. walk).

If you can't make it up to the Dadès Gorge itself by nightfall (a much nicer place to spend the night), the best place to stay in Boumalne is the **Hôtel Al Manadar,** five minutes up the hill from the main square. The terrace has a stunning view of the valley, and the rooms are newly renovated to include their own views as well as showers. (☎ 83 01 72. Doubles 130dh; triples 180dh.) Its **restaurant** serves good food with a minimal wait (*menu* 60dh; entrees 35dh). If you don't like to walk, the **Hôtel Adrar,** near the main square, is convenient and functional, if a bit shabby. (Hot showers 10dh. Singles 40dh; doubles 60dh; triples 90dh; quads 120dh.) Its **restaurant** serves decent food as well (entrees 35-40dh).

DADÈS GORGE ☎04

The winding ride up the Dadès Gorge rivals the unique rock formations, while towering kasbahs rise up on the slopes and dissolve into the surrounding land. At about the 27km mark, the road narrows and several hotels mark the beginning of a foot path through the gorge (directly across from the Hôtel la Kasbah de la Vallée, to the left of the camping driveway). The path crosses a stream and winds its way up the gorge, where the walls grow closer and closer together. An hour walk yields great scenery, though the physically fit will want to tackle the entire circuit (5hr.). To get here, take a right once you cross the river coming from Boumalne. Lorries run quite frequently to and from the gorge. There are several places to stay and eat, the best being the ◼Restaurant Hôtel La Gazelle du Dadès, which has a lodge-like atmosphere at great rates. (☎ 83 17 53. Doubles 30dh, with shower 60dh; triples 80dh; quads 100dh; sleeping on the terrace 10dh, in the *salon* 20dh; camping 5dh per person, shower included.) Through the hotel, hire a **guide** (200dh per day), arrange **rafting expeditions** when the water is high (Jan.-Apr.; 200dh per person per day), and rent **bikes** (60dh per day). Its **restaurant** also serves filling meals (3-course *menu* 45dh). Another option in the gorge is the **Auberge des Gorges du Dadès**, at 25km, in the valley above the river. The hostel arranges **treks** and has traditional rooms around a courtyard. (☎/fax 83 17 10. Singles 100dh; doubles 140dh.)

TINERHIR (TINGHIR) ☎04

Like Boumalne du Dadès, Tinerhir is mainly useful as a base for exploring the nearby Todra gorge. For those with time, however, the eastern part of town (on the right when coming from Ouarzazate) contains an old medina and *mellah* worthy of exploration. As you wind through the dark passages, look for the "cross of the south" above the windows, signifying the existence of an ancient trading route between central Africa and the Jews of Tinerhir. Every Sunday and Monday morning, a lively *souq*, well worth seeing, takes place 2km toward Ouarzazate.

◪ **PRACTICAL INFORMATION.** The highway turns into av. Mohammed V as it reaches the town. **Buses** arrive just off it, in pl. Principale. Parallel to av. Mohammed V is av. Hassan II, where most of the cheaper hotels and restaurants are located. Buses go to **Marrakesh** via Ouarzazate (CTM 9hr., 8am, 83dh; private lines 8am-6pm, prices vary) and **al-Rachidia** (CTM 2hr., 1:30pm, 31dh; private lines 7:30am-6pm, 28dh). **Grand taxis** running east and west and **lorries** going up the gorge (15-20dh) leave on the other side of the garden between the two main roads. **Banks** line av. Mohammed V. The **post office** is near the taxi stand on av. Hassan II.

◪◪ **ACCOMMODATIONS AND FOOD.** The most interesting place to stay in town is the ◼Hôtel Tomboktou, Av. Bir Anzarane; from Ourzazate, turn right onto the paved road before the center of town. The traditionally decorated rooms in this restored kasbah run a bit steep, but you'd pay three times the price for similar accommodations in any bigger town. (☎ 83 51 81; fax 83 35 05. Singles 89dh, with bath 250dh; doubles 156dh, with bath 350dh.) For a cheaper stay, budget hotels line the strip of av. Hassan II opposite the park. Next to the CTM office is the student-oriented **Résidence El Fath**, 56 av. Hassan II, which has earth-toned rooms with showers and soft beds. The owner will arrange **bike rentals** for exploring the gorge. (☎ 83 48 06. Bikes 100dh per day. Singles 40dh; doubles 80dh; triples 90dh.) **Hôtel Al Quods,** just down the road, is a bit cheaper but has fewer amenities. (☎ 83 46 05. 30dh per person.) Just outside of town toward Ouarzazate is **Camping Ourti**, av. Mohammed V, which has bungalow-type rooms (35dh per person) and a swimming pool which is 10dh but free for guests. (☎ 83 32 05. Camping 12dh per person, 10dh per tent, 8dh per car.) Camping Ourti will also arrange outings up the gorge and to palmeries. Hôtel Tomboktou probably has the best **restaurant** in town, with chicken *pastilla* for 80dh and other entrees for 15-80dh.

TODRA GORGE ☎ 04

The road out of Tinerhir snakes up the **Todra River Valley** for 14km before reaching
the mouth of the **gorge** (5dh entrance fee per car). From here, hike up between the
towering walls. Todra is more developed than the Dadès; while more extensive
facilities are available, privacy and the sense of wilderness are lost. Still, the hike
is spectacular. Almost 1000ft. high, the sienna walls frame a blue strip of sky above
and fall to a rocky riverbed below. A half-day hike is enough to appreciate the magnificence of the gorge, but a few days, or even a week, will allow you to climb well
into the High Atlas. Rock climbing is popular, but there are no agencies with equipment or guides. Along the way to the gorge are a trio of beautiful campgrounds.
Auberge de l'Atlas is slightly better than the other two facilities. Rooms are big and
bright with pine furniture, and the campsites are well shaded. (☎/fax 83 42 09.
Camping 10dh per person, 15dh per tent, 6dh per car. Doubles 90dh; triples 140dh;
Berber tent 20dh). Its **restaurant** serves standard fare (*menu* 50dh). ▇**Café-Restaurant Auberge Étoile des Gorges** has six worn rooms; alternatively, sleep on the roof
below the walls of the gorge. (☎ 83 51 58. Singles 30dh; doubles 60dh; roof 5dh;
Berber tent 15dh.) Its **restaurant** serves entrees for 35-40dh and a *menu* for 50-
60dh. At the end of the road is the pricey **Hôtel Les Roches,** which is frequented by
tour groups. The rooms are decent, but for a more enchanting night's rest, sleep on
the rooftop terrace under the high rock walls. (☎ 83 48 14; fax 83 36 11. Singles
100dh; doubles 150dh; triples 180dh. V, MC, AmEx.) The **restaurant** serves good
food at high prices (entrees 50dh for hotel guests, 70dh otherwise).

THE ZIZ VALLEY

AL-RACHIDIA الرشيد ية ☎ 05

Although named after the first Alawite sultan, Moulay al-Rashid, al-Rachidia was
founded by the French as an administrative capital and military outpost. Today, al-
Rachidia's university and successful businesses have brought the town an air of
prosperity and friendliness; it offers little to do or see, but the town makes a pleasant stop for travelers heading into the southern deserts and gorges.

All **buses** arrive in town at the main bus station (☎ 57 20 24) at pl. Principale, just
off the town's main street, av. Moulay Ali Cherif. Buses go to **Erfoud** and **Rissani**
(1hr.; CTM 5am, private companies 5 per day 7:30am-7:30pm; 15-20dh); **Meknes** (7
hr.; CTM 10pm, private companies 4 per day 6am-10pm; 80dh); **Fez** (8hr., private
companies 10 per day 7am-11:15pm); **Marrakesh** (11hr.; CTM 5:45am, private companies 8:30am and 7pm; 115dh); **Agadir** (12hr.; CTM 7am, private companies 5 per
day 10am-7pm; 168dh) via **Ouarzazate; Casablanca** (16hr.; CTM 8pm, private companies 5 per day 5:30-10pm; 133-160dh) via **Rabat.** To find **grand taxis,** walk down av.
Moulay Ali Cherif toward the center of town, turn right after Restaurant Imilchil,
and ask around. Taxis go to **Erfoud** (16dh); **Rissani** (20dh) and **Tinerhir** (about 50dh).
There are several **banks** in town, although none have ATMs. Services include **police**
(☎ 19), at the bus station; a dingy **Red Cross,** av. Moulay Ali Cherif next to Restaurant Imilchil; and the **post office,** av. Mohammed V, left off av. Moulay Ali Cherif
coming from the bus station (open daily 7am-2:30pm; in winter 7am-9pm).

Most budget hotels are, thankfully, near the bus station. **Hotel El Ansar,** 34 rue Ibn
Batouta, behind the bus station and to the left, has the best value, with sparkling
rooms and free hot showers. (☎ 57 39 19. Singles 40dh; doubles 60dh; triples
80dh.) The older and more run-down **Hotel Renaissance,** 19 rue Moulay Youssef,
directly across pl. Principale from the bus station has standard rooms, most with
showers. (☎ 57 26 33. Singles 30dh, with shower 46dh; doubles with shower 70dh;
triples with shower 90dh.) Most restaurants and **markets** cluster on av. Moulay Ali
Cherif. For fresh produce, try the **supermarket,** across from Hotel M'Daghra. (Open
Sa-Th 8am-1pm and 4-9:30pm.) **Café-Restaurant Echajara,** 38 av. Moulay Ali Cherif
(☎ 57 15 10), serves a complete *menu* for 30dh. Here you can also find Larbi Lam-
hamdi, who will arrange sunrise/sunset **tours** to the **Merzouga dunes** (250dh).

MOROCCO

ERFOUD ارفود ☎ 05

One of the last places to fall to the French (in 1932), Erfoud today has little of the spark of revolution left. Although famous for its marble fossils and its annual date festival (in October), and convenient as a base for exploring the Dunes of Merzouga, Erfoud itself has little to entertain visitors. At best, the town is a pleasant place to relax in winter before heading to the dunes or imperial cities.

CTM **buses** depart from av. Mohammed V, Erfoud's main street, and go to **Rissani** (2hr., 6am, 6dh); **al-Rachidia** (8:30am, 15dh); and **Meknes** (8hr., 8:30pm, 95dh). All other destinations require transit through al-Rachidia. More frequent private buses leave from pl. des F.A.R., at the far end of av. Mohammed V. **Grand taxis** go to **Rissani** (6dh) and **al-Rachidia** (16dh), departing from the intersection of av. Mohammed V and av. Moulay Ismail. **Banks**, a **hospital**, and the **post office** are there as well.

Erfoud's hotels are all on the expensive side. **Hôtel Merzouga**, 114 av. Mohammed V, outshines the rest, offering spotless and cheery rooms with showers. (☎ 57 65 32. Singles 60dh; doubles 80dh; triples 120dh; terrace 25dh.) The hotel's **restaurant** serves traditional Moroccan cuisine (3-course *menu* 40dh). Another option is the **Hôtel Lahmada,** down av. Moulay Ismail and to the left when facing the post office. The carpeting, imitation kasbah tiling, and well-stocked private bathrooms come with a price tag. (☎ 57 69 80; fax 57 60 97. Singles 121dh; doubles 140dh; triples 187dh). To really save money, stay at the newly renovated **campground,** not far from the center of town. Follow the signs from av. Moulay Ismail (10min.). The numerous sink, toilet, and shower facilities make up for the heat and lack of shade. (10dh per person and per tent; 15dh for electricity).

NEAR ERFOUD: THE DUNES OF MERZOUGA الشبي

About 50km south of Erfoud is one of Morocco's most enduring images: the monstrous ❖al-Chebbi dunes of Merzouga. The largest in the world—some claim they are up to 125m tall—they definitely warrant a visit. They are most enchanting at sunrise and sunset, when golden light and cooler air make for a captivating experience. Legend has it that the dunes have more than just aesthetic value—it is said that submersion in the sweltering sand will cure heart disease and rheumatism.

Arrange excursions from Erfoud—hire a 4x4 *grand taxi* (5-6hr., 400-500dh per taxi) in pl. des F.A.R. or join the air-conditioned package tour (600dh per car) leaving from Hôtel Merzouga. Those with their own vehicles should consider enlisting a guide to help navigate through the sand-blown roads. One highly recommended guide is **Ali** from **Abira Transport;** save money by booking directly through him. In the town of Merzouza, several Berber families rent out their camels for treks up and over the dunes (50dh per hr., 50dh per day). Ask any driver or hotel owner to point you to one of these spots; camels will be waiting.

"Hotels" near the dunes are mostly indistinguishable concrete block buildings; many travelers choose to spend the night on the sand under the stars instead. ❖Auberge-Restaurant-Camping La Caravane has a free campground-type enclosure, as well as small rooms with Berber blankets. (☎ 35 16 54; fax 57 52 19. Singles 50dh; doubles 100dh; triples 120dh.) Austere **Hotel Er-Chebbi** is no different from its neighbors, but it does have a telephone. (☎ 35 16 26. 60dh for 1 or 2 people.)

APPENDIX

CLIMATE

In the following charts, the first two columns for each month list the average daily minimum and maximum temperatures in degrees Celsius and Fahreinheit. The rain column lists the average number of days in that month with a reasonable amount of rain.

SPAIN

	JANUARY			APRIL			JULY			OCTOBER		
	°C	°F	Rain	°C	°F	Rain	°C	°F	Rain	°C	°F	Rain
Barcelona	6-13	42-55	5	11-18	52-64	9	21-28	70-82	4	15-21	42-70	9
Madrid	2-9	36-48	8	7-18	45-64	9	17-31	62-88	2	10-19	50-66	8
Málaga	8-17	46-62	7	13-21	55-70	6	21-29	70-84	0	16-23	61-73	6
Santiago de Compostela	5-10	41-50	21	8-18	46-64	7	13-24	55-75	1	11-21	52-70	10
Sevilla	6-15	42-59	8	11-24	52-75	7	20-36	68-97	0	14-26	57-61	6

PORTUGAL

	JANUARY			APRIL			JULY			OCTOBER		
	°C	°F	Rain	°C	°F	Rain	°C	°F	Rain	°C	°F	Rain
Faro	9-15	48-59	9	13-20	55-68	9	20-28	68-82	0	16-22	61-72	6
Lisbon	8-14	46-57	15	12-20	54-68	15	17-27	62-81	2	14-22	57-72	9
Porto	5-13	41-55	18	9-18	48-64	18	15-25	42-77	5	11-21	52-70	15

MOROCCO

	JANUARY			APRIL			JULY			OCTOBER		
	°C	°F	Rain	°C	°F	Rain	°C	°F	Rain	°C	°F	Rain
Fez	4-16	39-61	8	9-23	49-73	9	18-36	64-97	1	13-26	55-79	7
Marrakesh	4-18	39-64	7	11-26	52-79	6	19-38	66-100	1	14-28	57-82	4
Rabat	8-17	46-62	9	11-22	52-72	7	17-28	63-73	0	14-25	57-77	6
Tangier	8-16	46-61	10	11-18	52-64	8	18-27	64-81	0	15-22	59-72	8

TIME ZONES

Spain is 1 hour later than Greenwhich Mean Time (GMT) and 6 hours later than US EST. **Portugal** and **Morocco** are on GMT and 5 hours later than EST. Thus, when it is 3pm in New York, it is 8pm in Portugal and Morocco and 9pm in Spain. Spain and Portugal, together with the rest of Europe, switch to and from Daylight Savings Time about one week before the US does. Morocco does not switch, and is thus 4 hours later than US EST and 2 hours earlier than Spain in the summer.

ADDRESSES

Spain and Portugal: "Av.," "C.,""R.," and "Trav." are abbreviations for street, "Po." and "Pg." for promenade, "Pl." for square, and "Ctra." for highway. A building's number follows the street name. **Morocco:** "av.," "bd.," "rue," and "calle" mean street; "pl." is a plaza. The building number comes before the street name, when there is one. When hunting for an address, note that many streets are being renamed in Arabic; "rue" and "calle" may be replaced by "zankat," "derb," or "sharia."

SPANISH PHRASEBOOK

Spanish pronunciation is very regular. Vowels are always pronounced the same way: *a* ("ah" in father); *e* ("eh" in essence); *i* ("ee" in eat); *o* ("oh" in oat); *u* ("oo" in boot); *y*, by itself, is pronounced like *ee*. Most consonants are the same as English. Important exceptions are: *j* ("h" in "hello"); *ll* ("y" in "yes"); *ñ* ("gn" in "cognac"); *rr* (trilled "r"); *h* is always silent; *x* retains its English sound. The stress in Spanish words falls on the last syllable, unless the word ends in a vowel, an "s", or an "n". All exceptions require a written accent on the stressed syllable. *Let's Go's* Portuguese and Moroccan Arabic phrasebooks provide pronunciation tips (see below).

ENGLISH	SPANISH	ENGLISH	SPANISH
The Bare Minimum			
Yes/No	Sí/No	**Do you speak English?**	¿Habla (usted) inglés?
Hello	Hola (Sí on the phone)	**I don't understand**	No entiendo
Good morning	Buenos días	**I don't speak Spanish**	No hablo español
Good afternoon	Buenas tardes	**What/When**	¿Qué?/¿Cuándo?
Good evening/night	Buenas noches	**Where/How**	¿Dónde?/¿Cómo?
Goodbye	Adiós/Hasta luego	**Who/Why**	¿Quién?/¿Por qué?
Please/Thank you	Por favor/Gracias	**How are you?**	¿Cómo está (usted)?
Excuse me	Perdón/Perdóname	**Good/Bad/So-so**	Bién/Mal/Así así
Help	¡Socorro!	**What time is it?**	¿Qué hora es?
No smoking/Got a lighter (cigarette)?	No fumar/¿Tiene fuego (un cigarillo)?	**How much does it cost?**	¿Cuánto cuesta?
Here/There/Left/Right/Straight	Aquí/Allí/Izquierda/Derecha/Recto	**Can you drop me off here?**	¿Usted me puede dejar aqui?
Open/Closed	Abierto/Cerrado	**My name is...**	Me llamo...
Hot/Cold	Caliente/Frío	**What is your name?**	¿Cómo se llama?
Where is a late-night pharmacy?	¿Dónde está una farmacia de guardia?	**Is there a telephone that I could use?**	¿Hay un teléfono que podría usar?
Where is the toilet?	¿Dónde está el lavabo?	**I'm sick.**	Estoy enfermo/a.
Accommodation and Transportation			
I want/I would like	Quiero/Quisiera	**How do I reach...?**	¿Cómo llego a...?
I would like a room	Quisiera un cuarto	**One ticket to...**	Un billete para...
Do you have any rooms?	¿Tiene cuartos libres?	**Bus (Train) station/Airport**	Estación de Autobús (Tren)/Aeropuerto
I would like to reserve a room, please.	Quisiera reservar una habitación, por favor.	**How much is the fare to...?**	¿Cuánto vale el billete a...?
bath/shower/water	baño/ducha/agua	**train/plane/bus**	tren/avión/autobús
key/sheets	llave/sábanas	**round-trip**	ida y vuelta
air conditioning	aire acondicionado	**How long is the trip?**	¿Cuánto dura el viaje?
Hotel/Hostel/Campgrounds/Inn	Hotel/Hostal or Albergue/Camping/Posada	**At what time does it leave/arrive?**	¿A qué hora sale/llega?
Food and Dining (also see Glossary)			
breakfast	desayuno	**the check, please**	la cuenta, por favor
lunch	almuerzo	**drink**	bebida
dinner	cena	**dessert**	postre
Can I get this without the meat?	¿Me puede preparar este plato sin carne?	**Can you please bring me...?**	¿Me puede traer... por favor?"
Days			
Sunday	domingo	**today**	hoy
Monday	lunes	**tomorrow**	mañana
Tuesday	martes	**day after tomorrow**	pasado mañana
Wednesday	miércoles	**yesterday**	ayer
Thursday	jueves	**day before yesterday**	antes de ayer/anteayer
Friday	viernes	**week**	semana
Saturday	sábado	**weekend**	fin de semana

PORTUGUESE PHRASEBOOK

ENGLISH	PORTUGUESE	PRONOUNCIATION
Yes/No	Sim/Não	seeng/now
Hello	Olá	oh-LAH
Good day, afternoon/night	Bom dia, Boa tarde/noite	bom DEEer, BOAer tard/noyt
Goodbye	Adeus	ah-DAY-oosh
Please	Por favor	pur fah-VOR
Thank you	Obrigad(o)/(a) (to male/female)	oh-bree-GAH-doo/dah
Sorry	Desculpe	dish-KOOL-peh
Excuse me, please	Desculpe	dish-KOOLP
Do you speak English?	Fala inglês?	FAH-lah een-GLAYSH?
I don't understand	Não entendo	now ayn-TAYN-do
Where is...?	Onde é que é ...?	OHN-deh eh keh eh...?
How much does this cost?	Quanto custa?	KWAHN-too KOOSH-tah?
Do you have a single/double room?	Tem um quarto individual /duple?	tem om KWAR-toe een-DE-vee-DU-ahl/DOO-play?
Help!	Socorro!	so-ko-RO!

MOROCCAN PHRASEBOOK

ENGLISH	MOROCCAN ARABIC	FRENCH
Hello (polite)	assa-LAA-mu-'a-LEY-kum / 'a-LEY-kum as-sa-LAAM (response)	Bonjour (day) / Bonsoir (night)
Hello/How are you?	la-BAS?	Ça va?
Fine, thanks	la-bas, al-HAM-du-li-lah	Tres bien, merci
Yes/No	EE-yeh/LA	Oui/Non
Please	min FAD-lak (m), min FAD-lik (f)/'AF-fak (m), 'AF-fik (f)/al-LAH-yikhaleek	S'il vous plaît
Thank you	shukran/mercee	Merci
I want (I would like)...	bgheet...	Je voudrais...
I need/I don't need	khuss-NEE/ma-khuss-NEESH	J'ai besoin de/Je n'ai pas besoin de
Where is...?	feen...?	Où est...? / Où se trouve...?
When is...?	fo-QASH...?	A quelle heure est...?
Bus/Taxi/Train	ut-tu-BEES/TAK-see/al-MA-shina	Bus/Taxi/Train
Hotel/Bathroom	u-TEEL/TWA-let or ham-MAM	Hôtel/Toilette
Is there a room?	wesh kayn beet?	Est-ce qu'il y a une chambre libre?
I don't speak Arabic (French)	ma-kan-tkal-LAMSH al-'arabi (al-fransawee)	Je ne parle pas arabe (français)
Do you speak English?	wesh-kat-TKAL-lim in-GLEE-zee?	Parlez-vous anglais?
How much does it cost?	sh-HAL ta-MAN?	Combien ça coute?
Let's work on a better price.	DIR-l-na shee taman mezyan / wa-TSOW-wab m'ana (very colloquial)	Faites-moi un bon prix.
A lot/A little bit	bez-ZAF/sh-WEEY-ya	Beaucoup/Un peu
Cheap/Expensive	ri-KHEES/GHEH-lee	Pas cher/cher
I'm not interested	ma bagh-EESH	Je ne suis pas interessé
Excuse me	SMEH-li	Pardon
Help!	an-NAJ-da! an-qee-DOO-nee!	Au secours!

ARABIC NUMERALS										
0	1	2	3	4	5	6	7	8	9	10
•	١	٢	٣	٤	٥	٦	٧	٨	٩	١٠
sifir	waahid	itnayn	talaata	arba'a	khamsa	sitta	sab'a	tamaniya	tis'a	'ashara

APPENDIX

GLOSSARY

In the following glossary we have tried to include the most useful shortlist of common terms possible, particularly words we use in the text and those that you will encounter frequently in food menus. Non-Castilian Spanish words are specified as **C** (Catalan), **B** (Basque), or **G** (Gallego), respectively. In the Morocco glossary section, **A** stands for Moroccan Arabic and **F** refers to French.

SPAIN: TRAVELING
abadía: abbey
abierto: open
ajuntament (C): city hall
albergue: youth hostel
alcazaba: Muslim citadel
alcázar: Muslim palace
autobús: bus
avenida: avenue
avinguda (C): avenue
ayuntamiento: city hall
bahía: bay
bakalao: Spanish techno
baños: baths
barcelonés: of Barcelona
barrio viejo: old quarter
biblioteca: library
bodega: wine cellar
buceo: scuba diving
cajero automático: ATM
calle: street
cambio: currency exchange
capilla: chapel
carrer (C): street
casa particular: lodging in a private home
caseta: party tent for Sevilla's *Feria de Abril*
castell (C): castle
castillo: castle
catedral: cathedral
cerrado: closed
calabacín: zucchini
caldo gallego: white bean and potato soup
carretera: highway
churrigueresco: ornate Baroque architecture style
ciudad vieja: old city
ciutat vella (C): old city
colegio: school
consigna: luggage storage
Correos: post office
corrida: bullfight
cripta: crypt
croquetas: fried croquettes
encierro: running of the bulls
entrada: entrance
ermida (C): hermitage
ermita: hermitage
església (C): church
estación: station
estanco: tobacco shop
estanque: pond
estany (C): lake
extremeño: of Extremadura
fachada: façade
feria: outdoor market or fair
ferrocarriles: trains
fuente: fountain
gallego: of Galicia
gitano: gypsy
glorieta: rotary

iglesia: church
igrexa (G): church
IVA: value-added tax
jardín público: public garden
judería: Jewish quarter
kiosco: newsstand
librería: bookstore
lista de correos: poste restante
litera: sleeping car (in trains)
llegada: arrival
madrileño: Madrid resident
madrugada: early morning
manchego: from La Mancha
menú: full meal with bread, drink and side dish
mercado: market
mercat (C): market
mezquita: mosque
mirador: lookout point
monestir (C): monastery
monte: mountain
mosteiro (G): monastery
Mozárabe: Christian art style **Mudéjar:** Muslim architectural style
muelle: wharf, pier
muralla: wall
museo: museum
museu (C): museum
nezakalturismoa (B): rural tourism
palau (C): palace
parador nacional: state-owned luxury hotel
paseo, Po.: promenade
passeig, Pg. (C): promenade
plaça, Pl. (C): square
plateresque: architectural style noted for its facades
platja (C): beach
plaza, Pl.: square
praza, Pr. (G): square
puente: bridge
rastro: flea market
real: royal
REAJ: the Spanish HI youth hostel network
Reconquista: the Christian reconquest of the Iberian peninsula from the Muslims
refugio: shelter, refuge
reina/rey: queen/king
retablo: altarpiece
ría (G): estuary
río: river
riu (C): river
rua (G): street
sacristía: part of the church where sacred objects are kept
sala: room or hall
salida: exit, departure
Semana Santa: Holy Week, leading up to Easter Sunday
serra (C): mountain range
seu (C): cathedral

sevillanas: type of flamenco
sida: AIDS
sierra: mountain ranges
sillería: choir stalls
tienda: shop or tent
tesoro: treasury
torre: tower
universidad: university
v.o.: *versión original*, a foreign-language film subtitled in Spanish
valle: valley
zarzuela: Spanish light opera

SPAIN: FOOD & DRINK
a la plancha: grilled
aceite: oil
aceituna: olive
adabo: battered
aguacate: avocado
ahumado/a: smoked
ajo: garlic
al horno: baked
albóndigas: meatballs
alioli: Catalan garlic sauce
almejas: clams
almuerzo: midday meal
alubias: kidney beans
anchoas: anchovies
anguila: eel
arroz: rice
arroz con leche: rice pudding
asado: roasted
atún: tuna
bacalao: salted cod
bistec: steak
bocadillo: sandwich
bollo: bread roll
boquerones: anchovies
brasa: chargrilled
cacahuete: peanut
café con leche: coffee w/milk
café solo: black coffee
calamares: calamari, squid
caldereta: stew
calimocho: red wine and coke
callos: tripe
camarones: shrimp
caña: small beer in a glass
canelones: cannelloni
cangrejo: crab
carne: meat
cava (C): champagne
cebolla: onion
cena: dinner
cerdo: pig, pork
cereza: cherry
cervecería: beer bar
cerveza: beer
champiñones: mushrooms
choco: cuttlefish
chorizo: spicy red sausage
chuleta: chop, cutlet
chupito: shot
churros: fried dough sticks
cocido: cooked; meat and peas stew
conejo: rabbit
coñac: brandy
copas: drinks
cortado: coffee with little milk
crudo: raw
cuchara: spoon

cuchillo: knife
cuenta: the bill
desayuno: breakfast
dorada: sea bass
empanada: meat/pastry pie
ensaladilla rusa: vegetable salad with mayonnaise
entremeses: hors d'oeuvres
escabeche: pickled fish
espagueti: spaghetti
espárragos: asparagus
espinacas: spinach
fabada asturiana: bean soup with sausage and ham
flan: crème caramel
frambuesa: raspberry
fresa: strawberry
frito/a: fried
galleta: cookie
gambas: prawns
gazpacho: cold soup with garlic and tomato
guindilla: hot chili pepper
guisantes: peas
helado: ice cream
horchata: sweet almond drink
horneado: baked
huevo: egg
jamón dulce: cooked ham
jamón serrano: cured ham
jatetxea (B): restaurant
jerez: sherry
langosta: lobster
langostino: large prawn
lechuga: lettuce
lomo: pork loin
manzana: apple
manzanilla: dry, light sherry
mejillones: mussels
melocotón: peach
menestra de verduras: vegetable mix/pottage
merienda: tea/snack
merluze: hake
migas: fried breadcrumb dish
morcilla: blood sausage (black pudding)
muy hecho: well-done (steak)
natillas: creamy milk dessert
paella: rice and seafood dish
pastas: small sweet cakes
patatas bravas: potatos in spicy tomato sauce
patatas fritas: French fries
pavo: turkey
pechuga: chicken breast
pepino: cucumber
pescaíto frito: tiny fried fish
picante: spicy
pimienta: pepper
piña: pineapple
pintxo (B): Basque for tapa
plancha: grilled
plátano: banana
plato del día: daily special **plato combinado:** entrée and side order
poco hecho: rare (steak)
pollo: chicken
pulpo: octopus
queso: cheese
rabo de toro: bull's tail
ración: small dish
rebozado: battered and fried
refrescos: soft drinks
relleno/a: stuffed

APPENDIX

salchicha: pork sausage
sangría: red wine punch
seco: dried
sesos: brains
setas: wild mushrooms
sidra: cider
solomillo: sirloin
sopa: soup
taberna: tapas bar
tapa: bite-sized snack
tenedor: fork
ternera: beef, veal
terraza: patio seating
tinto: red (wine)
tortilla española: potato omelette
tostada: toast
trucha: trout
tubo: tall glass of beer
uva: grape
vaca, carne de: beef
verduras: green vegetables
vino: wine
vino tinto: red wine
xampanyería (C): champagne bar
yema: candied egg yolk
zanahoria: carrot
zarzuela de marisco: shellfish stew
zumo: fruit juice

PORTUGAL: TRAVELING

alto/a: upper
autocarro: bus
bairro: town district
baixo/a: lower
berroes: stone pigs found in Trás-Os-Montes
bicyclete tudo terrano: mountain bike
bilhete: ticket
bilheteria: ticket office
câmara municipal: town hall
camioneta: coach
capela: chapel
casa de abrigo: shelter-house, usually in parks
castelo: castle
centro de saúde: state-run medical center
chegadas: arrivals
cidade: city
claustro: cloister
conta: bill
coro alto: choir stalls
Correios: post office
cruzeiro: cross
Dom, Dona: courtesy titles, usually for kings and queens
domingo: Sunday
entrada: entrance
esquerda: left (abbr. E, Esqa)
estação rodoviária: bus station
estrada: road
feriada: holiday
floresta: forest
fortaleza: fort
grutas: caves
horario: timetable
igreja: church
ilha: island
intercidade: inter-city train
lago: lake
largo: small square
ligação: connecting bus/train
livraria: bookstore

miradouro: lookout
mosteiro: monastery
mouraria: Moorish quarter
mudança: switch/change
obras: construction
paco: palace
paragem: stop
partidas: departures
pelourinho: stone pillory
pensão (s.), pensões (pl.): pension(s)/guesthouse(s)
ponta: bridge
porta: gate
pousada da juventude: youth hostel
pousada: state-run hotel
praça: square
praça de touros: bullring
praia: beach
PSP: Polícia de Seguranca Pública, the local police force
quarta-feira: Wednesday
quarto de casal: room with double bed
quinta-feira: Thursday
quiosque: kiosk; newsstand
res do chao: ground floor, abbr. R/C
residencial: guesthouse, more expensive than *pensões*
retablo: altarpiece
ribeiro: stream
rio: river
romaria: pilgrimage-festival
rossio: rotary
rua: street
sábado: Saturday
saída: exit
sé: cathedral
segunda-fiera: Monday
selos: stamps
sexta-feira: Friday
terça-fiera: Tuesday
termas: spa
tesouro: treasury
torre de menagem: keep
tourada: bullfight
turismo: tourist office
vila: town

PORTUGAL: FOOD AND DRINK

açorda: thick soup with bread
adega: wine cellar, bar
aguardente: firewater
alface: lettuce
alho: garlic
almoço: lunch
ameijoas: clams
Antigua: aged grape brandy
arrufada de Coimbra: raised dough cake with cinnamon
assado (no forno): baked
azeitonas: olives
bacalhau: cod
bacalhau à Gomes de Sá: cod with olives and eggs
bacalhau à transmontana: cod braised with cured pork
balcao: counter in bar or café
batata: potato
batido: milkshake
bem passado: well done
bica: espresso
bifinhos de vitela: veal filet with wine sauce

bitoque de porco: pork chops
bitoque de vaca: steak
bolachas: cookies
café com leite: coffee with milk, in a mug
caldeirada: shellfish stew
caldo: broth/soup
caldo verde: cabbage soup
camarões: shrimp
caneca: pint-size beer mug
caracóis: snails
carioca: cafe mixed with hot water; like American coffee
carne: meat
carne de vaca: beef
cebola: onion
cerveja: beer
chourico: sausage
churrasqueira: BBQ house
cogumelos: mushrooms
conta: bill
couvert: cover charge added to bill for bread
cozido: boiled
ementa: menu
ervilhas: green peas
esacalfado: poached
espadarte: swordfish
espetadas: skewered meat served with melted butter
esturjão: sturgeon
fatia: slice
feijao: bean
frango: chicken
frito: fried
galao: coffee with hot milk
gasosa: lemonade
gelado: ice cream
grao: chick peas
grelhado: grilled
guisado: stewed
hamburger no prato: hamburger patty with fried egg
imperial: tall thin beer glass
jantar: dinner
lagosta: lobster
laranja: orange
linguica: very thin sausage
maca: apple
manteiga: butter
mariscos: shellfish
massapão: marzipan
mexilhões: mussels
no churrasco: barbequed
no forno: baked
padaria: bakery
panado: breaded
pao: bread
pastelaria: pastry shop
pequena almoço: breakfast
peru: turkey
pimentos: peppers
polvo: octupus
porço: pork
posta: slice of fish or meat
prato do día: dish of the day
presunto: ham
quiejo: cheese
recheado: stuffed
salmão: salmon
sande: sandwich
sobremesa: dessert
sopa juliana: soup with shredded vegetables

sumo: juice
tasca: bistro/cafe
tigelada: sweet egg dessert
tomatada: rich tomato sauce
tosta: grilled cheese
tosta mista: grilled ham and cheese sandwich
toucinho do ceu: "Bacon of Heaven," an egg dessert
verdures: vegetables
vinho branco: white wine
vinho de casa: house wine
vinho verde: young wine
vitela: veal

MOROCCO

adhan (A): call to prayer
agneau (F): lamb
aguelmane (A): lake
aourir (A): small mountain
aujourd'hui (F): today
azrour (A): rock
auberge de jeunesse (F): youth hostel
azib (A): shepherd's hut
bastilla (A): pigeon pie
bab (A): gate
beurre (F): butter
bière (F): beer
billet (F): ticket
birra (A): beer
blanc (F): white
boeuf (F): beef
borj (A): tower
boulettes de viande (F): meatballs
brochettes (F): shish-kebab, usually lamb
bus (F): bus
chambre (F): room
chameau (F): camel
chaud (F): hot
compris (F): included
consigne (F): left luggage
couscous (F): semolina grain
couscous bidaoui (A): couscous with 7 vegetables
cornes de gazelles (F): pastry horns with marzipan
coûter (F): to cost
crevettes (F): shrimp
demain (F): tomorrow
djebel (A): mountain peak
douche (F): shower
droite (F): right
ejben (A): cheese
erg (A): sand dune
fassi (A): resident of Fes
fermé (F): closed
forsheta (A): fork
frites (F): French fries
froid (F): cold
fromage (F): cheese
gare (F): train station
gare routière (F): bus station
gauche (F): left
glace (F): ice cream
hadj (A): Mecca pilgrimage
hammam (A): public bath
harira (F): Moroccan lamb-based soup
hier (F): yesterday
huile (F): oil
djellaba (A): traditional Moroccan garment
djoutia (A): flea market
kasbah (A): family fortress

kefta (F): Moroccan burger
l-habra (A): steak
l'houli (A): mutton
légume (F): vegetable
lehmama (A): pigeon
litham (A): veil
louer (F): to rent
louz (A): almonds
madrassa (A): school
makhzen (A): government
malka (A): spoon
mechoui (A): roast lamb
medina (A): old Arabic city
mellah (A): Jewish quarter
mihrab (A): prayer niche
msalla (A): prayer area
moos (A): knife
mosquée(F): mosque
moussem (A): festival
musée (F): museum
nouveau/nouvelle (F): new
oignons (F): onions
ouvert (F): open
pain (F): bread
palais (F): palace
pastilla (F): chicken, almond paste, and spices in a pastry

piscine (F): pool
poisson (F): fish
poste (F): post office
poulet (F): chicken
qahwa: coffee
qniya (A): rabbit
qsar, qsour (pl.) (A): fortified village with curved, white-washed houses
rouge (F): red
rue (F): street
salle de bain (F): bathroom
shrab (A): wine
souq (A): market
tajine (F): Moroccan stew
timbre (F): stamp
tmer (A): dates
toilette (F): toilet
train (F): train
viande (F): meat
vieux/vielle (F): old
ville (F): city
vin (F): wine
voiture (F): car
zelidj (A): decorative tiles

AVERAGE TRAVEL TIMES IN SPAIN AND PORTUGAL

	Algeciras	Badajoz	Barcelona	Bilbao	Córdoba	Granada	León	Málaga	Madrid	Pamplona	Salamanca	San Sebastián	Santiago	Sevilla	Toledo	Valencia	Zaragoza
Algeciras																	
Badajoz	10hr.																
Barcelona	19½hr.	13½hr.															
Bilbao	11-13hr.	10-11½hr.	8-11hr.														
Córdoba	5-6hr.	6hr.	11hr.	9-11hr.													
Granada	5-7hr.	7½-9½hr.	12-13hr.	10-12hr.	3hr.												
León	11hr.	8½hr.	11½hr.	7hr.	7-9hr.	10hr.											
Málaga	5½hr.	7-8hr.	13hr.	11-13hr.	2½-3hr.	2hr.	9-11½hr.										
Madrid	6hr.	4½hr.	7hr.	5-7hr.	2-6hr.	5hr.	4½-5½hr.	4-6hr.									
Pamplona	11hr.	9½hr.	6-8hr.	2hr.	9hr.	10hr.	4hr.	9-11hr.	5hr.								
Salamanca	9hr.	5½hr	11½hr.	5½-6½hr.	6-8hr.	8hr.	3hr.	7-9hr.	3hr.	6-7hr.							
San Sebastián	12-14hr.	10-12hr.	7-10hr.	11hr.	10-12hr.	11-13hr.	5¼hr.	12-14hr.	6-8hr.	1-2hr.	5½-6½hr.						
Santiago de Campostela	14hr.	12-13hr.	15hr.	11hr.	11-13hr.	13hr.	5½hr.	12-14hr.	7½-8hr.	12hr.	7-8hr.	12hr.					
Sevilla	4-5hr.	4½hr.	13-16hr.	8-11hr.	1½hr.	3-5hr.	7-9hr.	2½-3hr.	2½-3½hr.	8hr.	8hr.	9-11hr.	11hr.				
Toledo	6hr.	5hr.	7hr.	6-8hr.	3-5hr.	14hr.	6hr.	5-6hr.	1½hr.	9hr.	4hr.	7-9hr.	12hr.	3hr.			
Valencia	13-15hr.	10hr.	4-6hr.	12hr.	7hr.	8hr.	10-13hr.	11hr.	5-7½hr.	10hr.	8-10½hr.	10hr.	11hr.	9hr.	5-7½hr.		
Zaragoza	9hr.	8hr.	4hr.	4hr.	6-8hr.	8hr.	5½-6hr.	7-9hr.	3hr.	2hr.	7hr.	4hr.	11-12hr.	8½hr.	4hr.	6hr.	

	Braga	Coimbra	Évora	Faro	Fátima	Lisbon	Porto
Braga		4hr.	9-10hr.	12-15hr.	5½hr.	8½hr.	2hr.
Coimbra			6hr.	12hr.	1½hr.	3hr.	3hr.
Évora				6hr.	5½hr.	3hr.	7hr.
Faro					7½hr.	5hr.	8½hr.
Fátima						2½hr.	3½hr.
Lisbon							6hr.
Porto							

APPENDIX

INDEX

A

MAP INDEX

INDEX

Will you have enough stories to tell your grandchildren?

Yahoo! Travel

Do You YAHOO!?

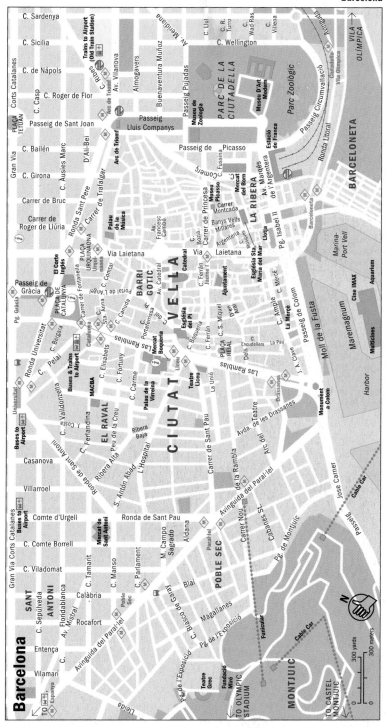

Madrid Metro

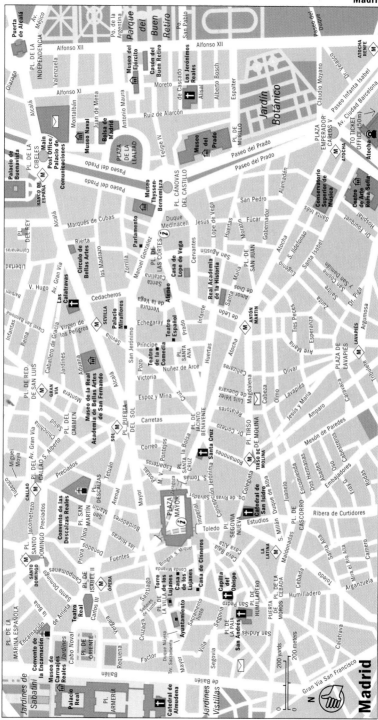

Madrid

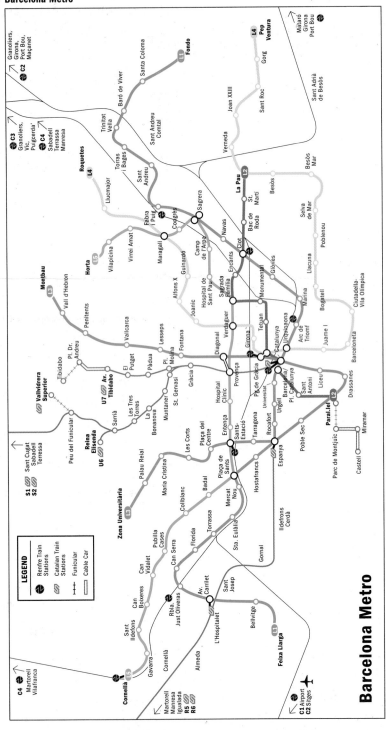

Barcelona Metro